LANGUAGE IN CULTURE AND SOCIETY

A Reader in Linguistics and Anthropology

LANGUAGE IN

HARPER & ROW, PUBLISHERS

CULTURE AND SOCIETY

A Reader in Linguistics and Anthropology

DELL HYMES
University of Pennsylvania

New York, Evanston, and London

 For information address Harper & Row, Publishers, Incorporated, 49 East 33rd Street, New York, N. Y. 10016.

C-1

Library of Congress Catalog Card Number: 64-15151

Contents

Part II. Equality, Diversity, Relativity

Part III. World View and Grammatical Categories

Part IV. Cultural Focus and Semantic Field

Part V. Role, Socialization, and Expressive Speech

Part VI. Speech Play and Verbal Art

Part VII. Social Structure and Speech Community

Part VIII. Processes and Problems of Change

Part IX. Relationships in Time and Space

Part X. Toward Historical Perspective

Acknowledgments

1. Reprinted from Franz Boas, Introduction, in Franz Boas (Ed.), *Handbook of American Indian Languages* (BAE-B 40, Part I), (Washington, D.C.: Smithsonian Institution, 1911), pp. 59–73. By courtesy of the Bureau of American Ethnology.
2. Reprinted from *Southwestern Journal of Anthropology*, 1948, *4*:140–147. By permission of the author and the editor.
3. Reprinted from Paul L. Garvin (Ed.), *Report of the Seventh Annual Round Table Meeting on Linguistics and Language Study* (Monograph Series on Languages and Linguistics, No. 9), (Washington, D.C.: Georgetown University, 1957), pp. 167–173. By permission of the author and the Institute of Languages and Linguistics, Georgetown University.
4. Translated by D. H. Hymes from Claude Levi-Strauss, *Anthropologie structurale* (Paris: Plon, 1958), chap. 2. By permission of the author and the publishers. An earlier version was published in French as L'Analyse structurale en linguistique et anthropologie, in *Word*, 1945, *1*:1–21.
5. Reprinted from *Estudios antropólogicos publicados en homenaje al doctor Manuel Gamio* (Mexico, D.F.: Sociedad Mexicana de Antropología, 1956), pp. 659–671. By permission of the author and the Sociedad Mexicana de Antropología.
6. Reprinted from *Nature*, 1937, *140*:172–173. By permission of the editor. The review appeared under the title retained here.
7. Extracted from J. R. Firth, The Technique of Semantics, *Transactions of the Philological Society* (London: 1935), pp. 36–72. The article has also been reprinted in J. R. Firth, *Papers in Linguistics 1934–1951* (London: Oxford University Press, 1957), pp. 7–35. By permission of the Philological Society and Miss Jean M. Wheeler.
8. Extracted from T. G. H. Strehlow, *Aranda Traditions* (Melbourne: Melbourne University Press, 1947), pp. xvi-xxi. By permission of the author and the publisher.
9. Reprinted in abridged form from *International Journal of American Linguistics*, 1952, *18*:172–177. By permission of the author and the editor.
10. Reprinted from *Word*, 1945, *1*:194–208. By permission of the author and the editors.

11. Reprinted from *Word*, 1946, *2:*103–112. By permission of Mrs. Jean Sapir, Morris Swadesh, and the editors.
12. Extracted from Franz Boas, Introduction, in Franz Boas (Ed.), *Handbook of American Indian Languages* (BAE-B 40, Part I), (Washington, D.C.: Smithsonian Institution, 1911), pp. 24–27, 42–43, 81.
13. Translated by D. H. Hymes from A. Meillet, Le Genre féminin dans les langues indo-européenes, *Journal de psychologie: normale et pathologique*, 1923, *20:*943–944. By the permission of the editor.
14. Translated by D. H. Hymes from Marcel Mauss, Discussion, *Journal de psychologie: normale et pathologique*, 1923, *20:*944–947. By the permission of the editors. This discussion and the preceding article are reprinted in A. Meillet, *Linguistique historique et linguistique générale* (Collection Linguistique, Societé de Linguistique de Paris, No. 60), (Paris: Klincksieck, 1952 [new printing], pp. 24–28.
15. Reprinted from *Science*, 1931, *74:*578. By permission of *Science* and Mrs. Jean Sapir.
16. Reprinted in abridged form from John B. Carroll (Ed.), *Language, Thought, and Reality: Selected Writings of Benjamin Lee Whorf* (New York: Wiley; Cambridge: Technology Press, 1956), pp. 65–86. By permission of the editor and the publishers.
17. Reprinted from *Language*, 1951, *27:*111–120. By permission of the author and the Linguistic Society of America.
18. Reprinted from *American Anthropologist*, 1962, *64:*340–350. By permission of the author and the American Anthropological Association.
19. Extracted in modified form from Franz Boas, *Geographical Names of the Kwakiutl Indians* (Columbia University Contributions to Anthropology, No. 20), (New York: Columbia University Press, 1934), pp. 9–21. By permission of the publishers.
20. Reprinted with slight revisions by the author from *International Journal of American Linguistics*, 1955, *21:*187–189. By permission of the author and the editor.
21. Reprinted with slight revisions by the author from Ward H. Goodenough, *Property, Kin, and Community on Truk* (Yale University Publications in Anthropology, No. 46), (New Haven: Yale University Press, 1951), pp. 61–64. By permission of the author, the Yale University Press, and the Department of Anthropology, Yale University.
22. Reprinted from *Southwestern Journal of Anthropology*, 1955, *11:*339–344. By permission of the author and the editor.
23. Reprinted from *American Anthropologist*, 1961, *63:*113–132. By permission of the author and the American Anthropological Association.
24. Reprinted from *The Uganda Journal*, 1948, *12:*166–171. By permission of the author and The Uganda Society.
25. Reprinted from *Language*, 1944, *20:*142–149. By permission of the author and the Linguistic Society of America.
26. Reprinted from *Journal of Abnormal and Social Psychology*, 1961, *62:*375–

385. By permission of the authors and the American Psychological Association.

27. Reprinted from *International Journal of American Linguistics*, 1948, *14*:11–14. By permission of the author and the editor.
28. Reprinted with an additional postscript by the author, from *Journal of Child Psychology and Psychiatry*, 1961, *1*:313–324. By permission of the author and Pergamon Press Ltd.
29. Reprinted from *Man*, 1954, *54*:55–57. By permission of the editor and The Royal Anthropological Institute.
30. Reprinted from *Word*, 1949, *5*:268–272. By permission of the author and the editors.
31. Extracted from John Boman Adams, Culture and Conflict in an Egyptian Village. *American Anthropologist*, 1957, *59*:225–235. By permission of the author and the American Anthropological Association.
32. Reprinted from *Studies in Linguistics*, 1958, *13*:1–12. By permission of the author.
33. Reprinted from *Language*, 1959, *35*:631–636. By permission of the author and the Linguistic Society of America.
34. Reprinted from *Journal of American Folklore*, 1957, *70*:173–175. By permission of the author and the American Folklore Society.
35. Reprinted from *Language*, 1948, *24*:280–286. By permission of the author and the Linguistic Society of America.
36. Reprinted from *Word*, 1945, *1*:217–238. By permission of the author and the editors.
37. Reprinted from *Journal of American Folklore*, 1958, *71*:312–324. By permission of the author and the American Folklore Society.
38. Reprinted in abridged form from *Journal of the Washington Academy of Sciences*, 1947, *37*:329–352. By permission of the author and the editor.
39. Reprinted in abridged form from Thomas A. Sebeok, Structure and Content of Cheremis Charms, Part One, *Anthropos*, 1953, *48*:369–388. By permission of the author and the Anthropos Institut; and from Thomas A. Sebeok, The Texture of a Cheremis Incantation, *Mémoires de la Société Finno-Ougrienne*, 1962, *125*:523–527 (Helsinki, 1962), by permission of the author and the Finno-Ugric Society.
40. Extracted from Ann H. Gayton and Stanley S. Newman, *Yokuts and Western Mono Myths* (UCP-AR, *5*:1), (Berkeley: University of California Press, 1940), pp. 4–11. By permission of the authors and the University of California Press.
41. Reprinted from *American Speech*, 1927, *2*:432–439. By permission of Columbia University Press.
42. Reprinted from *Southwestern Journal of Anthropology*, 1955, *11*:345–354. By permission of the author and the editor.
43. This article was the basis of a talk presented before the Association for Asian Studies in New York City on April 1, 1958. It has never before been published.

44. Reprinted from *American Anthropologist*, 1961, *63*:976–988. By permission of the author and the American Anthropological Association.
45. Reprinted from *Word*, 1959, *15*:325–340. By permission of the author and the editors.
46. Reprinted with slight revisions by the author from *Anthropological Linguistics*, 1959, *1*(3):34–41. By permission of the author and the editor.
47. Reprinted from *Language*, 1948, *24*:335–345. By permission of the author and the Linguistic Society of America.
48. Reprinted with slight revisions by the author from *International Journal of American Linguistics*, 1939, *9*:117–118. By permission of the author and the editor.
49. Reprinted with slight revision by the author from *Current Anthropology*, 1960, *1*(5–6):424–425. By permission of the author and the editor.
50. Reprinted with revisions by the author from *American Speech*, 1948, *23*:194–203. By permission of the author and Columbia University Press.
51. Reprinted from *Word*, 1958, *14*:47–56. By permission of the author and the editor.
52. Reprinted from *American Anthropologist*, 1957, *53*:338–341. By permission of the author and the American Anthropological Association.
53. Reprinted from *Language*, 1961, *37*:97–112. By permission of the author and the Linguistic Society of America.
54. Reprinted from *Language*, 1956, *32*:146–157. By permission of the author and the Linguistic Society of America.
55. Reprinted from *Anthropological Linguistics*, 1959, *1*(2):28–31. By permission of the author and the editor.
56. Reprinted from *International Journal of American Linguistics*, 1955, *21*:228–294. By permission of the author and the editor.
57. Reprinted from *Social Forces*, 1938, *17*:107–118. By permission of the author and the Williams and Wilkins Company.
58. Reprinted from *African Studies*, 1953, *12*:1–9. By permission of the author and the Editorial Committee.
59. Reprinted from *Language*, 1950, *26*:175–185. By permission of the author and the Linguistic Society of America.
60. Reprinted in slightly modified form from *Southwestern Journal of Anthropology*, 1959, *15*:20–35. By permission of the author and the editor.
61. This article was written especially for this volume and has never before been published.
62. Reprinted with slight revisions from *Language*, 1948, *24*:117–131. By permission of the author and the Linguistic Society of America.
63. Reprinted in abridged form from *Word*, 1956, *12*:175–210. By permission of the author and the editors.
64. Reprinted in slightly revised form from *Southwestern Journal of Anthropology*, 1951, *7*:1–21. By permission of the author and the editor.
65. Reprinted from *Word*, 1945, *1*:54–58. By permission of the author and the editors.

66. Reprinted from *Language*, 1956, *32:*3–16. By permission of the author and the Linguistic Society of America.
67. Extracted from A. L. Kroeber, Statistics, Indo-European, and Taxonomy, *Language*, 1960, *36:*1–21. By permission of Mrs. Theodora Kroeber and the Linguistic Society of America.
68. This article was written especially for this volume and has never before been published.
69. Reprinted with slight corrections and omission of the first and last sections from *Language*, 1961, *37:*1–28. By permission of the author and the Linguistic Society of America.

Foreword

AS AN ANTHROPOLOGIST who found his way into his profession by being shown how to analyze Boas' *Chinook Texts* into grammar, and whose first remembered purely intellectual pleasure, as a boy of ten, was the demonstration of pattern in the classes of English strong verbs, it is a pleasure to say something about Professor Hymes' reader.

It is a recognized problem whether we ought to say "language *and* culture" or "language *in* culture." As to the essential relevant facts, everyone is in agreement. When we need a term for that larger whole which is the common property of all groups of men and which distinctively sets off mankind from all other animals, there is no question: we call it culture. Even where special contexts favor or justify special terms, like "civilization" or "noesis" (derived from Sir Julian Huxley's "noetic evolution"), it is clearly culture that is meant. But an equally important consideration is that language is easily the most nearly autonomous, self-consistent, and self-contained unit which is discernible within the totality of culture. Why this is—why perhaps it had to be so—is something that we do not understand with clarity or conviction; and I shall therefore not try even to suggest an explanation, but accept the fact as something that students of language and students of culture both posit as a starting point, explicitly or implicitly.

It is, however, a fair question what language-study and culture-study share, if one is a part of the other. They share certain processes and properties and allegiances which the articles in this book touch on, avowedly or by reference, again and again, and which its reader will know something about when he has finished the perusal. There is however, one kind of content, one body of phenomena, which language and culture indubitably share—and that is meaning.

It is one of the tenets of modern linguistic science that as it has cast out psychologizing as something irrelevant, distracting, and likely to be misleading *to the linguist*, so also it must try to operate as far as possible without leaning unduly on meaning. Of course, every linguist knows that this is impossible. The fourth chapter of this very book is directed toward semantics. And yet the ideal is clear; a good descriptive grammar deals with strictly linguistic units, such as phonemes and morphemes, their forms and their distributions (these last being their place, order, combination, or any other mathematically expressible occurrence). Alas for the ideal! There regularly are less morphemes than different patterned distributions occurring in any language. And how do we keep them apart? By their meaning. And legitimately so; for the meanings are also facts adhering to the facts of morphemes and morpheme distributions. And that they can be relevant is obvious from the circumstance that whatever else language does, one of its patent uses is to convey information.

In short, the apparent antisemantic attitude of recent modern linguistics is the result of having developed an operational and pragmatic procedure that gives clean-cut immediate recognition of the elements, patterns, and structure of languages. No linguists deny meaning nor do they deny that ultimately the relation of linguistic structure and meaning is a problem which will have to be admitted and attacked. It is just that pure linguistic science is so much more developed and better organized than semantic science that linguists find they can travel faster and farthest with a minimum encumbrance of the semantic baggage.

Where anthropology is concerned in this is that anthropology is the particular science which is most immediately and wholeheartedly—holistically is the technical word for it—concerned with culture as such, culture in general, and in particular, but it is always more than some special aspect or part of culture such as economic culture or social culture or technological or religious or intellectual culture. Anthropology is therefore less ready than linguistic science to accept the astringent technique of purging out meaning as far as possible. Not that anthropologists are aficionados with special semantic interest; on the whole they are probably pretty innocent of that. But the meanings of words do attach to those very artifacts and mentifacts which constitute culture and which attach also to that nature in the frame of which every culture must be set. Linguists have an informal and nonprofessional way of saying that lexicon *is* merely culture. This is roughly quite true: a dictionary does exemplify or embody only a small part of the structure of its language; and nearly all of its content—all except the relatively small number of "grammatical words"—is of cultural relevance.

I want to say one more thing about "meaning": a caution. Anthropologists sometimes say that in all cultural phenomena there can be distinguished form (or sensory appearance), use, function, and meaning. This meaning is something quite different from linguistic meaning; it signifies more nearly the subjective emotional connotation of a phenomenon rather than its semantic denotation. For good measure and distraction I add the query whether the third member of this tetralogy, function, is ever anything else than either a purpose or a relation which the members of the culture are unaware of, but which the anthropologist is clever enough to discern.

Anthropological study, if sufficiently intensive, must include some linguistic forms and their range of meaning: all those forms, for one thing, whose range of meaning differs from that of the most nearly corresponding terms in our own speech—like *mana* or *taboo* or *totem*, for instance; or again like the

Japanese words which we half-translate and therefore mistranslate by *sincerity* or *obligation* or *reciprocation* or *thanks*. Or, even simpler, when a native word means not *blue* or *green*, but *blue or green*, or *ako* does not mean *brother* but *older brother, exclusive of younger, but inclusive of parallel cousin*.

However, the common roots of the study of language and culture go much deeper than such mere clarifications and safeguards. They are evidenced by men like Boas and Sapir being eminent in both anthropology and linguistics; and thus among Sapir's students, represented by passages in this book, there were some who took anthropological degrees and now hold linguistic positions as well as linguists now in anthropology departments. One might add that all major institutions of learning in the United States regularly include a linguist in their anthropological staffs.

It is also well to remember that as a matter of history our western civilization linguistic science grew out of philology, which was concerned with meanings and norms, and with texts and literature, and with culture in both the humanist's and the scientist's sense of the word culture. It was by clotting itself out from this little-differentiated continuum that pure or general linguistics originated; and the "revolt against meaning" is but one stage in the process. Yet the underlying relations of linguistics with humanism and philology remain; and when sufficient differentiation has been accomplished, we may anticipate a new reintegration, which will leave all participants more broadly based and more effectively equipped. One of the taproots of anthropology is humanistic, just as one of the currents that nourished linguistics is, in the strictest sense, scientific. This book should help keep alive past intellectual endeavors in their living present forms, as well as advance the day of future larger reconstitution.

A. L. Kroeber

General Introduction

WITH *Language in Culture and Society: A Reader in Linguistics and Anthropology*, I have tried to provide a book that will serve the needs of students and teachers, and also interest anyone concerned with the serious study of the topics named in the title.

Most obviously, of course, the book should be useful for courses in "Language and Culture"—that multifariously defined label under which topics associated with language are often introduced into the curriculum. Indeed, the book emerges mainly from my own experiences in teaching and research under that heading. As part of professional training at the graduate level, it provides the only single volume coverage of the field from an anthropological point of view. At the same time, I hope that it is a volume that can be put in the hands of students and colleagues, apart from courses, as a general guide to anthropological concerns with language. The contents have been made as ample as possible, and extensive bibliographies prepared, with that twin purpose in mind.

The perspective that informs the book can be summarized in a few paragraphs, directed at the reasons for including such material, and such a book, in the training of anthropologists. (Although I shall usually speak simply of "language," on the one hand, and "culture," on the other, the terms should be understood as implying, respectively, "and speech," and "and society," as well.)

Whatever one's views of the nature and goals of anthropology, clearly speech is so fundamental an activity of man, language so integral a part of his culture, that no teaching of anthropology worthy of the name could pass either by. Not only would our subject be incomplete without them, but speech and language provide useful, sometimes crucial, examples of general problems, whether we focus on how men differ, or how they are alike; on how cultures work, or how they change; on the scope of anthropology, or the skills of the anthropologist.

The area to which conversance with language and linguistics does not pertain seems small. Only the few whose work does not involve field ethnography, historical anthropology, or general theory, can safely ignore them. Such a general principle, however, is hard to separate from its most salient examples. Not only, as Levi-Strauss (1953) pointed out, must one distinguish the relationships between language and culture from those between *a* language and *a* culture, and between linguistics and anthropology; one must also distinguish the relations which may obtain between particular linguists (or departments of linguistics) and particular anthropologists, sociologists, literary scholars, etc.(or departments of same). The pertinence of linguistics will be judged by many anthropologists in terms of their experience with particular scholars and departments; and it is in these terms that they will judge the kind and amount of linguistic knowledge and training their anthropology students need. Thus the present book is intended as something of an argument and ostensive definition, designed to have a scope broader than may be manifest in particular programs of linguistic training, in or out of anthropology, in relation to anthropological concerns. The purpose is to show that there exists, apart from the particularities of given institutions, a broad, complex, and significant field of linguistic problems—one that intersects almost every concern of the anthropologist, as well as of students of related behavioral and humanistic disciplines; and to show that the field has a noteworthy history, a lively present, and a future of promise.

At the same time it must be noted that the book contains little or nothing of certain topics central to linguistics itself. This is partly so because such topics as the methods of formal descriptive linguistics are quite adequately handled at length in other books, and nothing would be gained by handling them tangentially here. The technique and perspective gained by training in such methods is prerequisite to active contribution to most of the anthropological interests represented in the present volume, of course, and just because such methods are not represented as such, I should like to underscore their importance. Partly, however, the exclusion has also a theoretical justification. It is simply that the status of such methods is usually different as between linguistics proper and anthropology. In present-day linguistics the methods and forms of descriptive statement loom large as ends in themselves. In anthropology they must always have the status of means.

This last distinction is but an aspect of the general thesis that the relation between anthropology and linguistics, historically and in present practice, is the same as that between anthropology and a number of other disciplines; there is overlap rather than inclusion of one by the other. On the one hand, the special discipline, such as linguistics, does not exhaust the interest of the anthropologist. While in principle committed to coordinating all scientific knowledge about a subject, it has its particular set of technical skills, its particular history, ideology, emphases, and professional organization, all subject to local variation in time and place. Linguistics as a discipline is, in fact, a congeries of subfields, whose orientations are conditioned by particular bodies of data, national backgrounds, leading figures, and favorite problems (as Malkiel points out and documents in the last section of the book). In consequence, it may very well occur that anthropologists make their own contributions of data and of theory, and their concerns may give rise to questions which the linguistics of their immediate environment may not at the time be asking, or to emphases which it may not care to make. On the other hand, the anthropological interest in language does not exhaust that of the linguist. On general intellectual principle, of course, nothing linguistic is alien to anthropology, but at any given time and place, anthropology's active interest is far from covering everything within the manifold domain of the scientific study of language. In short, the anthropological interest is always selective, grouping together facets of language that might not otherwise attract joint attention.

All this has a bearing on the training of anthropologists. Depending on the representation of special fields and interests, the teaching of linguistics will vary greatly from one institution to another, and some offerings will be of more relevance to anthropology than others. Moreover, in any case other departments cannot be expected to provide all the linguistic training and orientation toward language that anthropologists need. Departments of anthropology must themselves exercise responsibility for some of the linguistic knowledge their students need.

The general thesis can be put in terms of ideal goals. (1) It is the task of linguistics to coordinate knowledge about language from the viewpoint of language. (2) It is anthropology's task to coordinate knowledge about language from the viewpoint of *man*. Put in terms of history and practice, the thesis is that there is a distinctive field, *linguistic anthropology*, conditioned, like other subfields of linguistics and anthropology, by certain bodies of data, national background, leading figures, and favorite problems. In one sense, it is a characteristic activity, the activity of those whose questions about language are shaped by anthropology. Its scope is not defined by logic or nature, but by the range of active anthropological interest in linguistic phenomena. Its scope may include problems that fall outside the active concern of linguistics, and *always it uniquely includes the problem of integration with the rest of anthropology*. In sum, linguistic anthropology can be defined as *the study of language within the context of anthropology*.

The thesis has a bearing on the training of anthropologists, for when we teach about language in anthropology, to some extent we engage in linguistic anthropology in this sense. We are not teaching linguistics as it would or might be taught by a specialist who knew nothing of anthropology, just as in other cases we are not teaching economics, political science, or history of religions as these might be taught by their specialists. We are teaching as anthropologists concerned with subjects relevant to questions which anthropologists ask. Rather than adding one quantum of discipline A to set beside quanta of disciplines B, C, and, D, we are trying to consider the subject-matter of all those disciplines from some general point of view. This being so, we should approach the subject-matter of a particular field, such as speech and language, with emphasis on the fundamental questions it poses for anthropology, rather than on sheer information content; and we should approach such questions from a general ground held in common with the rest of anthropology, rather than leave them disjunct in terms couched only for specialists. (For example, the concepts of the phoneme, morpheme, and other units of descriptive linguistics could be approached in terms of the role of cultural factors in perception).

At this point the pedagogic and the scientific goals meet. To be able to teach easily and effectively in the way recommended above would presuppose a good deal of work in empirical organization and theoretical analysis that, in fact, has yet to be done. The present reader is a case in point. Ideally, such a collection would illustrate a well articulated body of theory, or a well defined set of problems having general acceptance. At present a reader in the area of language, culture, and society cannot wholly do so. The resurgent spread of linguistic interests in anthropology and related fields is too recent, and the strands and centers of interest too varied, for such consensus. A sense of the need for such a book has prompted me to go ahead, despite delays and difficulties, making the best choices my own awareness of the state of theory and relevance of problems would permit. The organization of the sections, and the introductions to them, do not pretend to be more than a step. If the book proves useful and stimulating, my hope, as that of Professor Kroeber in his Foreword, is that it may advance the day when a better integrated body of theory and problems exists.

Several of the most significant conceptual approaches that have been proposed so far are represented in Part I (cf. also Hockett's article in Part IX). Such treatments tend to assume the existence of two distinct disciplines, and/or subject matters, and to proceed to explore their interdependence, not only substantively, but also in part methodologically, as seen from the author's point of view. Here and in the rest of the book, the organization brings out the main foci of anthropological concern with language, not so much in terms of the filling in of a preconceived scheme as through an inductive reflection of existing types of work. The themes of the remaining parts can be summarized as follows: (II) the evaluation of differences and similarities among languages, especially of exotic languages in relation to our own; (III) the significance of linguistic patterns for the basic outlook of a people; (IV) the relation between a people's vocabulary and their other interests; (V) how speaking enters into norms of interaction among persons, and into the acquisition of such norms by children; (VI) how the motives of play and art are manifested linguistically—the ludic and aesthetic aspects of speech; (VII) the relation between levels or varieties of speech, on the one hand, and types of community and their boundaries, on the other; (VIII) how social factors enter into linguistic change; (IX) modes of classifying and interpreting resemblances among languages, especially as to their historical import; (X) awareness of our own scholarly and scientific activity as one conditioned aspect of the place of language in culture.

Beyond the foci of attention signaled by the sections, the reader should be aware of a number of other themes, and conceptual distinctions, that pervade anthropological concerns with language and are valuable for their interpretation, as pointers, or lines of explication. (For convenience of identification, the themes and distinctions are numbered consecutively.)

First, there are two themes which have to do with the vocation of anthropology, and which can be traced as keys to its history: (1) interpreting the relation of other ways of life (including other ways of speech) to our own, and (2) standing between the natural sciences and the humanities in method and subject matter. The first theme carries with it the danger of succumbing to one or the other of two temptations that dog the interpretive tasks; *failure of empathy*, the "classical" error, too readily assuming a single norm, often our own, by which to judge diversity; and *failure of identity*, the "romantic" reaction to diversity, giving one's heart too wholly or readily to another way of life, substituting its norm (real or imagined) for our own. The problem of maintaining a proper balance carries over into the second theme. Often enough the anthropologist find himself attacked from both sides, as too "humanistic," too "subjective," or impure in method to qualify as a scientist, and as too "mechanistic," too concerned with explicit method and objectifying materials to be acceptable to defenders of the humanities. Yet he is committed to honor the gods of both, the necessity of objectivity and generality on the one hand, of neglecting nothing of human value on the other. (On the perspectives of anthropology, for those unacquainted with them, two excellent succinct treatments are Clyde Kluckhohn, "Common Humanity and Diverse Cultures," in Daniel Lerner (Ed.), *The Human Meaning of the Social Sciences*, pp. 245–284 (New York: Meridian Books), and Alfred Kroeber, "The History of the Personality of Anthropology," AA, 1959, 61:3.398–404.)

Of equal importance are two linguistic themes, (3) the extension of the concept and method of structural analysis as the key to understanding language and language-linked phenomena, both descriptively and historically, and (4) the key role of language in human life, and hence of linguistics in its study. The first implies the distinction between (5) structure and variation, the second that between (6) structure and function. What one understands by the concept and method of structural analysis, and how one phrases the key role of language, of course may vary a good deal. In general, in fact, these distinctions, and those to follow, have their prime importance as guides to understanding differences of emphasis and approach, and what controversy may be about. What one counts as structure, as opposed to variation; as structurally relevant or irrelevant; how and where one expects to find structure; whether one sees certain phenomena as deviations from a structural norm, or sees the structure as inhering in the range of variation; to what extent one conceives structure as inherent in certain data, or as a model, perhaps an a priori one, of the analyst's devising (a contrast made famous in the profession by F. W. Householder, Jr., as "God's truth" vs. "hocus pocus")—questions such as these bring out significant differences in the views scholars take, for example, towards the relation of language and linguistic method to other phenomena of anthropological interest, and affect the work of anthropological interest that gets done. One of the most crucial questions is that of one's criteria for structural relevance and validity, a problem which Kenneth L. Pike has signaled as that of "emic" vs. "etic" classification (see his article in

Part I). A similar question deals with one's conception of the role of language in human life, for such a conception implies some assumption, explicit or not, as to what function or functions of language exist, or are primary, and as to how language enters into the history of the child or the species.

Related to the concept of structural analysis are three similar, but by no means identical, distinctions between (7) language and speech; (8) code and message; (9) habit and behavior. Assumptions about the nature of these distinctions, and what phenomena should be assigned to each, underlie a good deal of current work and controversy. Together they point to the fundamental questions of the locus, and the object, of what one describes and treats as "linguistic." Related also is the question of what linguistic phenomena one treats as (10) product and as process; (11) as historically given or as on-going activity; or, how one treats vis-a-vis each other the distinctions of (12) synchronic vs. diachronic, on the one hand, and (13) static vs. dynamic, on the other. A good deal of unconscious inconsistency and confusion is possible when moving between such distinctions, or between them and one or more of the preceding pairs.

One must keep in mind, of course, the distinctions noted earlier between (14) language and culture, (15) a language and a culture, and (16) linguistics and anthropology, the corresponding terms of which are sometimes unjustifiably merged. It is important also to note how the relations between the terms of one of the preceding three distinctions may be conceived. In particular, is the relation of language to other aspects of culture seen as that of (17) evidence, or instance? Is relationship sought in terms of correlation between the two, or in terms of linguistic phenomena as an index of something else? Or are linguistic phenomena treated as themselves a manifestation of the cultural point in question, whether or not they correlate in some particular way with other aspects? Both approaches may be appropriate in some contexts, and misleading in others.

Here we have often to deal with a deceptive slipping back and forth between two uses of the term "culture," between (18) its use as a theoretical or generic term (in which case its defining characteristics imply the inclusion of language), and its use as a convenient shorthand for aspects of culture, except language. The second use, of course, underlies such expressions as "language and culture." Such a use is paralleled with other aspects of culture, but not all; the exceptions are perhaps ethos and social structure. (Witness the use of "art and culture," "music and culture," "technology and culture," but not, say, "kinship and culture," in recent anthropological writing.) The criterion for the second use seems to be that the field in question involves some sort of study of physical objects (including texts here as objects) that has become associated with technical competence. What makes the slipping back and forth between the two uses of "culture" a rather vicious habit is the fact that the generality and prestige of the first use may be implicitly carried over into the second. Then the implicit parenthesis of "X and (other aspects of) culture" is erased, and the X relegated to a periphery, the burden of proving a relevance to the central term being its own. (No one asks in so many words about the relation between "kinship and culture," although it must sometimes seem as problematic as that of language.)

The second sense of "culture" is, of course, used in the title of the present book, and the distinction implied is likely to continue to be a useful one, given the ease with which language can be distinguished as a phenomenon; the continuation of a distinct discipline specializing in its study; and the awkwardness of longer phrases such as "language and other aspects of culture and society," as against the economy and familiarity of the formula, "language and X." No practical harm is done, and there are quite appropriate occasions for use of the formula, so long as one remembers that on a theoretical plane the situation is different. Failure to remember can confuse or impair anthropological thinking and research, setting up false antitheses and leaving significant phenomena unstudied.

Part of the problem is that there is a second, and similar familiar usage to cope with, the habit of referring to "word and deed," of saying that "actions speak louder than words," so that it is sometimes necessary for scientists to remind themselves that the use of words is itself an act, speaking itself a form of behavior.

The question of the relation between language and culture often involves a complex of issues that may be summed up under the heading of striking a balance between language as (19) a "help" and a "hindrance"—adopting two terms once used by Sapir (1933a; p. 11 in Mandelbaum (Ed.) (1949)). One may look at language as making thought possible, and one may also look at it as molding and hence restricting thought. One may see language as a powerful and essential means of human communication, and one may also view languages as artificial barriers to international understanding. And so on. Involved here are such issues as (20) the degree of interdependence between language and thought, or the rest of culture, or society, or personality, or behavior, and (21) the relative preponderance of influence in one or the other direction. Also involved is the distinction between (22) the potential of a language as an open system, and its actual capacity as learned and used at a given place and time; and the distinction already made (14, 15, 16) between the generic properties of language and culture, the particular properties of *a* language and *a* culture, and the particular properties of the material studied by certain linguists and anthropologists.

Another complex of issues may be characterized as involving the distribution relative to each other of languages, as named units, and other anthropological units, whether historically ("race, language, culture") or contemporaneously (multilingualism, boundaries of speech communities, etc.). Here often enters the question of (23) part in relation to whole. It is a question of what set of features, or sample, may be accepted as representative, so that one speaks of it, or takes it as identical with, a language on the one hand, and a culture, or society, or personality, on the other. Often enough a finding of lack of relation between language and culture, or between languages, depends upon the particular conception of one or the other term with which one begins, and may be an artifact of that partiality. Conversely, an equating of two units may be similarly based. Two recurrent examples of the problem are the equation of a "language" with that fraction of its features which, through retention from a common ancestor, give it its genetic classification, and the equation of a "language" with that aspect of linguistic phenomena which may be caught up in a linguist's description. The answer, of course, is to investigate beforehand the validity of the set of features, or sample, as a basis for the purpose in question.

Of general importance is the extent to which (24) uniformity, or difference, is stressed, whether as between languages, between a language and a culture, within a language, or whatever; and also, of course, the way in which uniformity and difference are conceived. Here we have a principal linguistic instance of the anthropological vocation to relate other ways of life to our own. The task can be put as accounting for the uniformities and differences in the natural condition of mankind. So phrased, it underlies not only many theoretical notions and cross-cultural studies, but also classificatory work generally. Changes of relative emphasis upon uniformity and difference, and the ways in which they have been conceived (evolutionary, historical, functional, and so forth) have played a great part in the history of linguistics and anthropology. (The dimension of part in relation to whole is again involved.)

Most important of all, perhaps, in the present connection is the distinction between (25) the interdependence of language and culture (or, a language and a culture, linguistics and anthropology), on the one hand, and their relative autonomy on the other. The emphasis in this book is of course on interdependence, but, as the preceding distinctions, and the contents themselves, make clear, there is a good deal of variation in opinion as to the nature of the interdependence.

These distinctions may be helpful in teaching and thinking about the study of speech and language in an anthropological context. Let me now explain further the plan and origin of the book.

In general the selections have been made with a view to showing the development, and the range, of anthropological concerns with language. (The list of contents, and their juxtapositions, may themselves be informative.) Each section has an introduction to point up these matters. In addition, each selection is followed by a reference note, giving background information from the original footnotes, and the article's own references, if any. The reference notes frequently contain further references, topically arranged, on the subject of the article. As a means of economy, recurrent references are given in full only once in a general bibliography at the end of the book, being identified elsewhere by author and year (e.g., Sapir, 1921). Thus an article, or the introductory comment of a reference note, may contain citations to be found both in the immediately following list and in the general bibliography. Together, the reference notes and general bibliography form something of a working bibliography of the entire field. An alphabetical guide to the topics for which special bibliography is given follows the general bibliography.

As to the contents themselves, each scholar would doubtless make a more or less different choice. My own conception of the book and of individual contents has changed a good deal since the project was first conceived (as a reader in American Indian linguistics), and since work on the broader scale first began at the Center for Advanced Study in the Behavioral Sciences, while I was a Fellow there in 1957–1958. The present contents reflect the helpful advice of a number of colleagues, who responded to a request for comment on a preliminary list. The final selection and responsibility, of course, remain mine, and there are no doubt biases, conscious and unconscious, that will variously please and displease; I am aware how much the modification of the list over the years since the book's inception reflects not only the advice of others, but also my own intellectual development during the period. In support of the present list, I may say that there has been a positive reason for every inclusion, and that as much has been included as has been practically possible. Moreover, the bibliographies can quickly lead to other literature and points of view. Also, good students find disagreement stimulating. Some of the articles have been included because I have found them useful starting-points for lectures and class discussion. If one of them provokes someone to plunge into the literature, or the field, to prove a point, or sets off a chain of thought that transcends the offending view, the hours of correspondence, editing, and proofreading will have been justified.

Several specific considerations affecting the selection should be explained. I have mostly avoided materials that have already been reprinted, or otherwise made easily available. In particular I have not used anything from the selected writings of Boas, Sapir, and Lee; the recently re-issued memorial volume to Sapir (*Language*, *Culture*, *Personality*, edited by Spier, Hallowell, Newman); and the *Language in Culture* volume discussing Whorf, edited by Hoijer and distributed as a memoir by the American Anthropological Association. The one exception is Whorf. All his significant writings in the field of language and culture have been collected by Carroll (*Language*, *Thought*, *and Reality*), and some of his essays have been reprinted many times, yet Part IV could hardly appear without him. I have chosen an early and little known piece, hitherto published only by Carroll, which sets Whorf's other writings in perspective, both as to the balance of his own views and interests, and as to his place in the tradition of American anthropology.

Except for some articles of historical significance, the contents have been chosen more for subject-matter, than for author, and the absence of a well known name is accidental, as is the recurrence of another. In one case it proved just not possible to obtain from one author an article for which I had hoped for some time. On the other hand, I have tried not to favor any one author unduly, and, other things equal, have chosen an article by someone not otherwise represented. Undoubtedly accidents of personal history have unconsciously influenced the outcome. Of course sometimes a scholar whose name is linked with a topic seems not to have happened to write an appropriate or available piece; sometimes articles have had to be omitted because of practical considerations of size, difficulty of editing, or cost. Such are the trials of an editor of an anthology, and indeed, some articles had been edited for inclusion before one problem or another forced reluctant omission.

I had at first thought to include nothing of my own, despite several suggestions, but finally decided that the historical account of Kroeber's work was the most useful piece available for pairing with that by Malkiel in the final section, as well as a complement to the Foreword and an appropriate conclusion for the book as a whole.

Just as easily accessible articles have been avoided, so those difficult of access have often been preferred. I have taken special pleasure in finding a pertinent but not well known article, especially if by a leading anthropologist not best known for his work with language. There has been an effort to have a reasonable geographical distribution, although my own specialization in the American field, and hence closer knowledge of its literature, may show. The proportion of articles dealing with the American Indian, however, reflects far more the concentration of American anthropology in that area until recently. A decade from now a revision of this book would be weighted much more toward Africa, Oceania, and Asia. I have tried to represent the anthropology-linked traditions of linguistic work in England and France, the two countries whose linguistics and anthropology are most influentially tied to those of the United States.

Finally, I hope that the inclusion of two reviews will help call attention to the importance of reviews in the development of the field, and the necessity of consulting them. It is especially true in linguistics that a review may be a significant publication in its own right.

As to the placing of articles in sections, the present arrangement has grown by trial-and-error from repeated shufflings. Some articles have ties with more than one topic. The index to topical bibliographies and the reference notes help make it possible to trace such connections, and should be useful to teachers wishing to make reading assignments in terms of a course organization of a different structure, and to students wishing to follow their own noses.

Certain points about the editing of the contents need to be noted. In most of the cases the present selection represents the complete original. There are two kinds of exception. In some cases the present selection represents a continuous portion of a book or longer article, whose other contents would have been less relevant or out of place. Such (in order of appearance in the book) are Boas on linguistics and ethnology; Firth's discussion of sociological linguistics; Strehlow's comments on Aranda traditions; the portion from Boas' monograph on Kwakiutl place names; the section from Goodenough's Truk monograph (revised for this book); the sections from Gayton and Newman's Yokuts monograph; and Kroeber's discussion of taxonomy. In a few cases an intervening part of the original has been omitted. Such cases (all with approval of the author, except in the cases of the deceased Boas and Whorf, of course) are Boas' remarks on grammatical categories; Hill's Cherokee analysis; Whorf's manuscript; Shimkin's account of Wind River Shoshone literature; Sebeok's analysis of Cheremis charms; and Gudschinsky's account of lexicostatistical technique. In the case of Sebeok's article, another section subsequently written, has been added. All such intervening omissions have been marked.

To present as uniform a volume as possible, avoiding clashes and vagaries of style, and to economize, footnotes to the original articles have frequently been incorporated into the main text, if of substantive relevance, or assembled in the reference note at the end, if bearing on the backgrounds of the material (sponsorship, source of data, orthography used). Citations have also been standardized, and incomplete references have been corrected insofar as practicable. In addition, orthography has been standardized where possible. The orthographic changes, primarily a question of conformity to contemporary American usage, have been explained in a separate Note on Orthography. Scholars must thus consult the original publication, should a question arise as to a point of form in these respects.

It is a pleasant task to be able to thank so many for their help in making the book a reality. To the late Alfred Kroeber, I am indebted in many ways, not least for his Foreword to this book, written at the expense of other commitments. To the late Clyde Kluckhohn, I should like to dedicate the book as a whole. It was conceived and carried near to completion during years at Harvard, when the opportunities given me were owed largely to him. All of us are indebted to him, as to Kroeber, for championing linguistics in anthropology during the last decade.

Actual work on the book began at the Center for Advanced Studies in the Behavioral Sciences during 1957–1958, and the use of its facilities for the purpose is but one of the reasons I have to remember the Center, and its guiding hands, Ralph Tyler and Preston Cutler, with gratitude. Bob Hogan there, Martha Robinson at Harvard, and Clay Denman and Grace Lee at Berkeley helped provide the material manuscript; Karl Reisman at Harvard, and Joseph McHugh, Bob Scholte, Laura Gould at Berkeley contributed to its editing. I am grateful to the Center; the Laboratory of Social Relations at Harvard and its late director, Sam Stouffer; the Peabody Museum of American Archaeology and Ethnology, its director J. O. Brew, and its librarian, Margaret Currier; the Faculty Research Committee of the University of California at Berkeley; and the Social Science Research Council (through an Auxiliary Research Award) for support and aid of my planning, delving, editing, and writing.

I should like to thank all those who have taken the time and trouble to answer inquiries and to give advice, especially the authors for their cooperation and assistance, and generally the authors, editors, and institutions who have generously granted the permission necessary to such a collection. I hope that they will regard the book as having justified their confidence.

Harry Hoijer must be singled out for special thanks; the book was first conceived as a joint undertaking with him. I should like also to mention Martin Joos, who suggested the appropriateness of "linguistic anthropology," rather than "anthropological linguistics," as name for the concerns represented here;

and Harold Conklin, who helped shape the present form of the title. My warmest thanks go also to Ethel Albert, Robert Austerlitz, Ignacio Bernal, William Bittle, Bernard Bloch, William Bright, Robbins Burling, Denzel Carr, John Carroll, Joseph Casagrande, Desmond Cole, Richard Dorson, Edward Dozier, Samuel Elbert, Murray Emeneau, Susan Ervin, John Fischer, Charles Frake, David French, Morton Fried, Paul Friedrich, Paul Garvin, H. A. Gleason, Jr., Walter Goldschmidt, Ward Goodenough, Joseph Greenberg, Sarah Gudschinsky, John Gumperz, Mary Haas, Eugene Hammel, A. A. Hill, Charles F. Hockett, Fred W. Householder, Jr., Melville Jacobs, Frederica de Laguna, Dorothy Lee, Alexander Leighton, Fang Kuei Li, Robert Longacre, Floyd Lounsbury, Daniel McCall, Norman McQuown, Samuel Martin, Laura Nader, Stanley Newman, Eugene Nida, Kenneth Pike, Frank H. Roberts, A. Kimball Romney, Irving Rouse, John Rowe, J. David Sapir, Bob Scholte, Thomas Sebeok, Milton Singer, Henry Lee Smith, Jr., Robert F. Spencer, Edward H. Spicer, Leslie Spier, Volney Stefflre, Theodore Stern, William Sturtevant, Morris Swadesh, Sol Tax, Douglas Taylor, Karl Teeter, Maner Thorpe, George Trager, Evon Vogt, Carl Voegelin, Florence Voegelin, Uriel Weinreich, Hans Wolff, William Wonderley, John Yegerlehner.

The last word of thanks must go to my wife, Virginia, and children, Robert and Alison. All helped. None can be happier to see the book completed.

DELL HYMES

Orthographic Note

The student of languages and what they disclose must adjust to a variety of orthographies. As one turns from one language to the next, or even from one publication about the same language to the next, the same sound may be found represented by different symbols, and the same symbol found representing different sounds.

Such variation is partly unavoidable, for scientific and practical reasons. To write each language as if its sounds had to be differentiated graphically from all other unlike sounds in all the languages of the world would be absurd. The alphabet of a given language would be required to express particularities irrelevant to both the system of the language and the needs of its users, swelling typography and printing costs, and impeding both scientific analysis and practical purposes such as literacy training and education. If we accept the scientific analysis of a language as a system, and consider the practical needs of the users of a language, then we accept the desirability of a simple orthography for each language. We accept also then, as consequence, the necessity of some special learning of the phonetic and phonemic values of the symbols used for each language, for our cultural tradition provides only a limited number of simple symbols.

There are, to be sure, universally recognized limits to the allocation of symbols to sounds: "p" and "b", for example, are used always for some sort of labial stop, not for any other position or manner of consonant, or for any kind of vowel. To continue the example, there are, however, a variety of kinds of labial stops, differing not only as to voicing, a difference often implied by "p" (voiceless) and "b" (voiced) themselves, but also as to aspiration, glottalization, length, tenseness, fortis quality. Two sources of variation in the values of symbols result.

In so far as such features are present but not pertinent to the phonological system of the language, there is no point in symbolizing them. Their presence is properly indicated, not in the orthography, but in the phonetic description of the language, and, to some extent, in the explanation of the values of the symbols used for representing the language in anthropological and other accounts.

In so far as such features are present and are pertinent, differences among the systems of languages may still lead to variation. Suppose two languages, for one of which the only relevant difference among stops is between voiceless and voiced (the voiceless series being also aspirated), and for the other of which, the relevant differences among stops distinguish voiceless aspirated, voiceless unaspirated, and voiced stops. (The situation would be the same for our purpose if the first language distinguished aspirated and unaspirated stops, the aspirated series being also voiceless.) The simplest orthographies, structurally and practically, will be "p", "b" in the first case, "p‘," "p", "b" in the second. In the second, "pʰ" might replace "p‘ ".) Similar considerations apply in many instances, dependent, as here, on an interrelation between the kind and number of symbols simple for the language in question, and the limited set of simple symbols cultural tradition provides. Explanation of the values of the symbols used for representing a language commonly will disclose variation of this sort.

There is another source of orthographic variation that is, in principle, avoidable. Sometimes the same sound is represented by different symbols, and the same symbol used for different sounds, not because of differences in the language concerned, but because of accidents of history and preference on the part of users or students of the language. The prestige attached to particular orthographic traditions, and the desire to resemble or to differ from them may play a part. Within the scientific community such differences exist, for example, as between the alphabet of the International Phonetic Association (1949), widely used in Europe and Africa; the principles adopted specifically for Africa by the International Institute of African Languages and Cultures (1930); and two orthographies widely used in American anthropology, the earliest formulation of modern standing by Boas and others (1916), and the more recent formulation by Sapir and some of his students (Herzog *et al.* 1934). There are also practical considerations of the type available to different printers, and of the symbols available on standard typewriters. Lounsbury (1953, pp. 402–403) and Gleason (1955, pp. 222–225; 1961, pp. 314–316) discuss orthographies likely to be encountered by anthropologists. The general problem of choice of orthography in a field situation is discussed by Pike (1947), Croft (1951), Garvin (1954), and Voegelin and Voegelin (1959). (See also the references on literacy, orthography, etc., with Bull's article in Part VIII, especially those by Berry, Gudschinsky, and Smalley; see also *The Bible Translator* in which orthographic problems are occasionally discussed. A systematic study of such problems among missionaries is under way by Andrée Sjoberg.)

There is no early prospect that orthographic differences dependent on tradition and preference will be resolved. For the sake of consistent style, and the beginning student, I have tried to standardize the use of symbols in this book, wherever a substitution of symbol could be made without impairing the accuracy or utility. (Where a standard orthography would have been made unrecognizable (e.g., Sanskrit), or reanalysis of the data would have been implied, the orthography has been left unchanged.) The charts accompanying this note show the symbols chosen for general use. The charts are limited in several respects. They show only symbols used in this book. They assume familiarity with the principles that underlie such charts. The position of a symbol in the charts cannot be taken as precise for its use in a given language, but only as indicating an approximate value; the fricative types of sound represented by Θ, ꞩ, and ɬ, for example, have a certain range as to position of articulator and point of articulation, "r"s come in a variety of forms, flapped, tapped, trilled, and as in "Dvorak." For symbols and sound types not required in this book, and understanding of the analytic bases and conventions of phonetic charts and symbols, see texts and manuals such as Pike (1947), Gleason (1955, 1961), Hockett (1955, 1958), and Trager (1958). Comparison of these texts and manuals will disclose some of the variation possible in the values of symbols and in the symbols for values, beyond that indicated here.

REFERENCE NOTE

BOAS, FRANZ, P. E. GODDARD, E. SAPIR, and A. L. KROEBER

1916. *Phonetic Transcription of Indian Languages: Report of Committee of American Anthropological Association.* (Smithsonian Miscellaneous Collections, 6:6.) Washington, D.C.: Smithsonian Institution.

HERZOG, G., S. NEWMAN, E. SAPIR, M. HAAS SWADESH, M. SWADESH, and C. VOEGELIN

1934. Some Orthographic Recommendations. *AA*, *36*:629–631.

INTERNATIONAL INSTITUTE OF AFRICAN LANGUAGES AND CULTURES

1930. *Practical Orthography of African Languages.* Revised Edition. (Memorandum I.) London: Oxford University Press.

INTERNATIONAL PHONETIC ASSOCIATION

1949. *The Principles of the International Phonetic Association*, being a description of the International Phonetic Alphabet and the manner of using it, illustrated by texts in 51 languages. London: International Phonetic Association, Department of Phonetics, University College.

TRAGER, GEORGE L.

1958. *Phonetics: Glossary and Tables.* (Studies in Linguistics, Occasional Papers 6.) Buffalo: University of Buffalo, Department of Anthropology and Linguistics.

VOEGELIN, C. F., and F. M. VOEGELIN

1959. Guide for Transcribing Unwritten Languages in Field Work. *AL 1*(6):1–28.

part I

THE SCOPE OF LINGUISTIC ANTHROPOLOGY

Introduction

THE SCOPE OF STUDY of language in an anthropological context depends most of all upon two things, the exigencies of field work and the nature of theoretical orientations. This has been true of the currents that have formed linguistic anthropology and holds true today.

The two main lines of development have been (1) the gradual growth of coordinated substantive knowledge about the world's languages since the Renaissance and Age of Discovery through the efforts of missionaries, explorers, travelers, administrators, philologists, and linguists and anthropologists proper, and (2) the participation of such linguistic knowledge in changes and varieties of intellectual outlook, as, for example, in the change from the Enlightenment to the Romantic movement, and in competing views of the character and nexus of linguistics as a psychological, historical, or sociological discipline.

We gain a useful perspective through awareness of the course of such developments, especially as a balance against the common tendency to take the latest as best and current reputations as fixed. Intellectual fashions shape a good deal of the work done in anthropology and linguistics and hence affect the scope of their intersection, often to the detriment of continuity and cumulativeness. Here brief note can be taken only of the three recent lines of development which have the greatest relevance to contemporary American anthropology: one English, one French, and one, of course, American.

Sir Edward Tylor's chapters on language in his *Primitive Culture* (1871) and *Anthropology* (1881) may be taken as the first major treatment of the subject as part of a conscious general anthropology that has continuity to the present day. Tylor had predecessors in England, of course, notably R. G. Latham, a great figure now unfortunately neglected, who also linked linguistic and ethnological interests. Latham closely anticipated the later views of Sweet, Malinowski, and Firth with his emphasis upon "living philology"—seeking general principles in the study of on-going speech communities. Tylor dealt mainly with language in its historical and theoretical aspects in relation to the nature and development of culture. Marett's *Anthropology* (1912) added the crucial importance of language in field work, a theme which was subsequently dramatized in English anthropology by Malinowski and reiterated by Nadel.

Malinowski is the founding father of concerns with language in contemporary British anthropology. The other major figure, Radcliffe-Brown, paid little attention to linguistics, considering it the most easily dispensable aspect of a "natural science of society," although he also voiced interest in a study of comparative epistemology which would have had an important linguistic dimension. Malinowski (1920) very early proclaimed "an urgent need for an Ethnolinguistic theory, a theory for the guidance of linguistic research to be done among natives and in connection with ethnographic study." Sound theory and extensive study of the facts were seen as interdependent, and theory was conceived as aiming at synchronic rather than historical relations. Such a theory "would show us what is essential in language and what therefore must remain the same throughout the whole range of linguistic varieties; how linguistic forms are influenced by physiological, mental, social, and other cultural elements; what is the real nature of Meaning and Form, and how they correspond; a theory which, in fine, would give us a set of well-founded plastic definitions of grammatical concepts."

In 1923 Malinowski's famous "Meaning in Primitive Languages" appeared, mixing empirical observation with questionable or mistaken evolutionary notions in support of Ogden and Richards' theory of communication and focusing on language as a mode of action, not a countersign of thought. Later in *Coral Gardens and Their Magic*, Part II (1935), Malinowski elaborated his ethnographic theory of language in chapters interspersed among concrete descriptions meant to exemplify a necessary method of linguistic presentation. The method was essentially the extended presentation of cultural commentary and context for a text. Malinowski was facile as a polyglot, but weak in descriptive linguistics. His specific accounts seem unsatisfactory today, partly for technical inadequacy, partly for certain hobby-horses, but his general orientation retains great importance. It has shaped the conviction in British social anthropology that one must use the native language in field work, and through the concept of context of situation and Malinowski's relationship with J. R. Firth, it has influenced the development of descriptive linguistics proper, contributing to the distinctiveness of the modern British school. Firth himself wrote: "Malinowski's contribution in English to the advancement of the study of such languages [exotic] from the point of view of a professional anthropologist is a brilliant enhancement of the English tradition and we can be proud to include him as one of the makers of linguistics as we now understand it in this country" (1957a, p. 94).

Other principal figures in the relations between linguistic and anthropological work in the British Isles in this century have been Hocart, Haddon, and, of course, A. H. Gardiner and J. R. Firth, both of whom were involved with Malinowski in the development of the point of view that is singled out here. (For their interrelations with Malinowski, see Gardiner, 1919, and Firth, 1957a.) Subsequently, Robins (1959), McIntosh (1952), and Hill (1958) have contributed on the linguistic side, and Nadel (1951, 1954) and Evans-Pritchard (1929 and other works cited in general bibliography) on the side of anthropology.

In the British point of view just sketched, the relation between language and other aspects of culture is seen as interdependence between different aspects of the same event or social action. Language itself is seen as primarily an activity and its engagement in social context as a necessary part of its description. Its use in communication tends to be seen primarily in terms of the function of controlling or influencing action.

In France the modern linking of anthropology and linguistics must be traced to four great scholars, the linguists de Saussure and Meillet, the sociologist Durkheim, and the anthropologist Mauss. (The difference of label can be minimized, for Durkheim and Mauss collaborated closely, Durkheim has influenced American and British anthropology even more than Mauss, and both could be termed "social anthropologists" today.) De Saussure is celebrated as the father of structuralism on the European continent; for successful advocacy of the existence and autonomy of a synchronic linguistics with a system as its object; and for his distinction between *la langue* and *la parole*, the former pertaining to the society and the collective norm, the latter to the individual person and event. (The proper interpretation of *la langue* vs. *la parole*—what de Saussure meant, or should have meant—has been one of the most controversial topics in linguistic theory.) Meillet is noted not only as a great figure of historical and comparative linguistics, but also for his forthright enrolling of linguistics in the ranks of social science, e.g., in the opening pages of the classic article in which he presents social stratification as a key to explaining semantic change (1906b). Linguistics is viewed in terms of Durkheim's conception of sociology as an autonomous study with "social facts" as its object; Meillet ranges the collective autonomous object of linguistics, *la langue*, as a social fact *par excellence*. (Cf. Sommerfelt, 1961, and Doroszewski's analysis [1933] of de Saussure's conception of *la langue* vs. *la parole* as an effort to mediate between the views of two sociologists, Durkheim and Tarde.)

Among the most noted linguists who have continued this French tradition of linguistics as a social science are Marcel Cohen and the Norwegian, Alf Sommerfelt, as well as those associated with the new journal *L'Homme*, e.g., Emile Benveniste (an editor) and André Haudricourt. Of anthropologists the outstanding figure is Claude Levi-Strauss.

In the viewpoint of this school the relation between language and other aspects of culture tends to be seen as one of congruence between parallel systems or products of collective psychology. Language itself is seen as primarily a shared, socially inherited system, the use of which in communication tends to be seen primarily in terms of the cognitive function of distinguishing or expressing meanings. (There have, of course, been

French (and Swiss) schools with strong emphasis on the affective function of expressing emotion, which Malinowski also stressed, but as derivative of a general pragmatic function, not as primary or autonomous).

It is of course unjust to impute exclusive emphasis in the two countries, within these two schools or without, on the points of view just sketched. But the contrast drawn is representative of the main thrust of each, as the papers included here by Malinowski and Firth, on the one hand, and Levi-Strauss and Mauss, on the other, indicate, and as other of their writings confirm. The contrast itself is an instructive one for any theoretical conception of the relation of language to culture. Put into a formula, both views interpret language and culture as modes or facets of a single underlying factor, but in the one the unity is that of the event, in the other that of the mind.

Turning to the United States, we can trace an involvement of linguistics in anthropological study to the early interest in American Indian languages as indicative of the origins and character of the natives of the New World, an interest which Jefferson and Thoreau, among other noted figures, actively shared. The scope of American linguistic anthropology continued to be defined in terms of the American Indian throughout the nineteenth century and into the twentieth. A roster of names would include Pickering, Barton, Gallatin, Hale, Gibbs, Gatschet, Whitney, Brinton, Powell, Henshaw, Dorsey, Mooney, Hewitt, Boas, Swanton, Dixon, Kroeber, Goddard, Sapir, Lowie, Radin, Mason, Harrington, Bloomfield, down to the generation preponderantly represented in this book. (In the more recent work other areas of the world begin to figure more notably.) That almost without exception each did some direct field work and concerned himself with unraveling genetic relationships (all did one or the other) is testimony enough to the two leading and enduring characteristics of American work during the period.

From early days field work was of practical value for information as to the character and relations of important Indian societies, or at least of scholarly value to preserve knowledge of disappearing ones, and subsequently it became a professional cachet as well. Genetic relationship among languages was seized upon rather early also, as the best basis for ordering the mass of New World tribes and ethnological data. Hence until recently, work on the classification of American Indian languages was of prime interest to almost every American anthropologist.

Of the other interests with considerable continuity in American anthropology, perhaps the chief one has been the interpretation of the origin and social significance of linguistic categories. Such an interest goes far back in the histories of linguistics and anthropology, even where Amerindian languages are concerned, at least to Europe and Wilhelm von Humboldt early in the nineteenth century. But as a focus for the role of language in culture, of linguistics in anthropology, the continuity and importance of the interest has a special prominence in American work.

American work has to a large extent shared the predisposition of the French school to see the unity of language and culture as one of cultural product or social heritage rather than as one of event or social action. Another notable trait of American linguistic anthropology, the collection of texts, has, like field work, a tradition with a long and distinguished history in other countries as well.

The major American figure and a watershed between an earlier and later period is, of course, Franz Boas. As a field investigator and analyst, he pioneered in the quality of his work, especially on the North Pacific coast. As a teacher and instigator of field work, he was relentless in setting students at linguistic research and in seeking funds to support it. As an editor, he brought out the *Handbook of American Indian Languages*, founded the *International Journal of American Linguistics*, and found outlets for native language texts in various scholarly series.

That Boas was practically the shaper of American professional anthropology, through his training of students at Columbia, is well known. That he was equally significant for general linguistics in the United States, beyond the Americanist field, is perhaps less widely realized, but the fact can be traced in his influence on three major figures of the first half of the century, Sapir, Kroeber, and Bloomfield. Sapir was Boas' student, inspired by Boas' shattering of accepted generalizations to move from comparative philology into anthropology, where he was perhaps the one authentic genius to grace it in this century (the judgment is Kroeber's). Kroeber was also Boas' student and has recorded the impact of Boas as fieldworker and teacher on him and the field at large.

As fieldworker:

> In the last decade of the nineteenth century, the linguistic investigations of Boas began to appear. The importance of these is twofold. Boas first clearly realized that it was indispensable for each language to be described in terms of its own configuration, instead of on a preconceived abstract scheme which in practice often came to little more than a modification of Latin grammar. Like Gatschet and Dorsey he also realized the necessity of grammars and lexica being supplemented by solid bodies of texts in the original language. These two realizations, coupled with an untiring energy and capacity for work, plus the ability to inspire others, have made him the dominant figure in the development of American native linguistic science (Kroeber, 1939b, p. 117).

And as teacher:

> University instruction in the subject commenced in the 1880's with Brinton at Pennsylvania, and Boas, first at Clark, then at Columbia. Brinton, not being a field worker, had necessarily to confine his teaching to discussion of already published results: it failed to elicit a lively response and soon dwindled away. Boas developed the method of empirical instruction, setting his students to discover the structure of a language by analysis of texts. This equivalent of laboratory method introduced the student to an attitude of independent research. It also served as specific training

for new field investigation, which was subsequently provided whenever possible. This method naturally proved to be intensely stimulating to capable students, and has been universally followed since (pp. 118-119).

Bloomfield, who with Sapir has shaped recent American descriptive linguistics, phrased a dedication as follows: "In our work we have thought of Franz Boas, the pioneer and master in the sudy of American languages and the teacher, in one or another sense, of us all" (in Hoijer, 1946, p. 6).

Part of Boas' great strength was the fact that he combined the interests of humanistic scholarship with the goals of science, reflecting and helping transmit the hybrid parentage of anthropology itself. (Whether we today can adopt his conception of the *means* of science is another matter.) Trained in physics and geography, he contributed importantly to biological anthropology and statistical method, yet he studied intensively language, folklore, and art. His interpretations of cultural process show a concern to weigh the natural determinants and conditions of human life, on the one hand, and man's creative achievements within them, on the other. The combination of perspectives shows explicitly and succinctly in a passage of an official report. Beginning with a strong humanistic motive, it concludes with as strong a statement of scientific reasons for linguistic study. (Although the passage is couched in terms of American languages, there is a general application.)

[*I. Scientific Position of the Work.*] The need for work in American native languages arises from the simple fact that different communities speak different languages. On our continent, north of Mexico, there are many stocks of apparently unrelated languages. Some of these consist of only a single language, others of many more or less closely related languages. Even if we did not know how to derive any further knowledge from the record of a language, we should feel a powerful and instinctive urge to record all these forms of speech, much as archaeologists study ancient civilizations or astronomers the distant bodies of the sky. Perhaps by an act of faith, civilized man regards this intellectual mastery of the universe as one of his very few most important activities.

Many among the American languages are spoken by a few old persons, sometimes by a single person. With their deaths the languages will be extinct. Not a few are gone, and there is no possibility of recovering them. It would seem a duty of our time to recover whatever can be saved in the two Americas, particularly in our own country.

Other nations and posterity will judge us more by our accomplishment of this task than by more practical achievements. Moreover, it is a task to be performed in limited time; we could not, if we would, delay the replacement by English of our native languages.

Our study, however, has a deeper scientific value than is implied by the mere mastery of the facts. From the records of languages we are able to derive far-reaching historical conclusions. Our knowledge of human speech in its varieties and development represents a strategic point, at the present time, in the advance of science.

Where two or more languages are evidently related, the comparative method of linguistic study—one of the major scientific achievements of the nineteenth century—enables us to trace their history in detail back to an early point in time. In the American field such studies have been begun with marked success in the case of the Algonquian and the Athapascan families; similar work for Siouan, Iroquoian, and Uto-Aztecan will probably soon be possible. The results of such comparative study carry us far into pre-Columbian time.

In the progress of science hitherto, there has been a painful contrast between our great achievement in physical and biological science and our failure to gain scientific understanding of human affairs. To the latter half of this contrast there is one striking exception, our ability to record languages scientifically and to derive scientific results from these records. We account for this by the consideration that language is the simplest and the basic feature among those which make up specifically human activity. Whatever our literary and artistic or our philosophical and religious grasp of human ways, the scientific understanding of man will in all likelihood grow from our understanding of language, and this understanding has already reached the scientific stage. From it we may reasonably hope to derive practical benefits comparable to those which have arisen from our scientific understanding and control of nonhuman things (Boas, 1939a, pp. 105-106).

The last paragraph above states a theme which has occupied a number of scholars concerned with the anthropological and social import of linguistics, such as Sapir (1929c), Bloomfield (1925, 1942a), Hockett (1948c), Trager (1949), Kroeber (1952), Hjelmslev (1953), Uldall (1957), Levi-Strauss (1958a).

With Boas almost the total scope of American linguistic anthropology until the present time became defined or adumbrated. Almost all the general topics of this book were taken up by him (Parts I, II, III, IV, VI, VIII, IX, X). The topics of part V gained importance through the work of Sapir and, with those of VII and the related aspects of VIII, became the focus of sustained study only after the Second World War, partly through the increased involvement of American anthropologists in the study of complex societies and the impact of developing sociological and social anthropological theory.

After Boas, the main shapers of the scope of linguistic anthropology have been Kroeber, Sapir, and Bloomfield. Kroeber and Sapir were Boas' students early in his career at Columbia and, as the quotation above has indicated, Bloomfield ranked Boas as his teacher as well. Less need be said here of these men, for the material to assess their contribution is more readily available than is the case with Boas and, indeed, their immediate students are now the present leaders of the profession. Kroeber's contribution is discussed at length in Part X. For Sapir's work, see especially the essay by Harris (1951a) and of course, his own *Language* (1921) and *Selected Writings* (Mandelbaun [Ed.], 1949). For Bloomfield, there is the article by Bloch (*Lg.*, 1949, *25:* 87-98) and Bloomfield's book *Language* (1933), the most influential linguistic treatise of the past generation, as well as Hockett's account of his Algonquian work in this volume (Part IX). But certain of the professional contributions of Sapir and Bloomfield should be singled out here.

Sapir, a superb fieldworker and analyst of linguistic form, made more substantial contributions to the description of more varied languages than perhaps any man or woman since. His flashing mind and ability to detect pattern, combined with his ability to focus on and recall detail, mark all his work, and fed into the second of his major contributions, that of applying and developing the comparative method in the unraveling of the genetic relationships of New World languages. He laid the groundwork for comparative study of a greater number of language families than perhaps any other person. Much of the continuing contribution of American anthropology to field description ("anthropological linguistics" proper) and comparative linguistics is due to his inspiration.

Sapir was also wide-ranging in his tastes and interests and alert to almost every vital implication of linguistic phenomena. His essay on "Language" (1933a) is a concise masterpiece, portraying the dynamics of speech in social life with an unrivaled trenchant skill. Sapir inspired the main American anthropological activity in these areas and until recently his students and associates were almost alone in their attention to speech and personality, semantic description and functioning, and social variation in speech.

Although he did not move from linguistics into anthropology as did Sapir, Bloomfield was always close to the other discipline. In his first general book (1914) he chided works on linguistics that neglected ethnology (p. 317), and showed the influence of Boas' "Introduction" (1911). Some years later in his paper launching the Linguistic Society of America and its journal *Language*, Bloomfield described linguistics as most closely related to ethnology among the other human sciences, although prior to them all, and remarked: "The work of directly observing and recording human speech is much like the work of the ethnologist; indeed, in our country, where such work has been best done, it has been performed chiefly by the ethnologic-linguistic school" (1925, pp. 1-2). (In its relations with ethnology, distinct yet concerned, Bloomfield's linguistics much resembles that of the great nineteenth-century American linguist, William Dwight Whitney.)

Together with Sapir, Bloomfield helped establish present standards for field work and description in anthropological ("ethnologic") linguistics and the effectiveness of the comparative method of Indo-European as a foundation for historical work in unwritten languages (cf. Sapir, 1931c, and Hockett in Part IX). Bloomfield's uncompromising effort to personify the scientific attitude in his work links him with Boas. Conscious development of descriptive methodology in American linguistics in the last generation has taken Bloomfield as its patron saint, chiefly in his behaviorist aspect, although the two most recent developments, those of Chomsky (1957) and Pike (1954, 1955, 1960) ("transformational" and "tagmemic" grammar, respectively) both hark back more to Sapir.

Although Sapir, like Kroeber, shared Boas' focal interest in language as a historical product embodying ways of thought, he ranged much further in his explicit conceptions of linguistic function, and hence in the implicit scope of linguistic anthropology, for example, stressing the expression of individual personality, as we have noted. In his first book (1914) Bloomfield also showed concern with cognitive categories, but in his *Language* (1933) he had become converted to a rather narrow version of behaviorism. An aggressively "scientific" approach, a rejection of "mentalism," and a focus on descriptive method per se pervaded American linguistics for almost a generation, with Bloomfield as its patron saint. In his *Language* Bloomfield's focus is upon the role of language as a surrogate for nonverbal behavior, controlling the action of others; but where Malinowski granted a wide range of functions and cultural connections as derivatives from such a view, opening outward into the whole range of social anthropology, Bloomfield was silent. Very restricted definitions of the concepts "language" and "linguistics" prevailed, and whatever did not fit them was put at a distance. In recent years, however, a concern with the spectrum of functional relations has gained new prominence.

One factor in the new prominence has been Roman Jakobson and those who share his views, associated with the Prague School. Jakobson has expounded a broad view of what is relevant to language and linguistics, and it is noteworthy he has ranged his work closely with anthropology in the United States. Indeed, he spent his first months in America living with Boas and has written two significant appreciations of Boas' work (1944, 1959) as well as playing a major role in interdisciplinary conferences.

On reviewing the three lines of thought which have been discussed, two characteristics stand out. A close link between linguistics and anthropology has entered into the formation of each, affecting conceptions both of the nature of language and linguistic description and of the place of language in culture.

So far, then, the histories of the two disciplines in the present century are inseparable. It is difficult to speak of the future, but it seems fair to say that the links between linguistics and anthropology in the United States are being not only sustained, but heightened. A generation of younger anthropologists, who take the recent developments in linguistic method for granted, are continuing the anthropological contribution to descriptive and historical linguistics in many areas of the world, and the psychological and sociological aspects of language use are receiving unprecedented attention. Indeed, the main foci of interest among younger anthropologists working with language would seem to be semantic description or sociolinguistics or both. It may be that the development of these foci of interest will lead historians of twentieth-century linguistics to say that whereas the first half of the century was distinguished by a drive for the autonomy of language as an object of study and a focus upon description of structure, the second half was distinguished by a concern for the integration of language in sociocultural context and a focus upon the analysis of function.

Let us turn now to the individual articles of the section.

The "Introduction" to the *Handbook of American Indian Languages* has become a classic and as close to a founding text as modern American linguistic anthropology possesses. In the section devoted to the relations between linguistics and ethnology (read "cultural anthropology" and "social anthropology" as well), Boas develops the first general arguments for the two basic themes of the practical and the theoretical necessity of linguistic work in ethnology.

Note that in the section on practical needs Boas discusses verbal art as examples of the "deeper problems of ethnology," just as later in his "Introductory" to the first number of *IJAL* (1917) he stated that "The problems treated in a linguistic journal must include also the literary forms of native production" (p. 7). Kroeber's view of the importance of Boas' stricture on the practical use of language has been quoted; to it should be added Lowie's ranking of the stricture as having "raised field work to an entirely new level" (1937, p. 132). It is worth noting that the practical need did not itself lead Boas to consider linguistics an integral aspect of ethnology, for a few years earlier he had noted a breaking up of anthropological research through specialization and, while demanding that the field worker be familiar with the principles of biology and linguistics, had foreseen their separation from ethnology-archaeology: "I think the time is not far distant when anthropology pure and simple will deal with the customs and beliefs of the less civilized people only, and when linguistics and biology will continue and develop the work that we are doing now because no one else cares for it" (1904). The change of view implicit in the argument of the section on "Linguistics and Ethnology" presented here (and in Boas' subsequent practice with doctoral candidates in his department) seems based on the theoretical consideration.

The identification here of ethnology with the study of mental phenomena, the emphasis on their unconscious patterning (though not along psychoanalytic lines), and the thesis that language is of special importance to the understanding of such patterning, all give the key to much of Boas' work and thought and to a good deal of the subsequent development of the field. The importance of these views is reiterated by Sapir (1927b), Jakobson (1944), Levi-Strauss (1953b, pp. 526-527), and Whorf (1956a) among others. Levi-Strauss writes that in the history of structural thought, Boas may be credited with having introduced the distinction between the conscious or unconscious charaeter of models of empirical reality.

Whereas Boas treats "culture" as a generic term for all the nonbiological aspects of human life, Greenberg treats it as but one of the three coordinate aspects of the object of ethnological study, the cultural, individual, and social. In doing so, he reflects the greater interaction and concern for integration among the social (or behavioral) sciences, particularly anthropology, sociology, and psychology, that emerged after the Second World War, contrasting with the emphasis of each discipline on autonomy and on the generality of its subject matter in the period in which Boas wrote. Greenberg's charting of eighteen types of ethnolinguistic investigation has the broadest articulated scope of any of the discussions of the subject. As an account of the field, the logical outline is, of course, partly programmatic; it would be a useful exercise to try to complete the list of examples from extant studies.

Note that in citing Morris' treatment of semiotic Greenberg also points out the other direction in which linguistics faces, toward such disciplines as logic and mathematics. The subject matter of ethnology has sometimes been claimed in principle as part of a semiotic with linguistics as its heart (cf. Trager, 1949; Hjelmslev 1953; Goodenough 1957a; Uldall, 1957) or as a coordinate member (cf. Levi-Strauss, 1953b, pp. 536 ff.).

Goodenough traces an interdependence of linguistic and other cultural phenomena that recalls the Boasian view. His explicit focus on methodology, however, reflects another concern that has risen to prominence since the Second World War. Like Boas and Kroeber, Goodenough locates the interdependence first in the study of meanings. Goodenough's way of handling cultural meanings, however, is distinctive. He defines an ethnography as a theory, a model of a particular case, and associates it with a predictive criterion: "what you have to know in order to operate as a member of the society." The goal of valid descriptions of particular cultures has long been shared by ethnographers, but by defining ethnography as a theoretical, predictive enterprise, Goodenough has stimulated a development which might be called "the new ethnography," in which linguistic data and methods play a central role.

Like Goodenough, Levi-Strauss sees linguistics as a stimulus to ethnological method, but here is concerned with comparative analysis rather than individual descriptions. In part the difference reflects a difference in dominant concern between recent American linguistics, emphasizing descriptive method, and the thrust of European structuralism, as manifest in the Prague school of Troubetzkoy and Jakobson, toward statement of necessary relations. This study by Levi-Strauss, like many of his works, is exemplary for its sense of continuity of problem, its incisive use of a wide range of relevant literature, and its novel insight. Note the conclusion in which the proper methodology for social anthropology and linguistics is taken as based on the symbolic nature of their object of study.

Pike combines several themes—the difference between the physical continua in nature and the discrete classifications made of them by human beings; the need to ground description of a body of cultural material in terms relevant to the data itself; the desire to extend the successes of linguistic analysis to analysis of other cultural data; and a desire to fit both into a common framework. In so doing, Pike develops the most thoroughgoing attempt so far toward a general structural analysis of human behavior grounded in linguistics. Two notable aspects of his work are the close attention to descriptive operations and the concern for practical relevance.

Both Pike's belief in the unity of theory and practice and his vocation as a teacher of workers in other cultures are reflected in this, but there is also a close parallel to Goodenough's view that "A proper definition of culture must ultimately derive from the operations by which we describe particular cultures" and the concern with social change and applied anthropology of many nonmissionary anthropologists. Pike's coinage of "emic" and "etic" has had increasing acceptance ("etic," derived from "phonetic," refers to units and classifications not validated in native reactions to the behavior in question, as opposed to "emic" units and classifications, which are). Equally striking is Pike's insistence that a unified theory or descriptive methodology is needed to account properly for composites of verbal and nonverbal behavior that are considered by their participants as single units of activity. The most prominent line of recent American concern with the relations of linguistic and nonlinguistic behavior has dealt with their matching, correlation, or summation, not with their "integrated synthesis . . . within a single [detailed] description." No ethnographic studies in other cultures derived from Pike's approach have yet been published, although some are underway.

Malinowski's short review makes manifest his principal themes, that language is first and foremost a mode of activity, that its main function is pragmatic control, and, throwing down the gauntlet, that linguists (and anthropologists) must fumble their subject unless they realize these truths and become wholeheartedly empirical in the study of them.

Firth's treatment of sociological linguistics forms part of a general view of linguistics as concerned with meaning, meaning being taken as the whole of the various functions which a linguistic form may have. From this point of view, the various branches of linguistic study, from phonology to specification of social context, are but different steps in one process of analysis, which Firth terms "serial contextualization." Such an approach might well meet Pike's requirement of integrated synthesis of a description of verbal and nonverbal behavior in some cases; but no requirement of unified methodology for both is made and the focus throughout is on linguistic forms rather than, as in Pike's approach, on behavior generally.

Note Firth's attention to linguistic aspects of life-history, social roles, and types of situation and his delineation of modes of use, from "wishing, blessing, cursing, boasting" to types of narrative. A full-scale description of the communication system of a society or community in such terms would bring into focus much that escapes the frames of reference of ordinary linguistic and ethnographic study as pursued separately. (For an elaboration of such an approach under the heading of the "ethnography of speaking," see Hymes, 1962a.)

Linguistics and Ethnology 1

FRANZ BOAS

IT SEEMS DESIRABLE TO SAY a few words on the function of linguistic researches in the study of the ethnography of the Indians.

PRACTICAL NEED OF LINGUISTIC STUDIES FOR ETHNOLOGICAL PURPOSES

First of all, the purely practical aspect of this question may be considered. Ordinarily, the investigator who visits an Indian tribe is not able to converse with the natives themselves and to obtain his information first-hand, but he is obliged to rely more or less on data transmitted by interpreters, or at least by the help of interpreters. He may ask his question through an interpreter, and receive again through his mouth the answer given by the Indians. It is obvious that this is an unsatisfactory method, even when the interpreters are good; but, as a rule, the available men are either not sufficiently familiar with the English language, or they are so entirely out of sympathy with the Indian point of view, and understand the need of accuracy on the part of the investigator so little, that information furnished by them can be used only with a considerable degree of caution. At the present time it is possible to get along in many parts of America without interpreters, by means of the trade-jargons that have developed everywhere in the intercourse between the whites and the Indians. These, however, are also a very unsatisfactory means of inquiring into the customs of the natives, because, in some cases, the vocabulary of the trade-languages is extremely limited, and it is almost impossible to convey information relating to the religious and philosophic ideas or to the higher aspects of native art, all of which play so important a part in Indian life. Another difficulty which often develops whenever the investigator works with a particularly intelligent interpreter is, that the interpreter imbibes too readily the views of the investigator, and that his information, for this reason, is strongly biased, because he is not so well able to withstand the influence of formative theories as the trained investigator ought to be. Anyone who has carried on work with intelligent Indians will recall instances of this kind, where the interpreter may have formulated a theory based on the questions that have been put through him, and has interpreted his answers under the guidance of his preconceived notions. All this is so obvious that it hardly requires a full discussion. Our needs become particularly apparent when we compare the methods that we expect from any investigator of cultures of the Old World with those of the ethnologist who is studying primitive tribes. Nobody would expect authoritative accounts of the civilization of China or of Japan from a man who does not speak the languages readily, and who has not mastered their literatures. The student of antiquity is expected to have a thorough mastery of the ancient languages. A student of Mohammedan life in Arabia or Turkey would hardly be considered a serious investigator if all his knowledge had to be derived from second-hand accounts. The ethnologist, on the other hand, undertakes in the majority of cases to elucidate the innermost thoughts and feelings of a people without so much as a smattering of knowledge of their language.

It is true that the American ethnologist is confronted with a serious practical difficulty, for, in the present state of American society, by far the greater number of customs and practices have gone out of existence, and the investigator is compelled to rely upon accounts of customs of former times recorded from the mouths of the old generation who, when young, still took part in these performances. Added to this he is confronted with the difficulty that the number of trained investigators is very small, and the number of American languages that are mutually unintelligible exceedingly large, probably exceeding three hundred in number. Our investigating ethnologists are also denied opportunity to spend long continuous periods with any particular tribe, so that the practical difficulties in the way of acquiring languages are almost insuperable. Nevertheless, we must insist that a command of the language is an indispensable means of obtaining accurate and thorough knowledge, because much information can be gained by listening to conversations of the natives and by taking part in their daily life, which, to the observer who has no command of the language, will remain entirely inaccessible.

It must be admitted that this ideal aim is, under present conditions, entirely beyond our reach. It is, however, quite possible for the ethnographer to obtain a theoretical knowledge of native languages that will enable him to collect at least part of the information that could be best obtained by a practical knowledge of the language. Fortunately, the Indian is easily misled, by the ability of the observer to read his language, into thinking that he is also able to understand what he reads. Thus, in taking down tales or other records in the native language, and reading them to the Indians, the Indian always believes that the reader also understands what he pronounces, because it is quite inconceivable to him that a person can freely utter the sentences in his language without clearly grasping their meaning. This fact facilitates the initial stages of ethnographic information in the native languages, because, on the whole, the northern Indians are eager to be put on record in regard to questions that are of supreme interest to them. If the observer is capable of grasping by a rapid analysis the significance of what is dictated to him, even without being able to express himself freely in the native language, he is in a position to obtain much information that otherwise would be entirely unobtainable. Although this is wholly a makeshift, still it puts the observer in an infinitely better position than that in which he would be without any knowledge whatever of the language. First of all, he can get the information from the Indians first-hand, without employing an interpreter, who may mislead him. Furthermore, the range of subjects on which he can get information is considerably increased, because the limitations of the linguistic knowledge of the interpreter, or those of the trade-language, are eliminated. It would seem, therefore, that under present conditions we are more or less compelled to rely upon an extended series of texts as the safest means of obtaining information from the Indians. A general review of our ethnographic literature shows clearly how much better is the information obtained by observers who have command of the language, and who are on terms of intimate friendship with the natives, than that obtained through the medium of interpreters.

The best material we possess is perhaps contained in the naïve outpourings of the Eskimo, which they write and print themselves, and distribute as a newspaper, intended to inform the people of all the events that are of interest. These used to contain much mythological matter and much that related to the mode of life of the people. Other material of similar character is furnished by the large text collections of the Ponca, published by the late James Owen Dorsey; although many of these are influenced by the changed conditions under which the people now live. Some older records on the Iroquois, written by prominent members of the tribe, also deserve attention; and among the most recent literature the descriptions of the Sauk and Fox by Dr. William Jones are remarkable on account of the thorough understanding that the author has reached, owing to his mastery of the language. Similar in character, although rendered entirely in English, are the observations of Mr. James Teit on the Thompson Indians.

In some cases it has been possible to interest educated natives in the study of their own tribes and to induce them to write down in their own language their observations. These, also, are much superior to English records, in which the natives are generally hampered by the lack of mastery of the foreign language.

While in all these cases a collector thoroughly familiar with the Indian language and with English might give us the results of his studies without using the native language in his publications, this is quite indispensable when we try to investigate the deeper problems of ethnology. A few examples will show clearly what is meant. When the question arises, for instance, of investigating the poetry of the Indians, no translation can possibly be considered as an adequate substitute for the original. The form of rhythm, the treatment of the language, the adjustment of text to music, the imagery, the use of metaphors, and all the numerous problems involved in any thorough investigation of the style of poetry, can be interpreted only by the investigator who has equal command of the ethnographical traits of the tribe and of their language. The same is true in the investigation of rituals, with their set, more or less poetic phrases, or in the investigation of prayers and incantations. The oratory of the Indians, a subject that has received much attention by ethnologists, is not adequately known, because only a very few speeches have been handed down in the original. Here, also, an accurate investigation of the method of composition and of the devices used to reach oratorical effect, requires the preservation of speeches as rendered in the original language.

There are also numerous other features of the life of the Indians which can not be adequately presented without linguistic investigation. To these belong, for instance, the discussion of personal, tribal, and local names. The translations of Indian names which are popularly known—like Sitting-Bull, Afraid-Of-His-Horse, etc.—indicate that names possess a deeper significance. The translations, however, are so difficult that a thorough linguistic knowledge is required in order to explain the significance adequately.

In all the subjects mentioned heretofore, a knowledge of Indian languages serves as an important adjunct to a full understanding of the customs and beliefs of the people whom we are studying. But in all these cases the service which language lends us is first of all a practical one—a means to a clearer understanding of ethnological phenomena which in themselves have nothing to do with linguistic problems.

THEORETICAL IMPORTANCE OF LINGUISTIC STUDIES: Language a Part of Ethnological Phenomena in General

It seems, however, that a theoretical study of Indian languages is not less important than a practical knowledge of them; that the purely linguistic inquiry is part and parcel of a thorough investigation of the psychology of the peoples of the world. If ethnology is understood as the science dealing with the mental phenomena of the life of the peoples of the world, human language, one of the most important manifestations of mental life, would seem to belong naturally to the field of work of ethnology, unless special reasons can be adduced why it should not be so considered. It is true that a practical reason of this kind exists, namely, the specialization which has taken place in the methods of philological research, which has progressed to such an extent that philology and comparative linguistics are sciences which require the utmost attention, and do not allow the student to devote much of his time to other fields that require different methods of study. This, however, is no reason for believing that the results of linguistic inquiry are unimportant to the ethnologist. There are other fields of ethnological investigation which have come to be more or less specialized, and which require for their successful treatment peculiar specialization. This is true, for instance, of the study of primitive music, of primitive art, and, to a certain extent, of primitive law. Nevertheless, these subjects continue to form an important part of ethnological science.

If the phenomena of human speech seem to form in a way a subject by itself, this is perhaps largely due to the fact that the laws of language remain entirely unknown to the speakers, that linguistic phenomena never rise into the consciousness of primitive man, while all other ethnological phenomena are more or less clearly subjects of conscious thought.

The question of the relation of linguistic phenomena to ethnological phenomena, in the narrower sense of the term, deserves, therefore, special discussion.

LANGUAGE AND THOUGHT

First of all, it may be well to discuss the relation between language and thought. It has been claimed that the conciseness and clearness of thought of a people depend to a great extent upon their language. The ease with which in our modern European languages we express wide abstract ideas by a single term, and the facility with which wide generalizations are cast into the frame of a simple sentence, have been claimed to be one of the fundamental conditions of the clearness of our concepts, the logical force of our thought, and the precision with which we eliminate in our thoughts irrelevant details. Apparently this view has much in its favor. When we compare modern English with some of those Indian languages which are most concrete in their formative expression, the contrast is striking. When we say *The eye is the organ of sight*, the Indian may not be able to form the expression *the eye*, but may have to define that the eye of a person or of an animal is meant. Neither may the Indian be able to generalize readily the abstract idea of an eye as the representative of the whole class of objects, but may have to specialize by an expression like *this eye here*. Neither may he be able to express by a single term the idea of *organ*, but may have to specify it by an expression like *instrument of seeing*, so that the whole sentence might assume a form like *An indefinite person's eye is his means of seeing*. Still, it will be recognized that in this more specific form the general idea may be well expressed. It seems very questionable in how far the restriction of the use of certain grammatical forms can really be conceived as a hindrance in the formulation of generalized ideas. It seems much more likely that the lack of these forms is due to the lack of their need. Primitive man, when conversing with his fellowman, is not in the habit of discussing abstract ideas. His interests center around the occupations of his daily life; and where philosophic problems are touched upon, they appear either in relation to definite individuals or in the more or less anthropomorphic forms of religious beliefs. Discourses on qualities without connection with the object to which the qualities belong, or of activities or states disconnected from the idea of the actor or the subject being in a certain state, will hardly occur in primitive speech. Thus the Indian will not speak of goodness as such, although he may very well speak of the goodness of a person. He will not speak of a state of bliss apart from the person who is in such a state. He will not refer to the power of seeing without designating an individual who has such power. Thus it happens that in languages in which the idea of possession is expressed by elements subordinated to nouns, all abstract terms appear always with possessive elements. It is, however, perfectly conceivable that an Indian trained in philosophic thought would proceed to free the underlying nominal forms from the possessive elements, and thus reach abstract forms strictly corresponding to the abstract forms of our modern languages. I have made this experiment, for instance, with the Kwakiutl language of Vancouver Island, in which no abstract term ever occurs without its possessive elements. After some discussion, I found it perfectly easy to develop the idea of the abstract term in the mind of the Indian, who will state that the word without a possessive pronoun gives a sense, although it is not used idiomatically. I succeeded, for instance, in this manner, in isolating the terms for *love* and *pity*, which ordinarily occur only in possessive forms, like *his love for him* or *my pity for you*. That this view is correct may also be observed in languages in which possessive elements appear as independent forms, as, for instance, in the Siouan languages. In these, pure abstract terms are quite common.

There is also evidence that other specializing elements, which are so characteristic of many Indian languages, may be dispensed with when, for one reason or another, it seems desirable to generalize a term. To use the example of the Kwakiutl language, the idea *to be seated* is almost always expressed with an inseparable suffix expressing the place in which a person is seated, as *seated on the floor of the house*, *on the ground*, *on the beach*, *on a pile of things*, or *on a round thing*, etc. When, however, for some reason, the idea of the state of sitting is to be emphasized, a form may be used which expresses simply *being in a sitting posture*. In this case, also, the device for generalized expression is present, but the opportunity for its application arises seldom, or perhaps never. I think what is true in these cases is true of the structure of every single language. The fact that generalized forms of expression are not used does not prove inability to form them, but it merely proves that the mode of life of the people is such that they are not required; that they would, however, develop just as soon as needed.

This point of view is also corroborated by a study of the numeral systems of primitive languages. As is well known, many languages exist in which the numerals do not exceed two or three. It has been inferred from this that the people speaking these languages are not capable of forming the concept of higher numbers. I think this interpretation of the existing conditions is quite erroneous. People like the South American Indians (among whom these defective numeral systems are found), or like the Eskimo (whose old system of numbers probably did not exceed ten), are presumably not in need of higher numerical expressions, because there are not many objects that they have to count. On the other hand, just as soon as these same people find themselves in contact with civilization, and when they acquire standards of value that have to be counted, they adopt with perfect ease higher numerals from other languages and develop a more or less perfect system of counting. This does not mean that every individual who in the course of his life has never made use of higher numerals would acquire more complex systems readily, but the tribe as a whole seems always to be capable of adjusting itself to the needs of counting. It must be borne in mind that counting does not become necessary until objects are considered in such generalized form that their individualities are entirely lost sight of. For this reason it is possible that even a person who has a flock of domesticated animals may know them by name and by their characteristics without ever desiring to count them. Members of a war expedition may be known by name and may not be counted. In short, there is no proof that the lack of the use of numerals is in any way connected with the inability to form the concepts of higher numbers.

If we want to form a correct judgment of the influence that language exerts over thought, we ought to bear in mind that our European languages as found at the present time have been moulded to a great extent by the abstract thought of philosophers. Terms like *essence* and *existence*, many of which are now commonly used, are by origin artificial devices for expressing the results of abstract thought. In this they would resemble the artificial, unidiomatic abstract terms that may be formed in primitive languages.

Thus it would seem that the obstacles to generalized thought inherent in the form of a language are of minor importance only, and that presumably the language alone would not prevent a people from advancing to more generalized forms of thinking if the general state of their culture should require expression of such thought; that under these conditions the language would be moulded rather by the cultural state. It does not seem likely, therefore, that there is any direct relation between the culture of a tribe and the language they speak, except in so far as the form of the language will be moulded by the state of culture, but not in so far as a certain state of culture is conditioned by morphological traits of the language.

UNCONSCIOUS CHARACTER OF LINGUISTIC PHENOMENA

Of greater positive importance is the question of the relation of the unconscious character of linguistic phenomena to the more conscious ethnological phenomena. It seems to my mind that this contrast is only apparent, and that the very fact of the unconsciousness of linguistic processes helps us to gain a clearer understanding of the ethnological phenomena, a point the importance of which can not be underrated. It has been mentioned before that in all languages certain classifications of concepts occur. To mention only a few: we find objects classified according to sex, or as animate and inanimate, or according to form. We find actions determined according to time and place, etc. The behavior of primitive man makes it perfectly clear that all these concepts, although they are in constant use, have never risen into consciousness, and that consequently their origin must be sought, not in rational, but in entirely unconscious, we may perhaps say instinctive, processes of the mind. They must be due to a grouping of sense-impressions and of concepts which is not in any sense of the term voluntary, but which develops from quite different psychological causes. It would seem that the essential difference between linguistic phenomena and other ethnological phenomena is, that the linguistic classifications never rise into consciousness, while in other ethnological phenomena, although the same unconscious origin prevails, these often rise into consciousness, and thus give rise to secondary reasoning and to re-interpretations. It would, for instance, seem very plausible that the fundamental religious notions—like the idea of the voluntary power of inanimate objects, or of the anthropomorphic character of animals, or of the existence of powers that are superior to the mental and physical powers of man—are in their origin just as little conscious as are the fundamental ideas of language. While, however, the use of language is so automatic that the opportunity never arises for the fundamental notions to emerge into consciousness, this happens very frequently in all phenomena relating to religion. It would seem that there is no tribe in the world in which the religious activities have not come to be a subject of thought. While the religious activities may have been performed before the reason for performing them had become a subject of thought, they attained at an early time such importance that man asked himself the reason why he performed these actions. With this moment speculation in regard to religious activities arose, and the whole series of secondary explanations which form so vast a field of ethnological phenomena came into existence.

It is difficult to give a definite proof of the the unconscious origin of ethnic phenomena, because so many of them are, or have come to be, subjects of thought. The best evidence that can be given for their unconscious origin must be taken from our own experience, and I think it is not difficult to show that certain groups of our activities, whatever the history of their earlier development may have been, develop at present in each individual and in the whole people entirely sub-consciously, and nevertheless are most potent in the formation of our opinions and actions. Simple examples of this kind are actions which we consider as proper and improper, and which may be found in great numbers in what we call good manners. Thus table manners, which on the whole are impressed vigorously upon the child while it is still young, have a very fixed form. Smacking of the lips and bringing the plate up to the mouth would not be tolerated, although no esthetic or other reason could be given for their rigid exclusion; and it is instructive to know that among a tribe like the Omaha it is considered as bad taste, when invited to eat, not to smack one's lips, because this is a sign of appreciation of the meal. I think it will readily be recognized that the simple fact that these habits are customary, while others are not, is sufficient reason for eliminating those acts that are not customary, and that the idea of propriety simply arises from the continuity and automatic repetition of these acts, which brings about the notion that manners contrary to custom are unusual, and therefore not the proper manners. It may be observed in this connection that bad manners are always accompanied by rather intense feelings of displeasure, the psychological reason for which can be found only in the fact that the actions in question are contrary to those which have become habitual. It is fairly evident that in our table manners this strong feeling of propriety is associated with the familiar modes of eating. When a new kind of food is presented, the proper manner of eating which is not known, practically any habit that is not in absolute conflict with the common habits may readily establish itself.

The example of table manners gives also a fairly good instance of secondary explanation. It is not customary to bring the knife to the mouth, and very readily the feeling arises, that the knife is not used in this manner because in eating thus one would easily cut the lips. The lateness of the invention of the fork, and the fact that in many countries dull knives are used and that a similar danger exists of pricking the tongue or the lips with the sharp-pointed steel fork which is commonly used in Europe, show readily that this explanation is only a secondary rationalistic attempt to explain a custom that otherwise would remain unexplained.

If we are to draw a parallel to linguistic phenomena in this case, it would appear that the grouping of a number of unrelated actions in one group, for the reason that they cause a feeling of disgust, is brought about without any reasoning, and still sets off these actions clearly and definitely in a group by themselves.

On account of the importance of this question, it seems desirable to give another example, and one that seems to be more deeply seated than the one given before. A case of this kind is presented in the group of acts which we characterize as modest. It requires very little thought to see that, while the feelings of modesty are fundamental, the particular acts which are considered modest or immodest show immense variation, and are determined entirely by habits that develop unconsciously so far as their relation to modesty is concerned, and which may have their ultimate origin in causes of an entirely different character. A study of the history of costume proves at once that at different times and in different parts of the world it has been considered immodest to bare certain parts of the body. What parts of the body these are, is to a great extent a matter of accident. Even at the present time, and within a rather narrow range, great variations in this respect may be found. Examples are the use of the veil in Turkey, the more or less rigid use of the glove in our own society, and the difference between street costume and evening dress. A lady in full evening dress in a streetcar, during the daytime, would hardly appear in place.

We all are at once conscious of the intensity of these feelings of modesty, and of the extreme repugnance of the individual to any act that goes counter to the customary concepts of modesty. In a number of cases the origin of a costume can readily be traced, and in its development no considerations of modesty exert any influence. It is therefore evident that in this respect the grouping-together of certain customs again develops entirely unconsciously, but that, nevertheless, they stand out as a group set apart from others with great clearness as soon as our attention is directed toward the feelings of modesty.

To draw a parallel again between this ethnological phenomenon and linguistic phenomena, it would seem that the common feature of both is the grouping-together of a considerable number of activities under the form of a single idea, without the necessity of this idea itself entering into consciousness. The difference, again, would lie in the fact that the idea of modesty is easily isolated from other concepts, and that then secondary explanations are given of what is considered modest and what not. I believe that the unconscious formation of these categories is one of the fundamental traits of ethnic life, and that it even manifests itself in many of its more complex aspects; that many of our religious views and activities, of our ethical concepts, and even our scientific views, which are apparently based entirely on conscious reasoning, are affected by this tendency of distinct activities to associate themselves under the influence of strong emotions. It has been recognized before that this is one of the fundamental causes of error and of the diversity of opinion.

It seems necessary to dwell upon the analogy of ethnology and language in this respect, because, if we adopt this point of view, language seems to be one of the most instructive fields of inquiry in an investigation of the formation of the fundamental ethnic ideas. The great advantage that linguistics offer in this respect is the fact that, on the whole, the categories which are formed always remain unconscious, and that for this reason the processes which lead to their formation can be followed without the misleading and disturbing factors of secondary explanations, which are so common in ethnology, so much so that they generally obscure the real history of the development of ideas entirely.

Cases are rare in which a people have begun to speculate about linguistic categories, and these speculations are almost always so clearly affected by the faulty reasoning that has led to secondary explanations, that they are readily recognized as such, and can not disturb the clear view of the history of linguistic processes. In America we find this tendency, for instance, among the Pawnee, who seem to have been led to several of their religious opinions by linguistic similarities. Incidentally such cases occur also in other languages, as, for instance, in Chinook mythology, where the Culture Hero discovers a man in a canoe who obtains fish by dancing, and tells him that he must not do so, but must catch fish with the net, a tale which is entirely based on the identity of the two words for *dancing* and *catching with a net*. These are cases which show that Max Müller's theory of the influence of etymology upon religious concepts explains some of the religious phenomena, although, of course, it can be held to account for only a very small portion.

Judging the importance of linguistic studies from this point of view, it seems well worth while to subject the whole range of linguistic concepts to a searching analysis, and to seek in the peculiarities of the grouping of ideas in different languages an important characteristic in the history of the mental development of the various branches of mankind. From this point of view, the occurrence of the most fundamental grammatical concepts in all languages must be considered as proof of the unity of fundamental psychological processes. The characteristic groupings of concepts in American languages will be treated more fully in the discussion of the single linguistic stocks. The ethnological significance of these studies lies in the clear definition of the groupings of ideas which are brought out by the objective study of language.

There is still another theoretical aspect that deserves special attention. When we try to think at all clearly, we think, on the whole, in words; and it is well known that, even in the advancement of science, inaccuracy of vocabulary has often been a stumbling-block which has made it difficult to reach accurate conclusions. The same words may be used with different significance, and by assuming the word to have the same significance always, erroneous conclusions may be reached. It may also be that the word expresses only part of an idea, so that owing to its use the full range of the subject-matter discussed may not be recognized. In the same manner the words may be too wide in their significance, including a number of distinct ideas the differences of which in the course of the development of the language were not recognized. Furthermore, we find that, among more primitive tribes, similarities of sound are misunderstood, and that ideas expressed by similar words are considered as similar or identical, and that descriptive terms are misunderstood as expressing an identity, or at least close relationship, between the object described and the group of ideas contained in the description.

All these traits of human thought, which are known to influence the history of science and which play a more or less important rôle in the general history of civilization, occur with equal frequency in the thoughts of primitive man. It will be sufficient to give a few examples of these cases.

One of the most common cases of a group of views due to failure to notice that the same word may signify divers objects, is that based on the belief of the identity of persons bearing the same name. Generally the interpretation is given that a child receives the name of an ancestor because he is believed to be a reincarnation of the individuality of the ancestor. It seems, however, much more likely that this is not the real reason for the views connected with this custom, which seems due to the fact that no distinction is made between the name and the personality known under the name. The association established between name and individual is so close that the two seem almost inseparable; and when a name is mentioned, not only the name itself, but also the personality of its bearer, appears before the mind of the speaker.

Inferences based on peculiar forms of classification of ideas, and due to the fact that a whole group of distinct ideas are expressed by a single term, occur commonly in the terms of relationship of various languages; as, for instance, in our term *uncle*, which means the two distinct classes of father's brother and mother's brother. Here, also, it is commonly assumed that the linguistic expression is a secondary reflex of the customs of the people; but the question is quite open in how far the one phenomenon is the primary one and the other the secondary one, and whether the customs of the people have not rather developed from the unconsciously developed terminology.

Cases in which the similarity of sound of words is reflected in the views of the people are not rare, and examples of these have been given before in referring to Max Müller's theory of the origin of religions.

Finally, a few examples may be given of cases in which the use of descriptive terms for certain concepts, or the metaphorical use of terms, has led to peculiar views or customs. It seems plausible to my mind, for instance, that the terms of relationship by which some of the eastern Indian tribes designate one another were originally nothing but a metaphorical use of these terms, and that the further elaboration of the social relations of the tribes may have been largely determined by transferring the ideas accompanying these terms into practice.

More convincing are examples taken from the use of metaphorical terms in poetry, which, in rituals, are taken literally, and are made the basis of certain rites. I am inclined to believe, for instance, that the frequently occurring image of *the devouring of wealth* has a close relation to the detailed form of the winter ritual among the Indians of the North Pacific coast, and that the poetical simile in which the chief is called the *support of the sky* has to a certain extent been taken literally in the elaboration of mythological ideas.

Thus it appears that from practical, as well as from theoretical, points of view, the study of language must be considered as one of the most important branches of ethnological study, because, on the one hand, a thorough insight into ethnology can not be gained without practical knowledge of language, and, on the other hand, the fundamental concepts illustrated by human languages are not distinct in kind from ethnological phenomena; and because, furthermore, the peculiar characteristics of languages are clearly reflected in the views and customs of the peoples of the world.

REFERENCE NOTE

This note is divided into two parts. References dealing with Boas, Sapir, Kroeber, and Bloomfield are discussed and presented in Part A. (For further references on the general history of linguistic anthropology and specific figures, see notes to the next article and others in this section.) References dealing with the question of linguistic field work are discussed and presented in Part B. (For references on the theoretical place of linguistics in ethnology, consult the Introduction to this section and the note to Pike's article on pp. 54-61.)

A. BOAS, SAPIR, KROEBER, BLOOMFIELD

Some additional passages from Boas' "Introduction," showing his views on grammatical categories, are brought together in Part III.

Boas and other shapers of linguistic anthropology in America have been discussed in the Introduction to this section. Here references scattered through the book are brought together and some additional references given, both to the work of each and to the evaluations their work has received.

For the work of Boas, see the bibliography in Kroeber *et al.* (1943). Most of his significant writing on linguistic questions, apart from individual descriptions and materials, is cited in the general bibliography, in references to his selection in Part IV, and in the references to Swadesh's second article in Part IX. Boas *et al.* (1916) defines a style that characterizes the field work of both Boas and a generation or more of American anthropological linguistics.

For general coverage of Boas' work, see Herskovits (1953), Goldshmidt (1959), and Kroeber *et al.* (1943). For recent discussion of his approach, see Kroeber (1956), Levi-Strauss (1953a, 1953b), Lowie (1937, 1956), Wax (1956); and with special reference to language, see Bloomfield (1943b), Emeneau (1943), Hall (1950), Harrington (1945), Hymes (1956a, 1961b, 1961f, 1963c), Jakobson (1944, 1959), Newman (1950), Voegelin (1952a), Wells (1962).

For the work of Sapir, see the nearly complete bibliography in Mandelbaum (1949, pp. 601-617). To it should be added Sapir (1931b), Sapir and Swadesh (1946), and Sapir (1925). Most of his significant writing on linguistic questions, apart from individual descriptions and materials, is cited in the general bibliography and in references to Swadesh's second article in Part IX. As noteworthy representatives of the development of his views and interests, see also Sapir (1907a, 1907b, 1911, 1917, 1930, 1944).

For general coverage of Sapir's work, see Harris (1951a), Mandelbaum (1949, pp. v-xii and editorial notes *passim*), and Swadesh (1939). With special reference to language, see the above and Aberle (1960), Boas (1939b), Haas (1953), Harris (1951a), Hjelmslev (1939), Hymes (1963c), and Voegelin (1942).

For Kroeber, see the article and references in Part X.

For the work of Bloomfield, see the bibliography in Bloch (1949). Several of his significant writings are included in the general bibliography. In addition, see especially Bloomfield (1913, 1922a, 1922b, 1924, 1927b, 1927c, 1929, 1930, 1931, 1933b, 1934, 1935, 1936, 1939, 1942c, 1946). (A collection of his selected papers is much needed.)

References not in the general bibliography:

BLOCH, BERNARD

1949. Leonard Bloomfield. *Lg.*, *25:* 87-98.

BLOOMFIELD, LEONARD

1913. Review of W. Wundt, *Elemente der Völkerpsychologie. American Journal of Psychology, 24:* 449-453.

1922a. Review of E. Sapir, *Language. The Classical Weekly, 15:* 142-143.

1922b. Review of O. Jespersen, *Language. American Journal of Philology, 43:* 370-373.

1924. Review of Ferdinand de Saussure, *Cours de linguistique générale. Modern Language Journal, 8:* 317-319.

1927b. On Some Rules of Pāṇini. *JAOS, 47:* 61-70.

1927c. On Recent Work in General Linguistics. *Modern Philology, 25:* 211-230.

1929. Review of B. Liebich, *Konkordanz Pāṇini-Candra. Lg., 5:* 267-276.

1930. Linguistics as a Science. *Studies in Philology, 27:* 553-557.

1931. Review of J. Ries, *Was ist ein Satz? Lg., 7:* 204-209.

1933b. The Structure of Learned Words. In *A Commemorative Volume Issued by the Institute for Research in English Teaching on the Occasion of the Tenth Annual Conference of English Teachers.* Tokyo. Pp. 17-23.

1934. Review of Havera, *Handbuch der erklarenden syntax. Lg., 10:* 32-40.

1935. Linguistic Aspects of Science. *Philosophy of Science, 2:* 499-517.

1936. Language or Ideas? *Lg., 12:* 89-95.

1939. *Linguistic Aspects of Science.* (International Encyclopedia of Unified Science, *1:* 4). Chicago: University of Chicago Press.

1942c. Linguistics and Reading. *The Elementary English Review, 19:* 125-130, 183-186.

1943b. Obituary of Franz Boas. *Lg., 19:* 198.

1946. Twenty-one Years of the Linguistic Society. *Lg., 22:* 1-3.

BOAS, FRANZ

1939b. Edward Sapir. *IJAL, 10*(1): 58-59.

BOAS, FRANZ *et al.*

1916. Phonetic Transcription of Indian Languages. Report of Committee of American Anthropological Association. *Smithsonian Miscellaneous Collections, 66*(6): 1-16.

EMENEAU, MURRAY B.

1943. Franz Boas as a Linguist. In A. L. Kroeber *et al., Franz Boas, 1858-1942.* (Memoirs of the American Anthropological Association, No. 61; Vol. 45, no. 3, part 2.) Menasha, Wis.: The Association.

HAAS, MARY R.

1953. Sapir and the Training of Anthropological Linguists. *AA, 55:* 447-449.

HALL, ROBERT A., JR.

1950. Review of F. Boas, *Kwakiutl Grammar with a Glossary of the Suffixes. IJAL, 16:* 101-102.

HARRINGTON, JOHN P.

1945. Boas on the Science of Language. *IJAL, 11:* 97-99.

HERSKOVITS, MELVILLE J.

1953. *Franz Boas. The Science of Man in the Making.* (Twentieth Century Library). New York and London : Scribner.

HJELMSLEV, LOUIS

1939 Nekrolog auf E. Sapir [In English]. *Acta Linguistica, 1:* 76-77.

KROEBER, A. L.

1956. The Place of Boas in Anthropology. *AA, 58:* 151-159.

KROEBER, A. L., *et al.*

1943. *Franz Boas, 1858-1942.* (Memoirs of the American Anthropological Association. No. 61; vol. 45, no. 3, part 2:) Menasha, Wis.: The Association.

LOWIE, ROBERT H.

1937. Franz Boas. *The History of Ethnological Theory.* New York: Rinehart. Pp. 128-155.

1956. Boas Once More. *AA, 58:* 159-164.

NEWMAN, STANLEY S.

1950. Review of F. Boas, *Kwakiutl Grammar with a Glossary of the Suffixes. IJAL, 16:* 99-101.

SAPIR, EDWARD

1907a. Preliminary Report on the Language and Mythology of the Upper Chinook. *AA, 9:* 533-544. [Also in Frederica De Laguna (Ed.), *Selected Papers from the American Anthropologist, 1888-1920.* Evanston: Row, Peterson.]

1907b. Herder's Ursprung der Sprache. *Modern Philology, 5:* 109-142.

1911. The Problem of Noun Incorporation in American Languages. *AA, 13:* 250-282.

1917. Linguistic Publications of the Bureau of American Ethnology, a General Review. *IJAL, 1:* 76-81.

1925. The Similarity of Chinese and Indian Languages. *Science, Supplement, 57:* xii.

SWADESH, MORRIS

1939. Edward Sapir. *Lg., 15:* 132-135.

1948. Review of F. Boas, *Kwakiutl Grammar with a Glossary of the Suffixes. Word, 4:* 58-63.

VOEGELIN, C. F.

1942. Sapir: Insight and Rigor. *AA, 44:* 322-324.

WAX, MURRAY

1956. The Limitations of Boas' Anthropology. *AA, 58:* 63-74.

WELLS, RULON

1962. Phonemics in the Nineteenth Century, 1876-1900. Unpublished ms.

B. FIELD WORK

The implications of language and linguistics for anthropological field work are brought out in many of the contributions to this book. For general references on the subject, see Hymes (1959b), Conklin (1961), Gleason (1961, chap. 18), and Phillips (1959-1960). Two flurries of discussion of the subject followed that by Boas: Mead (1939), Lowie (1940), Henry (1940), Elkin (1941), and Bohannon (1956), Beals (1957), Taylor (1958), Bohannon (1958). Some of the writings of most interest and practical value are: Bloomfield (1942b), Frake (1961), Gleason (1961, chap. 18), Harris and Voegelin (1953), Kluckhohn (1945), Lounsbury (1953), Malinowski (1923, 1935), Nida (1947a, 1949, 1952-1953), Pike (1947; 1948; 1952, pp. 120-121; 1954, 1956), Quine (1959), Reyburn (1958a), Swadesh (1937), Voegelin and Harris (1952).

References not in the general bibliography:

BEALS, RALPH L.

1957. Native Terms and Anthropological Methods. *AA*, *59:* 716-717.

BOHANNON, PAUL

1956. On the Use of Native Language Categories in Ethnology. *AA*, *58:* 557.

1958. Rejoinder. *AA*, *60:* 941.

CONKLIN, HAROLD C.

1961. Bibliography on Ethnographic Research (Theory, Method, Techniques). New York : Columbia University, Department of Anthropology. Mimeographed.

ELKIN, A. P.

1941. Native Languages and the Field Worker in Australia. *AA*, *43:* 89-94.

HARRIS, Z. S., and C. F. VOEGELIN

1953. Eliciting in Linguistics. *SJA*, *9:* 59-75.

HENRY, JULES

1940. A Method for Learning to Talk Primitive Languages. *AA*, *42:* 635-641.

LOWIE, ROBERT H.

1940. Native Languages as Ethnographic Tools. *AA*, *42:* 81-89.

MEAD, MARGARET

1939. Native Languages as Field Work Tools. *AA*, *41:* 181-205.

PIKE, KENNETH L.

1952. More on Grammatical Prerequisites. *Word*, *8:* 106-121.

TAYLOR, DOUGLAS

1958. On Anthropologists' Use of Linguistics. *AA*, *56:* 940-941.

Linguistics and Ethnology 2

JOSEPH H. GREENBERG

FOR PURPOSES OF the present discussion we define speech as the totality of speaking activities within human social groups. We thus exclude at once the artificial symbolic languages of logic, mathematics, and the sciences, and secondary languages derived from spoken languages, such as writing and codesignalling. The linguist's subject so defined recommends itself as a point of departure for a consideration of the many-faceted relations between ethnology, as the science of culture, and linguistics, as the study of natural language.

The special position of linguistics arises from its two-fold nature: as a part of the science of culture by virtue of its inclusion in the mass of socially transmitted tradition of human groups, and as a part of the nascent subject of semiotics, the science of sign behavior in general. That language should be included in both of these more general sciences is no more contradictory than, for example, the double status of physical anthropology with its simultaneous affiliation with a physiologically oriented zoölogy and with anthropology, the general study of man approached both physically and culturally. Since linguistics faces in these two directions, it should be aware of the implications for itself both of the semiotician's discussions of language and of the general science of culture. Linguists have, on the whole, been more aware of their affiliations with cultural anthropology than with semiotics, a state of affairs which is understandable in view of the recency of the semiotician's interest in the general features of language.

In view of the analytic interests of the semioticians, who have usually approached language with a background of logical training, it is natural to turn to them for an analysis of language on which to base our consideration of the relationships of linguistics to the rest of ethnology. At present a prime desideratum is the translation of the special terminology developed by the linguist into a general integrated language concerned with sign behavior. This task, moreover, is an essential step in the development of a unified language for the sciences.

The aspect of semiotics which I shall apply here is the analysis of language into the three dimensions of the pragmatic, the semantic, and the syntactic, first advanced by Morris, and now widely adopted. (This distinction was first broached by Morris, in his *Foundations of the Theory of Signs* [Chicago, 1938]. I am aware that Morris himself, in his recent book, *Signs, Language and Behavior* [New York, 1946], tends to deprecate the significance of this set of distinctions. However, its validity remains unimpaired and its usefulness for the problem treated here will be made apparent. In my formulation of the definitions of syntactic, semantic, and pragmatic I have closely followed R. Carnap, *Introduction to Semantics* [Cambridge, 1942], p. 7.) The basis of Morris' distinctions lies in a consideration of the sign situation as involving three factors: the user of the sign, the sign itself, and the *designatum* or that to which the sign refers. It is not necessary to include the speakers and the *designata*; we may abstract from one or both of them. This gives us three fields of investigation. If we include reference to the users of the language we are in the field of pragmatics. If we abstract from the user of language and consider only expressions and their *designata*, we have an investigation in semantics. If we abstract also from the *designata* and study only the relations between the expressions themselves, we have syntax. This use of the term syntax is qualified, when necessary, as logical syntax to distinguish it from syntax as used by linguists for the study of constructions involving words. All these three aspects of languages, according to the semiotician, are the concern of one who would scientifically analyze a given language. It is the syntactic aspect, which we may equate with the linguist's term structural, which has claimed the chief interest of linguistics, and this for essentially the same reasons which have led logicians to carry to greatest extent the analysis of the syntactic dimension of logical and mathematical language, namely their susceptibility to formulation in highly condensed and symbolic form. This is a marked tendency in contemporary descriptive linguistics. It has led to statements in some branches of analysis isomorphic with those which would arise from a recourse to the symbolism of modern mathematical logic; it is merely that a different traditional notation is employed. Present-day descriptive linguists strive towards formulations in which elements are defined by a purely formal procedure without reference to meaning. While it is in syntactics that recent linguistics has made its most significant methodologic progress, the remoteness of this aspect of language has led to the recurrent complaints of the cultural scientist against the irrelevance to his problem of a large portion of contemporary linguistics.

The semantic aspects of a large language are most conveniently stated in a lexicon in which each morpheme and construction is assigned a meaning. The production of such a lexicon is traditionally a part of the descriptive linguist's treatment of a language. Differences in meaning must be referred to as criteria at various stages of his analyses, notably at the phonemic level. Moreover general statements about phonemic patterning and in the morphology are approximations whose degree of probability increases as the lexion approaches completeness. For these reasons even a formal approach to language cannot disregard semantics. Since the *designata* of morphemes are objects in the cultural universe of the speakers, the linguist can only state meanings by referring to extralinguistic aspects of culture. As long as the cultural background of the language is not too diverse from that of the linguist himself, or not too unfamiliar to him, this creates no special difficulty, but when faced with basic cultural differences the linguist must either call in the ethnographer or acquire the relevant ethnographical information himself. Careful compilation of a lexicon is then a field in which the linguist and ethnologist can fruitfully collaborate. To the ethnologist, the semantics of the language of the people in whom he is interested is a subject of considerable interest since it presents him with a practically exhaustive classification of the objects in the cultural universe of the speakers. For certain morphemes whose *designata* are not sensually perceivable events in the space-time of the investigator the linguistic approach is crucial. That this has been realized in general by ethnologists is evidenced by the liberal use of native terms which characterize magical and other ideological components of culture, a practice which has resulted in the borrowing via the ethnographic literature of such words as *mana* and *taboo* into the European languages.

The lexicon of a language holds as it were a mirror to the rest of culture, and the accuracy of this mirror image sets a series of problems in principle capable of empirical solution. In certain instances, notably that of kinship terminology, this problem is a familiar one, and has occasioned a number of specific investigations. On the whole, however, the ethnographic problems presented by this aspect of language remain for the future.

With the pragmatic aspect of language we arrive at the point where the interest of the ethnologist is greatest and that of the linguist merely marginal. In general, the linguist is not interested in what the speakers of a language say on specific occasions. His own material is gathered, as such material must, from pragmatic observations of the language behavior of specific informants, but though these pragmatic aspects are primary in his actual research, formulation of results is made without reference to the speaker. The linguist has always been interested in *la langue*, not *la parole*, and this classic distinction in linguistics corresponds to the division of language into syntactics and semantics on the one hand, and pragmatics on the other.

To the ethnologist in the field, however, verbal behavior is as much an object of study; or should be, as non-verbal behavior. Like non-verbal behavior it is subject to varying degrees of patterning. The more obvious instances of highly stereotyped verbal behavior are frequently noted in ethnographies, for example formalized greetings and farewells. However, the description of the total gamut of such behavior is never attempted in ethnographic descriptions.

The slightest degree of patterning is shown on those occasions when all that may be confidently stated is whether speech will occur or not. For instance we may observe whether it is part of the standardized behavior of a people to speak at meals or keep silent. Usually the pattern is more definite in that there are limitations on the appropriate subject matter that may be mentioned in particular cultural contexts. On occasion we may go further and predict certain stylistic features, as when we state that a Sunday sermon will follow a certain organization beginning with a scriptural text and will employ a certain definable style. The highest degree of patterning is found in ritual where even the specific utterances may be predicted. Another example is found in standardized greetings which we are, revealingly enough, likely to call ritual.

Also a subject of great interest to the ethnologist are the specific statements of members of a culture intended to be general statements about their own patterns of behavior. These can be verified by reference to actual behavior and any discrepancies which may appear are of considerable interest. The difference between ideal patterns and real patterns of behavior is precisely that between verbalized patterns and actual behavior. The behavior referred to may itself be verbal, as when an informant states that people greet each other in the morning by asking "Have you slept well?", a statement capable of empirical verification.

If anything, ethnologists, a large portion of whose work consists of conversations with informants, have in the past overemphasized such verbal formulations and the demand has increasingly been made that such statements be checked by actual observation. Here, as in the case of the meaning-area in semantics, such inconsistencies may involve a cultural lag, invariably on the side of the linguistic component, it would appear. Such observations enable us at once to reconstruct the past and note the direction of culture change.

One instance of verbalized patterns is of particular interest in connection with the topic under discussion—statements by members of the community concerning language itself. In a culture with a developed linguistic science this will be linguistics as cultural activity as well as popular statements concerning language. Here the degree of knowledge of linguistics required of the ethnological observer may be compared to the knowledge of medicine needed to evaluate native ideas concerning curing practices.

As we pass from the pragmatic through the semantic to the syntactic dimension, we reach regions which are successively less obvious to the observer and more needful of special techniques of analysis. It is for this reason that the pragmatic aspect falls to the ethnologist whose work involves gross observations of cultural activities, that the semantic aspect is a middle ground in which both ethnologist and linguist may work, while the syntactic phase, which is the most recondite, is the natural focus of interest for the linguist. Interrelationships of language with other aspects of culture follow the same hierarchical progression. Syntactics apparently reflects nothing of the rest of culture and is inherently self-contained. Hence the linguist's contention that there is no such thing as a "primitive" language and that similar linguistic structures may appear under the most diverse cultural circumstances. In semantics, we find a direct reflection of the contents of culture, while in the field of pragmatics we deal directly with cultural behavior.

Thus far we have followed the semioticians in their formulation. This formulation, resting as it does mainly on a consideration of the symbolic languages evolved in logic and mathematics, abstracts from two most important aspects of natural languages. In treating artificial languages we are usually not interested in the history of the language or in the definition of the exact community which employs the language and the denotative relationships of the membership of that community with those of other communities using languages of less or greater degree of similarity.

The unit of the descriptive linguist is a speech community, taken more or less widely, as indicated by such rough terms as language, dialect, or sub-dialect. The definition of this community is often undertaken in the introductory portion of a linguistic description where the people are named, and population figures and geographical distributions are given. In his choice of a unit of description the linguist resembles the cultural anthropologist who describes cultural norms valid for a circumscribed group of people, a tribe, community, or nation. Such a treatment disregards—and justifiably so for the purpose in hand—relations in two directions, one towards the individual, and the other in the direction of the exact determination of the membership in this community and the relationship of its membership to others whose speech shows some degree of similarity to its own. This super-organic approach to linguistics I call cultural, as opposed to individual and social. Thus far all our discussion has been of cultural linguistics in the syntactic, semantic, and pragmatic phases.

In the field of individual speech we consider the relation of the speech habits of the individual to the rest of his personality, a problem primarily for the social psychologist, since it can only be meaningfully investigated by reference to the speech patterns of the community of which he is a member. Here, for example, within the semantic dimension, belongs the problem of individual variant connotations of morphemes.

Social linguistics, often called ethnolinguistics, involves in its synchronic aspect, a whole series of significant problems regarding correlations between population groupings as determined by linguistic criteria and those based on biologic, economic, political, geographical, and other non-linguistic factors. For example, in such a speech community as the Japanese, where specific verb and noun are found whose usage depends on the status of the individuals involved in verbal communication, we may compare groupings based on these usages with socio-economic strata defined by other criteria. As an example of correlation with biological groupings, we have studies of sex differences in speech. If we consider the relationship of speech communities to each other on a geographical basis we have the field of dialect area studies and here again it is possible to note correlations with non-linguistic factors. The study of isoglosses in relation to political, economic, or religious factors is an example of this type of investigation.

Up to now we have omitted the dimension of time. If a study describes the situation at one time level, abstracting from change, I shall call it, in accordance with the usual terminology, synchronic; if it takes into consideration change through a period of time I call it diachronic. The total field of language, as here defined, is composed of eighteen combinations, involving the syntactic, semantic, and pragmatic aspects, treated from the cultural, individual, or social point of view, either synchronically or diachronically.

If we consider the development of individual speech diachronically, we are again concerned with problems primarily of interest to the social psychologist, for we investigate the individual's acquisition of speech against a social background. Such problems as the factors influencing the particular form of speech that develops in an individual and the relative influences of family and other groupings in the determinations of the speech habits of the individual are within the scope of diachronic individual linguistics.

Cultural diachronic linguistics, particularly in its syntactic phase, is the field of historic linguistics, one of the chief activities of the professional linguist. The semantic subdivision is closely connected with the application of the historic and comparative methods insofar as it is only by resemblances both in form and meaning that the identity of specific linguistic forms can be recognized diachronically or that evidence for the relationship of diverse languages can be gathered. Some have attempted to cultivate the specific semantic aspect, notably Bréal who, in his pioneer attempt, applied the term *sémantique* to the historical study of meanings. The pragmatic dimension of cultural diachronic linguistics includes the historical approach to ritual and mythology, and thus includes comparative folklore. The study of specific literary forms within certain cultural traditions and the historical investigation of metrics are other examples of pragmatic historical research.

Social diachronic studies or historical ethnolinguistics is the phase of the interrelationships of ethnology and linguistics of which there has probably been the greatest awareness. The correlations between linguistic groupings of people and those derived on other bases, notably physical and cultural, is a standard problem in historic research. Examples of historical ethnolinguistic approaches are the tracing of former population distributions through linguistic groupings, the estimate of chronologic remoteness or recency of the cultural identity of groups on the basis of degree of linguistic divergence, the reconstruction of a partial cultural inventory of a proto-speech community on the basis of a reconstructed vocabulary, acculturational studies of the influence of one culture on another by the study of loan-words, and diffusionist studies of single elements of culture in which points of primary or secondary diffusion can be traced by a consideration of the form of the words which often point unequivocally to a particular language as the source.

It is perhaps worthwhile to note the extent to which our analysis of language is also applicable to culture traits in general. Obviously the distinction between synchronic and diachronic is relevant and it is possible to study cultures either descriptively or historically. The distinction between the cultural, the social, and the individual approaches is also valid. If we adopt Linton's convenient concept of status, then the behavior patterns themselves are the results of cultural analysis, while the manner of selection of individuals for given statuses, whether achieved or ascribed, together with factors of sex, age, geographical locations, etc., are social as here defined. The study of personality variations in the carrying out of the patterns is part of the individual approach.

On the other hand, the analysis into syntactic, semantic, and pragmatic is distinctly linguistic, but in a wider range than natural language. Sometimes we find what may be called quasi-languages. For instance, in describing the game of chess, the rules of the game are syntactic while the behavior of the players is part of the pragmatic aspect. Inasmuch as the individual moves of the game seem to have no reference to anything outside themselves, the semantic dimension is lacking, hence the term quasi-language. In art and religion, we may have symbolism in which individual elements have *designata* or reference to things outside themselves. In these instances pragmatic, semantic, and syntactic elements are all present, and we are wont, as a matter of fact, to call such fields of expression languages. To describe on what occasions, by what performers, and with what details of interpretations and audience reaction the opera "Die Walkuere" was performed is a pragmatic investigation. To refer a series of low descending notes to the majesty of Wotan is a statement in semantics, while to discuss the musical form of the opera is to treat its syntactics.

The foregoing analysis reveals the richness of language and the diversity of viewpoints from which it can be approached. It suggests that linguistic and extralinguistic segments of culture are intimately connected in a number of different ways. The ethnologist may view language merely as a tool, howbeit a vital one in his research, if he fastens his attention merely on the content of informants' statements, but he may go further and view each specimen of the informants' speech as an instance of verbal behavior revealing both personal and cultural aspects. He may, if he attains sufficient practical command of the language, observe language on its pragmatic side in the daily life of the people. He may also penetrate into the workshop of the linguist and come to understand the technical processes employed there and utilize the finished product which he produces. Altogether there is a rewarding field which awaits the linguistically oriented ethnologist and a mature science of culture is unlikely to emerge without the linguistic approach to culture having played a significant role.

REFERENCE NOTE

This paper was read at the meeting of Section H of the American Association for the Advancement of Science, Chicago, 1947. Greenberg notes that "Of previous treatments of this general topic, I have profited most from the two illuminating joint articles of C. F. Voegelin and Z. S. Harris" (1945, 1947).

While couched primarily in terms of ethnology, Greenberg's account of linguistic problems broaches many interests that have been cultivated by sociology and psychology as well. It is in effect a view of the relations between linguistics and anthropology, sociology, and psychology and between language and culture, society, and personality. References given here are to writings that deal with the relations between the disciplines and the most general relations between their subject matters. (More specific relationships are dealt with throughout the book.) The references are organized into three parts: (A) Linguistics and Anthropology, (B) Linguistics and Sociology, (C) Linguistics and Psychology.

A. LINGUISTICS AND ANTHROPOLOGY

The relationship between linguistics and anthropology, and to a large extent, correlatively, between language and culture, has been the subject of considerable discussion in the last two decades or so. The following references indicate the chief contributions, mostly in the American literature, but to some extent by English and French scholars as well. Specific contributions of Boas, Sapir, Kroeber, and Bloomfield are noted; the preceding article should be consulted, together with the Introduction to this section for a more general view of their work. The contributions of Levi-Strauss, Pike, Malinowski, and Firth are further cited and discussed with their articles in this part, and those of Trager with his article in Part V. Of those whose contributions are noted only here, Greenberg, Hoijer, and Voegelin should be singled out as the most prominent and influential on the American scene in addition to those just mentioned.

The references are: Aberle (1960), Bittle (1952, 1953), Bloomfield (1914, pp. 317 ff.; 1925; 1942a), Boas (1911, 1917, 1938b, 1939a, 1942), Firth (1935, 1950, 1957a), Gleason (1962), Greenberg (1948a, 1953, 1954b, 1957c, 1959a, 1959b); Harris (1940, 1951a), Hocart (1918), Hockett (1948a, 1948b, 1948c, 1950), Hoijer (1948c, 1951, 1953, 1954a, 1954b, 1962), Hymes (1962a, 1963a, 1963b, 1963c); Kroeber (1941, 1952), Kroeber and Kluckhohn (1952, pp. 115-124), Levi-Strauss (1951, 1953a, 1955, 1958a, 1960d, 1961), Levi-Strauss, Jakobson, Voegelin, Sebeok (1953), Lounsbury (1959, 1960, 1962), McQuown (1954a, 1954b, 1956), Meillet (1933), Olmsted (1950, 1955), Pike (1954-1955-1960, 1956, 1957-1958), Radin (1933), Reichard (1950), Robins (1959), Sapir (1912, 1916, 1921, 1927a, 1927b, 1929c, 1933a, 1947), Schmidt (1939, pp. 281-293), Silva-Fuenzalida (1949), Sommerfelt (1960a), Uhlenbeck (1960), Voegelin (1937, 1949a, 1949b, 1950, 1951, 1961a, 1961b), Voegelin and Harris (1945, 1947, 1952), Whorf (1956a).

References not in the general bibliography:

BITTLE, WILLIAM

1952. Language and Culture: A Comment on Voegelin's View. *SJA*, *8:* 466-471.

1953. Language and Culture Areas: A Note on Method. *Philosophy of Science*, *20:* 247-256.

HOCKETT, C. F.

1950b. Language "and" Culture: A Protest. *AA*, *52:* 113.

KROEBER, A. L., and C., KLUCKHOHN

1952. *Culture. A Review of Concepts and Definitions.* (Papers of the Peabody Museum of American Archaeology and Ethnology, Harvard University, vol. 47, no. 1.) Cambridge: The Museum.

LOUNSBURY, FLOYD G.

1959. Similarity and Contiguity Relations in Language and Culture. In Richard S. Harrell (Ed.), *Report of the Tenth Annual Round Table Meeting on*

Linguistics and Language Study. (Monograph Series on Languages and Linguistics, No. 12.) Washington, D.C.: Georgetown University. Pp. 123-128.

MCQUOWN, NORMAN A.

1954b. Cultural Implications of Linguistic Science. In Hugo Mueller (Ed.), *Report of the Fifth Annual Round Table Meeting on Linguistics Teaching*. (Monograph Series on Languages and Linguistics, No. 7.) Washington, D.C.: Georgetown University. Pp. 57-61.

1956. A Linguistics Laboratory Serves Cultural Anthropology. *AA*, *58:* 536-539.

OLMSTED, DAVID L.

1950. *Ethnolinguistics So Far*. (Studies in Linguistics, Occasional Papers, No. 2.) Norman, Okla.: Battenburg Press.

1955. The Science of Language. *Encyclopedia Americana*, *16 :* 718-724.

REICHARD, GLADYS A.

1950. Language and Culture Patterns. *AA*, *52:* 194-204.

SCHMIDT, WILHELM

1939. *The Culture Historical Method of Ethnology. The Scientific Approach to the Racial Question*. Translated by S. A. Sieber. Preface by Clyde Kluckhohn. New York: Fortuny.

SILVA-FUENZALIDA, ISMAEL

1949. Ethnolinguistics and the Study of Culture. *AA*, *51:* 446-456.

VOEGELIN, C. F.

1937. Anthropological Limits of Language. *Proceedings of the Indiana Academy of Science*, *46:* 57-64.

1949a. Linguistics Without Meaning and Culture Without Words. *Word*, *5:* 36-42.

1949b. Relative Structurability. *Word*, *5:* 44-45.

1950. A "Testing Frame" for Language and Culture. *AA*, *52:* 432-435.

1951. Culture, Language, and the Human Organism. *SJA*, *7:* 357-373.

1961a. Anthropological Linguistics in the Context of Other Fields of Linguistics. *A William Cameron Townsend en el vigesimo-quinto aniversario del Instituo Lingüístico de Verano*. Mexico, D.F.: The Institute. Pp. 673-686.

1961b. Centrifugal and Centripetal Directions of Field Work in Anthropology. *Plateau*, *34:* 50-59.

B. LINGUISTICS AND SOCIOLOGY

Discussions of the relation of linguistics to sociology and of language to society have been less common on the American scene than in European scholarship. Cf. the discussions by Bram (1955), Carroll (1953, pp. 112-132), Cohen (1956a, especially pp. 15-16, 25-32 for general European references and bibliography), Doroszewski (1933), Hertzler (1953), Hill (1958), Jespersen (1925), Leroy (1953), Lewis (1947), Leyton (1957), McDavid (1946), Parsons (1961), Pieris (1951), Putnam and O'Hern (1955), Radcliffe-Brown (1957, pp. 96, 107-109, 120, 142-143), Sapir (1927a, 1927b), Schlauch (1936), Sechehaye (1942), Segerstedt (1947), Sommerfelt (1932, 1938, 1956, 1961). See also the references in Parts V, VII, and VIII.

References not included in the general bibliography are:

BRAM, JOSEPH

1955. *Language and Society*. (Studies in Sociology, No. 8). New York: Random House.

LEROY, M.

1953. Le Social et l'individuel dans la science du langage. *Revue de Sociologie*, *4:* 475-489.

LEYTON, A. C.

1957. Semantic Aspects of Sociological Studies. *Synthèsè*, *10:* 270-278.

PIERIS, R.

1951. Speech and Society: A Sociological Approach to Language. *American Sociological Review*, *16:* 499-505.

SCHLAUCH, MARGARET

1936. The Social Basis of Linguistics. *Science and Society*, *1:* 18-44.

SECHEHAYE, ALBERT

1942. De la Définition de la phonème à la définition de l'entité de langue. *Cahiers de Ferdinand de Saussure*, *2:* 45-55.

SEGERSTEDT, T. T.

1947. *Die Macht des Wortes: Eine Sprachsoziologie*. Zurich: Pan-Verlag. [Translated from the Swedish.]

SEREBRENNIKOV, B. A.

1953. Le Problème des rapports des faits linguistiques avec l'histoire de la societe. *Voprosy jazykoznanija* (Questions de Linguistique), *1:* 34-51. Moscow.

SOMMERFELT, ALF

1932. La Linguistique, science sociologique. (Leçon d'inauguration de la chaire de linguistique générale à l'Université d'Oslo.) *Norsk Tidsskrift for Sprogvidenskap*, *5:* 315-331.

1956. Language, Society, and Culture. (Lectures at University of Michigan, 1953.) *Norsk Tidsskrift for Sprogvidenskap*, *17:* 1-81.

C. LINGUISTICS AND PSYCHOLOGY

The relation of linguistics and psychology and of language to psychological phenomena and research has been a recurrent subject for discussion throughout the history of the various social or behavioral sciences. For a number of the important earlier discussions, see references in Kantor (1936, 1952). The references given here, with one or two exceptions of special interest, include the more important and more useful recent treatments, often in historical or survey form, often programmatic (as are many of the discussions in the preceding two groups): Alkon (1959) Brown (1958), Carroll (1953, pp. 69-111; 1958), Delacroix (1924), Esper (1935), Gray (1939, pp. 92-93), Hymes (1961b), Janet and Dumas (1933), Kainz (1946-1954), Kantor (1936), Lounsbury (1962), Maccoby, Newcomb, Hardy (1958), Mead (1904), Miller (1951, 1954), Miller, Galanter, Pribram (1960), Mowrer (1960), Newman (1941), Olmsted (1955), Olmsted and Moore (1952), Osgood (1953), Osgood and Sebeok (1954), Pronko (1946), Roback (1954), Sanford (1942), Saporta (1961), Schlauch (1946), Skinner (1957), Sperber (1945), Vygotsky (1939, 1962), Weiss (1925), Werner and Kaplan (1956). For some of the most recent work, especially of anthropological interest, see references in Parts III, IV, V. Brown (1959), Hoch and Zubin (1958), Miller (1953), Miller, Galanter, Pribram (1960), Osgood and Sebeok (1954), Osgood, Suci, Tannenbaum (1957), Saporta (1961), and Skinner (1957) may be singled out as representing the work that has most stimulated recent anthropological interest.

References not in the general bibliography are:

ALKON, PAUL L.
1959. Behaviourism and Linguistics: an Historical Note. *Language and Speech, 2:* 37-51.

DELACROIX, H.
1924. Linguistique et psychologie. *Le Langage et la pensée*. Paris : Alcan (2nd., 1930.) [Also in Pierre Janet and Georges Dumas (Eds.), *Psychologie du langage*. Paris: Alcan. 1933. (*Journal de psychologie: normale et pathologique, 30* [1-4].)]

ESPER, E. A.
1935. Language. In C. Murchison (Ed.), *A Handbook of Social Psychology*. Worcester, Mass.: Clark University Press. Pp. 417-460.

MEAD, G. H.
1904. The Relation of Psychology and Philology. *Psychological Bulletin, 1:* 375-391.

MILLER, G. A., E. GALANTER, K. H. PRIBRAM
1960. *Plans and the Structure of Behavior*. New York: Holt.

MOWRER, O. H.
1960. *Learning Theory and the Symbolic Process*. New York: Wiley.

OLMSTED, DAVID L.
1955. Review of C. E. Osgood and T. A. Sebeok, *Psycholinguistics, A Survey of Theory and Research Problems*. *Lg., 31:* 46-59.

OLMSTED, DAVID L., and OMAR KHAYYAM MOORE
1952. Language Psychology and Linguistics. *Psychological Review, 59:* 414-420.

PRONKO, N. H.
1946. Language and Psycholinguistics. *Psychological Bulletin, 43:* 189-239.

ROBACK, A. A.
1954. *Destiny and Motivation in Language; Studies in Psycholinguistics and Glossodynamics*. Cambridge, Mass.: Sci-Art.

SANFORD, F. H.
1942. Speech and Personality. *Psychological Bulletin, 39:* 811-845.

SKINNER, B. F.
1957. *Verbal Behavior*. New York: Appleton-Century-Crofts.

SPERBER, HANS
1945. Behaviourism in Linguistics. *Monatshefte für deutschen Unterricht, 37:* 176-184.

WEISS, A. P.
1925. Linguistics and Psychology. *Lg., 1:* 52-57.

3 *Cultural Anthropology and Linguistics*

WARD H. GOODENOUGH

CULTURAL ANTHROPOLOGISTS try to do a number of different things, and a great many of them, at least, can be discussed in relation to linguistics. But the anthropologist's basic task, on which all the rest of his endeavors depend, is to describe specific cultures adequately. This aspect of anthropological work is known as ethnography. It provides the context for what I shall have to say this morning.

A proper definition of culture must ultimately derive from the operations by which we describe particular cultures. Because these operations are still in early stages of formulation and development, it is not yet possible to state precisely just what we mean when we speak of a society's culture. A working definition will be necessary, however, in order to discuss linguistics in relation to ethnography.

As I see it, a society's culture consists of whatever it is one has to know or believe in order to operate in a manner acceptable to its members, and do so in any role that they accept for any one of themselves. Culture, being what people have to learn as distinct from their biological heritage, must consist of the end product of learning: knowledge, in a most general, if relative, sense of the term. By this definition, we should note that culture is not a material phenomenon; it does not consist of things, people, behavior, or emotions. It is rather an organization of these things. It is the forms of things that people have in mind, their models for perceiving, relating, and otherwise interpreting them. As such, the things people say and do, their social arrangements and events, are products or by-products of their culture as they apply it to the task of perceiving and dealing with their circumstances. To one who knows their culture, these things and events are also signs signifying the cultural forms or models of which they are material representations, a fact to which I shall return shortly.

Given such a definition, it is obviously impossible to describe a culture properly simply by describing behavior or social, economic, and ceremonial events and arrangements as observed material phenomena. What is required is to construct a theory of the conceptual models which they represent and of which they are artifacts. We test the adequacy of such a theory by our ability to interpret and predict what goes on in a community as measured by how its members, our informants, do so. A further test is our ability ourselves to behave in ways which lead to the kind of responses from the community's members which our theory would lead us to expect. Thus tested, the theory is a valid statement of what you have to know in order to operate as a member of the society and is, as such, a valid description of its culture. Its acceptability beyond this depends largely on the esthetic criteria to which scientists and mathematicians customarily refer by the term "elegance."

Ethnographic description, then, requires methods of processing observed phenomena such that we can inductively construct a theory of how our informants have organized the same phenomena. It is the theory, not the phenomena alone, which ethnographic description aims to present.

Thus viewed, it seems to me that the methodological problem of ethnography is identical with that of descriptive linguistics. A phonetic transcription, for example, describes a particular material manifestation of a language by means of an *a priori* taxonomy of sounds; it does not describe the language or any segment of it. It does not indicate what the speaker said, but what a recorder heard before he had learned the language. (I defy you to make a phonetic transcription after you've learned the language.) It is the raw data from which statements describing the language may be induced, from which the language may be learned. The linguistic problem is to construct a theory as to what are the acoustical percepts with which the speakers of the language in question operate—the phonemes, combinations of phonemes, and arrangements of the combinations by which they discriminate speech behavior. Thus, phonemic description bears the same relation to speech as sounds and behavior that cultural description bears to the material world in general. Indeed, we may define a language in precisely the same terms in which we have already defined a culture. It consists of whatever it is one has to know in order to communicate with its speakers as adequately as they do with each other and in a manner which they will accept as corresponding to their own.

In this sense, a society's language is an aspect of its culture. This is contradicted in no way by the fact that two communities speaking what passes for the same language may otherwise have somewhat different cultures. Other major aspects of culture have a similar kind of semi-independence; societies sharing a common technological tradition may possess different religions. The frequent assertion that language and culture are independent, while properly cautioning against certain kinds of inference, is in other respects an unfortunate half-truth.

The relation of language to culture, then, is that of part to whole. Theory and method applicable to one must have implications for the other. With this in mind, let us examine the implications which the method of structural linguistics may have for ethnography.

It is a proud boast of structural linguists that by their methods they are able to describe the phonology, morphology, and syntax of a language without resort to the meaning of the utterances which they analyze. Because of the improper use to which meaning was formerly put and because of the apparently intuitive approach to meaning which earlier linguists employed, outlawing the use of semantic criteria for descriptive purposes and basing structural analysis on distributional criteria instead has served a very useful purpose. It would be a terrible mistake, however, to assume that structural linguistic method has nothing to do with meaning.

What structural linguistics has done is simply to disallow the use of meanings as entities already known and therefore available as criteria of structural analysis. By doing so, linguists have succeeded in developing a fairly precise method for deriving meanings as the end product of analysis, a fact which, as far as I am aware, has been obscured by an uncritical distinction between so-called structural and referential meaning. In order to clarify what I am suggesting here, let us see how the concepts and methods of structural linguistics may be fitted into sign theory.

For purposes of this discussion, we may distinguish between two different kinds of signs. The first type consists of any sign which is itself a member and, as such, representative of the class of phenomena signified. Thus, a particular safety-pin is a member and representative of a conceptual class of object. It must signify to us the criteria for being in that class before we can recognize it as a safety-pin. It does so by virtue of possessing the properties which we define as necessary for membership in the class. As material manifestations of the conceptual classes, the forms, which they signify, such signs have been aptly termed iconic (Morris, 1946). The second type of sign is non-iconic, consisting of all signs which themselves lack the properties delimiting the classes of phenomena they signify. Now, any material object, event, or act to which people respond is necessarily an icon signifying a conceptual form of some kind (or people wouldn't respond to it). For a sign to be non-iconic, then, it must be other than material. While non-iconic signs signify conceptual forms, they are themselves conceptual forms, which are in turn signified by iconic signs.

Language illustrates the two types very well. As a linguistic form, the word *stone* does not itself have the properties by which we recognize things to be stones. It is, therefore, a non-iconic sign. Each specific utterance of the word, however, is an iconic sign signifying the linguistic form which it materializes. Indeed—and this is the point I wish to emphasize—every uttered sound or "phone" is an iconic sign of a phoneme, itself possessing the properties by which we recognize the phonological class it represents. Every speech utterance is an iconic sign of a corresponding linguistic form or combination of forms. In this respect, linguistic forms are no different from all other cultural forms which have material representation or can be given such representation in iconic signs. A house is an icon of the cultural form or complex combination of forms of which it is a material expression. A tree, in addition to being a natural object of interest to a botanist, is an icon signifying a cultural form, the very same form which we also signify by the word *tree*. If, as I have already suggested, every object, event, or act has stimulus value for the members of a society only insofar as it is an iconic sign signifying some corresponding form in their culture, it follows that any method which enables us inductively to isolate and describe such cultural forms precisely and rigorously by virtue of operations performed on their icons will be of tremendous value to ethnographers.

It is here, of course, that structural linguists have made a notable contribution; for it is on utterances as iconic signs that they have concentrated their attention. By refusing to allow matters relating to the role of linguistic forms as non-iconic signs to enter their deliberations, they have developed rigorous methods for manipulating utterances as icons so that it is possible to isolate and make valid statements concerning the linguistic forms and sequences of forms which they signify. Structural linguistics is, in effect, a science of iconic signs, a method for describing what they signify, and in this sense, what they mean.

Once we recognize this fact, it is but a short step to apply the method to the problem of describing those concepts which are signified by linguistic and other cultural forms in their role as non-iconic signs. A demonstration of how linguistic method may be applied to this end is now in press and will appear in [Goodenough, 1956]. Without entangling us in the details and complexities, I can illustrate the fundamentals very simply in connection with writing.

Every letter that is actually written on a piece of paper is an icon signifying the conceptual model for the letter, a grapheme. The grapheme is in turn a non-iconic sign signifying a phoneme. (For the sake of simplicity, I am assuming the writing to be phonemic.) The phoneme, in turn, is materialized in speech as a sound which is an iconic sign of the phoneme. If someone unfamiliar with the language wishes to isolate and describe the phoneme represented by the grapheme, he asks an informant to pronounce for him a sample of written words and phrases, of which one group contains the grapheme in question in various positions in the words and phrases while a control group does not contain the grapheme. If he records each utterance in some kind of phonetic notation, he can then follow established methods for isolating the accoustical criteria which differentiate the phoneme in question from others. Having thus described the phoneme he has at the same time described what the grapheme signifies, because the already isolated grapheme was the point of reference for collecting the phonetic data for phonemic analysis. The investigator now knows, as well as he can ever know, what the grapheme means as a non-iconic sign in the culture of his informant.

Similarly, by getting an informant to show him a sample of things which, in the informant's meaning system, can be called stones as against a sample of things which cannot be called stones, someone learning to speak English can by virtue of the resulting series of contrasts establish a verifiable hypothesis as to what are the criteria for being a stone. Taken together, these criteria describe a concept, a cultural form, which each stone in his sample signifies as an iconic sign and which the word *stone* signifies as a non-iconic sign. The method of phonemic analysis, in which the object is to bring out systematically all points of contrast between groupings of icons as an informant sets them up and, thus, step-by-step to eliminate all but one hypothesis as to what they signify, is fully applicable here.

There are problems to be sure. We lack for other material phenomena the equivalent of a phonetic notation whereby we translate the icons into easily manipulated forms for analytical purposes. But this was once a problem in linguistics as well. It poses obstacles, but none that cannot be removed by applying a little effort. Another complication stems from the fact that non-iconic signs can, and, as I am beginning to discover, frequently do, signify more than one conceptual form, in the same way that a letter in an alphabet may signify more than one phoneme. One of the findings already emerging from preliminary analyses is the fact that nonlinguistic forms have systematic relationships to each other in paradigms and combine in accordance with principles analogous to those of linguistic morphology and syntax. Indeed, they seem generally to exhibit much the same kinds of structural relationships, however more widely ramified, with which we are becoming familiar in connection with linguistic forms—but I am getting beyond the scope of this paper.

The thing to note here is the fact that what non-iconic signs signify can be systematically gotten at only through analysis of icons and determination of the forms they signify. Out of the linguist's desire to commit hitherto unwritten languages to writing in such a way as accurately to reflect their phonic structures has come the necessary science of icons on which a general science of signs can be erected.

If we return now to our original point of departure, we may ask why a descriptive science of signs is crucial to ethnography. What have anthropologists been describing without such a science to help them, if not cultures?

It is in the course of learning his language and how to use it that every human being acquires the bulk of his culture. An ethnographer, himself a human being, can hope to acquire another society's culture only by learning and using its language. Thus, as a set of forms, language is not only a part of culture; as a set of easily manipulated non-iconic signs, it is a major intrument for learning it.

What I am saying, of course, is that we learn much of a culture when we learn the system of meanings for which its linguistic forms stand. Much descriptive ethnography is inescapably an exercise in descriptive semantics. It is true that ethnographers have so far been only a little more systematic about it than is the average layman as he learns a new culture. As a result, we have tended to talk *about* cultures instead of accurately describing them. Much of ethnography is taken up with a description of the material setting in which a culture exists and of its technological, social, mythological, and emotional artifacts. Relatively little attention is devoted—systematically, at least—to isolating the concepts or forms in terms of which the members of a society deal with one another and the world around them, and many of which are signified lexically in their language.

The great problem for a science of man is how to get from the objective world of materiality, with its infinite variability, to the subjective world of form as it exists in what, for lack of a better term, we must call the minds of our fellow men. We all of us succeed in doing so, somehow, or we couldn't learn to understand each other. That language exists at all is evidence enough of this. But the processes by which we do it have eluded our grasp. Structural linguistics has, I think, made us conscious, at last, of their nature, and has gone on to convert this consciousness into a systematic method.

Yesterday, Professor Hill said that he regarded linguistics as the best instrument yet devised for getting inside the human skin. He was speaking as a linguist. As a cultural anthropologist, I heartily endorse his opinion.

4 *Structural Analysis in Linguistics and in Anthropology*

CLAUDE LEVI-STRAUSS

ALTHOUGH UNQUESTIONABLY one of the social sciences, linguistics has a very special place among them. It is not a social science just as the others, but that which has by far made the greatest progress; the only one, in fact, which can claim the name of science and which has succeeded, at one and the same time, in formulating a positive method and in knowing thoroughly the nature of the facts subject to its analysis. This privileged situation brings with it certain obligations; the linguist will often see investigators from neighboring, but different, disciplines take inspiration from his example and attempt to follow his path. *Noblesse oblige:* a linguistic journal such as *Word* cannot limit itself to the illustration of strictly linguistic arguments and points of view. It should also welcome psychologists, sociologists and ethnographers anxious to learn from modern linguistics the path which leads to positive knowledge of social facts. As Marcel Mauss wrote twenty years ago: "Sociology would certainly be much more advanced if it had proceeded everywhere by imitating linguists. . . ." (1951). The close analogy in method between the two disciplines imposes on them a special duty of collaboration.

Since Schrader (1890, chap. XII, part 4), there is no need to demonstrate what assistance linguistics can bring to the sociologist in the study of problems of kinship. Linguists and philologists (Schrader, 1890; Rose, 1911) were those who showed the improbability of the hypothesis—to which so many sociologists in the same period still clung—of matrilineal survivals in the family of classical antiquity. (See also on this question the more recent works of George Thompson, favorable to the hypothesis of matrilineal survivals.) The linguist provides the sociologist with etymologies which permit establishing, between particular kinship terms, connections which could not be directly perceived. Conversely, the sociologist can inform the linguist of customs, of positive rules and prohibitions, which explain the persistence of certain traits of language, or the instability of terms or of groups of terms. During a meeting of the Linguistic Circle of New York Professor G. Bonfante illustrated this point of view by recalling the etymology of the term for "uncle" in certain Romance languages: Greek θετος becoming, in Italian, in Spanish and in Portuguese, *zio* and *tio;* and he added that in certain regions of Italy, the uncle is called *barba.* The "beard," the "divine" uncle, what these terms suggest to the sociologist! The research of the late Hocart on the religious character of the avuncular relation and the theft of the sacrifice by the maternal relatives also come to mind (1915, 1923, 1925, and others). Whatever may be the appropriate interpretation for the facts collected by Hocart (his own is surely not entirely satisfactory), it is certain that the linguist participates in solving the problem by detecting, in present-day vocabulary, the tenacious persistence of vanished relationships. At the same time, the sociologist explains to the linguist what underlies his etymology, and confirms its validity. More recently, it is while studying the kinship systems of South Asia as a linguist that Paul K. Benedict has been able to make an important contribution to the sociology of the family of that part of the world (1942, 1943).

But while proceeding in this way, linguists and sociologists each pursue their own paths quite independently. To be sure, they pause from time to time to exchange particular results; still these results come from different courses of development, and there is no attempt to benefit one group by the technical and methodological progress of the other. This attitude was understandable in a period when linguistic research concentrated on historical analysis. In relation to the ethnological research of the same period, the difference was more one of degree than of kind. Linguists had a more rigorous method; their results were better established; the sociologists could take inspiration from their example in "giving up the idea of taking the distribution in space of existing species as the basis for their classifications" (Brunschvicg, 1927, p. 562); but after all, anthropology and sociology expected only lessons from linguistics; nothing augured a revelation. (Between 1900 and 1920 the founders of modern linguistics, Ferdinand de Saussure and Antoine Meillet put themselves deliberately under the patronage of sociologists. It is only after 1920 that Marcel Mauss begins, as economists say, to reverse the trend.)

The birth of phonology overturned this state of things. It brought new perspectives not only to linguistics; a transformation of this scope is not confined to a particular discipline. Phonology cannot fail to play for the social sciences the same revitalizing role that nuclear physics, for example, played for the exact sciences. This revolution, whose most general implications we shall try to consider—of what does it consist? The renowned master of phonology, N. Troubetzkoy, provides us with an answer. In a programmatic article (1933), he reduces, in brief, the phonological method to four fundamental steps: in the first place, phonology passes from the study of *conscious* linguistic phenomena to that of their underlying *unconscious* structure; it refuses to take *terms* as independent entities, on the contrary it takes *relations* between terms as the basis of its analysis; it introduces the notion of *system:* "Present-day phonology does not limit itself to stating that phonemes are always members of a system, it *shows* concrete phonological systems and displays their structure" (1933, p. 243); finally, it aims at the discovery of *general laws* either found by induction "or ... deduced logically, which gives them an absolute character" (1933, p. 243).

Thus, for the first time, a social science succeeds in formulating necessary relationships. Such is the sense of this last phrase of Troubetzkoy, while the preceding rules show how linguistics should proceed in order to attain this result. It is not necessary for us to show here that Troubetzkoy's claims are justified; the great majority of modern linguists seem sufficiently in accord on this point. But when an event of this importance takes place in one of the sciences of man, representatives of neighboring disciplines are not only permitted but required to examine promptly its implications and its possible application to facts of another order.

Thus new perspectives open. It is no longer a question merely of an occasional collaboration, such that the linguist and the sociologist, each working in his own corner, from time to time toss across whatever each finds that might interest the other. In the study of problems of kinship (and undoubtedly also in the study of other problems), the sociologist is in a situation exactly like that of the linguist in phonology: like phonemes, kinship terms are elements which have a signifying function; like them, they acquire this function only by being integrated into systems; "kinship systems," like "phonological systems," are elaborated by the mind at the level of unconscious thought; finally, the recurrence, in distant regions of the world and in profoundly different societies, of forms of kinship, rules of marriage, attitudes similarly prescribed between certain types of kin, etc., leads one to believe that, in the one case as in the other, the observable phenomena result from the play of general, but hidden, laws. The problem can then be formulated in the following fashion: in *another order of reality*, the phenomena of kinship are phenomena of the *same type* as linguistic phenomena. Can the sociologist, utilizing a method analogous *in form* (if not in content) to that introduced by the phonologist, bring about in his science a progress like that which has just taken place in the linguistic sciences?

One will feel even more disposed to undertake this approach when one has noted an additional fact: the study of problems of kinship presents itself today in the same terms, and seems to suffer the same difficulties, as linguistics on the eve of the phonological revolution. There is a striking analogy between the older linguistics, which sought its principle of explanation above all in history, and certain efforts of Rivers: in both cases, an account of synchronic phenomena is to be rendered wholly—or almost wholly—by diachronic study. Comparing phonology and the older linguistics, Troubetzkoy defines the former as a "structuralism and a systematic universalism" which he opposes to the individualism and the "atomism" of previous schools. And when he envisages diachronic study, it is in a profoundly modified perspective: "The evolution of the phonological system is, at each given moment, directed by the *tendency toward an end*. . . . This evolution has then a meaning, an internal logic, that the historical phonologist is called upon to display" (1933, p. 245; Jakobson, 1931a; 1929, pp. 44 ff.). The "individualistic," "atomistic" interpretation, based solely on historical contingency that Troubetzkoy and Jakobson criticize, is very much the same, in point of fact, as that generally applied to problems of kinship (Rivers, 1914, *passim*; 1924, chap. IV). Each detail of terminology, each special rule of marriage, is connected with a different custom, as its consequence or vestige: one falls into a debauch of discontinuity. No one asks how kinship systems, considered as synchronic wholes, could be the arbitrary result of the coming together of a number of heterogeneous institutions (most of them moreover hypothetical), and nevertheless function with a certain regularity and effectiveness. (For a similar criticism, see Tax, 1937.)

Nevertheless, a preliminary difficulty interferes with the transfer of the phonological method to primitive sociology. The superficial analogy between phonological systems and kinship systems is so great that it immediately starts on a false trail. This is to assimilate kinship terms to the phonemes of language from the point of view of their formal treatment. One knows that to attain a law of structure, the linguist analyzes phonemes into "differential elements," which it is possible then to organize into one or more "pairs of oppositions" (Jakobson, 1939). The sociologist could be tempted to dissociate the kinship terms of a given system by following a method of the same sort. In our kinship system, for example, the term *father* is characterized positively with regard to sex (+ male: — female), relative age (+ older: — younger), generation (+ ascending: — descending); on the other hand, it has a null extension, and cannot express relationship by marriage. Thus one will ask, for each system, what relations are expressed, and for each term of the system, how is it characterized—positively or negatively with regard to each of these relations: generation, extension, sex, relative age, connection by marriage, etc. It is at this "microsociological" stage that one would hope to detect the most general laws of structure, just as the linguist discovers his at the infra-phonemic level of the distinctive features, or the physicist at the infra-molecular level, that is to say at the level of the atom. One could interpret in these terms the interesting effort of Davis and Warner (1937).

But a threefold objection soon appears. A truly scientific analysis must be realistic, simplifying and explanatory. Thus the differential elements, which are the end result of phonological analysis, possess an objective existence from a threefold point of view, psychological, physiological and even physical; they are less numerous than the phonemes formed by their combination; finally, they permit one to understand and reconstruct the system. Nothing of this sort would result from the preceding hypothesis. Such a treatment of kinship terms, as we have just imagined, only appears to be analytical; for in fact, the result is more abstract than the starting point; instead of going toward the concrete one withdraws from it, and the final system—if system there is—could be only conceptual. In the second place, the experience of Davis and Warner proves that the system obtained by this process is infinitely more complicated and difficult to interpret than the data of experience. (Thus at the end of the analysis by these authors, the term "husband" is replaced by the formula: $C^{2a/2d/0}SU^{1}ag/\text{Ego}$. Note here two recent studies, using a much more refined logical machinery, which have great interest both as to method and results: Lounsbury, 1956, and Goodenough, 1956.) Finally the hypothesis has no explanatory value; it does not make the nature of the system comprehensible; still less does it permit one to reconstruct its origin.

What is the reason for this failure? Too literal a fidelity to the method of the linguist has in reality betrayed its spirit. Kinship terms have not only a sociological existence; they are also elements of discourse. In hurrying to transfer the linguist's methods of analysis to them, one must not forget that inasmuch as they are part of vocabulary, they are subject to these methods, not in an analogical way, but directly. Now linguistics teaches precisely that phonological analysis does not have a direct grasp on words, but only on words previously dissociated into phonemes. *There are no necessary relations at the level of vocabulary*. (As one can see in chap. V [of *Anthropologie structurale*], I would today use a more qualified formulation.) This is true of all the elements of the vocabulary—and includes kinship terms. It is true in linguistics and must then be true *ipso facto* for a sociology of language. An effort of the sort whose possibility we are now discussing would then consist of extending the phonological method, while forgetting its foundation. In an article already old, Kroeber (1909) has prophetically foreseen this difficulty. And if at that time he inferred the impossibility of a structural analysis of kinship terms, it is because linguistics itself was then confined to a phonetic, psychological and historical analysis. The social sciences must, indeed, share the limitations of linguistics; but they can also profit from its progress.

One must not forget the very profound difference between the table of phonemes of a language and the table of kinship terms of a society. In the case of the first, there is no doubt as to the function: we all know what end a language serves; it serves communication. What the linguist a long time ignored, on the other hand, and what phonology alone allowed him to discover, is the means thanks to which language attains this result. The function was evident; the system remained unknown. In this regard the sociologist finds himself in quite the opposite situation: that kinship terms constitute systems we have known clearly since Lewis H. Morgan; on the other hand, we are still ignorant of the use for which they are intended. Misunderstanding of this initial situation reduces most structural analyses of kinship systems to pure tautologies. They show what is evident, and neglect what remains unknown.

This does not mean that we must give up the idea of introducing an order and of discovering a signifying function in kinship terminologies. But it is necessary at least to recognize the special problems which a sociology of vocabulary poses, and the ambiguous nature of the relationships which unite its methods to those of linguistics. For this reason, it would be preferable to limit discussion to a case where the analogy presents itself in a simple fashion. Fortunately we have this possibility.

What one generally calls "kinship system" comprises, as a matter of fact, two very different orders of reality. There are first the terms, by which the different types of family relationships are expressed. But kinship is not expressed only in a terminology: the individuals, or the classes of individuals who use the terms, feel themselves (or do not feel themselves, according to the case) bound to a well-defined mode of conduct with regard to one another: respect or familiarity, right or duty, affection or hostility. Thus, beside what we propose to call the *system of appellations* (and which constitutes, properly speaking, a system of vocabulary), there is another system, equally psychological and social in nature, which we designate the *system of attitudes*. Now if it is true (as has been shown above) that the study of systems of appellations is in a situation analogous but inverse to that of phonological systems, that situation is so to speak "turned right side up again," when it is a question of systems of attitudes. We divine the role played by these last, which is to assure the cohesion and equilibrium of the group, but we do not comprehend the nature of the connections existing between diverse attitudes, and we do not perceive their necessity. (One must except the remarkable work of Warner [1930-1931], where the analysis of the system of attitudes, debatable as to depth, none the less augurs a new phase in the study of problems of kinship.) In other words, just as in the case of language, we know the function, but it is the system which we lack.

Between *system of appellations* and *system of attitudes* we thus see a profound difference, and we part on this point from A. R. Radcliffe-Brown, if, as one has sometimes reproached him, he truly believed that the second is only the expression, or the translation on the affective plane, of the first (1935, 1941). In recent years, many examples have been given of groups where the table of kinship terms does not reflect exactly that of familial attitudes, and conversely (Opler, 1937; Halpern, 1942). One would be mistaken to believe that in every society the kinship system constitutes the principal medium by which individual relationships are regulated; and even in those societies where this role has devolved upon it, it does not everywhere fill it to the same degree. Moreover, it is necessary to distinguish always between two types of attitudes: first, the diffuse attitudes, uncrystallized and not institutionalized, which one can accept, on the psychological plane, as the reflection or the efflorescence of the terminology; and beside or in addition to the preceding, the attitudes which are stylized, obligatory, sanctioned by tabus or by privileges, and expressed through fixed ceremonial. Far from reflecting the terminology automatically, these attitudes often appear as secondary elaborations intended to resolve contradictions, and to surmount insufficiencies, inherent in the system of appellations. This synthetic character stands out in particularly striking fashion among the Wik Monkan of Australia; in this group, joking privileges arise to sanction a contradiction between the actual kinship relations uniting two men, prior to marriage, and the theoretical relation that would have to be supposed between them to account for their subsequent marriage with two women who do not have the corresponding relationship (Thomson, 1935). There is a contradiction between two possible systems of terminology, and the emphasis placed on the attitudes represents an effort to integrate, or to transcend, this contradiction among the terms. One will readily agree with Radcliffe-Brown's affirmation of the existence of "real relations of interdependence between the terminology and the rest of the system" (1941, p. 8); at least some of his critics have missed the mark in inferring, from the absence of a rigorous parallelism between attitudes and terminology, the mutual autonomy of the two orders. But this relation of interdependence is not a point-for-point correspondence. The system of attitudes constitutes rather a dynamic integration of the system of appellations.

Even on the hypothesis—to which we adhere without reserve—of a functional relation between the two systems, onc has the right, for methodological reasons, to treat the problems proper to each as separate problems. This is what we propose to do here for a problem rightly considered the point of departure for all theories of attitudes that of the maternal uncle. We will attempt to show how a formal transposition of the method followed by the phonologist throws a new light on this problem. If sociologists have given it particular attention, this is, as a matter of fact, only because the relationship between maternal uncle and nephew seemed the focus of an important elaboration in a very great many primitive societies. But it does not suffice to establish this frequency; it is necessary to discover the reason for it.

Let us recall rapidly the principal stages in the development of this problem. During the 19th century and until Sydney Hartland (1917), the importance of the maternal uncle was readily interpreted as a survival of a matrilineal system. This remained purely hypothetical, and its possibility was particularly doubtful in the face of European examples. In another connection, the attempt by Rivers (1907) to explain the importance of the maternal uncle in southern India as a residue from a marriage between cross-cousins led to a particularly heartbreaking result: the author himself had to recognize that this interpretation could not account for all the aspects of the problem, and he resigned himself to the hypothesis that *several* heterogeneous and now vanished customs (marriage of cousins being only one of them) would have to be invoked to understand the existence *of a single* institution. Atomism and mechanism triumphed (Rivers, 1907, p. 624). Indeed, it is only with an article of cardinal importance by Lowie on the matrilineal complex (1919) that what one would like to call the "modern phase" of the problem of the avunculate begins. Lowie shows that the correlation invoked, or postulated, between the predominance of the maternal uncle and a matrilineal system does not stand analysis; in fact, the avunculate is found associated with patrilineal systems as well as with matrilineal systems. The role of the maternal uncle cannot be explained as a consequence or a survival of a system of matriarchy; it is only the particular application "of a very general tendency to associate definite social relations with definite forms of kinship regardless of maternal or paternal side." This principle, introduced for the first time by Lowie in 1919, according to which there is a general tendency to *qualify attitudes* constitutes the only positive base of a theory of kinship systems. But at the same time, Lowie left certain questions unanswered: what is properly called avunculate? Are not different customs and attitudes confounded under a single term? And if it is true that there exists a tendency to qualify all attitudes, why are only certain attitudes found associated with the avuncular relation, and not, according to the groups considered, any possible attitude?

We digress here to underline the striking

analogy between the development of our problem and certain stages of linguistic thought: the diversity of possible attitudes in the domain of interindividual relations is practically unlimited; it is the same for the diversity of sounds which the vocal apparatus can articulate and produce effectively in the first months of life. Each language, however, retains only a very small number of all these possible sounds, and linguistics poses itself two questions in this regard: why have certain sounds been selected? What relations exist between one or several of the chosen sounds and all the others (Jakobson, 1942)? Our sketch of the history of the problem of the maternal uncle finds itself precisely at the same stage: the social group, like language, finds a very rich psycho-physiological material at its disposition; like language also, it retains only certain elements of which some at least remain constant across the most diverse cultures, and which it combines in ever diversified structures. One then asks what is the reason for the choice, and what are the laws of combination.

Concerning the particular problem of the avuncular relation, it is advisable to turn to Radcliffe-Brown; his celebrated article on the maternal uncle in South Africa (1924) is the first attempt to get at and to analyze the modalities of what we might call the "general principle of the qualification of attitudes." It will suffice to recall rapidly here the fundamental theses of this study that is now classic.

According to Radcliffe-Brown, the term "avunculate" comprises two antithetical systems of attitudes: in one case, the maternal uncle represents the familial authority; he is feared, obeyed and possesses rights over his nephew; in the other, it is the nephew who exercises privileges of familiarity with regard to his uncle, and can treat him more or less as a victim. Secondly, there is a correlation between the attitude toward the maternal uncle and the attitude with regard to the father. In both cases, we find two systems of attitudes, but reversed; in groups where the relation between father and son is familiar, that between maternal uncle and nephew is strict; and where the father appears as the austere repository of familial authority, it is the uncle who is treated with license. The two groups of attitudes form, then, as the phonologist would say, two pairs of oppositions. Radcliffe-Brown concluded by proposing an interpretation of the phenomenon: the line of descent determines, in the last analysis, the meaning of these oppositions. In the patrilineal system where the father, and the line of the father, represents the traditional authority, the maternal uncle is considered, sometimes even called, and generally treated as, a "male mother." The reverse situation occurs in a matrilineal system: there, the maternal uncle incarnates authority, and the relations of tenderness and familiarity are fixed on the father and on his line.

It would be difficult to exaggerate the importance of this contribution by Radcliffe-Brown. After the relentless critique of the evolutionist metaphysic so masterfully conducted by Lowie, this is the effort of synthesis undertaken on a positive base. To say that this effort did not attain its goal at a single stroke certainly does not lessen the homage due the great English sociologist. Let us recognize then that Radcliffe-Brown's article, it too, leaves open some very difficult questions: in the first place, the avunculate is not present in all matrilineal and patrilineal systems; and one finds it sometimes in systems which are neither the one nor the other. (Thus the Mundugomor of New Guinea, where the relation between maternal uncle and nephew is constantly familiar, while descent is alternatively patrilineal and matrilineal. See Mead, 1935, pp. 176-185.) In addition, the avuncular relation is not a relation in two, but in four terms: it assumes a brother, a sister, a brother-in-law, and a nephew. An interpretation like that of Radcliffe-Brown arbitrarily isolates certain elements of a global structure, one which must be treated as such. Some simple examples will show this double difficulty.

The social organization of the natives of the Trobriand Islands, in Melanesia, is characterized by matrilineal descent, free and familiar relations between father and son, and a marked antagonism between maternal uncle and nephew (Malinowski, 1929). On the other hand, the Circassians of the Caucasus, who are patrilineal, place the hostility between father and son, while the maternal uncle helps his nephew, and gives him a present of a horse when he marries (Dubois de Monpereux, 1839, cited in Kovalevski, 1893). So far, we are within the limits of Radcliffe-Brown's schema. But let us consider the other familial relationships which are implied: Malinowski showed that in the

Trobriand Islands, husband and wife live in an atmosphere of tender intimacy, and that their relations are reciprocal in character. On the other hand, the relations between brother and sister are dominated by an extremely rigorous tabu. What now is the situation in the Caucasus? It is the relation between brother and sister that is the tender relation, to such a point that among the Pschav, an only girl "adopts" a "brother" who will play for her the role, customary for the brother, of chaste bed companion (Dubois de Monpereux, 1839). But the situation between spouses is entirely different: a Circassian does not dare appear in public with his wife and visits her only in secret. According to Malinowski, there is no graver insult among the Trobrianders, than to tell a man that he resembles his sister; the Caucasus offers an equivalent of this prohibition, forbidding asking a man about the health of his wife.

When one considers societies of the "Circassian" or "Trobriand" type, it does not suffice to study the correlation of the attitudes: *father/son*, and *uncle/sister's son*. This correlation is only an aspect of a global system in which four types of relation are present and organically linked, namely: *brother/sister*, *husband/wife*, *father/son*, *maternal uncle/sister's son*. The two groups which have served us as examples show the two applications of a law which can be formulated as follows: in the two groups, the relation between maternal uncle and nephew is, to the relation between brother and sister, as the relation between father and son is to the relation between husband and wife. The result is that if one pair of relations is known, it will always be possible to deduce the other. (That is, if the relation between uncle and nephew, and between brother and sister, are both positive, the relation between father and son, and between husband and wife will both be negative; if the first pair are both negative, the second pair will both be positive; if one of the first pair is positive, the other negative, the relations in the second pair will be correspondingly one positive, one negative, the uncle-nephew relation having the same value as that between father and son, the brother-sister relation the same as that between husband and wife.

[See Figs. 1a and 1b, and Levi-Strauss' comment below on the former, reproduced from his article. Fig. 1b, devised by the editor, supplements the normal kinship chart mode of depiction used in Fig. 1a, in order to emphasize graphically the double orientation of each person, and the symmetry of the necessary relationships, in the structure discerned by Levi-Strauss. Usually, as in the Circassian, Trobriand, Tonga, and Siuai cases in Fig. 1a, each pair of relationships shown with parallel lines must share the same sign: if Wife: Husband is +, so must Uncle: Nephew be, and so forth.]

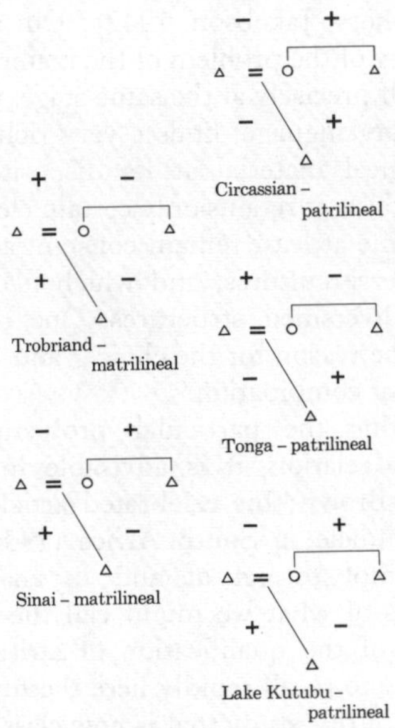

Figure 1a.

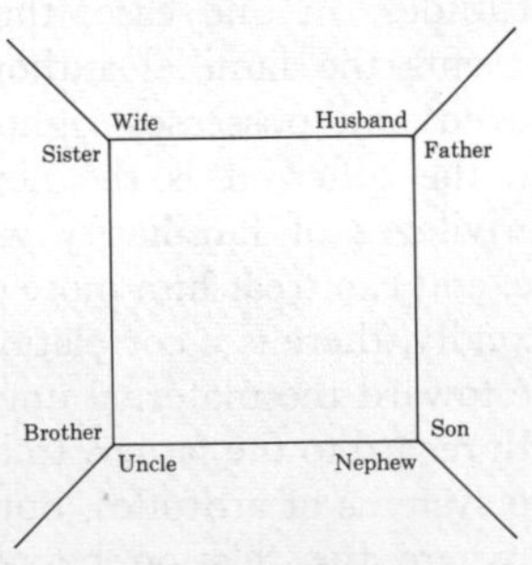

Figure 1b.

Let us consider, for the moment, some other cases. Among the Tonga, in Polynesia, descent is patrilineal as among the Circassians. Relations between husband and wife seem public and harmonious; domestic quarrels are rare and, although often superior in status to her husband, the wife "does not harbour the least thought of rebellion against him ... on all domestic matters, she yields willingly to his authority." Likewise, the greatest freedom reigns between the maternal uncle and the nephew: the latter is *fahu*, above the law, with respect to his uncle with whom all familiarities are permitted. To the freedom of these relationships are opposed those between a father and his son. The former is *tapu*, the son is forbidden to touch his head or his hair, to brush against him when he eats, to sleep on his bed or on his pillow, to share his drink or his food, to play with objects which belong to him. The strongest of all *tapu*, however, is that which prevails between brother and sister, who must not even find themselves together under same roof (Gifford, 1929, pp. 16-22).

Although they are also patrilineal and patrilocal, the natives of Lake Kutubu, in New Guinea, exemplify a structure which is the converse of the preceding: "I have never seen as intimate an association between father and son," writes F. E. Williams on this subject. Relations between husband and wife are marked by the very low status accorded the feminine sex, "the sharp separation between the masculine and feminine centers of interest." The women, says Williams, "must work hard for their master ... sometimes, they protest and receive a beating." Against her husband, the wife profits from the protection of her brother, and it is with him that she seeks refuge. As to relations between the nephew and the maternal uncle: "The term 'respect' best sums them up ... with a tinge of fear," for the maternal uncle has the power (as among the Kipsigi of Africa) to curse his nephew and afflict him with serious illness (Williams, 1940-1941, 1941-1942; 1941).

This last structure, derived from a patrilineal society, is nevertheless of the same type as that of the Siuai of Bougainville, who have matrilineal descent. Between brother and sister, "amical relations and reciprocal generosity." Between father and son. "nothing indicates a relation of hostility, of rigid authority or of fearful respect." But the relations of the nephew with his maternal uncle fall "between rigid discipline and an interdependence willingly recognized." Nevertheless, "informants say that all boys feel a certain fear of their maternal uncle and that they obey him better than their father." Concerning husband and wife, good feeling hardly seems the rule between them: "Few young spouses are faithful ... the young husbands are always suspicious, inclined to jealous rages ... marriage involves all sorts of difficult adjustments" (Oliver, 1955, *passim*).

The same picture, but still more marked, is found among the Dobu, who are matrilineal and neighbors of the matrilineal Trobrianders also, but with a very different structure. Dobuan households are unstable, they practice adultery assiduously, and husband and wife live always in fear of perishing from the sorcery of the other. Actually, Fortune's remark "that to allude to a wife's powers of sorcery so as to be understood by her husband is a grave insult" seems a permutation of the Trobriand and Caucasian prohibitions cited above.

In Dobu, the mother's brother is considered the harshest of all parents. "He beats his nephews long after their parents have ceased to do so," and it is forbidden to pronounce his name. Without doubt it is with the "navel," the husband of the mother's sister, that is to say a doublet of the father, that the tender relation exists, more than with the father himself. Nevertheless, the father is considered to be "less severe" than the uncle, and, contrary to the law of hereditary transmission, he seeks always to favor his son at the expense of his uterine nephew.

Finally, the tie between brother and sister is "the strongest of all social ties" (Fortune, 1932, pp. 8, 10, 45, 62-64, etc.).

What must be concluded from these examples? The correlation between forms of the avunculate and types of lineal descent does not exhaust the problem. Different forms of avunculate can coexist with the same type of descent, patrilineal or matrilineal. But we always find the same fundamental relation between the four pairs of oppositions which are necessary to the elaboration of the system. This will appear more clearly in diagrams which illustrate our examples, and where the + sign represents the free and familiar relations, the — sign the relations marked by hostility, antagonism or reserve (Fig. 1a). This simplification is not entirely justified, but one can make use of it in a provisional fashion. We will go further into the indispensable distinctions.

The synchronic law of correlation, thus suggested, can be verified diachronically. If one summarizes the evolution of family relations in the Middle Ages, as it appears from Howard's account, one obtains approximately the following plan: the power of the brother over the sister diminishes, that of the prospective husband increases. Simultaneously, the tie between father and son weakens, that between maternal uncle and nephew grows stronger (Howard, 1904).

This evolution seems confirmed by the documents assembled by L. Gautier, for, in the earliest texts (Raoul de Cambrai, Geste des Loherains, etc.), the positive relation becomes established between father and son, and it shifts only gradually toward the maternal uncle and the nephew (Gautier, 1890; on the same subject, one can consult with profit Gummere, 1901; Farnsworth, 1913). (The preceding paragraphs have been written in 1957, and substituted in the initial text, in response to the judicious observation by my colleague M. Luc de Heusch, of the Free University of Brussels, that one of my examples was materially incorrect. Let this acknowledge my thanks to him.)

We see then that the avunculate, to be understood, must be treated as a relation interior to a system, and that it is the system itself which must be considered in its entirety, in order to perceive its structure. This structure rests on four terms (brother, sister, father, son), united among themselves by two pairs of correlative oppositions, and such that, in each of the two generations implied, there exists always a positive relation and a negative relation. What, now, is this structure and what can be its ground? The answer is the following: this structure is the simplest kinship structure which can be conceived and which can exist. It is, properly speaking, *the element of kinship*.

In support of this affirmation, one can put forward a logical argument: for a kinship structure to exist at all, there must be present the three types of family relations always given in human society, that is to say: a relation of consanguinity, a relation of marriage, a relation of descent; in other words, a relation of sibling to sibling, a relation of spouse to spouse, a relation of parent to child. It is easy to understand that the structure considered here is that which permits satisfying this threefold requirement in accord with the principle of the greatest economy. But the preceding considerations have an abstract character, and a more direct proof can be invoked for our demonstration.

The primitive and irreducible character of the element of kinship such as we have defined it results, as a matter of fact, in a very direct way from the universal existence of the incest tabu. This is equivalent to saying that, in human society, a man can obtain a wife only from another man, who gives to him a daughter or sister. There is then no need to explain how the maternal uncle makes his appearance in the structure of kinship: he does not appear, he is immediately given, he is the condition of it. The error of traditional sociology, as of traditional linguistics, is to have considered terms, and not the relations between terms.

Before pushing further, let us quickly dispose of some objections which might come to mind. In the first place, if the relation of "brothers-in-law" forms the inevitable axis around which the structure of kinship is constructed, why bring the child produced by the marriage into the elementary structure? It must be understood that the infant represents perhaps just as well the born or unborn child. But, that said, the child is indispensable to testify to the dynamic and teleological character of the initial step which founded kinship on, and across, marriage. Kinship is not a static phenomenon; it exists only to perpetuate itself. We do not think here of the desire to perpetuate the race, but of the fact that, in most kinship systems, the initial disequilibrium which it produces, in a given generation, between those who give a woman and those who receive her, can stabilize itself only by counter-prestations taking place in later generations. Even the most elementary kinship structure exists simultaneously in the synchronic and diachronic orders.

Secondly, could one not conceive a symmetrical structure, of equal simplicity, but where the sexes were reversed, that is to say a structure implicating a sister, a brother, the wife of this last, and the daughter born of their union? Without doubt; but this theoretical possibility can be immediately eliminated on an experimental basis: in human society, it is men who exchange women, not the contrary. It remains to be discovered if certain cultures have not tended to realize a sort of fictitious image of this symmetrical structure. The case can only be rare.

We now reach a more serious objection. It could be that we have succeeded only in turning the problem inside out. Traditional sociology devoted itself to explaining the origin of the avunculate, and we have extricated ourselves from that quest by treating the brother of the mother, not as an extrinsic element, but as an immediately given fact of the simplest family structure. Why, then, do we not encounter the avunculate in every time and place? For if the avunculate has a very widespread distribution, it is nevertheless not universal. It would be vain to have avoided explaining the cases where it occurs only to run afoul of the cases where it does not.

Let us first observe that the kinship system does not possess the same importance in all cultures. To certain ones it supplies the active principle which rules all social relations, or the greater part of them. In other groups, as in our society, this function is absent or very diminished; in still others, such as the societies of the Plains Indians, it is only partially fulfilled. The kinship system is a language; it is not a universal language, and other means of expression and action can be preferred to it. From the point of view of the sociologist, this comes to saying that, given a particular culture, a preliminary question always poses itself: is the system systematic? Such a question, at first glance absurd, would be so actually only with regard to language; for language is the system of signification par excellence; it cannot *not* signify, and all its existence is in signification. On the other hand, the question must be examined, with increasing rigor, in proportion as one moves away from language to consider other systems, which also lay claim to signification, but for which the function of signification remains partial, fragmentary, or subjective: social organization, art, etc.

Besides, we have interpreted the avunculate as a characteristic trait of the elementary structure. This elementary structure, resulting from defined relations among four terms, is in our view the veritable *atom of kinship*. (It is doubtless superfluous to emphasize that the sort of atomism we have criticized in Rivers is that of classical philosophy and not the structural conception of the atom which is found in modern physics.) There is nothing which can be conceived of or understood short of the basic demands of its structure, and, on the other hand, it is the sole material for the construction of more complex systems. For there are more complex systems; either, to speak more exactly, the whole kinship system is elaborated by repeating this elementary structure, or it develops by integrating new elements. It is necessary, then, to consider two hypotheses: that where the kinship system being considered proceeds by simple juxtaposition of elementary structures, and where, consequently, the avuncular relation remains constantly apparent; and that where the system's unity of construction is already of a more complex order. In this last case, the avuncular relation, while still present, could be submerged within a more highly differentiated context. For example, one can conceive a system taking the elementary structure for its point of departure, but adding to it, on the side of the maternal uncle, his wife, and on the side of the father, first his sister, then her husband. One could easily demonstrate that such a development would bring with it, in the succeeding generation, a parallel twofold division: the child must then be differentiated into son and daughter, each united by a symmetrical and inverse relation to the terms occupying the other peripheral positions in the structure (the preponderant position of the father's sister in Polynesia, South-African *nhlampsa*, and inheritance of the mother's brother's wife). In a structure of this type, the avuncular relation continues to be manifest; but already it is no longer predominant. It can become effaced, or confused with others, in structures of still greater complexity. But precisely because it is dependent upon the elementary structure, the avuncular relation reappears clearly, even tends to stand out, each time the system being considered enters a critical period: whether because it is undergoing rapid transformation (North Pacific Coast); whether because it finds itself at the point of contact and conflict between profoundly different cultures (Fiji, South India); or whether because it is undergoing a fatal crisis (European Middle Ages).

It is necessary, finally, to add that the symbols, positive and negative, which we have used in the preceding diagram (Fig. 1a) represent an extreme simplification, acceptable only as a stage in demonstration. In reality the system of elementary attitudes comprises at least four terms: an attitude of affection, of tenderness and spontaneity; an attitude resulting from the reciprocal exchange of prestations and counter-prestations; and, in most bilateral relations, two unilateral relations, one corresponding to the attitude of creditor, the other to that of debtor. In other words: mutuality (=); reciprocity (±); right (+); obligation (—); these four fundamental attitudes can be represented in their reciprocal relations in the following fashion:

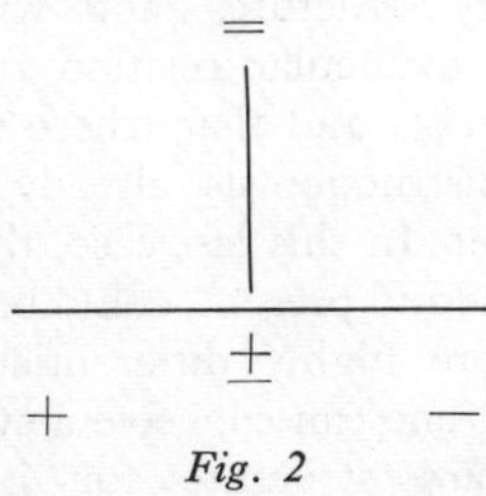

Fig. 2

In many systems, the relation between two individuals often expresses itself, not by a single attitude, but by several which form, so to speak, a bundle (thus, in the Trobriand Islands, between husband and wife one finds mutuality *plus* receiprocity). This is an additional reason why the fundamental structure can be difficult to lay bare.

We have tried to show all that the preceding analysis owes to the contemporary masters of primitive sociology. It is nevertheless necessary to underline that, on the most fundamental point, it has moved far from their teaching. Let us cite, for example, Radcliffe-Brown:

> The unit of structure from which a kinship is built up is the group which I call an "elementary family," consisting of a man and his wife and their child or children. . . . The existence of the elementary family creates three special kinds of social relationship, that between parent and child, that between children of the same parents (siblings), and that between husband and wife as parents of the same child or children. . . . The three relationships that exist within the elementary family constitute what I call the first order. Relationships of the second order are those which depend on the connection of two elementary families through a common member, and are such as father's father, mother's brother, wife's sister, and so on. In the third order are such as father's brother's son and mother's brother's wife. Thus we can trace, if we have genealogical information, relationships of the fourth, fifth or n^{th} order (1941, p. 2).

The idea expressed in this passage, according to which the biological family constitutes the point of departure from which every society elaborates its kinship system, is certainly not confined to the English master; there are not many points on which one would find today a greater unanimity. In our opinion, there is none more dangerous.

Undoubtedly the biological family is present, and is continued, in human society. But what gives kinship its character of social fact is not what it must retain from nature; it is the essential step by which it is separated from nature. A kinship system does not consist of objective ties of descent or of given degrees of consanguinity among individuals; it exists only in the consciousness of men, it is an arbitrary system of representations, not the spontaneous development of a situation of fact. This certainly does not mean that the situation of fact is automatically contradicted, or even simply ignored. Radcliffe-Brown has shown, in studies which today are classics, that even systems of the most rigid and artificial appearance, such as the Australian systems of marriage classes, take careful account of biological relationship. But an observation as unquestionable as his leaves intact the fact, decisive in our eyes, that in human society, kinship is allowed to establish and perpetuate itself only by, and across, modalities determined by marriage. In other words, the relations treated as "relations of the first order" by Radcliffe-Brown are functions of, and dependent on, those he considers secondary and derived. The primordial nature of human kinship is to require, as its condition of existence, the connection of what Radcliffe-Brown calls "elementary families." Thus, what is truly "elementary" is not families, which are isolated terms, but the relation between these terms. No other interpretation can account for the universality of the incest tabu, of which the avuncular relation in its most general aspect, is only a corollary, sometimes manifest and sometimes concealed.

Because they are systems of symbols, systems of kinship offer the anthropologist a privileged terrain on which his efforts can almost (and we insist on this: almost) overtake those of the most developed of the social sciences, i.e., linguistics. But the condition of this meeting, from which one can hope for a better knowledge of mankind, is never to lose sight of the fact that in sociological as in linguistic study, we are in the midst of symbolism. Now, if it is justified, and in a sense inevitable, to have recourse to a naturalistic interpretation in order to understand the emergence of symbolic thought, once this is given, the nature of explanation must change as radically as the newly appeared phenomenon differs from those which preceded and prepared for it. From this moment, any concession to naturalism would run the risk of compromising the immense progress already accomplished in the linguistic domain, progress which begins to take form also in family social structure, and of throwing this last away for an empiricism with neither inspiration nor fecundity.

REFERENCE NOTE

The reference note is organized into two parts. Part A contains the specific references cited by Levi-Strauss (if not included in the general bibliography). Part B contains discussion and indication of references regarding the work of Levi-Strauss, and also of the Prague school of linguistics, whose stimulus he discusses, in terms of the two leading figures who have most influenced linguistics and anthropology, Troubetzkoy and Jakobson.

A. SPECIFIC REFERENCES

BENEDICT, PAUL K.

1942. Tibetan and Chinese Kinship Terms. *Harvard Journal of Asiatic Studies, 6:* 313-337.

1943. Studies in Thai Kinship Terminology. *JAOS, 63:* 168-175.

BRUNSCHVICG, L.

1927. *Le Progrès de la conscience dans la philosophie occidentale.* Paris. F. Alcan. 2 vols.

DAVIS, K. and W. L. WARNER

1937. Structural Analysis of Kinship. *AA, 39:* 291-313.

FARNSWORTH, W. O.

1913. *Uncle and Nephew in the Old French Chanson de Geste.* New York: Columbia University Press.

FORTUNE, REO F.

1932. *The Sorcerers of Dobu.* London: Routledge.

GAUTIER, LEON

1890. *La Chevalerie.* Paris: Sanard and Derangeon.

GIFFORD, E. W.

1929. *Tonga Society.* (*B. P. Bishop Museum Bulletin*, No. 61). Honolulu.

GUMMERE, F. B.

1901. The Sister's Son. In *An English Miscellany Presented to Dr. Furnivall.* London.

HARTLAND, S.

1917. Matrilineal Kinship and the Question of its Priority. *Memoirs of the American Anthropological Association, 4:* 1-87.

HOCART, A. M.

1915. Chieftainship and the Sister's Son in the Pacific. *AA, 17:* 631-647.

1923. The Uterine Nephew. *Man, 23*(4): 11-13.

1925. The Cousin in Vedic Ritual. *Indian Antiquary, 54.*

HOWARD, G. E.

1904. *A History of Matrimonial Institutions*. Chicago. 3 vols.

KOVALEVSKI, M.

1893. La Famille matriarcale au Caucase. *L'Anthropologie*, *4:* 259-278.

LOWIE, ROBERT H.

1919. *The Matrilineal Complex*. (UCP-AAE, vol. 16, no. 2.) Berkeley and Los Angeles: University of California Press.

MALINOWSKI, B.

1929. *The Sexual Life of Savages in Northwestern Melanesia*. New York: Liveright.

MAUSS, MARCEL

1951. Rapports réels et pratiques . . . *Sociologie et Anthropologie*. Paris: Presses Universitaires de France.

MEAD, MARGARET

1935. *Sex and Temperament in Three Primitive Societies*. New York: Morrow.

OLIVER, DOUGLAS L.

1955. *A Solomon Island Society. Kinship and Leadership Among the Siuai of Bougainville*. Cambridge: Harvard University Press.

RADCLIFFE-BROWN, A. R.

1924. The Mother's Brother in South Africa. *South African Journal of Science*, *21:* 542-555.

1935. Kinship Terminology in California. *AA*, *37:* 530-535.

1941. The Study of Kinship Systems. *JRAI*, *71:* 1-18.

RIVERS, W. H. R.

1907. The Marriage of Cousins in India. *Journal of the Royal Asiatic Society*.

1914. *The History of Melanesian Society*. London, Cambridge. 2 vols.

1924. *Social Organization*. Edited by W. J. Perry. London. Kegan Paul, Trench, Trubner.

ROSE, H. J.

1911. On the Alleged Evidence for Mother-Right in Early Greece. *Folklore* *22:* 277-291.

SCHRADER, O.

1890. *Prehistoric Antiquities of the Aryan Peoples*. Translated by F. B. Jevons. London: Griffon.

TAX, SOL

1937. Some Problems of Social Organization. In Fred Eggan (Ed.), *Social Anthropology of North American Tribes*. Chicago: University of Chicago Press.

THOMSON, D. F.

1935. The Joking-Relationship and Organized Obscenity in North Queensland. *AA*, *37:* 460-490.

WARNER, W. LLOYD

1930-1931. Morphology and Functions of the Australian Murngin Type of Kinship. *AA*, *32:* 207-256; *33:* 172-198.

WILLIAMS, F. E.

1940-1941, 1941-1942. Natives of Lake Kutubu, Papua. *Oceania*, *11:* 121-157, 259-294, 374-401; *12:* 49-74, 134-154.

1941. Group Sentiment and Primitive Justice. *AA*, *43:* 523-539.

B. GENERAL REFERENCES

A number of the writings of Levi-Strauss show his conception of anthropology and anthropological problems as specially concerned with the place of language in culture and of linguistics in social anthropology. His general conception of a semiotic social science, embracing both language and other aspects of social life, is well brought out in Levi-Strauss (1960d). Other writings include several which deal with general correlations and approach (1949, 1951, 1953a, 1962) and a number of striking studies of myth, whose methodology, as that of the article translated here, has part of its roots in linguistics (1955, 1956, 1960a, 1960b, 1960c, 1961).

Moore and Olmsted (1952) criticize certain of the broad hypotheses early advanced by Levi-Strauss (1951); the hypotheses are given qualified support in Kluckhohn (1961).

For work of Troubetzkoy and Jakobson, see references in the general bibliography, as well as Jakobson and Halle (1956) and Jakobson, Fant, Halle (1952). Jakobson (1933) is a general account of the Prague school. Jakobson's writings on Boas (1944, 1959), which adopt the Boasian pairing of grammatical processes and grammatical categories (1957b), and his general and functional statements (1942, 1953, 1957a, 1960a) are of special importance for anthropology. For another anthropological influence from Jakobson's work, see references to Kluckhohn following the article by Pike (pp. 54-61). For Jakobson's bibliography through 1956, see *For Roman Jakobson* (1956).

References not in the general bibliography:

MOORE, OMAR KHAYYAM, and DAVID L. OLMSTED
1952. Language and Professor Levi-Strauss. *AA*, *54:* 116-119.

5 *Towards a Theory of the Structure of Human Behavior*

KENNETH L. PIKE

FOR MANY YEARS my esteemed friend Dr. Manuel Gamio has been attempting to study man through the simultaneous application of the techniques of numerous disciplines. This approach to the study of man within the context of the entire range of activities in which he participates is an emphasis which is essential if one wishes to understand man in order to be of service to him, as Dr. Gamio has devoted many years of his life in the service of the indigenous races of Mexico. It is with great pleasure, therefore, that I write this brief contribution to a volume honoring Dr. Gamio.

The thesis which for the past seven years I have been exploring is the following: that every purposeful activity of man is structured, and that certain basic characteristics are common to every such activity, so that it should be possible to develop a theory and a technique which would pass without jar from the study of the structure of one kind of activity of man to that of any other kind. Ideally, this would result in one basic theory of structure, one basic set of terms, and one basic methodology which could be applied to the analysis of language, the analysis of ritual behavior, the analysis of sports, the analysis of occupational activity, or even to the processes of thought itself. In 1954 I published the first part of a detailed development of this thesis in a work entitled *Language, in Relation to a Unified Theory of the Structure of Human Behavior* (Pike, 1954). In this present article I shall highlight a few of the general principles underlying the detailed presentation given in that volume.

WAVES VERSUS PARTICLES

In order to apply to the analysis of all human behavior a theory must on the one hand take account of the apparent irreconcilability between the fact that a behavior event is often a physical continuum with no gaps in which the movement is stopped, but on the other hand must take account of the fact that human beings react to their own behavior and to that of other individuals as if it were segmented into discrete chunks.

In order to treat this contrast in the present theory, we may first state that for every purposive unit of human behavior there is an underlying physical base which constitutes this continuum—as in the phrase "I know John" there is no pause between any of the sounds, or as the motions of a conductor's baton may constitute for some time a continuous motion without pause.

Next, we note that this continuum is not a steady nonfluctuating one, but that there are in it some "waves" of activity. These activity waves are waves of physical motion; there is a flow and ebb of activity, ups and downs of movement, steady states and change states of motion. Within these waves of motion one can detect nuclei (the steady state or the peak of a motion) and troughs of movement (which are the "change points" or transition areas where one activity is changed to another, or the relatively relaxed points within the continuum of activity). Thus, as the conductor moves his baton the beat movement constitutes the peak of such a wave, and the trough is constituted of the transition movement between beats. Similarly, a syllable is the peak of a movement, and the break between syllables is a trough between two such waves of movement.

There may be small waves superimposed upon larger waves of movement, furthermore, as ripples may be superimposed upon a large wave of water; a consonant or a vowel is a small wave of movement superimposed upon the larger wave of the syllable, or movements of the eyes may be ripples upon the larger wave of the movement of the head as it adjusts to see some object, and so on.

In addition to this basic point of view, however, the theory indicates that when people react to human behavior in their own culture they react to it as if it were a sequence of separate particles of activity; the actor in such activity and the native perceiver of this activity both tend to ignore or to be unaware of the transition states between the waves of activity. For this reason, a purely physical analysis of human behavior may analyse it as comprised of waves, but a cultural analysis of human behavior must treat it as comprised of particles—discrete behavioral entities. Our theory combines these two by retaining a physical base as postulated for every human event, and, in addition, a discrete structuring of that event in terms of smaller unitary events. The label which we shall apply to any such particle of activity is "eme" or "emic unit" (deriving the terms from the latter part of the word "phoneme" or the phrase "phonemic unit"). Emes occur not only in speech but in nonverbal activity of all kinds, so that as one basic assumption of our theory, designed to be applicable to all kinds of human behavior, we accept the principle of the simultaneous presence of movement waves and of experiential particles in the physical and cultural data.

STRUCTURE IN RELATION TO NATIVE REACTION TO IT

In the discussion of particles of activity as experienced by the participants in that activity, we were acting upon a further assumption which we now wish to make more explicit: the emic analysis of the emic units of human behavior must analyse that behavior in reference to the manner in which native participants in that behavior react to their own behavior and to the behavior of their colleagues. This principle implies that no adequate analysis of the structuring of human behavior can be made upon a physical basis only, since the physical basis can deal only with continua of various kinds without reference to the fact that natives (in many instances at least) react to that behavior as if it were comprised of discrete particles.

In addition, this point of view—that structure must be analysed in relation to native reaction to behavior—must be extended until purpose is included within the matrix within the data which is used to arrive at conclusions as to the nature of that structure, and must be included as one of the relevant structural components in many of the definitions of the basic units of the structure. Purpose, within this theory, may be rephrased as implying "elicitation of response" and response may be rephrased as implying "reactions to elicitation of response." In reference to language, for example, Professor Charles C. Fries has insisted "the question itself is part of the frame in which the answer as an utterance operates" (Fries, 1952, pp. 165-169).

In other words, the analysis of the response to a question cannot usefully be treated without reference to the fact that it is correlated with the prior occurrence of the question which elicits that response, whether the response be verbal or nonverbal. Similarly, in a football game, the feinting of a player, as a device to deceive the opposite side, is an elicitation of a response, which will put his opponents in a disadvantageous position; the feint elicits a deliberate reaction.

The studying of response is important, furthermore, because only within a framework of the elicitation of response and of the response itself can one determine the points in the physical continuum at which there are emic breaks. That is, only within such a framework can one determine what are the discrete particles from the point of view of the partipants themselves. The technique used is one of substitution frames, in which, within a large sequence of activity, one item can be withdrawn and another put in its place, in such a fashion that the response elicited differs for the two instances. Thus, the sentence "Shut the door" and the sentence "Shut the drawer" elicit different responses, and at the same time indicate that there is a break in the sequence before the words "door" and "drawer" which can be assumed to be an emic transition between emic units.

In order to cover all of behavior, it is convenient—at the early stages of analysis, at least—to equate purpose and meaning. Within the analysis of verbal material one will usually speak of the meaning of an emic unit, whereas in the analysis of nonverbal activity one will usually speak of the purpose of that event.

Purpose and meaning are here treated alike to the extent that both of them have reference to the elicitation by a participant of a reaction from another participant, or the predictable reaction of the second participant to his interpretation of the purposes of the first participant.

PREDICTABILITY OF DIFFICULTIES IN ACCULTURATION

Every person is chemically structured. He has grown up in an environment where the responses elicited from him by his colleagues have developed in him a set of responses to certain continua as if those continua were divided in a certain discrete way, and as if those discrete responses were related to a total system of such responses. This is an essential part of the structure of human behavior. If this were not a part of the structure of human behavior, no person would be able to elicit a reaction from another person, since the second person would be unable to understand the signals of the first; the first would not be able to elicit responses, and the second would not be able to give adequate responses.

As a result of this structuring, a community has developed useful and appropriate cultural norms of reaction of many different types, when within the limits of appropriate alternatives. When an individual in one community attempts to respond to an individual of a different community, however, a great deal of confusion may result: the activity which in the first community would elicit one response might in the second community elicit a very different response. This is most easily seen in such situations as that which I have encountered, for example, when waving good-bye in an American fashion to a Spanish-speaking friend—the friend has thought I was calling him over for an interview, since the calling gesture of the Spanish speaker from Latin America, and the gesture for waving good-bye in my own culture are sufficiently alike in their physical characteristics to be interpreted by a member of the other culture as constituting the quite different unit from his own culture.

The detailed clashing of two emic systems, however, may be much more subtle. In English, for example, the vowels of the word "mate" and "met" may occur in the same context (between the sounds "m" and "t"), such that the words which they in part constitute are distinct from the point of view (i.e., the response) of the English hearer, and for this reason the two vowels likewise come to constitute in English two discrete emic entities. Two Spanish vowels which are somewhat like the two English vowels of "mate" and "met" may be found in the Spanish words "pelo" ("hair") and "perro" ("dog"). In Spanish, however, the response elicitation of the two vowels is quite different from the response elicited by the somewhat similar English vowels, since the two vowels of Spanish are not contrastive but constitute just one emic unit in that language (i.e., just one Spanish phoneme).

In such a situation, one can predict with a very high degree of probability that the person coming from a system containing a pair of emically undifferentiated vowels to a language containing a physically similar pair of emically differentiated vowels will have a great deal of difficulty in responding to this emic constrast, precisely because he has trained himself by millions of practice sessions to ignore the distinction. (That is, by conversations over a long period of time, each of which constitutes a practice session in responding to the elicitation). The Spanish speaker could be expected to have difficulty, therefore, in learning to discriminate the words "mate" and "met." Some years ago, in one country in Latin America, for example, I was lecturing on English pronunciation to over one hundred teachers of high-school English and it was difficult to find a single one of them who did not have great difficulty in discriminating these sounds (and, along with these, "mit" and "mat"), even though some of these teachers spoke English fluently.

It is only through an emic analysis of the sounds or of the activities of a community that one can predict the difficulties which members of that community will have in passing to another community to learn its response patterns. But it is on the basis of such considerations that the best techniques for the teaching of foreign languages have recently been developed, especially under the leadership of Professor Fries of Michigan. He insists that textbooks must be prepared separately for every uni-directional language situation—that is, not only for every pair of languages, but for every pair of languages in reference to the direction in which the learning is to take place, so that a textbook for teaching

English to Spanish speakers might be quite inadequate if it were translated and used as a textbook to teach Spanish to English speakers, since the emic problems met may not be reciprocal. Certain elements may rather require much greater practice in the one direction than in the other, just as a Spanish speaker must be provided a great deal of practice material to learn to differentiate "mate" and "met," whereas the English speaker does not need practice to keep from making erroneous responses of a severe nature in pronouncing the corresponding vowels of "pelo" and "perro."

It is hoped that in the future similar predictions of emic clash and consequent problems of acculturation can be made not only in respect to language learning but also in respect to acculturation in the field of etiquette, or of ritual, or of law, commerce, and so on. A great deal of such prediction may already have been made by anthropologists, but if this theory could be developed in sufficient detail, such prediction might be established in a more systematic fashion and with a higher degree of reliability.

SPOT AND CLASS

One of the basic principles which was developed for our theory, and which has made it possible to go much further than has previously been considered possible by some persons, is the setting up of the correlation between "spot" and "class" as an integrated unit. By "spot" we mean the place at which substitution can occur, just as above we used the phrases "Shut the door" and "Shut the drawer" to show the substitution of the one word for the other. By this theory, all behavior is considered to contain significant spots at which behavior occurrences may be found. At each spot a series of alternatives is possible, so that if no such series of alternatives is to be found in any particular place within a continuum of behavior, it is assumed that no emic spot is covered by that particular area.

The spot may be one in which large emic units occur, or one in which small emic units occur. Smaller spots may in turn occur in sequence in a larger spot, in a hierarchical progression similar to the manner in which ripples can occur on waves within one of the physical continua. In a football game, for example, there are spots for the occurrence of plays, and at the spot for any one play there are a variety of possibilities, such as passing, kicking, or running; where alternatives for such plays exist, an emic spot is present. A certain sequence of spots makes up, as a whole, the larger spot for a series of "downs"; several such series of downs, under certain conditions, fill a larger spot, during which one side has control of the ball, etc.

The particular list of items which are appropriate to a spot constitutes, by virtue of its occurrence in that spot, an emic class of items which is pertinent to the language and not a mere arbitrary aggregation of the analyst. It is this appropriateness for occurrence in such a spot which constitutes one of the criteria for an emic class of items—although the actual delineation of such a class has to take account of numerous other criteria which are not relevant to the discussion here.

The spot-class combination, moreover, constitutes a correlation which, as such, may be considered an emic unit of a type related to but different from a particular emic event by itself. It is the development of this concept which constitutes one of the most useful parts of the theory and one of the greatest departures from traditional analysis. I am acquainted with no other major attempt to show how verbal and nonverbal culture could be integrated into a single theory. Probably the reason for this lack is the fact that persons who have wished to accomplish this goal have in general started from the point of view of attempting to find the cultural correlates of the phoneme and morpheme, which form a very difficult starting point for such integration. Beginning with the spot-class unit, however, this transfer of technique begins in a much more simple fashion, and in a way which can be appreciated with much less difficulty by persons outside of the linguistic field.

The very great advantage of the spot-class start is that, with it, one is able to by-pass the necessity for a *minimum* unit in the early stages of the analysis. At any point within behavior, whether the behavior event under consideration be large or small, the analyst can start looking for substitutable items which elicit, in conjunction with the matrix in which they are imbedded, differential responses from members of the community. Whenever such a situation is found, the investigator can begin his analysis with spot-class units—with a charting of the spots as they occur in sequence, and with a searching for the limits to the membership of the classes which occur in their respective spots. When he has done this with his starting matrix, or with a number of such matrices, he can choose either to advance up the hierarchy to larger units, or to turn his attention to smaller spot-class units within the unit which he has already discussed. He is, therefore, by this technique not stymied with the necessity for beginning at some kind of an assumed minimum such as the cultural equivalent of the phoneme or morpheme.

Another reason why the spot-class approach is helpful is that whereas in linguistics the threshold is quite stable (so that the minimum segmental units of sounds—the phonemes—are the minimum segments within almost any consideration of linguistics), the minimum of nonverbal culture which is useful to treat emically (as the natives react to it) changes with the purpose or attention of the actor. If the actor is an ordinary participant in a football game, for example, we may assume that his attention is usually focused on the plays or on the principal segments of the individual plays, and rarely would be consciously focused on units much smaller than that. When a football coach is teaching the players the rudiments of the game, however, this awareness threshold may be very sharply lowered, to such items as foot placement, and minor body movements in the processes of blocking, tackling, or passing. Within the current theory, this difference of participant type is seen to be an essential part of the formula of any activity, and an ignoring of this difference leads to chaos in the analysis. Since, however, this change of participant activity changes the threshold of attention of the participants, the minimum emic units of that activity may themselves change. In spite of these changes, however, the spot-class technique proceeds without jar either upwards or downwards in the hierachy until it comes to some threshold which seems to be relevant to that particular kind of activity with reference to the particular kind of participant attention being given to it.

HIERARCHICAL STRUCTURE, FOCUS, AND THRESHOLD

We now make more specific reference to a number of items treated indirectly in the preceding sections: language and all kinds of behavior are constituted of a hierarchical structure. Small units may make up large units, and large units make up still larger units. Small spots of an emic type occur within larger emic spots, and these larger ones occur in still larger ones. Units occur within units in the hierarchical structure. In addition, a theory which is to take account of behavior other than speech must certainly include within it a difference of participant focus, the changing attention given by a participant to his own activity or to the activity of other participants. This change of focus is relevant to the person's activity, since his responses vary enormously in reference to his change of focus. In the football game, for example, the attention of the fans in the stands may be directed to things widely different from those to which attention is directed by the coach. It would be folly to assume, therefore, that the emic structuring of the activity of a novice watching the game from the stands is structurally the same as the activity of the football coach as he watches the game analytically. The activity of the two must be treated differently, as their focus is different. One's attention, furthermore, may be focused to include larger units or smaller units of the hierarchy, and the threshold of attention, as we indicated previously, can change. Some kind of threshold enters the description of any emic event, and ultimately provides the limits such that minimum emic units of a hierarchy of a system may be postulated.

THE BEHAVIOREME AS A HIGH-LAYERED UNIT

It is convenient to have a label for a unit of behavior upon which the participants are at the moment putting conscious attention, or which they are performing with deliberate conscious awareness of some real or assumed purpose. Such a unit we shall call a "behavioreme." (Another possible term for this unit is "behavior cycle," a phrase used by S. F. Nadel [1951].) A list of some typical manifested behavioremes might include a football game, the reciting of a poem, or—with a lower threshold—a response to a question.

INTEGRATION THROUGH JOINT VERBAL AND NONVERBAL CLASSES

Behavioremes may be constituted either of nonverbal events, or of verbal events, or of composite nonverbal-verbal events. It is this last type which should now be seen to have considerable significance. An event comprised of both verbal and nonverbal activities could not be analysed by the linguist alone since his techniques do not allow him to analyse the nonverbal activity. Likewise, it could not be analysed by the nonlinguistic anthropologist alone, since his techniques do not include the analysis of the details of a sentence. We insist, moreover, that it could not be analysed by the combination of a linguist and a nonlinguistic anthropogist, since the current techniques of neither of them are integrated with the techniques of the other, and any joint analysis by the two of them would merely be an aggregate of conclusions, rather than an integrated synthesis of the materials within a single description in which the synthesis would proceed on the basis of a single theory, with a single set of terms, and a single kind of approach.

Consider, for example, a party game in which people sing the stanza of a song; on the repetition of that same stanza, one word is deleted and a gesture is put in its place. For example, from the phrase "Under the spreading chestnut tree" the word "spreading" may be deleted, and a gesture—the arms outspread—may be substituted for it. During the third singing of that stanza, a further word is replaced by another gesture: for the word "tree" a gesture with the arms upright may be substituted. This kind of replacement can continue, until practically all the words in the stanza are replaced by gestures.

What do we deduce from this incident? First, that it is certainly a single emic unit of activity—it is so considered by the participants, who call it a single game, not a composite of several games. They also identify it as a single unit by such statements as "Well, that was a good game, but we want another one now," and so on, in which the phrase "another one" indicates their treatment of the party game as a single unit. The integration of the verbal and nonverbal activity is here so complex however, that an attempt to describe it by the mere summation of an atomistic linguistic approach and an atomistic nonlingustic anthropological approach would utterly fail to reveal the structure of that unit. There is no escape, in describing this unit, from setting up spot-classes in which the emic classes are comprised of both verbal and nonverbal materials. It is precisely this substitutability of nonverbal materials for verbal materials—in the same class with them, occurring in the same spot, as structurally integrated in the identical fashion—which allows this party game to proceed as a functioning unit. Only a unified theory of the structure of human behavior, such as we have been attempting to develop, can possibly describe such a unitary instance as this and do it justice. Yet such a party game, though striking in this regard, is not necessarily different from a wedding in which the verbal "I will" may be integrated to other official parts of the service, such as the signing of his name by the officiating clergyman or other person. A unified theory of the structure of human behavior must allow for the integration—not just the summation—of verbal and nonverbal events.

SIMULTANEOUS MODAL STRUCTURING OF AN EVENT

The previous elements of the theory have lent themselves to discussion one at a time, with only a certain amount of overlap from one to another. We now come to a phase which is much more difficult to handle, inasmuch as it deals with that part of the theory which asserts that any emic event is simultaneously structured in three ways, i.e., in three "modes." (i.e., in "three dimensions." The use of the term "dimension" is suggestive of the general idea. It is misleading, however, in that it seems to ignore the physical component which is present in every mode.) The attempt to describe the manner in which each of these distinct components can be demonstrated in terms of differential native reaction is a very elaborate procedure which we cannot indicate in detail here. We will, however, hint at the direction in which it goes, and refer the reader to the larger volume for illustrative detail.

The manifestation mode is the hierarchical, segmental structuring of the physical material which is present in every human behavioral event. In language, this implies structure in terms of phonemes, which in turn enter a hierarchy with syllables, stress groups, and still higher units. A phoneme such as the consonant "t" is utterly different from a word such as "boy"; the structuring of the hierarchy in which the phoneme occurs is a hierarchy of physical units. It specifically is *not* a hierarchy comprised of the progression from phoneme, to word, to phrase (and hence it breaks here very strongly with much of the current linguistic theory) but is the structuring of a physical unit within a larger physical unit and so on as we have just indicated.

The feature mode of an emic unit of activity is, in general, comprised of the simultaneous identificational-contrastive components of that unit, with its internal segmentation (and one component of the whole unit) analysed with special reference to purpose or lexical meaning wherever these are detectable. It is in reference to this mode, therefore, that any over-all meaning of a sentence is treated, and the intonational and segmental components of the sentence as well. In addition, the internal segmentation of the feature mode of the sentence leads to the morpheme units as the minimum internal segmental components of its feature mode.

The third mode is the distribution mode, and here reference is made to the breaking up of the sentence into its pertinent major and minor spot-classes. Specifically, the distribution mode is not distribution abstracted as such, but the correlation of spots plus the classes filling those spots. This last statement is extremely important to the theory since, by it, a physical base is preserved not only for the manifestation mode itself, but for the distribution mode and for the feature mode. Within this theory, there is never an emic unit postulated without a physical base; the manifestation mode of the sentence is the physical base of that sentence, but the distribution mode of the sentence also has its own manifestation mode so that the distribution mode likewise has its physical base.

This results in modes within modes, so that every emic unit within every mode of a larger unit has in turn its components which likewise are comprised of a feature mode, a manifestation mode, and a distribution mode. In other words, there is a hierarchical structuring of components of modes within components of modes. The details of this modal hierarchical structuring constitute a kind of chain reaction which becomes extraordinarily complex, and beyond the possibility of illustration in a brief summary such as this.

The presentation of the modal characteristics of an emic unit can also be indicated by a formula—the formula basic to the theory as a whole, and the one which is applicable equally to verbal and to nonverbal behavior. With "U" for emic unit, "F" for feature mode, "M" for manifestation mode, and "D" for distribution mode, this central formula becomes

$$U = \begin{matrix} F \\ M \\ D \end{matrix}$$

CONCEPTUALIZED HYPOSTASIS

It is useful to point out one implication of the theory where it can be easily misrepresented. The theory insists that every emic unit has a physical base, a physical component. Yet the theory suggests that a thought can be such an emic unit. What is the physical base, then, to a thought? The answer which this theory gives, is that the neural activity within the brain constitutes the manifestation mode of a particular thought—and the theory does not leave room for thoughts "floating through the air" without being constituted of the specific neural activity of some specific individual at some specific time and place.

A further problem must be treated, however: what is the "meaning" of a word, when the meaning, for analytical purposes, is abstracted from the form, as indicated by such a sentence as "The word 'boy' is comprised of two parts, one of which is the sequence of phonemes and the other is the meaning?" Our answer here is that the abstraction of the meaning, as such, is similar to the "thoughts" referred to above—the manifestation mode of the *activity* of abstracting the meaning is comprised of the neural activity of the person doing the abstracting, and of his verbalization of that activity (such as "defining the meaning" of a word). Within the normal activity of participants as they operate, without a deliberate abstraction of the meaning, no abstracted unit of meaning, as such, is postulated by the theory. Similarly, no form is postulated as emically locatable, without reference to the total purposive content of some behavioreme—and system of components of behavioremes—of which it is a part. "Meanings," therefore, as such, are exclusively a "conceptualized hypostasis"—the abstracting activity of the analyst (or of a participant acting as an analyst—as the analyst himself is a participant, as a scientist, in the larger community) or the product of that activity—the neural activity of thinking of an abstraction of the responses of individuals.

Here, again, we find it vital to be certain of the kind of participant whose activity we are analysing. If we are analysing the activity of a nonreflective speaker, his emic units are treated as wholes without the abstraction of form and meaning, in the large majority of instances. On the other hand, if we are analysing the activity of the analyst, then we are certain to find many conceptualized hypostases of a very convenient type, which constitute the constructs of science. These, too, are trimodally structured, within the formula

$$U = \begin{matrix} F \\ M \\ D \end{matrix}$$

REFERENCE NOTE

The major presentation of Pike's interconnected views on the analysis of language and other aspects of human life is in the three volumes of his *Language in Relation to a Unified Theory of the Structure of Human Behavior.* Among the articles in which his ideas are developed are Pike (1952, 1958, 1959, 1960, 1961). A nontechnical presentation, relating Pike's views to practical and philosophical problems, has been reprinted as *Language and Life* (1957-1958).

French (1955) uses principles similar to those of Pike, and Mayers (1959) develops Pike's approach further; both deal with the analysis of ritual behavior.

Other recent essays in the extension or generalization of linguistic methodology to nonlinguistic materials, include Garvin (1949); Goodenough (1951, 1957a, both in this volume); Hall (1959), a generalization of principles developed with G. L. Trager; various writings of Levi-Strauss (see the preceding article); a number of writings by the late Clyde Kluckhohn (1956, 1958a, 1958b, 1959, 1961), adapting Roman Jakobson's principle of distinctive features (componential analysis of phonological units) to the comparative study of values; a concise statement by Trager (1959); and a development of the glossematic approach, associated with the Cercle Linguistique de Copenhagen and Louis Hjelmslev, by Uldall (1957). The critique of Pike by Gauthier (1960) bears on much of the linguistic approach, but is perhaps answered by the new ethnographic methodology of Goodenough (1957), Frake (1961, 1962a, 1962b), and others.

References not in the general bibliography:

FRENCH, KATHERINE STORY

1955. Culture Segments and Variation in Contemporary Social Ceremonialism on the Warm Springs Reservation, Oregon. Doctoral dissertation, Columbia University.

GARVIN, PAUL L.

1952. Structure and Variation in Language and Culture. In Sol Tax (Ed.), *Indian Tribes of Aboriginal America.* (Selected Papers of the XXIXth International Congress of Americanists, New York, 1949.) Chicago: University of Chicago Press. Pp. 216-221.

GAUTHIER, MICHEL

1960. Review of K. Pike, *Language in Relation to a Unified Theory of the Structure of Human Behavior. Word, 16:* 392-398.

KLUCKHOHN, CLYDE

1956. Toward a Comparison of Value-Emphases in Different Cultures. In L.

White (Ed.), *The State of the Social Sciences*. Chicago: University of Chicago Press. Pp. 116-132.

1958a. The Scientific Study of Values and Contemporary Civilization. *Proceedings of the American Philosophical Society*, *102*(5): 469-477.

1958b. The Scientific Study of Values. *University of Toronto Installation Lectures, 1958*, Toronto. Pp. 25-54.

1959. Common Humanity and Diverse Cultures. In D. Lerner (Ed.), *The Human Meaning of the Social Sciences*. New York: Meridian (M64). Pp. 245-284.

1961. *Anthropology and the Classics*. (The Colver Lectures in Brown University, 1960.) Providence: Brown University Press.

MAYERS, MARVIN

1959. Religious Activity Among the Pocomchi of Guatemala. Paper read at the Fifty-eighth Annual Meeting, American Anthropological Association, Mexico City.

PIKE, KENNETH L.

1958. Interpenetration of Phonology, Morphology, and Syntax. In Eva Sivertsen (Ed.), *Proceedings of the Eighth International Congress of Linguists* (*Oslo, 1957*). Oslo: Oslo University Press. Pp. 363-374.

1961. Stimulating and Resisting Change. *Practical Anthropology*, *8*: 267-274.

The Dilemma of Contemporary Linguistics 6

BRONISLAW MALINOWSKI

[REVIEW OF: M. M. Lewis. *Infant Speech: a Study of the Beginnings of Language.* (International Library of Psychology, Philosophy and Scientific Method.) London: Kegan Paul, 1936.]

Mr. Lewis introduces his excellent study of infant speech somewhat dramatically by reminding us how, exactly half a century ago, Max Müller's saying "No thoughts without words" left linguistic studies somewhat in the air. To some, the aphorism went too far; to others not far enough. For the psychologist it was going too far, for obviously symbolic thought without words does occur. Linguistically it did not go far enough, for words mean more than ideas, and in their most important function they are as much a form of human action as any type of bodily behaviour.

Today, linguists are faced by a similar dilemma. Once we recognize with Mr. Lewis that "language is a form of activity, a mode of human behaviour, perhaps the most important" (p. 5), the question arises: Can we treat language as an independent subject of study? Is there a legitimate science of words alone, of phonetics, grammar, and lexicography? Or must all study of speaking lead to sociological investigation, to the treatment of linguistics as a branch of the general science of culture? If the earliest and most fundamental function of speech is pragmatic—to direct, to control, and to correlate human activities—then obviously no study of speech except within the "context of situation" is legitimate. The distinction between *language* and *speech*, still supported by such writers as Bühler and Gardiner, but dating back to de Saussure and Wegener, will have to be dropped. Language cannot remain an independent and self-contained subject of study, once we recognize that it is only the general norm of human speech activities. Finally, we shall have to decide whether, with some recent German psychologists, we have to assign three separate functions to speech: the expressive, the evocative, and the representative; or whether we must be satisfied with the admission that speech has only one main function, that of pragmatic control, of co-ordinating human action; while all the other manifold uses and aspects of language are derivative.

The dilemma of contemporary linguistics has important implications. It really means the decision as to whether the science of language will become primarily an empirical study, carried out on living human beings within the context of their practical activities, or whether it will remain largely confined to deductive arguments, consisting of speculation based on written or printed evidence alone. The first view would insist on drawing the material of linguistics from the observation of infant speech, from the study of pathological phenomena in aphasia, from field work on the actual use of language by the various strata of civilized society, and among so-called primitive peoples.

The grammarian and the lexicologist may have in future to abandon their comfortable, two-dimensional world of parchment and paper, and either go into the field, or else rely on material documented not only by words, but also by those aspects of human life, activity, and social organization by which the use of words is determined. The present reviewer, like most modern anthropologists, would plead for the empirical approach to linguistics, placing living speech in its actual context of situation as the main object of linguistic study.

Mr. Lewis is not too dogmatic in the excellent theoretical introduction to his book. He gives there an impartial summary of most modern theoretical work. He himself, however, takes the empirical view that "the main function of language in human life as the mediator between man and man" must be taken as the guiding principle in any linguistic inquiry.

A cavilling critic might note some omissions in his choice of authorities. The absence of any reference to the work of Philipp Wegener, one of the forerunners of the modern movement; or to the American psychologist, G. H. Mead, who perhaps was the first clearly to formulate the principles of pragmatic symbolism; the relatively small space given to the work of Jespersen and Piaget; and the omission of John Dewey's most important contribution, that is, of chap. v in his *Experience and Nature* might be remedied in a future edition. On one or two formal matters I should like to suggest also an amendment. Thus to state that "speech is an instrument, a tool" is not, as the author supposes, a useful simile, but, like all analogies, an unnecessary handicap. Speech, obviously, is not a tool, but a habit, a standardized type of activity of the human organism. It is, therefore, not to be classed with the material products of man, but rather with the other modes of active human adjustment to the enviroment and to the mechanisms of culture. Again, Mr. Lewis speaks of "language as an institution." Whatever meaning be given the word "institution," the label again brings language as a fixed product into the realm of material achievements and leads us away from the study of speech customs within the living context of human activities.

But these are minor criticisms, and they are found only in the theoretical preliminaries of Mr. Lewis's treatise. When he comes to work, and enters his empirical laboratory, all the minor misconceptions vanish. Throughout, he studies the child's speech habits within the circumstances in which they occur. He conducts, in fact, all his observations, in the only admissible manner: he investigates *speech* and not *language;* and investigates it, not as a detached, purely linguistic transfusion of meaning, but as a means of action on adults by the child and conversely the influence of speech and other activities of the grown-up on the child.

This makes the author recognize that to regard the child's spontaneous utterance as merely "expressive" in its function is erroneous. In fact, through the whole range of the author's observation, the distinction between "expressive," "evocative," and "representative" falls to the ground. Mr. Lewis's results show that the only correct treatment is to study the total situation: the vocal act of the child, which is linked up with the circumstances; and the reactions of the adults which respond to the child's prelinguistic activity. The meaning of such a vocal act can only be defined as the change produced by the child's utterance in mobilizing its social environment, and making the adults obey its wishes. Obviously, an utterance like this is at the same time expressive, in that it corresponds to the child's feelings of discomfort or anxiety; it is representative, in so far as it is linked up with the situation; and it is evocative in so far as it makes the elders respond to the child's utterance. "Throughout all this the child will tend to use his cries more and more as an aid to the rest of his behaviour, and even as a substitute for it. . . ." In other words, from the very beginning, the human being uses his voice in prearticulate and later on in an articulate sense, in order to achieve, through the assistance given him by others, what he cannot do through his own bodily activity.

The work of Mr. Lewis is in many ways a great advance on all previous experimental studies on child speech and a valuable contribution to the theory of language. In his use of older sources, he is judicious, critical, and comprehensive. In the setting of his own observations, he has taken his inspiration from the most scientific, that is, the most empirical point of view in modern linguistics.

REFERENCE NOTE

For other statements by Malinowski of his views on language in culture, see particularly his articles of 1920 and 1923, and Volume II of *Coral Gardens and Their Magic* (1935). In this volume, Part Five ("Corpus Inscriptionum Agriculturae Quiriviniensis; or The Language of Gardens") and Part Seven ("Magical

Formulae") are mainly documentation. The arguments of Part Four ("An Ethnographic Theory of Language and Some Practical Corollaries") and Part Six ("An Ethnographic Theory of the Magic Word") should be part of the education of any anthropologically-oriented student of language, if critically read.

Malinowski's work as a whole is evaluated in Raymond Firth (1957). The article by J. R. Firth (no kin to the editor) is a good overview of his linguistic work; see also the contributions by Kaberry and Leach. The limitations to Malinowski's handling of native semantic categories and to his views on pragmatic function of speech are analyzed by Leach (1957); Malinowski's views are also criticized by Voegelin and Harris (1947, n. 4, pp. 589-592) and discussed theoretically by Spang-Hannsen (1954).

References not in the general bibliography:

KABERRY, PHYLLIS

1957. Malinowski's Contribution to Field-Work Methods and the Writing of Ethnography. In R. Firth (Ed.), *Man and Culture*. London: Routledge & Kegan Paul. Pp. 71-92.

LEACH, EDMUND R.

1957. The Epistemological Background to Malinowski's Empiricism. In R. Firth (Ed.), *Man and Culture*. London: Routledge & Kegan Paul. Pp. 119-138.

7 On Sociological Linguistics

J. R. FIRTH

THE CENTRAL CONCEPT of the whole of semantics considered in this way is the context of situation. In that context are the human participant or participants, what they say, and what is going on. The phonetician can find his phonetic context and the grammarian and the lexicographer theirs. And if you want to bring in general cultural background, you have the contexts of experience of the participants. Every man carries his culture and much of his social reality about with him wherever he goes. (An Englishman on "safari" in the wilds of Africa carries not only many English artifacts about with him, but even if there is no Englishman within a day's journey, he may have reason to exclaim in English when something suddenly goes wrong, or use his language to address animals, refractory Africans, and God, and in writing his own notes and to his friends, enemies, and government, and he will, of course, have a certain amount of reading to do.) But even when phonetician, grammarian, and lexicographer have finished, there remains the bigger integration, making use of all their work, in semantic study. And it is for this situational and experiential study that I would reserve the term "semantics." (Taking advantage of what Coleridge called the "desynonymizing" process, I would use the term "semasiology" for the historical study of changes of meaning. Another suggestion is that *phonetics* and *semantics* be regarded as branches of *general* linguistics, the corresponding fields in *special* grammar being *phonology* and *semasiology*.)

But even when we have arrived at the context of situation, we are not at the end of the "House that Jack Built." The rest of the contextualization process is the province of sociological linguistics.

Sociological linguistics is the great field for future research. In this short paper I can only indicate the difficulties and make a few tentative suggestions, first in connexion with the very difficult problem of describing and classifying typical contexts of situation within the context of culture, and secondly of describing and classifying types of linguistic function in such contexts of situation.

Our greatest difficulty at present is the absence of any really well documented work on how we acquire our speech as we grow up. We cannot lay the blame on psychologists or sociologists, because it is much easier for a student of linguistics to acquire sufficient psychology and sociology for this work than for a psychologist or sociologist to acquire the necessary linguistic technique. After all, we are not aiming at linguistic sociology, but building on the foundations of linguistics. And as we have seen, without phonetics there can be no morphology of a spoken language, without intonation no syntax. And unless these are sound, there can be no semantics.

An example from the Society's Dictionary will raise the problem of categories for types of linguistic function. When the word *set* came to be done, it occupied eighteen pages and a column, and it extends to 154 main divisions; the last of these, *set up*, has so many subdivisions that it exhausts the alphabet and repeats the letters again down to *rr*.

Multiplying illustrative contexts have gone on indefinitely and filled a whole volume. In practice, however, we find that these contexts can be grouped into types of usage; and even if we only employ the few social categories mentioned in the Dictionary, such as common, colloquial, slang, literary, technical, scientific, conversational, dialectal, and remember the principle of relative frequency however approximately, we shall be getting nearer to a practical handling of the social background of the usage of words in typical contexts.

What we need are more accurately determined linguistic categories for the principal types of sentences and of usage we employ in our various social roles. Every one of us starts life with the two simple roles of sleeping and feeding; but from the time we begin to be socially active at about two months old, we gradually accumulate social roles. Throughout the period of growth we are progressively incorporated into our social organization, and the chief condition and means of that incorporation is learning to say what the other fellow expects us to say under the given circumstances. It is true that just as contexts for a word multiply indefinitely, so also situations are infinitely various. But after all, there is the routine of day and night, week, month, and year. And most of our time is spent in routine service, familial, professional, social, national. Speech is not the "boundless chaos" Johnson thought it was. For most of us the roles and the lines are there, and that being so, the lines can be classified and correlated with the part and also with the episodes, scenes, and acts. Conversation is much more of a roughly prescribed ritual than most people think. Once someone speaks to you, you are in a relatively determined context and you are not free just to say what you please. We are born individuals. But to satisfy our needs we have to become social persons, and every social person is a bundle of roles or *personae;* so that the situational and linguistic categories would not be unmanageable. Many new categories would arise from a systematic observation of the facts.

We learn speech in the routine action of the daily round. Speech is very largely vocal action in control of things and people including oneself, action in relation or in adjustment to surroundings and situation. We establish ourselves on speaking terms with our environment, and our words serve our familiarity with it. "The study of words in cultural familiarity" might almost describe this aspect of semantics.

We are born into a vast potential cultural heritage, but we can only hope to succeed to a very small part of the total heritage and then only in stages. There would appear to be a need to emphasize that for each stage of childhood and youth, of each type of child, there are a relevant environment and relevant forms of language.

There is a vast field of research here in what may be called the biographical study of speech. There is material for all the branches of linguistics in the study of all the various components of meaning in this linguistic life-history of the young person as an active member of his age-group as well as a pupil, in his seven ages of childhood and youth.

There are great possibilities for "biographical semasiology" or the history of changes in meaning of such words as *father*, *mother*, *love*, *child*, *play*, *toy*, *work*, *money*, *clothes*, *drink*, etc. There have been a certain number of rather sketchy works on "biographical phonetics," and odd fragments of "biographical grammar"; but we are still without real knowledge on language development.

Connected with this biographical approach is the history of what we have called the accumulation of social roles. The grown man has to play many parts, functioning in many characters, and unless he knows his lines as well as his role he is no use in the play. If you do not know your part and your lines, there are no cues for the other fellow, and therefore no place or excuse for his lines either.

The multiplicity of social roles we have to play as members of a race, nation, class, family, school, club, as sons, brothers, lovers, fathers, workers, churchgoers, golfers, newspaper readers, public speakers, involves also a certain degree of linguistic specialization. Unity is the last concept that should be applied to language. Unity of language is the most fugitive of all unities, whether it be historical, geographical, national, or personal. There is no such thing as *une langue une* and there never has been.

This "free interlocking" of roles is a great conservative influence, for the "same" word may be used in many different roles, and may even be specialized in certain uses; but so long as the specialized use does not acquire great intensity by virtue of context, or extend in frequency, other uses do not suffer. The entry of the broadcast voice into the homes of the people will have just so much influence as the context of listening provides. But it is one of many new technical instruments of the age which are breaking down barriers of all sorts and promoting "free interlocking" of social and linguistic circles, tending to prevent further linguistic subdivision and to strengthen the forces of conservation. (See Lloyd-James, 1935, pp. 98-99, 110-113.)

For the adequate description and classification of contexts of situation we need to widen our linguistic outlook. Certain elementary categories are obvious, such as speaking, hearing, writing, reading; familiar, colloquial, and more formal speech; the languages of the Schools, the Law, the Church, and all the specialized forms of speech.

Then one might add such types of situation as those in which there is an "individual" or "monologue" use of language, and those in which there is a sort of "choric" use, as when vocal interchange merely promotes or maintains affective rapport. Malinowski has applied to this kind of linguistic behaviour the very happy phrase "phatic communion"—"a type of speech in which ties of union are created by a mere exchange of words" (1923, p. 315).

Malinowski has also insisted on the specially interesting types of situation in which vocal interchange is just part of a job of work in hand, such as fishing, hunting, loading a truck, or the co-operative handling of tools and materials. He says the meaning of such words is "their pragmatic efficiency." Most of our contemporary "eye-language" in notices and directions is of this kind.

A great deal of conversation or discussion may also be in preparation for concerted or socially determined action. All the language of public administration and government may be said to be the language of planning and regulation, the language of public guidance. The subsequent discussion of success or failure may be regarded both as "phatic communion" and as a situation in which something planned is either accomplished or ends in failure.

In more detail we may notice such common situations as

a. Address: "Simpson!" "Look here, Jones," "My dear boy," "Now, my man," "Excuse me, madam."

b. Greetings, farewells, or mutual recognition of status and relationship on contact, adjustment of relations after contact, breaking off relations, renewal of relations, change of relations.

c. Situations in which words, often conventionally fixed by law or custom, serve to bind people to a line of action or to free them from certain customary duties in order to impose others. In Churches, Law Courts, Offices, such situations are commonplace. Your signature or your word is a very important piece of linguistic behaviour. In passing, we may notice that, when other things fail, judges often have recourse to very rudimentary semantics in their interpretations. There is a great field for practical semantics in the contextualization of crucial words in judicial remarks and judgements, particularly in the lower courts.

Such words are made binding by law, but many other words and phrases are used with a similar binding effect in everyday life, because their use releases overwhelming forces of public opinion, of social custom. "Be a sport!" "I know you won't let us down." One of the magic words of the age is *plan*. The mere use of this word and its derivatives releases certain forces of opinion and experience and gives the word weight. Its association with certain influential contexts gives it a power over us in this age of uncertainty.

Many more types of situation will occur to the interested student, but there is an obvious need for a more accurate study of our speech situations in order that categories may be found which will enable us to extend such social studies all over the world.

It is perhaps easier to suggest types of linguistic function than to classify situations. Such would be, for instance, the language of agreement, encouragement, endorsement, of disagreement and condemnation. As language is a way of dealing with people and things, a way of behaving and of making others behave, we could add many types of function—wishing, blessing, cursing, boasting, the language of challenge and appeal, or with intent to cold-shoulder, to belittle, to annoy or hurt, even to a declaration of enmity. The use of words to inhibit hostile action, or to delay or modify it, or to conceal one's intention are very interesting and important "meanings." Nor must we forget the language of social flattery and love-making, of praise and blame, of propaganda and persuasion.

The valuation or judgement in appraisement or blame of people, nations, books, plays are all of the greatest interest and far more stereotyped or socially conditioned than most people imagine. Most Englishmen will know the various reactions to "a good man" "a good chap," "a good fellow," "a good sort," "a good scout." A study of the jargon of contemporary book reviewers in the press shows how all such routine situations involving public judgement tend to produce stereotyped forms of language. This does not mean that such reviews are become meaningless, but rather that a fairly simple set of stock indications are practically convenient.

A more formal and much broader classification of types of language function would notice various types of narrative—traditional narrative, sacred and profane, and the free narrative of ordinary intercourse. Narrative of this kind would include description, but exposition and argument might be examined also.

Finally it must be repeated that most of the give-and-take of conversation in our everyday life is stereotyped and very narrowly conditioned by our particular type of culture. It is a sort of roughly prescribed social ritual, in which you generally say what the other fellow expects you, one way or the other, to say.

It will be agreed that the adequate description of speech-behaviour, viewed in this way, necessitates a highly developed phonetic technique. The close connexion between the practical contextual view of speech and the scrupulous formal technique here described has recently been so well expressed by one of my pupils, Fritz Güttinger, that I take the liberty of quoting it at length. It follows also, of course, that loose linguistic sociology without formal accuracy is of little value.

Zu den nachhaltigsten Eindrücken, welche man von der programmatischen Schrift J. R. Firths über den Sprechvorgang, wie auch von seiner Lehrtätigkeit am University College London davonträgt, gehört die Einsicht, dass die Spielregeln der Sprache und des Sprechens im Grunde etwas viel Roheres sind, als man zu glauben gewohnt ist. Was für Folgen dies für die allgemeine Sprachtheorie hat, braucht hier nicht ausgeführt zu werden. Daraus, dass das Zweckhafte, Handlungsmässige der Worte und Sätze Betrachtung abgesondert wird, ergibt sich letzten Endes die Notwendigkeit, die Formenwelt nach streng formalen Gesichtspunkten zu beschreiben (*Neue Schweizer Rundschau*, July, 1935, pp. 176-177).

[To the lasting impressions, which one carries away from the programmatic writing of J. R. Firth about the speech event, as well as from his teaching at University College London, is due the insight that the rules of speech and of speaking are really a good deal rougher than one is accustomed to believe. What consequences this has for general linguistic theory does not need to be amplified here. Thence arises in the last analysis the necessity, if the goal-direction, activity-regulating aspect of words and sentences is to be isolated for consideration, to describe the sphere of linguistic forms from strictly formal viewpoints.]

The moment a conversation is started, whatever is said is a determining condition for what, in any reasonable expectation, may follow. What you say raises the threshold against most of the language of your companion, and leaves only a limited opening for a certain likely range of responses. This sort of thing is an aspect of what I have called contextual elimination. There is a positive force in what you say in a given situation, and there is also the negative force of elimination both in the events and circumstances of the situation and in the words employed, which are of course events in the situation. Neither linguists nor psychologists have begun the study of conversation; but it is here we shall find the key to a better understanding of what language really is and how it works.

On a much wider basis, but none the less a branch of linguistics, is the study of dialects and languages as organs of cultural *élites* or other special social groups, e.g., Medieval Latin, the English "governing voice," Swahili, Classical Arabic, and also as channels or vehicles of culture contacts, as mechanisms of culture diffusion, e.g., French in Egypt, English and Russian in Asia.

In studies such as these in the past there has been too much vague speculation about "influences," and not enough accurate investigation into the actual mechanisms and channels of culture contacts and culture "movements." Who are the "culture-makers"? Who are the "carriers" of the particular cultural tradition, of the particular pronunciation, word, dialect, or form of speech? Is the number of "carriers" increasing or decreasing, and why? What is the mechanism of "transmission" from "carrier" to "carrier"? Where is a particular culture trait or linguistic habit at its best, in its "optimum 'locale,'" and why?

The whole problem of translation is also in the field of semantics, but is much too vast to be entered upon here.

The above review of the wide field of general semantics implies rather a different general philosophical attitude towards speech from that which has set our scale of linguistic values hitherto. But I am convinced that the greatest need of linguistic scholarship at the present time is a new outlook over a much wider field of life in company with others looking through adjacent windows converging on the same scenes. The new philosophy, the new outlook, means new values in scholarship, but not necessarily in conflict with the older values.

The technique I have here sketched is an empirical rather than a theoretical analysis of meaning. It can be described as a serial contextualization of our facts, context within context, each one being a function, an organ of the bigger context and all contexts finding a place in what may be called the context of culture. It avoids many of the difficulties which arise if meaning is regarded chiefly as a mental relation or historical process.

By this time we are accustomed to the subdivision of meaning or function. Meaning, then, we use for the whole complex of functions which a linguistic form may have. The principal components of this whole meaning are phonetic function, which I call a "minor" function; the major functions—lexical, morphological, and syntactical—the province of a reformed system of grammar; and the function of a complete locution in the context of situation or the typical context of situation, the province of semantics.

REFERENCE NOTE

Firth's work is well represented in his *Papers* (1957b). Regarding anthropological perspective, see especially the essays on "Personality and Language in Society" (1950) and "General Linguistics and Descriptive Grammar" (1951), as well as his early book, *The Tongues of Men* (1937). See also his "Synopsis of Linguistic Theory, 1930-1955" (1957c). Bursill-Hall (1960a, 1960b) presents an excellent general review of Firth's approach, placing it in context of other schools, as well as a good bibliography of the group; see also Bursill-Hall (1960c) and Robins (1961). For Firth's relationship to Malinowski, see his own paper (1957a), as well as comments in Bursill-Hall's review.

References not in the general bibliography:

BURSILL-HALL, G. L.

1960a. Levels Analysis: J. R. Firth's Theories of Linguistic Analysis I. *The Journal of the Canadian Linguistic Association*, *6*(2): 124-135.

1960b. Levels Analysis: J. R. Firth's Theories of Linguistic Analysis II. *The Journal of the Canadian Linguistic Association*, *6*(3): 164-191.

1960c. The Linguistic Theories of J. R. Firth. *Thought from the Learned Societies of Canada, 1960*. Toronto: Gage. Pp. 237-250.

FIRTH, J. R.

1957c. A Synopsis of Linguistic Theory, 1930-1955. In *Studies in Linguistic Analysis*. (Special volume of the Philological Society.) Oxford: Blackwell. Pp. 1-32.

LLOYD-JAMES, A.

1935. *The Broadcast Word.*

ROBINS, R. H.

1961. John Rupert Firth. *Lg.*, *37:* 191-200.

part II

EQUALITY, DIVERSITY, RELATIVITY

Introduction

ANTHROPOLOGY AND LINGUISTICS, like other disciplines dealing with man, have had to overcome misconceptions and stereotypes in order to attain a footing for their work. Moreover, to maintain an objective, informed approach toward human similarities and differences, whether cultural, racial, or linguistic, remains a constant task. Mistaken notions find a constant source of renewal in ignorance and interest, affecting the public climate of opinion within which the professions work and sometimes their own members as well. The question is often one of correcting popular errors; sometimes the errors are of scholars' own making and persist in circles that should know better.

Direct field experience has played a major part in forming the anthropological approach, but we must not be misled into thinking it the sole and sovereign remedy. Many a prejudice has resisted exposure to countervailing facts or found support in a distorted selection of them, and many non-anthropologists have shared the attitude one might call "anthropological" from reflection or principle. (It has roots in the philosophy of history, for example). Within anthropology itself, only the accumulated weight of experience, together with its critical assessment and advocacy, have sufficed to establish the modern professional attitude. And it is important to notice that the opportunity to validate the attitude by direct experience is in some respects disappearing. While some peoples of the world, and ways of life, are coming closer to each other, through modern travel and communications, others recede. Anthropology is particularly affected by the fact that much of the world which dawned upon Europe in the Age of Discovery has almost set again. Soon the chance to refute errors as to human potentialities and accomplishments in types of cultures such as those of the North American Indian will be entirely gone, so far as direct experience is concerned. For the content and felt quality of such vanished ways of life, we shall have to rely on the scholar's care for such records as we have. Thus there will never come a time when patient concern for the full range of fact and detail will not be necessary safeguards against perpetuation of errors among others and ourselves.

Much of the problem of misconception has centered around notions of primitive languages, their supposed characteristics and value. The principles and supporting facts of the modern anthropological attitude are clear.

First, we know no natural languages with vocabularies so limited that their speakers must eke them out with gestures (and hence perhaps cannot communicate in the dark); which lack definite systems of sounds and grammar; which lack standards of usage; which, because of lack of system or of writing, change more rapidly in structure than other languages; which lack abstract terms or capacity for forming them; which cannot serve significant intellectual and aesthetic expression. We know, indeed, no demonstrated characteristics which would place together the languages of "primitive" peoples as against those of "civilized" peoples. Not that some such characteristics might not eventually be shown; but if so, they will not be of the generically disabling kind, either as to the inadequacy of such languages so far as their indigenous context and ultimate potential are concerned or as to their scientific interest.

This leads to the second point. The diversity of the world's languages is an irreplaceable laboratory for understanding the nature of language and hence something of the nature of man. The value of a language for this purpose does not depend on the political significance of the people who speak it nor on their numbers. It depends upon its distinctiveness as a type and, historically, as an independent case. From a scientific point of view, the speech habits carried about in the memory of an impoverished, grizzled Indian woman may be worth more than all the English spoken in the state in which she lives. (Note Whorf's concluding statement in Part III [pp. 129-141]; Sapir and Swadesh in this Part; and McQuown, 1960.) Of course, many sociolinguistic problems can be studied only in speech communities where the language in question is actively in use. But for problems of types and universal traits of languages, of range of variation and covariation of features in languages as historical products, one surviving speaker may be enough for a description that is a valuable scientific contribution. (See, for example, Boas' work with Chinook and Sapir's with Takelma cited with Sapir and Swadesh in this section.) Such a contribution may also help make possible demonstration and reconstruction of a language family, and the general validity and theoretical status of the principles of comparative linguistics (the great accomplishment of linguistic science in the nineteenth century) depend on their testing in other language families, such as those of the New World. (See Hockett's paper in Part IX, pp. 599-611.)

Anthropologists and linguists hold these views, not simply because of their democratic principles (although such are frequently present), but because misconceptions on such points interfere with their work. A science cannot afford to operate in terms of stereotypes that have no grip on reality or on the basis of a sample (say, languages of international importance only) that has only an accidental relationship to its universe of study.

At the same time, preoccupation with the proper characteristics and values of lesser known, often unwritten, languages, can carry with it a subtler hazard, that of meeting a stereotyped error with a response that becomes stereotyped in turn. The disproof of misattributed differences in adequacy and character may lead to denial of any functional differences at all; a focus on correct appreciation of diversity may obscure the commonality that exists. Much of recent outlook has combined presumptions that the world's languages are equivalent in social adequacy, equal in total complexity, and almost endlessly diverse in structure. In short, the *relativity* of function, as well as of form and meaning, to the particular language has been assumed. Relativity, of course, may mean many things, such as that phenomena should not be judged out of context; that dependence on context makes phenomena not comparable; that dependence on context makes phenomena equivalent (or in some sense, equal). Only the implications of the first meaning are scientifically necessary for anthropology and linguistics. The minimum platform for their work comprises equality in the sense of equality of scientific consideration and potential relevance; diversity and relativity in the senses of respect for the integrity of phenomena; openness to the discovery of difference; insistence on the cross-cultural testing of general assumptions; cultivation of the inductive bases for the validation of empirical statements "on the ground"; above all, recognition that judgments of similarity and difference are not all or nothing and vary not only with the facts; and recognition that the most difficult and perhaps precisely anthropological task is not to establish either similarities or differences, so much as to discover and demonstrate the relationships between them, in phenomena and in levels of explanation.

Thus, we know that the languages of "primitive" peoples are not inferior or of the same type or even validly measurable by criteria of the sort that have usually been invoked. On the other hand, we do *not* know that all languages are equal in every respect; that their structural differences cannot be subsumed under better general formulations; that they cannot be compared and measured as to complexity or as to adequacy for particular purposes.

Many people still make the original errors about the nature of "primitive" languages, as well as related errors about the nature of language generally, such as identifying the idea of "a language" primarily with its vocabulary or its written form. In consequence, if one questions the counteridentification of "a language" with its grammatical structure or its spoken manifestation, or raises the possibility of ranking languages validly in certain respects, one may seem to be lending aid and comfort to an enemy. Yet here, as in other aspects of anthropology, unless conventional refutation of earlier errors is transcended, vital problems remain uninvestigated.

Signs of change have begun to appear in recent years. The structural analysis of writing and its functional role are being discussed, with writing accepted as an intrinsic aspect of languages coordinate with their spoken forms. There is a good deal of fresh work that accepts the description of vocabulary as part of structural analysis, confusing a language neither with its dictionary (against which Sapir warned) nor with its grammar. The work of Hockett, Greenberg, Voegelin, and others in empirical typology has revived anthropological interest in universals and general laws. This interest has been stimulated also by an increased awareness of the work of European schools of structuralism, which have long been concerned with such questions. There is increased attention, too, to the dependence of individual analyses upon assumptions as to universal properties. (See Kroeber's outlook.)

The renewed spread of interest in evolution also plays a part here, for study of the origin of language—its evolutionary emergence—must always involve projecting into prehistory a conception of language's intrinsic, universal traits, as the entity whose emergence is to be explained. Moreover, the question has been approached (by Hockett, Sebeok, and others) by controlled comparison between the forms of communication in different species, a procedure which further highlights the generic properties of all languages.

Whether or not the end-product, language, can be treated in isolation, study of the *process* of emergence must take into account the dependence of linguistic traits on social and biological context. A central problem is to determine what stage of sociocultural development would have required what form and degree of communication. A focus on generic properties is likely to emphasize how much full-blown language *can* do, but a realistic theory of the evolution of human communication must take into account how little language *need* do. Here a comparative study of the differential functional involvements of languages in different societies is essential. Such a problem emphasizes the present lack of adequate discussion of languages in terms, not of their potential equivalence in complexity and functional adequacy, but in terms of their actual, achieved functioning at the present time. The framework of such discussion must be evaluative and implicitly evolutionary, and so may evoke the errors of old evolutionary views; but only such a framework, concerned with the social context of the emergence, adaptation, and fate of linguistic varieties, can enable anthropology to contribute to understanding of the problems of language development and competition in the contemporary world.

In sum, the developing anthropological attitude takes the theme of "equality, diversity, relativity" as its starting point and working assumption, so far as most conventional notions about language are concerned; but it is prepared to find inequality, sameness, and comparability where pertinent and valid.

The contents of Part II speak to the starting point described above. Strehlow's work is particularly appropriate, because of the role that conceptions of the Aranda have played in conceptions of the cultures and languages of "primitive" societies. In the selection from his preface to *Aranda Traditions*, Strehlow points to inadequate field contact as one source of misconception and to lack of linguistic control as the root of the inadequacy. His experience is a plea for the intimate acquaintance that requires knowledge of a people's language before one judges their accomplishments and share of common humanity.

Hill documents and corrects an example of another source of misconception, persistence of scholarly error. Whereas Strehlow emphasizes an accurate source of knowledge, Hill stresses the need for accuracy of analysis as well.

Nida presents a well-organized account of specific ways in which languages can differ, doing so within the context of the necessity of joint linguistic and ethnological work. His examples are drawn from an enterprise which provides perhaps our finest control case for comparative semantics, the translation of the Bible into languages throughout the world. The task of translating such a text poses the problems of discovering and balancing diversity and commonality in their full complexity. The maxim with which Nida ends, "A combination of analytical social anthropology and descriptive linguistics provides the key to the study of semantics," has both practical and theoretical importance, as shown in Part IV.

Sapir and Swadesh demonstrate diversity in a particular, and traditionally important, area, that of obligatory categories, by means of another translation control case, a single sentence. Their demonstration leads directly into the problem which forms the focus of Part III. Note the joining of emphasis upon diversity of structure with assertion of ultimate similarity or equivalence of function—differences reducible to a common psychological ground (Sapir), denial that structural gap shows lack of expressive power (Swadesh)—a combination which has characterized much of recent American linguistics and anthropology.

On Aranda Traditions 8

T. G. H. STREHLOW

I HAVE SOMETIMES FELT that the anthropologists of the past tended to over-emphasize the differences between the Australian natives and ourselves; and this, I venture to suggest, has been due largely to the language barrier between them and their informants. Too often traditions and customs were noted down in their barest outlines; and the details were later filled in by the scientists themselves according to their own conception of what the natives' ideas ought to have been on certain subjects. In other words, the parched skeletons brought back from necessarily brief field excursions were often covered with flesh and skin in the private studies of thc anthropologists, and then presented to the public as living representatives of Australian natives, voicing suitably primitive sentiments. This earlier "primitivist" attitude of scientists may be illustrated by a condensed paragraph from the introduction to the account of the well-known Horn Expedition to Central Australia in 1894. The Horn Expedition, which had the official backing of "the Colonies of Victoria, New South Wales and South Australia," included among its members such scientists of reputation as Professors Baldwin Spencer and Ralph Tate, Dr. E. Stirling, and Mr. J. Alexander Watt. The record of this expedition was compiled under the editorship of Professor (later Sir) Baldwin Spencer. The aboriginal data were obtained largely through the assistance of the Postmaster of Alice Spring, Mr. Gillen, the later collaborator of Sir Baldwin Spencer.

Here the scientific attitude to the aboriginals is summed up over Horn's own signature as follows:

> The Central Australian aborigine is the living representative of a stone age who still fashions his spear-heads and knives from flint or sandstone and performs the most daring surgical operations with them. His origin and history are lost in the gloomy mists of the past. He has no written records and few oral traditions. In appearance he is a naked, hirsute savage, with a type of features occasionally pronouncedly Jewish. He is by nature light-hearted, merry and prone to laughter, a splendid mimic, supple-jointed, with an unerring hand that works in perfect unison with his eye, which is as keen as that of an eagle. He has never been known to wash. He has no private ownership of land, except as regards that which is not over carefully concealed about his person. . . . Religious belief he has none, but is excessively superstitious, living in constant dread of an Evil Spirit which is supposed to lurk round his camp at night. He has no gratitude except that of the anticipatory order, and is as treacherous as Judas. He has no traditions, and yet continues to practise with scrupulous exactness a number of hideous customs and ceremonies which have been handed from his fathers, and of the origin or reason of which he knows nothing. . . . After an experience of many years I say without hesitation that he is absolutely untamable. . . . Verily his moods are as eccentric as the flight of his own boomerang. Thanks to the untiring efforts of the missionary and the stockman, he is being rapidly "civilized" off the face of the earth, and in another hundred years the sole remaining evidence of his existence will be the fragments of flint which he has fashioned so crudely.

Such an observation suggests that the Australian aboriginal was then regarded merely as a highly specialized offshoot of the human species—primitive and incapable of further development, and therefore inevitably and naturally doomed to total extinction from the day when the superior white man entered upon his domains. Today many people are beginning to doubt whether the passing of the aboriginals from great portions of our continent was due entirely to unavoidable natural forces; and even the general attitude of the scientist towards the natives has changed greatly: their social system, their customs, their languages, and their ceremonies have been and are being diligently studied, and in the event of their disappearance owing to avoidable neglect much more interesting evidence of their existence would be left behind than merely a few rudely fashioned fragments of flint.

The style used in the translation of the legends and chant verses calls for a few words of explanation. These legends and chants were recorded, not in English, but in Aranda, direct from dictation by native informants. Up to date only a small portion of them has been translated: Since the writer, by reason of his birth and upbringing, is able to think in Aranda as well as in English, he has sought to give a translation that will reproduce faithfully the same impression on the mind of the English reader that they would have in the original tongue upon the native listener.

It is impossible to give here even a brief outline of the various devices used to achieve this result. It must be emphasized, however, that the Aranda used by skilful native story-tellers and in the difficult, intricate, and archaic language of the chants is an instrument of great strength and beauty, which can rise to great heights of feeling.

The general Australian public is, on the whole, unaware of this fact. It has been led to believe that the native Australian languages are hopelessly poor and primitive in structure and vocabulary. There are two main reasons for this mistake. In the first place, the average white person who comes into close contact with the aboriginals, and thus acquires a smattering of their dialects, is himself rarely well-educated. His own English is often of a poorer type and much more limited in vocabulary than the language of the people whom he despises. Not even the master of his own tongue, he cannot do justice to the idiom of the people amongst whom he lives; and of course, there is not the slightest reason why he should take an interest in any uneconomic linguistic studies. Even more harm has been done, however, by some scientists who, in their efforts to find the "missing link" in the Australian aboriginals, have described their language as devoid of all ornaments and graces, and characterized by an almost sub-human simplicity.

This false popular idea of the Australian aboriginal dialects has been fed and encouraged by the universal use of pidgin English as the medium of intercourse between the natives and the whites. Northern Territory pidgin English is not English perverted and mangled by the natives; it is English perverted and mangled by ignorant whites, who have in turn taught this ridiculous gibberish to the natives and who then affect to be amused by the childish babbling of these "savages."

The following account is intended to bring home the ruinous effect of pidgin English on any moving story. The caricatured tale should be familiar to most readers.

Long time ago ole feller Donkey him bin big feller boss longa country. Alright. By an'by another feller —him name ole Muckbet—bin hearem longa three feller debbil-debbil woman: them feller debbil-debbil woman bin tellem him straight out—"You'll be big feller boss yourself soon." Alright. Him bin havem lubra, ole lady Muckbet.

Alright. That Muckbet an' him lubra bin askem ole man Donkey come longa them (i.e., their) place one night. While ole man Donkey bin lie down asleep, them two feller bin finishem that poor ole beggar longa big feller knife,—properly big feller knife, no more small one. Bykrise, that ole feller bin loosem too much blood altogether! That Muckbet him bin big feller boss then alright!

By an' by that Muckbet an' him lubra bin killem lubra an' piccaninny belonga Mucktap,—that Muckbet him too much cheeky beggar alright. That feller Mucktap him bin properly sorry longa him mate (i.e., wife) an' that lil' boy.

That ole woman, lady Muckbet, him (i.e., she) bin walk about night time. Him bin havem candle. Him bin sing out—"Me properly sorry longa that ole man, me bin finishem; him bin havem too much blood, poor beggar; me properly sorry longa him." Him (i.e., she) bin finish then; no more (i.e., she is no more she is dead),—finish altogether.

Alright. That Mucktap him bin come along then. Him bin havem big feller fight longa that Muckbet,— oh properly! Him bin killem that Muckbet, him bin choppem off him head, finishem him properly. That's all.

This pidgin English account of the tragedy of Macbeth reveals the injustice and the insult that is done to any story told in this medium. The old tale immediately becomes utterly childish and ridiculous. All details are omitted. Even the general outline of the story is by no means accurate. Only a few characters are mentioned by name; and their names are distorted till they become merely funny. The whole account is an inadequate, untruthful, and malicious caricature of a great story. It would be impossible, even for a great writer, to compose a serious tragedy from such material as this. Yet this is the medium in which most native legends have been noted down in the first instance by white scientists!

It may now be clear why, even after such ridiculous pidgin English versions have been smoothed out into good simple English, the native Australian Legends have still remained poor and childish tales of little interest to any save the anthropologists.

Thanks to the patience of his informants the writer was able to record his legends in Aranda without any false "assistance" from pidgin English.

The difficulties of translation from Aranda to English are considerable. The originals abound in archaic and obsolete words, no longer used in current diction, but traditionally preserved in these instances. The verb stem in Aranda can take about a thousand combinations of suffixes; and many of these change the original force of the verb in such a way that a whole sentence may be necessary in English in order to express the new shade of meaning. Again, in the chant verses, the original word components are always run together and then re-subdivided into metrical feet: this pattern of versification ensures that no uninitiated person can readily understand a verse that he has not had explained to him by his elders.

It follows that an English translation which tries to convey the artistic force of these chants and legends must often use a whole sentence where the Aranda version uses only one verb. It must also use archaic words or turns of expression where the native version employs them. It must frequently paraphrase native words for which there is no exact English equivalent. Since the translator cannot hope to run together archaic English words into a single verse-unit, and re-subdivide it into a regular verse pattern, he has to use inversion and certain poetical turns in an attempt to capture some of the dramatic effect of the original.

An instance of the application of these principles as regards chants is afforded by the translation of the opening verse of the Ulamba Chant:

/: (K)erare: / ǰariǰe: / kalbiǰe: /
/: Kaŋkinža: / batuare: / ulalbiǰe: /

These two lines must first be reduced to prose as

Erariǰariǰaka albuǰika
ŋkinžaba iturala albuǰika

Erariǰariǰaka is an archaic poetic term, meaning "full of longing for something that has been lost," or "filled with longing to return home." *Albuǰika* is an infinitive meaning "to go home," "to turn homeward." The translation "His heart is filled with longing to turn home" tries to express the force of this Aranda line; it uses the poetic phrase "his heart is filled with longing" in order to express the force of the archaic poetic term *erariǰariǰaka.* Again, *ŋkinza* means both "sun" and "afternoon", and the translation "afternoon sun" combines both these meanings. *Iturala* means either "in the heat of the sun" or "in the brightness of the sun." *ŋkinžaba iturala* means, then, "at that time in the afternoon when the sun is glowing in all its heat and brightness." The translation "High in the heavens gleams the afternoon sun" attempts to put this into poetic language. The original rhythm of the verse—which is very effective when it is being chanted mournfully—naturally defies all efforts at recapture.

Another instance is afforded by the translation, in the Curlew Myth, of the verb *atakeri-takerereperelatanguna.* This word is derived from the simple verb *atakererama*, which means "to become rested," "to spread out roots" (from *atakera*, N. A., = "root"; *erama* "to become"). This simple verb is strengthened by means of the reduplication of its element into *atakeri-takererama*, which may be translated as "to become full of roots," "to spread out roots everywhere." Next the *-erama* portion of the word is reduplicated, and the verb *erama* thus becomes *erep-erama. Atakeri-takerereperama* now means "to become a bundle of roots," "to spread and spread one's roots in every conceivable direction." This long verb is then put into the imperative of the positive active voice (*atakeri-takerereperelatana*); and the final touch is given to it by the addition of the N.A. emphasizing particle *-guna.* The complete word now has the force of "remain rooted down firmly for all time." (The whole complex structure of the Aranda verb has been set out in detail in the writer's *Aranda Phonetics and*

Grammar, an *Oceania* monograph published by the Australian National Research Council).

The purpose of a good translation is to reproduce faithfully both the matter and the spirit of the original. The writer hopes that his readers will enjoy these translated portions of Northern Aranda legends and chants as much as he did the original version.

REFERENCE NOTE

Specific discussion and references regarding the Aranda are given immediately below. Following that, discussion and references regarding "primitive" languages, evolution in language, and progress in language are given in Part A, while references regarding the evolutionary emergence, or origin, of language, are given in Part B.

The Aranda and their language have figured in anthropological theory and controversy for a number of decades. With particular reference to language, see Hocart (1933); Laycock (1960), with bibliography of Aranda linguistics; and Sommerfelt (1938a, 1960b). Note also that the discussion of language's general position in social life by Durkheim (n.d.) is in a book that draws heavily upon Australian data.

A. "PRIMITIVE" LANGUAGES AND EVOLUTION AND PROGRESS IN LANGUAGE

On translation of western literature into a pidgin as evidence for communicative adequacy (if not literary value), see Hall (1959).

On persistence of mistaken conceptions of so-called primitive languages, see, as examples, the remarks refuted by Bloch (1956, pp. 96, 345, 411), Entwhistle (1949), Gonda (1956), Tovar (1954, especially pp. 343, 345-349), Hockett's paper in Part IX, and Hill's paper which follows. See further the following works which are directed against particular misconceptions: the classic paper by Boas (1889) on "alternating sounds"; Codrington (1903), Hale (1903, p. x), and Powell (1891, p. 141) on supposed instability; Hockett (in Part IX) and Sapir (1931c) on supposed inapplicability of the comparative method; Boas (1907; 1911, pp. 64-66) on "concreteness," as well as Brown (1958, chap. 8), Hocart (1918), and Levi-Strauss (1962); Gluckman (1959) on one aspect of supposed poverty of vocabulary; Holmberg, as cited under Herzog's article in Part VI, regarding supposed absence of true language among a simple hunting people. Broad discussions of the concept of "primitive" languages and their supposed characteristics are given by Beals and Hoijer (1959, pp. 566-569), Cooper (1928), Driver (1961, chap. 25), Goldstein (1960), Kluckhohn (1957), Kroeber (1911), Nida (1947b, sections 1, 3), Sapir (1921, p. 234 and *passim*), Thalbitzer (1938). See also references to Hill's article on pp. 86-89.

On specific mechanisms and processes of evolutionary change in languages (better: microevolutionary change), see references in Part VIII.

On general conceptions of progress in language and evolutionary trends and aspects of languages, see Bally (1952, chap. 2), Bloomfield (1914, pp. 342-345; 1942a), Brosnahan (1960), Brown (1958, chap. 8), Cassirer (1923), Cohen (1950; 1956a, pp. 138), Durkheim (n.d., pp. 437-439, including critique of Levy-Bruhl's interpretations of linguistic data from unwritten languages), Ginsberg (1956, chap. 11 and p. 194), Greenberg (1957, 1959b), Hymes (1961a, 1961c, 1963b),

Jespersen (1894; 1922, Book IV, especially chaps. 17, 18; 1941), Lenneberg (1960), Leroy (1950), Martinet (1957), Paget (1933), Ray (1961), Sebeok (1962), Service (1960), Sommerfelt (1938, 1960a), Vendryes (1925, pp. 344-359), Werner and Kaplan (1956), Whitney (1874).

On the related question of evolutionary implications of language typology, see references to the article by Sapir and Swadesh on pp. 101-107.

References not in the general bibliography:

BEALS, RALPH L. and HARRY HOIJER

1959. *An Introduction to Anthropology.* (2nd ed.) New York: Macmillan.

BLOCH, BERNARD

1956. [Remarks]. In F. Norman (Ed.), *Proceedings of the Seventh International Congress of Linguists (London, 1952).* London: Under the auspices of the Permanent International Committee of Linguists, with the assistance of Unesco. Pp. 394-396.

BROSNAHAN, L.

1960. Language and Evolution. *Lingua, 9:* 225-236.

CODRINGTON, REV. R. H.

1903. On the Stability of Unwritten Languages. *Man, 3:* 25-26 (Article 11).

COOPER, JOHN M.

1928. Primitive Languages. *Primitive Man* [now, *Anthropological Quarterly*], *1:* 17-23.

DRIVER, HAROLD E.

1961. Language. *Indians of North America.* Chicago: University of Chicago Press. Chap. 25.

ENTWHISTLE, W. J.

1949. Pre-Grammar? *Archivum Linguisticum, 1:* 117-125.

GINSBERG, MORRIS

1956. The Concept of Evolution in Sociology. *On the Diversity of Morals. Essays in Sociology and Social Philosophy.* London: Heinemann. (Originally published, 1932.) Vol. I, chap. II.

GOLDSTEIN, KURT

1960. Concerning the Concept of Primitivity. In Stanley A. Diamond (Ed.), *Culture in History: Essays in Honor of Paul Rodin.* New York: Columbia University Press. Pp. 99-117.

GONDA, J.

1956. *The Character of the Indo-European Moods, with Special Regard to Greek and Sanskrit.* Wiesbaden: Harrassowitz. [Reviewed, Murray Fowler, *Lg.*, 1957, *33:* 50-54.]

GREENBERG, JOSEPH H.

1956. Language and Evolutionary Theory. *Essays in Linguistics.* (Viking Fund Publications in Anthropology, No. 24.) New York: Wenner-Gren Foundation for Anthropological Research; Chicago: University of Chicago Press. Pp. 56-65.

HALE, EDWARD EVERETT

1903. Introduction. In J. H. Trumbull, *Natick Dictionary.* (BAE-B 25.) Washington, D.C.: Smithsonian Institution. Pp. ix-xiv.

HOCART, A. M.
1933. Aranta Language: Strehlow vs. Spencer and Gillen. *Man, 33:* 92.

KAPLAN, BERNARD
1957. On the Phenomena of "Opposite Speech." *JASP, 53:* 389-393.

KLUCKHOHN, CLYDE
1957. General Semantics and "Primitive" Languages. *General Semantics Bulletin*, nos. 20, 21.

KROEBER, A. L.
1911. The Languages of the American Indian. *The Popular Science Monthly, 78:* 500-515.

LAYCOCK, D. C.
1960. Language and Society: Twenty Years After. *Lingua, 9:* 16-29.

LEROY, MAURICE
1950. *Sur le Concept d'évolution en linguistique.* Bruxelles: Office de Bruxelles.

MARTINET, ANDRÉ
1957. Phonetics and Linguistic Evolution. In L. Kaiser (Ed.), *Manual of Phonetics*. Amsterdam: North-Holland Publishing Co. Pp. 252-273.

PAGET, R. A. S.
1933. L'Évolution du langage. In Pierre Janet and Georges Dumas (Eds.), *Psychologie du langage*. Paris: Alcan. Pp. 92-100. [*Journal de psychologie: normale et pathologique, 30* (1-4).]

POWELL, J. W.
1891. Indian Linguistic Families North of Mexico. *BAE-AR, 7:* 1-142.

SOMMERFELT, ALF
1960b. Language and Society. *Lingua, 9:* 212.

THALBITZER, WILLIAM
1938. Is Eskimo a Primitive Language? *Actes du Quatrième Congrès International de Linguiste (Copenhague, 1936)*. Copenhagen: Manksgaard. Pp. 254-262.

TOVAR, ANTONIO
1954. Linguistics and Prehistory. *Word, 10*(2-3): 333-350. [=*Linguistics Today*].

WHITNEY, WILLIAM DWIGHT
1874. On Darwinism and Language. *North American Review, 119:* 61-88.

B. ORIGIN OF LANGUAGE

For surveys and critical reviews of theories on the origin of language, see Brown (1958, pp. 131-135), Carroll (1953, pp. 17, 100-101), Cassirer (1944, pp. 44-61, 142-175), Diamond (1959, chap. 20), Gray (1939, pp. 39-40, 420-421), Jespersen (1922, chap. 21), McQuown (1957), Paget (1951), Revesz (1956), Sapir (1933a), Sommerfelt (1954), Tovar (1954), Vendryes (1925, pp. 5-16). Original considerations of a general or particular nature contine to be advanced as well; on this score, see Brown (*idem*), Burke (1952-1953), Cassirer (*idem*), De Laguna (1927), Diamond (1959), Haldane (1952), Hockett (1958, chap. 64; 1959; 1960a), Jespersen (1922, chap. 21), Johannesson (1949), Langer (1942), Paget (1930, 1951), Pumphrey (1951), Revesz (1954-1955, 1956), Sebeok (1962), Sturtevant (1947, chap. 5), Swadesh (1960b), Thorndike (1943), White (1940). Among older views, note the originality of Hale (1887, 1888).

References not in the general bibliography:

BURKE, KENNETH

1952-1953. A Dramatistic View of the Origins of Language. *Quarterly Journal of Speech*, October, 1952; December, 1952; February, 1953.

DIAMOND, A. S.

1959. *The History and Origin of Language*. New York: Philosophical Library.

HALDANE, J. B. S.

1952. The Origin of Language. *The Rationalist Annual for the Year 1952*, 38-45.

HALE, HORATIO

1887. The Origin of Languages and the Antiquity of Speaking Man. *Proceedings, American Association for the Advancement of Science, 35:* 279-323.

1888. *The Development of Language*. (Proceedings of the Canadian Institute, Third Series, vol. VI.) Toronto: Copp, Clark. Pp. 1-44.

JOHANNESSON, ALEXANDER

1949. *Origin of Language: Four Essays*. Reykyavik, Iceland: Leiftar; Oxford: Blackwell.

MCQUOWN, NORMAN A.

1957. Review of G. Revesz, *The Origins and Prehistory of Language*. *AA, 59:* 747-748.

PAGET, R. A. S.

1930. *Human Speech*. London: Kegan Paul; New York: Harcourt, Brace.

1951. The Origin of Language. *Science News, 20:* 82-94.

PUMPHREY, R.

1951. *The Origin of Language*. Liverpool.

REVESZ, GEZA

1954-1955. The Psychogenetic Foundations of Language. *Lingua*, 4: 318-322.

1956. *The Origins and Prehistory of Language*. Translated from the German by J. Butler. New York: Philosophical Library. (First published, Berne, 1946.)

ROSENKRANZ, BERNHARD

1961. *Der Ursprung der Sprache; ein Linguistisch-anthropologischer Versuch*. Heidelberg: Winter.

SOMMERFELT, ALF

1954. The Origin of Language, Theories and Hypotheses. *Journal of World History, 1:* 885-902.

THORNDIKE, E. L.

1943. The Origin of Language. *Science, 98:* 1-6.

9 *A Note on Primitive Languages*

ARCHIBALD A. HILL

0.1. MOST MODERN LINGUISTS who have experience of preliterate languages would reject the idea of the inefficiency, formlessness, and over-particularity of primitive speech, which once seemed so well grounded in the evolutionary anthropology characteristic of the 19th century. Yet there are many who still hold such views; namely that primitive tongues have a multiplicity of forms, fail to generalize, and are almost exclusively concrete. The following passage, from a book by a professional linguist, published in 1951, is an example which has a familiar ring: "To have a separate word for all the things we may talk about would impose a crippling burden on our memory. We should be worse off than the savage (read Cherokee) who has special terms for 'wash oneself' . . . 'wash someone else,' . . . but none for the simple act of 'washing' (Ullmann, 1951, p. 49)." This paper will be devoted to trailing the washing Cherokee through books on general linguistics, proving that he is a ghost though one that still walks, and to laying him once for all.

1.1. The linguist who has done most to present the picture of Cherokee as inefficiently particular because it lacks a general term for washing is no less a figure than Otto Jespersen. The statement that there are thirteen different verbs for washing appears first in *Sprogets Oprindelse* in 1892 (p. 849), and for the last time in *Efficiency in Linguistic Change* (1941, p. 45). In between it can be found in *Progress in Language* (1894, p. 351), *Growth and Structure of the English Language* (1905, p. 54), and *Language* (1922, p. 430). It was a favorite example of primitive inefficiency to which he returned again and again, embedding it in books which still enjoy great prestige. Jespersen got the example from A. H. Sayce, though his acknowledgment is not perfectly clear, since what he acknowledges is material which adjoins the Cherokee forms in Sayce's books (Sayce, 1874, pp. 78-79). Sayce, in turn, quite properly acknowledges the source of his material, which is the starting point of the whole tradition, though he uses this source in the later of the two forms in which it appeared. The earliest form is an article by the pioneer Americanist, John Pickering (1823). The article forms a long appendix to a reprint of Edwards' "Observations on the Mohegan Language," (Edwards, 1823) and was made the basis of a later article by Pickering in 1831 in volume six of the *Encyclopedia Americana*. This second form was printed again in 1836 and several later editions of the encyclopedia, without change. It was the encyclopedia article (or rather a separate printing of it) that Sayce used. (Sayce [1874] gives only twelve forms, though he quotes the figure thirteen, in spite of the fact that there were fourteen in his source. Sayce erroneously says that all Cherokee verb forms are incorporating, "the object being never mentioned." The example is also used in Sayce's *Introduction to The Science of Language* [1890, 1.120 and 2.5-6]. It is to this latter book that Jespersen refers on p. 430 of his *Language*. It was primarily the quotation in Sayce [1874] that Jespersen used, since it alone quotes the actual verb forms. Sayce's forms are by no means accurately quoted, and Jespersen in turn adds several new errors, which he never corrected in his successive quotations of the Cherokee forms.)

1.2. It is not necessary to go into other uses of the Cherokee example which are off the main line of transmission, but one at least, deserves comment. This is the discussion by J. N. B. Hewitt, who alone shows scepticism. In 1893 he wrote: "An analyzation of the fourteen examples given shows that they are not all verbs denotive of washing; some signify 'to swim,' others 'to soak,' others 'to wet or sprinkle,' and still others 'to boil'." It is curious that Hewitt is the only scholar who took the trouble to count the forms, thereby correcting the original statement that there are thirteen verbs, though actually fourteen were given. It is even more curious that the verbs do not mean what Hewitt says they mean. He was either guessing, or was misled by the forms of Northern Iroquois which he knew well.

1.3. The passage from Pickering, in its early form, follows. The passage is found at p. 121, though there is an earlier reference at p. 114 to Mr. Buthrick as "present missionary to the Cherokees," and stating that Pickering was indebted to a "learned friend" for the communication from Buthrick. I have slightly modified the passage, by adding numbers for ease of reference, and omitting the repeated portions of the translations.

In the Cherokee (says the Rev. Mr. Buthrick) . . . thirteen different verbs are used to express the action of "washing" as follows:

1. *Cŭ tŭ wō* I am washing	myself, as in a river
2. *Cŭ lē stū lā*	my head
3. *Tsē stū lā*	another person's head
4. *Cŭ cŭ squō*	my face
5. *Tsē cŭ squō*	another's face
6. *Tā cà sā lā*	my hands
7. *Tā tśē yà su la*	another's hands
8. *Tā cō sū lā*	my feet
9. *Tā tsē yâ sū la*	another's feet
10. *Tā cŭng kē lâ*	my clothes
11. *Tā tse yŭng kē lâ*	another's clothes
12. *Tā cŭ tē yā*	dishes
13. *Tsē yŭ wâ*	a child
14. *Cô wē lâ*	meat

This difference of words prevents the necessity of mentioning the object washed. So also with the verbs 'love,' 'take,' 'have,' 'leave,' 'die,' 'weigh,' etc.

"Mr. Buthrick" was the Reverend Daniel Sabin Butrick, 1789-1851, missionary to the Cherokees from 1818 until his death, in the period both before and after the removal. He was the author of several manuscript volumes now in the Houghton Library at Harvard, and co-author of a Cherokee speller in the pre-Sequoyah roman developed by the missionaries. There is a good deal of rather engaging information about him in Starkey (1946).

. . . .

[Hill transliterates and identifies Butrick's words with the aid of the extensive Cherokee literature and a personal communication from Floyd Lounsbury. His detailed analysis gives:

1. *k-ata-wo*	I-reflexive-bathe (in a stream)
2. *k-ali-sdul-e*	I-reflexive-head-wash
3. *tsi-sdule-e*	I-head-wash (whose head unspecified)
4. *k-a-gə̃sk-wo*	I-him (or "it")-face-wash
5. *tsi-gə̃sk-wo*	I-face-wash (whose face unspecified)
6. *de-k-asul-e*	plural object-I-extremely-wash
7. *de-tsi-ya-(a)-sul-e*	plural object-I-him-extremely-wash
8, 9. identical with (6,7,).	
10. *de-g-ə̃gil-e*	plural object-I-him-clothing-wash
11. *de-tsi-y(a)-ə̃gil-e*	plural object-I-him-clothing-wash
12. *de-k-atiy-e*	plural object-I-dish (or spoon)-wash
13. *tsi-yə̃w(i)-e*	I-person (?)-wash
14. *g-owil-e*	I-meat-wash]

3.1. My analysis is by no means perfect, but it is sufficient to show that the forms are genuine and are systematic. Yet the complexity of the relation of these forms to Cherokee structure is made greater by the fact that Butrick's list of verbs ('love,' 'have,' 'weigh,' etc.) suggests that he was actually describing two different phenomena, but in a fashion so compressed as to be unintelligible. One of these phenomena is the existence of a score or so of "classificatory verbs" which take different forms according to whether the object of the action is round, animate, long and thin, etc. These forms have been described by Professor Haas (1948), and long ago by Worcester (1852), though it is interesting that the grammarians like Gabelentz missed them entirely. A second phenomenon is actual noun incorporation, which Professor Lounsbury tells me now occurs only with nouns for parts of the body and certain articles of clothing, though it is evident from forms quoted by Mooney (Myths of the Cherokee, *BAE-AR* [1897-1898], *19:* 509) that incorporation must once have been more widespread. The incorporated noun morphemes are now always bound, and usually differ altogether from the ordinary free forms for the same objects. The two phenomena can, but need not, be combined. It is worth noting that Sayce misunderstood Butrick's reasonably careful statement, and jumped to the conclusion that this very limited incorporation and classification was characteristic of all verbs.

3.2. It is clear that Cherokee, so far from being hopelessly over-specific, is a language like other languages, possessed of order and system, no matter if that system is different from our own. We do not find fourteen totally unrelated expressions for washing, but two morphemes only, which differ in meaning, and which enter into a whole series of systematic contructions. Even with less than perfect identification of the elements in our word list, we can see that they have a regular pattern. They follow each other in this fixed order: number prefix of the goal, pronominal actor prefix, pronominal goal prefix, incorporated goal morpheme, action morpheme. One or more of these, of course, may be absent, and it is not maintained that what is true of these constructions is necessarily true of all others in Cherokee. Thus for instance, in constructions which I have seen in texts, it is far commoner for the action morpheme to be followed by further formative elements, than it is for the action morpheme to end the construction as here. What is important, however, is that the order of morphemes is as systematic and as fixed as the order in English 'I wash my face.' The difference between the English and Cherokee constructions amounts to little more than that one set of morphemes is bound, and is a less than perfectly productive part of the linguistic structure; the other set of morphemes is free, and enters into an unlimited number of constructions.

4.0. As to the supposed lack of generalizing power, it is ironical that the list of forms before us generalizes in one instance more than does English. We can not content ourselves with a general term like extremity, but must specify hand or foot. I can cite still other forms which are constructed in a sufficiently generalized fashion so that Jespersen would have had to call them civilized, had he known them. The suffix *-ya*, 'real' or 'principal,' can be added to *ata*, 'tree,' to give *ataya*, 'principal tree, oak,' and to *yə̃wi*, 'man,' to give *yéwiya*, 'principal man, Indian.' I can think of no better example of a cultural lag than that the letter written by Butrick some time before 1823 is still having its effect in 1951 because linguists incorporated his statements in supposedly authoritative books without bothering to subject his list of forms to analysis.

REFERENCE NOTE

References for Hill's article are given immediately below (A), followed by additional comment and references on its subject (B).

A. REFERENCES SPECIFIC TO THE PAPER

EDWARDS, J.

1823. Observations on the Mohegan Language. *Collections of the Massachusetts Historical Society*, Series 2, Vol. 10, pp. 81-160. Cambridge, Mass.

HAAS, MARY R.

1948. Classificatory Verbs in Muskogee. *IJAL*, *14:* 242-245.

HEWITT, J. N. B.

1893. Polysynthesis in the Languages of the American Indian. *AA* (o.s.), *6* 381-407.

JESPERSEN, OTTO

1892. Sprogets Oprindelse.

PICKERING, JOHN (ED.)

1823. Dr. Edwards' Observations on the Mohegan Language. *Collections of the Massachusetts Historical Society*, Series 2, Vol. 10, pp. 135-160. Cambridge, Mass.

SAYCE, A. H.

1874. *The Principles of Comparative Philology*. London: Trübner.

1890. *Introduction to the Science of Language*. (4th ed.) London: Kegan Paul, Trench and Trübner.

STARKEY, MARION L.

1946. *The Cherokee Nation. New York*: Knopf.

ULLMANN, STEPHEN

1951. *Words and Their Use*. London: Muller.

WORCESTER, S. A.

1852. [Principles of the Cherokee Language]. In Henry Schoolcraft, *Historical and Statistical Information Respecting the History, Conditions, and Prospects of Indian Tribes of the United States*. Washington, D.C. Vol. 2, pp. 443-456.

B. GENERAL COMMENTS AND REFERENCES

On "primitive" languages, see the note to Strehlow's article on pp. 82-84.

On praise of such languages for excellence, or even superiority in some ways, see, as examples, Bishop Baraga: "In closing, let it be allowed that the Indian language is perfect in its own way, and has many beauties not to be found in our modern languages" (continuing with a peroration to the Ojibwa verb) (1878, p. 422); Boas: "We could read our newspapers with much greater satisfaction if our language would compel them to say whether their reports are based on self-experience, inference, or hearsay!" (as would some Indian languages) (1942, p. 182); Hale: "It seemed to them [European linguists who doubted Eliot's account of Natick, an Algonquian language of Massachusetts] impossible that languages so perfect in their systems and so carefully precise in their adaptations of those systems could maintain their integrity among tribes of savages who had no writing" (1903, p. x); Whorf: "The Hopi actually have a language better equipped to deal with such vibratile phenomena than is our latest scientific terminology" (1936, p. 131); "In this field and in various others, English compared to Hopi is like a bludgeon compared to a rapier" (1956a, p. 85).

References not in the general bibliography:

BARAGA, RT. REV. F.

1878. *A Theoretical and Practical Grammar of the Otchipwe Language for the Use of Missionaries and Other Persons Living Among the Indians*. (2nd ed.) Montreal.

HALE, EDWARD EVERETT

1903. Introduction. In J. H. Trumbull, *Natick Dictionary*. (BAE-B 25.) Washington, D.C.: Smithsonian Institution. Pp. ix-xiv.

10 *Linguistics and Ethnology in Translation-Problems*

EUGENE NIDA

THE LINGUIST AND THE ETHNOLOGIST are more or less conscious of the relationship between their respective fields of research. Almost all would recognize that language is best described as a part of culture, and it soon becomes evident to those doing field-work in descriptive linguistics that one who has had some training in social anthropology has a distinct advantage in dealing with many types of semantic problems, particularly those in which the culture under consideration is quite different from his own. Nevertheless, despite a well-recognized relationship between linguistics and ethnology on the part of some, the practical value of the relationship is often overlooked or vaguely defined. At any rate, it would seem that only partial use has been made of social anthropology in dealing with the many semantic problems with which the investigator of aboriginal languages is constantly confronted.

The person who is engaged in translating from one language into another ought to be constantly aware of the contrast in the entire range of culture represented by the two languages. Nevertheless, the problems of translation have seldom been studied from this standpoint. This situation is due to many factors. First, most translations with which we are familiar have been carried on within the Indo-European language-family, and, for the most part, the culture of this linguistic area is relatively homogeneous. Second, most translations which have involved data from widely differing cultures have been translations from languages representing simple cultures to languages representing complex cultures, for example, translations of folk-lore data from Zuñi to English. The complex cultures have so many alternates of behavior and have acquired such a knowledge of alternates in other cultures that the translation-task is not so complicated, nor is the translator so aware of the cultural features involved.

A third factor tending to obscure the cultural features involved in translation is our habit of discussing words almost wholly in terms of psychological entities rather than in terms of social ones. The study of semantics on the basis of certain psychological theories has too often resulted in the entire problem being enmeshed in theories of perception and the relationship between the "referent" and the "thought-complex." A fourth factor has been the emphasis upon the stylistic and literary factors of translation, so that one often receives the erroneous impression that translation is basically an art rather than a science.

In association with the Summer Institute of Linguistics and the American Bible Society, the writer has had occasion to become acquainted with problems of translation which reveal some very significant matters in the relationship between linguistics and ethnology. The data have been gathered from the examination of translations of the Bible into various aboriginal languages. These translations were made by both linguistically and non-linguistically trained individuals. The value of the data is of special significance because of several features. First, the Bible has been and is being translated into a great variety of languages. At the present time the Bible, or portions of it, have been published in 1064 different languages. Second, the subject-material of the Bible covers a wide range of cultural situations. In fact, there are few phases of life which are not mentioned in considerable detail. Third, the culture represented in the Bible is somewhat different from the core of our present Western culture. As a result, when one is translating the Bible into some aboriginal language, the problems of cultural equivalence are far more evident than if one were translating a literary product of our own culture. It is easier to see the problems when one's own culture is not involved, for there is too much about one's own patterns of behavior which is taken for granted.

The immediate importance of proper ethnological background for the translator can be seen in noting the two most common errors which translators make. One of these is literalness and the other is the desire to avoid foreign words. The ridiculous consequence of literalness is evident in the translation of the Semitic idiom "children of the bridechamber" (Matt. 9: 15; Mark 2: 19; Luke 5: 34). In one of the Bantu languages of Africa the translator had attempted to translate this idiom literally, and the result was "children of the house of the man who marries the woman." The translator thought that the children were in some way related to the bridegroom and not to the bride, so he chose the "house of the bridegroom" rather than the "house of the bride." Actually, however, the Bantu translation designated the children of the bridegroom by his other former wives, for among the people of that tribe polygamy was commonly practiced. There could be no other interpretation for the native. The translator was not aware of the Jewish marriage-customs nor of the idiom "children of the bridechamber," which designated either the guests who participated in the celebration, or, as other authorities contend, the friends of the bridegroom.

Almost the reverse type of tendency, but equally unguided, is to be found in the insistence of some translators upon preserving the native language and looking upon all borrowed words as some type of contamination. In one of the Indian languages of Latin America one translator went so far as to translate "ass" as "a small long-eared animal," even though the natives of the particular tribe were well acquainted with burros and used the Spanish name *burro*. The translation by "a small long-eared animal" did not make sense to the native, for it is as applicable to a rabbit as to a burro—in fact, somewhat more so.

Words are fundamentally symbols for features of the culture. Accordingly, the cultural situation in both languages must be known in translating, and the words which designate the closest equivalence must be employed. An examination of selected problems in various aspects of culture will make it possible for one to see more clearly the precise relationship of cultural information to the semantic problems encountered in descriptive linguistics. Translation-problems, which are essentially problems of equivalence, may be conveniently treated under (1) ecology, (2) material culture, (3) social culture, (4) religious culture, and (5) linguistic culture.

The extremity of ecological variation from territory to territory is seldom anticipated, and there is often considerable difficulty in finding some equivalence in terms which designate such ecological features. For example, in Yucatan, Mexico, practically no correspondence can be found to the four seasons of the temperate zones. In translating the passage in Mark 13: 28, which deals with the fig tree putting forth its leaves just before summer, there are several complications. The only fig tree that is known to the Mayas is a wild variety which does not produce fruit. Moreover, this tree, like practically all the other trees of the forest, loses its leaves entirely during the hot season, which usually lasts from February till the end of May. Then, within a few days after the rainy season begins, the fig tree and all the other trees of the forest put out their leaves. One must equate the summer with the rainy season, but in this case the rainy season must always precede the putting forth of the leaves. It is impossible to employ the Spanish word *verano*, which is used by the Spanish-speaking people to designate the calendrical summer in temperate zones, for the word *verano* has been borrowed by the Mayas to designate the hot season during March, April, and May. Ecological differences between the tropics and the semi-tropical or temperate zones necessitate many adaptations, but often, even at best, the equivalents are not too close. The only other possibility in the illustration just cited would be to designate a month instead of the summer as the time foretold by the leafing of the fig tree; but even this would be unsatisfactory, due to the considerable fluctuation in the beginning of the rainy season.

If is often difficult in tropical countries to render the word "desert" as a place which has sparse vegetation. It is absolutely inconceivable to a Maya Indian that any place should not have vegetation unless it has been cleared for a maize-field, and a cleared field is not the cultural equivalent of the desert of Palestine. Accordingly, one must translate "desert" as an "abandoned place," for culturally the two places are similar in that they both lack human population. In this case, the culturally significant features must be substituted for the ecological ones.

When some region is completely lacking in some topographical feature, it is frequently impossible to present exactly the feature of another region. For example, the inhabitants of some of the low limestone islands of the Pacific and the Indians of the peninsula of Yucatan find it almost impossible to conceive of "mountains" in the sense of the Palestinian equivalent. To the Maya Indian a *muul* "hill" is "an elevation of land," and at best it cannot be much more than one hundred feet high. If one uses "great hill" to designate "mountain," it may mean an elevation of as much as one hundred and fifty feet, but in no case does it approximate something which may rise several thousand feet into the air. Such a thing is quite inconceivable to a Maya, and any attempt to force him to imagine anything so large only makes him think that the source of such information is untrustworthy. A "great hill" is not a completely accurate designation of a "mountain" in Palestine, but it is the best cultural and ecological equivalent. To translate "river" by "flowing water," or "lake" by "large expanse of water," or to describe the operation of a boat to peoples who have never seen such things nor heard of them, often places as much strain upon their credulity as it does for us to be informed that eggs stand on end in China during a certain season of the year.

Problems involving material culture-features are often far more complex than those involving ecological features. On the other hand, there are many items of close equivalence between the Palestinian culture of Bible times and the cultures of many aboriginal cultures today. In many places in the world the "ox-goad," the "mill-stone," and the "stone water-jar" have almost exact equivalents. However, despite the number of situations of considerable cultural similarity, the differences are very great. For example, many of the illustrations of the New Testament include the processes and plants of agriculture. In many places in the New World wheat is completely unknown among the aboriginal population. Accordingly, in most places the illustrations must be made applicable to maize wherever this is possible. Nevertheless, in those parts of the New World where the dibble-stick is used for planting, the illustration of the sower who scattered seed on various types of ground seems completely incredible. Only considerable explanation can ever convince the Indian that the sower in the famous parable was not out of his mind.

The villages of many aboriginals are quite different from the walled cities of ancient times. Accordingly, the account in Acts 9: 24, in which the gates of the city are closed, appears almost inconceivable. The aboriginal language will probably not have a word for "gate," and if it should, the city or village would certainly not possess such. On the one hand, if one attempts to use "doors of the city," then the picture is more confused than ever, for the native would then think that the city was some gigantic thing built within one house having doors, or that there were some huge doors standing somewhere around the city. On the other hand, in many tribes, in order to apprehend criminals or to prevent men from going to their fields when there is public work to be done, the roads are closed by guards and no one can leave the city. This cultural situation has some meaning, and the translation may make use of it.

There is often a tendency in translating to attempt to indicate the same environmental feature, but to overlook the different cultural significance involved. In translating the well-known discourse on the vine in the fifteenth chapter of the Gospel According to John, some translators have used a word for "vine" which designates a vine-like plant, but one which is not necessarily cultivated nor bears fruit. The fact that the word designates a type of plant, as regards its habits of growth, is not the point in question. The entire meaning of the discourse turns upon the features of cultivation and the care given to such a plant. Equivalence of material form is not enough. The cultural significance is the vital matter.

It is not only necessary to examine ecological features, but also to determine how the natives interpret such environmental matters. For example, in the Totonac language if one translates literally the expression "from the uttermost part of the earth to the uttermost part of heaven," occurring in Mark 13: 27, the native is likely to be confused, or even to laugh, as one did. He commented that such a distance would be nothing at all. His explanation of the Totonac cosmogony was that the earth and the heavens (this is identical with "sky" in Totonac) are formed like the half of an orange. The earth's surface corresponds to the flat surface and the sky corresponds to the curved surface, but the farthest point of the sky and the farthest point of the earth would both be at the extended horizon, in other words, would be identical. The translation of this expression must be changed in Totonac to "from all over the earth to all over the sky," if it is to render the original correctly in terms of the closest cultural parallel.

In the complexities of social organization and social control, the translator is very frequently confronted by many difficulties in interpretation and equivalence. For example, in the Maya language there is no term for "brother" or "sister" as such, but one must designate whether the person is an older or younger brother or older or younger sister. Often in the Biblical account there is no indication as to the age-relationship. The only hint which we have is that the older brother's or sister's name normally occurs before the younger one's. Nevertheless, it is necessary to assign some age-relationship to every word which designates brothers or sisters.

The indication of class and caste is often quite difficult in translating. It is easy enough at times to obtain words for "ruler," "leader," and "rich," but an expression to designate "the common people" is not so easy. Such people are often the culturally insignificant and uncolorful, and a name for them is sometimes either negative or non-existent. In the Maya culture of Yucatan the social and economic stratification in the Indian villages is rather well determined by the distance which the inhabitants live from the center of town or village. Accordingly, the translator employed the phrase "the people in the back part of town" for the "common people." The natives immediately perceived the meaning of the social distinction.

A very similar type of problem is the one which involves a translation for "Gentiles" in contrast with "Jews." This is doubly difficult since in Latin America the word *Gentiles* has often been borrowed into various Indian languages with the meaning of "unbeliever" and "unbaptized person." It is sometimes possible to translate "Gentiles" by "those who are not Jews." However, in some contexts such a negative classification does not convey the meaning of the original. In the examination of almost any society, one will find a designation for the group which is considered to be the same as the central unit and another group which is considered to be different from or outside the central group. These are known to sociologists as the "in-group" and the "out-group." A designation for the second group is often similar to our usage of "foreigners," though in many instances one can find an expression which will emphasize the distinction in mode of life even more than a foreign point of habitation. A translation such as "the different peoples" usually makes it possible to convey the meaning of "Gentiles."

At times the problems of translation which involve social practices become very complex. For example, Jesus spoke of "a bill of divorcement" as sanctioned by the law of Moses (Mark 10: 4). Among the Totonacs of Mexico there has been no such thing as a legal document of divorce even though there is such a feature in the Mexican national culture. The Totonacs who desire to obtain a "legal divorce" pay the town-secretary to erase their name from the civil register. If both parties are agreeable, the fee is not large; but if only one party desires a divorce by erasure, then the fee is considerably higher, for the secretary can usually demand and obtain a larger payment. In Totonac the expression for obtaining a "legal" divorce is literally "to have one's name erased." The important thing about this transaction is that it is looked upon as having complete legal sanction. If one were to translate "bill of divorcement" by a phrase such as "letter stating that the man is leaving his wife" (there is no single word for "divorce"), the entire point of the passage would be missing, because such a man would be immediately condemned by his fellow Totonacs. The entire point of Jesus' statements about the "bill of divorcement" turns upon the legal sanction.

It may well be asked what may be the effect of

encroaching Mexican national culture with its different legal system. According to Mexican law, such name-erasing is illegal. On the other hand, the expression "to name-erase" has become so much a symbol for legal divorce that it is employed to designate types of divorce which do not involve the actual procedure of erasing names. It should be noticed, however, that successive editions of the Bible in an aboriginal language usually need to be brought up to date from decade to decade with reference to the degree of social and vocabulary-change induced through progressive contact with a national government and with western civilization.

The social implications of actions described in the Bible are always a subject of interest. When the Totonac people read about a man carrying a pitcher of water (Mark 14: 13; Luke 22: 10), they are tremendously amused. It seems very silly to the women to think of a man doing women's work, and the men are astonished at the man's ignorance of propriety.

In matters of religious culture the problems of translation are often the most perplexing. The names for deity are a continual difficulty. The native word may have a heavy connotative significance which makes it awkward to use. On the other hand, a foreign word often implies an "alien" God. Whether the translator is aware of it or not, the natives usually equate such a foreign term with one of their better-known and understood deities.

More difficult, however, than the titles for deity are the words for "sanctity" and "holiness." These words are so closely connected with the entire problem of tabu that it is quite difficult, in many instances, to find an adequate designation. One translator in Africa attempted to find an expression for "Holy Spirit." He rather naïvely asked for "holy" and then for "spirit," and combined the two words into a title for deity. The first word has the basic meaning of "tabu," but this tabu is usually produced by contact with an evil spirit. Only rarely do good spirits create a tabu. The word for "spirit" can designate either a good or an evil spirit, but in the particular culture the evil spirits are very much in the majority. If the spirit is a good spirit, it is usually necessary specifically to denote the fact by an attributive. The combination which the translator chose for "Holy Spirit" was doubly confusing. To the natives, the only meanings for this combination of words would be "a spirit (probably an evil one) which has acquired a tabu by contact with some other spirit (undoubtedly evil)" or "a spirit which makes objects tabu." This second type of spirit could only very rarely be a good spirit. The fact that the translator had such extreme difficulty in explaining to natives that a good God possessed such a spirit should have been evidence enough that the phrase did not make sense. It has generally been found that the concept of tabu involves so many other related aspects that the translator is usually forced to start with some such word as "pure" or "clean," and by a process of teaching to build up the concept of "holy."

At times a literal translation of the Greek text may have rather disastrous consequences in an aboriginal language. In the eastern dialect of Aztec the literal translation of Jesus' words "Abraham rejoiced to see my day" (John 8: 56), would be a declaration on the part of Jesus that he was a shaman with a basically animal nature. The Eastern Aztecs believe that a shaman or physically deformed person who appears to have some mystic power is actually an animal and walks about as such during the night. During the day, however, he assumes the guise of a man. The daytime-guise is called "his day." Jesus' statement would be interpreted by the Aztecs as being an explicit statement as to his being an animal and not a person.

In Acts 16: 16, a girl "possessed with a spirit of divination" is mentioned. In the Mazatec language of Mexico this is quite difficult to translate literally. There is no regular expression for divination, and no spirit is directly associated with this belief. The Mazatecs, however, do believe in certain types of divination, but the expression which denotes an individual who possesses such powers is "one who has two spirits." The one spirit is that which everyone possesses, but the second is a special supernatural spirit. To translate "a girl with a spirit of divination" one must actually say in Mazatec "a girl who has two spirits."

The phase of culture in which the greatest number of translation-problems arise is the linguistic one. Language is a part of culture, but translation from one language to another involves, in addition to the other cultural problems, the special characteristics of the respective languages. For example, some languages have only three types of words: noun-like words, verb-like words, and particles. It is impossible to approximate in such a language the types of attribution which exist in some Indo-European languages. Many languages express some concepts in verb-like words which we normally express in nouns. For example, in Mazatec there are no nouns corresponding to the English lexical items "food," "faith," "love," "baptism," and "repentance." All expressions which contain these English nouns must be translated into Mazatec by verbal expressions.

The differences which exist between languages and the resultant adaptations which must be made because of these differences may best be treated under (1) phonological, (2) morphological, (3) syntactic, and (4) lexical factors.

The translator must of necessity compare the phonological systems involved in the two languages, for it is necessary to transliterate proper names, and to do this scientifically and consistently one must be able to recognize the closest equivalents in sounds between the two languages. However, having made the proper transliterations in terms of the sound-systems, one has to be sure that the resultant forms are not homophonous, or nearly so, to some native word which may be quite objectionable or confusing. For example, in one of the Bantu languages a transliteration of *rabbi* proved to be too closely related in sound to an obscence native word, and the transliteration had to be modified.

The relationship of the phonological systems of two languages is especially prominent in the translation of songs. In tonal languages it is almost impossible to adapt the words to a Western melody and still preserve the meaning. In one of the tonal languages of Latin America the translators found to their amazement that their translation which they thought concerned "sinners" was actually directed at "fat people." The notes of the music proved to be opposite to the tones of the words.

In one instance a native Totonac Indian reacted quite violently to hymns which did not preserve the correspondence between the long and short vowels in the Totonac language and the long and short notes of the music. He proceeded to rectify the problem by his own translations, which he very ingeniously worked out. The results were exceedingly well received by his fellow Totonacs. Some rather similar attempts have been made by modern Chinese musicians in writing words to western tunes. Some translators have found it very valuable to employ the old chant-forms of the language, which normally preserve the meaning of the words and at the same time provide a melodic pattern.

The morphological structures of two languages often seem quite irreconcilable. Seldom do two languages have the same sets of obligatory categories in their morphology. A classification of forms according to number seems very important in the Indo-European languages, and yet in the Mazatec and Tarahumara languages of Mexico there is normally no indication of number whatsoever. In English the indication of possession is optional, but in the Maya and Athabascan languages there are certain words which must always occur with possessors. The indications of relative degrees of respect are very imperfectly indicated in a language such as Spanish, but in Aztec it is impossible to say anything to anyone without indicating precisely the relative degree of respect to which the speaker and hearer are entitled in the community. In some of the Aztec dialects these morphological categories are much more highly developed than in either Korean or Japanese. All such differences in the morphological systems pose real problems for the translator who wishes to represent adequately the "flavor" of the original. There is nothing in the Greek text to indicate which affixes of respect one must employ in Aztec. The only thing which can be done is to reconstruct the situation in terms of the Aztec social pattern and in the light of the social situation of Bible times. In such circumstances it is quite inconceivable that Jesus, who was a young man in his early thirties during his preaching career, would not have addressed the Pharisees, the Sadducees, and the scribes with terms of respect. These men were as a group undoubtedly older than Jesus, and their education and social position would have entitled them to a greater degree of "linguistic" respect than would be given Jesus.

The differences in the category of voice are often quite difficult for the translator. In the Eastern Aztec there is no passive voice. Hence, it is impossible to translate literally "Judge not, that ye be not judged" (Matt. 7: 1). The second verb must be in an active form and, as such, must have a subject and an object. The Greek text does not provide the subject by stating the agent. The subject must be supplied by the context. Accordingly, the sentence reads in Aztec: "Judge not that God may not judge you."

Some translators have felt called upon to attempt to invent such passive contructions in various languages which lacked them, but the result has been more than discouraging. The native speaker manages very well without such a passive voice. An attempt to force a new set of grammatical forms on a language has about as much chance of success as a Hindu attempting to introduce the turban as the standard head-dress among American farmers.

The variety of syntactic differences in languages provides many difficult problems for the translator. One of the greatest is the result of the special structure of Greek which permits long sentences made up of several clauses which are rather intricately combined. Few other languages can compare with Greek in this type of "style." One who translates into an aboriginal language often finds it necessary to cut many of the longer sentences into short ones, to repeat the subject- and object-nouns, and to express the conjunctives by rather cumbersome paraphrases.

The feature in which languages seem to differ to the greatest extent is in the use of pronominal expressions. Some languages have very elaborate systems and employ pronouns frequently. Other languages have quite limited pronominal systems and use pronouns much less frequently than does English. In still other languages there seems to be no correlation between the elaboration of the pronominal system and its frequency of use. There is nothing, however, that so marks the translation as the work of a foreigner or a novice as the improper use of pronouns.

Still other languages demand elaborate systems of lexical classifiers. One does not say in such languages "Jerusalem," "Jordan," or "synagogue," but rather, "city Jerusalem," "river Jordan," and "building synagogue." This means the addition of a considerable number of words to the text, but there is no alternative. Such changes are demanded by the syntactic structure of the language, and any translation which does not possess such classifiers does not represent the aboriginal language.

Without doubt the problems of equivalence and adaptation between languages are greatest in the lexical items. The area of meaning of a word in one language is never completely identical with the area of meaning of a similar word in another language; for example, English *ears* may be translated by Spanish *orejas* or *oídos*, depending upon whether the outer or inner ear is meant.

It is a common misapprehension about aboriginal languages that they have extremely limited vocabularies and much difficulty in expressing fine shades of meaning. It all depends upon the particular phenomena which are being considered. The Totonac language is not particularly rich in philosophical distinctions, but in classifying noises or odors, it is quite exceptional. For example, there are six different stems for "noise," which may be described as having the following meanings: "noise of children yelling," "noise of people talking," "noise of people arguing or turkeys gobbling," "noise of people talking and screaming in great anger," "a noise which grows increasingly worse," and, finally, "the noise of a funeral." Totonac also has some sixteen different stems for designating various odors.

Individual words are, nevertheless, not as confusing as combinations of words with specialized meanings. For example, in Acts 14: 11, the Spanish translation of the de Valera version reads *llevaba la palabra*, but the Mazatec literal translation of this, "he carried the word," actually means in Mazatec, "he was very smart." Figures of speech involve highly specialized meaning, as can be seen in a quick glance at any Indo-European language. The American expression "tickled to death" and "it burns me up" give evidence of considerable shift of meaning. The foreigner who complained about English because he had been told that the Americanisms "bologna," "applesauce," and "horse-feathers" all meant the same, had a real point. One must expect similar specializations of meaning in other languages. They are, of course, seldom to be found in parallel developments. This only adds to the ceaseless interest which can be derived from the study of lexical problems. Note a few of the specializations of meaning in Mazatec: "head-soft" means "smart"; "to carry softly" means "to steal"; an "embroidered lion" is a "tiger"; an "animal's wing" is his "liver"; and a "hand's beans" are its "fingers."

Some expressions in English which seem so commonplace as scarcely to be classed with specialization of meaning actually have no parallels in other languages. To say "he opened the eyes of the blind" would mean nothing in Aztec other than the process of pushing apart the eyelids. To say that "he lifted up his eyes to behold" means to the native that someone picked up his eyes to examine or carry. Saying that a man was "one of twelve" implies in Aztec that there were thirteen altogether. One must say rather, "one counted with the eleven."

In order to translate correctly into another language one must study the actual usage. The etymology may be of interest, but the descriptive linguist (and every translator should be such) must study each word on the basis of how native speakers use it, and not on the basis of what the investigator thinks it should mean or how he thinks it should be used. For example, in Maya the normal expression for "thank you" is *diosbootik*, which means literally, "God pay you." Moreover, this is the translation which almost any Maya Indian will give when he is asked about the literal meaning of the word. Nevertheless, when the Maya Indian prays to God, he gives thanks to God with this same term. The specialization of meaning is almost as great as in English *good-bye*. To the native investigator, however, it might seem that in saying *diosbootik* the Mayas are instructing God to pay himself for having done some favor to His suppliant. This is, of course, an absurd interpretation, but very illustrative of the problem of analysis on the basis of actual usage.

The meaning of any linguistic item must be considered in terms of the situations in which it may occur. For example, the meaning of the *-th* suffix in English which occurs in such words as *truth*, *wealth*, *health*, *stealth*, and *length* must be stated in terms of (1) the combinations in which it occurs and (2) the function of the suffix in these combinations. The meaning of *-th* is stated entirely in terms of linguistic situations. The meaning of the word *home* must likewise be stated in terms of the situations in which it may occur, but these situations may be defined in terms of linguistic and non-linguistic phenomena. The linguistic phenomena include the classes to which this word *home* belongs. The non-linguistic phenomena include the factors which define the significance of this word in the social structure. The ethnologist is best equipped to describe and define the cultural situations which provide the so-called "meaning" of the word *home*.

Languages are basically a part of culture, and words cannot be understood correctly apart from the local cultural phenomena for which they are symbols. This being the case, the most fruitful approach to the semantic problems of any language is the ethnological one. This involves investigating the significance of various cultural items and the words which are used to designate them. A combination of analytical social anthropology and descriptive linguistics provides the key to the study of semantics.

REFERENCE NOTE

References are organized into two parts, those dealing with diversity among languages in Part A, those with translation in Part B.

A. DIVERSITY

On diversity among languages, see, for general discussion and exemplification, Boas (1911), Firth (1937), Gray (1939), Nida (1947b), Sapir (1911b; 1921, chaps. 3-6), and Whorf's articles collected in Carroll (1956), especially Whorf (1940c, 1941a, 1942, 1956a). Further examples are found in many of the articles in this volume, especially in Parts III-VII. For diversity in connection with typology and surveys of language types, see the references to the article by Sapir and Swadesh on pp. 101-107.

Reference not in the general bibliography:

SAPIR, EDWARD

1911b. The History and Varieties of Human Speech. *The Popular Science Monthly*, *79:* 45-67.

B. TRANSLATION

The type of problem to which Nida calls attention, requiring both linguistic and ethnographic control, has had a continuous history; see, e.g., Chamberlain (1901, 1910), Mair (1935), Phillips (1959-1960). With special reference to Bible translation, see Chamberlain (1901, 1910), Gleason (1962), Kilgour (1939), Longacre (1958), McKaughan (1961), Nida (1947c, 1952, 1959, 1961), Wallis and Bennett (1959), Wright (1953a), and references to Bull's article on pp. 527-533.

For general surveys of problems and theories of translation, see also Amos (1920); Booth *et al.* (1958); Brower (1959); Harris *et al.* (1954); Locke and Booth (1955), with review by Joos (1956); Morgan (1959); Postgate (1922); Unesco (1957); and the journals *Babel*, *The Bible Translator*, and *MT* (*Machine Translation*). On mechanical translation, see further much of Garvin (1962). For a representative variety of specific contributions to the theory, critical analysis, and specifics of translation, note Edwards (1954), Empson (1935), Fang (1953), Furley (1958), Hollander (1959), Jakobson (1959), Longacre (1958), Matthiessen (1931), Nida (1963), Quine (1959), Richards (1953), Stern (1953), Wright (1953a). The anthropological problem and literature are well analyzed and demonstrated in Phillips (1959-1960).

References not in the general bibliography:

AMOS, F.

1920. *Early Theories of Translation*. New York: Columbia University Press.

[BABEL]

1955–. *Babel. Revue internationale de la traduction*. Bonn: La Fédération Internationale des Traductions and Unesco.

[THE BIBLE TRANSLATOR]

1950–. *The Bible Translator*. London: United Bible Societies.

BOOTH, A. D., *et al.*

1958. *Aspects of Translation*. (The Communication Research Centre, University College, London; Studies in Communication, No. 2.) London: Secker and Warburg.

CHAMBERLAIN, A. F.

1901. Translation: a Study in the Transference of Folk Thought. *JAF*, *14:* 165-171.

1910. Some Difficulties in Bible Translation. *Harper's Magazine*, *121:* 726-731.

EDWARDS, J.

1954. Pound's Translations. *Poetry*, *83:* 233-238.

EMPSON, WILLIAM

1935. The Need for "Translation" Theory in Linguistics. *Psyche*, *15:* 188-197.

FANG, ACHILLES

1953. Some Reflections on the Difficulty of Translation. In Arthur F. Wright (Ed.), *Studies in Chinese Thought*. (Comparative Studies of Cultures and

Civilizations, No. 1.) Chicago: University of Chicago Press. Pp. 263-287. [Also, The American Anthropological Association, Memoir 75.]

FURLEY, D. J.
1958. Translation from Greek Philosophy. In A. D. Booth *et al.*, Aspects of Translation. (The Communication Research Centre, University College, London; Studies in Communication, No. 2.) London: Secher and Warburg. Pp. 52-64.

GARVIN, PAUL S. C. (ED.)
1962. *Natural Language and the Computer*. New York: McGraw-Hill.

HARRIS, Z. S., *et al.*
1954. *Eight Papers on Translation.* (Reprint series of *IJAL*, *IJAL*, 1954, *20*(*4*): 259-340.) Bloomington.

HOLLANDER, JOHN
1959. Versions, Interpretations, and Performances. In Reuben A. Brower (Ed.), *On Translation.* (Harvard Studies in Comparative Literature, No. 23.) Cambridge: Harvard University Press. Pp. 205-231.

JAKOBSON, ROMAN
1959. On Linguistic Aspects of Translation. In Reuben A. Brower (Ed.), *On Translation.* (Harvard Studies in Comparative Literature, No. 23.) Cambridge: Harvard University Press. Pp. 232-239.

JOOS, M.
1956. Review of W. N. Locke and A. D. Booth, *Machine Translation of Languages*. *Lg.*, *32:* 293-298.

KILGOUR, R.
1939. *The Bible Throughout the World: A Survey of Scripture Translations.*

LOCKE, W. N., and A. D. BOOTH
1955. *Machine Translation of Languages: Fourteen Essays.* Cambridge and New York: Technology Press and Wiley.

MCKAUGHAN, HOWARD
1961. Bible Translation and Linguistics. *Journal of Christian Education*, *4:* 7-16.

MAIR, LUCY
1935. Linguistics Without Sociology: Some Notes on the Standard Luganda Dictionary. *BSO(A)S*, *7:* 913-921.

MATTHIESSEN, F. O.
1931. *Translation. An Elizabethan Art.* Cambridge: Harvard University Press.

MORGAN, BAYARD QUINCY
1959. A Critical Bibliography of Works on Translation. In Reuben A. Brower (Ed.), *On Translation.* (Harvard Studies in Comparative Literature, No. 23.) Cambridge: Harvard University Press. Pp. 271-293.

[MT]
1954. *Mechanical Translation.* Cambridge: Massachusetts Institute of Technology.

NICHOLSON, H. P. (ED.)
1961. *Proceedings of the National Symposium on Machine Translation* (Special volume of *MT*.) New York: Prentice-Hall.

NIDA, EUGENE A.

1959. Principles of Translation as Exemplified by Bible Translating. In Reuben A. Brower (Ed.), *On Translation.* (Harvard Studies in Comparative Literature, No. 23.) Cambridge: Harvard University Press. Pp. 11-31. *Toward a Science of Translating.* In press.

POSTGATE, J. P.

1922. *Translation and Translations, Theory and Practice.* London: Bell.

RICHARDS, I. A.

1953. Toward a Theory of Translating. In Arthur F. Wright (Ed.), *Studies in Chinese Thought.* (Comparative Studies of Cultures and Civilizations, No. 1.) Chicago: University of Chicago Press. Pp. 247-262. [Also, The American Anthropological Association, Memoir 75.]

STERN, R. G.

1953. Pound as Translator. *Accent, 13:* 264-268.

[UNESCO]

1957. *Scientific and Technical Translating and Other Aspects of the Language Problem.* Paris: Unesco.

WALLIS, ETHEL, and MARY BENNETT

1959. *Two Thousand Tongues to Go.* New York: Harper.

American Indian Grammatical Categories 11

E. SAPIR AND M. SWADESH

(THE FIRST PART OF THIS ARTICLE, up to and including the example sentences, was written by Sapir; the analysis of the sentences and what follows was written by me. Sapir must have begun the writing in 1929, just before his field trip to the Navaho, as suggested by the fact that a Sarcee example is used in the typescript while a handwritten note, evidently added later, gives the Navaho equivalent. Surely the Navaho and not the Sarcee would have been given if the paper had been composed after the summer of 1929. In completing the article, I have tried to follow Sapir's general plan as indicated in the early part of the paper and in a few handwritten notes attached to the typescript. In matters of detail I have not attempted to reproduce what Sapir might have written. Nevertheless I hope that my contribution may be of value by supplying data that otherwise might have to be sought in a number of scattered sources.—M. SWADESH)

Few people realize that within the confines of the United States there is spoken today a far greater variety of languages—not dialects, not slightly divergent forms of speech, but fundamentally distinct languages—than in the whole of Europe. We may go further. We may say, quite literally and safely, that in the state of California alone there are greater and more numerous linguistic extremes than can be illustrated in all the length and breadth of Europe. Such a group as German, French, Irish, Polish, Lithuanian, Albanian, Greek, Basque, Turkish, Hungarian, Finnish, and Circassian—to list European forms of speech with maximum distinctness—exhibits a lesser gamut of linguistic differences, as regards both phonetic elements and peculiarities of structure, than an equal number of languages that might be selected from among those spoken in California.

Needless to say, it is to the aboriginal languages of America that we have reference. Whether these all stem from a common origin or not—and we have as yet little tangible evidence that they do—they now present the most bewildering diversities of form. They are at once the delight and the despair of the linguistic student. It is saddening to reflect that many of them, doomed to extinction, may never be adequately recorded for want of a sufficient number of properly trained investigators. But we already know enough to be able to define some of the fundamental problems of American Indian linguistics. And we have the right to say that a small and devoted band of students, working far from the market place of science, have already rescued so much of these exceptionally difficult languages that general linguistic theory would be quite a different thing without their labors. It would be difficult to overestimate the value of these technical and seemingly detached studies for an eventual philosophy of speech. They have something of that apparent aloofness from, yet uncanny, subterranean relevance to, the psychology of thought and of patterned expression that a purely theoretical branch of mathematics possesses in relation to concrete physical problems which one would imagine to be safely beyond its reach. All forms of linguistic expression are reducible to a common psychological ground, but this ground cannot be properly understood without the perspective gained from a sympathetic study of the forms themselves.

It is clear at the outset that we have no right to speak of American Indian grammatical categories. The languages of our natives differ too much to make it possible to speak of the general presence or absence of particular categories. All our well-known types of formal patterning in speech can be illustrated in aboriginal America, and some that are not at all or not so well known to us, but there is hardly one that can be said to be universal. Certain American languages, like Chinook, recognize gender of a type that is not dissimilar to the masculine, feminine, and neuter of our classical tongues, but in a much larger number such distinctions are entirely wanting. An equivalent classification into animate and inanimate nouns is fairly widespread, particularly among the languages of the Algonkian stock.

Plurality of the noun is often expressed with as necessary a particularity as in English or French, but frequently there are no true plurals. Sometimes it is the verb rather than the noun which is inherently singular or plural. A vague idea of this apparently illogical and yet perfectly natural classification may be obtained by looking upon such English verbs as *to massacre* and *to troop* as inherently plural forms meaning 'to kill several' and 'to run (used of several subjects)' respectively. If we think of a sentence like *the dog trooped* as the factual equivalent of the normal sentence *the dogs ran,* the plurality of the noun being ignored while the complementary plurality of action, which we habitually ignore, is selected for explicit grammatical expression, we shall be able to get an approximate feeling for the idiom of inherently plural verbs. In many American languages what seems at first sight to be a true plural of the noun turns out on closer analysis to be a distributive. In such a language, say Nootka or Tsimshian, both spoken in British Columbia, the word *houses* of the English sentences *I have many houses* and *I have houses at the point and up on the hill* would not necessarily be rendered in the same way. In the former case Nootka might quite readily content itself with the absolute or singular form of the noun, leaving the logical plurality of the concept to be inferred from the inherent significance of the word for 'many.' In the latter case, however, it would be more idiomatic to employ a reduplicated form of the noun, expressing distribution, for the reference is not to a mere plurality of houses but to their presence at different points of space—some here, some there.

In the expression of case too there is a great variety of usage in America. While certain languages, like Yokuts and Wintun in California, possess syntactic and local cases that are analogous to the cases of the older Indo-European languages, many other American languages, perhaps the majority of them, are as innocent of cases as modern French. The relations expressed by the nominative, accusative, genitive, dative, and other analogous forms are naturally somehow provided for in these languages, just as they are provided for in French or in English. One method is the use of syntactic particles, like our *of* or *to*; word order is sometimes important, as in English; or various other morphological devices may be employed which make case affixes quite superfluous (the genitive relation, for instance, may be rendered with the help of possessive pronominal elements, as in Chinook, which expresses our English *the man's house* by *the-man his-house*). Where case elements are found, they do not necessarily correspond exactly to classical usage. Thus, the familiar contrast of nominative and accusative, or subjective and objective, is replaced in Eskimo by one between absolutive and "subjective," the former being used when the noun is in an objective relation or is the subject of an intransitive verb, while the latter at once defines the genitive relation and the subject of a transitive verb.

Needless to say, the variations of morphology are just as far-reaching in the verb as in the noun. To take the category of tense as an example, there are American languages that are very particular about temporal discrimination (Wishram, a Chinook dialect, has no less than four preterits, which differ in the remoteness of the time from the moment of speaking), while others seem hardly to worry about so fundamental a distinction as that between present and past (in Takelma, for instance, an obscure but most interesting language of southwestern Oregon, the future is carefully distinguished in both stem form and pronominal affixes from the present, but the latter tense is really an "aoristic" or indefinite tense which may apply equally well to the present or past).

It is obviously impossible in the face of such variety of structure to write about American Indian languages in general terms. It will be far more profitable to take up a few concrete instances and to analyze them with some care. What I propose to do in the remainder of this paper is, first, to see how a very simple English sentence is structurally transformed in its rendering into some half dozen selected languages of the American aborigines. In this way we shall gain a livelier idea of the realities of American Indian linguistic study and, at the same time, we shall learn how plastic a process is linguistic expression in itself. And, secondly, I shall draw attention to a few important grammatical categories that are either not expressed at all in languages nearer home or are expressed only fragmentarily or by implication.

The English sentence *he will give it to you* may be expressed as follows in Wishram, a Chinookan dialect of the region of the Dalles, on the Columbia river; in Takelma, an extinct or all but extinct language of southwestern Oregon; in Southern Paiute, a Shoshonean language of the semi-desert country north of the Grand Canyon of the Colorado; in Yana, which is spoken, or was until recently, by a handful of Indians in the upper drainage of the Sacramento in northeastern California; in Nootka, which is spoken on the west coast of Vancouver Island; and in Navaho, an Athabaskan language of northwestern New Mexico and northeastern Arizona:

Wishram: *ačimlúda* < *a-č-i-m-l-ud-a*
will-he-him-thee-to-GIVE-will

Takelma: *ˀòspink* < *ˀòk-t-xpi-nk* (*s* < *ktx* by regular contraction)
WILL·GIVE-to-thee-he·or·they·in·future

S. Paiute: *maγavaaniaak'aŋa'mi* < *maγa-vaania-aka-aŋa-'mi*
GIVE-will-visible·thing-visible·creature-thee

Yana: *ba·ǰamasiwaˀnuma* < *ba·-ǰa-ma-si-wa-ˀnuma*
ROUND·THING-away-to-does·or·will-done·unto-thou·in·future

Nootka: *ˀoyi·ˀa·qƛateˀic* < *oˀ-yi·-ˀa·qƛ-ˀat-eˀic*
THAT-give-will-done·unto-thou·art

Navaho: *neido·ˀá·ł* < *n-a·-yi-diho-ˀá·ł*
thee-to-transitive-will-ROUND·THING·IN·FUTURE

In the above examples hyphens show the formal analysis, and a schematic element-by-element translation gives a general idea of the notional structure. The stem is marked by small caps in the translation.

In these six languages, selected for grammatical variety, we find not only differences in the order and organization of the meaningful elements but also in the matter of what notions are included along with the main content. It may come as a surprise to some readers to find references to "round thing" and "visible," since our original sentence did not specify the nature or the location of the thing given. These are details that had to be added for natural translation in essentially the same way as supplying for French the gender of the object (*le* or *la*) and the general social setting of the statement (*te* or *vous*). We have concretized the object as a stone: of masculine gender in Wishram, inanimate in Southern Paiute, and of round-object classification in Yana and Navaho.

For some of the languages we had to decide whether to ignore or insist on the sex and number of the third-person subject. For example, in Takelma, third-person verbal endings make no sex or number distinctions. We could have shown the number by adding an independent personal pronoun, *ˀá·k* for the singular; to show both the sex and the number, we would have had to use a concrete nominal expression like 'male-person one' (*tˀi·ˀ-là·pha mi·ˀs*). However, this would have put a great deal of emphasis on these details. It would be comparable to amplifying our undifferentiated English second person reference to read *he will give it to just you yourself, a man.*

These considerations serve to emphasize a basic fact of language and speaking, namely, that no language response can be separated from the contextual pattern in which it occurs. Since languages differ in the way their forms are affected by concrete details, one cannot translate from one to another without constantly referring back to the context. In the process of translation, one must sometimes add details that are ignored in the first language and sometimes omit details that are definitely specified in the first.

Quite in contrast to the Takelma stands Wishram with a gender system that is reminiscent of English, recognizing masculine and feminine and neuter; however, in detail it is more on the order of Russian or German, since the classification of animals and objects is arbitrary. Differentiation into animate and inanimate classes is illustrated in Southern Paiute which combines this dichotomy with that of visibility, indicating whether the entity can or cannot be seen from the standpoint of the action's main setting.

Still another kind of classification is that of shape, reflected in the Yana and Navaho examples. However, it is the verb-stem and not the pronoun that is involved. Both of these languages, though genetically unrelated and structurally very different, happen to coincide in treating our notion of giving as a handling operation involving an object classified as long, round, sheet-like, etc. The bare stem refers to any kind of movement of the given type of object, and the affixes define the movement. In Yana, one says that a round thing is moved away from someone and to someone else, expressed by the subject and object. The Navaho speaks of handling (indicated by the transitive element) a thing to or for someone.

An interesting phenomenon illustrated in our material is the use of zero forms for expressing one of the grammatical categories in a set. The Navaho has no specific element for the third person subject, but it is nonetheless definitely implied by the absence of any first or second person element. The same is largely true in Yana and Nootka, but the fact does not appear in our examples because of the passive formation used. For third-person object, zero forms are even more common.

Case relations, differentiating giver and gift and receiver, are found expressed in our six languages by every conceivable means: by the order of elements, by the use of different forms, by relational markers, by relational implications of concrete elements. Wishram illustrates three of these methods: The subject and object (if third person masculine or feminine) are doubly distinguished, by form and by position. The second person object form is the same as the subject but the relative position (subject preceding, object following) serves to mark the difference. The indirect object, in addition to its fixed position, is clearly marked by the relational element *-l-*, meaning 'to' or 'for.' Similar indirect-object markers, placed either before or after the pronominal element, are found in Takelma and Navaho. Also possible are subject and object markers, though they are not illustrated in our example sentences. It may be interesting to add the Yokuts for *he will give it to you*, showing an object representing the recipient, and a locative for the gift (third person subject is normally omitted); the meaning is, as it were, 'will present thee at (or with) it.'

ma-m wa·n-en ṭa·-ni
THEE-obj. GIVE-will THAT-at

Passive signs, in Yana and Nootka, constitute another type of relational element helping to distinguish between the actor and the affected entity. In the case of Yana the use of the passive is entirely formalized, since it is the only method ever used for a third person acting upon a first or second person. In Nootka the passive is stylistic: it serves to give greater syntactic prominence to the psychologically important entity.

A particularly interesting syntactic relation is that between the Nootka stem *ʔo-* 'that, that one' and the suffix *-yi·* (or *-i·*) 'to give.' The latter element belongs to a class of suffixes known as governing, which stand in a definite relation to any stem with which they may be used. The relation with the pronouns contained in the paradigmatic modal endings is less definite. Thus, the subject after the passive could be interpreted either as the recipient or the gift, but the stem can refer only to the gift.

The number of pronominal elements that can enter into the paradigmatic complex is three in the case of Wishram and Navaho, two in Takelma and Yana, one ordinarily in Nootka, none in Yokuts. Our Southern Paiute form has three pronominal elements attached to the verb, but they are loose enclitics that could just as readily be attached to some other word in the sentence, replaced by independent pronouns, or omitted altogether. Our Yana form, with two pronominal elements, could be interpreted either 'he will give to you' or 'he will give you (to someone)'; however, in view of the meaning conveyed by the stem, the latter interpretation would be possible only if one happened to be talking to a round object. Takelma actually has two separate verb themes' *ʔokù-t-* (future *ʔòk-t-*) means 'to give (something) to' while the irregularly related *ʔoyón-* (future *ʔóyn-*) means 'to give': The two stems respectively form *ʔòspink* 'he will give to you' and *ʔóynxpink* 'he will give you away.'

The Southern Paiute example shows some formal ambiguities that may serve as a basis for general comment. The different enclitics of third person have only one form each and the order in which two of them are joined is determined by class (inanimate precedes animate) and not by case relations. For the second person, subject and object are different in form but there is no formal distinction between direct and indirect object. Thus, from the strictly formal viewpoint, our sentence can mean either 'creature will give thing to thee' or 'thing will give creature to thee' or 'creature will give thee to thing' or 'thing will give thee to creature.' In the nature of things and creatures, the first is the most likely interpretation. Or, putting it otherwise, it is not likely that the sentence would be used in just this form unless the most natural order of events is involved or unless the context is such as to indicate clearly the meaning. Southern Paiute does not want for alternate and less ambiguous modes of expression. For example, one can say:

maŋa-su-aka-'mi maγa-vaania
VISIBLE·CREATURE·ACTING-just-visible·thing-thee GIVE-will

imi-ncuγʷa maγa-vaania-ak'-aŋa
THEE-to GIVE-will-visible·thing-visible·creature

maŋa-su maγa-vaania-aka imi-ncuγʷa
VISIBLE·CREATURE·ACTING-just GIVE-will-visible·thing THEE-to

In addition to devices shown here, another common method for clearing up ambiguities is that of adding elements without changing the ambiguous form. The technique is that used in Spanish *se la dará a Usted* amplifying the ambiguous *se la dará*.

Our six languages agree with English in showing future time, but there are important differences in the over-all scheme of time classification. Nootka has two autonomous systems of time categories. Tense is of secondary importance, involving two mechanically added elements, for future and past, whose use is largely optional. By contrast, aspect is an obligatory category. Every normal word (exclusive of relational particles and interjections) requires an aspect classification, marked by suffix or internal change or a combination of the two. The extensive system of categories includes: durative, inceptive, momentaneous, graduative (similar to English progressive), pregraduative, iterative, iterative inceptive. (The form used in our example, *ʔoyi·* 'give that,' is momentaneous.) Neither tense and aspect have anything to do with the modal paradigms, which alone are inflected for person. The Navaho system of verbal categories is essentially one of aspect, including: perfective, imperfective, iterative, progressive, future, optative. Wishram has a pure tense system, including future, present, and four kinds of past, distinguished according to their remoteness from the present. The Takelma system mixes tense and mode, since it includes: aorist, future, potential ('can do so'), inferential ('evidently does so'), and imperative. As points of comparison we may note that the English set of verbal categories is largely one of tense and aspect, while the French combines tense and aspect and mode.

Turning now for a moment to formal structure, our examples illustrate very nicely the contrast between agglutinative and fusional techniques of expression. The Wishram is a remarkably clear-cut example of agglutination, since the words are analyzable into elements each of which expresses a single notion. The Takelma involves two interconnected fusions, in the stem and in the suffix. The stem combines tense-mode with its lexical value, and the endings combine tense-mode with person. As expressed in the stem, tense-mode is ambiguous since what we call the future stem is actually used for all categories other than the aorist; likewise it is ambiguous in the suffix, since some of the modal forms coincide. However, stem and suffix together give an unambiguous expression. We can illustrate this with some forms of 'to give to,' whose stem-forms are *ʔokù-t-* for aorist and *ʔòk-t-* for the non-aorist categories. With endings we have:

ʔokúspi gives *or* gave it to you
ʔòspink will give to you
ʔòspi can give to you
ʔòspik evidently gave to you

It will be seen that the general pattern is comparable to that of the Latin verb. Similar fusion is found in Navaho where the vowel and the stem-final consonant change to mark the aspects while inflectional prefixes also mark them. Yana stems vary according to voice (*ba·-* is static or passive, *bo·-* is the form for causative or active transitive). Southern Paiute has consonantic changes, affecting a few stems, to mark aspect, but mostly uses mechanical suffixation. Nootka has fusion in aspect formation and in modal paradigms. It is interesting that prevailingly agglutinative languages, even of polysynthetic type, as are Yana and Nootka, may nevertheless employ fusion for certain limited purposes.

Among the agglutinative languages, there are wide differences in structural flexibility. Our sentence can be expressed in Wishram only in the form given (except of course that independent pronouns may be used along with it). Within the verb, precisely the given affixes and stem must be used and in exactly this order. By contrast, Southern Paiute allows a number of different possibilities based on the fact that the suffixes of person are loose enclitics that may be included or omitted and, when used, may be added to any word in the sentence; independent pronouns may be used in place of or in addition to the enclitics. Nootka, also, admits of varying expressions of the same general idea: one has the option of passive or active construction, of inclusion or omission of an explicit object, of relative synthesis (combining much into one word) or analysis (using several words).

On first seeing our six translations, which all render *he will give it to you* as a single word, the reader could have gotten the impression that all American Indian languages are extremely synthetic. Of course, such a generalization does not hold true, as may be seen in some of the comments and examples subsequently brought forward. Certainly synthesis is common among American Indian languages, but it would not be easy to judge just how much above average they are in this trait. Incidentally it may be observed that, by usual criteria of independence of elements, the French verb might be regarded as synthetically constructed: *il te la donnera* could just as well be written *itladonra*, emphasizing its structural similarity to Wishram.

We have by now demonstrated the considerable variety that exists among American Indian grammatical categories. It is safe to say that any grammatical category to be found elsewhere in the world is sure to have a near analog somewhere in the native languages of the new world. And surely there are no exclusively American traits that are not to be found anywhere else. This does not mean it is impossible to generalize in any way upon American Indian grammatical categories. There certainly seem to be features that are to a significant degree less common or more common in America than elsewhere. Thus, some general characterization in terms of relative scarcity or frequency should be possible but must be made with consideration and caution. In the present paper, we do not attempt to go beyond a general examination of the problem.

One important negative fact should be evident even from this brief survey, namely, that there is nothing that can be seriously called "primitive" about these languages. True, we had to bring in some grammatical categories in our translations that were not present in the English, but these categories are neither more nor less necessary, from the standpoint of absolute logic, than a gender classification. True also that some English categories are ignored in other languages. This does not prevent them from expressing all sorts of ideas without undue ambiguity, and they have sufficient expressive means to eliminate ambiguities when necessary. It would be naïve to imagine that any analysis of experience is dependent on pattern expressed in language. Any concept, whether or not it forms part of the system of grammatical categories, can be conveyed in any language. If a notion is lacking in a given series, it implies a difference of configuration and not a lack of expressive power.

SAPIR'S NOTES

[These are the jottings found attached to the unfinished typescript. They may be of interest in showing points Sapir planned to include in the discussion.—M. SWADESH]

Adequacy of expression in America. Naïveté of imagining that any analysis of experience is dependent on pattern expressed in language. Lack of case or other category no indication of lack functionally. Given situation $A \ldots N$, expressed as $A_1 \ldots N_1$ symbolically in which there is no one to one correspondence. Absence of member C_1 simply means difference of configuration, not lack of C.

In any given context involving use of language, lang. response is not to be split up into its elements grammatically nor sensorimotorly but kept as unit in contextual pattern. Each unit has its own relatively autonomous pattern.

Orientation as to psychological interest (Nootka) . . . nouns—verbs.

Verbal categories of tr.: intr., act.: stat. (Yana method).

Importance of aspects in America: Nootka, Paiute.

Polysynthetic tendency: Nootka, Yana.

[The notes also include two of the variant translations, the first and third, mentioned in the discussion of S. Paiute.

Variant translations for Nootka, with analysis added by M. S.:]

ˀo-yi:-ˀa:qƛ-ma so:t-il
THAT·ONE-give-will-does THEE-to

hin-i:- (same form with empty stem *hin-* instead of pronominal stem *ʔo-*).
[Sapir's Sarcee translation:] *na-γa-yi-na-ʔa.*

My reason for selecting these six languages is partly that they well illustrate differences of structure, partly that they happen to be languages with which I have had some first-hand acquaintance in the field. —E. SAPIR

SWADESH'S NOTES

The Eskimo contrasting cases are also called "absolute" and "relative." See, for example, William Thalbitzer, "Eskimo," in Boas (1911, p. 1016).

Sapir has shown how such matters [as general characterization of American Indian grammatical categories in terms of relative scarcity or frequency] can be treated in his paper, "The Problem of Noun Incorporation in American Languages" (*AA*, 1911, *13:* 250-282).

Of the phonetic symbols, the following may need explanation: *ɬ* for voiceless lateral spirant; *ƛ* for voiceless lateral affricate; (') for glottalization; grave accent (\`) in Takelma for stress with falling pitch, acute (´) for stress with high or rising tone; in Navaho unmarked syllables are low-level in pitch, acute sign is for high-level pitch.

I have departed from Sapir's original writing in several details, most of them in accordance with his own later usage and recommendations: *č*, *ǰ*, *ƛ* for *tš*, *dj*, *tl*; double vowels instead of length sign in Southern Paiute; omitting indication of voiceless vowels in S. Paiute (voicelessness is positionally determined, applying to odd-numbered vowels before *p t k c s* and to final vowels of polysyllables); omitting accent mark in S. Paiute (it falls on second syllable of trisyllabic and longer words, on first syllable of short words). In Takelma, I have introduced some innovations as a result of my own study of some phonemic problems which Sapir pointed out to us: I have treated the aspirates and the glottalized consonants as clusters (*ph* etc., *pʔ* etc.) and therefore used *p* etc. for the simple stop. As to the accents, I have adopted two signs after concluding that Sapir's original rising and high-level represent one phonemic type.

Sapir's original footnote on phonetics reads: "I have simplified the phonetics as far as it seemed possible to do so without destroying the essential pattern of the native words." The wording reflects the time of writing; Sapir could not then count on his anticipated readers, anthropologists and linguists, to understand an explicit reference to phonemics. —M. SWADESH

SELECTED BIBLIOGRAPHY

Wishram and Chinook: E. Sapir, Preliminary Report on the Language and Mythology of the Upper Chinook, *AA*, 1907, *9:* 533-544; E. Sapir, *Wishram Texts* (Publications of the American Ethnological Society, No. 2), 1909; F. Boas, Chinook, *Handbook of American Indian Languages* (BAE-B 40, Part I), 1911, pp. 423-677, including a few passages on Wishram by Sapir.

Takelma: E. Sapir, The Takelma Language of Southwestern Oregon, *Handbook of American Indian Languages* (BAE-B 40, Part II), 1922, pp. 1-296.

Southern Paiute: E. Sapir, *The Southern Paiute Language* (grammar, texts, dictionary) (Proceedings of the American Academy of Arts and Sciences, Vol. 65), 1930.

Yana: E. Sapir, *The Fundamental Elements of Northern Yana*, (UCP-AAE 13), 1922, pp. 215-234.

Nootka: E. Sapir and M. Swadesh, *Nootka Texts* (with brief grammatical description and stem and suffix lists) (William Dwight Whitney Linguistic Series, Linguistic Society of America), 1939; M. Swadesh, Nootka Internal Syntax, *IJAL*, 1939, *9:* 77-102.

Navaho: E. Sapir and H. Hoijer, *Navaho Texts* (William Dwight Whithey Linguistic Series, Linguistic Society of America), 1942; Berard Haile, *A Manual of Navaho Grammar*, St. Michael's, Arizona, 1926. [See now references to Hoijer's article in Part IV—D. H. H.].

American Indian structural variety: H. Hoijer and others, *Linguistic Structures of Native America* (Viking Fund Publications in Anthropology, No. 6), 1946.

REFERENCE NOTE

On questions of grammatical typology as such, see references to Kroeber's article in Part IX. On its cognitive implications, see Part III.

This note is organized in two parts. Part A deals with language universals and general linguistics, Part B deals with communication and functions of speech.

A. LANGUAGE UNIVERSALS AND GENERAL LINGUISTICS

For discussions and presentations of language universals, see Aginsky and Aginsky (1948), Asch (1958), Casagrande (1963), Greenberg (1962), Greenberg (Ed.) (1963), Hockett (1955, section 2; 1959, 1960a), Hymes (1960d), Jakobson (1942, 1958, 1963), Jespersen (1924), Kroeber (1916), Lenneberg (1960), Osgood (1960, 1963), Robins (1952), Sapir (1933a), Weinreich (1963).

On universal properties of languages, as qualifying all languages for scientific study, see references to the articles by Strehlow and Hill on pp. 79-82 and 86-88, and note the position taken by Bloomfield: "A principle such as the regularity of phonetic change is not part of the specific tradition handed on to each new speaker of a given language, but is either a universal trait of human speech or nothing at all, an error," (1925, p. 130, n. 1). On the role of universal properties in the analysis of individual cases, cf. Jakobson (1958), Kroeber (1916).

On the relevance and importance of all languages to the study of general linguistics, see, for example, Uhlenbeck (1960) and Whorf (1940c, 1941a, 1942, 1956a).

On various aspects of general linguistics and its aims, see Ellis (1958), Frei (1948), Gabelentz (1901), Gardiner (1932), Greenberg (1957c, chap. 8; [Ed.] 1963), Hjelmslev (1928, 1935, 1937), Jakobson (1958), Kroeber (1916), Malkiel (1962a, 1964), Martinet (1960), McQuown (1960), Meillet (1906a, 1918), Reichling (1948), Sapir (1947).

Both language universals and general linguistics are often involved, of course, if sometimes implicitly, in discussions of language typology (again, see Kroeber's article in Part IX), of descriptive and historical linguistics, and of the scope and methods of linguistics as a field, including its relations to other disciplines; see, e.g., Bloomfield (1926), Joos (1950), Pike (1943, 1959), Sapir (1929c), Trager (1949), Whorf (1956b), among American statements.

On the nature of structural, or descriptive, linguistics in regard to its general aims, see Bally (1952), Bazell (1954), Bloomfield (1926, 1933, and reviews listed on p. 24), Boas (1911, 1917, 1938a, 1938b), Bühler (1934), Cassirer (1944, chap. 8), Chomsky (1957), Firth (1951), Garvin (1953, 1954b), Greenberg (1957c), Harris (1940, 1951b), Haudricourt (1959), Hjelmslev (1928, 1944, 1953, 1959), Hockett (1958), Jakobson (1962), Jakobson and Halle (1956), Jespersen (1922, 1924), Joos (1957), Levi-Strauss (1958a), Lotz (1950), Martinet (1953, 1960, 1962), Pike (1954-1955-1960, 1956, 1959), Sapir (1921, 1924a, 1929c, 1933a), Trager (1949, 1955a, 1956), Troubetzkoy (1939, 1949b).

References not in the general bibliography:

AGINSKY, BURT and ETHEL

1948. The Importance of Language Universals. *Word. 4:* 168-172.

BLOOMFIELD, LEONARD

1925. On the Sound-System of Central Algonquian. *Lg., 1:* 130-156.

CASAGRANDE, JOSEPH B.

1963. Language Universals in Anthropological Perspective. In Joseph H. Greenberg (Ed.), *Universals of Language*. Cambridge: M.I.T. Press.

FREI, HENRI

1948. De la Linguistique comme science de lois. *Lingua, 1:* 25-33.

GABELENTZ, G. VON DER

1901. *Die Sprachwissenschaft.* (2nd ed.) Leipzig: Tauchnitz.

GARVIN, PAUL L.

1953. Review of R. Jakobson, C. G. Fant, M. Halle, *Preliminaries to Speech Analysis. Lg., 29:* 472-482.

1954b. Review of L. Hjelmslev, *Prolegomena to a Theory of Language. Lg., 30:* 69-96.

GREENBERG, JOSEPH

1962. Is the Vowel-Consonant Dichotomy Universal? *Word, 18:* 73-81.

HAUDRICOURT, ANDRÉ

1959. Méthode scientifique et linquistique structurale. *L'Année sociologique,* (3ième Série.) Paris: Presses Universitaires de France. Pp. 31-48.

HJELMSLEV, LOUIS

1928. *Principes de Grammaire Générale.* (Det Kgl. Danske Videnskabernes Selskab. Historisk-filologiske Meddelelser *16:* 1). Copenhagen: Høst.

1944. Editorial. *Acta Linguistica. 4* (3): *v-xi.* [Also in Hjelmslev, *Essais Linguistique.* (Travaux du Cercle Linguistique de Copenhague, No. 12.) Copenhagen: Nordisk Sprog—og Kulturforlag, 1959. Pp. 21-26.]

JAKOBSON, ROMAN

1963. Implications of Language Universals for Linguistics. In Joseph H. Greenberg (Ed.), *Universals of Language,* Cambridge: M.I.T. Press. Pp. 208-219.

KROEBER, A. L.

1916. *Araphao Dialects.* (UCP-AAE 12.) Pp. 71-138; cf. pp. 90 ff.

OSGOOD, CHARLES E.

1960. The Cross-Cultural Generality of Visual-Verbal Synesthetic Tendencies. *Behavioral Science, 5:* 146-149.

1963. Language Universals and Psycholinguistics. In Joseph H. Greenberg (Ed.), *Universals of Language.* Cambridge: M.I.T. Press. Pp. 236-254.

REICHLING, ANTON

1948. What is General Linguistics? *Lingua, 1:* 8-24.

ROBINS, R. H.

1952. Noun and Verb in Universal Grammar. *Lg., 28:* 289-298.

B. COMMUNICATION AND FUNCTIONS OF SPEECH

The general topic of "communication" and its functional analysis, like that of the functional analysis of speech, is a vital one and yet at the same time diffuse, so far as development and representation in the scientific and scholarly literature is concerned. Almost any specific topic in the present book is germane to some degree. General views on the field of linguistics and the study of language, such as noted above, and general discussions of the sort included and cited in Part I are especially pertinent, as are many of the references to Parts V, VI, and VII. No attempt is made here to give more than some indication of the range of interests and viewpoints discussed under the headings of "communication" and "functions of speech." More than for most topics, a satisfactory bibliographic guide would have to be closely annotated and deal not merely with works explicitly labeled as treating the topic, but also frequently with passages and implications scattered throughout the rest of the literature.

On communication, cf. Berelson (1952), Berelson and Janowitz (1950), Bloomfield (1942a), Boas (1938b), Carpenter and McLuhan (1960), Carroll (1953, chap. 7 and *passim*), Cherry (1957), Deutsch (1952), Doob (1961), Duncan (1962); Fearing (1953), Frank (1958), Gleason (1961, chap. 23), Goodenough (1957b), Edward T. Hall (1959), Harrah (1960), Hayakawa (1958), Hockett (1953), Jakobson (1961), Kecskemeti (1954), Keesing and Keesing (1956), Kluckhohn (1961, with comment by Kroeber), Lacy (1961), Levi-Strauss (1960d), Lewis (1947), Lomax (1959), Mandelbrot (1954), McLuhan (1962), Miller (1951), Morris (1946), Nida (1960), Peterson (1955), Pierce (1961), Pool (1959), Ruesch and Bateson (1951), Ruesch and Kees (1956), Sapir (1931a), Shannon and Weaver (1949), Slama-Cazacu (1961), Verburg (1962), Žinkin (1962).

Assumptions and preferences as to the various functions of speech are at once a fundamental problem of general linguistics and the study of language universals and a determinant of activity in linguistics proper and the analysis of communication generally, as well as a guide to explicating major differences of approach. On functions of speech, cf. Bally (1952, pp. 13-33), Barker (1945), Bernstein (1961), Black (1949), Brown (1958), Bühler (1934), Burke (1958, 1961, 1962), Cassirer (1923, 1944), Cohen (1956a), De Laguna (1927), Estrich and Sperber (1952), Gardiner (1919, 1932), Garvin (1944), Harrah (1960), Hjelmslev (1953), Hymes (1961c, 1962a), Jakobson (1960a), Kluckhohn (1954), Luria (1959a, 1959b), Maccoby, Newcomb, Hartley (1958), Malinowski (1923, 1935), Ogden and Richards (1923), Parsons (1961), Pike (1961), Potter (1960), Sapir (1933a), Sebeok (1962), Sinclair (1951), Skinner (1957), Slama-Cazacu (1961), Spang-Hannsen (1954), Van Holk (1962), Verburg (1952), Vygotsky (1939, 1962), White (1940). Note especially Jakobson (1960a), Sapir (1933a), and Sebeok (1963) for comprehensive accounts.

References not in the general bibliography:

BERELSON, BERNARD

1952. *Content Analysis in Communication Research*. Glencoe: Free Press.

BERELSON, BERNARD, and MORRIS JANOWITZ (EDS.)

1950. *Reader in Public Opinion and Communication*. Glencoe: Free Press.

DEUTSCH, KARL

1952. On Communication Models in the Social Sciences. *Public Opinion Quarterly*, *16*: 356-380.

DOOB, LEONARD W.

1961. *Communication in Africa. A Search for Boundaries*. New Haven: Yale University Press.

FEARING, FRANKLIN

1953. Toward a Psychological Theory of Human Communication. *Journal of Personality*, *22*: 71-88.

FRANK, LAWRENCE K.

1958. Tactile Communication. *ETC.: A Review of General Semantics*, *16*: 31-79. Reprinted from *Genetic Psychology Monographs*, *56*: 209-255.]

GARVIN, PAUL L.

1944. Referential Adjustment and Linguistic Structure. *Acta Linguistica*, *4*: 53-60.

HAYAKAWA, S. I.

1958. Communications and the Human Community. *ETC.: A Review of General Semantics. 16:* 5-16.

HOCKETT, C. F.

1953. Review of Shannon and Weaver, *The Mathematics of Communication. Lg., 29:* 69-93.

JAKOBSON, ROMAN

1961. Linguistics and Communication Theory. In *Structure of Language and Its Mathematical Aspects.* (Proceedings of Symposia in Applied Mathematics, Vol. 12.) Providence: American Mathematical Society. Pp. 245-252.

KECSKEMETI, PAUL

1954. *Meaning, Communication and Value.* Chicago: University of Chicago Press.

LACY, DAN

1961. *Freedom and Communication.* Urbana: University of Illinois Press.

MANDELBROT, BENOÎT

1954. Structure formelle des textes et communication: deux études. *Word, 10:* 1-27.

NEHRING, ALFONS

1946. The Functional Structure of Speech. *Word, 2:* 197-209.

PETERSON, GORDON E.

1955. An Oral Communication Model. *Lg., 31:* 414-427.

PIKE, KENNETH L.

1961. Strange Dimensions of Truth. *Christianity Today, 5:* 690-692.

PIERCE, JOHN ROBINSON

1961. *Symbols, Signals, and Noise: The Nature and Process of Communication.* New York: Harper & Row.

SHANNON, CLAUDE L., and WARREN WEAVER

1949. *The Mathematical Theory of Communication.* Urbana: University of Illinois Press.

SNELL, BRUNO

1952. *Der Aufbau der Sprache.* Hamburg: Claassen Verlag. [Reviewed, W. Winter, *Lg.*, 1953, *29:* 193-195.]

VAN HOLK, ANDRÉ

1962. Referential and Attitudinal Constructions. *Lingua, 11:* 165-181.

VERBURG, PIETER A.

1952. *Taal en Functionaliteit.* Wageningen: Veennans.

1962. Some Remarks on "Communication" and "Social" in Language Theory. *Lingua, 11:* 453-568.

ŽINKIN, N. I.

1962. Four Communication Systems and Four Languages. *Word, 18:* 143-172.

part III

WORLD VIEW AND GRAMMATICAL CATEGORIES

Introduction

TO WHAT EXTENT AND IN WHAT WAYS is a language related to the world view of those who speak it? This question has gained prominence in American anthropology in association with the work of Benjamin Whorf and Dorothy Lee, but Whorf himself saw his work as part of a tradition formed by Boas and Sapir. In fact, interest in the question can be traced backwards through the work of Daniel Brinton in the late nineteenth century to that of Wilhelm von Humboldt at its beginning. (Humboldt drew extensively upon American languages, as in his "Essay on the Character of the American Verb," which Brinton later translated.)

With "world view" we must range here such other terms as have been used for some general or pervasive aspect of a culture—ethos, configuration, pattern, theme, metaphysics, logico-meaningful integration, and the like. And we must recognize, as did Whorf, that the linguistic phase of such an aspect of culture should be sought in "fashions of speaking" that cut across conventional boundaries between grammar and vocabulary. Likewise, Boas developed the principle of selective linguistic classification by proceeding from "phonetic groups expressing distinct ideas" to grammatical concepts proper. But the linking of world view particularly with grammar has a long and special history which warrants singling out.

It is easy to see how the linking might arise and persist in western thought. Grammar has seemed to occupy a special place, central or basic to the linguistic scheme of things, because it is relatively more stable, both through time and across dialects, than vocabulary and phonology often are; because it contains features that are relatively more general and fundamental, since, unlike individual words and sounds, they "*must* be expressed" (quoting Boas); and because the concepts associated with general grammatical features often pertain to general categories that find a place in metaphysics—space, time, act, person, thing. Join this to views of language and thought, or of language and logic, as interdependent, perhaps two sides of the same coin; confront it with the dramatic diversity in grammar that is apparent in the languages of the world; and it is understandable how grammar might seem to go to the heart of the problem of interpreting other ways of life or thought in relation to our own.

In his seminal work, Wilhelm von Humboldt interpreted types of grammatical structure as manifesting the intellectual development of men in different conditions of culture. Such linking of grammar to mode of thought persisted throughout the nineteenth century, especially in a typological tradition that shared the linguistic stage with the development of comparative Indo-European, becoming linked with a concept of "inner form." As the last quotations from Boas' article in this part show, he indeed undertook his great contributions to descriptive linguistics in America in terms of a conception of ethnology as the science of mental phenomena and of the inner form of languages as a key to native forms of thought, undisturbed by later rationalization. His objective determined the form of the grammars in the famous *Handbook of American Indian Languages*, with their introductory essays on "Grammatical Categories" and "Ideas Expressed by Grammatical Processes," for Boas intended a comparative psychological study to follow the individual sketches. In Europe the subject attracted the efforts of the leaders of French sociology and anthropology, Durkheim and Mauss.

The Boasian interest waned in American anthropology and linguistics; Bloomfield, for example, had shared it in his first general book (1914; compare pp. 321-322 with the selections from Boas here and in Part I) but apparently abandoned it. But the phenomena and the problem posed remained. How indeed could the diversity of grammatical categories of the languages of the world be accounted for? And how should their relation to individuals and cultures be interpreted? A renewal of interest such as that sparked by Whorf's writings is not surprising.

The renewed interest shows an increased concern with the problems inherent in describing and interpreting individual cases. There have been reformulations of the general problem, including a number of discussions of its methodological basis, and efforts to improve the empirical basis in semantic description. The broader implications for philosophy, psychology, logic, and the history of culture have receded before analytic examinations such as that of the conference reported in Hoijer (1954a) and the testing of particular hypotheses such as represented by the work of Brown (1957), Brown and Lenneberg (1958), and the Southwest Project in Comparative Psycholinguistics, preliminary results of which are discussed by Carroll (its director) and Casagrande (1958).

The present status of the problem can be assessed by restating the fundamental questions somewhat as follows: Are linguistic habits related to other habits and behavior? Do people with different linguistic habits differ also in other linguistically related habits and behavior? Can the linguistic habits and differences be taken as determining the others? Most would agree that the answer to all three questions is, to some extent, yes. There would be considerable disagreement as to what that extent is and as to what is acceptable as evidence for it. Clearly the answer depends partly on the sector of linguistic habits being examined, phonological, lexical, grammatical (some of the clearest cases having to do with recognition of speech sounds and lexically named shapes and objects); on the nature of the other habits and behavior to which language is being related, since some are more likely to be mediated linguistically than others; and partly, too, on the level at which habits are being described and interpreted. The more one abstracts from semantic particulars, the more alike languages are likely to seem. But the empirical evidence is determinative only within broad lines, and one's answer depends too on other considerations, such as the extent to which one is prepared to find peoples and languages radically different or much alike and the importance of the role one is prepared to give to language at all.

In striking a balance, it is clear that linguistic determinism and linguistic relativity cannot be absolute in the face of the known facts of linguistic change, multilingualism, and cultural diffusion. People do make new discriminations and find linguistic expression for them, often by borrowing; they do learn other languages, translate, and understand each other across language boundaries; the distribution of philosophical outlooks in space and time does not coincide with that of languages. On the other hand, it is clear that language habits are not merely interchangeable frostings but enter into the composition of the "cake of custom." The known facts of interference in the speech of bilinguals, of reshaping of linguistic borrowings, of difficulties in translation and in establishing terminology and syntactic usages for new ideas attest to this, as does a good deal of experimental evidence.

In exploring the broad spectrum of "partial linguistic determinism," two things must be born in mind. One is that our explorations and findings can be no better than the accounts of linguistic habits, particularly semantic habits, from which we start; and these are often not very good. Only recently has American linguistics and anthropology given painstaking attention to semantic description, Whorf having been a notable exception in the preceding period. Also, the role of semantic habits is dependent upon sociocultural context. The significance of semantic habits must depend on the modes and situations of use of language. A particular personality, society or cultural tradition may differ in the opportunities it offers such habits to have effect—to pick an extreme case, the effect of Latin, now pretty much restricted to use as an ecclesiastical language, is probably different for those who speak it today than for its speakers in late republican Rome.

The important distinction between *habitual* and *potential* behavior enters here. The potential range of perception and thought is probably pretty much the same for all men. However, we would be immobilized if we tried to notice, report, and think of all possible discriminations in experience at each moment of our lives. Most of the time we rely on the discriminations to which our language is geared, on what Sapir termed "grooves of habitual expression." Groups and individuals differ both in the nature of these grooves and in the extent and circumstances of employing them and of calling them into question. A great range of variation is possible, and the effect of language on culture and the individual, except within broad limits, is largely a matter of particular cases.

The discussion so far reflects the prevailing interest in the significance of differences in linguistic categories in terms of their effect on behavior. Psychologists have played a major role in research on the problem. Psychological testing, however, presupposes the accounts of what *are* the differences in linguistic categories and their appropriate cultural contexts—and these accounts must come from the skills of linguistics and anthropology. And there is a second significance to such differences which anthropology must take into account. Semantic patterns, whatever their role in present perception and cognition, reflect past acts of perception and cognition, which, collectively repeated and approved, have passed from individual experience into cultural habit. Consistent differences between languages in productive semantic patterns can be described as historically derived differences in cognitive style, and their significance can be interpreted in relation to general anthropological concepts, such as those of drift and tradition trend (see Hymes, 1958b, 1961a; Newman in Part VI).

All the preceding points make clear the importance of distinguishing between the effect of a language on a culture, on the one hand, and on individual life-histories and experiences, on the other.

The main lines along which interest has developed in American anthropology are brought out in the papers selected here. Boas' "Introduction" to the *Handbook of American Indian Languages* has come to symbolize the fact of diversity in grammatical categories, highlighting, as it does, the inadequacy of familiar Indo-European notions to account for the New World data. Boas, as we have seen, stressed description of each language according to its own genius and considered linguistic analysis essential to study of the deeper problems of ethnology. But it seems fair to say that he saw language as inextricably involved in a culture, rather than as a major determinant of it. He noted ways in which a language may affect particular characteristics of a culture, but held the view that the general state of a culture has the long-run determining effect on its language.

Meillet and Mauss here represent the interest of French anthropology in the problem of social aspects of cognition and *la pensée sauvage* (to use the title of a recent book by Levi-Strauss), as well as in the pertinence of New World data to its solution. Meillet gives an early demonstration of one of the main hazards in interpreting the significance of categories, the danger of anachronism; and Mauss adds the principle that major linguistic and social categories need not match one another at all. At the same time Mauss speaks to the fascination and theoretical importance of linguistic categories and the need to explain them.

The brief, little known abstract included here is Sapir's chief published expression of two theses later prominently associated with Whorf: "the tyrannical hold that linguistic form (once constituted and acquired) has upon our orientation in the world," and the incommensurability of differing languages. Sapir's concern with fundamental concepts as the key to types of languages, which he shared with Boas, and the theme of the autonomy of linguistic form had been developed in his book *Language* (1921). But in *Language* the autonomy of linguistic form had been linked with a negative attitude toward correlations between such form and culture (1921, pp. 221-235), an attitude repeated in a posthumous piece (1947). It is not clear whether Sapir felt that the view expressed here was consistent with that in his book or marked a change.

Whorf's article puts his concern with grammatical categories into perspective in the development of anthropology. It brings out his scientific goal of an adequate taxonomy of languages and his concern with diversity, not for its own sake but as an instrument of understanding. It must be remembered that he stressed linguistic relativity so that it might be transcended (1942) and that what he denied was not the possibility of calibrating different linguistic backgrounds, but that agreement and a common picture of the world could be reached *unless* there were calibration. And in the chief article he published for an anthropological audience (1941b), relating the Hopi language to Hopi habitual thought and behavior, Whorf insisted that correspondence could develop only where the language and culture had been together for a long time, that is, that such correlations would not be universal, but dependent upon historical circumstances.

Whorf's writings have attracted attention for the trenchant skill with which he dramatized the notions of linguistic structure and differences; for the novel theme that an exotic language might be not only different and equal, but superior, when compared to the Indo-European type; and for sometimes extreme and debatable assertions. But a proper assessment of his place in the history of anthropology must see him as the leading and, for a time, almost sole representative of some of its principal linguistic objectives, general taxonomy and semantic description, and, through his advocacy and research, as a major contributor to progress in both.

Hoijer's study of Navaho categories and culture is perhaps the soundest, best documented of its kind in the anthropological literature, joining careful linguistic analysis to equally thorough cultural studies. Such individual ethnolinguistic complexes as that of the Navaho depicted here need to be compared and contrasted within general frameworks that will allow their significance to be more fully assessed, but the development of such a framework depends on the accumulation of further, well-documented studies such as this (cf. Hymes, 1961a). Here Mathiot's paper is noteworthy. She takes individual form-classes as guides, painstakingly seeks to discover and delineate their semantic correlates, and weights the relative standing of the results. Of special importance is her use of native speaker reactions; her success in finding semantic correlates suggests that the main difficulty in finding them is to start looking properly. Note also her recurrent relating of Papago results to Whorf's work with Hopi and "Standard Average European." All this represents an encouraging continuation and advance in basic research in the tradition that extends through Whorf from Boas.

On Grammatical Categories 12

FRANZ BOAS

DIFFERENCES IN CATEGORIES OF DIFFERENT LANGUAGES

In all articulate speech the groups of sounds which are uttered serve to convey ideas, and each group of sounds has a fixed meaning. Languages differ not only in the character of their constituent phonetic elements and sound-clusters, but also in the groups of ideas that find expression in fixed phonetic groups.

LIMITATION OF THE NUMBER OF PHONETIC GROUPS EXPRESSING IDEAS

The total number of possible combinations of phonetic elements is also unlimited; but only a limited number are used to express ideas. This implies that the total number of ideas that are expressed by distinct phonetic groups is limited in number.

Since the total range of personal experience which language serves to express is infinitely varied, and its whole scope must be expressed by a limited number of phonetic groups, it is obvious that an extended classification of experiences must underlie all articulate speech.

This coincides with a fundamental trait of human thought. In our actual experience no two sense-impressions or emotional states are identical. Nevertheless we classify them, according to their similarities, in wider or narrower groups the limits of which may be determined from a variety of points of view. Notwithstanding their individual differences, we recognize in our experiences common elements, and consider them as related or even as the same, provided a sufficient number of characteristic traits belong to them in common. Thus the limitation of the number of phonetic groups expressing distinct ideas is an expression of the psychological fact that many different individual experiences appear to us as representatives of the same category of thought.

This trait of human thought and speech may be compared in a certain manner to the limitation of the whole series of possible articulating movements by selection of a limited number of habitual movements. If the whole mass of concepts, with all their variants, were expressed in language by entirely heterogeneous and unrelated sound-complexes, a condition would arise in which closely related ideas would not show their relationship by the corresponding relationship of their phonetic symbols, and an infinitely large number of distinct phonetic groups would be required for expression. If this were the case, the association between an idea and its representative sound-complex would not become sufficiently stable to be reproduced automatically without reflection at any given moment. As the automatic and rapid use of articulations has brought it about that a limited number of articulations only, each with limited variability, and a limited number of sound-clusters, have been selected from the infinitely large range of possible articulations and clusters of articulations, so the infinitely large number of ideas have been reduced by classification to a lesser number, which by constant use have established firm associations, and which can be used automatically.

It seems important at this point of our considerations to emphasize the fact that the groups of ideas expressed by specific phonetic groups show very material differences in different languages, and do not conform by any means to the same principles of classification. To take again the example of English, we find that the idea of WATER is expressed in a great variety of forms: one term serves to express water as a LIQUID; another one, water in the form of a large expanse (LAKE); others, water as running in a large body or in a small body (RIVER and BROOK); still other terms express water in the form RAIN, DEW, WAVE, and FOAM. It is perfectly conceivable that this variety of ideas, each of which is expressed by a single independent term in English, might be expressed in other languages by derivations from the same term.

Another example of the same kind, the words for SNOW in Eskimo, may be given. Here we find one word, *aput*, expressing SNOW ON THE GROUND; another one, *qana*, FALLING SNOW; a third one, *piqsirpoq*, DRIFTING SNOW; and a fourth one, *qimuqsuq*, A SNOWDRIFT.

In the same language the SEAL in different conditions is expressed by a variety of terms. One word is the general term for SEAL; another one signifies the SEAL BASKING IN THE SUN; a third one, a SEAL FLOATING ON A PIECE OF ICE; not to mention the many names for the seals of different ages and for male and female.

As an example of the manner in which terms that we express by independent words are grouped together under one concept, the Dakota language may be selected. The terms *naxtáka* TO KICK, *paxtaka* TO BIND IN BUNDLES, *yaxtaka* TO BITE, *ičáxtaka* TO BE NEAR TO, *boxtaka* TO POUND, are all derived from the common element *xtaka* TO GRIP, which holds them together, while we use distinct words for expressing the various ideas.

It seems fairly evident that the selection of such simple terms must to a certain extent depend upon the chief interests of a people; and where it is necessary to distinguish a certain phenomenon in many aspects, which in the life of the people play each an entirely independent role, many independent words may develop, while in other cases modifications of a single term may suffice.

Thus it happens that each language, from the point of view of another language, may be arbitrary in its classifications; that what appears as a single simple idea in one language may be characterized by a series of distinct phonetic groups in another.

The tendency of a language to express a complex idea by a single term has been termed "holophrasis," and it appears therefore that every language may be holophrastic from the point of view of another language. Holophrasis can hardly be taken as a fundamental characteristic of primitive languages.

We have seen before that some kind of classification of expression must be found in every language. This classification of ideas into groups, each of which is expressed by an independent phonetic group, makes it necessary that concepts which are not readily rendered by a single one among the available sound-complexes should be expressed by combinations or by modifications of what might be called the elementary phonetic groups, in accordance with the elementary ideas to which the particular idea is reduced.

This classification and the necessity of expressing certain experiences by means of other related ones, which by limiting one another define the special idea to be expressed, entail the presence of certain formal elements which determine the relations of the single phonetic groups. If each idea could be expressed by a single phonetic group, languages without form would be possible. Since, however, ideas must be expressed by being reduced to a number of related ideas, the kinds of relation become important elements in articulate speech; and it follows that all languages must contain formal elements, and that their number must be the greater, the fewer the elementary phonetic groups that define special ideas. In a language which commands a very large, fixed vocabulary, the number of formal elements may become quite small.

. . . .

The few examples that I have given here illustrate that many of the categories which we are inclined to consider as essential may be absent in foreign languages, and that other categories may occur as substitutes.

INTERPRETATION OF GRAMMATICAL CATEGORIES

When we consider for a moment what this implies, it will be recognized that in each language only a part of the complete concept that we have in mind is expressed, and that each language has a peculiar tendency to select this or that aspect of the mental image which is conveyed by the expression of the thought. To use again the example which I mentioned before, *The man is sick*. We express by this sentence, in English, the idea, *a definite single man at present sick.* In Kwakiutl this sentence would have to be rendered by an expression which would mean, in the vaguest possible form that could be given to it, *definite man near him invisible sick near him invisible.* Visibility and nearness to the first or second person might, of course, have been selected in our example in place of invisibility and nearness to the third person. An idiomatic expression of the sentence in this language would, however, be much more definite, and would require an expression somewhat like the following, *That invisible man lies sick on his back on the floor of the absent house.* In Eskimo, on the other hand, the same idea would be expressed by a form like (*single*) *man sick*, leaving place and time entirely indefinite. In Ponca, one of the Siouan dialects, the same idea would require a decision of the question whether the man is at rest or moving, and we might have a form like *the moving single man sick.* If we take into consideration further traits of idiomatic expression, this example might be further expanded by adding modalities of the verb; thus the Kwakiutl, whose language I have used several times as an example, would require a form indicating whether this is a new subject introduced in conversation or not; and, in case the speaker had not seen the sick person himself, he would have to express whether he knows by hearsay or by evidence that the person is sick, or whether he has dreamed it. It seems, however, better not to complicate our present discussion by taking into consideration the possibilities of exact expression that may be required in idiomatic forms of speech, but rather to consider only those parts of the sentence which, according to the morphology of the language, *must* be expressed.

We conclude from the examples here given that in a discussion of the characteristics of various languages different fundamental categories will be found, and that in a comparison of different languages it will be necessary to compare as well the phonetic characteristics as the characteristics of the vocabulary and those of the grammatical concepts in order to give each language its proper place.

. . . .

It was originally intended to give a somewhat elaborate introduction, setting forth the essential psychological characteristics of American languages; but with the development of the plan of work it was found necessary to relegate this discussion to the end of the whole work, because without a somewhat detailed discussion of the various languages the essential points can not be substantiated by reliable evidence.

. . . .

In accordance with the general views expressed in the introductory chapters, the method of treatment has been throughout an analytical one. No attempt has been made to compare the forms of the Indian grammars with the grammars of English, Latin or even among themselves; but in each case the psychological groupings which are given depend entirely upon the inner form of each language. In other words, the grammer has been treated as though an intelligent Indian was going to develop the forms of his own thoughts by an analysis of his own form of speech.

REFERENCE NOTE

For other expressions of Boas' views on grammatical categories and their interrelations with culture, see Boas (1917; 1920b, p. 320; 1938b; 1942). For an interpretation of Boas' views, see Jakobson (1959).

For general references on the analysis of grammatical categories, see those following the article by Mathiot (pp. 154-163). For general references on their relation to culture and world view, see those following the article by Hoijer (pp. 142-153).

13 The Feminine Gender in the Indo-European Languages

A. MEILLET

THE FEMININE GENDER provides a good example of a grammatical category that plays (in a good many of the modern Indo-European languages) a considerable role in morphology without answering, most of the time, to a definite meaning. One says: "une *table*" and "un *guéridon*." (The two French nouns, though marked by the preceding articles as of feminine gender, in the first case, and masculine, in the second, both designate kinds of tables.) Indeed, the femine gender had already lost its semantic import in Latin.

In the prehistoric language of which Latin and the other Indo-European languages are developments, the feminine gender, on the contrary, probably had a semantic force.

It appears as a subdivision of the "animate" gender, which is opposed to the "inanimate" gender, called "neuter." The feminine form is obtained by derivation from the masculine form by means of a suffix *-â-* or *-yâ-*. The feminine is thus a subdivision of the "animate gender." It is not marked in the noun itself, but only in the adjective which occasionally occurs with it.

For names of living beings, the feminine serves to designate the female. But it is not a matter of living beings alone. The notion is extended to everything that is considered "animate"; for example, "earth," feminine, is opposed to sky (male). Tree (feminine) is opposed to the fruit that it bears, which is something "inanimate," of neuter gender. An active organ is animate: thus the "hand" which receives is feminine, in opposition to "foot," masculine. [Notation of forms and glosses is as in the original.—D.H.H.]

But all the cases cannot be directly explained. Once the category has been created, one is led to apply it throughout the language. The grammatical machinery compels all animate nouns to be either masculine or feminine. And the apportionment between the two genders can sometimes depend on very little. It is then often difficult to distinguish between cases in which the distinction had a clear meaning and those in which a gender was attributed to this or that word, simply because the language assigned every noun to one of a fixed number of "genders."

On Language and Primitive Forms of Classification 14

MARCEL MAUSS

I SHOULD LIKE TO ADD some observations, complementary, not critical, to those of my master, M. Meillet.

First, if it is true that form, in language, is fundamentally distinct from the substance of thought, is even relatively independent of it, then one must add that here is no characteristic peculiar to language, but a characteristic diagnostic of most social phenomena of the nonmorphological type, of nearly all the workings of collective consciousness. (Roughly, of phenomena of social psychology or cultural content, as opposed to those of social relations or social structure.) Most can be unfailingly recognized by this arbitrary, symbolic nature, as being selected, so to speak, for no reasons other than historical. The form of rites and customs, those of money or esthetic representations, are wholly as dependent, one might say, on collective wills and habit and have as little of necessity as those which clothe language. In any case one is always dealing with a social phenomenon when there is arbitrariness of symbolism, just as much as when there is constraint exercised by such symbolism, once established.

This leads to consideration of all classifications pertaining to collective representations, of which those of masculine and feminine gender, specific to two or three groups of languages, are but an instance. They bear precisely this unmistakable feature of symbolism and arbitrariness so symptomatic of these beginnings of human reason. We have attempted, Durkheim and I, to describe a certain number of them in our essay on primitive forms of classification ("De quelques formes primitives de classification," *L'Année sociologique*, 1900-1901, *6*: 1-172). Mention of this work does not suffice, however, and it must be expanded to show that the same principle applies here.

To begin with, one must note that linguistic facts are effects rather than causes. On the one hand, the categories of collective thought are not necessarily expressed in the categories of language, and, on the other hand, those which are expressed by language are not necessarily those which are the most conscious or most important. For instance: there are few civilizations where the division of labor between the sexes and the apportionment of things among them which is parallel to it, the distinction of "male" and of "female," is more dominant, more conscious, more tyrannical than among the Polynesians or among the Chinese. It regulates occupations, and rites, and laws, and theology, and divination, and aesthetics. Now, it is not expressed in the languages of these civilizations, which, so to speak, do not know distinctions of gender. On the other hand, if the Indo-European civilizations have been preceded by civilizations among which these divisions had a meaning, such as that which M. Meillet endeavors to reconstruct, the modern European civilizations on the contrary no longer credit it. For them the genders correspond to nothing more than a sort of linguistic etiquette, this being only an effect, a survival. Thus we have notions strongly expressed by means other than language, on the one side; notions that are weak, or even broken down, but linguistically tyrannical, on the other; we witness a complete divorce between linguistic forms and the substance of thought. And this divorce is normal, because language is but one of the means of expression of collective thought and not the adequate expression of that thought itself.

In the second place, one must note that the division into masculine and feminine genders has, in certain cases, a close correspondence with quite definite social phenomena. One must recall here the work of Sir James George Frazer on "The Origin of Gender" (*Fortnightly Review*, 1900). Sir James thought it possible to connect that origin with exogamy and the fact that the wife, normally of another clan than her husband, spoke another dialect. Sir James's theory raises numerous questions and objections which were posed in their time. But Sir James cites an incontestable fact, that M. Meillet and M. Rivet know well: among the Caribs, ancient and modern, the wife speaks another language than the husband. However, Sir James does not mention—and the fact is important—that the second language, that of the women, belongs to another family of languages, Arawakan. Here, it is no longer words which are categorized, it is the entire linguistic apparatus which changes with the sex, not of things, but of the persons who speak.

Elsewhere, it changes with classes, for example in Polynesia and in Japan, where the language varies at one and the same time with the person who speaks and the person to whom one speaks. These variations, which are moreover less than that of the two languages of the Caribs, are none the less appreciable; quite as the division among the various Prakrits and Sanskrits spoken by the various personages of the classical drama in India is appreciable. Elsewhere it is both the languages of the speakers and the things which are divided at one and the same time. For—and it is on this point that we wish to conclude the first part of our observations—it is not only according to clans and sexes, but also according to all sorts of other social categories that things have been classed or apportioned by language. Thus we still have simultaneously noble and common speakers, on the one hand, of noble and common things, on the other.

The social origin of all these forms of classification is clear. In other cases, it is less so. One must study all of them, or the most essential, at least. We should like to recall that it was to this problem that our regretted student, collaborator and friend, A. Bianconi, devoted himself. He had begun the *Study of the Categories of Thought Through the Classifications of the Bantu Languages*—a wonderful subject on which he had already assembled a considerable number of documents, that an heroic death prevented him from utilizing. It is known that the Bantu divide things into eight to fourteen categories, which they designate by different prefixes. Bianconi was going to disengage the principles of that remarkable apportionment, sufficiently uniform in all the various Bantu languages and societies, and nevertheless varied enough from one to the other for comparisons to be instructive. Perhaps, at the moment at which we were robbed of our friend, he was a little too much under the influence of those of our ideas which we had voiced, and of those of the ethnographer Dennett, which he had moreover elegantly discussed. Perhaps he tied the classes of words too closely to the clans, districts, and social classes (especially the court and feudal hierarchy). Alas! We are deprived of his contribution, one that might have been definitive. The subject remains to be taken up, and must be taken up.

Nevertheless, it should be further generalized and at the same time made more profound. Indeed, one must realize the number and dimension of the facts whose consideration is necessary in order to accomplish this social—and, in virtue of being social, real—history of the principal processes of human reason constituent of these genders. We have indicated so far only a very small number of facts, and these have been facts of slight proportions. But there are others, great and numerous, such as M. Boas has so well described in his *Handbook of American Languages* (*Bulletin of the Bureau of American Ethnology*). The consideration of the American languages will be essential here. What is to be said, indeed, of these languages of the American northwest, such as Chinook, Kwakiutl, where things, acts, ideas are aligned—with verbs, nouns—in several dozen categories that cross-cut one another and are signified by prefixes, infixes, suffixes and variations of form? What is to be said of those categorizations in which are expressed simultaneously the relationships of the one who speaks with the one to whom one speaks and with the thing of which one speaks (present or absent, real or unreal, large or small, this last category being also that of the abstract and feminine)?

Nowhere are the relations between sociology and psychology clearer than in these matters. On the one hand, here as elsewhere, the social facts furnish one of the richest repertoires of facts, the most numerous and most notable that the psychologist has to consider. A psychology which took no account of them would immediately have lost its validity. And on the other hand, psychology is certainly incapable, without joining with sociology, of describing—much less of explaining—the detail of these facts, the modes of constituting these categories, and the apportionment of ideas among them. One thing is well demonstrated: it is impossible to write the history of the abstracting, the categorizing activity of the human mind, without taking these facts of linguistics and collective psychology into account and, above all, without taking into account the way in which these phenomena, being simultaneously social as well as psychological, are interdependent with the other phenomena of the history and very structure of societies.

REFERENCE NOTE

Meillet's views on grammatical categories are further expressed in his article "Linguistique et Anthropologie" (1933a). For his role in establishing the relations of linguistics, sociology, and anthropology, see Meillet (1906a, 1906b), Sommerfelt (1938a, 1961); and Cohen (1956a, 1956b).

On Mauss' point about the lack of mirror relationship between linguistic and social categories, see the article by Goodenough in Part V. On such parallelism generally, see Cohen's review of such concerns in European linguistics and anthropology in this century (1956a, 1956b) and many of the references to the articles by Hoijer and Mathiot in this section.

On the general importance of the data shared by linguistics and the social sciences from the viewpoint of social psychology or the collective working of the human mind, see Sapir (1921, chap. 10, especially p. 235), and see Levi-Strauss (1960d), in which he critically reviews developments in structural linguistics and social anthropology in this century.

15 Conceptual Categories in Primitive Languages

EDWARD SAPIR

The relation between language and experience is often misunderstood. Language is not merely a more or less systematic inventory of the various items of experience which seem relevant to the individual, as is so often naïvely assumed, but is also a self-contained, creative symbolic organization, which not only refers to experience largely acquired without its help but actually defines experience for us by reason of its formal completeness and because of our unconscious projection of its implicit expectations into the field of experience. In this respect language is very much like a mathematical system, which, also, records experience, in the true sense of the word, only in its crudest beginnings but, as time goes on, becomes elaborated into a self-contained conceptual system which previsages all possible experience in accordance with certain accepted formal limitations. Such categories as number, gender, case, tense, mode, voice, "aspect" and a host of others, many of which are not recognized systematically in our Indo-European languages, are, of course, derivative of experience at last analysis, but, once abstracted from experience, they are systematically elaborated in language and are not so much discovered in experience as imposed upon it because of the tyrannical hold that linguistic form has upon our orientation in the world. Inasmuch as languages differ very widely in their systematization of fundamental concepts, they tend to be only loosely equivalent to each other as symbolic devices and are, as a matter of fact, incommensurable in the sense in which two systems of points in a plane are, on the whole, incommensurable to each other if they are plotted out with reference to differing systems of coordinates. The point of view urged in this paper becomes entirely clear only when one compares languages of extremely different structures, as in the case of our Indo-European languages, native American Indian languages, and native languages of Africa.

REFERENCE NOTE

For the apparent shift in Sapir's views, compare his *Language* (1921, pp. 221-235) and a posthumously published article (1947) with the often quoted opening paragraphs of (1929c) and the present statement. The difference is at least one of emphasis, if not of basic outlook.

A Linguistic Consideration of Thinking in Primitive Communities

16

BENJAMIN LEE WHORF

I

THE ETHNOLOGIST ENGAGED in studying a living primitive culture must often have wondered: "What do these people think? How do they think? Are their intellectual and rational processes akin to ours or radically different?" But thereupon he has probably dismissed the idea as a psychological enigma and has sharply turned his attention back to more readily observable matters. And yet the problem of thought and thinking in the native community is not purely and simply a psychological problem. It is quite largely cultural. It is moreover largely a matter of one especially cohesive aggregate of cultural phenomena that we call a language. It is approachable through linguistics, and, as I hope to show, the approach requires a rather new type of emphasis in linguistics, now beginning to emerge through the work of Sapir, Leonard Bloomfield, and others, though Boas enunciated it decades ago in his introduction to the *Handbook of American Indian Languages*.

One of the clearest characterizations of thinking is that of Carl Jung, who distinguishes four basic psychic functions: sensation, feeling (*Gefühl*), thinking, and intuition. (To the reader who may not be prepared to accept all of Jung's views, I might say that his conception of these functions is essentially that of earlier psychologists such as Wundt, to which, however, he adds his own penetrative insight and clarification of fundamentals. A distinctive feature in Jung's viewpoint is that his four functions are distinguished not merely qualitatively but as separate energy systems of operation of an energic principle, the Jungian libido, which feature contrasts them with mere processes and complexes. They are relatively closed systems. In other words, if I understand Jung rightly, none of the libido or energy available for thinking can pass over into the form of feeling or sensation and vice versa, except by going into the unconsious and receding so far therein that it reaches the primitive undifferentiated state. This libido concept has proved itself of psychiatric value, and it may also have significance for the "linguistics of thinking" if it is true that the psychic energy available for linguistic processes, included in the thinking function, is a differentiated energy, entrained in a closed system and not transferable between such systems. However, such a Jungian viewpoint is by no means necessary for the linguistic approach to thinking which I am here dealing with. These views of Jung will be found in his *Psychological Types*, translated by Baynes, New York and London, 1923.—J.B.C.) It is evident to a linguist that thinking, as defined by Jung, contains a large linguistic element of a strictly patterned nature, while feeling is mainly nonlinguistic, though it may use the vehicle of language, albeit in a way quite different from thinking. Thinking may be said to be language's own ground, whereas feeling deals in feeling values which language indeed possesses but which lie rather on its borderland. These are Jung's two rational functions, and by contrast his two irrational functions, sensation and intuition, may fairly be termed nonlinguistic. They are, it is true, involved in the processes of talking, hearing, and understanding, but only in an infinitesimal part of their entire range. We are thus able to distinguish thinking as the function which is to a large extent linguistic. (Some have supposed thinking to be entirely linguistic. Watson, I believe, holds or held this view, and the great merit of Watson in this regard is that he was one of the first to point out and teach the very large and unrecognized linguistic element in silent thinking. His error lies in going the whole hog; also, perhaps, in not realizing or at least not emphasizing that the linguistic aspect of thinking is not a biologically organized process, "speech" or "language," but a cultural organization, i.e., *a* language. Some linguists may also hold the idea that thinking is entirely linguistic.)

The linguistic side of SILENT thinking, thinking without speaking, is of a nature as yet little appreciated. Silent thinking is basically not suppressed talking or inaudibly mumbled words or silent laryngeal agitations as some have supposed. (No text is available for a note Whorf indicated should go here. Whorf may have intended to refer again to Watson, who identified thought with subvocal movements of the speech musculature. See his article, "Is thinking merely the action of language mechanisms? [V]," *British Journal of Psychology*, 11.87-104 [1920].—J.B.C.) Such an explanation merely appears plausible to the linguistically unsophisticated "common sense" view. "Common sense" is unaware that talking itself means using a complex cultural organization, just as it is unaware of cultural organizations in general. Sense or meaning does not result from words or morphemes but from patterned relations between words or morphemes. Isolations of a morpheme, like "John!" or "Come!" are themselves patterns or formulas of a highly specialized type, not bare units. (Apparent isolations of words in a vocabulary list also derive what meaning they have from the patterned "potentials of linkage," which ramify from them and connect them with complex patterns of linguistic formulation.) Words and morphemes are motor reactions, but the factors of linkage BETWEEN words and morphemes, which make the categories and patterns in which linguistic meaning dwells, are not motor reactions; they correspond to neural processes and linkages of a NONMOTOR type, silent, invisible, and individually unobservable. (The pronounced materialist may still be granted leave to regard this matrix of relations as consisting of paths and chains of brain cells or what-not which link and relate themselves by physicochemical processes, but no clue to the nature of the RAPPORT, the structure of the matrix relations, can be obtained in this way, any more than the social organization of a tribe could be worked out from the blood groups of its individuals. It can only be determined by a penetrating study of the LANGUAGE spoken by the individual whose thinking process we are concerned with, and it will be found to be FUNDAMENTALLY DIFFERENT for individuals whose languages are of fundamentally different types. Just as cultural facts are only culturally determined, not biologically determined, so linguistic facts, which are likewise cultural, and include the linguistic element of thought, are only linguistically determined. They are determined not merely by language, but by languages. If the thinkers who are being studied speak our own language, let us say English, then the necessary penetrating study of the English language which is required can be made only by an investigator who has studied and is able to contrast widely differing types of language from English, for only in this way can there be brought into the forefront of consciousness an awareness of the existence of mere bare RELATIONS that do not correspond to any verbalized concepts but nevertheless govern absolutely the linkages of morphemes and shape the channels of thinking. [This note is extracted from a preliminary draft, and appears to represent what Whorf intended at this point.—J.B.C.]) It is not words mumbled, but RAPPORT between words, which enables them to work together at all to any semantic result. It is this rapport that constitutes the real essence of thought insofar as it is linguistic, and that in the last resort renders the mumbling, laryngeal quiverings, etc., semantically *de trop*. The nonmotor processes that are the essential thing are, of their nature, in a state of linkage according to the structure of a particular language, and activations of these processes and linkages in any way, with, without, or aside from laryngeal behavior, in the forefront of consciousness, or in what has been called "the deep well of unconscious cerebration," are all linguistic patterning operations, and all entitled to be called thinking.

Moreover, an analysis of silent thinking into motor quiverings corresponding to suppressed words and morphemes would no more be a real analysis of thinking than the analysis of a language into actual words and morphemes would be a real analysis of the language. The crudest and most amateurish grammar analyzes more effectively than that, and any scientific grammar is necessarily a deep analysis into relations.

For example, gender in English is a system of relations that has an almost minimal outward representation in morphemes. Its only motor reactions are the two pronouns 'he' and 'she' (including, of course, 'his, him, her, hers'). The motor processes which actualize the gender-linked nouns are undifferentiated in gender, but the linkage between such a motor process and another motor process actualizing the proper pronoun, 'he' or 'she,' is (1) differentiated in gender, (2) a nonmotor process, since the two motor processes are discrete and may even be separated by a prolonged period of rest. The gender nouns, such as boy, girl, father, wife, uncle, woman, lady, including thousands of given names like George, Fred, Mary, Charlie, Isabel, Isadore, Jane, John, Alice, Aloysius, Esther, Lester bear no distinguishing mark of gender like the Latin *-us* or *a-* within each motor process; but nevertheless each of these thousands of words has an invariable linkage bond connecting it with absolute precision either to the word 'he' or the word 'she,' which however does not come into the overt-behavior picture until and unless special situations of discourse require it. (A marginal note in the MS shows that Whorf intended to point out, in a footnote, that use of gender-linked nouns is not dependent upon knowing any particular individual to which they may refer, although it inevitably classifies such individuals as to sex.—J.B.C.) These thousands of linkage processes rallying around the common point of the pronoun and ramifying to all the thousands of nouns of one gender form a sort of psychic complex belonging to (1) the nonmotor and nonactualized realm, (2) the thinking function in Jung's definition, (3) the linguistic and cultural order.

There is no evident reason why such a complex should not enter into various functional relations with other material of thought without necessarily requiring the activation of any of the individual words or class marks with which it is connected. We can be thinking of, say, the division of labor between the sexes in a certain culture without having to think of the rather bookish words 'female' and 'male' and to refer continually to them in our meditations upon such a subject. What we more probably do as we run over such a question in our minds is sift the facts in terms of a sort of habitual consciousness of two sex classes as a standing classificatory fact in our thought-world, something which is quite different from sex as a concept or sex as a feeling-value. The basis of this shadowy, abstract, and wordless adumbration of a sex classification is not a word like 'sex' or 'female' or 'woman'; it is a linguistic RAPPORT as distinguished from a linguistic UTTERANCE. In English it is probably a rising toward fuller consciousness of the two great complexes of linkage bonds pertaining to the linguistic sex-gender system. It is, one might say, the total pronominal-linkage pressure of the George, Dick, and William class of words, or of the Jane, Sue, and Betty class, that functions in the meditation and NOT a VERBAL concept like 'male' or 'female.' But in a language without sex gender, like Chinese or Hopi, any thinking in terms of a sex classification could not be of this nature; it would presumably operate around a word, or a feeling, or a sexual image, or a symbol, or something else.

A linguistic classification like English gender, which has no overt mark actualized along with the words of the class but which operates through an invisible "central exchange" of linkage bonds in such a way as to determine certain other words which mark the class, I call a COVERT class, in contrast to an OVERT class, such as gender in Latin. Navaho has a covert classification of the whole world of objects based partly on animation and partly on shape. Inanimate bodies fall into two classes which linguists have styled "round objects" and "long objects." (Actually, the Navaho verb system provides for MORE than two classes of inanimate bodies, a fact which makes Whorf's point, if anything, more valid.—J.B.C.) These names, of course, misrepresent; they attempt to depict the subtle in terms of the gross, and fail. Navaho itself has no terms which adequately depict the classes. A covert concept like a covert gender is as definable and in its way as definite as a verbal concept like 'female' or feminine, but is of a very different kind; it is not the analog of a word but of a rapport-system, and awareness of it has an intuitive quality; we say that it is sensed rather than comprehended. It is possibly the kind of concept or idea which in Hindu philosophy is called *arūpa*, formless. The Navaho so-called "round" and "long" nouns are not marked in themselves nor by any pronouns. They are marked only in the use of certain very important verb stems, in that a different stem is required for a "round" or a "long" subject or object. Many other verb stems are indifferent to the distinction. A new object, for which the Navaho has no name, will be put into one or the other class by analogy, not analogy as it would seem to us, but as guided by the contents of the two Navaho complexes.

A covert linguistic class may not deal with any grand dichotomy of objects, it may have a very subtle meaning, and it may have no overt mark other than certain distinctive "reactances" with certain overtly marked forms. It is then what I call a CRYPTOTYPE. It is a submerged, subtle, and elusive meaning, corresponding to no actual word, yet shown by linguistic analysis to be functionally important in the grammar. For example, the English particle UP meaning 'completely, to a finish,' as in 'break it up, cover it up, eat it up, twist it up, open it up' can be applied to any verb of one or two syllables initially accented, EXCEPTING verbs belonging to four special cryptotypes. One is the cryptotype of dispersion without boundary; hence one does not say 'spread it up, waste it up, spend it up, scatter it up, drain it up, or filter it up.' ('Burst' belongs to this cryptotype; the colloquial 'bust' does not.) Another is the cryptotype of oscillation without agitation of parts; we don't say 'rock up a cradle, wave up a flag, wiggle up a finger, nod up one's head,' etc. (In a marginal note, Whorf cites 'shake up,' apparently to point out that this verb implies agitation of parts. The reader should note, incidentally, that this whole discussion concerns only transitive verbs, as is made explicit at the end of the paragraph.—J.B.C.) The third is the cryptotype of nondurative impact which also includes psychological reaction: kill, fight, etc.; hence we don't say 'whack it up, tap it up, stab it up, slam it up, wrestle him up, hate him up.' (In a marginal note, Whorf alludes to such expressions as 'strike up [a band],' 'hit it up,' but states that they are not true transitives and are not considered. He also refers to verbs such as 'sing, shout, cry' in the same way.—J.B.C.) The fourth is the verbs of directed motion, move, lift, pull, push, put, etc., with which UP has the directional sense, 'upward,' or derived senses, even though this sense may be contradicted by the verb and hence produce an effect of absurdity, as in 'drip it up.' Outside this set of cryptotypes, UP may be freely used with transitives in the completive-intensive sense.

Another English cryptotype is that of the transitive verbs of a covering, enclosing, and surface-attaching meaning, the reactance of which is that UN- may be prefixed to denote the opposite. Hence we say 'uncover, uncoil, undress, unfasten, unfold, unlock, unroll, untangle, untie, unwind,' but not 'unbreak, undry, unhang, unheat, unlift, unmelt, unopen, unpress, unspill.' With the exception of a few words mostly semiarchaic, e.g., 'unsay, unthink, unmake,' the use of UN- as a reversive prefix in true verbs coincides with the centripetal enclosing and attaching meaning. (From a marginal note, it is evident that Whorf intended to consider the words 'unstart,' 'unbalance,' and 'undo' in a footnote. Whorf might also have cautioned the reader against being misled by participial or adjectival forms such as 'unbroken, unheated, unopened,' etc., in which the prefix 'un-' does not denote the reverse of an action, but of an adjectivally expressed condition. It is interesting to speculate on the possibility that the reason that words such as 'unsay, unthink, unmake' are now obsolete may be precisely the fact that they had to yield to the pressure of the cryptotype represented by such words as 'uncover, uncoil, undress,' etc.—J.B.C). We have no single word in the language which can give us a proper clue to this meaning or into which we can compress this meaning; hence the meaning is subtle, intangible, as is typical of cryptotypic meanings. Nevertheless this formless idea delimits a quite definite class of words and grammatical forms, and may be dredged up from its own plane of thought formations and grasped in a semi-intuitive way. To do this, one needs only meditate on the meaning of the cryptotype, e.g., of the typical verbs which take UN-, or to use methods of free-analogizing akin to the "free-association" methods of Freud and Jung. Thus I can imagine a newly coined verb *flimmick*. If *flimmick* means, let us say, 'tie a tin can to,' then it falls into the cryptotype and I can say, e.g., 'he *unflimmicked* the dog.' But, if it means 'to take apart,' there will be no tendency for anyone to make a form *unflimmick* meaning 'put together'; e.g., 'he *unflimmicked* the set of radio parts.' Such a form will appear strange and unacceptable. Similarly a knowledge of this cryptotype previous to the adoption of the new words 'camouflage' and 'wangle' would have enabled us to predict that it would be possible to say 'uncamouflage it,' but not 'unwangle it.'

In contrast to the cryptotype I give the name PHENOTYPE to the linguistic category with a clearly apparent class meaning and a formal mark or morpheme which accompanies it; i.e., the phenotype is the "classical" morphological category. The meanings of 'up' and 'un-' are phenotypes, and so are the various tenses, aspects, voices, modes, and other marked forms which all grammars study. Grammatical research up to the present time has been concerned chiefly with study of phenotypes. A certain type of grammar proceeds as if linguistic meaning dwelt wholly in them. The anthropologist should not be satisfied with such a grammar, any more than with an ethnology that described only positive behavior and ignored the patterning of taboos and avoidances. It can be shown that, in some languages at least, linguistic meaning results from the interplay of phenotypes and cryptotypes, not from phenotypes alone.

Thus in Hopi the use of the aspect and tense forms is often governed by cryptotypes. They govern, for instance, the way of expressing the beginning of an action or state, the English 'begins to do,' or 'begins to be' form. First, a different form (phenotype) is used, depending on whether the verb is active or inactive (either passive or static), and this is a cryptotypic distinction, for the formal apparatus of Hopi grammar does not set up any active-versus-inactive contrast. Hopi, moreover, classes being 'in, at, over,' or in some other spatial relationship as ACTIVE, but being 'red, long, little, pretty, turned around, shot,' as INACTIVE. Causal and incausal are really better terms here than active and passive. Next, if the verb is active, the phenotype for beginning depends on which of three active cryptotypes is involved. With most verbs one can use either the inceptive aspect or the future tense. Analysis seems to indicate that Hopi regards the subject of these verbs as working into and through the action by a process of dynamic adjustment. The subject progressively adjusts himself into the action, and throughout the action is maintaining this adjustment either to develop or to stabilize and continue the effect. Hopi includes here (Marginally, Whorf notes that this is "strange at first, but illuminating."—J.B.C.) sleeping, dying, laughing, eating, as well as most organic functions and most alterative operations, e.g., cutting, bending, covering, placing, and thousands of others. The second cryptotype uses only future tense to express beginning, and includes verbs of straight-line uniform motion, running, fleeing, going, coming, being in or at a place or in any spatial relationship, opening, closing, and certain others. Analysis indicates that here the subject is classed as instantly assuming a full-fledged new status, not as dynamically working into and through a process. The third cryptotype expresses beginning by means of the projective aspect, a phenotype which used elsewhere means 'does with a forward movement.' This cryptotype implies that the subject is seized and assimilated by a field of influence, carried away by it, as it were; and it consists of gravitational and moving-inertia phenomena; 'falling, tumbling, spilling, jumping, whirling,' and also, strange though it seems to us, 'going out' and 'going in.' According to the logic of Hopi linguistics, a person about to enter a house or go outdoors launches off and yields himself to a new influence like one who falls or leaps.

What needs to be clearly seen by anthropologists, who to a large extent may have gotten the idea that linguistics is merely a highly specialized and tediously technical pigeonhole in a far corner of the anthropological workshop, is that linguistics is essentially the quest of MEANING. It may seem to the outsider to be inordinately absorbed in recording hair-splitting distinctions of sound, performing phonetic gymnastics, and writing complex grammars which only grammarians read. But the simple fact is that its real concern is to light up the thick darkness of the language, and thereby of much of the thought, the culture, and the outlook upon life of a given community, with the light of this "golden something," as I have heard it called, this transmuting principle of meaning. As I have tried to show, this amounts to far more than learning to speak and understand the language as the practical language teacher conceives these ends. The investigator of culture should hold an ideal of linguistics as that of a heuristic approach to problems of psychology which hitherto he may have shrunk from considering—a glass through which, when correctly focused, will appear the TRUE SHAPES of many of those forces which hitherto have been to him but the inscrutable blank of invisible and bodiless thought.

II

Awareness of psychological undercurrents is the last thing to arrive in the conquest of linguistic understanding, both in the individual and in history. The attempt to teach one's language to a foreigner results in some awareness of OVERT formal patterns; paradigms and inflected stems. The earliest grammars known are cuneiform wordlists of this kind, giving equivalents as between Sumerian and the Semitic Akkadian. A further step did not occur until philosophy, in both Greece and India, discovered a relation between reasoning and linguistic patterns; this resulted for philosophy in a formal logic, and for grammar in the discovery of at least the more outstanding categories in the classical Indo-European tongues. In the Semitic world, grammar remained largely formal, the classical Hebrew and Arabic grammars consisting mostly of paradigms, known by code names which made no attempt even to characterize, much less penetrate, the meanings of these linguistic classes. Even Latin grammar, with its terms like indicative, subjunctive, passive, etc., was psychological by comparison. The discovery of ancient Hindu grammar by Western scholars in the early nineteenth century impressed these scholars chiefly by its formal perfection. But it also revealed certain psychological subtleties, such as the recognition of different covert ideas within word-compounding technique, and the classification of compounds as *tatpurusha*, *dvandva*, *bahuvrihi*, and so on. (See William Dwight Whitney, *Sanskrit grammer* [Harvard University Press, 1931, Chapter XVIII].—J.B.C.)

Even the greatest European grammarians of the nineteenth century did not go much beyond formal and covert structures except for riding the classical grammatical and philosophical concepts to the limits of travel in the languages they studied. To this statement there is one grand exception—one of those amazing geniuses who baffle their contemporaries and leave no successors. The real originator of such ideas as rapport-systems, covert classes, cryptotypes, psycholinguistic patterning, and language as part and parcel of a culture was, so far as I can learn, a French grammarian of the early nineteenth century, Antoine Fabre d'Olivet (1768-1825), who investigated Semitic languages and particularly Hebrew, though his work, like that of Mendel in genetics, made no impress whatsoever on the thought of his time. Unfortunately for its comprehension either then or now, its author was a mystical and religious metaphysician who mingled this side of his nature with the workings of one of the most powerful linguistic intellects of any age. The result was to produce a mystical and gnostic "translation" of Genesis, or rather, an Upanishadic paraphrase that was like some shocking vision of cosmic space alive with terrific hieroglyphs—that got itself promptly placed on the Index. Nor did this repudiation by orthodoxy win any encomiums from what was then the radical left, for his Biblical views were at the same time too iconoclastic and too transcendental to satisfy any possible school of exegesis. But the strictly linguistic part of Fabre d'Olivet's work, embodied in *La langue hébraïque restituée*, which appeared in 1815-16, when separated from his extraordinary Upanishad upon Genesis, can be seen today to be based on purely linguistic criteria and to show great psychological penetration, and ideas far in advance of his time. (I have supplied the dates which Whorf left blank in the manuscript. The full title of this scarce work is *La langue hébraïque restituée, et le véritable sens des mots hébreux rétabli et prouvé par leur analyse radicale.* Copies are to be seen in the Library of Congress, the Cornell University Library, and perhaps a few other libraries in the United States. It is probable that Whorf knew the work chiefly from the translation into English by Nayán Louise Redfield, *The Hebraic tongue restored* [New York and London, G. P. Putnam's Sons, 1921].—J.B.C.) It must be added that, although mystical almost to the point of a Jacob Boehme or a William Blake, Fabre d'Olivet steered absolutely clear of the cabalistic and numerological hocus-pocus with which the old Jewish tradition of Hebrew was laden. And, while he threw overboard the whole formalistic Hiphil-Hophal conception of grammar, he also declined to foist Latin and Greek patterns upon Hebrew. His Hebrew stands on its own feet as completely as does Boas's Chinook. He reorganized the treatment of verb conjugations on a psycholinguistic basis, considered individual prefixes and suffixes from the standpoint of their meaning and function, went into the semantics of vowel patterns and the semantic coloring of vowels, and showed how many Hebrew stems can be resolved into meaningful fractions, as, e.g., such English words as 'flash, flicker, clash, click clack, crack, crash, lick, lash' can be so resolved. Refusing to identify the letters of Hebrew writing with the actual phonetic elements and yet perceiving that these elements are not mere sounds, but stereotyped, codified, and patterned semantic sounds, he advanced to a conception of the phoneme, which he called the "sign" or the "vocal sign"—struggling with terminology but showing real insight into linguistic actualities. He stressed the fact of a complex rapport between signs and between words. A phoneme may assume definite semantic duties as part of its rapport. In English the phoneme ð (the voiced sound of *th*) occurs initially only in the cryptotype of demonstrative particles (the, this, there, than, etc.). Hence there is a psychic pressure against accepting the voiced sound of *th* in new or imaginary words: *thig*, *thag*, *thob*, *thuzzle*, etc. not having demonstrative meanings. Encountering such a new word (e.g., *thob*) on a page, we will "instinctively" give it the voiceless sound θ of *th* in "think." But it is no "instinct." Just our old friend linguistic rapport again. Assign a demonstrative meaning, let *thag* equal 'over the fence,' for instance, and we will substitute the voiced phoneme ð of "there." Fabre d'Olivet knew all about such things.

Moreover, Fabre d'Olivet thought in an anthropological and not simply a grammatical way; to him, speech was not a "faculty" exalted on its own perch, but something to be understood in the light of human behavior and culture, of which it was a part, specialized but involving no different principle from the rest. The vocal sign (phoneme) was a highly specialized gesture or symbolic act, language a development of total somatic behavior becoming symbolic and then diverting its symbolism more and more into the vocal channel—such is his teaching put into the modern idiom.

No figure so significant for the linguistic approach to thinking again appears until we come to the Irish linguist James Byrne (1820-97). His studies were based on the exceedingly valuable idea of a worldwide survey of grammatical structures in all languages known. His great work—it at least deserves to be called great in conception, even though perhaps not in execution—in two volumes, called *General Principles of Structure of Language*, appeared in 1885. It had the remarkable feature of presenting condensed grammatical sketches of languages all over the globe, from Chinese to Hottentot. Almost every linguistic stock outside of America is represented, and a good number of American ones. On this survey Byrne based his psychological theory. And it seems to me at least rather significant that Byrne found, on the basis of language structure, a similar contrast of two fundamental psychological types to that which Jung much later found from psychiatry and called the types of extraversion and introversion. Jung also showed how, all down through history, the irreconcilable opposition of two such types has resulted in fundamental controversies and schisms in successive philosophies and religions. Byrne independently found, or thought he found, a correlation between language structure and two types of mentality, one quick-reacting, quick-thinking, and volatile, the other slow-reacting, slow-thinking, but more profound and phlegmatic. His slow-thinking mentality, suggestive of Jung's introvert, he thought went, on the whole, with languages of a synthetic type having a complex overt morphology and much derivation and word-building, the extreme of the type being polysynthesis. His quick-thinking (extraverted) type went, on the whole, with a simpler morphology, lack of synthesis, an analytic or in the extreme an isolating type of language.

But, while I am sympathetic to the possibility of such a finding, which would indeed be a mighty achievement, and also impressed by Byrne's anticipation of Jung, I find Byrne's general thesis unconvincing, chiefly because I can see how Byrne was working with utterly inadequate materials. It is of the greatest importance to man's knowledge of his own intellectual makeup, especially in future times, that the really colossal task that Byrne so rashly attempted be done as well as possible. This would require not only a survey of many more languages, particularly American ones, than Byrne used, but a grammar of each language worked out scientifically and on the basis of the language's own patterns and classes, and as free as possible from any general presuppostitions about grammatical logic. Byrne got his materials from old-fashioned grammars, formal and even "classical" in cut. These grammars might at any juncture quarter a regiment of alien patterns and ideas on the unfortunate tongue. Not one of these grammarians, nor Byrne himself, could have made a *sui generis* configurative report on a language as Fabre d'Olivet had done; that ability had died. But until it again lives as a well-developed scientific technique and is applied to another world survey and comparison, man will remain ignorant of the roots of his intellectual life. He will be debarred from any consideration of human thought on a planetary scale, of what it is in respect to the species.

That ability began to live again with and after the attack made by Boas on the American Indian languages, and especially his statement of principles, and ideals of method, in his justly celebrated introduction to the *Handbook* (1911). And, with Boas, it reappeared in a modern scientific form, and in terms of the acceptable science CULTUS, not as before in terms of an exuberant mystically disposed creative imagination. Boas showed for the second time in history, but for the first in a scientific manner, how a language could be analyzed *sui generis* and without forcing the categories of "classical" tradition upon it. The development of an adequate technique for this new outlook had to come haltingly. When under Boas the American languages first began to reveal the unparalleled complexity and subtlety of their thought categories, the phonemic calculus was still unborn. The American field linguist could not, like Fabre, intuit the phoneme and morphophoneme in a brilliant tour de force of imaginative insight. He had to wait for these concepts to be developed by specialized phoneticians, working at first in the modern-language field, and at first he lacked in psychological penetration.

The new era passes into a second phase, into the truly modern linguistic point of view, with the appearance on the scene of Sapir, and particularly with the publication of his *Language* in 1921. Sapir has done more than any other person to inaugurate the linguistic approach to thinking and make it of scientific consequence, and moreover to demonstrate the importance of linguistics to anthropology and psychology. From this point on it would be a task to mention individual contributors to this dawning realization and growing idea that linguistics is fundamental to the theory of thinking and in the last analysis to ALL HUMAN SCIENCES.

III

This linguistic consideration of thinking as applied to primitive communities is of significance for anthropology in two ways. First, the ethnological and the psychological-linguistic insights into the same primitive community, especially if made by the same investigator, can be reasonably expected to have a very fertilizing effect upon each other. We have the testimony and the enlightening teaching of Sapir and others that this is so. The very essence of linguistics is the quest for meaning, and, as the science refines its procedure, it inevitably becomes, as a matter of this quest, more psychological and cultural, while retaining that almost mathematical precision of statement which it gets from the highly systematic nature of the linguistic realm of fact.

Let us suppose that an ethnologist discovers that the Hopi speak about clouds in their rain prayers, etc., as though clouds were alive. He would like to know whether this is some metaphor or special religious or ceremonial figure of speech, or whether it is the ordinary and usual way of thinking about clouds. Here is the sort of problem to which language might be able to give a very meaningful answer, and we immediately turn to it to see if it has a gender system that distinguishes living from nonliving things, and, if so, how it classes a cloud. We find that Hopi has no gender at all. The traditional grammar of the pre-Boas period would stop at this point and think it had given an answer. But the correct answer can only be given by a grammar that analyzes covert as well as overt structure and meaning. For Hopi does distinguish an animate class of nouns AS A CRYPTOTYPE and only as a cryptotype. The crucial reactance is in the way of forming the plural. When members of the Flute Society, e.g., are spoken of as Flutes, this (covertly) inanimate noun is pluralized in the animate way. But the word *ʔo:'mâw* 'cloud,' is always pluralized in the animate way; it has no other plural; it definitely belongs to the cryptotype of animateness. And so the question whether the animation of clouds is a figure or formality of speech or whether it stems from some more deep and subtly pervasive undercurrent of thought is answered, or at the least given a flood of new meaning.

Language thus should be able to analyze some, if probably not all, of the differences, real or assumed, between the mentality of so-called primitive peoples and modern civilized man. Whether the primitives constitute a unit class of mentality over against modern man, apart from the differences between their cultures and his, as is implied in Lévy-Bruhl's concept of PARTICIPATION MYSTIQUE (Lévy-Bruhl, 1912—J.B.C.) and in the equation of "primitive" to "infantile" used by Freud and Jung; or whether (again apart from general culture) the CIVILIZED MODERN is the unit class of mentality because of the great structural similarity of all the modern civilized Western languages, while over against it are many diverse types of mentality reflecting a rich diversity of speech structure: This is only one of the great psychological world-questions that fall into the domain of linguistics and await the impersonal and positive type of answer that linguistic research can give. We are accustomed to think of such a mentality as is implied by PARTICIPATION MYSTIQUE as less of a thinking mentality, as less rational, than ours. Yet many American Indian and African languages abound in finely wrought, beautifully logical discriminations about causation, action, result, dynamic or energic quality, directness of experience, etc., all matters of the function of thinking, indeed the quintessence of the rational. In this respect they far outdistance the European languages. (See for example the Hopi treatment of repetitive and vibrational phenomena in my paper, "The punctual and segmentative aspects of verbs in Hopi," or the instances of [*lacuna*] in Watkins' Chichewa. [Probably Whorf intended to allude to the Chichewa verb system, which is extremely sensitive to the causative aspects of acts. For example, there are several past tenses, use of which depends not only on the remoteness of the past time being referred to (before or since last night) but also on whether the act continues to have an influence on the present. There are also seven "voices," which express different kinds of relations among subject, verb, and predicate (including object). See pp. 49-57, 72-81 in *A grammar of Chichewa, a Bantu language of British Central Africa*, by Mark Hanna Watkins, *Language Dissertation* no. 24. 1937. See also Whorf's later discussion in his article, "Language, mind, and reality" (1942, pp. 265 f.).—J.B.C.]) The most impressively penetrating distinctions of this kind often are those revealed by analyzing to the covert and even cryptotypic levels. Indeed, covert categories are quite apt to be more rational than overt ones. English unmarked gender is more rational, closer to natural fact, than the marked genders of Latin or German. As outward marks become few, the class tends to crystallize around an idea—to become more dependent on whatever synthetizing principle there may be in the meanings of its members. It may even be true that many abstract ideas arise in this way; some rather formal and not very meaningful linguistic group, marked by some overt feature, may happen to coincide very roughly with some concatenation of phenomena in such a way as to suggest a rationalization of this parallelism. In the course of phonetic change, the distinguishing mark, ending, or what not is lost, and the class passes from a formal to a semantic one. Its reactance is now what distinguishes it as a class, and its idea is what unifies it. As time and use go on, it becomes increasingly organized around a rationale, it attracts semantically suitable words and loses former members that now are semantically inappropriate. Logic is now what holds it together, and its logic becomes a semantic associate of that unity of which the CONFIGURATIVE aspect is a bundle of nonmotor linkages mooring the whole fleet of words to their common reactance. Semantically it has become a deep persuasion of a principle behind phenomena, like the ideas of inanimation, of "substance," of abstract sex, of abstract personality, of force, of causation—not the overt concept (lexation) corresponding to the WORD causation but the covert idea, the "sensing," or, as it is often called (but wrongly, according to Jung), the "feeling" that there must be a principle of causation. Later this covert idea may be more or less duplicated in a word and a lexical concept invented by a philosopher: e.g., CAUSATION. From this point of view many preliterate ("primitive") communities, far from being subrational, may show the human mind functioning on a higher and more complex plane of rationality than among civilized men. We do not know that civilization is synonymous with rationality. These primitive tribes may simply have lacked philosophers, the existence of whom may depend on an economic prosperity that few cultures in the course of history have reached. Or perhaps too much rationality may defeat itself, or arouse some strong compensatory principle. These are all questions, essentially anthropological, to which a liaison between ethnology and psychological linguistics would seem to offer the soundest approach.

The second way in which linguistic consideration of thinking is significant for anthropology has more reference to the future, and perhaps most of all to the far distant future of the human species when it will have developed into something other, and let us hope far higher, than present-day man. Turning first to the nearer future, it is desirable that anthropology collaborate in preparation for the time, which cannot be too far postponed, when it will be both possible and urgently necessary to make the cultural and psychological world-survey of languages that is envisioned in the work of James Byrne—this time in a way which will enrich our science with the prodigal wealth of new truth that lies in that field waiting to be discovered.

As time goes on, the type of knowledge that such a survey would unlock becomes more and more a matter of concern and interest outside the world of scholarly pursuits—for it may play a very important part in world history that is now in the making. The problems of achieving mutual understanding, of language barriers, of propaganda and advertising, of education, of the technique of managing human affairs without undue friction, of an intelligence in human relations that can keep pace with the changes brought about by the physical sciences, all run afoul of this matter of language and thought. Everyone is naturally interested in questions of language, although they either do not know it, or know it and think they know all about it. There is for example a movement for the extended use of Ogden's ingenious artificial language called Basic English, which has met with much sympathy among businessmen, educators, people interested in international affairs, and social prophets like H. G. Wells. There is no use sitting aloof and loftily condemning such linguistic movements as unscientific. Unscientific or not, they are linguistic phenomena of today, and why should linguistic science, which alone can handle the vital underlying principles of such movements, stand by in sequestered unconcern and let them blunder along, exercising their crude but vast power to change the thinking of tomorrow? Basic English appeals to people because it seems simple. But those to whom it seems simple either know or think they know English—there's the rub! Every language of course seems simple to its own speakers because they are unconscious of structure. But English is anything but simple—it is a bafflingly complex organization, abounding in covert classes, cryptotypes, taxemes of selection, taxemes of order (The marginal notation appears: "memberships in covert categories of a certain type," and there is a reference to Bloomfield [1933] where the subject of taxemes is taken up in Chapters 10,12, and elsewhere.—J.B.C.), significant stress patterns and intonation patterns of considerable intricacy. English is indeed almost in a class by itself as regards prosodic complexity, being one of the most complex languages on earth in this respect; on the whole, it is as complicated as most polysynthetic languages of America, which fact most of us are blissfully unaware of. The complex structure of English is largely covert, which makes it all the harder to analyze. Foreigners learning English have to absorb it unconsciously—a process requiring years—by dint of constant exposure to bombardment by spoken English in large chunks; there exists at this moment no grammar that can teach it. As with Basic English, so with other artificial languages—underlying structures and categories of a few culturally predominant European tongues are taken for granted; their complex web of presuppositions is made the basis of a false simplicity. We say 'a large black and white hunting dog' and assume that in Basic English one will do the same. How is the speaker of a radically different mother tongue supposed to know that he cannot say 'hunting white black large a dog'? The English adjectives belong to cryptotypes having definite position assignments, and their formula is a definite and complex one, but lo, the poor Indian organizes his thinking quite differently. The person who would use Basic English must first know or learn the immensely intricate covert structure of actual "English as she is spoke."

We see here the error made by most people who attempt to deal with such social questions of language—they naïvely suppose that speech is nothing but a piling up of LEXATIONS, and that this is all one needs in order to do any and every kind of rational thinking; the far more important thought materials provided by structure and configurative rapport are beyond their horizons. It may turn out that the simpler a language becomes overtly, the more it becomes dependent upon cryptotypes and other covert formations, the more it conceals unconscious presuppositions, and the more its lexations become variable and indefinable. Wouldn't this be a pretty kettle of fish for the would-be advocates of a "simple" international tongue to have had a hand in stewing up! For sound thinking in such fields we greatly need a competent world-survey of languages.

IV

And now, turning to the more distant future, one may perhaps be permitted to essay a broader view, to look at the subject of linguistics and its bearing upon thinking from the standpoint of the whole human species. In order to do this we must not be afraid to begin with a platitude. Man is distinguished from other animals by language, and by his great development of thinking. So far as we can envision his future, we must envision it in terms of mental growth. We cannot but suppose that the future developments of thinking are of primary importance to the human species. They may even determine the duration of human existence on the planet earth or in the universe. The possibilities open to thinking are the possibilities of recognizing relationships and the discovery of techniques of operating with relationships on the mental or intellectual plane, such as will in turn lead to ever wider and more penetratingly significant systems of relationships. These possibilities are inescapably bound up with systems of linguistic expression. The story of their evolution in man is the story of man's linguistic development—of the long evolution of thousands of very different systems of discerning, selecting, organizing, and operating with relationships. Of the early stages of this evolutionary process, the REALLY PRIMITIVE ROOTS of language, we know nothing. What we are at least in a position to find out is the RESULTS of this evolution as they exist broadcast about the planet in our present day. Only the beginnings of such a knowledge of worldwide linguistic taxonomy are in evidence. In our armchair generalizations about grammar, and the related fields of logic and thought-psychology, we are in the same position as pre-Linnaean botany. We have not yet got anything like a description of existing linguistic species, to use a biological metaphor.

Fortunately for biology, a worldwide systematic taxonomy preceded and laid a foundation for the historical and evolutionary approach. In linguistics as in other cultural studies, we have had unfortunately the reverse situation. The evolutionary concept, having been dumped upon modern man while his notions of language and thought were based on knowledge of only a few types out of the hundreds of very diverse linguistic types existing, has abetted his provincial linguistic prejudices and fostered the grandiose hokum that his type of thinking and the few European tongues on which it is based represent the culmination and flower of the evolution of language! This is as if a pre-Linnaean botanist who had conceived the idea of evolution should suppose that our cultivated wheat and oats represent a higher evolutionary stage than a rare aster restricted to a few sites in the Himalayas. From the standpoint of a matured biology, it is precisely the rare aster which has the better claim to high evolutionary eminence; the wheat owes its ubiquity and prestige merely to human economics and history.

The eminence of our European tongues and thinking habits proceeds from nothing more. The relatively few languages of the cultures which have attained to modern civilization promise to overspread the globe and cause the extinction of the hundreds of diverse exotic linguistic species, but it is idle to pretend that they represent any superiority of type. On the contrary, it takes but little real scientific study of preliterate languages, especially those of America, to show how much more precise and finely elaborated is the system of relationships in many such tongues than is ours. (At this point in the manuscript appears a marginal notation: "Conclusion—error supposing function of language to be only the COMMUNICATION of thought." By emphasizing the word communication, Whorf apparently meant to convey the implication that language not only communicates thought but functions in its very inception, a conclusion to which we are forced if we accept the main thesis of this article.—

J.B.C.) By comparison with many American languages, the formal systematization of ideas in English, German, French, or Italian seems poor and jejune. Why, for instance, do we not, like the Hopi, use a different way of expressing the relation of channel of sensation (seeing) to result in consciousness, as between 'I see that it is red' and 'I see that it is new'? We fuse the two quite different types of relationships into a vague sort of connection expressed by 'that,' whereas the Hopi indicates that in the first case seeing presents a sensation 'red,' and in the second that seeing presents unspecified evidence from which is drawn the inference of newness. If we change the form to 'I hear that it is red' or 'I hear that it is new,' we European speakers still cling to our lame 'that,' but the Hopi now uses still another relater and makes no distinction between 'red' and 'new,' since, in either case, the significant presentation to consciousness is that of a verbal report, and neither a sensation per se nor inferential evidence. Does the Hopi language show here a higher plane of thinking, a more rational analysis of situations, than our vaunted English? Of course it does. In this field and in various others, English compared to Hopi is like a bludgeon compared to a rapier. We even have to think and boggle over the question for some time, or have it explained to us, before we can see the difference in the relationships expressed by 'that' in the above examples, whereas the Hopi discriminates these relationships with effortless ease, for the forms of his speech have accustomed him to doing so.

CARROLL'S NOTES

This paper was found by me in handwritten manuscript form, undated, among the papers left by Whorf to his wife and recently turned over to his son, Robert Whorf. The manuscript appeared to be complete (except for certain footnotes), but it was generally in a somewhat unfinished state, necessitating some editorial work on my part. Notes on the manuscript indicate that Whorf intended to prepare it for publication. He even listed individuals to whom he planned to send reprints including Jung, N(ayán) L(ouise) Redfield, Sapir, Carroll, Wayne Dennis, (Claude) Bragdon, H. G. Wells, and H. L. Mencken. We may date the writing of this article as taking place about late 1936, from two facts: first, it must have occurred after the publication, in early 1936, of his article, "The Punctual and Segmentative Aspects of Verbs in Hopi," to which he refers, and, second, it probably preceded the writing (in late 1937) of his article, "Grammatical Categories," which gives a somewhat more fully developed notion of cryptotype than occurs in the present paper.—J.B.C.

[Carroll also supplied the dates of Fabre d'Olivet, Byrne, and their works, as well as the references in the text to Boas, Sapir, and Lévy-Bruhl. These emendations have been silently incorporated into the present text.]

BIBLIOGRAPHY

At the end of the manuscript appears a section entitled "Bibliography (Notes)" which is merely a skeleton of a bibliography; it consists chiefly of names. I have already given footnote references for the following names: Bloomfield, Boas, Byrne, Fabre d'Olivet, Jung, Sapir, Watkins, and Watson. Below I give the citations that Whorf most probably had in mind for the other names; in several cases he was explicit.—J.B.C.

De Angulo, Jaime. Tone Patterns and Verb Forms in a Dialect of Zaptoec. *Lg.*, 1926, *2*: 238-250.

Flournoy, Théodore. *Métaphysique et psychologie.* Geneva: 1890. [? This may not be the relevant work.]

Haas, Mary. [Whorf probably referred to unpublished material which he had seen. See her sketch of Tunica, an American Indian language, in H. Hoijer *Linguistic Structures of Native America*. New York 1946.—J.B.C.]

Jones, William, and Truman Michelson. Algonquian (Fox). In Franz Boas (Ed.), *Handbook of American Indian Languages, Part* 1. Washington, D.C.: 1911. Pp. 735-873.

Koffka, K. *Principles of Gestalt Psychology*. New York: Harcourt, Brace, 1935.

Lévy-Bruhl, Lucien. *Les fonctions mentales dans les sociétés inférieures*. Paris: Alcan, 1912. [Translated as *How Natives Think*. London: Allen and Unwin, 1926.]

Lowes, John Livingston. *Road to Xanadu*. Cambridge: Harvard University Press, 1927. [Whorf misremembered the author's name as Dickinson. He comments, "Interesting for illustrations of the dredging up of linguistic material from the unconscious."]

Murdock, George P. *Our Primitive Contemporaries*. New York: Macmillan, 1934.

Newman, Stanley S. *A Grammar of Yokuts, an American Indian Language of California*. Unpublished Ph.D. dissertation, Yale University, 1932.

[Also, *Yokuts Language of California*. (Viking Fund Publications in Anthropology, No. 2.) New York: 1944.]

Morice, Adrian G. *The Carrier Language (Dene Family); A Grammar and Dictionary Combined.* St. Gabriel-Modling near Vienna: 1932.

Ogden, Charles K. *Basic English: A General Introduction with Rules and Grammar.* London: Kegan Paul, Trench, Trubner, 1930). [Whorf's citation is to Ogden and Richards, but I believe he meant to refer to this book about Basic English.]

Swadesh, Morris. [Whorf probably referred to unpublished material which he had seen. See Swadesh's sketch of South Greenland Eskimo in H. Hoijer, *Linguistic Structures of Native America.* New York, 1946.—J.B.C.]

Trager, George L. The Phonemes of Russian. *Lg.*, 1934, *10:* 334-344.

REFERENCE NOTE

For the full range and import of Whorf's views, see his articles (1936, 1938, etc.) as collected by Carroll (1956). For discussions of Whorf's views, see especially Brown (1958, chap. 1), Fishman (1960), Hoijer (1953, 1954a, 1954b), Hymes (1961b), Lenneberg (1953), Longacre (1956), Trager (1959), Waterman (1957), among other references listed with Hoijer's article on pp. 142-153.

17 *Cultural Implications of Some Navaho Linguistic Categories*

HARRY HOIJER

SOME YEARS AGO, in an article called "The Status of Linguistics as a Science" (1929c), Edward Sapir made an interesting statement describing language in part as "a guide to 'social reality.'" The statement goes on to say:

Though language is not ordinarily thought of as of essential interest to the students of social science, it powerfully conditions all our thinking about social problems and processes. Human beings do not live in the objective world alone, nor alone in the world of social activity as ordinarily understood, but are very much at the mercy of the particular language which has become the medium of expression for their society. It is quite an illusion to imagine that one adjusts to reality essentially without the use of language and that language is merely an incidental means of solving specific problems of communication or reflection. The fact of the matter is that the "real world" is to a large extent unconsciously built up on the language habits of the group. No two languages are ever sufficiently similar to be considered as representing the same social reality. The worlds in which different societies live are distinct worlds, not merely the same world with different labels attached (p. 209).

One of Sapir's students, Benjamin L. Whorf, followed this lead in a series of brilliant papers, recently re-issued in a pamphlet published by the Foreign Service Institute of the Department of State under the title *Four Articles on Metalinguistics*. In the longest and most important of these, "The Relation of Habitual Thought and Behavior to Language," Whorf compares the language patterns of Hopi, an Indian tongue spoken in Arizona, with those of modern European languages, mainly English, French, and German. His purpose is stated as follows:

The portion of the whole investigation here to be reported may be summed up in two questions: (1) Are our own concepts of "time," "space," and "matter" given in substantially the same form by experience to all men, or are they in part conditioned by the structure of particular languages? (2) Are there traceable affinities between (a) cultural and behavioral norms and (b) large-scale linguistic patterns? (Spier, Hallowell, and Newman (Eds.), 1941, p. 78)

Incidentally, and to avoid possible misunderstanding, Whorf explicitly denies (*ibid.*) "that there is anything so definite as 'a correlation' between culture and language, and especially between ethnological rubrics such as 'agricultural,' 'hunting,' etc., and linguistic ones like 'inflected,' 'synthetic,' or 'isolating.'"

We need not summarize Whorf's discussion of the problems he sets, but I should like to quote from his conclusions:

Concepts of "time" and "matter" are not given in substantially the same form by experience to all men but depend on the nature of the language or languages through the use of which they have been developed. They do not depend so much upon *any one system* (e.g., tense, or nouns) within the grammar as upon the ways of analyzing and reporting experience which have become fixed in the language as integrated "fashions of speaking" and which cut across the typical grammatical classifications, so that such a "fashion" may include lexical, morphological, syntactic, and otherwise systemically diverse means coordinated in a certain frame of consistency. . . .

As for our second question . . . There are connections but not correlations or diagnostic correspondences between cultural norms and linguistic patterns. Although it would be impossible to infer the existence of Crier Chiefs from the lack of tenses in Hopi, or vice versa, there is a relation between a language and the rest of the culture of the society which uses it (pp. 92-93).

It seems likely that Whorf is understating the significance of the "connections" he elucidates between language and other aspects of culture. It is altogether probable that there may be "diagnostic correspondences," not in the specific fashion of Whorf's example, but in a more abstract or remote sense. If a study of a language, a set of patterns of speaking, uncovers a certain framework for reality characteristic of its speakers, and if a study of non-linguistic cultural patterns lays bare similar fundamental concepts, there is more than just a non-diagnostic connection between the several aspects of a culture. But this is a problem as yet uninvestigated; Whorf's analysis does no more than suggest certain lines of research.

My purpose in this paper is to apply Whorf's technique of analysis to a quite different culture, that of the Navaho Indians of New Mexico and Arizona. In passing, it is not without interest that the Navaho, though they lived as neighbors of the Hopi for more than 400 years and have taken over many of the overt patterns of Hopi culture, are nevertheless very different from them in their basic cultural assumptions and outlook. The world of social reality characteristic of the Navaho, and reflected in their language, is no more like that of the Hopi than it is like our own.

Before we investigate the Navaho fashions of speech germane to our purpose, it is necessary to outline briefly the major structural characteristics of the Navaho language, and in particular of the verb. Navaho morphological constructions, however they may be subdivided, are fundamentally much alike in structure. Each consists of a theme—composed of a stem or set of stems with or without a thematic prefix—which may occur either alone or with one or more non-thematic prefixes. Many constructions also include one or more proclitics and enclitics, semi-independent elements which usually have syntactic function.

Three major form classes may be recognized: particles, nouns, and verbs. These differ mainly in the amount and kind of grammatical inflection they undergo. Particles—e.g., pronouns, numerals, modifiers, conjunctions—are not inflected, though they often take one or more proclitics or enclitics. Nouns occur as free themes (i.e., in absolute contructions), preceded by a possessive pronoun prefix (i.e., in possessive constructions), and in compounds or complex phrase-like constructions which function as nouns. A small number of noun themes, together with all independent postpositions, appear only in possessive constructions or in compounds; these have no free forms. Another but very small set of themes appears both as nouns and as verbs: thus, the theme *nát'òh* in absolute and possessive noun constructions has the meaning 'tobacco' and, in verb constructions, the meaning 'to smoke (a cigar or cigarette).'

Verb themes never occur as free forms and are usually provided with from three to seven or more distinctive stems, with or without a thematic prefix. Non-thematic verb prefixes are of two kinds, derivational and paradigmatic. The former are mainly adverbial in function, while the latter denote concepts of aspect, mode, tense, number, and the pronouns for the subject, object, and indirect object.

Some verb themes can be made into verb constructions solely by the addition of one or more appropriate paradigmatic prefixes to one of its stem forms. Most verb themes, however, require one or another set of derivational prefixes in addition to the appropriate paradigmatic elements. Such derivations (i.e., verb themes plus derivational prefixes) are called verb bases. Many themes appear in several bases and some, like the theme 'one round object moves,' in more than a hundred bases (see Hoijer, 1949, pp. 17-21). The term "verb base" applies, however, to any verb segment to which paradigmatic prefixes may be added to form a free verb construction, whether this consists of a theme alone or of a theme plus derivational prefixes.

Verb bases fall into two major categories, neuter and active. Neuter bases are conjugated for person and number in only one paradigm (the stem is invariable throughout the paradigm), but active bases have seven required paradigms: imperfective, perfective, progressive, future, iterative, customary, and optative. Active bases may have as many as five distinctive stems (e.g., one each for imperfective, perfective, progressive and future, iterative and customary, and optative), but some have fewer (i.e., where a single stem appears in more than one paradigm), and, in a few instances, one stem may occur in all seven paradigms.

Verb bases built on the same theme occasionally employ different though related sets of stems. Compare, for example, the bases *di-. . .bá:h, -bà:ˀ, -bàh* 'begin to go on a raid' and *nà-. . .-bà:h, -bà:ˀ, -bàh, -bá:h* 'go about raiding.' Contrasts such as these testify that particular stem configurations denote specific aspects, cutting across the division into the categories listed above. Thus *di-. . .-bá:h, -bà:ˀ, -bàh* is a base defining momentaneous action as contrasted with *nà-. . .-bà:h, -bà:ˀ, -bàh, -bá:h*, which defines continuative action. The numerous verb bases employing the theme 'a round object moves' are divided into no less than seven aspectival categories, each with a distinctive set of stems (Hoijer, 1949, pp. 13-17).

Turning our attention now to the meanings of these verbal categories, we find that neuter verbs in general report states or conditions. Neuter verbs contain no morpheme denoting tense, mode, or aspect, but simply report a state of being (an absence of movement or action) like 'being at rest,' 'standing,' or 'sitting.' Some neuter verbs define qualities: to be 'blue,' 'white,' 'thin,' 'fat,' or 'tall.'

Active verbs, on the other hand, report events, movements, and actions. These are reported, not necessarily in relation to tense categories, but mainly in respect to aspect and mode. In an imperfective verb, the event is moving toward fulfillment; the third person imperfective *nìǹdà:h*, for example, means 'he moves to a sitting position.' Note that the emphasis lies not on the present tense (unavoidable in the English translation) but on the uncompleted nature of the movement. The same verb in the third person perfective, *nìńdá*, means 'he has moved to a sitting position,' that is, the movement to a sitting position has been completed or achieved. Both these expressions can be given tense by adding appropriate but optional enclitics: *nìǹdà:h-dò:* (*-dò:*, future tense enclitic) 'he will be moving to a sitting position' and *nìńdá-dò:* 'he will have moved to a sitting position.' But although such tense enclitics as *-dò:* may or may not be used, the active verb cannot avoid aspectival or modal denotation, for it must be expressed in one or another of the seven required paradigms.

In the progressive aspect—e.g., *nò:dà:l* 'he goes along moving to a sitting position'—events are reported in continuous process without reference to a beginning or end. A better example is found in *yò:ˀà:l*, roughly 'he is carrying a round object,' which, upon analysis, turns out to mean 'he moves along handling a round object.' Again note the emphasis on the state rather than the time of the action; compare *yò:ˀà:l-nìˀ* (*-nìˀ*, past tense enclitic) 'he was moving along handling a round object.'

Iterative forms of the active verb have clearly aspectival denotation; the third person iterative of 'one moves to a sitting position' (the verb base cited above) is *ǹnádà:h* 'he moves to a sitting position repeatedly.' Emphasis here lies solely on the repetition of the event, a repetition which has no end. The customary, a paradigm made up by combining the imperfective prefix complex with the iterative stem, while it also emphasizes repetition, carries the further denotation that such repetition is a matter of habit or custom. Such forms are particularly numerous in reports of customs, habitual modes of group behavior, where, for example, the Navaho will say (Sapir and Hoijer, 1942, p. 404). *nà:dą́:ˀ* ('corn') *déiɣìš* ('they customarily gather it') *ˀá:dó·* ('and') *déiλàˀ* ('they customarily husk it').

The optative is purely a modal category. For example (NT 20), Coyote, because the weather is hot, says: *k'òs* ('clouds') *hólèˀ* ('let there be!'), *ǹˀdóžòł* ('let it sprinkle [with rain]!'); and when the water from the rain is high, *šìłdóˀè:l* ('let [the water] begin to float with me!').

Only the future paradigm expresses tense in Navaho (e.g., *nìdò:dà:l* 'he will move to a sitting position'), and even here there is some evidence, too tentative to introduce in this paper, that the future, so-called, is better interpreted as an inceptive progressive—that is, as an aspect rather than a tense category.

While at first sight the Navaho division of verb bases into neuters and actives appears to represent a sharp dichotomy, further analysis reveals both a structural and a semantic relation between them. Neuter verb bases, though never conjugated in more than one paradigm, are not all conjugated in the same paradigm. There are, in fact, five neuter paradigms, each with its own meaning, as follows:

(1) The *s*-neuter, structurally identical with the *s*-perfective of active verb bases, which reports a position at a point in space or time, (an object) in a given position. Thus, *ʒìł* ('mountain') *sìˀą́* ('a round solid object lies at rest') = 'a mountain lies at rest'.

(2) The *n*-neuter, structurally identical with the *n*-perfective of active verb bases, which reports a position extending in a line from one

point to another. Thus, *ʒìl* ('mountain') *ńˀą́* ('round solid objects lie in a row') = 'a range of mountains lies extending from one point to another.'

(3) The *y*-neuter, structurally identical with the *y*-perfective of active verb bases, which reports a position extending indefinitely from a fixed point. Thus, *cé* ('rock, stone') *yí:ˀá* ('a rigid object has extension from a fixed point') = 'a [slender pinnacle of] stone extends [upward].' This phrase is also a noun, referring to the slender, phallus-like rocks so common in the Navaho country.

(4) The imperfective neuter, structurally identical with the imperfective of active verb bases, which reports qualities similar to those denoted by adjectives in English. Thus, *lìgài* 'it is white.'

(5) The progressive neuter, structurally identical with the progressive of active verb bases. We find only one example: *yò:ˀí* 'he has him in view, he sees him.'

These several forms of the neuter category strongly suggest that the neuter represents semantically a phase of events characterized by the withdrawal of motion: the state of being that remains when movement of a particular kind ends.

To summarize this phase of our investigation, it would appear that Navaho verb categories center very largely about the reporting of events, or better, "eventings." These eventings are divided into neuters, eventings solidified, as it were, into states of being by virtue of the withdrawal of motion, and actives, eventings in motion. The latter are further subdivided into imperfectives, eventings in process of completion; perfectives, eventings completed; progressives, eventings moving along; and iteratives, eventings repeated over and over again. The customary reports eventings repeated by force of habit or custom; the optative, a desire that an eventing take; and the future, the expectation that an eventing will occur.

But this is not all. A careful analysis of the meanings of Navaho verb bases, neuter and active, reveals that eventings themselves are conceived, not abstractly for the most part, but very concretely in terms of the movements of corporeal bodies, or of entities metaphorically linked with corporeal bodies. Movement itself is reported in painstaking detail, even to the extent of classifying as semantically different the movements of one, two, or several bodies, and sometimes distinguishing as well between movements of bodies differentiated by their shape and distribution in space.

To illustrate, there are four basic and different verb themes which report the unspecified movement of human beings, other animate beings, and certain natural objects classed as animate. Of these, *-há:h* means 'one (member of this class) moves,' *-ˀà:š* means 'two or a few move,' *-ká:h* means 'several move,' and *-zé:h* means 'a group moves en masse.' If movement is more precisely specified, still other themes must be employed: *-λó:š* 'move on all fours, trot,' *-γè:d* 'move at a run,' *-t'á:h* 'move by flying,' *-ˀè:l* 'move by floating on water,' *-bą́:s* 'move by rolling [as a hoop or wheel].' In the five themes last cited, the number moving is not specified; the theme is the same for one, two, or more.

An especially vivid example of the Navaho pattern of reporting movement in terms of an object or objects moving is revealed by a literal analysis of the meaning 'he picks something up' or 'he chooses or selects something.' Twelve verbs express this meaning. All have the same prefix complex: *nâidì:-* 'third person causes it [to move] upward,' but each has a different theme, depending on the nature of the referent of 'it.' If 'it' refers to a round solid object, the theme (in its imperfective form) is *-ˀà:h*; thus, *nâidì:ˀà:h* 'third person causes a round solid object to move upward.' Long slender objects require the theme *-tį̀:h*, one animate object the theme *-tè:h*, a set of objects the theme *-ní:l*, a rigid container with contents the theme *-kà:h*, a fabric-like object the theme *-có:s*, a bulky object the theme *-zò:d*, a set of parallel objects the theme *-žó:š*, an unspecified mass the theme *-ǰā:h*, a wool-like mass the theme *-ǰò:l*, a rope-like object the theme *-lé*, and a mud-like mass the theme *-λè:h* (Hoijer, 1945a).

As I have indicated previously, the meaning of a verb base may be denoted by a theme alone or by a theme with one or more deivational prefixes. Prefixes and prefix combinations, like the themes we have just cited, also refer in large part to movement. To illustrate, let us cite a few of the more than one hundred verb bases formed on the theme *-há:h* 'one animate object moves [in an unspecified fashion].' I quote only the prefix complexes plus the meanings of the completed verb bases: *Oà:-di-...* 'one moves away from, outwalks,' *Oà:-na-. . .* 'one comes back to,' *Oà:-. . .* 'one comes or goes to,' *Oà:-ná:-. .* 'one again comes or goes to,' *ʔa-. . .* 'one moves away, out of sight,' *ʔa-hé-. . .* 'one moves in a circle back to the starting point,' *dàh-di-. . .* 'one starts off on a journey,' *tá-di-. . .* 'one moves to one place after another,' *tà:h-. . .* 'one moves into the water,' *na-. . .* 'one moves across,' *ha-. . .* 'one moves out of an enclosed space,' *há-di. . .* 'one starts off to fetch,' *yàh-ʔa-. . .* 'one goes inside [e.g., a house],' *O-c'á-. . .* 'one moves away from,' *O-č'ą́:h-ʔa-...* 'one moves in between', *č'í-. . .* 'one moves outside [e.g. of a house]' (*O* represents any pronominal prefix) (see also Hoijer, 1949, esp. pp. 18-21).

But this high degree of specificity in the reporting of movement is not confined in Navaho to verbs having particular reference to motion of one sort or another. On the contrary, it permeates the Navaho lexicon in the sense that many verbs, not at first sight expressive of movement, prove to be so on more detailed analysis. For example, the theme *-há:h* 'one animate object moves [in an unspecified fashion]' is easily recognized in a large number of bases, the meanings of which appear to be far distant from any concept of movement. The following examples are typical: *Oà:-nà-. . .-há* 'be busy, preoccupied,' literally 'one moves continuously about with reference to it'; *ʔé:h-... -há:h* 'one dresses,' lit. 'one moves into clothing'; *ho-. . .-há:h* 'a ceremony begins,' lit. 'a happening moves'; *ná-. . .-hā* 'one lives,' lit. 'one moves about here and there'; *ʔánį̀:-nà-. . . -há* 'one is young,' lit. 'one moves about newly'; *yìsdá-. . .-há:h* 'one is rescued, saved,' lit. 'one moves to safety.'

Similar examples follow, based on the theme *-ʔà:h* 'a round object moves': *O-dá:h-. . .-ʔà:h* 'greet someone with a message,' lit. 'move a round solid object to meet someone'; *nà-ho-. . . -ʔá* 'make plans,' lit. 'move happenings about here and there'; *Oè:nì-ho-. . .-ʔà:h* 'decide upon, make a rule about,' lit. 'move a rule down to rest by means of [it]'; *ha-di-...-ʔà:h* 'sing,' lit. 'move words out of an enclosed space'; *č'í-ho-. . .ʔ-à:h* 'make [it] known,' lit. 'move an event outside.'

A third Navaho speech pattern further emphasizes movement; this is the technique of reporting substantive concepts in terms of some characteristic action or movement of an object or set of objects. Structurally, this means that finite verb forms or larger expressions containing finite verb forms may have two grammatical functions—nominal and verbal (see Hoijer, 1948b, pp. 183-184). Thus, *hànì:bą́:z* 'full moon' or 'a hoop-like object has rolled out' (act. pf.), *ʔàdìłdìł* 'stave game' or 'several objects move repeatedly through space' (act. ipf.), *nà:lcò:s* 'a paper, letter' or 'a fabric-like object is moved about' (pass. ipf.) *cìnà:bą̀:s* 'wagon' or 'wood rolls about hoop-like' (*cìn* 'wood' + *nà:bą̀:s* 'it rolls about hoop-like,' act. prog.).

Neuter verb bases parallel those in the active category, for states or conditions, like eventings, are often reported only in reference to specified classes of objects. For each of the twelve active verb themes earlier cited in translating 'he picks it up' we have a corresponding neuter theme which denotes the same class of object at rest. Thus, *sìʔą́* 'a round solid object is at rest,' *sìtą́* 'a long slender object is at rest,' *sìtį́* 'an animate object lies,' *sìnìl* 'a set of objects lie,' *sìką́* 'a rigid container with contents is at rest,' *sìłcò:z* 'a fabric-like object is at rest,' *sìžò:d* 'a bulky object is at rest,' *sìzò:ž* 'a set of parallel objects is at rest,' *sìǰà:* 'an unspecified mass is at rest,' *sìǰò:l* 'a wool-like mass is at rest,' *sìlá* 'a rope-like object is at rest,' and *sìƛé:ʔ* 'a mud-like mass is at rest.'

To summarize: in three broad speech patterns, illustrated by the conjugation of active verbs, the reporting of actions and events, and the framing of substantive concepts, Navaho emphasizes movement and specifies the nature, direction, and status of such movement in considerable detail. Even the neuter category is relatable to the dominant conception of a universe in motion; for, just as someone is reported to have described architecture as frozen music, so the Navaho define position as a resultant of the withdrawal of motion.

Parallels to this semantic theme may be found in almost every aspect of Navaho culture taken as a whole. Even today the Navaho are fundamentally a wandering, nomadic folk, following their flocks from one pasturage to another. Myths and legends reflect this emphasis most markedly, for both gods and culture heroes move restlessly from one holy place to the next, seeking by their motion to perfect and repair the dynamic flux which is the universe. As illustration, the reader may consult any of the tales recorded in Navaho Texts, especially perhaps that entitled The Origin of Horses, the tale of Turquoise Boy as he seeks out a mode of transport for man (NT 108-125).

To turn now to another aspect of verb structure: what is the precise relationship, in semantic terms, between the subjects and goals of a Navaho verb on the one hand and the verb base on the other? We have already noted that the finite verb form, active and neuter, is a syntactic construction in microcosm, for inevitably included in such forms are anaphoric pronouns referring to words or phrases outside the verb which define its subject, object, and indirect object.

In neuter intransitive verbs the subject pronoun prefix refers to an object which (a) belongs to the class of objects defined by the verb theme and (b) is characterized by the state or condition denoted by the verb base. An example: from *-tį́* 'one animate object lies' we may form *sítį́* 'I lie,' *síńtį́* 'you lie,' and *sìtį́* 'he lies.' *si-* is a prefix used with neuters, and the pronoun prefixes (*į́-* first person, *ń-* second person, and zero third person) refer to single beings characterized by the condition of lying.

In neuter transitives, however, the subject pronoun prefix denotes, not a member of the class defined by the verb theme, but some thing or being outside this class. It is the direct-object prefix that refers to an object in the class defined by the verb theme and characterized by the state or condition denoted by the verb base. Furthermore, the subject pronoun prefix refers to an agency conceived as responsible for the object denoted by goal pronoun. Thus, if we transitivize the forms quoted above, and add to them respectively the goal pronouns *ǹ-* second person, *ši-* first person, and *yi-* third person, we obtain: *ǹsìłtį́* 'I have you lying,' *šìsíńłtį́* 'you have me lying,' and *yìstį́* (< *yi-si-ł-tį́*) 'he has him lying.'

A more concrete illustration of this contrast comes from the following two phrases *ƛ'é:ˀǰí sìˀą́* 'the Night Way [a ceremony] is in progress' *ƛ'é:ˀǰí* 'Night Way' plus *sìˀą́* 'a round solid object is in position' (ceremonials are included in the category of round solid objects) and *ƛ'é:ˀǰí yìsˀą́* 'he is responsible for [this] performance of the Night Way' (*yìsˀą́* < *yį̀-si-ł-ˀą́*). In the first phrase *ƛ'é:ˀǰí* is the subject of the verb *sìˀą́*, but in the second it is the goal of *yìsˀą́*, and the subject, an agency referred to by the third-person subject prefix, is conceived in a state of responsibility for the ceremony.

In active intransitive verbs, the subject pronoun prefix refers to an object which (a) belongs to the class of objects defined by the verb theme and (b) participates as actor in the action denoted by the verb base. Note this significant detail: that the object denoted by the subject pronoun does not perform the action; it is, rather, included in the action of a set of objects to which it belongs. An example: from the base *ni-. . .-tè:h* 'one animate object moves to a lying position (i.e., lies down),' we may form the imperfectives *nìštè:h* 'I lie down,' *nítè:h* 'you lie down,' and *nìtè:h* 'he lies down.' *ni-* is a derivational prefix (the prefix for the imperfective is zero), and the subject pronouns (*š-* first person, high tone second person, and zero third person) refer to actors included by virtue of their animateness in the meaning of the verb base.

Active transitive verbs introduce the notion of agency. Here the subject pronoun prefix refers to an agent who initiates the action denoted by the verb base in reference to a specified object, symbolized by the goal pronoun, included in the class of objects defined by the verb theme. An example: from the causative base *di-. . .-ł-tè:h* 'begin to cause an animate object to move (i.e., begin to carry an animate object),' we may form the following imperfectives: *ǹdìštè:h* (< *nì-di-š-ł-tè:h*) 'I begin to carry you,' *šìdíłtè:h* 'you begin to carry me,' and *yìdìłtè:h* 'he begins to carry him.' *di-* is a derivational prefix 'begin to . . .' and *ł-* functions as a causative prefix. The subject pronouns (*š-* first person, high tone second person, and zero third person) denote agents who initiate the movement of the objects referred to by the goal pronouns (*nì-* second person, *ši-* first person, and *yi-* third person). These objects, being animate, are of course included in the meaning of the verb theme, 'an animate object moves.

This analysis of the relation of subject to verb and verb to goal illustrates a second basic theme of Navaho culture, one that is clearly related to the Navaho division of objective reality into a number of sharply defined object classes in motion or at rest. Both movement and position, in terms of Navaho semantic and grammatical categories, are inherent in and specific to an object class; they are not extraneously produced by an actor, nor imposed as a force upon a goal. Accordingly, in Navaho intransitive verbs, the subject is not reported as performing an action, but as a person or other entity associated with an action or position. The third-person neuter verb *sìdá*, roughly 'he sits,' means literally that the entity symbolized by the third-person subject pronoun, by virtue of its membership in the object class 'one animate being' assumes the kind of sitting position characteristic of this class. Similarly, in the third-person active intransitive verb *nà:yá*, roughly 'he wanders about,' the third person referred to by the subject pronoun, again by reason of its membership in the object class 'one animate being,' participates in the action 'wander about' as specified for this class. In forms like these, the events are reported as if object-class positions and actions existed independently and the so-called 'actors' merly hitched a ride on them.

But if men and other beings may not, in the Navaho world of reality, produce or perform actions, they can and do relate themselves as agents to object classes in position or in motion. In a construction previously cited, *ƛ'é:ʔjí yìsʔą́* 'he is responsible for [this] performance of the Night Way,' the agency referred to by the subject pronoun sponsors a performance of the Night Way as a specific instance of a round solid object in position. He does not perform it nor cause others to do so; he simply, as it were, ties a particular performance of the Night Way to a round object position already in the universe. Similarly, in active transitive verb expressions, as in *cé yìdìʔà:h*, roughly 'he begins to carry a stone,' the agency referred to by the subject pronoun of *yìdìʔà:h* makes *cé* 'stone' a particular member of the round object class in this kind of motion. Again the agency does not of itself produce the motion, nor act upon the goal; it simply links a given round object with a movement of round objects already extant.

In conclusion, it is of interest to note that this relationship of subject, action, and goal, and its implications for the world view of the Navaho, are strikingly paralleled by a conclusion drawn by Kluckhohn, mainly from non-linguistic data. Kluckhohn abstracts from his studies of Navaho culture a number of basic cultural premises, covert assumptions or postulates underlying Navaho behavior. One of these postulates is: "Nature is more powerful than man"; it is amplified by Kluckhohn in the following words:

> Navahos accept nature and adapt themselves to her demands as best they can, but they are not utterly passive, not completely the pawns of nature. They do a great many things that are designed to control nature physically and to repair damage caused by the elements. But they do not even hope to master nature. For the most part The People [i.e., the Navaho] try to influence her with songs and rituals, but they feel that the forces of nature, rather than anything that man does, determine success or failure. . . .
>
> Many white people have the opposite view; namely, that nature is a malignant force with useful aspects that must be harnessed, and useless, harmful ones that must be shorn of their power. . . . Their premise is that nature will destroy them unless they prevent it; the Navahos' is that nature will take care of them if they behave as they should and do as she directs (Kluckhohn and Leighton, 1946, pp. 227-228).

Again we note a cultural premise which may be illustrated in both the language and the non-linguistic aspects of culture. It is my suggestion that this phenomenon connotes a functional interrelationship between socially patterned habits of speaking and thinking and other socially patterned habits, of the utmost importance for the student of language who proposes to do more than merely describe linguistic structures. Contrastive analyses of habits of speaking yield much understanding of many wholly subconscious aspects of human behavior, undetectable by any other means. But more important, it is by reason of such correlations between language and non-linguistic culture that we shall come to understand how and why linguistic structures change, and to understand, moreover, the still unexplained relationships between overt behavior and the numerous symbolic systems that men set up as a screen between themselves and the objective universe in which they live.

REFERENCE NOTE

This paper was presented as a forum lecture at the Linguistic Institute in Ann Arbor, Michigan, July 20, 1950.

References on Navaho linguistics and categories, from Hoijer's paper and supplementing it, are given in A below. References on the relation of language to cultural values and world view, generally, and regarding Whorf, are given in B below.

A. NAVAHO LINGUISTICS AND CULTURAL CATEGORIES

Details of Navaho linguistic structure will be found in Hoijer (1945a, 1945b, 1946a, 1946b, 1948a, 1949) with special reference to the verb. For further details on the noun, see Hoijer (1948b). Text forms are cited from Sapir and Hoijer (1942); the number in parentheses refers to the page on which the citation appears.

For further support of Hoijer's inference as to the importance of motion in Navaho language and culture, see Astrov (1950); Kluckhohn (1960); Landar (1959, pp. 303-306), in which the literature on the theme (except for Reichard's work) is summarized; and Reichard (1949). On the cultural premise regarding nature, see Lee (1944b) and Redfield (1952, 1953).

References not in the general bibliography:

ASTROV, MARGOT

1950. The Concept of Motion as the Psychological Leitmotif of Navaho Life and Literature. *JAF*, *63:* 45-56.

HOIJER, HARRY

1945a. Classificatory Verb Stems in the Apachean Languages. *IJAL*, *11:* 13-23.

1945b. The Apachean Verb. Part I: Verb Structure and Pronominal Prefixes. *IJAL*, *11:* 193-203.

1946a. The Apachean Verb, Part II: The Prefixes for Mode and Tense. *IJAL*, *12:* 1-13.

1946b. The Apachean Verb, Part III: The Classifiers. *IJAL*, *12:* 51-59.

1948a. The Apachean Verb, Part IV: Major Form Classes. *IJAL*, *14:* 247-259.

1948b. The Structure of the Noun in the Apachean Languages. In *Actes du 28ᵉ Congrés international des Americanistes*, Paris. Pp. 173-184.

1949. The Apachean Verb, Part V: The Theme and Prefix Complex. *IJAL*, *15:* 12-22.

KLUCKHOHN, CLYDE

1960. Navaho Categories. In Stanley A. Diamond (Ed.), *Culture in History*. New York: Columbia University Press. Pp. 65-98.

KLUCKHOHN, CLYDE, and DOROTHEA LEIGHTON

1946. *The Navaho.* Cambridge: Harvard University Press.

LANDAR, HERBERT J.

1959. Four Navaho Summer Tales, Part III. *JAF*, *72:* 298-309.

LEE, DOROTHY DEMETRACOUPOULOU

1944b. Linguistic Reflection of Wintu Thought. *IJAL*, *10:* 181-187. [Also, in *Explorations*, 1956, *6:* 6-14, somewhat revised.]

REDFIELD, ROBERT

1952. The Primitive World View. *PAPS*, *96:* 3-36.

1953. *The Primitive World and Its Transformation.* Ithaca: Cornell University Press.

REICHARD, GLADYS

1949. The Character of the Navaho Verb Stem. *Word*, *5:* 55-76.

B. LANGUAGE, CULTURAL VALUES, AND WORLD VIEW

Some of the history of the general subject in American anthropology is traced in Hymes (1961a); in French linguistic sociology, in Cohen (1956a, especially pp. 137-138, 157-167; 1956b); for anthropological involvement, note also Durkheim (n.d., pp. 75-76, 435-438), Hocart (1917), the comments by Mauss on pp. 125-127; and Radcliffe-Brown (1957, pp. 119 ff.) on comparative epistemology.

Some of the further history of the topic, especially in European thought, is analyzed by Cassirer (1923); it is indicated here by such works as the pioneering essay of von Humboldt (1836), Steinthal (1850, 1860), Finck (1899), Cassirer (1923, 1933, 1944), Vossler (1913), Baudoin de Courtenay (1929), Weisgerber (1929, 1950a, 1950b, 1953-1954), Öhman (1951, 1953), Hartmann (1957a, 1957b), and some of the references cited with Newman's article in Part VI.

On Whorf, his views, and the issues raised by him, see the varied evaluations of Bedau (1957), Black (1959), Brown (1958, chap. 7), Carroll (1958), Fearing (1954), Fishman (1960), Gastil (1959), Greenberg (1954b), Heidbreder (1958), Henle (1958), Hoijer (1953, 1954a, 1954b), Hymes (1961b), Kluckhohn (1961), Lenneberg (1953), Longacre (1956), Osgood and Sebeok (1954, section 7: 4), Radnitzky (1961), Trager (1959), Waterman (1957). For another influential contribution to current interest, see the work of Lee (1938, etc.), as well as comment on it by Graves (1957) and Hoijer (1953). Hoijer (1954a) is a significant point in American anthropological discussion; cf. reviews by Garvin (1956), Goodenough (1955), Kluckhohn (1956), Malkiel (1956).

For recent experimental studies, see Brown (1956, 1957), Brown and Lenneberg (1958), Carroll and Casagrande (1958), Casagrande (1960), Ervin (1961-1962), Lenneberg and Roberts (1956), and discussion of their import in Greenberg (1959a) and Hymes (1961b).

Others who have posed the importance of the topic include Alexander (1936); Basson and O'Connor (1947), regarding philosophy; Sommerfelt (1938a), out of a long-standing interest of the school of Durkheim, Mauss, and Meillet; Ullmann (1957), in the context of semantics generally; Vygotsky (1962), a significant Russian and Werner and Kaplan (1956), both in regard to cognitive psychology. For a critique with special reference to philosophical thought, see Feuer (1953); on the much discussed relation of grammatical categories to philosophical thought compare Wells (in Levi-Strauss, *et al.* [1953], pp. 64-65) with Cassirer (1923, pp. 126-127, 254-255; 1942) and the discussions of Chinese cited below.

Whole-language and culture combinations and discussions of the case history sort include, besides Hoijer, Lee, and Whorf, Bally (1950, pp. 345 ff.); Capell (1960); Evans-Pritchard (1954a); Garvin (1949); Hymes (1961a, section 5); Muller (1945); Vossler (1925); and, especially regarding Chinese, Chang (1952), Chao (1959), Granet (1934, especially pp. 21, 31-34), Hockett (1954b), and Luh (1948).

On further aspects of the relation of language to culture, thought, and behavior, especially concerning vocabulary and semantic fields, see the references to articles in Part IV. On the problems of semantic description and analysis, see references to the article by Mathiot on pp. 154-163 and to the article by Frake on pp. 193-206.

References not in the general bibliography:

ALEXANDER, HUBERT G.

1936. Linguistic Morphology in Relation to Thinking. *Journal of Philosophy*, *33:* 261-269.

1937. Language and Metaphysical Truth. *Journal of Philosophy*, *34:* 645-652.

BASSON, A. H., and D. J. O'CONNOR

1947. Language and Philosophy: Some Suggestions for an Empirical Approach. *Philosophy*, *22:* 49-65.

BAUDOIN DE COURTENAY, J.

1929. *Einfluss der Sprache auf Weltanschauung und Stimmung*. Warsaw.

BEDAU, H. A.

1957. Review of J. B. Carroll (Ed.), *Language, Thought, and Reality*. *Philosophy of Science*, *24:* 289-293.

BLACK, MAX

1959. Linguistic Relativity: The Views of Benjamin Lee Whorf. *Philosophical Review*, *68:* 228-238. [Also in Black, *Models and Metaphors*. Ithaca: Cornell University Press, 1962. Pp. 244-258.]

CAPELL, A.

1960. Language and World View in the Northern Kimberley, Western Australia. *SJA*, *16:* 1-14.

CASAGRANDE, JOSEPH B.

1960. The Southwest Project in Comparative Psycholinguistics: A Preliminary Report. In Anthony F. C. Wallace (Ed.), *Men and Cultures*. Philadelphia: University of Pennsylvania Press. Pp. 777-782.

CASSIRER, ERNST

1933. Le Langage et la construction du monde des objets. In Pierre Janet and Georges Dumas (Eds.), *Phychologie du language*. Paris: Alcan. Pp. 18-44. [*Journal de Psychologie: normale et pathologique*, *30* (1-4).]

1942. The Influence of Language Upon the Development of Scientific Thought. *Journal of Philosophy*, *39:* 309-327. [Also, in *Journal de psychologie: normale et pathologique*, 1946, *39:* 129-152.]

CHANG, TUNG-SUN

1952. A Chinese Philosopher's Theory of Knowledge. *ETC.: A Review of General Semantics*, *9:* 203-226.

CHAO, YUEN-REN

1959. How Chinese Logic Operates. *AL*, *1:* 1-8.

ERVIN, SUSAN

1961-1962. Abstracts of Articles on Psycholinguistics. *IJAL*, *27:* 259-263; *28:* 205-209.

FEUER, LEWIS S.

1953. Sociological Aspects of the Relation Between Language and Philosophy. *Philosophy of Science*, *20:* 85-100.

FINCK, F. N.

1899. *Der deutsche Sprachbau als Ausdruck deutscher Weltanschauung*. Marburg.

FISHMAN, JOSHUA

1960. A Systematization of the Whorfian Hypothesis. *Behavioral Science*. *5:* 232-239.

GARVIN, PAUL L.

1956. Review of H. Hoijer (Ed.), *Language in Culture*. *AA*, *58:* 568.

GASTIL, RAYMOND D.

1959. Relative Linguistic Determinism. *AL*, *1* (9)*:* 24-38.

GIPPER, HELMUT (ED.)

1959. *Sprache, Schlüssel zur Welt. Festschrift für Leo Weisgerber*. Düsseldorf: Pädagogischer Verlag Schwann.

GOODENOUGH, W. H.

1955. Review of H. Hoijer (Ed.), *Language in Culture*. *Lg.*, *31:* 241-245.

GRAVES, ROBERT

1957. Comment on D. Lee, Lineal and Non-Lineal Codifications of Reality; Symbolization and Value. *Explorations*, *7:* 46-51, 67-73.

HARTMANN, PETER

1957a. *Wesen und Wirkung der Sprache im Spiegel der Theorie Leo Weisgerbers*. Heidelberg: Winter.

1957b. *Probleme der sprachlichen Form*. (Untersuchen zur allgemeinen Grammatik, No. 3). Heidelberg: Winter.

HEIDBREDER, EDNA

1958. Woodworth and Whorf on the Role of Language in Thinking. In G. S. Seward and J. P. Seward (Eds.), *Current Psychological Issues: Essays in Honor of Robert S. Woodworth*. New York: Holt.

HENLE, PAUL

1958. Language, Thought, and Culture. In Paul Henle, (Ed.), *Language, Thought, and Culture*. Ann Arbor: University of Michigan Press, Pp. 1-24.

HOIJER, HARRY

1959. Semantic Patterns of the Navaho Language. In Helmut Gipper (Ed.), *Sprache—Schlüssel zur Welt*. Düsseldorf: Pädagogischer Verlag Schwann. Pp. 369-373.

KLUCKHOHN, CLYDE

1956. Review of H. Hoijer (Ed.), *Language in Culture*. *AA*, *58:* 569-574. [A corrected version was circulated by Kluckhohn privately.]

LEE, DOROTHY DEMETRACOUPOULOU

1938. Conceptual Implications of an Indian Language. *Philosophy of Science*, *5:* 89-102.

1940a. A Primitive System of Values. *Philosophy of Science*, *7:* 355-378.

1940b. The Place of Kinship Terms in Wintu Speech. *AA*, *42:* 604-616.

1940c. Noun Categories in Wintu. *Zeitschrift für Vergleichende Sprachforschung*, *67:* 197-210.

1941. Some Indian Texts Dealing with the Supernatural. *Review of Religion*, May, pp. 403-411.

1943. The Linguistic Aspect of Wintu Acculturation. *AA*, *45:* 435-440.

1944a. Categories of the Generic and Particular in Wintu. *AA*, *46:* 362-369.

1944b. Linguistic Reflection of Wintu Thought. *IJAL*, *10:* 181-187. [Also in *Explorations*, 1956, *6:* 6-14, somewhat revised.]

1946. Stylistic Use of the Negative in Wintu. *IJAL*, *12:* 79-81.

1949. Being and Value in a Primitive Culture. *Journal of Philosophy*, *46:* 401-415.

1950a. Lineal and Non-lineal Codifications of Reality. *Psychosomatic Medicine*, *12:* 89-97. [Also in *Explorations*, 1957, *7:* 30-45.]

1950b. Notes on the Conception of the Self Among the Wintu Indians. *JASP*, *45:* 538-543.

1957. Symbolization and Value. *Explorations*, *7:* 56-66.

1959. *Freedom and Culture*. Englewood Cliffs, N.J.: Prentice-Hall (Spectrum Book S-6). [Includes 1944b, 1949, 1950a, 1950b, 1957 listed above.]

LONGACRE, ROBERT E.

1956. Review of W. Urban, *Language and Reality*, and B. L. Whorf, *Four Articles on Metalinguistics*. *Lg.*, *32:* 298-308.

LUH, CHIH-WEI

1948. Language Forms and Thought Forms. *Yenching Journal of Social Studies*, *4* (1): 107-119.

MALKIEL, YAKOV

1956. Review of H. Hoijer (Ed.), *Language in Culture*. *IJAL*, *22:* 77-84.

MILEWSKI, TADEUSZ

1954. Switaspoglad kilku plemion Indian polnocnoamerykanskich w swietle analizy kategorii rodzaju ich jezko. *Lud*, *41:* 153-182. [English summary: Tribal [Yuchi] Mentality and Grammatical Categories, pp. 1374-1376].

RADNITZKY, G. A.

1961. Some Remarks on the Whorfian Hypothesis. *Behavioral Science*, *6:* 153-157.

SAUVAGEOT, A.

1939. Problème de la structure interne et du bilinguisme. *Rapports du Ve Congrès International des Linguistes* (Brussels). Pp. 19-39.

STEINTHAL, H.

1850. *Die Classification der Sprachen, dargestellt als die Entwickelung der Sprachidee*. Berlin.

1860. *Charakteristik der hauptsächlichsten Typen des Sprachbaus*. Berlin.

VOSSLER, KARL

1913. *Frankreichs Kultur im Spiegel seiner Sprachentwickelung*. Heidelberg: Winter. (2nd ed., 1930.)

1925. *Geist und Kultur in der Sprache*. Heidelberg: Winter. (Translated by Oscar Oeser, as *The Spirit of Language in Civilization*. London: Routledge and Kegan Paul, 1932.)

WEISGERBER, LEO

1929. *Muttersprache und Geistesbildung*. Göttingen.

1950a. *Die Muttersprache im Aufbau unsrer Kultur*. Düsseldorf: Schwann.

1950b. *Vom Weltbild der deutschen Sprache*. Düsseldorf: Schwann.

1953-1954. *Vom Weltbild der deutschen Sprache I: Die inhaltbezogene Grammatik; II. Die sprachliche Erschliessung der Welt*. (2nd ed.) Düsseldorf: Schwann.

18 Noun Classes and Folk Taxonomy in Papago

MADELEINE MATHIOT

THE PURPOSE of this paper is not simply to test the Whorf hypothesis in the sense of asking whether there are "traceable affinities" between language and culture. Some such affinities can now be taken for granted. I would rather like to examine how such affinities can be traced and the degree of reliability with which this can be done on the basis of a pilot study rather than an extensive field investigation.

The language concerned is Papago, a Uto-Aztecan language of Arizona. The data under investigation are two sets of linguistic phenomena: a grammatical category and a set of word sub-classes partially defined in terms of this category, as further specified below. The grammatical category is that of number. It is formally marked by a morphemic process of reduplication. This morphemic process is not limited to nouns, but affects verbs and modifiers as well. The present discussion will, however, be limited to nouns. With nouns, the grammatical category of number contains three terms: singular, plural, and distributive.

The nouns considered in this study include only those which fit into the distributional frames mentioned below. For reasons of a common semantic property of these frames, such nouns are called quantifiable nouns. (Compare with Whorf's chapter on "Nouns of Physical Quantity in SAE and Hopi" [1941b].) On the basis of a casual survey of the lexicon, they seem to include the majority of the nouns in the language. These nouns constitute several sub-classes in terms of their participation in the category of number, which is a morphological criterion, and in terms of their occurrence in certain phrase-syntactic frames. Details are given in Table 1.

The classes of quantifiable nouns are: mass nouns, aggregate nouns, and individual nouns, as well as two mixed classes of aggregate-individual nouns. (This is a question similar to that asked by Whorf in regard to Hopi, but the Papago situation is more highly differentiated.)

TABLE 1

DIAGNOSTIC FRAMES FOR DEFINING NOUN CLASSES

Frame		
1:	ha (some, a little) hé?es (how much?)	+Noun nonreduplicated
2:	há?i (some, a few) hé?es (how many?)	+Noun nonreduplicated
3:	há?i (some, a few) hé?es (how many?)	+Noun reduplicated
4:	smú?ij (there is a lot of) há?akiaj (there is a certain number of)	+Noun nonreduplicated

Mass nouns fit frame 1 only.
Aggregate nouns fit frame 2 only.
Individual nouns fit frame 3 only.
Mixed (aggreg.-indiv.) nouns (type 1) fit either frame 2 or 3.
Mixed (aggreg.-indiv.) nouns (type 2) fit both frames 3 and 4.

What are then the cultural correlates, if any, of the grammatical category of number and what are those of the classes of quantifiable nouns? Of these two questions the one concerning noun classes seems to be more readily answerable for two reasons: (1) Nouns can be investigated lexically and one could expect correlations with more specific and therefore more readily ascertainable features of the culture than in the case of a grammatical category, since such a category is usually assumed to be related to more abstract characteristics of the culture. (2) We are here dealing with a more limited universe of data by comparison with the grammatical category which affects a large segment of the language.

Two methodological directions are possible in

relating linguistic to cultural data. (1) One can go from language to culture, i.e., examine the cultural content of linguistic classes. (2) One can go from culture to language, i.e., examine the linguistic content of cultural classes. Since our point of departure is a hypothesis about the cultural function of linguistic phenomena, the first methodological direction is primary, and only if it fails to yield satisfactory results will the second direction have to be tried.

With the class of mass nouns, the first technique gives immediate results. The class is small and a mere inspection of the members of the class is enough to suggest that there is a classificatory criterion for these nouns. Whorf's definition of English mass nouns applies here perfectly. "Mass nouns denote homogeneous continua without implied boundaries" (1941b). This cultural criterion is perceptual rather than conceptual, in that it is based on observable outward characteristics rather than on implied properties.

The perceptual boundary between mass nouns and other nouns is illustrated by the different class membership of "sand" (*ʔóʔohia*) and "gravel" (*ʔóʔoḍ*). "Sand" is a mass noun, whereas "gravel" (just as "beans") is an aggregate noun. Examples appear on Table 2.

TABLE 2

EXAMPLES OF MASS NOUNS
(PERCEPTUAL CRITERION: TEXTURE)

šúudaghi "water"	váaga "dough"
kavhíi "coffee"	gíighi "fat, tallow"
návait "wine"	múuñ hídoḍ "cooked beans"
ʔátol "gravy"	pósol "corn gruel"
kúlañ "medicine"	tókhi "cotton"
cúʔi "flour"	cévaghi "clouds"
ʔásugal "powdered granulated sugar"	mámḍhoḍ "water skum"
ʔón "salt"	hével "wind"
mátai "ashes"	júukhi "rain"
kúubs "dust"	gévhi "snow, ice"
ʔóʔohia "sand"	cúukug "meat"
jévuḍ "soil, ground"	páan "bread"
ʔía "saguaro fruit pulp"	lóoba "material"

Each of the two classes of individual and aggregate nouns, on the other hand, has a very large inventory. They include such heterogeneous entities as "coyote," "nose," "stone," "pennies," "wife," or "Mexican" among individual nouns, and "deer," "hair," "hailstones," "money," "servant," or "Papago" among aggregate nouns.

The two noun classes share one perceptual characteristic which differentiates both of them from the class of mass nouns, namely, they "denote bodies with definite outlines," (which is Whorf's definition of English individual nouns; see (1941b) [= Carroll (1956), p. 140]. It is interesting to note that in cases where there is a choice, that is to say, when the entity could be regarded either in terms of its texture or in terms of its shape, sometimes texture prevails, sometimes shape. Thus, both "cloud" and "cotton" are mass nouns, whereas "whirlwind" is an individual noun.

Unlike the above distinction, no principle of classification differentiating individual from aggregate nouns is apparent from a mere inspection of the members of each class. There is no apparent reason why entities of such similar nature as "deer" and "antelope," or "quail" and "woodpecker" should belong to different noun classes. Moreover, in testing the various nouns of the language in the diagnostic frames, no hesitation was ever observed on the part of the informant in regard to mass nouns, whereas some hesitation was observed in regard to aggregate and individual nouns. In addition, the language has mixed aggregate-individual classes but no mixed classes involving the mass nouns. We can therefore infer that the distinction between aggregate and individual nouns is more covert than that between mass nouns and the other nouns.

Since the first methodological direction of going from language to culture did not yield any results, the second, that of going from culture to language was explored. In trying to assign members of cultural classes to the two linguistic classes, the main problem was to decide what kind of cultural classes to select.

As a first attempt, certain common sense functional categories of entities were tried out. The selection of these categories was influenced by the concept then held of the nature of the distinction between individual and aggregate nouns. This conception was undoubtedly affected by the linguistic terminology employed. The lexical inventory of the following categories was inspected in the hope of finding a correspondence between them and the linguistic classes: domesticated vs. wild animals, animals living in groups vs. animals living individually, animals playing the role of human beings in myths and tales vs. nonhumanized animals, plants and animals used for food or medicinal purposes vs. those that are not, and so on.

No simple correlation emerged in terms of these categories. It was then decided to look instead for cultural categories which were independent of the investigator's frame of reference. Such cultural categories are given by folk taxonomy. Folk taxonomy, as discussed by H. Conklin (1962, p. 13), is the grouping of entities in terms of the category labels given to them by the culture, rather than by the observer's common sense or scientific knowledge. A technique for eliciting folk taxonomy can be based on the semantic substitution technique proposed by E. Nida (1961, p. 316).

Instead of ascertaining relations of substitutability, a relation of inclusion was used as the basis for an elicitation procedure. First a set of lexical units with the most general meanings relevant to a potential taxonomy were selected from the lexical file. These were utilized as the superior categories (X) of an inclusion hierarchy. The relation of inclusion was tested by submitting to the informant questions of the kind: Is A an X?, where A stands for any lexical unit with a meaning more specific than that of X, but still related to it.

By the use of this technique, three sets of folk taxonomic data were elicited: (1) broad taxonomic classes, (2) narrow taxonomic classes, and (3) taxonomic labels.

All three sets of data will now be examined in terms of the possible correlation of their lexical inventories with the classes of individual and aggregate nouns. These inventories are shown on Table 3.

TABLE 3

RELATION OF NOUN CLASSES TO FOLK TAXONOMY

I. Taxonomic Classes

Birds (ʔú ʔ uhhig)

Implicit folk taxonomy (perceptual criterion: flight habits)

Individual nouns	Aggregate nouns
báˀag "eagle"	kákaicu "quail"
ñúvhi "buzzard"	cúcul "chicken"
cúkuḍ "owl"	táḍai "road runner"
víšag "hawk"	kúukuˀul "burrowing owl"
ñépoḍ "nighthawk"	kóokoḍ "pelican (?), seagull (?)"
hávañ "crow"	šášañ "blackbird"
híkvig "woodpecker"	civicúuc "sandpiper"
ˀókokoi "white-winged dove"	pápalho "pigeon"
hógkaḍ "cactus wren"	vípismal "hummingbird"
šúug "mocking bird"	
hóhoi "mourning dove"	
kúḍuvic "bee martin"	
palóoma "dove"	

Plants (háˀicu mo vúušañ, lit.: "thing(s) that grow(s)")

Explicit folk taxonomy

1. Trees and bushes (háˀicu ˀúˀus, lit.: "stick things")
2. Cacti (hóˀi, lit.: "sticker(s)")
3. Cultivated seasonals (háˀicu ˀéˀes, lit.: "things planted from seeds")
4. Wild seasonals (héjel vúušñim, lit.: "growing by itself")
5. Unlabeled (wild perennials which are neither cacti nor trees and bushes)

Implicit folk taxonomy (perceptual criterion: shape)

1. Trees and bushes

Mixed (type 2) nouns	Aggregate nouns
kúi "mesquite"	ˀáan "desert broom"
ˀáuppa "cottonwood tree"	kóˀokmaḍk "a variety of paloverde"
ˀúupaḍ "catclaw"	kúkhi céhedaghi "a variety of paloverde"
hóˀidkam "ironwood"	mélhog "ocotillo"
šégai "greasewood, creosote bush"	kúavul "hackberry"
	ˀáago "crown-of-thorns"
	ˀúuḍvis "grapevine"
	hóhovai "jojoba bush"
	ˀónk "salt bush"
	tóhavs "brittlebush"
	taḍššaghi "bur-sage"

TABLE 3 *(continued)*

2. Cacti		
Mixed (type 2) nouns		Aggregate nouns
háašañ "saguaro"		cúcuis "organ pipe cactus"
		hánamhi "any variety of cholla cactus"
		náv "prickly pear cactus"
		ʔíisvig "hedgehog cactus"
		jíavul "barrel cactus"
3. Cultivated seasonals		
Mixed (type 2) nouns		Aggregate nouns
ʔíhug "devilsclaw"		pílkañ "wheat"
		múuñ "beans"
		húuñ "corn"
		víhol "peas"
		géphi "watermelon"
		háal "a variety of squash"
		šáʔaškaḍk "a variety of squash"
		ñépi "a variety of squash"
		ʔúuv hál "canteloupe"
		míloñ "melon"
		káañu "sorghum"
		kálvaš "chickpeas"
		láanji "lentils"
		sívul "onion"
		báabas "potatoes"
4. Wild seasonals		
Mixed (type 2) nouns		Aggregate nouns
ʔáḍavhi "buffalo-gourd"		šáaḍ "wild potatoes"
		hívijjul "canaigre"
		ban víivga "wild tobacco"
		cúhuggia ʔíivaghi "a variety of wild spinach"
		ʔópon "a variety of wild spinach"
		vépeghi vášai "tangleweed"
		víibam "milkweed"
		bíibhiag "morning glory"
5. Unlabeled		
		Aggregate nouns
		hói "Spanish bayonet"
		ʔáʔuḍ "agave, century plant"
		tákvui "yucca"
		móho "beargrass"
		ʔúmug "sotol"
		ʔúḍuvhag "cattails"
		váapk "reeds"
II. Taxonomic Labels		
Aggregate nouns		Individual nouns
hémajkam "people"	vs.	ʔáli "child"
		ʔúvhi "woman"
hájuñ "relative"	vs.	all kinship terms
háʔicu dóakam "animal"	vs.	most specific varieties of animals
ʔúʔuvhig "bird"	vs.	most specific varieties of birds
haivañ "cattle"	vs.	tóolo "bull"
		nóviu "castrated bull"
		vísilo "calf"
tótoñ "ant"	vs.	kúaḍaghi "a variety of ant"
tátam "tooth"	vs.	máccuḍ "molar"
ʔóʔohonakuḍ "instrument to write with"	vs.	láabis "pencil"
but:		Individual nouns
		ʔúus "tree or bush"
		vámaḍ "nonvenomous snake"
		múuval "fly-type or bee-type of insect"
		hújuḍ "lizard"

If we examine the distribution of aggregate and individual nouns in two broad taxonomic classes, on the one hand "living things" (*háʔicu dóakam*) which include animals, birds, and people, and on the other hand "growing things" (*háʔicu mo vúušañ*), i.e., plants, we note the following: (1) The class of "living things" contains both aggregate and individual nouns, although the great majority are individual nouns. (2) The class of "plants" contains no individual nouns. Most of the nouns are aggregate and only a few are mixed aggregate-individual (type 2) nouns.

In this set of data, there is thus a strong statistical trend towards a correspondence between cultural classes and linguistic classes. Living things are preponderantly individual nouns, plants are preponderantly aggregate nouns.

It appears from the above that the linguistic distinction between individual and aggregate nouns is utilized as a covert reinforcement of the overt taxonomic distinction between living things and plants. This distinction is close to the common grammatical distinction of animate vs. inanimate. There is, however, no morphological category of animateness in Papago. But there is this close statistical correspondence of individual to animate and aggregate to inanimate. (Compare with Whorf's discussion of of animateness as a cryptotype in Hopi [1956a, p. 79].) It was therefore reasonable to look for a formal criterion distinguishing animate from inanimate on a level of linguistic structure higher than the morphological. Such a formal criterion was found on the level of clause syntax.

A set of predicates was found which allows the unambiguous distinction between animate and inanimate subjects. These predicates are shown in Table 4.

TABLE 4
PREDICATES USED AS TEST FRAMES

to be standing pl. subject	animate nouns take "gégok" inaminate nouns take "cúuc"
or	
to be lying down pl. subject	animate nouns take "vóophi" inaminate nouns take "véec"

In terms of these criteria, plants are exclusively inanimate, whereas living things are exclusively animate. Thus, noun classes as defined on the clause syntax level turn out to be in a one-to-one correspondence to a broad folk taxonomic distinction. This, however, does not answer the question of the cultural significance of the distinction between individual and aggregate nouns, although it does provide us with a more restricted cultural universe of data within which to examine it further. As a next step, the further subdivision of both "living things" and "plants" in the folk taxonomy was examined.

The following subdivision of the broad class of "living things" was obtained:

1. "people" (*hémajkam*)
2. "birds" (*ʔúʔuvhig*)
3. "animals" (*háʔicu dóakam*). (Note that the same label applies to both "animals" and "living things.")

The following subdivision of "plants" was obtained:

1. "cacti" (*hóʔi*, lit.: sticker(s))
2. "trees and bushes" (*háʔicu ʔúʔus*, lit.: stick things). They include all plants with woody stems or trunks.
3. "cultivated seasonals" (*háʔicu ʔéʔes*, lit.: things planted from seeds)
4. "wild seasonals" (*héjel vúušñim*, lit.: growing by itself). Both "cultivated" and "wild seasonals" include plants with hollow or pithy stems for which there is a special name, "*váʔug*,' which is never applied to a tree, bush, or cactus.
5. A fifth subclass of plants exists, although no taxonomic tag was found for it. They are the wild perennials which can be defined negatively as not belonging with either cacti or trees and bushes.

For purposes of this paper, of all the subclasses of "living things," only "birds" were examined in some detail. All subclasses of "plants" were considered.

The question which arose was: Is there any significance to the fact that some birds are aggregate rather than individual nouns, and that some plants are mixed rather than aggregate nouns? In other words, what is the function of the linguistic distinction within a taxonomic class?

A second question was whether the linguistic distinction between two clearly distinct classes (individual vs. aggregate) has cultural correlates similar to that between two partially disctinct classes (agrregate vs. mixed)?

The class of "birds" and the various classes of "plants" will now be examined in turn. The lexical inventory of "birds" is illustrated in

Table 3. It can be seen that bird names which are aggregate nouns refer to birds that do not fly much, such as the road runner, the quail, and the chicken, whereas birds that "really" fly are individual nouns. Note that the distinction implicit in the linguistic difference is based on a perceptual criterion and that the distinction is one of degree.

In regard to plants, even the simple matter of the percentage of mixed nouns in the various narrow taxonomic classes is differential. Only one class, that of "trees and bushes," contains a sizable inventory of mixed nouns. The other three classes, those of "cacti," "cultivated seasonals," and "wild seasonals," have only one mixed noun each. The fifth class, that of wild perennials, has none.

In the case of the cacti and cultivated seasonals, an effort was made to get a fairly exhaustive collection; thus, the ratio of aggregate to mixed nouns is not simply a result of inadequate sampling.

The class of "trees and bushes" is distributed over the noun classes of aggregate and mixed as follows: Mixed nouns are the names for plants such as "mesquite," "cottonwood," and "catclaw." Most of them seem to share the characteristic of being tree-like plants, i.e., they have a trunk and real leaves. Aggregate nouns are the names for plants such as "ocotillo," "desert broom," and all the bushes. Most of them seem to share the characteristic of being bush-like plants, i.e., they grow from the ground up in an undifferentiated mass of branches and leaves. Note that this distinction is again perceptual. It is again one of degree.

In the case of the three other taxonomic classes of plants, the names of the following plants stand out as mixed nouns in each class: (a) the saguaro among the "cacti," (b) the devilsclaw among the "cultivated seasonals", (c) the buffalo-gourd among the "wild seaonals."

Each of these three plants has some unique characteristics as compared to the other plants in its class: (a) the saguaro cactus has a strikingly different appearance as compared to other cacti, (b) the devilsclaw bush has pods unlike any other cultivated seasonals, (c) the buffalo-gourd is the only wild seasonal to have gourds. In each of these classes, one member is linguistically contrasted with the rest, and also turns out to have a unique characteristic of shape.

The two questions asked about the relation of noun class to narrow folk taxonomic class were answered as follows, although these answers are as yet far from being conclusive: (1) The linguistic class distinction appears to indicate a further subdivision of the narrow taxonomic class in terms of a perceptual criterion. It thus constitutes an implicit taxonomic difference, in addition to the explicit folk taxonomy which can be elicited through informant work. (2) Linguistic class distinctions appear to have the same type of cultural correlates, whether they are clear-cut or mixed.

In view of the connection between noun classes and folk taxonomy, and in view of the function of taxonomic labels in establishing taxonomic classes, it was considered a logical next step to examine the linguistic class membership of these labels.

The examination showed the following rough statistical breakdown of folk taxonomic labels in terms of noun classes: (a) none of them are mass nouns, (b) most of them are aggregate nouns, (c) a few are individual nouns.

As can be seen in Table 3, for a number of cases outside of plant names, it seems that when the taxonomic label is an aggregate noun, the names grouped under it tend to be individual nouns. From the above it can be inferred that another function of the linguistic distinction between individual and aggregate nouns is to provide a means of distinguishing between different levels of abstraction. This hypothesis, although suggestive, remains as yet unverified.

I will now turn to a discussion of the category of number. As was stated previously, the grammatical category of number, for the nouns, consists of three terms: singular, plural, and distributive, and is formally expressed by the morphemic process of reduplication. (Compare with Whorf's chapter on "Plurality and numeration in SAE and Hopi," 1941b.)

The plural is limited to a single noun class, that of individual nouns. The distributive can occur with any noun. The semantic distinction between plural and distributive can best be studied with the class of individual nouns, in which both occur in contrast. Both plural and distributive express the quantitative distinction of one versus more than one. They contrast in that the plural indicates more than one entity in the same location or time, whereas the distributive indicates more than one entity in different locations or at different times.

The distinction between plurality and distributiveness is therefore "geometric" rather than "arithmetic." It involves degrees of multiplicity, viewed, however, not from a numerical standpoint (as in the case of the well-known distinction between dual and plural), but from the standpoint of dispersion: several entities in the same location or at the same time are less dispersed than several entities in different locations or at different times. Thus the plural can be regarded as an intermediate step between complete collocation (the singular) and complete dispersion (the distributive).

It is interesting to note that the opposition between collocation and dispersion, which seems to manifest the Papago conception of multiplicity, is a perceptual rather than a conceptual one, since it is tied to the basic perceptual categories of time and space (which, incidentally, are not differentiated in Papago).

I will now compare the results of my examination of the cultural correlates of noun classes and of the category of number. A first observation relates to the importance of perceptual criteria in the classification of experience in Papago language and culture. This is borne out not only by the singling out of mass nouns, but also by the criteria used in implicit folk taxonomy as well as by the semantic nature of the number category. A second observation is that the two linguistic patterns investigated in this paper, the noun classes and the category of number, each show gradual rather than yes/no binary oppositions. Whether this is a characteristic feature of the entire system remains to be investigated. It is tempting, however, to suggest that if this turned out to be the case, i.e., if the system indeed showed a preponderance of gradual over binary oppositions, then one might infer a possible correlation between this characteristic on the one hand, and culturally conditioned perception and behavior on the other. Such an inference would imply that Papago perception and behavior are along a sliding scale rather than in terms of a two-valued logic.

Let me cite an anecdotal corroboration of this inference: I was told of a Papago who quit his job of sorting oranges because he found it impossible to make up his mind about good and bad oranges.

In conclusion, it is important to stress the varying degrees of reliability of our findings. Four general types of inferences were drawn in the course of this study: one relating to implicit folk taxomony, one relating to the geometric rather than arithmetic conception of the number category, one relating to the sliding-scale rather than two-valued nature of Papago thinking, and finally, one relating to the predominance of perceptual over conceptual criteria in the Papago classification of experience. (Ruth Underhill, in a personal communication [April 26, 1961], tells me: "From a psychological standpoint, I agree decidedly with your suggestion of a 'sliding' approach in Papago thinking, rather than yes or no propositions. I met it often.

"Your other statement as to perceptual criteria is probably correct also. At least, I met nothing to the contrary. I was impressed by the fact that Papagos would make no judgements of people by report or by letters from Washington. They had to watch an individual in action. For instance, when a new person came to live in a village, he might be a refugee from some other place where he had misbehaved. I asked: 'Would you send someone to the other village to ask about him?' This surprised the informant who answered: 'Oh no. We would just wait and watch him.' ")

The first two inferences are, in essence, an elaboration of a statement of linguistic meaning. They are verifiable, and have been partially validated, by direct manipulation of linguistic and cultural behavior. They are, in addition, strengthened by supportive evidence from other linguistic levels. The third inference, at this stage, constitutes no more than a generalization suggested by the characteristics of particular linguistic patterns, which has been only incidentally related to some cultural observations. However, as was stated above, this inference is capable of further verification by additional linguistic and cultural research. The fourth inference, on the other hand, is based entirely on the observer's own interpretation of the cultural correlates of linguistic phenomena. This last inference represents an additional level of abstraction, since it is a second-order inference based on the first two inferences. It is therefore furthest removed from direct linguistic and cultural observation, and will allow definitive verification only by means of specifically designed psychological tests.

In terms of the above, two closely related criteria of reliability can be set forth: (1) the extent to which a given inference has already been validated; (2) the extent and nature of additional verification needed to validate a given inference.

At the present stage of the analysis, therefore, these criteria permit an ordering of the four inferences in terms of reliability as follows: although none of them is conclusive, (1) and (2) are more reliable than (3), and (3) in turn is more reliable than (4).

REFERENCE NOTE

This paper was presented in the session on language and culture of the Annual Meeting of the Southwestern Anthropological Association, Santa Barbara, March 31-April 1, 1961. The data were collected under contract to the Franciscan Province of St. Barbara, Office of the Provincial, Oakland, California.

On the analysis of vocabulary and general approaches to meaning, see the references in Part IV.

On the description and analysis of GRAMMATICAL CATEGORIES, with particular reference to systems of pronouns, see Austerlitz (1959), Conklin (1962, pp. 133-136), Harris (1948), Hjelmslev (1957), Hocart (1918), Householder (1955), Jakobson (1957b), Krupa and Altmann (1961), McKaughan (1959), Merrifield (1959), Thomas (1955), Trager (1961), and Wonderly (1952). With particular reference to cases and prepositions, see Benveniste (1949), De Groot (1956), Hjelmslev (1935-1937), Jakobson (1936, 1958), Lotz (1949), Sebeok (1946), and Velten (1932). With particular reference to verbal categories, see Bull (1960), Garey (1957), Householder (1954), Jakobson (1957b), Lotz (1962), Ruiperez (1953), Van Holk (1953), and Velten (1931). Some implications of Jakobson (1957b) are suggested in Hymes (1961a).

For discussions of the origins of grammatical categories, note also Boas (1920b, 1942), Cassirer (1923), Durkheim (n.d.), Fodor (1959), Malinowski (1923), Sommerfelt (1942), and Velten (1932).

For general treatments and surveys, see Gleason (1961, chap. 14), Gray (1939), Hockett (1958, chap 27), Jespersen (1924), Kantor (1936, pp. 324-328 [bibliography]), Leopold (1929), Sapir (1921, chaps. 4-5), Vendryes (1925, Part 2, chaps. 2-3), Voegelin (1952a), and Whorf (1938, 1945.)

On points of method and approach, see, in addition to many of the studies already cited, Garvin (1958), Hoijer (1954b, 1959). Meillet (1928), Newman (1954), Sørensen (1958), Trager (1961), Voegelin (1948, 1952b), and references to Frake's article in Part IV.

References not in the general bibliography:

AUSTERLITZ, ROBERT

1959. Semantic Components of Pronoun Systems: Gilyak. *Word, 15:* 102-109.

BENVENISTE, EMILE

1949. Le Système sublogique des prepositions en Latin. *Travaux du Cercle Linguistique de Copenhague, 5:* 177-184.

BULL, WILLIAM E.

1960. *Time, Tense, and the Verb: A Study in Theoretical and Applied Linguistics, with Particular Attention to Spanish.* (University of California Publications in Linguistics, No. 19.) Los Angeles: University of California Press.

DE GROOT, A. W.
1956. Classification of Cases and Uses of Cases. *For Roman Jakobson*. The Hague: Mouton. Pp. 187-194.

FODOR, I.
1959. The Origin of Grammatical Gender, I, II. *Lingua*, *8:* 1-41, 186-218.

GAREY, HOWARD B.
1957. Verbal Aspect in French. *Lg.*, *33:* 91-110.

GARVIN, PAUL L.
1958. A Descriptive Technique for the Treatment of Meaning. *Lg.*, *34:* 1-32.

HARRIS, ZELLIG S.
1948. Componential Analysis of a Hebrew Paradigm. *Lg.*, *24:* 87-91.

HJELMSLEV, LOUIS
1957. Animé et inanimé; personnel et non personnel. *Travaux de l'Institut de Linguistique* (Université de Paris), *1:* 155-199. [Also Hjelmslev, *Essais Linguistiques*. (Travaux du Cercle Linguistique de Copenhague, No.12.) Copenhagen: Nordisk Sprog—og Kulturforlag, 1959. Pp. 211-219.]

HOIJER, HARRY
1959. Semantic Patterns of the Navaho Language. In Helmut Gipper (Ed.), *Sprache—Schlüssel zur Welt*, Düsseldorf: Pädagogischer Verlag Schwann. Pp. 361-374.

HOUSEHOLDER, FRED W.
1954. Review of E. A. Hahn, *Subjunctive and Optative*. *Lg.*, *30:* 389-399.
1955. Review of P. Forchheimer, *The Category of Person in Language*. *Lg.*, *31:* 93-99.

JAKOBSON, ROMAN
1936. Beiträge zur allgemeinen Kasuslehre. *Travaux du Cercle Linguistique de Prague*, *6:* 240-288.
1958. Morofologiceskie nablujudenija nad slavjanskim skloneniem (Sostav russkix padeznyx form). In *American Contributions to the Fourth International Congress of Slavicists* (Moscow, 1958). (Slavistic Printings and Reprintings, No. 21.) 's-Gravenhage: Mouton. [Reviewed, A. M. Schenker, *Lg.*, 1959, *35:* 656-666.]

KRUPA, V., and G. ALTMANN
1961. Semantic Analysis of the System of Pronouns in [the] Indonesian Language. *Archiv Orientální*, *29* (4): 620-625. Prague.

LEOPOLD, WERNER
1929. Inner Form. *Lg.*, *5:* 254-260.

LOTZ, JOHN
1949. The Semantic Analysis of the Nominal Bases in Hungarian. *Travaux de Cercle Linguistique de Copenhague*, *5:* 185-197.
1962. Semantic Analysis of the Tenses in Hungarian. *Lingua*, *11:* 256-262.

MCKAUGHAN, HOWARD
1959. Semantic Components of Pronoun Systems: Maranao. *Word*, *15:* 101-102.

MEILLET, A.
1928. Sur la Terminologie de la morphologie générale. *Revue des études hongroises*. Pp. 9 ff. [Also in Meillet, *Linguistique Historique et Linguistique*

Générale. (2nd ed.) (Collection Linguistique, La Société de Linguistique de Paris, No. 8.) Paris: Champion, 1926-1936. (Reprinted 1938-1948.) Vol. 2, pp. 29-35.]

MERRIFIELD, W. R.
1959. The Kiowa Verb Prefix. *IJAL, 25:* 168-176.

NEWMAN, S. S.
1954. Semantic Problems in Grammatical Systems and Lexemes: A Search for Method. In Harry Hoijer (Ed.), *Language and Culture* (Comparative Studies of Cultures and Civilizations, No. 3.) Chicago: University of Chicago Press, 1954. Pp. 82-91. [Also, The American Anthropological Association, Memoir 79.]

RUIPEREZ, M. S.
1953. The Neutralization of Morphological Oppositions as Illustrated by the Neutral Aspect of the Present Indicative in Classical Greek. *Word, 9:* 241-252.

SEBEOK, THOMAS A.
1946. Finnish and Hungarian Case Systems: Their Form and Function. *Acta Instituti Hungarici Universitatis Holmiensis.* (Series B, Linguistica 3.) Stockholm.

SOMMERFELT, ALF
1942. The Social Origin of Linguistic Categories. *Man, 52:* 137.

SØRENSEN, HELGER STEEN
1958. *Word-Classes in Modern English, with Special Reference to Proper Names, with an Introductory Theory of Grammar, Meaning, and Reference.* Copenhagen: Gad.

THOMAS, DAVID
1955. Three Analyses of the Ilocano Pronoun System. *Word, 11:* 204-208.

TRAGER, GEORGE L.
1961. Taos IV: Morphemics, Syntax, Semology in Nouns and in Pronominal Reference. *IJAL, 27:* 211-222.

VAN HOLK, G. F.
1953. *The Semantic Spectrum of the Russian Infinitive.* Leiden: A. W. Sijthoff's Uitgeversmaatschappij N. V. [Reviewed, F. J. Whitfield, *Lg.*, 1954, *30:* 521-522.]

VELTEN, H. V.
1931. On the Origin of the Categories of Voice and Aspect. *Lg., 7:* 229-241.
1932. The Accusative Case and Its Substitutes in Various Types of Languages. *Lg., 8:* 255-270.

VOEGELIN, C. F.
1948. Distinctive Features and Meaning Equivalence. *Lg., 24:* 132-135.
1952b. Linguistically Marked Distinctions in Meanings. In Sol Tax, (Ed.), *Indian Tribes of Aboriginal North America.* (Selected Papers of the 29th International Congress of Americanists.) Chicago: University of Chicago Press. Pp. 222-233.

WONDERLY, WILLIAM L.
1952. Semantic Components in Kechua Person Morphemes. *Lg., 28:* 366-376.

part IV

CULTURAL FOCUS AND SEMANTIC FIELD

Introduction

SINCE BEFORE BOAS FIRST MENTIONED four Eskimo words for "snow," anthropologists have taken elaboration of vocabulary as an indication of the interests of particular cultures and of differences among them. The fundamental question asked has been, In what way is a language an index of its associated culture?

One must stress that the answer is an interesting and not obvious one. If language were an exact mirror of culture, to use an image often cited, so that entries in a complete dictionary and the contents of a complete ethnography were in one-to-one relationship, ethnography, indeed, might dispense with linguistic work, since the results of the latter would be isomorphic, after all, with ethnography done without it. If, on the other hand, language were a perfect and inseparable symbolism of culture, to use another frequent interpretation, then ethnography might reduce to a branch of linguistics. In point of fact, ethnography can neither eschew lexicography nor become identical with it. The heart of the matter is that cultural categories are lexically expressed, not automatically, but selectively. The relation between cultural categories and language is problematic. In a particular culture a language serves as a sort of "metalanguage," a cultural way of communicating about much, but not all, of the culture. Thus, the modified question, To what extent and in what ways is a language an index of its associated culture, should be of considerable interest.

Cases of lexical elaboration have tended to be noticed especially in terms of response to matters of environmental and ecological importance (e.g., baskets, cattle, reindeer, yams, snow), but some elaborations of vocabulary would enable one to place a culture geographically and some would not. For example, the many Yana terms for baskets and acorns by themselves would identify a California Indian tribe; but the many terms having to do with eyes and sight indicate an individual concern, one that so far as I know would not have been predicted and does not depend on environment. (The Yana are not reported to have had more eyes, or kinds of eyes, than other people.) Beyond such subtler differences of foci, peoples may differ in the degree to which they exploit the "metacultural," more strictly, referential, function of language, not only in particular areas, but across the board. Contrastive analyses of similar and adjacent peoples would be revealing and lead to a knowledge of the variables involved in lexical formation and elaboration that gross contrasts between distant groups do not afford. Presumably the net result in a given case is a balance struck between selective interest and adaptive need. The question is important for the renewed interest in studying culture and personality in the light of their cognitive aspects.

In pursuing such problems, one broaches the related question, To what extent and in what ways is the vocabulary of a language structured (or amenable to structural analysis)? This question is inseparable from the task of developing methods of semantic analysis and lexicographic statement along structural lines, a task in the forefront of interest for many anthropologists and linguists at the present time (e.g., recent work of Voegelin, Lounsbury, Goodenough, Conklin, Frake, Nida, Joos, Haugen, Weinreich, and others).

Much of the existing work has been done in terms of the concept of semantic field (or in Voegelin's usage, "domain"), a concept developed mainly in Europe. In American anthropology the field of kinship has been the most extensively studied, followed perhaps by numerals and color terms, with lesser attention to names of persons, places, and creatures. The concentration of attention on fields whose structuring seems more obvious, or more obviously grounded in extralinguistic factors, should not obscure the fact that the basic problem and principle of structural analysis can and does apply to all sectors of vocabulary (as Frake's analysis of disease terms in this part shows so well).

In the field of kinship, much of the anthropological dispute has turned on two issues: (1) the extent to which kinship terminology matches social categories and (2) the extent to which the structure of one is to be accounted for in terms of that of the other. Alongside the significance of grammatical categories, the significance of kinship terms has been anthropology's "language-and-culture" problem *par excellence* (see the analysis by Levi-Strauss in Part I), as well as a favorable and favored testing-ground for methods of structural and semantic analysis.

Some sectors of vocabulary have been cultivated independently, although usually not structurally, especially by European scholarship, under special headings such as toponymy, anthroponymy, *Wörter-und-Sachen*, or onomastics or onomatology. The linking of this detailed experience with structural perspective will be fruitful for both anthropology and linguistics.

In considering the concept of cultural focus, so named and defined by Herskovits (1950, pp. 542 ff.), one must go beyond the static index aspect of vocabulary to a broader range of questions of process and function. Herskovits suggests that a focal area of culture will receive greater elaboration and be more subject to change. A second question is whether or not the presence or degree or kind of structuring in a lexical domain depends upon its being a focus of interest for a particular culture or group.

(Weinreich has put this in terms of the extent to which an area of vocabulary is "terminologized" [1963].) A third question is the lexical counterpart of that posed in Part III, the role played by linguistic categories in daily life. Structural analysis delineates the categories, and attention to elaboration brings out their character as reflections of, or better, adaptations to, social and natural environments (cf. Sapir, 1912). Such lexical categories, however, can also exercise a determinative role in individual experience and culture. Moreover, this may be quite apart from presence of special elaboration. (For a theory of cognition and personality which incorporates new approaches to semantic analysis as an integral part, see Wallace, 1961.)

In one of the few detailed toponymic studies in American anthropology, Boas investigates the interplay of environment, cultural life, and linguistic form. After surveying the content of terms among the Kwakiutl, he compares several American Indian groups, particularly the Kwakiutl and Eskimo, regarding the link between types of term and available linguistic processes. The conclusion would seem to be that cultural interests are the major factor in terminology, but that the selectivity of linguistic form affects the kinds of terms that occur and their frequency, and hence, by implication, perhaps something of the concepts and experience of the speakers of the language.

Lotz points out how the structure of one semantic field, numerals, can shape the goals striven for in a major cultural activity, such as sports. His analysis suggests the pervasive influence of favored numerical units in other aspects of our lives. (Note Boas' mention of other lexical influence on culture in Part I.)

Goodenough first shows the danger in imputing a particular semantic field and cultural content to grammatical classifications, especially on the a priori basis of conventional ("etic") labels such as "possession." Indicating with examples the actual Truk conceptual use of nominal "possession," he turns to Truk property and exchange relations proper and supports in a more specific and empirical way the principle argued by Mauss (in Part II), that major social categories need not find regular linguistic expression and hence language is indeed a selective index to culture. At the same time Goodenough reports that if linguistic forms and categories could not help in making the cultural analysis, structural concepts drawn from linguistic methodology did.

Conklin demonstrates that languages may differ not only in their segmentation of a semantic field, such as color, but also in the dimensions of the semantic fields themselves. His work shows that it is essential procedure to discover the questions members of the cultures themselves would ask in classifying objects and the dimensions such questions imply, to study contrast in well-defined situations with indigenous stimuli, and to recognize the existence of levels of categorization.

Frake presents a semantic analysis sparked by the necessity of coping with certain fields as foci of conversation in the culture he studied. The paper is important for its procedural care, the handling of levels of contrast in relation to native questions and responses, and the sociolinguistic hypothesis that "the greater the number of distinct social contexts in which information about a particular phenomenon must be communicated, the greater the number of different levels of contrast into which that phenomenon is categorized." (See Meillet, 1906b, for a complementary hypothesis concerning the number of distinct senses a term acquires.) Frake offers this as an explanation for cross-cultural differences in hierarchical elaboration of terminology in a field, as opposed to notions of different capacity for abstract thought. Note also the critical discussion of use of western scientific taxonomies in analyzing folk taxonomies, and the difference between Subanun agreement on the criteria defining categories of diseases and their disagreement regarding application to a particular case.

19 On Geographical Names of the Kwakiutl Indians

FRANZ BOAS

INTRODUCTORY

F. J. Egli in his *Nomina geographica* (Leipzig, 1893, 2nd ed.) has demonstrated that geographical names, being an expression of the mental character of each people and each period, reflect their cultural life and the line of development belonging to each cultural area. To this statement should be added, that the form of each language limits the range of terms that can be coined.

In the following pages the geographical nomenclature of the Kwakiutl Indians of British Columbia will be discussed from these points of view. At the same time the localization of the legendary history of the tribe will be briefly described [omitted here].

THE MEANINGS OF NAMES OF PLACES

The geographical terminology of the Kwakiutl is that of a sea-faring people to whom the forms of land and water and the dangers of the sea are all-important and who obtain their subsistence both from the sea and from the land.

Instead of the points of the compass they orient themselves according to the direction of the coastline and rivers. Down river and down along the coast (in the sense of northward or westward); up river and up the coast (in the sense of southward or eastward); inland, away from sea or river; and seaward, away from land, are the principal directions which appear commonly in geographical terms. (Cf. *gwa-* "down river"; *n'əl-* "up river"; *a:ƛ-* "inland"; *ƛ'a:s-* "seaward.") According to this terminology the extreme north is also "at the mouth of the river."

Geographical terms refer often to the specific location of a place. This is often defined according to its position relative to the principal directions. Such are "down river"; "down river corner beach"; "beach facing down river"; "hind end down river" (i.e., westward); "behind the part downstream" (cf. *gwa-*);—"up river side"; "beach facing up river"; "hind end up river" (i.e., eastward) (cf. *n'əl-*);—"inland side"; "region alongside inland"; "facing inland" (cf. *a:λ-*); —"seaward point"; "seaside"; "beach seaward opposite" (cf. *λ'á:s-*).

In some cases the term *nəq-* "straight," may be used to designate location, as in "beach straight in front"; "right in the middle on the water"; "middle of the beach"; "middlemost"; "straight out to sea"; —or *ma:ky-* "near," as in "near rock"; "near ground"; "near end"; —*ge:'-* "across," as in "lying across on rock"; "end lying across"; "lying across behind"; —*ma:s-* "lengthwise," as in "rock lying lengthwise"; "stretching lengthwise inside (a bay)"; "hind end lying lengthwise."

The structure of the language permits the expression of the terms "down river, up river, landward, seaward," by means of suffixes; but local names based on such compositions are rare, probably because the suffixes express primarily movement. Examples are *é:wult'ala*, of somewhat doubtful derivation (*-ult'a:la* "movement out towards the open sea"); *ó:sde:səla* "going up the beach."

Among terms expressing location may be mentioned the innumerable terms for islands. The term for island *m'əkyɔ́la* is derived from *m'əkw-* "a round thing is somewhere"; and *-ɔla* "on the water." Derived from *m'əkw* —we have "island at point"; "island in opening"; "island at foot (of mountain)";

"body of island in front"; "island in neck (of river)." All these indicate the position of an island in reference to its position, or the position of points in reference to islands near by.

Some locations are designated as points from which a prominent place, or the goal of a journey may be sighted: *dó:x'walic'e:ne:'* "the seeing of the beach (namely at the head of Knight Inlet)"; *dó:gune:gwis* "seeing the corner of the beach"; *do:xc'ɔ'las* "place of looking inside"; *dá:doqwanage:səla* "looking all around (?)."

A large number of terms are descriptive of form or appearance, so much so that from the topographical features the name might often be guessed, unless it so happens that specific interests attached to the place interfere with the descriptive nomenclature. Thus a long inlet is called "long inside"; and we have "long beach"; "long body"; "long point" (cf. *gyilt-*); —"small, round beach"; "small round (passage) through"; "having small, round opening in middle" (cf. *t'o:qw-*); —"high point"; "high corner" (cf. *e:ky'*); —"wide inside" (cf. *le:x-*).

Here belong particularly the numerous terms formed from the indefinite nominal *o:-* (*aw-* before vowels) with attached locative suffixes. As examples may be mentioned "point"; "passage"; "inside"; "mouth of river"; "hind end"; and compounds of *o:-* with several suffixes, such as "beach at forehead"; "meadow at small opening"; "rocky flat." Names taken from parts of the body occur in this group, but they are not very common. We find "cheek"; "back"; "forehead"; "body"; "neck"; and compositions of *o:-* with body part suffixes that are otherwise not used as independent nouns: "foot (of mountain)"; "end on hand (i.e., branching delta of river, or branching mountain ridges)."

The description of places depends not only upon their form, but also upon the aspect from which they excite interest. Among these the demands of navigation are the most important. Places with heavy swell are designated accordingly: "having swell"; "swell inside" (cf. *t,o:xw-*); —"breakers at rear end"; "breakers" (cf. *λ'əky-*) are names of this kind. Related are terms expressing the occurrence of foam, "foam beach"; "foam site" (cf. *axw-*). The winds appear in names like "having wind"; "receptacle of northwest wind"; "(sail) tearing place"; the tides in "tide point"; "tide on beach"; "tide running alongside." The depth of water characterizes places like "deep inside"; "deep beach at hind end" (cf. *wunq-*); —shallowness, places like "shallow rock"; "shallow in middle on water"; "shallow in places inside" (cf. *q'axw-*); —places running dry, "dry behind"; "dry in middle beach" (cf. *se:q-*). Travel by water is directly referred to in terms like "place of paddling to end of beach"; "place of paddling through" (cf. *se:xw-*). Shelter against wind and sea gives names to many places: "having shelter"; "having shelter alongside"; "shelter point"; "calm water" (cf. *q'o:qw-*); —*hé:naxc'ə'was* "place of refuge inside."

Here may also be mentioned names of campsites that are frequented in canoe travel: "campsite" (= "fire"); "place of fire (camp) in middle"; "place for stopping on the way."

Travel by land is not unimportant as indicated by the numerous place names of trails: "trail"; "place of trail"; "trail behind neck (of mountain)."

Rivers are specified as large or small, sometimes according to their location, but few seem to have true names. One of these is *gwá'ne:*, the river flowing out of Nimkish Lake. Generally they are called "river of such and such a place." We find "little river"; "little river" (a second diminutive); "principal river"; "real river"; "river behind" (cf. *wa*).

Lakes also are generally merely specified as to position: "lake on ground"; "lake in middle (of river)."

Prominent mountains have names; some according to striking features, like "gulches"; "raven face"; or on account of their size, like "elder brother" (i.e., the greatest mountain).

Many names indicate the material characteristic of the place, or peculiarities of its appearance. We have, for instance, "having sandstone"; "sandstones on surface"; "quartzite"; "rocky surface"; "rolled (stones)"; "sandy beach." Color is sometimes expressed: "red ground"; "red beach"; "place with green patches"; "white beach"; "grey faced"; "having grey color"; "painted"; "striped hollow place (lit.: stripe receptacle)." Places characterized by trees or being bare of trees are named accordingly: "(trees) standing on surface of beach"; "having (trees) standing on rock"; "(tree) standing on beach"; "(tree) standing at rear end"; "bare in middle"; "bare rock."

Burnt woods appear quite often: "burnt surface"; "burnt rock"; "burnt inside beach." Evidently many of these names cannot be very old, since in course of time on burnt places woods will spring up again. The same may be said of places on which deciduous trees grow; like "alder beach"; "birch trees at mouth of river," although in some cases the soil may favor such growth to the exclusion of coniferous trees. Here belong also place names derived from *ky'e:t-* "grass": "grassy beach"; "grassy point"; "grass body."

Cascades and rapids have on the whole, only generic names. Rockslides are used as designations: "rockslide on beach"; "rockslide"; and "trembling place" (on account of rock slides); "place of rumbling noise."

Other names taken from local forms are: "gulches" (mentioned before); "forked end"; "forked top"; "parted hair (name of a mountain)"; "bad smell coming up from beach"; "bad smell coming out of it"; "squeaking beach" (because the sand squeaks when walked upon); "two heads" (so called from two stones of peculiar shape); "scarred" (a mountain in Knight Inlet); "raven face" (a mountain with a form resembling a raven, mentioned before).

A large number of names designate places as those where useful objects may be found, particularly food and useful trees. It is not surprising that river fish, fruits, shellfish, and land animals are principally so used, because most sea animals are not as sharply localized as the salmon in rivers, fruits and trees in patches, clams on beaches. It is hardly necessary to enumerate many of these: with the ending *-ad* "having," we find "having humpback salmon"; "having olachen"; "having sockeye salmon"; "having spring salmon"; "having trout"; —"having horse clams"; "having clams"; "having mussels"; "having sea eggs"; "having spider crabs"; "having herring spawn"; also "having poisonous clams." For fruits we have: "having blueberries"; "having elderberries"; "having salal berries"; "having salmon berry shoots"; "having Viburnum berries"; "having berry picking." For trees we find for instance "having yellow cedar"; "having cedar bark."

With the ending *-as* "place of," we have: "place of mussels on rock"; "place where one tries to get grizzly bears"; "porpoise place"; "land otter place"; "halibut fishing beach place"; "mountain goat place"; "place for fishing humpback salmon."

With the ending *-ac'* "receptacle," we have: "receptacle for Viburnum berries"; "elderberry receptacle."

House sites, or rather village sites, are often so named: "house site on rock"; "house site on beach"; "house site on ground"; "house site at foot (of mountain)"; "house on rock"; "house in middle." We have also "hunter's lodge."

The houses are sometimes built on foundations of crossed logs: "piled crosswise"; "piled crosswise on beach"; "piled crosswise on rock". Some of these may not refer to foundations, although the Indians so interpret them, but rather to the masses of driftwood piled up on the beach.

Villages have their forts, *x̣usə́la*, which are named according to their positions: "fort-point"; "fort on flat beach"; "fort at mouth."

Graveyards of the villages are often named: "having grave on point"; "grave on ground"; "grave on chest (i.e., halfway up a hill)"; "having grave on side."

The number of names that refer to the social customs and beliefs of the people is small. *Yílx̣ume:'* "head hanging from stake" and *yílx̣wdə'ma* "site where heads are hung on rock," refer to the war custom of cutting of the heads of slain enemies and hanging them from stakes or from horizontal poles resting on a frame work.

A few places are called "place of shredded cedarbark on rock," from the custom of burying infants' bedding there under stones.

"Place of *Há:naƛe:'no*" refers to the ancestor of one of the subdivisions of the *Q'ó:moyɔ'ye:* (*Kwé:xa*) of the *Kwá:gyuł*, who is said to have originated at that place.

Among names referring to mythical beings, *nó:mas* "old man," is the most common. Almost every dangerous point is so called, and the Indians explain that the name refers to the sea monsters that are supposed to dwell at these places. Compounds of *nó:mas* also occur: "old man point"; "old man site on rock"; "old man on rock." We find also "having sea monsters." The name *nú:x̣wne:'mis*, the term for the mythological beings before they became animals, is also applied to a place.

References to personages occuring in mythology and folk tales are *dzó:nogwade:h* "having *dzó:noq̣'wa*"; "house of snoring woman"; "grave of mink" (as mythical person); "mink's seat on the rocks" (see Boas, *The Religion of the Kwakiutl Indians* [Columbia University Contributions to Anthropology, vol. X, part 1], 1930, p. 75); "fort of *kwé:xagyi'la*"; "Copper at hind end," the name of a place where the ancestor of the *Nú:nəmasəqəlis* division of the *λá:wic'e:s* pushed his copper plate under a rock; "having (the fabulous) man of the woods."

A few names refer to supernatural power: "supernatural power"; "supernatural power on rock"; "place of supernatural power on rock"; "container of supernatural power"; "supernatural ground"; "supernatural power on side."

Others refer to ghosts: "ghost place"; "meeting of ghosts"; "container (i.e., house) of ghosts."

THE LINGUISTIC FORM OF NAMES OF PLACES

Geographical terminology does not depend solely upon cultural interests, but is also influenced by linguistic structure. Kwakiutl has a very large number of suffixes expressing location and similar concepts. Many of these appear in the geographical terminology and the concepts expressed by these suffixes limit the range of names that can be expressed by single words.

I give here a number of examples of suffixes which will indicate the range of concepts that find expression. [There follow some sixty-two entries of suffixes, together with examples of their use in place names. The range of concepts among the suffixes can be indicated by presenting their glosses; place, receptacle; site; an open place surrounded by woods, beach; rock, stone; on ground; inside; surface of round thing; middle; flat; hind end; bottom end; point; point, nose; on top; side; side of head, temples; through (a channel); into; up from the beach; out to sea; out to sea; moving on water; on water; into a hole; into a hole (Koskimo); around; here and there, about; opposite; between; superlative; top of head; abdomen; head; mouth; forehead; cheek, i.e., side of a hill; neck, narrow part of river; nape of neck; chest, i.e., middle part of front of hill; back; body; crotch; hand; thigh; foot (of mountain); tooth; corner; round opening, color; mouth of river; water; tree, bush; a suffix of unknown meaning, occurring in "place of ghosts"; principal; real;ordinary; noise, sound; to make; smell; having.]

A comparison of the geographical nomenclature of two tribes living largely by sea hunting and fishing may illustrate the influence of language upon the formation of place names. Let us compare Kwakiutl and Eskimo nomenclature.

The Kwakiutl have innumerable terms for islands, almost all of which refer to their location in regard to the configuration of the neighboring land, such as "island at the point, island in the middle, island in front," etc. The Eskimo cannot form words of this type, because parallel locative suffixes are missing. Since many of the locative suffixes of Kwakiutl are stem words in Eskimo, and since the nominal suffixes of Eskimo are attributive, the descriptive terms necessarily represent a different kind of imagery. In Eskimo we have derived from *ako* "the middle part," names like: "the middle place"; "the little middle one"; "the most central one." In Kwakiutl the term "middle" is ordinarily a suffix and we find "pond in the middle"; "hole in middle"; etc., terms that cannot be formed in Eskimo except by long phrases that do not lend themselves well to the demands of a succinct nomenclature. The words for islands, discussed before, are in Kwakiutl such as "island at point"; "island in neck (of river)"; etc. Eskimo terms describe islands as small, large, lesser, very large, ordinary, peculiar, etc. Some of these terms might be formed in Kwakiutl, but they seem to occur rarely, if at all. Words like a large, small, largest island might be formed, while other attributive ideas hardly exist in the form of suffixes. The same observation may be made in regard to the terms for "point of land." In Kwakiutl this is almost always the suffix-*ba*; in Eskimo it is expressed by the independent stem *nuvuk*. This may be specialized by the attributive suffixes of Eskimo which are limited in number, while the Kwakiutl suffix may be attached to any descriptive stem. The number of terms designating points of land is, therefore, much more varied in Kwakiutl than in Eskimo.

When there is agreement in linguistic form we find also similar terms. Thus both Eskimo and Kwakiutl have suffixes which express "place of" and "having" and we find quite analogous terms, such as "winter place, spring place; having houses, having reindeer bucks," in Eskimo; and "winter place, house site, having olachen," in Kwakiutl.

Formation of local names is again different in languages that compound with ease, as in Mexican [Nahuatl] *Ajuchitán*, from *atl* "water," *xocitl* "flower," *tlan* "at, in"; or *Mecacalco*, from *mecatl calli* "house," *-co* "place"; *Popocatepetl*, "smoking mountain"; *ixtaxzo quitlan*, from *ixtac* "white," *zoquitl* "clay," *-tlan* "near, in"; *Xochicalco*, from *xochitl* "flower," *calli* "house," *-co* "place"; *Temilpa* from *tetl* "stone," *milli* "field," *-pa* "in", *Hueyxaltepec*, from *huey* "large," *xalli* "sand," *tepetl* "mountain," *-c* "in." (According to Antonio Peñafiél, *Nomenclatura geográfica de México* [1895]. The Nahuatl forms are cited in conventional orthography.)

Similar compositions, although more loosely formed, are used by the Tewa: *Pimpijetsiweki' iŋkwage* "northern mesa where canyon is narrow," from *piny* "mountain," *pije* "toward" (= "north"), *tsi'i* "canyon," *weki* "narrowness," *'iwe* "locative," *'i'i* "locative and adjectival suffix," *kwage* "mesa"; *p'i'oge'oŋwi'keji* "pueblo ruin down at the woodpecker place," *p'i'o* "woodpecker," *-ge* "down at," "*-'oŋwi* "pueblo," *keji* "ruin"; *top'op'awe'i'* "place of the piñon tree which has a hole through it," *to* "piñon," *p'o* "hole," *p'awe* "pierced," *'i'i* "locative and adjectival suffix." (From Harrington [1916], pp. 266, 203, 287, respectively. Harrington's orthography is retained.)

Keresan names are of a similar character. The linguistic habit admits names consisting of several independent words. Near Cochiti we find "rabbit mountain" (see also Harrington, 1916, p. 421); "choke cherry corner inner place" (see also Harrington, 1916, p. 429); in the Laguna dialect "south below spring"; "north corner of swampy place"; "north gap"; "turquoise house"; "white paint spring"; "Kangaroo-rat House." [From Boas, *Keresan Texts* (1925), p. 32, line 11; 32, line 26; 34, line 2; 36, line 15; the preceding all from Part II; and from Part I, pp. 240 and 92, line 7, respectively, the remainder; forms omitted.—D.H.H.]

Navaho names are also compounds of several short words: "mountain black"; "star (constellation) lies there"; "two went-for water." [Examples from Gladys Reichard with forms omitted—D.H.H.]

The same habit prevails in Zuñi where both firmer and looser combinations of words occur: *a't'iwulapnakwin* "where rocks lie scattered about," from *a'* "rock," *t'i* "to lie," *ulapna* "around," *kwin* "at"; *wemp'oakwin* "where wild beasts crouch", from *wema* "wild beast," *p'oa* "to crouch," *kwin* "at"; *co'łuwayällakwi* "standing arrow mountain," from *co'* "arrow," *łuwa* "many stand," *yälla* "mountain," *kwi(n)* "at." The following are more loosely combined: *hecot'a ts'inakwi* "painted house," from *hecot'a* "house," *ts'ina* "design, mark," *kwi* "at"; *aince k'änakwi* "bear spring," from *aince* "bear," *k'äna* "spring," *kwi* "at"; *akämoliya tepokäłan* "gravel hill," from *a'* "stone," *kämoliya* "ball," *tepokäłan* "hill." (Examples from Ruth L. Bunzel. Her orthography has been retained; her "c" = š, her "ä" = ɛ.)

Dakota nomenclature even admits whole sentences nominalized as names: "buffaloes that return running"; "tree standing on rocks"; "hill wearing blue robe"; "they who find a woman"; "the river that bends on itself"; "jealous ones who fight each other"; "four trees, made red, standing"; "smoke arises from the ground (hot springs)."

There are also many others that are purely descriptive: "roily water (the Missouri)"; "water flowing along"; "bad river"; or those named from the occurrence of useful products, "little flint creek"; "cherry creek"; "little blue grass creek"; "digging pipestone"; "black pipestone"; "oak growing in abundance." There are also places referring to supernatural experiences: "holy butte"; "holy water"; "owl maker hill" (referring to a tale of the child-stealing owl); "the thunder's hunting ground". (Examples from Ella Deloria. As nominalized, the names are not sentences.)

In linguistic form this whole group is differentiated from the Kwakiutl and Eskimo terminology by the ease with which close compounds are formed, as in Nahua, or by the readiness with which loosely compounded sentence words are accepted for the purposes of nomenclature. The Kwakiutl does not seem to accept a term like "bad river" as a name. His terminology is confined within the range of the possibilities of composition. The sentence "he finds a woman" (used as a name in Dakota) can be formed but such forms are not in use. The only groups of words that are found are possessive combinations, like "the river of *Dzo·dzade'*," or "the seat of mink."

The particular line of cultural interest has a considerable influence upon the choice of local terms. The Dakota are decidedly historically minded and name places after prominent persons or from historical events like "Flying-By's encampment"; or "Four-Bear's camp"; "abandoned site of the Pawnee"; "they caused the enemies to swim." References to legendary events also occur. These occupy a prominent place in the nomenclature of all the southwestern tribes. Place names referring to incidents in mythology and in religious ritual are numerous among all the pueblos as well as among the Navajo. Their great rarity in the northwest forms a striking contrast to the southwest.

[The monograph is completed by a short discussion of difficulties of translation and interpretation of Kwakiutl names, a section on "References to Names of Places in Mythology" (pp. 22-37), an "Alphabetical List of Names of Places" (pp. 38-83), and twenty-two detailed maps showing the location of named places in various sections of Kwakiutl territory. It is reported that the monograph was recently used by a contemporary Kwakiutl to discover halibut-fishing grounds whose location had been forgotten by himself and his peers.]

REFERENCE NOTE

Special references cited by Boas have been incorporated in the preceding text.

This note is organized in two parts, concerning (A) toponymy and spatial orientation, and (B) the field of onomastics generally. For discussion of work in the Romance field, see Malkiel's article in Part X and Malkiel (1959, p. 182). For other related work and problems, see the references on semantic description and lexicography with Frake's article on pp. 193-206 and references on the corresponding question of the grammatical expression of cultural focus and selective elaboration in Part III.

A. TOPONYMY AND SPATIAL ORIENTATION

As the area of Boas' article, toponymy is singled out here from among other semantic fields to indicate the range of interests and problems that may impinge upon anthropological pursuit of any one of them. Toponymy proper can be taken as the study of linguistic designations for places and other aspects of geographical reference. Often the interest is historical or local curiosity, but especially when approached in terms of structural analysis, involving the organization of such designations into sets and on the basis of underlying components, the topic broaches the problems of spatial orientation in general, both as a cognitive activity and a factor of social life and cultural values.

On these problems, see especially Carpenter (1955), Cassirer (1923, pp. 198-214), Diamond (1960), Dixon (1899), Durkheim (n.d., pp. 11-12), Gaster (1950, chap. 1), Hallowell (1955), Levi-Strauss (1962), Lynch (1960), Silverman (ms.), and Waterman (1920, p. 192). (For comparison of the Yurok world view, discussed by Waterman, to the Greek view, see Theodora Kroeber, 1959.) For American Indian documentation of Gaster's concept of topocosm (the joint sociogeographical frame of reference of communities), note Boas' section on localization of mythological events, cited at the end of his article (1934, pp. 22-27); the myth in Jacobs (1934, Part I, pp. 228-237); and cf. Harrington (1916) and Waterman (1920), regarding the close-grained lexical mesh of the (literal) cognitive map interwoven with the life of such communities. (Waterman states: "The principal feature treated in this paper is the distribution of primitive [=Yurok] place names. Several thousands of such names are listed, representing probably [*only*—DHH] a fourth, if not a third, of the total number known to the Yurok" [1920, p. 179].)

For other problems, including those more particularly concerned with the long-established field of place-name research, as well as locational and directional terms, see Beeler (1961), Bright (1962), Buck (1929), Charency (1899), Dauzat (1946, 1957), Harrington (1916), Haugen (1957), Kronasser (1952, chap. 18), Lamont (1957), Lounsbury (1960c), McDavid (1958), Morice (1933), Silverman (ms.), Smith (1956), Stewart (1945), Trager (1946), Trager and Mutziger (1947), Whorf (1941b, 1950, 1953), Wonderly (1946). Allen (1958), Beeler, Bright, Haugen, Lounsbury, Trager, Whorf (1953), and Wonderly are especially to be noted on various points of method and procedure.

On the general study of names, including geographical names, see Allen (1958), Cortés, Garcia Blanco, Tovar (1958), and the journals *Names* (reviewed by H. Hoijer, *IJAL*, 1953, *19:* 315-316) and *Onoma* (reviewed by A. Martinet, *Word*, 1952, *8:* 262-264), as well as European work in folklore and dialectology generally.

References not in the general bibliography:

ALLEN, W. S.

1958. "Proper Names" in Onomastics and Linguistics. In L. Cortés, M. Garcia Blanco, A. Tovar (Eds.), *Cinquième Congrès international de toponymie et d'anthropologie, actes et mémoires.* (Acta Salamanticensia iussu senatus universitatis edita, Filosofia y Letras, Vol. 11, Nos. I, 2.) Salamanca.

BEELER, MADISON S.

1961. Review of V. Madison and H. Stillwell, *How Come It's Called That?* *JAF*, *74:* 178-180.

BRIGHT, WILLIAM

1962. Review of B. H. Granger, *Will C. Barnes' Arizona Place Names*, and E. G. Gudde, *California Place-Names. JAF*, *75:* 77-82.

BUCK, CARL DARLING

1929. Words for World, Earth and Land, Sun. *Lg.*, *5:* 215-227.

CARPENTER, EDWARD

1955. Space Concepts of the Aivilik Eskimo. *Explorations*, *5:* 130-145.

CHARENCY, HYACINTHE

1899. Noms des points de l'espace dans divers dialectes américains. *JSAP* *2:* 109-178.

CORTÉS, L., M. GARCIA BLANCO, A. TOVAR (EDS.)

1958. *Cinquième Congrès international de toponymie et d'anthroponymie, actes et mémoires.* (Acta Salamanticensia iussu senatus universitatis edita, Filosofia y Letras, Vol. 11, Nos. 1, 2.) Salamanca.

DAUZAT, ALBERT

1946. *La Toponymie francaise.* (2nd ed.) Paris: Payot.

1957. *Les Noms de lieux. Origine et évolution.* (5th ed.) Paris; Librairie Delagrave. (1st ed., 1926.)

DIAMOND, STANLEY A.

1960. Anaguta Cosmography; The Linguistic and Behavioral Implications. *AL*, *2* (2): 31-38.

DIXON, R. B.

1899. The Color-Symbolism of the Cardinal Points. *JAF*, *12:* 10-16.

GASTER, THEODOR H.

1950. *Thespis. Ritual, Myth and Drama in the Ancient Near East.* New York: Schuman.

HALLOWELL, A. IRVING

1955. Cultural Factors in Spatial Orientation. *Culture and Experience*. Philadelphia: University of Pennsylvania Press. Pp. 184-202.

JACOBS, MELVILLE

1934. *Northwest Sahaptin Texts*. (Columbia University Contributions to Anthropology, No. 19.) New York: Columbia University Press.

KROEBER, THEODORA

1959. *The Inland Whale*. Bloomington: Indiana University Press.

LAMONT, W. D.

1957. Old Land Denominations and "Old Extent" in Islay. *Scottish Studies, 1:* 183-203.

LOUNSBURY, FLOYD G.

1960c. Iroquois Place-Names in the Champlain Valley. In *Champlain Basin—Past, Present, Future*. (Report of the New York-Vermont Interstate Commission on the Lake Champlain Basin; New York Legislative Document, No. 9.) Albany. Pp. 21-66.

LYNCH, K.

1960. *The Image of the City*. Cambridge: Harvard University Press.

MCDAVID, RAVEN I., JR.

1958. Linguistic Geographic and Toponymic Research. *Names, 6:* 65-73.

SILVERMAN, MARTIN G.

Ms. Concepts of Direction. (Based on a Harvard University Senior Honors' Thesis, 1960.)

SMITH, A. H.

1956. *English Place-Name Elements*. (Publications of the English Place-Name Society, Nos. 25, 26). Cambridge: Cambridge University Press.

STEWART, GEORGE A.

1945. *Names on the Land. A Historical Account of Place-Naming in the United States*. New York: Random House.

TRAGER, GEORGE L.

1946. Review of G. A. Stewart, *Names on the Land. IJAL, 12:* 108-110.

TRAGER, GEORGE L., and J. G. MUTZIGER

1947. The Linguistic Structure of Mongolian Place Names. *JAOS, 67:* 184-195.

WATERMAN, T. T.

1920. *Yurok Geography*. (UCP=AAE *16* [5].) Berkeley and Los Angeles: University of California Press. Pp. 177-314.

WONDERLY, WILLIAM

1946. Zoque Place-Names. *IJAL, 12:* 217-228.

B. ONOMASTICS

Onomastics, or the study of names, can be taken, or subdivided (as the case may be) to deal with all the vocabulary of a language. The writings which deal with one or another lexical aspect of culture or cultural aspect of vocabulary are almost innumerable. The references selected below illustrate well the range of both subject matter and descriptive problems in work dealing with particular cultural foci and semantic fields.

On the concept and study of semantic fields as such, see especially Ducháček (1960), Guiraud (1958a, pp. 70 ff.; 1956), Kronasser (1952, chap. 13), Öhman (1951, 1953), Ullmann (1957, pp. 152-170, 309-315), Voegelin and Voegelin (1957), Waterman (1957). On semantic fields and analysis in relation to kinship, see especially Burling (1962), Goodenough (1956), Lounsbury (1956), Wallace and Atkins (1960), and references to Evans-Pritchard's article in Part V.

Many of the references, like Frake's article on pp. 193-206, are exemplary for their combination of descriptive control and cultural interest. Marsh and Laughlin (1956) is especially noteworthy, combining analysis of the productivity and elaboration of a field of terminology with analysis of the values, beliefs, and practices in which it is imbedded. See also the following: Asch (1958), Aschmann (1946, to which cf. McQuown [1954a]), Beneveniste (1953), Boas (1927), Bohannon (1953), Burke (1962), Chao (1953), Conklin (1957, 1958, 1962), Cowan (1946), Crosland (1962), Dieterlen (1952), Edmonson (1958), Evans-Pritchard (1929; 1934a; 1940, pp. 41-48), Flugelman (1932), Ghirlanda (1956), Gluckman (1959), Goodenough (1953), Guiraud (1958a, pp. 70 ff.), Herculano de Carvalho (1953); Hoernle (1923); Keesing and Keesing (1956), Kluckhohn (1956), La Barre (1947), Levi-Strauss (1962), Lounsbury (in Hoijer, 1954a, p. 211); McQuown (1954a), Mahr (1962; and previous articles in the series), Malkiel (1957, 1959), Mandler and Kessen (1959), Matoré (1951), Nicolaisen (1957), Nida (1958), Öhman (1951), Reichard (1948), Robbins, Harrington, Freire-Marreco (1916), Sapir (1912), Scott (1958), Stout (1947), Vendryes (1925, Part III), Voegelin and Hymes (1953), Watson (1943), Whorf (1953), Zinsli (1945).

References not in the general bibliography:

ASCHMANN, HERMANN

1946. Totonac Categories of Smell. *Tlalocan, 2:* 187-189.

BENVENISTE, EMILE

1953. Le Vocabulaire de la vie animale chez les indiens du haut Yurok (Alaska). *Bulletin de la Société Linguistique de Paris, 49:* 79-106. [Kutchin Athapaskan.]

BOAS, FRANZ

1927. Religious Terminology of the Kwakiutl. *Festschrift Meinhof*. Hamburg: Friedrischen. Pp. 386-392. [Also in Boas, *Race, Language and Culture*. New York: Macmillan, 1940. Pp. 612-618.]

BOHANNON, PAUL

1953. Concepts of Time Among the Tiv of Nigeria. *SJA, 9:* 251-262.

CHAO, YUEN-REN

1953. Popular Chinese Plant Words. *Lg., 29:* 379-414.

CONKLIN, HAROLD C.

1958. *Betel Chewing Among the Hanunóo.* (Proceedings of the Fourth Far Eastern Prehistory Congress, No. 56.) Quezon City: National Research Council of the Philippines.

COWAN, GEORGE M.

1946. Mazatec House Building. *SJA, 2:* 375-390.

CROSLAND, M. P.

1962. *Historical Studies in the Language of Chemistry*. Cambridge: Harvard University Press.

DIETERLEN, G.

1952. Classification des vegetaux chez les Dogons. *Journal de la Société des Africanistes, 22:* 115-158.

DUCHÁČEK, OTTO

1960. *Le Champ conceptuel de la beauté en français moderne.* (Opera Universitatis Brunensis, Facultas Philosophica.) Praha: Státni Pedagogické, Nakladatelství.

EDMONSON, M. S.

1958. *Status Terminology and the Social Structure of North American Indians.* (Publications of the American Ethnological Society.) Seattle: University of Washington Press.

FLUGELMAN, F.

1932. Moral Vocabulary of an Unwritten Language. *Anthropos, 27:* 213-248.

GHIRLANDA, ELIO

1956. *La Terminologia Viticola nei Dialetti della Svizzera Italiana.* (Romanica Helvetica, No. 61). Berna: Edizioni A. Francke S. A. [Reviewed, R. A. Hall, Jr., *Lg.*, 1957, *33:* 79-80.]

GOODENOUGH, WARD H.

1953. *Native Astronomy in the Central Carolines.* (Museum Monographs, University Museum, University of Pennsylvania.) Philadelphia.

GUIRAUD, PIERRE

1956. Les Champs morpho-sémantiques. *Bulletin de la Société Linguistique de Paris, 52:* 265-288.

HERCULANO DE CARVALHO, JOSE GONÇALO C.

1953. *Coisas e palavras: Alguns problemas etnograficos e linguisticos relacionados com os primitivos sistemas de debulha na Peninsula Iberica.* (Biblos, No. 29.) Coimbra.

HOERNLE, A. W. T.

1923. The Expression of the Social Value of Water Among the Naman of Southwest Africa. *South African Jounal of Science, 20:* 514-526.

LA BARRE, WESTON

1947. Potato Taxonomy Among the Aymara Indians of Bolivia. *Acta Americana, 5:* 83-103.

MAHR, AUGUST C.

1962. Delaware Terms for Plants and Animals in the Eastern Ohio Country: A Study in Semantics. *AL, 4* (5).

MALKIEL, YAKOV

1957. Review of J. Herculano de Carvalho, *Coisas e palavras. Lg., 33:* 54-76.

1959. The Skein-Winding Reel in Gallo-Romance. Studies in Etymology, Dialect Geography, and Material Civilization. *Romance Philology, 12:* 262-282.

MANDLER, GEORGE, and WILLIAM KESSEN

1959. *The Language of Psychology.* New York: Wiley.

MATORÉ, G.

1951. *Le Vocabulaire et la société sous Louis-Philippe.* Geneva-Lille: Droz.

NICOLAISEN, W. F. H.

1957. The Semantic Structure of Scottish Hydronomy. *Scottish Studies, 1:* 211-240.

REICHARD, GLADYS A.

1948. Navajo Classification of Natural Objects. *Plateau, 21:* 7-12.

ROBBINS, W. W., J. P. HARRINGTON, BARBARA FREIRE-MARRECO

1916. *Ethnobotany of the Tewa Indians.* (BAE-B 55.) Washington, D.C.: Smithsonian Institution.

SCOTT, W. H.

1958. Some Calendars of Northern Luzon. *AA, 60:* 563-570.

WATSON, J. B.

1943. How the Hopi Classify Their Food. *Plateau, 15:* 49-52.

ZINSLI, P.

1945. *Grund und Grat; die Bergwelt im Spiegel der schwiezerdeutschen Alpenmundarten.* Bern: Francke.

20 *On Language and Culture*

JOHN LOTZ

"IDEAL TARGETS" for records in sports provide a case-study in the currently fashionable discussion on the interrelation between language and culture. The difference between Anglo-Saxon countries and countries using the metric system may further elucidate the role of the linguistic factor.

In May 1954, when Bannister ran the "dream mile" (one mile in less than 4 minutes), the newspapers listed a number of other ideal objectives in sports: 9 seconds for the hundred-yard dash, 7 feet for the high-jump, 16 feet for the pole-vault, 60 feet for the shot-put (this one was achieved a few days later). These objectives were for male athletes; one can also add the "dream mile" for women: one mile in less than 5 minutes (also reached in the same month).

All such "ideals" aim at lowering the record time for running certain standard distances to a fixed number of seconds or minutes, or, in field events, at raising the length or height of the existing record to a fixed number of length units. The numbers involved are simple integers when the target number is low, and 'round figures' when the number is higher (4 minutes, 12 feet, 60 feet, but not $3\frac{3}{4}$ minutes for the mile or 61 feet for the shot-put). Such targets of course exist in other sports as well (e.g., in weight-lifting, or the 0.300 batting average in baseball as a more modest aim).

That these targets depend on the use of language and not on other factors is demonstrated by the difference between the formulations of such targets in Anglo-Saxon countries and in countries using the metric system. The latter list as ideal targets: 10 seconds for 100 meters, 20 kilometers for the one-hour race, 80 meters for javelin-throwing, etc. Because of this dependence on language, such targets cannot be "adequately" translated; to try to run 1609 meters in 4 minutes is not the same thing as shooting for the 4-minute mile.

These targets must be within reasonable reach, just above the present records, and therefore an ideal target can normally be formulated in only one measuring system; for instance in the high jump the target in Anglo-Saxon countries is 7 feet, half an inch above the present world record of 212 centimeters: 220, or even 225, is neither "round" enough, nor realistic enough.

When such an ideal target is fashionable in the world of sports, as e.g., the 4-minute mile, the number of occasions on which that event is put on the program also increases (e.g., the one-mile race was often run in the "metric" countries of Europe). When the ideal is achieved, that target gradually becomes obsolete; this has happened to the 30-minute 5 kilometers, and it will happen to the dream mile.

It seems clear that these ideal targets for sports records presuppose a general cultural setting of a non-verbal sort: appreciation of number and quantity, high valuation and meticulous recording of top physical performance, a realistic appraisal of man's physical abilities using the present top achievement as a reference point and extrapolating from there. But these targets must also be formulated verbally. The verbal expression is an attributive phrase consisting of a number followed by measures of time, length, and weight. These expressions of the ideal targets readily lend themselves to analysis and interpretation by reason of their morphemic simplicity and semantic-conceptual transparency.

The second part of the verbal expression, the measure of time and length, is determined by tradition and convention. The foot-yard system, because of the larger number of basic units, allows a much greater variety of ideal targets than the metric system. The expressions for these measuring units are either single morphemes (second, minute, hour, inch, foot, year, mile, meter) or, in the metric system, consistently formed complex morphemes with a unifying stress pattern (centimeter, kilometer, etc.).

The number part of the phrase poses two linguistic problems with psychological and cultural implications: (a) the low, fundamental numbers, and (b) the round numbers.

The beginning of the integer series is said to be the cultural possession of all mankind, although in some cultures only the very first integers occur. They are single morphemes in English and in many languages. The round numbers, on the other hand, imply the selection of certain numbers, the base numbers, from the sequence of the integers (e.g., ten, a thousand, the "-illion" numbers, etc.), which make the manipulation of large numbers possible. The base numbers vary in different cultures (or they may be missing altogether); they may also vary within the same culture for different objects (e.g., in the Western culture twelve is used for eggs and paper; *tjog* (twenty) is used in Sweden for crayfish; the Akkadian 12 and 60 survive in time measures; in general use, the decimal system prevails in pure numbers, but not in measurements in Anglo-Saxon countries). Round numbers are either base numbers alone, or in simple combinations with the fundamental numbers. There are various degrees of "roundness": any fundamental number in combination with any base number yields a round number (60, 200,000, etc.); certain repetitive types, such as 110, 880, or the 666 of the Apocalyptic Beast, are also regarded as round, as are 5, 50, etc., and 25, 250, etc., in the decimal system. The feeling of what is round may vary in different countries, e.g., 16 is felt to be more round in Anglo-Saxon countries than in Continental Europe because it is a base in measurement—16 ounces to the pound. In all these numerical expressions the purely linguistic part is morphemically simple and the expression consists of a few differing morphemes: this is psychologically axiomatic; the reference, on the other hand, is determined by historical-cultural accident. The status of expressions like *quatre-vingt-dix* (four score and ten) and problems such as that of notation and its influence on the verbal expression are beyond the scope of these notes. (The counterpart of the round number is the simple fraction, especially binary divisions like half, quarter, etc., and in the decimal system the fractions ending in .5 or .25 etc., the decimal equivalents of successive halvings, which accounts for the feeling of roundness associated with 5, 25, etc., mentioned above.)

The fundamental and the round numbers play a prominent part on the "desiderative-imperative" aspects of our culture: in law, age limits, length of fish permitted to be caught, speed limits (with their implications for the problems of transportation); in sports: distances to be run specified in round numbers (the marathon distance, 26 miles, 385 yards, is a quasi-traditional distance introduced at the first Olympic Games); in social events: wedding anniversaries, college class reunions, bicentennials; in prices and salaries (the American $9.95 price tag is a deliberate avoidance of such numbers, aimed of course at having the customer psychologically class the article as within the range of the next lower "round" price). In actual measurements, any degree of accuracy may be used that seems reasonable (running times are generally given in tenths of a second, distances in yards or fractions of miles; in the metric system, jumps and throws are measured only in whole centimeters), but even in actual reporting of numbers, rounding is common: on old tombstones ages are generally given in round tens, with fives next in frequency. Thus, it is the morphemic-conceptual simplicity and not the objective reference that is decisive.

The use of numbers in such targets determines cultural aims and behavior dependent on these. The simplicity of the linguistic expression and the correlated simple conceptual organization seem to account for the setting up of ideal aims and these cannot be explained by non-linguistic references, biological properties, or the like. The simplicity of the linguistic expression seems to be the organizing principle in other semantic fields also (such as colors, kinship, spatial organization, movements, etc.) in which simple morphemes or morpheme-combinations are set against expressions which might yield a more exact description and identification, but are linguistically complicated and cumbersome.

REFERENCE NOTE

On the role of LEXICON AS A DETERMINANT OF BEHAVIOR or cultural pattern, see references to Hoijer's article on pp. 142-149, especially work by Brown, Carroll, Casagrande, Lenneberg, and MacClay; Bally (1952, chap. 7); and many of the references on semantics to Frake's article on pp. 193-206. A number of experimental psychological and other results are discussed in Hymes (1961b); see references and discussion also in Kluckhohn (1954) and Miller (1956). Also, note Burke (1962) and the priority of lexical examples in Sapir (1929c) and Whorf (1941b) and compare the material tested by Carmichael, Hogan, and Walter (1932) in a classic experiment to Sapir (1929c) and the restudy by Herman, Lawless, and Marshall (1957).

On the role of numbers, there has been little recent anthropological discussion. See Cassirer (1923, chap. 3, part 3); Levi-Strauss (1962, chap. 5); Thomas (1907), with reference to Brinton, regarding the origin of the related phenomena of sacred numbers; Boas (1914, p. 489), for one factor underlying sacred or ritual numbers; Lowie (1924, pp. 284-285) for two such factors; Lowie (1925); and Granet (1934, chap. 3) for extended treatment of the role of conventional numerical patterns in a high civilization.

References not in the general bibliography:

BRINTON, D. G.
1894. On the Origin of Sacred Numbers. *AA* (o.s.), *7:* 168-173.

CARMICHAEL, L., H. P. HOGAN, A. A. WALTER
1932. An Experimental Study of the Effect of Language on the Reproduction of Visually Perceived Forms. *Journal of Experimental Psychology*, *15:* 73-86.

HERMAN, DAVID T., RICHARD H. LAWLESS, RICHARD W. MARSHALL
1957. Variables in the Effect of Language on the Reproduction of Visually Perceived Forms. *Perceptual and Motor Skills*, *7* (Monograph Supplement, *2:* 171-186). [Also in Sol Saporta (Ed.), *Psycholinguistics*. New York: Holt, Rinehart, and Winston, 1961. Pp. 537-551.]

LOWIE, ROBERT H.
1924. *Primitive Religion*. New York: Boni and Liveright.
1925. Five as a Mystic Number. *AA*, *27:* 578.

THOMAS, CYRUS
1907. Counting. In F. W. Hodge (Ed.), *Handbook of American Indians North of Mexico*. (BAE-B 30.) Washington, D.C.: Smithsonian Institution. Pp. 353-354. [Reissued, New York: Pageant Books, 1959.]

Language and Property in Truk: Some Methodological Considerations 21

WARD H. GOODENOUGH

IN THE ANALYSIS of property relationships two fundamentally different approaches are possible. The first is to isolate specific configurations of rights, privileges, and powers (and their counterparts: duties, lack of rights, and liabilities), and to classify types of ownership and title accordingly. The second is to start with linguistic forms which indicate the relations of persons to owned objects, to isolate semantic criteria which determine the use of the forms, and to derive types of possessive relationships therefrom. Our analysis of property on Truk has been based primarily on the first approach, though we have used the second to get helpful clues as we went along.

An analysis based exclusively on the linguistic approach has recently been published by Capell (1949). In discussing ownership throughout the Pacific area, Capell draws certain conclusions about its expression on Truk. Briefly, he classifies ownership on Truk as follows:

1. Simple ownership, expressed by suffixing a possessive pronoun to the word for the object possessed, e.g., *wa-* 'canoe,' *wæ:y* 'my canoe'; *wu:f* 'clothes,' *wufey* 'my clothes'; *fəni* 'land,' *fəniwey* 'my land'; *sa:m* 'father,' *semey* 'my father.'

2. Ownership from the standpoint of the object owned, expressed by suffixing a possessive pronoun to a classifying word which is then followed by the word for the object owned. Capell makes two subdivisions here: (a) by the use to which an object will be put, e.g., *yeney mæ:y* 'my-cooked-portion-to-eat breadfruit,' *wocay wu:c* 'my-uncooked-portion-to-eat banana,' *winimey ni:* 'my-drink coconut'; (b) by class of object owned without reference to use, e.g., *wæ:y citosa* 'my-canoe automobile,' *wufey sə:c* 'my-clothes shirt,' *semey səmwon* 'my-father chief,' *neyi nayif* 'my-child knife,' *yæ:y rawises* 'my-general-object trousers.'

It is not our purpose here to evaluate Capell's analysis with regard to Oceania generally, but there are good grounds for suspecting its validity as far as Truk is concerned. Capell's distinction between simple and classificatory modes of possession is misleading. All possessive formation in Trukese is classificatory, in that in any expression involving a possessive, the pronoun is always suffixed to a word which denotes the class of the object possessed. It is entirely optional as to whether or not this classificatory word is followed by a modifier which specifies the possessed object more exactly. Thus, the expressions *neyi nwæ:n* 'my child adult-male,' i.e., 'my adult son,' *neyi nayif* 'my-child knife,' i.e., 'my knife,' and *neyi kikkin* 'my-child little,' i.e., 'my little child,' are syntactically identical. If the context were clear, one could simply say *neyi* 'my-child object' of all these without the following modifier.

Similarly, one can simply say *wæ:y* 'my-canoe-object' for either a canoe or an automobile, or one can differentiate the two by saying *wæ:y wa:* 'my-canoe canoe' for the one, and *wæ:y citosa* 'my-canoe automobile' for the other. There is indeed a distinction in Trukese, but, as this last example shows, it is not between simple and classificatory modes, but between forms such as *wa:*, which can occur both as a class-term and as a modifier following a class-term, and forms such as *citosa*, which in possessive constructions occur only as a modifier. In short, there is but one mode of possessive formation in Trukese, namely, suffixation of pronominal forms to classifying forms, not two as proposed by Capell.

Capell's analysis, however, is still suggestive, for by his reasoning, when a Trukese speaks of an object as *neyi* 'my-child object,' he means that he possesses it in a different way than when he speaks of it as *wæ:y* 'my-canoe object' or *yæ:y* 'my general class of object.' Such a difference is certainly reflected in the contrast between *neyi mwæ:n* 'my-child adult male,' i.e., 'my adult son,' and *yæ:y mwæ:n* 'my-general-object adult-male,' i.e., 'my older brother,' or between *yeney mæ:y* 'my portion of cooked breadfruit for me to eat' and *yæ:y mæ:y* 'my breadfruit for other than eating purposes.' Unquestionably the possessor signifies something about the kind of relationship between himself and an object such as a breadfruit, by his choice of preceding classifier. The fact that the same word may be differently classified, with a difference in meaning accordingly, is proof of it.

How does this relate to concepts of ownership within the framework of property relationships? Very little, if at all. Differences in Trukese behavior depend on whether the property concerned is productive or non-productive of food. This distinction cuts right across the use of classifying forms in the language. One says both *neyi pi:k* 'my-child pig' and *neyi nayif* 'my-child knife,' but pigs are classed with productive, knives with non-productive property. As we have seen, one also says *neyi mwæ:n* 'my adult son,' but persons are not objects of ownership in the way that animals and material things are. A father cannot subject his son to any property transaction nor enjoy the rights, privileges, and powers of full, residual, or provisional title with respect to him. (Trukese property law distinguishes two forms of ownership, which we have called *full* and *divided ownership*. In the first the rights, privileges, and duties of the owner viz-à-viz the community constitute a *full title*. In the second, resulting from a form of gift called *niffag*, the rights, privileges, and duties of the recipient make up a *provisional title*, while those of the donor constitute a *residual title*.)

We obtain similar results when we seek to correlate other possessive classifiers with property relationships. While differences in classifier unquestionably reflect differences in the ways in which the subject and object of a possessive pronoun are conceived to be related, the criteria on which these differences are based fall outside the realm of ownership in a property sense. They are not part of the social structure as such.

The question remains as to how Trukese concepts of property ownership *are* reflected in their language, if not in possessive formations. Of immediate importance to a Trukese are holdings from which he gets his food. Such a holding is called a *yæpar* (*yæpari* 'my-land holding'). This word would never be used for something to which one held only residual title; it indicates actual possession or control for purposes of food exploitation, whether one is full or provisional title holder. In speaking of property in land, another frequent expression is *fənɨwey* ('my-land,' 'my-home island,' depending on context). As 'my-land,' it means simply that a person has some kind of interest in the plot in question, either as full, residual, or provisional title holder, or as member of a corporation holding any of these titles. (Title may be held by groups of siblings together with their matrilineal descendants as well as by individuals. Kin groups which are themselves parties to property relationships as distinct from their individual members are labeled *corporations*.) A third expression is 'my land with (or from) so-and-so,' as in *fənɨwey me kinɔwus* ('my land from Kinɔwus,' or 'Kinɔwus and my land'). It means that the speaker holds the land under provisional title from Kinɔwus, who is residual title holder, or that the speaker and Kinɔwus hold the land jointly as a minor corporation in which Kinɔwus is *mwæ:ni:ci* (senior member). It may also mean that the speaker owns a garden on soil which he exploits on loan from Kinɔwus. This expression is regularly used as the polite way of speaking about a holding in the presence of its residual title holder. As far as the writer knows, these are the standard ways of expressing "ownership" of land. It is important to note that none of them indicates the precise nature of legal ownership, and that there are no Trukese words which can be translated by what we have called full ownership, divided ownership, full title, residual title, or provisional title. Neither are there any grammatical forms functioning in this way. These basic property concepts are lexically unexpressed.

To acquire property as a result of sale, inheritance, *ki:s* or *niffag* is expressed by suffixing the form *-ni* to the word denoting the class of object acquired, e.g., *wufeni* 'acquire clothes' (*wu:f*), *wæ:ni* 'acquire a canoe' (*wa:*), *nəwɨni* 'acquire a child-object,' as a knife, *yæ:ni* 'acquire something not otherwise classified' (*ya:-*). Use, under loan or otherwise, is expressed by doubling the word denoting the class of object borrowed, e.g., *wufowuf* 'use or wear clothes,' *wa:wa* 'use or ride in a canoe,' *nəwɨnəw* 'use a child-object,' such as a knife, *ya:ya* 'use something otherwise not classified.' Elbert (1947, p. 85) gives the following sentence showing the difference between acquisition under some form of title and simple use: *wɨwa fəffəni ye:y fəni gə wɨse wesewesen fəniweni* 'I'm using this land but I-have-not really acquired-title-to-it.' (It will be noted that the forms to which *-ni* can be suffixed and the forms which may be doubled to indicate use are the same ones that can take a suffixed possessive pronoun.) This difference in meaning applies, however, only to objects which can be owned within the framework of the property system. When parents get a child, they also *nəwɨni* (acquire) it, just as they *nəwɨni* a knife. When they behave as parents to a child, they also *nəwɨnəw* it, just as when they behave in ways appropriate to the use of a knife. But as we said before, a parent does not acquire title to a child in the same way that he acquires title to a knife, nor does he have the same rights, powers, and privileges with respect to it. In its broader sense, *-ni* simply means that one has entered into a relationship with an object or person such that one enjoys certain rights in that relationship which are denied to others, without any implication as to the nature of these rights or their alienability, except as may be inferred from the total context.

The linguistic forms which proved most helpful in our analysis of property were those denoting transactions. Analysis of their use provided an initial opening for isolating the different configuations of rights, privileges, and powers to which objects other than persons are subject on Truk. Our primary aim, however, was to get at the latter by whatever means possible, so that our analysis is not based on these words alone.

Our aim was that the conceptual framework finally arrived at for describing property relations should account fully for all of our data, leaving as few exceptions to any rule as possible. Wherever exceptions were encountered, our framework was modified accordingly. In this connection, the criterion of economy has been consistently employed. No more forms of ownership have been established than proved necessary to account for the different configurations of rights and privileges presented by our data. To this end we have found the linguistic criterion of "complementary distribution" (Bloch and Trager, 1942, pp. 42-45) exceedingly helpful, though applied to non-linguistic data. This can be illustrated in connection with *niffag*.

The type of gift which the Trukese call *niffag* can result in radically different relationships between the parties concerned. With one set of *niffag* a recipient has permanent and formalized obligations to the giver, with another his obligations are informal and impermanent. Within the first there is additional variation in the form which a recipient's obligations take, as reflected in the different kinds of food he gives a residual title holder (donor) in connection with canoes, pigs, chickens, and land. Does this mean that we have to distinguish two or more distinct transactions, all called *niffag* in Trukese, or that we are dealing with different aspects of a single transaction, analogous to the allophones of a phoneme in language? It was found that of the various configurations of obligations resulting from *niffag* only one could occur with any one form of property and that it occurred with this one constantly. The forms of obligation resulting from *niffag* were thus in complementary distribution with respect to forms of property, and could be classed as different expressions of a single type of transaction. Contrariwise, the occurrences of *ki:s* (another type of gift) and *niffag* were applicable in part, at least, to the same forms of property. Since they contrasted with each other, it was necessary to consider *ki:s* and *niffag* as distinct transactions.

In conclusion, it appears that there is no necessary one-to-one correspondence of forms of ownership with linguistic forms. To assume that grammatical distinctions in forming the possessive must parallel concepts of ownership is not warranted. The content of language was useful in providing a clue to property concepts in connection with terms for transactions. But most significant for the relationship between language and culture were the operations performed in analysis. Functionally significant types of title and ownership were inferred from the distribution of rights and duties with respect to points of difference in objects of ownership and in transaction vocabulary, just as phonemes are inferred from the distribution of speech sounds with respect to points of difference in meaning. In each case, it is the fact of relevant difference for the informant, not merely the content of the difference.

It is a canon of structural linguistics that phonological and grammatical forms are independent structures to be analyzed without regard to the content of semantic categories. The data presented here suggest that the canon should hold in reverse, that behavioral and legal forms, along with other things which languages talk about, are also independent structures to be analyzed without regard to the content of linguistic categories. When both kinds of structure have been described in their own terms, how they relate to one another becomes susceptible of study.

REFERENCE NOTE

For the phonemic system and orthography adopted by Goodenough, see his "Linguistic Note," pp. 26-28 of the original monograph. There is some minor variation from island to island and community to community within the Truk lagoon in the shape of vocabulary items, as regards the selection both of individual phonemes and of whole forms. The native words cited are those of the Romonum dialect, except where otherwise indicated.

The questions raised by Capell, as to the personal and possessive relationships expressed in Pacific languages, go back in one or another form as far as Wilhelm von Humboldt's treatment of the Kawi-language of Java and his famous introduction to that work (1836). For a clustering of discussions, involving points of general theory and method, see Cassirer (1923, chap. 3, part 4:2), Hocart (1917, 1918), Levy-Bruhl (1916), Ray (1919), and see the recent areal survey in Emeneau (1953, p. 349, n. 23). On inferences from vocabulary, cf. Greenberg (1954b), Hockett (1954b), Hoijer (1953), McQuown (1954a), Newman (1954), Trager (1955b).

References not in the general bibliography:

CAPELL, A.

1949. The Concept of Ownership in the Languages of Australia and the Pacific. *SJA*, *5:* 169-189.

COOK, W. W.

1933. Ownership and Possession. *Encyclopedia of the Social Sciences*, *11:* 521-525.

ELBERT, S. H.

1947. *Trukese-English and English-Trukese Dictionary*. Pearl Harbor: U.S. Naval Military Government.

LEVY-BRUHL, L.

1916. L'Expression de la possession dans les langues mélanésiennes. *Mémoires de la société de linguistique*. *19:* 96-104.

RAY, SIDNEY R.

1919. The Melanesian Possessives and a Study in Method. *AA*, *21:* 347-360.

Hanunóo Color Categories 22

HAROLD C. CONKLIN

IN THE FOLLOWING brief analysis of a specific Philippine color system I shall attempt to show how various ethnographic field techniques may be combined profitably in the study of lexical sets relating to perceptual categorization.

Recently, I completed more than a year's field research on Hanunóo folk botany (Conklin, 1954a, 1954b). In this type of work one soon becomes acutely aware of problems connected with understanding the local system of color categorization because plant determinations so often depend on chromatic differences in the appearance of flowers or vegetative structures—both in taxonomic botany and in popular systems of classification. It is no accident that one of the most detailed accounts of native color terminology in the Malayo-Polynesian area was written by a botanist (Bartlett, 1929). I was, therefore, greatly concerned with Hanunóo color categories during the entire period of my ethnobotanical research. Before summarizing the specific results of my analysis of the Hanunóo material, however, I should like to draw attention to several general considerations.

1. Color, in a western technical sense, is not a universal concept and in many languages such as Hanunóo there is no unitary terminological equivalent. In our technical literature definitions state that color is the evaluation of the visual sense of that quality of light (reflected or transmitted by some substance) which is basically determined by its spectral composition. The spectrum is the range of visible color in light measured in wave lengths (400 [deep red] to 700 [blue-violet] milimicrons [Osgood, 1953, p. 137]). The total color sphere—holding any set of external and surface conditions constant—includes two other dimensions, in addition to that of spectral position or hue. One is saturation or intensity (chroma), the other brightness or brilliance (value). These three perceptual dimensions are usually combined into a coördinate system as a cylindrical continuum known as the color solid. Saturation diminishes toward the central axis which forms the achromatic core of neutral grays from white at the end of greatest brightness to black at the opposite extremity. Hue varies with circumferential position. Although technically speaking *black* is the absence of any "color," *white*, the presence of all visible color wave lengths, and neutral *grays* lack spectral distinction, these achromatic positions within the color solid are often included with spectrally-defined positions in the categories distinguished in popular color systems.

2. Under laboratory conditions, color *discrimination* is probably the same for all human populations, irrespective of language; but the manner in which different languages classify the millions (estimates range from 7,500,00 to more than 10,000,000 [Optical Society of America, 1953; Evans, 1948, p. 230]) of "colors' which every normal individual can discriminate *differ*. Many stimuli are classified as equivalent, as extensive, cognitive—or perceptual—screening takes place (Lounsbury, in Levi-Strauss *et al.*, 1953, pp. 47-49). Requirements of specification may differ considerably from one culturally-defined situation to another. The largest collection of English color names runs to over 3,000 entries (Maerz and Paul, 1930), yet only eight of these occur very commonly (Thorndike and Lorge, 1944). Recent testing by Lenneberg and others demonstrates a high correlation in English and in Zuñi between ready color vocabulary and *ease in recognition*

of colors (Lenneberg, 1953, pp. 468-471; Lenneberg and Roberts, 1956; Brown and Lenneberg, 1954). Although this is only a beginning it does show how the structure of a lexical set may affect color perception. It may also be possible to determine certain nonlinguistic correlates for color terminology. Color terms are a part of the vocabulary of particular languages and only the intracultural analysis of such lexical sets and their correlates can provide the key to their understanding and range of applicability. The study of isolated and assumed translations in other languages can lead only to confusion (Lenneberg, 1953, pp. 464-466; Hjemslev, 1953, p. 33).

In the field I began to investigate Hanunóo color classification in a number of ways, including the eliciting of linguistic responses from a large number of informants to painted cards, dyed fabrics, other previously prepared materials (cf. Ray, 1952, 1953), and the recording of visual-quality attributes taken from descriptions of specific items of the natural and artificial surroundings. This resulted in the collection of a profusion of attributive words of the nonformal—and therefore in a sense "color"—type. There were at first many inconsistencies and a high degree of overlap for which the controls used did not seem to account. However, as the work with plant specimens and minute floristic differentiation progressed, I noted that in *contrastive* situations this initial confusion and incongruity of informants' responses did not usually occur. In such situations, where the "nonformal" (i.e., not spatially organized visible quality) of one substance (plant part, dyed thread, or color card) was to be related to and contrasted with that of another, both of which were either at hand or well known, terminological agreement was reached with relative ease. (The lack of a term similar in semantic range to our word "color" makes abstract interrogation in Hanunóo about such matters somewhat complicated. Except for leading questions [naming some visual-quality attribute as a possibility], only circumlocutions such as *kabitau ti:da nu pagbanta:yun*? "How is it to look at?" are possible. If this results in description of spatial organization or form, the inquiry may be narrowed by the specification *bukun kay ?anyu?* "not its shape [or form].")

Such a defined situation seemed to provide the frame necessary for establishing a known level of specification. Where needed, a greater degree of specification (often employing different root morphemes) could be and was made. Otherwise, such finer distinctions were ignored. This hint of terminologically significant levels led to a reëxamination of all color data and the following analysis emerged.

Color distinctions in Hanunóo are made at two levels of contrast. The first, higher, more general level consists of an all-inclusive, coördinate, four-way classification which lies at the core of the color system. The four categories are mutually exclusive in contrastive contexts, but may overlap slightly in absolute (i.e., spectrally, or in other measurable) terms. The second level, including several sublevels, consists of hundreds of specific color categories, many of which overlap and interdigitate. Terminologically, there is "unanimous agreement" (Lenneberg, 1953, p. 469) on the designations for the four Level I categories, but considerable lack of unanimity—with a few explainable exceptions—in the use of terms at Level II.

The four Level I terms occur as attributes with the prefix *ma-* "exhibiting, having," as indicated in parentheses, or as free words (abstracts). They are:

1. *(ma)bi:ru* "relative darkness (of shade of color); blackness" (black)
2. *(ma)lagti?* "relative lightness (or tint of color); whiteness" (white)
3. *(ma)rara?* "relative presence of red; redness" (red)
4. *(ma)latuy* "relative presence of light greenness; greenness" (green)

The three-dimensional color solid is divided by this Level I categorization into four unequal parts; the largest is *mabi:ru*, the smallest *malatuy*. While boundaries separating these categories cannot be set in absolute terms, the focal points (differing slightly in size, themselves) within the four sections, can be limited more or less to black, white, orange-red, and leaf-green respectively. In general terms, *mabi:ru* includes the range usually covered in English by black, violet, indigo, blue, dark green, dark gray, and deep shades of other colors and mixtures; *malagti?*, white and very light tints of other colors and mixtures; *marara?*, maroon, red, orange, yellow, and mixtures in which these qualities are seen to predominate; *malatuy*, light green and mixtures of green, yellow, and light brown. All color terms can be reduced to one of these four but none of the four is reducible. This does not mean that other color terms are synonyms, but that they designate color categories of greater specification within four recognized color realms.

The basis of this Level I classification appears to have certain correlates beyond what is usually considered the range of chromatic differentiation, and which are associated with nonlinguistic phenomena in the external environment. First, there is the opposition between light and dark, obvious in the contrasted ranges of meaning of *lagtiʔ* and *bīru*. Second there is an opposition between dryness or desiccation and wetness or freshness (succulence) in visible components of the natural environment which are reflected in the terms *raraʔ* and *latuy* respectively. This distinction is of particular significance in terms of plant life. Almost all living plant types possess some fresh, succulent, and often "greenish" parts. To eat any kind of raw, uncooked food, particularly fresh fruits or vegetables, is known as *pag-laty-un* (<*latuy*). A shiny, wet, brown-colored section of newly-cut bamboo is *malatuy* (not *mararaʔ*). Dried-out or matured plant material such as certain kinds of yellowed bamboo or hardened kernels of mature or parched corn are *mararaʔ*. To become desiccated, to lose all moisture, is known as *mamaraʔ* (<*paraʔ* "desiccation"; and parenthetically, I might add that there are morphological and historical reasons—aside from Hanunóo folk etymologizing—to believe that at least the final syllables of these two forms are derived from a common root). A third opposition, dividing the two already suggested, is that of deep, unfading, indelible, and hence often more desired material as against pale, weak, faded, bleached, or "colorless" substance, a distinction contrasting *mabi:ru* and *mararaʔ* with *malagtiʔ* and *malatuy*. This opposition holds for manufactured items and trade goods as well as for some natural products (e.g., red and white trade beads, red being more valuable by Hanunóo standards; indigo-dyed cotton sarongs, the most prized being those dyed most often and hence of the deepest indigo color—sometimes obscuring completely the designs formed originally by *white* warp yarns; etc.). Within each of these Level I categories, increased esthetic value attaches as the focal points mentioned above are approached. There is only one exception: the color which is most tangibly visible in their jungle surroundings, the green (even the focal point near light- or yellow-green) of the natural vegetation, is *not* valued decoratively. Green beads, for example, are "unattractive," worthless. Clothing and ornament are valued in proportion to the sharpness of contrast between, and the intensity (lack of mixture, deep quality) of "black," "red," and "white."

Level II terminology is normally employed only when greater specification than is possible at Level I is required, or when the name of an object referred to happens also to be a "color" term (e.g., *bula:wan* "gold; golden [color]"). Level II terms are of two kinds: relatively specific color words like *(ma)dapug* "gray" (<*dapug* "hearth; ashes"), *(ma)ʔ arum* "violet," *(ma)dilaw* "yellow" (< *dilaw* "turmeric"); and constructions, based on such specific terms—or on Level I names—but involving further derivations, such as *mabirubiru* "somewhat *mabi:ru*" (more specific than *mabi:ru* alone only in that a color which is *not* a solid, deep, black is implied, i.e., a color classed within the *mabi:ru* category at Level I, but not at or near the focal point), *mabi:ru (gid)* "very *mabi:ru*" (here something close to the focal center of jet black is designated), and *madi:lawdi:law* "weak yellow." Much attention is paid to the texture of the surface referred to, the resulting degree and type of reflection (iridescent, sparkling, dull), and to admixture of other nonformal qualities. Frequently these noncolorimetric aspects are considered of primary importance, the more spectrally-definable qualities serving only as secondary attributes. In either case polymorphemic descriptions are common.

At Level II there is a noticeable difference in the ready color vocabulary of men as compared to women. The former excel (in the degree of specification to which they carry such classification terminologically) in the ranges of "reds" and "grays" (animals, hair, feather, etc.); the latter, in "blues" (shades of indigo-dyed fabrics). No discernible similar difference holds for the "greens" or "whites."

In short, we have seen that the apparent complexity of the Hanunóo color system can be reduced at the most generalized level to four basic terms which are associated with lightness, darkness, wetness, and dryness. This intracultural analysis demonstrates that what appears to be color "confusion" at first may result from an inadequate knowledge of the internal structure of a color system and from a failure to distinguish sharply between sensory reception on the one hand and perceptual categorization on the other.

REFERENCE NOTE

Field work among the Hanunóo on Mindoro Island (1952-1954) was supported by grants from the Social Science Research Council, the Ford Foundation, and the Guggenheim Foundation.

References not in the general bibliography:

BARTLETT, HARLEY HARRIS

1929. Color Nomenclature in Batak and Malay. *Papers, Michigan Academy of Science, Arts and Letters, 10:* 1-52.

CONKLIN, HAROLD C.

1954a *The Relation of Hanunóo Culture to the Plant World.* Doctoral dissertation, Yale University.

1954b. An Ethnoecological Approach to Shifting Agriculture. *Transactions, New York Academy of Sciences*, Series II, *17:* 133-142.

EVANS, RALPH M.

1948. *An Introduction to Color*. New York: Wiley.

MAERZ, A., and M. R. PAUL

1930. *A Dictionary of Color*. New York: McGraw-Hill.

OPTICAL SOCIETY OF AMERICA, COMMITTEE ON COLORIMETRY

1953. *The Science of Color*. New York: Crowell.

RAY, VERNE F.

1952. Techniques and Problems in the Study of Human Color Perception. *SJA*, *8:* 251-259.

1953. Human Color Perception and Behavioral Response. *Transactions, New York Academy of Sciences*. Series II, *16:* 98-104.

THORNDIKE, E. L., and I. LORGE

1944. *The Teacher's Word Book of 30,000 Words*. New York: Bureau of Publications, Teacher's College, Columbia University.

The Diagnosis of Disease Among the Subanun of Mindanao 23

CHARLES O. FRAKE

ALTOUGH MY ORIGINAL FIELD WORK among the Eastern Subanun, a pagan people of the southern Philippines, was focused on a study of social structure, I found it exceedingly difficult to participate in ordinary conversations, or even elicit information within the setting of such conversations, without having mastered the use of terminologies in several fields, notably folk botany and folk medicine, in which I initially had only marginal interest. Effective use of Subanun botanical and medical terminologies required more knowledge of verbal behavior than linguists typically include in their conception of a structural description. To generate utterances which were grammatical (Chomsky, 1957, pp. 13-17) but not necessarily meaningful or congruent (Joos, 1958a) did not suffice. Yet descriptive linguistics provides no methods for deriving rules that generate statements which are semantically as well as grammatically acceptable. Having acquired only an unsystematic and intuitive "feel" for the use of certain portions of the Subanun lexicon during a first field study, I attempted during a second study a more rigorous search for meanings. This investigation became a major focus of my field work. Presented here is a partial analysis of one of the less numerous terminologies: 186 'disease names.' (Single quotation marks enclose *glosses*, English labels which substitute for, *but do not define*, Subanun terms.)

THE SUBANUN

Some 50,000 Eastern Subanun inhabit the eastern portion of Zamboanga Peninsula, a 130 mile-long extension of the island of Mindanao in the Philippines. Most of this population practices swidden farming in the mountainous interior of the peninsula, leaving the coasts to Christian immigrants of recent decades from the Bisayan Islands to the north. Prior to this century the coasts were controlled, and sporadically occupied, by Philippine Moslems, who established an exploitative hegemony over the pagan Subanun in certain locales (Christie, 1909; Frake, 1957b).

In terms of segmentation and stratification, Subanun society displays remarkable simplicity. Each nuclear family is the focus of a partially unique and variable network of social ties with kin and neighbors which constitutes, for that family, the "total society." This maximal, nondiscrete, sphere of social relationships has no corporate organization and is not segmented into lineages, age-sets, secret societies, territorial districts, political factions, or the like. Despite this simplicity of their social structure, the Subanun carry on constant and elaborate interfamily social activities: litigation, offerings, feasts—all well lubricated with ample quantities of rice wine. Warfare is lacking (Frake, 1961).

All Subanun are full-time farmers. Special statuses are few in number, filled by achievement rather than ascription, restricted in domain, and limited in economic rewards. The status of legal authority has been discussed elsewhere (Frake, 1957a). In the sphere of making decisions about disease, differences in individual skill and knowledge receive recognition, but there is no formal status of diagnostician or even, by Subanun conception, of curer. Everyone is his own 'herbalist' (*memuluŋ*). There are religious specialists, 'mediums' (*belian*), whose job it is to maintain communications with the very important supernatural constituents of the Subanun universe. Mediums hold curing ceremonies, but the gods effect the cure. They make possible verbal communication with the supernaturals, but again the information received comes from the gods. The medium is but a channel for the divine message.

A consideration of disease etiology, together with etiologically derived therapy, would require extended discussion of Subanun relations with the supernatural world. In limiting ourselves to diagnosis, on the other hand, we can largely ignore information derived from very noisy, supernaturally-produced signals.

DISEASE CONCEPTS

"Am I sick?" "What kind of disease do I have?" "What are my chances?" "What caused this disease?" "Why did it happen to me (of all people)?" Illness evokes questions such as these among patients the world over. Every culture provides a set of significant questions, potential answers, and procedures for arriving at answers. The cultural answers to these questions are *concepts* of disease. The information necessary to arrive at a specific answer and eliminate others is the *meaning* of a disease concept.

The Subanun patient, no matter how minor his illness, rarely depends upon introspection to answer these questions. He solicits the readily proffered judgment and advice of kin, neighbors, friends, specialists, deities, and ethnographers. Sickness comprises the third most frequent topic of casual conversation (after litigation and folk botany) among Subanun of my acquaintance, and it furnishes the overwhelmingly predominant subject of formal interviews with the supernaturals.

Because disease is not only suffered and treated, but also talked about, disease concepts are verbally labelled and readily communicable. Their continual exposure to discussions of sickness facilitates the learning of disease concepts by all Subanun. Subanun medical lore and medical jargon are not esoteric subjects; even a child can distinguish *buni* from *buyayag*—two fungous skin infections not, to my knowledge, differentiated by Western medical science—and state the reasons for his decision.

This corpus of continually emitted and readily elicitable verbal behavior about disease provides our evidence for the existence and meaning of culturally defined disease concepts. We begin with actual disease cases—instances of 'being sick' (*miglaru*) by Subanun identification. We note the kinds of questions *the Subanun ask* about these cases, we record the alternative (or *contrasting*) replies to each kind of question, and then we seek to differentiate the factors by which a Subanun decides one reply, rather than an alternative, applies in a particular situation.

Among the questions evoked by a disease case, there invariably appears one of a set of utterances which demands a 'disease name' (*ŋalan mesait en*) in response. Answering a question with a 'disease name' is *diagnosis*. Subanun diagnosis is the procedure of judging similarities and differences among instances of 'being sick,' placing new instances into culturally defined and linguistically labelled categories. Diagnostic decisions pertain to the selection of 'medicinal' (*kebuluŋan*) therapy, to prognosis, and to the assumption of an appropriate sick role by the patient. They do not answer, nor depend upon, the crucial etiological questions that guide the search for 'ritual' (*kanu*) therapy in severe and refractory cases. The Subanun thus discriminate among the various constellations of disease symptoms and react differentially to them. They diagnose *kinds* of disease.

DISEASE NAMES

The fundamental unit of Subanun diagnosis is the *diagnostic category* (or "disease") labelled by a 'disease name.' Whereas an *illness* is a single instance of 'being sick,' a diagnostic category is a conceptual entity which classifies particular illnesses, symptomatic or pathogenic components of illness, or stages of illness. The course of an illness through time and its symptomatic components at any one time do not always fit into a single diagnostic category. Consequently, a single illness may successively or simultaneously require designation by several disease names.

Although not all illnesses can be diagnosed by a single disease name, every disease name can diagnose a single illness. Disease names thus differ from designations of kinds of symptoms, such as 'itch' (*matel*), or kinds of pathogenic agents, such as 'plant floss' (*glaŋis*,) which do not function as diagnostic labels for illnesses.

The question "What kind of illness is that?" (*dita? gleruun ai run ma iin*) will always elicit a diagnostic description. Actually, however, a Subanun rarely states this question explicitly; rather he implies it when making an assertion such as "I feel sick" (what do you think is wrong with me?); "You look sick" (what is the matter with you?); "I hear he's sick" (do you know what he's got?). When accompanied by the proper intonation and inserted particles to express worried concern, such utterances invariably stimulate diagnostic discussions resulting in a consensual linguistic description of a particular illness.

If none of the linguistic components of a description of an illness can by itself describe a disease case, then the description as a whole constitutes a disease name, labelling a single diagnostic category. Thus the description *mesait gulu* 'headache' labels a single diagnostic category, for neither *mesait* 'pain' nor *gulu* 'head' can alone diagnose an illness. On the other hand, the description *mesait gulu bu? mesait tian* 'headache and stomach ache' constitutes two diagnostic categories because each component can itself serve as a description of an illness. A single disease name is a *minimal* utterance that can answer the query "What kind of illness is that?"

At the most specific level of contrast (see below), we have recorded 186 human-disease names (apart from referential synonyms), and the productivity of Subanun disease terminology permits the formation of an indefinite number of additional names. For example, we never recorded *mesait kuleŋkay* 'little-finger pain' as a disease name, but should a Subanun find occasion to communicate such a concept he could unambiguously do so by constructing this label.

Standard descriptive phrases of the productive (polylexemic) type, such as *mesait tian* 'stomach ache' and *meŋebag gatay* 'swollen liver,' label a number of common ailments. A few other disease names, which one might call "suggestive" rather than "descriptive," have constitutents not productive in the formation of new disease names: for example, the derivative *penabud* 'splotchy itch' <*sabud* 'to scatter, as chicken feed.' There remain 132 diagnostic categories which possess unique, single-word labels. The Subanun must consequently rote learn unique and distinctive labels for the vast majority of his diseases, a situation paralleled even more markedly in the botanical lexicon of well over one thousand items. The fact that all Subanun do, in fact, learn to use a copious vocabulary of disease and plant terms with great facility reflects the prominent place of these terminologies in daily conversation.

LEVELS OF CONTRAST

In a given diagnostic situation, a Subanun must select one disease name out of a set of contrasting alternatives as appropriately categorizing a given set of symptoms. Before considering his criteria of selection, we must determine which disease categories, in fact, contrast with each other. Two disease names *contrast* if only one can correctly diagnose a particular set of symptoms. (We consider later the question of disagreement about "correctness.") A particular illness may require the diagnoses of more than one set of symptoms for complete description, as with the case of 'being sick' with both a 'headache' and a 'stomach ache.' In such cases the linguistic contruction with 'and' (*bu?*) makes it clear that the illness comprises a conjunction of two contrasting diagnostic categories. With reference to the set of symptoms of pains in the head, only one of the contrasting responses is applicable. Any difficulties caused by conjunctive descriptions of illnesses can be obviated by taking evidence for contrast only from illnesses described by a single disease name.

When the same set of symptoms elicits different single-disease-name responses, and informants consider each response to be correct, two things may be responsible. The disease names may be referential synonyms; i.e., the categories they designate are mutually inclusive or equivalent. This happens when, for example, the terms are dialect variants or variants appropriate to different kinds of discourse, such as casual as opposed to formal speech. The second possibility, and the one that concerns us here, is that one category totally includes another; it is superordinate and operates at a less specific *level of contrast*.

An example from English illustrates the meaning of *levels of contrast*. If we confront English-speaking informants with a dog, say a poodle, and collect designations applicable to it, we would eventually have a corpus of words such as poodle, dog, animal, and (from the zoologically sophisticated) canine, mammal, vertebrate. Since all of these words correctly designate the same object, they do not contrast at the same level. Neither are they referential synonyms, for whereas all poodles are dogs, the converse is not true. The category "dog" totally includes the category "poodle." A poodle is a kind of dog, a dog a kind of mammal, a mammal a kind of vertebrate, and so on. Arranging classes by inclusion produces a hierarchy of levels, each ascending level being less specific and including more than its predecessor.

Now suppose, still pointing to a poodle, we ask our (zoologically unsophisticated) informants the following questions:

1. Is it a plant?
2. Is it a cat?
3. Is it a collie?

The responses are, respectively:

1. No, it's an animal.
2. No, it's a dog.
3. No, it's a poodle.

Animal thus contrasts with plant, dog with cat, and poodle with collie.

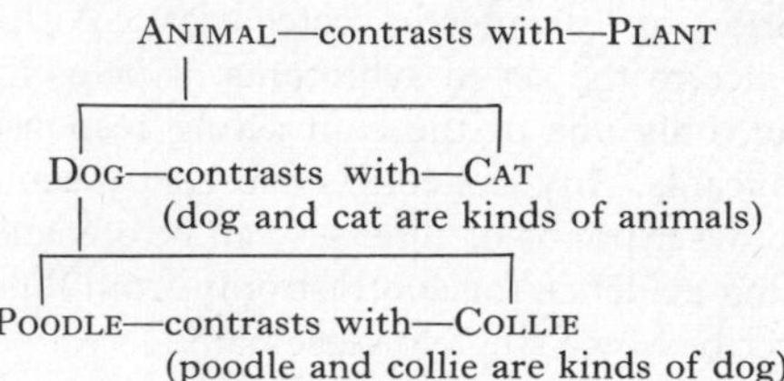

We could, of course, elicit many more contrasts at each level, and, working with zoologists or dog lovers as informants, we could isolate additional levels.

A *taxonomic hierarchy* comprises different sets of contrasting categories at successive levels, the categories at any one level being included in a category at the next higher level. Taxonomies divide phenomena into two dimensions: a horizontal one of discrimination (poodle, collie, terrier) and a vertical one of generalization (poodle, dog, animal).

The importance of recognizing levels of contrast in Subanun disease nomenclature first became apparent when, early in the field work, I had an infectious swelling on my leg. I asked all visitors for the name of my ailment and received a variety of different answers (all single disease names) from different people or even from the same people on different occasions. Subanun disease naming seemed to be an inconsistent and unpredictable jumble. Further interrogation, together with closer attention to the sociolinguistic contexts of responses, soon made it clear that all respondents were right; they were just talking at different levels of contrast. Some—especially those who wished to avoid a detailed medical discussion of my ills in favor of another subject—were simply telling me I had a 'skin disease' (*nuka*) and not another kind of external disease. Others were informing me that I had an 'inflammation' (*meyebag*) and not some other 'skin disease.' Still others—habitual taxonomic hair-splitters and those who had therapeutic recommendations in mind—were diagnosing the case as 'inflamed quasi bite' (*pagid*) and not some other kind of 'inflammation.'

Fig. 1 diagrams the taxonomic structure of a

<table>
<tr><td rowspan="4">samad 'wound'</td><td colspan="15">nuka 'skin disease'</td></tr>
<tr><td rowspan="3">pugu 'rash'</td><td rowspan="3">nuka 'eruption'</td><td colspan="3">meyebag 'inflammation'</td><td colspan="6">beldut 'sore'</td><td colspan="2">buni 'ringworm'</td><td rowspan="3">bugais 'spreading itch'</td><td rowspan="3"></td></tr>
<tr><td rowspan="2">pagid 'inflamed quasi bite'</td><td rowspan="2">bekukay 'ulcerated inflammation'</td><td rowspan="2">meyebag 'inflamed wound'</td><td colspan="2">telemaw 'distal ulcer'</td><td colspan="2">baga? 'proximal ulcer'</td><td rowspan="2">beldut 'simple sore'</td><td rowspan="2">selimbunut 'spreading sore'</td><td rowspan="2">buyayag 'exposed ringworm'</td><td rowspan="2">buni 'hidden ringworm'</td></tr>
<tr><td>telemaw glai 'shallow distal ulcer'</td><td>telemaw bligun 'deep distal ulcer'</td><td>baga? 'shallow proximal ulcer'</td><td>begwak 'deep proximal ulcer'</td></tr>
</table>

Fig. 1

LEVELS OF CONTRAST IN 'SKIN DISEASE' TERMINOLOGY

portion of the twenty-nine specific 'skin disease' (*nuka*) categories. Superordinate categories stand above their subordinates. A given category contrasts with another category at the level at which the two share an upper horizontal boundary not crossed by a vertical boundary. Any case, for example, diagnosed as *telemaw glai* 'shallow distal ulcer' can also be labelled *telemaw* 'distal ulcer,' *beldut* 'sore,' or *nuka* 'skin disease' depending on the contrastive context. If, pointing to a 'shallow distal ulcer,' one asks:

1. Is it a *telemaw glibun* ('deep distal ulcer')?
2. Is it a *baga?* ('proximal ulcer')?
3. Is it a *meŋebag* ('inflammation')?
4. Is it a *samad* ('wound')?

The predictable responses are respectively:

1. No, it's a *telemaw glai* ('shallow distal ulcer').
2. No, it's a *telemaw* ('distal ulcer').
3. No, it's a *beldut* ('sore').
4. No, it's a *nuka* ('skin disease').

The clearest examples of different levels of contrast appear when a disease category subdivides into "varieties." Systemic conditions producing discolored urine, for example, known generally as *glegbay*, have 'red' (*glegbay gempula*) and 'white' (*glegbay gemputi?*) subcategories. The 'distal ulcer' *telemaw* subdivides into *telemaw glai* 'male (i.e., shallow) ulcer' and *telemaw glibun* 'female (i.e., deep) ulcer.' Although in these examples, subordinate levels of contrast are indicated by attaching attributes to superordinate disease names, such linguistic constructions are not necessarily evidence of inclusion. Thus *beldut pesui* 'sty,' literally, 'chick sore,' is not a kind of *beldut* 'sore' but a kind of 'eye disease' (*mesait mata*). It is the way linguistic labels are applied to phenomena and not the linguistic structure of those labels that points to levels of contrast.

As a matter of fact, when we systematically investigate the contrasts of each Subanun disease term, we find a number of cases in which the same linguistic form appears at different levels of contrast. The term *nuka* 'skin disease,' for example, not only denotes a general category of ailments which includes conditions like *baga?* 'ulcer,' but it also denotes a specific kind of skin condition, a mild 'eruption' that contrasts with *baga?* (see Fig. 1). In all such cases, if the context (especially the eliciting utterance) does not make the level of contrast clear, respondents can indicate the more specific of two levels by means of optional particles: e.g., *tantu nuka* 'real *nuka*,' i.e., 'eruption,' not *any* 'skin disease.'

The use of the same linguistic form at different levels of contrast, while a source of confusion until one attends to the total context in which a term is used, should not surprise us. It is common enough in English. The word *man*, for example, designates at one level a category contrasting with nonhuman organisms. At a more specific level, *man* designates a subcategory of human organisms contrasting with *woman*. Subordinate to this we find the contrast: *man* (adult male)—*boy*. *Man* can even appear at a still more specific level to designate a kind of adult male human, as in Kipling's " . . . you'll be a man, my son."

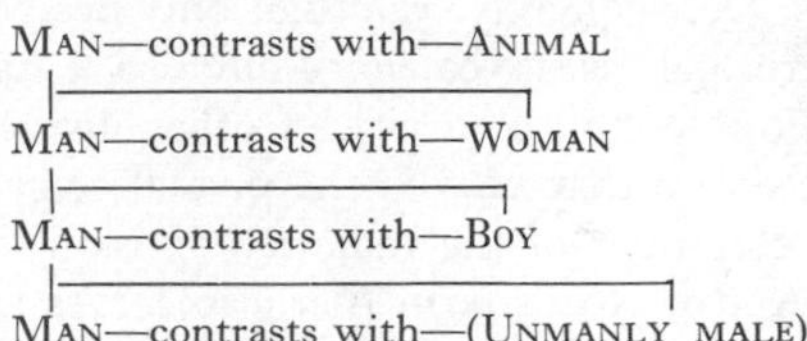

(There is no standard lexeme labelling the category that contrasts with *man* in the sense manly male. The most likely polylexemic designation is probably "not a real man.")

This use of single forms at several levels of contrast seems particularly characteristic of Subanun disease terminology. It appears elsewhere as well, in botanical nomenclature and kinship terminology for instance, but not so extensively. The reasons for its use in disease terminology become, in part, explicable when we consider the use of disease names to designate sequential stages of illness.

The changing and unpredictable course of disease symptoms considerably complicates diagnosis. Of course other phenomena also change. A plant, passing from seedling to mature tree, changes radically in appearance. But a seedling of one kind invariably produces a mature plant of the same kind. A papaya seedling never grows into a mango tree. Consequently, the members of a plant category can be identified at any stage of growth, and terminological distinctions of growth stages do not affect classifications of kinds of plants. Given an illness at a particular stage of development, on the other hand, its symptoms may proceed along a variety of different courses or it may heal altogether. Just as one illness sometimes requires several disease names for complete description at any one time, so its course over time may pass through several distinct diagnostic categories.

Every disease name designates a potential *terminal* stage: a stage of 'being sick' immediately preceding 'cure' (or 'recuperation') or 'death.' But some disease stages, potentially terminal, may also be prodromal stages of other terminal diagnostic categories. This situation occurs especially among the skin diseases. Each sequential stage leading to an ulcer or an itchy skin disease is, in itself, a potential terminal stage designated by a disease name. A case of *nuka* 'eruption,' for example, sometimes heals without complication; at other times it eventually develops into one of 23 more serious diseases. Consequently, *nuka* not only designates a terminal disease category but also a stage of development in a variety of other diseases.

Fig. 2 shows that *nuka* is the pivotal stage in the development of the majority of 'skin diseases.' And it is this term that also serves as a general designation for 'skin diseases,' including some for which *nuka* 'eruption' is not a prodrome.

The term *nuka* thus has three uses:

1. As a general designation for 'skin disease,' applicable to any skin disease at any stage of development.
2. To designate a prior stage of some, but not all, 'skin diseases.'
3. To label a terminal diagnostic category, 'eruption,' which contrasts with other 'skin-disease' categories.

The reader will find further examples of multiple semantic uses of single linguistic forms by comparing Fig. 1 and 2.

Subanun disease terminology well illustrates the proviso, often stated but rarely followed through in semantic analysis, that the meaning of a linguistic form is a function of the total situation, linguistic and nonlinguistic, in which the form is used. Essentially it is a matter of determining with what a term contrasts in a particular situation. When someone says, "This is an *x*," what is he saying it is *not?* (cf. Kelly, 1955, pp. 59-64).

Fig. 1 and 2 reveal a partial relation between levels of contrast and stages of development in 'skin disease' terminology. Among 'skin diseases,' where the course of development *through*

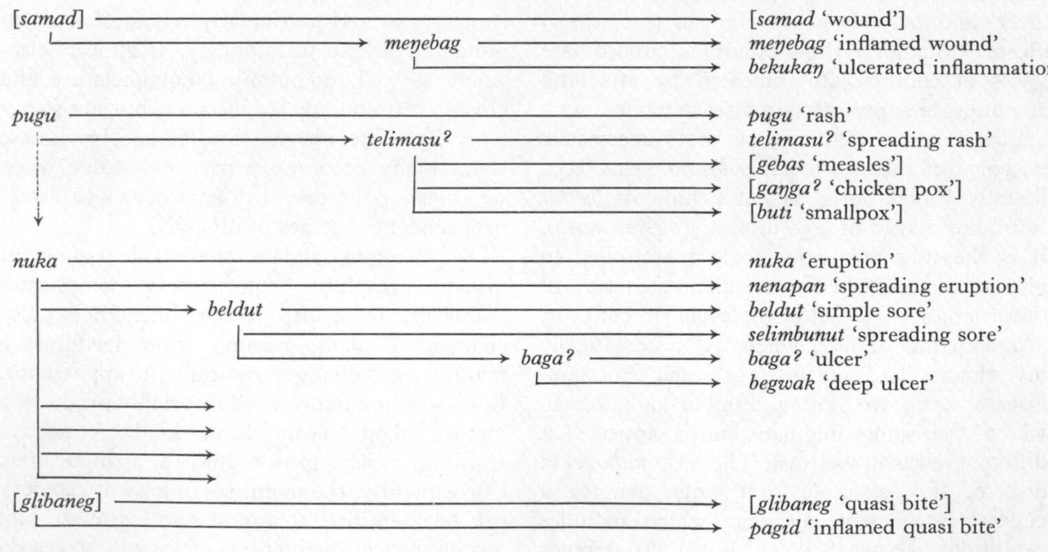

Fig. 2
SKIN DISEASE STAGES

Only a few of the diseases arising from *nuka* 'eruption' are shown.
Diseases enclosed in brackets are not classifiable as *nuka* 'skin disease.'

different diagnostic categories is most complex, the segregation of different levels of contrast is more elaborate than elsewhere in the disease taxonomy. But the terminological complexity of skin disease development does not suffice to explain why this area of the disease vocabulary exhibits more levels of contrast than other areas. A similar variability of number of levels in different segments of a taxonomy, not correlated with the designation of developmental stages, also occurs in botanical and zoological nomenclature.

To explain why some areas of a folk taxonomy subdivide into a greater number of superordinate-subordinate levels than other, we advance the following hypothesis: the greater the number of distinct social contexts in which information about a particular phenomenon must be communicated, the greater the number of different levels of contrast into which that phenomenon is categorized. Skin diseases, for example, enter into a wide variety of social contexts, apart from therapeutically oriented discussions. They can influence bride-price calculations. Here, the concern is over the degree of disfigurement and the contagiousness of the disease. They can be used to justify, perhaps to one's spouse, a failure to perform an expected task. Here the disabling properties of the disease must be communicated. Skin disease terms figure prominently in competitive joking and maligning, thus entering into special kinds of discourse such as drinking songs and verse. In many of these situations it is imperative to speak at just the level of generality that specifies the pertinent information but leaves other, possibly embarrassing, information ambiguous.

The same hypothesis should hold cross-culturally. If the botanical taxonomy of tribe A has more levels of contrast than that of tribe B, it means that the members of tribe A communicate botanical information in a wider variety of sociocultural settings. It does not mean that people in tribe A have greater powers of "abstract thinking." As a matter of fact it says nothing about general differences in cognition, for when it comes to fish, tribe B may reveal the greater number of levels of contrast.

Folk taxonomies are cultural phenomena. Their structural variation within and between cultures must be explained by the cultural uses to which a taxonomy is put, and not by appeal to differences in the cognitive powers of individual minds (cf. Brown, 1958, pp. 284-285).

DIAGNOSTIC CRITERIA

A 'disease name,' it will be recalled, is a minimal, congruent (i.e., meaningful) answer to the question, "What kind of illness is that? (*dita? gleruun ai run ma iin*)." Alternatively, it is a congruent insertion in the frame, "The name of (his) disease is ——— (*ŋalan en ig mesait en* ———)." Since different *illnesses*, that is, different instances of 'being sick' (*miglaru*), may elicit the same disease-name response, a disease name labels a class of illnesses: a *diagnostic category*.

Given a set of contrasting disease names, the problem remains of determining the rules which govern the assigning of one name rather than another in a particular diagnostic situation. Rules of use may be analytic, perceptual, or explicit in derivation.

Analytic derivation of meanings ideally yields *distinctive features:* necessary and sufficient conditions by which an investigator can determine whether a newly encountered instance is or is not a member of a particular category. The procedure requires an independent, *etic* (Pike 1954, p. 8) way of coding recorded instances of a category. Examples are the "phone types" of linguistics and the "kin types" of kinship analysis. (Lounsbury, 1956; pp. 191-192). The investigator classifies his data into types of his own formulation, then compares "types" *as though* they were instances of a concept. From information already coded in the definitions of his "types," he derives the necessary and sufficient conditions of class membership. Thus by comparing the kin types of English "uncle" (FaBr, MoBr, FaSiHu, etc.) with the kin types in every other English kin category, the analyst finds that by scoring "uncle" for features along four dimensions of contrast (affinity, collaterality, generation, and sex) he can state succinctly how "uncles" differ from every other category of kinsmen. (English kinship classification requires a special definition of affinity to contrast "in-laws" with other kin, some of whom [like FaSiHu] are connected to ego by a marriage link but are categorized with consanguineals [like FaBr]. This definition provides that kin of different generations connected by a marriage link qualify as affinals only if the marriage link is in the lower generation.) The definition of "uncle"as "nonaffinal, first-degree collateral, ascending generation, male" suffices to enable an investigator to predict whether any new kin type he encounters (such as FaMoSiHu) is or is not an uncle. This is not, however, the same thing as a definition which states how people in the society in fact, categorize persons as "uncles" (Wallace and Atkins, 1960, pp. 75-79). (When analytically derived features are probabilistically, rather than necessarily and sufficiently, associated with category membership, then we may speak of *correlates* rather than of distinctive features. A correlate of the uncle-nephew relation is that uncles are usually, but not necessarily, older than their nephews.)

To arrive at rules of use one can also direct attention to the actual stimulus discriminations made by informants when categorizing. What perceptual information enables one to distinguish an oak tree from a maple tree, a cold from the flu? Perceptual attributes relevant to categorization, whether distinctive or probabilistic, are *cues*. Discovering cues in ethnographic settings requires as yet largely unformulated procedures of perceptual testing that do not replace the culturally relevant stimuli with artificial laboratory stimuli (cf. Conklin, 1955, p. 342).

Finally, one can simply ask his informants about meanings: "What is an uncle?" "How do you know he is an uncle and not a father?" Such procedures yield the culture's explicit definitions or *criteria* of categories (cf. Bruner's [Bruner *et al.*, 1956, p. 30] "defining attributes" and Wittgenstein's [1958, pp. 24-25] use of "criteria" and "symptoms," the former being distinctive, the latter probabilistic).

These different procedures for determining rules of use are not equally applicable to every system of contrasting categories. Distinctive feature analysis becomes impractical without an economical, minimally redundant, and highly specific etic coding device. Explicit criteria may be lacking or highly inconsistent where category discriminations and decisions do not require verbal description. In some cases, consistent criteria may be present, yet provide an unsatisfactory description of behavior: compare the inutility of seeking informants' explanations in certain tasks of formal linguistic analysis. Yet there are categories—like those pertaining to supernatural phenomena—which are known only through verbal descriptions by informants. The difference between a 'deity' (*diwata*) and a 'goblin' (*menemad*) can only be what my informants tell me it is.

Our choice of procedures for arriving at meanings of disease names is, in part, a function of the kind of category such names label, and, in part, of the kind of field data we succeeded in obtaining about diagnostic behavior.

Distinctive-feature analysis is ruled out on both counts. The preliminary denotative definitions would require a listing of illnesses assigned to each disease category in recorded diagnoses. The only meaningful etic units available for such a list are the diagnostic categories of Western medicine. Practical and methodological problems prevent their use. We had neither facilities nor personnel to make competent Western diagnoses of all disease cases we observed. Yet, as useful as such information would be for many other purposes, it would, in fact, prove of little help in defining Subanun diagnostic categories. For one thing, too few illnesses actually occurred during our stay in the field to sample adequately a sufficient proportion of Subanun diagnostic categories. Moreover, even if one could match each Subanun diagnostic category with a series of Western diagnoses, the latter would still provide very deficient etic types. We cannot assume, as we can when working with phone types or kin types, that every Western diagnostic category will be totally included by some Subanun category. Every case diagnosed by Western criteria as tuberculosis will not receive the same Subanun diagnosis. Furthermore, a Subanun category such as *peglekebuun* 'chronic cough,' which sometimes matches with tuberculosis, will not always do so. The criteria and cues of the two diagnostic systems are too disparate for one-to-one or one-to-many matching. The problems presented to the analyst by this overlapping of categories in the two systems are compounded by the superabundance of information encoded in a Western diagnostic category. Knowing only that Subanun disease *X* partially matched Western diagnostic categories *a*, *b*, *c*, and that Subanun disease *Y* partially matched Western categories *d* and *e*, one could not easily extract from medical knowledge about, *a*, *b*, *c*, *d*, and *e* distinctive features defining the contrast between *X and Y*. For all of these reasons, distinctive-feature analysis from lists of matched native and scientific names is not feasible for folk taxonomies of disease nor, for that matter, of plants, animals, and most other natural phenomena as well.

Inadequacies of our data largely prevent confident definition of Subanun diagnostic categories by distinctive stimulus attributes, or cues, of illnesses. The discovery of what cue discriminations informants are making when contrasting one disease with another is exceedingly difficult. Many apparently pertinent cues, such as the ones that enable a Subanun patient to distinguish 'headache' (*mesait gulu*) from 'migraine' (*tampiak*) are known only by verbal descriptions. A disease "entity" such as 'headache' is not something that can be pointed to, nor can exemplars of diseases ordinarily be brought together for visual comparison and contrast as can, say, two plants. Moreover, situational features other than stimulus attributes of the illness bear on the final diagnostic decision. The same degree of pain, if objectively measured, could probably lead to a diagnosis of either 'headache' or 'migraine' depending on current social or ecological role demands on the patient. Nevertheless, very few diagnostic decisions are made by the Subanun without some apparent appeal to stimulus properties of illness; and in the majority of diagnoses these are the overriding considerations.

It is difficult, then, to define Subanun diagnostic categories in terms of analytic or perceptual attributes of their denotata. On the other hand, these very difficulties facilitate recognition of diagnostic criteria: explicit defining attributes of disease categories. Since one cannot point to a disease entity and say 'That's a such and such," as one can with a plant specimen, and since no one individual ever personally experiences but a fraction of the total number of diseases he can, in fact, differentiate, the Subanun themselves must learn to diagnose diseases through verbal description of their significant attributes. It is thus relatively easy for a Subanun to describe precisely what makes one disease different from another. He can tell us, for example, that the ulcer *begwak* produces a marked cavity, unlike the ulcer *baga?*. He can describe the difference in appearance between *glepap* 'plaque itch' and *penabud* 'splotchy itch,' the difference in locale between the 'ringworms' *buni* and *buyayag*, the difference in pathogenesis between *meŋebag*, an 'inflamed wound,' and *beldut*, a spontaneous 'sore.' This is not to say that the evaluation of the cues of a particular illness as exemplars of diagnostic criteria is always easy or consistent. Informants operating with identical diagnostic concepts may disagree about the application of these concepts in a particular case, but rarely disagree in their verbal definitions of the concepts themselves.

The procedures for eliciting and analyzing diagnostic criteria parallel those used to determine the system of nomenclature: we collect contrasting answers to the questions the Subanun ask when diagnosing disease. By asking informants to describe differences between diseases, by asking why particular illnesses are diagnosed as such and such and not something else, by following discussions among the Subanun themselves when diagnosing cases, and by noting corrections made of our own diagnostic efforts, we can isolate a limited number of diagnostic questions and criterial answers.

A classification of Subanun diagnostic criteria follows from (1) the questions which elicit them and (2) the status of the answers as diagnostic labels.

1. By eliciting question
   - 1.1. Pathogenic criteria.
   - 1.2. Prodromal criteria.
   - 1.3. Symptomatic criteria.
   - 1.4. Etiological criteria.
2. By status of the answer as a diagnostic label
   - 2.1. Elementary criteria.
   - 2.2. Complex criteria.

1.1. *Pathogenic criteria* are diagnostically significant responses to questions of 'pathogenesis' (*meksamet*), which is different from '*etiology*' (*melabet*). 'Pathogenesis' refers to the agent or mechanism that produces or aggravates an illness, 'etiology' to the circumstances that lead a particular patient to contract an illness. Thirty-four elementary diagnostic categories require pathogenic information for diagnosis. Examples are 'wound' (*samad*), 'burn' (*pasu?*), 'intestinal worm' (*pasemu*). (Latin Americanists should recognize this term [see Redfield and Redfield, 1940, p. 65]. Disease names adopted from Spanish *pasmo* or *pasma* are widespread in the Philippines. This was the only Subanun disease name of obvious Spanish origin that we recorded.) In such cases, where the identification of a pathogen is criterial to diagnosis, the association between the pathogen and the illness is relatively obvious both to the investigator and to his informants.

In addition, the Subanun posit the existence of many pathogens—such as 'plant floss' (*glaŋis*), 'microscopic mites' (*kamu*), 'intrusive objects' (*meneled*), 'symbolic acts' (*pelii*), 'stress' (*pegendekan*), 'soul loss' (*panaw i gimuud*)—which are not diagnostically criterial. These noncriterial pathogens, whose presence generally must be determined independently of diagnosis, provide clues in the search for etiological circumstances and serve as guides to prophylactic measures. But standard, named pathogens, whether criterial or not, have a limited range of pertinence. In the cognitive decisions occasioned by an illness, pathogenic mechanisms are significant only when they are necessary appurtenances to diagnosis or to etiological explanations. Otherwise they are of little interest. Like Western physicians, the Subanun do not know the pathogenic agents of many of their diseases, but, unlike the former, the Subanun consider this lack of knowledge to be of trivial rather than of crucial therapeutic significance. Consequently a large number of Subanun diseases lack standard pathogenic explanations, and many disease cases go by without any effort (except by the ethnographer) to elicit them from consultants or supernaturals.

1.2. *Prodromal criteria* are diagnostically significant responses to questions of the origin or 'prodrome' (*puunan en*) of a given illness, the 'prodrome' always referring to a prior and diagnostically distinct condition. A *derivative* disease is one whose diagnosis depends on its having a specified prodrome. When referring to a derivative disease, a query about its prodrome *must be* answered by another disease name, previously applicable to the illness. A *spontaneous* disease, in contrast, is one for which the response to a query about prodromes *can be* 'there is no prodroma' (*ndaʔ ig puunan en*).

Fig. 2 shows a number of illnesses whose diagnoses depend on their having passed through specific other stages. One cannot have *begwak* 'deep ulcer' unless one has previously, as part of the same 'illness,' had *nuka* 'eruption,' *beldut* 'sore,' and *bagaʔ* 'ulcer,' in that order. 'Eruption' (*nuka*), on the other hand, need have no prodrome, though it sometimes begins as 'rash' (*pugu*). The latter disease is always spontaneous.

For any derivative disease, a given prodrome is a necessary but not a sufficient diagnostic criterion. If the evidence of other criteria overwhelmingly points to a contrary diagnosis, one must conclude—since the criteriality of the prodrome cannot be discounted—that the previous diagnosis, or current information about it, is erroneous. Thus an informant insisted that an inflammation on my leg was an inflamed insect bite (*pagid*) rather than an inflamed wound (*tantu meŋebag*), even though I had told him I thought it originated as a 'minor cut.' I simply, according to him, had not noticed the prodromal bite. In such cases the existence of the prodrome is deduced from its criteriality to a diagnosis actually arrived at on other grounds. Our data would have been much improved had we earlier recognized the importance of these *ex post facto* classificatory decisions as evidence of criteriality.

1.3. *Symptomatic criteria* are diagnostically significant responses to a variety of questions about the attributes of an illness currently perceptible to patient or observer. These are the most frequent, wide-ranging, and complex of diagnostic criteria. Our data are not, in fact, complete enough to list, or even to enumerate, all the questions, with all their contrasting responses, necessary to define in explicit Subanun terms the symptomatic differences among all disease categories. Moreover, we can present here, in analyzed form, only a small proportion of the data we do have.

To exemplify symptomatic criteria we shall discuss several major questions that occur repeatedly in the diagnosis of a variety of illnesses; then we shall illustrate how these and other criterial contrasts intersect to define a segment of skin-disease terminology.

Specifications of locale along several dimensions provide fundamental criteria of Subanun diagnosis, closely relating to selection of appropriate therapeutic measures, to prognostic judgment, and to the evaluation of the disabling potential of an illness. First of all, disease symptoms can be located along a dimension of depth or penetration with two basic contrasts 'external' (*dibabaw*) and 'internal' (*dialem*), depending on the presence or absence of visible lesions on the surface of the body. An external disease may penetrate to produce internal symptoms as well as external lesions, in which case the disease has 'sunk' *(milegdaŋ)*. Rarely, a disease may penetrate to the other side of the body producing 'balancing' *(mitimpaŋ)* or 'pierced' *(milapus)* lesions. Penetration is prognostic of seriousness; the therapy of a number of skin diseases aims at preventing 'sinking.'

Those diseases which may be pinpointed anatomically (in Subanun terms, of course) are *localized* diseases. Should an initially localized condition begin to spread to adjacent areas within the same penetration level, then it will often fall into a new and distinct disease category. The distinction between circumscribed and spreading conditions pertains especially to external lesions. If a 'sore' (*beldut*) becomes multilesional (*misarak*), it is no longer *beldut*, but *selimbunut* 'spreading sore.' Other diseases for which spreading is an important diagnostic criterion are 'spreading rash' (*telimasu?*), 'spreading eruption' (*nenapan*), 'yaws' (*buketaw*) and 'spreading itch' (*bugais*). The Subanun describe an external condition that covers all or most of the body surface as *mipugus* or *miluup*, the latter term also designating a completely dibbled rice field.

Degree of penetration and spreading correlate closely with prognostic severity, hence their diagnostic importance. Distinctions of specific locales seem to reflect in part the disabling potential of a disease. Thus, lesions on the hands and feet often receive different designations from similar lesions elsewhere on the body; compare *baga?* 'proximal ulcer' with *telemaw* 'distal ulcer.' Among itchy skin diseases which seldom cause severe discomfort, distinctions of locale correspond with unsightliness. Thus the Subanun, who regard these diseases as extremely disfiguring, distinguish lesions hidden by clothing from those visible on a clothed body: compare *buni* 'hidden ringworm' with *buyayag* 'exposed ringworm.'

Specifications of interior locales usually refer to the area below an external reference point: the 'head,' 'chest,' 'xiphoid,' 'side,' 'waist,' 'abdomen,' and so on. The only internal organs commonly named as disease locales are the 'liver' and the 'spleen.' The liver in Subanun anatomical conceptions is somewhat akin to the heart in popular Western notions. (We recorded no Subanun diseases attributed to the heart.) The choice of the spleen as a disease locale seems to represent an instance of Subanun medical acumen. The term for spleen, *nalip* (identified during dissections of pigs), names a disease characterized by externally visible or palpable swelling attributed to this organ. The Subanun regard *nalip* as a complication of actual or latent malaria (*taig*). In Western medicine, an enlarged spleen (splenomegaly) may indicate malaria infection (Shattuck, 1951, p. 50).

Most peoples probably single out disorders of sensation as one of the most pertinent characteristics of diseases: witness our own stock query, "How are you feeling?" The Subanun ask "Does it hurt?" (*mesait ma*). The contrasting replies to this question are, first, an affirmative, "Yes, it hurts"; second, a denial of pain followed by a specification of a contrasting, nonpainful, but still abnormal sensation, "No, it doesn't hurt; it itches"; and, third, a blanket negation implying no abnormal sensation. Thus the Subanun labels a number of contrasting types of sensation and uses them to characterize and differentiate diseases.

The contrast between 'pain' (*mesait* or *megeel*) and 'itch' or 'irritation' (*matel*) has special relevance to skin lesions. 'Sores' 'hurt,' whereas scaly lesions 'itch.' But should a sore-like lesion both 'itch' and at the same time multiply and spread, a distinctive and serious disease is indicated: *buketaw* 'yaws.' The type of sensation also indicates possible pathogenic agents. Pain usually follows some kind of trauma so if the patient has suffered no obvious injury, the supernaturals have very likely inflicted an invisible wound. Itchiness signals the presence of an irritating agent, often *glaŋis* 'plant floss.' Once a condition has been labelled 'painful' in contrast to other possibilities, the kind of pain can be specified at a subordinate level of contrast. However, the Subanun make such specifications more in contexts of complaining about discomfort than in diagnosing. Consequently the terms descriptive of pain are often chosen for their rhetorical rather than denotative value. Such terms resemble English metaphors: 'burning,' 'piercing,' 'splitting,' 'throbbing.'

There are, of course, many other sensations criterial to diagnosis and a long list of diagnostic questions referring to appearances and to bodily functions. Rather than attempting to

LEVELS OF TERMINOLOGICAL CONTRAST	*beldut* 'sore'					
	telemaw 'distal ulcer'		*bagaʔ* 'proximal ulcer'			
	telemaw glai 'shallow distal ulcer'	*telemaw glibun* 'deep distal ulcer'	*bagaʔ* 'shallow proximal ulcer'	*begwak* 'deep proximal ulcer'	*beldut* 'simple sore'	*selimbunut* 'multiple sore'
depth	sh	dp	sh	dp		
distality	distal		proximal			
severity	severe				mild	
spread	single					mult
DIAGNOSTIC QUESTIONS	RANGE OF CONTRASTING ANSWERS					

Fig. 3

CRITERIAL CONTRASTS DIFFERENTIATING THE 'SORES'

discuss each of these, it will be of greater methodological advantage to illustrate how a series of questions with their contrasting answers defines one small segment of the disease terminology. Fig. 3 diagrams the criterial definitions of the types of 'sores' (*beldut*) distinguished by the Subanun (cf. Fig. 1). The 'sores' contrast with 'inflammations' (*meŋebag*) in having the prodrome *nuka* 'eruption.' 'Inflammations' and 'sores,' on the other hand, fall together in contrast to many other skin diseases in being 'painful' (*mesait*) rather than 'itchy' (*matel*). Answer to questions of spread, severity, distality (hands and feet vs. rest of body). and depth differentiate all the sores.

Depth, and especially severity, are not sharply defined by distinctive cues. In the case of 'sores,' size, persistence, and a variety of specific symptoms may point to severity: suppuration (*dun ig mata nen*), opening (*miterak*), hot sensation (*minit*), throbbing pain (*kendutendut*), intermittent burning pain (*metik*). Although not explicitly stated, judgment of severity is, in fact, partially a function of social-role contingencies. Do the patient and his consultants wish to emphasize the former's crippling disability, which prevents him from discharging an expected obligation? Or do they wish to communicate that the patient's lesion is not serious enough to interfere with his duties? Diagnosis is not an automatic response to pathological stimuli; it is a social activity whose results hinge in part on role-playing strategies.

1.4. *Etiological criteria* are diagnostically significant responses to questions of 'etiology'; how did the patient 'encounter' (*melabet*) his illness? These questions ask "Why did it happen to me?" rather than "What causes this kind of disease?" Diagnostic knowledge of the kind of disease does not give knowledge of 'etiology' in this sense. Confident determination of etiological circumstances requires communication by divination or seance with the supernaturals. Since this kind of communication tends to be costly, patients reserve etiological searching for cases when ordinary 'medicinal' (*kebuluŋan*) treatments predicated on diagnosis have not met with success. Etiological determination generally enables the patient to undertake propitiatory rituals (*kanu*) with therapeutic value. But some etiological circumstances, notably those involving human agency, cannot be counteracted by propitiations to supernaturals. These cases require treatment with specially acquired 'medicines' such as 'charms' (*pegbeliŋen*), 'amulets' (*buluŋ penapu*), 'potions' (*gaplas*), and 'antidotes' (*tekuli?*). When illnesses have a medicinally treatable etiology, the disease is then *named* for the etiological circumstance regardless of previous symptomatic diagnosis. There are seven such diseases, only two of which were recorded as diagnoses during my two years in the field: *mibuyag* 'bewitched' and *pigbuluŋan* 'poisoned.'

In view of other descriptions of primitive medicine, the surprising fact about Subanun diagnosis is that in naming all but seven of the 186 human disease categories, diagnostic questions refer directly to the empirical evidence of the disease itself and its history. The exceptional cases result from these few etiological circumstances whose determination by divination or seance necessitates renaming the illness they caused. Otherwise the results of etiological determinations do not affect previously determined empirical diagnoses. A deity may have to inform a Subanun how and why he got sick, but the symptoms themselves normally provide the information to name the disease, and by naming it, the Subanun is well on the road to prognosis and preliminary therapy.

2.1. *Elementary criteria* are those whose linguistic expression is not a disease name. 'Pain' (*mesait*) is an elementary criterion because *mesait*, by itself, cannot function as a disease name.

2.2. *Complex criteria* are themselves diagnostic categories labelled by a disease name. 'Malaria' (*taig*), for example, is diagnosed by the presence of the *disease* 'fever' (*panas*) plus the elementary criterion of 'periodic chills' (*seleŋaun*). The disease 'fever' (*panas*) is, in turn, diagnosed by the presence of the disease 'malaise' (*mesait glawas*) plus the elementary criterion of 'feeling feverish' (*mpanas*). Earlier we noted that some illnesses require a simultaneous conjunctive description by more than one disease name, e.g., 'stomach ache and headache.' A few conjunctive combinations diagnose distinct disease categories. The diseases 'stomach ache' (*mesait tian*), 'difficult breathing' (*bektus*), and 'chest pains' (*mesait gegdeb*) function as complex criteria in the diagnosis of *ba?us*, a systemic disease for which we have devised no satisfactory gloss.

THE SIGNIFICANCE OF DIAGNOSIS

The diagnostic criteria distinguishing one Subanun disease from another, in their explicit verbal formulation by informants, define conceptually distinct, mutually exclusive categories at each level of contrast. Informants rarely disagree in their verbal descriptions of what makes one disease different from another. This does not mean, however, that they are equally consistent in their naming of actual disease cases. Two informants may agree that the ulcers *baga?* and *begwak* differ in degree of penetration, yet disagree on whether a particular ulcer they are examining exhibits sufficient depth to exemplify *begwak*. The "real" world of disease presents a continuum of symptomatic variation which does not always fit neatly into conceptual pigeonholes. Consequently the diagnosis of a particular condition may evoke considerable debate: one reason a patient normally solicits diagnostic advice from a variety of people. But the debate does not concern the definition of a diagnostic category, for that is clear and well known; it concerns the exemplariness of a particular set of symptoms to the definition (cf. Goodenough, 1956, p. 215).

Conceptually the disease world, like the plant world, exhaustively divides into a set of mutually exclusive categories. Ideally every illness either fits into one category or is describable as a conjunction of several categories. Subanun may debate, or not know, the placement of a particular case, but to their minds that reflects a deficiency in their individual knowledge, not a deficiency in the classificatory system. As long as he accepts it as part of his habitat and not 'foreign,' a Subanun, when confronted with an illness, a plant, or an animal, may say he does not know the name. He will never say there is no name. The conceptual exhaustiveness of the Subanun classification of natural phenomena contrasts with the reported situation among many other peoples.

Diagnosis—the decision of what 'name' to apply to an instance of 'being sick'—is a pivotal cognitive step in the selection of culturally appropriate responses to illness by the Subanun. It bears directly on the selection of ordinary, botanically-derived, medicinal remedies from 724 recorded alternatives. The results of this selection, in turn, influence efforts to reach prognostic and etiological decisions, which, in their turn, govern the possible therapeutic need for a variant of one of 61 basic, named types of propitiatory offerings. All of these decisions and resulting actions can have far-reaching social and economic consequences.

In this paper we have presented some methodological devices which we feel are effective in delimiting the basis for decisions underlying terminological systems. Unfortunately, while in the field we did not reach even the methodological sophistication of this article. Consequently, our data have proved deficient at a number of critical points.

REFERENCE NOTE

The reference note is organized into four parts: (A) the author's note and references specific to the paper that are not in the general bibliography; (B) General Orientations Toward Meaning; (C) Problems of Semantic Description; (D) Lexicography and Dictionary Making.

A. AUTHOR'S NOTE

Field work among the Subanun, conducted in 1953-1954 and 1957-1958, was supported by grants from the U.S. Government, Yale Southeast Asia Studies Program, and Smith, Kline, and French Co. The bulk of the data upon which this analysis is based were obtained in 1957-1958 in the Gulu Disakan and Lipay regions northeast of Sindangan Bay in the interior of Zamboanga del Norte Province. All linguistic forms cited are from the Eastern Subanun dialect of this region. The frequent use of the first person plural in this article is not a rhetorical device but reflects the indispensable participation of my wife, Carolyn M. Frake, in the collection of field data. Handling of this material has profited from lengthy discussions with Harold Conklin and Volney Stefflre. Dell Hymes and Clyde Kluckhohn made helpful criticisms of an earlier draft of this paper.

References specific to the paper and not in the general bibliography:

CHRISTIE, E. B.

1909. *The Subanun of Sindangan Bay*. (Bureau of Science, Division of Ethnology Publications, No. 6.) Manila.

FRAKE, C. O.

1957a. Litigation in Lipay: A Study in Subanun Law. *Ninth Pacific Science Congress, Proceedings*. Bangkok. [In press.]

1957b. The Subanun of Zamboanga: A Linguistic Survey. *Ninth Pacific Science Congress, Proceedings*. Bangkok. [In press.]

1961. The Eastern Subanun of Mindanao. In G. P. Murdock (Ed.), *Social Structure in Southeast Asia*, (Viking Fund Publications in Anthropology, No. 29.) Chicago: Quadrangle Books. Pp. 51-64.

KELLY, G.

1955. *The Psychology of Personal Constructs*. New York: Norton. Vol. I.

REDFIELD, R., and M. P. REDFIELD

1940. *Disease and Its Treatment in Dzitas, Yucatan* (Contributions to American Anthropology and History, No. 32; Carnegie Institution of Washington, Publication no. 523.) Washington, D.C.

SHATTUCK, G. C.

1951. *Diseases of the Tropics*. New York: Appleton-Century-Crofts.

WITTGENSTEIN, L.

1958. *Blue and Brown Books*. New York: Harper & Row.

B. GENERAL ORIENTATIONS TOWARD MEANING

In pursuing semantic analysis as a part of ethnography and theory, some awareness of the different general orientations to the study of meaning, especially as treated by our society's specialists in such discussion—philosophers and their psychological, literary, and other congeners—is necessary.

Among the major orientations and most useful references, in addition to those cited in Part III, may be noted: Barr-Hillel (1954, 1959), Basilius (1952), Black (1949, 1962), Bloomfield (1933, pp. 139-169; 1943a), Brough (1953), Brown (1956; 1958, especially pp. 82-109), Bühler (1934, pp. 79-255), Burke (1945, 1951a, 1957, 1958, 1961, 1962), Burks (1948-1949), Cassirer (1923), Carnap (1959), Chomsky (1955), Goodenough (1957a), Guiraud (1958a), Fries (1954), Hjelmslev (1953), Hoijer (1954a, *passim*), Hymes (1961a), Jespersen (1924), Kronasser (1952), Langer (1942), Lenneberg and Roberts (1956), Levi-Strauss (1960d, 1962), Linsky (1952), Lounsbury (1955), McQuown (1954a), Malinowski (1923, 1935), Morris (1939, 1946), Naess (1953), Ogden and Richards (1923), Osgood, Suci, Tannenbaum (1957), Quine (1953, 1959, 1960), Read (1948), Saporta (1961, chap. 5), Schlauch (1946, 1947), Sinclair (1951), H. L. Smith (1952), Stern (1931), Ullmann (1957), Wallace (1961), Weinreich (1963), Wells (1954), Wittgenstein (1953), Ziff (1961). The following are useful surveys and critiques: Black (1949), Brown (1958), Guiraud (1958a), Kronasser (1952), Linsky (1952), Read (1948), Saporta (1961), Ullmann (1957), and Wells (1954).

References not in the general bibliography:

BARR-HILLEL, Y.

1954. Logical Syntax and Semantics. *Lg.*, *30:* 230-237.

1959. Review of R. M. Martin, *Truth and Denotation*. *Lg.*, *35:* 311-314.

BROUGH, J.

1953. Some Ancient Indian Theories of Meaning. *Transactions of the Philological Society* (London). Pp. 161-176.

BURKS, A. W.

1948-1949. Icon, Index, and Symbol. *Philosophical and Phenomenological Research*, *9:* 673-689.

CARNAP, RUDOLPH

1959. *Introduction to Semantics*; *Formalization of Logic*. (Rev. ed.) Cambridge: Harvard University Press. (1st ed., 1942.)

CHOMSKY, N.

1955. Logical Syntax and Semantics. *Lg.*, *31:* 36-45. [Also in Sol Saporta (Ed.). *Psycholinguistics*. New York: Holt, Rinehart and Winston, 1961. Pp. 261-268.]

FRIES, C. C.

1954. Meaning and Linguistic Analysis. *Lg.*, *30:* 57-68.

LINSKY, LEONARD (ED.)

1952. *Semantics and the Philosophy of Language*. Urbana: University of Illinois Press.

LOUNSBURY, FLOYD G.

1955. The Varieties of Meaning. In Ruth Hirsch Weinstein (Ed.), *Report of the Sixth Annual Round Table Meeting on Linguistics and Language*

Teaching. (Monograph Series on Languages and Linguistics, No. 8.) Washington, D.C.: Georgetown University. Pp. 158-164.

NAESS, ARNE

1953. *Interpretation and Criticism*. Oslo: Dybwad.

QUINE, WILLARD VAN ORMAN

1953. *From a Logical Point of View*. Cambridge: Harvard University Press.

1960. *Word and Object*. New York and London: Wiley.

READ, ALLEN WALKER

1948. An Account of the Word "Semantics." *Word*, *4:* 78-97.

SCHLAUCH, MARGARET

1947. Mechanisms and Historical Materialism in Semantic Studies. *Science and Society*, *12:* 254-259.

WITTGENSTEIN, L.

1953. *Philosophical Investigations*. Translated by G. E. M. Anscombe. Oxford: Blackwell.

ZIFF, PAUL

1961. *Semantic Analysis*. Ithaca: Cornell University Press.

C. PROBLEMS OF SEMANTIC DESCRIPTION

On the particular problems of semantic description, in addition to references above, those listed in Part III, and those listed for the articles in this part, see the following: Bally (1951), Bazell (1953), Firth (1935, 1951), Frake (1962a), Goodenough (1955, 1956), Greenberg (1954b), Hattori (1956), Haugen (1957), Hjelmslev (1957), Jakobson (1957b, 1959), Jespersen (1937), Joos (1958a), Leach (1958), Nida (1958, 1961), Öhman (1951, 1953), Oliver (1949), Osgood (1959), Phillips (1959-60), Robins (1952), Sapir (1930, 1944), Ullmann (1952, 1953, 1957), Voegelin and Voegelin (1957), Weinreich (1955, 1958, 1959, 1963), Wells (1954, 1958), Whorf (1956b).

References not in the general bibliography:

BAZELL, C. E.

1953. La Semantique structurale. *Dialogues*, *3:* 120-132.

FIRTH, J. R.

1951. Modes of Meaning. *Essays and Studies*, 118-149. [Also in Firth, *Papers in Linguistics, 1934-1951*. London: Oxford University Press, 1957. Pp. 190-215.]

GOODENOUGH, WARD H.

1955. Review of H. Hoijer (Ed.), *Language in Culture*. *Lg.*, *31:* 243-245.

HATTORI, SHIRO

1956. The Analysis of Meaning. *For Roman Jakobson*. The Hague: Mouton. Pp. 201-212.

HJELMSLEV, LOUIS

1957. Dans quelle Mesure les significations des mots peuvent-elles être considérées comme formant une structure ? In Eva Sivertsen (Ed.), *Proceedings of the Eighth International Congress of Linguists* (*Oslo, 1957*). Oslo: Oslo University Press, 1958. Pp. 636-654. [Also in Hjelmslev, *Essais Linguistiques*. (Travaux du Cercle Linguistique de Copenhague, No. 12.) Copenhagen: Nordisk Sprog—og Kulturforlag, 1959. Pp. 96-112.]

JESPERSEN, OTTO

1937. *Analytic Syntax*. Copenhagen: Munksgaard.

OSGOOD, C. E.

1959. Semantic Space Revisited. *Word, 15:* 192-199.

ROBINS, R. H.

1952. A Problem in the Statement of Meanings. *Lingua, 3:* 121-137.

SAPIR, E.

1944. Grading: A Study in Semantics. *Philosophy of Science, 11:* 93-116. [Also in David G. Mandelbaum (Ed.), *Selected Writings of Edward Sapir in Language, Culture, and Personality*. Berkeley and Los Angeles: University of California Press, 1949. Pp. 122-149.]

WEINREICH, URIEL

1958. Travels Through Semantic Space. *Word, 14:* 346-366.

1959. A Rejoinder. *Word, 15:* 200-201.

WELLS, RULON S.

1958. To What Extent Can Meaning Be Said To Be Structured? In Eva Sivertsen (Ed.), *Proceedings of the Eighth International Congress of Linguists (Oslo, 1957)*. Oslo: Oslo University Press, 1958. Pp. 655-666.

D. LEXICOGRAPHY AND DICTIONARY-MAKING

Semantic analysis and lexicography, or dictionary-making, are inextricably involved with each other. Conceptions and availability of one markedly affect those having to do with the other. As to types of dictionaries, note such examples and analyses as Buck (1949), Conklin (1953), The Franciscan Fathers (1910), Hallig and Wartburg (1952), Hoijer (1949), Kennedy (1953), Le Cœur (1950), Lekens (1952), Malkiel (1962), Sapir (1930-1931), Sebeok (1962), Voegelin and Voegelin (1957), Westphal (1959).

On the problems and procedures of making dictionaries, cf. Allen (1958, Part VI, pp. 371-392), Bloomfield (1933, pp. 274 ff.), Casares (1950), Conklin (1962), Empson (1951, especially chap. 21), Garvin (1947, 1955), Hiorth (1955a, 1955b, 1956), Householder and Saporta (1962), Joos (1958b), Kovtun (1957), Kurath (1952), Matoré (1953), Nida (1958), Starnes (1954), Voegelin (1959), Voegelin and Hymes (1953), Voegelin and Voegelin (1957), Weinreich (1962b).

References not in the general bibliography:

BUCK, CARL DARLING

1949. *A Dictionary of Selected Synonyms in the Principal Indo-European Languages*. Chicago: University of Chicago Press.

CASARES, JULIO

1950. *Introducción a la lexicografía moderna*. (Revista de filologia espanola, anejo 52.) Madrid.

CONKLIN, HAROLD C.

1953. *Hanunóo-English Vocabulary*. (University of California Publications in Linguistics, No. 9.) Berkeley and Los Angeles: University of California Press.

FRANCISCAN FATHERS, THE

1910. *An Ethnologic Dictionary of the Navaho Language*. Saint Michaels, Ariz.: The Franciscan Mission of the Southwest.

GARVIN, PAUL L.

1947. Review of L. V. Shcherba, *Opy obščej teorii leksikografii*. *Word*, *3:* 128-130.

HALLIG, R., and W. V. WARTBURG

1952. *Begriffssystem als Grundlage für die Lexikographie. Versuch eines Ordnungsschemas.* (Abhandlungen der deutschen Akademie der Wissenschaften zu Berlin, 4.) Berlin.

HIORTH, FINNGEIR

1955a. On the Subject Matter of Lexicography. *Studia Linguistica*, *9:* 57-65.

1955b. Arrangement of Meaning in Lexicography. *Lingua*, *4:* 413-424.

1956. On the Relation Between Field Research and Lexicography. *Studia Linguistica*, *10:* 57-66.

HOIJER, HARRY

1949. *An Analytical Dictionary of the Tonkawa Language.* (University of California Publications in Linguistics, No. 5.) Berkeley and Los Angeles: University of California Press.

JOOS, MARTIN

1958b. Review of Eric P. Hamp. *A Glossary of American Technical Linguistic Usage, 1925-1950. Lg.*, *34:* 279-288.

KENNEDY, GEORGE A.

1953. *ZH Guide: An Introduction to Sinology.* (Yale University Sinological Seminar.) New Haven: Yale University Far Eastern Publications. [Reviewed, *Lg.*, *29:* 568-576.]

KOVTUN, L. S.

1957. On the Construction of a Lexicographic Article. In O. S. Axmanova *et al.* (Eds.), *Leksikograficeskiy sbornik*, *1:* 68-97. Moscow.

KURATH, HANS

1952. Introduction. In Kurath and Sherman M. Kuhn (Eds.), *Middle English Dictionary*. Ann Arbor: University of Michigan Press. Part E. 1.

LE CŒUR, C.

1950. *Dictionnaire ethnographique Teda, précéde d'un lexique Français-Teda.* (Memoires de l'Institut Francais d'Afrique Noire, No. 9.) Paris.

LEKENS, P. BENJAMIN

1952. *Dictionnaire ngbandi* (*Ubangi-Congo belge*). (Annales de Musée Royal du Congo Belge, Sciences de homme, Linguistique, No. 1.) Anvers: Editions de Sikkel.

MALKIEL, YAKOV

1962. A Typological Classification of Dictionaries on the Basis of Distinctive Features. In Fred W. Householder and Sol Saporta (Eds.), *Problems in Lexicography*. (RCAFL-P 21; *IJAL*, *28* (4): Part 4.) Bloomington.

MATORÉ, G.

1953. *La Méthode en lexicologie*. Paris.

SAPIR, EDWARD

1930-1931. *The Southern Paiute Language: Southern Paiute, A Shoshonean Language*; *Texts of the Kaibab Paiutes and Uintah Utes*; *Southern Paiute Dictionary*. (Proceedings. American Academy of Arts and Sciences, No. 65.) Part 1, pp. 1-296; Part 2, pp. 297-535; Part 3, pp. 537-730.

SEBEOK, THOMAS A.

1962. Materials for a Typology of Dictionaries. *Lingua*, *11:* 363-374.

STARNES, DEWITT T.

1954. *Renaissance Dictionaries*, *English-Latin and Latin-English*. Austin: University of Texas Press. [Reviewed, S. M. Kuhn, *Lg*., 1954, *30:* 551-554.]

VOEGELIN, CARL F.

1959. Review of S. Newman, *Zuni Dictionary*. *AA*, *61:* 162-163.

WEINREICH, URIEL

1962b. Lexicographic Definition in Descriptive Semantics. In Fred W. Householder and Sol Saporta (Eds.), *Problems in Lexicography*. (RCAFL-P 21; *IJAL*, 28 (4): Part 4.) Bloomington.

WESTPHAL, E. O. J.

1959. *Kwangari: An Index of Lexical Types*. London: School of Oriental and African Studies, London University.

part V

ROLE, SOCIALIZATION, AND EXPRESSIVE SPEECH

Introduction

Whatever the angle of vision, all study of language and speech as part of social life is basically one, rooted in the interdependence within social life itself. The linguistic aspects of adaptation to environment and circumstance, formation and expression of personality, social structure and interaction, cultural values and beliefs—all are facets of an on-going whole. Taken as disciplinary foci, each is a standpoint from which to describe and interpret the same behavioral reality. This basic principle must be kept in mind, however convenient and necessary it is to select and group together particular aspects of the subject at a given time.

If there is a major division to be made, it is that between a primary focus on the content of language and a primary focus on acts of speech. The first underlies descriptive linguistics as usually conceived, including its extension by way of semantic description into the topics of Parts III and IV. The second underlies much of what is contained in the next four Parts, V-VIII. Although study of one must involve or lead into consideration of the others, and there are obvious connections to be traced in the articles presented in this book, the intimacy of content within each side is on the whole much greater than between them. Parts III and IV deal primarily with the relation of language content to the content of culture and the world of experience and with the degree to which they reflect and affect each other. The function of reference is the central concern. This part and the next three deal primarily with the relation of speech event to social interaction and with speech as an instrument for the acquisition and maintenance of personality, role, and status. The functions of expression, persuasion, and identification become of central concern.

In the study of such functions one becomes concerned with the *selective variation* of linguistic resources in relation to person, motive, and situation. (The term "selective variation" is put forward by Whatmough [1956].) If particular studies are to reinforce each other cumulatively, however, and a general theory be built up, then the fundamental notion of an act of speech, or *speech event*, must be explicated. Jakobson (1960a) has provided the best account so far, and the following is an adaptation of it.

A speech event implies a set of constitutive factors and functions. The strength of a general anthropological study of speech as part of behavior depends upon the adequacy with which such factors and functions are conceived as a framework for analysis. In the individual case, of course, what counts as a speech event, what factors are present, and what hierarchy of functions are served must be determined empirically if the results are to have validity. In general, however, major types can be defined as a heuristic starting-point.

As factors of a speech event, one can distinguish seven major types: (1) sender, (2) receiver, (3) channel, (4) message-form, (5) code, (6) topic, (7) context or scene. Of course each type subsumes further distinctions, such as, in (1-2) between intended addressor and addressee, and senders and receivers who are intermediary or unintended; (6) between explicit and implicit topic; (7) between physical and psychological context. Functions of speech events can be distinguished into major types by association with a principal focus on each of the above factors in turn: (1) expressive and identificational, (2) directive, persuasive, etc., (3) contact, (4) poetic, (5) metalinguistic, (6) referential, (7) contextual or situational. Of course, each type subsumes further distinctions: (1-2) between what a speech event expresses for the sender or how it affects the receiver, on the one hand, and what it reveals (intentionally or not) of the identity and state of either; (3) between physical and psychological contact; (4) between the attention to the form of the message that poetry (and advertising slogans, etc.) attract, the poetic function proper, and attention to message-form for other reasons (such as proofreading).

In using a classification of components of speech events, one asks what can be told about a component from the event or what difference would result if it varied while the other components were held constant. Thus, regarding (1), what can be told about the age, sex, nationality, motive, attitude, etc. of the sender—what would be different if the sender or his state were different? (2) What can be told about the recipients of the message? (3) What changes or effect would result from a different physical channel (voice, writing, instrument, or mode of manipulation of any of the three) or from a different psychological nexus between the participants? This might be the perspective of the communications engineer, the analyst of speech surrogates (Stern, 1957), or the psychiatrist. (4) What would be different if the choice of form were different? By what means is attention attracted to the form itself? (5) What can be told about the code which the message presupposes? This is often the focus of the descriptive linguist and of the child or foreigner learning the language. (6) What can be told about the topic of the speech event? What would be different if it were different? (7) How would the speech event differ if it occurred in a different context?

There are two ways to pursue such an inquiry. One can note features associated with a certain component and isolate and study them as such: features diagnostic of certain types of speaker and hearer or speaker-hearer contact; expressive, rhetorical, poetic features; the repertoire of metalinguistic devices (e.g., the query, "How do you spell that?") for communicating about a code; features diagnostic of particular channels, topics, situations; and the like. One can also view the whole of a speech event in terms of a particular function, for example,seeing the entire act as variously expressive of the sender.

A full study would, of course, also inventory kinds of speech events, partly through analysis of terminology (cf. Part IV), and would consider all of the social structure in this light (cf. Part VII, the articles by Conklin, Cowan, Herzog, Emeneau, and Sebeok in Part VI, and those by Fischer and Haas in Part VIII).

The general analysis of the functions of speech within a community helps bridge the gap between descriptions of language in terms of grammar, texts, and dictionary, and descriptions of behavior (of which speech is part) in terms of ecology, personality, social structure, religion, and the like. It also contributes to the comparative study of the role of speech in different societies (and types of personality). In a general analysis of communication and action, speech is but one mode among others, and the degree and way in which it is used varies among groups and individuals. Not only are there cross-cultural differences, but there are significant class differences within a single society (see Bernstein's article in this section). The value attached to speech activity or to a language; conceptions about them; settings in which speech is required, forbidden, or, being optional, informative; attention to speech in the definition and evaluation of groups and roles; how and how much speech enters into the socialization which shapes personalities, into the learning of roles and skills, and into expression and perception of personality; the relative status of "words" and "deeds," of channels such as speech and writing, of functions such as referential and expressive—all these may differ cross-culturally as markedly and significantly as religion and sex.

The articles in this part represent three aspects of the role of speech in interpersonal relationships which have received particular attention: forms of address, the process of acquisition, and expressive use. Since forms of address may constitute a well-defined semantic field and involve kinship terms, their study is linked closely to the history of the concerns represented in both Part IV and Part VII, and has received impetus from the recent developments in structural ("componential") analysis in both.

The study of the acquisition of speech has lagged in anthropology; there is very little adequate cross-cultural data, let alone systematic comparative study. Structural linguistics has given a fresh impetus and sharpness to its description, however, and the renewed concern for the study of intellectual development in children enhances its interest. Except for Sapir and his student, Stanley Newman, the linguistic aspects of personality were almost ignored in American linguistics and anthropology until recently. The concentration of linguists on descriptive method and formal structure and the ignorance among anthropologists of the necessary linguistic techniques divorced both from the subject. In one of his series of studies, Newman speaks of the problem, echoing Sapir (1929c):

> A study of this peripheral language material offers the linguist an opportunity to broaden the scope of his science into a less schematic and more realistic approach to language phenomena, and to discover relations between linguistics and other sciences that could result in a mutual exchange of contributions and insights. The sharp separation which exists between linguistics and other disciplines is, at best, an arbitrary one, based upon the development of an isolated methodology and not upon any empirical division of its subject matter (1941, pp. 94-95).

Recent cooperative research by psychiatrists, linguists, and anthropologists has concentrated a wide range of attention on the subject and brought progress in the basic task of identifying the full range of vocal features which serve personality.

In "Nuer Modes of Adress," Evans-Pritchard shows the detailed correlation between usages in address and aspects of social structure. In doing so, he succinctly validates a postulate proposed by Emeneau (1950), which has underlain much anthropological attention to forms of address, as well as to other semantic fields: "Some forms are ordered in classes or subclasses corresponding to systems or subsystems within the environment." But whereas some would propose first to determine the classes of linguistic forms and then to seek external correlates, Evans-Pritchard presents a case in which the forms are grouped together as a class only because of a prior knowledge of their common social function, a knowledge which is necessary also to explain the variety and dimensions of choice among them. Emeneau's postulate is a two-way street: sometimes the ordering of linguistic forms is a guide to structure in other aspects of life; here the converse is true.

Haas delineates a case in which the distinction of male and female roles has penetrated the grammatical core of a language and then compares other reported cases, setting up types in terms of the participants in the speech events in which the sex distinction is made.

Note that she relates the types to the particular linguistic means which implement them, including whether the men's or women's form can be taken as basic to the other. (It may be significant that the cases in which the women's form appears basic are from tribes with matrilineal descent—Koasati, Greek, Muskogee.)

Brown and Ford extend the important work of Brown and Gilman (1960), interpreting American usage in address in terms of two major dimensions, intimacy and status, and relating usage to more general aspects of the place of the dimensions in social relations. Evidence suggests that the dimensions and the characteristics of their use have great generality and can be usefully applied to the patterning of a great many phenomena of linguistic choice.

Casagrande's study is a rare detailed account of baby talk in a nonwestern language. The importance of the subject is highlighted by

Casagrande's concluding observations and by the implications of the fact that a child must first learn the baby forms, then repress their use. Further information also suggests that baby forms may be no easier than adult forms and that some societies lack baby talk altogether. Casagrande's query as to the length of time required for children to learn different languages takes on added significance in terms of current debate as to what extent a child's acquisition of language is dependent on experience and to what extent on the unfolding of a species-specific capacity. Study of language acquisition has tended to seize upon such relatively external features as vocabulary size and utterance length, but work has now turned to the child's own linguistic system and his acquisition of its rules.

Bernstein's work demonstrates the existence and importance of major differences in language function within a single culture. Different patterns of social structure are seen as stressing and shaping different possibilities inherent in language use, with marked consequences for the children who acquire each. Indeed, speech is interpreted as the major means through which social structure becomes part of individual experience. The two patterns described, a *formal* (= *elaborate*) and a *public* (= *restricted*) code, are related to a wide range of behavior and attitudes, not least to prospects in education and therapy.

Nadel describes an African case of interplay between cultural values, language content, and a child's experience. Note the concluding validation of the inferences by the Nupe's own intense interest in the phenomena of their language.

The Mohave, as described by Devereux, provide a sharp three-way contrast among themselves, the Nupe, and, over-all, the United States. The Nupe eschew sexual reference and sharply divide polite from impolite expressions; we have over-all at least three levels of such vocabulary, technical, "vulgar," and intermediate euphemism, each appropriate to some situations and inappropriate to others; and the Mohave have a vocabulary which is both extensive and single, the terms carrying no implication of profanity or obscenity in themselves. Something else must so define the situation. Thus, one child may learn an incomplete, intrinsically tainted set of terms for such matters; another may learn a large, intrinsically neutral vocabulary; a third may learn terms of several levels, how much of each level is learned and the sense of naturalness or appropriateness with which it is used varying with background and situation. One can speculate about differences in personality that may be entailed; there is enough variation in our own society for controlled studies.

Devereux's article is valuable as well for the wide range of phenomena, often psychiatric in implication, to which it draws attention. Note, for example, the Mohave belief that infants understand speech. It is remarkable that this and other articles by Devereux (e.g., Devereux, 1951) are almost alone in recent American linguistic and anthropological literature in having a psychoanalytic orientation toward speech. Verbal behavior is, of course, the stock in trade of psychoanalysis, and Freud found etymology also grist to his mill (a notable example using both is Stone [1954]). Although psychoanalytic articles sometimes display outdated conceptions about linguistic phenomena, some anthropological and linguistic conceptions of human motivation must seem equally naïve to the psychoanalyst. Some integration of psychiatric work with linguistics has begun, however, in connection with the research represented by Trager's article in this section.

Like Devereux's article, the excerpt by Adams is an empirical account of phenomena toward which the technical developments reported by Trager are directed. Adams provides a succinct analysis of a situation of cultural dominance of expressive over referential function in normal communication and of the practical consequences of the fact.

Trager sets forth the background of the present study of paralinguistics and offers a systematic framework for analyzing communication. Within the framework he details the advances that have been made in analyzing the range of speech phenomena outside of language, what Sapir (1927a) termed "the linguistically irrelevant habits of speech manipulation which are characteristic of a particular group." The work is still very much in progress. It has only begun to be extended to speech communities other than English, a necessary step if a general etic framework is to be standardized and used in the way that a phonetic alphabet can be now. With focus necessarily on identifying and describing the phenomena, little has been done in determining how they occur relative to each other and how their occurrences interrelate with such things as situation, role, and personality.

Even so, the present state of the work alerts the fieldworker to the significance of paralinguistic phenomena in any group with which he is concerned, the dimensions of the difference between the "what" and the "how" of what is said. Much of what would be coded by observers of behavior, for example, as aggression, nurturance, succorance and the like, may be communicated paralinguistically, absent from a transcription of what is said in ordinary orthography, at best perhaps impressionistically characterized (in a foreign language) by adverbs such as "tenderly," "curtly." And paralinguistic phenomena may play an important part in the process of socialization.

Nuer Modes of Address 24

E. E. EVANS-PRITCHARD

THIS ARTICLE DESCRIBES different ways in which persons are addressed among the Nilotic Nuer of the Anglo-Egyptian Sudan, apart from the use of kinship terms. The forms of address described are all employed in salutations; they may be used also to attract a person's attention and in the course of conversation, though in ordinary conversation Nuer do not constantly reiterate a person's name or other title of address.

The study of names and titles of address has some importance because, as will be seen from the notes recorded below, they symbolize a man's social position in relation to the people around him, so that, by the use of one or other of them, the status of the speaker to the person addressed is readily recognized. Like kinship terms, these modes of address thus emphasize social relationships and serve to evoke the response implied in the particular relationship so indicated. They are often used among relatives, especially among very close kinsmen, instead of kinship terms.

Every Nuer has a personal or birth name. This is *cotdu pany*, your true name. It is given shortly after birth and without ceremony by the parents, sometimes on the suggestion of a relative, though the father has the final decision in the matter. The personal name is retained through life and is preserved in the names of the children, particularly of the sons, each of whom is often referred to, and addressed, as "son of so-and-so." The personal name eventually becomes a point in lineage structure.

A boy is addressed by this personal name by everyone in his paternal village. When he is grown up members of his family and close paternal kinsfolk and friends of about his own age, that is to say of his age-set or of sets immediately above and below his own set, continue to use it. It might be regarded as unduly familiar were a man to address a man much senior to himself by his personal name. He should address him as *gwa*, "father," and he would be so addressed himself by very much younger men. Married women with children are seldom either addressed or referred to by their personal names, although there is no impropriety in doing so. Out of respect one generally uses the teknonymous mode. Unmarried girls may be freely addressed by their personal names by everyone. Small children, till they have learned the correct usages, call everyone, including their parents and other elders by their personal names.

A number of these personal names are recorded by H. C. Jackson (1923, pp. 142, 171). They refer as a rule to events which took place before or at the time of birth, or to the place of birth; and a man generally knows the circumstances which led to his being given the name he bears. I list a few names as examples of this form of nomenclature:

Reath, 'drought'; *Nhial*, 'rain'; *Nyout*, 'heavy rainstorm'; *Pet*, 'the name of a month'; *Nyaluaak*, *nya* 'feminine prefix,' *luaak* 'cattle byre'; *(Nya)wec*, 'cattle camp'; *(Nya)puol*, 'pool of water'; *(Nya)pun*, 'wild rice'; *Duob* 'path.' The "*juoli*" class of names, those given to children whose elder brothers and sisters have died; *Bath*, 'to be lost'; *Cuol*, 'to compensate'; *Bilieu*, 'you will die'; *Mun*, 'earth'; *Lul*, 'to cry'; *Gac*, 'to be dismayed'; *(Nya)mer*, 'tear'; *Ruei*, 'spittle' (the mother had not conceived so the father's kinsfolk spat into a gourd and her belly was rubbed with the spittle and a prayer was offered that she might conceive); *Deng* (a prophet, in whom dwelt the spirit *Deng*, performed a similar rite); (*Nya*) *gaak*, 'quarrel' (the child was born at the time of a dispute); *Met*, 'to deceive' (when the child's father was wooing his mother he boasted of the number of cattle he could give as bridewealth for her hand, but when it came to handing them over he began to make excuses, saying that the black cow had died, that the white cow had been eaten by a lion, and so on).

A child is often given a second personal name by his maternal grandparents. The maternal grandparents are expected to bring up the eldest child of their daughter and it is a common practice to wean other children by leaving them for a few months at the home of their maternal grandmother. When a person is in his maternal kinsmen's district he is addressed by this second name, by which also his maternal kinsmen habitually refer to him. Hence both men and women commonly have two personal names, one in use among their paternal kinsmen and the other in use among their maternal kinsmen. These two names have often a similar meaning, e.g., *Lul*, 'cry'; *Wia*, 'cry of warning'; *Mun*, 'earth'; *Tiop*, 'earth mixed with cattle manure and ashes'; *Nhial*, 'rain (sky)'; and *Deng*, 'a sky-god.'

Personal names sometimes recur in lineal descent. I have only met one man called after his father, and in this case the child was probably named after his father's death. Occasionally a man is called after his paternal grandfather or great-grandfather so that his ancestor's name may be remembered in daily speech. When this is done, Nuer say of the boy, *Ce cung ni wic gwandongde*, "He stands on the head of his (great) grandfather." It is possible that women are likewise sometimes named after their grandmothers and great-grandmothers, but I have no information on this point.

Twins have special personal names so that one knows at once when hearing a certain name that the bearer of it is a twin. The senior twin is generally called *Both* (*Nyaboth*), 'the one who goes ahead,' and the junior is generally called *Duoth* (*Nyaduoth*), 'the one who follows.' They are also sometimes called *Gwong*, 'guinea-fowl,' and *Ngec*, 'francolin,' or simply *Dit* (*Nyadiet*), 'Bird,' for Nuer say that twins are birds. Children born of the same mother after twins also have stereotyped names. The one who comes after the twins is called *Bol* (*Nyibuol*) or *Bicock* and the next child is called *Tot* (*Nyatot*) or *Cuil*.

Every Nuer child inherits a *cot paak*, the honorific, or praise name of his clan. Although any man or woman may be addressed by this name, in practice it is little used and then mostly on ceremonial occasions and by women. When women address men in this way it is generally on some formal occasion, such as the return of a man to his home after a long absence, or at weddings and initiation ceremonies. Thus when a youth comes back from a long journey it would be correct for his mother or any senior woman of his home to greet him by his clan honorific name in reply to his salutation. Younger women on such an occasion would use his ox-name (see below). Women address one another by their clan names more often, though their use is always formal. It is a recognized form of address by a mother-in-law to her son's wife. I have heard women employ it to their small children when pleased with them. I have recorded a number of these clan names elsewhere (1934b).

The women of a man's (or woman's) paternal district address him by the honorific name of his father's clan and the women of his maternal district use that of his mother's clan. Thus a man of the Gaatagankiir clan born of a woman of the Gaatnaca clan will be addressed in Jinkany tribal area, in which the father's clan are predominant, as *gat* (son of) *you* and in the Lou tribal area, where the mother's clan is predominant, as *gat* (son of) *nya* (daughter of) *gun*. In the case of a woman she would be addressed as *nya you* in Jinkany country and as *nya nya gun* in Lou country.

Personal names are acquired shortly after birth and honorific clan names are inherited from parents. Men and women later in life acquire other titles of address. Boys are often addressed by their playmates by names derived from male calves of the cows they milk, but their elders would not so address them and other boys would not use the names in the presence of their elders. But when a boy is initiated to manhood his father or paternal uncle gives him an ox (or a bull calf which he later castrates), and this ox, which he describes as *thak gareda*, "the ox of my initiation," becomes his favorite in the herd. From its colors, distribution of markings, shape of horns, and other peculiarities, he takes his *cot thak*, ox-name. He may later take a different name when he acquires a new ox which he prefers, or when the old one dies; the new name either then takes the place of the old or both are used. Most men seem to keep for life the ox-names they acquire at the time of their initiation. A man may say by which ox-name he wishes to be addressed but usually the people of his home give him the name after the ox of his initiation. However, if they see that he pays particular attention to an exceptionally fine ox in his herd, perhaps rubbing ashes on its back and singing and prancing behind it in the early mornings in the dry-season cattle camps, they will call him after that one. At first only the age-mates of a freshly initiated lad may know his ox-name but the older people soon get to know it in the cattle camps which are formed soon after his initiation. There he frequently displays himself with the ox and shouts out his new name; this is heard by the whole camp, and his age-mates greet him by it when their elders are present. A man shouts out the name of the favorite ox (*thak moc*) from which he has taken his name when he spears a man in war or an animal or fish in hunting. Also young men of about the same age call out their ox-names (with many embellishments) to one another at dances, often after a bout of duelling with clubs; and two lines of youths stand opposite each other and shower ox-names on one another preparatory to a spectacular jump into the air in unison.

A man is addressed by his ox-name, especially in salutations, by his age-mates: it is their privilege to address him in this way. Nevertheless there is no objection to men of about the same age greeting one another by their ox-names even if they belong to different age-sets so long as the sets are adjacent in the age-set system. It would be presumptuous to address a much senior man by his ox-name. The younger man would call him *gwa*, 'father,' and the older man would call the younger, *gatda*, 'my son.' If a stranger wishes to greet a man of about his age by an ox-name and does not know his ox-name, it is permissible for him to use any of the commoner ox-names, such as Kurjok. Ox-names are generally, though not always, forgotten after a man's death and normally it is the personal name which survives in the genealogies. I have written a paragraph on the formation of ox-names in my book on the Nuer (1940, p. 46).

Nuer maidens also take ox-names, in their case from the bulls calved by the cows they milk, and they address one another by these names. Youths sometimes address girls with whom they are flirting by their ox-names, and the girls sometimes address the youths similarly, but men do not in public so address their sweethearts, nor girls their lovers. A man rarely addresses his sisters or the other girls of his home by their ox-names; only when he is very pleased with them. Ox-names of girls are thus in the main used only among the girls themselves, when they are alone together, and are therefore seldom heard except at dances, when the girls call them out to one another, combining the names with fanciful elaborations such as *toar mathda*, 'beer strainer, my friend'; *gwith mathda*, 'pride, my friend'; *thiau*, 'arm-rings' (for a girl who is wearing them). Married women take cow-names from their favorite cows in the family herd, and they use cow-names among themselves. Men do not address women by these names.

It has been remarked that at dances men call out their ox-names with many embellishments, and that girls call out theirs with fanciful elaborations. These embellishments and elaborations are dance-names. The dance-name (*cot bual*) precedes the ox-name with which it is generally, if not always, used. Married women's cow-names are also coupled with dance-names at dances. Usually there does not seem to be any connection between the meanings of the dance-names and the cattle-names. The dance-names are sometimes nick-names (used only at dances), given to their bearers by their friends, but are more often traditional names chosen for reasons of euphony, e.g., *Yar* (sulky) *Joklieth* (ox-name), and *Rang* (good spearsman) *Boipar* (ox-name), for men; *Pun* (wild rice) *Rolnyang* (ox-name), and *Keat* (a riverside shrub) *Nyinyar* (ox-name), for girls; *Biet* (silent) *Wityan* (cow-name), and *Rier* (the white pith of reeds) *Kuaar Nyang* (cow-name), for married women.

A man who is getting on in years is very often addressed as *gat*, 'son of,' followed by the name of his father, and this is the correct mode of address for young men to their seniors if they do not use *gwa*, 'father.' Anyone who wishes to be polite to a man, whether a kinsman or an unrelated person, may address him in this way; it is, too, a suitable mode of salutation for a man who is not old enough to be called *gwa* but is too senior to saluted by his ox-name. There is no reason, however, why an older man should not make use of this complimentary mode to a younger if he wishes to do so, and younger men are sometimes addressed in this way. In referring to a man, one can couple his name directly with that of his father, e.g., while *Wia* son of *Cam* would be saluted as *gat* (son of) *Cam* he might be referred to as *Wia Cam*, though the usage is not common. A man may also be addressed by reference to his father's ox-name, which name takes the place of his personal name.

As I have explained elsewhere (1945, pp. 39-42), a man (or woman) may, according to where he is living, who addresses him or refers to him, and the occasion of address or reference, be called after his pater, his genitor, his foster-father, his pro-pater in ghost-marriage, and his pro-pater in leviratic marriage, though the pater's name is the one that is said to survive in lineage structure. Thus a boy who is living with his mother and his mother's lover by whom he was begotten is called after his genitor and foster-father in that man's village and district, but in the country of his pater he is called after his pater. A boy born in ghost-marriage is called after his pro-pater except on ceremonial occasions when his place in lineage structure needs to be indicated by reference to his pater's name.

Girls are addressed by their father's names much less than men, and for women in general the mode is occasional and definitely expresses a compliment to the speaker. It would be considered correct, for instance, though it is not obligatory, for a man to address a wife of his father other than his own mother by *nya*, 'daughter of,' followed by the ox-name of her father, if he were not using a kinship term.

If a man is living among or visiting his maternal relatives they salute him by his mother's name instead of, or as well as, that of his father. Women in similar circumstances are addressed by their mothers' names.

The teknonymous usage, the naming of a man after his eldest child—*gwan* (father of) so-and-so—is not so common as the corresponding use of patronymics whereby a man is named after his father. It is, however, just as complimentary and is the correct way of addressing in-laws, particularly the addressing of a husband by his wife's kinsmen. People try to avoid the use of proper names when speaking of their relatives-in-law, especially shortly after the marriage ceremonies. I was told that some men, while they consider themselves still young, do not care to be addressed by the names of their eldest children since this might suggest that they are old men.

The parallel usage—*man* (mother of) so-and-so—is the normal way of addressing and speaking about a married woman. The eldest child's name is generally used, whether boy or girl, but occasionally a second child's name is used if the second is a boy and the first is a girl. Should a man be ignorant of the name of the eldest child it is not a breach of manners to use the name of the child he does know.

The way in which these modes of address show the social status of the person concerned can be seen clearly in a comparison between the teknonymous usage and the use of patronymics. The Nuer have a patrilineal mode of descent and residence is normally patrilocal. A woman has status in her husband's home in virtue of her having borne him a child, so that the usual way of addressing a married woman by the people of her husband's social group is by the name of her eldest child, the link which joins her to them. Before she has borne a child there is no way of addressing her in her husband's home but as she lives with her parents till after the birth of her first child this does not cause inconvenience. A man is not often addressed among his own people by the name of his eldest child but his wife's people normally address him in this manner for his link with them is through the child he has begotten by their daughter. On the other hand, a man is attached to his paternal home and lineage through his father, and it is consistent that he should be addressed by a patronymic; women go to their husbands' homes and lineages, so it is understandable that in their case the use of patronymics is rare. A grown man is by preference addressed as son of so-and-so and a married woman as mother of so-and-so. But in a person's maternal grandparents' home his social link with the people is through his mother and a matronymic is commonly used by them when addressing him. The bonds between a man and his maternal kinsmen are further emphasized by their use of a special personal name and the honorific name of their clan.

When a boy is living in the village of a man who stands to him in some respect as a father, but who is not his pater, his social link with this man's people is indicated by calling him after the "father's" name, though he is called after his pater's name in his pater's village. Age status is also expressed in modes of address, particularly by the use of ox-names among coevals and by their omission between seniors and juniors. As we have seen, the use of some modes of address indicate sex, others show the peculiar relationships set up in a family by the birth of twins, and others are indicative of special social situations.

REFERENCE NOTE

For other ethnolinguistic studies of African groups by Evans-Pritchard, see his articles (1929, 1934a, 1949, 1954a, 1956) and his book, *The Nuer* (1940, pp. 41-48).

Among the best analyses of the complex involvements of naming and address with social structure and cultural values—often as part of analyses of broader systems of kinship and role terminology—may be cited those of Aberle and Austin (1951), Beals (1961), Befu and Norbeck (1958), Brown and Gilman (1960), Chao (1956), Conant (1961), Emeneau (1938; 1941; 1950; 1953, with an important survey of the special grammatical status for kinship terms on pp. 345-350), Garvin and Riesenberg (1952), Goodenough (1951, 1956), Grimes and Grimes (1962), Halpern (1942), Lee (1940), Levi-Strauss (1943), Lounsbury (1956), Martin (1958), Mbaga and Whiteley (1961), Milner (1961), Murdock (1934), Needham (1954), Opler (1937), Pittman (1948), Schneider (1953), Schneider and Homans (1955), Schneider and Roberts (1956), Service (1960), Shimkin (1941), Swartz (1960), Trager (1943), Voegelin and Voegelin (1935).

Many of the analyses just cited have importance for methodological problems and for the general relation of language to culture or behavior. Of methodological interest, note also Burling (1962), Dozier (1955), Greenberg (1949), Landar (1962), Leach (1958), Levi-Strauss (1953b, p. 545), Oliver (1949), Romney and Epling (1958), Wallace and Atkins (1960), together with Frake's paper in Part IV and references cited there. Concerning evidence for the relation of language to culture or behavior, besides Beals, Goodenough, Lounsbury, Opler, Schneider and Roberts, Service, and Wallace and Atkins cited above, see Levi-Strauss (1951, 1953a) and the review of the problem in Levi-Strauss' article in Part I. Kroeber's part is discussed in the article on him in Part X, n. 37.

On address, see the articles by Newman and Gumperz in Part VII and their references.

Regarding naming practices and the social content of names, see, besides many of the studies just listed, Dauzat (1956), Hilger (1958), Morice (1933), Pettitt (1946), Sapir (1924c), Turner (1949, pp. 31-42), Voth (1905), Wachtmeister (1956), Wieschhoff (1937, 1941), and especially, Levi-Strauss (1962, pp. 226-286).

On the onomatopoetic, or "baby-talk," shape of kin-terms, see Murdock (1959) for statistical proof of the cross-cultural significance of such correlations as the shape *ma*(*ma*), *na*(*na*) for "mother," *pa*(*pa*), *ta*(*ta*), etc., for "father"; see Jakobson (1960b) for linguistic discussion; and see the significant but neglected article by Freire-Marreco (1915), a participant in some of the earliest ethnolinguistic work in the American southwest, for a sociological principle to explain the use of such terms for particular kin.

Among recent studies of the place of names in acculturation, note Casagrande (1955) and Ritzenthaler (1945) for a description of social adaptation among

American Indians, Garvin (1947) for a description of linguistic adaptation, Spencer (1961) for a contemporary situation in the Old World, Turner (1949, pp. 31-190) for covert survival of African names among American Negroes.

References not in the general bibliography:

ABERLE, D. F., and W. M. AUSTIN

1951. A Lexical Approach to the Comparison of Two Mongol Social Systems. *Studies in Linguistics, 9:* 79-90.

BEALS, RALPH L.

1961. Kinship Terminology and Social Structure. *Kroeber Anthropological Society Papers, 25:* 129-148.

BEFU, HARUMI, and EDWARD NORBECK

1958. Japanese Usages of Terms of Relationship. *SJA, 14:* 66-86.

CONANT, FRANCIS P.

1961. Jarawa Kin Systems of Reference and Address: A Componential Comparison. *AL, 3* (2): 19-33.

DAUZAT, ALBERT

1956. *Les Noms de personnes. Origine et évolution.* (4th ed.) Paris: Delagrave. (1st ed., 1925.)

EMENEAU, MURRAY B.

1938. Personal Names of the Todas. *AA, 40:* 205-223.

EVANS-PRITCHARD, E. E.

1934b. The Nuer: Tribe and Clan, Parts iv-vii. *Sudan Notes and Records, 17:* 28-29.

1945. *Some Aspects of Marriage and the Family Among the Nuer.* (Rhodes-Livingstone Papers, No. 11.) Livingstone and Cape Town.

FREIRE-MARRECO, BARBARA

1915. A Note on Kinship Terms Compounded with the Postfix 'e in the Hano Dialect of Tewa. *AA, 17:* 198-202.

GARVIN, PAUL L.

1947. Christian Names in Kutenai. *IJAL* 13. 69-77.

GRIMES, JOSEPH E., and BARBARA F. GRIMES

1962. Semantic Distinctions in Huichol Kinship Terminology. *AA, 64:* 104-114.

HILGER, SISTER INEZ

1958. Naming a Chippewa Indian Child. *Wisconsin Archaeologist, 39:* 120-126.

JACKSON, H. C.

1923. Nuer of the Upper Nile Province, Parts 1, 2, *Sudan Notes and Records, 6:* 59-107; *6:* 123-189.

JAKOBSON, ROMAN

1960b. Why "Mama" and "Papa?" *Selected Writings, I: Phonological Studies.* The Hague: Mouton, 1962. Pp. 538-545.

LEE, DOROTHY DEMETRACOPOULOU

1940. The Place of Kinship Terms in Wintu Speech. *AA, 42:* 604-616.

LEVI-STRAUSS, CLAUDE

1943. The Social Use of Kinship Terms Among Brazilian Indians. *AA, 45:* 398-409.

MBAGA, K., and W. H. WHITELEY

1961. Formality and Informality in Yao Speech. *Africa, 31:* 135-146.

MURDOCK, G. P.

1934. Kinship and Social Behavior Among the Haida. *AA, 36:* 355-385.

1959. Cross-Language Parallels in Parental Kin Terms. *AL, 1* (9): 1-6.

NEEDHAM, RODNEY

1954. The System of Tekonyms and Death-Names of the Penan. *SJA, 11:* 416-431.

RITZENTHALER, ROBERT

1945. The Acquisition of Surnames by the Chippewa Indians. *AA, 47:* 175-177.

ROMNEY, A. KIMBALL, and P. J. EPLING

1958. A Simplified Model of Kariera Kinship Systems. *AA, 60:* 59-74.

SAPIR, EDWARD

1924c. Personal Names Among the Sarcee Indians. *AA, 26:* 109-119.

SCHNEIDER, DAVID M.

1953. Yap Kinship Terminology and Kin Groups. *AA, 55:* 215-236 (esp. 229-230).

SCHNEIDER, DAVID M., and JOHN ROBERTS

1956. *Zuni Kin Terms.* (Laboratory of Anthropology, Notebook No. 3, Monograph 1.) Lincoln: University of Nebraska.

SHIMKIN, D. B.

1941. The Uto-Aztecan Systems of Kinship Terminology. *AA, 43:* 223-245.

SPENCER, ROBERT F.

1961. The Social Context of Modern Turkish Names. *SJA, 17:* 205-218.

SWARTZ, MARC J.

1960. Situational Determinants of Kinship Terminology. *SJA, 16:* 393-397.

VOEGELIN, C. F., and ERMINIE WHEELER-VOEGELIN

1935. Shawnee Name Groups. *AA, 37:* 617-635.

VOTH, H. R.

1905. *Hopi Proper Names.* (Field Columbian Museum, Publication 100; Anthropological Series, *6* [3].) Chicago.

WACHTMEISTER, ARVID

1956. Naming and Reincarnation Among the Eskimos. *Ethnos, 21:* 130-142.

WHITE, LESLIE A.

1958. What Is a Classificatory Kinship Term? *SJA, 14:* 378-385.

WIESCHHOFF, H. A.

1937. Names and Naming Customs Among the Mashona in Southern Rhodesia. *AA, 39:* 497-503.

1941. The Social Significance of Names Among the Ibo of Nigeria. *AA, 43:* 212-222.

25 *Men's and Women's Speech in Koasati*

MARY R. HAAS

Koasati has certain well-defined differences between the speech of men and of women. Other Muskogean languages, such as Muskogee and Hitchiti, also had such differences formerly, and here and there throughout the world one meets with similar instances. Sometimes the differences affect vocabulary items, sometimes the pronunciation of particular words.

I

Koasati is a Muskogean language now spoken in southwestern Louisiana. One of the most interesting features of the language is the fact that the speech of women differs in certain well-defined respects from that of men. The differences may be described by means of a fairly simple set of rules, and the most concise way to formulate them is to set up the forms used by women as basic and to derive the forms used by men from these. While this procedure is preferred because of the greater expediency it offers in the formulation of the rules, it is in most instances arbitrary. In a few instances, however, the speech of women is seen to be somewhat more archaic than that of men and to this extent it is possible to justify the procedure on historical grounds.

The differences between the two types of speech are confined to certain indicative and imperative forms of verbal paradigms. In order to simplify the statement of the rules governing the forms which differ in these paradigms, the rules governing the identical forms are presented first. These are as follows:

1. If the women's form ends in a vowel, the men's form is the same. Examples:

W or M	
lakawwilí	'I lifted it'
oktawhiská	'you stirred it'
iskó	'he drank'

2. If the women's form ends in *č*, the men's form is the same. Examples:

W or M	
lakáwč	'you are lifting it'
hí:č	'he is looking at it'
ča:kháč	'you (pl.) are chopping it'

The remaining rules take care of the instances in which the forms used by men differ from those used by women. The first three of these provide for the cases in which the men's forms substitute an *s* for the nasalization of a final vowel or for certain final consonants of the women's forms.

3. If the women's form ends in a nasalized vowel, the men's form substitutes an *s* for the nasalization. Examples:

W	M	
lakawtakkó	*lakawtakkós*	'I am not lifting it'
lakawwą·	*lakawwá·s*	'he will lift it'
ką·	*ká·s*	'he is saying'

4. If the women's form has the falling pitch-stress on its final syllable and ends in a short vowel followed by *l*, the men's form substitutes the high pitch stress for the falling pitch-stress and an *s* for the *l*. Examples:

W	M	
lakawwîl	*lakawwís*	'I am lifting it'
molhîl	*molhís*	'we are peeling it'
lakawhôl	*lakawhós*	'lift it!' (addressed to second person plural)

5. If the women's form has the falling pitch-stress on its final syllable and ends in a short vowel followed by *n*, the men's form retains the falling pitch-stress but substitutes an *s* for the *n* and lengthens the preceding vowel. Examples:

W	M	
lakawčîn	*lakawčî·s*	'don't lift it!'
tačilwân	*tačilwâ·s*	'don't sing!'
iltočihnôn	*iltočihnô·s*	'don't work!'

The last rule takes care of the instances in which the men's forms differ from the women's by the simple addition of an *s*.

6. If the women's form ends in a short or long vowel plus one or two consonants, the men's form adds an *s* except under the following circumstances: when the women's form ends in *č*, rule 2; when the women's form has the falling pitch-stress on its final syllable and ends in a short vowel followed by *l*, rule 4; when the women's form has the falling pitch-stress on its final syllable and ends in a short vowel followed by *n*, rule 5. (It should also be noted that *t* + *s* regularly contracts to *č*.) Examples:

W	M	
lakáw	*lakáws*	'he is lifting it'
lakáwwitak	*lakáwwitaks*	'let me lift it'
mól	*móls*	'he is peeling it'
lakáwwilit	*lakáwwilič*	'I lifted it'
í:p	*í:ps*	'he is eating it'
ta·l	*ta·ls*	'he is weaving it'
tačílw	*tačílws*	'you are singing'
iltolí:hn	*iltolí:hns*	'we are working'
mí:sl	*mí:sls*	'he is blinking'

(The *l* is not lost in *mols* because the word does not have the falling pitch-stress; contrast with rule 4.)

This completes the rules governing the differences between the speech of men and of women. The table below summarizes these rules by showing in condensed form the final part of the word. Note that *a* stands for any vowel, *k* for any consonant, while other letters and diacritics have their proper phonetic value.

W	M	W	M
a	*a*	*ân*	*â:s*
č	*č*	*ak*	*aks*
ą	*as*	*a:k*	*a:ks*
ą·	*a·s*	*akk*	*akks*
âl	*ás*	*a:kk*	*a:kks*

It sometimes happens that several of these rules operate within the same paradigm and in such a case the differences between the speech of the two sexes is particularly striking. This is illustrated in the three singular paradigms given below:

W	M	
o:tîl	*o:tís*	'I am building a fire'
ó:st	*ó:sč*	'you are building a fire'
ó:t	*ó:č*	'he is building a fire'
lakawwîl	*lakawwís*	'I am lifting it'
lakáwč	*lakáwč*	'you are lifting it'
lakáw	*lakáws*	'he is lifting it'
ka:hâl	*ka:hás*	'I am saying'
í:sk	*í:sks*	'you are saying'
ka:	*ká:s*	'he is saying'

As has been mentioned, in some instances the speech of women appears to be more archaic than that of men. In rule 4 it is pointed out that when the women's form has a falling pitch-stress on the final syllable and ends in a short vowel followed by *l*, the men's form substitutes a high pitch-stress for the falling pitch-stress and an *s* for the *l*. In the cases that fall under this rule the women's forms are more archaic than those of men. In a first person singular present progressive form like *lakawwîl* (w. sp.) the *-l* is the first person singular sign and is related to the suffix *-li* which is used in the aorist and certain other paradigms; compare *lakawwîl* (w. sp.) 'I am lifting it' with *lakawwilí* (w. or m. sp.) 'I lifted it.' The men's form corresponding to *lakawwîl*, however, is *lakawwís* and in it the personal sign is missing. The archaism of women's speech is further illustrated in a first person plural present progressive form like *lakawhîl* (w. sp.). Here the personal sign is *-hil*, related to the first person plural sign *-hilí* which is used in the aorist and certain other paradigms; compare *lakawhîl* (w. sp.) 'we are lifting it' with *lakawhilí* (w. or m. sp.) 'we lifted it,' The men's form corresponding to *lakawhîl* is *lakawhís*; the *l* of the ending *-hil* has been lost.

This concludes the technical discussion of the differences between men's and women's speech in Koasati. It is of interest to note that at the present time only middle-aged and elderly women use the women's forms, while younger women are now using the forms characteristic of men's speech. The attitude of older Indians toward the two forms of speech is also interesting. One of my men informants thinks that the speech of women is better than that of men. He said that women talk "easy, slow, and soft. It sounds pretty. Men's speech has too much *ssss*."

Members of each sex are quite familiar with both types of speech and can use either as occasion demands. Thus if a man is telling a tale he will use women's forms when quoting a female character; similarly, if a woman is telling a tale she will use men's forms when quoting a male character. Moreover, parents were formerly accustomed to correct the speech of children of either sex, since each child was trained to use forms appropriate to his or her sex.

II

Other Muskogean languages appear to have had at one time differences between the speech of men and of women similar to those preserved in Koasati down to the present day. Creek men and women of the present day speak in exactly the same way, both using the forms which were once used only by men. But occasionally the archaic women's forms are preserved in tales where a female character is talking. At first these strange forms were puzzling to me—they were like nothing in ordinary speech; but after I discovered the phenomenon of sex differences in speech in the related Koasati language and learned the nature of these differences, it became clear that these puzzling forms were those formerly used by women. The matter was then carefully checked with some of the older people and these were also able to identify the forms as archaic women's speech.

The examples that I found in Muskogee in this way are not very numerous, but here again the women's forms appear to be basic. The only rule discovered is as follows: Women's forms end in a long vowel with a falling pitch-stress while the corresponding men's forms shift the stress to the penultimate syllable, altering it to a high pitch-stress, and in addition shorten the long vowel and add *s*. If the shortened vowel is *i* it is often dropped altogether. Examples:

W	M	
okikâ·	*okíkas*	'he was'
ó·kickî·	*ó·kíckis*	'you are'
o·kakaŋkî·	*o·kakáŋks*	'I meant' (short *i* dropped)
apo·kiphoykâ·	*apo·kiphóykas*	'let him stay'

These few examples are practically all that have been discovered; but when coupled with the evidence from the Koasati, the evidence here seems conclusive for the postulation of a former special women's speech among the Creeks.

Gatschet (1884) tells us that Hitchiti also once had special forms of speech used by women and he gives brief but convincing proof of this fact when he speaks of "the ending *-i* of the verbs, standing instead of the *-is* of the male dialect." Gatschet also thinks that the forms used by women were merely more archaic and that long ago men used these forms also; but he offers no proof for this assumption and I think it is more reasonable to assume that the so-called "ancient" language was actually used only by women. That it was considered "ancient" by the Hitchiti themselves probably means no more than that women no longer regularly used these forms in ordinary conversation.

Evidence for the presence of a difference between the speech of men and of women has been brought forth for three of the Muskogean languages. In a paper on "The Classification of the Muskogean Languages," I presented the evidence for classifying these languages into two primary divisions, the Western and the Eastern (Haas, 1941a). The Western division consists only of Choctaw and Chickasaw, but the Eastern division may be divided into three subdivisions, namely Alabama plus Koasati, Hitchiti plus Mikasuki, and Muskogee (Creek) plus Seminole. It is thus seen that evidence for sex differences in speech comes entirely from the Eastern division and that each of the main subdivisions is known to have possessed the trait. Whether or not it was at one time present in the languages of the Western division also is not now known.

III

Languages which contain major or minor differences between the speech of men and of women are not so rare as might be supposed. From the evidence that has been given in the two preceding sections it appears that most of the Muskogean languages, originally spoken throughout a large part of the southeastern United States, may have had such differences. Sapir (1929b) has published evidence that such differences existed in Yana, an Indian language of California, while Jenness (1932) speaks of their occurrence among the aboriginal languages of Canada, saying: "More strange to Europeans were the slight differences in speech between men and women that appeared in a few languages. There were sometimes mere differences in vocabulary, certain words being used by women only; but in Siouan and in the Eskimo dialect of Baffin Island there were also slight differences in grammatical form."

That this phenomenon occurred also in South America is evidenced by the fact that Carib has become almost the classical example of sex differences in speech. The phenomenon occurs also in Asia. Bogoras (1922) has demonstrated its existence in Chukchee, spoken far to the north in eastern Siberia, and it is also found in less extensive form in Thai, spoken far to the south in the Indo-Chinese peninsula.

An interesting trait apparently related to this is that in which the sex of the hearer is of grammatical importance. Taking both traits together we find that there are three main types in which the sex of speaker and/or hearer is grammatically relevant. These three types are shown in the following table.

	SPEAKER	HEARER
Type I	M	M or W
	W	M or W
Type II	M or W	M
	M or W	W
Type III	M	M
	M	W
	W	M
	W	W

The ways in which these types of differences may be actualized are varied, but most of them fall into one or the other of the two following categories: (1) differences in vocabulary, possible in all three types shown in the diagram; and (2) differences in the pronunciation of many or most words, common in Type I.

A few examples of these three types of differences and the ways in which they are actualized may be presented here.

In Thai there are two important differences which fall into Type I and which are actualized by a difference in vocabulary items. The first of these differences is seen in the use of the pronoun *phǒm* 'I' by men and the use of the pronoun *dìchǎn* 'I' by women. There are many other pronouns that can be used, depending on the relative rank of speaker and hearer, the degree of intimacy between speaker and hearer, or the kinship between speaker and hearer. The pronouns *phǒm* and *dìchǎn* are used in ordinary polite conversation (not intimate) when speaker and hearer are of equal rank.

The second difference in the speech of men and of women in Thai is in the use of certain polite particles. These are placed at the end of the sentence, particularly in questions and answers and in certain formulaic expressions such as those meaning 'Thank you,' 'Excuse me,' and the like. The polite particle used by men is *khráb*; those used by women are *khá* (in questions) and *khâ* (in answers or statements).

Although Type I differences are shown by only four vocabulary items (two for men and two for women), the polite particles are used frequently and, because of this frequency, an ordinary conversation is characterized by considerable difference in men's and women's speech.

In Yana the forms used by women are shortened and altered at the end so that in this case (in contrast to Koasati) the men's forms appear to be basic. Thus where a man says *ʔauna* a woman says *ʔauh* 'fire.'

In Chukchee also sex differences in speech are indicated by altering the words; Bogoras (1922) mentions two varieties of this, presumably occurring in different dialects. In the first variety the men's form appears to be basic and the rule for determining the women's form, according to Bogoras, is as follows: "Women generally substitute *š* for *č* and *r*, particularly after weak vowels. They also substitute *šš* for *rk* and *čh*." Therefore where a man says *rámkɪčhɪn* 'people,' a woman says *šámkɪššɪn*. And, quoting Bogoras again, "The sounds *č* and *r* are quite frequent; so that the speech of women, with its ever-recurring *š*, sounds quite peculiar, and is not easily understood by an inexperienced ear."

In the second variety of differences in Chukchee the women's forms appear to be basic. According to Bogoras, "The men, particularly in the Kolyma district, drop intervocalic consonants, principally *n* and *t*. In this case the two adjoining vowels are assimilated." Example: *nɪtváqênat* (w. sp.) vs' *nɪtváqaat* (m. sp.)

Instances of Type II, where the sex of the hearer is of importance, are not so common as instances of Type I. One interesting instance, though, is found in the Tunica language of Louisiana (Haas, 1941b). Here the differences are found only in the pronominal system, and consist in the use of different words, prefixes, or suffixes. Moreover, the differences are maintained in three numbers, singular, dual, and plural, though in certain paradigms the dual and plural forms have fallen together.

Altogether these differences occur in eight different paradigms. Examples:

	HEARER	SINGULAR	DUAL	PLURAL
Semelfactive	M	*-ˀa*	*-wi′na*	*-wi′ti*
Suffixes	W	*-ˀi*	*-hi′na*	*-hi′ti*
Independent	M	*má*	*wi′nima*	
Pronouns	W	*hɛ′ma*	*hi′nima*	

Instances where Type II is combined with Type I to produce Type III are found in some of the Siouan languages, such as the now extinct Biloxi. Here there was an elaborate system of Type III forms in use—for example in the imperative of verbs. The following sample set, worked out by Dorsey (Dorsey and Swanton, 1912), means 'Carry it!'

	SINGULAR	PLURAL
M to M	*ki-kaŋko′*	*ki′-takaŋko′*
M or W to W	*ki-tki′*	*ki′-tatki′*
W to M	*ki-tate′*	*ki′-tatute′*

The Biloxi picture is complicated not only by a full set of Type III forms in both singular and plural but by an additional set of singular and plural forms which are used by both sexes when speaking to children, thus: *ki* 'carry it!' (sing.) and *kitu′* 'carry it!' (pl.).

AUTHOR'S NOTE

The collection of materials on the Koasati language comprised a part of the work done on the history of the towns of the Creek Confederacy under a grant from the Penrose Fund of the American Philosophical Society in 1938-1939.

Other languages mentioned in this paper for which the materials quoted are taken from my own notes are Muskogee (Creek), Tunica, and Thai. Linguistic materials on Muskogee were collected during field work among the Creek Indians (in Oklahoma) in 1936 and 1937 through two grants made by the Department of Anthropology, Yale University. Linguistic materials on Tunica (in Louisiana) were obtained principally in 1933 under the auspices of the Committee on Research in American Native Languages of the American Council of Learned Societies. Work on Thai was done for the Committee of the National School of Modern Oriental Languages and Civilizations of the American Council of Learned Societies. For the Jenness reference, I am indebted to Dr. Erminie Wheeler-Voegelin.

Briefly described, the sounds of the Koasati language are as follows: The vowels are *i*, *a*, and *o*; they may occur either with or without the length phoneme. Short *i* = [I] (but [e] finally), *a* = [ə], *o* = [U]; long *i:* = [e:], *a:* = [a:], *o:* = [o:]. All vowels occur also nasalized. Consonants are as follows: voiceless stops *p*, *t*, *k*; voiceless affricate *č*; voiced stop *b*; voiceless spirants *f*, *ł*, *h*; semivowels *y*, *w*; lateral *l*; nasals *m*, *n*. There are two pitch-stresses in Koasati, the high (′) and the falling (ˆ). All syllables preceding the stressed syllables are high in pitch, except that an open syllable containing a short vowel is low.

The sounds of the Muskogee language are similar to those of Koasati, except that the Muskogee stops are voiceless lenes and there is an additional nasal *ŋ*. A fuller description is given in (Haas, 1940). The rules for the pitch-stresses are also similar to those of Koasati; but in Muskogee, when two high pitch-stresses occur in the same word, the level of the second is lower than that of the first. Unstressed final syllables are very low in pitch.

The phonetic symbols used in the Thai examples quoted here have their usual values except that *ph* stands for [pʻ], *ch* for [*č*ʻ], and *kh* for [kʻ]. There are five tones, the even or middle (unmarked), the low (ˋ), the falling (ˆ), the high (′), and the rising (ˇ). (A fuller description of Thai sounds is found in Haas [1942, n. 2], and on p. 303 and following.)

The phonetic symbols used by Bogoras in the examples quoted here have their usual values except that *ś* is [c] (or, as he says "like *z* in German *Zeit*") and that *ê* is (ᴇ). Bogoras also indicated that the consonant *ś* [c] is used only by women (1922, p. 645).

I have made a few changes in the spelling used by Dorsey and Swanton so that the phonetic symbols used would correspond to those in common use today. I have also put the M-to-W and the W-to-W forms together, since they are identical, though Dorsey listed them separately.

REFERENCE NOTE

On men's and women's speech, in addition to the references given by Miss Haas, see Chamberlain (1912), Cohen (1956, pp. 112-114, 117-119), Flannery (1946), Furfey (1944), Grootaers (1952a, 1952b), Jespersen (1921, chap. 13), and *Orbis*, vols. 1, 2 (1952, 1953).

References not in the general bibliography:

BOGORAS, WALDEMAR

1921. Chukchee. In Franz Boas (Ed.), *Handbook of American Indian Languages*. (BAE-B 40, Part 2.) Washington, D.C.: Smithsonian Institution. Pp. 631-903.

CHAMBERLAIN, ALEXANDER F.

1912. Women's Languages. *AA. 14:* 579-581.

DORSEY, JAMES O., and JOHN R. SWANTON

1912. *A Dictionary of the Biloxi and Ofo Languages*. (BAE-B 47.) Washington, D.C.; Smithsonian Institution.

FLANNERY, REGINA

1946. Men's and Women's Speech in Gros Ventre. *IJAL, 12:* 133-135.

FURFEY, P. H.

1944. Men's and Women's Language. *American Catholic Sociological Review, 5:* 218-223.

GATSCHET, ALBERT S.

1884. *A Migration Legend of the Creek Indians*. Philadelphia: Brinton.

GROOTAERS, WILLEM A.

1952a. Quelques Remarques concernant le langage des femmes. *Orbis, 1:* 82-83.

1952b. Différences entre langage masculin et feminin. *Orbis, 1:* 84-85.

HAAS, MARY R.

1940. Ablaut and Its Function in Muskogee. *Lg., 16:* 149-150.

1941a. The Classification of the Muskogean Languages. In L. Spier, A. I. Hallowell, and S. S. Newman (Eds.), *Language, Culture, and Personality*. Menasha, Wis.: Banta. Pp. 41-46.

1941b. Tunica. In Franz Boas (Ed.), *Handbook of American Indian Languages, Part 4*. (BAE-B 40.) Washington, D.C.: Smithsonian Institution. Pp. 1-143.

1942. The Use of Numeral Classifiers in Thai. *Lg., 18:* 201-202.

JENNESS, DIAMOND

1932. *The Indians of Canada*. (National Museum of Canada, Bulletin 65.) Ontario.

26 *Address in American English*

ROGER BROWN AND MARGUERITE FORD

When one person speaks to another, the selection of certain linguistic forms is governed by the relation between the speaker and his addressee. The principal option of address in American English is the choice between use of the first name (hereafter abbreviated to FN) and use of a title with the last name (TLN). These linguistic forms follow a rule that is truly relational. Their use is not predictable from properties of the addressee alone and not predictable from properties of the speaker alone but only from properties of the dyad. Kinship terms of address (e.g., dad, mom, son) are also relational language, but they constitute a restricted language of relationship since most dyads that might be created in America would not call for any sort of kinship term. Proper names, on the other hand, constitute a nearly universal language of relationship; the semantic dimensions involved serve to relate to one another all of the members of the society.

Much of our knowledge of the dimensions that structure interaction has been obtained from paper-and-pencil performances such as the status ranking of acquaintances or the sociometric choice from among acquaintances. There can be no doubt that the dimensions revealed by such data are genuinely functional in ordinary life. However, performances elicited by the social scientist are not the everyday performances that reveal dimensions of social structure and cause each new generation to internalize such dimensions. It is always possible that a paper-and-pencil task imposes a dimension or encourages an unrepresentative consistency and delicacy of differentiation. It is desirable to study social structure in everyday life, but much of the everyday behavior that is governed by social dimensions is difficult to record and involves an uncertain number of significant contrasts (e.g., influencing decisions, smiling at someone, warmth of manner). Forms of address are speech and so there is a recording technique called writing which preserves most of the significant detail. English forms of address are reasonably well described by a single binary contrast: FN or TLN. These forms are ubiquitous and for any set of interacting persons it is possible to obtain a collection of address dyads from which the latent structuring dimensions can be inferred. This paper provides an example of the application of semantic analysis to the study of social structure. We begin by describing the norms of American address, then point out a certain pattern in these norms which is to be found in the forms of address of all languages known to us. This abstract speech pattern suggests a feature of social structure that may possibly be universal.

METHOD

MATERIALS

To discover the norms of address in American English we require a large sample of usage. The range of the subject population is vast but the uniformity must be great. Some sensible compromise is required between the stratified national sample dictated by the scope of the problem and the unsystematic observation of one's friends dictated by the probable simplicity of its solution. Four kinds of data have been used.

Usage in modern American plays. There are more instances of address in plays than in any other form of literature. Thirty-eight plays written by American authors, performed since 1939, and anthologized in three volumes of *Best American Plays* (Gassner, 1947, 1952, 1958) were used. Of the plays in these volumes we omitted only those set in some remote time or in a country other than the United States. Without listing all the titles it is possible to indicate the range of American usage that it represented. By geographic region we move from *The Philadelphia Story* to the Southland of *The Member of the Wedding* through the midwest of *Picnic* to the Far West of *The Time of Your Life*, by social class from *The Rose Tattoo* and *A View from the Bridge* through *Death of a Salesman* and *Tea and Sympathy* to *The Solid Gold Cadillac*. For military usage there are such plays as *Mister Roberts* and *No Time for Sergeants*. The speech of Jewish, Italian, and Negro minorities is represented and also that of such groups as politicians, corporation executives, narcotics addicts, college professors, and policemen.

Of course these materials are not a record of actual speech from the characters named but are the speech constructed for such characters by playwrights. Probably playwrights accurately reproduce the true norms of address, and it is possible to check one author against another. In addition, however, there are three other kinds of data to catch possible inaccuracies in this first set.

Actual usage in a Boston business firm. For 2 months a man employed in a drafting firm took advantage of leisure moments to jot down for us instances of linguistic address overheard from his fellow workers. He collected address terms for 214 different dyads in which 82 different people are involved either as speaker or addressee. Each person is identified by full name, sex, age, and position in a 12-level occupational hierarchy. In addition, we benefited from our informant's good knowledge of friendship patterns among the dramatis personae.

Reported usage of business executives. Each year there is at MIT a group of Alfred P. Sloan Fellows; these are business executives between 30 and 38 years of age, who are nominated by their respective employers to study for one year at the institute. The 34 Sloan Fellows designated for 1958-1959 served as informants for this study. They come from many different parts of the country, most of them from very large corporations but a few from small companies.

By the time the Sloan Fellows served as informants the general pattern of the norms had become sufficiently clear to make possible the writing of a questionnaire designed to elicit the most important information. Each man was asked to write down the full names and positions of four persons whom he was accustomed to see nearly every day at his place of business, and he was to distribute his selections so as to include: one person equal to himself in the organization hierarchy with whom he was on close or intimate terms, one person equal to himself with whom he was on distant or formal terms, one person superior to himself in the organization hierarchy, one person subordinate to himself in the hierarchy. After listing the names the informant was asked to write down for each person listed the exact words that he (the informant) would customarily speak in greeting that person for the first time each day. In addition, the Sloan Fellows were asked some other questions that will be described when they become relevant.

Recorded usage in Midwest. The Psychological Field Station of the University of Kansas directed by Roger G. Barker and Herbert F. Wright (1954) kindly allowed us to make an extended study of 10 "specimen records," each of which record the events and conversation in a full-day of the life of a child. The station has also allowed us to work with a set of brief "behavior settings observations" made on 56 children in the town called Midwest and on 56 children in Uredale, England, matched with those in Midwest by sex and age. In these materials we have been primarily concerned with a grammatical analysis of the kinds of "mands" addressed to children (for another study of the language of social relationship) but have, in addition, taken the opportunity to check our conclusions about American address against the Midwest records.

PROCEDURE

For each of the 38 plays every instance of address was recorded, together with an identification of the speaker and addressee. The method of study is a sort of controlled induction. (Since address involves two persons and, very often, a choice between two linguistic forms, we believe it should be possible to treat the complete set of address dyads for any group of persons as a matrix of paired comparisons from which the dimensions structuring the group could be rigorously derived. We are at present trying to develop such a method.) Approximately one-third of the plays were first examined in an effort to discover rules that would summarize all of the instances of address they contained. The resulting provisional rules were then tested against a second set of plays and underwent some revision. The revised rules proved adequate to the description of all instances of address in a third and final set of plays, The supplementary data from a business firm, from the Sloan Fellows, and from the Midwest records were used as additional checks on the rules induced from the plays and also to test several particular hypotheses.

MAJOR PATTERNS OF ADDRESS

If we consider only the FN and TLN there are just three logically possible dyadic patterns: the reciprocal exchange of FN, the reciprocal exchange of TLN, and the nonreciprocal pattern in which one person uses FN and the other TLN. All three patterns occur with high frequency and the problem is one of inducing the semantic factors invariably associated with a given pattern and serving to distinguish it from the others.

In classifying instances of address into the three classes, FN was taken to include full first names (e.g., Robert), familiar abbreviations (e.g., Bob), and diminutive forms (e.g., Bobbie). It may be said at once that male first names in American English very seldom occur in full form (Robert, James, or Gerald) but are almost always either abbreviated (Bob, Jim) or diminutized (Jerry) or both (Bobbie, Jimmy). Female first names are more often left unaltered. Titles for the purpose of this classification include, in addition to Mr., Mrs., and Miss, such occupational titles as Dr., Senator, Major, and the like.

TWO RECIPROCAL PATTERNS

The vast majority of all dyads in the plays exchange FN (Mutual FN). Indeed, where the actual name is not known there occur sometimes what may be called generic first names; these include the Mack, Jack, and Buddy of taxi drivers. Mutual TLN is most commonly found between newly introduced adults. The distinction between the two patterns is primarily one of degree of acquaintance with the degree required for the Mutual FN being less for younger people than for older people and less where the members of the dyad are of the same sex than where they are of different sex.

It seems likely that the two reciprocal patterns are on a dimension that ranges from acquaintance to intimacy. However, in modern American English the distance between the two points is small with the Mutual FN usually representing only a very small increment of intimacy over the Mutual TLN; as small sometimes as 5 minutes of conversation. Because the segment of the line that lies between the two patterns is usually so very short, it is not easy to make out its exact character. However, in English of the past and in cognate languages today the Mutual FN is farther displaced from the Mutual TLN, and from these cases and other materials later to be presented we can hazard a characterization of intimacy. (In six American plays [Quinn, 1917] written between 1830 and 1911 the reciprocal FN between adults clearly implies a much longer and closer acquaintance than it does in contemporary usage.) Intimacy is the horizontal line between members of a dyad. The principal factors predisposing to intimacy seem to be shared values (which may derive from kinship, from identity of occupation, sex, nationality, etc., or from some common fate) and frequent contact. Among the behavioral manifestations of intimacy, a relatively complete and honest self-disclosure is important.

NONRECIPROCAL PATTERN

In this case one member of the dyad says FN and the other TLN. There are two kinds of relation that can generate this pattern. The first is a difference of age: children say TLN to adults and receive FN; among adults an elder by approximately 15-or-more years receives TLN and gives FN to his junior. The second is a difference of occupational status: this may be a relation of direct and enduring subordination (e.g., master-servant, employer-employee, officer-enlisted man); it may be a relation of direct but temporary subordination, involving someone in a service occupation (e.g., waiter, bootblack) and a customer; it may be an enduring difference of occupational status that does not involve direct subordination (e.g., United States senators have higher status than firemen). If the intimacy dimension that governs reciprocal address is the horizontal of social relationship, then the status dimension that underlies the nonreciprocal pattern may be called the vertical of social relationship. (Kinship terms of address in American English (Schneider & Homans, 1955) also show a nonreciprocality of status. Members of ascending generations are commonly addressed with kinship titles (mother, father, grandmother, grandfather, uncle, aunt) but respond by calling their children, grandchildren, nephews, and nieces by FN.)

Age and occupational status are correlated and most instances of nonreciprocal address involve congruent differences on the two dimensions. There is, however, proof that a difference on either dimension alone is able to generate the nonreciprocal pattern. The proof is the existence of nonreciprocal dyads matched on one dimension but not on the other.

Because there are two criteria for the assignment of status and, in addition, the correlation between the two criteria is not perfect, we must ask what happens to address in dyads where the elder has the humbler occupation. There are in the plays numerous instances in which the criteria oppose one another: an adolescent girl and her family's middle-aged cook, a young navy ensign and a middle-aged enlisted man, a young executive and an elderly janitor. In all such cases address is in accordance with occupational status and so it would appear that there is a normative rule of priority for the two criteria. It is to be expected in a society whose values are more strongly linked to achieved personal attributes than to ascribed attributes (Parsons, 1951) that occupation would prevail over age in the determination of deference.

The three sets of data in addition to the plays confirm the generalizations made above. Sloan Fellows call almost all of their business acquaintances by FN and expect this address to be reciprocated. In the few cases where one of these men would say TLN and expect to receive FN the other member of the dyad was invariably an organizational superior and was also the elder. In the Boston drafting firm, also, most address is on the pattern of Mutual FN. The few cases of Mutual TLN involved persons who were scarcely acquainted and who were well matched by age and position. There were 40 different instances of nonreciprocal address. In 36 of these the recipient of TLN was the organizational superior and elder; in 28 cases he was a member of one of the four top executive ranks whereas the recipient of FN was a member of one of the eight unionized ranks. In three cases the organizational superior was younger than his subordinate and it was the superior, not the elder, who received TLN. The single remaining case involved a pair matched by rank but not by age and in this case the elder received TLN. Midwest children participate in nonreciprocal address dyads with parents and teachers and in Mutual FN dyads with other children.

VARIANT FORMS OF ADDRESS

In this section are offered tentative characterizations of the several common forms other than FN and TLN. At a later point in the paper we will return to these variants and suggest the nature of their relationship with the major patterns.

TITLE WITHOUT NAME

Commonly used titles (T) include sir, madam, ma'am, and Miss. In general these forms are used like TLN; either reciprocally between new acquaintances or nonreciprocally by a person of lower status to a person of higher status. The address form T is probably a degree less intimate and a degree more deferential than TLN. It may, for instance, be used reciprocally where acquaintance is so slight that the last name is not known. In nonreciprocal military usage between ranks the TLN may be used to immediate superiors but the T to remote colonels, generals, commanders, and admirals even though the names of these superiors are well known.

Beyond this general characterization as a minimally intimate and maximally deferential form particular varieties of T have their specialized uses. The form ma'am is most commonly heard from young men to mature women. Schoolchildren in Yoredale, England, preface almost all address to a teacher by saying: "Please, Miss . . ." In parallel circumstances Midwest children use TLN.

LAST NAME ALONE

An occasional person is regularly addressed by LN. This seems usually to occur where the FN is polysyllabic and has no familiar abbreviation whereas the LN is either a monosyllable or easily transformed into a monosyllable. In these circumstances LN is simply a substitute for FN and patterns in identical fashion.

Where the LN is not the usual form for an addressee it represents a degree of intimacy greater than TLN but less than FN. In military usage enlisted men receive the LN from officers when they are little acquainted; increased familiarity leads to the FN downward though not upward. Elderly and very distinguished professors sometimes begin letters to junior colleagues whom they know fairly well: "Dear Jones . . ." The form is not reciprocated in this case.

Reciprocal LN is common between enlisted men until they become acquainted. The enduring reciprocal LN seems always to go with a mutual antagonism that blocks progression to intimacy. In *The Caine Mutiny Court Martial*, for instance, Greenwald and Keefer exchange LN though the degree of acquaintance and their ages would normatively produce Mutual FN. In the climax of this play Greenwald dashes a drink in Keefer's face. In *The*

Philadelphia Story Kittredge and Haven exchange LN; the former is the husband-to-be of Tracy Lord and the latter her former-but-still-interested husband.

MULTIPLE NAMES

A speaker may use more than one form of the proper name for the same addressee, sometimes saying TLN, sometimes FN or LN or a nickname, sometimes creating phonetic variants of either FN or the nickname. We are not here interested in the business of temporal progression through the possible forms where earlier terms are dropped as new terms are taken up. The case of multiple names (MN) is the case in which two or more versions of the proper name are used in free variation with one another.

The instances of MN in the plays suggested that this form represented a greater degree of intimacy than the FN, but degrees of intimacy are not easily judged and so we decided to put the hypothesis to a more direct test. The test involved individual interviews with 32 MIT male undergraduates. Each subject was asked to think of four men of about his own age all of whom he had met for the first time approximately one year ago. In addition, it was to be the case that the subject had had about equal opportunity to get to know all of these men and yet now was to find himself on close, friendly terms with some of them and on more distant terms with others. The subject was asked to write down the full names of the four men and then to record the name by which he usually addressed each one. When this had been done, the subject was asked, for each acquaintance, whether he ever addressed the man in any other way and all the names currently being used were noted down.

In an earlier paragraph it was suggested that one of the meanings of intimacy is a relatively complete and honest disclosure of the personality. Jourard and Lasakow (1958) have devised a Self-disclosure questionnaire which requires the subject to indicate whether or not he has discussed with a designated other person each of 60 topics classifiable under the headings: Attitudes and opinions, Tastes and interests, Work (or studies), Money, Personality, and Body. Our 32 subjects filled out this questionnaire for each acquaintance. For each subject, then, we ranked the four acquaintances in order of decreasing Self-disclosure and we take this to be an order of decreasing intimacy. It generally corresponds with the subjects' ordering of the four into friends and acquaintances.

Across all subjects we combined the 32 closest friends, those eliciting highest Self-disclosure scores (Self-disclosure 1) and also the 32 acquaintances with Self-disclosure rank orders 2, 3, and 4. For each rank group we determined the number of cases addressed by MN (2 or more proper names) and the number addressed by FN alone. The results appear in Table 1. The cases of MN decline as intimacy declines. Using the sign test and a one-tailed hypothesis it was determined that the Self-disclosure 1 group contained more cases of MN than did the next most intimate group (Self-disclosure 2) with $p = .020$. The difference between the most intimate and the least intimate (Self-disclosure 4) group shows more cases of MN in the former group with $p < .004$.

TABLE 1

FREQUENCIES OF TWO FORMS OF ADDRESS TO ACQUAINTANCES AT DIFFERENT LEVELS OF SELF-DISCLOSURE

	Self-disclosure 1	*Self-disclosure* 2	*Self-disclosure* 3	*Self-disclosure* 4
Multiple Names	18	10	7	3
First Name	14	22	25	29

NOTE. Self-disclosure 1 vs. Self-disclosure 2 by sign test, $p = .020$; Self-disclosure 1 vs. Self-disclosure 4 by sign test, $p < .004$.

One informant addressed his closest friend whose name is Robert Williams as Williams or Robert or Bob or Willie and his next closest friend whose name is James Scoggin as Scoggin, James, Jim, or Scoggs. Many informants reported that they sometimes playfully addressed a good friend by TLN. Others used playful, and usually pejorative, phonetic variations: Magoo for Magee, Katool for Katell, Lice for Leis.

The tendency to proliferate proper names in intimacy is interesting because it accords with a familiar semantic-psychological principle. For language communities the degree of lexical differentiation of a referent field increases with the importance of that field to the community. To cite a fresh example of this kind of thing, Conklin (1957) reports that the Hanunóo of the Philippine Islands have names for 92 varieties of rice which is their principal food. In naming ferns and orchids, with which they are little concerned, the Hanunóo combine numerous botanical species under one term whereas the rice they differentiate so finely is for the botanist a single species. Within a language community Brown (1958) has pointed out that a speaker more concerned with a given referent field will make finer lexical distinctions than a speaker less concerned with that field (botanists have more names for plants than do psychologists). In the referent field composed of other persons we have seen that where contact and concern are minimal and distance greatest, titles alone are likely to be used in address. To call someone Miss or sir is to address the person on a categorical level which does not establish the addressee's individual identity. The proper name constitutes the individual as a unique organism. Beyond the single proper name, however, where interest is still greater the individual is fragmented into a variety of names. Perhaps this differentiation beyond individuality expresses various manifestations or ways of regarding someone who is close (Brown, 1959).

A GENERAL SYSTEM OF ADDRESS

How are these various forms of address related to one another? Consider first only the three major patterns. The Mutual TLN goes with distance or formality and the Mutual FN with a slightly greater degree of intimacy. In nonreciprocal address the TLN is used to the person of higher status and the FN to the person of lower status. One form expresses both distance and deference; the other form expresses both intimacy and condescension. Within the limits of two dyadic address forms there is a formally or logically possible alternative pattern. The form used mutually between intimates could be used upward to superiors and the form used between distant acquaintances could be directed downward to subordinates. Because there is an alternative the pattern actually found is not a formal necessity but rather an empirical fact; a fact, we shall see, of great generality.

Several years ago we began our general studies of the language of social relationship with a selection point that does not occur in modern English but which does occur in the other Indo-European languages. In French, for example, a speaker must choose between two second person singular pronouns; his addressee may be addressed as *tu* or as *vous*. In German the comparable forms are *du* and *Sie*; in Italian *tu* and *Lei*. In English of the past, from about the 13th century until the 18th, there was a cognate option of address; the choice between *thou* and *ye*. We have studied the semantic rules governing these pronouns in 20 languages of Europe and India, comparing one language with another and the usage of earlier centuries with later (Brown & Gilman, 1960). For our present purposes the important point is that these pronouns in all the languages studied follow the same abstract pattern as the FN and TLN.

In discussing the pronouns of address let us use T as a generic designator for pronouns of the type of *tu* and *du* and V as a designator for pronouns of the type of *vous* and *Sie*. Mutual V is the form of address for adult new acquaintances; it begins where TLN begins – at the temporal point of origin of the dyad. Mutual T like Mutual FN is an expression of increased intimacy but it is, for most Europeans, much farther along the line than is the Mutual FN of Americans. From medieval times into the present century nonreciprocal T and V was the pattern for those unequal in status with the superior receiving the V and the subordinate the T. In recent times the nonreciprocal use of the pronouns has much declined because of a conscious egalitarianism. The important point is, however, that when the nonreciprocal pattern has been used anywhere from southern India to Scandinavia the downward directed form has been the intimate T and the upward directed the distant V.

It may be that the abstract linkage in personal address of intimacy and condescension, distance and deference is a linguistic universal, but we certainly do not know that as yet. We do know that the linkage occurs also in some non-Indo-European languages (e.g., Japanese second person pronouns). Indeed, in those few languages for which we have found adequate descriptions of the semantics of address, no violations of the abstract pattern have yet appeared.

It seems also that the pattern applies to more than names, titles, and pronouns. The Sloan Fellows' greetings to their business associates almost invariably used the FN. However, the greetings themselves were quite varied; including Hi, Morning, Good Morning, Hello, Howdy, etc. Only Hi and Good Morning occurred with sufficient frequency to make possible the discovery of a pattern. The Sloans reported on greetings to four classes of associate: Equal and Intimate, Equal and Distant, Superior, and Subordinate. In Table 2 appear the frequencies of Hi and Good Morning for these various categories. Hi is more common to intimates and to subordinates while Good Morning is for distant acquaintances and superiors. Using the McNemar test for the significance of changes in related samples with the Yates correction for continuity, the difference between intimates and acquaintances is significant with $p <$ .0025 and the difference for subordinates and superiors with $p < .025$. In both cases a one-tailed test was used since the direction of the differences was predicted by the abstract pattern of address. The records of actual usage in a Boston firm accord with this finding. In one revealing instance a workman was greeted "Hi" and promptly answered "Hi," but as he turned and recognized the boss, he added "Good morning."

TABLE 2

TWO FORMS OF GREETING FOR FOUR CLASSES OF ASSOCIATE

	Equal and Intimate	
	Good Morning	Hi
Equal and Distant		
Hi	0	4
Good Morning	4	10
	Subordinate	
	Good Morning	Hi
Superior		
Hi	1	3
Good Morning	13	8

NOTE. With McNemar test for the significance of changes in related samples (employing Yates correction) χ^2 for Intimate vs. Distant = 8.10, $p < .0025$ and χ^2 for Subordinate vs. Superior = 4.00, $p < .025$.

Why should the abstract pattern described govern address between two persons? A curious fact about contemporary use of T and V provides a clue. While the nonreciprocal pattern for pronouns has generally been abandoned in Europe, inequality of status continues to affect one aspect of usage. Dyads begin at the Mutual V and, with time, may advance to the intimacy of Mutual T. For many the shift from V to T is an important rite of passage. The Germans even have a little informal ceremony they call the *Bruderschaft*. One waits for a congenial mood, a mellow occasion, perhaps with a glass of wine, and says: "Why don't we say *du* to one another?" The new usage is, of course, to be reciprocal. However, there is one necessarily nonreciprocal aspect of the occasion—someone must make the suggestion. When there is a clear difference of status between the two the right to initiate the change unequivocally belongs to the superior—to the elder, the richer, the more distinguished of the two. The gate to linguistic intimacy is kept by the person of higher status.

The norms of English address also make a pattern in time. A dyad must, with time, either increase its total amount of contact or else dissolve. Since the Mutual TLN represents less contact than the Mutual FN if Mutual TLN is to occur in a given dyad it must occur at an earlier time than the Mutual FN. The place of the nonreciprocal pattern in time is between the other two and it may be understood as a step from Mutual TLN in the direction of Mutual FN; a step which, like the suggestion of the *Bruderschaft* is taken first by the superior. Many dyads will linger for a very long time—possibly the life of the dyad—in the nonreciprocal pattern. In this circumstance the pattern gives enduring expression to an inequality of status.

Consider a familiar sort of example. A prospective graduate student arrives at a university to meet some of the faculty of the psychology department and is interviewed by the chairman. Probably the two will initially exchange TLN. In the course of the day or, if not, shortly after the student enrolls, the chairman will begin to call him by FN. He extends the hand of friendship, but the student knows that it behooves him not to grasp it too quickly. The student will continue with the TLN for several years (4 is probably the mode) and in this period the nonreciprocality of speech will express the inequality of status. If the chairman is neither very elderly nor very august the student will eventually feel able to reciprocate the FN and the dyad will have advanced to Mutual FN. The three patterns may be described as a progression in time (see upper portion of Fig. 1) if we add several important qualifications.

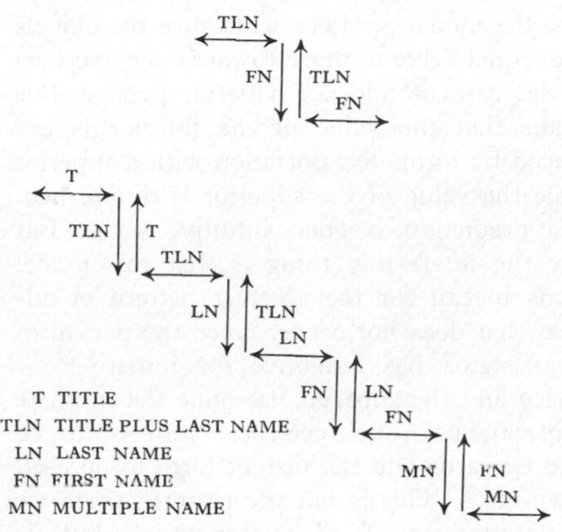

Fig. 1.

Graphic models of the progression of address in time (from left to right). (The upper portion of the figure represents the major progression; the lower portion represents the full progression.)

Not every dyad passes through all three steps. There are some that begin at each of the three points: adults of equal status with Mutual TLN, master and servant with nonreciprocality, young people with Mutual FN. In addition, not every dyad that continues to exist will necessarily advance to Mutual FN. In North Carolina until 1860 the Negro slave said TLN to his master and was told FN (Eliason, 1956), and there was no change with time. There is a final qualification concerning the progression of address in time. Even when relationships do develop in intimacy they will not necessarily pass through the intermediate nonreciprocal stage. When the members of a dyad are not of clearly unequal status, they will advance at the same time to Mutual FN.

The general statement that can be made is: if an address pattern changes in time it will change in the direction of Mutual TLN → nonreciprocal TLN and FN → Mutual FN though a step may be skipped. Even this statement cannot stand without a little more explanation. There are special circumstances in which the direction of movement of address can be reversed. If a person of lower status seems to move too fast to the reciprocation of the FN a superior may step back from his use of FN to TLN. The day after a convivial office party a breezy young clerk calls out to the president: "Morning, Jack!" and in icy tones the president replies: "Good morning, *Mr.* Jones." The person of lower status must never use a more familiar form of address than the person of higher status and the backstep by the superior puts the subordinate in just that position from which he will usually withdraw to the propriety of TLN.

The variant forms of address discussed at an earlier point in this paper seem to function as additional optional steps in the progression of address. (This paper does not discuss all American English forms of address but only those that have clear positions in the intimacy and status pattern. There is, for instance, the use of the complete name [*John Jones* or even *John Montgomery Jones*] which is used as an intensifier and is particularly favored by mothers "manding" disobedient children.) Title alone (T) probably is the formal extreme since we find in our data that dyads which begin as Mutual T often change with time to nonreciprocal TLN downwards and T upwards. The last name alone (LN) must be intercalated between TLN and FN since LN downwards is found in combination with TLN upwards and LN upwards is found in combination with FN downwards. The use of multiple names (MN), we have seen, represents the intimate extreme. Making these additions to the major three-step progression we arrive at the full progression of Fig. 1 (lower portion) in which each new step towards intimacy is initiated by the superior who is, therefore, not just the gatekeeper to Mutual FN but the pacesetter for all linguistic advances in intimacy.

The qualifications that apply to the major progression apply also to the full progression. Dyads may begin at any point, need not move at all, and if they move may skip steps. There is an additional qualification that results from the multiplication of forms. Any less formal term may be used downwards in a nonreciprocal pattern with any more formal term being used upwards. Thus we find not only the TLN with the LN but also the T with LN or even with FN as when a captain calls an enlisted man *Jones* or *John* but is called *captain.*

Is there any way to test the accuracy of the full progression pictured in Fig. 1? We have found no dyads that pass through the entire progression but only dyads moving in one or another limited region. By the time the third and final set of plays was ready for analysis, the full progression had been constructed. If the progression, with all its qualifications, is accurately descriptive of American English practice, one should find certain kinds of address combinations and not others. Any address form can be used mutually (5 possible combinations). When there is a clear difference of status we may have any nonreciprocal pattern that combines a less formal term downward with a more formal term upwards (10 possible combinations). With a clear status difference we may not have any nonreciprocal pattern that combines a more formal term downwards with a less formal term upwards (10 impossible combinations). In the last set of plays instances of all the possible combinations occur and no instances of the impossible combinations. The static predictions of the model are validated.

The construction also generates a set of dynamic predictions. When address changes (if there is not either a reproving or a jocular intent) movement must be in the direction from left to right in the drawing of Fig. 1 though it need not be to the immediately adjacent position. Changes of address in the plays are surprisingly infrequent and seldom involve more than two steps. Only seven different kinds of change occurred but all of these are included among those defined as possible by the model. One "impossible" change occurred in the play *Born Yesterday*. Billie Dawn, the junk dealer's mistress, in speaking with the wife of a United States Senator who is many years her senior initiates movement from Mutual TLN to a more intimate form. This violation of the norms is greeted with general shock and is a device that helps to establish Billie Dawn's ingenuous vulgarity. Insofar as the limited occurrences of change in address permit, then, the model is confirmed in its dynamic aspect.

STATUS AND INTIMACY IN SOCIAL RELATIONS

Two persons of unequal status may be conceived as two points on a generalized value scale of the sort used by Osgood and Tannenbaum (1955) for the congruity model which they have used to predict attitude change. The person of superior status has, of course, the greater value on such a scale. Movements towards intimacy of address in terms of the congruity model are acts of association. Such acts, the model predicts, will cause the objects of unequal value to move towards one another; in the case of address between persons this means that the value of the inferior is enhanced by intimate association with a superior while the value of the superior is diminished. The prediction is good intuitive sense. But now the interesting thing is that this model seems to call for the abstract pattern of address that does not occur. Since the person of lower status has a motive for initiating intimacy and the superior has none the intimate form ought, in nonreciprocal address, to be used upwards and the distant form to be used downwards. This is not the pattern which we have found in all of our materials but, is rather, the formal alternative to that pattern and we have nowhere found this alternative to be the operative norm.

The abstract design of address is not a direct expression of the realities of status and intimacy but is rather a denial of the realities. The pattern might have been designed to minimize the pain of invidious status distinctions. The person of lesser value may be presumed to be ever ready for association with a person of higher value but the person of higher value must be presumed to be less ready. If the person of lesser value were to initiate associative acts, he would run the risk of rebuff; if the person of higher value initiates such acts there is no such risk. The superior, then, must be the pacesetter in progression to intimacy. If there is to be no progression but rather an enduring nonreciprocal expression of inequality, this expression is not so disagreeable as it might be since the superior offers intimate address and it is the inferior who demurs. The abstract pattern minimizes the pain that could be involved when persons are to be related on two dimensions: the horizontal of intimacy and the vertical of status.

The person of higher status is, we believe, the pacesetter not in linguistic address alone but in all acts that increase intimacy. The Sloan Fellows who served as informants for us responded to two questions that concern nonlinguistic moves towards intimacy. Each question was answered with reference to each of the four persons listed by the informant. One of these persons, you may remember, was a Superior, one a Subordinate, one Equal and Intimate, one Equal and Distant. The informant indicated on a scale from 1-5 how willing he would be to behave in the designated manner with reference to each person. The Number 1 represents maximal willingness ("Definitely would") and 5 minimal willingness ("Definitely would not"). The questions are:

1. In ordinary circumstances would you be willing to ask "X" for the loan of his comb?
2. Suppose "X" were feeling very unhappy about something or other. Would you put your hand on his shoulder in a reassuring way?

The results appear in Table 3 and show a familiar pattern. Informants were more willing to borrow a comb from, and to put a hand on the shoulder of, an associate who was Equal and Intimate than one Equal and Distant and also more willing to initiate these acts of intimacy with Subordinates than with Superiors. Using a sign test and a one-tailed hypothesis the comb question differentiates intimate from remote associates with a $p = .008$ and Subordinates from Superiors with a $p = .033$; the hand-on shoulder question differentiates intimate from remote associates with a $p = .029$ and Subordinates from Superiors with a $p < .002$. These nonspeech acts follow the pattern of TLN and FN; of T and V; and of Hi and Good Morning. Perhaps all kinds of associative behavior can be placed on a rough scale of intimacy and in the progression over this scale of a dyad the superior may always be in advance.

TABLE 3

COMPARATIVE WILLINGNESS TO INITIATE ACTS OF INTIMACY WITH FOUR CLASSES OF ASSOCIATE

	More Willing with Equal and Intimate Than with Distant Associate	*More Willing with Equal and Distant Than with Intimate Associate*	*More Willing with Subordinate Than with Superior*	*More Willing with Superior Than with Subordinate*
Borrow Comb	7	0	9	2
Hand on Shoulder	11	3	24	1

NOTE. By sign test Intimate vs. Distant on Borrow Comb, $p = .008$; on Hand on Shoulder, $p = .029$. Subordinate vs. Superior on Borrow Comb, $p = .033$; on Hand on Shoulder, $p < .002$.

With a good sized inequality of status the use of FN by the higher does not, of course, justify immediate reciprocation from the lower. The lower must wait for the initiation of additional acts of intimacy before taking a step on his own. It is very likely that the normative lag in intimacy increases with the degree of status inequality. However, the norms are not always perfectly clear; graduate students will sometimes be uncertain whether the time has come to say FN to a professor, employees will wonder whether they know their bosses well enough to use the familiar form. When someone is in this region of uncertainty, we find that he avoids the use of any sort of personal name and makes do with the uncommitted omnibus *you.*

SUMMARY

The semantic rules governing address in American English are worked out from a varied collection of data that includes usage in American plays, actual usage in a Boston business firm, reported usage of business executives from various cities in the United States, and usage recorded in a midwestern American town. The most common address forms are the first name (FN) and the title plus last name (TLN). These function in three sorts of dyadic pattern: the Mutual TLN, the Mutual FN, and the nonreciprocal use of TLN and FN. The semantic distinction between the two mutual patterns is on the intimacy dimension with Mutual FN being the more intimate of the two patterns. In the nonreciprocal pattern a distinction is made in terms of status with the higher saying FN and the lower TLN. The practice of using the intimate form to a subordinate and the distant form to a superior also governs the use of pronouns of address in many languages as well as the use of certain conventional greetings. It is suggested that this very general pattern prevails because in the progression towards intimacy of unequals the superior is always the pacesetter initiating new moves in that direction. The superior is the pacesetter because the willingness of the person of lower status to enter into association can be taken for granted and there is little risk that a superior will be rebuffed whereas the risk would be great if the inferior were to initiate acts of association. Such variant forms of address as the title alone, the last name alone, and the use of multiple names are fitted into a model that purports to describe the temporal progression of address from acquaintance to friendship. Each new step towards friendship is, in this model, initiated by the person of higher status.

REFERENCE NOTE

In addition to references cited by Brown and Ford. see those listed with Evans-Pritchard's article on pp. 221-225, especially Befu and Norbeck (1958), Garvin and Riesenberg (1952), Mbaga and Whiteley (1961), Milner (1961), and Pittman (1948). Note also Law (1948), comments on Brown's work in Lounsbury (1962), and references with Martin's article in Part VII. Rubin (1962) reports a case in which the dimensions used by Brown and Ford are manifested in a choice between whole languages (Guarani, Spanish).

References not in the general bibliography:

BROWN, ROGER W.

1959. Humbert's Idiography. *Contemporary Psychology*, *4:* 172-174.

CONKLIN, HAROLD C.

1957. *Hannunóo Agriculture*. Rome: Food and Agriculture Organization of the United Nations.

ELIASON, N. E.

1956. *Tarheel Talk: An Historical Study of the English Language in North Carolina to 1860*. Chapel Hill: University of North Carolina Press.

GASSNER, J. (ED.)

1947. *Best Plays of the Modern American Theater: Second Series*. New York: Crown.

1952. *Best American Plays: Third Series*. New York: Crown.

1958. *Best American Plays: Fourth Series*. New York: Crown.

JOURARD, S. M., and P. LASAKOW

1958. Some Factors in Self-Disclosure. *JASP*, *56:* 91-98.

LAW, HOWARD W.

1948. Greeting Forms of the Gulf Aztecs. *SJA*, *4:* 43-48.

OSGOOD, C. E., and P. H. TANNENBAUM

1955. The Principle of Congruity in Attitude Change. *Psychological Review*, *62:* 42-55.

QUINN, A. H. (ED.)

1917. *Representative American Plays*. New York: Century.

Comanche Baby Language 27

JOSEPH B. CASAGRANDE

THE COMANCHE LANGUAGE reveals an unusually rich and formalized vocabulary of special baby words which were used in teaching the child to speak. Their use began when the child was old enough to understand, at about one year according to informants, and dropped off as the child matured and learned the normal, adult locutions at the age of 3 to 4. If a child persisted in using these words after the age of 5 or so, it would be laughed at and ridiculed for its babyish ways. Today English holds sway and these baby words no longer function actively, although children in those families or households where there are older persons who speak only Comanche may have some knowledge of them. So of necessity these data were recorded from the lips of adult speakers, most of whom, however, maintain a lively memory of the baby forms.

The following list was checked with eight informants and is probably exhaustive. Where known, the adult form or derivation is given in brackets after the translation of the baby word or words.

ʔáʔh, ʔáx, ʔáʔhA 'something nasty or dirty; feces, urine, penis, a smell; warning to get away from something dirty; I have wet, dirtied myself; command for baby to defecate.'

ʔaʔhá:ʔ 'no good!' (said to baby).

The next two forms are used in speaking to and by older children. They are derived from the baby words, but with regular verbal suffixes.

ʔáʔhi:kwhA 'go off and defecate!'

ʔáʔhI, ʔáʔhinɨʔ 'I have dirtied myself.'

ʔaná:, ʔanó: 'it hurts!' (pointing to place); sore place, cut; command to child to get away from thing or place where it might get hurt.'

ʔasí:, ʔaʔsí: 'rectum; feces, defecation; anything nasty.'

ʔeroró:ʔ, ʔeró:ʔ, ʔetó:ʔ 'white man' [*táivo:ʔ* 'white man'].

ʔɨt':ʔ, ʔɨtɨtɨtɨ́ʔ 'it's hot!; command to stay away from something hot; fire, lamp, lightning, sun, flashlight, firewood; anything that will burn' [*ʔɨrɨ́:ʔ, ʔɨrɨrɨrɨ́:ʔ*].

ʔɨ:kétaʔ 'don't; let me alone.'

ʔɨ́: 'exclamation of surprise' (women or babies).

hɨ́:, hɨ:kétaʔ as above; also used by adults; 'don't' (scared).

ʔɨcɨ́:ʔ, ʔɨcɨcɨcɨ́:ʔ 'cover me, dress me, I'm cold; it's cold; command to stay away from something cold' [*ʔɨcɨ́:* used only as an exclamation].

ʔɨnɨ:ʔ 'insect; any small noxious animal, to babies when one wants child to be afraid of something or leave it alone; bug, snake, scorpion, ant, person; exclamation of fright' [*ʔɨ́nɨ:*].

ʔúʔtU 'give it to me!' [*ʔúhtU*].

ʔum:áʔ 'good! nice! beautiful' (said by mother when she wants to comb child's hair, dress it; said to attract child's attention to clothes, toy); 'anything bright or colorful that attracts the child; red, yellow, blue.'

umó:ʔ, mó:ʔ 'cattle, cow, bull' (onomatopoeia).

papá:ʔ 'I want a drink'; water [*pá:* 'water'].

papó:ʔ, popó:ʔ 'dog.'

pepé:ʔ 'ball' (it was said by one informant that this word was used only by girls as boys didn't play with balls) [*naʔ sihpé:ʔ*].

pikí:ʔ 'pig' (English: pig, piggy).

tatá:ʔ 'something to eat, especially meat; I want, give me . . .; eat!' [*tíhkap* 'food, meat'].

tató:ʔ 'shoes, moccasins' [*ta-* is a prefix meaning 'foot'; *tàhtokó:ʔ* 'toe'].

táʔsi 'vagina' (*táʔsip* to baby when bouncing

it on the knees; a personal name: 'one who has a vagina') [*táʔI*].

tutú:ʔ 'automobile, train, anything that whistles' (onomatopoeia).

kaká:ʔ, *kaká* 'bird; headlouse.'

kani:ʔ 'house, tipi' [*kánh*I].

kokó:ʔ 'fruit, candy cookies; any snack between meals'; give me . . .

ciki:ʔ 'chicken' (English).

cici:ʔ 'breast, bottle, milk, I want to be suckled!' [*pícip* 'milk, breast'].

cíʔciʔ, *píciʔ* said by mother to child when she is going to nurse it.

mamá:ʔ 'horse'; said by child when it wants to be carried on someone's back.

mamá:ʔ 'mother' (English).

mukí:ʔ, *mu:kí:ʔ* 'giant, owl, bogey' (to scare child) [related to *mú:pic*, the legendary 'giant owl'].

mumú:ʔ used to scare child; 'child's exclamation of fright; the dark, thunder; cow.'

naná:ʔ 'it might hurt, get away; blood, sore, hurt'; said if baby doesn't feel well; if it is bitten or hurt by another child (see *ʔaná:*).

nɨní:ʔ 'doll; baby; little ones of animals; little . . .'

nɨnici:ʔ 'dear little doll, baby' [related to the pronominal prefix, *nɨ-* 'I, me'].

waʔó:ʔ, *wa:ʔó:ʔ* 'cat' [*wáʔo:*].

ʔɨʔsI, *níʔɨsik* 'cover me!' [*ʔɨhɨkI*, *niʔɨhɨkI*].

wɨʔasI 'penis' [*wɨʔA* (*wɨʔasiʔ* male personal name 'one who has a penis')].

The *sI* here, and also in the baby word for 'vagina', *táʔsI*, is probably derived from the diminutive suffix, *-cI*.

RELATIONSHIP TERMS

piá 'mother' (the regular adult word; there is no special baby word in common use).

pipiá said by some babies.

ʔapɨ:ʔ 'father, father's brother, father's *haic* ('friend') [*ʔápɨ* address form; *ʔáhpɨʔ* reference form].

ʔatá:ʔ 'mother's brother, husband of mother's friend' [*ʔárhA* address form; *ʔáraʔ* reference form].

paci:ʔ 'older sister' [pácI address form; *páciʔ* reference form].

nami:ʔ 'younger sister' (*námI* address form; *námiʔ* reference form).

taká:ʔ 'sibling' (*tákA* address form; *tákaʔ* reference form).

tami:ʔ 'younger brother' (*támI* address form; *tamiʔ* reference form).

pavi:ʔ 'older brother' (*pávI* address form; *páviʔ* reference form).

pahá:ʔ 'father's sister' (*páhA* address form; *páhaʔ* reference form).

kakú:ʔ 'grandmother' ('mother's mother' is the adult meaning; *kákU* address form; *kákuʔ* reference form).

tokó:ʔ, *totó:ʔ* 'grandfather,' sometimes 'father' (this form used by a younger child) ('mother's father' is the adult meaning; *tókO* address form; *tókoʔ* reference form).

The following terms may also be used if the child is old enough to make the distinction: *kɨnú:ʔ* 'father's father' (*kɨnU* address form; *kɨnuʔ* reference form); *huci:ʔ* 'father's mother' (*húcI* address form; *húciʔ* reference form).

These kinship terms, other than those used for 'father,' 'mother,' and 'grandparents,' probably appear relatively later in the child's vocabulary. Just how far they are extended to include those relatives normally subsumed under them in adult usage is not certain, but they may be taken to apply primarily to those persons designated above or their surrogates. It is interesting to note that the maternal grandparental terms are those first used for all grandparents. This suggests matrilocal residence, or at least more intimate contact with the mother's parents than with the father's.

In addition to the above list of formal baby words several characteristics of Comanche children's speech may be mentioned. There is a tendency for children to add the diminutive-endearing suffix, *-cI* and the related *-sI* to words: e.g., *haici:ʔ* for *haic* 'friend.' Reduplication, as might be inferred from the above list, is another feature: *tɨtɨi* is said by little girls for *tɨ:i* 'girl friend'; *pipiá* for *piá* 'mother,' etc. (Kroeber mentions this tendency to reduplicate in the speech of a Zuni child of 23 months whom he observed; his paper [Kroeber, 1916] is the only published account of the speech development of a primitive child.) Although reduplication is present in Comanche as a grammatical process, it performs no ostensible grammatical function in the child's speech. Various phonemic substitutions are made; *p* for *kw* as *pɨhI* for *kwɨhI* 'wife'; *pánA* for *kwánA* 'odor, smell'; also *i* for *ɨ* as *tiás* for *tɨas*, etc. One person carries the personal name, *pitá:siʔ* 'one who always defecates,' a "baby name," where a *p* is substituted for the *kw* in *kwitA* 'defecate!' and the suffix *-sI* is also added. These substitutions are not regular, but are commonly made by children learning to speak. Somewhat more regular is the substitution of *t* for *r* (see examples in the word list)

Several facts become apparent upon study of the above list of baby words. First, it must be recognized that these function not as single, simple words, but as whole sentences with many different, albeit related, possible meanings (exclamatory, imperative, declarative, interrogative) which are elucidated by gestures, intonations, and the context of the situation. They are really sentence-words. Phonetically, the baby words are simple: there are no pre-aspirated consonants; the sonants plus *h* does not appear; whispered vowels and the defective (i.e., found in only a few words) phonemes, *r* and *v*, are rare and their appearance is probably late in the speech development of the child. The *x* phoneme and the long *m* are unique to the baby vocabulary.

Reduplication is evident and appears to be especially common in those words generic to the baby language and basic to it. The baby word phonetic pattern of two syllables with the second vowel accented, long, and usually ending in a glottal stop occurs in most of the examples. Words derived from the adult vocabulary are put into this pattern, as may be seen from the relationship terms. Presumably it is in this phonetic form that words are first presented to the child. This seems consistent with our practice of carefully enunciating words when teaching them to a child.

Language development poses several problems for the generic psychologist and anthropologist as well as the linguist. Some baby words are to be found in all languages, written and unwritten, though not commonly as formalized and in such abundance as in Comanche. In all these baby words two facts claim attention: the universality of reduplication and the use of simple phonemes, especially the labials *p*, *b*, *m*, the stops *t*, *d*, *k*, *g*, and "cardinal" vowels (*i*, *e*, *ɛ*, *a*, *ɔ*, *o*, *u*). The use of simpler phonemes is probably explained in terms of the baby's limited ability to manipulate his speech organs, since learning to speak even one's native tongue involves the induction of an intricate set of motor habits and is a maturational process comparable to acquiring such other skills as walking or skipping. But the problem of reduplication is not so easy of solution. Jespersen has this to say, "It is simpler and more natural to refer these reduplications to the pleasure always felt in repeating the same muscular action until one is tired" (Jespersen, 1922, p. 109). But this seems an oversimple explanation. A natural tendency to reduplicate may perhaps be granted and seems to be supported by the oft-made observation of the infant's babbling repetition of the same sound. This proclivity seems to have been tacitly recognized by adults and conventionalized by them in reduplicated baby words. (Margaret Mead [1930, pp. 36 ff.] discusses the child's speech education in Manus, and mentions the endless repetition back and forth between adult and baby of the same monosyllable. She says, "This random affection for repetitiousness makes an excellent atmosphere in which the child acquires facility in speech" [p. 37].)

As the growth of speech facility parallels to a marked degree the maturation of the child's intellectual capacities, one might ask how comparative speech phenomena reflect this. Does it take longer for a primitive child who has to learn a highly complex language, such as many North American Indian languages, to gain control of his language than, say, a Chinese or American child? (Clyde Kluckhohn, who has made extensive observations on Navaho children, feels that the Navaho child, as compared with the English-speaking child of the same age, is somewhat retarded in acquiring equal facility with his extremely difficult language.) At what age is the primitive child capable of making the subtle analogical formations that many primitive languages require?

Some knowledge of children's speech development and baby words seems essential for the anthropologist or psychologist interested in problems of personality development and character structure. From the vocabulary itself one can form some idea of the child's world in a given culture; what objects and affects impinge upon it. Discipline and attitudes are reflected, as in Comanche where feces, urine, and the genitalia and feelings of disgust are equated, and where there are words used to frighten the child, admonish it, and control its movements. It seems likely that conscious speech training might be correlated with later educational procedures and attitudes towards children. This seems true for the Comanche where the position of children was high as was general on the Plains. It also seems important to know how long baby words are used and, if they are reverted to later in life, under what conditions. (Persistence in using baby talk was an important symptom of personality disturbances among Pilaga children where in extreme cases, those of half or full orphans, baby talk persists until the ninth year. In the most severe cases of personality disturbances a pattern of phonetic substitution is rigidly followed through and at times results in serious phonetic distortion [Henry and Henry, 1940].) The extension of kinship terms, the child's induction into their use, and the varying importance of the different relatives or classes of relatives to the child are all relevant. (See Hogbin, 1939, pp. 38-42, for an admirable start in this direction.)

REFERENCE NOTE

The material for this paper was gathered on a field trip sponsored by Columbia University to the Comanche Indians living near Indiahoma, Oklahoma, during the summer of 1940. A, I, O, U represent voiceless vowels.

See Herzog (1949, p. 97) for further comment on Comanche child language.

Baby words are listed by Chamberlain (1890, 1893); Dennis (1940, p. 35), including words from Shungopavi, Zuni, and Cochiti (personal correspondence); Frachtenberg (1917); Jespersen (1922); Kroeber (1916); and Sapir (1929d). [For recent comparative data, see Austerlitz (1956), Burling (1959), Ferguson (1956) and Larsen (1949)].

On CHILD LANGUAGE generally, especially on the child's own linguistic system, see Applegate (1961), Halle (1962, pp. 64-65), Jakobson (1941), and Leopold (1953-1954). Halle and Applegate discuss the problem from a transformational viewpoint. Modern descriptive, or structural, principles are important also in the work of Berko (1958), Berko and Brown (1961), Brown (1957), Ervin and Miller (1963), Pike (1949), Velten (1943), Weir (1962), and work in Bellugi and Brown (1964).

For general surveys and discussions, see Brown (1958, chap 6), Carroll (1960), Cohen (1952), Ervin and Miller (1963), Gregoire (1937-1947, 1950), Hockett (1958, chap. 4), Jakobson (1941), Jespersen (1922, Book II), Leopold (1948, 1952a, 1952b, 1953-1954), Lewis (1947, pp. 12-70; 1951), McCarthy (1954), Malinowski (1937), and Saporta (1961, pp. 331-375), which includes Berko (1958), Carroll (1960), and Leopold (1953-1954).

On social and cultural aspects, see references to Bernstein's article on pp. 251-260.

References not in general bibliography:

APPLEGATE, JOSEPH R.

1961. Phonological Rules of a Subdialect of English. *Word, 17:* 186-193.

AUSTERLITZ, ROBERT

1956. Gilyak Nursery Words. *Word, 12:* 260-279.

BERKO, JEAN

1958. The Child's Learning of English Morphology. *Word, 14:* 150-177.

BERKO, JEAN, and ROGER W. BROWN

1961. Psycholinguistic Research Methods. In Paul H. Mussen (Ed.), *Handbook of Research Methods in Child Development*. New York: Wiley. Pp. 517-577.

BURLING, ROBBINS

1959. Language Development of a Garo and English Speaking Child. *Word*, *15*: 45-68.

CARROLL, JOHN B.

1960. Language Development in Children. *Encyclopaedia of Educational Research*. New York: Macmillan. Pp. 744-752.

CHAMBERLAIN, ALEXANDER F.

1890. Notes on Indian Child-Language. *AA* (O.S.), *3*: 237-241.

1893. Notes on Indian Child-Language. *AA* (O.S.), *6*: 321-322.

COHEN, MARCEL

1952. Sur l'Étude du langage enfantin. *Enfance*, *5*: 181-249.

DENNIS, WAYNE

1940. *The Hopi Child*. New York: Appleton-Century.

ERVIN, SUE, and WICK MILLER

1963. Language Development. In Harold Stevenson (Ed.), *Child Development*. (Yearbook of the National Society for the Study of Education.)

FERGUSON, CHARLES

1956. Arabic Baby Talk. *For Roman Jakobson*. The Hague: Mouton. Pp. 121-128.

FRACHTENBERG, LEO J.

1917. Abnormal Types of Speech in Quileute. *IJAL*, *1*: 295-299.

GREGOIRE, ANTOINE

1937-1947. *L'Apprentissage du langage*. Paris: Droz.

1950. La Renaissance scientifique de la linguistique enfantine. *Lingua*, *2*: 355-398.

HENRY, JULES, and ZUNIA HENRY

1940. Speech Disturbances in Pilaga Children. *American Journal of Orthopsychiatry* 10. 362-369.

HOGBIN, H. IAN

1939. *Experiments in Civilization*. London. Routledge.

JAKOBSON, ROMAN

1941. *Kindersprache, Aphasie und allgemeine Lautgesetze*. (Uppsala Universitets Arsskrift 1942: 9, Sprakvetenskapliga Sällskapets i Uppsala Förhandlingar, Jan., 1940-Dec., 1942, Bil. A.) Uppsala: Almquist and Wicksell. [Reviewed, W. Leopold, *Lg.*, 1942, *18*, 253-254.]

KROEBER, A. L.

1916. The Speech of a Zuni Child. *AA*, *18*: 529-534.

LARSEN, KAY

1949. Huasteco Baby Talk. *El México Antiguo*, *7*: 295-298.

LEOPOLD, WERNER F.

1939-1949. *Speech Development of a Bilingual Child: A Linguist's Record*. (Northwestern University Studies, Humanities Series, Nos. 6, 11, 18, 19.) Evanston: Northwestern University Press. 4 vols. [Reviewed, P. L. Garvin, *Word*, 1950, *10*: 75-78; H. V. Velten, *Lg.*, 1949, *25*: 215-219.]

1952a. *Bibliography of Child Language*. Evanston: Northwestern University Press.

1952b. Anton Grégoire and the Revival of Child Linguistics. *Lingua*, *3:* 224-226.

1953-1954. Patterning in Children's Language Learning. *Language Learning*, *5:* 1-14.

LEWIS, M. M.

1951. *Infant Speech. A Study of the Beginnings of Language.* (2nd rev. ed.) London and New York: Routledge & Paul.

MCCARTHY, DOROTHEA

1954. Language Development in Children. In Leonard Carmichael (Ed.), *A Manual of Child Psychology*. (2nd ed.) New York: Wiley. Pp. 492-630.

MEAD, MARGARET

1930. *Growing Up in New Guinea*. New York: Morrow.

PIKE, EVELYN G.

1949. Controlled Infant Intonation. *Language Learning*, *2:* 21-24.

SAPIR, EDWARD

1929d. Nootka Baby Words. *IJAL*, *5:* 118-119.

VELTEN, H. V.

1943. The Growth of Phonemic and Lexical Patterns in Infant Language. *Lg.*, *19:* 281-292.

WEIR, RUTH HIRSCH

1962. *Language in the Crib*. (Janua Linguarum, Series Maior 14.) The Hague: Mouton.

Aspects of Language and Learning in the Genesis of the Social Process 28

BASIL BERNSTEIN

INTRODUCTION

A MAJOR THEORETICAL PROBLEM is the relationship between the social structure and individual experience. Through what means is the social process learned and what are the implications of such learning? These questions raise, critically, the problem of the relationship between sociology and psychology. The sociologist's attempt to derive personality statements is often considered by the psychologist as crude and insensitive; whilst to the sociologist, psychological statements relating to social process, particularly institutional behaviour, often have an air of joyous naïveté. It seems that neither discipline has reached a level of theorctical sophistication such that integration becomes possible. An approach to this question may be made if one examines an intervening variable which is limited and shaped by a given type of social organization and yet conditions the form of a basic learning process. I would like to examine the possibility that spoken language, or rather specific linguistic forms, fit these criteria. Speech, as Luria points out (1961), can be considered as a complex of additional signals which leads to marked changes in the field of stimuli. It is proposed that forms of spoken language, in the process of their learning, initiate, reinforce and synthesize special types of relationship with the environment and thus create particular dimensions of significance.

Studies of the language development of institutionalized children indicate that they may be grossly retarded in vocabulary, complexity of sentence contruction and type and power of abstraction (Bernstein, 1960a). Although the relationship between I.Q. and language ability is one of complex reciprocity the studies clearly indicate that the functional level of general performance and social effectiveness may be greatly reduced in an environment detrimental to the development of language skills. It is also clear that linguistic differences occur in the normal environment, e.g., in the language use of children in their peer group, combat units in the armed services, criminal sub-cultures, and between status groups. Linguistic differences between status groups is most marked where the gap between them is very great. Studies of the language habits of children indicate that these differences are revealed almost from the beginnings of speech. (Irwin, 1948a, 1948b; Sampson, 1956.) I suggest that the measurable inter-status linguistic differences between the lower working-class and the middle-class, rather than reflecting differences in innate capacity, result from entirely different modes of speech which are dominant and typical within these strata. More formally, different social structures place their stress on different possibilities inherent in language use, and once this stress is placed, then the resulting linguistic form is one of the most important means of eliciting and strengthening ways of feeling and thinking which are functionally related to the social group.

DEFINITION OF SPEECH FORMS

Before characterizing the linguistic usages typical of the two social strata I want to contrast two types of linguistic utterance. Following Hughling Jackson's (1932) distinction between well-organized and now-organizing speech and the refined use of this distinction by Dr. F. Goldman-Eisler (1958a) I would like to contrast what may be called highly-coded with now-coding utterances. A now-coding utterance is one in which speech is specially and often newly created to fit a particular referent. A highly-coded utterance consists of attaching ready-made terms or phrases as well-organized sequences to designate a referent (e.g., comments about the weather; the opening gambit at a cocktail party). Now-coding utterances are individuated. The sequences have a low transition probability and are therefore relatively individual and unexpected. Highly-coded utterances tend to be utterances which are the result of common conditioning and learning. They are shared by a given language community and possess a relatively high transition probability. In the case of now-coding utterances the individual is emitting a series of signals which symbolize the speaker's separateness and difference. These utterances are symbolic of an individuated experience. This is not the case with highly-coded utterances, for the signals tend to symbolize the normative arrangements of a group. Social symbols are created, which are reinforced in the speaking. Highly-coded utterances will tend to be short, fast, fluent and relatively unpaused and, because of their well-organized or automatic character, permit high affective ventilation and the use of gross expressive symbolism. They will also tend to refer to, and become a vehicle for, concrete rather than analytic thought processes. On the other hand, now-coding utterances will tend to be slower, longer, utterances with relatively longer pauses within the speech sequences and become a vehicle for analytical thought processes (Goldman-Eisler, 1958b, 1960). Finer graduations of expressive symbolism may accompany this form of utterance than in the case of highly-coded utterances.

Although an individual will naturally shift from one type of utterance to another, depending upon the context of a social situation, there may well be a series of diverse social contexts which are dominated by the use of one type rather than the other. The language of the child in his peer group, judging from the material in the Opies' recent book (Opie and Opie, 1959), may be considered as a system of highly-coded utterances which, as the child learns, regulates his behaviour by preparing him to respond to and emit particular types of signals in relation to a specific stimuli pattern. In this way the adequacy of his socialization to the norms of his sub-culture is revealed and reinforced every time he speaks. I shall call a system of communication dominated by highly-coded utterances the *pure* form of a *public* language, whilst a system which permits and encourages now-coding utterances, or one where they may be frequently signalled and elicited, the *pure* type of a *formal* language. [See the Postscript on pp. 258-260 for a revised formulation.]

Certain problems arise from this analysis of speech. It is clear that an analysis of speech in terms of highly-coded and now-coding utterances takes as its unit the word, and then seeks statistical frequencies and the transition probabilities of the units. The analysis can be fruitfully extended to the consideration of larger units such as particular speech sequences. The language of children, as presented by the Opies, enables us to make certain predictions of such sequences, because a code is now available for a relatively large and diverse area of communication. It is also possible to make some statements about the psychological and sociological dimensions of relevance, facilitated by speech which is regulated by highly-coded utterances (Bernstein, 1960b). However, when a code is not available because the permutations and units are either too large or unknown, then a word or a given speech sequence is an inadequate unit for analysis. It becomes necessary to shift, at this point, from a micro-level analysis of particular words or speech sequences to a macro-level analysis of linguistic structure. On this level I propose to characterize the general forms of the two distinct linguistic usages mentioned earlier. [See now the Postcript.]

The general form of a *public* language is a mode of communication, which is marked off from other modes of speech by the rigidity of its syntactical structure and the limited and restricted use of structural possibilities for sentence organization. It is a form of condensed speech in which certain meanings are restricted and the possibility of their elaboration is reduced. Whilst it may not be possible to predict any one content of this language, it is suggested that the structural organization and syntax is highly predictable. The class of the content is also predictable. A *formal* language, by contrast, is one in which the structure and syntax is potentially less predictable for any one individual. The formal possibilities of sentence organization are used to clarify meaning and make it explicit. Its chief characteristics are:

1. Accurate grammatical order and syntax regulate what is said.
2. Logical modifications and stress are mediated through a grammatically complex sentence construction, especially through the use of a range of conjunctions and subordinate clauses.
3. Frequent use of prepositions which indicate logical relationships as well as prepositions which indicate temporal and spatial contiguity.
4. Frequent use of impersonal pronouns, 'it,' 'one.'
5. A discriminative selection from a range of adjectives and adverbs.
6. Individual qualification is verbally mediated through the structure and relationships within and between sentences.
7. Expressive symbolism discriminates between meanings within speech sequences rather than reinforcing dominant words or phrases, or accompanying the sequence in a diffuse generalized manner.
8. It is language use which points to the possibilities inherent in a complex conceptual hierarchy for the organizing of experience.

These characteristics must be considered to give a *direction* to the organization of thinking and feeling rather than to the *establishing* of complex modes of relationships. The characteristics are relative to those of a *public* language.

The individual, when he speaks a *public* language, operates within a mode of speech in which individual selection and permutation are grossly restricted; whilst in the case of a *formal* language the speaker is able to make a highly individual selection and permutation. I am not arguing that a *formal* language speaker always does this. I am simply stating that the possibility exists. A *formal* language is considered the dominant and typical speech form of the middleclasses.

(Whilst it is obvious that certain aspects of children's speech development must necessarily hold irrespective of the social structure, the organization of the language used and responded to, is of critical importance whatever the age of the child. The following conversation took place in a middle-class nursery. Two little girls of 4 were arguing about their respective heights—"I'm bigger than you." "No, I'm bigger than you"—when the conversation suddenly took this turn:

S: "Well, my sister's seven and a half."
K: "Well, but she's not you."
S: "No, everyone's theirselves."

An example of the subordination of behaviour to verbal control is the following: A middle-class grandmother was visited by her 2-year old grand-daughter, who was found alone in the drawing-room. The grandmother, by the door, saw the child look round the room, firmly repeating: "That's a don't, and that's a don't, and that's a don't! . . ." It is unlikely that a *public* language would induce this regulative function in a child so young. It is more probable that the impulse would have been acted out.

It is not easy to give briefly examples of *public* language usage, but the reader is referred to Hoggart [1957], and to the writer's own work and tape-recordings. See also Bossard, 1945.)

I suggest that where an individual is *confined* to a *public* language certain cognitive and affective processes are differentiated in a particular manner forming a relatively coherent functional system sensitized to a special stimuli pattern (Bernstein, 1961a). I further suggest that this linguistic usage is a function of a sub-culture, not of individual psychology. The characteristics of a *public* language (the major speech form of the lower working class) are as follows:

1. Short, grammatically simple, often unfinished sentences with a poor syntactical form.
2. Simple and repetitive use of conjunctions ('so,' 'then,' 'and,' 'because').
3. Little use of sub-ordinate clauses to break down the initial categories of the dominant subject.
4. Inability to hold a subject through a speech sequence, so that a dislocated informational content is facilitated.
5. Rigid and limited use of adjectives and adverbs.
6. Infrequent use of impersonal pronouns as subjects of conditional clauses or sentences.
7. Frequent use of statements where the reason and conclusion are confounded to produce a categoric statement.
8. A large number of statements/phrases which signal a requirement for the previous speech sequence to be reinforced: "Wouldn't it? You see? You know?" etc. This process is termed "sympathetic circularity."
9. Individual selection from a group of idiomatic phrases or sequences will frequently occur.

10. *The individual qualification is implicit in the sentence organization: it is a language of implicit meaning.*

These criteria refer to an ideal linguistic structure. What will be found empirically is an orientation to this form of language use. It is clear that some of these characteristics will occur in most forms of language use but a *public* language is a form of usage in which all the characteristics will be found. It is possible to consider approximations to a *public* language to the extent that other characteristics do not occur. (Approximations to a *public* language will be spoken in the peer group of children and adolescents, criminal sub-cultures, combat units in the armed services, and in rural groups.) (See the characteristics of a *formal* language.) Although any one example of a *public* language will be associated with a particular vocabulary and sequence frequency, it is worth while emphasizing that the definition and characterization is independent of vocabulary. I am concerned with the implications of a general mode, not with the isolated significance of particular words, or speech sequences. I am not arguing for a mechanical relationship between language and other forms of behaviour; rather for a gradual modification of learned responses, through language, which stabilizes and strengthens perceptions. Stability is maintained by the development of inter-related systems of responses held together and sustained by the act of speech. Speech, as Luria has pointed out (Luria and Yudovich, 1959), is not only a means of indicating corresponding objects or relationships in the external world but abstracts, isolates, generalizes perceived signals and relates them to certain categories. *Language marks out what is relevant, affectively, cognitively and socially, and experience is transformed by that which is made relevant.*

PSYCHOLOGICAL IMPLICATIONS OF A PUBLIC LANGUAGE

Where an individual is limited to a *public* language, the possibilities signalled by language are perceived in a distinctive manner. Language is perceived *not* as a set of possibilities which can be fashioned sensitively to facilitate the expression of a unique individual experience. Language, in this case, is *not* a means to verbalize, relatively precisely, the experience of separateness and difference. Rather, with a *public* language, an individual inter-acts within a linguistic form which maximizes the means of producing *social* rather than individuated symbols. The early linguistic relationship between a mother and a child is one which maximizes the direct experience of affective inclusiveness, rather than that of verbally conditioned cognitive and affective differentiation. As speech marks out a pattern of stimuli to which the child adapts, so, in the learning of this pattern, his perception is organized, structured and reinforced. The adequacy of his response is rewarded or punished by the adult model until the child is able to regulate his own responses independently of the adult. In this way the child learns, and so internalizes his social structure from the very beginnings of speech.

Luria has shown the importance of the impelling, or starting and planning function of speech: a *public* language focuses on the *inhibiting* function of speech by directing our attention (that is the attention of the observer) to potential referents which carry no stimulus value for the speaker. A *public* language narrows yet intensifies the range of stimuli to which the child learns to respond; the dimension of significance created by the speech is restricted. Vygotsky (1939) made the interesting observation that abbreviated, condensed speech is a function of a social relationship where the subject of the dialogue is held in common. This is the case with a *public* language, where the subject is a special type of unifying sub-culture which renders unnecessary and irrelevant, complex verbal procedures. The implications of such a speech form are critical for behaviour.

It is suggested that where an individual is restricted to a *public* language, speech does *not* become an object of special perceptual activity, *neither* does a theoretical attitude develop towards the structural possibilities of sentence organization. The speech is epitomized by poor syntactical organization and a severely limiting structural organization. It is a vehicle for expressing and receiving concrete, global, descriptive relationships organized within a relatively low level of conceptualization. The speech delivery, within a normal environment, is composed of fast, fluent, short, relatively unpaused sequences, accompanied by a diffuse affective discharge. Affect is not used to discriminate among meanings carried within speech sequences. It is used to reinforce specific dominant words or accompanies the utterance in a generalized diffuse manner. It can be seen that this pattern of expressive and verbal signals will decide how effective is any process of communication. The release of affect is further facilitated by the fact that the median and final consonants in a word will tend to be unvoiced. Thus the mode of speech itself will elicit and reinforce a special affective correlate. The affective potential is not differentiated, stabilized and made specific by being linked by the language to a relatively wide range of referents. Affect which is regulated by the speech is conditioned by the concreteness of the language. This means that much affect is unconventionalized by language, and is available to be triggered off in a diffuse manner.

It has been suggested that the number and type of new relationships available to an individual is limited as a result of the learned sensitivity to descriptive, global concepts, but equally important is the fact that a particular cluster of relationships are not of great relevance to the speaker. These are relationships which are initiated by considerations of *subjective intent* (Kohn, 1959a, 1959b). Subjective intent refers to the conditions of, and reflections upon, the motivations of self and other. This must not be taken to mean that this never occurs. Such statements will be made, but they will be of a restricted and global nature. In information theory terms, these relationships will not be adequately coded, for a *public* language signals the normative arrangements of a group rather than the individuated experience of its members. Sensitivity to subjective intent is not suddenly acquired; it arises out of experience which has been conditioned to its relevance and importance. This sensitivity reinforces the recognition of separateness and difference. The ability to verbalize relatively precisely subjective intent does not necessarily create a greater sympathy for others; but it makes available to an individual a means whereby a group of experiences can be the subject of rational control and manipulation. Planning functions are extended. Of equal importance, once such questions have relevance then a whole order of potential learning is made available. It follows that, where the verbal elaboration of considerations of intent is relatively well-developed, the number of referents which condition the response of an individual to his environment are greatly increased. New areas of curiosity are stimulated. A heightened sensitivity to the motivation of self and others facilitates the development of a low guilt threshold, and opens the way to the control of behaviour by eliciting feelings of guilt. A *public* language which minimizes the verbal elaboration and the making explicit of subjective intent, raises the guilt threshold in relation to particular classes of experiences.

A corrollary of the fact that subjective intent is not adequately coded in this linguistic form is the somewhat paradoxical result that, despite the warmth and vitality which so often goes with this mode of speech, the language remains *impersonal* in the literal sense of that term. Warmth and vitality arise out of an immediacy which the use of the language facilitates, for the terms are global, direct, concrete and activity-dominated, whilst the well-organized character of the structure permits high affective ventilation. But the words and speech sequences refer to broad classes of contents rather than progressive differentiation within a class. In a sense the referents are too abstract. (The reverse is also possible. A range of items belonging to a class may be specified without the concepts which summarizes the class being known.) The categories referred to are rarely broken down and this has critical implications if the referent to be designated is a subjective state of the speaker. The other side of the appearance of *affective* elements like warmth and vitality is impersonality of language. It is perfectly possible, despite the restricted vocabulary which is a symptom of the form of speech, to create speech which fits individuated experiences, but the orientation induced by this mode of communication does not make such characterization appropriate.

SOCIAL FUNCTION OF THE PUBLIC LANGUAGE

The factor of impersonality opens the way to a form of social behaviour which is controlled by a rigid, explicit and authoritarian social structure where status, role, age-grades and the customary connections between these elements become strategic orientating cues. This social structure channels and focuses the diffuse affective potential which the use of the language, itself, helps to create. Conformity to symbols of solidarity will then be intense and the level of activity may be much reduced if they are concretely absent; and these symbols are absent if the language is used in an inappropriate context. Such a situation may raise considerably the level of anxiety.

The impersonality allows for two almost contradictory types of response. On the one hand, the mechanical solidarity which it facilitates creates loyalty to the group, its functions and aspirations; it creates a social relationship of a warm, vital and inclusive form; yet it leads to a large measure of dependency on these symbols and so to an inherent *passivity*. On the other hand, the impersonality protects or insulates the speaker from responsibility, personal involvement and guilt for what he has said or done. A whole range of verbal behaviour and action is made available, particularly forms of behaviour which are often called "acting-out." From the point of view of *non-public* language users the behaviour may appear anti-social. This must not be understood to mean that such responses are necessarily frequent or dominant, but only that this form of behaviour is liable to be released particularly if the level of tension is raised. These circumstances are likely to arise in frustrating situations or when the social structure no longer creates realizable expectations. Blame is more likely to be attributed to the environment than to the speaker, and this reinforces the development of the mechanisms of displacement and denial (Miller and Swanson, 1960). The latter arise also because of the general rigidity of the personality induced by the speaking of the language.

The psychological and sociological *status quo* of a speaker limited to a *public* language is accomplished by protective devices built into the linguistic medium. Perhaps the most important of these protective functions, is that other forms of language use (i.e., *formal* language) cannot be directly comprehended but will be mediated through the *public* language. In other words a *formal* language will be translated, and in this process an alternative orientation which would sensitize the speaker to a different dimension of significance is neutralized. Where a translation cannot be made there is no communication and thus absolute protection. The structure of the language inhibits verbal expression, and so the learning attendant on such expression, of those experiences of separateness and difference which would isolate the speaker from his group. It channels cognitive and affective states which, if expressed, might constitute a potential threat to the equilibrium. For example, curiosity is limited and focused by the relatively low level of conceptualization and a concern with the immediate prevents the development of a reflective experience. The primacy of mechanisms of displacement and denial act to preserve the *status quo*. A resistance to change or rigidity is partly related to the way authority is justified or legitimized. For the signals of authority will inhere in the *form* of the social relationship rather than in complex principles.

I think at this point it will be useful to make the implicit hypotheses explicit. The behaviour referred to throughout this paper is contrasted with that associated with the speaking of a *formal* language. The classification of the hypotheses is one of convenience.

COGNITIVE

The individual who is limited to a *public* language will tend to possess a relatively closed perceptual system. The number of new relationship available to him will be restricted. It follows that there will be a high degree of perceptual rigidity.

He will be oriented towards a relatively low order of conceptualization which will set the limits to the matrix of relationships within which he operates. The Piagetian developmental sequence from *concrete* to *formal* operations may not be inevitable in the case of a child restricted to a *public* language. The child may well be limited to *concrete* operations (Inhelder and Piaget, 1958; Bruner, 1959).

The individual will have difficulty in structuring certain types of unstructured situations. He will be insensitive to the means whereby generalization becomes possible.

There will be a low tolerance of ambiguity.

A distinct relationship will be found between verbal and non-verbal measures of intelligence; language scores are depressed in relation to scores obtained on the higher ranges of the non-verbal test (Bernstein, 1958; Bernstein, 1960c; Venables, 1959).

AFFECTIVE

It will be difficult for the user to elaborate subjective intent verbally and make it explicit.

A situation in which this is required will raise considerably the level of anxiety. This will in turn inhibit further verbalization.

Affect will be relatively unconventionalized by language. A high potential for motor discharge will be available for expression under particular conditions.

PERSONALITY

The language use will facilitate the development of tough- rather than tender-mindedness, and conservatism rather than radicalism.

Although the experiences of anxiety and guilt occur in all social groups, the speaker of a *public* language will tend to possess a relative inability to tolerate anxiety and guilt. It is suggested that behaviour is subordinate to *shame* rather than guilt. Shame indicates a felt diminution of *respect* accorded to conduct by a *group*.

The typical form of break-down will tend to be delinquent, especially where the existing social structure no longer provides effective, realizable expectations.

CLINICAL

The speaker will be highly resistant to a form of therapy which inheres in the process of communication. If the therapy is successful the speaker will no longer be restricted to a *public* language.

Typical defence modes will be denial and displacement.

Behaviour associated with speakers of this language is often labelled hysterical. It is suggested that the apparently similar behaviour derives from a different dynamic.

Projective tests are more likely to reveal normative orientation than significant pathology unless the pathology is florid.

The incidence of stammering will tend to be relatively low.

SOCIOLOGICAL

The customary form of social relationship will be one in which communication is direct and immediate.

The speaker will be sensitive to an authority which is legitimized by the form of the social relationship rather than by complex principles.

The social structure will maximize identification with others rather than the significance of individuated differences.

There is likely to be a state of tension and conflict with the major society of which this social structure is a part. There will be a considerable resistance to formal education and a high degree of failure unless other special conditions are present.

Age and sex roles will be efficiently distinguished and separately defined.

The gang will be a typical and important unit for the child and adolescent.

In terms of Parsons' schema, the social value orientation will be collective rather than self, particularistic rather than universalistic, diffuse rather than specific, ascriptive rather than achieving, affective rather than neutral (Parsons, 1952).

PROBLEMS OF LINGUISTIC CHANGE IN EDUCATION AND THERAPY

One important issue concerns the question of the reversibility of behaviour regulated by the implications of spoken language. There is little evidence to draw upon, but it is common sense to suppose that the later linguistic change is attempted the more difficult it becomes. It is also possible that critical learning periods occur in the development of the child, and what is not learned at one period prejudices the efficiency of future learning. This can be seen in the day-to-day practice of formal education. I am inclined to believe that a crucial stage in development is the period between the acquisition of *concrete* operations and their transformation into *formal* operations. Equally important as the problem of reversibility are the conditions under which linguistic change is possible. Resistance, especially unconscious resistance, to such change in the case of a *public* language speaker is likely to be very high, for there is every probability that attempts to modify the linguistic orientation will be perceived by the speaker as attempts to change the means whereby he has been socialized. Such language change may involve for the speaker the experiences of isolation, bewilderment and defencelessness; whilst the structure of the "teaching" situation may well be felt as persecutory. The individual's normal orientating system will no longer be appropriate and the level of anxiety will be raised considerably. This inhibits new learning. Unless the social relationship is defined by both speaker and "teacher" as one of trust and mutual respect the process is unlikely to be successful. The *public* language of the speaker must not be disvalued, for this mode of speech psychologically unites the speaker to his kin and on a sociological level to his local traditions, and so risk of alienation is high.

It is thought that the situation of language change may have a bearing on the length of psychoanalytic treatment. This may partly be a function of the need for a *public*-language speaking patient to acquire a new language. The psychoanalytic situation maximizes the pressure on the patient to structure and re-structure his experiences verbally in an individuated manner. The patient's normal language system and the conventional relationships which the system signals and symbolizes are *inappropriate*, and from the point of view of the analyst are something to be "worked through.' New referents have to be designated and related within the changing context of the transference relationship. As the patient's conventional language system is disrupted, so the learning which the language stabilizes disintegrates and, with this, affect which attaches to the learning, is released. A new potential for relationships is created and with it the possibility of affective transformation and re-orientation. It is likely that this process of language change will be lengthy under normal circumstances. When the patient speaks a *public* language this process will be extremely difficult to effect.

CONCLUSIONS

There is some danger of creating the impression that the mode of speech discussed in this paper produces entirely standardized and uniform behaviour in the speakers. This is not the case, for such a form of communication creates a vast potential of responses. All that is meant is that the behaviour which it releases will possess many significant and common features. It also follows that personality differences between speakers occur and are significant in their effect upon behaviour, but it is of critical importance to separate out sociologically relevant aspects of development. This is equally necessary for practical as well as theoretical considerations. The conclusion of a paper is no place to discuss the relationships between sociology and psychology, but it does seem that the relationships between these disciplines are illuminated if the process by which the individual internalizes his social structure is conceptualized. If this were to be accomplished successfully, then we would have a theory of social learning. It is hoped that an analysis of spoken language may be a step in such a direction.

If the theory of language behaviour put forward in this paper is substantiated, then the operation of sociological factors upon development is profound. Different social structures will emphasize or stress different aspects of language potential, and this in turn will create for the individual particular dimensions of relevance. As the child learns his speech, so he will learn his social structure, and the latter will become the sub-stratum of his innermost experience through the effects of linguistic processing. The major role of speech, from this point of view, is to sensitize the child progressively towards the demands that will be made upon him by the normative arrangements of his group, by modifying his experience and so stabilizing his perceptions. *And this process is reinforced every time he speaks.* It does not make sense to talk of mechanical cause and effect; rather, what takes place is a progressive modification of learned responses, which become differentiated and stabilized by interrelated functional systems, initially created and later co-ordinated by speech.

SUMMARY

Speech is regarded as the major means through which the social structure becomes part of individual experience. Two modes of speech, associated with the lower working class and middle class, have been suggested which elicit and sustain particular forms of relationships to the environment and so establish different orders of learning and relevance. Behaviour maintained and released by a *public* language has been considered, and a series of hypotheses offered. Some comments have been made related to the problem of linguistic change.

POSTSCRIPT, 1961

[Dr. Bernstein's formulation of the distinction between two modes of speech has continued to develop in the course of his on-going research, and he has provided an additional statement of his latest views to accompany his article. The statement which follows has not been published elsewhere as such. For a specific experimental result employing it, see Bernstein, 1962.]

I think it is possible to present the ideas developed in the paper in a more economic and general manner. The concepts *formal* and *public* are not good analytic distinctions; they operate at too low a level of abstraction and they are probably semantically confusing. They will be replaced by the terms *elaborated* and *restricted* codes.

These two codes may be distinguished on the linguistic level in terms of the probabilities of predicting, *for any one speaker*, which structural elements will be used to organize meaning. In the case of an *elaborated* code the speaker will select from a relatively extensive range of alternatives, therefore the probability of predicting the pattern of organizing elements in *any one sequence* is considerably reduced. If a speaker is using a *restricted* code then the range of these alternatives is severely limited and the probability of predicting the pattern is greatly increased.

On a psychological level the codes may be distinguished in terms of the extent to which each facilitates or inhibits the orientation to symbolize intent in a verbally explicit form. Behavior processed by these codes will develop different modes of self-regulation and thus different forms of orientation.

The codes, themselves, are a function of particular forms of social relationships, or more generally, qualities of social structures.

The pure form of a *restricted* code would be one where the lexicon is wholly predictable and therefore, also, the organizing structure. Examples of this pure form would be ritualistic modes of communication. An actor, also, would be using a pure form of a *restricted* code, although from the point of view of the audience it would be an *elaborated* code. In fact his success in the role would be the extent to which he maintained these two definitions. In contemporary society what is found more often is a *restricted* code where prediction is possible *only* at the structural level. The simplification of structural alternatives is a function of the shared identifications which create the form of the social relationship. Those reduce the tension to verbalize intent and make it explicit. The intent of the speaker using a *restricted* code will tend to be signalled by acoustic and expressive means. A limiting case of a *restricted* code is one where the speaker is linguistically, wholly constrained by the code. This is the condition which corresponds to the analysis of a *public* language.

The following model and brief analysis may be helpful in drawing attention to the relationship between these codes and to verbal planning and modes of orientation.

In this model there is a *signal store* in which inter-related *verbal* and *non-verbal* signals are contained. There are also the usual *encoding* and *decoding* processes controlled and integrated by the *verbal planning* function.

When A signals to B, I suggest that at least the following takes place:

Orientation: B scans the incoming message for a pattern of dominant signals. (This is the beginning of the verbal planning sequence.)

Association: Associations to the pattern of dominant signals control selection from the signal store, which interacts both with such associations and with the third process, organization.

Organization: Organization and integration of signals to produce a sequential reply.

The term code as I use it implies the principles which regulate these three processes. It follows that *restricted* and *elaborated* codes will establish different kinds of control which crystallize in the nature of verbal planning. The latter is a resultant of the conditions which establish the patterns of orientation, association and organization. The originating determinants of this trio would be the form of the social relationship or more generally the quality of the social structure. This would allow the following postulate: The form of the social relationship acts selectively on the type of code which then becomes a symbolic expression of the relationship, *and* proceeds to regulate the nature of the inter-action. Simply, the *consequences* of the form of the social relationship are transmitted and sustained by the code on a psychological level. Strategic learning would be elicited, sustained and generalized by the code which would mark out *what* has to be learned and would constrain the *conditions* of successful learning.

I should like to indicate very briefly four aspects of verbal planning control where the code is restricted and the individual is limited to this code.

1. The sequences will tend to be dislocated, disjunctive, relatively well organized (high transition probabilities) but with relatively poor syntactic control, stressing the active rather than the passive voice, and point to the concrete, the descriptive and the narrative. Non-verbal signals will be an important source of significant changes in meaning as by definition the verbal sequences are impersonal, i.e., not individuated and serve as social symbols reinforcing the form of the social relationship rather than increasing the tension to signal individualized intent.

2. An example will best indicate the second aspect. When A meets B whom he does not know A will yet have some idea of B. This idea will be translated in terms of the verbal planning of A's original signals to B. If B's return signals indicate that A's original idea is inadequate, or, perhaps, inappropriate, A will modify his idea and through verbal planning control send different signals and note B's response. After an interval some type of equilibrium regulating the relationship will have become established with occasional fluctuations damped down by feedback achieved via verbal planning control, V. P.–transmission–return signals–check– verbal planning–transmission. By this process A will have internalized the "intent" of B (G.H. Mead) via speech (V. + N.V.). If the code is *restricted*, by definition so is verbal planning; consequently the range and type of others who can be so internalized is limited. By implication the social tie to those who can be so becomes a very powerful bond which is both positively and negatively strengthened by the code.

3. The third aspect relates to problem solving and the role of speech in orientating and thus changing the quality of the environment for the speaker.

As the problem to be solved moves in the direction of the relatively abstract it is likely that inner verbal sequences will be evolved (not necessarily threat movements, perhaps below the threshold of incipient articulation) which will proceed to orient the thinker and change the quality of the signals responded to in the environment. When the thinker is limited to a *restricted* code the verbal sequences evoked may direct perception to the more gross aspects of the environment and so his solution will become more and more inappropriate in direct relation to the degree of abstraction of the problem. This verbal feedback in some problem solving activities will be continuously reinforced. The bond relating the thinker to the concrete and descriptive will become progressively tighter with the cumulative effect of the use of the *restricted* code.

4. The fourth aspect refers to the time dimension of verbal planning, that is, to the delay between impulse and signalling. If the speaker can use an *elaborated* code or is oriented to its use, he can tolerate the anxiety associated with delay in selection. Subsequent signalling is likely to be more appropriate and the anxiety generated will tend to be reduced by the appropriateness of the signals. In this way (delay ↔ anxiety → appropriate signals → reduction in anxiety ↔ reinforcement of the sequence), a channel for the reduction of anxiety through verbal control is forged by the continued use of an *elaborated* code.

In a *restricted* code the delay between impulse and signal will be shorter in a normal environment. Raising the level of coding difficulty, thus increasing the delay potential, may lead to a break-down in signalling or the signalling may not adjust to the new demands. The first solution results in a total drop in output; the second avoids increasing the delay between impulse and signal. Either way the code does not facilitate the toleration of anxiety and the reduction of anxiety by appropriate signalling. In a *restricted* code the channel for the release of anxiety will tend to be changed in somatomotor expressive set (cf. Bernstein, 1962].

REFERENCE NOTE

On various aspects of the social context and cultural content of LANGUAGE ACQUISITION in addition to the references cited by Bernstein, see Belluzi and Brown (1964), Bossard (1954), Brown (1958, chap. 6), Chamberlain (1896), Church (1961), De Laguna (1927), Fearing (1954), Hymes (1961b, 1961c, 1962a), Leopold (1948), Luria (1959), Piaget (1924), Schachtel (1947), Steward (1960), Voegelin and

Robinett (1954,) Vygotsky (1962), Waterhouse (1949). On the role of generic factors, see Lenneberg (1960).

On cross-cultural variation, see Pettitt (1946) for a continental survey, and B. Whiting's bibliographic guide in Heinecke and Whiting (1953), as well as theoretical discussion in Hymes (1961b, 1961c, 1962a).

On method and approach in the study of socialization, including verbal behavior, see Heinecke and Whiting (1953, consult subject index headings, "Language; speech," "Oral behavior," "Stuttering"); Hilger (1960, pp. 12, 17, 20, 22-25, 30, 31-46, 47), Mead and Wolfenstein (1955), Mussen (1961), Whiting and Child (1953, p. 255), Whiting *et al.* (1953, p. 18; 1954).

On bilingualism as it affects the child, see references to Diebold's article in Part VIII, especially Arsenian (1937), Barker (1951), Bossard (1945), Buxbaum (1949), Hall (1951), Lambert *et al.* (1960), Leopold (1939-1949; 1948), and Lowie (1945).

BERNSTEIN, BASIL

1958. Some Sociological Determinants of Perception. *British Journal of Sociology*, *9:* 159-174.

1959. A Public Language: Some Sociological Implications of a Linguistic Form. *British Journal of Sociology*, *10:* 311-326.

1960a. Sozio-Kulturelle Determinanten des Lernens. Mit besonderer Berücksichtigung der Rolle der Sprache. *Kölner Zeitschrift für Soziologie und Sozialpsychologie*. Sonderheft 4. 52-79. [Review article]

1960b. Review of I. Opie and P. Opie, *The Lore and Language of Schoolchildren*. *British Journal of Sociology*, *11:* 178-181.

1960c. Language and Social Class: Research Note. *British Journal of Sociology*, *11:* 271-276.

1961a. Social Class and Linguistic Development: A Theory of Social Learning. In A. H. Halsey, J. Floud, and A. Anderson (Eds.), *Society, Economy and Education*. Glencoe: Free Press.

1962. Linguistic Codes, Hesitation Phenomena and Intelligence. *Language and Speech*, *5:* 31-46.

BOSSARD, JAMES H. S.

1945. Family Modes of Expression. *American Sociological Review*, *10:* 226-237.

1954. *The Sociology of Child Development*. New York: Harper & Row.

BRUNER, J. S.

1959. Inhelder and Piaget's *The Growth of Logical Thinking, I.* A Psychologist's Viewpoint. *British Journal of Psychology*, *50:* 363-370.

CHAMBERLAIN, A. F.

1896. *The Child and Childhood in Folk-Thought*. New York: Macmillan.

CHURCH, JOSEPH

1961. *Language and the Discovery of Reality. A Developmental Psychology of Cognition*. New York: Random House.

GOLDMAN-EISLER, F.

1958a. Speech Analysis and Mental Processes. *Language and Speech*, *1:* 59-75.

1958b. Speech Production and the Predictability of Words in Context. *Quarterly Journal of Experimental Psychology*, *10:* 96-106.

1958c. The Predictability of Words in Context and the Length of Pauses in Speech. *Language and Speech*, *1:* 226-231.

1960. Hesitation and Information in Speech. Paper read at the Symposium on Information Theory. London.

HEINECKE, CHRISTOPH, and BEATRICE B. WHITING

1953. *Bibliographies on Personality and Social Development of the Child.* New York: Social Science Research Council.

HILGER, SISTER INEZ

1960. *Field Guide to the Ethnological Study of Child Life.* (Behaviour Science Field Guides, No. 1.) New Haven: Human Relations Area Files Press.

INHELDER, B., and J. PIAGET

1958. *The Growth of Logical Thinking.* London: Routledge and Kegan Paul.

IRWIN, O. C.

1948a. Infant Speech: The Effect of Family Occupational Status and of Age on Sound Frequency. *Journal of Speech and Hearing Disorders, 13:* 320-323.

1948b. The Effect of Family Occupational Status and of Age on the Use of Sound Types. *Journal of Speech and Hearing Disorders, 13:* 224-226.

JACKSON, J. H.

1932. *Selected Writings.* London: Hodder and Stoughton. Vol. 2.

KOHN, M. L.

1959a. Social Class and Parental Authority. *American Sociological Review, 24:* 352-366.

1959b. Social Class and Parental Values. *American Journal of Sociology, 64:* 337-351.

LURIA, A. R.

1959. The Directive Function of Speech, I, II. *Word, 15:* 341-352, 453-464.

1961. *The Role of Speech in the Regulation of Normal and Abnormal Behavior.* London: Pergamon.

LURIA, A. R., and F. I. YUDOVICH

1959. *Speech and the Development of Mental Processes in the Child.* London: Staples. [Reviewed, Roger W. Brown, *Word,* 1960, *16:* 125-130.]

MEAD, MARGARET

1946. Research on Primitive Children. In L. Carmichael (Ed.), *Manual of Child Psychology.* New York: Wiley. Pp. 667-706.

MEAD, MARGARET, and MARTHA WOLFENSTEIN (EDS.)

1955. *Childhood in Contemporary Cultures.* Chicago: University of Chicago Press.

MILLER, D. R., and G. E. SWANSON

1960. *Inner Conflict and Defense.* New York: Holt.

MUSSEN, PAUL H. (ED.)

1961. *Handbook of Research Methods in Child Development.* New York: Wiley.

OPIE, IONA, and PETER OPIE

1959. *The Lore and Language of Schoolchildren.* Oxford: Oxford University Press. [Reviewed, Beatrice Whiting, *JAF,* 1961, *74:* 278-279.]

PARSONS, TALCOTT

1952. *The Social System.* London: Tavistock.

PIAGET, J.

1924. *La Langue et la pensée chez l'enfant*. Neuchatel and Paris: Delachaux and Niestlé. (Translated as *The Language and Thought of the Child*. New York: Harcourt, Brace, 1926.)

SAMPSON, O. C.

1956. A Study of Speech Development in Children 18-30 Months. *British Journal of Educational Psychology, 26:* 194-202.

SCHACHTEL, E. G.

1947. On Memory and Childhood Amnesia. *Psychiatry, 10:* 1-26. [Also in Schachtel, *Metamorphosis*. New York: Basic Books, 1959. chap. 12.

VENABLES, E. C.

1959. *Fifteen to Eighteen. Report of the Central Advisory Council for Education in England*. London: Ministry of Education. Vol. 1.

VOEGELIN, C. F., and F. M. ROBINETT

1954. "Mother Language" in Hidatsa. *IJAL, 20:* 65-70.

WHITING, J. W. M., and CHILD, I. L.

1953. *Child Training and Personality*. New Haven: Yale University Press.

WHITING, J. W. M., *et al.*

1953. *Field Manual for the Cross Cultural Study of Child Rearing*. (Preliminary Draft.) New York: Social Science Research Council.

1954. *Field Guide for a Study of Socialization in Five Societies*. Cambridge: Laboratory of Human Development, Palfrey House, Harvard University.

29 *Morality and Language Among the Nupe*

S. F. NADEL

IN VARIOUS PUBLICATIONS on the Nupe I have had occasion to comment on the prudishness of the people and, more particularly, on their severe disapproval of language savouring of obscenity or immodesty (Nadel, 1942, p. 396; 1949, p. 181; 1954, pp. 113, 118, 218, 219). Any open reference to sex and to certain bodily organs or physiological processes would fall under this ban. In this brief note I propose to adduce further evidence for this moral attitude, exemplifying it in the current vocabulary of the people and so demonstrating its firm and far-reaching institutionalization.

The prudish morality reveals itself in the linguistic usage in several ways. To begin with, the Nupe distinguish sharply between expressions which are suitable for polite conversation and others which are not. The former usually take the form of euphemisms or circumlocutions, while the latter, being direct or outspoken, are considered fit only for "dirty" stories and jokes or for the more careless talk of young people. At the same time certain specific, non-circumlocutory terms are used in the manner of a technical vocabulary, respectable but restricted to a particular class of speakers—the *mallam* or scholarly person. In the conversation both of "laymen" and "scholars" the indelicate character of the topic is frequently disguised by the use of loan words from Hausa-Arabic, i.e., from a language knowledge of which is itself considered a sign of refinement. In the extreme case, Nupe language may altogether lack the corresponding terms.

Thus Nupe has no specific word for cohabitation. In general conversation or in stories one uses the phrase 'sleeping together' or, metaphorically, the word for eating (*gī*). The word *chį* which means generally to love, to be in love, to desire, may also be used to indicate the sexual act, though it is never employed in this sense by older people or "scholars." The latter speak instead of *jemayi*, 'to connect,' a word of Arabic derivation. Again, there is no Nupe word for sexual desire save the Hausa word *jaraba* (trial? temptation?). The word for penis, *eba*, is rarely heard even though there is no accepted metaphor for it. The vagina, on the other hand, can be described, more or less indirectly, by a whole series of words. The specific name *dzuko*, which has no second meaning, is definitely a "dirty" expression and is usually replaced by *enya* ('thing') or *yeta* ('in front'); scholars use the Hausa word *kafa* ('opening'). For anus one says *biye*, which means 'buttocks' as well as 'base,' 'foundation.' The specific term 'to urinate', *jį lori*, is taboo in polite company, though the Hausa, for example, use the corresponding phrase *yi boli* quite freely. A more "refined" expression, which can be used even in front of the other sex, is *najesa*, which is the Hausa word for excrements. For 'defecate' one invariably uses the circumlocution 'to go outside.' To be pregnant is *de nwą*—a nondescript phrase since *de* merely means 'to have' and *nwą* has many meanings (to lay hold, catch, seize, adhere to). But a more polite usage is to say of a woman that she 'has a belly' (*u de gbako*). Young men among themselves sometimes use a crude and indelicate allusion, saying of a woman that *nw'a gi 'zo*, 'she has eaten beans' (which 'blow up the belly'). Menstruation is described by a Hausa-Arabic term, *alada*, lit. 'the customary,' or by the circumlocutions 'the month' or 'the woman's thing.' For semen, too, there is only an Arabic "technical" term, used by scholars—*mayini*. Otherwise one speaks of *tiya*, an unspecific term derived from *ti*, to drip, bleed, flow (as a spring), etc. Some of my uneducated informants simply spoke of 'water from the penis.' The absence of a specific term for semen seems to indicate an uncertain physiological knowledge apart from a prudish use of language, for the same informants also believed that conception was caused by the infusion of male urine into the womb. (This qualifies a somewhat too sweeping statement [1954, p. 21].)

The avoidance of suggestions of obscenity equally characterizes Nupe folklore of all kinds. The Nupe distinguish between two kinds of stories, *etą*, 'serious' stories, i.e., mythical or historical accounts of instructive value told by the old men or scholars, and *echį*, 'mere tales,' fables and other stories, moralizing or humorous, which serve mainly for the entertainment of the young people. The first kind of tale, of which I have what I believe is a complete record, contains not a single obscene reference. My collection of *echį*, though not perhaps complete, is yet sufficiently large to substantiate the claim made above. Of the 21 stories I collected only two contain "indelicate" references, both of a humorous kind and approximating to what the Nupe would regard as "smutty jokes." In both cases the obscene allusions are toned down through being embodied in (easily understood) puns.

The first story, called "The Rich Man," tells how the friend of a rich man was able to read the thoughts of the latter ('the speech in his heart') owing to a magic medicine which he had acquired. The owner of the medicine eventually made a present of it to his friend, who at the time had no clothes on and did not know where to put the medicine. It slipped from his hands and fell to the ground. Before the man could get hold of it, it was swallowed up by the ground. Now, the word for 'ground' is the same as for 'penis'; thus the story concludes with this jocular "moral": "In this fashion the ground [penis] acquired the secret of the medicine. Thus when a woman pleases you, the penis [or the ground] understands the speech of your heart at once [i.e., becomes erect]."

The second story is called "How Men Became Husbands" and goes as follows. At one time there was a town where there were only men, and another where there were only women. The king of the Town of Men sent a clever young man to the Town of Women to obtain wives, and the young man did so by the following stratagem: he placed the handle of a hoe in a pot filled with the sweet and potent sediment from sorghum beer, and peddled it in the Town of Women, claiming that it was a new kind of food, called *kparaba* (an invented word, which can, however, be understood to mean 'skin of the penis'). Describing the beer as 'sediment of the penis,' he induced the women to lick the handle, which they found so tasty that they were keen to have more of the new food. After having consumed it all the women became so intoxicated that they followed the young man to the Town of Men, where they were captured and made the wives of the inhabitants. The conclusion of the story makes use of another pun based on the identity of *eba*, 'penis,' and *eba*, 'husband,' thus: "In this fashion the young man brought it about that the men now had wives . . . He brought it about that the women tasted the sweetness of husbands [or of the penis], of beer, and of the food called Skin of Penis, so that they will never again give up that taste.'

The existence of stories of this kind, even though they are few, and the accepted convention of jokes employing "dirty" words, clearly represent an escape from and a highly conscious reaction to the normal restraint. And this breaks down also, as I have described elsewhere (1949, p. 183), in the songs sung at one annual festival whose whole character indicates a unique occasion for sexual licence. Apart from this instance and one further sexual allusion in the rules of divining (which are, however, only known to the expert [1954, p. 44]), the large number of songs, riddles and proverbs current in Nupe are entirely without any mention of obscene or even "indelicate" topics.

With a language so circumscribed it is difficult to imagine any planned instruction of the young in sexual matters. Nor does it exist. Children learn the "facts of life" in the same haphazard manner as they do with us, and Nupe parents consider this state of affairs not only normal but adequate. To certain undesirable facts one simply shuts one's eyes. Thus my informants denied, when directly questioned, that Nupe boys ever masturbated; when confronted with incontrovertible evidence they admitted that parents did sometimes observe this kind of "play" and would warn their boys that it was a "bad thing."

From this tacit disregard for sex, too, there is some escape: thus in certain crude drawings made by young boys I found the private parts of men or women prominently displayed. But this "escape" does not crystallize in any firm convention. Nor has the taste for realistic drawings much chance of survival in a culture by and large devoid of representational art. The few (non-indigenous) examples of realistic art which have been preserved in Nupe are, incidentally, nearly all highly decorous.

In conclusion it is relevant to emphasize that the inferences here drawn from linguistic usage are justified by the intense interest which the Nupe show in the semantic aspect of their language. One illustration of this is the predilection for puns, which is widely characteristic of Nupe folklore; another, the general readiness of the people to engage in etymological speculations (1954, *passim*). It can be said without exaggeration that the Nupe are truly fascinated by the meanings of words and their exploration. When they employ metaphors or otherwise manipulate expressions, they are always fully aware of the semantic implications. Thus the words which we here assumed to reveal (or conceal) a particular meaning, bearing on standards of taste and morality, have precisely this significance for the users also.

REFERENCE NOTE

For other references having to do with puns, folk tales, and the like, see Part VI. For further studies having to do with the social context and cultural content of language acquisition, see references to Casagrande's article on pp. 245-250 and Bernstein's article on pp. 251-263, as well as Haas' article in Part VI.

References not in general bibliography:

NADEL, S. F.

1942. *A Black Byzantium*. (International Institute of African Languages and Cultures). London: Oxford University Press.

1949. The *Gani* Ritual of Nupe: A Study in Symbiosis. *Africa, 19:* 177-186.

1954. *Nupe Religion*. Glencoe: Free Press.

Mohave Voice and Speech Mannerisms 30

GEORGE DEVEREUX

THERE IS AN EXTREME PAUCITY of data pertaining to the management of the voice in non-Indo-European languages. Hence it may be of some interest to describe the vocal behavior of the Mohave Indians during conversations dealing with sexual topics. Since the Mohave discuss sexual matters, especially those not pertaining to the process of gestation, rather freely—being, in this respect, as in many others, different from their non-Yuman neighbors (Kroeber, 1925)—the following data also shed some light on the overall vocal behavior of the Mohave. A detailed discussion of Mohave phonetics is not necessary in the present context, since this problem is adequately covered by Kroeber's monograph (1911).

The Mohave are a talkative people, who admire skilled orators, witty conversationalists (Devereux, 1948a) and expert swearers (Devereux, 1951), though they have no liking for people who are merely coarse or verbally sadistic (Devereux, 1941). Their enjoyment of talk is so great that one frequently finds oneself following with great interest the conversation between one's informant and interpreter, without being able to understand more than one word in a hundred, simply because they give the impression of being wholly absorbed by, and involved in, the act of communication.

It is, hence, not surprising that elaborate precautions should be taken to prevent the birth of mute children, by means of a meticulous compliance with the relevant taboos (Devereux, 1950). Yet, the ability to speak is not thought of as a criterion of intelligence, since even fetuses about to be born, as well as twin infants and nursing babies are believed to be capable of understanding, and responding to, rational verbal admonitions, even though they are manifestly incapable of speech (Devereux, 1947).

The Mohave of both sexes have pleasing voices, which they manage with consummate skill. They exploit to the utmost the musical and expressive potentialities inherent in a language possessing pitch, and transfer even to English some of the musical qualities of Mohave speech, without approximating the sing-song impression produced by Swedes.

Despite their skilful management of the voice, the Mohave do not seem to be *consciously* interested in sound-production. Thus, the date at which the male puberty rite occurs is not determined by the cracking of the adolescent's voice (Devereux, 1949b). Furthermore, unlike the kindred Yuma the Mohave deny that the laughter of women differs from that of men, except in its pitch, and perhaps also its volume.

It is also striking that, despite the intensity of the Mohave Indian's participation in the act of verbal communication, extreme forms of voice-production are rare or absent. In other words the Mohave are seldom shrill and do not whisper frequently. It is also significant that I have never met, or heard of, an individual possessing several "voices," although in Western society certain latently homosexual and grandiose individuals frequently have three distinct 'voices': a basso boom, a shrill scream and an aggressive, low-pitched whisper. The avoidance of extremes of voice-production is especially conspicuous when a Mohave man quotes and imitates the speech of a woman or of a transvestite: The narrator does not change to falsetto but uses his normal voice, suggesting, rather than mimicking, nuances of female speech, even in imitating a male transvestite's use of the female expletive *peleley* (Devereux 1937).

Imperfections of voice-production and of speech are obstacles to communication which are sometimes rooted in neurotic mechanisms and represent, among other things, an aggression toward, or a repudiation of, one's interlocutor (Ferenczi, 1927).

a. Whispering. Although the Mohave may whisper for reasons of discretion (Devereux, 1950), I have never observed the type of whispering well known to psychiatrists, which is at once a reaction formation against the urge to scream at one's interlocutor, and a hostile act, which defeats the listener's desire to understand what the speaker *allegedly* "intends" to tell him.

b. Disregard for the hearing range is relatively frequent among the Mohave, who sometimes continue to talk even after their erstwhile intelocutor has passed beyond the effective hearing range. This mannerism appears to be due to inertia, rather than to unconscious aggressions (Devereux, 1949a).

c. *Mumbling.* Mohave informants, conversing with the interpreter about matters of which they are not quite certain, sometimes cease to speak in a manner which obviously subsumes an audience, and engage in a sort of musing pseudo-monologue, marked by a blurring of pronunciation, and sometimes also by a lowering of the pitch of the voice and a slowing down of the normal tempo of speech. The mumbler's behavior gives one the impression that he is re-testing and re-appraising his knowledge by means of verbalization: He utters his sentences hesitantly, and seems to listen to his own voice, as though he were thinking "This doesn't sound quite right" or else "This does sound right, doesn't it?" I have never heard an informant use mumbling in a hostile or resistive manner.

d. *Rhythm and tempo.* The Mohave have a traditional staccatto, strongly accented and rather rapid manner of delivering traditional memorized texts which are usually couched in brief sentences (Densmore, 1932; Kroeber, 1925). This characteristic method of delivery is so completely a part of the recited text, that it is very difficult, even for the most willing informant, to slow down to the point where the text can be conveniently recorded. Although adhesions between a traditional text and its usual manner of delivery are, of course, to be expected in a non-literate society, they can be exploited for the purpose of resisting communication. Thus, when working with the rather timid and not overly willing old Nyahwera, in the presence of a shaman whom he feared, my interpreter and I found it impossible to induce him to utter slowly the archaic text of the "recitativo" songs of the initiation ritual for transvestites. On the other hand my friends and willing informants Hivsu Tupoma and Ahma Humare always managed, after a few false starts, to dictate native texts at a speed which made it possible for me to record their recitations verbatim.

e. *Text of songs.* Everyone is familiar with the difficulty of reciting the text of a song without singing, at the same time, the musical part thereof. This difficulty is so genuine that, when Ahma Humare taught me his weylak curing songs, I had to stop him from time to time to record certain half-heard words. In order to do so, I had to pronounce first what I *believed* the word to be, in order to enable him to repeat it after me in the *correct* manner. Likewise, after recording an entire sentence, and after reading it back to him, Ahma Humare was usually able to repeat this sentence without singing it because, for the first time in his life, he had heard it recited without music. This observation underscores the significance of auditory factors in learning, in a non-literate society. The adhesion of the text to the music does not appear to be exploited for the purpose of inhibiting communication because of unconscious resistances and aggressions.

f. *Pseudo-communication* does not, properly speaking, belong in a study of voice-production, and is, hence, mentioned only because it also exemplifies defective communication. The shaman T.B., reputed to be a witch, managed to confuse completely both my very competent interpreter and myself. Not merely did he skip from topic to topic, not merely did he contradict himself periodically but even went so far as to utter what seemed to be long series of non-sequiturs. On re-reading the recorded conversation I am forcibly reminded of the ramblings of a moderately well-preserved schizophrenic, although there is no reason whatsoever to suspect T.B. of being a schizophrenic, or of having been in a dreamstate induced by a conversation about the shamanistic and esoteric aspects of mental disease, as seen from the shamanistic point of view, since—significantly enough—his voice-production and speech mannerisms were not in the least unusual or deviant. In the end both my interpreter and myself independently reached the conclusion that T.B. was deliberately confusing us.

g. *Suppression of means of communication.* The Mohave show a singular reluctance to speak English, unless they speak English well. On the other hand they do not seem to pretend not to understand it when, in reality, they do happen to know a little English. Thus old Mrs. Chach who knew only scraps of English, always made a genuine effort to understand what I said to her, or in her presence—even to the point of laughing out loud even before some affectionate jibe of mine (Devereux, 1948a) was interpreted to her—although, except on one occasion, she never attempted to utter a single English word. In 1938, however, when I visited her to bid her goodbye before leaving the reservation, after asking the interpreter to translate several of her affectionate parting remarks to me, she took my hands and with great warmth bade me "Goodbye." The formal English words were pronounced very hesitatingly, clearly indicating that she barely knew them. She probably used them only because she admittedly had a premonition that she would not see me again, and, hence, presumably wanted to speak to me directly at least once in her life. (Significantly enough, the same [correct] premonition also caused her to violate the taboo on being photographed. After my departure she asked a young Mohave to take her picture and to send it to me, so that I would not forget her (Devereux, 1948a].) The shaman Hivsu Tupoma, one of my closest friends and most willing informants, readily admitted that he knew a few words of English, but insisted on using an interpreter. On one occasion, however, when, under the influence of alcohol he decided to speak to me of his acts of witchcraft, he saw me in private, and thus revealed that he spoke broken, though intelligible English. I know of no English-speaking Mohave who, because of his contempt for whites, or for some other reason, pretends not to speak that language, although e.g. Pueblo Indians are known to use this mode of evasion. (A person who had just experienced a major trauma and was trying to tell people about it, is reported to have been speechless from sheer excitement.)

h. *Temporary mutism.* The Mohave Indian, who is not addicted to sulking, does not refuse to communicate by simply assuming an attitude of stolid silence, or by playing dumb, which is the traditional defense of less proud and less mercurial minority groups. On the other hand, although all young people speak English fairly well, shy youngsters, and especially young schoolgirls, sometimes become almost speechless with embarrassment. A little genuine friendliness generally suffices, however, to induce them to converse in a cheerful, easy and animated manner. (According to Róheim [1932] the kindred Yuma are sometimes referred to by local whites as veritable "sphinxes." This does not jibe with my own impressions of the Yuma, nor have I ever heard a white inhabitant of Parker, Arizona, describe the Mohave as stolid, silent or mysterious.)

A severely neurotic prepubescent Mohave schoolboy, who spoke good English, tended to answer embarrassing questions which I asked *in English* in the negative. The same questions repeated *in Mohave* by my able teen age interpreter were generally answered in the affirmative. This may be due to the fact that the matters about which he was being questioned were known to him to be disapproved of by the only English-speaking people he knew—his teachers—though they were not disapproved of by Mohave society at large. Another reason may be that the acts about which he was being questioned (masturbation, etc.) were experienced "in Mohave" (relative lack of guilt feelings being part of the experience) and could therefore be reproduced (answered in the affirmative) only in Mohave. Stated in English (with an externally imposed halo of guilt and sin) the "negative answer" was affectively correct, though behaviorally untrue. [This paragraph has been added by the author to the originally published article.]

The expression of emotions is a notoriously elusive matter. The following observations may, hence, be of some interest.

a. *Merriment.* When discussing scabrous matters, or when engaged in affectionately obscene banter (Devereux, 1948a), speech tends to speed up and to alternate with guffaws, though never with giggles, snickers and salacious whispers. The transition from speech to guffaw is a swift, though a gradual one, and many Mohave almost, though not quite, manage to laugh and to speak at the same time. The face becomes relaxed and the features expand into a mobile and infectious smile.

b. *Embarrassment.* On rare occasions, especially when I had just begun to work with my octogenarian friend, Mrs. Chach, I was able to detect a certain amount of embarrassment in her speech. Once or twice she even clapped her hand before her mouth, a gesture also known to be used by embarrassed men. During one of our early interviews she repeatedly pronounced the word *modhar* (penis) as *mo:dha:r*, greatly ejaggerating the length of both vowels. When I naively inquired whether this was an archaic or idiosyncratic manner of pronouncing the word in question, both Chach and my interpreter laughed and explained that the old lady was merely a trifle self-conscious. Her embarrassment also manifested itself in a slightly greater meticulousness in reproducing the regular pitches and stresses of ordinary pronunciation. This peculiarity of speech disappeared very rapidly, and, later on, when we exchanged affectionate insults Mrs. Chach gave me rapid-fire tit for tat, without the least trace of embarrassment. On a subsequent field-trip, on hearing her pronounced *hispan* (vagina) as *hišpan*, I asked whether she again felt embarrassed. Both Chach and my interpreter guffawed and told me that her pronunciation was due solely to the absence of upper incisors. She even put her right index in her mouth to show me the gap in her teeth.

c. *Solemnity and reserve.* When discussing the serious side of sexuality, i.e., gestation, my informants' voices tended to become more resonant, and were a trifle lower pitched than usual. Pronunciation also tended to be unusually meticulous. At the same time they displayed a tendency to use short, clipped, "preaching-style" sentences, and the characteristic staccatto delivery of orators, or of persons narrating a major myth, which has already been described above. When speaking in this manner their faces bore a frown of concentrated attention.

Summary. The Mohave are expert speakers and conversationalists, who manage their voices with consummate skill and tasteful restraint. Gross abnormalities of speech-production and obstacles to communication were absent.

REFERENCE NOTE

References not in the general bibliography:

DENSMORE, F.

1932. *Yuman and Yaqui Music.* (BAE-B 110.) Washington, D.C.: Smithsonian Institution.

DEVEREUX, G.

1937. Institutionalized Homosexuality of the Mohave Indians. *Human Biology*, *9:* 498-527.

1947. Mohave Orality. *Psychoanalytic Quarterly, 16:* 519-546.

1948a. *Mohave Etiquette.* (Southwest Museum Leaflets, No. 22.) Los Angeles: Southwest Museum.

1948b. The Function of Alcohol in Mohave Society. *Quarterly Journal of Studies on Alcohol, 9:* 207-251.

1949a. Some Mohave Gestures. *AA, 51:* 325-326.

1949b. The Mohave Male Puberty Rite. *Samiksa: Journal of the Indian Psychoanalytical Society, 3:* 11-25.

1950. Heterosexual Behavior of the Mohave Indians. In G. Roheim (Ed.), *Psychoanalysis and the Social Sciences.* New York: International Universities Press. Vol. II, pp. 85-128.

1951. Mohave Indian Verbal and Motor Profanity. In G. Roheim (Ed.), *Psychoanalysis and the Social Sciences,* New York: International Universities Press. Vol. III, pp. 99-127.

1957. A Primitive Slip of the Tongue. *Anthropological Quarterly*, *30*: 27-29.

FERENCZI, S.

1927. Psychogenic Anomalies of Voice Production. *Further Contributions to the Theory and Technique of Psycho-Analysis*. New York: Boni & Liveright

FORDE, C. D.

1931. *Ethnography of the Yuma Indians*. (UCP-AAE 28.) Berkeley and Los Angeles: University of California Press. Pp. 83-278

KROEBER, A. L.

1911. *Phonetic Elements of the Mohave Language*. (UCP-AAE 10.) Berkeley and Los Angeles: University of California Press. Pp. 45-96.

1925. *Handbook of the Indians of California*. (BAE-B 78.) Washington, D.C.: Smithsonian Institution.

ROHEIM, GÉZA

1932. Psycho-Analysis of Primitive Cultural Types. *International Journal of Psycho-Analysis*, *13*: 1-224.

31 On Expressive Communication in an Egyptian Village

JOHN BOMAN ADAMS

ORDINARILY, THE MEMBERS of the opposed factions met socially and disagreed no more violently than is usual among the normally argumentative villagers. Contravention seldom degenerated into conflict because of the control exercised by certain mechanisms that were, at that time, still powerful enough to check hostility. Especially important in controlling discussion was that part of the strict code of manners which prescribed not only that discussion should be temperate, but that whatever its content, the voices of the discussants should be moderately pitched, their faces friendly, and their gestures graceful. Any discussant who did not observe these prescriptions would "lose face" and his arguments would be discounted. If conflict threatened, the Omdah and the *shuyyuk il balad* were inclined, from long practice, to mediate between the discussants, though ordinarily they took sides.

These prescriptions of the code of manners suggest that the villagers' interpretation of communications depends on something more than their discursive content. The villager is ordinarily conditioned to give and receive communications whose content is so stereotyped that he pays little attention to it other than to note that it conforms to the norms of traditional utterances and that the speaker is hence socially acceptable. His interpretation of what is said depends largely upon his attitude toward the speaker. If the speaker is a "friend," then what he says is generally accepted as "friendly." Even if the content is not complimentary, the listener assumes that his friend "doesn't mean what he says" or is "only teasing." If the speaker is an "enemy," then everything he says, however conciliatory, is suspect. The villager has few merely neutral relationships.

In view of the suspicions and easily injured sensibilities of the villagers, it is not always easy for an individual to determine at a given moment just who his friends and enemies are. These statuses are often established in the exchange of stereotyped expressions of esteem and concern that are obligatory whenever two or more persons meet. Since the same expressions are always uttered, interpretations of "friendliness' or "enmity" depend upon meanings conveyed by subtle qualities of tone, pitch, and melody. These qualities, in their different modes, are interpretable to one who is acquainted with their culturally defined meanings. Certain melodic patterns connote, e.g., "sincerity," others "irony," "sarcasm," or even "hostility." Certain tones, ways of accenting, abbreviating, or elongating words convey similar meanings.

In addition to establishing the basic relationship between the communicants, these non-discursive aspects of speech convey a host of other meanings that establish the unique interpretations of stereotyped communications. Even when communications are not stereotyped, interpretations depend as much upon these meanings as upon the discursive content. In this sense, the villager is more of a poet than a logician in his understanding and use of language.

Recent communications from the government tend to be interpreted in these terms. In prerevolutionary times the government was usually considered to be unfriendly by the villagers, and the "popular" efforts of the revolutionary government have not entirely eliminated this feeling. Considerable discussion of governmental communiqués is devoted to such questions as: "Did the speaker sound friendly?" "Do you think he was sincere?" "What did he mean when he said (so and so) in that way?" The problem of interpretation is complicated by the fact that (at the time of my study) there are few radios in the village and that most governmental communications are printed in the newspapers. These are read aloud in the coffee-house by the literate villagers, who convey their own reactions to the news by manipulating their voices, gestures, and facial expressions.

When communications are from or with persons of other cultures, they are likely to be misinterpreted entirely. Each culture defines its own presentational meanings, and a sound, color, or form that has a particular meaning in one culture may have a different and even a contradictory meaning in another. The speech melody and rhythm that connote "sincerity" in Egypt usually seems to an American to sound "cross" or "belligerent.' Conversely, the melody and rhythm that connote "righteous indignation" to an American is often interpreted by Egyptians as "hostile," "vengeful," and "nervous (uncontrolled)".

I attended a discussion in which a number of villagers, an Englishman, and an American were present. The Englishman was newly arrived from Oxford University, where he was a lecturer, and although he was an authority on Islamics he was relatively unacquainted with village life. The American was well acquainted with village ways but knew less than the Englishman about the theoretical aspects of the culture. In the course of the discussion—dealing with imperialism—the Englishman, as representative of a great imperial power and therefore a potential "enemy," was at a disadvantage. His speech was sincerely complimentary but, unfortunately, he spoke with a decided "Oxford accent" that made him seem to "sneer," even to the American. The tone of his speech was that of one who is "talking down to the great unwashed." Of course, he did not intend to convey these meanings. His accent would have been differently interpreted in his own culture, where it would have had favorable status connotations. The villagers concluded that he was an "enemy" and that his stated concern for the Middle East was a hypocritical device to gain his, and England's, selfish ends.

The American had had considerable experience with ingratiating devices, both in his own culture and in the Egyptian village. His remarks were less complimentary than those of the Englishman, and he even made one or two that might have been interpreted as insults. However, he spoke in a friendly, humble way, frequently consulted the opinions of the villagers, smiled constantly, and laughed whenever he made a slighting remark—usually following it with a joke about himself. His "friendliness" was assumed as a matter of course by the villagers, though not by the puzzled and slightly disgusted Englishman.

I do not mean to imply that all of the villagers interpret communications in the same way. They share certain cultural understandings, but they differ in others. The differences are determined by their various experiences in institutions that have been changing in structure and functions for a considerable time.

32 Paralanguage: A First Approximation

GEORGE L. TRAGER

0. INTRODUCTION

For many years linguists and other students of language and of communication as a whole have been aware that communication is more than language. They have known that all the noises and movements entering into the activity of people talking to each other and exchanging communications needed to be taken into account if a total picture of the activity was to be arrived at. At the same time it was known, by a sort of tacit consent, that much of what went on was not accessible to study by such scientific methods as had yet been devised. Accordingly, linguists limited themselves to examination of such parts of linguistic structures as they could define and examine objectively, and other communication systems than language proper remained undefined.

0.1. With the development of techniques of phonemic analysis, it became possible to include accentual phenomena of many kinds in linguistic study. The present author in "The Theory of Accentual Systems" (Trager, 1941) set forth the necessity of treating accentual phenomena—stress, pitch, quantity, and others—by the same techniques as had been applied for centuries to vowel and consonant phenomena. A few years later English pitch phonemes were analyzed (Wells, 1945). Then the study of intonation phenomena in English was begun on a large scale (Pike, 1946): in this work and the practical applications that have stemmed from it, many phenomena were alluded to that were not strictly analyzable in terms of the phonemes of pitch, or any other phonemic entities in the system set forth, but which were clearly parts of the total utterances being examined and analyzed.

In *The Field of Linguistics* (Trager, 1949), the study of language and its attendent phenomena was designated as macrolinguistics, which was subdivided into prelinguistics, microlinguistics, and metalinguistics (p. 2). Prelinguistics was said to include "physical and biological events from the point of view of the organization of the statements about them into systems of data useful to the linguist" (p. 2). And the statement of the "relations between language and any of the other cultural systems . . . will constitute the metalinguistics. . . ." (p. 7).

Following this programmatic statement, a first application to the actual material of English speech was made in *An Outline of English Structure* (Trager and Smith, 1951). Part III, Metalinguistics, of that work (pp. 81-88) set forth some preliminary considerations of "metalinguistic phonology" and "metalinguistic morphology," and attempted to describe some of the factors that could lead to a definition of style.

In the spring of 1952, Birdwhistell, Smith, and Trager engaged in a research seminar at the Foreign Service Institute which led Birdwhistell to define and delimit his preliminary material on body motion and to publish the results (1952).

As another result of the same seminar, and in pursuit of some of the suggestions in *An Outline of English Structure*, Smith put out in prepublication mimeographed form *An Outline of Metalinguistic Analysis* (1952). The principal concerns were with items to be included under a "metalinguistic phonology." Categories were established, symbols provided, and suggestions made as to how the phenomena might be described. As will be seen below, the categories have been almost completely rearranged as a consequence of work since that time.

In the fall of 1952, Smith and Trager engaged in another research seminar with Edward T. Hall, Jr., which led to a preliminary publication (Hall and Trager, 1953). There it was pointed out that language was accompanied by other communication systems, one of motion kinesics (see 3, below), and one of extralinguistic noises—vocalizations. This idea was expanded and revised by Trager and Hall in their "Culture and Communication . . ." (1954). There communication was placed in a larger setting, called symbolics. Included in symbolics were the phenomena allocated (above) to prelinguistics, identified by such terms as cerebration, encoding, voice set, voice quality, body set, and motion quality. Communication itself was divided into language, vocalizations, and kinesics.

0.2. In the summer of 1956 research was conducted at the Center for Advanced Study in the Behavioral Sciences at Stanford, California, by a group of psychiatrists and anthropologists on material from psychotherapeutic interviews recorded on tape and film. The group has continued its association, has involved Trager and Smith in the project, and is preparing an extensive publication (Bateson, *et al.*, 1958). In this work a great deal of new material was gathered in the areas so far designated as vocalizations and kinesics. One publication has already resulted (McQuown, 1957).

Similar work by Smith with R. E. Pittenger resulted in a publication containing some even more precise statements about the kinds of events being recorded in the area of vocalizations (Pittenger and Smith, 1957).

In preparation for the publication alluded to (Bateson, *et al.*, 1958). and for further work under a joint project of the Upstate Medical College of the State University of New York and the Institute for Research in Human Communication of the University of Buffalo, as well as for other research being engaged in by the the various persons so far named, it seems appropriate at this time to set forth as a first approximation to definitiveness a statement of the fields we are working in, the kinds of events being observed, the tentative classification of these events in terms of a postulated frame of reference, the terminology being used, and other pertinent matters.

The author is responsible for the detail of this presentation, but he has developed it in constant communication with the colleagues mentioned, all of whom agree with the statement in general, though necessarily reserving the right to differ in many details and even in major classifications. The whole area is still too new for anything more precise. As virtual co-authors must be mentioned Henry Lee Smith, Jr., Norman A. McQuown, and Ray L. Birdwhistell.

1. *THE COMMUNICATION SYSTEMS*

It is taken as a given that language is the principal mode of communication for human beings. It is further assumed that language is always accompanied by other communication systems, that all culture is an interacting set of communications, and that communication as such results from and is a composite of all the specific communication systems as they occur in the total cultural complex.

1.1. *Language* will be described here only to the extent of saying that it is the cultural system which employs certain of the noises made by what are called the organs of speech, combines them into recurrent sequences, and arranges these sequences in systematic distributions in relation to each other and in reference to other cultural systems. That is, language has sound, shape, and sense. This brief description is based upon the extended discussion presented by the author in his article "Language" (Trager, 1955a), and further commented on in the article "Linguistics" (Trager, 1956).

When language is used it takes place in the setting of an act of *speech*. Speech ("talking") results from activities which create a background of *voice set* (1.2, below). This background involves the idosyncratic, including the specific physiology of the speakers and the total physical setting; it is in the area of prelinguistics (Trager, 1949, pp. 2-3). Against this background there take place three kinds of events employing the vocal apparatus: language (as described); variegated other noises, not having the structure of language—*vocalizations*; and modifications of all the language and other noises. These modifications are the *voice qualities*. The vocalizations and voice qualities together are being called *paralanguage* (a term suggested by A. A. Hill, who has been interested in the development of these studies). Paralanguage is part of the metalinguistic area of activity.

The setting of language and paralanguage may be diagrammatically depicted thus:

Voice set
[*as a background against which are measured*:]

voice qualities
[and]
vocalizations } [*These being termed*] paralanguage

[*found in systematic association with*]
language.

The words *paralinguistic* and *paralinguistics* are self-explanatory.

Voice set is briefly discussed in 1.2 and voice qualities are taken up in 1.3. Then section 2 and its subdivisions (2.1-2.3) are devoted to the vocalizations.

1.2. *Voice set* as here delimited is, as stated, a matter of prelinguistics. It involves the physiological and physical peculiarities resulting in the patterned identification of individuals as members of a societal group and as persons of a certain sex, age, state of health, body build, rhythm state, position in a group, mood, bodily condition, location. From the physical and physiological characteristics listed are derived cultural identifications of gender, age grade, health image, body image, rhythmic image, status, mode, condition, locale—and undoubtedly others.

In analyzing and recording the paralinguistic phenomena to be described, it is necessary to state what the voice set back of them is. Such a statement is at least in part an abstraction going back from the actual observation of the paralanguage. But it is not the intention here to discuss the exact nature of voice set and its relation to paralanguage—this being a large separate task. The notation of voice set accompanying a paralinguistic analysis is then to be made in whatever ordinary descriptive terms are available, and to be understood preanalytic.

1.3. *Voice qualities* are recognizable as actual speech events, phenomena that can be sorted out from what is said and heard.

The voice qualities noted so far are these: *pitch range*, *vocal lip control*, *glottis control*, *pitch control*, *articulation control*, *rhythm control*, *resonance*, *tempo*. Pitch range may be identified as *spread* upward or downward, or *narrowed* from above or below. Vocal lip control ranges from heavy *rasp* or hoarseness through slight rasp to various degrees of *openness*. Glottis control deals with *sharp* and *smooth* transitions in pitch. Articulation control covers *forceful* (precise) and *relaxed* (slurred) speech. Rhythm control involves *smooth* and *jerky* setting off of portions of vocal activity. Resonance ranges from *resonant* to *thin*. Tempo is described as *increased* or *decreased* from a norm.

These voice qualities as described seem to involve paired attributes, but the pairs of terms are more properly descriptive of extremes between which there are continua or several intermittent degrees. Symbols are suggested in section 4 below.

2. *VOCALIZATIONS*

By contrast with voice set and voice qualities, which are overall or background characteristics of the voice, the *vocalizations* are actual specifically identifiable noises (sounds) or aspects of noises. Yet they are all different in scope and in concatenation from the sounds of language. Every investigator of language has found it necessary to allude to such sounds but to separate them from the actual linguistics material he describes.

We have found it convenient to discuss three kinds of vocalizations. There is a group of items whose number is yet not delimited, and which have a wide scope over or between linguistic material; these are called *vocal characterizers*—discussed in 2.1. A second group, the *vocal qualifiers*, again have rather wide scope and may be combined with the characterizers; they are discussed in 2.2. The third group is composed of sounds that are much like the sounds of language, but again differ from them in scope and concatenation; these are the *vocal segregates*, taken up in 2.3. Symbols for all vocalizations are suggested in 4 below.

2.1. The vocal characterizers are first of all *laughing* and *crying*, which appear to be much alike and may represent extremes of a continuum, something like the voice qualities; intermediate (and possibly involving other vocalizations) would be giggling, snickering, whimpering, sobbing. Then comes a group involving *yelling* and *whispering* as extremes, with muffled sounds and muttering in between. Other groups involve *moaning* and *groaning*, *whining* and *breaking*, *belching* and *yawning* and probably others. With all these, one "talks through" them.

All of these, as stated, can cover large areas of talking, surrounding, as it were, the language material, or they can occur between bits of language. Together with language, they are embedded in and modified by the voice qualities and voice set.

2.2. Vocal qualifiers were at one time considered by some of us as including many of the voice qualities and vocal characterizers. But working with the material has made it clear that there is a small set of sound characteristics that can be separated out and handled very precisely, and which "qualify" large or small stretches of language material as well as of the other vocalizations.

We now hold that there are three kinds of vocal qualifiers, those of *intensity*, *pitch height,* and *extent.* Within each of these we establish a dichotomy, a range up and a range down from a norm or zero point. And for each range up or down we identify three degrees. The total set-up is as follows:

intensity:	overloud / oversoft	: somewhat / considerably / very much
pitch height:	overhigh / overlow	: slightly / appreciably / greatly
extent:	drawl / clipping	: slight / noticeable / extreme

2.3. Attention was first drawn to what we now call vocal segregates by the necessity of treating such items as English *uh-uh* for negation, *uh-huh* for affirmation, the *uh* of hesitation, *sh*, the Japanese hiss, and other sounds that did not seem to fit into ordinary phonological frames in a language. The *uh-uh* and *uh-huh* noises were at first thought to be alone in this category, called "vocal identifiers" by Pittenger and Smith (1957). The term *vocal segregates* was suggested by Bateson.

Some of these noises, such as *uh*, *sh*, or the various clicks, seemed in many ways to be identical with actual language sounds, in the language being studied, or in some other. But they did not appear in the kinds of sequences that can be called words, and it became increasingly evident from the work alluded to in 0 above that they would have to be analyzed separately and by a scale less fine-grained than that of phonetics.

The number of different noises of this type that came out in the data we examined led the present writer to establish a table, something like those used in phonetics. The classification turns out to be multi-dimensional, requiring special arrangment if depicted on paper. One dimension is that of articulating organs or areas, with closure and release, or as continuant; then comes a dimension of manners of articulation, including vowel-like resonance, and then there is a final dimension dealing with voice and with clicking.

The articulating organs and areas recognized are: spread lips, puckered lips, dental, alveolar, palatal, dorsal, glottal, velic, bronchial. The manners of articulation are: closed-lip nasalization, open-lip nasalization, lateral, trill, vowel-like resonance (higher, lower), inspiration, expiration. The final categorization is as voiced, voiceless, or clicked. A category of non-phonation (zero phonation, "pause") seems to be necessarily included under segregates. A table of vocal segregates, with suggested symbols, is found below in 4.

It will be useful to describe in the terms just given some of the noises that are dealt with here. The usual *uh-uh* of negation has higher vowel-like resonance, with internal (and often initial) glottal closure; it may or may not be accompanied by closed-lip or open-lip nasalization. The *uh-huh* of affirmation is just like the negation except for glottal continuant internally instead of glottal closure. The reported *ha*, or the like, as the word for "yes" in many American Indian languages, is probably the segregate complex of the glottal continuant, lower vowel-like resonance, and open-lip nasalization. The Japanese hiss is the alveolar continuant, with inspiration. The shushing sound is the palatal continuant. Coughs, snorts, sniffs, imitations of animal cries, all seem to be analyzable in these terms.

3. *PARALANGUAGE AND KINESICS*

Kinesics was first delineated as an area for anthropological investigation, as stated, by Birdwhistell in 1952. Since the summer of 1956 Birdwhistell has had the opportunity to conduct extended series of observations on films, in the presence of or with the collaboration of one or more linguists. The theoretical description of the field has gone along with that of paralanguage, and it appears that in their overall structure these two fields of human behavior may be largely analogous to each other, as contrasted with language. Thus there seems to be no subdivision of either kinesics or paralinguistics exactly analogous to the phonology-morphology-semology division of language. Just how the structures of paralanguage and kinesics will work out eventually is not yet clear, however. One important correlation is between kinesic "markers" and points of occurrence of zero-segregates. Another is the coincidence of such motions as head nods with the occurrence of vocal qualifiers.

The research projects now going on should make possible a more nearly definitive statement of kinesics before long, and should also bring added refinements to the description of paralanguage.

4. *SUMMARY*

This article has presented a synthesis of the now available data on the phenomena, which accompany language, usually referred to by such terms as "tone of voice." These phenomena, the necessity of analyzing which was pointed up by research on filmed and tape-recorded psychotherapeutic interviews and similar materials, are now handled under the term paralanguage.

Paralanguage is divided into voice set as background for, and voice qualities and vocalizations as accompaniments of, language proper.

In analyzing a communication, one must, to cover all the data, include material in the areas of paralanguage and kinesics as well as in language. In the research alluded to above various applications of this injunction have been made. The analyses of the material observed that have been presented here arose from this research, and various practical solutions of problems of symbolization and keeping apart of levels were reached. We conclude this presentation by suggestions for symbols.

It is emphasized that the presentation is not definitive, and the symbols especially are to be taken as the most tentative of suggestions.

4.1. Symbols for the main categories are:

Voice set [*precedes*]	VS
Speech [*which includes*]:	Sp
Paralanguage [*divided into*]	PL
Voice qualities [*and*]	VQ
Vocalizations	Vz
Language. [The whole accompanied by]	L
Kinesics	K

If one is doing recording on large sheets of paper, it is probably best to arrange the lines so that an orthography line (Or) comes first, then L with any necessary subdivisions (Ph phonology—Pht phonetics, Phm phonemics; Mp morphology—Mpp morphophonemics, Mpm morphemics; Sy syntax; Se semology [with subdivisions as they are developed]). After this can be placed PL with subdivisions, then VS, and finally K. All should be correlated with a time line, in divisions appropriately small (1/24 second for film, and so on).

VS, as said, is best handled in the present state of development by descriptive terms.

VQ includes categories for which letter symbols combined with mnemonic visual symbols are proposed:

pitch range	Pr
spread upward	-↑̬
downward	-↓̆
narrowed from above	-↑
below	-↓̂
vocal lip control	Lc
rasp—heavy (hoarseness)	-8̩
plain	-o̩
openness—slight	-o
full	-8
glottis control	Gc
voicing—over	-ˇ
under	-̬
breathiness—slight	-ʿ
heavy	-ʿʿ
pitch control	Pc
sharp transition	-↱ or -↴
smooth transition	-↱ or -↴
articulation control	Ac
forceful	-F
rexlaxed	-R̸
rhythm control	Rc
smooth	∾
jerky	≠
resonance	Re
resonant	-r̲
thin	-t̲
tempo	Te
increased	-<
decreased	->

The principal symbols should be used with the subsidiary ones. Symbols should be placed at the beginning and end of each stretch affected, thus: Te-<...>. VQ is a category in which several items may appear at once, so several lines should be allowed.

The vocalizations, Vz, are subdivided into:

Vch	vocal characterizers
Vqu	vocal qualifiers
Vsg	vocal segregates

The Vch categories are probably best represented by letter abbreviations for the present, thus:

laughing	Lf	
giggling		-gi
snickering		-sn
crying	Cr	
whimpering		-wh
sobbing		-so
yelling	Ye	
muffled		-mf
whispering	Wh	
muttering		-mt
moaning	Mn	
groaning	Gr	
whining	Wn	
breaking	Br	
belching	Bl	
yawning	Yn	

These are used as are the VQ symbols: Lf . . . Lf.

Vqu categories have these symbols:

intensity	In-
overloud	^ ^^ ^^^
oversoft	ˇ ˇˇ ˇˇˇ
pitch height	PH-
overhigh	↑ ⇑ ⤊
overlow	↓ ⇓ ⤋
extent	Ex-
drawl	⌢ ∓ ∓∓
clipping	⌣ ± ±±

The symbols are placed at the beginning and end of the stretch affected: ↑ . . . ↑ .

The Vsg table is as follows:

	spread lips	puckered lips	dental	alveolar	palatal	dorsal	glottal	velic	bronchial
Closure and release	P	P.	T̨	T	C	K	ʔ	V	⊖
Continuant	Φ	Φ.	Ş	S	$	X	H	╳	⊕

Closed-lip nasal	M	} ← combined with (the Closure and release / Continuant symbols above)
Open-lip nasal	N	
Lateral	L	
Trill	R	
Vowel-like-higher	Ǝ	
lower	A	
Inspiration	≯	→ [are modified by
Expiration	≮	
Voiced	v̄	} ← (modify the above)
Voiceless	ʌ̄	
Clicked	c̀	
Zero-segregate	∅	

These symbols are used more or less like phonetic symbols, sequentially: *uh-huh* ƎHƎ, *ɪh-hunh* ƎHƎN, *hm* HM, *brrr* (referring to cold) PRv̄, *tsk-tsk* Tc̀, etc.

REFERENCE NOTE

Trager's work, like Devereux's ethnographic observations, broaches a complex area of interrelations among linguistic phenomena, personality, and expressive communication. The references are organized according to the following categories:

A. Expressive Language and Its Analysis
   1. General
   2. Sound Symbolism

B. Nonverbal Expressive Phenomena
   1. Gestures
   2. Special Gestural Codes
   3. Communicative Motor Habits and Expressive Movement Generally

C. Speech Disturbances

D. Speech and Personality
   1. General
   2. Person Perception
E. Expressive and Persuasive Uses of Language
   1. General
   2. Oaths, Profanity, and Insult
   3. Petition, Prayer, and Praise

Trager's references, if not in the general bibliography, are in (A). For the development of Trager's view on a general theory of language as part of culture, and linguistics in anthropology, see Trager and Smith (1951); Trager (1949, 1955a, 1956, 1959); and Trager and Hall (1954); cf. also Smith (1952).

A. EXPRESSIVE LANGUAGE AND ITS ANALYSIS

1. *GENERAL*

In addition to the references listed below, see Adams (1957), Bally (1950; 1951; 1952, chap. 4 "Mecanisme de l'expressivité linguistique."), Black (1949, pp. 201-220, "Questions about emotive meaning,"), Cohen (1956a, pp. 227-270), Doob (1961), Estrich and Sperber (1952, chaps. 13-15), Osgood, Suci, Tannenbaum (1957), Sebeok (1960b, Part 8; 1962), Troubetzkoy (1949b, chap. 2), Vendryes (1925, pp. 137-154).

References not in the general bibliography:

BATESON, GREGORY, RAY L. BIRDWHISTELL, HENRY W. BROSIN, CHARLES F. HOCKETT, NORMAN A. MCQUOWN

1958. *The Natural History of an Interview.* [In manuscript].

BERQUE, JACQUES

1961. Expression et signification dans la vie arabe. *L'Homme, 1:* 50-67.

BIRDWHISTELL, RAY L.

1952. *Introduction to Kinesics. An Annotation System for Analysis of Body Motion and Gesture.* Washington, D.C.: Department of State, Foreign Service Institute.

DESPERT, J. L.

1941. Emotional Aspects of Speech and Language Development. *Journal of Psychiatry and Neurology, 105:* 193-222.

GOLDMAN-EISLER, FRIEDA

1961. Comparative Study of Two Hesitation Phenomena. *Language and Speech, 4:* 18-26.

HAAS, MARY R.

1946. Techniques of Intensifying in Thai. *Word, 2:* 127-130.

HAMP, ERIC P.

1957. Stylistically Modified Allophones in Huichol. *Lg., 33:* 139-142.

HENRY, JULES

1936. The Linguistic Expression of Emotion. *AA, 38:* 250-256.

JAKOBSON, ROMAN

1956. The Metamorphic and Metonymic Poles. In Roman Jakobson and Morris Halle, *Fundamentals of Language.* The Hague: Mouton. Pp. 76-82.

KLUCKHOHN, CLYDE

1945. The Personal Document in Anthropological Science. In Louis Gottschalk, Clyde Kluckhohn, Robert Angell, *The Use of Personal Documents in History, Anthropology, and Sociology*. (Social Science Research Council. Bulletin 53.) Washington, D.C. Pp.79-173.

MAHL, G. F.

1959. Exploring Emotional States by Content Analysis. In Ithiel de Sola Pool (Ed.), *Trends in Content Analysis*. Urbana: University of Illinois Press. Pp. 83-130.

1960. The Expression of Emotions on the Lexical and Linguistic Levels. Paper presented at Symposium on "Expression of the Emotions in Man," American Association for the Advancement of Science, December 29-30. New York.

MAROUZEAU, J.

1923. Langage affectif et langage intellectuel. *Journal de psychologie: normale et pathologique, 20:* 560-578.

MCQUOWN, NORMAN A.

1957. Linguistic Transcription and Specification of Psychiatric Interview Material. *Psychiatry, 20:* 79-86.

MEAD, MARGARET, and RHODA METRAUX (EDS.)

1953. *The Study of Culture at a Distance*. Chicago: University of Chicago Press.

PEAR, THOMAS H.

1957. *Personality, Appearance and Speech*. London: Allen and Unwin.

PIKE, KENNETH L.

1946. *The Intonation of American English*. (University of Michigan Publications in Linguistics, No. 1.) Ann Arbor: University of Michigan Press.

1957. Abdominal Pulse Types in Some Peruvian Languages. *Lg., 33:* 30-35.

PITTENGER, ROBERT E., CHARLES F. HOCKETT, JOHN J. DANEHY

1960. *The First Five Minutes. A Sample of Microscopic Interview Analysis*. Ithaca: Martineau.

PITTENGER, ROBERT E., and HENRY SMITH, JR.

1957. A Basis for Some Contributions of Linguistics to Psychiatry. *Psychiatry, 20:* 61-78.

SAUVAGEOT, A.

1957. *Les Procédés expressifs du français contemporain*. Paris: Klincksieck.

STANKIEWICZ, EDWARD

1954. Expressive Derivation of Substantives in Contemporary Russian and Polish. *Word, 10:* 457-468.

1960a. The Consonantal Alternations in the Slavic Declensions. *Word, 16:* 183-203.

1960b. Expressive Language. In Thomas A. Sebeok (Ed.), *Style in Language*. New York: Wiley; Cambridge: Technology Press. Pp. 96-97.

TRAGER, GEORGE L.

1941. The Theory of Accentual Systems. In L. Spier, A. I. Hallowell, S. S. Newman (Eds.), *Language, Culture, and Personality*. Menasha, Wis.: Banta. Pp. 131-145.

1960. Taos III: Paralanguage. *AL, 2* (2): 24-30.

1961. The Typology of Paralanguage. *AL, 3* (1): 17-21.

WELLS, RULON S.
1945. The Pitch Phonemes of English. *Lg.*, *21:* 17-39.

WERNER, HEINZ (ED.)
1955. *On Expressive Language*. Worcester, Mass.: Clark University. [Reviewed, Roger Brown, *Lg.*, 1955, *31:* 543-549.]

2. *SOUND SYMBOLISM*

In addition to the references listed below, see Brown (1958, chap. IV), Hockett (1958, chap. 35), Hymes (1960b, pp. 111-114), and Smithers (1954).

BOLINGER, DWIGHT P.
1950. Rime, Assonance, and Morpheme Analysis. *Word*, *6:* 116-136.

BRINTON, DANIEL GARRISON
1894. On the Physiological Correlations of Certain Linguistic Radicals. *Proceedings American Oriental Society* (March). Pp. cxxxiii-cxxxiv.

BROWN, ROGER W., A. BLACK, A. HOROWITZ
1955. Phonetic Symbolism in Natural Languages. *JASP*, *50:* 388-393.

BÜHLER, KARL
1933. L'Onomatopée et la fonction representative du langage. In Pierre Janet and George Dumas (Eds.), *Psychologie du langage*. Paris: Alcan. Pp. 101-119. [*Journal de psychologie: normale et pathologique*, *30* (1-4).]

MARCHAND, HANS
1959. Phonetic Symbolism in English Word-Formation. *Indogermanische Forschungen*, *64:* 146-168, 256-277. Berlin

MARKEL, NORMAN N., and ERIC P. HAMP
1961. Connotative Meanings of Certain Phoneme Sequences. *Studies in Linguistics*, *15:* 47-61.

MIRON, MURRAY S.
1961. A Cross-Linguistic Investigation of Phonetic Symbolism. *JASP*, *62:* 623-630.

B. NONVERBAL EXPRESSIVE PHENOMENA

1. *GESTURE*

In addition to the references listed below, see Cohen (1956, p. 74).

BIRDWHISTELL, RAY L.
1954. Kinesics and Communication. *Explorations*, *3:* 31-41. [Also in Edmund Carpenter and Marshalls McLuhan (Eds.), *Explorations in Communication: An Anthology*. Boston: Beacon. Pp. 54-64.]

BREWER, W. D.
1951. Patterns of Gesture Among the Levantine Arabs. *AA*, *53:* 232-237.

CRITCHLEY, MACDONALD
1939. *The Language of Gesture*. London: Arnold; New York: Longmans, Green.

EFRON, DAVID

1941. *Gesture and Environment. A Tentative Study of Some of the Spatio-Temporal and "Linguistic" Aspects of the Gestural Behavior of Eastern Jews and Southern Italians in New York City, Living Under Similar as Well as Different Environmental Conditions.* With sketches by Stuyvesant Van Ween and a Preface by Franz Boas. New York: King's Crown. [Reviewed, A. M. Tozzer, *AA*, 1942, *44:* 715-716.]

HAYES, FRANCIS

1957. Gestures: a Working Bibliography. *Southern Folklore Quarterly*, *21:* 218-317.

LABARRE, WESTON

1947. The Cultural Basis of Emotions and Gestures. *Journal of Psychology*, *16:* 49-68.

SCHLAUCH, MARGARET

1936. Recent Soviet Studies in Linguistics. *Science and Society*, *1:* 152-167.

VENDRYES, J.

1950. Langage oral et langage par gestes. *Journal de psychologie; normale et pathologique*, *43:* 7-33.

2. *SPECIAL GESTURAL CODES*

BRUNVAND, JAN

1960. More Non-Oral Riddles. *Western Folklore*, *19:* 132-133.

HUGHES, RUSSELL M.

1941. *The Gesture Language of the Hindu Dance.* New York: Columbia University Press.

MESSING, SIMON D.

1960. The Nonverbal Language of the Ethiopian Toga. *Anthropos*, *55:* 558-560.

PEAR, THOMAS

1935. Suggested Parallels Between Speaking and Clothing. *Acta Psychologia*, *1:* 191-201.

RIJNBECK, G. VAN

1954. *Le Langage par signes chez les moines.* Amsterdam.

STOKOE, WILLIAM C., JR.

1960. *Sign Language Structure. An Outline of the Visual Communication Systems of the American Deaf.* (Studies in Linguistics, Occasional Papers 8.) Buffalo: University of Buffalo, Department of Anthropology and Linguistics. [Reviewed, H. Landar, *Lg.*, 1961, *37:* 269-271.]

TERVOORT, B. T. M., S.J.

1953. *Structurele Analyse van Visueel Taalgebruik binnen een Groep Dove Kindern.* Amsterdam. 2 vols. [Reviewed, B. Spang-Thomsen, *Word*, *12:* 454-467 (1956).]

3. *COMMUNICATIVE MOTOR HABITS AND EXPRESSIVE MOVEMENT GENERALLY*

In addition to the references listed below, see Goffman (1961, pp. 85-152).

ALLPORT, GORDON W., and P. E. VERNON

1933. *Studies in Expressive Movement.* New York: Macmillan.

BAILEY, FLORA L.
1942. Navaho Motor Habits. *AA, 44:* 210-234.

DEUTSCH, FELIX
1947. Analysis of Postural Behavior. *Psychoanalytical Quarterly, 16:* 192-213.

FRANK, LAWRENCE K.
1957. Tactile Communication. *Genetic Psychology Monographs, 56:* 209-255. [Also in *ETC.: A Review of General Semantics*, 1958, *16:* 31-79.]

HALL, EDWARD T., JR.
1955. The Anthropology of Manners. *Scientific American, 192:* 84-90.

HEWES, GORDON W.
1955. World Distribution of Postural Habits. *AA, 57:* 231-244.
1957. The Anthropology of Posture. *Scientific American, 196:* 122-132.

MAUSS, MARCEL
1935. Les Techniques du corps. *Journal de psychologie: normale et pathologique, 32:* 271-293.

MEAD, MARGARET, and FRANCES MACGREGOR
1951. *Growth and Culture. A Photographic Study of Balinese Childhood.* New York: Putnam.

REUSCH, JURGEN, and WELDON KEES
1956. *Nonverbal Communication. Notes on the Visual Perception of Human Relations.* Berkeley: University of California Press.

C. SPEECH DISTURBANCES

In addition to the references listed below, see Hymes (1961b), Jakobson (1942), Klausner (1955), Kluckhohn (1954), May (1956), Sapir (1915), Saporta (1961, Section 7), Steward (1960), Vygotsky (1939).

CUTTEN, GEORGE BARTON
1927. *Speaking with Tongues, Historically and Psychologically Considered.* New Haven: Yale University Press.

DE SAUSSURE, RAYMOND
1946. On Personal Metaphors in Psychiatric Cases. *Word, 2:* 188-190.

DEVEREUX, GEORGE
1957. A Primitive Slip of the Tongue. *Anthropological Quarterly, 30:* 27-29.

FREUD, SIGMUND
1938. *The Psychopathology of Everyday Life.* (From the 4th German Edition.) New York: Macmillan. [Also, New York: New American Library (Mentor Book), 1951; and in *The Basic Writings of Sigmund Freud.* Edited by A. A. Brill. New York: Modern Library, 1938.]

GOLDSTEIN, KURT
1946. On Naming and Pseudo-Naming. *Word, 2:* 1-7.
1948. *Language and Language Disturbances.* New York: Grune and Stratton.

GOODGLASS, HAROLD, and JEAN BERKO
1960. Agrammatism and Inflectional Morphology in English. *Journal of Speech and Hearing Research, 3:* 257-267.

GOODGLASS, HAROLD, and J. HUNT
1959. Grammatical Complexity and Aphasic Speech. *Word, 14:* 197-207.

HEAD, H.
1926. *Aphasia and Kindred Disorders of Speech*. New York: Macmillan. 2 vols.
HOCH, P., and J. ZUBIN (EDS.)
1958. *Psychopathology of Communication*. New York: Grune and Stratton.
JAKOBSON, ROMAN, and MORRIS HALLE
1956. Aphasia as a Linguistic Problem. *Fundamentals of Language*. The Hague: Mouton. Pp. 55-67. [Also in Heinz Werner (Ed.), *On Expressive Language*. Worcester, Mass.: Clark University Press. Pp. 69-81; and Sol Saporta (Ed.), *Psycholinguistics*. New York: Holt, Rinehart and Winston, 1961. Pp. 419-427.]
1959. Linguistic Glosses to Goldstein's "Wortbegriff." *Journal of Individual Psychology*, *15:* 62-65.
KAINZ, F.
1954. *Physiologische Psychologie der Sprachvorgänge* (2nd ed). (Psychologie der Sprache, Vol. III.) Vienna. (1st ed., Stuttgart: 1943.)
KAPLAN, BERNARD
1957. On the Phenomena of "Opposite Speech." *JASP*, *55:* 389-393.
LANDAR, HERBERT J.
1961. Reduplication and Morphology. *Lg.*, *37:* 239-246.
LEMERT, EDWIN M.
1962. Stuttering and Social Structure in Two Pacific Societies. *Journal of Speech and Hearing Disorders*, *27:* 3-10.
LENNEBERG, ERIC H.
1960. Review of W. Penfield and L. Roberts, *Speech and Brain-Mechanisms*. *Lg.*, *36:* 97-112.
MAHL, G.
1957. Disturbances and Silences in the Patient's Speech in Psychotherapy. *JASP*. *42:* 3-32.
MCCARTHY, DOROTHEA A.
1954. Language Disorders and Parent-Child Relationships. *Journal of Speech and Hearing Disorders*, *19* (4).
OSTWALD, PETER
1961. The Sounds of Emotional Disturbance. *Archives of General Psychiatry*, *5*: 587-592.
PENFIELD, WILDER, and LAMAR ROBERTS
1949. *Speech and Brain-Mechanisms*. Princeton: Princeton University Press. [Reviewed, Eric Lenneberg, *Lg.*, *36:* 97-112 (1960).]
ROBERTSON, J. P. S., and S. J. SHAMSIE
1959. A Systematic Examination of Gibberish in a Multilingual Schizophrenic Patient. *Language and Speech*, *2:* 1-8.

D. SPEECH AND PERSONALITY

1. *GENERAL*

In addition to the references listed below, see Estrich and Sperber (1952, chaps. 13-14), Goffman (1959), Hymes (1961b).

ALLPORT, GORDON W., and H. CANTRIL
1934. Judging Personality from Voice. *Journal of Social Psychology*, *5:* 37-55.

ASCH, SOLOMON
1946. Forming Impressions of Personality. *JASP*, *41:* 285-290.

CHAO, YUEN REN
1953. Introduction to Discussion of Speech and Personality. In Levi-Strauss *et al.*, *Results of the Conference of Anthropologists and Linguists.* (*IUPAL*; Memoirs of *IJAL*, No. 8.) Bloomington: Indiana University.

NEWMAN, STANLEY S.
1939. Personal Symbolism in Language Patterns. *Psychiatry*, *2:* 177-182.
1941. Behavior Patterns in Linguistic Structure: A Case Study. In L. Spier, A. I. Hallowell, S. S. Newman (Eds.), *Language, Culture and Personality.* Menasha, Wis.: Banta. Pp. 94-106.
1944. Cultural and Psychological Features in English Intonation. *Transactions of the New York Academy of Sciences*, *7:* 45-54.

NEWMAN, STANLEY S., and VERA G. MATHER
1938. Analysis of Spoken Languages of Patients with Affective Disorders. *American Journal of Psychiatry*, *94:* 913-942.

SANFORD, FILLMORE H.
1942. Speech and Personality. *Psychological Bulletin*, *39:* 811-845.

SAPIR, EDWARD
1927. Speech as a Personality Trait. *American Journal of Sociology*, *32:* 892-905. [Also in David G. Mandelbaum (Ed.), *Selected Writings of Edward Sapir in Language, Culture, and Personality*. Berkeley and Los Angeles: University of California Press, 1949. Pp. 533-543.]

WISHNER, JULIUS
1960. Reanalysis of "Impressions of Personality." *Psychological Review*, *67:* 96-112.

2. *PERSON PERCEPTION*

On social perception of persons as having particular traits because of linguistic characteristics, see references in (D1) above, and Klausner (1955), Lambert *et al.* (1960); McCormack (1960), McDavid (1952-1953), Putnam and O'Hern (1955); see also the references with Gumperz' article in Part VII, pp. 416-428.

LAMBERT, W. E., R. C. HODGSON, R. C. GARDNER, S. FILLENBAUM
1960. Evaluational Reactions to Spoken Languages. *JASP*, *60:* 144-151.

E. EXPRESSIVE AND PERSUASIVE USES OF LANGUAGE

1. *GENERAL*

In addition to the references listed below, see Brown (1958, chaps. IX-X), Burke (1945, 1951a, 1957, 1961), Duncan (1962), Pool (1959), Richards (1936). See also references on verbal contest with Conklin's article (pp. 295-300), on poetic language with Sebeok's article (pp. 356-371), and on ceremonial language with Newman's article (pp. 397-406). Consult also discussions of curses, oaths, praise names, prayer, etc., in Leach (1949-1950). Many of the preceding references to this article and references to the articles in Part VI are also relevant.

BRYANT, DONALD C.
1958. *The Rhetorical Idiom*. Ithaca: Cornell University Press.

CUYLER, CORNELIUS M. (ED.)
1960. *Speech Training in the Minor Seminary*. Washington, D.C.: Catholic University of America Press.

HAYAKAWA, S. I.
1941. *Language in Action*. New York: Harcourt, Brace.

HOWES, RAYMOND F. (ED.)
1961. *Historical Studies of Rhetoric and Rhetoricians*. Ithaca: Cornell University Press.

LASSWELL, HAROLD, NATHAN LEITES, *et al.*
1949. *Language of Politics: Studies in Quantitative Semantics*. New York: Stewart.

2. *OATHS, PROFANITY, AND INSULT*

In addition to the references below, see Devereux (1951), Evans-Pritchard (1929, 1949, 1956), and Nadel (1954). Ransom (1946, pp. 54-55) shows joint diffusion of obscenity and cursing with an expressive morphological process, to but one group of Aleuts. On verbal contest, see also p. 299.

BURRIDGE, KENELM O. L.
1957. Disputing in Tangu. *AA*, *59:* 763-780, especially pp. 764 ff.

DORSON, RICHARD M. (ED.)
1962. Symposium on Obscenity in Folklore. *JAF*, *75:* 189-265.

KIRK-GREENE, A. H. M.
1955. On Swearing: An Account of Some Judicial Oaths in Northern Nigeria. *Africa*, *25:* 43-53.

LOWIE, ROBERT H.
1959. Crow Curses. *JAF*, *72:* 105.

RANSOM, JAY ELLIS
1946. Aleut Linguistic Perspective. *SJA*, *2:* 48-55.

RITZENTHALER, ROBERT
1945. Totemic Insult Among the Wisconsin Chippewa. *AA*, *47:* 322-324.

SWADESH, MORRIS
1933. Chitimacha Verbs of Derogatory or Abusive Connotation with Parallels from European Languages. *Lg.*, *9:* 192-201.

3. *PETITION, PRAYER, AND PRAISE*

Discrete studies are rare, and one almost has to go back to Tylor for a systematic discussion in anthropology. Some of the references illustrate the subject: Gifford (1958), Lessa and Vogt (1958), Lowie (1933), Mason (1917), Nellis (1947), Reichard (1944); M. G. Smith (1957); see also Astrov (1946), Day (1951), and other references with Shimkin's article (pp. 344-355), as well as references to Evans-Pritchard's article (pp. 221-227), Gumperz' (pp. 416-428). Other references make points of method and perspective: Burke (1957, esp. pp. 241-243), Gifford (1958), Mead (1933, especially p. 3), Smith (1957).

GIFFORD, E. W.
1958. Karok Confessions. *Miscellanea P. Rivet, Octogenario Dicata.* (Thirty-first International Congress of Americanists.) Mexico City: Universidad Nacional Autónoma de México. Pp. 245-255.

LESSA, WILLIAM, and EVON VOGT

1958. *Reader in Comparative Religion*. New York: Harper & Row.

LOWIE, ROBERT H.

1933. Crow Prayers. *AA, 35:* 433-442.

MASON, J. ALDEN

1917. Tepecano Prayers. *IJAL, 1:* 91-153.

MEAD, MARGARET

1933. More Comprehensive Field Methods. *AA, 35:* 1-15.

REICHARD, GLADYS

1944. *Prayer: The Compulsive Word*. New York: Augustin.

TYLOR, EDWARD B.

1958. Rites and Ceremonies. *Religion in Primitive Culture*. New York: Harper Torchbooks. Chap. 18, especially pp. 450-460. (Part II of *Primitive Culture*. London: John Murray, 1871.)

part VI

SPEECH PLAY AND VERBAL ART

Introduction

THE LUDIC AND AESTHETIC MOTIVES are part of all speech as an activity and all language as a product. Indeed, we find in Burke (1958) the suggestion that such motivation generally underlies the elaboration and rounding out of verbal patterns, and Newman, in his article on pp. 372-381, analyzes a whole language as embodying a style, and hence, by inference, an aesthetic preference. Jakobson has called for the study of *poetic function*, defining that function by situations in which the *shape* of a message becomes a focus of attention, perhaps exploited for its own sake. Such study would have a wide range, for devices serving poetic function occur in many uses of language besides poetry proper, as Jakobson points out in an analysis of the slogan "I like Ike."

On the whole, studies with this specific orientation have been lacking in American linguistics and anthropology. Speech play and verbal art have come to attention mainly by obtruding upon the ordinary course of linguistic and ethnographic analysis and through the collection and analysis of texts.

When, in some culture, either motive has found specialized verbal form and a cultural niche, attention is likely to be directed at several correlated questions: What are the distinctive linguistic traits? How do they relate to the general structure or ordinary use of language in the group? What are the functions of the specialized use? How do they relate to the rest of the social structure and culture? Beyond this are questions of comparative study and the development of hypotheses and general theories.

Several aspects of the subject can be illustrated by excellent studies. Still, too little work has been done, especially regarding speech play, for much in the way of hypotheses or generalizations. (Roberts and Sutton-Smith [1962] are an exception, although they do not focus on verbal games.) Verbal art, in the sense of oral literature, has been more fortunate, for its study has often accompanied, or been made possible by, the anthropological habit of collecting texts. Although many texts have been collected specifically for linguistic and folkloristic purposes, many have also been collected for their value as authentic documents of native culture. Such collection was a principle of procedure with Boas and became for Radin (1933) the chief criterion by which to judge ethnological work. In this respect anthropology has been, as Levi-Strauss has put it, the third wave of the humanistic revolution, carrying to the whole of the world the concerns first directed by the Renaissance toward the classical antiquity of Greece and Rome, and then by the Romantic movement toward the Orient. In effect, anthropology is the philology of peoples who had no philological tradition of their own.

The collection and publication of texts has waned, partly due to decline of linguistic competence among ethnographers, partly due to shifts of interest, but also partly because of past failures to complete the philological task of making native text materials usable by others. Mere publication of text is of little value when few if any others are conversant with the language. With the increase of linguistic competence among ethnographers and the possibility of computer programs to handle some of the philological work (concordances, for example), collection and publication of texts may again expand, especially if it is remembered that an analyzed and edited text fit for publication is not mere data, but a scholarly product. Interest in the interpretation of folklore texts has already revived through work in structural analysis and interpretation by Jakobson, Levi-Strauss, Sebeok (represented here), Jacobs, and others.

One can hope that the study of verbal play and art will be extended by the structural analysis of many more individual cases and by the development of cross-cultural typologies and frameworks for controlled comparison. Both activities require close cooperation between linguistic and ethnographic work, for the phenomena are essentially sociolinguistic, and general questions are likely to focus on the interrelations between linguistic form and cultural function or on the complex units comprised by both.

Such uses of language often employ a special channel or make specialized use of a common one, and so the general subject of alternative types and uses of channels—whistling, drumming, horn-calling, singing, chanting, writing, and the like—can be subsumed here. There is further reason in the fact that analysis of both channel-linked and other specialized forms usually requires the same starting-point, comparison with a base form of the message in the ordinary code. But the subject of channels obviously also has a close relation with social structure and boundaries among speech-communities (Part VII) and the general study of the communication system of a group.

Needless to say, linguistic accuracy is the only solid basis for all such work. (Recall Strehlow's remarks in Part II.) It is unfortunate how often injunctions of Boas, Sapir, Radin, and others to this effect have been ignored. To paraphrase Sapir, we would not think much of an expert on French culture who controlled no French. Beyond the matter of cultural interpretation through texts and direct communication, it is clear that questions about special modes of communication—how they work, what they can express, and what effects they have—cannot be answered except with reference to linguistic detail. Regarding verbal art in particular, material not collected in the integrity of its own language is obviously suspect on grounds of validity, and such material makes the necessary attention to linguistic form impossible.

In general, there are two anthropological maxims for the study of speech play and verbal art: unlike some forms of art (1) their medium is itself already culturally structured and (2) they are universal. Hence the need, stated above, to consider the structure of the language which is their mode of existence. Hence also an ethnographic query applicable to any group: to what extent, in what ways, and for what purposes is speech manipulated for its own sake or for kinds of effect recognized as play and art? Work directed to such queries serves two of anthropology's long-range goals: a truly comparative literature, wherein the concepts employed in studies of metrics, structure, genre, style, function, and the like are conceived and articulated on an adequate cross-cultural basis; and comparative analysis of cultures as systems of communication.

The articles in Part VI differ in many respects, but they repeatedly bring out two types of relationship, that between linguistic form proper and the form of a particular genre and that between a particular genre and its cultural context.

Conklin's article is notable for its detailed correlation between special modes of speech and social roles. The attention here and in Conklin (1955) to specific mechanisms makes his work valuable for a general typology. Devices of speech disguise are apparently more varied in these two Philippine cases than in any other cases encountered in the literature. Haas presents brief but precise statements of two nonwestern children's word games. Note their relevance to socialization (Part V) and bilingualism (Part VIII).

Cowan gives an unusually full picture of the nature and use of a speech surrogate. His account is particularly interesting for its demonstration of the extensive functional capacity a highly restricted code may have, at least within a close-knit social group. Herzog's paper also raises questions of functional capacity. Like Conklin's it shows a special coding (here based on reduction rather than metamorphosis of basic shape) used for concealment and involved in social prestige; and together with his other papers (1934, 1935) it indicates how complex the system of alternative channels and associated linguistic devices may become in even a small tribe.

Emeneau relates aesthetic use of language to cultural focus, showing in detail how an oral poetry works, both structurally and socially, and justifying its claim as literature. Shimkin shows how aesthetic interest can be elaborated through language in even a relatively simple hunting society. Whereas Emeneau gives precise analysis of metrical patterns and Shimkin illustrates stylistic devices, Sebeok develops a statement of generality and simplicity out of relations of content, achieving a formal definition of the genre of charms in Cheremis.

The discussions by Newman and Gayton suggest some of the problems of Part III, but as interpreted in terms of a comparative stylistics of grammar rather than a comparative metaphysics. The key sentence is Newman's aphorism about the ordinary grammar, "It tells what a language can do but not what it considers worthwhile doing." The final paragraph recalls Sapir's statement that "Language is the most massive and inclusive art we know, a mountainous and anonymous work of unconscious generations" (1921, p. 235).

Linguistic Play in Its Cultural Context 33

HAROLD C. CONKLIN

1. METHODS OF MODIFYING the normal patterns of speech for purposes of entertainment or concealment are perhaps universal. Where such practices abound in both type and incidence, one may assume that considerable cultural importance is associated with the contexts in which they occur, and that the statuses of the most frequent users are also of particular significance. The following is a brief analysis of the linguistic and sociocultural aspects of such a situation recently noted in the Philippines among the Hanunóo.

2. The most common form of salutation in Hanunóo consists of a request for betel chew ingredients. One of many ways of expressing this greeting is an indirect statement like:

ba:raŋ may bu:ŋa qa:san sa kanta katagbuq

'Perhaps the people we have just met have some arcca nuts.' In producing such an utterance, however, a speaker may intentionally change its phonological content and shape considerably without modifying the narrowly defined linguistic meanings of its component elements. In this sense, the following alternative renderings of the sample sentence—however different they may be pragmatically—are semantically and syntactically identical:

A *ra:baŋ may ŋa:bu sa:qan sa tanka kabugtaq*
B *ba:raŋ may bu:ŋaŋ qa:saŋ sa kantaŋ katagbuŋ*
C *qaybar qaymay qaybuŋ qayqas qaysa qaykan qaytag*
D *bansuwayb may buŋsuwayb qansuwayb sa kansuwayb kataŋsuwayb*
E *baba tag sa raraq, may bubu tag sa ŋaŋa tag sa qaqa tag sa sasaq, sa kaka tag sa tataq, katata tag sa bubuq*

The first type, exemplified by A, results from simple REARRANGEMENT of the phonemic content of polysyllabic forms so that the initial CV of the first stem syllable is transposed with the first CV of the second syllable. Prefixes, monosyllabic particles, and vowel length position remain unchanged. In trisyllabic stems, the first and last (third) CV are transposed: a form such as *balaynun* 'domesticated' is pronounced *nulayban*.

In the second type, as in B, there is a simple SUBSTITUTION of a particular consonant phoneme (in this instance *ŋ*) for the final consonant phoneme of each polysyllabic form.

The third type, as in C, involves short PREFIXATION WITH PARTIALS, i.e., with only the first CVC of each word.

The fourth type, as in D, involves SUFFIXATION WITH PARTIALS, i.e., with only the first CV of each polysyllabic form, not counting prefixes.

The fifth type, E, involves REDUPLICATIVE SUFFIXATION WITH PARTIALS (which consist of the intitial CV of each stem syllable of polysyllabic forms), and the addition of the segment *tag sa* 'goes to," or pause, between the resulting forms.

The basic changes involved in these five pig-Latin-like kinds of alternation can be reduced to very simple stem formulae:

	C V C C V C 1 2 3 4 5 6	*r i g n u k* 'tame' 1 2 3 4 5 6	*b i · ŋ a w* 'nick' 1 2 3 4 5 6	*q u s a h* 'one' 1 2 4 5 6
A	453126	*nugrik*	*ŋa:biw*	*saquh*
B	12345*C*	*rignuŋ*	*bi:ŋaŋ*	*qusaŋ*
C	*CVC*123/4	*qayrig*	*qaybiŋ*	*qayqus*
D	12*CCVC*(*VCC*)	*rinsiŋ, rinsuwayb*	*biŋsiŋ, biŋsuwayb*	*qunsiŋ, qunsuwayb*
E	12*12 tag sa* 4545*q*	*riri tag sa nunuq*	*bibi tag sa ŋaŋaq*	*ququ tag sa sasaq*

These examples also illustrate how rules for modifying dissyllabic stems with open syllables are derived from those for stems of the CVCCVC pattern.

The changes noted so far are known collectively to the Hanunóo as *sinulih* 'turned wrong-side-up.' They consist mostly of reordering, substituting, and adding segmental phonemes within the bounds of normally discrete, free forms or smaller units. A Hanunóo speaker, however, may choose to alter the sample sentence by changing the over-all manner of articulation or vocalization in one of four ways:

F *yanas*, barely audible WHISPERING

G *paliksih*, i.e., CLIPPED pronunciation typified by greater speed, greater glottal tension, the expansion of intonational contours, and shortening of long vowels

H *padiqitun*, i.e., FALSETTO

I *paha·gut*, any sequence of articulations during which the direction of air flow in normal speech is reversed, i.e., in which the air flow is produced entirely by INHALATION instead of by exhalation

Any of these four techniques involving voice qualifiers may be used in combination with any type of *sinulih* (e.g., *paha:gut* plus suffixation with partials). Such COMBINATIONS are referred to as cases of *quruŋdan*, which can be considered a special type, J.

Other Hanunóo forms of linguistic play include:

K *qinuman*, i.e., DISCONTINUOUS SUBSTITUTION, in which there is modification of particular isolated words by vowel or consonant change (e.g., *pa:ray, qinu:mih, ba:li dur, hi:raw* for *paray, qinumih* (girls' names), *ba:li duy* 'fine, pal,' *hi:rak* 'jealousy')

L *pinaqu:maŋ*, or DISCONTINUOUS (LEXEMIC) INVERSION, i.e., the use of a form the meaning of which is the opposite of what one actually wishes to express, with or without additional phonological changes (e.g., *da:qut qay waydiq* 'very bad indeed' instead of *mayad waydiq* 'very good indeed'; *hayga pinabi:lug nimu kanmu bayqun?* 'why did you make your basket round?' for *hayga qinaŋa:baŋ kanmu bayquŋ?* 'why is your basket flatsided?')

These last two techniques were not included with the preceding sets, A-E, F-I, and J, because they apply to only a small number of items in any continuous discourse; and even where they occur, not all sentences are affected.

3. The striking thing about these twelve types of speech modification is not so much their variety as their unexpected frequency in recorded text materials. Linguistic description alone cannot explain either the proliferation or the frequency, and hence one is led to ask with what nonlinguistic cultural features, if any, these practices are correlated. A correct general answer to this inquiry would be simply CUSTOMARY COURTING BEHAVIOR. And as might be expected, the most frequent users of these techniques are those Hanunóo occupying the status of marriageable but unmarried youth, a combined marital-status-and-age-group category called *layqaw* (or *balwas*).

If one divides the society into three groups—pre-*layqaw*, and post-*layqaw*—it is easy to demonstrate a positive correlation between such language play and the *layqaw* status position. I have shown this in Table 1 by plotting the occurrence of modified speech conversations

TABLE 1

INCIDENCE OF HANUNÓO LINGUISTIC PLAY

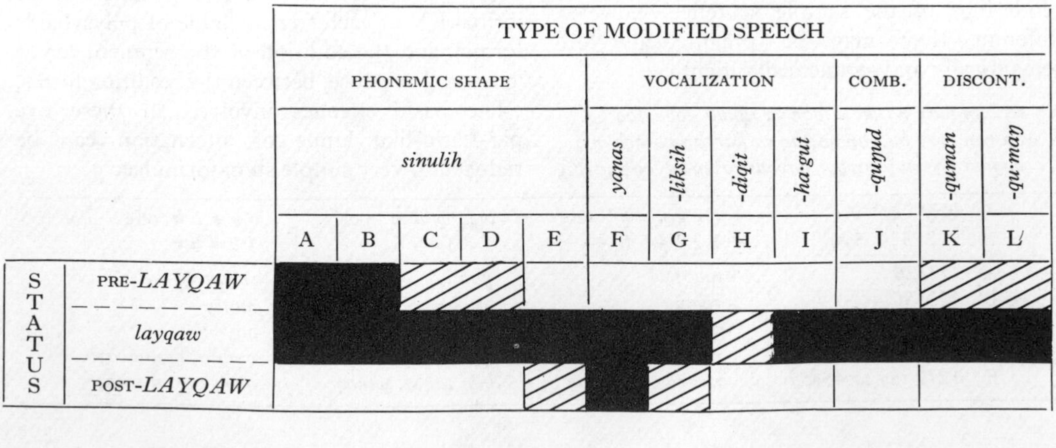

	TYPE OF MODIFIED SPEECH											
	PHONEMIC SHAPE					VOCALIZATION				COMB.	DISCONT.	
	sinulih					*yanas*	*-liksih*	*-diqit*	*-ha·gut*	*-quruŋd*	*-quman*	*-qu·maŋ*
	A	B	C	D	E	F	G	H	I	J	K	L/
STATUS: PRE-*LAYQAW*												
STATUS: *layqaw*												
STATUS: POST-*LAYQAW*												

recorded during a year's field study. On this chart, blank spaces indicate nonoccurrence, solid filled-in areas indicate continuous or very frequent occurrence, single-hatched areas indicate sporadic or infrequent occurrence (less than five recorded instances in each case). Monolexemically delimited Hanunóo categories are labeled in lower-case italics (an initial hyphen indicating that the following is the stem of the full label).

In describing the specific circumstances under which these types occur it will help to review first those sections of Hanunóo ethnography which deal with courting and the roles associated with the *layqaw* status.

The Hanunóo are pagan jungle farmers living in small hamlets dispersed over a mountainous area of about 800 square kilometers in southern Mindoro, in the Philippines. Their society is predominantly egalitarian, loosely stratified, weakly integrated politically, and structured primarily by the principles of ambilateral descent and the neighborhoodlike organization of local groups. The independent nuclear or polygamous family is the only corporate kin group; it is also normally equivalent to the basic residential and economic unit.

Marriage is traditionally proscribed within the bounds of personally-focused, bilateral, kindredlike categories, which are maximally extended to include all of Ego's consanguineals, their spouses, and the consanguineals of the latter (if not previously more closely related). Because the members of Hanunóo settlements are usually linked by close bonds of cognatic kinship and the population of Hanunóo hamlets is small (usually less than 50), this prohibition results in strict local exogamy at the hamlet level. However, a marked tendency toward regional endogamy at higher levels leads to frequent intrakindred marriages, requiring ritual cleansing, for which the payment is commensurate with the closeness of the kin tie. There is no formal wedding rite or bride price, though marriage is usually preceded by a long period of courting and bride service, and followed by at least initial uxorilocality.

While most economic specializations in Hanunóo culture are subsidiary to their system of subsistence agriculture, or dependent upon it, many if not most noneconomic activities (including music, art, and literature) center around their patterns of premarital courtship and the associated *layqaw* roles of *kanqakan*, young marriageable male, and *dara:gah*, the female counterpart. To perform these roles fully and successfully Hanunóo youths must (1) have their eyebrows shaved and their teeth filed and blackened, wear decorative garments and beads in a very tight fashion, and use abundant amounts of fragrant herbs and perfumes; (2) be extremely agile and quick in household chores, in preparing betel quids, and in other body movements; (3) know how to make and play one or more of the traditional musical instruments used in serenading; (4) memorize as large a repertory as possible of chanted verses used in courting; (5) learn the Hanunóo syllabary, of which the main use is to record and hence facilitate the memorizing of such verses; (6) attend all socioreligious feasts, occasions on which serenading contests are held and *layqaw* from distant settlements gather; (7) master the art of facile, rapid conversation, in which the highest value is placed on the most indirect method of statement; and (8) engage in nightly courting activities, preferably in small, often elevated sleeping-houses built expressly for such purposes.

Courting involves the traveling of *kanqakan*, singly or in small groups, to other hamlets where *dara:gah* are known to live. On arrival, which is usually after most of the settlement is asleep, the *kanqakan* remain outside the unlit house, playing their stringed instruments and engaging the *dara:gah* in conversation, asking for betel ingredients, and waiting for an invitation to enter. They conceal their identity by wearing a blanket over the head and by speaking in a unusual manner. If the girl's parents or other suitors are present, and especially if a known close kin tie exists between the *dara:gah* and the newly arrived *kanqakan*, this concealment is particularly advisable. Once indoors, an extended exchange of metaphorical lyrics ensues, chanted to the intermittent accompaniment of flute, jew's-harp, or rebablike violin. If the visit is not an initial one, there may also be an exchange of decorated betel containers, embroidered shirts, neckbeads, or other gifts. If no difficulty develops, the couples lie down next to each other on sleeping mats provided by the *dara:gah* and continue the serenading for several hours until they stop to sleep, converse quietly, or engage in sexual play, the extent of which is usually a measure of the degree of intimacy achieved on previous visits. The *kanqakan* pack up their blankets, herbs, and spears, arrows, or swaggersticks (for protection against jealous suitors), and head for their own settlement before the rest of the *dara:gah*'s hamlet is awake.

Both *kanqakan* and *dara:gah* are expected to participate in this kind of activity maximally until marriage. They are allowed great freedom of movement and are approvingly encouraged, jostled, and teased by elders and by younger siblings alike, with reference to all manner of courting experiences. The highest and most prominent structure in a settlement is usually that made exclusively for *layqaw*. In short, to be admired as a real *kanqakan* or *dara:gah* is the acme of Hanunóo social existence.

The importance of this cultural focus is accentuated by a high degree of role anticipation and considerable role regression, as is typified most dramatically at any socioreligous feast. Here everyone dresses and appears to act as if he or she were a young dandy or a marriageable maiden, irrespective of actual age-group or other status affiliations. Although speech disguise and skill in other forms of linguistic play remain the specialty of the *layqaw*, courting instruments are carried by elders and youngsters alike. A small girl may compete with her older siblings and grandparents in a dancing and gong-beating contest, while a mother of four may surpass a young *kanqakan* in the latter's own game—repartee in chanted allegoric verse.

4. Against this cultural background, it is now possible to state more precisely the circumstances under which the previously noted forms of speech modification occur.

The first four types of *sinulih* (A, B, C, D) are used primarily among *layqaw* in daytime conversations for amusement and as a test of their ability to avoid or obscure direct statements, especially in the presence of eavesdropping kinsmen. One learns these techniques in early adolescence but only *layqaw* have been observed to use them productively. Elders occasionally object to excessive use of these forms of *sinulih* in their presence. The fifth *sinulih* type (E) differs from the first four in that it is used particularly to hide speech content from younger associates, and requires a knowledge of the Hanunóo script. This is actually a form of ORAL SPELLING. In other words, *ququ tag sa sasaq* can be translated literally as 'the-character-for-/qu(C)/ followed by the-character-for-/sa(C)/' in one context, and as 'one (i.e., *qusah*)' in another. It is used most often by younger *layqaw* who have only recently mastered the syllabary.

Hushed, barely audible *yanas* (F) is a simple technique perfected by *layqaw* in nocturnal courting situations in crowded surroundings. Fast *paliksih* (G) is perhaps the most common, the almost constant trademark of *layqaw* speech. It parallels neatly the high positive value placed on physical, i.e., bodily, agility. Frequently it is combined with types of *sinulih* voice disguise. When used alone it serves less to hide than to identify the speaker as a full-fledged *layqaw*. Some individuals continue to practice *paliksih* even after marriage. High-pitched, falsetto *padiqitun* (H) is rare. The only recorded cases show it to be a substitute for *paha:gut* (I) where the speaker was incapable of producing the latter. *Paha:gut*, finally, is the most effective means of voice disguise known to the Hanunóo. It is used exclusively by *layqaw*, and only during the initial stages of courting when maximum concealment of the speaker's identity is required. This technique parallels the *kanqakan*'s use of a blanket head covering as described above.

Combinations (J) of these nine techniques occur only in courting contexts where the *layqaw* involved desire secrecy or disguise.

The other two forms of linguistic play, *qinuman* (K) and *pinaqu:maŋ* (L) are used either for simple amusement (as in the humorous distortion of people's names or common phrases) or for the same reasons as noted above for *paliksih* (G). All groups sometimes participate, but *layqaw* are the most frequent users.

5. In analyzing their initially recognized high correlation with courtship behavior it has now been possible to place these speech modifications within the context of the total culture, and to show how an apparently esoteric part of language description may help to define a major status differentiation within the wider social structure. In summary, and within this wider frame of reference, these types of linguistic play and the ability to use them can be considered important and sometimes criterial attributes of the culturally prominent, complementary roles of *dara:gah* and *kanqakan*.

REFERENCE NOTE

The materials analyzed in this paper were recorded in 1952-1954, and checked in 1957. During these periods the author was engaged in ethnographic and linguistic field work, facilitated by grants from the Social Science Research Council, the Ford Foundation, the National Science Foundation, and the Columbia University Council for Research in the Social Sciences.

The consonants in Hanunóo are *p, t, k, b, d, g, m, n, ŋ, l, r, s, h, q, y, w*; of these, *q* is the glottal catch. The vowels are *i, u, a*. Vowel length is indicated by (:). All C (consonants) occur singly between vowels and in syllable-initial or in syllable-final position, with the following exceptions: *q, h* do not occur before C, and *y,w* do not occur in syllable-final position after *i, u* respectively.

Of general accounts of SPEECH PLAY among particular groups, note especially Arnott (1957), Freud (1938, pp. 35-178), Lowie (1914; 1935, pp. xviii-xx, 104-118), and the series of papers by Simmons (1955b, etc., listed here; 1960a; 1960c). The *pun* has received a certain amount of attention cross-culturally; note Emeneau (1948), Hoa (1955), Pike (1945a, 1946), Quirk (1951), Sapir (1932), Simmons (1955b), and cf. Pike (1945b) and Susman (1941). On both speech play and puns particularly, see Cohen (1956a, pp. 116, 226-269). *Humor* in language has been discussed in general by Estrich and Sperber (1952, chap. 15), and Freud (1938, pp. 633-803); it has been discussed with reference to specific nonliterate groups by W. W. Hill (1943), Jacobs (1960), and Skeels (1954a, 1954b). Speech play in the form of *verbal contest* has been described for the ancient Aryans by Kuiper (1960), cf. Renou (1960); for the Eskimo by Chamberlain (1910); for Hawaii by Beckwith (1922); for Mexican-Americans by Romano V. (1960); and for the Waiwai by Fock (1958). For general literature and principles, see also Cohen (1956a, pp. 252-253, 260-261) and Radcliffe-Brown (1949).

Conklin (1956) presents an exemplary description of a specific pattern of speech modification, the most complex such pattern so far adequately analyzed, one used for purposes of concealment. On the principles of analysis of such patterns, see Halle (1962, section 5). Other forms of linguistic concealment are involved in the articles in this part by Cowan, Herzog, and Newman and Gayton, and some of the references thereto. On such generally, see especially the references on argot, slang, and the like to Newman's article in Part VII. References on games are cited with Haas' article and on genres such as riddle, proverb, and the like with the article by Shimkin. See also part (E) of the reference note to Tragers' article in Part V, pp. 274-288.

References not in the general bibliography:

ARNOTT, D. W.

1957. Proverbial Lore and Word-play of the Fulani. *Africa, 27* (4): 379-396.

CHAMBERLAIN, A. F. C.

1910. Nith-songs. In F. W. Hodge (Ed.), *Handbook of American Indians North of Mexico*. (BAE-B 30.) Washington, D.C.: Smithsonian Institution. Part Two, p. 77.

EMENEAU, M. B.

1948. Homonyms and Puns in Annamese. *Lg., 23:* 239-44.

HOA, NGUYEN ĐINH

1955. Double Puns in Vietnamese, A Case of "Linguistic Play." *Word*, *11*: 237-244.

JACOBS, MELVILLE

1960. Humor and Social Structure in an Oral Literature. In Stanley A. Diamond (Ed.), *Culture in History*. New York: Columbia University Press. Pp. 181-189.

KUIPER, F. B. J.

1960. The Ancient Aryan Verbal Contest. *Indo-Iranian Journal*, *4*.

LOWIE, ROBERT H.

1914. Crow Rapid Speech Puzzles. *JAF*, *27*: 330-331.

1935. *The Crow Indians*. New York: Rinehart.

PIKE, K. L.

1945a. Tone Puns in Mixteco. *IJAL*, *11*: 129-139.

1945b. Mock Spanish of a Mixteco Indian. *IJAL*, *11*: 219-229.

1946. Another Mixteco Tone Pun. *IJAL*, *12*: 22-24.

QUIRK, RANDOLPH

1951. Puns to Sell. *Studia Neophilologica*, *23*: 81-86.

RADCLIFFE-BROWN, A. R.

1949. A Further Note on Joking Relationships. *Africa*, *19*: 133-140.

RENOU, LOUIS

1960. The Enigma in the Ancient Literature of India. *Diogenes*, *29*: 32-41.

ROMANO V., OCTAVIO IGNACIO

1960. Donship in a Mexican-American Community in Texas. *AA*, *62*: 966-976.

SAPIR, E.

1932. Two Navaho Puns. *Lg.*, *8*: 217-219.

SIMMONS, DONALD C.

1955b. Specimens of Efik Folklore. *Folklore*, *66*: 417-424.

1956a. Efik Riddles. *The Nigerian Field*, *21*: 168-171.

1956b. Erotic Ibibio Tone Riddles. *Man*, *56* (Article 78).

1958a. Efik Games. *Folklore*, *69*: 26-33.

1958b. Cultural Functions of the Efik Tone Riddle. *JAF*, *71*: 123-138.

1960b. Ibibio Topical Ballads. *Man*, *60* (Article 73).

SKEELS, DELL

1954a. A Classification of Humor in Nez Perce Mythology. *JAF*, *67*: 57-64.

1954b. The Function of Humor in Three Nez Perce Indian Myths. *American Imago*, *11*: 248-261.

SUSMAN, A.

1941. Word Play in Winnebago. *Lg.*, *17*: 342-344.

Thai Word Games 34

MARY R. HAAS

THAI SCHOOLCHILDREN between the ages of ten and eighteen often amuse themselves by playing games based upon a knowledge of words or vocabulary. There are two principal types of games. The first type may be called the Identical Initial Syllable Game and is based upon a knowledge of Thai words only. The second type may be called the Rhyming Translation Game since it is a game in which each successive Thai word must rhyme with the English translation of the preceding word. Or it may be played by starting with an English word and then each successive English word must rhyme with the Thai translation of the preceding English word.

The first type of game is particularly popular with younger children whose vocabulary in Thai is still somewhat limited. It is a good game to be played when it is raining outdoors or when the children prefer to sit and talk instead of exercising. The second type of game, since it is more complicated and involves a knowledge of two languages, is more likely to be preferred by the older children.

The principal purpose of both games is to enlarge the children's vocabulary, the first in Thai, the second in English. But more immediate incentives are also often provided in the form of a reward for the winner and penalties for the losers. The first loser is the first one who fails to supply an additional word when his turn comes around. One after another of the players drops out and the last child left is the winner. A penalty for the loser or losers is usually decided upon in advance. A loser may have to wash the dishes or clean up the room for the winner. Or perhaps he has to drink a bottle of water or sing a song. Another type of penalty permits the winner to knock on the knees of the loser for five or ten times, depending on what has been stipulated in advance.

The Identical Initial Syllable Game is considered easier than the Rhyming Translation Game and it is most often played by younger children as an aid to enlarging their vocabulary in their own language. The game always involves Thai disyllabic, or less commonly, polysyllabic words. Thai has many disyllabic words beginning in syllables like *ka-*, *kra-*, *kha-*, *pra-*, *ta-*, *tha-*, *ma-*, *ra-*, *la-*, *wi-*, *sa-*, and *ʔa-*. (If these syllables are pronounced in isolation, that is, other than as the first syllables of longer words, they are pronounced as *kàʔ*, *kràʔ*, *khàʔ*, *pràʔ*, *tàʔ*, *tháʔ*, *máʔ*, *ráʔ*, *láʔ*, *wíʔ*, *sàʔ*, *and ʔàʔ*.) Therefore the game can be played many times without any repetition of vocabulary items involved. The child who starts the game has the advantage of being able to select a word beginning in a syllable which he favors. If he starts out with a word like *sabaaj* 'to be well, comfortable,' the other player must quickly start thinking of other words beginning in *sa-*, e.g., *sabùu* 'soap,' *sadùag* 'to be convenient,' *sadɛɛŋ* 'to show,' *saʔàad* 'to be clean,' *sadùd* 'to stumble,' etc.

Sometimes further refinements are introduced to make the game more interesting and also more difficult. Of the literally dozens of Thai words which begin in the syllable *kra-*, only a limited number refer to birds and animals. To make the game more exciting, then, the children may limit the permitted words to those which have this type of reference, e.g., *kracɔ̀ɔg* 'sparrow,' *kratàaj* 'rabbit,' *krarɔ̂ɔg* 'squirrel,' *krasǎa* 'heron,' *krabyy* 'water buffalo,' etc. Other types of words beginning in *kra-*, such as *krapǎw* 'pocket,' *kradàad* 'paper,' *kradùug* 'bone,' *krasǔn* 'bullet,' etc., would not be permissible. (Terms referring to birds are normally preceded by the word *nóg* 'bird.' Hence one would normally say *nógkracɔ̀ɔg* 'sparrow,' and *nógkrasǎa* 'heron.' For the purposes of this variety of the Identical Initial Syllable Game, however, the term *nóg* is dropped. The names of the animals are not preceded by any generalizing term.)

Another popular game consists in trying to think of words which begin in the syllable *ma-* and refer to plants or trees bearing edible fruit. One reason for the popularity of this game is that there are a large number of words which come in this category and so the game can be kept going longer. (The syllable *ma-* [*máʔ*] as the first syllable of the name of a tree or plant bearing edible fruit is actually, etymologically speaking, a generalizing term referring to edible fruits, and that is why there are so many words beginning in this syllable which come in this category. Compare the use of *nóg*.) Examples are *mamûaŋ* 'mango,' *makhyǎ* 'eggplant,' *makhǎam* 'tamarind,' *maphráaw* 'coconut,' *maráʔ* 'bitter melon,' *manaaw* 'lemon, lime,' *madỳa* 'fig,' etc. This variety of the game is sometimes brought to an end in a way peculiar to it alone. The child who can think of no more names of fruits beginning in *ma-* says *maŋèeg*. This is not the name of a fruit but a threat to knock someone on the head. As the losing player utters this word he holds up his clenched fist in a threatening gesture. The winner, however, still exacts whatever penalty was agreed upon, e.g., knocking upon the knees of the loser.

A more difficult variety of the Identical Initial Syllable Game involves words beginning in the syllable *cam-*. Words beginning in this syllable are mostly elegant and learned and literary, and many of them would not be known to Thai children until they have entered a more advanced stage in their study of their own language. (Most, if not all of them, are probably of Cambodian origin.) There is no semantic limitation set when playing the game with this syllable. Since the semantic categories of the words beginning in *cam-* are quite varied, such a limitation would not be feasible. Examples are: *camnuan* 'amount, quantity,' *camnáb* 'to overtake, arrest,' *camphûag* 'species, kind,' *camdəəm* 'origin, originally,' *camləəj* 'defendant,' *camrəən* 'to improve,' *camrúʔ* 'to be beautiful' (rare and literary), etc.

Older children who have begun the study of English are more likely to amuse themselves by playing the Rhyming Translation Game. The one who starts the game again has a certain advantage since he may begin either in Thai or in English, though both languages are involved no matter which language is used in starting. If he chooses Thai, he gives a Thai word and its English translation. The next player must produce another Thai word which rhymes with the English translation of the first word. The game then proceeds in this fashion until only one player is left. An example of the way the game may be played when starting with Thai is as follows:

1st player:	'*kòb*'	*plɛɛwâa*	(means)	'frog'
2nd player:	'*hɔ̀ɔg*'	"	"	'spear'
3rd player:	'*mia*'	"	"	'wife'
4th player:	'*hâj*'	"	"	'give'

For variety the game may also be played by starting out in English. An example of this method of playing is as follows:

1st player:	'eat'	*plɛɛwâa*	(means)	'*kin*'
2nd player:	'sin'	"	"	'*bàab*'
3rd player:	'harp'	"	"	'*phin*'
4th player:	'fin'	"	"	'*khrîib*'

Perfect rhymes between two different languages are often difficult if not impossible to achieve. And the reader unfamiliar with Thai phonetics may be puzzled by one or two points involved in the rhymes occuring in the examples cited. English "spear" can be rhymed with Thai *mia* because the Thai vowel cluster *ia* is very close in sound to the British pronunciation of *-ear*, *-ere*, etc. English "wife" can be rhymed with Thai *hâj* because in Thai only one consonant can stand in syllable-final position and it would therefore be impossible to find any closer rhyme in Thai. (When English words are borrowed into Thai they also conform to this same pattern. Thus the English word "mile" has been borrowed into Thai as *maj*.)

Both types of games, besides providing amusement for the children who play them, are also of considerable educational value. It is easy to see why the Rhyming Translation Game is preferred by older children. It obviously requires considerably more skill and quicker thinking than the Identical Syllable Game. In the latter game the child with a good memory can plan ahead and think up a large number of words beginning in the chosen syllable while the other players are giving their words. In the Rhyming Translation Game, on the other hand, it is impossible to plan ahead. Therefore the best player will be the one who has a large enough vocabulary in English to be able to come up with a rhyming word on a moment's notice.

REFERENCE NOTE

The author's first information about Thai word games was obtained more than ten years ago from Ubol Huvanandana, who also supplied examples of words used in the Identical Initial Syllable Game. Additional information, particularly about the Rhyming Translation Game, was given to her by Waiwit Buddhari, who was working as Thai Linguistic Informant on the Thai Dictionary Project, Institute of East Asian Studies, University of California, Berkeley. He also provided examples of words used in the Rhyming Translation Game.

The Thai consonants are voiced stops *b*, *d*, *-g;* voiceless unaspirated stops *p*, *t*, *c* (palatal stop), *k*'; voiceless aspirated stops *ph*, *th*, *ch*, *kh;* voiceless spirants *f*, *s*, *h;* voiced semivowels *j*, [*y*], *w;* voiced nasals *m*, *n*, *ŋ;* voiced liquids *l*, *r*. The vowels are front unrounded *i*, *e*, *ε* [*æ̂*]; central unrounded *y*, [*ɨ*], *ə*, *a*; back rounded *ɔ'n o*. All nine of these vowels may occur doubled (phonetically lengthened), e.g., *ii*, *ee*, *εε*, etc., and the heterophonous vowel clusters *ia*, *ya*, *ua* also occur. There are five tones: middle (unmarked), low (\`), falling (ˆ), high (ʹ), and rising (ˇ). For further information, see Haas (1955).

The latest and most extensive treatment of CHILDREN'S GAMES AND SPEECH PLAY in English is Opie and Opie (1959); for an estimate of the significance of the Opies' work, see Whiting (1961). Among the many accounts of children's games and speech play in other parts of the world, those of Best (1925), Sutton-Smith (1959a), and Brewster (1951) for New Zealand may be singled out, since together they treat the indigenous tradition, the imported cultural tradition, and the interaction of the two; see also Brewster's review (1961) of Sutton-Smith (1959a). Aufenanger (1958) may also be cited. In general, one should consult the invaluable "Annual Bibliography of Folklore" compiled by W. Edson Richmond, and published in the Supplement to the *Journal of American Folklore*.

Among more recent studies on general theory, classification, and interpretation, see Caillois (1955, 1957, 1961) and Goffman (1961); Keri (1958) and Roheim (1943) give psychological interpretations; Höfer (1954) compares children's speech with standard speech and hints of ritual origin of games throughout; Roberts, Arth, and Bush (1959) test the hypothesis that favored type of game (strategy, chance, skill) correlates with type of culture and socialization process, the favorite types of game being considered as expressive exercises in mastery of the social system, the supernatural, and the self or environment, respectively; Sutton-Smith (1959b) gives a sociological analysis; and Roberts and Sutton-Smith (1962) extend the classification of Roberts, *et al.* (1959) and add conflict as a dimension of interpretation. On the general problem of interpenetration of verbal and nonverbal behavior, Browne (1955) has methodological interest, classifying verbal behavior (jump-rope rhymes) according to motor habits (jumping pattern).

References not in the general bibliography:

AUFENANGER, H.

1958. Children's Games and Entertainments Among the Kumongo Tribe in Central New Guinea. *Anthropos*, *53* (3-4): 575-584.

BEST, ELSDON

1925. *Games and Pastimes of the Maori.* Wellington: Whitcombe and Tombs.

BREWSTER, PAUL L.

1951. The Meeting of Maori and European Cultures and Its Effects Upon the Unorganized Games of Maori Children. *Journal of the Polynesian Society, 60:* 93-107.

1961. Review of B. Sutton-Smith, *The Games of New Zealand Children. JAF, 74:* 83-85.

BROWNE, RAY B.

1955. Southern California Jump-Rope Rhymes: A Study in Variants. *Western Folklore, 14:* 3-22.

CAILLOIS, ROGER

1955. The Structure and Classification of Games. *Diogenes, 12:* 62-75.

1957. Unity of Play: Diversity of Games. *Diogenes, 19:* 92-121.

1961. *Man, Play, and Games.* Glencoe: Free Press.

GOFFMAN, ERVING

1961. Fun in Games. *Encounters. Two Studies in the Sociology of Interaction.* Indianapolis: Bobbs-Merrill. Pp. 17-81.

HAAS, MARY R.

1955. *The Thai System of Writing.* Washington, D.C.: American Council of Learned Societies.

HÖFER, LEOPOLD

1954. Notizen zur Wiener Kindersprache. *Österreichische Zeitschrift für Volkskunde, 8:* 33-42.

KERI, HEDVIG

1958. Ancient Games and Popular Games: Psychological Essay. *The American Imago, 15* (1): 41-89.

ROBERTS, JOHN M., MALCOLM J. ARTH, ROBERT B. BUSH

1959. Games in Culture. *AA, 61* (4): 597-605.

ROHEIM, GÉZA

1943. Children's Games and Rhymes in Duau (Normandy Island). *AA, 45:* 99-119.

SUTTON-SMITH, BRIAN

1959a. *The Games of New Zealand Children.* (University of California Folklore Studies, No. 12.) Berkeley and Los Angeles: University of California Press.

1959b. A Formal Analysis of Game Meaning. *Western Folklore, 18* (1): 13-24.

WHITING, BEATRICE

1961. Review of I. Opie and P. Opie, *The Lore and Language of Schoolchildren. JAF, 74:* 278-279.

Mazateco Whistle Speech 35

GEORGE M. COWAN

1. THE PURPOSE of this paper is to describe a highly developed but little known type of communication as practised by the Mazateco Indians of Oaxaca, Mexico. The texts presented show the importance of tone in the language, and indicate that conversation can be carried on with a very wide range of lexical possibilities without the segmental phonemes of normal speech. The Mazatecos frequently converse by whistling to one another. The whistles are not merely signals with limited semantic value arrived at by common agreement, but are parallel to spoken conversations as a means of communication. Eusebio Martinez was observed one day standing in front of his hut, whistling to a man a considerable distance away. The man was passing on the trail below, going to market to sell a load of corn leaves which he was carrying. The man answered Eusebio's whistle with a whistle. The interchange was repeated several times with different whistles. Finally the man turned around, retraced his steps a short way and came up the footpath to Eusebio's hut. Without saying a word he dumped his load on the ground. Eusebio looked the load over, went into his hut, returned with some money, and paid the man his price. The man turned and left. Not a word had been spoken. They had talked, bargained over the price, and come to an agreement satisfactory to both parties—using only whistles as a medium of communication.

2. Whistled conversations correspond very closely to spoken conversations. When asked what a person "said" when he whistled, the natives will respond with a very specific and literal rendering in the spoken language. The spoken Mazateco equivalents of the whistled texts which appear below are the exact translations given by the informant himself. When the whistled texts were checked later with Fortino Cortés from Huautla de Jiménez, and a translation into spoken Mazateco was obtained, the translations were identical.

In distinction from this conversational whistling, whistles are also used as signals to animals. When driving burros or mules on the trail the Mazateco Indians use a slow, upgliding whistle to keep the animals in motion (§13, text 1). They call their dogs by whistling (§13, text 2). But for these whistled signals they can give no equivalent in the spoken language. They are signals, nothing more.

3. Only males whistle. Boys learn to whistle almost as soon as they learn to talk. They cannot tell when they first began to talk with whistles. Until middle age they use whistling constantly. Old men have seldom been heard whistling conversationally. Women have never been heard whistling except on one occasion when the subject of whistling was under discussion. There were no native men present to illustrate, so Herlinda Martinez de Concha, one of the native women, undertook to show how it was done by whistling a commonly used whistle phrase. It was so completely unnatural to her that she was quite embarrassed when she heard herself.

But the women, although they do not whistle themselves, understand what is whistled by the men. (The Mazateco language is homogeneous so far as sex is concerned, there being no difference between the speech of men and of women.) One day Chumi was standing idly in the doorway of our hut. Irene Flores was working around the hut. No one, it seemed, was paying any attention to the quiet, random whistlings of the boy so nonchalantly leaning against the doorpost. All of a sudden however, Irene whirled and launched out in a terrific scolding in spoken Mazateco. The whistling had not been as aimless and innocuous as it appeared. The mischievous boy had actually been whistling very meaningful things to the girl, until she could stand the teasing no more. (Observed and reported by Eunice V. Pike, Summer Institute of Linguistics.)

Ordinarily men and boys whistle only to other men or boys. The exceptions to this are rare; but, as indicated in the paragraph above, they do occur. Such taunting or teasing is not in the nature of the American "wolf call" so far as the whistle itself is concerned, but is an actual whistled phrase which the girls understand and to which they will give a spoken reply, if they deign to pay any attention to it all. Another exception to the general custom occurs when young boys whistle a reply to their mothers' spoken summons (§13, text 3).

4. Occasions. The most frequent occasion for whistling is perhaps in speaking at a distance, when the spoken words would perhaps not carry as well. Men scattered widely over a mountainside, each working in his own plot of ground, will often talk to one another with whistles. Travelers on the trails will keep in touch with one another by whistling, though separated by considerable distance.

When wishing to call or get the attention of someone, even though he be within easy speaking distance, the Mazatecos will often whistle his name. The village shoemaker often calls passersby into his shop with a whistle to chat with him while he works. A man may come to a friend's hut on a visit. While approaching or when he has actually arrived at the door of the hut, he will frequently whistle rather than call his friend's name. If the friend is at home, he may respond from within with a whistle, then come out to greet his visitor, or he may remain inside and whistle to his visitor to come in (§13, text 4).

When wishing to converse without disturbing or interfering with the spoken conversation of their elders, boys will chatter back and forth in whistles. Not once but several times in my hearing, in a room full of talking or singing people, the young boys, quite oblivious to what was going on around them, have talked back and forth across the room, not in whispers, but in subdued whistles. On similar occasions boys have been heard carrying on a whistled conversation with other boys outside, coaxing them to come in and join in the fun. The whistles were clearly audible, yet did not seem to interfere particularly with the adult conversation or singing in progress at the time. (On one occasion Eusebio Martínez was talking with Erasto Jiménez, a local carpenter of Huautla de Jiménez. Erasto talked so steadily that Eusebio was unable to interrupt and make his contribution to the conversation. He was observed, however, humming very abbreviated remarks into the conversation while Erasto kept on talking aloud—apparently without noticeable interference with Erasto's flow of speech.)

Much less frequently they whistle for secrecy. In the presence of a non-Mazateco, they have been heard making softly whistled asides to one another, even though the stranger would probably not have understood them had they spoken.

A Mazateco will whistle a warning to others when he sees strangers approaching. Whole villages as well as workers in the fields along the trail will thus be alerted and informed that someone is coming, long before the traveler actually puts in an appearance.

5. Frequency. Whistling may be heard daily, if not hourly, from early dawn until late at night. In a journey of but three or four hours, if the day is bright and sunny and the workers are in their fields, one may hear dozens of snatches of whistled conversation.

6. Distances whistled. Two men within a few feet of each other may whistle rather than speak. As mentioned above, they will whistle from within to a person just outside their hut. Men working in the fields may whistle to travelers passing on trails several hundred feet above or below. They whistle across the valley bottom to laborers a quarter of a mile away on the opposite mountainside. So far as is known, the distance whistled is limited only by the actual carrying-power of the whistle and the acuteness of their ears to hear.

7. Duration. Whistled conversations may consist of a single question and a single answer (§13, text 5). Dialogs have been recorded up to six or seven exchanges between two parties (thirteen separate utterances: §13, text 14). Conversations have been heard lasting perhaps

as long as three minutes. The single utterances tend to be short. So far as the actual whistling is concerned, there is no known reason why single utterances could not be much longer, nor why whistled dialogs could not continue indefinitely.

8. There are no known LEXICAL LIMITATIONS. (George Herzog, speaking of similar phenomena in the African drum calls, says: "On some signalling instruments communication is restricted to a limited number of signals, perhaps from ten to fifty; on others there is practically unlimited conversation between two players over a long distance. That this should be feasible with the apparently restricted means of the system, and with the great number of words sharing the same pitch, can easily be, and has been, doubted; especially since in West African languages, as in Chinese, the majority of the words consist of only one syllable. It would lead us too far afield, however, to go into detail on the question within the frame of this article. I must be content merely with testifying that it is done" [1934, pp. 455-456].) An informant trained to whistle out of natural context can upon request whistle without hesitation any utterance or fraction thereof that can be spoken independently. Quite frequently Fortino Cortés, who is such an informant, upon hearing me use a wrong tone in speaking Mazateco, has corrected me on the spot by simply whistling the correct tones. Even untrained informants, given a natural context, can whistle any given word. The limitations with such untrained informants are no more than those found in the spoken language. Although small boys, when asked to whistle some particular phrase, may reply "I can't," this indicates, not a lexical limitation as such, but a vocabulary limitation due to age; for given the spoken phrase, they can and will whistle it (observed by Eunice V. Pike).

9. AMBIGUITIES. Many words and phrases in Mazateco have identical tonal patterns. In the spoken language segmental phonemes usually distinguish tonally identical words and phrases. In the whistled language the absence of the segmental features gives opportunity for ambiguities, provided the context will permit two or more of the possible meanings.

The whistling of proper names is one of the most frequent causes of ambiguity. Once, when a whistled conversation was in progress with several boys participating, confusion arose as to who was calling whom. The boys openly admitted the difficulty, and one of them who had worked as an informant and was analytically conscious of tone in his language explained that several names had identical tonal patterns (observed by Eunice V. Pike). This stems from the fact that the Mazatecos use Spanish names, and the assimilation of Spanish words and names to the Mazateco tonal system follows a very definite pattern. The stressed syllable of the Spanish word becomes semi-high in tone, syllables preceding the stressed syllable become semi-low, syllables following the stressed-syllable become low. The words loses its Spanish stress and takes a Mazateco stress on the last syllable of the word. Thus names such as *Modesto*, *Gustavo*, *Frederico*, and *Ricardo* would all take an identical tone pattern: semi-low, semi-high, low. There is no way, aside from the context of the company present, to tell which name is being whistled.

In spite of the probability of ambiguity, the actual instances where confusion occurs are amazingly few. This is due to the fact that whistling is most frequently (though not necessarily) concerned with topics immediately obvious to both parties to the conversation, and used in situations where cultural context plays a much greater part than in the spoken language.

A large proportion of Mazateco whistled conversations begin with one of a rather limited number of topics. An easily identifiable cultural context is thus quickly established, and the possibility of ambiguities is at once reduced. Some of these lead-off whistles are: "Come here" (§13, text 4), "Where are you going?" (§13, texts 7.A, 9.A), "Where are you coming from?" (§13, text 6.A), "What are you doing?" (§13, texts 10.A1, 11.A1, 12.A1), and "What are you carrying?" (§13, text 14.A1). Farewells have been heard at the conclusion of whistled conversations (§13, text 9.A5), but the customary opening greetings and salutations of spoken conversations have not yet been heard.

10. Culturally, whistling is treated as a natural and integral part of conversation. What begins as a whistled conversation at a distance may conclude as a spoken one as the two parties draw closer together. In this case the usual formal greetings that serve as preludes to

spoken conversations may be ignored in passing from whistling to speaking, or the conversation may be interrupted by spoken greetings, thereafter proceeding from where it was interrupted at the termination of the whistling.

11. The whistle is obviously based upon the spoken language. It follows the same tonal system with regard both to registers and to lexically, morphologically, and syntactically significant glides. In one respect only do the glides of the whistle differ from the glides of the spoken language. In rapid whistling, the tones of two separate syllables of speech at times appear as a lengthened glide from the tone of the first syllable to the tone of the second. Thus, in §13, text 9.B2, the spoken form *-hmi^{3}-hą^{1}* appears in the whistle as a lengthened 3-1 glide; in text 3 *hme^{1}-ni^{3}* appears as a lengthened 1-3 glide (but not in text 13); and in text 5.A, *hme^{1}-kʔoa^{4}-* appears as a lengthened 1-4 glide. This phenomenon never occurs in speech, regardless of speed. Similarly, two successive syllables of speech with the same tone may appear in the whistle as a single lengthened punch; thus, in text 14.A7, the spoken form *čhi^{1}-nko^{1}* is represented by such a punch on tone 1. With these exceptions, every whistle punch (or syllable) corresponds to one syllable of the spoken language.

In both types of speech, the main word-stress falls on the last syllable of the stem. Both have stress-timed sentence rhythm. Occasionally, perhaps to ensure clarity over a considerable distance, the whistled utterances become more deliberate, almost syllable-timed. In both, the greater the distance being whistled or spoken, the greater the intensity and the spread between the registers. In both, the key is established by the first speaker. (This is confirmed also by the experience of Eunice V. Pike, who, when first learning to whistle, was not always able to strike the same key as her informant. Her informant, realizing her difficulty, would shift pitch, accommodating his pitch to hers.) Failure to stay in pitch causes difficulty for the other party to the conversation. An utterance, correct as to contour but off-key, may be misunderstood. This is especially true in whistling in contrast to speaking, where the presence of the segmental phonemes helps to establish the basic meaning in spite of the unnaturalness that results from straying from the key. When whistling or shouting long distances, the key is raised. When whistling or speaking over a short distance or in a secretive manner, it is lowered.

12. The Mazateco whistle, so far as has been observed, is always produced bilabially, with quite well rounded and somewhat protruded lips.

13. Texts. Each text is numbered as a separate paragraph. Within each paragraph, the letters A and B represent two different speakers. The successive utterances of each speaker are numbered A1, A2, etc., or B1, B2, etc.

The whistled utterances are cited between square brackets. Tones are represented by numerals from 1 (high) to 4 (low). Individual punches or syllables of whistle are separated by a comma; a medial pause is indicated by a semicolon. A glide from one tone to another is marked with a dash (3-1, 1-3, 2-4, 3-4, etc.). A glide or whistled syllable that is long in duration is marked by a following colon.

1. [3-1, 3-1, 3-1] (call to burro or mule; no spoken equivalent).

2. [1, 3, 1, 3, 1, 3] (call to dog; no spoken equivalent).

3. [1-3:] *hme^{1}-ni^{3}* 'What?'

4. [4, 2-4, 3-4] *ha^{4}-vi$^{2-4}$-ri$^{3-4}$* 'Come here, friend!'

5. A: [1-4:, 2, 3, 3, 3, 3-4] *hme^{1} kʔ oa^{4}-sʔį^{2} khi^{3}-ma^{3}-ni^{3} nthao$^{3-4}$* 'What is there such a wind for?' B: [1, 4, 4] *hɨ̨^{1}-la^{4} kʔoa^{4}* 'It will probably rain.'

6. A: [1, 2, 4, 3] *hña^{1} khoa^{2}ʔ ai^{4}-ni^{3}* 'Where are you coming from?' B: [3, 2, 2, 4, 3] *ni^{3}ʔya^{2} khoa^{2}ʔai^{4}-nia^{3}* 'I am coming from Huautla.'

7. A1: [1, 3, 3, 4] *hña^{1} ti^{3}-ʔmi^{3} ntʔai^{4}* 'Where are you going now?' B1: [4, 2, 3, 4] *i^{4} ti^{2}-vhia^{3}-vi^{4}* 'I am going here.' A2: [3, 2, 2, 3] *ni^{3}ʔya^{2}ti^{2}-vhia^{3}* 'I am going to Huautla.' B2: [1, 3, 2, 4, 3, 4] *ho^{1} čǫ^{3} khoa^{2}ʔai^{4}-ni^{3} sʔai^{4}* 'What time this afternoon will you come?' A3: [2, 3, 4, 2, 4, 3, 3-2, 4, 2, 4] *li^{2}-koi^{3}-la^{4} khoi^{2}ʔe^{4} ʔnta^{3} nčąǫ$^{3-2}$-la^{4} khoi^{2}ʔe^{4}* 'I will probably not come until tomorrow.' B3: [1, 3, 2, 4, 3, 3-2] *ho^{1} čǫ^{3} khoa^{2}ʔ ai^{4}-ni^{3} nčąǫ$^{3-2}$* 'What time tomorrow will you come?' A4: [3, 3, 4, 2, 4] *nči^{3}sę^{3}-la^{4} khoi^{2}ʔe^{4}* 'I will probably come at noon.'

8. A1: [1, 3, 3] *hña^{1} ti^{3}-ʔmi^{3}* 'Where are you going?' B1: [3, 1, 2, 3, 4-3] *či^{3}kį^{1} ti^{2}-vhi^{3}kʔa$^{4-3}$* 'I am going to get firewood.' A2: [2, 3, 2, 3, 1-3] *ɨ̨^{2} khoi^{3}čʔa^{2} či^{3}kį$^{1-3}$* 'Shall we both not go and

get firewood?' B2: [4, 2, 3, 3, 2] *sʔai^{4}-la^{2}-ni^{3} khoi^{3}čʔa^{2}* 'We'll go together later and get it.' A3: [1, 3, 2, 1-3:] *čo^{1}ya^{3}-la^{2}-nai$^{1-3}$* 'Wait for me.' B3: [4, 3, 3-2, 2, 3-4, 3] *to^{4}-nka^{3} he$^{3-2}$-ti^{2}-vhia$^{3-4}$ -ʔni^{3}* 'But I'm already going.' A4: [4, 3, 2, 2, 1, 3, 1 3] *to^{4}-hnko^{3}tho^{3}-la^{2} čo^{1}ya^{3}-nai$^{1-3}$* 'Just a minute wait for me.'

9. A1: [1, 3, 3] *hña^{1} ti^{3}-ʔmi^{3}* 'Where are you going?' B1: [2, 3, 2, 1-3] *ti^{2}-vhi^{3} si^{2}ša$^{1-3}$* 'I am going to work.' A2: [1, 3, 3, 2, 1-4, 3] *hña^{1} ti^{3}-ʔmi^{3}ni^{2}šai$^{1-4}$-ʔni^{3}* 'Where, then, are you going to work?' B2: [1, 1, 3, 3-1:, 2, 3, 2, 1-3] *hą^{1}-nta^{1} šo^{3}hmi^{3}-hą^{1} ti^{2}-vhi^{3}si^{2}ša$^{1-3}$* 'I am going to work there at the spring *šohmi*.' A3: [1, 3, 2, 4] *ho^{1} čǫ^{3} khoa^{2}ʔai^{4}* 'What time will you come?' B3: [2, 2, 4, 2, 4] *kǫą^{1} šǫ^{2}-la^{4} khoi^{2}ʔe^{4}* 'I will come when it is afternoon probably.' A4: [1, 3, 3-4, 3, 3, 2, 4] *hña^{1} ti^{3}-ʔmi$^{3-4}$-ʔni^{3} nka^{3} khoa^{2}ʔai^{4}* 'Where will you go then when you come?' B4: [2, 3, 2, 3] *li^{2}-hña^{3} ti^{2}-vhia^{3}* 'I am going nowhere.' A5: [3, 2, 2, 3-4, 3] *tʔį^{3}la^{2}na ntai$^{3-4}$-ʔni^{3}* 'Well, may you go well then.'

10. A1: [1, 3, 3, 2, 4] *hme^{1} ši^{3} ti^{3}-ñʔąi^{2}-ve^{4}* 'What are you doing there?' B1: [3, 2, 2, 3, 3] *ka^{3}vhe^{2} ti^{2}-va^{3}te^{3}* 'I am picking coffee.' A2: [3, 2, 2, 3, 3-4, 3] *ʔa^{3}-kǫą^{1} nkhį^{2} ti^{3}-li$^{3-4}$-ʔni^{3}* 'Well, have you picked a lot?' B2: [3, 3, 2, 4, 4, 3-2, 3] *sʔa^{1} hnko^{3} la^{2}-ta^{4}-la^{4} ti$^{3-2}$-na^{3}* 'I have probably picked only one *lata*.' A3: [3, 4, 2-3, 3, 3, 2-3, 3, 3, 3, 2-4, 4] *ʔa^{3}-ȼi^{4}-ni$^{2-3}$-ʔni^{3} ka^{3}vhe$^{2-3}$ ši^{3} ti^{3}-vi^{3}čai$^{2-4}$-ve^{4}* 'Is it your own coffee that you are picking there?' B3: [2, 3, 2-3; 4, 4, 2, 3, 4] *li^{2}-ȼʔą^{3}-hią$^{2-3}$ to^{4}-čo^{4}ʔnta^{2} ȼo^{3}ʔva^{4}* 'It is not mine; I am only working as a hired man.'

11. A1: [1, 3, 3, 2-3] *hme^{1} ši^{3} ti^{3}-ñʔąi$^{2-3}$* 'What are you doing?' B1: [3, 2, 2, 3, 1-3] *ka^{3}vhe^{3} ti^{2}-vʔe^{3}škoa$^{1-3}$* 'I am gathering coffee.' A2: [3, 2, 3, 3, 2, 3, 2, 1-3] *ʔa^{3}-nkhį^{2} ma^{3} ka^{3}vhe^{2} ši^{3} vʔe^{2}škoi$^{1-3}$* 'Are you gathering a lot of coffee?' B2: [2, 3, 3] *nkhį^{2} ma^{3}-ni^{3}* 'A lot.' A3: [1, 1-3, 3-4, 3, 3] *ho^{1} thį$^{1-3}$ roa$^{3-4}$ ma^{3}-ni^{3}* 'How many *roa* are there?' B3: [3, 3, 2, 4, 3, 3] *hnko^{3} ki^{3}nta^{2}-la^{4} ma^{3}-ni^{3}* 'Probably one *quintal*.'

12. A1: [1, 3, 3, 2-3, 4] *hme^{1} ši^{3} ti^{3}-ñʔąi$^{2-3}$-ve^{4}* 'What are you doing there?' B1: [2, 3; 3, 1, 2, 3, 3] *li^{2}-hme^{3}, či^{3}kį^{1} ti^{2}-va^{3}te^{3}* 'Nothing; I am cutting firewood.' A2: [3, 1, 3, 1, 4, 4] *ʔa^{3}-thį^{1} či^{3}kį^{1} ya^{4}-ve^{4}* 'Is there firewood there?' B2: [1, 1] *thį^{1}-ni^{1}* 'There is.'

13. [1, 3-4, 2, 3, 2] *hme^{1}-ni$^{3-4}$ li^{2}-koi^{3} ncʔoe^{2}* 'What is it? I did not hear.'

14. A1: [1, 1, 3, 3, 2, 4] *hme^{1} čʔa^{1} ši^{3} ki^{3}-čʔai^{2}-ve^{4}* 'What did you bring there?' B1: [1, 4, 1, 1] *čʔa^{1} na^{4}hme^{1}-ni^{1}* 'It is a load of corn.' A2: [1, 3, 3, 4, 3] *hña^{1} ti^{3}-ʔmi^{3}koai^{4}-ʔni^{3}* 'Well, where are you going with it?' B2: [3, 2, 4, 2, 3, 4] *te^{3}na^{2}nko^{4} ti^{2}-vhi^{3}koa^{4}* 'I am taking it to Tenango.' A3: [3, 3, 3, 3, 2, 3, 2-4, 3] *ʔa^{3}-ti^{3}-ʔmi^{3}ka^{3}te^{2}na^{3}-ni$^{2-4}$ʔni^{3}* 'Are you going to sell it then?' B3: [2, 3, 3, 2, 2-3] *ti^{2}-vhi^{3}ka^{3}te^{2}na$^{2-3}$* 'I am going to sell it.' A4: [1, 1, 3, 2, 4, 4, 2, 3, 1-3, 4] *ho^{1} thį^{1} čʔai^{3}-ʔni^{3} ʔi^{4}-ta^{4}te^{2}na^{3}-nai$^{1-3}$-vi^{4}* 'How much will you take then? Sell it to me here.' B4: [4-3, 4, 3, 3, 3, 2, 4] *ka$^{4-3}$ tąǫ^{4} kʔoa^{3} nka^{3} hnko^{3} ka^{2}ša^{4}* 'I will take \$2.50 a box.' A5: [3, 3-2, 2, 2, 2, 4, 4, 2, 3, 2-3] *ʔa^{3}-kai$^{3-2}$-li^{2} hao^{2} vi^{2}šo^{4} ka^{4}-hao^{2} ȼhoa^{3}-le$^{2-3}$* 'Won't you take \$2.25? I will give that to you.' B5: [3, 2, 2, 4, 2, 3; 3, 3, 2, 3, 4] *nka^{3} hą^{2} vi^{2}šo^{4} vʔai^{2}-na^{3}; hña^{3} nka^{3} ti^{2}-vhi^{3}koa^{4}* 'Three pesos are given to me where I am going with it.' A6: [4, 3, 3-2, 3, 3, 4, 3] *to^{4}-nka^{3} khį$^{3-2}$ ti^{3}-ʔmi^{3}koai^{4}-ʔni^{3}* 'But that is far you are going with it then.' B6: [4, 4, 3, 4, 3] *to^{4}-ya^{4} sʔe^{3}-la^{4}-na^{3}* 'I will just drop the matter now.' A7: [1:, 4, 3] *čhi^{1}-nko^{1} čʔai^{4}-ʔni^{3}* 'Well, you sure want a lot.'

AUTHOR'S NOTE

This paper was presented in part at the summer meeting of the Linguistic Society of America, August 1, 1947, at Ann Arbor, Michigan.

The Mazateco tribe is located in the northern tip of the State of Oaxaca, along the southern edge of the State of Puebla, and in the municipio of Zongolica, State of Vera Cruz, Mexico. The tribe numbers perhaps 60,000, with 55,743 monolingual speakers (not including children under five years of age) according to the 1940 census figures. It is a member of the Popoloca-Mazateco language family, which also includes Ixcateca and Chuchon. [See Gudschinsky (1958b), which sets up a Popotecan family, whose Popolocan member is the family designated as "Popoloca-Mazateco" by Cowan.]

The author, under the auspices of the Summer Institute of Linguistics, lived in Huautla de de Jiménez, Oaxaca, during the winters of 1943-1944 through 1946-1947. The data for the texts were gathered at Rio Santiago, a ranch pertaining to the municipio of Huautla de Jiménez and located three hours east of it. Modesto García, a lad of about 17 years, was the informant. The texts were later checked with

Fortino Cortés, a boy of 14 years, who lived in Huautla.

The same phenomenon is reported among the Zapotecos of Yatzachi el Bajo by Otis Leal of the Summer Institute of Linguistics, and among the Chinantecos by R. J. Weitlaner of the National School of Anthropology and History, Mexico City. Both the foregoing are tonal languages of Oaxaca, Mexico. [Sarah Gudschinsky (1958a, p. 341) reports its absence among the Soyaltepec Mazatec, who do not focus on abstracted tone without specific teaching.] George Herzog (1934, p. 454) refers to a similar phenomenon observed in Africa: "The use of musical instruments for communication over long distances is very common in Africa. . . . studies indicate that the musical elements of speech are transferred to the instrument and that this is the essence of the technique."

The segmental phonemes of spoken Mazateco (Huautla dialect) are as follows: voiceless stops *t*, *k*,'; voiceless affricates *ȼ*, *č*, *c̣* (sibilant, shibilant, retroflexed); voiced nasals *m*, *n*, *ñ*; voiceless fricatives *s*, *š*, *h*; voiced fricative *v*; lateral *l*; glide *y*; flap *r*; oral vowels *į*, *ę*, *ą*, *ǫ*; nasalized vowels *i*, *e*, *a*, *o*. For further description of these phonemes and a statement of what constitutes a phonemic syllable in spoken Mazateco, see Pike and Pike (1947, sections 2, 3, 5). Mazateco has four phonemic registers, indicated by superior numbers after the vowels as follows: 1 high, 2 semi-high, 3 semi-low, 4 low. For an analysis of the glides, with examples from spoken Mazateco, Pike (1948, pp. 95-165).

It is of interest to note that the spoken language has a retroflexed sibilant phoneme *š*, which, with some speakers, is frequently whistled in normal speech. This retroflexed tongue whistle is never used in the conversational whistling described in this article, nor is there ever any significant pitch to it.

REFERENCE NOTE

Ritzenthaler and Peterson (1954) and Hasler (1960) report other occurrences of WHISTLED SPEECH in Meso-America, Hasler noting that where the base language is tonal, the whistling reproduces tones only, and where the language does not have phonemic tone levels, the whistling reproduces intonation, but involves articulations of tongue and lips as well. Hasler also observes that in all cases whistled speech aids communication in mountainous terrain. Holmberg (1950, p. 23) describes the Siriono (Eastern Bolivia) use of whistling for communication while hunting, a practice combined with their relative uncommunicativeness, apparently mistaken by Wegner (1928) as evidence of a primitive group lacking articulate language altogether (see Holmberg, 1950, p. 10). Classe (1957) describes the whistled language (Spanish) of the Canary Islands, which suggests to Hasler a prehistoric link between Africa and America! Chao (1956) and Simmons (1960a) discuss aesthetic aspects of oral use of phonemic tone, and Ostwald (1959) considers some socio-psychological associations. A general survey with classification and historical considerations is provided by Theodore Stern (1957).

References not in general bibliography:

CHAO, YUEN-REN

1956. Tone, Intonation, Singsong, Chanting, Recitative, Tonal Composition, and Atonal Composition in Chinese. *For Roman Jakobson*. The Hague: Mouton. Pp. 52-59.

CLASSE, A.

1957. The Whistled Language of La Gomera. *Scientific American*, *196:* 111 ff.

GUDSCHINSKY, SARAH

1958b. *Proto-Popotecan, A Comparative Study of Popolocan and Mixtecan.* (Indiana University Publications in Anthropology and Linguistics; *IJAL*, Memoir 15.) Bloomington.

HASLER, JUAN A.

1960. El lenguaje silbado [Whistle speech]. *La Palabra y el Hombre.* (Revista de la Universidad Veracruzana, No. 15.) Xalapa. Pp. 25-36.

HOLMBERG, ALLAN R.

1950. *Nomads of the Long Bow. The Siriono of Eastern Bolivia.* (Institute of Social Anthropology, Publication No. 10.) Washington, D.C.: Smithsonian Institution.

OSTWALD, PETER F.

1959. When People Whistle. *Language and Speech, 2* (3): 137-145.

PIKE, KENNETH L., and EUNICE V. PIKE

1947. Immediate Constituents of Mazateco Syllables. *IJAL, 13:* 78-91.

RITZENTHALER, R. E., and F. A. PETERSON

1954. Courtship Whistling of the Mexican Kickapoo Indians. *AA, 56:* 1088-1089.

WEGNER, RICHARD N.

1928. Die Quruñqu'a, ein neuentdeckter Stamm primitivster Kultur ohne artikulierte und grammatikalische sprache in Ostbolivien. *Phœnix, Zeitschrift Deutsche Geistesarbeit für Südamerika, 14* (4-5): 369-384.

36 *Drum-Signaling in a West African Tribe*

GEORGE HERZOG

THE USE OF musical instruments for purposes of signaling is very widespread, and definite systems of communication are or were based on it in native Africa, Middle and South America, and the Pacific. The African systems are the most elaborate and often serve for free conversation; their existence is well known to the anthropologist and the traveler, but they have been little investigated from the linguistic point of view, and still less in their social setting. The few studies we have establish beyond doubt that in Africa this signaling, usually on drums, is based on a direct transfer into a musical medium of spoken language-elements: pitch or tone, which is of fundamental importance in most African languages, and some other phonetic features. Consequently, we do not deal here with a code such as the Morse code, in which the ascription of meaning to a series of symbols is purely conventional, nor with an intertribal code (as has been reported erroneously time and again). Communication between tribes speaking different dialects or languages is, of course, feasible, and is practiced, but all it requires is that the drummers in the border-area be to some extent bilingual. They can even learn to identify a number of signals in the neighboring language together with their approximate meanings, without knowing the text in the other language, or its exact translation. In exceptional cases, however, signaling does function like a conventional code. For instance, the Ewe of the Togo Mandate who learned drum signaling from their Twi neighbors do not transpose the Twi signals into Ewe; they drum Twi signals, but give them Ewe meanings (Westermann, 1907). If the drummer is bilingual, or if he understands at least the Twi texts, he is not involved with a code; otherwise he is, and so are his listeners. Naturally, signals constitute a code for any native listener who is not sufficiently familiar with the technique.

I had the opportunity in 1930 to study the signaling of a West African tribe, the Jabo of Eastern Liberia, in full detail. The late Edward Sapir began a study of this language with the assistance of a native speaker resident in the United States who came from the township of Nimiah, a politically independent subdivision of the Jabo. Sapir found unusually complex tonal phenomena not reported from Africa hitherto—4 tone-registers, utilization to an unusual degree of tone-differences for grammatical purposes, a large number of tonal changes due to the interaction of neighboring tones, and the existence of "tone-classes" (morphophonemic word-classes displaying differences in tone-behavior). He felt that these findings should be checked with other speakers in Africa and had the inspiration, characteristic of his particular imagination, that an investigation of drum-signaling would also serve as a further check on the language-data. The subsequent expedition in which Sapir's informant participated substantiated Sapir's brilliant work on both levels, and added a considerable body of new linguistic material.

The main results of this study are: signaling in Eastern Liberia follows linguistic features closely and in unusual detail; it is practiced on a great variety of instruments, some of which do not serve for communicating over a distance, but only for other purposes; signaling as a technique is intricately interwoven with phenomena of social life and structure; it displays the same type of sophistication which we know of African music and folklore; and it shows complex and subtle transitional forms between language and music. The language of signaling is, to some extent, a technical language. It is highly poetic, which is connected with the heroic connotations of warfare in this region, and with the elevated style of the language-symbols that surround offices of worldly authority or are embodied in dealings with supernatural powers. Signaling is employed in all these contexts. But, curiously enough, the very requirements of rational intellegibility also call for the employment of poetic forms. In Jabo, as in many languages of the Sudanese family, most stems are monosyllabic. Thus the bare occurrence in a signal of a beat for the name of a person, an animal, or an object could mean a large number of different things, so that it becomes exceedingly useful to expand the context of the word with a paraphrastic formula, such as a proverb or an honorary title which characterizes the person or animal. Then it is no longer a single beat, but a particular rhythmic and melodic motif which identifies the subject. The rich African development of honorary appellations, names, titles, and proverbs, highly poetic in themselves and used extensively in songs and stories, thus saturates the style of signaling (see Herzog and Blooah, 1936, and cf. Rattray, 1916); but even so, and partly just because of the high aesthetic requirements, the bulk of signaling is apt to be practiced and fully understood only by specialists.

These observations are likely to hold, on the whole, for much, if not most, of Negro Africa. It is probably a specialized local phenomenon that in Eastern Liberia a very large number of signals have texts which are or pretend to be in neighboring languages; and this also makes signaling difficult for the average person. The predilection for foreign material may indicate that signaling spread comparatively recently in this region; it may reflect comparatively recent population-movements. Yet it is also bound to be connected with the constitution of the population; the region is thickly studded with innumerable small tribes who hold intensive intercourse with each other, and regard the stronger tribes with wholesome respect. Much of the Jabo signaling and poetic material is in Kru or in *soi-disant* Kru, the language of a powerful tribe to the West; much of it in Grebo, a tribe to the East who settled on the coast before the Jabo and influenced the culture of the latter in many ways. Jabo drummers of Nimiah are still supposed to go for the study of signal-drumming to Trembo, where a different Jabo dialect is spoken. In the following study, only the summary results are submitted. Since the differences between the sytems on the different instruments are not negligible, only drum-signaling is treated here; the more technical detail is given under "The Technique of Jabo Drum-Signaling" (pp. 315-317). (For the geographic distribution, see the map in Thilenius, Meinhof, Heinitz, 1916, p. 180.)

The signal-drums of Eastern Liberia are of two types. The first are the wooden forms without a skin head, usually hollow cylinders, which are found in so many places of the world, with or without a signaling function. Technologically, they are not drums, but bells. (They are not to be considered drums proper, since they have no tensed membrances, but bells, since the vibrations decrease from the periphery —in this case the lips—toward the dead center.) The others are skin-covered drums, single-headed. In contrast with much of West-Africa, the use of skin-covered drums for signaling is quite restricted in Eastern Liberia, but that of the wooden drums is elaborate.

The wooden signal-drum or "slit-drum" consists of a hollowed-out tree-trunk with a longitudinal slit, the lips of which vary in thickness between themselves and in different places of the same lip, thus providing a number of points for producing various tones. Two straight sticks are used for beating, and different tones are also produced by different positions of the sticks in the hands, or by striking with a different part of the stick. A large instrument, over eight feet in length, may be used alone or in conjunction with a smaller drum about half of its size, but both played by the same drummer. The drums are the property of the military and policing organization of the town which includes all males, and which holds periodic assemblies and social gatherings. The drummer, a regular official of this organization, signals to a distance when he summons a member who may be in the fields to come to the village, or when an assembly is called unexpectedly. But the main duty of this drum is to serve somewhat like a chairman's gavel. The drummer regulates the meetings; he calls for order or dismisses the meeting, and so on, with special signals. In addition, on special occasions when war-like celebrations are held, he plays the praising titles of warriors or eminent men, who then advance and boast of their deeds, holding a dialogue with the drum, in which a horn-player may also join. Their female relatives are expected to come forth and offer gifts to the instrumentalists. Every mature man of some standing has a special title on this drum by which he is called, and which may refer to his deeds, character, or social status; although the title may equally well be teasing or gossipy, in harmony with the fact that the men's organization functions also as a social club. More martial and serious titles are given to men on the horn, in praising songs, and in formal greeting.

The bulk of the material which the drummer employs consists, then, of a large number of fixed formulas, variations, and additions to the fixed formulas. The latter are frequently repeated during one "communication," with variants and other forms interspersed. There is no exchange of communications between villages on these drums, or on the skin-covered ones, a technique so common elsewhere in Africa. Single signals can be conveyed from village to village, but this is rare. Naturally, when a village hears these drums from the next village or tribe, it is at once clear that something is "going on," either a meeting, or a war-like celebration, including a war dance, or actual preparations for war. A town or a small tribe will have only one set of these drums, and two or three individuals who play them well enough to be able to substitute for the regularly appointed drummer. The Jabo-speaking tribe of Nimiah, in which the study was made, consists of the Upper and the Lower Town (the latter on the seashore), with about 600 souls each, and a few smaller settlements. Although there is considerable rivalry and duplication of political institutions between the two towns, only the Upper Town, which is older and is the residence of the tribal chief, had these drums. The lower town could, technically, borrow them, but only against a sizable fee.

Signal-drumming is considered difficult by the natives. In the course of the study, I learned how to play every signal, first on one drum then on two, wrote them down in notation, and recorded them also acoustically—accomplishments equally astounding to the natives, although the finer points of variation and ornamentation were not mastered. The bare signals are fairly simple according to our musical standards, but local Whites or Americo-Liberians, unacquainted with the linguistic foundation, naturally cannot find their way in the system.

The skin-covered signal-drum is slightly personified; it has an honorary title. Elsewhere in West Africa, drums of this type have personal names and have sex ascribed to them according to their size. (The large Jabo wooden signal-drum has the name of God's wife.) The drum is a large hollowed wooden trunk, six to eight feet long; every village has one, and it is the official signaling instrument of the village, with its official player. It is usually lashed to the side of a house and slanted at an angle so that the player standing facing the skin head can play it. If need be, a similar drum may be used instead which, together with a set of smaller drums, is normally played for women's dances. In this case it stands upright on the ground, and the drummer stands behind it on a little platform. It is beaten with two quite heavy, straight wooden sticks. Different tones are produced by beating either the center of the head or a place nearer the edge, which gives a higher tone since the skin is more taut; and the two sticks are unequal in weight, which also enters into the tone-difference. Only a limited number of signals are used—the drummers knew only five—and no conversation is feasible. The signal is preceded by a series of evenly spaced rapid beats, to call for quiet and attention; this is repeated three times. Then comes the signal, three times, then again the call for attention, and so on as long as necessary. This call does not represent word-meaning. (The Yaounde of the Cameroons also have such a call-signal, according to material in the Berlin State Library recorded by M. Heepe and transcribed by me. See also Betz, 1898.) The signals are all short; some in surrounding languages.

Dance-drums. Various smaller drums of both types are used in dancing, with or without a large one. They play, for the most part, strictly musical rhythms without word-meaning; they "sing," to use the native expression, although word-meaning has been read into some of these musical rhythms. Four wooden slit-drums and one small skin-covered drum are used, without the singing voice, to accompany the war-dance of the men, which is a highly acrobatic affair as far as the dancing and the drumming of the leading drummer are concerned. The natives take considerable pride in the excellence of these performances, good teams visiting neighboring tribes and performing for them in exchange for copious gifts, food, and acclaim. The leading drummer of such a team uses two small wooden drums, one of them being the optional adjunct to the signal-drum in signaling, and the large signal-drum itself being demoted in this ensemble to playing a purely musical, simple rhythmic role. (The natives deplored repeatedly my great loss in not being able to hear one of their leading musicians who had the rare accomplishment of playing on three of these drums at the same time; he was in voluntary exile.) Every piece consists of an arrangement of definite musical rhythms in a loosely fixed order, but before the end of the piece, as a signal of its approaching end, the leading drummer beats out a few times a set motif which has word-meaning, while the other drummers pause. As with the xylophone pieces, the text of this motif is the name of the piece itself; it is apt to revile enemy tribes and to refer to old, successful wars and battles. The leading drummer also signals brief snatches to the dancers in which he praises or teases them; these have reference to their manner of dancing. Other snatches, some of them purely musical, serve as signals for the dancers so that they may shift the dance-movements, the latter being regulated in all dancing by the drumming and the leading drummer. In other dances only skin-covered drums are used; the small ones are beaten by the hands and can convey brief signals.

The Technique of Jabo Drum-Signaling

Jabo is a language spoken by five or six small independent tribes of about 6,000 speakers near Cape Palmas, on the seashore and in the interior. It belongs to a group of languages in Eastern Liberia and on the Ivory Coast which are designated as *groupe éburnéo-libérien* by Delafosse in his "Langues du Soudan et de la Guinée" (1924), and by Westermann (1927, 1935) as the subdivision "Kru languages" in the Kwa group of the Western Sudanese languages. It is a tone-language, meaning, as in most so-called Sudanese and in many Bantu languages, that every word and syllable has its inherent tone which is as integral a part of the word as its other phonetic constituents of vowels and consonants; the tone many change only according to set phonemic, morphophonemic, or grammatical rules. The system of these rules in Jabo—and in the whole "Kru" or "éburnéo-libérien" group no doubt represents one of the most richly elaborated formal systems in language. Jabo is, to a large extent, a monosyllabic language, and thus the number of words distinguishable only by tone is exceedingly large; even so, there are many homonyms. There is considerable "tonal suffixation," i.e., the addition of suffixes which consist only of lengthening the final stem-vowel and of tone (probably due to the loss of the full phonetic content of the suffix-syllable). Many grammatical distinctions are conveyed by tonal change only. To illustrate with a few examples, *ba*^{1} is "namesake," *ba*^{2} is (a) "to be broad," (b) "to be ruddy," (c) "you" pl. in the imperative, etc., *ba*^{3} is (a) "tail," (b) "we" imperative, etc., *ba*^{4} is a particle of impatient command. *tu*^{1} is "tree, wood" in particular, *tu*^{2} "tree, wood" in general. *blɛ*^{33} is "to be adjacent to," complete aspect, *blɛ*^{22} "to be adjacent to," incomplete aspect. *kli*^{1} is "foot-race," *pi*^{4}*li*^{4} is "grass"; since the relative of the noun is a suffix which consists of lengthening the final stem-vowel and of high tone, *kli*^{11} is "foot-race which," *pi*^{4}*li*^{41} is "grass which."

The practice of marking length (and tone) in African languages only when there is an obvious semantic difference, as has been recommended in various publications of the International Institute of African Languages and Cultures in London, is deplorable. It is rather likely that the situation is frequently as in Jabo: a long syllable (with long vowel) is to be interpreted as a dissyllabic unit; "lengthening" of a vowel often results from the presence of an identifiable syllabic suffix, the meaning of which is not always transparent. To do justice to this patterning and to other considerations, Sapir introduced the concept of the *mora* to complement that of the syllable. The mora in Jabo is a basic unit or segment which has, for its minimum content, tone, duration (the average time-duration of the "short syllable"), and voicing. The Jabo mora may be such an "empty mora," or it may contain a vowel, or a vowel-diphthong, a consonant plus a vowel, or a cluster of two consonants plus a vowel. Cases of the last type are all *clv* (consonant, *l* or one of its positional variants, and vowel). There are a few cases in which consonants function as syllabics; actually, they arise in free variation from nasal consonant plus vowel by elision of the vowel; tone and duration remain unimpaired.

Since some of the intricacies leave their imprint on signaling, it is necessary to submit here a cursory sketch of Jabo phonetics. Besides the four basic tones, which are independent phonemes, there are a number of quick glides, falling or rising between various of the four tones. Some of these are phonemic, some morphophonemic, some positional variants of the four tones; their time-value is equal to that of a single mora, and syllables which carry them count as single morae. The vowels fall in two series: one a "plain" set *e*, *ɛ*, *a*, *ɔ*, *o*; and the other, slightly velarized and closer, distinguished by a dot below, with the addition of *i* and *u*. Nasalization gives two additional sets, although some of the vowel-contrasts are suspended within these sets. There are a number of true diphthongs—vowel-combinations with single-mora value—and a number of permissible vowel-clusters. The diphthongs may have one of the four basic tones, or a quick glide. The members of the vowel-cluster do not, of course, need to have the same tone.

The consonants, in Sapir's phonetic description, fall into five sets: surds (slightly aspirated), sonants, consonants with "anacrusis" (this set includes all surds and sonants of the previous two sets), "emphatic" consonants, and "heavy" consonants (both latter sets are sonant, though not fully voiced). Phonemic reduction of these five sets is called for by introducing some principle which would not otherwise be necessary, for instance, the assumption of phonemic stress, of different degrees, of non-moraic tone, or some other device of pattern-interpretation. For the purposes of this article, the five sets are treated as such, the more so since the signaling phenomena do not too clearly support the more convenient of the phonemic interpretations. The "anacrusis"-set results most frequently, though not exclusively, from morphophonemic variation. Objectively, this set is actualized with quick-rising tone; if the consonant is sonant, it is slightly more tensed and longer than the regular sonant. The "emphatic" consonant is somewhat more stressed and longer still; it has initial pre-voicing. The "heavy" consonant has the pre-voicing of the emphatic, and still more stress and length. The last three sets have similar tonal features: pre-voicing on tone 3 before tone 2 or 3; on tone 4 before tone 4 or 1.

In signaling, the essential organization of this system, around the mora, remains intact. Normally, each mora is represented by a single beat or musical tone; the time-value of these tends to remain the same within a given signal or piece. Double morae are rendered with two beats or tones, or a long tone. Pauses are used at places where syntactic or expressive pauses are apt to occur in speech. The tone-system may be reduced to three or even two tones, but on some instruments the four-tone system is fully preserved. Special treatment is given those features which complicate the otherwise very consistent picture of Jabo sound-patterning: to diphthongs, quick-gliding tones, anacrusis, emphatic and heavy consonants, and to consonant-clusters. These features can be treated by several devices, the use of which is variable and optional, depending a good deal on the position of the element in the signal and the relation of position to the manual convenience of the player. In addition, the player has considerable aesthetic freedom in dealing with these features; they are, on the whole, looked upon as optional ornaments, although some occur quite consistently.

On the wooden signal-drums, every mora is given, as a rule, by a beat of its own. When two full vowels follow each other, the beat for one may be omitted, or both beats may be shortened. The use of two quick beats, given by the two sticks in alternation, is called "scraping" the drum; it is considered specifically an ornamental device and occurs in a few cases where linguistic reasons do not seem to account for it. True diphthongs may be represented by "scraping" or by a single beat; the same word in the same signal may have once one form, once another. Other cases where the term "scraping" applies are mentioned in the notes to the music-examples. An extra-short beat joined to the next shows up in a few cases in which it could not be explained on any linguistic grounds. Double morae with the same vowel-timbre are usually represented with their proper beats, whether their tones are the same or not. In a few cases they receive single beats; in every such instance on record, the word has also a single-mora form which is morphologically related and would fit into the signal-text almost as well. The drummers, in translating the signals, would, in some cases, give the grammatically more appropriate prose-forms, in others, the shorter forms which agree better with the signal.

The four-tone register-system is somewhat reduced; on the whole, it turns into a three-tone system, since tones 3 and 4 usually coincide, and this despite the fact that there would be no technical difficulty in keeping the two lower tones apart on these drums. The following qualifications hold, however. Tone 3 can be beaten at two places on the drum, one of which gives a lower pitch. Although the choice of these two musical variants of drum-tone 3 depends on the drummer's convenience and on aesthetic factors, the contrast between speech-tones 3 and 4 is thus to some extent preserved. Tones 3 and 2 are kept apart the most consistently. In a few cases where morphologically related forms of a word have tone 3 and 2, forms with tone 3 may be drummed with drum-tone 2, but rarely the converse. For the actual meaning the difference is apt to be negligible in the drumming-context. Tones 2 and 1 are not distinguished as consistently as 3 and 2; tone 1 is often given with drum-tone 2. In most cases, this seems to be due to the drummer's convenience. Drum-tone 1 can be beaten either to the right of drum-tone 2 (on the upper lip of the slit), or still further out (beyond the slit), or on the lower lip, or on the smaller drum, placed to the right of the larger. In either case, moving for tone 1 far to the right or down on the drum may not be convenient; tone 2 is then substituted, and this despite the fact that there is still a fifth way of producing tone 1: by striking the lip with a point near the tip of the stick; the further away from the hand is the point of the stick which is struck, the higher the tone. The treatment of quick-gliding tones on one-mora elements is not too consistent either. The most common tone of this type is the glide from 2 to 1, a phonemic or morphophonemic variant of tone 2. On the drum this glide is given either with tone 1 (which in speech is an occasional free variant for this glide), or it is given by a short beat on tone 2 followed by a regular beat on 1.

Morae with "anacrusis," with emphatic or heavy consonants, and such of the *clv* type (where the first consonant may or may not be emphatic) are treated chiefly by converting the beat into two short beats ("scraping"), or by prefixing a very short beat to the main beat, or by striking two tones at the same time. In most cases, the two sticks are used. It is, no doubt, because of this technical fact that the devices tend to be fairly regular when the word is in initial position in the signal or in a phrase; they are less apt to occur if the word is preceded by others, where the drummer may find them awkward. The emphatic consonants, if on tone 2—emphatics do not occur with tone 1—are usually given a short beat on tone 3, followed by the regular beat. If on tone 3 or 4, they are usually rendered with a single beat. Only two cases of heavy consonants occurred in the signals; they were treated like emphatics. The *clv* type, if it has tone 1 or 2, is beaten by the short beat plus regular beat-figure, especially if in initial position. If the tone is 3, the mora is given, in initial position, by a simultaneous double-beat. (Drummers find it awkward to beat with the left hand—which is used preferentially for low tones—in quick succession.) If the tone is 4, the mora is given by a single beat in both positions, this being one of the few cases in which tones 3 and 4 are kept apart. The extra-short beat is always on the same tone as the following regular beat, which is in harmony with the fact that the *clv* syllable is homogeneous in tone. The simultaneous double-beat for tone 3 may be also a carry-over from the xylophone technique which is much more free and where such a beat is used for a variety of linguistic and musical purposes. In a few cases, a simple mora on tone 3 or 4 was represented by the simultaneous double-beat. (See examples 1-7, p. 321.) (Similar intricacies of signal-drumming have been recorded elsewhere in West Africa; their interpretation, in the absence of correlation with phonetic and phonemic data, is not always clear as yet. In Ashanti, as shown by Rattray's material, the figure of short beat joined to the regular beat is used consistently for *crv* syllables—*r* is a variant of *l* in Sudanese languages—, also for long vowels, and very often for vowel clusters, which may actually be diphthongs. In Duala, in the Cameroons, simultaneous double-beats are used for onomatopoetic elements and exclamations; and figures of short plus regular beat and of two short beats occur; see the notations in Betz [1898].)

The skin-covered signal-drum gives only two tones. Only tones 2 and 3 occur in the texts of the signals which were known to the drummers. Yet, even within this limitation, the agreement between speech-tones and drum-tones is not too good. The reasons may well be technical. The force required for beating the drum effectively is very great, so that the drummer tends to use the right-hand and left-hand sticks in alternation, which is likely to result in a mechanical alternation of tones 3 and 2. In addition, some of the signals are in neighboring dialects, but the drummers may not have been aware of this in every case. On the other hand, emphatic consonants and *clv* syllables were all given the extra-short prefix-beat, which gives the limited number of signals sufficient variety to make them distinguishable from each other. The short prefix-beat is higher in pitch than the main beat, because the drummer stresses the main beat and cannot gather enough force for the former. (See examples 8-9.)

On the wooden dance-drums, tones 3 and 4 coincide again; 3, 2, and 1 are kept apart well enough; the quick glide 2-1 is apt to be beaten with drum-tone 1; *clv* clusters and emphatic consonants are apt to be treated as they are on the signal-drum proper. (See examples 10-11.) For the technique on the skin-covered dance-drums see the notes (examples 12-13).

Jabo signal-drumming presents a fundamentally simple and consistent system. Drum-treatment departs from the routine of this system and becomes both complex and variable *pari passu* with those elements which complicate the texture of the language and its sound-patterning. Elements containing diphthongs, consonants with anacrusis, emphatic or heavy consonants, and consonant-clusters are essentially equivalent to phonetically simpler morae in Jabo, but they all can be viewed as elements with a double or twin content. This is neatly reflected in their preferential treatment with two short beats, or with simultaneous double beats, or with the figure of a very short beat followed by the regular beat. Their equivalence to simple morae is expressed in the fact that these drum-figures are equal in time-value to the single beats which stand for simple morae.

Turning to historical considerations, it is not unlikely that the genesis of these special drum-features is connected with the development of their linguistic parallels. Most diphthongs in Sudanese languages may be assumed to go back to original full-vowel clusters. The *clv* is apt to come from old dissyllabic forms with petrified *-lv* suffixes, the old stem-vowel having dropped out (see Westermann, 1911, pp. 29-39; 1927 *Passim*). Anacrusis in Jabo in most cases clearly compensates for a lost nasal prefix. Emphatic consonants occupy a special position of interest. Similar consonants, at times called "implosives," have been reported from various West African languages. In Jabo they may well arise from a system of lost prefixes; in many Sudanese languages there are clear parallels, with obvious phonetic similarities, to the well-known Bantu prefix-system, as has been shown conclusively by Westermann's studies (see especially Westermann, 1927). The origin of the Sudanese tone-classes, undoubtedly present also in languages outside the Liberian-Ivory-Coast group, is probably tied up with the reduction or phonemic reinterpretation of the Bantu-Sudanese prefix-system. These problems and the relationship of Sudanese to Bantu will appear in a clearer light with increased attention to phonetic and phonemic principles, and especially to phenomena of tone, stress, and length. The suspension of the contrast in drumming between Jabo tones 3 and 4 should be understood in the light of the relationship of these tones in speech. The contrast is not fully maintained: tone 3 becomes 4 before 1; optionally it becomes 4 before or after tone 4. Historically the Jabo four-tone system, no doubt, grew out of an older three-tone system by splitting the lowest register. Most of the surrounding languages have three tones only, among them the Grebo, from whom the Jabo took over a good deal of their signaling material and music. The reduction to two tones on the skin-covered signal-drum, however, does not necessarily reflect an old two-tone system, but, rather, the impoverishment of signaling on these drums; elsewhere in West Africa the three tones are produced on such drums by using a smaller drum in conjunction with the larger.

As against the large mass of material in which communication is achieved by a direct transfer of formal speech-elements into the musical medium, there are a few cases in Jabo in which signals reflect emotional affect in speech, or use symbolic effects for "sound-painting," or acoustically represent non-vocal sounds. Emphatic stress is reflected in the signal, "Stop ye the noise, speak ye one by one!" (example 3); the words for "speak ye!" are treated as if the consonants were emphatic. One signal on the wooden signal-drum consists of rubbing a drum-stick repeatedly back and forth along its lower lip; this is said to represent "the anger of the army." (The "anger" of the men's assembly is sounded before it takes some mob-action sanctioned by law, such as destroying the house of the perpetrator of a grave crime, or collecting by force fines imposed by the native court, and the like.) The playing of the antelope-horn is said to "frighten" the enemy; it has no word-meaning. Non-vocal sounds are imitated on the xylophone.

Native theory and terminology. The Jabo have developed a technical terminology for signaling, although the musicians, the only ones who are apt to know it, make mistakes in its use. The vagaries in the use of the terminology contrasted with the unerring assurance with which drummers and horn-players reproduced at my request correctly and on the spur of the moment words which they had never played before. A man who does not play the drums, although he is proficient on the xylophone, was even quicker. Higher and lower registers are called by the terms *kẹ*^{22} and *Do*^{3}*lo*^{2}, respectively. These are unanalyzable stems, said to be the names of two birds which "keep company together and answer each other's calls," the first being a smaller bird with a higher voice, the second a larger bird with a lower voice. In signaling as in music the metaphors are not our "high" and "low"; occasionally "large" and "small" vọice is used. (Not the regular adjectives for "large" and "small," but words used either comparatively, or in the sense of "larger than" expected, etc., respectively.) The four registers are designated by expressions which combine *kẹ*^{22} and *Do*^{3}*lo*^{2} with the regular words for "large" and "small." In another scheme, the two words are compounded, the first qualifying the second, for the in-between registers. (It is noteworthy that the system provides for four registers, since on the signal-drums essentially a three-tone system is functioning.) But the distinction between tones 3 and 4 is not too clear, and most players become confused in the use of the terminology in either system for that very reason. It contributes to their uncertainty that on the wooden signal-drum there is such a variety of places and positions for the various tones. The highest tone can be beaten on three different spots which are progressively higher; the use of two higher ones is primarily ornamental, at times due to manual convenience. These two are designated by special terms formed by adding diminutives to *kẹ*^{22}.

The terms *kẹ*^{22} and *Do*^{3}*lo*^{2} are applied also to the registers representing higher and lower speech-tones on the horn, the musical bow, the xylophone, the dance-drums, and in signal-calling with the voice; and they are also applied to musical usage, for instance on the native harp. This is a strictly musical instrument, mounted on a large gourd the neck of which has been cut off. The open cavity is periodically placed on the chest and lifted off again; when it is off, the sound is stronger and an octave higher; now the instrument is said to play in *kẹ*^{22}, otherwise in *Do*^{3}*lo*^{2}. In singing, the terms refer to the higher as contrasted with the lower melodic sections; many types of songs are based on the consistent alternation of such sections. Finally, the terms are used in connection with the device of transposition on the horn and on the musical bow, by which words or phrases can be played in alternation in a higher or lower register than the one in which they are properly placed.

A word or syllable, taken out of a signal or offered at random without any context, was identified as to its register without any trouble by drummers and horn-players, at least whether it was in *kẹ*^{22} or *Do*^{3}*lo*^{2}, although there was no awareness whatsoever that these differences were in some fashion actually present in the spoken *words* themselves. The player would not give his judgment upon hearing the word; he would first play it and then classify it according to register or registers. When I asked just where *kẹ*^{22} and *Do*^{3}*lo*^{2} in signaling came from, the players offered craftsmen's rationalizations which were as ingenious as they were incorrect. The drummers' theory was that *kẹ*^{22} and *Do*^{3}*lo*^{2} were "in the sticks," and that the left-hand stick was heavier than the right-hand stick. This theory was based on two facts: such a difference does exist, but only on the skin-covered signal-drum—which the drummers in question did not play—is it large enough to make any difference in tone. Further, on the wooden signal-drum the lower registers are played on the left-hand side, preferably by the left hand; the higher ones on the right-hand side, preferably by the right hand. The theory disregarded the fact, however, that the drummers on the wooden signal-drum do not always distinguish the two sticks, which are almost equal in size and all other respects. When this was demonstrated to them, another explanation was offered: that the difference in registers was "in the hands"; the left hand being more awkward and "heavier." When I offered the suggestion that *kẹ*^{22} and *Do*^{3}*lo*^{2} were "in the words" themselves, only the drummer who served as my main informant grasped the idea. He accepted the theory as feasible; but when he came on a visit a month after work with him discontinued, it turned out that he went back, though apologetically, to the old theories of the drummers. Also the theory of the horn-players depended on instrumental factors and positions for explaining the register-differences.

Partial as these native theories are, they are not without interest. They indicate a degree of intellectual and technical sophistication which is not rare in "primitive" Africa. They demonstrate how terminology and technical theory may well develop where there is an object or instrument on which an otherwise abstract system can be observed in visible operation; the growth of musical theory and of scale-systems also is connected with observations on musical instruments, not on the singing voice or on acoustic phenomena in the abstract. The use of the Jabo terminology is shaky just because aesthetic and technical elaboration on the instrument resulted in a system more complex than the tone-system of speech itself; the signaling-theory stopped short exactly at the connection with the speaking voice. This, no doubt, likewise reflects a division of interests. The signalers are also musical instrumentalists, but they are not specialists in language and word-lore, as are singers, storytellers, or individuals whose preoccupation is with proverbs or native law. (For some of these connections, see Herzog and Blooah, 1936, "Introduction" and "Sayings.")

Several of these observations suggest that the element of pitch is not clearly isolated from its setting within other factors. This, again harmonizes with observations on primitive music. (A further example of the connection with music—or, rather, dancing— is the Jabo use of the expression "foot" for a phrase or short segment of a signal, reminiscent of the Greek metric concept of "foot." Except once in a while, and then for fun, one does not dance to a signal, but the connections between signal-drums and dance-drums make the choice of the image clear.) That the pitch-contrast is merely one phase of a complex contrast experienced by the listeners was demonstrated in one connection rather dramatically. In the beginning of the study I observed that what I expected to sound as high tones sounded rather consistently as low, and vice versa. This was at first ascribed to faulty hearing; the pitch of beaten wooden containers or tubes is identified less easily than that of other sound-sources. The recordings made on the spot showed the same discomforting anomaly. This was ascribed to vagaries of overtones registering on the rather inferior cylinder-records. Solicitous inquiries on my part, whether the drum sounded all right, brought the answer that it was rather old and that a new one ought to be made, should have been made years before; but that while it did not sound too well, the drum was good enough. After growing bafflement and uneasiness, I finally hit upon the notion that the drum might have been turned around at one time, and had it turned around again against some mild protests against tampering with the venerable object, which was said to be fifty years old. Then came the startled comment. "But how did you know?" It transpired that the right-side lower lip of the drum had become quite worn down in time, that being the spot where drummers prefer to hit a final tone 1 by bouncing the hand down from the upper lip with a flourish. To remedy the situation, the drum—which lies on the ground, facing with its slit the drummer who sits before it—was some years before this incident simply turned around so that a much less used upper lip now became the lower lip. Since the lower lip is thinner than the upper and thus produces higher tones, this operation, like Columbus' egg in its simplicity, meant that henceforth many low tones were higher, and many high tones lower, than the central tone 2. The reversal was not consistent because the pitch-contrasts are often achieved by using different spots on the same lip, or different hand-and-stick positions. The players were undoubtedly saved some feeling of confusion by the fact that their visual and motor experiences remained the same. The listeners, no doubt, satisfied themselves with the renewed acknowledgment that "It is difficult to understand the words of the drums." The comparative lack of disturbance at the reversal of the pattern, however, may shed some light on the curious phenomenon that in neighboring languages of the region groups of low-tone words of one language may be found to have high tone in another, and vice versa.

Drum-signaling in Eastern Liberia may be said to render the tonal and length-factors of speech accurately enough. It reflects quite faithfully the essential structural pattern of the language, including some of the more intricate details of the constitution of the "mora" or syllable. Among the local systems, it is the technically most elaborate, and the representation of phonetic detail is the most minute. This elaboration, however, is hardly to be blamed on attempts or tendencies to make communication easier to follow; the language of signal-drumming being highly conventionalized, and the material communicated restricted, the players are a comparatively few specialists. In other local signaling-systems, free conversation is practiced, in some by all persons including women and children, although the systems are technically less differentiated, less easy to follow. This situation compares with other regions in West Africa, for instance the Cameroons or the Congo-region, where many men know the use of the signal-drum and free conversation is feasible on it. Whether, as it would seem now to be the case, the Eastern Liberian developments are singularly rich and sophisticated, or whether they are a good sample of what is typical of African signal-communication, will become clearer when we have more studies of a detailed nature.

The technical, artistic, and social elaboration of signaling and signal-drumming in Africa is characteristic of that continent, and its study seems equally rewarding for understanding the synchronic patterns of African languages and for contributing to a knowledge of linguistic historical processes in Africa generally. One of the many interesting problems to which it points is comparison with the American

Wooden signal-drum

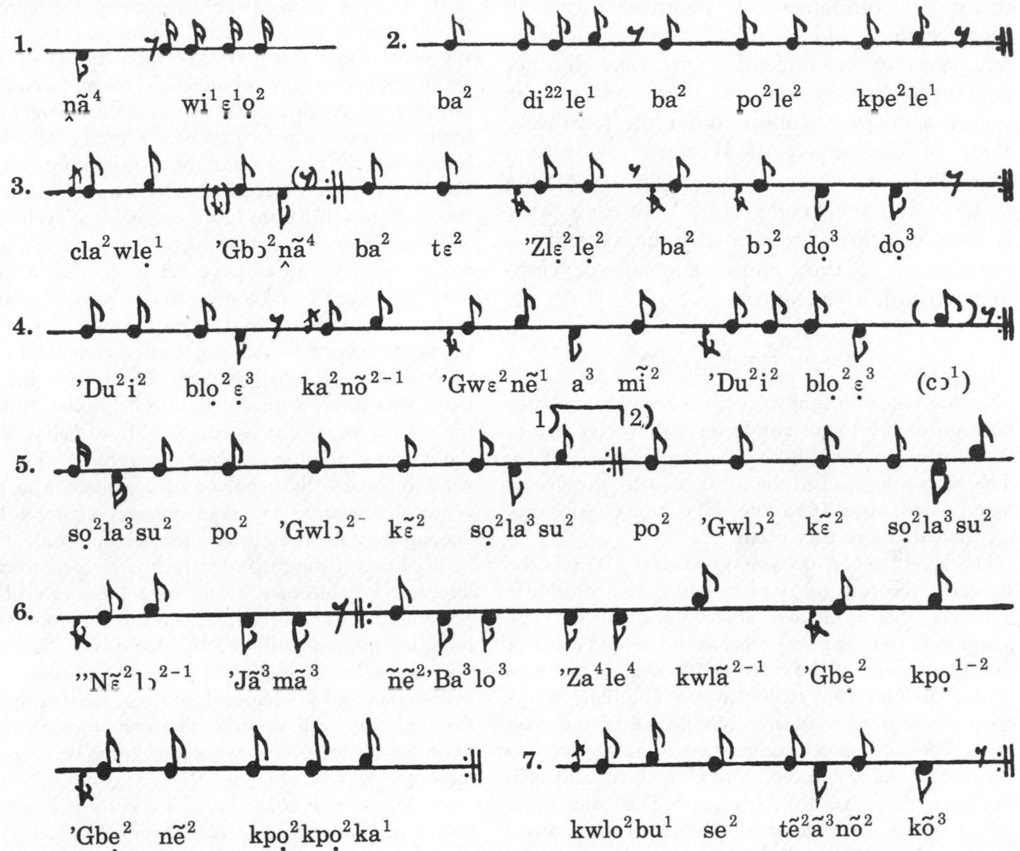
1. nã4 wi1ɛ̣1ọ2
2. ba2 di22le1 ba2 po2le2 kpe2le1
3. cla2wle1 'Gbɔ2nã4 ba2 tɛ2 'Zlẹ2lẹ2 ba2 bɔ2 dọ3 dọ3
4. 'Du2i2 blọ2ɛ3 ka2nõ2-1 'Gwɛ2nẽ1 a3 mĩ2 'Du2i2 blọ2ɛ3 (cɔ1)
5. sọ2la3su2 po2 'Gwlɔ2- kɛ̃2 sọ2la3su2 po2 'Gwlɔ2 kɛ̃2 sọ2la3su2
6. "Nɛ̃2lɔ2-1 'Jã3mã3 ñẽ2'Ba3lo3 'Za4le4 kwlã2-1 'Gbẹ2 kpọ1-2
'Gbẹ2 nẽ2 kpọ2kpọ2ka1
7. kwlo2bu1 se2 tẽ2ã3nõ2 kõ3

Skin-covered signal-drum

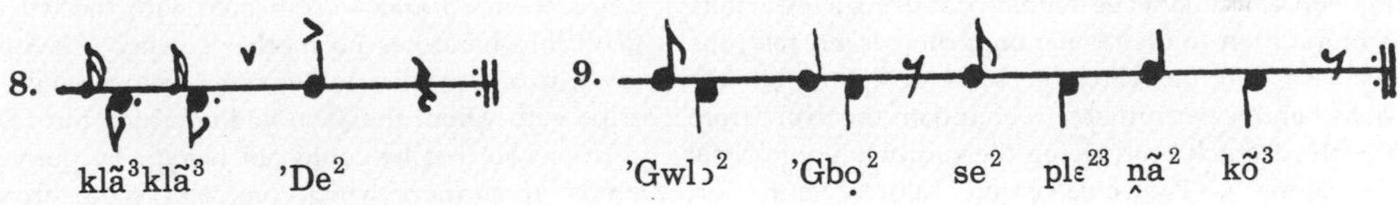
8. klã3klã3 'De2
9. 'Gwlɔ2 'Gbọ2 se2 plɛ23 nã2 kõ3

Wooden dance-drum

10. 'Gbe4la4 'Gbẹ2 dɛ2 klɛ̃2n1

11. tu3lu3 'Gbɛ4 wla2-1 'Gla2 bi2

Skin-covered dance-drum

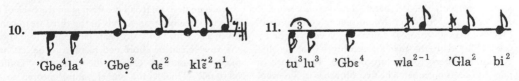

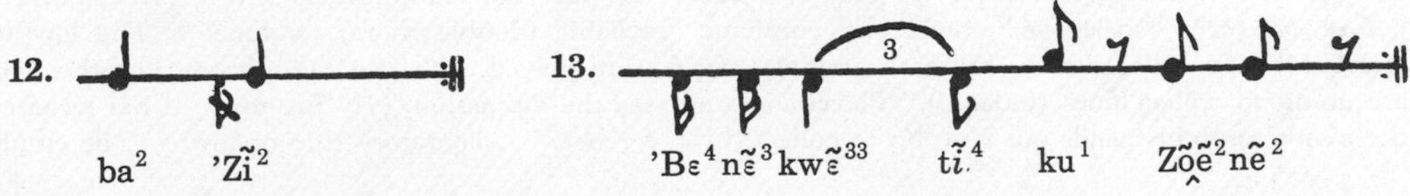
12. ba2 'Zĩ2
13. 'Bɛ4nɛ̃3kwɛ̃33 tĩ4 ku1 Zõẹ2nẽ2

Indian and the Pacific systems. The signal-drum has fundamentally identical forms in these regions, which could be due to diffusion from a common source of origin. Like all other content of native cultures, these systems are bound soon to disappear under the increasing force of the impact of Western civilization. The linguistic study of the various signaling systems and their comparison with each other is bound to throw light on the genesis and the psychology of this unique language-development in primitive cultures.

Notes to the Examples

For the sake of a simpler notation, only the relative position of the tones is indicated; the exact size of the musical intervals has no bearing on the pattern. The texts are given in the form used by the drummers; departures from the Jabo prose-forms are mentioned where they occur.

(1) "Greetings!" (lit., "your greetings!") This is the standard greeting of respect, which the drummer may use when a member enters the assembly. The pause does not represent a pause in the spoken form but lengthening of the first word, which in this case is permissible; the accompanying emphatic stress on the next word is apparently reflected by the extra beat. Tone 2 is not distinguished from 1, probably because of the fast speed. The first, third, and fifth beats are played with the left hand. The quick beats reflect actual pronunciation; the first two vowels are apt to be pronounced quite short, as also the third. Variants: (a) the first three beats form a triplet of sixteenths; the last is an eighth; (b) the first syllable is given a simultaneous double-beat using a lowertone 3 in addition to the regular one; there is no rest; the last beat is omitted; (c) the same as before, but the right hand is permitted to rebound on the drum from the third quick beat, giving the additional quick beat ("scraping"). (2) "Come ye quick! put ye your effort there!" Part of several signals, used also with the first part of example 3. The two parts of the signal may each be repeated a number of times. Beats 1, 2, 5, and 6 are with the left hand. The second word is Kru or Grebo; in Jabo it would mean "come again!" (3) "Soldiers all! Stop ye the noise; speak ye one by one!" Played in the men's assembly when the discussion threatens to get out of hand. The pause in parentheses is optional. The first phrase is in Trembo, a related dialect. The short up-beat for the emphatic consonant of the second word may be left out, or it may be on tone 2 instead of 3. The up-beats before *ba*^{2} *bɔ*^{2}, "speak ye," represent emphatic stress. (4) "To collect fines,—hunger is raging—we are going to collect fines (indeed!)." Played before the men's assembly sends out a group to collect, by force if necessary, fines imposed by the court; these in the form of foodstuffs, chickens, etc., the men will consume themselves. "Indeed" at the end is optional; the word comes from the Trembo dialect of Jabo and is appended to many signals at the end to make it possible for the drummers to finish the signal with a high-tone beat which they prefer there. The short beat before the first word of the second phrase, "hunger," seems purely ornamental ("scraping"), although the word has this form in other signals as well. This and the next word are possibly not in Jabo; the latter would be more apt to have the form *'Gwɛ*^{2}*n*^{2} here, although tone 1 could also be due to musical analogy with the preceding word. The two sections of the signal are repeated in various combinations. The low tones and short up-beats are played with the left hand, the others with the right. (5) "Solasu, throws (herself) upon the city, solasu." A "title of all women; the gossip of the men against the women." The first word refers to the behavior of a woman who goes about all the time and does not stay at home long enough to make it enjoyable for her husband; it can be used as a teasing name or nickname for a woman. The last syllable may be on tone 1 because of the preference for ending a signal on the high tone. Only tone 3 is played with the left hand. (6) Title of a man whose name is given in the first phrase, "The man-servant takes a handful (of rice); the dog shouts; the dog may well shout!" The man took this title as he was contemplating what it meant to be a servant, although he was not one. Rice is a native luxury; even the dog will object when a servant presumes to take some, according to the image. The 2-1 glides are represented with tone 1; the first can be optionally tone 1 also in speech. The last word and the third from the last are Kru forms; the Jabo have different tones. Tones 3 and 4 are beaten with the left hand. (7) "Shin-bone has no mother's gens." Playful title given to a man; his mother came from a neighboring tribe with whom the Jabo had anything but friendly relations so that he could not benefit by the various kinds of support which one can claim from his mother's gens. The title is also used as a proverb. "Shin-bone" is symbolic of hard luck and also of the grumpiness of a person who has hard luck "because there is no flesh on it; all the flesh is on the back of it." The two neighboring vowels in the third word can be given also with two short beats (sixteenths); in speech the vowels can be shortened likewise. The left hand plays all tones 3 except the last. (8) "Difficult matters!" This is the signal calling people to the town from the fields when there is grave trouble, death, and the like. The first word more often does not have the reduplicated form in prose, but a long syllable (double mora) on tone 3. The low tones were played with the right hand. For the figures, see the discussion. (9) "Big town, it has no circumference." A laudatory title of towns. The emphatic

consonant of the second word is represented by a long beat, while the third word is given with a short beat and the two morae of the next word by one beat only; perhaps all for the sake of establishing musical analogy between the two phrases of the signal. (10) "Mangy dog, is ailing." "Title" in honor of a dog; its owner, the warleader, picked it up during a battle with the neighboring Fishtown and brought it home with him although he was advised against it since the dog had the mange. Two regular beats represent *clv*. The last element is given with the tone of some neighboring language; in Jabo it would have tone 2 here. The third and sixth beats are played by the left hand. (11) "The snare spills the dance(ing) feet." "Title" played when a dancer stumbles or falls, to mock him or her. "To spill" is the expression for getting out of rhythm or for causing someone to get out of rhythm in music, signaling, or dancing. The 2-1 glide-tone is represented here exactly. For the next word, two sixteenths-beats are also used. (12) "Pass ye!" A dance-signal; to "pass" or to "pass the dance" refers to that movement in all group-dances in which the dancers file past the drums after having danced for a while before them. (13) "The people of Cape Palmas, picking up rotten corpses!" Taken from a piece for the war-dance in which the leading drummer plays this sentence toward the end, reviling a native tribe near Cape Palmas who are said to have been badly defeated in war at one time. The double-mora is represented by a long beat. The third word would have in this context tone 4-1 or 2-1 in Jabo; the latter could be represented by tone 1. Speech-tones 3 and 4 are beaten on these skin-covered drums by the cupped hand, preferably by the left, tones 2 and 1 by the right; 2 with the middle phalanges of the fingers; 1 with the fingertips.

REFERENCE NOTE

The author's expedition was under the auspices of the Department of Anthropology, University of Chicago, and of the Rockefeller Foundation. A sketch of the language, with a different orthography, was given by Sapir (1931). For further material, see Sapir and Blooah (1929) and the collection of proverbs cited (Herzog and Blooah, 1936). In the present study, the four registers are represented by the numbers 1 to 4, descending from the highest to the lowest. Length is not marked but implied by double tone-numbers so that each number stands for a mora. The quick-glide tone-combinations are denoted by numbers with a connecting hyphen. Consonants with "anacrusis" are marked with (') before them; "emphatic" consonants with capitals and the mark ('); "heavy" consonants with capitals and two marks (''). *Gb*, *kp*, and *nm* represent the well-known African labiovelar phonemes. The sounds written with *c* and *J* are somewhat fricative palatalized *t* and *d*, respectively; *n* with a semicircle beneath is a dental *n*; *ñ* is palatalized.

For a recent general classification of African languages, including Jabo and its congeners, see Greenberg (1948b, 1949-1954, 1963).

The bibliographic references are divided into two parts. References pertaining to Herzog's article and additional references concerning drum-signaling and other oral-aural codes are listed in Part A. Part B contains references concerning writing and other manual-visual codes.

A. DRUM-SIGNALING AND OTHER ORAL-AURAL CODES

A brief discussion of the horn-signaling system of the Jabo, with transcriptions of a few signals, is found in Herzog (1934, 1935). Among the special studies of this type of signaling are Betz (1898), Burssens (1939), Eboué (1935), Nekes (1912), Rattray (1916). For more general discussions see Thilenius, Meinhof, Heinitz (1916) and Labouret (1923). Labouret's study contains much excellent comparative material; cf. Rattray for the Ashanti. The above references were given by Herzog. To these may now be added: Armstrong (1953), Dugast (1960, pp. xix-xx [bibliography], 567-702), Jones (1959, chaps. 8-10), Lush (1935a, 1935b), Simmons (1955a, 1960a), Valen (1955). Theodore Stern (1957) is the only recent general survey and classification. Simmons (1960a) is good on the exact ways in which the tonal code functions, and Simmons (1960c) reports another case in which users of a tonal code show no awareness of its nature.

References not in general bibliography:

ARMSTRONG, ROBERT G.

1953. Talking [Musical] Instruments in West Africa. *Explorations, 4:* 140-153.

BETZ, R.

1898. Die Trommelsprache der Duala. *Mitteilungen aus den Deutschen Schutzgebieten, 11:* 1-86.

BURSSENS, A.

1939. Le Luba, langue à intonation, et le tambour-signal. *Proceedings, Third International Congress of Phonetic Sciences* (Ghent, 1938). Pp. 503-507.

DELAFOSSE, M.

1924. Langues du Soudan et de la Guinée. In A. Meillet and M. Cohen (Eds.), *Les langues du monde.* Paris: Societé de Linguistique de Paris. Pp. 548-552. [See now: M. Delafosse and A. Caquot. Langues du Soudan et de la Guinée. Meillet and Cohen (Eds.), *Les langues du monde* (Rev. ed.) Paris: Centre National de la Recherche Scientifique, 1952. Pp. 737-846.]

DUGAST, IDELETTE

1960. *Monographie de la tribu des Ndiki (Banen du Cameroun).* (Travaux et Memoires de l'Institut d'Ethnologie, Université de Paris, No. 63.) Paris: Institut d'Ethnologie and Centre National de la Recherche Scientifique. Vol. II.

EBOUÉ, F.

1935. La Clef musicale des langages tambourinés et sifflés. *Bulletin du Comité d'Études Historiques et Scientifiques de l'Afrique Occidentale Française, 18:* 353-360.

JONES, A. M.

1959. *Studies in African Music.* London and New York: Oxford University Press. Vol. I.

LABOURET, H.

1923. Langage tambouriné et sifflé. *Bulletin du Comité d'Études Historiques et Scientifiques de l'Afrique Occidentale Française,* pp. 120-158.

LUSH, A. J.

1935a. Kiganda drums. *Uganda Journal, 3:* 7-20.

1935b. Proverbs Based on Drums; Idiomatic Phrases Derived from Drums; Technical Terms Used in Connection with Drums; Drum Beats Peculiar to Clans. *Uganda Journal, 3:* 21-25.

NEKES, H.

1912. Trommelsprache und Fernruf bei den Jaunde und Duala in Südkamerun. *Mitteilungen des Seminars für Orientalische Sprachen, 3* (15): 69-83.

RATTRAY, R. S.

1916. The Drum Language. *Ashanti.* Oxford: Oxford University Press. Pp. 242-286.

SAPIR, EDWARD

1931. Notes on the Gweabo Language in Liberia. *Lg., 7:* 30-41.

SAPIR, EDWARD, and C. G. BLOOAH

1929. Some Gweabo Proverbs. *Africa, 2:* 183-185.

SIMMONS, DONALD C.

1955a. Efik Iron Gongs and Gong Signals. *Man, 55:* 107-108.

THILENIUS, G., C. MEINHOF, and W. HEINITZ

1916. Die Trommelsprache in Afrika und in der Südsee. *Vox, 26:* 179-208.

VALEN, LEIGH VAN

1955. Talking Drums and Similar African Tonal Communication. *Southern Folklore Quarterly, 19* (4): 252-256.

WESTERMANN, D.

1907. Zeichensprache des Ewevolkes in Deutsch-Togo. *Mitteilungen des Seminars für Orientalische Sprachen, 3* (10): 1-4.

1911. *Die Sudanensprachen, eine sprachvergleichende Studie.* (Abhandlungen des Hamburgischen Kolonialinstituts, No. 3.) Hamburg.

1927. Die westlichen Sudansprachen und ihre Beziehungen zum Bantu. *Mitteilungen des Seminars für Orientalische Sprachen, 30:* 52 ff.

1935. Charakter und Einteilung der afrikanischen Sprachen. *Afrika, 8:* 129-148.

B. WRITING AND OTHER MANUAL-VISUAL CODES

Although writing is not listed by Stern (1957) as a speech surrogate, it falls within the rubrics of such a classification and focuses attention on the general problems of specifying the relative autonomy and interdependence of alternative modes of speech-linked communication. On the status of written communication and its social role, see recent discussions by Brown (1958, chap. 2), Garvin (1954b, pp. 91-93), Gleason (1961, chaps. 25, 26), Hockett (1952; 1958, chap. 62), Uldall (1944), Vachek (1939, 1944-1949, 1948), Vendryes (1925, pp. 313-343). Other articles bearing on the analysis of written language as a signaling system include Bazell (1956), Bolinger (1946), Crossland (1956), Edgerton (1941), Francis (1958, pp. 436-437, 441-447), R. A. Hall (1963), Hamp (1959), Pulgram (1951). Instances of writing in partly or newly literate societies have been treated by Chamberlain (1906), Conklin (1949), Fletcher (1889), Ibarra Grasso (1953), Radin (1924), Ransom (1945), and Riesenberg and Kaneshiro (1960); see also Foreman (1938) and McLean (1890). On social consequences, see McLuhan (1962) and Sjoberg (1960, pp. 285-293).

One aspect of writing is its status as an object of aesthetic interest in visual form; see trenchant comments by Sapir (Mandelbaum [Ed.], 1949, pp. 383-384), linking it to concepts of drift and style; and such books as Degering (1952, 1954), Denholm (1954), and Roberts (1956).

For history, classification, and decipherment of writing systems, see Gleason (1961), the surveys and individual cases listed below, and Pedersen (1931). Schmitt (1952) interprets the development of script by Eskimo as recapitulating the general evolution of writing systems. The inventors of two systems for Amerindian languages are discussed by Foreman (1938) and McLean (1890). Also compare references to Bull's article in Part VIII.

For other manual-visual codes, see Kroeber (1958), Mallery (1881), Mooney (1910a), and Voegelin (1958) on the Plains Indian sign language; Mooney (1910a, 1910b), for Amerindian signaling generally; Locke (1923) for a particular method;

and Polunin (1959) for description of a community in Oceania. Ransom (1941) treats an interesting case of stimulus diffusion of such a code. Graphic devices other than writing are also surveyed by Croft (1949), Mallery (1886, 1893), and Steward (1936). Cases are analyzed by Hellinga (1954), Munn (1962), Nordenskiöld (1928-1930), and Stout (1947). Questions of theoretical interpretation and typology of such systems are considered in some of the general books on writing. For gesture as expressive communication and its description, see references following Devereux and Trager in Part V. References for whistling as a speech surrogate have been given with Cowan's article on pp. 305-311.

References not in general bibliography:

BARTHEL, T. S.

1958. Grundlagen zur Entzifferung der Osterinselschrift. *Abhandlung aus dem Gebiete der Auslandskunde*, *64* (B).

BAZELL, C. E.

1956. The Grapheme. *Litera*, *3:* 43-46.

BOLINGER, DWIGHT

1946. Visual Morphemes. *Lg.*, *22:* 333-340.

CHADWICK, JOHN

1958. *The Decipherment of Linear B*. Cambridge: Cambridge University Press.

CHAMBERLAIN, A. F.

1906. Acquisition of Written Language by Primitive Peoples. *American Journal of Psychology*, *17:* 69-80.

COHEN, MARCEL

1959. *La Grande invention de l'écriture et son évolution*. Paris: Klincksieck. 3 vols.

CONKLIN, HAROLD C.

1949. Bamboo Literacy on Mindoro. *Pacific Discovery*, *2* (4): 4-11.

CROFT, KENNETH

1949. Graphic Mechanisms of Communication in Native North America. *Indiana Magazine of History*, *45:* 339-352.

CROSSLAND, R. A.

1956. Graphic Linguistics and Its Terminology. *Mechanical Translation*, *3:* 8-11.

DEGERING, H.

1952. *Die Schrift. Atlas des Schriftformer des Abendlandes vom Altertum bis zum Ausgang des 18. Jahrhundert.* (3rd ed.) Tübingen.

1954. *Lettering: A Series of 240 Plates illustrating Modes of Writing in Western Europe from Antiquity to the end of the 18th Century; with Introduction.*

DENHOLM, YOUNG N.

1954. *Handwriting in England and Wales. From Earliest Times to the 17th Century.*

DIRINGER, DAVID

1948. *The Alphabet. A Key to the History of Mankind*. New York: Philosophical Library. [Reviewed, A. L. Kroeber, *AA*, 1951, *53:* 258-259.]

1958. *The Story of the Aleph Beth*. New York: Yoseloff.

1962. *Writing*. (Ancient Peoples and Places, Vol. 25.) London: Thames and Hudson.

DOBLHOVER, ERNST

1961. *Voices in Stone; The Decipherment of Ancient Scripts and Writings.* Translated from the German, *Zeichen und Wunder*, by Mervyn Savill. New York: Viking. (Original edition, Vienna, 1957.)

DRIVER, G. R.

1954. *Semitic Writing from Pictograph to Alphabet.* (Rev. ed.) (The Schweich Lectures of the British Academy, 1944.) London: Published for the British Academy.

EDGERTON, W. F.

1941. Ideograms in English Writing. *Lg.*, *17:* 148-150.

FÉVRIER, JAMES G.

1948. *Histoire de l'écriture.* Paris. Payot.

FLETCHER, ALICE C.

1889. The Phonetic Alphabet of the Winnebago Indians. *Proceedings, American Association for the Advancement of Science*, *38:* 354-357.

FOREMAN, GRANT

1938. *Sequoyah.* Norman: University of Oklahoma Press.

FRANCIS, W. NELSON

1958. *The Structure of American English.* New York: Ronald.

FRIEDRICH, JOHANNES

1957. *Extinct Languages.* Translated from the German, *Entzifferung Verschollener Schriften und Sprachen*, by Frank Gaynor. New York: Philosophical Library (The Wisdom Library, WL 90).

GARVIN, PAUL

1954b. Review of L. Hjelmslev, *Prolegomena to a Theory of Language. Lg.*, *30:* 69-96, esp. pp. 91-93.

GELB, I. J.

1952. *A Study of Writing. The Foundations of Grammatology.* Chicago: University of Chicago Press.

1958. *Von der Keilschrift zum Alphabet.* Stuttgart. (Revised translation of Gelb, *A Study of Writing*). [Reviewed, H. H. Paper, "The Study of Writing," *Lingua*, 1954-1955, *4:* 89-96; W. F. Edgerton, "On the Theory of Writing," *Journal of Near Eastern Studies*, 1952, *11:* 287-290.]

HALL, ROBERT A., JR.

1963. Graphemics and Linguistics. In Wallace Chafe (Ed.), *Aspects of Language and Culture.* (Proceedings, American Ethnological Society, Washington D.C., 1962.) Seattle: University of Washington Press.

HAMP, ERIC P.

1959. Graphemics and Paragraphemics. *Studies in Linguistics*, *14* (1-2): 1-5.

HELLINGA, W. G.

1954. Petroglyphs Caraïbes: Problème sémiologique. *Lingua*, *4:* 121-166.

HEWITT, J. N. B., and W. N. FENTON

1945. Some Mnemonic Pictographs Relating to the Iroquois Condolence Council. *Journal of the Washington Academy of Sciences*, *35:* 301-315.

HIGOUNET, CHARLES

1955. *L'Écriture.* ("Que Sais-je.") Paris: Presses Universitaires de France.

HOCKETT, C. F.

1951. Review of J. de Francis, *Nationalism and Language Reform in China. Lg.*, *27:* 439-445.

1952. Speech and Writing. *Report of the Third Annual Round Table Meeting on Linguistics and Language Teaching*. Washington, D.C.: Georgetown University Press. Pp. 67-76.

IBARRA GRASSO, DICK EDGAR

1953. *La escritura indigena andean.* (Biblioteca Paceña.) La Paz, Bolivia: Alcaldía Municipal.

JENSEN, HANS

1935. *Die Schrift in Vergangenheit und Gegenwart.* Gluckstadt und Hamburg. (2nd ed. Berlin: Deutscher Verlag der Wissenschaften, 1958.)

KARLGREN, BERNHARD

1923. *Sound and Symbol in Chinese.* London: Oxford University Press.

1940. *Grammatica Serica: Script and Phonetics in Chinese and Sino-Japanese.* Stockholm. [Reviewed Y. R. Chao, *Lg.*, 1941, *17:* 60-76.]

KNOROZOV, Y. V.

1958. The Problem of the Study of the Maya Hieroglyphic Writing. *American Antiquity*, *23:* 284-291. [Cf. Norman A. McQuown, American Indian and General Linguistics. *AA.*, 1960, *62:* 318-326.]

KROEBER, A. L.

1958. Sign Language Inquiry. *IJAL*, *24:* 1-19.

LOCKE, LESLIE L.

1923. *The Ancient Quipu or Peruvian Knot Record.* New York: American Museum of Natural History.

MCLEAN, JOHN

1890. *James Evans. Inventor of the Syllabic System of the Cree Language* [Text title: James Evans, the Canadian Cadmus.] Toronto: Methodist Mission Rooms.

MALLERY, G.

1881. Sign Language Among North American Indians. *BAE-AR* (1879-1880), *1:* 263-552.

1886. Pictographs of the North American Indians. *BAE-AR* (1882-1883), *4:* 3-256.

1893. Picture-Writing of the American Indians. *BAE-AR* (1888-1889), *10:* 1-822.

MOONEY, JAMES

1910a. Signals. In F. W. Hodge, (Ed.), *Handbook of American Indians North of Mexico.* (BAE-B 30.) Washington, D.C.: Smithsonian Institution. Vol. 2, pp. 565-567.

1910b. Sign Language. In F. W. Hodge (Ed.), *Handbook of American Indians North of Mexico.* (BAE-B 30.) Washington, D.C.: Smithsonian Institution Vol. 2, pp. 567-568.

MOORHOUSE, ALFRED C.

1953. *The Triumph of the Alphabet. A History of Writing.* (Life of Science Series Library, No. 28.) New York: Schuman.

MUNN, NANCY

1962. Walbiri Graphic Signs: An Analysis. *AA.*, *65:* 972-984.

NORDENSKIÖLD, E.

1928-1930. *Picture Writings and Other Documents.* (Comparative Ethnographical Studies, No. 7, Parts 1, 2.) Göteborg.

POLUNIN, IVAN

1959. A Note on Visual Non-literary Methods of Communication among the Muruts of North Borneo. *Man, 59:* 97-99.

PULGRAM, ERNST

1951. Phoneme and Grapheme: A Parallel. *Word, 7:* 15-20.

RADIN, PAUL

1924. The Adoption of an Alphabet by an Aboriginal People. *Cambridge University Reporter* (Proceedings of the Cambridge Philological Society), Nov. 25, pp. 24-31.

RANSOM, JAY ELLIS

1941. Aleut Semaphore Signals. *AA, 43:* 422-427.

1945. Writing as a Medium of Acculturation Among the Aleuts. *SJA, 1:* 333-344.

RIESENBERG, SAUL H., and SHIGERU KANESHIRO

1960. A Caroline Islands Script. (Anthropological Papers, No. 60; BAE-B 173.) Washington, D.C.: Smithsonian Institution. Pp. 269-334.

ROBERTS, C. H.

1956. *Greek Literary Hands, 350 B.C.-A.D. 400.* (Rev. ed.) Oxford: Clarendon.

SCHMITT, ALFRED

1952. *Die Alaska-Schrift und ihre Schrift-geschichtliche Bedeutung.* Marburg.

SJOBERG, GIDEON

1960. *The Pre-Industrial City.* Glencoe: Free Press.

STEWARD, JULIAN A.

1936. Petroglyphs of the United States. *Annual Report of the Board of Regents of the Smithsonian Institution.* Washington, D.C.: Smithsonian Institution. Pp. 405-425.

THOMPSON, J. ERIC S.

1960. *Maya Hieroglyphic Writing: An Introduction.* (2nd ed.) Norman: University of Oklahoma Press.

ULDALL, HANS

1944. Speech and Writing. *Acta Linguistica, 4:* 11-16.

VACHEK, JOZEF

1939. Zum Problem der geschriebenen Sprache. *Travaux du Cercle Linguistique de Prague, 8:* 94 ff.

1944-1949. Some Remarks on Writing and Phonetic Transcription. *Acta Linguistica, 5:* 86-93.

1948. Written Language and Printed Language. *Recueil Linguistique de Bratislava, 1:* 67-74.

VOEGELIN, C. F.

1958. Sign Language Analysis, on One Level or Two? *IJAL, 24:* 71-77.

VOEGELIN, C. F., and F. M. VOEGELIN

1961. Typological Classification of Systems with Included, Excluded and Self-Sufficient Alphabets. *AL, 3* (1): 55-96.

[WALAM OLUM]

1954. *Walam Olum or Red Score. The Migration Legend of the Lenni Lenape or Delaware Indians.* A New Translation, interpreted by linguistic, historical, archaeological, ethnological, and physical anthropological studies. Indianapolis: Indiana Historical Society.

37 *Oral Poets of South India — The Todas*

MURRAY B. EMENEAU

A CRITIC OF English literature once wrote that literature, "simply defined, is memorable speech placed on record" (Quiller-Couch, 1930, p. 188). Much discussion and expansion would be required to make this a really serviceable definition—e.g., what are to be the criteria of "memorability." But for our purpose, the critic Quiller-Couch has said something useful in his identification of two factors: the speech, which is primary, and the placing on record, which is secondary, but which has provided literature with its name.

The student of the earliest literary works of our Western culture, those of Greece, soon learns that not all of them are literature in the strict sense. The Homeric poems are not works that were composed with the aid of writing materials. They bear within themselves very patently the marks of oral composition and recitation, and the Greek traditions about them are hardly intelligible on any other interpretation. European poetry, however, soon exchanged oral composition for that based on the use of writing materials, and our literatures in the Western world are to the present day predicated in an extraordinarily intimate fashion on this newer technique and its consequences. So much is this so, that for many scholars over many centuries the implications of oral composition for the understanding of Homer were forgotten. Not all had been oblivious, to be sure—one need mention only Gilbert Murray and the Chadwicks to refute that—but there was a need for some new impulse to make the matter vivid enough to be vital in Homeric studies. This new impulse was external and analogous, as it turned out. An American classical scholar originally of the University of California, Milman Parry, knew well enough the method of composition of the Homeric poems and knew too that there existed in the modern world and in a geographical area not far removed from Greece an oral epic. In the comparatively peaceful period between the two World Wars he went to Yugoslavia and in the mountains of the southern part of that country and of Albania he recorded and investigated the South Slav epic. He and his collaborators and pupils found there a technique remarkably similar in many details to that which had been postulated for Homer. It was possible to go on and to apply profitably to Homeric interpretation other details of the technique of the South Slav epic singers. Much of the needed reexamining of several of these literatures based on oral composition has been done by Maurice Bowra in his masterly and suggestive book *Heroic Poetry*, which was published in 1952. His title shows how he has restricted himself to one of the genres that he persuasively distinguishes, namely the heroic epic, whether Homeric Greek, Mesopotamian and Hittite, Old Germanic and Old Romance, or South Slav, East European, Uzbek, Yakut, or Ainu. Other genres still require detailed treatment of the same kind; several of these will be referred to in what follows. But we must gratefully say that very much of Bowra's treatment of the oral technique applies just as well, *mutatis mutandis*, to some other genres as it does to the heroic epic.

Other oral literatures have long been known. In fact, it has been clearly recognized that, in the long millennia of human life before the comparatively recent times when writing became commonplace, all memorable speech, or literature, if it may be called such for lack of a better term, was composed orally and transmitted orally, without benefit of writing.

When writing was beginning, some of this oral literature was recorded, as we believe happened with Homer. The problem for literary scholars has been to distinguish in the oldest records what was written down from the mouths of oral composers and what was composed on paper (or cuneiform bricks, or palmleaves, or birchbark, or whatnot) in imitation of oral composition. That the latter happened we know —witness the Hellenistic Greek epic and its Latin successor. This must certainly be a problem in dealing with such Hebrew literature as the Psalms of David and the prophetic books of the Old Testament. It is likewise a problem in dealing with the old Germanic literatures—those of Iceland, the earliest Anglo-Saxons, the speakers of Old High German—or with the poetic literatures in the oldest stages of the Romance languages, e.g., that of Provence and that centering around the song of Roland.

To mention a literary corpus which is closer to the subject of this symposium than is Homer—the problem of oral composition arises in Sanskrit literature at more than one point. Old as is writing in the history of the culture of India in its classical form, there is literature there that is even older than writing. The Vedas, the oldest religious texts of Hinduism, contain in their earliest layers hymns and other ritual utterances, the beginning of which can be conservatively placed in the second millennium B.C. These texts present clear evidence that they are oral compositions. Perhaps the most striking kind of evidence is the extensive repeated use, in the verses, of traditional poetic units. Maurice Bloomfield in his intensive study of the phenomenon in the two volumes called *Rig-Veda Repetitions* found that in the Rigvedic collection of over 1000 hymns, approximately one-fifth of the lines are involved in this repetitive use. He and his pupil, Franklin Edgerton, who was my teacher, carried on further studies of this repeated material in the whole of the Vedic literature, with profit for the interpretation of these texts. The result was the three volumes of *Vedic Variants*, in the third of which I had the honor of collaborating in 1931-32.

More important than the details is the tradition that the whole immense corpus of Vedic literature was both composed and transmitted without any recourse to writing. Oral transmission down to the present day by memorization is undoubted—but at the same time suspect, since it is clear that there has at times been recourse to good old manuscripts to correct corrupted oral tradition. This only illustrates the tenacious hold of traditional ways of doing things in India. It does not invalidate the necessity of treating the oldest Vedic texts as examples of oral composition before writing was usual in India, since this in effect is what the tenaciously held tradition means for us in this connection. Our suspicions must lead us to close examination of each text to determine, as was said before, what is the record of oral composition and what the imitation. The safeguards which the Hindus invented very early against change in their holy texts make this determination on the whole easy for the earliest Vedic texts and not too difficult even for the latest.

Another Sanskrit literary corpus that traditionally was both composed and transmitted orally is the epic, consisting of two enormous works, the *Mahābhārata* and the *Rāmāyaṇa*. The marks of oral composition and of a very early synthesis of numerous oral recitations into one unified text are clearly evident in both these epics (as they are in Homer). The tradition of the transmittal of the *Mahābhārata* (and of the *Rāmāyaṇa* too) even illustrates the postulate that in a living oral tradition and barring special conditions, no two oral recitations of what purports to be the same work are identical, but each recitation is a fresh composition. For we are told in the *Mahābhārata* itself that its length is not always the same (Book 1, adhyāya 1) and that the text as we have it is the third recitation in a succession of famous recitations of different lengths. This oral characteristic (which we know very well from Bowra's work) did not come to an end even after the *Mahābhārata* was written down, perhaps in the fourth century A.D., perhaps somewhat earlier. The copyists have never ceased to add more good, bad, or indifferent passages or stories to their versions when they could do so. It is only recognition of the oral technique of composition and its implications that makes it possible to deal with the Sanskrit epic in any but the most fumbling way. Bowra excluded this enormous corpus from his study as being not strictly heroic epic; he said (p.v): "a truly heroic foundation is overlaid with much literary and theological matter." But the truth is that the

Mahābhārata at least, is an amalgam of several different genres of oral poetry. One is truly heroic in Bowra's sense. Another is the theological or moralistic oral genre, for which there is much evidence outside the epic—in the latest Vedic texts, in the early law books, in the early texts of Buddhism, and in many works of later date which draw much from the oral traditions of Hinduism. Still another genre, closely related to the last, is that which states in verse form the laws, the manners and customs, of Hinduism. Again there is much evidence for an oral tradition, probably even a tradition of free oral composition, in this genre. There may also be other types of oral composition to be identified as part of the epic combination. And in all probability we must recognize that the same composers worked in all or most of the techniques. Bowra was really defeated by the complexities of the Hindu epic, rather than justified logically in excluding it from his work.

In 1935, after undergraduate and graduate training that had included study of Homer and the Sanskrit epics and Vedas, as well as study of linguistics, I went to India to apply my linguistics to several of the non-literary languages of South India. I worked first on the Todas of the Nilgiris. They were already very well known to anthropologists through a lengthy account published by W. H. R. Rivers in 1906. Their language, however, though known to be one member of the Dravidian family, was a problem, for the solution of which there was only poor and scanty evidence, and indeed it turned out to be the most aberrant of the languages of the family and very difficult to analyze, both descriptively and comparatively.

The culture of the Todas is just as divergent from its Indian roots as is their language, because of their long isolation (since the beginning of the Christian era, as I think I have now proved) from the general streams of Hindu culture. This isolation was produced both by their geographical situation on a lofty, 8000-foot-high plateau and by the general framework of the Hindu caste system within which they and their few neighbors live. This social framework favors diversity within unity, and on the Nilgiri plateau, an area of forty by twenty miles, has allowed four communities to live symbiotically, but with four remarkably different cultures and four mutually unintelligible languages.

The linguistic scholar working in the field has perforce to be or become something of an anthropologist, so that he may understand what his informants are talking about in the language he is studying. It was no different in my own case. I soon learned much about the life of the Todas, some, though very little of it, not already known to Rivers. They are a remarkably attractive looking people—even if one makes all allowance for a field investigator's personal preference for his first tribe. They are aware of it—they sing that "in the Nilgiris live a black-headed people," referring to their distinctive and attractive coiffures; they spend much time over these with the aid of butter, which is, alas, all too often rancid and evil smelling. And their neighbors, the Kotas, admit that "the Todas are useless, but so beautiful." In the local caste system of the Nilgiris, the Todas rank highest. Small as the community is, numbering approximately 600 people, it has a most complex social structure. It is usual within Hindu endogamous castes to find subcastes which are also endogamous, i.e., which do not intermarry. So with the Todas, who have two nonintermarrying subcastes, one ranked higher than the other. Within each subcaste there are a number of exogamous clans; members of a clan may not marry each other but must marry members of other clans within the endogamous subcaste. The Todas complicate matters by having the members of each subcaste completely divided into two different systems of clans, one system on a patrilineal basis, the other on a matrilineal basis; each Toda, therefore, belongs to a patrilineal clan and to a matrilineal clan and must avoid marriage with two different sets of kin—the matrilineal clans were not known to Rivers (Emeneau, 1937, 1941).

This is by no means the end. There are subdivisions of clans, right down to the individual family, and all the divisions and subdivisions are identifiable and definable in terms of specific functions apart from those connected with marriage. When we reach the family, it is prevailingly polyandrous, several brothers having a common wife. Paternity of children within a polyandrous family is determined by a ceremony during which the pregnant wife is given a toy bow and arrow by one of her husbands; he is the socially accepted father of all children born to the woman until the occasion arises sometime to change the paternity by having another brother give the bow and arrow. The economic side of marriage arrangements is complex. Divorce and regularized wife-stealing are possible and even common. Alongside of marriage within the subcaste, there are also socially approved and regularized arrangements between individuals of the two subcastes; in theory, each man has a regular sexual partner in the subcaste not his own, and so has each woman. It is considered bad manners to mention it if a woman's child looks like her partner in the other subcaste. And besides all these regularized arrangements, there are also more casual love affairs.

The Todas are a community of buffalo herders. All their economic life is based on the dairy products of the herds and consequently on the pasture lands. The herds and pastures are inherited within the patrilineal clans. Even in the social structure, the number of the polyandrous husbands in a family depends on the relation between the size of the family's herd and the number of buffaloes that can be sustained by any one clan pasture location; if the herd becomes too large, the brothers must split up to utilize two different locations, and each group of brothers then needs a separate wife to do the housework.

The care of the buffaloes has been made the basis of religion. Every item of dairy practice is ritualized, from the twice daily milking and churning of butter to the great seasonal shifting of pastures, the burning over of the dry pastures, and the giving of salt to the herds. Periodical rebuilding of dairies and the ordination of dairymen are all occasions for ritual. The holy entities of the religion are the pasture locations with their necessary dairy buildings, pens, calf sheds, streams, and herds. The ritualization has been carried to extreme lengths, in the sanctification of locations and the avoidance of ceremonial impurity, in ritual practices, and in the accompanying ritual utterances. In general the sacred herds (they are not the only herds) belong to the clans of the higher subcaste, and the sacred dairymen are drawn from the lower subcaste (it is general Hindu practice that Brahmans who are officiant priests of temples are lower in rank than those who are not).

One other conspicuous feature of Toda culture can be mentioned—the funerals. Regulations and practices are complicated, and center about the dispatch of the dead person to the afterworld with a proper complement of buffaloes, which are slaughtered so that they may accompany him on his path. The chase and capture of the buffaloes is an opportunity for men to show prowess, and the funeral in general is an opportunity for a great gathering in best clothes and for festivity and dancing.

In this sketch we have not exhausted all the the themes of Toda life; we have not even attempted to clothe the themes in the elaborate detail that fills so much of Rivers' book. The total impression given by the Todas is that in the course of centuries they have produced a culture marked by extreme elaboration of a smallish number of basic themes, and that little of the detailed elaboration is not obligatory. There is variation possible, to be sure; there are choices and alternatives; but once one theme is chosen rather than another, there is little freedom of choice in the way in which the theme is carried out in actions and even in utterances. This is a culture of the kind that has been called "closed." (See, e.g., Dodds, 1951, esp. pp. 237, 255 [note 1], and the bibliography contained in the latter reference.) It is so nearly closed, so little open to option or conscious choice ("open-ended" is the fashionable word) that it has proved difficult in the last century for the Todas to acculturate or to admit any but the most inconsequential changes. Once any major theme should go awry because of pressure from outside the group or because of a novel preference that is pushed by a strong personality within the group, the whole fabric of embroidered detail would disintegrate. This is especially true of the economic basis on which so much of Toda culture is founded. The pasture lands on which their herds depend are coveted by surrounding agriculturalists and have been alienated to a small extent to one or another pressure group, the Badaga farmers or the English town builders or tea growers. In spite of this, alienation has on the whole been sparingly allowed by the local government. But it is instructive that when one of the clans (*ïṇkity*) lost its nuclear dairy locations, it lost its ritual, its singleminded emphasis on pastoralism, and its desire to follow through all the obligations and rights that tied it to the unchanged remainder of the tribe. A funeral of a member of this clan that I attended was marked by more pugnacious, ill-natured quarreling than any other in my experience, and the Todas of this clan hardly seemed in their preoccupations or even in their appearance to be Todas any longer.

It was not long after my work started on the Toda language that I found that the utterances of greatest interest to the Todas themselves were their songs, and that here was a new example of oral poetry. If I have reverted to study of the Toda songs again and again in the last twenty years, it is not only because, as I said before, one has a preference for his first tribe, but also because of the intrinsic interest of the songs and because there seems always to be something new to say about them. (A preliminary account was given in Emeneau, 1937.)

Part of my current research is the preparation of over 250 song texts for publication. These were recorded from dictation as part of linguistic research that covered a period totaling about eight months made up of shorter intervals within a total of three years spent in India. I would leave the Nilgiris at times to work elsewhere, and when I returned, the accumulation of notable songs composed during my absence would be dictated; or, while I worked on another Nilgiri language, Todas would come to me once a week or so and would dictate new songs or songs that they remembered. Unfortunately, this was in the times before tape recorders, or in fact before any reasonably good recording apparatus of a portable character, and no records of this kind are in my possession, although I hope that tape recordings can be made in the near future. It will be only when such recordings are available that work can be done on the music of the songs, and I hope that the Todas and their song art will not become extinct before this happy event. I am not trained in the requisite type of musicology, much to my regret; there are very few who are. My work, then, consisted only in taking down at dictation, as if it were prose, the words of the songs. There is perhaps the less regret for this, since the singing of songs is only one of two manifestations of the Toda art. Identically the same types of words are used also as a shouted accompaniment to the men's dancing, and although samples of this also should be recorded on tape, little would result from it of musicological interest apart from the metrical distribution of the words with reference to the dance rhythm. The words on these dance occasions are all important, and my records suffice.

I shall describe the essentials of the verbal structure of the Toda songs, a structure that is, as I have said, identical for both the songs as sung and the dance songs. The metrical structure is the simplest that I know of in any elaborate poetic art. Each sung unit consists of three syllables, which may comprise one or two or three words. This is all—no rules of accent, quantity, alliteration, rhyme, or the like, are discoverable. It is a syllable-counting meter and nothing more. From this simple beginning, however, there is built up a complicated structure on principles other than metrical. Sentences consist of from one sung unit to as many as five or six or even seven, with a possibility of quite complicated syntax. But, one very striking feature of the structure, no such sentence may be uttered without being paired with another sentence exactly parallel to it in syntactic structure and in number of units. And the second characteristic feature: all the paired units are rigorously dictated within the technique (with only the most minor of qualifications, which I shall present later). For example, if a man is to be identified by mention of his patrilineal clan, each clan of the higher subcaste has a pair of three-syllable names for use in the songs—similarly for many other entities that are mentioned in song. On the other hand, many entities are sung of only in pairs, e.g. in describing a wife-stealing affair that is settled by discussion before the assembly of chief men, there is a song-pair formed by the words for wife (*mox*) and the compensation that is paid to a husband by a man who has stolen his wife (*ter*): *te̱r wïd̲ o·ṭk öštyïθs̱ïk* 'you (pl.) settled compensation for each man' /*mox wïd̲ o·ṭk kïsïθs̱ïk* 'you (pl.) made a wife for each man.' Thorn bushes and fallen stones mark the disrepair of a neglected dairy, and are mentioned as a pair: *u·r̲yïθ muṭ po·ṇyïθs̱ïk* 'you (pl.) cleared the thorns that had grown up' /*pïḍθïθ xas̱ tu·kyïθsïk* 'you (pl.) lifted the stones that had fallen.' Pen bars (*tošt*) and pen posts (*tüṭy*) are always mentioned together, as are the dairy bell (*moṇy*) and ax (*mošt*), the dairyman-priest's garment (*tüṇy*) and the cane (*peṭ*) that he uses to drive the buffaloes. Children and buffalo calves are mentioned together, either as the crying child (*ʋṛyïθ mox*) and the bellowing calf (*karθïθ xoṟ*), or as the child on the lap (*moṛyïš mox*) and the calf in the calf pen (*kaṛïṣ xoṟ*). The technique also dictates all the syntactic constructions that may occur on the basis of the paired words and units. There is, in effect, a stereotyped two dimensional poetic language—the syntactic construction is one dimension, the required paired construction the other. One occasional complication is the interweaving of two such structures; the two first halves are sung, and then the two second halves.

The subjects of the songs are a close match for the Toda culture and the interests of the Todas. Every event in their lives is likely to be sung about on the spot or immediately afterwards, either by the participants or bystanders, or by specialists in the song technique. A really notable event will become the subject for more than one song. Some songs will be remembered for weeks or years or generations, usually because the events they commemorate are of sufficient note to come to mind again and again; and this, of course, includes the small number of songs that deal with the lives of the legendary culture heroes. We do not know much about the history of the song technique, but it became clear after a large number of songs had been recorded, that in the course of the presumably long development of the technique, every theme in Toda culture and every detail of the working out of every theme have been provided with one or several set patterns of words and turns of phrase for use in song. We have seen that though Toda life is complicated in its patterns, these are limited and rather tightly closed. The song technique provides a rich verbification of all Toda life, but rich as it is, the basic features that characterize it and that I have sketched out, ensure that it also is a limited and tightly closed technique. Its themes, its set pieces, are in part covered by the sketch of Toda culture that I have given. Funerals and their accompanying dance-songs and sung laments bulk largest in the record. These rehearse in outline the life of the deceased—a man's marriages and children, his prosperity through the increase of his herds, a career as a dairyman-priest who starts as a poor servant boy and ends as the owner of many buffaloes after service in many dairies, or a man's repute as a person of wisdom in settling disputes, or whatever else he may have been notable for in his lifetime; a woman's beauty and many husbands, or her careful attention to her family's needs, or her brood of children may be celebrated. The provision of the buffaloes to accompany the dead is a matter of emulation as well as of dispute, many quarrels occur over them, and the buffaloes figure prominently in the funeral songs. Weddings and the wife-stealing or the negotiations that precede them are sung about at length. So are other domestic ceremonials, like the giving of the bow and arrow to legitimize children, or the ceremonial piercing of the ears if it should by chance be delayed until adulthood. The dairy ceremonials of a seasonal nature are accompanied by dance-songs, as are the rebuilding and reconsecration of a dairy. Love songs are common. There is a popular song that details all the important places of the Nilgiris—hills, valleys, streams, villages, etc. Fragments from it, as well as many other geographical phrases, are found in most songs. All this geographical nomenclature is a verbification of the love for familiar places that is not unknown as a subject for poetry in the literatures well-known to us. That this is the Toda emotion is clear from the song composed by two homesick small girls whose father, because of drought, had to pasture his buffaloes away from the familiar places among people and places strange to them.

Given the technique and the interest in the songs, a corollary but perhaps unexpected consequence is that every Toda can and does compose songs. The two little girls who were homesick did not do it very well, since their knowledge of the technique was imperfect. Many adults too have an imperfect mastery of the art. It is surprising, however, how many are competent and how many different names occur in my records as composers. The best, of course, are those who work hard at it, and the impression that I got was that there were a few men and women who had made a high reputation for themselves as singing composers, and that the best composers were those who officiated during the dances, since they had to work hardest to acquire a technique that would carry them through the fast moving dance without stumbling over what to sing.

Solo composition is only one of the manners of delivery, and perhaps not the commonest. It must be obvious that with all details of composition closely dictated by the technique, duet and choral delivery is always possible. All the performers will have a good knowledge of the technique and will know what is being sung about. The first unit, even the first syllable of the first unit that is uttered by the chief performer almost always gives a certain clue to the limited possibilities of the two dimensional structures that he intends to use; a quick intelligence on the part of his accompanists does the rest. In the dances there is usually a chief composer assisted by one companion; they shout in unison. If a song is being sung, the composer whistles the tune first, and those who sing with him can then accompany him in unison, or he may sing the first half of each two dimensional structure and a single accompanist may sing the other half antiphonally, or a large group may likewise split up to perform antiphonally. My impression is that group performances are preferred to solo work.

A striking feature of all Toda singing is its enigmatic and allusive character. Traditionally, no person is identified in song by his or her name. When the song is addressed to a person, alive or dead, a buffalo name is used in a vocative form instead of a personal name. All the identification that is provided consists of allusion to the patrilineal clan membership by means of the paired units that I have mentioned earlier. When the song is composed on a public occasion, a funeral, a wedding, or the like, this is sufficient for the Todas. They all know exactly who and what is being sung about. If the song is sung again on a later occasion, a minimum of explanation is needed. This indirection of reference is compounded for the outside observer by the set phraseology. Even in a tightly closed culture like that of the Todas, no two events are identical, and the fixed song units are not really closely fitted to any actual event, but only to the generalized themes of the culture. They are, in fact, counterparts of the ethnologist's abstractions from a number of similar but not identical events within a culture. The Toda verbalizations then, like the ethnologist's generalized descriptions, need much comment to point out their relevance to particular manifestations of the cultural themes. The relevance, I must emphasize, is not overtly provided in the song words. It must be recognized by the audience of the songs, and life-long practice in hearing and in composing makes them expert at this. It is this recognition of the relevance of old words to the slightly differing recurrence of old themes that in all probability stimulates the Todas' aesthetic pleasure in their songs. I should suppose that the greater the range of relevances a composer can bring to bear on a particular situation, the more he is appreciated as a composer. However, even though the external observer finds that all Toda singing is an exercise in the enigmatic, the Todas themselves recognize a sub-class of their songs as being particularly enigmatic. These are the love songs. The occasions of these are, in general, not a matter of public knowledge, the personae are not identified even by mention of their clan membership, and in the outcome no one but the composer, his or her beloved, and perhaps their most intimate friends who assist in furthering the affair, know what it is all about. These songs are identified by a pair of song units: *wariṭy xe·ḷf*, *wariṭy foṇt*, as "riddling words." This distinction is for the Todas, of course, a valid one. For us it is only a matter of degree, and the technique as a whole must be characterized as enigmatic and allusive.

This then is oral poetry, with all the marks that we have learned to recognize as characteristic of oral poetry.

One such mark is that every performance, even of what purports to be the same song, is a free composition and that there cannot be two identical performances. This has been amply demonstrated in all accounts of modern living oral literatures, it is clear within the Vedic corpus, and I have already alluded to it as a tradition about the transmission of the *Mahābhārata* that is contained within the frame material of that epic itself. The time available for performance will dictate the length of the song, as will the interest of the singer or of the audience; or, if one singer's song is repeated by another singer, their differing tastes and capabilities will determine different handling of the phraseology. Setpieces will be expanded or cut down, alternative possibilities in the choice of formulaic phrases will be adopted, and so on. The subject matter will, however, be the same, and usually the overall organization of the song—and the song can be said to be the same. And yet the differences between two renditions of the same song by the same singer at a long interval may be enormous, as I found when in a number of instances I took down the same song twice with an interval between. This happened even when very old traditional songs were concerned. The most patent instance was that of the song of the homesick girls. A practiced composer overheard them, liked the tune, and expanded the words until they satisfied him as a worthy effort. I did not record the girls' version, but I am sure the two versions would hardly have been recognizable as the same song, and yet within the Toda rules of the game they were the same.

Another alleged characteristic of oral poetry is concerned with the language. The poetical language is often (it has been said, always) different, and often markedly so, from the vernacular of the singer. This needs no demonstration to be evident to the student of Homer. The dialect of the Homeric poems is not merely different from the everyday dialect of all Homeric singers, no matter what their vernacular; it is clear that it could never, in the form in which we see it, have been the vernacular of anyone at all, because of historical accidents in the transmission of the technique. Bowra was content to mention this, and to add a little about similar situations in some of the other poetries that he treated. It might have been discussed by him at greater length, but he probably was justified in his sketchy treatment, first by the limitations of his linguistic training (no one is well enough at home in twenty-five or more languages to produce a comparative treatment of the desired detailed kind), and secondly, by the danger of exhausting the interest of his audience. I shall take my cue from him, and merely say that the Toda poetic language is different from the everyday language. I cannot go into details, nor do I know the answers to all questions that arise. The syntax of the songs is looser than in the colloquial, perhaps as a function of the formulaic nature and the metrically defined shortness of the song units. The morphology, especially of the verb, is different, whether more archaic or merely a contrived difference I cannot yet say. In a few points, by comparison with related languages, it has been possible to identify archaisms of morphology or of vocabulary. But at the same time, by the same method it is possible to identify very numerous borrowings from the language of the neighboring Badagas, who have been in the Nilgiris for roughly five centuries, and whose song technique, if they have one, is quite unknown for purposes of comparison. Much detailed study is still necessary before it will be possible to make useful generalizations about this matter of language. It suffices to note that Toda poetry does agree with other oral poetries in using a language that has features differentiating it from the language of everyday life. But I should add the proviso that this is true of all poetry, oral or written; it is part of the definition (or rather of some definitions) of poetry that something of the sort should be so. We do not yet really know all the criteria that distinguish the two varieties of poetry.

The last mark of oral poetry that I shall mention is the use of fixed phraseology that has been studied so extensively and profitably in Homer, the Vedas and Sanskrit epics, and the South Slav epics. I have met it also in the songs which the Coorgs compose at harvest festivals and on other religious occasions. They also live in South India, in the mountains between the Malabar coast and Mysore state. Their technique is very different from that of the Todas, and if there is a historical connection between the two, it can be only of the most remote nature. I must say no more about their songs, interesting as they are. The Toda technique is of extreme interest in this matter of fixed phraseology, since it seems to and actually does operate almost completely with formulaic language, as does no other oral composition that we know of so far. The corpus that I am operating with consists of roughly 10,000 or or 11,000 couplets, i.e., two dimensional structures, and I doubt whether in this sizeable body of material there is found any paired song unit which does not recur at least once. Most paired units recur again and again. Certainly this almost complete failure to use unique units is not characteristic of any other of the oral poetries that I have mentioned. Each of them, moreover, except the Coorg material, exceeds my Toda corpus in volume by anything from two to ten or a great many more times. The unique repetitiousness of the Toda songs is not to be explained away by the relative proportions of the material examined. The Toda technique is really virtually a closed one, as none of the others is. Bowra (1952), in examining various heroic poetries, found (p. 233) that the Homeric language comes closest to this. I quote a small part of what he has to say:

> In the first twenty-five lines of the *Iliad* there are at least twenty-five formulae of one kind or another, and in the first twenty-five lines of the *Odyssey* there are about thirty-three. Nor are these passages exceptional; they give a fair sample of how the poems are composed. There is hardly a passage in either poem in which there are not many small formulae, while about a third of each poem consists of lines and blocks of lines repeated elsewhere . . . . It is clear that the formula plays a more important part in ancient Greek heroic poetry than in any oral poetry which we have examined . . . . It is present equally in the machinery of narrative and in the highest flights of poetry, though here it is managed with uncommon tact and seldom makes itself noticeable. Homer clearly derives his art from a powerful tradition which has worked out formulae for almost every occasion, and his task was to make good use of them.

So Bowra on Homer. If my findings for Toda poetry are correct in this respect, as I feel sure they are, it exceeds even Homer.

Can there be no broadening of the Toda technique in this matter? The answer is certainly yes. One of the composers, during the period that I was observing, boasted repeatedly that he was innovating by introducing the names of persons into his songs, and lamented that it was not catching on. If he was correct in claiming this as his own invention, it was certainly being used by others also in imitation of him, in spite of his lament. If he was incorrect in his claim, at least the use of personal names must have been so infrequent before him that this was for all practical purposes an innovation. For our present purpose it means of course an expansion of the permissible phraseology. Occasionally the provision of a paired unit for a name was clever, e.g., the name of the boy, Piḽyfo · to · w, has *piḽy* 'silver' as its first element; the paired unit in a song was Pïnfo · to · w, in which the first element is *pïn* 'gold.'

I repeatedly inquired whether there were any new song units in songs that were being dictated to me, and seldom was told that there were. Those few that were identified as such were usually not impressive. They are indications, however, that the formulaic language is still being added to, if only very slowly. I must admit, however, that this impression of slowness is only to be expected from inspection of a selection of the songs composed over the short period of three years. Innovation must have gone on steadily in the past, but at what rate or rates we cannot hope to know. When the English first came to the Nilgiris, new phraseology was certainly added so that they and some of their innovations in Nilgiri life could be sung about. And the total of the poetical language could only have been achieved by such a process. But it still remains true, I think, that this technique is, of all that have been examined carefully so far, the one most formulaic in character.

Having treated Toda poetry as typically oral composition, it remains to ask whether it fits into the typology of oral poetry offered by the Chadwicks in their voluminous work *The Growth of Literature*. They have set up a category of personal or occasional poetry, which, as they exemplify it, is certainly the one into which Toda poetry fits. They find it, as they say, "probably everywhere," and they cite notable examples of extempore topical poetry among the Kirghiz Tatars, the Polynesians, and various East African communities, including Yoruba, Galla, and the Amhara of Abyssinia. Unfortunately, the Chadwick book does not discuss this type at sufficient length, probably because there is not on record a sufficient body of authentic material. Perhaps when the Toda corpus is published and a few others similar in content, it will be possible for some scholar to give us a treatment of this type parallel to Bowra's book on the heroic epic, and to show fully its role as a type of lyric poetry.

I cannot close without a slight discussion of values. What part does their poetry play in the life of the Todas, and what are their attitudes towards it? Can we justly and fruitfully examine it in a wider, more universal frame of reference?

I have already said something about the occasions for songs, and need only repeat that all the events of Toda life seem to be the subjects of song and that there is a tendency for every event of note to be celebrated on the spot. This is in truth an occasional poetry. It is so intimately connected, however, with all Toda life that its character is very different from that of the verses written by a poet laureate to celebrate a coronation or whatever other state occasion is so celebrated. Every Toda can be his own poet laureate. No event is complete without its accompanying song or shower of songs. No action is perfect without its highly stylized verbal accompaniment in the traditional terms that praise, blame, or merely comment. Few past actions of note are remembered without a notable comment in song being remembered and recomposed. Most cultures are given to discussion of events after they have happened. Few can be so given to highly formalized statements about past events, or can have the directions of discussion so tightly controlled as they would seem to be among the Todas, for whom the judgments on events are so rigorously channeled into traditional phraseology. If the culture is as nearly closed as I have said earlier, one of the factors making for this situation, perhaps only a minor one but still worth identifying as such, is, in all probability, the role that the songs fill as a censor. This is the judgment of an external observer, and I have nothing in my record of Toda utterances to back it up. It is a matter worth futher investigation.

Certainly the songs are an aesthetic factor of importance in the Todas' lives. They draw from them tremendous pleasure. Bowra commented on the heroic singers (p. 29): "The poet wishes not to instruct but to delight his audience." And this is true too of the Toda lyricists, with the corollary that they delight themselves as well. No one can watch the dance song composers without recognizing this: the rapidly circling, shouting ring of dancers, the flashing teeth and thrown back heads of the composer and his accompanists, their eyes gleaming with the excitement of the words they are uttering, are warrants for this conclusion. On occasion my interpreter came to me in the morning still excited by the virtuosity of the composers at the funeral dances of the previous day, and all agog to dictate the dance songs to me. And I have found them equally exciting, though this is perhaps not fair evidence, since I was affected also by my own scholarly excitement as an observer.

I should add that when songs are sung, another aesthetic factor is involved, that of the music, with which I could not deal. I was told, however, that ideally every new song that is sung should have a new tune. One composer went so far as to tell me that only the tunes matter; anyone can compose the words. This is a statement that must be taken into account in judging the total aesthetic effect. But he was being very onesided. The verbal utterances that are common to the sung compositions and the dances are unquestionably an important element in both. They add an aesthetic moment to the tunes of the one and the dance movement of the other. This moment is surely the combined effect in the song words of the social comment and the noncolloquial language in which it is phrased.

Can we find in these songs poetical values which make them worth notice in a world survey of literatures? I am no expert in these matters, but I should attempt what I can, since no one else is likely to examine Toda poetry very intensively for a while.

It is especially difficult to discuss the matter, since there have been so many differing definitions of poetry. Leaving aside all others, it is perhaps useful, with some of the Hindu poets and critics, and occasionally with Western critics, to think of poetry as marked by "suggestion," which is fitted "to move by words unspoken," by implications (Rattigan, 1953, I, xx; Edgerton, 1936; and the work of Lascelles Abercrombie referred to by Edgerton; see also Ingalls, n.d.). Toda poetry, with its enigmatic-allusive technique, might seem to possess this characteristic. And in a way, I think, it does. As the Hindu critics developed the theory, the suggestion is one of an emotion which is to be communicated to an audience, not by a bald statement of the emotion, but by suitable statement of all the factors and the accompanying situation that produce the emotion. This the Toda words are fitted to do, if the emotion is taken to be one of a range that includes social values as well as the individual's private emotions. The panegyric for a dead man suggests, by stereotyped, but noncolloquial statements about his buffaloes and the disputes that he settled, that he was a person of consequence in the community. This, I think, is poetical suggestion. But the Toda range is limited, and its suggestion is, as we have seen, so imprecise and so stereotyped and inflexible, that this poetry cannot with any justice be ranked high in a universal scale.

Toda poetry, with its insistence on the single

situation spoken of in terms of a generalization of Toda cultural themes, hardly allows of generalization into universal human terms. But can we expect more than a minimum of this in any nationally or geographically delimited culture, even if it is carried by millions rather than by a few hundreds of people? European literature at times attempts to generalize for all European experience, but does not always succeed. And its results are seldom applicable to the Chinese, or to the Australian tribesman, except in the most minimal way. Toda poetry does not attempt it. If the Englishman or the visiting anthropological linguist has to be sung about, he is treated in Toda terms—he is living away from his familiar places, as were the homesick girls; he knows the clan buffaloes, as does the Toda clansman; and so on. Occasionally something better may be achieved, by reuse of those traditional phrases that allow it. The breakers of the ocean, seen by two Todas at a distant place of pilgrimage, were poetically sung about by a transfer of the language applicable to the rapids of the Nilgiri rivers and to the driving monsoon: *ï xömo · s̱ pa · we θwïlg pïsxwïθïn* 'one wave beats like the rapids of the river' *ï fiṭymo·s̱ kwa-re θo·št pïsxwïθïn* 'one wave beats like gusts of monsoon rain and wind.' One Christian Toda composer succeeded in adapting the old song units to the theme of the Benedicte in his prayerbook ("O all ye works of the Lord, bless ye the Lord; praise him and magnify him forever"); the result had values which I venture to think approached universality. But these values were won by acculturation, and could hardly have emerged unprompted from Toda culture as such.

We must come to the conclusion that the Todas in their poetry aim neither at universality nor at the poet's individual expression of his own psyche. The technique, as it has been evolved, has as its aim a generalization of all that makes the Todas Todas. They are a peculiar, even a self-consciously peculiar, people, as befits a segment at the top of a local caste system of the Hindu type. There is in their world view no urge to universalize the themes of their culture and the verbal expression of them. At the same time there is no urge towards self-expression; it is, in fact, an urge that would be out of place and might even be divisive in the closed culture of a small community. Their poetry then is strictly a miniature and provincial, even parochial, art with many limitations. But it has no obnoxious features and has numerous aesthetically pleasing ones both for its practitioners and for the external observer. For the Todas it is an enrichment of every facet of their experience, and an art that produces such abundant achievement deserves respect and admiration. As an expression of the values and emotions of a culture in memorable speech, it is poetry.

REFERENCE NOTE

This paper was delivered as the Faculty Research Lecture on the Berkeley campus of the University of California in 1955-1956. Among other publications of the author on the Toda, note Emeneau (1937a, 1941, 1950). On Parry, see Parry, and Lord, p. 342 below.

A. REFERENCES SPECIFIC TO THE PAPER

BOWRA, MAURICE
1952. *Heroic Poetry*. London: Macmillan.

CHADWICK, H. M., and N. K. CHADWICK
1932, 1936, 1940. *The Growth of Literature*. 3 vols. London.

DODDS, E. R.
1951. *The Greeks and the Irrational*. Berkeley and Los Angeles: University of California Press.

EDGERTON, FRANKLIN
1936. Indirect Suggestion in Poetry: A Hindu Theory of Literary Aesthetics. *PAPS*, *77*: 687-706.

EMENEAU, MURRAY B.
1937b. Songs of the Todas. *PAPS*, *77:* 543-560.

INGALLS, DANIEL H. H.
n.d. Sanskrit Poetry and Sanskrit Poetics. *Indiana University Conference on Oriental-Western Literary Relations*, pp. 3-24.

QUILLER-COUCH, A.
1930. *Studies in Literature, Third Series*. New York: Putnam.

RATTIGAN, TERENCE
1953. *The Collected Plays of Terence Rattigan*. London: Hamilton. Vol. 1.

B. GENERAL REFERENCES ON THE STUDY OF LITERATURE

General treatments of the study of literature, or verbal art are listed below. See also Boas (1925); Bogatyrev and Jakobson (1929); Estrich and Sperber (1952, chap. 14); Hockett (1958, chap. 63); Johansen (1949); Sapir (1921, chap. 11); Schlauch (1955, chap. 9); Sebeok (1960b, especially pp. 337-434); with statements from the viewpoints of linguistics (Householder, Jakobson), psychology (Brown, Miller), and literary criticism (Hollander, Wellek).

Studies of the verbal art of particular peoples and studies in particular genres are cited on pp. 351-355, following Shimkin's article. Many of these represent general viewpoints, as do many of the analyses of style and structure, especially those which are linguistically based, which are cited with Sebeok's article on pp. 357-359, 364-371. The list includes studies of metrics, content-analysis, and quantitative measures. Some studies of correspondence between linguistic, narrative, and cultural style are noted after the article by Newman and Gayton on pp. 372-381. Cf. also pp. 403-406 below on special languages.

Among literary critics and theorists whose work and scope has general pertinence for linguistics, anthropology and folklore, one may cite here Burke (1931, 1935, 1937, 1945, 1951a, 1957, 1958, 1961, 1962), Empson (1951, 1955), Pollock (1942), Richards (1942, etc.), Wellek and Warren (1949), and Wimsatt (1954).

References not in the general bibliography:

ALLEN, HAROLD B.
1958. Linguistics and the Study of Literature. In Allen (Ed.), *Readings in Applied English Linguistics*. New York: Appleton-Century-Crofts. Pp. 393-420.

BASCOM, WILLIAM B.
1955. Verbal Art. *JAF*, *68:* 245-252.

BOAS, FRANZ
1927. Primitive Literature, Music, and Dance. *Primitive Art*. (Instituttet for Sammenlignende Kulturforskning, Series B, vol. 8.) Oslo. Chap. 7. (New York: Dover Edition, 1955, with new name index.)
1938c. Mythology and Folklore. In F. Boas, *General Anthropology*. New York: Heath. Pp. 609-626.

BOWRA, C. M.
1962. *Primitive Song*. London: Chatto and Windus; Cleveland: World.

BURKE, KENNETH

1931. *Counterstatement*. New York: Harcourt, Brace. (Los Altos: Hermes, 1953; Chicago: Phoenix Book P14, 1957.)

1935. *Permanence and Change: An Analysis of Purpose*. New York: New Republic. (Los Altos: Hermes, 1954.)

1937. *Attitudes Toward History*. New York: Editorial Publications. (Los Altos: Hermes, 1959; Boston: Beacon, 1962.)

DUNCAN, HUGH DALZIEL

1953. *Language and Literature in Society*. Chicago: University of Chicago Press.

DUNDES, ALAN

1962. Earth Diver: Creation of the Mythopoeic Male. *AA*, *64:* 1032-1051.

EHRLICH, VICTOR

1955. *Russian Formalism, History-Doctrine*. The Hague: Mouton.

EMPSON, WILLIAM

1955. *Seven Types of Ambiguity*. (3rd ed.) New York: Meridian (Noonday Press). [Reviewed, S. B. Chatman, *Word 12* (2): 289-293 (1956)].

FISCHER, JOHN L.

1963. The Sociopsychological Analysis of Folktales. *CA*, *4:* 235-295.

GARVIN, PAUL L.

1955. *A Prague School Reader on Esthetics, Literary Structure, and Style*. Publications of the Washington Linguistics Club, No. 1.) Washington, D.C. [Reviewed, René Wellek, *Lg.*, 1955, *31:* 584-587.]

HARKINS, WILLIAM E.

1951. Slavic Formalist Theories in Literary Scholarship. *Word*, *7:* 177-185.

JACOBS, MELVILLE

1959. Folklore. In Walter Goldschmidt (Ed.), *The Anthropology of Franz Boas*. (The American Anthropological Association, Vol. 61, No. 5, Part 2; Memoir 89.) Menasha, Wis.; San Francisco: Chandler. [Reviewed, D. H. Hymes, *JAF*, 1961, *74:* 87-90.]

JUILLAND, A. G.

1954. Stylistique et linguistique: Review of C. Bruneau, *L'Époque réalistique*. *Lg.*, *30:* 313-338.

LORD, A. B.

1960. *The Singer of Tales*. Cambridge: Harvard University Press. [Reviewed, M. B. Emeneau. *JAF*, 1962, *75:* 67-69; discussion in *JAF*, 1961, *74:* 97-115.]

MESSING, GORDON H.

1951. Structuralism and Literary Tradition. *Lg.*, *27:* 1-12.

PARRY, MILMAN

1930. Studies in the Epic Technique of Oral Verse-Making.
I: Homer and Homeric Style. *Harvard Studies in Classical Philology*, *41:* 73-147.

1932. II. The Homeric Language as the Language of an Oral Poetry. *Harvard Studies in Classical Philology*, *43:* 1-50.

POLLOCK, T. C.

1942. *The Nature of Literature*. Princeton: Princeton University Press.

RICHARDS, I. A.

1926. *Principles of Literary Criticism*. London: Kegan Paul, Trench and Trübner. (2nd ed., 1938.)

1929. *Practical Criticism*. New York: Harcourt, Brace.

1932. *Mencius on the Mind*. London: Kegan Paul, Trench and Trübner.

1938. *Interpretation in Teaching*. New York: Harcourt, Brace.

1942. *How to Read a Page*. New York: Norton.

1955. *Speculative Instruments*. Chicago: University of Chicago Press. [Reviewed, S. B. Chatman, *Lg.*, 1957, *33:* 505-518.]

SEBEOK, T. A.

1959. Folksong Viewed as Code and Message. *Anthropos*, *54* (1-2): 141-153.

SHUMAKER, WAYNE

1960. *Literature and the Irrational. A Study in Anthropological Backgrounds.* Englewood Cliffs, N. J.: Prentice-Hall.

SIMMONS, DONALD C.

1961. Analysis of Cultural Reflections in Efik Folktales. *JAF*, *74:* 126-141.

STENDER-PETERSON, A.

1949. Esquisse d'une theorie structurale de la literature. *Recherches structurales.* (Travaux du Cercle Linguistique de Copenhague, No. 5.) Copenhagen Pp. 277-287.

STUTTERHEIM, C. F. P.

1953. *Problemen der Literatuurwetenschap*. Antwerpen-Amsterdam.

UTLEY, FRANCIS LEE

1961. Folk Literature: An Operational Definition. *JAF*, *74:* 193-206.

WIMSATT, W. K., JR.

1954. *The Verbal Icon. Studies in the Meaning of Poetry*. Lexington: University of Kentucky Press. (New York: Farrar, Straus & Cudahy, 1960.)

38 Wind River Shoshone Literary Forms: An Introduction

D. B. SHIMKIN

THIS PAPER SKETCHES the main forms of unwritten literature among the Wind River Shoshone of Wyoming: the myth (in its two forms of heroic novelette and incidental story or personality sketch), the anecdote, the poetic song, the public prayer, minor invocations, and the jokes of daily life. These materials illustrate the inherent and distinctive artistry, the breadth of individual variability, and the depth of emotional expressiveness which may exist among a simple folk. My illustrations are limited by a paucity of materials and warped by incomplete knowledge of the language. They can but hint at the full richness and vitality of Shoshonean traditions, both at Wind River and elsewhere.

Other subsidiary goals exist within the the framework of this essay. One is the typological delineation of the principal Shoshone literary forms in regard to structure, content, and style. Another is the characterization of the relations between mythology and the rest of culture: the social setting and social functions of storytelling, the nature and variations of attitudes toward mythology, and the reflections of archaic and modern culture in the myth. A third is the indication of interactions between narrators and the tales they tell; how each narrator tends to pattern myth-stuff according to his mood, and how, in doing so, he reveals much of his basic personality.

. . . .

THE MYTH: LITERARY DEVICES

Artifices of sound and of meaning are employed by narrators to enhance the beauty and dramatic vividness of their tales. They flow from six main sources: play on sounds, play on sequential devices, variations of expression, visual imagery, appeals to emotions, and special devices of mythical significance.

The *play on sounds* involves two phases of artistic endeavor, the patterning of the normal speech-sounds and the use of special sound effects to add particular vividness. The patterning of speech-sounds is intimately connected with the phonetic peculiarities of the Shoshone language. The consonants are simple: spluttering velar, lateral or glottalized sounds do not occur. Furthermore, consonants can not combine into clusters. Tongue-twisters of the typical Crow sort (Lowie, 1935) are therefore absent. The constant alternation of consonants and vowels, the phonemic differentiation of two vocalic lengths, and the regular patterning of three distinct degrees of stress infuse Shoshone with a distinct rhythmical swing.

In general, the initial vowel of each verbal stem in a word is stressed, with secondary stresses on succeeding odd vowels. This, of course, follows the old Uto-Aztecan pattern which is noticeable in its most rigid form in Southern Paiute (Sapir, 1930, pp. 39 ff.). In Shoshone, many true and apparent exceptions are to be found to this rule, so that regularity does not crystallize into monotony. For example:

surə mba'hanɨ wɨ' uza'wašaru^{i} *gə'tank*^{w}||
pənurəza'wašaruˀ in^{i} *sur wupi' x*^{w}||

(They, the father's sisters now are swinging him hard; he whom they are swinging leaps off.)

Speakers of the language clearly appreciate its melody, for the rules of good elocution, in myth-telling and oratory alike, demand a smooth, continuous flow of words elided into one another. They demand a flow that pulsates in waves of ever-rising pitch, and is broken by the metronome of stress. They permit no stoppages or changes in that flow, or, in fact, phonetic contrasts of any sort, as media of artistic expression.

The small number of initial consonantal phonemes and the paucity of basic stems result in constant alliteration in Shoshone. Quite typical is the following phrase:

su''ni sur yɨ'gwɨnɨd yi:k də'a kw:d|| surewɨ'' ukwɨdak sit sɔ'gupza'nak^{w}*|| su'khwent surədə'a urəna'yanuk urena' yanu'kiar.*

(When it has become evening, again she defecates. As she was defecating, it was the earth that mended. From there, she again is tracking them, is their tracker.)

On the other hand, various phonetic rules in regard to the sonancy, spirantization, and other alterations of intervocalic consonants save the tongue from monotonous cacophony. This is an especially dangerous potentiality in Shoshone, which uses reduplication as a normal grammatical mechanism. Thus it is that theoretical *mi'mian* and *do'do'in*^{i} become *mi'wian* (they went) and *do'ro'in*^{i} (they are climbing).

The combination of rhythmical and alliterative qualities in the language makes the narrator's emphasis upon rhyme wholly natural. Most descriptions, even by one so artless as Charley Nipwater, are in rhymed prose (as in the constant rhymed prose (*es-Saj*) of descriptions in classical Arabic belles-lettres). An illustration will make the point clear.

pa:'rhi du:'parhi mu'zambia so'guria zuk^{w} *hu'kaβagia na'yɨgwɨt*

(Elk, moose, mountain sheep, mule deer, Virginia deer, in the willows may they be!)

The special sound effects are either formal jugglings of words or imitations of natural noises. In the former category are such nonsense words as *e:'βimɔ'mɔgusɔ*, Coyote's magic name (an English approximation of this might be clay-nose-ose), as well as puns and similar plays on words. Puns, however, are typical of everyday joking but not of myths. An instance of mythological punning occurs, nevertheless, on the occasion of Blind Coyote's finding that his two female companions were named Waving Person and Sage-Brush Girl. "Strange," he said, "some people call me Waving Pretty-Boy, and others Sage-Brush Pretty-Boy. So we should be together, for our names are the same."

The imitations of natural noises are an integral part of the Shoshone language but to a small degree. Outside of interjections, onomatopoeia has originated only a few verbs, e.g., *wɔ'wɔ-*, to bark, and nouns, e.g., *šu'akwukwu*, robin. Most other onomatopoeic words, e.g., *hi:'to*, meadowlark, are really remnants of a Plateau Shoshonean past. On the other hand, unformalized imitations abound. An example of stuttering has been noted on a previous page. Baby talk also occurs to give coy effects.

ik ba:'bawuci də'as uyu'yuhuci əm ba'bawiči be:'kapuci

(Here's an 'ittle bit of water and some itsy-bitsy fat from your buddy's 'ittle kill.)

The Shoshone teller of tales does not even disclaim to imitate plain noises. He mimics the sounds of beasts, monsters, and particularly birds: Mourning Dove as she sorrows for her lost son, and pipsqueak Meadow-Lark as he gives aid to the enemy. He strains the capabilities of the human voice to give the sound of a knife as it slits a throat or of an anus as it breaks wind.

The ordinary *sequential devices* of Shoshone myths are four in number: parallel development to a climax, simple reiteration or repetition, sharp contrast, and parenthetical incorporation. As has been shown before, parallel development is the principal characteristic of plots, although reiteration is used in at least two ways. Characters relate adventures *in extenso* to others, either before or after their occurrence. Also, the plots of the longer incidental stories are largely repetitive. The anticlimaxes so common in tales exemplify contrast. Since virtually all details contribute directly to the development of the total plot the parenthetical incorporation of incidents is less usual than the other devices. Exceptions in a certain sense are the unessential elaborations of the emotions of minor human actors and the somewhat similar lavish descriptions of tools.

The structures of incidents within plots abundantly illustrate all four types of sequential devices. Parallel development is ubiquitous; the main form in which it occurs is the description of a series of actions in time. The Shoshone language makes such temporal seriation particularly tempting by offering the narrator his choice of many slightly differing suffixes of tense and aspect. Consequently, constancy in the stems used and variation in the suffixes easily and concisely create parallelisms. A textual example illustrates the superiority of Shoshone to English in this respect: Weasel's adoptive grandfathers start, in turn, to tow his boat. [Shoshone and English parallelisms are matched by numbers following phrases. Hyphens join English words which paraphrase a Shoshone word.]

suβe sur pa:'nʒux ba:'gar wɨtɨ'gwax sum tu:'nkunt gə'karix|| *uge'yagunaik^w* (1) *suβe sur sa:k gunai'k^w* (2) || *suβe uge'yagunai'gant* (3) || *suβe·sur ba:'rukaigun-aigɨn* (4) *sur sa:k ba:'' aβaigunaigɨn* (5)|| *sur pa:'nʒux suβe gwa'yax* (6) *suβ̇e sur gwa'yaβit* (7) || *bitus su'βa sa:'kiwa ma'rtoro'ɨn^i*.

(Then he, Mink, hits the water with rope in mouth. He sped-chasing-it (1); then it, the boat, sped (2). Then he is-in-the-state-of-speeding-in-chase-of-it (3). Then he is-speeding-under-water (4); then it, the boat, is-speeding-on-the-water (5). Then he, Mink, tires (6); then he is-one-who-is-made-tired (7). Again, he is-hoisting-himself-upon-the-boat.

Parallelism in logical or causal sequences occurs with less frequency. Typical, however, is the following instance:

It is he, Coyote, who is not eating; through not eating he starves.

Repetition is also a very important artifice. It forms, of course, an essential part of the parallelisms and is also relished for its own sake. Most activities and phrases must be repeated four or five or ten times, according to individual taste. Repetition in the form of enumeration is popular. Thus, a frightened man has run to tell Coyote:

They now—they who are mosquito-fly, big-fly, gray-fly, black-fly, yellow-fly, all dangerous—are arriving at my people's home.

Furthermore, the narrator often stresses important facts before and after their results. This happens when Water Ghost Woman has bullied Uncle Vulture into revealing the whereabouts of Mourning Dove and her son.

He now, having felt fear of her, is relating it: "Already, I, myself, in this way, blowing my nose, have snorted them far a way." This is that which he is relating, having felt fear of her.

Contrast forms a part of several descriptions of actions. Coyote, for instance, runs up the mountains chasing mountain sheep, then down again; then up again, and so on until he is exhausted. Only one type of contrast, however, seems to be an integral part of Shoshone style: antithetical orders, with the negative preceding the positive injunction. Weasel's Elder Brother furnishes an illustration as he directs the youngster, preparing for their trip.

You, having gone—that obsidian over there is worthless; two buttes beyond it, there now it's all good—from there you will now fetch much, all you can carry.

Similarly, Weasel's adoptive grandfathers tell him:

"You will in no possible case whatsoever sleep in a straight burrow," (they) told him, "and you will sleep in a crooked burrow."

The incorporation of parenthetical ideas is characteristic of many passages. Here, as in the case of parallelism, the Shoshone language is largely responsible. Polysynthesis combines many elements into a single word, which the speaker can readily analyze, e.g., *u-gə-rɨ-ka-'ma-xwa-c*, equivalent to ten long English words, "having just finished destroying something (or someone) invisible by eating with teeth." Syntax also permits the loose joining of such catch-all words to the substance of the sentence by prefixed personal pronouns. It matters little that the logical connection must often remain obscure. One may translate "*urəmi'wiak —wɨ' du:'wunaix*" by "as they are walking—because they are walking—, in their walking—a black spot appears." Syntax likewise permits demonstratives to assume relative functions; a single, compound demonstrative may tie two or three independent clauses. For example, Coyote directs:

Ke gəmbu''it ke də'as wə'səgindar! *su'kura bu''iha də'as wə'segɨndai gu'tido*!

(Don't be lookers or peekers either! At *him whosoever* might either look or peek someone will shoot!)

Finally, even completely disjointed flows of thought are but extensions of good Shoshone usage. Thus, when Coyote has started his Circle Dance, he watches the participants.

It is he now—as they are dancing the foremost one of them appears fat—he is now looking at that fat one.

The principal *mechanisms for achieving variety of expression* are synonyms, metaphors, similes, and special phonetic and syntactic alterations.

Only the first of these mechanisms will be discussed here. A later section on visual imagery will take up metaphors and similes. Among the Shoshone the non-functional phonetic and syntactic alterations are devices of poetry and not of prose. Consequently, the section on poetic songs will deal with them.

Synonyms of slightly differing meaning abound in Shoshone. They may have entirely different stems as in some nouns, e.g., *nɔ:r* (ridge), *dɔ'ya* (mountain), and innumerable verbs, e.g., *pɨ'di* (to arrive), *gim* (to come), *gɔ''i* (to return), *ya 'i* (to enter), *dɔ'i* (to enter or go out). They may simply vary suffixes. For instance, many interchangeable verbal suffixes express continuous action, e.g., *mi' ano:* (he keeps on going), *mi'axant* (he is in the state of going), *mi' agwai* (he is gone, and will be gone indefinitely). Nouns, pronouns, adverbs, and adjectives may also receive modal suffixes for emphasis or depreciation, e.g., *ni'ʒa* (I, indeed), *nu:'nə* (I, perhaps). They may change from independent words to adverbial or adjectival prefixes of the same stem. Semantic differences often accompany such changes. The word *na'riand* (dangerous), for example, combines with the verb meaning "to fall," and yields a compound *na'ria'ani-* (to faint in horror); but it also combines with the verb meaning "to cause to think," and yields a compound *na'riasu'aŋg-* (to esteem). Finally, they may form completely different grammatical structures. Thus, emphasis may be expressed by suffixes of many sorts added to the words stressed, or by the use of the negative particle and the unreal mood. An illustration of the last method is the following: *ni'ʒa ke ha'gap əgai''iwait* (It is impossible that I shall not be a stayer with you, i.e., I will remain with you at all costs.)

The Shoshone narrator and his audience are extremely interested in words as such, and extremely appreciative of good usage and accurate shading. They demand both idiomatic and exact expressions. For example, Guy Robertson, an older and more conservative man, scornfully rejected Lynn St. Clair's anglicized description *tom'boni-waiki* (in a circle) as an innovation for the correct *gu'na hɔ'ig* (around the fire). Both narrator and audience quickly grasp the delicate nuances of thought expressed by slightly differing synonyms. Almost every expression, every word, indeed, may have its peculiar connotation, unique, yet lucid. In short, variety of expression, especially when coupled with parallelism, is a main artifice of the Shoshone litterateur. It is an artifice, however, which no outsider can truly appreciate; translation grasps its shadow, not its substance.

Visual imagery accentuates important aspects of the action or background of a myth by making them especially vivid and picturesque. The Shoshone narrator uses three types of such imagery: direct descriptions, metaphors, and similes; pantomime is an occasional accompaniment of anecdotes. Descriptions of emotional scenes and of tool-making are very common, as preceding pages have shown, but other descriptions are exceedingly rare. Thus, there is only one representation of a landscape in all my material. Its simple beauty makes quotation worth while. When Weasel and his brother approach the "Water-Buffalo's" lair, the narrator describes the scene thus:

Here is water
Here is the Water Buffalo's lair,
Here is blue-edged water
Here many trees are standing.

Simple metaphors abound in Shoshone myths. Most of the animal characters are called both by their ordinary names and by descriptive terms, some of them derogatory. For example, Beaver is sometimes known as Big-Tail Owner; Bat, as Tobacco-Black-Mouthed One; Coyote, as Daylight Anus. Actions also may be metaphorically depicted. For instance, when Bat runs fast, he "becomes a white streak." Similes occur less frequently than metaphors. Some of them are unimaginative: When Weasel's Elder Brother reproaches the youngster for having disguised himself in Cannibal's skin, he says, "Even if I be like a woman (because he had become panic-stricken and shot at the supposed monster), it is one who might kill someone." Other similes, however, are exceedingly picturesque, e.g., hospitable Owl's piercing of his eye causes nutritive liquid to "flow from it like egg yolk."

It is hard to know what emotions myths arouse in Shoshone audiences. Only direct observation can tell us. The *emotional significance* of a given incident may be very different to them and to us. Two of my informants found great amusement in a very grim account of a murder. Where most of us would only have seen horror, they saw ridiculousness. Because of these differences in reactions, I will discuss here only those manifestations which I have actually seen.

Humor is an important characteristic of Shoshone tales. To achieve it, the narrator most often establishes ridiculous situations, relates pranks, tells obscenities, or plays on sounds. A rarer technique is irony, which may be illustrated by Weasel's conversation with Monster Owl. The boy is gorging himself at a forbidden hour, while she watches him silently. He offers her some meat, then taunts her for not taking it: "Why, are you going to become sick, having come to me on purpose?" She claws at him suddenly, but he avoids her, and scoffs, "You're clawing as though for a husband!"

Most listeners find the battle scenes of the tales tense and exciting. They are sympathetic toward such mothers as Mourning Dove, who yearns for her lost child, or such brothers as Weasel, who fears for his brother's safety. Coyote's perversions and vilenesses arouse revulsion in some.

Few special *devices of mythical significance* are found in Shoshone tales in comparison with those of many other peoples. The recitatives of the Southern Paiute and Eskimo (Rasmussen, 1930) have no parallels among the Shoshone, nor do the special voices and intonations peculiar to Nez Perce myth (Phinney, 1934, pp. 10 ff.). The mythological era is not emphasized as distinctive by the use of any special, indefinite mythological verbal aspect (Leenhardt, 1937), or the habitual use of a quotative—"it is said" (Deloria, 1932)—or by specific reference, e.g., "already only a short time away the human race comes" (Phinney, 1934). No special mythical sentence structure exists (Harris and Voegelin, 1939).

To be sure, Shoshone myths do have some artifices of this type. There are special mythical names for some animals. Weasel is called *pə'pəranʒ ugupə* (which I cannot analyze) rather than the usual *pa:'biǯi*. Various fantastic beings likewise have unanalyzable names, e.g., *gip*, a "water-buffalo," and *honowikhono*, a "buttocks-bouncer." Some, like the Water-Ghost-Beings, make characteristic noises, e.g., *wi:ho*! In addition to the peculiarities of name-giving, the myths have a stock of stereotyped actions and situations. Illustrative of a whole series of awakenings from death is the following incident. Bat has restored Coyote from death by frightening him with his magical arrows. The latter does not appreciate the true situation, and grumbles:

"Darned Bat, Tobacco-Black-Mouthed One! When I had been sleeping well, he woke me up," Coyote said it.

"No. You were not sleeping. You were killed. Look at your hide," (they) said it. Then as he looked at his own scabby hide, he felt badly.

Other stereotyped actions are reviving a comrade from death by rasping a wild rose branch vigorously in his mouth or anus, killing a monster by shooting him in the anus with a firedrill, fooling a monster with flies in a pot which buzz like human voices, or taking refuge from him by shrinking magically and hiding in a friendly relative's nose. A final device of mythological importance is the persistence of some animal characteristics in the personalities of the main actors. Thus, Badger can burrow underground and Kingfisher can fly.

. . . .

POETIC SONGS

So far as I know, true poetry occurs among the Wind River Shoshone only in songs. Most of these are meaningless vocalizations, as in the Sun Dance, war songs, and Peyote songs, but some have intelligible verses. To this latter class belong Ghost Dance, mocking and gambling songs, as well as songs with popular American tunes but Shoshone words. Unfortunately, I have examples of only the Ghost Dance and mocking songs from the second class.

Elsewhere, I have discussed Sun Dance songs in some detail (Shimkin, 1953); war songs are much like them. A brief text will illustrate the typical vocalizations of Peyote songs. They are sung during the ceremony with the accompaniment of a gourd rattle shaken about one hundred and sixty times a minute. They are sung in a distinctly falsetto voice; accented phrases rise sharply in pitch, whispered ones drop:

ɔ'hanininí c'hanininí
ɔ'haneni yana c'haneni yana
ɔ'haneni
yanawe:' yanawe:'
ra'ra yuwanuyana hininu[e]

The Ghost Dance, which the Shoshone call "Shuffling" (*Na'rayar*) is a simple ceremony performed during the winter months at full moon, and two or three nights thereafter. Its purpose is to shake away illness. Other, closely related dances, such as the Warm Dance and the Father Dance, have such functions as improving the weather and averting disaster.

As evening comes a fire is built. Often a pine tree is set up close to it. A leader stands by the fire and sings without accompaniment. Another replaces him when the first tires. Around the fire and the leader is a ring of dancers, men and women alternately. The dancers dance clockwise, dragging their feet sidewise, holding hands with intertwined fingers. Their only special article of dress is a blanket with which they shake away illness. This shaking and a ritual pounding of breasts normally conclude the rite. Periodically, however, and even in recent years, fainting, messianic frenzies, and prophecies have taken place during the performances.

The singers are shamans who dream or compose their songs. The music is a mere alternation of two themes of simple structure and narrow tonal range sung slowly in a high-pitched, nasal voice. The texts are cryptic descriptions of visions, fully understood only by their authors. (Cf. Kelly, 1939, p. 159, and Natches, 1923, p. 259.) These texts are built up of units of single lines which rhyme through simple, final repetition, through alliteration or assonance, or through true rhyme. Two varieties of Ghost Dance texts exist, one, which simply repeats each line, and another, more complicated in structure, which repeats each verse. Some examples follow.

Yellow willow is waving
Yellow willow is waving
Grass, big grass is waving
Grass, big grass is waving
Alder is waving
Alder is waving, etc.

Again:

Sage-brush goose's son
Sage-brush goose's son, etc.

Representative of the second group is

White-rock rivers
All kinds of rivers
Warm rivers
(Repeat whole verse)

A final example shows some interesting peculiarities. This is a song dreamt by a powerful shaman now deceased, Frank Perry.

pa:'rutɨ'mbi
pa:'ru ʒɨga:''yu
pa:'šoni pe'ŋgwinux
pa:'ŋgə maβi'

Water-black rock,
Water-black shining;
Two water-grass fishes
On the water's edge.

In this instance meter and stress are well balanced. The lines are of five, seven, seven, and five morae, respectively. The stresses are on the second and fourth, second and sixth, second and fifth, and second and fifth morae. But such balance is accomplished only through poetic license. In normal Shoshone the adjective precedes the modified noun; the suffix *a'yu* is short and unaccented; intervocalic *m* becomes a nasalized *w*; and so on.

In function and structure the mocking songs differ profoundly from the Ghost Dance songs. The former were composed and sung by gangs of young warriors in derisive serenades of fops who neither worked nor fought in battle, who indulged in extravagances of adornment such as the artificial lengthening of hair with horse hair glued on with pitch, and who—worst of all—could entice all women. The young men would go as quietly as possible in front of the fop's door. Then, suddenly, they would start drumming and singing at the tops of their voices. The music resembles that of the war songs but, unfortunately, I have recorded none of it. The text of one mocking song sung by Tassitsie is as follows:

ən ŋga'nhi tų'iwič i
mak nə hu:'awain^{i}
ke ən o'ar ndo'iwaix^{w}
mak nə hu:'awain^{i}
ən ŋga'nhi tų'iwič i
mak nə hu:'awain^{i}
ke ən o'ar ndo'iwaix^{w}
mak nə hu:'awain^{i}
a'ya hanǯ dičir gwə'kant
nan mawi:'yahant
dɔ'yawant no:'mia'^{yu}
keha nə:'cidə^{i}
əŋgwə'gwə'pain^{i} *nə wiǯa wən'*
du'koβ^{i} *utuwek'*

You('re) at home, Pretty Youth,
While I a-foresting go
Nowhere to did you go out,
While I a-foresting go.
You('re) at home, Pretty Youth,
While I a-foresting go.
Nowhere to did you go out
While I a-foresting go.
Oh Friend! Bad husband!
Just as well to keep her tied,
Among the mountains (you) keep on moving:
Won't you be ill?
(With) your wife for a wife I would stand,
A black face, bringing it.

The structure of this poem is quite regular, the odd lines having seven morae; the even, six. The even lines, furthermore, are, with the exception of the last, uniformly accented on the third (double) mora. Actually there are three verses here, the first two having the same refrain. The ninth and tenth lines rhyme, while the other pairs of lines share an identical final accentuation.

The term *tu'iwiči*, basically "youth," has a connotation of foppishness and excessive elegance in direct address and in proper names (cf. *pu'hutų'iwiči*, "Sage-brush-pretty-youth"). The word *gwë'kant*, literally "wife-owner," is poetic license for *gu:'xapë* (husband). The "black face" refers to the facial paint of a warrior who returns from combat after having achieved a battle honor or coup.

THE PUBLIC PRAYER

Public prayer comprises the most serious and majestic phase of Shoshone oratory. It takes place especially in the Sun Dance and the Peyote ritual. It is for the public good, to achieve the release of someone or of everyone from illness, to give them long life, or to accomplish successfully some ritual act, such as cutting down the tree for the Sun Dance outer pole.

Stylistically these prayers (which are not fixed in form) maintain a similar pattern. They begin with an invocation: "All right, my Father, having looked down on us from above . . ." Then follows a statement of the suppliant's condition: they are about to kill the sacred buffalo, to chop down the tree for the outer pole or they are here with a sick man. After this passage the prayer itself, e.g., "May you make him well." Often a prayer for spectators or the populace at large follows, with its statement of condition and its hope. Finally, comes "it is ended."

The prayers of some individuals differ. Quitan Quay is curt and omits the invocation. The prayer which Dick Washakie thought he might give was marked by its highly personal character.

Inasmuch as several of the texts appear elsewhere (Shimkin, 1953), a single illustration will suffice for the Sun Dance prayers:

> All right, My Father, having looked down toward me from above, by means of you I achieve a benediction. I make a supplication. Here is now a sick man, may you make him well! My prayer to you also Our Elder Brother Jesus: save him! The person whom you bless, for him your blessing is great. All right, I supplicate. That is all.

The Peyote prayers are peculiar enough to deserve more extended quotation. Gilbert Day prays in this manner on entering the tipi at the beginning of the ceremony:

> Our Father, looking toward us, and Our Elder Brother, "lower spirits," all together having looked toward us, may they pity us!

The first person plural here ("exclusive," i.e., "they and I") seems, as in other prayers, to have a general meaning, "everyone." The concept of "lower spirits" is peculiar; I know nothing more concerning it.

After midnight a recess takes places in the ceremony, and the paraphernalia are cleaned at this time. A water-bearer brings in a bucket from which all drink. Then, following some other ritual acts, the equipment is returned to its place, and the leader of the meeting goes outside to blow his whistle to the cardinal directions. He may also pray. Gilbert Day gives a sample text. After an introduction similar to that above, he says:

Eastward steadily, its breeze keeps blowing
Southward, its breeze keeps blowing
Westward, its breeze keeps blowing
Northward, its breeze keeps blowing
All well, here inside let them become!
Finished.

MINOR FORMS

Even every-day life is by no means lacking in little formulas, plays on words, and other elements of unwritten literature. A few examples will give some idea of their use.

When one wishes help from a noted shaman he must address him in a fixed way. With Moguca, Lynn St. Clair tells me, one must say

Prayer-Boy, I have just come for (you); pray for one of us right away! ("Prayer-Boy is an unusual term for shaman; the ordinary word means "owner of supernatural power" [*bɔ'xagant*].)

Then one hands him three dollars and he accepts the case.

Or again, when a child loses a deciduous tooth, he goes to a wildrose bush, digs a hole under it, and drops in the tooth. Then he mutters the following formula:

Wild Rose, you thrived well; in just this way my tooth should grow.

Finally, clever remarks may arise on any social occasion. When I was giving some Rorschach tests, a young man, Meyers Coopooie, cracked this pun on seeing the first plate:

hiniwič u—s hɔ'nɔwič
What is it—'tis Bat!

Members of the household roared with laughter.

CONCLUSIONS

1. The folk literature of a simple culture may be surprisingly rich, varied, and developed. Consequently, in assessing the total achievements of cultural groups with scanty material culture and loose social organization, considerable attention should be paid to their mythology and allied forms of artistic and philosophical expression.

2. The richness of Wind River Shoshone literary forms indicates that comparable developments may exist amongt he other Plateau Shoshoneans. The meager records available for those groups are no proof to the contrary, since they have been collected largely in English, and often with poor interpreters. Steward's tales imply orginal mythological forms of considerable length and complexity (Steward, 1936). Sapir's main informant was a schoolboy, who admitted imperfect knowledge (Sapir, 1930); St. Clair's (Ms. in BAE) and Marsden's materials are incomplete and poorly translated. Obviously, a great deal more exploration of this potentially rich field should be undertaken.

3. Among the Wind River Shoshone, the myth, the poetic song, and the public prayer comprise the finest forms of verbal expression. The primary function of the myth is the edification of the audience, while poetic songs are either social, or mystical in character, as in the case of the Ghost Dance songs.

4. On the basis even of incomplete and imperfect materials, it is clear that significant correlations exist between the styles of narrators and their individual personalities.

REFERENCE NOTE

The original article has been condensed to that portion which deals primarily with linguistic features. The sections reprinted are [Introduction] (p. 329), "The Myth: Literary Devices" (pp. 338-347), "Poetic Songs" (pp. 350-351), "The Public Prayer" (pp. 351-352), "Minor Forms" (p. 352), "Conclusion" (p. 352). Omitted are "Myth and Culture" (pp. 329-332), "The Myth: Plots" (pp.332-335), "The Myth: Characters" (pp. 335-338), "The Narrator and the Myth" (pp. 343-347), "Anecdotes" (pp. 347-349).

The elements of the Wind River Shoshone Peyote Cult are presented by Shimkin in Stewart (1944, pp. 104-121), and his study of their Sun Dance has now been published (Shimkin, 1953). The stories from which examples are taken remain unpublished, and the original citations from examples to them by narrator and title are omitted here, together with a few comparative observations. Shimkin states that "The orthography follows strict Americanist usage" (presumably referring to the practices advocated in "Phonetic Transcription of Indian Languages," *Smithsonian Institution-Miscellaneous Collections*, *66* [6] (1916)). No attempt has been made to revise the transcription, except that the symbols ə and ɨ been substituted throughout for ë and ï.

Among other treatments of the verbal art of individual peoples, either generally or in regard to particular genres, see Beckwith (1922), Boas (1914, 1916), Bunzel (1930), Chafe (1961), Chamberlain (1896), Cole-Beuchat (1957), Demetracopoulou and Du Bois (1932), Elbert (1951), Harries (1950, 1952, 1956, 1962), Herskovits and Herskovits (1958), Hymes (1958a, 1959a), Jacobs (1957, 1959, 1960, 1962), Jansen (1957), Kroeber (1948, 1951), Lowie (1932, 1933), Messenger (1959, 1960 [to which cf. *JAF*, *74:* 245-246 (1961)]), Nygard (1958), Paulme (1961), Propp (1958), Radin (1915, 1926, 1945, 1948, 1949, 1950, 1954-1956a, 1956b), Reichard (1930, 1947), Roberts and Swadesh (1955), Sapir (1910), Simmons (1960c), M. G. Smith (1957), Sokolov (1950), Spencer (1957), Voegelin and Euler (1957), Wolff (1962), and areal and topical surveys in Maria Leach (1949-1950). Studies of traditional African verbal art and its adaptation to modern circumstances, are regularly noticed in some detail in *African Abstracts* (London, 1950). Among such studies, see, e.g., Green (1948), Harries (1950, 1952, 1956), Hopgood (1948), Jordan (1957), Kalanda (1959), Malcolm (1949), Williamson (1958).

Many of the individual studies express general viewpoints, e.g., regarding a dramatistic perspective on oral narrative. Compare the studies of Jacobs (1959) and Radin (1945) with the theoretical approach of Burke (1945, 1951b).

On the need for such studies in the typological delineation of literary forms, Shimkin cites Taylor (1940, p. 18). On the process of defining genres in general, see Burke (1951b), as well as Wellek and Warren (1949); also Wolff (1962). For general studies of particular genres, see, for folktale and myth, the standard works by Thompson (1946, 1955-1958, 1961) and cf. Dundes (1963). For proverbs, see the standard work by Taylor (1962); for riddles, Taylor (1951) and Georges and Dundes (1962); for ballad and folksong, the best single reference for anthropologists is Wilgus (1959), a critical and historical study of scholarship with extensive bibliography. Reeves (1958) has special interest from a linguistic viewpoint, as does the work of Lomax (1959). For collections of Amerindian oral poetry with extensive bibliographies, see Astrov (1946) and Day (1951); for Amerindian tales, Coffin (1961) and Thompson (1929).

In general, on folkloristic topics, see the excellent "Annual Bibliography of Folklore" by W. Edson Richmond in the Supplement to the *Journal of American Folklore;* the publications of the American Folklore Society, including that journal; and consult Leach (1949-1950).

References not in the general bibliography:

ASTROV, MARGOT

1946. *The Winged Serpent. An Anthology of American Indian Prose and Poetry.* New York: Day.

BOAS, FRANZ

1916. Tsimshian Mythology. *BAE-AR*, *31:* 29-979.

BUNZEL, RUTH

1930. Introduction to Zuni Ceremonialism; Zuni Origin Myths; Zuni Ritual Poetry. *BAE-AR*, *47:* 467-544, 545-609, 611-835.

BURKE, KENNETH

1951b. Three Definitions. *Kenyon Review*, *13* (2): 173-192.

CHAFE, WALLACE L.

1961. *Seneca Thanksgiving Rituals.* (BAE-B 183.) Washington, D.C.: Smithsonian Institution.

CHAMBERLAIN, A. F.
1896. The Poetry of American Aboriginal Speech. *JAF, 9:* 43-47.
1903. Primitive Woman as Poet. *JAF, 16:* 205-221.

COFFIN, TRISTRAM P. (ED.)
1961. *Indian Tales of North America.* (Bibliographical and Special Series, No. 13.) Philadelphia: American Folklore Society. [Reviewed, D. H. Hymes, *AA*, 1962, *64:* 676-679; Alan Dundes, *JAF*, 1962, *76:* 69-71.]

COLE-BEUCHAT, P. D.
1957. Riddles in Bantu. *African Studies, 16:* 133-149.

DAY, A. GROVE
1951. *The Sky Clears. Poetry of the American Indians.* New York: Macmillan.

DELORIA, ELLA
1932. *Dakota Texts.* (Publications of the American Ethnological Society, No. 14.)

DEMETRACOPOULOU, DOROTHY, and CORA DU BOIS
1932. A Study of Wintu Mythology. *JAF, 45:* 373-500.

ELBERT, SAMUEL H.
1951. Hawaiian Literary Style and Culture. *AA, 53:* 345-354.

GEORGES, ROBERT A., and ALAN DUNDES
1962. Toward a Structural Definition of the Riddle. *JAF, 76:* 111-118.

GREEN, M. M.
1948. The Unwritten Literature of the Igbo-speaking People of South-eastern Nigeria. BSO(A)S, *12:* 838-846.

HARRIES, LYNDON
1950. Swahili Epic Literature. *Africa, 20:* 55-58.
1952. Popular Verse of the Swahili Tradition. *Africa, 22:* 158-164.
1956. Cultural Verse-Forms in Swahili. *African Studies, 15:* 176-187.
1962. *Swahili Poetry.* Oxford: Oxford University Press.

HARRIS, Z. S., and C. F. VOEGELIN
1939. Hidatsa Texts Collected by Robert H. Lowie. *Prehistory Research Series.* Indianapolis: Indiana Historical Society. Vol. I, pp. 173-239, esp. pp. 231-232.

HERSKOVITS, MELVILLE J., and FRANCES S. HERSKOVITS
1958. *Dahomean Narrative: A Cross-Cultural Analysis.* Evanston: Northwestern University Press. [Reviewed, D. F. McCall, *JAF*, 1959, *72:* 255-257.]

HOPGOOD, C. R.
1948. Language, Literature and Culture. *Africa, 18:* 112-119.

JACOBS, MELVILLE
1957. Titles in an Oral Literature. *JAF, 70:* 157-172.
1959. *The Content and Style of an Oral Literature. Clackamas Chinook Myths and Tales.* (Viking Fund Publications in Anthropology, No. 26.) New York: Wenner-Gren Foundation; Chicago: University of Chicago Press.
1960. *The People are Coming Soon: Analyses of Clackamas Chinook Myths and Tales.* Seattle: University of Washington Press. [Reviewed, D. French, *JAF*, 1961, *74:* 277-278.]
1962. The Fate of Indian Oral Literatures in Oregon. *Northwest Review, 5:* 90-99.

JANSEN, WILLIAM HUGH

1957. A Culture's Stereotypes and Their Expression in Folk Clichés. *SJA*, *13:* 184-200.

JORDAN, A. C.

1957. Towards an African Literature. II: Traditional Poetry. *Africa South*, *2:* 97-105.

KALANDA, A.

1959. Bartholomée Dipumba ou les perspectives nouvelles de la poésie congolaise. *Kongo-Overzee*, *25* (2-3): 77-85.

KELLY, ISABELLE T.

1939. Southern Paiute Shamanism. *UCP-AR*, *2:* 151-167.

KROEBER, A. L.

1948. Seven Mohave Myths. *UCP-AR*, *11:* 1-70.

1951. A Mohave Historical Epic. *UCP-AR*, *11:* 76-171.

LEENHARDT, M.

1937. Le Temps et la personalité chez les Canaques de la Nouvelle-Calédonie. *Revue Philosophique*, *62:* 43-58.

LOWIE, ROBERT H.

1932. Proverbial Expressions Among the Crow Indians. *AA*, *34:* 739-740.

1933. Crow Prayers. *AA*, *35:* 433-442.

MALCOLM, D. MCK.

1949. Zulu Literature. *Africa*, *19:* 33-39.

MESSENGER, JOHN C., JR.

1959. The Role of Proverbs in a Nigerian Judicial System. *SJA*, *15:* 64-73.

1960. Anang Proverb-Riddles. *JAF*, *73:* 225-235.

NATCHES, G.

1923. Northern Paiute Verbs. *UCP-AAE*, *20:* 243-259.

PAULME, DENISE

1961. Littérature orale et comportements sociaux en Afrique noire. *L'Homme*, *1* (1): 37-49.

PHINNEY, A.

1934. *Nez Perce Texts*. (Columbia University Contributions to Anthropology, No. 25.) New York: Columbia University Press.

RADIN, PAUL

1915. *Literary Aspects of North American Mythology*. (Canada Geological Survey, Anthropological Series, No. 6; Museum Bulletin, No. 16.) Ottawa: Government Printing Bureau.

1926. Literary Aspects of Winnebago Mythology. *JAF*, *39:* 18-52.

1945. *The Road of Life and Death: A Ritual Drama of the American Indians*. (Bollingen Series, No. 5.) New York: Pantheon Books.

1948. *Winnebago Hero Cycles: A Study in Aboriginal Literature*. (IUPAL; Memoirs of IJAL, No. 1.) Bloomington.

1954, 1956a. *The Evolution of an American Indian Prose Epic: A Study in Comparative Literature*. (Special Publications of the Bollingen Foundation, Nos. 3, 5.) Basel: Ethnographic Museum. Parts I, II.

1956b. *The Trickster: A Study in American Indian Mythology*. London: Routledge; New York: Philosophical Library.

RASMUSSEN, KNUD

1930. *Iglulik and Caribou Eskimo Texts*. (Reports of the Fifth Thule Expedition, Vol. 7, No. 3.) Copenhagen.

REEVES, JAMES

1958. *The Idiom of the People*. New York: Macmillan.

ROBERTS, HELEN, and MORRIS SWADESH

1955. *Songs of the Nootka Indians*. (Transactions of the American Philosophical Society, Vol. 45, No. 3.) Philadelphia: American Philosophical Society.

SHIMKIN, DMITRI

1953. Wind River Shoshone Sun Dance. (BAE-B 151.) Washington, D.C.: Smithsonian Institution. Pp. 397-484.

SPENCER, KATHERINE

1957. *Mythology and Values: An Analysis of Navaho Chantway Myths*. (Memoirs of the American Folklore Society, No. 48.) Philadelphia: American Folklore Society.

STEWARD, JULIAN H.

1936. Myths of the Owens Valley Paiute. *UCP-AAE, 34:* 5. Pp. 355-440.

STEWART, OMER C.

1944. Washo-Northern Paiute Peyotism. *UCP-AAE, 40:* 3. Pp.63-136.

TAYLOR, ARCHER

1940. Some Trends and Problems in Studies of the Folk-Tale. *Studies in Philology, 37:* 1-25.

1951. *English Riddles from Oral Tradition*. Berkeley: University of California Press.

1962. *The Proverb; An Index to "The Proverb."* (3rd ed.) Hatboro, Pa.: Folklore Associates. (1st ed., 1930; 2nd ed., 1934.)

THOMPSON, STITH

1929. *Tales of the North American Indian*. Cambridge: Harvard University Press.

1946. *The Folktale*. New York: Dryden. (Reissued by Holt, 1960.)

1955-1958. *Motif-Index of Folk-Literature*. (Rev. and enlarged ed.) Bloomington: Indiana University Press; Copenhagen: Rosenkilde and Bagger. 6 Vols.

1961. *The Types of the Folktale. A Classification and Bibliography*. (2nd Rev. and enlarged ed.) (Folklore Fellows Communication, No. 184.) Helsinki: Academia Scientarium Fennica.

VOEGELIN, C. F., and ROBERT C. EULER

1957. Introduction to Hopi Chants. *JAF, 70:* 115-136.

WALTON, E. L.

1930. Navajo Song Patterning. *JAF, 43:* 105-118.

WILGUS, D. K.

1959. *Anglo-American Folksong Scholarship Since 1898*. New Brunswick, N.J.: Rutgers University Press.

WILLIAMSON, S. G.

1958. The Lyric in the Fante Methodist Church. *Africa, 28* (2): 126-133.

39 The Structure and Content of Cheremis Charms

THOMAS A. SEBEOK

I. THE CORPUS AND ITS FUNCTION

The word "charm," as used in this paper, is equivalent to the Latin phrase *incantamentum et adjuratio magica*, or to the German word *Segen*, which has been defined with varying emphasis; in the concluding portion of this paper a formal definition will be offered, but here we adopt the definition of J. Grimm, according to whom *Segen* are "*Formeln im ausserkirchlichen Gebrauch, christlicher und nicht-christlicher Art, denen eine übernatürliche Wirkung und zwar meist schützender, heilsamer Art zugeschrieben wird*" [Formulas in use outside the Church, of both Christian and non-Christian sort, to which a supernatural effect and indeed mostly one of a protecting, healing kind is ascribed] (cited after F. Ohrt, "Segen," *Handwörterbuch des deutschen Aberglaubens*, 1935-1936, 7: 1582-1620).

This excellent definition includes at once historical, functional, and formal dimensions, all of which are important for a complete understanding. For our purposes, however, the third aspect will be paramount. This is because the effectiveness of a charm depends on its literally exact citation, and, conversely, because any departure from its precisely set mechanism may render the magic wholly ineffective. It goes without saying that the effect depends ultimately on the psycho-cultural valuation of the charm, that is to say, it must be firmly believed in by the speaker, and that a strong belief may, under certain circumstances, allow for minor variations in certain details of the text, though such variations do not of course alter the structural outlines of the charm.

In historical perspective, Cheremis charms are not especially problematic. They are, on the one hand, altogether different from the magic runes of Finnish folklore, both as to content and as to form. On the other hand, Cheremis charms are very like Russian ones, most of them sharing with the latter, among other diagnostic features, what may be called the "motif of an extremely improbable eventuality" (see p. 361). It can be safely concluded that among the Cheremis (and also among their linguistic congeners the Mordvins and Votyaks, as well as among their close neighbors the Chuvash) the now extant charms are of relatively recent origin, having diffused in Christian times, and, specifically, from Russian sources.

In the text collections which constitute our corpus, charms appear under functional headings. These may be classified in summary, with some inevitable overlapping, into four major categories: (1) charms having to do with medicine, both human and veterinary; (2) charms having to do with human relations, such as love or adversaries; (3) charms that are directed against witchery in general, including the Evil Eye, or certain specific spirits; and (4) charms having to do with the fauna or flora.

. . . .

[There follows an account of a type of Cheremis magician called *šübedəšə* literally "the one who spits," who cures by spitting and makes use of charms. (One Cheremis word for "charm" is *šübedəme*). The four major functional categories of charms are then elaborated by a subclassification which provides for each charm in the corpus, e.g., 1. Charms having to do with medicine; 1.1. For the cure of human ailments; . . . 1.1.3. Snakebite (two variants, .1 and .2); . . 1.1.5 Bleeding (four variants, .1-.4).]

Though functional classifications of the sort outlined above are of undoubted cultural interest, and are useful as a practical device, they do nevertheless tend to obscure the basic formal identities or similarities which underlie Cheremis charms. Furthermore, one recalls Olbrechts' criticism of Mooney's arrangement of Cherokee formulas "in a systematic sequence, in a logical order, 'logical' from the white man's point of view . . . This classification is quite foreign to Cherokee knowledge and use . . ." (Mooney and Olbrechts, 1932, p. 2). Since the cultural matrix in which the Cheremis charms function is known only sketchily at best, such a classification ought not to be insisted upon. On the other hand, a structural analysis is entirely in terms of the texts being analyzed. After some preliminary remarks on structural analysis in folklore, we hope to show how such an analysis could be applied to the charms in the present corpus.

II. STRUCTURAL ANALYSIS IN FOLKLORE

Structural analysis in folklore rests on an assumption, namely, that all the products of verbal behavior may, in the last analysis, be reduced to terms of symbolic logic. Respectability to this assumption is lent by a philosophical tradition epitomized by Alfred North Whitehead, who went even further when he suggested "that Symbolic Logic, that is to say, the symbolic examination of pattern with the use of real variables, will become the foundation of aesthetics . . . when in the distant future the subject has expanded, so as to examine patterns depending on connections other than those of space, number and quantity . . . ." (Whitehead, 1937, p. 186. For an attempt in the latter direction, see Johansen, 1949. See now also A. A. Hill, 1951, and Empson, 1951.)

It has been generally recognized that the techniques whereby, in actual practice, we study verbal behavior differ, by and large, from those whereby we study non-verbal behavior. (Cf. the statement of Voegelin and Harris, 1947, pp. 590-592, that "the techniques of linguistics and cultural anthropology are in general different," and elaboration thereof.) This is true in spite of occasional attempts to apply techniques of the former kind to the study of behavior which is verbal only in part, such as systems of kinship, which are in part systems of terminology (verbal) and in part systems of attitudes (non-verbal), the two parts being functionally interdependent; but, at any rate, such behavior was explicitly identified as being both systematic and symbolic. (Lévi-Strauss, 1945. Greenberg, 1949, shows how kinship can be defined by logical methods. Emeneau, 1950, p. 209, postulates that "some forms are ordered in classes or subclasses corresponding to systems or subsystems within the environment.")

Among the several other possible approaches to verbal behavior, it is linguistics that studies communication systems which are symbolic par excellence, i.e., codes and messages. The method of modern linguistics may be regarded as a kind of discrete or discontinuous mathematics. (Joos, 1950. On linguistics as algebra, see especially Hjelmslev, 1943.) Folklorists, too, have of late "increasingly turned their attention to the study of patterns, forms, and devices" (Wellek and Warren, 1949, p. 39, and corresponding references on p. 303), though such can hardly be characterized as their focal interest, since folklore has sundry pressing problems peculiar to it—such as those of transmission, and function in a natural and cultural setting (see, for example, the sort of topics discussed by Herskovits, 1950, chap. 24. Sebeok, 1951, tried to show how the folksongs of the Cheremis provide clues for an understanding of certain aspects of their social organization)—which have not encouraged the development of a rigorous technique of formal analysis.

It may be worth digressing at this point to recall that linguistics and folklore study have common roots in the nineteenth century and were pursued with equal vigor by such scholars as Jacob Grimm, Max Müller, Theodor Benfey, and others. Linguistic preoccupation with Proto-Indo-European reconstructions naturally led the brothers Grimm to assume tales to be a detritus of early Indo-European myths; and Müller's search for tale origins by way of Sanskrit etymologies illustrates the once intimate relationship between comparative linguistics and comparative mythology (Thompson, 1946, pp. 368 ff., and Pedersen, 1931; [see also Nygard, 1958]). Sydow (1945; 1948) is now critical in retrospect, and stresses the distinction between the methods of philological and folklore research; but while he points to a certain lack of understanding on the part of philologists in their attitude to the work of folklorists, he nonetheless concludes that collaboration between the two fields is of supreme importance.

Franz Boas and some of his students have, in more recent times, emphasized the necessity of studying the stylistic qualities of folklore texts, an impossible endeavor without a knowledge of linguistics: ". . . no one can pretend to study a people authentically without this knowledge. . . . The structure of a language and its vocabulary are so obviously fundamental for the proper appreciation and understanding of cultural and societal expressions that he who remains in ignorance of them does so at his own peril" (Radin, 1949, p. II).

The two disciplines have also crossed paths here and there with regard to certain specific methodological procedures, principally historical ones. For instance, the historic-geographic or Finnish method of folktale study (Krohn, 1926) utilizes techniques which are in a good many particulars the same as those of a school of linguistics, rather controversial, which goes by the name of "neolinguistics" (Bonfante, 1947; Bonfante and Sebeok, 1944; Robert A. Hall, Jr., 1946).

Now the interest of many linguists has shifted from historical to descriptive investigations, at least for the time being; moreover, linguistic statements—whether descriptive or historical—tend to be exact, rigorous, compact, and internally consistent, in terms of elementary units and their patterned relations; in other words, they tend to be structural. (Voegelin and Harris, 1947, pp. 594 ff., summarize trends. On the notion of structure in linguistics and the background thereof, see, among others: Jakobson, 1933; Pos, 1939; Harris, 1940; Brøndal, 1943; Cassirer, 1945; Hjelmslev, 1947.) "It seems that a major movement of this kind is now affecting many branches of science: the decline of what may be called atomism, or atomistic thought in general, and the emergence of theories based on the conception of pattern." (Whyte, 1950, p. 25. Cf. Whyte 1951, and Bertalanffy, 1950. For a further excellent summary of this point of view, see Ruesch and Bateson, 1951, chap. 10.) The notion of structure is thus unmistakably in the air. This is so despite the fact that as yet we do not know what exactly is meant by a "structure" in general, beyond the recognition of its being something purely formal and purely relational. Especially unclear is the connection between structures posited by the different sciences, but, at any rate, a structural statement is everywhere one which says something about relations rather than about the relata themselves. (Carnap, 1928, pp. 11-6. According to Langer, 1937, p. 24, the notion of structure is the "bridge that connects all the various meanings of form from geometric form to the form of ritual or etiquette . . . ." For a specific comparison between two branches of science, see Kroeber, 1943.)

In folkloristic texts, too, there are certain regularly recurrent units which permit experimentation along methodological lines which might be regarded, in these broad terms, as structural. This should surprise no one who has reflected on the close analogy between the language-speech dichotomy of Saussurean linguistics, and the relationship of a given folkloristic type and its actual variations as presented by specific informants. (Cf. Bogatyrev and Jakobson, 1929.)

It was realized long ago, for example, that folktales and myths frequently open and close with conventional formulas. German Märchen formulas have received attention half a century ago (Petsch, 1900); and Bolte and Polívka have assembled a great many of them (1930, pp. 13-36). More recently, a collection of fourteen Tübatulabal tale texts were examined for such formulas explicitly, in the words of the author of the article herself, "from a structural viewpoint" (Erminie Voegelin, 1948.). Such was also the approach of Vera Mae Alleman in her study of two hundred and seventy Cheremis tale texts (Sebeok, 1952, pp. 115-117). In the Cheremis materials, two hundred and seven tales were found to have initial formulas as against sixty-three which did not, and a hundred and forty-eight final formulas, as against a hundred and twenty-two which did not. The formulas turned out to be either elementary units which could not further be meaningfully subdivided from a folkoristic point of view but only linguistically, or were simply conjunctions of the basic units. The latter were surprisingly few for such a relatively large corpus, and were easily classifiable under a small number of such headings as attention indicators, time elements, introducers of characters (initials); termini, personal elements, and statements as to the further fate of characters (finals).

Other strikingly formulistic features in the tale have been suggested, though these have not been approached from a structural point of view. Such are: cumulative stories, where a whole series of items are repeated, plus one more; or, as in the Gaelic tales, certain recurring prose patterns known as "runs," which describe in a conventionalized fashion some series of events, in a contrasting style of speech. (Thompson, 1946, pp. 458-459. Cumulative tales are common in Cheremis; see Sebeok, 1952, p. 112.) The Soviet folklorist V. Propp reached his remarkable conclusion that "All fairy tales are uniform in their structure" on the basis of studies designed to show the laws which govern the interconnections and temporal sequence of the highly limited number of functions of the dramatis personae occurring in fairy tales (1958). Above all, a program for a structural investigation of the folktale must include a study of the patterning of motifs. The impulse to classify them has hitherto taken precedence over the impulse to search for the manner of their workings. A linguist would ask: given a particular tale type, what relationships prevail between motifs of which each complete tale is composed? It seems more than likely—to a linguist—that the motifs will occur in a relatively fixed order and that particular motifs will necessarily co-occur, while others will be in complementary distribution; some motifs will occur in variant forms and such variations will be either free, or conditioned by context, or by other specific factors, and hence as predictable as any other dependent variable.

The simpler forms of folklore are particularly accessible to structural investigations, though these have but barely begun. In his work on Jabo proverbs, Herzog has hinted that "certain formal features would also lend themselves to classification," and pointed out those that are the most frequent in that language, but did not utilize such a systematization in the body of his book (Herzog and Blooah, 1936, pp. 3 ff.). Bascom devised a system of symbols to represent the forms of Yoruba riddles, though the total number of his generalized formulas is slightly over a half of the total number of his riddles (1949). Reichard's analysis of the intricate structure of Navajo prayers shows especially how fruitful such an approach can be in raising further subtle questions about the material (1944, chap. V). The metric structure of the Mordvin folksong is one of the few rigorous statements available in this field. (Jakobson and Lotz, 1941. An English translation of this paper has now appeared in the *Acta Instituti Hungarici Universitatis Holmiensis*. [Series B, Linguistica 1.] Stockholm: 1952, pp. 5-13.) Herzog has also pointed to the special problems inherent in the analysis of the folksong where the structure of the verse interacts with the musical pattern. (Herzog, 1946 [followed by discussion by Roman Jakobson and Morris Swadesh], 1950, pp. 1039-1041. See also Sapir, 1910, for a pioneer article in this field.) An attempt was made at a structural analysis of a body of highly stereotyped Cheremis dream portents; all instances were found to be reducible to a single equation, $f(S_n) = i_n$, where each interpretation was expressed as the function of a given set of symbols (Sebeok, 1950b). In the present paper, the structure of still another body of Cheremis texts, namely, charms, will be subjected to analysis. (Mooney and Olbrechts, 1932, pp. 159-160, have a section on "Structure of the Formulas" among the Cherokee. The general pattern which is outlined there is, however, an ideal one, to which perhaps not one formula corresponds exactly.)

III. SAMPLE ANALYSIS

Charm 1.1.5.3 is arbitrarily selected for the purpose of this sample analysis. This charm, spoken in order to stop the flow of blood from a wound, is here reproduced first in a phonemic transcription; (the bracketed numerals are for ease of reference only):

[1] *olma-pu* [2] *kuze* [3] *peledən* [4] *šińčeš*, [5] *tug-ak* [6] *tidə* [7] *püčmə* [8] *kuškən* [9] *šičšə!* ([10] *buige* [11] *peledəšəm* [12] *kalasaš* [13] *küleš*.) [14] *büt* [15] *kunam* [16] *peled* [17] *kerteš*, [18] *tunam* [19] *ižə* [20] *məjəm* [21] *seŋə!*

Literal translation: [1] "apple-tree"; [2] "as"; [3] "blossoming"; [4] "stands"; [5] "just so"; [6] "this"; [7] "wound"; [8] "growing"; [9] 3d sg. imperative of the verb "to stand"; [10] "all"; [11] acc. of "blossom"; [12] "to mention"; [13] "it is necessary"; [14] "water"; [15] "when"; [16] "blossom"; [17] "can"; [18] "then"; [19] "first"; [20] "me"; [21] 2d sg. imperative of the verb "to overcome".

Free translation: [1-9] "As the apple-tree blossoms forth, just so let this wound heal!

[10-13] (All blossoms must be mentioned.) [14-21] When water can blossom forth, only then overcome me!"

Our analytical procedure will be an application of binary opposition as a patterning principle: that is, we shall repeatedly divide sequences dichotomously until the ultimate constituents are reached.

The first operation yields two immediate constituents, namely, I. [1-13] "As the apple-tree blossoms forth, just so let this wound heal! (All blossoms must be mentioned)," and II. [14-21] "When water can blossom forth, only then overcome me!" Since the entire charm consists of three grammatical sentences, namely, [1-9, 10-13, 14-21], it may well be asked why the first operation yields [1-13] and [14-21] rather than, say, [1-9] and [10-21]; the reasons for this will be clarified as we proceed with the analysis of the first immediate constituent. (Cf. Wells, 1947, on the use of this term in linguistics. The principal criterion for determining immediate constituents is substitutability.)

I. The sequence [1-13] consists of two sentences, namely, [1-9] and [10-13]. Now let the symbol o represent the word "tree," and let further a numeral subscript represent the kind of a tree involved; thus, let the subscript 1 stand for an "apple." Hence o_1 will symbolize "apple-tree." The second sentence can be regarded as equivalent to saying: "As the o_2 blossoms forth, just so let this wound heal! As the o_3 blossoms forth . . ." and so forth, until "As the o_n blossoms forth, just so let this wound heal!" Thus we have here a finite number of sentences precisely alike in construction; the number of sentences is equal to the number of ethno-botanically conceived species of tree.

The internal structure of all these sentences is the same. Each sentence may be divided into two clauses, one independent and one dependent. Using sentence [1-9] as the model, the independent clause is [5-9] "just so let this wound heal," and the dependent clause is [1-4] "as the apple-tree blossoms forth."

Both clauses can be further subdivided into an actor-action phrase, namely, [6-9] "let this wound heal" in the independent clause, and [1, 3-4] "the apple-tree blossoms forth" in the dependent clause; and a subordinating conjunction, namely, [5] "just so" in the independent clause, and [2] "as" in the dependent clause.

Now the actor-action phrase in the independent clause differs from the actor-action phrase in the dependent clause in the construction of the verb, namely, while the former, [9] "let . . . heal" is in the imperative mode (in Cheremis), the latter, [4] "blossoms forth" is in the indicative mode. The two verbs are practically identical: they both happen to be constructed on the same base, since *sińč-* and *sič-* are allomorphs; both are singular in number, and both in the third person. However, they are opposed as to mode. We regard this contrast of indicative versus imperative as the crucial and fundamental feature which distinguishes the two actor-action phrases from one another in each sentence of this immediate constituent.

Let all actor-action phrases with a verb in the imperative mode be symbolized by S, and the particular phrase [6-9] "let this wound heal" by s. S corresponds to what Ohrt has called, without precise definition, the sorcerer's expression of will, or the "subjective" element in the charm.

Let further all actor-action phrases with a verb in the indicative mode be symbolized by O. O corresponds to what Ohrt has called the "objective" element in the charm which, as we have seen, consists of a magically circumspect enumeration of all the facts which are relevant. The particular phrases, i.e., the individual facts, are distinguishable only in terms of the actor, as o_1, o_2, o_3, . . . o_n, hence the entire phrase [1, 3-4] "the apple-tree blossoms forth" may be represented by o_1.

Finally, let an arc symbolize both words, [2] and [5] of the subordinating conjunction "as . . . just so."

The entire first sentence can now be expressed in terms of a simple binary propositional operation, namely, implication, thus: $o_1 \supset s$. With the use of an additional symbol, namely, a dot to express conjunction, the entire first immediate constituent, that is, the first and second sentences together can be expressed thus: $(o_1 \supset s) \cdot (o_2 \supset s) \cdot (o_3 \supset s) \ldots (o_n \supset s)$; but this is equivalent to (symbolized by $\equiv$) $(o_1 \cdot o_2 \cdot o_3 \cdot \ldots o_n) \supset s$; and since $(o_1 \equiv O) \cdot (o_2 \equiv O) \cdot (o_3 \equiv O) \cdot (o_n \equiv O)$, and since, further, $s \equiv S$, we arrive at the expression $O \supset S$. The latter is regarded as equal by definition to the sequence [1-13].

II. The sequence [14-21] consists of but a single sentence. This sentence consists of two parts: one, [18-21] "only then overcome me," is an independent clause; the other, [14-17] "when water can blossom forth," is a dependent clause.

Both clauses can be further subdivided into an actor-action phrase, namely, [20-21] "overcome me" in the independent clause, and [14, 16-17] "water can blossom forth" in the dependent clause; and a subordinating conjunction, namely, [18-19] "only then" in the independent clause, and [15] "when" in the dependent clause.

In the first actor-action phrase, the verb [21] "overcome" is in the imperative mode (in Cheremis), whereas, in the second actor-action phrase, the verb [17] "can" is in the indicative mode. This opposition is the same which we have encountered in the first immediate constituent. However, let us now compare the imperative verb [9] "let . . . heal" of the first immediate constituent with the imperative verb [21] "overcome" of the second immediate constituent. We perceive at once that there is a special relationship between these two verbs, namely, "overcome" is a negation of "let . . . heal"; it is equivalent to "let not heal." The negation of a proposition can be symbolized with a line above the expression; since "let . . . heal" was s, "let not heal" or "overcome" is $\bar{s}$.

The internal structure of the actor-action phrase in the dependent clause of II., that is, [14, 16-17] "water can blossom forth" is very like the internal structure of the model phrase [1,3-4] "the apple-tree blossoms forth" of I. The two phrases are not, however, absolutely identical. We must refer back at this point to the "motif of an extremely improbable eventuality" mentioned earlier in this paper. It will be observed that an assertion such as [1, 3-4] "the apple-tree blossoms forth" is true; that is, apple-trees do in fact blossom forth. Contrariwise, the assertion [14, 16-17] "water can blossom forth" is—within ordinary experience—false, that is, water does not in fact blossom forth. The verb [17] "can" is the linguistic means whereby this difference in the truth-value of the two phrases is signalized. Let a superscript⁻ represent the extreme improbability of such a fact as water blossoming forth. The phrase [14, 16-17] can therefore be symbolized by $\bar{o}$.

Let an arc again symbolize the words [15] and [18-19] of the subordinating conjunction "when . . . only then."

The entire last sentence can now be expressed in terms of the same operation—implication—as all preceding sentences, thus: $\bar{o}\overset{\frown}{\supset}\bar{s}$. Since $\bar{o} \equiv O$, and, further, $\bar{s} \equiv S$, we arrive at the expression $O \supset S$. The latter is regarded as equal by definition to the sequence [14-21].

Since the sequence [1-13] as well as the sequence [14-21] are each equal by definition to the expression $O \supset S$, the entire charm 1.1.5.3 can be expressed thus: $(O \supset S) \cdot (O \supset S)$ which again $\equiv 2(O \supset S)$. It must be recalled, however, that in the first immediate constituent the propositional function of O is chosen so that for any O, $f(O)$ is true; and in the second it is chosen so that for any O, $f(O)$ is—within ordinary experience—false.

In sum, it appears that our sample charm is ultimately composed of two, and only two, basic elements, namely, O and S; and that these two elements are in opposition, in such a way that O implies S. (Pos, 1938, p. 245, characterizes the concept of "opposition" this way: "*L'opposition n'est pas un fait isolé: c'est un principe de structure. Elle réunit toujours deux choses distinctes, mais qui sont liées de telle façon que la pensée ne puisse poser l'une sans poser l'autre. L'unité des opposés est toujours formée par un concept, qui, implicitement, contient les opposés en lui et se divise en opposition explicite quand il est appliqué à la réalité concrète. . . .*" ["Opposition is not an isolated fact: it is a principle of structure. It always joins two things which are distinct, but linked in such a way that thought cannot entertain the one without the other. The unity of the things opposed is always formed by a concept, which, implicitly, contains them in itself and subdivides in overt opposition when applied to concrete reality. . . ."])

IV. THE HISTORIOLA

The elements O and S are basic to Cheremis charms: each of them consists of one set or a succession of sets of these two elements, and they are always related by the operation of implication.

In a few charms, however, an additional element must be taken into consideration. It will be called "historiola" here, and symbolized by H. Such an element occurs in much fuller shapes in the magic charms of many other cultures in the same tradition, including particularly Russian, and is often referred to as the "epic motif." It is essentially an introductory reference of some sort to a past helpful deed by a beneficent power, to whom the rest of the charm is anchored. In the Cheremis texts, however, its historical origins are barely recognizable, though this circumstance does not of course vitiate its status in the structure.

Charm 1.1.3.1 may be used for illustration. It opens with this statement (h_1): "Upon the summit of a high mountain there is a gold chest, in the gold chest a gold goblet, in the gold goblet a silk ball," which is then immediately followed by an $O \supset S$ proposition. The charm being a cure for snakebite, this proposition reads: "if the snake can penetrate therein, bite it, grasp it, eat it up and drink it down [viz., the silk ball], then only may he bite me!" Now h_1 is repeated verbatim, except that, in this second version (h_2), the word "silver" appears wherever h_1 has "gold." The identical $O \supset S$ proposition is then repeated. This is followed by a third version of H (h_3), which is the same as h_1 or h_2, except that the word "mother-of-pearl" appears whereever h_1 has "gold" or h_2 "silver." Finally, the identical $O \supset S$ proposition is repeated for the third time. The entire charm can now be expressed thus: $[(h_1 \cdot \bar{o}) \supset \bar{s}] \cdot [(h_2 \cdot \bar{o}) \supset \bar{s}] \cdot [(h_3 \cdot \bar{o}) \supset \bar{s}]$. Since, however, $h_1 \equiv H$, $h_2 \equiv H$, $h_3 \equiv H$, $\bar{o} \equiv O$, $\bar{s} \equiv S$, therefore 3 $[(H \cdot O) \supset S]$. We may regard an expression like $H \cdot O$ simply as an expanded variety of O itself, and symbolize it by P. Hence we arrive at the expression 3 $(P \supset S)$.

The symbolic content of a historiola is rather obscure, and can be partially elucidated only by recognizing historical connections and by observing the function of a given symbol in Cheremis folklore as a whole. In historical perspective, for instance, the high mountain mentioned in the historiola of charm 1.1.3.1 is a symbolic reference to Mount Calvary, that is to say, to Christ, though it seems virtually certain that the Cheremis are totally unaware of this. The place where Christ was crucified is regarded, in New Testament tradition, as the temple where God meets man, hence a safe refuge, which "the snake" is unlikely to reach. As to the symbol of the silk ball, this functions conventionally in Cheremis folklore as a representation of human life. It is so used in the following folksong, for example, where its relationship to the "gold" and "silver" images is especially noteworthy:

> The morning sun emerges,
> It emerges gold-like.
> The evening sun descends,
> It descends silver-like.
> Our lives pass away,
> They pass away silk-thread-like.
> We flow and go flowing-water-like.

In other words, the historiola asserts that human life is secure from evil attack under the protection of Christ, and it is therefore safe to set the conditions stated in O, for, within ordinary experience, they are sure to be unrealizable.

The internal form of the historiola in the above example is one encountered frequently in a type of Cheremis folksong. Elsewhere (Sebeok, 1949, p. 143), we have called it a "spiral construction" of images: ball inside the goblet inside the chest atop the mountain. A given spiral might be spatial, as here, or numerical, pertaining to quality or family relationship, and so forth.

The proportion of h_1 to h_2 to h_3 is that of "gold" to "silver" to "mother-of-pearl." In formula 1.2.1.1—which is absolutely identical in structure with 1.1.3.1—the same proportion recurs: h_1 "a gold-lump comes out of the gold-furnace sparkling, sizzling"; h_2 "a silver-lump . . . out of the silver-furnace . . ."; h_3 "a mother-of-pearl-lump . . . out of the mother-of-pearl-furnace. . . ." Further triadic proportions which occur in the corpus are as follows: "gold" to "silver" to "copper" in 3.1.4; "wood" to "earth" to "iron" in 2.1.1; "great god" to "god the creator" to "thunder god" in 3.1.4 and 3.4.2. Slightly different is the historiola of 1.1.3.2, where the triadic proportion is within the same statement: "snake-khan, tree-khan, earth-khan." Again slightly different is the historiola of 1.1.4: h_1 "the morning sun rises and approaches . . ."; h_2 "(the light) shines and approaches . . ."; h_3 "dawn appears and approaches . . ." The remaining historiolalike statements in the corpus are not triadic: 1.1.2.1 "fire comes burning, rolling, like a dry tree-trunk" (ter); and 2.1.4 "there are forty-one armies behind forty-one mountains" ("forty-one" is a favorite number also in the folksong).

V. THE TEXTURE OF A CHEREMIS INCANTATION

A *narrator* addresses—or a singer sings to—a palpable *audience*, spinning a *text* which, to be effective, requires: a *context* molding his recitation; a *tradition* fully, or at least partially, in common to the speaker and his listeners; and, finally, a physical and psychological *nexus* enabling them to enter and remain in contact. Emphasis on one or another of these six factors focuses upon this or that aspect of folklore study, but a sensitive folklorist will take each into account, and will do so in awareness of the more comprehensive information theoretical model of any communication network which involves the same dimensions: an *addresser* who encodes, according to specific statistical constraints, a *message* out of a *code* which, to permit decoding, must be shared by an *addressee*; the message also requires a *referent* and a *channel* tying the participants into a semistable unit. (This hexagonal model is discussed, and illustrated in Fig. 1, of Sebeok, 1962, where further references are given.)

Among the Cheremis, when the addresser functions as a *šübedəšə*—a "spitter"—his addressee may be a non-person, that is, an inanimate supernatural. Although this grammatical device of personification is a criterion shared by two genres in the Cheremis repertoire, namely, incantations (*šübedəmə*) and prayers, if the object of the message is supposed always to obey the command, as an automatic consequence of the speaker's words, the text belongs in the former category; whereas a prayer is merely a means to an end the outcome of which is held to be uncertain. In an incantation, therefore, where the message as such is the instrument of power, its form assumes paramount importance. This observation has been documented in a detailed study of a substantial corpus of Cheremis charms, where it was shown that every text belonging to this genre is ultimately composed of just two basic elements and that these two stand in opposition such that one term implies the other (Sebeok, 1956b). The interpretation of any Cheremis incantation then depends on two sources of information: the text (or input), and the set of rules applied to it (in brief, the code). (Cf. Ebeling, 1960, pp. 9, 13.)

Much in the sense in which Vladimir Propp (1958) argued that all fairy tales are uniform in structure, one is compelled to recognize that every Cheremis incantation belongs to the same structural type. At the same time, however, each text is marked by a unique set of features which impart to it a certain particularity and concreteness or—to borrow a label from literary criticism—texture (Wellek and Warren, 1949, p. 7). An extremely interesting fact about the data is this: that striking symmetries are found to characterize each message no less than the code itself. To illustrate this, we propose to analyze the *individual texture* of the same incantation—recorded by Yrjö Wichmann—the *general structure* of which was dissected above.

Take note, to begin with, of the number of the syllables and their distribution. In the opening sentence [1-9], divided syntactically (where marked by the comma), the dependent clause [1-4] and the independent clause [5-9] contain ten syllables each. The construction of the second sentence [10-13]—a parenthetic metastatement, giving a procedural prescription of how to continue—is different. Then, in the third sentence [14-21], the dependent clause [14-17] contains seven and the independent clause [18-21], with a deviation of one, eight syllables.

Symmetry also governs the selection and distribution of the phonemes: the second word of the first sentence [2] and the second word of the third sentence [15] both begin in *k*, whereas the third word in each [3, 16] begins in *p*. On the other hand, the fourth words in the two sentences [4, 17] are drawn together by a quasi-rhyme.

Beyond this, there is the peculiarly impressive distribution of the initial consonants. The most frequent initial consonant here is the compact grave discontinuous *k*. There are six of them [2, 8, 12, 13, 15, 17]; and they are distributed in almost perfect symmetry: the first sentence has two, the second has two, and the third has two. Only the final clause [18-21] has none—and this is not by chance.

Almost the same distribution prevails with the diffuse grave *p/b*. There are also six of these [3, 7, 10, 11, 14, 16], and again two per sentence. The high frequency of word-initial bilabials in this text is particularly noteworthy because both *p/b* occupy relatively low rank in the order of Cheremis phonemes. One must recall that, as Wichmann's informant explained, *šübedəšə šübeden paremda*, that is, the "spitter" cures by spitting; and assume that these are employed with special density here because of their suggestive value. (Cf. *pʿū·* 'Das Spucken imitierender Laut,' cited in another incantation [Ö. Beke, *Tscheremissische Texte*. Budapest: 1961. Vol. 3, p. 183].) But the final clause has none—and this also can not be fortuitous.

Then there is a remarkable feature that the two independent clauses which contain the imperative verbs [9, 21] pivotal in the analysis of the code correspond to each other—but by a different pair of initial consonants: in each clause there is one initial diffuse acute discontinuous *t* [5, 18]; then each clause ends [9, 21] with a word beginning with an acute continuous sibilant *š/s*.

The alliterative pattern may be diagrammed as follows:

[2- 3- 4]	*k - p - š*
[7- 8- 9]	*p - k - š*
[11-12-13]	*p - k - k*
[15-16-17]	*k - p - k*

In addition to this symmetric distribution of alliteration and the regulation in number of syllables, the grammatical parallelism is striking: there is a consistent morphological symmetry between the first dependent clause [1-4] and the last [14-17]. The opening words in each instance are substantives [1, 14]; the next are auxiliaries [2, 15], viz., different forms of the same interrogative pronoun; the next are a pair of etymological figures [3, 16]; the next are dissyllabic rhymed verbs [4, 17] having all grammatical categories in common. In similar fashion, there is morphological symmetry between the first independent clause [5-9] and the last [18-21]. Here, the opening words in each instance are auxiliaries [5, 18], viz., different forms of the same demonstrative pronoun; and the closing words are again dissyllabic verbs [9, 21] having all grammatical categories in common, save one (person).

It is clear that this text—at first glance so deceptively simple—is imbued with a multilevel network of balanced symmetries. In the earlier study, all Cheremis charms were shown to be coded on four levels of discourse: magical, logical, rhetorical, and linguistic. In these brief supplementary remarks, we tried to display still further symmetries as are embodied in a single message on the levels of morphology and phonology. The interpreter of these multiform equations and antinomies—of grammatical categories and morphemes (roots as well as suffixes), of phonemic bundles, their components (the distinctive features) and elementary sequences (the syllables)—perceives them, in the output, as semantic relationships. As such, they may be transcoded, for example, from one object language into another, or from Cheremis into a meta-language. As the entangled constituents of the verbal texture, however, they are inherently untranslatable: they are, in short, the ingredients of poetry.

Finally, one is tempted to wonder why there is this overpowering disposition to produce an esthetic equilibrium. The multiplication of mutually reinforcing symmetries serves to communicate, indeed, to impress the structure of incantations in general; but their incarnation in the texture forges this message into a functional tool—an instrument with which the healer is capable of ordaining the future.

REFERENCE NOTE

This article has had to be condensed by omission of some sections dealing with folkloristic background and classification by use; these are summarized in the text. The article has been expanded, on the other hand, by section V, written as a supplement to the original analysis of the sample charm. For Part II of the article (written with Louis Orzack), see Sebeok (1953b). Sebeok's references on structuralism are incorporated in the bibliography below.

For further studies of the Cheremis and their verbal art, see Sebeok (1950a) and other works listed and Sebeok and Zeps (1961).

On the problem of formal or structural analysis of folklore, either in general or with reference to texts other than verse, see Armstrong (1959), Bogatyrev and

Jakobson (1929), the title essay in Burke (1957, especially "On Methodology"), Dorfman (1956), Dundes (1962, 1963), Felice (1958), Fischer (1960), Harris (1949, 1952a, 1952b), A. A. Hill (1958), Levi-Strauss (1955, 1956, 1960a, 1960b, 1960c, 1961), Nygard (1958), Propp (1958), Rickert (1927), Saporta and Sebeok (1959), Sebeok (1956c), Erminie Voegelin (1948), Wolff (1962), Yen (1960).

On the closely related problem of stylistic analysis and criticism, see Bally (1951), Guiraud (1961), Hatzfeld (1949, 1952), Juilland (1954), Riffaterre (1959, 1960), Sebeok (1960b), Spitzer (1948), Stutterheim (1948b, 1952), Ullmann (1957, 1963), Voegelin and Yegerlehner (1957).

With particular reference to poetry and poetic language, see Bray (1925), De Groot (1957), Fónagy (1961), Frye (1957), Guiraud (1953a, 1953b, 1961), A. A. Hill (1951, 1953, 1955, 1956), Hulme (1962), Hymes (1960b,) Jakobson (1960a), Jespersen (1905, chap. 10), Levin (1962), Marouzeau (1949), Meillet (1913, Part 2), Nowotny (1962), Nygard (1958), [Polish Academy of Sciences] *Poetics, Poetyka, Poetika* (1961), Sebeok (1956a, 1960a), Sebeok and Zeps (1961), Žinkin (1962, pp. 162-172), and references on special languages, pp. 397-406. Note Bloomfield's comment (1933, p. 443) vis-à-vis Greenough and Kittredge (1961), and the fundamental point made by Kenner (1958, p. 178), making explicit in syntactic and grammatical terms the essential perspective of the title essay in Burke (1957). (In general, note also the critical writers cited with Emeneau's article on pp. 330-343, especially Burke, Richards, and Wimsatt.)

On metrics and prosody, see Austerlitz (1958), Emeneau (1958), Epstein and Hawkes (1959), Fischer (1959), Frye (1957), Greenberg (1960), Hrushovski (1954, 1960), Jakobson (1933), Jakobson and Lotz (1941), Lanier (1893), Lehmann (1956), Lotz (1942, 1954, 1960), Montgomery (1922), Sebeok (ed.) (1960b, pp. 133-209), Simmons (1960c); Stutterheim (1948a), Whitehall *et al.* (1956), Wimsatt and Beardsley (1959).

On quantitative approaches, see Guiraud (1953a, 1953b, 1954a, 1954b), Herdan (1956, 1960), Miles (1951, 1960; cf. Kroeber, 1958), Reed (1949), Sebeok (1957), Yule (1944).

On text analysis as a task of editing and enabling further research, see references to examples in recent work in Hymes (1959b, section 4); comments in Boas (1911), Garvin (1955), Nida (1947a, 1949), Radin (1933, 1949), and Strehlow (1947), together with references to Nida's article on translation in Part II. Hulme (1962) is a painstaking philological example with narrow focus (on specific lexical occurrences and meanings) and broad context; for larger focus, note the references above on problems of formal or structural analysis, such as Burke (1957). On textual criticism or the establishing of a text, a field with an extensive literature of its own, see, e.g., Ham (1959).

References not in the general bibliography:

ARMSTRONG, ROBERT P.

1959. Content Analysis in Folkloristics. In Ithiel de Sola Pool (Ed.), *Trends in Content Analysis*. Urbana: University of Illinois. Pp. 151-170.

AUSTERLITZ, ROBERT

1958. *Ob-Ugric Metrics*. (Folklore Fellows Communications, No. 174.) Helsinki: Academia Scientiarum Fennica. [Reviewed, A. A. Hill, *Lg.*, 1959, *35:* 567-569; D. H. Hymes, *Anthropos*, 1960, *55:* 574-576.]

BERTALANFFY, LUDWIG VON
1950. An Outline of General System Theory. *The British Journal for the Philosophy of Science, 1:* 1-32.

BOLTE, JOHANNES, and GEORG POLÍVKA
1930. *Anmerkungen zu den Kinder- und Hausmärchen der Brüder Grimm.* Leipzig. Vol. 4.

BRAY, DENYS
1925. *The Original Order of Shakespeare's Sonnets.* London: Methuen.

BRØNDAL, VIGGO
1943. Linguistique structurale. *Essais de linguistique générale.* Copenhagen. Pp. 90-97.

CARNAP, RUDOLF
1928. *Der logische Aufbau der Welt.* Berlin: Schlachtensee.

DE GROOT, A. W.
1957. Phonetics in Its Relation to Aesthetics. In L. Kaiser (Ed.), *Manual of Phonetics.* Amsterdam: North-Holland Publishing. Pp. 385-400.

DORFMAN, E.
1956. The Structure of the Narrative: A Linguistic Approach. *The History of Ideas News Letter, 2:* 63-67.

DUNDES, ALAN
1962. From Etic to Emic Units in the Structural Study of Folktales. *JAF, 75:* 95-105.

EBELING, C. L.
1960. *Linguistic Units.* The Hague: Mouton.

EPSTEIN, E. L., and TERENCE HAWKES
1959. *Linguistics and English Prosody.* With an Introduction by Henry Lee Smith. (Studies in Linguistics, Occasional Papers, No. 7.) Buffalo: University of Buffalo, Department of Anthropology and Linguistics.

FELICE, ARIANE DE
1958. Essai sur quelques techniques de l'art verbal traditionnel. *Arts et traditions populaires.* Paris. Pp. 41-50.

FISCHER, J. L.
1959. Meter in Eastern Carolinian Oral Literature. *JAF, 72:* 47-52.
1960. Sequence and Structure in Folktales. In Anthony F. C. Wallace (Ed.), *Men and Cultures.* Philadelphia: University of Pennsylvania Press. Pp. 442-446.

FÓNAGY, IVÁN
1961. Communication in Poetry. *Word, 17:* 194-218.

FRYE, NORTHRUP (ED.)
1957. *Sound and Poetry.* (English Institute Essays.) New York.

GREENBERG, JOSEPH H.
1960. A Survey of African Prosodic Systems. In Stanley A. Diamond (Ed.), *Culture in History.* New York: Columbia University Press. Pp. 925-950.

GUIRAUD, PIERRE
1953a. *Langage et versification d'après l'œuvre de Paul Valéry. Étude sur la forme poétique dans ses rapports avec la langue.* (Collection Linguistique, Société de Linguistique de Paris.) Paris: Klincksieck.

1953b. *Index du vocabulaire du symbolisme*. Paris: Klincksieck.

1954a. *Les Caractères statistiques du vocabulaire*. Paris: Presses Universitaires de France.

1954b. *Bibliographie critique de la statistique linguistique*. Revised and completed by T. D. Houchin, J. Puhvel, C. W. Watkins under the direction of J Whatmough. (Comité International Permanent de Linguistes, Publications du Comité de la Statistique Linguistique, No. 2.) Utrecht/Anvers: Spectrum.

1961. Pour une Sémiologie de l'expression poétique. *Langue et littérature*. (Actes du Huitième Congrès de la Fédération Internationale des Langues et Littératures Modernes.) Liège. Pp. 119-134.

HAM, EDWARD B.

1959. Textual Criticism and Common Sense. *Romance Philology*, *13:* 198-215.

HARRIS, ZELLIG S.

1949. Culture and Style in Extended Discourse. In Sol Tax (Ed.), *Indian Tribes of Aboriginal America*. (Selected Papers of the 29th International Congress of Americanists.) Chicago: University of Chicago Press. Pp. 210-215.

1952a. Discourse Analysis. *Lg.*, *28:* 1-30.

1952b. Discourse Analysis; A Sample Text. *Lg.*, *28:* 474-494.

HATZFELD, HELMUT

1949. Stylistic Criticism as Art-Minded Philology. *Yale French Studies*, *2:* 62-70.

1952. *A Bibliography of the New Stylistics*. Chapel Hill: University of North Carolina Press. (Expanded Spanish version, Madrid, 1955.)

HERDAN, GUSTAV

1956. *Language as Choice and Chance*. Groningen: Noordhoff. [Reviewed, R. W. Brown, *Lg.*, 1957, *33:* 170-181.]

1960. *Type-Token Mathematics*. The Hague: Mouton

HERZOG, GEORGE

1936. *Jabo Proverbs From Liberia*. London: Oxford University Press.

1950. Song: Folk Song and the Music of Folk Song. In Maria Leach (Ed.), *Funk and Wagnall's Standard Dictionary of Folklore, Mythology and Legend*. New York: Funk and Wagnall, 1949-1950. Vol. 2, pp. 1032-1050.

HILL, A. A.

1951. Toward a Literary Analysis. In F. Bowers (Ed.), *English Studies in Honor of James Southall Wilson*. Charlottesville: University of Virginia Press. Pp. 147-165.

1953. A Sample Literary Analysis. *Monograph Series on Languages and Linguistics*, *4:* 87-93. Washington: Georgetown University.

1955. An Analysis of *The Windhover:* An Experiment in Structural Method. *PMLA*, *70:* 972-73.

1956. *Pippa's Song:* Two Attempts at Structural Criticism. *Studies in English*, *35:* 51-56. Austin: The University of Texas. [Also in Harold B. Allen (Ed.), *Readings in Applied English Linguistics*. New York: Appleton-Century-Crofts, 1958. Pp. 402-406.]

1958. A Program for the Definition of Literature. *Studies in English*, *37:* 46-52. Austin: The University of Texas.

HJELMSLEV, LOUIS
1947. Structural Analysis of Language. *Studia Linguistica* 1. 69-78.

HRUSHOVSKI, BENJAMIN
1954. On Free Rhythms in Modern Yiddish Poetry. In Uriel Weinreich (Ed.), *The Field of Yiddish*. New York: Linguistic Civile of New York. Pp. 219-266.
1960. On Free Rhythms in Modern Poetry. In Thomas A. Sebeok (Ed.), *Style in Language*. New York: Wiley; Cambridge: Technology Press. Pp. 173-190.

JAKOBSON, ROMAN, and JOHN LOTZ
1941. Axiomatik eines Verssystems am mordwinischen Volkslied dargelegt. *Thesen zu einem Vortrag im Ungarischen Institut*. Stockholm.
1952. Axioms of a versification system exemplified by the Mordvinian folksong. *Acta Instituti Hungarici Universitatis Holmiensis, Series B. Linguistica. 1:* 5-13. Stockholm.

JUILLAND, A. G.
1954. Review of F. Bruneau, *L'époque realiste*. *Lg.*, *30:* 313-338.

KENNER, HUGH
1958. In the Wake of the Anarch. *Gnomon. Essays on Contemporary Literature*. New York: McDowell, Obolensky. Pp. 171-179.

KROEBER, A. L.
1958. Parts of Speech in Periods of Poetry. *PMLA*, *73:* 309-314

KROHN, KAARLE
1926. *Die folkloristische Arbeitsmethode*. Oslo: Aschehoug.

LANGER, SUZANNE K.
1937. *An Introduction to Symbolic Logic*. Boston: Houghton-Mifflin.

LANIER, SIDNEY
1893. *The Science of English Verse*. New York: Scribner.

LEHMANN, W. P.
1956. *The Development of Germanic Verse Form*. Austin: University of Texas Press. [Reviewed, G. J. Metcalf, *Lg.*, 1960, *36:* 236-244.]

LEVIN, S. P.
1962. *Linguistic Structures in Poetry*. (Janua Linguarum, No. 23.) The Hague: Mouton.

LOTZ, JOHN
1942. Notes on Structural Analysis in Metrics. *Helicon*, *4:* 119-146.
1954. Kamassian Verse. *JAF*, *67*: 369-377.
1960. Metric Typology. In Thomas A. Sebeok (Ed.), *Style in Language*. New York: Wiley; Cambridge: Technology Press. Pp. 135-148.

MILES, JOSEPHINE
1951. *The Continuity of Poetic Language: Studies in English Poetry from the 1540's to the 1940's*. Berkeley: University of California Press.
1960. *Renaissance, Eighteenth-Century, and Modern Language in English Poetry. A Tabular View*. Berkeley and Los Angeles: University of California Press.

MONTGOMERY, G.

1922. A Method of Studying the Structure of Primitive Verse, Applied to Songs of the Teton Sioux. *University of California Publications in Modern Philology, 11:* 269-283.

MOONEY, JAMES, and FRANS M. OLBRECHTS

1932. *The Swimmer Manuscript. Cherokee Sacred Formulas and Medicinal Prescriptions.* (BAE-B 99.) Washington, D.C.: Smithsonian Institution.

NOWOTNY, WINIFRED

1962. *The Language Poets Use.* New York: Oxford University Press.

PETSCH, R.

1900. *Formelhafte Schlüsse im Volksmärchen.* Berlin.

[Polish Academy of Sciences, Literary Research Institute]

1961. *Poetics, Poetyka, Poetika.* Warsaw: Polish Scientific Publishers; The Hague: Mouton and Co.

POS, H. J.

1938. La Notion d'opposition en linguistique. *Onzième Congrès International de Psychologie.* Paris: University of Paris. Pp. 246-247.

1939. Perspectives du structuralisme. *Travaux du Cercle Linguistique de Prague, 8:* 71-78.

REED, DAVID W.

1949. A Statistical Approach to Quantitative Linguistic Analysis. *Word, 5:* 235-247.

RICKERT, EDITH

1927. *New Methods for the Study of Literature.* Chicago: University of Chicago Press.

RIFFATERRE, MICHAEL

1959. Criteria for Style Analysis. *Word, 15:* 154-174.

1960. Stylistic Context. *Word, 16:* 207-218.

1961a. Problèmes d'analyse du style litteraire. *Romance Philology, 14:* 216-227.

1961b. Vers la definition linguistique du style. *Word, 17:* 318-344.

SAPORTA, SOL, and THOMAS A. SEBEOK

1959. Linguistics and Content Analysis. In Ithiel de Sola Pool (Ed.), *Trends in Content Analysis.* Urbana: University of Illinois Press. Pp. 131-150.

SEBEOK, THOMAS A.

1949. The Cheremis Folksong: A Soviet Viewpoint. *The Slavonic and East European Review, 28:* 130-151. (With Evelyn Lane.)

1950b. Cheremis Dream Portents. *SJA, 6:* 273-285.

1951. Levirate Among the Cheremis as Reflected by Their Songs. *AA, 53:* 285-291.

1952. *Studies in Cheremis.* Vol. 1, *Folklore.* (Indiana University Publications, Folklore Series, No. 6.) Bloomington.

1953b. The Structure and Content of Cheremis Charms, Part Two. *Anthropos, 48:* 760-772. (With Louis Orzack.)

1955. *Studies in Cheremis.* Vol. 5, *The Cheremis.* New Haven: Human Relations Area Files.

1956a. Sound and Meaning in a Cheremis Folksong Text. *For Roman Jakobson.* The Hague: Mouton and Co. Pp. 430-439.

1956b. *Studies in Cheremis*. Vol. 2, *The Supernatural*. (Viking Fund Publications in Anthropology, No. 22.) New York: Wenner Gren Foundation for Anthropological Research. (With Frances Ingemann.)

1956c. Structural Analysis in Folklore Research. In Sebeok (1956b).

1957. Toward a Statistical Contingency Method in Folklore Research. *Studies in Folklore Presented to Stith Thompson*. Indiana University Publications, Folklore Series, No. 9.) Bloomington.

1959a. Approaches to the Analysis of Folksong Texts. *Ural-Altaische Jahrbücher*, *31*: 392-399.

1956b. On Non-Random Distribution of Initial Phonemes in Cheremis Verse. *Lingua*, *8*: 370-384. (With Valdi J. Zeps.)

SEBEOK, THOMAS A., and VALDIS J. ZEPS

1961. *Concordance and Thesaurus of Cheremis Poetic Language*. (Janua Linguarum, No. 8.) The Hague: Mouton.

SMITH, HENRY LEE, JR.

1959. Toward Redefining English Poetry. *Studies in Linguistics*, *14*: 68-76.

SPITZER, LEO

1948. . *Linguistics and Literary History*. Princeton: Princeton University Press.

STUTTERHEIM, C. F. P.

1948a. Review of A. De Groot, *Algemene Versleer*. *Lingua*, *1*: 104-117.

1948b. 1952. Modern Stylistics I: Style and Style-Class; II. *Lingua*, *1*: 410-426; *3*: 52-68.

SYDOW, C. W.

1945. Nagra synspunker på sagoforskning och filologi, øst og Vest. *Afhandlinger tilegnede Prof. Arthur Christensen*, pp. 140-166. Copenhagen.

1948. Folk-Tale Studies and Philology. Some Points of View. *Selected Papers on Folklore*, pp. 189-219. Copenhagen.

ULLMANN, STEPHEN

1957. *Style in the French Novel*. Cambridge: Cambridge University Press. [Reviewed, M. Riffaterre, *Word*, 1959, *15*: 404-413.]

VOEGELIN, C. F., and JOHN YEGERLEHNER

1957. Toward a Definition of Formal Style, with Examples from Shawnee. *Studies in Folklore Presented to Stith Thompson*. (Indiana University Publications, Folklore Series, No. 9.) Bloomington. Pp. 141-150.

VOEGELIN, ERMINIE WHEELER

1948. Initial and Final Elements in Tubatulabal Myths. *SJA*, *4*: 71-75.

WELLS, RULON S.

1947. Immediate Constituents. *Lg.*, *23*: 81-117.

WHITEHALL, HAROLD

1951. From Linguistics to Criticism. *Kenyon Review*, *13*: 710-714. [Also in Harold B. Allen (Ed.), *Readings in Applied English Linguistics*. New York: Appleton-Century-Crofts, 1958. Pp. 398-401.]

WHITEHALL, H., S. CHATMAN, A. STEIN, JOHN CROWE RANSOM

1956. English Verse and What It Sounds Like. *Kenyon Review*, *18*: 411-477.

WHITEHEAD, ALFRED NORTH

1937. Remarks. *The Philosophical Review*, *46*: 178-186.

WHYTE, LANCELOT LAW

1950. Simultaneous Discovery. *Harper's Magazine*, February, pp. 23-26.

1951. *Aspects of Form. A Symposium on Form in Nature and Art*. London.

WIMSATT, W. K., JR., and MONROE C. BEARDSLEY

1959. The Concept of Meter: An Exercise in Abstraction. *PMLA* 74. 585-598.

YEN, ISABELLA Y

1960. *A Grammatical Analysis of Syau Jing*. (RCAFL-P 16; IJAL 26: 4, Part IV.) Bloomington.

YULE, G. UDNEY

1944. *The Statistical Study of Literary Vocabulary*. Cambridge: Cambridge University Press.

40 Yokuts Narrative Style

STANLEY S. NEWMAN AND ANNA H. GAYTON

Linguistic Aspects of Yokuts Style

STANLEY S. NEWMAN

To THE EXTENT THAT language is a medium for communicating ideas and for recording experience, appropriate equivalents in one language can always be supplied for those of another. On this colorless level a language has no style; it is merely what a dictionary implies it is—a bundle of lexical units for referring to things and events and relations, an instrument for conveying the brute content of experience.

But we are intuitively aware that our own native tongue, at least, is more than a group of speech symbols for referring to chairs and tables. We know, for instance, that there are a number of ways of saying essentially the same thing, that similar notions can be expressed by different stylistic uses of the language. Our intimate association with our native mode of expression has made us so acutely sensitive to these minute differences of style that we can frequently identify speakers or writers by the manner in which they draw upon the resources of the language. But our ability to make such fine discriminations within one language medium carries with it the seeds of an illusion, for inevitably we get the feeling that there is no limit to the potential variations of style in our language. And we are encouraged in this illusion by literary artists, whose task it is to convince us that they are working with a perfectly flexible medium that can be molded to any desired shape.

The process of translation helps to correct such illusions. In translating we come to the unhappy realization that each language, instead of shaping itself to our will, governs and directs the trend of our expression. We are sharply reminded that languages have an inner resistance. Their materials are already shaped into a system of formal and conceptual patterns. Within the patterns of a language other than our own, we are forced to make uncongenial distinctions and to ignore other distinctions that seem imperative to us. In Yokuts, for example, it is necessary to discriminate in all tenses an event which is in the process of transpiring from one that has already taken place and exists only as a resultant state or condition: a fundamental contrast is expressed in "he is walking" as against "he is in a condition subsequent to walking." Such a distinction is pedantic in English. Plurality need not be expressed in most nouns unless there is some special point to it; the form "house" can do the work of referring to the plural as well as the singular.

These patterns, however, are merely the potentialities of style. A grammar deals with them directly, describing their forms and their conceptual functions. It is not concerned with the selective tendencies operating in actual usage to favor certain potentialities and to neglect others. It tells what a language can do but not what it considers worthwhile doing. To the native a grammar is always unconvincing, for it ignores the most vital and intimate part of his language—the intricate network of values, of attitudes and expectancies that guides his selection of expressive tools.

It would be a sentimental presumption to suppose that we, as outsiders, can respond significantly to the values locked within the Yokuts language. The values and anticipations that we have developed in our own language will not be satisfied in Yokuts. In spite of this, we can escape our bias to some degree by following the selective trends of Yokuts as manifestations of the stylistic values proper to that language and by examining the manner in which Yokuts arrives at an integrated style through the exploitation of certain of its latent resources and the rejection of others.

A striking uniformity of style is to be found in Yokuts, and the personal narratives collected in the field show the same stylistic qualities as the myths and tales. In these stories there is no tendency to indulge in the elaboration of concrete details. The notions expressed remain on a highly generalized level. This bareness and simplicity of expression can be traced to a number of grammatical factors. Suffixation is practically the only grammatical technique of Yokuts that augments the meaning of word roots. The addition of a suffix, however, sets in motion a chain of formal operations. Principal among these are the vowel processes: in addition to occasional vowel changes that occur under special conditions, the root vowels undergo constant changes dictated by an intricate system of vowel classes; and the vowels of the suffix itself must then be changed to harmonize with the vowels of the root. To add the durative present *-ʔan*, for example, the roots *ʔe:pi*, "swim," and *de:yi*, "lead, take the lead," change their vowels in the stems *ʔipa:-ʔan*, "he is swimming" and *diya:-ʔan*, "he is leading." But the suffix must also change its vowel when it is appended to a stem of the "o" class: parallel to the forms quoted above, the root *yo:wo* "go home," undergoes vowel changes and also affects the vowel of the suffix in *yowo:-ʔon*, "he is going home."

But all of this shifting and balancing of vowels is completely devoid of any referential function. The vowel changes have a purely formal relevance and carry with them no increments of meaning. They are not like our vowel changes in "sing, sang, sung" or in "man, men," which have a clearly assignable function. They resemble the nonfunctional vowel changes in the stressed syllables of "grateful, gratitude" or "volcano, volcanic." Whereas changes of this type affect only a minute portion of the English vocabulary, in Yokuts they are deeply embedded in the language system and accompany every process applied to the word.

In its organization of morphological elements, Yokuts shows the same disregard for external function. The tightly organized and interrelated classifications of word types and subtypes, of stems, and of suffixes are not based upon any rationale of their conceptual content. These elements are classified according to their phonetic form and the way they behave as morphological units, not according to their meaning.

Every language possesses a certain amount of formal machinery that does not generate meaning. Of this type are the occasional vowel changes of English, mentioned above, and some scattered consonant changes ("invade, invasion; equate, equation"). But there is a scrupulous and unremitting attention given to form for its own sake in Yokuts. Throughout its grammatical system Yokuts reveals a degree of neatness and consistency in organization, a formal balance and symmetry, that is rare among languages. Although this formal emphasis contributes feebly to the creation of meanings, it is by no means insignificant as a stylistic factor. Formal movements that take place below the level of tangible meanings carry their own esthetic satisfactions. But they are the most subtle and indigenous aspects of a language; they can never be captured in a translation.

The suffixing system, which bears the heaviest burden of functional work in Yokuts, does not provide the means for an elaborate development of concepts within the word. There are no more than a hundred suffixes in Yokuts. Although English possesses about the same number, it does not rely primarily upon suffixation; such techniques as word order, compounding, prefixation carry as much, if not more, of the functional load. Yet, in spite of the fact that Yokuts depends almost exclusively upon suffixes, it is remarkably restrained in exploiting the possibilities of suffix combination. Every word in Yokuts, except the uninflected particle, must have at least one suffix, and the great majority of words occurring in the several volumes of text dictated by my informants do not go beyond this minimum requirement. Words containing two suffixes are fairly common; but words with three suffixes are relatively rare, and those with more than three are practically nonexistent in the texts. This is not a matter of mere statistics; it is a manifestation of selective forces in Yokuts that limit the free application of its grammatical resources. There is no analogous tendency in English to set upper and lower limits to the use of suffixation and to demand that a uniform degree of suffix elaboration be applied to words. As a matter of fact, English does not seek economy or uniformity in the use of any of its grammatical materials. In spite of the fact that we generally look outside the word unit to syntax for the creation of notional complexes, we feel no more strain in a lavishly suffixed word, such as "nationalistically" with its six suffixes, than in a suffixless word, such as "state."

An instructive exercise that I indulged in during my Yokuts field work was to construct words having four or five suffixes and to ask the informant for a translation. Although such words complied with the grammatical rules and could be translated by my informant without any difficulty, they seldom failed to provoke his amusement. It was obvious that these words were impossibly heavy and elaborate. To the Yokuts feeling for simplicity they were grammatical monstrosities.

The concepts expressed by the suffixes are abstract in nature. Yokuts does not possess the types of formative element, so familiar in many American Indian languages, that convey notions of concrete instrumentality, such as "with the hand" and "with a stick," or notions of specific location, such as "on the shore" and "in the house." The suffixes of Yokuts have more the character of algebraic symbols; their content is schematic rather than material. Among the verb suffixes, for example, are those defining an event as durative, continuative, repetitive, causative, reciprocal, passive, subordinate, undifferentiated past or present, future. The most common noun suffixes refer to case relations, marking the subject, direct object, and indirect object, or denoting possession, location, and the like. Particularized and concrete meanings are not expressed through the suffixes in Yokuts.

Even the stems, which are the only elements in Yokuts that can specify the material details of reference, show a strong tendency to carve out broad and comprehensive meanings from the referential field. The vocabulary of verb stems is largely made up of such diffuse and generalized notions as "come," "go," "walk," "run," "hear," "see," "smell." When suffixes with their abstract meanings are joined to stems whose referential content is so inclusive, the resulting words contain notions that are generalized. Although English is well stocked with words expressing notions of this kind, it also has an extensive vocabulary whose words are packed with delicate overtones of meaning. It can add subtle nuances to the general notion of "walk" by using such terms as "stroll," "saunter," "stride," "pace," "march," "tread," "plod," "hobble," "limp," "toddle." There is nothing like this in Yokuts. A book of Yokuts synonyms would be poor indeed. The language is not well equipped, either in its stems or in its formative elements, to build word units that are conceptually detailed or that express refinements and shadings of meaning.

Nor are the broad concepts of Yokuts words sharpened by special figurative uses. A stubborn literalness of reference invades the entire language. The shifts and extensions of meaning that add pungency and vigor to English play no part in Yokuts style. Such phrases as "to strike the eye," "to strike a bargain," "a sharp tongue," "a sharp appetite," "the family tree," "the tree of knowledge" illustrate the English genius for employing terms transferred from their literal sense. But in Yokuts a tree is a tree and nothing more. The language does not permit its words to cut metaphorical capers.

By exploiting the metaphorical possibilities of English words and by drawing upon our vocabulary of finely nuanced words, we can achieve variety and nicety of expression. Manuals of English style are merely underlining the potentialities inherent in the language when they encourage the student in his frantic efforts to avoid repetitions of the same word in close proximity. Although we may regard variety as an absolute virtue of style and repetition as a universal sin, it is obvious that Yokuts cannot be driven in this direction. The broad area of reference covered by Yokuts words gives them a wide range of application, and their literal significance holds them austerely within their proper boundaries of reference. It would be flying in the face of these forces in Yokuts to seek variety by ringing delicate changes upon a recurring notion. When a notion is to be repeated, there is no need to avoid verbal repetition. A passage such as, "And he walked home. And his friend also walked home. And the people walked home," however monotonous and slovenly it may appear to English sensibilities, is stylistically appropriate in Yokuts.

Yokuts possesses a special class of verbs which, in contrast to the generalized concepts typical of the language, express notions that are narrowly defined and specific. The following examples illustrate the kind of notions conveyed by this class of verbs.

kʔubwiyi "strike a flat object to the ground"
wipʔwiyi "make a slow bending motion upward" (as branches bending upward in the wind)
bidinwiyi "tumble from a high place"
xapapwiyi "get spread out in a fanlike formation"
no:mno:mwiyi "make puckering motions in and out"

The stylistic possibilities of these verbs for creating vivid images in a concentrated manner is obvious; but not so obvious to English feeling, which delights in flashes of sharp imagery, is the sense of violence and bizarreness which these verbs suggest to the Yokuts stylistic consciousness.

From the perspective of Yokuts, these verbs are linguistic freaks. Their grammatical form, as well as their content, is anomalous in the Yokuts system. These verbs are composed of two elements, a stem of the verb *wiyi*, "do, do thus," being added to another stem defining the nature of the activity. The technique of stem composition, displayed in these "do" verbs, occurs nowhere else in the language. Furthermore, a number of the "do" verbs, particularly those referring to specific sounds, contain a stem having an onomatopoetic force: *ga:gwiyi*, "cackle," *tuhwiyi*, "spit," *ʔuhwiyi*, "cough," *hikʔwiyi*, "make a hiccuping sound," miwwiyi, "whistle through the air." Such mimetic play with sounds is not only absent elsewhere in the language, but it is out of keeping with the severe formalism of Yokuts. In their meanings, in their form, and in their phonetic mimicry, these verbs seem to be cut to the pattern of a foreign idiom. They are like an ornate Byzantine mosaic set in a Calvinistic church.

It is a significant comment on the directive tendencies of historical drift in language that these eccentric "do" verbs have been leveled out of most of the modern Yokuts dialects. Only a few petrified noun derivatives are left in these dialects to indicate that the "do" verbs were formerly common throughout Yokuts. Only in one dialect, Yauelmani, have they been found as a fully operative and productive set of verbs. But they have a peculiar status in this dialect: they are regarded as the linguistic property of children. I did not become aware of this class of verbs until, after two or three weeks of field work, I overheard some remarks which my informant's eight-year-old son was addressing to himself. Only with the greatest difficulty could I coax my informant to explain the "do" verb which his child had used and to give me further examples of this class. It was evident that he regarded words of this type as being too silly for serious discussion and totally out of keeping with the essential sobriety of adulthood. Not until some time later did he tell me that these words were used primarily by children. But even after he had overcome his reluctance to discuss the "do" verbs, he was never able to treat them seriously. A spirit of facetiousness always accompanied our work with them.

The myths do not contain many examples of the "do" verbs. As a stylistic device these verbs are limited in their usefulness to contexts where an implication of startling and ludicrous extravagance is appropriate. In the story of Condor and Falcon only two examples occur. The first one describes the ineffectual booming sound made by Thunder in his efforts to move, the use of a "do" verb in this case suggesting not only the violence of the noise but its incongruity as coming from so helpless a person as Thunder. In the incident dealing with Crow, another "do" verb is employed to refer to his sudden transformation of color. Again the verb adds a touch of characterization, for Crow turns black as a result of stupidly gorging himself with black seeds. Stories dealing with Coyote as a trickster and a dupe offer the most favorable conditions for the use of these verbs. And yet, despite their effectiveness for describing the clownish antics of Coyote, they are not very frequent even in stories of this type. There still remains the feeling that the "do" verbs belong to a lunatic fringe of the language.

Someting of the same flavor pervades the various sets of reduplicated words in English—"putt-putt" and "toot-toot," "pitter-patter" and "tittle-tattle," "piggy-wiggy" and "ducky-wucky." Like stem composition in Yokuts, reduplication is so exceptional and aberrant in English that it strikes the native form-feeling as a piece of ingenuous frivolity, proper to childish speech and appropriate on an adult level only when a frivolous reference is intended. But the values which color a grammatical technique are relative to the individual patterning of each language. To reverse the analogy, reduplication is felt as a thoroughly respectable technique in Yokuts, just as stem composition in English, as illustrated in "blackbird" or "noteworthy," has nothing of the outlandish character that it possesses in Yokuts. Even onomatopoeia, whose apparently spontaneous and direct symbolism might be expected to find a universal response, carries a different stylistic tone in the two languages: in Yokuts, it is associated only with the eccentric "do" verbs; in English, though it occurs in many of the low-caste reduplicated words, it is also found extensively throughout our vocabulary of image-creating words, such as "clink," "hush," "squeak," "squeal," where it serves to sharpen the vividness and specificity of reference.

Words are convenient but arbitrary units by means of which to examine the kinds of notions that a language expresses and the style of its expression. The limits of a word are determined by the morphological factors peculiar to each language, not by any notional criteria. Although Yokuts words, with the notable exception of the "do" verbs, tend to sketch only the bare and generalized outlines of a reference, the language possesses syntactic resources for combining words in such a way that its sentences could attain any degree of notional intricacy and richness. A passage of Macaulay's prose, with its long and involved periods, could be translated into grammatically correct Yokuts. But the result would be a grammarian's idle fancy, a distortion of the syntactic idiom of Yokuts. The language is as diffident in applying its means of elaboration in syntax as in suffixation.

Adjectival notions, for example, can be expressed by means of a simple syntactic device. A noun functions as an adjectival term augmenting or delimiting the meaning of any other noun by being linked in parallel series with it, and theoretically any number of such adjectival nouns can be juxtaposed to the noun they modify. The English predication, "he entered the small gray house," could be paraphrased in Yokuts: *go:binhin ṭew gudew pʔahlikʔniw*, "he entered the house, the small one, the gray one." But one will search far in a body of Yokuts myths to find any such double use of adjectival terms modifying a noun. With the exception of demonstratives ("this one, that one") and quantifiers ("one, two, all, many"), even a single modifying term is rarely juxtaposed to a noun. Yokuts prefers to make separate sentences of its qualifications. More in line with the stylistic habits of Yokuts would be *go:binhin ṭew* / *ʔamaʔ ṭa gudiʔ* / *ʔamaʔ ṭa yow pʔahlikʔin*, "he entered the house. / And that one was a small one. / And that one was also a gray one."

In the same spirit Yokuts avoids expressing subordinate and superordinate relations between its predications. It possesses particles indicating temporal and modal subordination, such as "when" and "if," and suffixes forming subordinate verbs, but these are syntactic tools that Yokuts employs only on rare occusions. Its favorite device for relating predications to one another is the particle *ʔamaʔ*, that can best be translated as "and" or "and then," an element that achieves only the loosest and most ambiguous type of coordination. The great majority of sentences in a Yokuts text begin with this feeble coordinator. Occasionally a tighter cohesion is attained by the use of another particle meaning "also, again." But the language seldom goes beyond this in its efforts to connect and relate its predications.

These items of syntactic behavior reflect the general tendency in Yokuts to demand a severe simplicity of content from its units of expression. In contrast to English, Yokuts does not pack its individual words with a wealth of meaning, nor does it compensate for the conceptual thinness of its words by an elaborate display of syntactic processes. Notions are sparsely distributed over a sequence of predications, and the predications themselves are broken up into independent, loosely joined sentences.

To the English imagination, rooted in its own habits of expression, the total effect of Yokuts style is anything but stimulating. The mode of expression undoubtedly appears drab, colorless, monotonous. Instead of a sentence structure that is varied, that presents smooth contours in passing from one predication to another, the progression is a series of bumps and jerks; statements are made in the abrupt manner of a telegram. The brevity of the sentences suggests a cryptic style, but one searches in vain for evidences of concentrated expression, for latent implications, for subtle metaphors playing beneath the surface of overt meanings. The broadly generalized notions have a literal reference. But the absence of nicety and richness of expression in Yokuts is not the symptom of meager grammatical resources; it is, rather, the result of wilful selective forces within the language, for those resources which are the most powerful for the creation of meanings and for the development of notional complexes in words and in sentences are employed the most sparingly.

But, by the same token, the stylistic features of English cannot appeal to the intuitions of a Yokuts native. To him English must appear erratic, lacking in those qualities of restraint and consistency which he finds in his own language. He will see no uniformity in the pattern of English sentences: some are short, and some are tediously long; some are lucid and immediately comprehensible, and some are so over-loaded with subordinated and sub-subordinated notions, with qualifications and involutions of meaning, that the mind is wearied in trying to follow the labyrinthine twists and turns. Behind this unevenness of expression there seems to be a strident and feverish energy, obsessed with the need of expressing nuances that could best be left to contextual inference. To the native accustomed to the casual and quiet dignity of Yokuts style, English hammers too insistently upon the sensibilities with its succession of garish images, its interminable sleight-of-hand tricks with meanings that pass through sudden metaphorical changes, its insatiable taste for onomatopoetic mimicry. The language lacks balance and symmetry even in its grammatical system, wich is a tangle of sprawling patterns. And English practices no economy in exploiting its motley resources; it draws upon its forms of expression with a prodigal hand.

Each of these appraisals is based upon the use of an irrelevant frame of values. It is no more valid than applying the principles of realistic painting to geometric art. Each language is like a particular art form in that it works with a limited range of materials and pursues the stylistic goals that have been and are constantly being discovered in a collective quest. Yokuts is a type of collective expression that values balance of inner form and restraint in the representation of meanings. In spite of the spurious impression that can hardly be avoided in an English translation, Yokuts is not a peculiar and imperfect kind of English.

Narrative Style

ANNA H. GAYTON

It is not that phase of style which concerns itself with "character building," "plot development," "attainment of effects"—so-called "literary style"—which we wish to discuss here. Only an intense intimacy, such as Professor Lowie's with Crow life, language, and narrators (Lowie, 1935, pp. 105-118), or Dr. Reichard's with the Coeur d'Alêne (Reichard 1930, 1947), would permit comment along those lines. Certainly neither Newman nor myself knows what may be the "literary" goals consciously or unconsciously sought in the telling of a Yokuts tale. The style we are concerned with is that which shows on the face of the stories: what materials are used in tale construction.

The narrative style of Yokuts myths is no less restrained than the grammatical style of Yokuts language. One wonders if thought processes, habituated to precise grammatical forms, conform to an analogous pattern in arranging a series of ideas. The simplicity of the myths in Kroeber's collection was borne out by my own collection made twenty years later, and corroborative testimony is furnished by Newman's group of Dumna and Yauelmani texts.

This simplicity or directness is not so marked

in the Western Mono myths; they have a tendency to ramble. There is a difference between a series of self-contained episodes which may be amalgamated as a composite myth or remain discrete, and the episode which depends upon a prior action and in turn leads to another. Broadly speaking, the former is Yokuts, the latter Mono, when their tales achieve length. With Yokuts align Lake Miwok and Pomo of the Central California region, and with Mono align Achomawi-Atsugewi, Shasta, and Klamath along the eastern highlands.

With few exceptions the stories collected are myths in the sense which Boas has defined (Boas, 1914, p. 378). They are concerned with persons and events of an era before the appearance of man, when birds, animals, insects, and even plants, were active denizens of this world. There are one or two stories of human beings which are really in the myth category. Such is the tale of the man who followed his wife to the land of the dead. It explains the nature of the afterworld, why the dead cannot be visited, just as other myths explain how land was made or how fire was obtained. The characters have to be human: their animal predecessors were immortal or revived by easy means. The other story is that of the Pleiades, the group of discontented young wives who rose to the sky. Both stories are localized by tribe in accordance with the narrator's tribal affinity. Of tales which are believed to record recent historical events, Newman obtained two, one the narrative of an actual war between several tribal groups (which is not included here) and *The Gamblers*. Gayton recorded two, *The Boastful Man* and *A Bear Transformation*. One of Kroeber's tales, *The Man and the Owls*, appears to have been regarded as an actuality.

That mysterious necessity, whether psychic, neurological, or emotional, which makes culture persist, seems more palpably in effect in mythology than in other aspects of culture. (This "necessity" was manifested individually by a Wobonuch man, who, though consistently refusing to act as an interpreter, always worked near by while his daughter interpreted for my informant. One day he suddenly threw down his ax, strode menacingly toward the young woman, and said, "If you're going to tell it, you tell it right!") There is little or no ritual usage of myths by Yokuts and Mono: out of a world compiled of thousands of objects, acts, and ideas, the narrator is theoretically free to choose his literary materials, yet he persistently tells his story according to traditional form. This observation is an old one, but it can never be overemphasized. And it is recalled here because the stylistic simplicity of Yokuts tales is a case in point. The usual stock-in-trade of North American Indian narrators—the *inexhaustible dish*, *kill-all arrow*, *life-token*, *Symplegades*, and such—were known to the Yokuts and appear in their tales. But instead of being used frequently, as in Pomo or more extremely as in Northwest Coast myths, they are used sparingly, one in one tale, another in another. Now, this may be narrative restraint, or it may be conforming to tradition, or both. But simplicity is maintained in spite of the possibility for florescence.

Although ritualistic pressure did not bear upon Yokuts tales, two constraining factors may be noted. The first was the rôle of these myths as traditional lore, that is, sheer historical information. The myths are repeated to the young as historic fact—this *was* the way land was made, fire was obtained, evil cannibals overcome, and so on. The explanatory element is frequent. (The presence of explanatory elements in myths, however, may not necessarily indicate an etiological motivation [cf. Waterman 1914].) This aspect of the myths should necessitate adherence to general plot even though details might be altered or augmented. The second factor, which actually would affect the relative importance of characters, rather than plot, is the reflection of social organization in the myths which makes Eagle the chief, Dove his messenger, and Coyote and Cougar influential people. (The integration of mythical and actual social forms is discussed in Gayton, 1930, pp. 369-371.) In Newman's text material all these persons are referred to as "the great ones." But again, while holding the characters in place, this factor would not prevent the addition of many minor actors were such elaboration desired.

It is conceivable that the constant retelling of certain very popular tales is another phase of the Yokuts trend toward simplicity and restraint: novelty and variety were not sought. Our collection is not sufficiently exhaustive to prove this point.

In the native texts there is no tendency to be explicit in referring to characters or to cultural features. If an episode has to do with several characters, the speaker or actor in each instance is not always named. The listener is expected to know who is talking or acting, for it is apparently assumed that he is already familiar with the details of the story. (We have no check on the possibility of a greater specificity in the case of a new story being related to an unfamiliar audience.) Nor are there individual speech styles to identify certain characters.

The number of cultural features appearing in the myths are few as compared with Basin tales, wherein many material objects are mentioned, or with Pomo myths which recount Coyote's creations and institutions. In Yokuts and Western Mono myths are items or incidents which may be understood through the culture, but are not always self-evident. The most important of these is the social pattern, Eagle as chief, Dove and Road Runner as messengers, Owl as doctor. A little episode describing an assembly called by Eagle to decide upon a seed-gathering expedition introduces two tales; and Eagle's judiciary rôle also appears in *Condor Steals Falcon's Wife*. Shamans' mercenary practices are exposed, and the slamming of their trays upon the ground is their usual method of "shooting power." The power of jumping great distances, a shaman's ability, is directly mentioned in a Western Mono myth, and is inferential in several others. Fasting or observing a meat taboo is mentioned in various tales, especially in one referring to the Jimson-weed ritual. Ceremonials such as the annual mourning ceremony, shamans' contest, snake dance, and bear dance are not mentioned, although one obscure reference is made to the feather ornaments worn by bear dancers. Falcon's ill-luck at gambling is not due to the fact that his wife is betrayed, but to her pregnancy as a consequence of the betrayal. The "confession feast," the ritualistic recounting of an exotic experience, climaxes the Orpheus tales.

The rôle of parents-in-law as mediators in domestic quarrels is indicated in the Pleiades tales.

The great gambling game, particularly for spectacular rivalry, was shinny. Of secondary importance, arrow shooting, lance throwing, racing, and the hand-game are mentioned as forms of contests.

Hunting adventures and exploits, which are frequent in stories from the Basin, are ignored, as are almost all mundane occupations. The eating of clover and wild onions, and seed gathering are spoken of, but rarely.

Custom required one to call out when approaching a house. To draw near unannounced would arouse suspicion (mentioned in an abstracted text).

The sacred quality of tobacco is brought out by Falcon's exclusive use of it as food and occasional references to its usage for accomplishing some superhuman task. The common sacred talisman, a strand of eagle down, is mentioned. Contact with one's supernatural power or guardian spirit through song is indicated in a few tales.

It is not rewarding to recount further the incidents of culture in the stories: this résumé indicates the general nature of the cultural features exhibited.

Formalized structure of the tales is not always followed. The most common opening of a Yokuts story is with a statement: "people were living there" (*ṭaw xo:xo:hin maniʔ yokotʔs*) or "So-and-so was there" or "so-and-so was going along." Western Mono myths more often refer to the time rather than the place, saying, "In olden times" or "Long ago" (*manatí'čoʔin*) before taking up the action.

Closing phrases are not necessary. A few of Newman's texts end with "That is the end" or my own, taken in English, with "And that's all." But there is no indication of the "tying up" of a story reported for some people or a "call for an early spring." The taboo on summer story-telling was known but thought of as unimportant, or as a logical consequence of habits rather than as a taboo at all. All of Newman's texts were recorded in the summer. My Michahai informant said that people naturally told stories in the winter evenings, in the summer young people stayed outside and played. According to the same informant, any visitor in a house might tell stories or adventures. Boys and girls would ask for them if they dared, or hoped that conversation would evoke such recountings. Adolescent Michahai would go to a well-known storyteller's house in the early evening and stay till they were "chased home."

It is apparent, however, that the "animal transformation" episode serves as a closing incident. While this event is the subject of complete tales, fully developed, it appears in contracted form at the end of almost any myth. This is true of Yokuts and Western Mono particularly, and is somewhat less characterestic of Owens Valley Paiute, Miwok, and Pomo. As tales of more northerly groups are examined, this ending, describing a group transformation which signified the ending of one era and the beginning of the present, gives way to single transformations, either of one's self or another. This individual transformation blends into the Transformer Concept of Plateau-Northwest Coast distribution.

Songs are more frequently introduced in Western Mono myths than in Yokuts, one trait among many which show the close kin of Mono tales with those of the Basin Shoshoneans (Sapir, 1910). On the other hand, conversation appears more often as a stylistic device in Yokuts myths.

The persons participating in the tales are few, almost exclusively those "great ones" whose lineages are important in actuality: Eagle, Falcon, Cougar, Coyote, Dove, Crow. Eagle is the creator, but is seldom an actor; there is never a hint that he is anything but wise, just, and powerful. Wolf is the creator or a participant in Western Mono and Yauelmani creation tales. Coyote plays a dual role, that of creator or, more often, assistant creator, and that of a dupe. Falcon, the fighter and gambler, is the only person to be favored with a metaphorical title: he is often called "The Fearsome One" (*ṭanyiṭit*).

(The simple form "Falcon" has been used throughout as there is doubt in any given instance whether it is the prairie falcon or the peregrine falcon (duck hawk) which is meant. The Yokuts *li'mik* is supposed to be the prairie falcon (Falco mexicanus] which is identified with *kini'*, the duck hawk [Falco peregrinus anatum], by the Western Mono. For the foothill Yokuts and the Mono mountaineers it is possible that the duck hawk is thought of as the hero. The two birds are not readily distinguishable: "The Prairie Falcon resembles the Duck Hawk in size and actions, though it is not as courageous and 'noble' as the latter. . . . Both Falcons nest on ledges or in caves of cliffs but the Duck Hawk's aerie commonly overlooks water, while the Prairie Falcon frequently nests in very arid country" [May, *Hawks of North America*, p. 107]. The peregrine falcon [duck hawk] ". . . is, perhaps the most highly specialized and superlatively well-developed flying organism on our planet today, combining in a marvellous degree the highest powers of speed and aerial adroitness with massive, warlike strength. A powerful, wild, majestic, independent bird, living on the choicest of clean, carnal food, plucked fresh from the air or the surface of the waters, rearing its young in the rocks of dangerous mountain cliffs, claiming all the atmosphere as its domain, and fearing neither beast that walks nor bird that flies, it is the very embodiment of noble rapacity and lonely freedom" [May, *Hawks of North America*, p. 109, quoting G. H. Thayer].)

His association with Crow is notable. The animal characteristics of these persons are occasionally pointed by their actions, as Buzzard's searching of ravines or Bottlefly's sniffing in all directions. Falcon's abstention from food, his eating of tobacco for supernatural power, and the fastidious eating of a little liver by Cougar's child while Coyote's brats glut themselves, reflect cultural attitudes as well as describing characteristic animal action. (Although "character study" is rarely the object of native tales, there is a Miwok myth [Gifford, 1917, p. 323] which seems to have no other purpose than the vivid description of a number of animals. It is superbly done.)

REFERENCE NOTE

Cross-references to the location of tales and abstracts in the monograph have been omitted.

The symbol *o* has been substituted for Newman's use of *ɔ* and glottal stop and vowel length marked as elsewhere in this volume. The phonetic key is otherwise as follows: *i*, as in English *beet*; *e*, as in English *bet; a*, as in German *Mann; o*, as in French *note; u*, as in English *boot; p*, *t*, *k*, aspirated surds, as in English *pill*, *till kill; b, d, g,* unaspirated surds as in French *pas, tas, cas; p', t', k'*, like *b, d, g,* but with simultaneous glottal release; . , (as *ṭ, ṣ*, etc.) indicates that the consonant is articulated with the tip of the tongue against the alveolar ridge, somewhat farther back along the palate than the articulation for English *t, s*, etc. Other phonetic symbols can be read with their English value.

For a similar concern with spare narrative style, see Jacobs (1945). On some of the general questions of characterizing the style of a language, see Bally (1950; 1952, pp. 53-74), Croce (1909), Fowkes (1957), Hatzfeld (1952, section on "Idiomatology"), Levi-Strauss (1951, 1953a), Roberts (1944), Rose (1919), Schmidt-Hidding (1957), Vossler (1925), and Wells (1960). Hymes (1961a) gives a general survey and prognosis.

References not in the general bibliography:

CROCE, BENEDETTO

1909. *Aesthetic. As Science of Expression and General Linguistic.* Translated from the Italian by Douglas Ainslie. New York: Macmillan. (Rev. ed., 1922; Reprinted Noonday Press (N 102), 1953.)

FOWKES, ROBERT A.

1957. Review of Peter Hartmann, *Nominale Ausdruckformen im wissenschaftlichen Sanskrit. Word, 13* (3): 515-519.

GAYTON, ANNE H.

1930. Yokuts-Mono Chiefs and Shamans. *UCP-AAE, 24:* 361-420.

GIFFORD, E. W.

1917. Miwok Myths. *UCP-AAE, 12:* 283-338.

HATZFELD, HELMUT

1952. *A Critical Bibliography of the New Stylistics.* (The University of North Carolina Studies in Comparative Literature, No. 5.) Chapel Hill: University of North Carolina Press.

JACOBS, MELVILLE

1945. *Kalapuya Texts.* (University of Washington Publications in Anthropology, No. 11.) Seattle: University of Washington Press.

ROBERTS, MURAT H.

1944. The Science of Idiom: A Method of Inquiry into the Cognitive Design of Language. *PMLA, 59:* 291-306.

ROSE, H. A.

1919. Comparative "Idiomatology." *Man, 19:* 133-137 (#73).

SCHMIDT-HIDDING, W.

1957. Das Verhältnis von Idiomatik und Grammatik: Grundzuge einer Idiomatik. *Der Deutschunterricht, 9* (3): 43-58.

VOSSLER, KARL

1925. Die Nationalsprachen als Stile. *Jahrbüch für Philologie, 1:* 1-23. [Incorporated in his *The Spirit of Language in Civilization* (1932).]

WATERMAN, T. T.

1914. Explanatory Elements in the Folk-Tales of the North American Indians. *JAF, 27:* 1-54.

WELLS, RULON

1960. Nominal and Verbal Style. In Thomas A. Sebeok (Ed.), *Style in Language.* New York: Wiley; Cambridge: Technology Press. Pp. 213-220.

part VII

SOCIAL STRUCTURE AND SPEECH COMMUNITY

Introduction

One would expect a fundamental question of social anthropology to be: How is a language related to the social structure of the community in which it is spoken? But while the social aspects of language and communication in the case of the major national states have received considerable attention, it has been as much or more from historians, political scientists, and sociologists; and anthropologists have done relatively little in the areas of the world in which they predominantly work. Most studies, whatever the source, are case histories with little attention to controlled comparison cross-culturally. The development and application to individual studies of an over-all perspective or theory is rare. However, a good deal of work has begun to analyze particular dimensions of the relations between language and social structure and to broach general issues, couched in terms of facts of speech variation. Among the notions involved, two—*speech community* and *speech situation*—should be singled out. (*Speech community* is used here as the familiar term, although *linguistic community* would be more exact [cf. Gumperz, 1962].)

Speech community is a fundamental concept for the relation between language, speech, and social structure. Like many fundamental concepts, it is more often assumed than analyzed or explained.

As long as one operates in terms of languages and cultures conceived as isolates, internally homogeneous and externally discrete, it is common to speak of "the" language and "the" culture of "a" people. The term speech community is then little more than a stylistic alternative for referring to such a unit, implicitly interchangeable in its referent with the others. If the equation of a language, culture, and people is not taken for granted, but seen as problematic, the identification of a speech community becomes a serious empirical and theoretical issue. Particularly is this so if the non-coincidence of language, culture, and people is seen, not only as a problem of the occurence of a definable language or culture *beyond* the limits of a given community, but also as a problem of the co-occurrence of more than one *within* a given community.

In linguistic anthropology increased attention to more complex societies and to the complexities of relationships among social groups of all kinds and sizes within larger "social fields" (see Lesser, 1961) has worked together with a trend toward treating culture and social structure in terms of communication (cf. Edward T. Hall, 1959; Levi-Strauss, 1953b). The question of defining one's object of study is more clearly posed. Instead of referring a description to a named language or culture almost automatically, one is likely to refer it, linguistically, to a delimited dialect or style and culturally, to a particular community. From this it is but a short step to an entirely new point of departure, such that one begins by identifying one's object of study as a community and correlated communication matrix (cf. Gumperz, 1962) within some broader social field. The occurrence or distribution of homogeneous sets of linguistic and cultural habits relative to such a unit becomes a matter to be empirically determined.

The implications and promise of such an approach for linguistic anthropology are great. Whereas primary focus on a single language or grammatical code tends to make variation seem peripheral or intrusive, primary focus on the speech habits of a community as a unit lets forms of variation fall into place. Variation, competition, differential use, and survival among speech habits, whether within one language, between several languages, or both, can be described naturally as part of the linguistic picture of the population as a whole. Indeed, such a sociolinguistic unit, the speech habits of a population or community, seems the natural unit for study of processes of sociolinguistic change and evolution (see Part VIII). Moreover, what appears as variation from the standpoint of a single, homogeneously defined code may show patterning of its own. Analysis of the ways in which linguistic features covary with other factors of speech events shows that such variation is not random, but follows rules of use. If the generality of the concept, speech habits of a community, is exploited, and taken to include the formulation of such rules then one moves from the realm of variation (largely statistical in conception) to a realm of structure and to the constitution of a new, second, qualitative and descriptive science of language, beside that of the linguistic code per se.

In so moving, one breaks sharply with the widespread view that assigns structure exclusively to language (*la langue*) and only variation to speech (*la parole*), replacing it by the assumption that the full range of the speech activity of a community is structured. The patterning of language, as manifested in grammar, is but one phase, and to some extent, a dependent one, of the patterning of speech activity in general. Research based on the new approach (which may be termed the ethnography of speaking; see Hymes, 1962) brings into focus a good deal that has escaped attention, not being caught up in the frame of reference of either linguistics or ethnography as usually practiced. The whole of behavior is approached from the point of view of discovering the relevant classes of speech events, the factors constituting them, the range of functions served by speech in the particular community, and the relations existing among them.

A general knowledge of the kinds of events, factors, and functions whose relations may make up the speech economy of a group is only beginning to emerge. The introduction to Part V has sketched an approach in terms of speech events, and what is involved can be indicated further in two ways. First, consider the fact that it is not the case that anyone can say anything, by any means, in any manner, to anyone else, on any occasion, and to any purpose. This shows one of the ways in which a community's speech activity constitutes a system. Not everything can co-occur, or, to put it positively, what occurs as one factor of a speech event is interdependent with what occurs as another. Second, think of a stranger to a community, concerned with anticipating and interpreting the behavior of its members and learning to observe the norms which govern it. Think perhaps of a stranger entering the community by being born into it as a child. Suppose the child learns the rules of the community's language or languages. He now has the ability to produce and interpret grammatical utterances and to judge the grammaticality of utterances by others. To some theorists, this ability is what the first descriptive science of language seeks to account for. Yet with this ability, the child remains a partial stranger. Although he can produce any grammatical utterance, he does not know *which* grammatical utterance to choose at a given time. Such a child would lack the ability for which an ethnography of speaking seeks to account, one which children do in fact normally acquire, the ability to produce and understand utterances as appropriate to a situation and to judge appropriateness. The child learns what the ethnographer seeks to discover and state explicitly—the classes of speech events recognized in the community and the rules governing relations among them, their constitutive factors, and the functions subserved.

The study of speech communities, empirically defined in terms of populations and structures of communication, would seem to underlie almost every aspect of anthropological interest in the relations between language, personality, society, and culture. A crucial nexus lies in another concept more often assumed than analyzed or explained, that of *speech situation*. As with the concept of speech community, the problem is one of determining boundaries. Just as speech community has often been taken for granted as the reference for description of a linguistic code, so speech situation has often been taken for granted as the reference for accounts of linguistic variation. Also, as the article by Firth in Part I indicates, the concept of *context of situation* has become a technical term in British linguistics, warranting the validity of a described text, and, by being specified, "permitting renewal of contact with reality." Relatively little has been done to show how to identify, structurally, where one situation ends and another begins or, indeed, how to map a community internally in terms of situations, as the settings for speech events, for use of particular channels and codes or specialized subcodes, for the play of particular functions, and the like. Obviously things depend on the situation;

but on what does the situation depend? Progress in this regard is as much an ethnographic as a linguistic problem.

In the description of social structure in relation to speech community, then, two leading themes are (1) boundaries—external with regard to speech communities and internal with regard to speech situations, and (2) co-variation among linguistic features, as in the delineation of speech levels or speech varieties, and between linguistic features and social features. Studies of sociolinguistic variation are the primary avenue, beside that of semantic description, along which the principle of structural description is being extended outward from the linguistic code itself into the analysis of social function. While many studies are couched in particularistic terms, this new general perspective on sociolinguistic variation is emerging.

Few generalizations can be hazarded at the present time, but there are two which are essential to proper understanding of the scope of the problem. First, variations in speech are recognized and evaluated in *every* community. As the essays by Bloomfield and Newman make clear, even a small and tight-knit hunting or horticultural society will recognize differences in linguistic competence and prestige and distinct levels of usage. Just as there are no "primitive" languages without grammar, so there are no "primitive" speech-communities without socially recognized standards of speech. In short, contrary to views sometimes held, speech variation and evaluation are universal, and no groups can be excused from receiving fresh and careful attention in the greatly needed work of constructing an empirically adequate taxonomy of speech communities or types of communication structure. Second, the phenomena in question, whether of boundaries or variation, are *sociolinguistic* in nature. Accounts in terms of linguistic features alone cannot suffice to identify lines of cleavage in communication or levels of speech. Sociocultural attitudes and values, as well as context of situation, are important as well. In short, the social and linguistic factors are interdependent, and in the work of descriptive analysis of individual cases, both must be taken into account from the outset.

Bloomfield's essay is perhaps the first careful analysis of speech standards in a nonliterate tribe. Its significance is enhanced by posing the problem in terms of the folk attitudes towards correctness in our own society. Note that the two sources of attitudes first examined, consciousness of writing habits, and spread of standard or literary languages, as well as the general explanation in terms of models of conduct and of speech, all have in common that the merit of the preferred forms is secondary. The merit is secondary, acquired by social context, not primary, i.e., intrinsic to the linguistic form. Even such a careful study cannot resolve all aspects of the vexed question of correct and incorrect usage, but it lays much of the foundation of a sound attitude and points toward further comparative study. Note also the charming individual speech portraits of Menomini speakers.

Newman shows the presence of both sacred and slang levels of usage in a compact pueblo community and the dependence of each on situational determinants and cultural attitudes. Again the status of the terms is largely secondary, rather than intrinsic. A point of possible comparative importance is the inverse relation of sacred and slang terms to ordinary usage, the one using specialized words for ordinary meanings, the other introducing specialized meanings for ordinary words. Newman's concluding analysis of speech variation as differentiated in terms of the status of age and situation, despite absence of classes or castes, reinforces and extends Bloomfield's concluding generalization.

In a well-knit contrastive study, Martin examines speech levels in one of the best known cases, the complex social structures of Japan and Korea. The focus is upon obligatory choices within the grammatical core of the language, although lexical choices figure as well; but, whereas in Sapir and Swadesh's article in Part II, and in Part III generally, the choice implied something of world view or ontology, here it is social attitude. The analysis of underlying dimensions and hierarchy of dimensions represents an important step, both for understanding the semantic structure of the forms in question and for making use of such forms diagnostically in the study of contemporary variation and historical change in social relations.

Gumperz takes an over-all view, both of recent study of speech variation in linguistics and anthropology, and of the place of various types of speech variation in the Indian subcontinent. Note particularly his reference to the accumulated European experience, so far little tapped by contemporary American anthropologists. In tracing the links between speech variation, lines of communication, and sociocultural taxonomy, Gumperz pinpoints a number of problems for study, together with appropriate methods, while developing a general distinction between vernacular and argot or special parlance.

In his paper on "Diglossia," Ferguson pioneers in the important task of identifying and analyzing cross-cultural types of speech community, drawing on Europe, North Africa, and the Caribbean. Note the variety of historical origins which have converged in manifestations of the same detailed sociolinguistic complex. Diglossia is an excellent example of coexistence in the same community of mutually unintelligible codes, correlated with values and situations, and of the necessity of taking the community as frame of reference to avoid distorting the communication situation (as native attitudes do in denying that the Low form "exists"). The analysis of origins and the prognosis of alternative developments relate the paper to the problems of Part VIII (e.g., the paper by Bull) and make it of considerable general interest by suggesting answers to contemporary problems and prospects of linking sociolinguistic types to general historical and evolutionary processes.

Drawing on research for Unesco in Nigeria, Wolff presents fresh evidence as to the dependence of speech community boundaries, and lines of communication, on cultural values and attitudes, as much as, or more than, upon linguistic relationship or degree of objective linguistic similarity. The paper well illustrates the fact that the results of such research can be of theoretical importance, as well as significant for the practical needs out of which they arise. Note the concluding series of general hypotheses about the interrelationships of linguistic and cultural factors in interlingual communication.

Literate and Illiterate Speech 41

LEONARD BLOOMFIELD

I

LITERATE AND ILLITERATE SPEECH in a language like English are plainly different. We find it easy, aside from occasional points of detail, to judge of "incorrect" or "faulty" locutions, "bad grammar," "mispronunciation," and the like. This, in fact, is the layman's chief interest in linguistics.

When we try, however, to define what we mean by these judgments, to state the causes of "mistakes," or to set up a standard, we run into great difficulties. The popular explanation of these matters is certainly wrong; scientific students of language have dealt little with them explicitly, somewhat more by implication, and never in a satisfactory way. In this paper I shall give some facts from a speech-community where conditions differ from ours to so great an extent as to provide a kind of check, and shall try to draw conclusions; I may say at the outset that these conclusions are neither decisive nor complete enough to be satisfactory.

II

The popular explanation of "correct" and "incorrect" speech reduces the matter to one of knowledge versus ignorance. There is such a thing as correct English. An ignorant person does not know the correct forms; therefore he cannot help using incorrect ones. In the process of education one learns the correct forms and, by practice and an effort of will ("careful speaking"), acquires the habit of using them. If one associates with ignorant speakers, or relaxes the effort of will ("careless speaking"), one will lapse into the incorrect forms.

It would be easy, but would require much space, to show that these notions do not correspond to the facts. There is no fixed standard of "correct" English; one need only recall that no two persons speak alike, and that, take it as a whole, every language is constantly changing. At the time when we learn to speak we are all ignorant babies, yet many children of five or six years speak "correct" English. Even some ignorant adults speak "good" English; on the other hand, there are highly educated people, even teachers and professors, who speak "bad" English. All speaking, good or bad, is careless; only for a few minutes at a time can one speak "carefully" and when one does so, the result is by no means pleasing. In fatiguing effect and in ungracefulness, "careful" speaking is like walking a chalk-line or a tight-rope.

If we leave aside all this, there is one error in the popular view which is of special interest. The incorrect forms cannot be the result of ignorance or carelessness, for they are by no means haphazard, but, on the contrary, very stable. For instance, if a person is so ignorant as not to know how to say *I see it* in past time, we might expect him to use all kinds of chance forms, and, especially, to resort to easily formed locutions, such as *I did see it*, or to the addition of the regular past-time suffix: *I seed it*. But instead, these ignorant people quite consistently say *I seen it*. Now it is evident that one fixed and consistent form will be no more difficult than another: a person who has learned *I seen* as the past of *I see* has learned just as much as one who says *I saw*. He has simply learned something different. Although most of the people who say *I seen* are ignorant, their ignorance does not account for this form of speech. On the other hand, I once knew a school-teacher who, when she spoke carefully, sometimes said *I have saw it*; in normal speech she said *I have seen it*. In short, what we find is not well-informed and regulated activity opposed to ignorant and careless, but rather a conflict of definite, fixed locutions, one of which, for some reason, is "good," while the others are "bad."

Mistaken as are the popular notions on this subject, they are interesting because they throw some light on our attitude to language. The popular explanation of incorrect language is simply the explanation of incorrect *writing*, taken over, part and parcel, to serve as an explanation of incorrect speech. It is the writing of every word for which a single form is fixed and all others are obviously wrong. It is the spelling of words that ignorant people, or better, unlettered people, do not know. It is writing that may be done carefully or carelessly, with evident results as to correctness. With all this it accords that popular comment on a wrong form of speech is often given in terms that properly apply to writing, not to speech; for instance, he who says *git* instead of *get*, or ketch instead of catch, is popularly said to be substituting one *letter* for another, to be mistaking the *spelling* of the word. In sum, the popular ideas about language apply very well to writing, but are irrelevant to speech.

Now, writing, of course, is merely a record of speech. Making this record is an activity very different from the activity of speaking. This is especially striking among us, since our writing is not entirely parallel with speech, but contains numbers of such spellings as *go: throw: sew: beau: though*, where different spellings represent one sound-type, and such as *though: through: bough: cough: rough*, where one spelling represents different sound-types. Writing, like telegraphy or short-hand, is an activity that deals with language, but it is quite different, far less practised and ingrained, far more superficial in our make-up, than speech. Until quite recently only very few people knew how to read and write; even today many peoples do not write their language. Writing is based on speech, not speech on writing.

The fact that almost anyone except a professed student of language explains matters of speech by statements which really apply only to writing, is of great psychologic interest. In infancy, when we learned to speak, we necessarily had no words with which to describe what we were doing. After we had learned to speak, we had no occasion to acquire such words or to make such a description. Consequently, as adults, we cannot state what we do when we talk: we are unconscious of the movements we make with our tongue or vocal chords, of the sound-pattern or the grammatical structure of our speech. (This appears in the difficulty with which school-children learn the few and fairly superficial facts of English grammar that have found a place in the school curriculum. To give anything like a full description of even his native language is a difficult undertaking for any linguist.) Writing, on the other hand, we learned after we knew how to speak; in fact, we learned it through the medium of speech. The teacher told us, in words, what to do, and trained us to state it; we learned the names of the letters, and to spell words, that is, to state which letters we use for a given word. Consequently, ever after, we are able to describe what we do when we write: we are conscious of our movements in writing, and of the forms and succession of the letters. It is on the basis of such contrasts that some psychologists make out a very good case for the view that a "conscious" action is simply one which we are able to describe in words. Whether one accepts this view or not, it is easy to see why a normal person, when asked to explain something about language, really talks about writing; to see why it took generations of students to develop a set of technical terms about speech, and why it now takes a long time to learn the use of these terms, in case one wants to enter upon the scientific study of language.

III

The popular view of "good" and "bad" English has led us a good way round and has shown us some interesting outlooks, but it has brought us back to where we started. The scientific view, though not satisfactory, will bring us farther. It has the advantage of being based on a more extensive survey of various languages and of their history than any one person could make; also it has the advantage of a methodical approach. This last means that we shall not operate with the terms "good" and "bad" language, or their equivalents, since it is precisely these which we are trying to define.

We observe, to begin with, that in every group of people, savage or civilized, ignorant or educated, the infants learn, by imitation, the speech-habits of the older people round them. Even the child learning to speak does not use haphazard forms: he approaches more and more closely the forms used by his elders, and finally talks just like them. Speech defects after early childhood are individual abnormalities; aside from these, the individual's peculiarities of speech are minute. Through the rest of his life he seems to speak uniformly, so far as an observer could note.

History, however, shows that there is a constant and gradual, imperceptibly slow, change in the language of every community. This change is uniform within a group of people who are constantly talking with one another, say, within a single village. But where communication is less frequent, the changes are sure to be different. For instance, if people of the same speech settle so as to form two mountain villages, with a big valley between, then, in a few generations, different changes will have taken place in the two groups. In time they may find it hard to understand each other when they meet; if they stay apart long enough, they may finally be speaking mutually unintelligible languages. When some of the Angles and Saxons left the Continent in the fifth century A.D., they spoke the same language as the less enterprising members of their tribes who stayed at home. Since then, however, both the language of the emigrants and that of the stay-at-homes have changed, and, since there has necessarily been little communication across the North Sea, they have changed in different ways, until today an Englishman and a Dutchman or a North German do not understand each other's speech. In this way, wherever there are lines across which communication is hampered, —water, mountains, deserts, political boundaries, and the like,—we find differences of speech, even though history may tell us that once upon a time, say, at the original settlement, there was uniformity.

Now, as civilization progresses, the population grows denser, means of communication improve, and petty political boundaries lose their importance. More and more often people from different parts of the country, speaking different local dialects, have occasion to converse with each other. They soon learn, on these occasions, to avoid forms of speech that are misleading or unintelligible to the other fellow. Usually, too, there is some city which serves as a center for the larger activities of the nation. The contact of persons from different regions occurs more in this city than elsewhere; the provincial has more occasion to speak with natives of this city than with speakers of any one other dialect. In the history of English, London played this part. Thus there arises a *Standard Language* of more or less definite form. Finally, civilization leads to the widespread use of writing. Since writing is a very deliberate activity, it is easy to adapt one's writing to the requirements of wide communication: one avoids provincialisms and, if there is a metropolis, imitates the writing of the city. Thus it happens that the *Standard Language* is most definite and best observed in its written form, the *Literary Language.* The next step is popular education: children are taught in schools to write and, if possible, to speak in the forms of the Standard Language.

It is at this point that the science of language gives its explanation, if I understand it aright, of "good" and "bad" language. The child, growing up in the province, say, in some mountain village, learns to speak in the local dialect. In time, to be sure, this local dialect will take in more and more forms from the standard language, but so far in the history of mankind complete standardization seems nowhere to have taken place. The child, then, does not speak the standard language as its native tongue. It is only when he reaches school, long after his speech-habits are formed, that he is taught the standard language. No language is like the native speech that one learned at one's mother's knee; no one is ever perfectly sure in a language afterward acquired. "Mistakes" in language are simply dialect forms carried into the standard language. The "bad" English for *I saw it* is not any haphazard error, but the perfectly fixed and definite form, *I seen it*, the form used in most American dialects of English. So far as age is concerned, *Do you want out?* is more respectable than *Do you want to go out?*— but the latter happens to be the form of Standard English: questions of age, of logical or esthetic value, or even of consistency within the system of the language are irrelevant. Dialect forms in the standard language are "bad."

Since only part of the population lives in the metropolis (when there is one, as in England), and since, even there, different social classes communicate little, and since the standard language, closely tied up with the literary language, tends to become archaic (that is, to ignore the changes of the last generations), it results that only relatively few children speak Standard Language as their real mother tongue. Almost everybody's standard speech will show dialect coloring and occasional lapses into dialect.

Sometimes a large dialect group will re-assert itself; thus an Englishman will say that all Americans speak bad Standard English (that is, dialectally colored Standard), but we, finding the British standard too unlike our native forms, have developed a standard of our own, which deviates decidedly in pronunciation and to some extent in word-forms and constructions. The situation is all the more complicated in that we have no one center, like London. But, with the literary language in its usual function as a kind of guide to the standard speech, we have worked out in practice a fairly definite American standard, and are able, except for small details, to agree on what is and what is not "good",—that is, Standard,—American English.

Beside mixing dialect into standard speech, we are likely to distort the latter in some other ways. Native speakers of dialect are prone, once in a while, to speak carefully, that is, to worry about their speech, and go too far in substituting school forms for native forms. A person whose native speech says *I see: I seen: I have seen*, after learning in school to say *I saw*, may occasionally go too far in substituting *saw's* for *seen's* and say *I have saw it*,—a "hyper-urban" form. Knowing that the standard language is close to the written form, we are likely to go too far in guiding ourselves by the latter, for instance, to pronounce a t-sound in *often*,—"spelling-pronunciation." Or again, many words common in writing are rare in speech; when, for once, we speak them, we may violate the habit of those who know the spoken form. Sometimes the spoken tradition of a fairly rare word in this way dies out: *author*, *Gothic* used to be pronounced *autor*, *Gotic*; the th-sound is due to lapse of the oral tradition.

These details could be elaborated, but in the main the scientific diagnosis of "bad" language seems to be: standard language with dialect features. In the local dialect one native speaker would thus be as good as another, and "mistakes" or "bad" forms impossible.

IV

According to the scientists' view of the matter, then, a small community of people speaking a uniform language, and above all, a community without schools or writing, would not distinguish "good" and "bad" language. When I first studied such a community, I found, to my great surprise, that these distinctions were made, if perhaps less frequently than among us.

The Menomini Indians of Wisconsin, a compact tribe of some 1700 people, speak a language without dialectal differences and have no writing. Yet the Menomini will say that one person speaks well and another badly, that such-and-such a form of speech is incorrect and sounds bad, and another too much like a shaman's preaching or archaic ("the way the old, old people talked").

To a surprisingly large extent, considering how slight my acquaintance with their language, I was able to share in these judgments of the Menomini. A foreigner who recorded English as though it were an unwritten language, might obtain several forms of a locution, as, for instance,

You'd better do that,
You had better do that,
You would better do that,
You ought better do that.

His written record would probably fail to give him any distinction between the value of these forms. But if he listened to us long enough, and if fortune favored him, he might learn that the normal good form is the first; that the second is more deliberate and elevated; that the other two strike us as unidiomatic, vulgar, pedantic, or what you will,—in short, as incorrect. So in Menomini we have, for "What are you laughing at?"

wǽki? wǽh-ayǽniyan?
wǽki? aya:yó:sinaman?
tá:ni? wætǽ:hpiyan?

The first form is illiterate, childish, stupid; the second is normal; the third elevated, poetic, archaizing.

Some people say *tsí:pin* instead of *kí:spin* for "if"; this sounds as bad as *git* and *ketch* in English.

Here is a sketch of the linguistic position of some of the speakers whom I knew best:

Red-Cloud-Woman, a woman in the sixties, speaks a beautiful and highly idiomatic Menomini. She knows only a few words of English, but speaks Ojibwa and Potawatomi fluently, and, I believe, a little Winnebago. Linguistically, she would correspond to a highly educated American woman who spoke, say, French and Italian in addition to the very best type of cultivated, idiomatic English.

Her husband, Storms-At-It, a shaman, is half Potawatomi, and speaks both languages. Of English he knows not even the cuss-words. In Menomini he often uses unapproved,—let us say, ungrammatical,—forms which are current among bad speakers; on the other hand, slight provocation sets him off into elevated speech, in which he uses what I shall describe as spelling-pronunciations, together with long ritualistic compound words and occasional archaisms. He corresponds, perhaps, to a minister who does not put on much "dog," speaks very colloquially in ordinary life, but is at the same time very intelligent and able to preach or exhort in the most approved semi-biblical language.

Stands-Close, a man in the fifties, speaks only Menomini. His speech, though less supple and perfect than Red-Cloud-Woman's, is well up to standard. It is interlarded with words and constructions that are felt to be archaic, and are doubtless in part really so, for his father was known as an oracle of old traditions.

Bird-Hawk, a very old man, who has since died, spoke only Menomini, possibly also a little Ojibwa. As soon as he departed from ordinary conversation, he spoke with bad syntax and meagre, often inept vocabulary, yet with occasional archaisms.

White-Thunder, a man round forty, speaks less English than Menomini, and that is a strong indictment, for his Menomini is atrocious. His vocabulary is small; his inflections are often barbarous; he conctructs sentences of a few threadbare models. He may be said to speak no language tolerably. His case is not uncommon among younger men, even when they speak but little English. Perhaps it is due, in some indirect way, to the impact of the conquering language.

Little-Docter, a half-breed, who died recently in his sixties, spoke English with some Menomini faults, but with a huge vocabulary and a passion for piling up synonyms. In Menomini, too, his vocabulary was vast; often he would explain rare words to his fellow-speakers. In both languages his love of words sometimes upset his syntax, and in both languages he was given to over-emphatic diction, of the type of spelling pronunciation.

Little-Jerome, a half-breed, now in the fifties, is a true bilingual. He speaks both English (the dialectal type of the region) and Menomini with racy idiom, which he does not lose even when translating in either direction. He contrasts strikingly with the men (usually somewhat younger) who speak little English and yet bad Menomini.

To recite the features of good and bad Menomini would be to annotate almost every item of the grammar, and many of the lexicon. In the pronunciation of good speakers, Menomini has, of course, its typical cadence and glide-sounds. Young people who speak English often diverge in Anglicizing the pronunciation. Older bad speakers exaggerate certain glide-sounds and miss some of the cadences, confusing short and long vowels. Over-elegant speech, on the other hand,—as from the lips of shamans or of the well-educated Little-Doctor,—displaces the stress-accent toward the end of the word, and gives full long quantity to vowels which in good, idiomatic speech are not entitled to it. This last feature is a fairly close parallel to our "spelling-pronunciations," such as the full form *fore-head* for *forrid* and the now perhaps accepted *waist-coat* and *seam-stress*, for *weskit* and *semstress*. Only, there is no writing in Menomini, hence no spelling to explain "spelling-pronunciations." Sometimes there is a clear analogic basis. Thus the word *niná:tumik* "he calls me" may be distorted to *niná:tomik* or even to *nina:tó:mik*, the *o*: being the long vowel that corresponds in Menomini to the short *u*. Now, these distorted forms are probably due to the influence of other inflectional forms which properly have the long *o*:, such as *nina-nató:mik* "he will call me." But in other cases this explanation seems not to hold, as when *atǽhimin* "strawberry" is in spelling-pronunciation *atǽhe:me:n* where the long *e*: corresponds to short *i*.

As a whole, this phenomenon is due to the fact that Menomini has a living morphologic alternation of long and short vowels; in emphatic or rhetorical speech the long vowels are carried into forms where normally they do not belong.

In inflection, Menomini, like the other Algonquian languages, has an *obviative* form for subsidiary third persons. Thus, if our story is of a man meeting another man and of the ensuing occurrences, our first man will be spoken of in the normal third person form, and the other man in the obviative form. The good Menomini speaker has no such difficulty as we have with our single pronoun *he*. But bad Menomini speakers profit not at all from this distinction, but get as tangled in their two forms as a bad speaker of English with his one ambiguous *he*.

Whatever is hearsay and not the speaker's own experience has the predicate verb or particle in a special *quotative* form. Hence in traditional narrative all predicates are in this form, unless they be actual thoughts or speeches of the actors in the story, or parenthetic insertions of the narrator; these exceptions, indeed, make possible some nice shadings of sense and style. In ordinary speech even the bad speaker will use his quotatives correctly, but as soon as he embarks on a longer story, he may lapse into non-quotatives for whole sentences at a time, which make the story sound as though he had been present when it took place.

Many archaisms of the medicine-man's language are pinchbeck,—distortions in the direction of Ojibwa, or of Triballian. Others are genuine, as comparison with related languages will show. Still others are circumlocutions. No doubt the starting-point for these was in cases where the normal word was tabu during ritual. The Algonquian word for "bear" is lost in Menomini, and is replaced by a word which used to mean "little animal"; in ritual other terms are used, such as "ant-eater," "berry-gatherer," "Bruin." But the habit has been extended to words where there is no tabu; the shaman uses long compounds or derivatives, such as "extensive woman" or "grandmother-expanse" for "earth," and "standing-men" for "trees," and "eternal men" for "stones."

V

It would be useless to seek the criterion of good and bad Menomini by gauging the alternative forms as to consistency with the general system of the language, for Menomini, like English, contains many irregularities. It is often the irregular form that is the proper one, just as in English *You had better do it* is preferred to *You ought better (to) do it*, although the latter accords with the general forms of our syntax. Similarly, *forrid* is preferred to the logically more explicable *fore-head*. On the other hand, the irregular form may be less acceptable than a regular one: *I dove* is not so good as *I dived*, *I ain't* not so good as *I'm not*. A good Menomini speaker will say for "medicine-man" *maski:hkí:wineniw*, a form which has the accent on a syllable that in almost any other word would be incapable of stress, and has vowel-shortening in the last element; yet only a bad speaker will use the logical combination of the words "medicine" and "man," and speak horrid-sounding *maskí:hkiw-inǽniw*.

The nearest approach to an explanation of "good" and "bad" language seems to be this, then, that, by a cumulation of obvious superiorities, both of character and standing, as well as of language, some persons are felt to be better models of conduct and speech than others. Therefore, even in matters where the preference is not obvious, the forms which these same persons use are felt to have the better flavor. This may be a generally human state of affairs, true in every group and applicable to all languages, and the factor of Standard and Literary Language versus dialect may be a superadded secondary one.

Vocabulary Levels: Zuñi Sacred and Slang Usage 42

STANLEY NEWMAN

NATIVE MEMBERS of English-speaking communities are sensitively aware that certain words and expressions in their language carry overtones of high or low status. Synonyms are often differentiated by such distinctions in ranking. *To desire* and *to want* have much the same denotative meaning, but one is on a relatively high and dignified level in contrast to the neutral tone of the other; *isn't* fulfills on a colloquially neutral plane the same referential function as the low-class *ain't*.

Although the phenomena of vocabulary levels are not well understood, it is clear that they cannot be treated purely in terms of linguistic form of derivation. Some high-toned English words are morphologically complex, but others are not. Slang expressions may be either monosyllabic or elaborate in form and in metaphorical circumlocution. Certain English words derived from Latin or French have acquired dignity, but others are part of our everyday vocabulary (*suit*, *dress*), and still others are substandard (*a dame*, *a joint*). Similarly, forms of Anglo-Saxon derivation range from the archaic poetical and biblical words to the vulgar four-letter words.

Interest in such stylistic features of vocabulary has been largely confined to lexicographers and to the literary specialists of our society, who have recognized that these features are the reflections of cultural norms. But it has also been assumed that stylistic phenomena of any kind are the product of literary refinement, particularly as developed in the traditions and standards of belletristic writing. Yet, non-literate societies without a specialized tradition of *belles lettres* have their high-valued words and phrases, which occur in myths or other sacred discourse, oratorical language, and the verbal forms of etiquette. (The literature on sacred language is as vast as it is fragmentary, but see especially Bunzel [1932, pp. 617-620], and White [1944]. Oratorical style is discussed in Boas [1897, p. 346]. Some of the Aztec *huehuetlatolli*, a genre of oral narrative illustrating the forms of politeness to be used in appropriate situations, are published with Spanish translations in Angel Ma. Garibay K. [1943]. For verbal etiquette in the use of greetings and titles, see Nellis [1947] and Pittman [1948].)

Although much has been written about taboo words, information is sparse on the occurrence in primitive groups of the lower levels of speech, such as substandard or slang usage. (Most of the sources dealing with substandard usage limit themselves to specific types of verbal conventions, such as puns and nicknames. For a general treatment of verbal humor in one non-literate society, see W. W. Hill [1943, pp. 16-20]. The linguistic devices employed to characterize the physical or psychological peculiarities of individuals are described in Sapir [1915].) In our own culture substandard language is usually defined as the usage of the low occupational, socio-economic, or educational classes: slang is "below the standard of cultivated speech . . . the special vocabulary of thieves, vagabonds, etc." or "language consisting either of new words or phrases, often of the vagrant or illiterate classes, or of ordinary words or phrases in arbitrary senses, and having a conventional but vulgar or inelegant use." (These definitions are, respectively, from *The American College Dictionary* and *Webster's Collegiate Dictionary*, 3rd ed.) If graded levels of usage, both high and low, occur in societies without a specialized tradition of literary cultivation and without a class stratification, then these stylistic phenomena must rest upon a broader cultural base than would appear from the evidence in our own culture. It is the purpose of this paper to describe the characteristics of Zuñi sacred and slang usage, as evidence of vocabulary levels in a non-literate society.

Zuñi sacred terms are used in prayers, myths, songs, and traditional sayings. They also occur in conversations within the kiva, where special proprieties must be observed in language as in other forms of behavior.

As one aspect of their wisdom, old people are reputed to have the most thorough knowledge of sacred language. The younger informants with whom I worked were consistently modest about their ability to explain religious terms; they frequently did not know the narrative details or the names of personages in the myths to which the terms alluded. Whether young or old, however, Zuñi adults can unhesitatingly identify particular words and phrases as belonging to the sacred, in contrast to the everyday, vocabulary. And even young Zuñis understand the denotative meaning of most sacred terms, though they may be ignorant of their allusions and implications.

Semantically, the forms identified as sacred are characterized by specialization of meaning when used in religious contexts. In everyday usage, for example, the stem *pinna-* means "to blow (of the wind)"; in prayers the singular noun form *pinnanne* refers, not to "wind," but to "life, breath."

Accompanying this semantic specialization is the feature of lexical distinctiveness: sacred terms are substitutions for everyday terms with similar denotative references. Insofar as its denotative meaning is concerned, *pinnanne* in the sacred meaning of "life, breath" replaces the neutral forms of *hoʔʔi-*, "to be alive," and *yanhaku-*, "to breathe." Similarly, the ordinary word for "frogs" is *takka*; in sacred songs "frogs" are *woliye tinan kʔayapa*, literally "several-are-in-a-shallow-container (such as a dish, puddle, lake) they-sitting they-are-in-liquid." Lest the apparently elaborate circumlocution in this example be misinterpreted as a mark of poetic style, it should be pointed out that phrasal lexemes of this type are common throughout Zuñi vocabulary: "gila monster" is *čittol ʔasipa*, "rattlesnake it-has-hands"; a man's nickname is *ʔa:na tenna ponławe*, "going-along almost-disappeared he-moves-rapidly-with-head-down."

Most sacred terms are merely the conventional equivalents of such truly neutral words as *takka*, "frogs." There is no unfavorable connotation attached to *takka* which would make it unacceptable in sacred contexts. Only the particular histories of word usage could explain why some everyday animal names, for example, have developed sacred substitutes while others have been accepted without substitution in religious discourse. But certain everyday words, it is true, carry connotations which would be inappropriate in religious situations, and substitute terms are therefore essential. In daily speech *nowe*, "beans," *kʔola*, "chile," or *pola*, "cottonwood tree," may be used in an extended meaning for uncomplimentary reference to "Spanish-Americans"; a similar reference to "Spanish-Americans" is made by such compounds as *nopolo:wa*, composed of *no-*, the stem for "bean," and *-polo:wa*, a form of the stem for "cottonwood tree," or *cipolo:wa*, containing *ci-*, the stem for "body hair." Such words, informants explain, are mildly insulting and too undignified to be proper in kiva language. Likewise, obviously borrowed words, such as *melika*, "Anglo-American," cannot be used in the kiva. This prohibition against loan words is obviously not to be equated with the tradition of linguistic purism, whereby organizations in many of the modern national states legislate against foreignisms that threaten to adulterate the native language. It stems, rather, from the general Zuñi injunction against bringing unregulated innovations into ceremonial situations: using a word like *melika*, as one informant expressed it, would be "like bringing a radio into the kiva." Officially constituted clowns may deliberately make use of radios and telephones, borrowed words, and even foreign pronunciations of Zuñi words for purposes of ceremonial humor, but this license is permitted only to clowns. For other persons the prohibition is leveled against employing certain words, not against referring to foreigners, while speaking in the kiva. If a Zuñi wishes to refer to Spanish-Americans or Anglo-Americans in kiva conversations, he may do so by using the substitute term *poʔya: kʔapa*, literally "wide hats," for this purpose. But the function illustrated here, that of supplying replacements for undignified words of the everyday vocabulary, applies to only a few of the religious terms and cannot be established as an explanatory principle of sacred usage.

Not only do most of the sacred terms replace neutral words, they are also composed of forms that occur in the neutral vocabulary of daily speech. Some exceptions, of course, can be cited. It is possible to find words which are unique to sacred discourse. But such unanalyzable forms, whether native archaic words or words borrowed from the ceremonial vocabularies of neighboring groups, are extremely rare among the Zuñi religious terms I collected. Likewise, words which contain elements denoting specifically religious concepts can be found, but they are few in number. An example is *ʔoneyalanne*, which is sometimes translated as "road, path" and explained as a prayer word substituting for the everyday term *ʔonanne*; sometimes it is translated as "road of life, sacred road." The word is composed of *-nne*, the singular noun ending, preceded by two stems: *ʔoneya-*, "cornmeal, pollen," and *yala-*, "to be stretched across." The denotations contained in the word are clearly religious, being associated with the ceremonial sprinkling of cornmeal to form a path from the altar to the entrance of the kiva.

Only a few of the Zuñi sacred terms, then, can be explained as replacements for the more undignified words of everyday usage or as uniquely sacred words containing forms not used in daily discourse and forms with distinctively religious denotations. For the most part, the vocabulary of religious words replaces the neutral vocabulary and is composed of the same forms. A sacred term is marked, however, by discriminable lexical and semantic features: it is lexically distinct from an everyday term with an equivalent denotative meaning; having a specialized meaning in religious contexts, it is semantically distinct from the same form as used in secular situations. Cultural attitudes provide the content and background for these verbal differentiations. Because the realm of religion carries high value in Zuñi culture, the words habitually employed in sacred contexts acquire connotations of dignity and high status. Furthermore, these words belong to the province of sacred knowledge best understood by old people, and it is this age group which carries the greatest prestige in Zuñi society.

For purposes of definition, slang will refer to those low-valued words and expressions which enjoy only a very brief period of currency. In contrast to the sacred vocabulary, the ephemeral vocabulary of slang is said to be understood and used only by Zuñi children and young adults. Old people are supposed to ignore such "nonsense talking"—*penakʔammeʔ peye*, literally "not-fit-to-be-spoken is-talking," an expression which covers slang, punning, telling tall stories, and other frivolous uses of language. Slang, however, does not carry strong disapproval. It is merely one of the types of foolish behavior normally indulged in by young people, and among members of this age group it can be tolerantly excused.

Specialization of meaning applies to slang as well as to sacred terms. Thus, *wapli-* in everyday speech denotes "to scratch up the ground, to gouge holes in the ground"; as a slang term popular in the early 1940's it acquired the meaning "to run away, to dash off." The standard word for "a spring (of water)" is *kʔanak^{w}ayinanne*, which gained a brief currency among young men as a somewhat rakish word denoting "a woman"; the shift of meaning in this example follows the cultural association, expressed in other Zuñi contexts, between thirst and sexual desire.

The feature of lexical replacement is also characteristic of Zuñi slang. The stem *ʔanʔá:-*, "to run away," is the neutral equivalent of *wapli-* in its slang meaning. Replacing the slang usage of *kʔanak^{w}ayinanne* are several words in the everyday vocabulary, such as *ʔoka*, "a female," or other terms which classify females into specific age groups.

The denotative meaning of many slang terms, however, is difficult to define and seemingly irrelevant to the connotative function of indicating the speaker's intention and attitude. Zuñi slang abounds in expressions used for taunting and chiding or for responding verbally to the reprehensible behavior of others. Most exclamatives are lexical forms whose denotative content approaches the vanishing point and whose meaning function must be largely described in terms of the attitudes they are understood to convey. Zuñi possesses, in addition to its standard exclamatives, several others that have suffered the faddish fate of slang terms. An example is *maʔana*, an exclamative of reproach current about ten years ago as a response to teasing from the opposite sex. The form might be analyzed as *maʔ*, a particle variously translated as "well, so, all right," and *ʔana*, another particle expressing uncertainty or negation, as "possibly, hardly, not quite, but no." In this exclamative, as in others, however, there is no identifiable denotation which can be analyzed or literally translated. All that can be proposed as a definition of *maʔana* is that it was an exclamative, implying reproach or mild rebuke, employed by young people for a short period as a fashionable way of making a verbal response to teasing.

Similarly indeterminate in denotative content are the formulaic utterances of Zuñi slang, each of which begins with a fixed sequence of words and ends with one of several alternative words or phrases. An expression of this type, used by boys fifteen or twenty years ago to convey an attitude somewhat akin to the English "all right for you," is illustrated in *wans tom* ——, "just you (objective case) ——." Some of the alternative endings for this utterance are *mišo*, "lizard," *šola*, "scorpion," *čʔikʷa sa:koni*, "Chikwa Short-Legs" (the proper name and nickname of a Zuñi man), or *kʷʔačʔi sa:niko*, a playful reversal of syllables on the preceding form. Informants were unable to explain whether "lizard," "scorpion," and "Chikwa Short-Legs" were based upon allusions to stories or local events, or how these references might be related to the meaning of the total utterance. A young Zuñi asserted, with thorough reasonableness, that he had used the expression as a boy simply because he had heard other boys using it. Evidently the denotations contained in the utterance were irrelevant to its intentional meaning, which was tacitly understood. Another utterance of this type, in vogue five or ten years ago, functioned as a snappy comeback to discourage unwarranted curiosity. If a young person were asked what he had bought at the store or what he was carrying in a parcel, he might reply *maʔ hinik ʔana* ——, "well, maybe possibly ——," completing the sentence with *wa:kaši*, "cow," *kʔakʷenne*, "house," or *kʷaʔholi*, "something." In this instance, at least, the denotative content of the utterance can be roughly translated as "Well, it might just possibly be a cow (a house, a something)." But the denotations are somewhat oblique and secondary to the meaning conveyed in the speaker's intention, that of making a fantastic reply to an unseemly question.

The denotative significance of some apparently meaningless expressions might be made meaningful if the situations in which they arose were known. A number of slang expressions have reference to specific local events, but the denotative relevance of any such expression will be understood only by the user who is familiar with the incident to which it refers. One of the slang terms which informants were able to clarify was *łuntašaʔa*, literally "body-lengthens," with a meaning equivalent to "he is girl-crazy." The origin of the term was attributed to a cartoon movie, in which a wolf, on seeing a pretty girl, lengthened its body to approach her. Another example is *tohsit ʔutteka*, "spider bit-him," one of the many expressions meaning "he is drunk." It has reference to a Zuñi trial, held several years ago, in which this statement is said to have been offered as a defense by the relatives of a young man charged with drunkenness and disorderly conduct. It is obvious, however, that a knowledge of the origin of an expression or its transferred meaning is not necessary for its proper usage and understanding. A Zuñi learns to apply terms like *łuntašaʔa* in their specialized slang meanings—and to use the denotatively meaningless expressions illustrated previously—by observing how other members of his culture react to these verbal cues in various situational contexts. In the same way, a native speaker of English at the turn of this century could successfully employ such slang terms as *rubberneck*, "a prying person," whether or not he was aware of its connection with *rubberneck-wagon*, "a sight-seeing bus"; and he would learn the intentional sense of *twenty-three skidoo*, whose origin and denotative connection with the meaning "go away" is obscure even to lexicographers.

Finally, another characteristic peculiar to the slang vocabulary of Zuñi lies in the prevalence of unique forms, forms not appearing at any other level of usage. Especially common among these unique elements, which in my data represent the slang of only the last generation, are forms borrowed from English. An example is the taunting *piš piš piš*, from English "fish," used by Zuñi boys some twenty years ago; a variant of the taunt was *piš no*ʔ*li*, "fish nose," *no*ʔ*li* being the Zuñi word for "nose." The insulting allusion here, according to one informant, was to the fish-like nose on the White man's portraits of Indians, as found in calendar pictures or on the buffalo nickle. Another borrowing which also illustrates the Zuñi's adoption of the White man's Indian is the expression *su:ča* ʔ*intiyan*, from English "such an Indian," applied as a joking rebuke to a person excessively awkward in performing some ordinary chore, such as riding a horse or carrying a pail of water. The exclamative *su:*, which conveys the same attitude, is merely a first-syllable abbreviation of the total expression and exemplifies a linguistic device fairly common in Zuñi.

As compared with sacred language, the rapidly changing vocabulary of Zuñi slang shows some distinctive peculiarities: a large proportion of slang words and expressions are denotatively meaningless or indeterminate and possess a communicative function that is largely intentional; slang contains many unique forms, not used in everyday neutral discourse; many of its expressions are based upon specific local incidents; it is a low-valued level of language primarily associated with the usage of young people. But, like sacred language, slang usage is also characterized by specialization of meaning and by the employment of substitute forms to convey the meanings expressed by other forms in everyday usage.

To the native speaker of Zuñi, the sacred vocabulary carries overtones of dignity and prestige; slang is regarded as a low-valued type of behavior. Both levels of language are distinguishable from everyday usage. Expressed in terms of a formula, a given lexeme (e.g., *k*ʔ*anak*^{w}*ayinanne*) has denotative meaning I ("a spring of water") in neutral usage but denotation II ("a woman") in slang; a given denotative reference (e.g., "frogs") is expressed by lexeme I (*takka*) in neutral usage but by lexeme II (*woliye tinan k*ʔ*ayapa*) in sacred language. These are overtly discriminable features of verbal behavior which aid in serving to distinguish one level of language from another.

The demarcation between these levels, of course, is not sharp and absolute. Many lexical forms overlap all levels without undergoing any specialization of meaning: the pronouns, in addition to their extensive use in everyday speech, are woven into prayers as well as slang utterances. Furthermore, the levels shade into one another by infinite gradations, and they cannot be reduced to a set of neatly separated categories through the device of definition. There are Zuñi forms, near either end of the subtly graded scale of usage, which might be regarded as semi-sacred and semi-slang. Thus, *yehču-*, "to draw in the breath, to inhale," has religious implications outside of ceremonial contexts in such words as ʔ*i:yehčuk*ʔ*akka*, literally "they caused each other to inhale," but actually having the transferred reference "they greeted each other (in the traditional Zuñi manner)." The transferred meaning is based upon the cultural association between the concept of breath and that of life and spiritual force derived from the divinities: people greet each other by placing their clasped hands upon each other's mouth and thereby passing breath and life to one another.

At the other end of the scale of usage are a host of nearly slang, slightly substandard, or somewhat informal words and expressions. Some Zuñi puns have become part of the standard stock of traditional jokes; but others, which have their source in local incidents and disappear from usage after a short life, should perhaps be classed as slang or semi-slang. A neutral reference to "my wife" is *hom* ʔ*ill* ʔ*ona*, "the one who has me"; ʔ*okaccik*ʔ*i* conveys the same denotative reference, but it is usually translated as "the old lady, the old woman" and though part of traditional usage, is a decidedly substandard word which must be used with circumspection. Many terms referring to persons—the words for "Spanish-American" mentioned earlier, nicknames, kinship terms in their humorously extended meanings—imply attitudes ranging from mild joshing to insult. They are neither slang nor neutral but belong to an intermediate region of substandard and familiar usage.

These intricate levels of usage are learned by the native speaker as part of his cultural experience. He not only acquires a semantic knowledge of the arbitrary denotations assigned to verbal forms, that area of meaning which is relatively easy to translate from one language to another. He also learns that certain conceptual fields, to which the words of his language refer, are highly valued in his culture, while others carry various degrees and shades of undignified overtones. Words referring to "wind," "breath," "inhaling," "blowing the breath upon" have denotative equivalents in English and Zuñi. But these concepts to a Zuñi are linked in a network of religious beliefs, and, through the mediation of these beliefs, words referring to such concepts are potentially loaded with sacred connotations. Similarly, a person foreign to English can be taught the denotative reference of *lamb* without much difficulty; but, unless he has also become culturally conditioned to Christian ideology with its associated pastoral images, he will be unable to react to the potentially religious connotations of such words as *lamb*, *flock*, *pasture*, *pastor*, *shepherd*. In fact, if the foreigner has been differently conditioned to these ideas in his own culture, he may react in the wrong way. English-speaking missionaries found that the pastoral references of the Old Testament evoked hostile connotations among their Chinese listeners, whose cultural experience had taught them "to regard herding as an inferior way of life of frontier barbarians, and herdsmen as the natural enemies of Chinese farmers" (Wright, 1953a, p. 301).

The native speaker likewise learns to respond to the additional connotations which words assume by virtue of the cultural status of the people who use these words and the situations in which they are habitually used. In a stratified society, such as that in which English is spoken, the verbal habits distinctive of each class acquire connotations of approval or disapproval, depending on the status of that class. In a culture which has accorded high prestige to the written word, especially to the esthetic forms of writing, the vocabulary traditionally encountered in poetry and belle-tristic prose becomes imbued with overtones of refinement and dignity. But these appear to be merely special cultural conditions in which behavior, verbal or otherwise, reflects the values associated with status groups and prestige situations.

In Zuñi culture there are no class or caste strata against which verbal forms take on a spectrum of values. But status differentiation is applied to age groups; and the speech peculiar to young people is low-valued, while that associated with old people is prestigeful. There is no specialized tradition of esthetic writing to give an aura of prestige to its distinctively literary forms and no contrast with the vulgate of forms used only in speech. But a comparable differentiation is applied in Zuñi to its cultural situations; the verbal usage characteristic of sacred places and practices is marked as the dignified level of vocabulary, in contrast to the usage distinctive of the movies, the school playground, and the practices of taunting and teasing.

It would appear, then, that vocabulary levels reflect cultural phenomena of a very general nature. Words acquire connotative gradations in accordance with the cultural values assigned to ideas, status groups, and situations. This area of meaning is difficult to translate from one language to another, especially when the languages are set in cultures which are widely different. For translation in this sense involves finding equivalents for the values associated with the ideas, status groups, and situations in two different cultural systems.

REFERENCE NOTE

The author's study of Zuñi language and culture was aided by a grant from the Wenner-Gren Foundation for Anthropological Research.

The vowel symbols used in transcribing Zuñi represent sounds much like the Spanish or Italian vowels. Zuñi vowels, however, may be phonemically short or long, length being indicated by a colon after the vowel. *P*, *t*, and the glottal stop (ˀ) are always unaspirated and voiceless, the remaining stops and affricates being aspirated before vowels and unreleased before consonants; furthermore, *k* is a palatalized velar, phonetically *ky*, before *a*, *e*, *i*, or before a glottal stop followed by these vowels. Zuñi *c* represents phonetic *ts*, the *č* is similar to the initial consonant of *church*, the *ƚ* is a lateral spirant, and the remaining consonant symbols have approximately their English values. Stress, which is not marked, occurs on the first syllable of the Zuñi word. A more detailed description of the Zuñi system of sounds occurs in Newman's "A Practical Zuñi Orthography" in Smith and Roberts (1954; pp. 163-170).

References are organized into two parts: (A) specific to Newman's article and (B) concerning argots, slang, ceremonial and sacred languages, and other aspects of the topic of "special languages." The topics of speech levels and speech variation as such are treated following Gumperz' article on pp. 416-428. For much pertinent material, see all the articles and references in Parts V and VI and the references to Bright's article in Part VIII.

A. NEWMAN'S REFERENCES NOT IN THE GENERAL BIBLIOGRAPHY

BOAS, FRANZ

1897. The Social Organization and Secret Societies of the Kwakiutl. *United States National Museum, Report (1895)*, pp. 311-738. Washington, D.C.

BUNZEL, RUTH

1932. Zuñi Ritual Poetry. *BAE-AR* (1929-1930), *47:* 611-835.

MA. GARIBAY K., ANGEL

1943. *Huehuetlatolli: Documento A.* Sacramento: Tlaloc.

SMITH, WATSON, and JOHN ROBERTS

1954. *Zuni Law: A Field of Values:* (Papers of the Peabody Museum of American Archaeology and Ethnology, Vol. 43, No. 1.) Cambridge: Harvard University Press.

B. SPECIAL LANGUAGES

On argots as a special object of study, see the general studies by Dauzat (1929), Guiraud (1958b), and the discussion and references in Cohen (1956a, chap III, especially pp. 116, 189, 208-211). A case in the southwestern United States is analyzed by Barker (1950) and Braddy (1956, 1960). See also Chao (1931), Chéon (1906), Goldin *et al.* (1950), Grove (1950), Leiris (1948), Leslau (1949, 1952), May (1956), Niceforo (1912), and Ullmann (1952, p. 249 and *passim*).

On slang as a special object of study, note the various discussions and documentation by Bloomfield (1933, *passim*). Evans-Pritchard (1954b), with subsequent correspondence in *Man* (1956, *56:* 15-16); Greenough and Kittredge (1961, chap. 6); Jespersen (1925, chap. 8); Mencken (1936, 1945), with extensive guide to literature and materials of slang in English; Partridge (1948, 1961); Stanzel (1956); Stern (1960); Thomas (1914); Vycichl (1959); Wentworth and Flexner (1960); and especially the analytic review of Wentworth and Flexner by Mathiot (1962b).

On ceremonial languages, see the various documentations and analytical points in Carrington (1947), Dozier (1958), Fock (1958), French (1958), Hymes (1958a), Ittmann (1959), Kroeber (1960b); Ma. de Barral (1958), Marouzeau (1949, chap. 4), May (1956), Opler and Hoijer (1940), Parker (1925), Radin (1950), Salisbury (1962), Stout (1947), Thompson (1961), Voegelin (1942, 1960). Note the analysis by White (1944), a functional interpretation contra historical interpretations such as Speck (1931, esp. pp. 62-63); the general treatment by Van Gennep (1908); and the context of this general treatment in Van Gennep (1960, p. 169).

Special languages are further discussed as general types by Cohen (1956a, chap.

3), Ferguson and Gumperz (1960, pp. 1-18), Vendryes (1925, Part IV, Ch. II), and, as noted, by Van Gennep (1908).

The prevalent categories for such forms of language use are not entirely discrete. In particular, any such "special language" may involve the use of speech play or disguise, and function as a language of partial or complete concealment. On children's special languages, used for concealment, note especially Jespersen (1922, pp. 180-188) and the special studies by Forchhammer (1939) and Hirschberg (1913).

References not in the general bibliography:

BRADDY, HALDEEN

1956. Smugglers' Argot in the Southwest. *American Speech*, *31:* 96-101.

1960. The *Pachucos* and Their Argot. *Southern Folklore Quarterly*, *24:* 255-271.

CARRINGTON, J. F.

1947. The Initiation Language: Lokele Tribe. *African Studies*, *6:* 196-207.

CHÉON, A.

1906. L'Argot Annamite. *Revue Indochinoise* (August), pp. 1269-1297.

COHEN, MARCEL

1939. *Nouvelle Études d'Éthiopien Méridional*. Paris: Champion. Pp. 357-371.

DOZIER, EDWARD P.

1958. Cultural Matrix of Singing and Chanting in Tewa Pueblos. *IJAL*, *24:* 268-272.

EVANS-PRITCHARD, E. E.

1954b. A Zande Slang Language. *Man*, *54:* 289.

FORCHHAMMER, EGIL

1939. Über einige Fälle von eigentümlichen Sprachbildungen bei Kindern. *Archiv. Ges. Psychol*, *104:* 395-438.

FRENCH, DAVID

1958. Cultural Matrices of Chinookan Non-Casual Language. *IJAL*, *24:* 258-263.

GOLDIN, H. E., *et al.*

1950. *Dictionary of American Underworld Lingo*. New York: Twayne

GRANET, M.

1922. Le Langage de la douleur en Chine. In *Études Sociologiques sur la Chine*. (Paris, 1953).

HIRSCHBERG, L. R.

1913. "Dog Latin" and Sparrow Languages Used by Baltimore Children. *Pedagogical Seminar*, *20:* 257-258.

ITTMANN, JOHANNES

1959. Outline of the Language of the Water Spirit Society on the Cameroon Mountain [Skizze der Sprache des Nixenkultbundes am Kamerunberg]. *Afrika und Uebersee*, *43:* 161-190.

LEIRIS, M.

1948. *La Langue secrète des Dogons de Sanga* (*Soudan français*). (Travaux et Mémoires de l'Institut d'Ethnologie, No. 50.) Paris.

LESLAU, WOLF

1949. An Ethiopian Merchant's Argot. *Lg.*, *25:* 22-28.

1952. An Ethiopian Minstrel's Argot. *JAOS*, *72:* 102-109.

MA. DE BARRAL, FR. BASILIO

1958. Vocabulario Teurgico Mágico de los Indios Guaraos. *Anthropológica*, *4:* 27-36.

MATHIOT, MADELEINE

1962b. Review of Wentworth and Flexner, *Dictionary of American Slang*. *AA*, *64:* 672-676.

NICEFORO, A.

1912. *Le Génie de l'argot*. Paris: Mercure de France.

OPLER, MORRIS, and HARRY HOIJER

1940. The Raid and War-Path Language of the Chiricahua Apache. *AA*, *42:* 617-634.

PARKER, ROSCOE E.

1925. Spenser's Language and the Pastoral Tradition. *Lg.*, *1:* 80-87.

PARTRIDGE, ERIC

1948. *Shakespeare's Bawdy. A Literary and Psychological Essay and a Comprehensive Glossary*. London. (New York: Dutton [Everyman Paperback, D55], 1960.)

1961. *A Dictionary of Slang and Unconventional English*. (Rev. ed.) New York: Macmillan.

RADIN, PAUL

1950. *The Origin Myth of the Medicine Rite: Three Versions*. (IUPAL; Memoirs of IJAL, No. 3.) Bloomington.

RUSIĆ, BRANISLAV

1956. The Mute Language in the Tradition and Oral Literature of the South Slavs. *JAF*, *69:* 299-309.

SPECK, FRANK G.

1931. *A Study of the Delaware Indian Big House Ceremony*. (Publications of the Pennsylvania Historical Commission, No. 2.) Harrisburg.

STANZEL, FRANZ

1956. Zur Herkunft des Rhyming Slang. *Die Sprache*, *3:* 193-202.

STERN, H. H.

1960. The Language of the German Service Man of World War II and the Nature of Slang. *German Life and Letters*, *12:* 282-297.

THOMAS, N. F.

1914. "Slang" in Southern Nigeria. *Man*, *14* (1): 3-4 (Article 3).

THOMPSON, BARD

1961. *Liturgies of the Western Church*. Cleveland and New York: World.

VAN GENNEP, ARNOLD

1908. Essai d'une théorie des langues spéciales. *Revue des études ethnographiques et sociologiques*, *1:* 327-337. [Also in *Religions, mœurs et légendes*. (2nd series.) Paris; 1913.]

1960. *The Rites of Passage*. Translated from the French by Monika B. Vizedom and Gabrielle L. Caffee. Chicago: University of Chicago Press. (Originally published, 1909.)

VOEGELIN, C. F.

1942. Word Distortions in Delaware Big House and Walam Olum Songs. *Proceedings of the Indiana Academy of Science*, *51:* 48-54.

VYCICHL, WERNER

1959. A Forgotten Secret Language of the 'Abbādi Sheikhs and the Slang of the Halab is-Sudān. *Kush*, *7:* 222-228.

WENTWORTH, HAROLD, and STUART BERG FLEXNER (COMPS. and EDS.)

1960. *Dictionary of American Slang*. New York: Crowell.

YEGERLEHNER, JOHN

1958. Structure of Arizona Tewa Words, Spoken and Sung. *IJAL*, *24:* 264-267.

Speech Levels in Japan and Korea 43

SAMUEL E. MARTIN

INTRODUCTION

This paper is one of several preliminary studies with the aim, first, to pinpoint certain areas of ethnolinguistic structure shared by Korea and Japan and, then, to explore these areas for keys to similarities and differences in national character. Let me briefly mention the several areas that I am investigating.

1. In SYNTAX we find a remarkable similarity, almost a unit-for-unit correspondence, between the two languages. Small points of difference do exist, however. For example: (A) Korean freely sticks nouns together to make long agglutinative compounds, but colloquial Japanese prefers analytical constructions broken up by the word *no*, equivalent to either the Korean copula modifier in 'which is' or the Korean particle *ui* 'of.' (B) Korean and Japanese both have a particle of de-emphasis (*wa* in Standard Japanese, *un/nun* in Korean), but in Japanese the function of this particle is often reduced to little more than a sentence-opener. (C) Few Koreans have any feeling for a clear-cut "model" language behind their many colloquial abbreviations; Japanese, on the other hand, are used to seeing and hearing the formal "models" for such abbreviations as *zya* = *de wa*, *site 'ru* = *site iru*, *sit' oku* = *site oku*.

2. Korean has perhaps the richest and most extensive system of SOUND SYMBOLISM in the world; each of over a thousand lexemes occurs not as an isolated item, but as a set of words with systematic variations in shape that correspond to subtle but structured differences in connotation. The Japanese system is feeble by comparison. In addition, Korean has a variety of vulgar and deprecatory synonyms for many common nouns and verbs, permitting a flavor of earthiness hard to match in Japanese.

3. Korean has a number of ASPECT SUBTLETIES that Japanese lacks: the past-past *-ess.ess-ta*, the various retrospective forms (*ha-tun*, *ha-tula*, *ha-p.tita*), the casual constructions (*ha-ci*, *ha-ci yo*), the apperceptive forms (*ha-kwun*, *ha-kwumen*). On the other hand, Japanese offers a handy set of final particles (*né*, *sa*, *yo*, etc.) that often evade the Korean translator.

4. Japanese has an elaborate set of POLITE FORMULAS, stock phrases designed to smooth every conceivable social situation. A foreigner who memorizes about twenty or thirty of the common situational exchanges can circulate in Japanese society with surprising success, even if he knows no other expressions; he soon gets the feeling that Japanese conversation is all formula, with no content. Korean, of course, has a few such formulas, too—but no one would claim that *mian hamnita* is heard with any thing like the frequency of Japanese *sumimasén* 'excuse me; thank you.' In a number of situations the Japanese has an explicit (and often very effective) way to soothe people's feelings; in many of these same situations, the Korean, like the American, says nothing at all. Both are apt to suspect the sincerity of the Japanese, and this is unjust, since it is virtually impossible to say "thank you" all day long and not end up with a vague feeling of gratitude, or to excuse yourself time after time without a certain humility setting in of itself.

1. OBLIGATORY CATEGORIES

Every language forces upon the speaker certain choices before he can make an utterance; these are the OBLIGATORY CATEGORIES of the language. In English, we cannot talk about something—let us say that 4-legged animal that the Japanese call *néko*, the Koreans *kwayngi*—

without deciding immediately whether the something is to be singular or plural, definite or indefinite. We have to make our choice among the expressions 'the cat, the cats, a cat, some cats'; we can't just say 'cat' as the Korean or Japanese does. We have two quite arbitrary axes of distinction: an AXIS OF NUMBER and an AXIS OF SPECIFICITY (see Fig. 1).

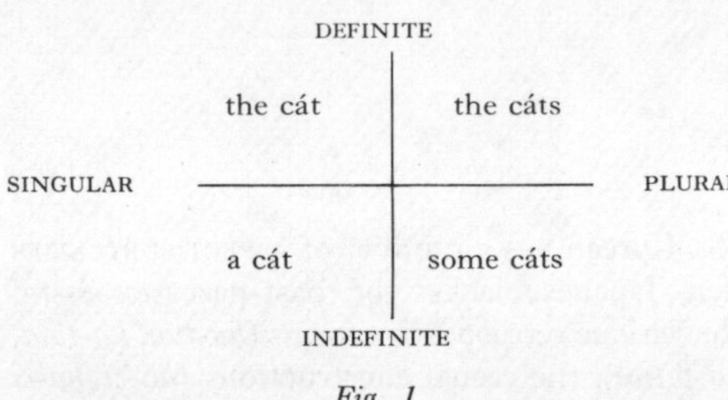

Fig. 1

In addition, there is a third axis, that of generality: 'the cat' (a type of animal) versus 'the cat' (this or that cat), each singular definite; 'a cat' versus 'any cat,' each singular and indefinite; 'the cats' (a type of animal) versus 'the cats' (these or those cats), each plural and definite; 'cats' (a type of animal) versus 'some cats,' each plural and indefinite.

The arbitrary nature of such categories comes home to us at once when we try to explain the proper use of the articles to our Far Eastern colleagues, or to account for the fact that "the United States" is singular on this side of the Atlantic but plural in England.

To add a certain piquancy to English inscrutability the same sound, an *-s*, will make a sentence plural when attached to the noun, but singular when attached to the verb:

the cat*s* jump
the cat jump*s*

It is small wonder that learning English has been called "the yellow man's burden."

2. *SPEECH LEVELS*

Japanese and Koreans are fortunately spared a number of these distinctions that are forced upon us. They need not even have a subject in their sentences, so they are spared the strangely shapeless 'it' of 'it seems to me' and 'it rains' or the peculiar 'there' of 'there's someone here.' Sentences in Korean and Japanese are quite complete with just a predicate, often nothing more than a verb form. But before they can utter the verb form, the Japanese and the Koreans are forced to make a choice alien to us: that of speech levels. In both languages there are two axes of distinction: the AXIS OF REFERENCE and the AXIS OF ADDRESS (see Figs. 2 and 3).

STANDARD JAPANESE

1. *Axis of address*

	PLAIN :	POLITE :	DEFERENTIAL
Copula	dá	désu	—
	de áru (formal)	de arimásu (formal)	de gozaimásu
Verb forms	...-(r)u	...(i)-másu	— (gozaimásu)

2. *Axis of reference*

	Copula	Verb forms
HUMBLE	—	o-...-i suru
NEUTRAL	dá	...-(r)u
EXALTED	de irassyáru	o-...-i ni náru

3. *Donatory verbs* ('gives')

HUMBLE	ageru	} (out-giving)
NEUTRAL	{ yaru	} (out-giving)
NEUTRAL	{ kureru	} (in-giving)
EXALTED	kudasáru	} (in-giving)

4. *Euphemistic verbs*

	'does'	'says'	(etc.)
HUMBLE	itasu	móosu	
NEUTRAL	suru	iu	
EXALTED	nasáru	ossyáru	

Fig. 2

STANDARD KOREAN

1. *Axis of address*

INGROUP

PLAIN :	INTIMATE :	FAMILIAR
-ta	-na	-e
		-ci

OUTGROUP

POLITE :	AUTHORITATIVE :	DEFERENTIAL
-e yo	-(s)o	-(su)p.nita
-ci yo		

2. *Axis of reference*

NEUTRAL	-ta
EXALTED	-(u)si-

3. *Euphemistic verbs*

	'eat'	'sleep'	'stay'
NEUTRAL	mek-	ca-	iss-
EXALTED	capswu-(si-)	cwumusi-	kēysi-

Fig. 3

The choice of plain, polite, or deferential STYLE in Japanese depends on the speaker's attitude toward the person that he is addressing. The choice of humble, neutral, or exalted EXPRESSIONS—in any of the three styles—depends primarily on the speaker's attitude toward the subject of the expression. I am simplifying the picture here by limiting the discussion to verb forms; for Japanese, but not for Korean, the situation is further complicated by the spectrum of meaning covered by the deferential noun prefix *o-*.

In the meaning 'to give,' Japanese, unlike Korean, has not one, but two neutral verbs: *yaru*, a verb for giving to the OUT-GROUP and *kureru*, a verb for giving to the IN-GROUP. By definition, the humble form, *ageru*, is out-giving, the exalted form, *kudasáru*, is in-giving (Fig. 2). "In-group" and "out-group" are flexible, relative terms; when 'I give to you,' YOU are in the out-group; but when 'you give to him,' YOU are absorbed in my in-group as opposed to HIM, unless he is an intimate of mine. When 'he gives to him,' we have to decide from the situation which of the two—HE or HIM—is closer to ME and belongs in the in-group.

3. *JAPANESE SHAPES*

The Japanese diagram shows, for each style and type of expression, typical shapes taken by the copula (*dá, désu, de irassyáru* 'it is') and by verb forms. There is no humble copula, and there is no way to make a verb form *per se* deferential, with the exception of *áru* 'exists' (which becomes *gozaimásu*). The modern trend is to use *de gozaimásu* as the humble copula only, and eliminate the deferential style from predicates altogether. This produces a neater, 2-way opposition of plain vs. polite, humble vs. exalted, with the neutral form neutralizing the opposition between humble and exalted (see Fig. 4).

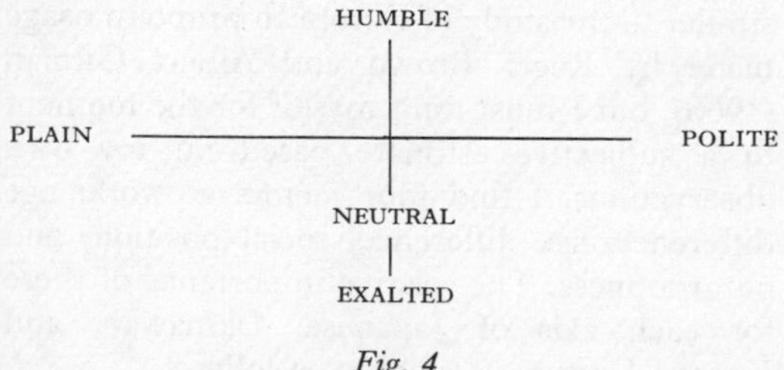

Fig. 4

The use of *de gozaimásu* as humble is probably responsible for the use of *de irassyaimásu* and other exalted verbs with subjects that are inanimate objects pertaining to exalted persons, a growing habit much deplored by Japanese observers.

In addition to the regularly formed humble and exalted verb expressions, there are about 20 or 30 euphemistic verbs; each of these either takes the place of the expected regular form (*oide ni náru* or *irassyáru* for the non-existent **o-i ni naru* 'stays') or serves as an elegant synonym alongside the regularly formed humble or exalted (*mesiagaru* alongside *o-nomi ni náru* 'drinks').

4. *KOREAN CATEGORIES*

When we compare the Korean distinctions, the first thing that strikes us is the absence of a humble form. It is sometimes claimed that such a form once existed, but I suspect that the meaning of the suffix in question (*-saop-*) was merely deferential. With the exception of one euphemistic humble verb *poyw-* 'to see' (corresponding to neutral *po-*, exalted *po-si-*) which occurs only in a few set expressions, the nearest equivalent of the Japanese humble forms is use of the deferential style. Korean makes its exalted forms neatly and regularly with the so-called honorific infix *-usi-/-si-*, and there are only a few euphemistic verbs alongside the regular exalted forms.

The next thing we notice is that the axis of address divides up into six styles; this compares with only three in Japanese, with those three perhaps in the process of reduction to two. The first three styles (plain, intimate, familiar) can be lumped together as "in-group address" and the last three as "out-group address"; notice that these terms are used here with respect to ADDRESS, not to REFERENCE (as with the Japanese verbs for giving). We see that Korean has a rich variety within these two groups; there is leeway to show intimacy or familiarity within the in-group, and to show authority or special deference within the out-group. The relationship between in-group address and out-group address, like the relationship between plain address and polite address in Japanese, is analogous to the use of the pronouns *du* and *Sie* in modern German or of *tu* and *vous* in modern French. In Seoul, the use of the authoritative address (by a person taking command of a situation: policeman to traffic offender, customer to laundry-man, guest to hotel-clerk, passenger to taxi-driver, etc.) seems to be undergoing replacement by either the polite or the deferential. New information indicates that in Seoul the local-dialect form of the authoritative *-swu/-wu* is used within the family circle to elders (including servants), while the intimate *-e* and the plain *-ta* are used to juniors; the familiar *-ney* is used to friends. For a somewhat different interpretation, see Ooe (1958, pp. 25-29). Some Koreans would like to standardize the *-sup.nita* style as analogous to the Japanese *désu* style; actually, it corresponds more closely to the Japanese *de gozaimásu* style, and is probably destined for a similar fate—eventual replacement by the polite style, except for formal cliches.

5. *RYUKYU SYSTEMS*

There is probably no dialect of Japanese or Korean that does not have some such system as those outlined. I have given data for two systems from the Ryukyus: one from Okinawa and one from Amami Oshima (see Figs. 5 and 6).

OKINAWA (SHURI)

1. *Axis of address*

	PLAIN :	POLITE :	DEFERENTIAL
Copula	ya-n	ya-ibii-n	deebiru (du ya-ibii-ru)
Verb forms	-yu-n,-i-n	-(y)abii(r)-, -ibi(ir)	—

2. *Axis of reference*

	Copula	Verb forms
HUMBLE	—	qu-...-i s-yun
NEUTRAL	ya-n	-yu-n,-i-n
EXALTED	1. qwaa nsèe-n*	1. ...(-i) nsèe-n*
	2. qwaa misèe-n	2. ...(-i) misèe-n
	3. quya(-i) nsèe-n	3. qu-...-i nsèe-n
	4. quya(-i) misèe-n	4. qu-...-i misèe-n
	5. —	5. qu-...-i nsyoo-rari-in
	*(Noble to older farmer)	qu-...-i misyoo-rari-in

3. *Donatory verbs* ('gives')

HUMBLE	qusagi-yu-n	out-giving (humble, neutral)
NEUTRAL	qagi-yu-n / kwí-yu-n	
EXALTED	qu-tabi-i misèe-n	in-giving (neutral kwí-yu-n, exalted)

Fig. 5

AMAMI OSHIMA (*Shodon*)

1. *Axis of address*

	PLAIN	POLITE
Copula	dya, #, da	daroo(wo)m
Verb forms	-um, -un, -ur	-oo(wo)m, -aawom

2. *Axis of reference*

	Copula	Verb forms
HUMBLE	—	qu-...-i sy-um
NEUTRAL	dya, #, da	-um, -un, -ur
EXALTED	1. daryi n syom	1. -i n syom (n syaawom)
	2. —	2. -i qumoo(r)y-um
	3. —	3. -i qumoory-i n syom

Fig. 6

The Oshima system is somewhat simpler than that of Standard Japanese, but the two axes are still very much present. The Okinawan system is much the same as Standard Japanese, but it gets quite complicated with levels of exaltation. This is undoubtedly due in large part to the complex caste structure that existed within the relatively small community of Shuri until recent days. Pronouns and certain interjections (of the 'yes'-and-'no' type) reflect this same complexity. In both Ryukyu systems there are many euphemistic and exalted verbs, and both have special donatory verbs, of which the Okinawa (Shuri) forms are given in Fig. 5.

6. *FACTORS OF CHOICE*

We now come to the problem of finding out what factors operate to influence a speaker's choice of reference and address forms. We expect the factors to obtain relatively, of course, for the speaker and the person spoken to or of; and we are not surprised at an overlap of factors in any given situation. I wish that I could present a statistically based description of the factors and their relative importance, similar to the study of European pronoun usage made by Roger Brown and Albert Gilman (1960), but I must limit myself for the moment to a subjective estimate based on my own observations. I find four factors at work: age difference, sex difference, social position, and outgroupness. The relative importance of these for each axis of Japanese, Okinawan, and Korean I estimate roughly as follows:

	Reference	Address
Standard Japanese	position age difference sex difference outgroupness	outgroupness position age difference sex difference
Standard Korean	outgroupness position age difference sex difference	outgroupness position sex difference age difference
Shuri Okinawan	age difference position outgroupness sex difference	age difference outgroupness position sex difference

I am not too happy with these estimates, and I should be interested to hear other people's reactions to them. I suspect that much of the dissatisfied feeling among older people that "politeness levels" are changing is due to changes in the relative importance of the various factors and perhaps also to changes in feelings of what constitutes an in-group and an out-group. Age and sex differences were undoubtedly more important factors in the past than they are today; in 19th-century Okinawa, a difference of one day in age was sufficient to call for different levels of speech. Outgroupness and position seem far more important in Standard Japanese and Korean today. One reason is the preference to avoid direct pronominal reference, since this involves one with still another axis of distinctions, in some ways more complex. An effective use of verb forms makes pronouns largely unnecessary.

It has been noted by Japanese investigators that politeness increases with distance, size, and impersonality of the audience; you are more polite to a person on the telephone than face-to-face, you are more polite to a group of individuals than to each one separately, you are more polite in letters than in speaking (*Gengo Seikatu*, 1957, p. 9). It has also been noted that the use of any Standard Japanese forms is considered more polite than even the most honorific of local dialect forms (*Gengo Seikatu*, 1957, p. 7). In a given speech situation, several styles often alternate with each other; a Korean may open up a conversation with the deferential style, slip into the polite style, and then occasionally throw in a deferential form. Yamasita Syoosei of the Japan Broadcasting Company (*Gengo Seikatu*, 1957, p. 55) suggests that the normal maximum frequency for *gozaimásu* is about once in 5 sentences for a male speaker, once in 3 sentences for a female speaker, with the other sentences in polite style. It seems to me that the former figure corresponds rather well to the frequency with which a Yale undergraduate inserts 'sir' in sentences addressed to his teachers; the latter figure is close to the obsequious frequency with which an American salesman inserts the name of his prospective customer into the sales-pitch.

The best statistical study available is the report on attitudes in non-standard dialect areas made by the Kokuritu kokugo kenkyuuzyo (National Language Research Institute), called *Keigo to keigo isiki* (Honorifics and consciousness of them; 1957); this came to my attention after writing the preceding section. The principal conclusions of the Japanese study (pp. 376-378) are presented here in a free translation:

1. Honorific forms incorporating negatives (analogous to our 'wouldn't you like to') are generally felt to be more polite than those without negatives.

2. An individual does not show marked idiosyncratic preference for a particular one of several competing honorific forms in his usage.

3. The longer the utterance, the more polite it is felt to be. [*Sóo na n desu* '(it is a fact that) it is so' somehow just "sounds" more deferential than *Sóo desu* 'it is so' (cf. *Gengo Seikatu*, 1958, p. 11).]

4. Utterances with local dialect in them are considered less polite.

5. Utterances with at least a few Chinese loanwords in them are considered more polite than those without.

6. Politeness of usage seems to be in inverse proportion to feeling that one has the upper hand in a situation.

7. Actual usage is often at variance with ideal usage.

8. Strangers are accorded more polite usage than acquaintances.

9. Distinctions of usage toward the addressee are more finely drawn as one moves geographically from East to West.

10. One's sex is the most important social factor determining one's honorific *usage*; one's age is the least important.

11. There is a tendency for men to discrimi-

nate different situations calling for honorific usage, for women to use honorifics all the time.

12. *Knowledge* of honorific forms is primarily controlled by education background. One's sex has little to do with it.

13. *Attitudes* toward honorifics differ greatly with age level.

14. In general, people like the more polite honorific forms.

15. Honorific speech incorporating dialect forms is displeasing, both from oneself or from others.

16. Those who favor the more polite honorific forms are more polite in their own usage.

17. Situations of address where more politeness is expected are: women to men, the young to the old, lower classes to upper classes.

18. Of these three factors, class difference is generally felt to be the overriding one.

19. One's sex is no factor in one's ability to discriminate honorific speech behavior on the part of others.

20. There is considerable psychological resistance to the rule suggested by the Ministry of Education's guide *Kore kara no keigo* (*Honorifics From Now On*) that one should not use honorifics in speaking to outsiders of one's own work superiors (bosses).

21. There is considerable opposition in the abstract to the overuse of the deferential prefix *o-*, but in actual conversation situations the resistance weakens.

22. In speaking of one's own relatives, there is a strong consensus that honorifics are inappropriate; yet actual usage contradicts this.

23. Young people are more easy-going in their usage of honorifics. (Cf. *Gengo Seikatu*: "it is difficult to smile when you say *gozaimásu*" [1958, p. 11].)

24. People who strive to be polite tend to use honorific forms.

25. The "rigid" personality type (i.e., the one slow to grasp a change of situation in a psychological test) is poor at using honorifics.

7. SOME PROBLEMS

One difficulty in investigating both Okinawan and Korean attitudes is the extent to which these have been influenced by Japanese ways. A shrewd Seoulite once explained attitude conflicts in modern Korea to me in this way. There are, he says, three groups of people: First, there are the old folks who are often in positions of power and authority; they, together with the farmers, have the old *yangpan* feudal outlook. Second, there are the middle-aged urban people, who gained the technical skills to run the country through their Japanese educations; these people will damn the Japanese in public, but deep inside they feel more at home with Japanese social attitudes than with the old Korean ones. Finally, there are the young people, who have come under the sway of international ideas, largely American in origin.

Now it has been suggested that perhaps the complications of speech levels are due to the Tokugawa dictatorship in Japan on the one hand, and to an over-exposure to Confucianism in Korea on the other. There may be something to this; we can certainly attribute the special complications of the exalted forms in Shuri to the stratified society there. But the actual axes of reference and address themselves are too widespread, and also too well attested in early Japanese literature, to be traced to any one external cause. Kindaiti (according to *Kokugogaku ziten*, 1955, p. 586) has suggested that speech levels developed in three stages: a stage of taboo, a stage of "absolute honorifics" (in which a high-status person uses exalted forms for himself and humble forms for the low-status person), and a stage of "relative honorifics." He says that Ainu exemplifies the second stage and that Old Japanese had a strong touch of it. I find his evolutionary bias a bit suspect; the origin of speech levels, like the ultimate origin of all language categories, is probably moot. In any event, it would be unwise to make a prediction that the present system will die out as feudalism is replaced by democracy; after all, no one expects IBM machines to kill off the English number category. We shall probably have speech levels in Japanese and Korean as long as we have plurals in English.

REFERENCE NOTE

In this paper the Japanese forms are cited in the Yale Romanization, Korean forms in the orthography of Martin (1954), and Ryukyu forms in phonemic transcription, the *q* representing the glottal stop. The paper is based partly on field work aided by a travel grant from the Social Science Research Council in 1953-1954; it was first presented before the Association for Asian Studies in New York on April 1, 1958.

References not in the general bibliography:

JAPANESE

EKOYAMA TUNEAKI
1943. *Keigohoo* [Honorific Usage]. Tokyo.

GARDNER, E. F., and S. E. MARTIN
1952. *Honorific and Familiar Speech in Japanese*. New Haven.

[GENGO SEIKATU]
1954. Articles on women's speech. *28* (January): 1-25, 40-41, 56-63.
1957. Articles on honorific speech. *79* (July): 2-57.
1958. Discussion of employee-customer usages. *82* (July): 2-14.

HOOZYOO TADAO
1951. Toohoku hoogen ni okeru taisya-sonkei "su" no honsitu [The Nature of the Honorific "su" in the Northeast Dialects]. *Kokugogaku*, *6:* 65-82.

IMAIZUMI TADAYOSI
1943a. Nihongo no keigo [Japanese Honorifics]. *Gendaigohoo no syosoo*. Tokyo.
1943b. Gendai no keigo [Modern Honorifics]. *Gendaigohoo no syosoo*. Tokyo.

ISIBASI SYOOZOO
1944. *Keigo si ronkoo* [A Disquisition on the History of Honorifics]. Osaka. Keigo-teki zinsyoo no gaimen [Observations on Honorific Appellation]. *Hoobun ronsoo*.

JORDEN, E. H.
1963. *Beginning Japanese*. New Haven. 2 vols.

KOKUGO-GAKU ZITEN [Dictionary of Japanese Studies].
1955. Articles on: Aisatu [Greetings] 1-2; Keigo [Honorifics] 276-8; Zidoo-go [Children's Speech] 504; Zyosei-go [Women's Speech] 545; Zettai keigo [Absolute Honorifics] 586; Sondai-go [Self-Elevating Words] 609, Teinei-go [Polite Speech] 660-1; Dansei-go [Men's Speech] 628; Nyooboo kotoba [Women's Words] 731-2. Tokyo.

KOKUGO SINGIKAI
1952. *Kore kara no keigo* [Honorifics from Now On]. In Hirota Eitaroo, *Yoozi yoogo ziten*. (12th ed.) Tokyo: 1956. Pp. 274-280.

KOKURITU KOKUGO KENKYUU-ZYO [National Language Research Center]
1957. *Keigo to keigo isiki* [Honorifics and Consciousness of Them]. Tokyo.
1953-1954-1955. *Nenpoo* [Annual Report]. *4:* 33-41; *5:* 59-110; *6:* 66-77.

KINDAITI KYOOSUKE
1933. *Kokugo kenkyuu*. [National Language Studies] (Rev. ed.) Tokyo.

MARTIN, S. E.
1962. *Essential Japanese*. (3rd ed.) Tokyo.
Ms. *Materials for a Japanese Reference Grammar*.

MARUYAMA RINPEI
1941. *Nihon keigohoo* [Japanese Honorific Usage]. Tokyo.

MASIMO SABUROO
1948. *Huzin-go no kenkyuu* [Study of Women's Speech]. Tokyo.

MIO ISAGO
1958. *Hanasi-kotoba no bunpoo* [Colloquial grammar]. Tokyo.

MIYAKE TAKEROO
1948. *Gendai keigohoo* [Modern Honorific Usage]. Tokyo.

TUZIMURA TOSIKI
1955. Keigo no ayamari ni tuite [On the Misuse of Honorifics]. *Kokugogaku, 21:* 30-43.

YAMADA YOSIO
1931. *Keigohoo no kenkyuu* [Study of Honorific Usage]. (Rev. ed.) Tokyo.

YAMAZAKI HISAYUKI
1955. Kokugo no taiguu hyoogen taikei to sono rekisi [The System of Japanese Honorific Expressions and Its History]. *Kokugogaku, 21:* 17-29.

KOREAN

CHOY HYENPAY
1946. Insa hanun mal [Greeting Expressions]. *Hankul, 11* (2).
1955. *Wuli mal pon* [Korean Grammar]. (Rev. ed.) Seoul. 777-792; 230, 345-348, 365-368

HE WUNG
1954. The Honorifics in the Korean Language—Past and Present. *Journal of Sengkyun-kwan University*, no. 1 (February).

I HUISUNG
1955. *Kwuk-e-hak kaysel* [Introduction to Korean Linguistics]. Seoul. Pp. 296-297.
1962. Phonetic symbolism in Korean. *American Studies in Altaic Linguistics.* Bloomington. Pp. 177-189.

I THAK
1946. Chingho ui mal wa insa ui mal ey tay-ha.ye [On Titles and Greetings]. *Hankul, 11* (1).

KIM HYANGKYU
1947. Kyengnyangsa ui yenkwu [Study of Honorific and Humble Expressions]. *Hankul, 12* (4).

MARTIN, S. E.
1954. *Korean Morphophonemics*. Baltimore: Linguistic Society of America.
Ms. *A Korean Reference Grammar.*

OOE TAKAO
1958. On the Indicative Endings in Modern Korean. *Gengo kenkyuu, 34:* 1-40.

OGURA SINPEI
1938. *Tyoosengo ni okeru kenzyoo-hoo sonkei-hoo no zyodoosi* [Humble and Honorific Auxiliary Verbs in Korean].

YEL WUN
1947. Nam ul pulul ttay ssunun kyenge [Honorifics Used When Calling Others]. *Hankul, 12* (1).

RYUKYU

HARING, DOUGLAS G.

1953. Japanese National Character. *Yale Review, 42:* 375-392.

HATTORI SIROO, and HIGA SYUNTYOO

1955. Ryuukyuu-go [The Ryukyu language]. In *Sekai gengo gaisetu* [Languages of the world], vol. 2.

KANESIRO TOMONAGA

1944. *Naha hoogen gaisetu* [Outline of the Naha dialect]. Tokyo.

MARTIN, S. E.

Ms. *The Shodon Dialect of Amami Oshima; The Shuri Dialect of Okinawa.*

44 Speech Variation and the Study of Indian Civilization

JOHN J. GUMPERZ

ALTHOUGH ENQUIRY into the relationship between language and culture has grown considerably in recent years, most modern American work in this field so far operates with unit languages and cultural isolates. The Whorf hypothesis has focused attention on the relationship between linguistic structures and native ways of categorizing cognitive experience and led to important advances in structural semantics. In cross-cultural analyses of such structures, however, each system is treated as a homogeneous "linguistic and cultural whole" (Kroeber, 1939a) regardless of internal social or geographical differences in speech and behavior patterns. Studies of linguistic diffusion similarly emphasize borrowings between distinct and often unrelated languages. Less attention has been devoted to Bloomfield's "dialect borrowing" (1933, p. 476), the spread of features within a speech area. Furthermore, historically oriented structural linguists confine their research to historical linguistics or internal language history, the formal reconstruction of hypothetical parent varieties from a series of distinct languages or dialects, in contrast to external language history, the study of linguistic change in relation to the social currents which effect it. The great body of nineteenth and twentieth century research on speech variation within single speech communities has as yet evoked little interest among either structural linguists or social scientists in the United States. Yet, much of this work is of central relevance for the studies of complex civilizations or "intermediate societies" as they have recently been termed (Casagrande, 1959), which are becoming more and more common in modern anthropology.

In contrast to many modern American linguists, who because of their concern with methodology, have often found it difficult to communicate with other students of culture, dialectologists—and especially those trained in the European tradition—tend to think of themselves primarily as cultural geographers, folklorists, or social historians. They regard linguistic analysis not as an end in itself but rather pursue it for the information it provides about the history and culture of a region. Thus, of the earlier work, the investigations of the German scholars Fischer, Haag, and Wrede have produced convincing evidence for the relationship between present-day dialect isoglosses and certain German territorial boundaries of late medieval and early modern times (Bach, 1950, pp. 81 ff.). Gilliéron, the author of the *Linguistic Atlas of France* (Gilliéron and Edmont, 1903-1910) and his students, although their primary concern was with phonetic change, have given us many new insights into the manner in which the rise and spread of certain words or pronunications reflect the social forces and intellectual currents of a period. More recently, the *Linguistic Atlas of Italy and Southern Switzerland* by Karl Jaberg and Jacob Jud (1928-1940) provides maps which show the distribution of linguistic forms, along with their changes in meaning. It furthermore gives detailed drawings of the objects of material culture which these forms represent and their regional variations in shape. The most extreme position on the relation between dialect study and cultural phenomena is that of the German, Theodore Frings, who coined the slogan "*Sprach-geographie ist Kulturgeographie*" and dropped the term *Sprachraum* (linguistic region) in favor of *Kulturraum* (cultural region) (Bach, 1950, pp. 63 ff.).

Frings' cultural regions were defined in collaboration with teams of social historians, geographers, and folklorists. These same regions then became the units for detailed enquiries into the conditions leading to the rise of new linguistic forms and into the geographical and social itineraries by which these forms spread both within regions and from one region into another. In these studies, speech features were treated as units of social communication and were surveyed along with such other traits as housing types, dress, ritual, and folklore. The general orientation of European dialectologists also carried over into the planning of the *Linguistic Atlas of the United States*, which was done in cooperation with social historians and anthropologists and which employs a stratified sample including upper, middle, and lower class speakers (McDavid, 1958). Although this work is as yet incomplete, the results obtained so far indicate a close connection between speech and land settlement and migration patterns.

Aside from geographical surveys, we also have a number of studies showing correlations between speech and social groupings. Jaberg and Jud, in the course of their investigations of Italian dialects, found considerable differences between speakers of different social classes in urban Florence (Jaberg, 1936). Marcel Cohen's *Pour une sociologie du langage* (1956a) constitutes a detailed but somewhat discursive and uncritical review of the literature in this field. Bach (1950, pp. 227 ff.) gives a somewhat better organized account of German work on the subject. In the United States there have been several recent highly suggestive studies on social speech differences and on the function of speech variants as class and status signals (McDavid, 1958; Putnam and O'Hern, 1955).

The methodological approach of much dialect research so far is open to criticism. Linguistic data were too often collected through mail questionnaires or recorded by means of impressionistic phonetic notations which omit information crucial for phonemic analysis (Bloomfield, 1933; Smith, 1952). There is furthermore, as a rule, little concern with adequate methods of sampling and with problems of reliability and validity (Pickford, 1957). In spite of these and many other shortcomings, the general concepts used in the study of speech variation are quite applicable to modern research problems. A combination of the analytic methods of structural linguistics with the sampling and interviewing techniques of modern social scientists should provide new scope for cooperative research in language and culture.

In a recent publication an effort was made to bring together some modern linguistic studies on social and functional intra-language variation in India, along with an introduction discussing the place of such studies in modern linguistic theory (Ferguson and Gumperz, 1960). The present paper is a more general effort to relate the analysis of speech variation to current research trends in the study of Indian civilization. An attempt will be made to point out problem areas where linguistic data might help to clarify relationships and to suggest ways in which linguistic tools can be utilized for relevant research.

LEVELS OF SOCIAL COMMUNICATION

We begin with the problem of delineating cultural subdivisions. Most early efforts in this direction have employed the concept of the culture area as developed for tribal cultures of the North American subcontinent (Kroeber, 1939a; Wissler, 1938), in which diversity was conceptualized in terms of a series of distinct cultural wholes. Bacon's attempts to utilize this concept in classifying both tribal cultures and complex civilizations on the entire Asian continent have met with a number of criticisms (Bacon, 1946; Kroeber, 1952). There is even less agreement in regard to the culture areas of the South Asian subcontinent, where the variety of criteria available for such subdivision is so great as to give rise to many conflicting classifications (Cohn, 1957). As Berreman states in examining the applicability of the culture area concept to a highly diversified Himalayan Hill area:

> In discussing cultural affiliations of Sirkanda residents, one could defend as valid their membership in any or all of the following culture areas: North India, Pahari, Central Pahari, Garwal, Tehri Garwal, Bhatbair. Others could be delimited including some crosscutting these. Groups peripheral to some of these areas might be located centrally in culture areas defined by different criteria. . . . The crude groupings which result from culture area studies are subject either to the limitation inherent in the study of a few elements or patterns selected from the universe of cultural data and divorced to some extent from

their cultural context or to the limitations inherent in the subjective comparison of total configurations (1960).

In suggesting an alternative framework of analysis, Cohn and Marriott (1958) bypass the problem of isolating cultural wholes and, following the guidelines set down by Redfield and others, focus on the communicative processes which tie together the diverse components of Indian civilization. They view these processes in terms of four levels of communal relations of different geographical extent. These are: (1) the all-India level, defined by the subcontinent; (2) the region, defined by literary language and distinctive caste patternings; (3) the subregion defined by certain spoken dialects; and showing some peculiar cultural distinctiveness and characteristic castes; and (4) the local level, which may constitute either a single village or a group of villages tied by common kinship or other social ties. The integrative processes which tie together these levels are two: supra-local networks of relationships, such as marriage, pilgrimage and trade networks, and relationship with centers, where various sources of innovations are concentrated.

Stratified distribution models like the above find their clearest illustration in speech variation. European scholars regularly differentiate between dialects and the standard speech of the educated and urban population. Recently writers have pointed to additional distinctions between local varieties ("patois" or "Mundart") and supra-local varieties ("regional dialects," "dialects," or "Halbmundart") (McIntosh, 1952; Martinet, 1954; Moser, 1950). It is also commonly understood that these levels are at least partly independent of each other and correspond to different networks of social communication. An often cited example is that of the "dialect continua" (Ferguson and Gumperz, 1960; Trevor Hill, 1958) such as the chain of similar Germanic dialect running from Switzerland to the North Sea and including the German, Dutch, and Flemish language areas, or the various Romance dialects found along the shores of the Mediterranean in a region including Italy, France, and Spain. Within a dialect continuum mutual intelligibility is proportional to geographical distance and not directly related to political and standard language boundaries. Rural populations on both sides of such a boundary usually have no difficulty in understanding each other while they might be unable to comprehend geographically distant varieties spoken in their own language area. The relationship between standard language and local speech in such speech communities has recently been termed one of "superposition" (Ferguson, 1959a, Ferguson and Gumperz, 1960). They serve as special styles used on formal occasions or for communication with outsiders and local populations are for all intents and purposes bilingual or, to coin a new term, "bilectal."

In India, Cohn and Marriott's generalized levels parallel distinctions between regional languages, reflecting the urban and national trends of the last hundred years, regional or subregional dialects which serve as the media for the traditional hinge groups, and local varieties spoken around the home and farm (Gumperz, 1958a; Gumperz and Naim, 1960). The diversity of networks integrating these levels is reflected in further variations such as those between Hindi and Urdu normative styles (Gumperz and Naim, 1960), the various forms of standard Bengali, literary and colloquial Tamil (Chowdhury, 1960; Dimock, 1960; Pillai, 1960), the many subregional dialect literatures, trade languages and in caste dialects on the local scene (Bright, 1960a; Gumperz, 1958a).

Linguistic studies illustrating these networks may take two forms: they may either trace the distribution of a single dialect or variety, or focus on the relations between systems through comparison of two or more dialects or styles. While the linguistic methods used for this purpose will be generally those of dialectology, they will have to be specially adapted and modified for the task at hand. We will first discuss distribution at the local level since the bulk of anthropological research so far has centered around village communities and then deal with the relationship of local to other superposed levels.

LOCAL VARIATION

The problem of isolating distinct speech or culture areas becomes less complex if supra-local features are excluded from consideration. This is accomplished in dialect studies by concentrating on rural districts and emphasizing speech forms used around the home and farm. Although changes in mutual intelligibility in a dialect continuum are gradual, it is possible to draw certain relatively sharp boundary lines by mapping historical or typological isoglosses, thus separating out areas of greater or lesser uniformity. Different isoglosses do not necessarily coincide, however, and dialectologists as a rule do not attempt to assign each single locality to one or another dialect area. They distinguish between "focal areas," that is, zones that are relatively free from major isoglosses, and "transition zones," that is, those that are cut by large bundles of isoglosses. The focal area transition zone model thus draws a distinction between areas of uniformity and areas of diversity where two or more behavioral alternatives are possible, a distinction which could fruitfully be applied to the study of other cultural phenomena.

Speech communities differ in the ease with which they lend themselves to subdivision. Scholars working in Italy have found little difficulty in defining large relatively homogeneous dialect regions, such as Piedmont and Liguria, which are sharply cut off from others by series of important isoglosses. In central France, on the other hand, speech is much less diverse and changes are so gradual that some of the early Romance dialectologists have categorically stated that since each word has its own history and distribution, it is impossible to separate out distinct dialect areas (Bach, 1950; Jaberg, 1936). The opposite is the case in southwest Germany, where diversity is so great that many villages can be said to have dialects of their own. The problem of evaluating dialect boundaries has been solved in part by distinguishing between more or less important bundles of isoglosses, but there is little agreement on criteria to be used for this. Already in 1931 Troubetzkoy (1949a) pointed out that the use of phonemic in place of the usual phonetic or lexical isoglosses might lead to a clearer definition of speech boundaries. Since Troubetzkoy's time, structural linguists have developed a number of conceptual schemes suitable for comparing phonemic structures of dialects. Best known among these are the overall pattern developed for English by Trager and Smith (1951) and the related common core approach which was recently illustrated by J. C. Catford (1958). Another approach is the distinctive feature analysis as developed by Jakobson and others which has recently been applied to the study of Slavic dialects by Stankiewicz (1956). So far, however, these methods have been used primarily for the comparison of dialect areas. They have not been applied to the study of particular dialect boundaries.

A preliminary survey of three village dialects in the Hindi area of North India utilizing a technique of grading isoglosses adapted from that suggested by Troubetzkoy discovered a number of isoglosses of varying degrees of structural importance (Gumperz, 1958b). The data suggest that transition from one type of phonemic structure to another is not as abrupt as one might suppose. Phonemic contrasts tend to show a decrease in functional load and phonetic distinctiveness as one approaches an isogloss. Thus, for example, in the case of the retroflex and dental nasals *n* and *ṇ* which contrast in the western portion of the region studied and not in the eastern section, we find that the number of words with the retroflex nasal decreases as we go east. Furthermore, whereas in the west the retroflex and the dental are clearly distinguishable phonetically, when we come closer to the boundary this phonetic distribution becomes more and more difficult to hear. The phonetic interval decreases until the distinction is audible only in slow speech. Similar phenomena were observed by Moulton in his recent study of Swiss dialects (1960). There is therefore little reason to believe that the use of structural in place of phonetic or lexical isoglosses will obviate the need for distinguishing between focal areas and transition zones.

The cultural correlates of local village dialects may be studied either from the historical point of view or from the point of view of present-day social relationships. The social historian might ask: What are the connections with territorial boundaries and settlement and migration patterns? Is it possible to find clear relationships such as exist in Europe? Grierson's dialect survey for the Hindi area as a whole shows many north-south isoglosses and few boundaries going from east to west (1916). This could be a reflection of the direction of Aryan colonization, or the spread of Brahminical influences which proceeded east along the Ganges and then fanned out to the north and south. One recent study seems to confirm this view (Agraval, 1959). There are many aspects of

Indian civilization, however, which should keep us from drawing overhasty conclusions. Cohn and Marriott point to the diversity of administrative, economic, and religious centers and of market and pilgrimage networks which seems much greater than in other parts of the world. Possibly this diversity is also reflected in language boundaries.

The present-day social correlates of language isoglosses are usually described in terms of communication density. Bloomfield's illustration of this concept has a great deal of similarity with the sociogram of the modern social psychologist (1933, p. 46). But it does not seem likely that a conventional sociogram compiled on the basis of research with small groups will coincide with important speech boundaries. Work in Germany seems to point to connections with larger networks such as those dominated by administrative and market centers (Bach, 1950). For India it might be of interest to investigate correlations of local dialects with marriage networks such as those described by Rowe (1961), geographical distribution patterns of dominant caste groups or with trading and pilgrimage networks. Since traders and pilgrims do not ordinarily occupy high positions in the local caste hierarchy, it is doubtful whether their contacts with the village have as profound an effect as kinship ties. But this is a matter for further study. Cooperative surveys by anthropologists and linguists covering both focal areas and transition zones which would sample highly diversified hill areas such as that described by Berreman (1960), as well as the more uniform plains regions, might provide some important insight into the basic processes of social change.

LOCAL AND SUPERPOSED SYSTEMS

Although most dialect surveys concentrate on the speech of the home and farm, it is well known that local varieties coexist with supra-local or superposed styles or dialects. Even small rural communities are rarely completely uniform, but usually show a diversity of speech styles. Angus McIntosh, in illustrating this problem in Scotland states:

> . . . there may exist in any given community a complex linguistic situation, for members of the community may differ greatly . . . in the way they talk. At one end of the scale, there is in many places the "broad" local dialect speaker who is least affected by influence from the outside; at the other there may be someone whose speech has no perceptible regional characteristics at all. In between these extremes there may be intermediate types of speech and some people will have more than one at their command, each available for appropriate occasions (1952, p. 29).

He also speaks of "a network of dialects each inevitably influencing the other." The coexistence of local and supra-local forms within the same locality finds its behavioral correlate in the anthropologist's concepts of "levels of sociocultural integration" (Steward, 1951). The systematic treatment of the linguistic phenomena involved has so far been considered outside the scope of dialectology, but as McIntosh suggests and as we will attempt to show below it can be of great importance for the study of civilizational processes.

In a general discussion of the problem of coexistent styles, Trevor Hill (1958) suggests a distinction between two types of varieties: "vernaculars" transmitted by parents to children, and "koinée" such as trade languages and standard languages. We will adopt Hill's distinction. The term "vernacular" will be employed for the form of speech used in the home and in the local peer group. This is not always the same as that transmitted to children by parents since it is quite possible that age grading is as important as family background in shaping basic speech patterns (Hockett, 1950). For all other styles of speech found in the village we will use the term "argot" and define it as any speech variety distinct from that used around the home and the local peer group, which serves as the norm in one or more socially definable communication situations.

Linguistic diversity in rural South Asia is relatively greater than in Europe. The local dialects discussed above serve as vernaculars for most villagers. There may also be some untouchable groups with distinct vernaculars of their own (Gumperz, 1958a). In addition to the vernaculars there will be several argots. One form of the sub-regional dialect is used with traders from nearby bazaar towns. Other different forms may be employed with wandering performers or religious ascetics. There is some evidence to show that in earlier times two or three different sub-regional literary dialects cultivated by different groups of literati coexisted in the same region. Thus, wandering ascetics of the Krishna cult might use Braj

Bhasa while worshipers of Rām would use Avadhi. Standard Hindi is the norm for intercourse with educated outsiders. We also find it used in certain religious caste or village uplift meetings. On other occasions, especially in business transactions or when talking to educated Muslims, Urdu is called for. Furthermore, a few of the more educated people know English and there are others who have at least some knowledge of Sanskrit. These two languages although not directly related to the local forms function as integral parts of the village stylistic web. Educated speakers tend to switch freely from one language to another when conversing about urban subjects, often inserting entire English phrases into their Hindi discourse. Others who do not have a command of English use a large number of English loan words in similar situations. Sanskrit is an essential component of certain Brahminical communication roles. The distinction between bilingualism and "bilectalism" thus becomes blurred in social situations of this type.

In the small urban centers the sub-regional dialect serves as the vernacular of the trading and service castes. Argots aside from standard Hindi, Sanskrit, and English might also include one or more of the local dialects. Similarly, standard Hindi is the vernacular of a few of the highly urbanized big-city residents. These individuals, however, will usually be familiar with English as one argot and will also command one or another of the sub-regional dialects for contacts with the local population.

The ordinary villager or small city dweller of course does not control all the above argots, but he recognizes their function as ideal speech behavior: if he does not have command of the stylistic norm associated with a social situation, he will at least attempt to modify his speech in the direction of this norm by borrowing features of pronunciations, verb or noun endings, or lexical items associated with it. Similarly, traveling performers learn to modify their literary style so as to adapt to the local speech of their audience. Stylistic variation seems least pronounced in the speech of those individuals who tend to their own farms. It is greater with those who have outside economic interests or are active in religion and greatest with those who seem to have political ambitions. This suggests that, as in the case of the talking chiefs of Samoa, ability to manipulate argots might be one of the attributes of leadership in village India. The need for command of diverse styles increases as we go up the scale to the sub-regional and regional speech strata.

Some European scholars have utilized lexical data to trace the local effect of specific cultural movements. Thus, Frings (1948) has given us some studies on Roman influence in ancient Germany and on the itinerary of the Reformation in Germany in early modern times. Such studies, however, usually come as by-products of dialect surveys and are rarely specially planned. Furthermore, linguistic indices employed have been based on loan words in vernaculars only and correlations applied only to social history. More detailed surveys covering the entire range of styles could find much wider application.

The effect of a new dialect or language, introduced into a speech community as a result of a change in the social system, can be traced by studies of bilingualism or of borrowings into the local speech. Widespread community bilingualism is equivalent to the creation of a new argot. The effect of the social change in question will be directly proportional to the number of speakers of this new argot, and the number and type of communication roles in which it is employed. It will be inversely proportional to the amount of linguistic interference in the speech of local users of the argot as measured against that of the innovating group. Thus, in most Indian urban communities English is the argot associated with the process of Westernization. Western influence in India is greatest in centers like Bombay, Calcutta, and Madras where we find the highest proportion of English bilinguals, many of whom carefully cultivate pronunciations modeled on Oxford English and use their English in formal as well as informal situations.

In the case of borrowing, the effect varies with the items borrowed. Lexical terms and certain syntactic patterns are more easily adopted than phonemic contrasts or morphemes and indicate less of a social change. The use to which these loans are put is also important. If the borrowed items become part of a new argot and are employed in limited situations only, the effect is less than if they enter into the vernacular itself. We may illustrate this by examining the spread of the Persian loan phonemes *z*, *f*, *x*, *ḳ*, *g* in the so-called Hindi language area of North

India. These phonemes are integral parts of the vernacular only in certain urbanized Muslim homes. Elsewhere we find different degrees of adoption. In the Delhi and Lucknow urban circles the vernaculars include *z*, *f* but *x*, *g*, *ḳ* are used only on formal occasions. In Bihar where Islamic penetration is less deep *ḳ*, *g*, *x* are not ordinarily found and *f*, *z* are rare. The sub-regional and local dialect strata do not show any Persian loan phonemes, however the number of commonly used Persian lexical borrowings is greater in the West than in the East. Similar studies on the spread of modern urban Hindi in rural areas, for example, might form a basis for scalar indices for the measurement of social change and of the relative integration of rural areas in modern Indian national life.

LINGUISTIC MEASURES OF ARGOTS AND VERNACULARS

The methods used in the study of argots should be quite different from those of the dialect survey of the linguistic geographer, which attempts to cover all variations in a single questionnaire and rarely contains safeguards against style switching. To begin with, distribution of argots does not follow the same pattern as that of vernaculars. Two social groups having the same argot may have different vernaculars. A high-caste villager may speak the same form of urban Hindi as his untouchable neighbor. Their vernaculars are likely to be quite distinct. Similarly, speakers of the same vernacular may use different argots depending on their training and occupation.

Linguistic characteristics also differ. Differences between vernaculars may appear on all levels of structure: phonetic, phonemic, morphological, syntactic, or lexical (Trevor Hill, 1958). Between adjacent vernaculars, transitions are gradual. Phonetic differences often pattern, so that if in a dialect the front vowel [*i*] is slightly tenser than the equivalent front vowel [*I*] in another dialect, similar variations are likely to exist for other front vowels such as [*e*]. Such differences are best discovered and most easily classified on the basis of detailed phonetic studies, using a highly-refined system of transcription.

Argots, on the other hand, tend to be symbolized by the presence or absence of distinct allophones, phonemic contrasts, morphemes, or lexical features. There is less of a gradual transition. Furthermore, a great deal of variation is permissible within the same argot. Trevor Hill (1958) mentions the fact that there are some Enlishmen who say [*bæš*], [*hæt*], others [say *baš*], [*hat*] for 'bash' and 'hat'; both groups count as speakers of standard English. An argot is ordinarily learned after childhood often as a result of conscious effort; and its patterns are, so to speak, superimposed over those of the vernacular. To give a phonological example, a speaker of Hindi, residing in Delhi, will be phonetically similar to that of his Urdu-speaking neighbor. The two will differ to the extent that the Urdu speaker has learned to distinguish between *f*, *z*, *ḳ*, *g*, *x*, and *ph*, *j*, *k*, *g*, *kh*, whereas the Hindi speaker does not make all these distinctions but does distinguish between *ṇ* and *n*. When we compare our Urdu speaker from Delhi with another Urdu speaker from Bihar we find that while they agree with respect to the above phonemic distinctions, the overall phonetic aspects of the latter's speech will be closer to that of Hindi-speaking Biharis.

The total set of features which the linguist utilizes in identifying vernaculars, furthermore, includes both those which are known and recognized by natives as characteristic of that vernacular as well as others that ordinarily are not noticed. Thus, the pronunciation [*bəyd*] for 'bird' is regularly identified as characteristic of Brooklyn speech. Fewer laymen are aware of the fact that there are some Americans who pronounce the words 'cot' and 'caught' with the same vowel while others distinguish the two. The dialectologist's techniques guard against the effect of popular preconceptions about dialects. Items are elicited by round-about methods designed to keep the informant from being self-conscious, so as to obtain natural, unguarded speech responses. The resulting scientific classifications of dialects often come up with groupings which have little relation to popular notions of speech boundaries. Linguistic features characteristic of an argot are generally recognized as such within the speech community. As a matter of fact, they are the signals by which natives judge and receive advance information about the nature of a communication situation. Their social function is in every sense equivalent to the sociologist's "symbols of social status." It is the task of linguistic studies first to establish the nature of these symbols and then test for their presence or absence in certain well-defined communication contexts. Detailed analyses of the total phonetic system are less relevant. New methods will have to be devised for work with argots, incorporating controls of the type used in social science surveys and utilizing linguistic techniques derived from dialectology as well as bilingual studies.

CONCLUSION

The analysis of speech variation should form an integral part of the study of South Asian civilization. Speech distribution within a single speech community in India may be studied in terms of vernaculars, or of argots. Differences in vernaculars are attributable to breaks in overall communication density, and may reflect geographical or social distance. Differences in argot are related to such concepts as level of integration, role, reference group, and the like, and may be utilized to study the interrelation between local and supra-local networks. While vernaculars can be studied by traditional methods of dialectology, new methods will have to be developed for the study of argots.

REFERENCE NOTE

The first draft of this paper was presented at the Fifty-eighth Annual Meeting of the American Anthropological Association, Mexico, D.F., 1959, under the title, "Speech Variation as an Index in the Study of South Asian Civilization.".

The following note appeared with the paper: "I would like to thank Roman Jakobson, Susan M. Ervin, and Bernard Cohn for their helpful comments. Roman Jakobson suggests that the term 'argot' as employed in this paper is somewhat awkward since it is most commonly used in the more restricted meaning of 'secret language.' Possibly 'special parlance' would be a better term."

References are organized into three parts. (A) References specific to the present paper, not found in the general bibliography; (B) references concerning speech levels, including perception of social status and identity by means of speech; and (C) references concerning speech variation and diversity, in relation to both the speech community and speech situations. For further references or related topics, see the reference notes following the other articles in this part and in Part VIII.

A. REFERENCES SPECIFIC TO THIS PAPER

AGRAVAL, RAMESH P.

1959. *A Descriptive Analysis of Bundeli Dialect*. Doctoral dissertation, Lucknow University.

BACH, ADOLF

1950. *Deutsche Mundartforschung*. Heidelberg: Winter.

BACON, ELIZABETH

1946. A Preliminary Attempt to Determine the Culture Areas of Asia. *SJA*, *2:* 117-132.

BERREMAN, GERALD D.

1960. Cultural Variability and Drift in the Himalayan Hills. *AA*, *62:* 774-794.

CASAGRANDE, JOSEPH B.

1959. Some Observations on the Study of Intermediate Societies. *Intermediate Societies, Social Mobility and Communication*. Seattle: American Ethnological Society. Pp. 1-10.

CATFORD, J. C.
1958. Vowel Systems of Scots Dialects. *Transactions of the Philological Society* (London, 1957). London: The Society. Pp. 107-117.

COHN, BERNARD S.
1957. India as a Racial, Linguistic and Culture Area. *Introducing India in Liberal Education.* Chicago: University of Chicago Press.

COHN, BERNARD S., and MCKIM MARRIOTT
1958. Networks and Centers in the Integration of Indian Civilization. *Journal of Social Research, 1:* 1-9. (Ranchi, Bihar)

FRINGS, THEODORE
1948. *Grundlegung einer Geschichte der Deutschen Sprache.* Halle (Saale): Niemeyer.

GILLIÉRON, J., and E. EDMONT
1903-1910. *Atlas linguistique de la France.* Paris.

GRIERSON, GEORGE ABRAHAM
1916. *Linguistic Survey of India.* Calcutta: Government of India. Vol. 9.

MCDAVID, RAVEN
1958. American English Dialects. In Francis W. Nelson, *The Structure of American English.* New York: Ronald. Pp. 480-543.

MOSER, HUGO
1950. *Deutsche Sprachgeschichte.* Stuttgart: Schwab.

ROWE, WILLIAM L.
1961. The Marriage Network and Structural Change in a North Indian Community. *SJA, 16:* 299-311.

SMITH, HENRY L.
1952. Review of Hans Kurath, *A Word Geography of the Eastern United States. Studies in Linguistics, 9:* 7-12.

STEWARD, JULIAN H.
1951. Levels of Socio-Cultural Integration: An Operational Concept. *SJA, 7:* 374-390.

WISSLER, CLARK
1938. *The American Indian.* 3rd. ed. New York: Oxford University Press.

B. SPEECH LEVELS

For perception of social status or identity by means of speech, see De Camp (1961), Ferguson and Chowdhury (1960), Fischer (1958), Gumperz (1958a), Klausner (1955, 1956), Lambert *et al.* (1960), McCormack (1960), McDavid (1952-1953), Putnam and O'Hern (1955) and the review of their monograph by Evans (1956), and Spencer (1957).

On levels and varieties of usage, and attitudes toward them, in our own society, note Allen (1958, Part IV) and Dean and Wilson (1959, Part IV). The furor over the Third Edition of Webster's International Dictionary has been analyzed by Sledd and Ebbett (1962) and Dykema (1963), despite the refusal of some critics to enter into discussion. On such attitudes, see Bloomfield (1944). For evidence that other major and accepted dictionaries are, in effect, constructed on the same principles that broke the storm about the head of Merriam-Webster, see Fries' discussion in Dean and Wilson (1959, pp. 271-278). On "ain't," see Estrich and Sperber (1952, chap. 16) and Malone (1958).

Much of the material cited under (C) below is pertinent to the topic of speech levels, broadly conceived, as is material cited in Parts VI and VIII, particularly regarding verbal art in the former and dialectology, bilingualism, standard languages and literacy in the latter. See also the material on modes of address in Part V, some of which is cited here also.

On speech levels proper, see Bernstein (1961), Bloch (1910), Bright (1960a), Brown and Gilman (1960), Chowdhury (1960), Cohen (1956a; 1956b, pp. 175-180), Currie (1952), De Camp (1961), Dimock (1960), Estrich and Sperber (1952), Ferguson and Gumperz (1960, Introduction), Fock (1958), Furfey (1944), Garvin and Riesenberg (1952), Geertz (1960, pp. 248-260) and report of it by Frake (1962), Gonda (1948), Greenough and Kittredge (1961, chaps. 3-9), Gumperz (1958a), Hodge (1957), Jackson (1953) and review by Graves (1955), Jespersen (1925, chaps 3-8), Joos (1962), Keesing and Keesing (1956), Kenyon (1948), McKenzie and Harrington (1948, p. 11), Marouzeau (1949, chap. 1), Martin (1958), Martinet (1960, chap. 5), Meillet (1913, Parts II, III), Milner (1961), Pillai (1960), Sjoestedt-Jonval (1938), Spencer (1957), Strauss and Schatzmann (1955), Verguin (1957), Voegelin (1960), Weinreich (1955, p. 538), Wolff (1952, p. 63, n. 3).

References not in the general bibliography:

CURRIE, HAVER C.

1952. A Projection of Socio-Linguistics. The Relationship of Speech to Social Status. *Southern Speech Journal*, *18:* 28-37.

DYKEMA, KARL W.

1963. Cultural Lag and Reviewers of Webster III. *AAUP Bulletin*, *49* (4): 364-369.

EVANS, ROBERT

1956. Review of G. N. Putnam and E. M. O'Hern, *The Status Significance of an Isolated Urban Dialect*. *Lg.*, *32:* 822-825.

FRAKE, CHARLES O.

1962. Review of C. Geertz, *The Religion of Java*. *IJAL*, *28:* 66-67.

FURFEY, PAUL H.

1944. The Sociological Implications of Substandard English. *American Catholic Sociological Review*, March.

GEERTZ, CLIFFORD

1960. *The Religion of Java*. Glencoe: Free Press.

GRAVES, E.

1955. Review of Jackson, *Language and History in Early Britain*. *Word*, *11:* 318-326.

HODGE, CARLETON T.

1957. Some Aspects of Persian Style. *Lg.*, *33:* 355-369.

JOOS, MARTIN

1962. *The Five Clocks*. (RCAFL-P 22; *IJAL*, *28* [2], Part V.) Bloomington.

LAMBERT, W. E., R. C. HODGSON, R. C. GARDNER, S. FILLENBAUM

1960. Evaluational Reactions to Spoken Languages. *JASP*, *60:* 144-151.

MCKENZIE, PARKER, and JOHN P. HARRINGTON

1948. *Popular Account of the Kiowa Indian Language*. (Monographs of the School of American Research, No. 12.) Santa Fe, N.M.: School of American Research and Museum of New Mexico.

MALONE, KEMP

1958. Ain't. *Inside the ACD, 11* (1): 1, 3. New York: Random House.

SJOESTEDT-JONVAL, M.

1938. Les Langues de culture en celtique. *Conférences de l'Institut de Linguistique de l'Université de Paris*, 6.

SLEDD, JAMES, and WILMA R. EBBITT

1962. *Dictionaries and* That *Dictionary*. Chicago.

STRAUSS, ANSELM, and LEONARD SCHATZMANN

1955. Cross-Class Interviewing: An Analysis of Interaction and Communicative Styles. *Human Organization, 14* (2): 28-31. [Also in R. N. Adams and J. J. Preiss (Eds.), *Human Organization Research. Field Relations and Techniques*, Homewood, Ill.: Dorsey. Pp. 205-213.]

VERGUIN, JOSEPH

1957. Deux Systèmes de vocabulaire parallele à Madagascar. *Word, 13:* 153-156.

WOLFF, HANS

1952. Osage I: Phonemes and Historical Phonology. *IJAL, 18:* 63-68.

C. SPEECH VARIATION AND DIVERSITY

The terms "variation" and "diversity" have been used to subsume the widest variety of phenomena, especially of a social, cultural, or person-linked sort. Hence most of the contents of this book have some degree of pertinence, but especially those relating to dialectology. In the references below, attention is focused on work which treats variation as such and which relates to conceptions of the speech community or the speech situation as the context within which speech habits and their variation are examined.

1. *VARIATION*

On variation as such, see Akhmanova (1961), Allen (1958, Parts III, IV), Blanc (1960), Bright (1960b), De Camp (1961), Fischer (1958), Gleason (1961, chap. 24), Greenberg (1956), Greg (1927), Hulme (1962), Klausner (1955, 1956), Kučera (1955), Landar (1962), Maclay and Sleator (1960), Mayers (1960), McDavid (1952-1953), Meillet (1925, chap. 10), Mencken (1936, 1945), Moulton (1960, section 8), Pap (1956), Reichard (1945), Reichstein (1960), Reyburn (1956), Salisbury (1962), Sapon (1953), Ulvestad (1956), Vachek (1960), Weinreich (1957b).

References not in the general bibliography:

AKHMANOVA, OLGA

1961. Sociolinguistic Variation in Modern English. *CA, 2* (3): 269.

BLANC, HAIM

1960. Stylistic Variations in Spoken Arabic. A Sample of Interdialectical Educated Conversation. In C. A. Ferguson (Ed.), *Contributions to Arabic Linguistics*. (Harvard Middle Eastern Monographs, No. 3.)

Distributed for the Center for Middle Eastern Studies, Harvard University. Cambridge: Harvard University Press.

GREENBERG, J. H.
1956. The Measurement of Linguistic Diversity. *Lg.*, *32:* 109-115.

GREG, W. W.
1927. *The Calculus of Variants*. Oxford: Oxford University Press.

KUČERA, HENRY
1955. Phonemic Variations of Spoken Czech. *Word*, *11:* 575-602. [= *Slavic Word* 4].

MACLAY, HOWARD, and MARY D. SLEATOR
1960. Responses to Language: Judgments of Grammaticalness. *IJAL*, *26:* 275-282.

MAYERS, MARVIN K.
1960. *The Pocomchi. A Sociolinguistic Study*. (Dissertation Abstract.) Chicago: University of Chicago, Department of Anthropology.

PAP, LEO
1956. Review of J. Dias and J. Herculano de Carvalho, *O falar de Rio de Onor*. *Lg.*, *32:* 738-743.

REICHSTEIN, RUTH
1960. Études des variations sociales et géographiques des faits linguistiques. *Word*, *16:* 55-95. [Conclusion by André Martinet, pp. 96-99.]

SAPON, STANLEY
1953. A Methodology for the Study of Socio-Economic Differentials in Linguistic Phenomena. *Studies in Linguistics*, *11:* 57-68.

ULVESTAD, BJARNE
1956. *An Approach to Describing Usage of Variants in Language*. (IUPAL; Memoirs of *IJAL*, No. 12.) Bloomington.

VACHEK, JOSEF
1960. On Social Differentiation of English Speech Habits. *Philologica Pragensiy*, Roc 3, Cislo 4: 222-227.

2. *SPEECH COMMUNITY*

On the speech community in some of its general aspects, a topic which has been less often analyzed than assumed, see Bloomfield (1933, chap. 3), Cohen (1956a, pp. 105-226), Deutsch (1956), Estrich and Sperber (1952, chaps. 5, 6) Ferguson (1962), Friedrich (1962), Grove (1950), Gumperz (1962), Hymes (1962a), Kluckhohn (1961), Lesser (1961), Oliver (1958).

References not in the general bibliography:

DEUTSCH, KARL
1956. Autonomy and Boundaries According to Communications Theory. In Roy R. Grinker (Ed.), *Toward a Unified Theory of Human Behavior*. New York: Basic. Pp. 278-297.

OLIVER, DOUGLAS
1958. An Ethnographer's Method for Formulating Descriptions of "Social Structure." *AA*, *60:* 801-826.

3. *SPEECH SITUATIONS*

On situations as contexts for the description and variation of speech habits, see the varied dimensions and approaches represented in Aberle (1960), Barker and Barker (1961), Barker and Wright (1954), Bazell (1954), Bossard (1943, 1945), Burke (1945, 1951, and the title essay of 1957), Cherry (1957, p. 107), Conklin (1959), Cowan (1948), Evans-Pritchard (1948), Ferguson (1959a), Ferguson and Gumperz (1960, Introduction), Firth (1935, 1950, 1957a), Frake (1962b), Friedson (1956), Gastil (1961), Gluckman (1959), Goffman (1959, 1961), Goodenough (1957b), Guiraud (1961), Gumperz (1958a, 1962), Hall (1959), Hartung (1956), Trevor Hill (1958), Hulme (1962), Hymes (1962a), Joos (1958a), Kenyon (1948), Kluckhohn (1945, 1956), Lantis (1960), Lomax (1959), Longacre (1958), McIntosh (1952), Malinowski (1923, 1935), Morris (1946), Riffaterre (1959), Robins (1959), Ruesch (1956), Ruesch and Bateson (1951), Sapir (1931c), Skinner (1957), Slama-Cazacu (1961), M. G. Smith (1957), Spencer (1957), Sumby (1960).

References not in the general bibliography:

BOSSARD, JAMES H. S.

1943. Family Table Talk—An Area for Sociological Study. *American Sociological Review*, *8:* 295-301.

1945. Family Modes of Expression. *American Sociological Review*, *10:* 226-237.

FRIEDSON, ELIOT

1956. The Varieties of Individual Speech. *Quarterly Journal of Speech*, *42:* 355-362.

GASTIL, RAYMOND D.

1961. The Determinants of Human Behavior. *AA*, *63:* 1281-1291.

HARTUNG, CHARLES V.

1956. Doctrines of English Usage. *The English Journal*, *45:* 517-525. [Also in Harold B. Allen (Ed.), *Readings in Applied English Linguistics*. New York: Appleton-Century-Crofts, 1958. Pp. 235-245.]

LANTIS, MARGARET

1960. Vernacular Culture. *AA*, *60:* 202-216.

RIFFATERRE, MICHAEL

1959. Review of S. Ullmann, *Style in the French Novel*. *Word*, *15:* 404-413.

RUESCH, JURGEN

1956. The Observer and the Observed: Human Communication Theory. In Roy R. Grinker (Ed.), *Toward a Unified Theory of Human Behavior*. New York: Basic. Pp. 36-54.

SUMBY, WILLIAM H.

1960. The Control Tower Language: A Case Study of a Specialized Language-in-Action. *Language and Speech*, *3* (2): 61-70.

Diglossia 45

CHARLES A. FERGUSON

IN MANY SPEECH COMMUNITIES two or more varieties of the same language are used by some speakers under different conditions. Perhaps the most familiar example is the standard language and regional dialect as used, say, in Italian or Persian, where many speakers speak their local dialect at home or among family or friends of the same dialect area but use the standard language in communicating with speakers of other dialects or on public occasions. There are, however, quite different examples of the use of two varieties of a language in the same speech community. In Baghdad the Christian Arabs speak a "Christian Arabic" dialect when talking among themselves but speak the general Baghdad dialect, "Muslim Arabic," when talking in a mixed group. In recent years there has been a renewed interest in studying the development and characteristics of standardized languages (see esp. Kloss, 1952, with its valuable introduction on standardization in general), and it is in following this line of interest that the present study seeks to examine carefully one particular kind of standardization where two varieties of a language exist side by side throughout the community, with each having a definite role to play. The term "diglossia" is introduced here, modeled on the French *diglossie*, which has been applied to this situation, since there seems to be no word in regular use for this in English; other languages of Europe generally use the word for "bilingualism" in this special sense as well. (The terms "language," "dialect," and "variety" are used here without precise definition. It is hoped that they occur sufficiently in accordance with established usage to be unambiguous for the present purpose. The term "superposed variety" is also used here without definition; it means that the variety in question is not the primary, "native" variety for the speakers in question but may be learned in addition to this. Finally, no attempt is made in this paper to examine the analogous situation where two distinct [related or unrelated] languages are used side by side throughout a speech community, each with a clearly defined role.)

It is likely that this particular situation in speech communities is very widespread, although it is rarely mentioned, let alone satisfactorily described. A full explanation of it can be of considerable help in dealing with problems in linguistic description, in historical linguistics, and in language typology. The present study should be regarded as preliminary in that much more assembling of descriptive and historical data is required; its purpose is to characterize diglossia by picking out four speech communities and their languages (hereafter called the defining languages) which clearly belong in this category, and describing features shared by them which seem relevant to the classification. The defining languages selected are Arabic, Modern Greek, Swiss German, Haitian Creole. (See references on pp. 438-439.)

Before proceeding to the description it must be pointed out that diglossia is not assumed to be a stage which occurs always and only at a certain point in some kind of evolution, e.g., in the standardization process. Diglossia may develop from various origins and eventuate in different language situations. Of the four defining languages, Arabic diglossia seems to reach as far back as our knowledge of Arabic goes, and the superposed "Classical" language has remained relatively stable, while Greek diglossia has roots going back many centuries, but it became fully developed only at the beginning of the nineteenth century with the renaissance of Greek literature and the creation of a literary language based in large part on previous forms of literary Greek. Swiss German diglossia developed as a result of long religious and political isolation from the centers of German linguistic standardization, while Haitian Creole arose from a creolization of a pidgin French, with standard French later coming to play the role of the superposed variety. Some speculation on the possibilities of development will, however, be given at the end of the paper.

For convenience of reference the superposed variety in diglosia will be called the H ("high") variety or simply H, and the regional dialects will be called L ("low") varieties or, collectively, simply L. All the defining languages have names for H and L, and these are listed in the accompanying table.

	H is called	L is called
	ARABIC	
Classical (=H)	*'al-fuṣḥā*	*'al-ᶜāmmiyyah, 'ad-dārij*
Egyptian (=L)	*'il-faṣīḥ, 'in-naḥawi*	*'il-ᶜammiyya*
	SW. GERMAN	
Stand. German (= H)	*Schriftsprache*	[*Schweizer*] *Dialekt, Schweizerdeutsch*
Swiss (= L)	*Hoochtüütsch*	*Schwyzertüütsch*
	H. CREOLE	
French (= H)	*français*	*créole*
	GREEK	
H and L	*katharévusa*	*dhimotikí*

It is instructive to note the problems involved in citing words of these languages in a consistent and accurate manner. First, should the words be listed in their H form or in their L form, or in both? Second, if words are cited in their L form, what kind of L should be chosen? In Greek and in Haitian Creole, it seems clear that the ordinary conversational language of the educated people of Athens and Port-au-Prince respectively should be selected. For Arabic and for Swiss German the choice must be arbitrary, and the ordinary conversational language of educated people of Cairo and of Zürich city will be used here. Third, what kind of spelling should be used to represent L? Since there is in no case a generally accepted orthography for L, some kind of phonemic or quasi-phonemic transcription would seem appropriate. The following choices were made. For Haitian Creole, the McConnell-Laubach spelling was selected, since it is approximately phonemic and is typographically simple. For Greek, the transcription was adopted from the manual *Spoken Greek*, since this is intended to be phonemic; a transliteration of the Greek spelling seems less satisfactory not only because the spelling is variable but also because it is highly etymologizing in nature and quite unphonemic. For Swiss German, the spelling backed by Dieth (1938), which, though it fails to indicate all the phonemic contrasts and in some cases may indicate allophones, is fairly consistent and seems to be a sensible systematization, without serious modification, of the spelling conventions most generally used in writing Swiss German dialect material. Arabic, like Greek, uses a non-Roman alphabet, but transliteration is even less feasible than for Greek, partly again because of the variability of the spelling, but even more because in writing Egyptian colloquial Arabic many vowels are not indicated at all and others are often indicated ambiguously; the transcription chosen here sticks closely to the traditional systems of Semitists, being a modification for Egyptian of the scheme used by Al-Toma (1957).

The fourth problem is how to represent H. For Swiss German and Haitian Creole standard German and French orthography respectively can be used even though this hides certain resemblances between the sounds of H and L in both cases. For Greek either the usual spelling in Greek letters could be used or a transliteration, but since a knowledge of Modern Greek pronunciation is less widespread than a knowledge of German and French pronunciation, the masking effect of the orthography is more serious in the Greek case, and we use the phonemic transcription instead. Arabic is the most serious problem. The two most obvious choices are (1) a transliteration of Arabic spelling (with the unwritten vowels supplied by the transcriber) or (2) a phonemic transcription of the Arabic as it would be read by a speaker of Cairo Arabic. Solution (1) has been adopted, again in accordance with Al-Toma's procedure.

1. *FUNCTION*

One of the most important features of diglossia is the specialization of function for H and L. In one set of situations only H is appropriate and in another only L, with the two sets overlapping only very slightly. As an illustration, a sample listing of possible situations is given, with indication of the variety normally used:

	H	L
Sermon in church or mosque	x	
Instructions to servants, waiters, workmen, clerks		x
Personal letter	x	
Speech in parliament, political speech	x	
University lecture	x	
Conversation with family, friends, colleagues		x
News broadcast	x	
Radio "soap opera"		x
Newspaper editorial, news story, caption on picture	x	
Caption on political cartoon		x
Poetry	x	
Folk literature		x

The importance of using the right variety in the right situation can hardly be overestimated. An outsider who learns to speak fluent, accurate L and then uses it in a formal speech is an object of ridicule. A member of the speech community who uses H in a purely conversational situation or in an informal activity like shopping is equally an object of ridicule. In all the defining languages it is typical behavior to have someone read aloud from a newspaper written in H and then proceed to discuss the contents in L. In all the defining languages it is typical behavior to listen to a formal speech in H and then discuss it, often with the speaker himself, in L.

(The situation in formal education is often more complicated than is indicated here. In the Arab world, for example, formal university lectures are given in H, but drills, explanation, and section meetings may be in large part conducted in L, especially in the natural sciences as opposed to the humanities. Although the teachers' use of L in secondary schools is forbidden by law in some Arab countries, often a considerable part of the teacher's time is taken up with explaining in L the meaning of material in H which has been presented in books or lectures.)

The last two situations on the list call for comment. In all the defining languages some poetry is composed in L, and a small handful of poets compose in both, but the status of the two kinds of poetry is very different, and for the speech community as a whole it is only the poetry in H that is felt to be "real" poetry. (Modern Greek does not quite fit this description. Poetry in L is the major production and H verse is generally felt to be artificial.) On the other hand, in every one of the defining languages certain proverbs, politeness formulas, and the like are in H even when cited in ordinary conversation by illiterates. It has been estimated that as much as one-fifth of the proverbs in the active repertory of Arab villagers are in H (JAOS, 1955, *75:* 124 ff.).

2. *PRESTIGE*

In all the defining languages the speakers regard H as superior to L in a number of respects. Sometimes the feeling is so strong that H alone is regarded as real and L is reported "not to exist." Speakers of Arabic, for example, may say (in L) that so-and-so doesn't know Arabic. This normally means he doesn't know H, although he may be a fluent, effective speaker of L. If a non-speaker of Arabic asks an educated Arab for help in learning to speak Arabic the Arab will normally try to teach him H forms, insisting that these are the only ones to use. Very often, educated Arabs will maintain that they never use L at all, in spite of the fact that direct observation shows that they use it constantly in all ordinary conversation. Similarly, educated speakers of Haitian Creole frequently deny its existence, insisting that they always speak French. This attitude cannot be called a deliberate attempt to deceive the questioner, but seems almost a self-deception. When the speaker in question is replying in good faith, it is often possible to break through these attitudes by asking such questions as what kind of language he uses in speaking to his children, to servants, or to his mother. The very revealing reply is usually something like: "Oh, but they wouldn't understand [the H form, whatever it is called]."

Even where the feeling of the reality and superiority of H is not so strong, there is usually a belief that H is somehow more beautiful, more logical, better able to express important thoughts, and the like. And this belief is held also by speakers whose command of H is quite limited. To those Americans who would like to evaluate speech in terms of effectiveness of communication it comes as a shock to discover that many speakers of a language involved in diglossia characteristically prefer to hear a political speech or an expository lecture or a recitation of poetry in H even though it may be less intelligible to them than it would be in L.

In some cases the superiority of H is connected with religion. In Greek the language of the New Testament is felt to be essentially the same as the *katharévusa*, and the appearance of a translation of the New Testament in *dhimotikí* was the occasion for serious rioting in Greece in 1903. Speakers of Haitian Creole are generally accustomed to a French version of the Bible, and even when the Church uses Creole for catechisms, and the like, it resorts to a highly Gallicized spelling. For Arabic, H is the language of the Qur'an and as such is widely believed to constitute the actual words of God and even to be outside the limits of space and time, i.e., to have existed "before" time began with the creation of the world.

3. *LITERARY HERITAGE*

In every one of the defining languages there is a sizable body of written literature in H which is held in high esteem by the speech community, and contemporary literary production in H by members of the community is felt to be part of this otherwise existing literature. The body of literature may either have been produced long ago in the past history of the community or be in continuous production in another speech community in which H serves as the standard variety of the language. When the body of literature represents a long time span (as in Arabic or Greek) contemporary writers—and readers—tend to regard it as a legitimate practice to utilize words, phrases, or constructions which may have been current only at one period of the literary history and are not in widespread use at the present time. Thus it may be good journalistic usage in writing editorials, or good literary taste in composing poetry, to employ a complicated Classical Greek participial construction or a rare twelfth-century Arabic expression which it can be assumed the average educated reader will not understand without research on his part. One effect of such usage is appreciation on the part of some readers: "So-and-so really knows his Greek [or Arabic]," or "So-and-so's editorial today, or latest poem, is very good Greek [or Arabic]."

4. *ACQUISITION*

Among speakers of the four defining languages adults use L in speaking to children and children use L in speaking to one another. As a result, L is learned by children in what may be regarded as the "normal" way of learning one's mother tongue. H may be heard by children from time to time, but the actual learning of H is chiefly accomplished by the means of formal education, whether this be traditional Qur'anic schools, modern government schools, or private tutors.

This difference in method of acquisition is very important. The speaker is at home in L to a degree he almost never achieves in H. The grammatical structure of L is learned without explicit discussion of grammatical concepts; the grammar of H is learned in terms of "rules" and norms to be imitated.

It seems unlikely that any change toward full utilization of H could take place without a radical change in this pattern of acquisition. For example, those Arabs who ardently desire to have L replaced by H for all functions can hardly expect this to happen if they are unwilling to speak H to their children. (It has been very plausibly suggested that there are psychological implications following from this linguistic duality. This certainly deserves careful experimental investigation. On this point, see the highly controversial article which seems to me to contain some important kernels of truth along with much which cannot be supported—Shouby [1951].)

5. *STANDARDIZATION*

In all the defining languages there is a strong tradition of grammatical study of the H form of the language. There are grammars, dictionaries, treatises on pronunciation, style, and so on. There is an established norm for pronunciation, grammar, and vocabulary which allows variation only within certain limits. The orthography is well established and has little variation. By contrast, descriptive and normative studies of the L form are either non-existent or relatively recent and slight in quantity. Often they have been carried out first or chiefly by scholars OUTSIDE the speech community and are written in other languages. There is no settled orthography and there is wide variation in pronunciation, grammar, and vocabulary.

In the case of relatively small speech communities with a single important center of communication (e.g., Greece, Haiti) a kind of standard L may arise which speakers of other dialects imitate and which tends to spread like any standard variety except that it remains limited to the functions for which L is appropriate.

In speech communities which have no single most important center of communication a number of regional L's may arise. In the Arabic speech community, for example, there is no standard L corresponding to educated Athenian *dhimotikí*, but regional standards exist in various areas. The Arabic of Cairo, for example, serves as a standard L for Egypt, and educated individuals from Upper Egypt must learn not only H but also, for conversational purposes, an approximation to Cairo L. In the Swiss German speech community there is no single standard, and even the term "regional standard" seems inappropriate, but in several cases the L of a city or town has a strong effect on the surrounding rural L.

6. *STABILITY*

It might be supposed that diglossia is highly unstable, tending to change into a more stable language situation. This is not so. Diglossia typically persists at least several centuries, and evidence in some cases seems to show that it can last well over a thousand years. The communicative tensions which arise in the diglossia situation may be resolved by the use of relatively uncodified, unstable, intermediate forms of the language (Greek *mikti*, Arabic *al-luġah al-wusṭā*, Haitian *créole de salon*) and repeated borrowing of vocabulary items from H to L.

In Arabic, for example, a kind of spoken Arabic much used in certain semiformal or cross-dialectal situations has a highly classical vocabulary with few or no inflectional endings, with certain features of classical syntax, but with a fundamentally colloquial base in morphology and syntax, and a generous admixture of colloquial vocabulary. In Greek a kind of mixed language has become appropriate for a large part of the press.

The borrowing of lexical items from H to L is clearly analogous (or for the periods when actual diglossia was in effect in these languages, identical) with the learned borrowings from Latin to Romance languages or the Sanskrit *tatsamas* in Middle and New Indo-Aryan. (The exact nature of this borrowing process deserves careful investigation, especially for the important "filter effect" of the pronunciation and grammar of H occurring in those forms of middle language which often serve as the connecting link by which the loans are introduced into the "pure" L.)

7. *GRAMMAR*

One of the most striking differences between H and L in the defining languages is in the grammatical structure: H has grammatical categories not present in L and has an inflectional system of nouns and verbs which is much reduced or totally absent in L. For example, Classical Arabic has three cases in the noun, marked by endings; colloquial dialects have none. Standard German has four cases in the noun and two non-periphrastic indicative tenses in the verb; Swiss German has three cases in the noun and only one simple indicative tense. *Katharévusa* has four cases, *dhimotikí* three. French has gender and number in the noun, Creole has neither. Also, in every one of the defining languages there seem to be several striking differences of word order as well as a thorough-going set of differences in the use of introductory and connective particles. It is certainly safe to say that in diglossia *there are always extensive differences between the grammatical structures of H and L*. This is true not only for the four defining languages, but also for every other case of diglossia examined by the author.

For the defining languages it may be possible to make a further statement about grammatical differences. It is always risky to hazard generalizations about grammatical complexity, but it may be worthwhile to attempt to formulate a statement applicable to the four defining languages even if it should turn out to be invalid for other instances of diglossia. (Cf. Greenberg, 1954a.)

There is probably fairly wide agreement among linguists that the grammatical structure of language A is "simpler" than that of B if, other things being equal,

1. the morphophonemics of A is simpler, i.e. morphemes have fewer alternants, alterna-

tion is more regular, automatic (e.g., Turkish *-lar*~*-ler* is simpler than the English plural markers);

2. there are fewer obligatory categories marked by morphemes or concord (e.g., Persian with no gender distinctions in the pronoun is simpler than Egyptian Arabic with masculine-feminine distinction in the second and third persons singular);
3. paradigms are more symmetrical (e.g., a language with all declensions having the same number of case distinctions is simpler than one in which there is variation);
4. concord and rection are stricter (e.g., prepositions all take the same case rather than different cases).

If this understanding of grammatical simplicity is accepted, then we may note that in at least three of the defining languages, the grammatical structure of any given L variety is simpler than that of its corresponding H. This seems incontrovertibly true for Arabic, Greek, and Haitian Creole; a full analysis of standard German and Swiss German might show this not to be true in that diglossic situation in view of the extensive morphophonemics of Swiss.

8. *LEXICON*

Generally speaking, the bulk of the vocabulary of H and L is shared, of course with variations in form and with differences of use and meaning. It is hardly surprising, however, that H should include in its total lexicon technical terms and learned expressions which have no regular L equivalents, since the subjects involved are rarely if ever discussed in pure L. Also, it is not surprising that the L varieties should include in their total lexicons popular expressions and the names of very homely objects or objects of very localized distribution which have no regular H equivalents, since the subjects involved are rarely if ever discussed in pure H. But *a striking feature of diglossia is the existence of many paired items, one H one L, referring to fairly common concepts frequently used in both H and L, where the range of meaning of the two items is roughly the same, and the use of one or the other immediately stamps the utterance or written sequence as H or L.* For example, in Arabic the H word for 'see' is *ra'ā*, the L word is *šāf*. The word *ra'ā* never occurs in ordinary conversation and *šāf* is not used in normal written Arabic. If for some reason a remark in which *šāf* was used is quoted in the press, it is replaced by *ra'ā* in the written quotation. In Greek the H word for 'wine' is *inos*, the L word is *krasí*. The menu will have *inos* written on it, but the diner will ask the waiter for *krasí*. The nearest American English parallels are such cases as *illumination* ~ *light*, *purchase* ~ *buy*, or *children* ~ *kids*, but in these cases both words may be written and both may be used in ordinary conversation: the gap is not so great as for the corresponding doublets in diglossia. Also, the formal-informal dimension in languages like English is a continuum in which the boundary between the two items in different pairs may not come at the same point, e.g., *illumination*, *purchase*, and *children* are not fully parallel in their formal-informal range of usage.

A dozen or so examples of lexical doublets from three of the sample languages are given below. For each language two nouns, a verb, and two particles are given.

GREEK

H		L
íkos	house	*spíti*
ídhor	water	*neró*
éteke	gave birth	*eyénise*
alá	but	*má*

ARABIC

H		L
ḥiðā'un	shoe	*gazma*
'anfun	nose	*manaxīr*
ðahaba	went	*rāḥ*
mā	what	*'ēh*
'al'āna	now	*dilwa'ti*

CREOLE

H		L
homme, gens	person, people	*moun* (not connected with *monde*)
âne	donkey	*bourik*
donner	give	*bay*
beaucoup	much, a lot	*âpil*
maintenant	now	*kou-n-yé-a*

It would be possible to present such a list of doublets for Swiss German (e.g., *nachdem* ≅ *no* 'after,' *jemand* ≅ *öpper* 'someone,' etc.), but this would give a false picture. In Swiss German the phonological differences between H and L are very great and the normal form of lexical pairing is regular cognation (*klein* ≅ *chly* 'small,' etc.).

9. PHONOLOGY

It may seem difficult to offer any generalization on the relationships between the phonology of H and L in diglossia in view of the diversity of data. H and L phonologies may be quite close, as in Greek; moderately different, as in Arabic or Haitian Creole; or strikingly divergent, as in Swiss German. Closer examination, however, shows two statements to be justified. (Perhaps these will turn out to be unnecessary when the preceding features are stated so precisely that the statements about phonology can be deduced directly from them.)

1. *The sound systems of H and L constitute a single phonological structure of which the L phonology is the basic system and the divergent features of H phonology are either a subsystem or a parasystem.* Given the mixed forms mentioned above and the corresponding difficulty of identifying a given word in a given utterance as being definitely H or definitely L, it seems necessary to assume that the speaker has a single inventory of distinctive oppositions for the whole H-L complex and that there is extensive interference in both directions in terms of the distribution of phonemes in specific lexical items. (For details on certain aspects of this phonological interference in Arabic, cf. Ferguson, 1957.)

2. *If "pure" H items have phonemes not found in "pure" L items, L phonemes frequently substitute for these in oral use of H and regularly replace them in tatsamas.* For example, French has a high front rounded vowel phoneme /*ü*/; "pure" Haitian Creole has no such phoneme. Educated speakers of Creole use this vowel in *tatsamas* such as *Luk* (/*lük*/ for the Gospel of St. Luke), while they, like uneducated speakers, may sometimes use /*i*/ for it when speaking French. On the other hand, /*i*/ is the regular vowel in such *tatsamas* in Creole as *linèt* 'glasses.'

In cases where H represents in large part an earlier stage of L, it is possible that a three-way correspondence will appear. For example, Syrian and Egyptian Arabic frequently use /*s*/ for /*q*/ in oral use of Classical Arabic, and have /*s*/ in *tatsamas,* but have /*t*/ in words regularly descended from earlier Arabic not borrowed from the Classical. (See Ferguson, 1957.)

Now that the characteristic features of diglossia have been outlined it is feasible to attempt a fuller definition. DIGLOSSIA *is a relatively stable language situation in which, in addition to the primary dialects of the language (which may include a standard or regional standards), there is a very divergent, highly codified (often grammatically more complex) superposed variety, the vehicle of a large and respected body of written literature, either of an earlier period or in another speech community, which is learned largely by formal education and is used for most written and formal spoken purposes but is not used by any sector of the community for ordinary conversation.*

With the characterization of diglossia completed we may turn to a brief consideration of three additional questions: How does diglossia differ from the familiar situation of a standard language with regional dialects? How widespread is the phenomenon of diglossia in space, time, and linguistic families? Under what circumstances does diglossia come into being and into what language situations is it likely to develop?

The precise role of the standard variety (or varieties) of a language vis-à-vis regional or social dialects differs from one speech community to another, and some instances of this relation may be close to diglossia or perhaps even better considered as diglossia. As characterized here, diglossia differs from the more widespread standard-with-dialects in that no segment of the speech community in diglossia regularly uses H as a medium of ordinary conversation, and any attempt to do so is felt to be either pedantic and artificial (Arabic, Greek) or else in some sense disloyal to the community (Swiss German, Creole). In the more usual standard-with-dialects situation the standard is often similar to the variety of a certain region or social group (e.g., Tehran Persian, Calcutta Bengali) which is used in ordinary conversation more or less naturally by members of the group and as a superposed variety by others.

Diglossia is apparently not limited to any geographical region or language family. (All clearly documented instances known to me are in literate communities, but it seems at least possible that a somewhat similar situation could exist in a non-literate community where a body of oral literature could play the same role as the body of written literature in the examples cited.) Three examples of diglossia from other times and places may be cited as illustrations of the utility of the concept. First, consider Tamil. As used by the millions of members of the Tamil speech community in India today, it fits the definition exactly. There is a literary Tamil as H used for writing and certain kinds of formal speaking, and a standard colloquial as L (as well as local L dialects) used in ordinary conversation. There is a body of literature in H going back many centuries which is highly regarded by Tamil speakers today. H has prestige, L does not. H is always superposed, L is learned naturally, whether as primary or as a superposed standard colloquial. There are striking grammatical differences and some phonological differences between the two varieties. (There is apparently no good description available of the precise relations of the two varieties of Tamil; an account of some of the structural differences is given by Pillai [1960]. Incidentally, it may be noted that Tamil diglossia seems to go back many centuries, since the language of early literature contrasts sharply with the language of early inscriptions, which probably reflect the spoken language of the time.) The situation is only slightly complicated by the presence of Sanskrit and English for certain functions of H; the same kind of complication exists in parts of the Arab world where French, English, or a liturgical language such as Syriac or Coptic has certain H-like functions.

Second, we may mention Latin and the emergent Romance languages during a period of some centuries in various parts of Europe. The vernacular was used in ordinary conversation but Latin for writing or certain kinds of formal speech. Latin was the language of the Church and its literature, Latin had the prestige, there were striking grammatical differences between the two varieties in each area, etc.

Third, Chinese should be cited because it probably represents diglossia on the largest scale of any attested instance. (An excellent, brief description of the complex Chinese situation is available in the introduction to Chao [1947, pp. 1-17].) The *weu-li* corresponds to H, while Mandarin colloquial is a standard L; there are also regional L varieties so different as to deserve the label "separate languages" even more than the Arabic dialects, and at least as much as the emergent Romance languages in the Latin example. Chinese, however, like modern Greek, seems to be developing away from diglossia toward a standard-with-dialects in that the standard L or a mixed variety is coming to be used in writing for more and more purposes, i.e., it is becoming a true standard.

Diglossia is likely to come into being when the following three conditions hold in a given speech community: (1) There is a sizable body of literature in a language closely related to (or even identical with) the natural language of the community, and this literature embodies, whether as source (e.g., divine revelation) or reinforcement, some of the fundamental values of the community. (2) Literacy in the community is limited to a small elite. (3) A suitable period of time, on the order of several centuries, passes from the establishment of (1) and (2). It can probably be shown that this combination of circumstances has occurred hundreds of times in the past and has generally resulted in diglossia. Dozens of examples exist today, and it is likely that examples will occur in the future.

Diglossia seems to be accepted and not regarded as a "problem" by the community in which it is in force, until certain trends appear in the community. These include trends toward (1) more widespread literacy (whether for economic, ideological or other reasons), (2) broader communication among different regional and social segments of the community (e.g., for economic, administrative, military, or ideological reasons), (3) desire for a full-fledged standard "national" language as an attribute of autonomy or of sovereignty.

When these trends appear, leaders in the community begin to call for unification of the language, and for that matter, actual trends toward unification begin to take place. These individuals tend to support either the adoption of H or of one form of L as the standard, less often the adoption of a modified H or L, a "mixed" variety of some kind. The arguments explicitly advanced seem remarkably the same from one instance of diglossia to another.

The proponents of H argue that H must be adopted because it connects the community with its glorious past or with the world community and because it is a naturally unifying factor as opposed to the divisive nature of the L dialects. In addition to these two fundamentally sound arguments there are usually pleas based on the beliefs of the community in the superiority of H: that it is more beautiful, more expressive, more logical, that it has divine sanction, or whatever their specific beliefs may be. When these latter arguments are examined objectively their validity is often quite limited, but their importance is still very great because they reflect widely held attitudes within the community.

The proponents of L argue that some variety of L must be adopted because it is closer to the real thinking and feeling of the people; it eases the educational problem since people have already acquired a basic knowledge of it in early childhood; and it is a more effective instrument of communication at all levels. In addition to these fundamentally sound arguments there is often great emphasis given to points of lesser importance such as the vividness of metaphor in the colloquial, the fact that other "modern nations" write very much as they speak, and so on.

The proponents of both sides or even of the mixed language seem to show the conviction—although this may not be explicitly stated—that a standard language can simply be legislated into place in a community. Often the trends which will be decisive in the development of a standard language are already at work and have little to do with the argumentation of the spokesmen for the various viewpoints.

A brief and superficial glance at the outcome of diglossia in the past and a consideration of present trends suggests that there are only a few general kinds of development likely to take place. First, we must remind ourselves that the situation may remain stable for long periods of time. But if the trends mentioned above do appear and become strong, change may take place. Second, H can succeed in establishing itself as a standard only if it is already serving as a standard language in some other community and the diglossia community, for reasons linguistic and non-linguistic, tends to merge with the other community. Otherwise H fades away and becomes a learned or liturgical language studied only by scholars or specialists and not used actively in the community. Some form of L or a mixed variety becomes standard.

Third, if there is a single communication center in the whole speech community, or if there are several such centers all in one dialect area, the L variety of the center(s) will be the basis of the new standard, whether relatively pure L or considerably mixed with H. If there are several such centers in different dialect areas with no one center paramount, then it is likely that several L varieties will become standard as separate languages.

A tentative prognosis for the four defining languages over the next two centuries (i.e., to about A.D. 2150) may be hazarded:

SWISS GERMAN: Relative stability.

ARABIC: Slow development toward several standard languages, each based on an L variety with heavy admixture of H vocabulary. Three seem likely: Maghrebi (based on Rabat or Tunis?), Egyptian (based on Cario), Eastern (based on Baghdad?); unexpected politico-economic developments might add Syrian (based on Damascus?), Sudanese (based on Omdurman-Khartoum), or others.

HAITIAN CREOLE: Slow development toward unified standard based on L of Port-au-Prince.

GREEK: Full development to unified standard based on L of Athens plus heavy admixture of H vocabulary.

This paper concludes with an appeal for further study of this phenomenon and related ones. Descriptive linguists in their understandable zeal to describe the internal structure of the language they are studying often fail to provide even the most elementary data about the socio-cultural setting in which the language functions. Also, descriptivists usually prefer detailed descriptions of "pure" dialects or standard languages rather than the careful study of the mixed, intermediate forms often in wider use. Study of such matters as diglossia is of clear value in understanding processes of linguistic change and presents interesting challenges to some of the assumptions of synchronic linguistics. Outside linguistics proper it promises material of great interest to social scientists in general, especially if a general frame of reference can be worked out for analysis of the use of one or more varieties of language within a speech community. Perhaps the collection of data and more profound study will drastically modify the impressionistic remarks of this paper, but if this is so the paper will have had the virtue of stimulating investigation and thought.

REFERENCE NOTE

A preliminary version of this study, with the title "Classical or Colloquial, One Standard or Two," was prepared for presentation at the symposium on Urbanization and Standard Languages: Facts and Attitudes, held at the meeting of the American Anthropological Association in November, 1958, in Washington, D.C. The preliminary version was read by a number of people and various modifications were made on the basis of comments by H. Blanc, J. J. Gumperz, B. Halpern, M. Perlmann, R. L. Ward, and U. Weinreich.

A. REFERENCES ON THE FOUR DEFINING LANGUAGES

The judgments of this paper are based primarily on the author's personal experience, but documentation for the four defining languages is available, and the following references may be consulted for further details. Most of the studies listed here take a strong stand in favor of greater use of the more colloquial variety since it is generally writers of this opinion who want to describe the facts. This bias can, however, be ignored by the reader who simply wants to discover the basic facts of the situation.

1. *MODERN GREEK*

HATZIDAKIS, G. N.
1905. *Die Sprachfrage in Griechenland*. Athens. Chatzedaka.

KAHANE, H., R. KAHANE, and R. L. WARD
1945. *Spoken Greek*. Washington.

KRUMBACHER, K.
1902. *Das Problem der modernen griechischen Schriftsprache*. Munich.

PERNOT, H.
1898. *Grammaire Grecque Moderne*. Paris. Pp. vii-xxxi.

PSICHARI, J.
1928. "Un Pays qui ne veut pas sa langue," *Mercure de France*, October 1, pp. 63-121. [Also in Psichari, *Quelque travaux* .... Paris: 1930. Vol. I, pp. 1283-1337.]

STEINMETZ, A.
1936. Schrift und Volksprache in Griechenland. Deutsche Akademie (Munich), *Mitteilungen*, pp. 370-379.

2. *SWISS GERMAN*

DIETH, E.
1938. *Schwyzertütsch Dialäkschrift*. Zurich.

GREYERZ, O. VON
1933. Vom Wert und Wesen unserer Mundart. *Sprache, Dichtung, Heimat*. Berne. Pp. 226-247.

KLOSS, H.
1952. *Die Entwicklung neuer germanischer Kultursprachen von 1800 bis 1950*. Munich: Pohl.

SCHMID, K.
1936. Für unser Schweizerdeutsch. *Die Schweiz: ein nationales Jahrbuch 1936*. Basle. Pp. 65-79.

SENN, A.

1935. Das Verhältnis von Mundart und Schriftsprache in der deutschen Schweiz. *Journal of English and Germanic Philology, 34:* 42-58.

3. *ARABIC*

AL-TOMA, S. J.

1957. The Teaching of Classical Arabic to Speakers of the Colloquial in Iraq: a Study of the Problem of Linguistic Duality. . . . Doctoral dissertation, Harvard University.

CHEJNE A.

1958. The Role of Arabic in Present-Day Arab Society. *The Islamic Literature, 10* (4): 15-54:

LECERF, J.

1932-1933. *Littérature Dialectale et renaissance arabe moderne* (Damascus, 1932-33), pp. 1-14; *Majallat al-majma^c al-^{c}ilmī al-^{c}arabī* (Dimashq), Vol. 32:1 *^{c}Adad xāṣṣ bilmu'tamar al-'awwal lilmajāmi^c al-lugawiyyah al-^{c}ilmiyyah al- ^{c}arabiyyah* (Damascus, January, 1957).

MARÇAIS, W.

1930-1931. Three articles. *L'Enseignement Public, 97:* 401-409; *105:* 20-39, 120-133.

4. *HAITIAN CREOLE*

COMHAIRE-SYLVAIN, S.

1936. *Le Créole haitien.* Wetteren and Port-au-Prince.

HALL, R. A., JR.

1953. *Haitian Creole.* Menasha, Wis.

MCCONNELL, H. O., and E. SWAN

1945. *You Can Learn Creole.* Port-au-Prince.

B. OTHER REFERENCES SPECIFIC TO THE ARTICLE

CHAO, YUEN REN

1947. *Cantonese Primer.* Cambridge: Harvard University Press.

FERGUSON, CHARLES A.

1957. Two Problems in Arabic Phonology. *Word, 13:* 460-478.

SHOUBY, E.

1951. The Influence of the Arabic Language on the Psychology of the Arabs. *Middle East Journal, 5:* 284-302.

46 Intelligibility and Inter-Ethnic Attitudes

HANS WOLFF

1. DATA ON INTELLIGIBILITY between two linguistic media has been used primarily for two purposes: (1) it has served as a convenient criterion for distinguishing the concepts of *language* and *dialect*; (2) in recent years extensive use has been made of such data for the purpose of determining "dialect distance," i.e., the degree of divergence between dialects of the same language or between closely related languages. The present paper explores the significance of linguistic intelligibility and the conclusions that may possibly be drawn from its occurrence. It will be shown that intelligibility data, whether obtained by asking or by testing informants, does not always provide conclusive evidence concerning the linguistic proximity of two dialects or languages; moreover, it is here submitted that linguistic proximity—as established by the comparative method—seems to be of only secondary importance in the establishment and maintenance of interlingual communication. The term "interlingual communication" will be used here to include the meanings of "intelligibility" and "transfer of information," as used by Hickerson, Turner, and Hickerson (1952). On the other hand, intelligibility data may be useful in revealing—at least in certain linguistic areas—the existence of certain inter-ethnic relationships and attitudes, as well as a hierarchy of functional value between different languages or dialects of the same language. Finally, it will be noted from the examples given that the problem of intelligibility is frequently related to the general problem of bilingualism.

Methods for determining degrees of intelligibility between dialects were discussed a number of years ago in a paper by Voegelin and Harris (1951), in which the authors introduced the technique of "testing" the informant The purpose of such testing is, of course, to determine dialect distance; the technique consists of letting the informant listen to mechanically recorded portions of discourse in another dialect and measuring the amount of correctly translated material. It thus represents a considerable improvement over the older method of simply asking the informant. This method was first successfully used in the field by Hickerson and Turner with languages of the Iroquoian family and has since become an accepted method of solving the language-dialect question (cf. Hickerson, Turner, and Hickerson, 1952; Pierce, 1952; Biggs, 1957). As a measure of dialect distance, however, it also has serious drawbacks.

The principal difficulty arising from the technique—granting, for the moment, that it does indeed provide information on dialect distance—seems to be that several uncontrollable factors enter into the testing situation. We seem to be measuring primarily the informant's ability to react to a strange linguistic medium by more or less appropriate behavior, which we term "translation." While ability to translate obviously presupposes some type of intelligibility, the reverse is not necessarily true. Moreover, the translation or "rendition" is usually made into a third language—English, in the cases known to the writer—thus introducing an additional uncontrollable factor, proficiency in the target language. As a matter of fact, ability to translate appears to involve far more than mere intelligibility. For instance, the writer is thoroughly familiar with Spanish, but finds it difficult—upon sudden demand—to "translate" portions of Spanish discourse into English, partly for reasons of temperament: he dislikes having to translate. It would be absurd to suggest that this proves anything about intelligibility between Spanish and English, about the linguistic "distance" between Spanish and English, or about anything else, for that matter. It seems clear, then, that an informant's ability to translate literally or render freely what he has heard is not a fair test of intelligibillity and hence of dialect distance.

Two points are involved here. Anyone who dislikes translating will do less well in rendering language A into language B, no matter how well he may know both A and B. Moreover, he will do less well in rendering dialect X into dialect Y, although, in this case, there is no question as to whether he actually knows (in the sense of having learned Y, being a native speaker of X). However, in either case, the choice is between "ask the informant" and "test the informant." The crucial point is whether the informant—be he asked or tested—has, in his personal life, begun with language A (or dialect X) and has learned, or not learned, language B (or dialect Y). Dialect distance testing is effective under two conditions: (1) that the informant has not, prior to the test, learned the non-native dialect; (2) that the informant is free from any temperamental resistance to translating between his native dialect and one or more dialects with which he is unfamiliar.

Still another factor entering into informant testing is the latter's psycho-cultural reactions to a different linguistic medium and, possibly, to the people who customarily speak it. That such reactions can materially affect intelligibility will be seen from some of the examples cited below. Furthermore, since the test is administered with the aid of recorded materials, the informant's reaction to hearing speech from a lifeless box, rather than in a normal sociolinguistic situation, constitutes another uncontrolled variable.

The problem of dialect distance often arises in areas with a high incidence of bilingualism. In such cases the test will not permit us to distinguish between intelligibility due to linguistic proximity alone and intelligibility due to a language learning process. Finally, the test yields little useful information, when we are faced with the baffling phenomenon of "non-reciprocal" intelligibility (Olmsted, 1954).

From the foregoing it may be seen that several variables affect and determine the degree of linguistic intelligibility or interlingual communication. Since rather more seems involved than equivalence of linguistic units, such as phonemes and morphemes, the question naturally arises what the true significance of intelligibility is. In the following paragraphs we shall discuss several cases of different types of intelligibility and attempt to draw some useful conclusions therefrom.

2.1. While engaged in setting up orthographies for some of the languages of Nigeria a number of years ago, the writer often needed accurate information concerning intelligibility between several dialects spoken in a given area. There were several reasons for this concern. For one, orthography work requires standardization, and it is desirable to choose the standard from among those dialects which enjoy intelligibility over the widest possible area. Moreover, if two linguistic communities claim that there is little or no intelligibility between their respective speech forms, it may be necessary to set up different orthographies or at least to distribute different literacy materials. In connection with his investigations the writer encountered two features which were of interest: (1) the incidence of bilingualism is extremely high all over Nigeria; this is by no means a phenomenon peculiar to Nigeria, but it may well be that some of our conclusions are valid only for areas with a high incidence of bilingualism; (2) in some areas there is a very low correlation between similarity in vocabulary and grammar on the one hand and intelligibility, claimed or proven, on the other. In other words, two dialects might prove to be extremely close when subjected to comparative linguistic analysis, while, at the same time, speakers of these dialects would claim that they could not understand each other. More puzzling, even, was the phenomenon of non-reciprocal intelligibility between two such closely related dialects. Both "asking" and "testing" techniques were used, whenever possible, but the correlation remained low. It became obvious that more than linguistic similarity was involved in insuring a flow of communication between two dialects. The phenomenon might be stated as follows: linguistic (phonemic, morphemic, lexical) similarity between two dialects does not seem to guarantee the possibility of interlingual communication; similarly, the existence of interlingual communication is not necessarily an indication of linguistic similarity between two such dialects. We illustrate these statements by the series of examples which follow below.

2.2. Nembe and Kalabari of the Eastern Niger Delta belong to the linguistically very homogeneous group of Ijaw languages. On the basis of linguistic comparison Nembe and Kalabari are so similar as to justify their classification as dialects of the same language; the territory occupied by the two groups is geographically contiguous. The intelligibility data curiously contradicts expectations based on comparability. The Nembe freely acknowledge the similarity of the Kalabari dialects to their own and claim to be able to understand speakers of Kalabari. The latter, however, claim that Nembe is a very different language, unintelligible except for scattered word recognition. They answer Nembe claims of intelligibility by maintaining that this would be possible only if any given speaker of Nembe had taken the trouble to learn Kalabari. At the same time they haughtily dismiss as extremely unlikely and farfetched the idea that any Kalabari should bother to learn Nembe. All efforts of the writer to reach some kind of compromise in this area were fruitless, and separate orthographies had to be set up for the two groups. Since the Nembe-Kalabari situation is by no means unique in Nigeria, certain non-linguistic factors are worth mentioning.

The Kalabari are by far the largest and economically most prosperous group in the eastern Delta. They regard the Nembe—and, for that matter, all other Ijaw speaking groups—as poor country cousins, definitely inferior to themselves. They alone, among eastern Delta groups, boast several large towns, such as Abonnema and Buguma; because of their proximity to Port Harcourt and the shipping approaches to that harbor, they have access to much of the lively commercial activity in this area. Nembe and Brass—the two towns of the Nembe territory—have been reduced to the status of miserable fishing villages by the shifting sandbars of the lower Niger. In other words, one might term the Kalabari an "up-and-coming" society, enjoying an economic boom and having access to the more profitable features of civilization, despising the backwater Nembe, whose political power was broken during the Brass Rebellion several decades ago. Thus, the intelligibility evidence merely seems to underscore Kalabari ascendancy. Whether the Kalabari actually do understand Nembe and merely claim lack of intelligibility for prestige reasons, is, of course, irrelevant. Linguistic communication from Nembe to Kalabari, by means of the Nembe dialect, seems to be non-existent. There is evidence to the effect that either Kalabari or Pidgin English is used in all linguistic communication between Kalabari and Nembe.

2.3.Edo (the language of the kingdom of Benin), Ishan (to the northeast of Benin), and Etsako (in Kukuruku Division, north of Ishan) are three closely related languages of southwestern Nigeria. On the comparability level there are sufficient differences to consider them separate languages, and intelligibility seems to be, at best, fragmentary. Several years ago a group of Benin notables, under the leadership of the Oba, claiming mutual intelligibility for all three groups, proposed to fuse them into one lingua franca under the name of "Universal Edo," which was to contain elements—presumably vocabulary—of all three "dialects." Actually, Edo informants never claimed to understand Ishan and Etsako, but they did claim that the latter all understood Edo. Ishan and Etsako informants denied the existence of mutual intelligibility, but admitted that many of them understood Edo, because they had lived in Benin City and found employment there. Moreover, Ishan as well as Etsako informants claimed that Edo speakers would understand their languages only when spoken to in a halting, "broken" way, a sort of "pidgin" Ishan or Etsako. All Ishan and Etsako informants were unanimous in their denunciation of the Universal Edo Project as a piece of ill-camouflaged linguistic imperialism, an attempt on the part of Benin to extend its political control. The "Universal Edo Project," since it would make mass education for a large area much more economical and easier, was rather enthusiastically endorsed by British authorities on the spot. This support served to point up the fact the problem was political rather than linguistic.

The evidence here, as in the preceding example, seems to point up the fact that intelligibility, or interlingual communication, is a function of intercultural or interethnic trends and relationships. Benin seems to want to extend its cultural prestige, while Ishan and Etsako speakers—happy enough to recognize the Oba of Benin as their spiritual leader—jealously try to guard their linguistic along with their political independence.

2.4. In the Urhobo area of southwestern Nigeria we find an example of what might be termed "vanishing" intelligibility. Urhobo, spoken in several dialects in the western Niger Delta, belongs to the Edo Group and is therefore related to Edo and Benin. However, there is no intelligibility, demonstrated or claimed, between Urhobo and Edo. The Okpe-Isoko dialects are rather divergent from the rest of Urhobo, but until recently there was general agreement that mutual intelligibility was relatively high among all Urhobo dialects. Lately, however, speakers of Isoko have been claiming that their language is different from the rest of Urhobo, and that intelligibility between Urhobo and Isoko is not sufficient for normal linguistic communication. This claim has coincided with Isoko demands for greater political autonomy and ethnic self-sufficiency. Surprisingly enough, the speakers of the Okpe dialects—almost identical with Isoko—continue to consider themselves ethnically part of the Urhobo area and claim mutual intelligibility with the majority of Urhobo dialects.

2.5. Our last example, though different from the preceding ones, may aid in further clarifying the problem.

Abuan is a language spoken in the town and surrounding countryside of Abua on the mainland portion of the eastern Niger Delta. Structurally, it is quite different from other languages in the Delta. Outside the town of Abua there is a small settlement of Degema speakers, engaged in fishing in the creek, an activity in which the yam-growing Abuans are not interested. Degema is a splinter language of the Edo Group, totally unintelligible to Abuan. The homeland of the Degema speech community, one of several Edo splinter groups in the eastern Delta, is at Opu Degema, near the Kalabari capital of Abonnema. However, since the Degema sell some of their fish in the Abua market, there is, of course, some linguistic communication. It is entirely in Abuan. Learning Abuan is simply the price the Degema pay in return for being permitted residence and economic activity in the area. Such linguistic communication is commented on by the Abuans as follows: "the Degema can understand us and talk to us; therefore, our languages must be related." This linguistically naïve comment is nevertheless significant, since it presents the problem in a nutshell: linguistic communication, involving a certain type of intelligibility (non-reciprocal), exists because cultural factors provide a basis for it. Comparability does not enter into the picture. Moreover, no sane Abuan would dream of learning Degema. Many more cases illustrating this phenomenon could be mentioned, such as intelligibility data from Bura-Pabir, Kilba, Margi and Higi of Adamawa and Bornu Provinces, the Kana-Gokana speech area of Ogoni Division in the eastern Delta, and the different Chamba speaking groups of the northern Cameroons and Adamawa.

3.1. The foregoing illustrations raise a number of questions, not only as to the nature of intelligibility or the factors requisite for establishing and maintaining it, but also as to the significance which the existence of intelligibility has. Furthermore, in a given geographic area, does the occurrence of differential intelligibility—i.e., the fact that it exists between some groups mutually, between others non-reciprocally, between still others not at all—yield any useful non-linguistic information about such an area? To what extent is there a correlation between bilingualism and different types of intelligibility? What, if anything, does the absence of interlingual communication between two closely related linguistic media indicate? We shall have to limit ourselves, in the following, to a few tentative suggestions.

Obviously, intensive research into the nature of intelligibility and into the linguistic as well as non-linguistic requisites of interlingual communication is needed. At this point we can only draw the simplest working diagram to indicate what is going on. When an informant admits or claims that he understands another linguistic medium, he merely indicates that information travels to him via this other medium. Schematically, X → A, where A is the informant, and X represents a language other than his own. Similarly, a claim that the informant's language is understood by others means that information travels to others via his language; schematically, A → X, where A is the informant's language and X the speaker(s) of another language. In the same manner, mutual intelligibility could be represented as X ⇆ A and total lack of intelligibility as X — (zero) — A. Admittedly, these are unsatisfactory diagrams. What is meant by "information"? Is it what the speaker meant to convey, or merely information as to what language or dialect is involved? Could the informant react intelligently and properly to such information? Could he, or would he want to, talk to the person who sent this information? None of these questions can be answered until we have an operational model of linguistic intelligibility.

As to the question of the significance of intelligibility, the following answers suggest themselves. On the basis of the evidence presented above we may say that the existence of interlingual communication (involving various types of intelligibility) indicates the presence of certain non-linguistic factors which make such communication possible (or feasible or desirable). The evidence does not suggest, however, that linguistic similarity is a decisive requisite. Such similarity may, of course, determine the facility, viz., the speed with which interlingual communication is established, as well as being a factor in determining the number of individuals involved in such communication. Thus, if the languages are entirely unrelated, only a limited number of speakers—those participating in the cultural contact—may actually participate in the linguistic communication, being the only ones with opportunity to hear and learn the other language. The exact nature and variety of the above extra-linguistic factors is another problem for future research. At any rate, intelligibility data would not seem sufficient for determining linguistic proximity between dialects of the same language nor a sound basis for distinguishing dialect differences from language differences.

A further factor which deserves consideration in this connection is the existence, in many areas of the world, of languages with a high functional value, in the sense that the speaking and understanding of such languages entails certain specific advantages. An acquaintance of the writer's recently classified languages into "practical" and "impractical" languages, assigning Hungarian, her native language, to the impractical group and refusing to teach it to her children. This is exactly what is meant here. Such languages are likely to command far greater intelligibility than others, regardless of the degree of lexical or morphemic similarity which may be involved. Thus, speakers of Angas, in the Nigerian Plateau, will overwhelmingly admit the intelligibility of Hausa, though the similarity is very slight, apparent only to the trained comparativist. On the other hand, very few Angas understand Sura, which is geographically adjacent and linguistically very close to Angas. A European parallel would be for most Germans to claim that Persian was intelligible, while only a few admitted that they could understand Dutch. The point of the Nigerian example is, of course, that Hausa, the lingua franca of the Northern Region, has a very high functional value: it is the language of the market place and of communication with outsiders in general.

3.2. The following statements are submitted as a summary. Whether they are generally applicable or have validity only in certain linguistic areas, will depend on further research in the field of intelligibility in general and in different linguistic areas in particular.

1. In a given area, interlingual communication—involving any one of different types of intelligibility—takes place, when cultural factors are favorable to such communication. Linguistic similarity, although it may play a limiting or boosting role, is not a decisive factor. The phrase "cultural factors favorable . . ." is deliberately vague. Obviously, a great variety of factors and circumstances come into play; these should be the subject of future research.

2. As a corollary to (1), the existence of interlingual communication is indicative of the existence of the above favorable cultural factors. Linguistic proximity may be involved here, but it can not be predicated on the existence of intelligibility alone.

3. In an area with high incidence of bilingualism the absence of intelligibility between two linguistically close dialects is indicative of the presence of "negative" factors which prevent interlingual communication.

4. When intelligibility is non-reciprocal, the language or dialect spoken by the culturally dominant group, or the language or dialect with the greater functional value, seems to be the preferred medium for interlingual communication.

In conclusion, we put forward the following query: is it possible to determine the culturally dominant group in a given area by determining which language or dialect has the most widespread intelligibility? In other words, is it possible to speak of a "pecking order" of intelligibiliy?

REFERENCE NOTE

On related aspects of the problem of boundaries, see references on dialectology with McDavid's article in Part VIII. On related aspects of the problem of selective intelligibility and measurement of distance, see Garde (1961), Hockett (1958, chap. 38), McQuown (1958), Moser (1954), Reyburn (1956), Salisbury (1962), Stankiewicz (1957), and Weinreich (1962). Note also the article by Ferguson and its references on pp. 429-439 and those by Haas, Diebold, and Dozier in Part VIII.

References not in the general bibliography:

BIGGS, BRUCE

1957. Testing Intelligibility Among Yuman Languages. *IJAL*, *23:* 57-62.

HICKERSON, H., GLEN D. TURNER, NANCY P. HICKERSON

1952. Testing Procedures for Estimating Transfer of Information Among Iroquois Dialects and Languages. *IJAL*, *18:* 1-8.

MCQUOWN, NORMAN A.

1958. Measures of Dialect Distance in Tzeltal-Tzotzil. *Report on the Ninth Annual Round Table Meeting on Linguistics and Language Teaching.* (Monograph Series on Languages and Linguistics, No. 11.) Washington, D.C.: Georgetown University.

MOSER, HUGO

1954. Sprachgrenzen und ihre Ursachen. *Zeitschrift für Mundartforschung*, *22:* 87-111.

OLMSTED, DAVID L.

1954. Achumawi-Atsugewi Non-Reciprocal Intelligibility. *IJAL*, *20:* 181-184

PIERCE, JOE E.

1952. Dialect Distance Testing in Algonquian. *IJAL*, *18:* 203-210.

1954. Crow vs. Hidatsa in Dialect Distance and in Glottochronology. *IJAL*, *20:* 134-136.

part VIII

PROCESSES AND PROBLEMS OF CHANGE

Introduction

Dante may have first enunciated the principle that languages change, and inherently so; later in the Renaissance a compatriot, Tolomei, seems to have first recognized that the processes of linguistic change had regularity and could be used for historical inference. It was not until the eighteenth century, however, that sustained study began to lay the foundations for the historical disciplines, made famous especially in Indo-European work, that were to dominate linguistic study in the nineteenth and early twentieth centuries. After that crest of prominence, historical work receded somewhat before synchronic concerns, occasionally into isolation or neglect. In the strongest centers of linguistic work, however, and in anthropological interest in language, the historical and the descriptive or structural disciplines together form the twin bases of modern linguistics.

The first step in the study of change is to identify it, and the problem of discovery of historical connections between languages and linguistic elements as products of change occupies a major part of the history of the subject and the current work in much of the world. Such problems of classification and reconstruction are represented in Part IX; this part is devoted to the ongoing processes of change. The two are, of course, interdependent. The work of tracing relationships and classifying provides materials for the systematic study of processes of change, and at the same time assumptions and discoveries as to the latter underlie the various calculi of probabilities involved in the former.

An achievement of the nineteenth century was to establish processes or principles, such as those of sound change, analogy, and borrowing, as keys to unraveling the development of languages (see Meillet, 1906a). Such processes, and the consequences of their interaction, continue to raise questions for practice and basic research, and scholars continue to differ as to which should be given most weight, or, even admitted as explanations. Their general characteristics, however, especially as phenomena internal to languages, have been mapped. The same cannot readily be said for the articulation such processes have with other aspects of sociocultural change.

Progress in understanding the processes of linguistic change and applying the results to questions of relationship in space and time seems to depend ultimately on three factors. The first is accumulation of relevant cases. Anthropology makes a necessary contribution to this task, but its degree of relevance depends upon the degree to which the analysis of the cases is affected by the factors that follow: the progressive reinterpretation of the systematics of internal change in the light of structural theory as to the nature and functioning of the linguistic code; and the integration of internal with external change, historical linguistics with language history, that is, the effort to bridge the gap between the history of linguistic features and the history of linguistic communities.

Anthropology has a particular opportunity and responsibility in the effort to integrate internal and external change, for field studies of the ongoing processes of linguistic change, microevolutionary studies, as it were, are essential. Part VII has indicated that the proper focus of such studies is the speech habits of a defined population, a communication matrix, within which linguistic and other sociocultural traits cohabit.

Sometimes, indeed, even in phonology, a specific change can be explained as motivated directly by social interaction. For example, the "compromise vowel" *ȯ* of Bengali occurs phonemically in certain environments when speakers wish to avoid either of the social connotations associated with the choice between the normally contrasting *ɔ* or *o*; the *ɔ*: of certain varieties of Swiss German is used by some speakers to avoid a clear use of either *a*: or *o*: (Ferguson and Chowdhury, 1960, p. 39; Moulton, 1960, pp. 179-180). The size of the inventory of phonemes, and hence the underlying system of distinctive features and their functional load, may be dependent on the size of the speech community, relative to the size of adjoining speech communities with which communication must be maintained (Haudricourt, 1961). Or a particular process involved in sound change may be specific to particular sociolinguistic conditions. The true complexity of such change is suggested in the conclusion to an excellent, recent study: "Paradigmatic resistance to sound change is most likely to be at work where a new morphological pattern is in the process of crystallizing and where, conversely, the phonological pressure is at its weakest, as when a newly established speech community uses a bundle of dialects traceable to diverse backgrounds and not yet completely welded into a single, thoroughly integrated language" (Malkiel, 1960, p. 346).

Indeed, the view has been forcefully argued that the presumed regularity of individual sound changes is in fact but the diachronic reflection of the regularity of synchronic phonological norms or canons of word-shape (always and only within well-defined speech communities). And many scholars have recognized that even when internal linguistic conditions explain the likelihood or the fact of the appearance of a sound-change, only social conditions can explain the likelihood or the fact of its spread, establishment, and maintenance within a community. These examples have been drawn from phonology, because it is the sector of language on which historical linguistics has concentrated most intensively and to greatest effect, and because it is the sector from which explanatory dependence on social factors has been most nearly excluded. The point applies *a fortiori* to grammar, as in the selective development of grammatical categories in a language, and to lexicon. Linguistic change is, in fact, sociolinguistic change.

Valuable results can, of course, be obtained from the "internal" study of the history of a language, for their own sake, for their contribution to specific historical problems, and as part of the study of the theory and universals of linguistic change in general linguistics. And it is necessary, and sufficient for some purposes, to locate past stages in the development of a language in time and space, independently of other lines of change, and only then proceed to correlate such stages with sociocultural characteristics and external circumstances. In favorable cases, such analysis can lay bare the cambium of the connection (as in the study by Malkiel cited above), especially if the focus is on the linguistic product and not on the total process. Often it cannot, however, especially if we lack documents from the periods in question. Thus, even though the historically known cases are an invaluable part of the corpus on which a general theory of linguistic change must be based, they must be supplemented by the study of contemporary cases, in which our ability to test and validate theories of change is limited only by our ability to select and use the data that exists. Dialectologists have done much already, and linking the perspectives of structural linguistics and social anthropology will accomplish much more.

The essential thing is to treat the present as more than a prospective past. If linguistic and sociocultural studies are conducted separately, to be correlated only later, or, if being conducted together, the focus is only on products of past processes of change, then the opportunity at hand is missed. To establish the mutual articulation between change in linguistic and other social phenomena, "What is possible and highly desirable is that social dialects and their interactions in contemporary societies should be studied in minute detail, bearing hypotheses . . . in mind" (Bright, 1960b).

If we are to see clearly the social character of linguistic change, we cannot equate the diachronic with the dynamic, the synchronic with the static, respectively and exclusively. The four must be seen as autonomous and cross-cutting dimensions, generating in effect a four-fold table of perspectives on phenomena. In particular, the synchronic analysis of dynamics, of patterned variation and on-going change, and the diachronic analysis of "statics," of what is historically persistent and stable, take equal place beside synchronic invariance and diachronic flux.

To a great extent, then, the topic of the sociolinguistic character or matrix of change forms the heart of one consistent perspective on the gamut of linguistic phenomena. Most of the contents of this book are pertinent to the question: what is the interplay of social and linguistic factors in the process of change? Moreover, such a perspective integrates linguistics and the rest of anthropology in both theory and practice. Anthropology and other social or behavioral sciences control the theory and procedure necessary for dealing with the sociocultural variables that must be taken into account. And the study of ongoing change directs attention to the practical linguistic problems of the contemporary world. Such problems are not only part of the data, but sometimes manifest processes not otherwise encountered; and the exigencies of practical work often reveal phenomena and insights that might have been missed in purely academic or theoretical work.

Indeed, the study of linguistic change today must take place almost wholly within the context of the series of sociolinguistic phenomena that have become so marked since the rise of European mercantilism and the Industrial Revolution: the widespread extinction of languages; the recurrent subordination of once autonomous languages within novel and restricting social contexts; for many languages, the emergence of new and varied functional demands, in association with acculturation, standardization, and a national, sometimes international role; the continuous expansion and diversification of lexical and syntactic resources in certain languages; the emergence of a variety of pidgins and creoles; the recurrent efforts to construct, modify, and promote languages as international media—in general, the marked alterations in the relevant contexts or social fields within which the processes of change in a language must be considered.

In his discussion of linguistic and cultural change, Hoijer clearly poses the problem of discovering the connections between the two. He indicates some of the particular ways in which sociocultural change may influence sound change, especially in relation to the degree of stability of the pertinent speech community.

In a short, well-pointed paper, Trager shows that adaptation to a common environment can result in the sharing of a common trait by languages of disparate origins. Such convergence indicates a source for linguistic areas (cf. Emeneau in Part IX) possibly apart from bilingual contact and borrowing. He reminds us that rejection of simplistic environmental explanations (cf. Sapir, 1912) and recognition of the major importance of cultural interests and linguistic means (Boas, 1934), should not lead to blanket denial of environment's role in change as a partly autonomous, partly constraining or inducing factor.

Briefly reviewing types of linguistic variation, Bright refines the thesis advocated by Hoijer by going on to suggest specific types of sound change in association with specific types of social relationship. The more active part ascribed to members of the speech community, in innovation as well as in spread and maintenance of changes, engages linguistics in considerations of role and social structure.

McDavid deals also with the spread and maintenance of a feature of pronunciation, where its presence or absence is diacritic of social affiliation. Focusing on a detailed knowledge of the present incidence of postvocalic *-r*, he shows that the distribution cannot be explained in terms of geography alone, that the spread of the linguistic trait is not due to contiguity as such, but to the spread of a socioeconomic pattern.

Fischer, like Bright and McDavid, analyzes a specific linguistic difference associated with prestige, but one of morphemic shape, rather than of articulatory habit, and with detailed attention to personality and attitudinal correlates. His pinpointing of factors influencing preference for a linguistic variant, his statistical testing of their existence and significance, and his analysis of the implications of findings as to synchronic variation for the general theory of processes of change make this a noteworthy study.

In "Interlingual Word Taboo," Haas calls attention to a type of phenomenon in which it is the perception of identity, not of difference, that leads to preferential choice among alternative forms and consequent shift in the locus and frequency of occurrence of each. In sound ethnological fashion, several cases are brought together for comparison and contrast.

Bilingualism is a mechanism fundamental to many aspects of the social role of language and linguistic change (including the kind of interference treated by Haas). After a review of the nature and study of bilingualism, Diebold analyses certain cases in Mexico and demonstrates that the definition of such phenomena cannot be narrow and normative, but must be broad and inductive, to avoid excluding part of the data essential to analysis of the actual processes of change. Diebold goes on to draw the sociolinguistic implications of the contrast between the emergence of compromise forms of speech in some parts of the world and their absence in the Mexican situation.

In a detailed controlled comparison, Dozier analyzes the differential impact of bilingualism in the same imposed language on two indigenous forms of speech and concludes that the nature of the contact situations, rather than the characteristics of the languages themselves, determined the extensive assimilation in the one, the compartmentalized resistance in the other.

Garvin considers succinctly the problem of analyzing the emergence of standardized forms of speech in terms of a necessary complex of functions and correlated attitudes. The functions and attitudes that he identifies are of general interest and can be applied to the analysis of the position of language generally in any sociocultural situation, not only situations of acculturation and nationalism.

In his review article, Bull confronts the hard choices posed by the educational needs of the world in a situation of historically derived great linguistic diversity. He contrasts the child's initial ease of learning to read in his first language with his later linguistic needs; the potential equality of all languages with the real differences among them in their present states of development; and the conflicting claims of language pride and loyalty on the one hand, economic and political exigencies on the other.

Reinecke and Cole explore the theoretical and practical importance of the unplanned crystallization of new forms of speech in certain extreme situations of language contact, Reinecke with primary attention to the range of cases and their social involvements, Cole with concentration upon disentangling the actual history and functioning of a particular auxiliary language from the misperceptions of social prejudice and linguistic ignorance.

McQuown, reviewing the problems of a planned auxiliary language, brings into focus the linguistic requirements of such a solution to the needs of interlingual communication, as well as some of the social dimensions.

Linguistic and Cultural Change 47

HARRY HOIJER

Culture, to employ Tylor's well known definition, is "that complex whole which includes knowledge, beliefs, art, morals, law, custom, and any other capabilities and habits acquired by man as a member of society." It is clear that language is a part of culture: it is one of the many "capabilities acquired by man as a member of society."

Despite this obvious inclusion of language in the total fabric of culture, we often find the two contrasted in such a way as to imply that there is little in common between them. Thus, anthropologists frequently make the point that peoples sharing substantially the same culture speak languages belonging to disparate stocks, and, contrariwise, that peoples whose languages are related may have very different cultures. In the American Southwest, for example, the cultures of the several Pueblo groups, from Hopi in the west to Taos in the east, are remarkably alike. Puebloan languages, however, belong to four distinct stocks: Shoshonean, Zunian, Keresan, and Tanoan. The reverse situation—peoples speaking related languages but belonging to different culture areas—is illustrated by the Athapaskan-speaking groups in North America. Here we find languages clearly and unmistakably related, spoken by peoples of the Mackenzie area, the California area, and the area of the Southwest, three very different cultural regions.

The fact that linguistic and culture areas do not often coincide in no way denies the proposition that language is part and parcel of the cultural tradition. Culture areas result from the fact that some traits of culture are easily borrowed by one group from neighboring groups. In essence, then, the similarities in culture which mark societies in the same culture area result from contact and borrowing, and are limited to those features of culture which are easily transmitted from one group to another.

Language areas, on the other hand, are regions occupied by peoples speaking cognate languages. The similarities in language between such peoples are due, not to contact and borrowing, but to a common linguistic tradition. Traits of language are not readily borrowed and we should not expect to find linguistic traits among those cultural features shared by peoples in the same culture area.

If whole cultures could be grouped genetically as we now group languages into stocks and families, the culture areas so formed would be essentially coincident with language areas. This is difficult to do, since much of culture does not lend itself to the precise comparison necessary to the establishment of genetic relations. Among the Apachean-speaking peoples of the American Southwest, however, it is notable that groups so widely divergent in some of their more overt cultural traits as the Navaho, Chiricahua, and Kiowa-Apache nevertheless share a core of covert cultural items among which, of course, we find language. Thus Dr. Opler, after a careful consideration of the kinship systems of the Apachean-speaking tribes, says:

> The conclusion from ethnographic evidence seems inescapable that there was an early dichotomy of Southern Athabaskans [= Apacheans], and that the Navaho, Jicarilla, Kiowa Apache, and Lipan on the one hand, and the Western Apache, Chiricahua, and Mescalero on the other, are the fruits of further differentiation and movement after such a division. The cultural evidence for such a dichotomy makes intelligible the existence of the two kinship types.

> The implication seems to be that the impetus toward the development of the Jicarilla kinship type occured largely after the division of the proto-Southern Athabaskan-speaking peoples into two main bodies, but while the tribes which now use the Jicarilla type system were still much more closely connected than was the case at the time of first white contact (Opler, 1936a).

This conclusion is much the same as my own, based on purely linguistic evidence, as to the subdivisions of the Apachean-speaking peoples (Hoijer, 1938).

The interrelation of language and other aspects of culture is so close that no part of the culture of a particular group can properly be studied without reference to the linguistic symbols in use. As illustration we need only consider social organization, the complex of cultural traits which governs the relations of individuals and groups in human society. To determine the precise nature of those relations it is always necessary to analyze not only the meanings but often the grammatical form as well of the terms employed to symbolize intra-group relationships.

An interesting example may be taken from the Chiricahua Apache, among whom relatives are divided into several groups in terms of the degree of familiarity or respect displayed in their relations with one another (Opler, 1941, pp. 140-185). At one extreme we find the relations between siblings of the same sex, who treat each other with a friendliness and cordiality not paralleled elsewhere in Chiricahua society. At the other extreme are the relations of an individual with the relatives of his spouse, which are marked by extreme deference and studiously maintained respect observances. This distinction is faithfully reflected in the language, which possesses not only a considerable vocabulary of respect terms to be used in reference to one's in-laws but also employs a special third person pronoun for respect relatives and a special second person form when such kin are addressed directly. A man calls his wife's relatives, taken as a group, *káˀìšxéhé* 'those for whom I carry burdens,' a relative form of *káˀìšxé* 'I carry burdens for them' where *ká-* 'for them' is the respectful third person pronoun *go-* (combining form *k-*) plus the postposition *-á* 'for benefit of.' If the indirect object in such a construction had reference to a relative not of the respect group, the form would be *báˀìšxé* 'I carry burdens for them': *bá* < *bi-*, familiar third person, plus *-á* 'for benefit of.'

Among the Navaho, the intense, almost pathological avoidance of the dead is similarly reflected in the language. If, in telling historical tales, the Navaho must mention individuals who are no longer living, he almost always adds the enclitics *-ńt'é:ˀ* 'it used to be' or *-nìˀ*, past time, to their names to indicate that the persons referred to belong to the past (Sapir and Hoijer, 1942, text 30; see also n. 30.59 [p. 538]).

As a final example, it is noteworthy that both Apachean and Tewan, in common with many other American Indian languages, distinguish three number categories in the verb: singular, dual, and plural. In Apachean, indeed, the dual is far more frequently used than the plural (more precisely, the distributive plural), which is employed only rarely. This linguistic device is paralleled by the widespread custom, especially among the Indians of the Southwest, of conceiving of supernatural personalities as twins or otherwise paired individuals. Among the Navaho, almost every supernatural being and culture hero has a sibling or twin, and even such inanimate but sacred objects of ritual as the corn, the winds, thunder and lightning, and the firmament are rarely mentioned except in pairs (Sapir and Hoijer, 1942, text 15). It should be added that I am not suggesting that the dual number arose because of these cultural factors; it is the parallelism, not the possible causal relation, that is here emphasized.

Despite the obvious and necessary interrelation of language and other facets of culture, little research has as yet been done which would lead to an understanding of this relationship. Yet such an understanding would appear necessary to any study of linguistic change that is not confined to a compilation of the results of change in a particular language or group of languages. If this statement sounds extreme it is because, as linguists, we take the cultural context of language for granted. Descriptive studies of language, synchronic or diachronic, can be undertaken without detailed discussion of the cultures in which the languages described are so deeply imbedded. But linguistics, as the science of language, is not concerned alone with description; this is only a necessary first step to setting up scientific generalizations or laws. To understand and generalize on linguistic change, we must see it as part of the wider process of cultural change. Because linguistics is the oldest of the sciences dealing with culture, and because its descriptive techniques have gained an objectivity and a precision far beyond that produced by other sciences of culture, its contributions to the problem of cultural change should be far greater than is actually the case. That such contributions have not been made, results in part from the linguist's extreme concentration on language alone and his neglect of the problem of determining the role of language in the total culture.

Anthropologists, too, have until recently been more concerned with the study of specific aspects of culture than with the problem of cultural integration. This has led, especially among those primarily interested in culture history, to the conclusion that culture is a mere assemblage of traits, held together only by the accident of existing in the same society at the same time. With such a view of culture, the study of cultural change becomes, like much of historical linguistics, a record of the results of change rather than a study of the forces responsible for change.

Within the past twenty-five years, however, anthropologists have increasingly turned their attention to the development of concepts which will not only better describe individual cultures taken as wholes but will also account for their integration (for a review, see Opler, 1948). As a result, it has become clear that a culture is more than a fortuitous assemblage of traits; each culture possesses, in addition to its trait content, a unique organization in terms of which its distinct components are significantly related to one another.

The culture of the Chiricahua Apache well illustrates this point. Opler (1936) describes them as hunting and food-gathering nomads who lived in the semiarid regions of the American Southwest. Their artifacts were few and crude. Because of their meager technology and because the territory in which they lived was none too rich in food resources, the Chiricahua were few in number but spread over a considerable area. It was necessary for them to be well scattered, since the available food supply would soon have been exhausted by a denser population. At the same time a certain concentration of population was necessary to guard against invaders and to provide the labor necessary to subsistence.

With this technology, it is not surprising to find that

> the central unit of Apache social organization was the extended domestic family. Residence after marriage among the Apaches was matrilocal, and so the extended domestic family ordinarily included an older married couple, their married and unmarried daughters, their sons-in-law, their married daughters' children, and their unmarried sons. The individual dwellings of the several families comprising this group were scattered a short distance from one another; altogether those camps composed a cluster of related families who shared the varied fortunes of battle, feast, work, and ceremony (Opler, 1936b, p. 105).

In brief, the social organization of the Chiricahua had a form consistent with their technology and the resources of the environment in which they lived. Similar consistencies may be noted throughout this culture, as indeed is true of any culture which has not been thoroughly demoralized.

In consequence of this view of culture as an integrated whole, changes in the several departments of a culture cannot be regarded as distinct and unrelated but must be viewed as different aspects of a single process. Changes in one aspect of a culture must inevitably result, sooner or later, in changes in all other aspects. This may be illustrated in any instance of cultural change where there are enough data to view the process as a whole.

When, for example, machine tools were first introduced to Western European civilization, shifts in the economic system followed almost immediately. Capital accumulations derived from industry and trade rapidly replaced land and agriculture as the major wealth-producing sources. This in turn reordered the relations between individuals and groups in Western European society: the earlier paternalistic and relatively more intimate relations between the lord of the manor and his dependents were gradually replaced by the more impersonal and complicated relations of employer and employee. Ultimately every aspect of Western European civilization underwent drastic change, an occurrence amply attested by the fact that we today find the civilizations of feudal Europe almost as strange in their fundamental traits as any non-European civilization.

Given this conception of cultural change, it follows that changes in language, since language is an important part of the cultural pattern, must take place, in part at least, in response to cultural changes in general. Our problem may be stated as follows: (1) Can we establish that linguistic change—and by this we mean not only semantic change but phonemic and grammatical change as well—is a part of the pattern of cultural change in general and not independent of it? and (2) Can we determine precisely the particular mechanisms which relate language to the rest of culture and through which such co-ordinated changes take place?

In respect to the first of these problems, there are a number of observations which suggest that periods of significant change in culture are roughly coincident with marked shifts in linguistic structure. It is surely no accident that the radical linguistic changes which mark the transition from Anglo-Saxon to Modern English are roughly paralleled in time by the change from the relatively isolated rural English culture of the Anglo-Saxon period to the highly urbanized industrial civilization of England today. Note, however, that no direct connection between a specific linguistic type and a given level of cultural development is here proposed. We are not suggesting, for example, that the rise of mercantilism in England led specifically to the loss of endings in the English verb or to the formation of a relatively analytic linguistic structure from one that was relatively synthetic. We mean only to say that the rapid and far-reaching changes in other features of culture that took place in England between 900 and 1900 stimulated an equally widespread change in the linguistic features of that culture.

In the same way it is notable that the period of development of the Romance languages from the parent Italic dialects is paralleled by numerous and extensive changes in non-linguistic culture which affected southwestern Europe in essentially the same period. And in more recent times, Spanish, brought to the Americas in the early 1500's, developed along very different lines in each of the culturally distinctive areas in which it is now spoken. Ethnological researches in Latin America have revealed that the present-day folk cultures of these regions are complex blends of 15th- and 16th-century Spanish cultural themes and those of the local American Indian cultures. It is not at all improbable that these diverse cultural changes have been responsible for at least some of the diversification of New World Spanish.

Other interesting and challenging examples appear in the relative degrees of change which may be noted among languages belonging to the same linguistic family. It is notable, for example, that Lithuanian, in comparison with English, has preserved much more of the Proto-Indo-European grammar. Similarly, Lithuanian-speaking peoples, taken as a whole, have been far less affected than English-speaking peoples by the cultural innovations which mark the rise of modern European civilization.

Again, the Apachean languages divide into two groups, western and eastern. Navaho is linguistically the most divergent member of the western group and the speakers of Navaho have also diverged farthest from what we may call the basic culture of the Apachean-speaking groups. In the eastern group, the Kiowa-Apache, who adopted a Plains-like culture through their intimate association with the Kiowa and so diverged greatly from their earlier cultural base, are also far removed linguistically from the other languages of the eastern division.

These examples are of course not conclusive. Nevertheless, they do suggest that linguistic change tends to slow down where the culture of a people is relatively static or slow to change, and that, when a group undergoes rapid changes in its non-linguistic culture, linguistic change may similarly increase in tempo.

Care must be taken, however, not to read into this tentative generalization more than is actually there. It is not suggested that divergent tongues tend to become alike merely because their speakers come to share a similar culture. Neither complete nor partial linguistic assimilation need take place, and we have of course much evidence to this effect. Hungarian, Finnish, and Basque have survived as distinctive linguistic entities among the surrounding Indo-European languages in spite of considerable assimilation in other features of culture. Many examples of a like nature occur among American Indians. The Kiowa-Apache, Athapaskan in speech, have lived in intimate association with the Kiowa for centuries, but there is no evidence that either language has in the least approached the other in basic type. In brief, an increase in the rapidity of linguistic change by virtue of cultural changes stimulated by outside contacts need not result in an assimilation to the language of the outside group.

We may turn now to the second phase of the problem before us: Can anything be said of the manner in which features of language are linked to non-linguistic culture? More precisely, what are the mechanisms, if any, by means of which changes in non-linguistic cultural patterns set into motion changes in language?

An obvious relation exists of course between semantic change and cultural change. As a people acquire, by invention or borrowing, cultural innovations of any sort, there are inevitable additions to their vocabulary. In some cases, especially when the cultural innovations come by diffusion, the linguistic additions consist of borrowed terms, often taken from the same sources as the borrowed cultural items. Though in most cases such borrowed forms take on the phonemic and grammatical peculiarities of the language which receives them, it not infrequently happens that the borrowings alter both the phonemic and the grammatical patterns of the receiving language. This has apparently happened in English, where both phonemic and grammatical patterns have been affected by borrowings from French.

An interesting example of phonemic alteration caused by borrowing is found in an Apachean language, Chiricahua. Native Chiricahua words never begin with *l* or *ž*; these phonemes occur only medially and in final position. When, however, Chiricahua borrowed the Spanish words *loco* 'crazy' and *rico* 'rich,' which were nativized as *lô:gò* and *ží:gò* respectively, both *l* and *ž* acquired new positions of occurrence, so far confined to these words and their several derived forms.

Borrowings of this sort have undoubtedly occurred many times in the history of the world's languages. The two best-known examples are found in the probable diffusion of the so-called clicks from Bushman-Hottentot to the neighboring Bantu languages of South Africa, and in the fact that the Wakashan, Na-Dene, Salishan, and Tsimshian languages of British Columbia, which belong to four distinct stocks, have a surprising similarity in phonetic form, probably due to extensive borrowing. Unfortunately, we lack detailed data with which to demonstrate the precise manner in which these borrowings took place.

Cultural innovations may also result in shifts of meaning in older native terms. Navaho *łį́:ˀ*, which today means 'horse,' is a case in point. Comparative evidence, together with the analysis of certain Navaho compounds, reveals that *łį́:ˀ* originally referred to the dog, the only domestic animal the Navaho possessed before they took over the horse from the Europeans. The same is true of Navaho *bé:š*, formerly 'flint' but now 'metal,' a material obviously introduced by European contact.

A third way in which vocabulary reflects cultural change is by the formation of compounds and similar derivations to express newly acquired elements of culture. Navaho again provides many examples. One of the more interesting is *nà:dą́:ˀ*, the modern word for corn. Ethnological evidence demonstrates that the Navaho aquired corn only recently and that the borrowing was made from their Pueblo neighbors, their hereditary enemies. Linguistic analysis and comparative study confirms this conclusion; for it can be shown that *nà:dą́:ˀ*, which Navaho speakers of today cannot etymologize, is an old compound of *nà:-* 'enemy' and the possessed form *-dą́:ˀ* 'food.' *nà:dą́:ˀ*, historically interpreted, has the literal significance 'food of the enemy' (Sapir, 1936; Sapir gives a number of instances of the point made here).

It is clear, however, that semantic changes, however extensive, need not of themselves exert a profound influence on the basic structure of language. Sapir points out:

> It goes without saying that the mere content of language is intimately related to culture. A society that has no knowledge of theosophy need have no name for it; aborigines that had never seen or heard of a horse were compelled to invent or borrow a word for the animal when they made his acquaintance. In the sense that the vocabulary of a language more or less faithfully reflects the culture whose purposes it serves it is perfectly true that the history of culture and the history of language move along parallel lines. But this superficial and extraneous kind of parallelism is of no real interest to the linguist except in so far as the growth or borrowing of new words incidentally throws light on the formal trends of the language. The linguistic student should never make the mistake of identifying a language with its dictionary (1921, p. 234).

But though a language should not be identified with its dictionary, it is not altogether certain that we may wholly ignore the lexical content of a language in the determination of its essential structure, phonemic or grammatical. It is after all by examining and comparing the utterances of a speech community that we determine linguistic structure. And these utterances are composed of morphemes and words, the meanings of which are conditioned very largely by the non-linguistic culture of the group which speaks the language. As this culture changes, the lexical features of a language, as we have seen, may be added to or rearranged. Our problem may be restated, then, as follows: Does the addition of lexical features by borrowing, change in meaning, and the formation of compounds and phrase words exert enough influence on the utterances peculiar to a speech community to affect the phonemic and grammatical structure of the language? If we can show that the lexical content of a language does bear some relation to linguistic structure, then we have a link, however indirect and tenuous, between linguistic and cultural change.

It is at this point in our analysis that modern linguistic science fails to provide pertinent data. We have little or no precise information on the effect of semantic change upon the phonemic and grammatical patterns of a language. Our studies are for the most part more or less painstaking descriptions of a language at a particular period in its history or of the results of changes which have taken place in a language or a group of languages between two particular periods in its history. In brief, we lack studies on the processes of linguistic change and on the possibilities of relating these to the processes of change in the non-linguistic aspects of culture.

It is precisely such studies that are necessary to our problem. The factors which are responsible for linguistic change will never be uncovered by descriptions of phonetic correspondences or by comparative grammars. These provide only the data on linguistic change, abstracted very largely from the cultural contexts which might have given them the significance for which we are searching. Causes of linguistic change must be sought in these cultural contexts; for it is here that the complex fabric of language is made to fit the numberless meaningful situations provided by the daily experiences of the members of a society. Just as a people faced with new problems in the production of food and other necessities will devise new technical means and reorganize their social structure to meet these problems, so it is likely that the introduction of new meanings and the corresponding expansion of vocabulary will bring about changes in the essential formal structures by means of which vocabulary items are organized into units of speech.

Despite the deficiencies in our knowledge, it is still possible to suggest ways in which linguistic change may be specifically related to changes in other aspects of culture. As we have seen, the vocabulary of a language varies in response to cultural changes; and so our problem becomes one of determining the effect of semantic change upon the phonemic and grammatical patterns of language. In this discussion, however, I shall attempt only to link semantic changes with phonetic change.

We arrive at a description of the phonemes of a language by a comparison and analysis of meaningful utterances made by members of the speech community. These utterances include, among others, linguistic forms having special cultural significance, such as words and other locutions defining artifacts, processes of manufacture, social forms, or religious beliefs and practices. As the culture changes, such linguistic forms may be increased in number, changed in meaning, or otherwise varied. During a period of relative cultural stability, however, the utterances current in a given speech community attain a phonetic equilibrium in the sense that sounds are combined in definable arrangements. It is this fact that enables us to make a phonemic analysis, for we describe each phoneme in terms of its allophones, the particular phonetic forms it assumes in each of the positions in the utterance which it may occupy.

Among the phonetic features in which the allophones of a phoneme differ are some which derive from the phonetic contexts in which the phoneme may be present. In Navaho, for example, the phoneme *t* has a back palatal aspiration when it precedes a back vowel, a front palatal aspiration when it precedes a front vowel, and a mid-palatal labialized aspiration when it precedes a rounded back vowel. Since the phoneme *t* occurs only as a syllable initial and is followed only by a vowel, the allophones, in this instance, vary only by reason of differences in phonetic context.

To the extent that a phoneme is phonetically describable in terms of the contexts in which it appears, it follows that a phoneme may change phonetically as these contexts are altered in any way. In Chiricahua Apacha, as we have said, it is interesting to note that the phonemes *l* and *ž* occur only medially and finally in native words. But in a number of borrowed forms, the words *lô:gò* 'crazy' and *ži:gò* 'rich' and their derivatives, *l* and *ž* appear as word initials. The introduction of *lô:gò* and *ži:gò*, then, produced a phonetic change in Chiricahua: it gave *l* and *ž* new positions of occurrence, although their incidence is limited.

But this is not all. The occurrence of *l* and *ž* as word initials also altered in a minor way the phonetic equilibrium of Chiricahua utterances; it provided, in short, a new phonetic context for all the phonemes in Chiricahua which may occupy the final position in the word. None of these could previously have occurred, as word finals, before *l* and *ž*; but now such combinations became possible. This occurrence, which as far as I know produced no subsequent phonetic changes, nevertheless illustrates what is meant by a disturbance of the phonetic equilibrium in the utterances of a speech community.

Similar disturbances may well be caused when native words change in meaning as a result of changes in non-linguistic culture. When a word changes in meaning, it will not only occur in utterances which it could not previously have entered, but it may also form compounds not previously possible. Navaho *łį:ˀ*, formerly 'dog' but now 'horse,' combines in the latter meaning with *-γé:ł* 'burden' to give 'saddle'; and Navaho *bé:š*, earlier 'flint' but now 'metal,' combines with *c'à:ˀ* 'basket' to give the meaning 'bucket.'

The same is true when changes in non-linguistic culture result in the formation of compounds. In such instances, native forms may well enter into combinations previously unknown or even combine with borrowed forms. An interesting example of the latter is found in the Navaho compound *nà:kì-žá:lí* 'twenty-five cents,' where the native *nà:kì* 'two' unites with *-žá:lí*, from Spanish *real* plus the native ending *-í*.

As new linguistic forms become current in a given speech community, whether these be borrowings, native words changed in meaning, or newly coined compounds, it is evident that any of them may provide new phonetic contexts and so conceivably produce sounds which have not previously existed in the language. It is true, of course, that at particular periods in the history of a language we are able to say that some phonemes combine and that others do not. But such rules are merely descriptive of current habits of pronunciation; they do not govern the speakers of a language, who are indeed unaware of their existence. When cultural change brings about linguistic innovations, it is not likely that the speakers of a language will be bound by current habits of expression. They may well be compelled by new lexical circumstances to unite forms in an utterance in a way that will bring together phonemes (or, more precisely, their allophones) which have not previously occurred in sequence.

It is not contended, of course, that every phonetic change, or even the majority of them, has its origin in lexical and hence ultimately cultural change. There are many phonetic changes which are clearly the result of strictly linguistic factors; for example, a change in one feature of a phonemic system may well set in motion a whole series of shifts representing the integration of the newly developed phoneme to the system as a whole. It is only the initial disturbance of the phonetic equilibrium that is brought about by changes in non-linguistic culture, insofar as these affect the lexicon of a language. Once such a stimulus to phonetic change has taken place, it may well bring in its train a whole series of compensatory shifts which eventually, like the first Germanic consonant shift, may lead to change in almost every aspect of the phonemic system.

Unfortunately, there appear to be no data by means of which this hypothesis can be given a thorough testing. We need for this purpose detailed studies of speech communities over a considerable period of time, such studies to include both linguistic and non-linguistic aspects of the culture. More important, the linguistic studies must be based, not only on formal literary texts, whether oral or written, which are at present the base for most of our descriptive linguistics, but also on ordinary everyday conversational material. It is largely in the speakers' application of their linguistic techniques to the constantly shifting patterns of their non-linguistic behavior that we shall find the contexts resulting in change.

Despite our lack of data, however, it is worth noting, in conclusion, that our hypothesis meets the conditions imposed by the nature of phonetic change. These are four:

1. Phonetic change is usually regular in that it affects all the occurrences of a phoneme in certain clearly definable positions in the utterance. The hypothesis suggested is posited on this fact, since it proposes that phonetic change begins when a phoneme or one of its allophones is, by virtue of vocabulary changes, made to occur in phonetic contexts which have not previously existed.

2. Phonetic change affects all the speakers in a given speech community together; it does not begin with one speaker and spread from one individual to another. It is, in brief, a social phenomenon, not one that can be resolved into a series of individual occurrences. The same is true of changes in non-linguistic culture.

3. The speakers of a given community are unaware of sound change; innovations in habits of pronunciation are not made consciously, as some theories of change have suggested. Our hypothesis implies that speakers are guided in their use of language by the meanings to be expressed as well as by their unconsciously acquired habits of speech. When the speech context requires combinations of forms which run counter to speech habits, this need will take precedence and so modify the speech habits of the community.

4. Sound change is specific, affecting only certain sounds in a given language at a specific period in its history. The cultural concomitants of sound change, as here described, are similarly specific, occurring in a particular period in the history of a society.

REFERENCE NOTE

The substance of this paper was presented to the staff and students of the Linguistic Institute at one of the forums held during the summer of 1948 at the University of Michigan.

This note is organized in three parts: (A) references specific to Hoijer's article; (B) references concerning the sociolinguistic character or basis of linguistic change; and (C) references having to do with processes of linguistic change, with the focus on historically specific consequences and relationships within the linguistic system (sound change, grammatical change, semantic change). Ideas on evolutionary processes are noted in Part II.

A. REFERENCES SPECIFIC TO HOIJER'S ARTICLE

OPLER, MORRIS

1936a. The Kinship Systems of the Southern Athabaskan-speaking Tribes. *AA, 38:* 620-633.

1936b. An Interpretation of Ambivalence of Two American Indian Tribes. *Journal of Social Psychology, 7:* 103-105.

1941. *An Apache Life-way.* Chicago: University of Chicago Press.

1948. Some Recently Developed Concepts Relating to Culture. *SJA, 4:* 107-122.

B. SOCIOLINGUISTIC MATRIX OF CHANGE

On social factors as basic to or characteristic of linguistic change, see Brunot (1947, Introduction), Cohen (1956a, pp. 271-354), Diebold (1961, p. 97), Hymes (1960a, 1961c, 1962b), Jespersen (1922, chaps. 14-15; 1925); Meillet (1906a, p. 17), L'Hermitte (1954), Paul (1960, Introduction), Sommerfelt (1957, 1960b), Trim (1959), Vachek (1962), Weinreich (1953), Whitney (1875), Wils (1948).

On the initiation of change in phonological features by social factors, see Bright (1960b), Ferguson and Chowdhury (1960, pp. 37-39), Fischer (1958), Haudricourt (1961), Moulton (1960), Spencer (1957), Stankiewicz (1957). On the importance of social factors in spreading or maintaining change, see the above references and De Groot (1948), Hoenigswald (1960, 1962), Kurylowicz (1945-1949, pp. 36-37), Schogt (1961), and Sommerfelt (1945-1949, 1961). On social factors as initiating semantic and lexical change, see especially Meillet (1906b) and compare with Frake (1961).

On synchronic analysis as comprising dynamics, and processes of change see Jakobson and Halle (1957, pp. 249-250), Meillet (1925, chap. 10), Pulgram (1961), Spencer (1957), Stankiewicz (1957, 1962), Trim (1959). For an account of an English tradition on this subject, consult Quirk (1961) regarding Latham, Sweet, Firth.

References not in the general bibliography:

BRUNOT, FERDINAND

1947. *Histoire de la langue française des origines à 1900*. Vol. 7. *La Propagation du français en France jusqu'à la fin de l'ancien régime*. (2nd ed.) Paris: Colin. (1st ed., 1926.)

DE GROOT, A. W.

1948. Structural Linguistics and Phonetic Law. *Lingua, 1* (1): 175-208.

JAKOBSON, ROMAN, and MORRIS HALLE

1957. Phonology in Relation to Phonetics. In L. Kaiser (Ed.), *Manual of Phonetics*. Amsterdam: North-Holland. Pp. 215-251.

L'HERMITTE, R.

1954. Les Problèmes des lois internes de developpement du langage et la linguistique soviétique. *Word, 10* (2-3): 189-196.

PULGRAM, ERNST

1961. French ə: Statics and Dynamics of Linguistic Subcodes. *Lingua, 10:* 305-325.

QUIRK, RANDOLPH

1961. The Study of the Mother Tongue. (Inaugural lecture delivered at University College, London, February 21, 1961.) London: Lewis (Published for the College).

SCHOGT, H. G.

1961. La Notion de loi dans la phonétique historique. *Lingua, 10:* 79-92.

SOMMERFELT, ALF

1945-1949. Le Point de vue historique en linguistique. *Acta Linguistica, 5* (3): 113-124.

1957. Phonetics and Sociology. In L. Kaiser (Ed.), *Manual of Phonetics*. Amsterdam: North-Holland. Pp. 364-371.

1960b. External Versus Internal Factors in the Development of Language. *Norsk Tidsskrift for Sprogvidenskap, 19*.

STANKIEWICZ, EDWARD

1962. The Interdependence of Paradigmatic and Derivational Patterns. *Word, 18* (1-2): 1-22.

TRIM, J. L. M.

1959. Historical, Descriptive and Dynamic Linguistics. *Language and Speech,* 2 (1): 9-25.

VACHEK, JOSEF

1962. On the Interplay of External Factors in the Development of Language. *Lingua, 11:* 433-488.

WILS, J.

1948. In Memoriam: Jacques van Ginneken. *Lingua, 1* (1): 133-139.

C. PROCESSES OF CHANGE

For general treatments of processes of linguistic change, consult Bloomfield (1933, chaps. 20-24), Catalán (1957-1958), Cohen (1950), Hockett (1958, chaps. 42-54, 55-61), Hoenigswald (1960), Jespersen (1922, chaps. 14-21), Lehmann (1962), Martinet (1960, chap. 1), Meillet (1911, 1918, 1929), Paul (1960), Sapir (1921, chaps. 7-9), Sturtevant (1947, 1961), Vendryes (1925).

On various aspects of sound change, see, besides the above, Brown and Hildum (1956, note p. 419), Estrich and Sperber (1952, chap. 7); Garde (1961), Halle (1962, pp. 66-72), Haudricourt and Juilland (1949), A. A. Hill (1936), Householder (1962, p. 73), Jakobson (1929, 1931a, 1949), Jones (1950, chap. 32), Juilland (1953), Kent (1936), Kurylowicz (1948), Malkiel (1960a, 1962b), Martinet (1952, 1955, 1957, 1960), Penzl (1957), Smithers (1954), Stankiewicz (1957), Vachek (1961), Zipf (1929), and references above on social factors initiating change.

For arguments that genetic factors may play a part in sound change, see Brosnahan (1961) and compare the earlier views of Van Ginneken as described by Wils (1948.)

On certain functional aspects of grammatical change, see, besides the general references above, Garde (1961), Kurylowicz (1945-1949), Malkiel (1957-1958, 1960b), Mańczak (1958), Meillet (1912), Stankiewicz (1960, 1961, 1962). On drift, see Sapir (1921, chap. 7), McIntosh (1961, pp. 335-336), and Vachek (1961); McQuown (1956), and Cowgill (1963); cf. Meillet (1918; 1934, chap. 9, section 2) and also the considerations in Hymes (1958b, 1961a). See also references in Part IV.

On various aspects of semantic and lexical change, see, besides the general references above, Dozier (1955), Estrich and Sperber (1952, chaps 7-12), Greenough and Kittredge (1961, chaps. 9-26), Guiraud (1958a, chap. 4), Haas (1941), Hoenigswald (1960), Kronasser (1952), Marouzeau (1949), Gustav Stern (1931), Ullmann (1957, pp. 171-257). On adaptive aspects of lexical and semantic change, see also Part V and articles by Dozier, Garvin, and Bull and their references in this part.

For taboo, borrowing, bilingualism, acculturation, development of standard languages, and the like as processes of change, see references to subsequent articles in this Part. Many aspects of change are discussed or implied in Part IX, including some not treated here, such as rate of change, substratum, and areal relationship.

For useful accounts of the operation of processes of change (with attention to social context) in terms of the development of whole languages, note, on English, Baugh (1935), Bryant (1962), Jackson (1953), and Jespersen (1905); on French, Brunot (1905-); on Greek, Meillet (1913); and various works in the series "The Great Languages" (see listings under Palmer on p. 466). For a valuable account of a perspective on processes of change, recognized as distinctive, see Malkiel (1964).

References not in the general bibliography:

BAUGH, ALBERT C.

1935. *A History of the English Language.* New York: Appleton-Century. [Reviewed, R. G. Kent, *Lg.*, 1936, *12:* 73-75.]

BROSNAHAN, L.

1961. *The Sounds of Language. An Inquiry into the Role of Genetic Factors in the Development of Sound Systems.* Cambridge: Heffer.

BROWN, ROGER W., and DONALD C. HILDUM

1956. Expectancy and the Perception of Syllables. *Lg., 32:* 411-419.

BRUNOT, FERDINAND

1905-1953. *Histoire de la langue française des origines à 1900.* Paris: Colin. Vols. 1-15. (Incomplete) (Volumes 11-15 by Charles Bruneau.)

COWGILL, W.

1963. A Search for Universals in Indo-European Diachronic Morphology. In J. Greenberg (Ed.), *Universals in Language.* Cambridge: The M.I.T. Press. Pp. 91-113.

HAAS, MARY R.

1941. A Popular Etymology in Muskogee. *Lg., 17:* 340-341.

HAUDRICOURT, A., and A. G. JUILLAND

1949. *Essai pour une histoire structurale du phonetisme français.* Paris. Klincksieck.

HILL, A. A.

1936. Phonetic and Phonemic Change. *Lg., 12:* 15-22. [Also in Martin Joos (Ed.), *Readings in Linguistics.* Washington. D.C.: American Council of Learned Societies, 1957. Pp. 81-84.]

HOUSEHOLDER, F. W., JR.

1962. Review of H. Hoenigswald, *Language Change and Linguistic Reconstruction. IJAL, 28:* 69-97.

JONES, DANIEL

1950. *The Phoneme: Its Nature and Use.* Cambridge: Heffer.

JUILLAND, A. G.

1953. Bibliography of Diachronic Phonemics. *Word, 9:* 198-209.

KENT, R. G.

1936. Assimilation and Dissimilation. *Lg., 12:* 245-258.

KURYLOWICZ, J.

1948. Le Sens des mutations consonantiques. *Lingua, 1:* 77-85.

MCINTOSH, ANGUS

1961. Patterns and Ranges. *Lg., 37:* 325-337.

MCQUOWN, N. A.

1956. Evidence for a Synthetic Trend in Totonacan. *Lg., 32:* 78-80.

MALKIEL, YAKOV

1957-1958. Diachronic Hypercharacterization in Romance. *Archivum Linguisticum, 9:* 79-113; *10:* 1-36.

1960b. A Tentative Typology of Romance Historical Grammars. *Lingua, 9:* 321-416.

MAŃCZAK, W.

1958. Tendances générales des changements analogiques, I, II. *Lingua, 7* (3): 298-325; *7* (4): 387-420.

MARTINET, A.

1952. Function, Structure and Sound Change. *Word, 8:* 1-32.

1957. Phonetics and Linguistic Evolution. In L. Kaiser (Ed.), *Manual of Phonetics.* Amsterdam: North-Holland. Pp. 252-273.

MEILLET, A.

1911. Différenciation et unification dans les langues. *Scientia* (Rivista di scienzia) *9.* In Meillet, *Linguistique historique et linguistique générale.* (2nd ed.) (Collection Linguistique, Société de Linguistique de Paris, No. 8.) Paris: Champion, 1926-1936. 2 vols. (Reprinted, 1938-1948.)

1912. L'Évolution des formes grammaticales. *Scientia, 12.* [In Meillet, 1926-1936, vol. I pp., 130-148.]

1918. Convergence des développements linguistiques. *Revue Philosophique,* February. [In Meillet, 1926-1936, vol. I, pp. 61-75.]

1929. Le Développement des langues. In *Continu et Discontinu.* Paris: Bloud and Gay. Pp. 119 ff. [In Meillet, 1926-1936, vol. II, pp. 70-83.]

PALMER, L. R. (GENERAL ED.)

"The Great Languages" (Series). London: Faber and Faber; New York: Macmillan.

1948. R. A. D. Forrest. *The Chinese Language.*

1954. L. R. Palmer. *The Latin Language.* [Reviewed, E. Pulgram, *Lg.*, 1954, *30:* 499-503.]

1955. T. Burrough. *The Sanskit Language.* [Reviewed, P. Thieme, *Lg.*, 1955, *31:* 428-448.]

1958. R. Priebsch and W. E. Collinson. *The German Language.* (4th ed.)

1960. W. D. Elcock, *The Romance Languages.*

PENZL, H.

1957. The Evidence for Phonemic Changes. In Ernst Pulgram (Ed.), *Studies Presented to Joshua Whatmough.* The Hague: Mouton. Pp. 193-208.

STANKIEWICZ, EDWARD

1960. The Consonantal Alternations in the Slavic Declensions. *Word, 16:* 183-203, esp. pp. 184-193.

1961. Grammatical Neutralization in Slavic Expressive Forms. *Word, 17:* 128-145.

1962. The Interdependence of Paradigmatic and Derivational Patterns. *Word, 18* (1-2): 1-22.

STURTEVANT, E. L.

1961. *Linguistic Change. An Introduction to the Historical Study of Language.* Chicago: University of Chicago Press (Phoenix Books, 60). (1st ed., 1917.)

VACHEK, JOSEF

1961. Some Less Familiar Aspects of the Analytical Trend of English. *Studies in the Linguistic Characterology of Modern English.* (Brno Studies in English, No. 3.) Praha: Státní Pedagogické Nakladatelství. Pp. 9-78.

1962. On the Interplay of External Factors in the Development of Language. *Lingua, 11:* 433-448.

WILS, J.

1948. In Memoriam: Jacques van Ginneken. *Lingua, 1* (1): 133-139.

ZIPF, G. K.

1929. Relative Frequency as a Determinant of Phonetic Change. *Harvard Studies in Classical Philology, 40:* 1-95 [Reviewed, R. G. Kent, *Lg.*, 1930, *6:* 86-88.]

"Cottonwood" = "Tree": A Southwestern Linguistic Trait 48

GEORGE L. TRAGER

IN THE SOUTHWEST of the United States, the only deciduous trees that grow in abundance outside of the forests on the mountain slopes are the cottonwoods (*Populus angustifolia*, *P. acuminata*, *P. Sargentii*, and probably other species). They are to be found along every watercourse, whether it be a large river or a dry arroyo. Under such circumstances it would be natural for natives of the region to identify linguistically the concept "cottonwood" with that of "(deciduous) tree," and a number of Southwestern languages actually show this identification.

In the language of the Taos Pueblo in New Mexico (Tiwa branch of the Tanoan family) there is a word *łȍʔóne* which means 'wood, forest'; it is collective in form, and a singular in *-na* is used to mean 'piece of wood, stick,' and may also be used for 'tree.' However, the ordinary word for 'tree' is *tûłȍną*, which is the word also for 'cottonwood.' In form the word is a compound, consisting of an element *tû-* which seems to mean 'stick, log,' followed by *łô-* 'wood' (*-ną* being a nominalizing suffix); in this respect it is like other specific tree names, such as *tʔówłȍną* 'pinon' from *tʔów-* 'nut,' *kwę́łȍną* 'oak' from *kwę-* 'hard,' etc.; but that the general meaning 'tree' is basic is shown by the term *tȕłȍčǫleʔéne* 'deciduous tree' (*čǫ́l-* 'green'). In Isleta and Sandia (southern Tiwa dialects not very different from the nothern Taos and Picuris) the word *tûła* means 'tree, cottonwood'; in Picuris there is no exact cognate of *tûłȍną*.

In Tewa (the forms cited are from San Juan pueblo, but it appears that the facts are the same in all the dialects), *te* 'cottonwood' (cognate with Taos *tû-*) is used as an equivalent for English 'tree' and Spanish 'arbol' (but see below), 'in case no particular species is referred to.' The word *sǫ-*, cognate with Taos *łô-*, means 'firewood, trees felled for firewood.' Tewa is a branch of Tanoan.

In the Uto-Actecan languages there are usually specific terms for 'cottonwood' and a general term, quite different, for 'tree.' But in Hopi, which is in the Southwestern culture area, we find the same word, *söhő̂vi*, used for both. Hopi and Tanoan are related, but not very closely (Whorf and Trager, 1937).

In Kiowa, in western Oklahoma, the word for 'tree' is *ʔádw*, and that for 'cottonwood' is *ʔà-hį́* 'tree-real.' Other specific names of trees consist of a specifying element followed by *ʔádw*; the basic identification of 'tree' and 'cottonwood' is thus found here too. Kiowa is distantly related to Tanoan and Uto-Aztecan (Whorf and Trager, 1937, p. 609).

Finally, there is New Mexican Spanish, a language with a very different tradition in tree nomenclature, but spoken by a people who lived in comparative isolation from other speakers of their language for about two centuries. The Spanish word *álamo*, meaning the European poplar, and thus applied to American cottonwoods, has come to be the usual word for any deciduous tree not specifically identified, and the word *árbol*, meaning 'tree' in standard Spanish, is usually restricted in non-literate New Mexican and Coloradan Spanish to the meaning 'fruit tree.'

We have in the tendency here illustrated from a number of Southwestern languages an interesting example of the uniform influence of environment on languages of widely different structure, origin, and cultural traditions.

REFERENCE NOTE

In Taos and Isleta-Sandia the stress-tone is marked thus: (ʹ) primary; (ˆ) primary low; (ˋˋ) medial low; with weak stress-tone unmarked. In Kiowa stress is marked thus: (ʹ) primary; (ˋ) medial. In Taos *e*, *ę* are lower mid vowels; *o*, *ǫ* are low back; *a* is low front. In Tewa *e*, *ǫ* are higher mid vowels. In Kiowa *a* is higher-low front, *w* a higher-low back vowel. In Hopi *ö* is a mid front rounded vowel. The orthography has been modified from the original publication to represent Dr. Trager's present usage and analysis. Through Dr. Trager's courtesy a few typographical errors in the original publication also have been corrected.

For another example of adaptive linguistic response to the American West, see the discussion in Marckwardt (1942). The point documented by Trager has, of course, nothing to do with speculative and simplistic theories about the role of environment, such as that of Raglan (1929).

Special sources and references not in the general bibliography:

MARCKWARDT, A. H.

1942. Review of E. H. Criswell, *Lewis and Clark, Linguistic Pioneers. Lg., 18:* 151-154.

RAGLAN, LORD

1929. The Influence of Environment on Language. *Man, 29:* 171-172. [Subsequent discussion in *Man, 31:* 55, 96, 109, 130, 176.]

ROBBINS, W. W., J. P. HARRINGTON, B. FREIRE-MARRECO

1916. *Ethnobotany of the Tewa Indians.* (BAE-B 55.) Washington, D.C.: Smithsonian Institution.

TRAGER, GEORGE L.

Ms. Field notes from Taos (1935-1936, 1937); from Isleta, Sandia, Picuris, Kiowa (1937); observations of New Mexican Spanish (1934-1936).

WHORF, BENJAMIN L.

Ms. Personal communication on Hopi and Uto-Aztecan.

WHORF, BENJAMIN L., and GEORGE L. TRAGER

1937. The Relationship of Uto-Aztecan and Tanoan. *AA, 39:* 609-624.

Social Dialect and Language History 49

WILLIAM BRIGHT

Within any recognizable speech community, variations are normally found on all levels of linguistic structure—phonological, grammatical, and lexical. Some of these variations are correlated with geographical location: there are systematic differences, for instance, between the English of London and the English of New York. This type of linguistic variation has been studied in detail by dialectologists. Other types of linguistic variation, however, have received less attention. Some of this variation may be said to depend on the identity of the person spoken to or spoken about; the classical instances are those in Nootka, where separate linguistic forms are used in speaking to or about children, fat people, dwarfed people, hunchbacks, etc. (Sapir, 1915). Other variations are correlated with the identity of the speaker. These include cases of difference between men's and women's speech, e.g., in Koasati (Haas, 1944). More typically, linguistic variation is correlated with the social status of the speaker; this may be termed a variety of sociolinguistic variation. An instance which has recently received considerable attention is that involving "U" (upper-class) and "non-U" (middle-class) speech in England; it is claimed that the difference in speech has now become virtually the only overt mark of difference between these two classes (Ross, 1954, pp. 20-23). This type of variation thus provides a potential diagnostic index to social status, though sociologists have exploited this potential very little so far.

It should be noted that some cases of linguistic variation are correlated simultaneously with the identity of the person spoken to and the identity of the person speaking. Thus "female speech" in Yana was used not only *by* women, but also by men in speaking *to* women; "male speech" was used only by men speaking to men (Sapir, 1929b). In the sociolinguistic area, linguistic variation often reflects the relation between the status of the speaker and the status of the person addressed, rather than the absolute status of either; an example is Vietnamese (Emeneau, 1950, pp. 206-209).

Still other cases of linguistic variation are correlated not primarily with the identity of persons, but with other factors in the social and cultural context. For instance, a special type of speech was used by the Chiricahua Apache when on the war-path (Opler and Hoijer, 1940). A type of variation which is familiar in most societies is correlated with the difference between formal and informal situations—"formality" and "informality" being defined, of course, in terms of each particular society. Thus, as most Americans can confirm, pronunciations like *huntin'* are found more commonly in informal situations, while pronunciations like *hunting* are more common in formal situations (Fischer, 1958, p. 50). Variations such as this one in English are, to be sure, usually correlated with other factors besides that of formality. In some languages, however, the styles of speech used in formal vs. informal situations are highly standardized and strictly differentiated. Ferguson (1959a) has applied the term *diglossia* to this type of linguistic variation, and has described it in the Arabic, Swiss German, Haitian French, and modern Greek language communities. We may consider this another type of sociolinguistic variation, correlated with the varying social context within which an individual communicates. Here too, the linguistic differences provide a potential means for definition and recognition of social situations.

The Indian subcontinent is an exceptionally good field for the study of both types of sociolinguistic variation, and a volume describing such phenomena in several South Asian languages is now being issued (Ferguson and Gumperz 1960). First of all, the Indian caste system makes for easy recognition of the social levels with which linguistic variation is correlated. Thus, in the Dharwar District of Mysore State, "there appear to be three styles of conversational Kannada which correspond to the three main cleavages in the social system ... the Brahmin, the non-Brahmin, and the Harijan ['untouchable']" (McCormack, 1960). Secondly, several of the languages of South Asia show a clear difference between formal style (usually equated with the "literary language") and informal or colloquial style. Thus, in Kannada, overlying the dialect differences which correspond to caste and to geography, there is a single formal style which all educated people use in certain situations—in lecturing, in dramatic performances, and in all written composition. See Table 1 for a few comparisons between the formal style, on the one hand, and two colloquial dialects, the Brahmin speech and the middle-caste speech of the Bangalore area, on the other hand.

TABLE 1

	Formal	*Brahmin Colloquial*	*Non-Brahmin Colloquial*
"name"	hesaru	hesru	yesru
"man"	manušya	manšya	mansa
"friend"	snēhita	snēyta	sinēyta
"excuse me"	kšamisu	kšemsu	čemsu
"for doing"	māḍuvudakke	māḍokke	māḍakke
"doesn't do"	māḍuvudilla	māḍolla	māḍalla
"to a wedding"	maduvege	madvege	maduvke
"in a cart"	baṇḍiyalli	baṇḍīli	baṇḍyāgi

It seems likely that distinct caste dialects have existed in India for a long period, always remaining similar enough to preserve mutual intelligibility. Yet both the Brahmin and non-Brahmin dialects of modern Kannada show historical changes from the Old Kannada and Medieval Kannada languages. In some respects the two dialects show different changes, but they agree in many changes, as in the loss of medial vowels. To explain the cases of identical change in the two dialects, we may consider three hypotheses: (1) the Brahmin dialect inaugurated the changes, and the non-Brahmin dialect followed suit; (2) the non-Brahmin dialect was the innovator, and the Brahmin followed suit; (3) the two dialects independently developed in the same directions. Putting the possibilities in the form of a more general question, we may ask: In the over-all history of a language, are changes initiated predominantly by the higher social strata or by the lower?

It has been suggested that phonetic change, and perhaps linguistic change in general, are initiated by the upper strata, in order to "maintain a prestige-marking difference" from the lower strata (Joos, 1952, p. 229). The lower classes are said to narrow the gap again by imitating their social superiors, who are then forced to innovate once more. Thus language change is explained as a "protracted pursuit of an elite by an envious mass, and consequent 'flight' of the elite" (Fischer, 1958, p. 52). For a test of this hypothesis, we may consider the Kannada evidence. It can be shown that the Brahmin dialect does indeed innovate more as regards vocabulary change (Bright, 1960a). Thus in the middle-caste dialect, "curry" is *yesru*, from Old Kannada *esar* (attested from the 13th century); but the Brahmin form is *huli*, originally meaning "sour, a sour substance," and used to mean "curry" only in recent times. Much vocabulary change involves borrowings from Sanskrit or English, and the Brahmin dialect here often introduces foreign sounds along with the foreign words. Thus the Brahmin dialect introduces *z* in words like *dazan* from English "dozen," where non-Brahmins say *dajan*. On the other hand, the non-Brahmin dialect shows more sound-change within native vocabulary: cf. non-Brahmin *ālu* "milk," Brahmin *hālu* (Medieval *hāl*, Old Kannada *pāl*); non-Brahmin *gombe* "doll," Brahmin *bombe* (Old Kannada *bombe*). In the realm of grammar, the non-Brahmin dialect again seems to have innovated more, showing for example a locative suffix *-āgi* as against Brahmin and Old Kannada *-alli*. In general, the Brahmin dialect seems to show great innovation on the more *conscious* levels of linguistic change—those of borrowing and semantic extension—while the non-Brahmin dialect shows greater innovation in the less conscious types of change—those involving phonemic and morphological replacements.

Some evidence is available of a similar pattern in the caste dialects of Tamil. For instance, Old Tamil had a retroflex fricative which may be transcribed *ẓ*; this is preserved in Brahmin dialects, but merges with *y*, *ḷ*, *l* or zero in most non-Brahmin dialects. Thus Brahmin *kīẓe* "down" corresponds to *kīye* and *kīḷe* in several middle-caste dialects, and to *kī* in a Pariah dialect (Bloch, 1910, pp. 5-7; and my own observations). On the other hand, Brahmin dialects often innovate by adopting loan words, where non-Brahmin dialects preserve native Tamil vocabulary: "water" is Brahmin *tīrtham* or *jalam* (both from Sanskrit), where most non-Brahmin dialects use *taṇṇi* (from older *taṇ-ṇīr* "cold water"; Bloch 1910, p. 22). Fuller material on Tamil dialects which is now being published should make the picture much clearer (Zvelebil, 1959).

Both in Kannada and in Tamil, it is understandable that Brahmins' familiarity with foreign languages and their more active intellectual life should favor innovation on what I have called the more conscious level. It is less apparent, however, why the Brahmin dialect should be more conservative than others in the less conscious types of change. A possible hypothesis is that literacy, most common among Brahmins, has acted as a brake on change in their dialect—that the "frozen" phonology and grammar of the literary language have served to retard change in Brahmin speech. A possible test of this hypothesis lies in a consideration of the Tulu society of South India, on the coast west of the Kannada-speaking area. Brahmin and non-Brahmin dialects exist in Tulu, as in other South Indian languages; but there is no established writing system for any form of Tulu, and literacy among the Tulu people exists only for their second languages—Sanskrit, Kannada, and English. Material on the Tulu caste dialects is scanty, but suggestive: the Brahmin and non-Brahmin dialects show phonemic change in approximately equal degree (Bright, 1960a). When further Tulu data become available, they may give strong support to the hypothesis that although "conscious" linguistic change comes largely from higher social strata, "unconscious" change is natural in all strata where the literacy factor does not intervene.

Finally, we should consider the possible role of social dialects in the process of sound change itself. It has recently been suggested that the locus of phonemic change may be not within individual dialects, but the process of large-scale borrowing from one dialect to another. "No speaker of English can easily see himself giving up the contrast between, say, *clip* and *lip* . . . Yet that is more or less what happened to *knight* and *night* . . . a few centuries ago." It is hypothesized that some members of the English-speaking community may have pronounced *knight* with, let us say, an unreleased *k*; other speakers, attempting to imitate "the source dialect of their high-prestige neighbors," *misheard* the *kn* as *n* and initiated the new pronunciation, homonymous with *night* (Hoeningswald, 1960, p. 55). This hypothesis can be applied to the Kannada material: When Old Kannada *pāl* "milk" became Medieval Kannada *hāl*, the initial *h* presumably at first retained the voicelessness of its prototype. In modern Kannada, however, the *h* of Brahmin *hālu* is at least partly voiced. It is possible that this subphonemic change, occurring in the Brahmin dialect, was misapprehended by non-Brahmins; so that attempting to imitate *hālu* with voiced *h*, they said *ālu* instead. Such an explanation would change the picture previously presented of Brahmin and non-Brahmin roles in linguistic innovation: The upper class would now appear to originate sound change on the *phonetic* level; the lower class, imitating this inaccurately, produces change on the phonemic level.

Needless to say, we cannot now be certain that such a process operated in any particular historical change. What is possible and highly desirable is that social dialects and their interactions in contemporary societies should be studied in minute detail, bearing hypotheses like the above in mind. South Asia appears to provide an exceptionally rich field for this type of sociolinguistic investigation.

REFERENCE NOTE

On literacy as a retarding factor in rate of change, see Politzer (1961) and Zengel (1962). On various types of variation discussed, consult articles and references in V-VIII.

References not in the general bibliography:

POLITZER, ROBERT L.

1961. The Interpretation of Correctness in Late Latin Texts. *Lg.*, *37:* 209-214.

ZENGEL, MARJORIE S.

1962. Literacy as a Factor in Language Change. *AA*, *64:* 132-139.

ZVELEBIL, KAMIL

1959. Dialects of Tamil I, II. *Archiv Orientálni*, *27:* 272-317, 572-603.

Postvocalic -r in South Carolina: A Social Analysis 50

RAVEN I. MCDAVID, JR.

THE RELATIONSHIP between speech forms and the cultural configurations and prestige values within a civilization has been indicated by linguistic scientists, but so far most of the study of that relationship has been directed toward languages outside the Indo-European family. (See, for example, the work of the late Benjamin L. Whorf, particularly 1941b.) It is, however, just as proper to utilize the data of linguistics, as derived from a study of dialects of our own language, in analyzing some of the problems within our own culture (McDavid, 1946).

As an example of a situation in which linguistic data and other cultural data must be correlated, one may examine the distribution in South Carolina and the adjacent parts of Georgia of postvocalic *-r* as constriction in such words as *thirty, Thursday, worm, barn, beard, father.* (The term "constriction" includes turning up of the tongue tip [retroflexion, perhaps the rarest type of constriction in English], retraction of the tongue, spreading of the tongue, and other tongue movements providing friction during the articulation of a vowel. Traditionally, "retroflexion" has been used where this paper uses "constriction." In popular terminology, speakers lacking constriction in words of these types are said not to pronounce their *-r*.) A social analysis proved necessary for this particular linguistic feature, because the data proved too complicated to be explained by merely a geographical statement or a statement of settlement history. In this particular problem, moreover, the social analysis seems more significant than it might seem in others, because the presence or absence of postvocalic *-r* as constriction becomes an overt prestige symbol only on a very high level of sophistication. With little experience a speaker learns that the folk forms ['laItɚd], *lightwood*, and ['faɚboɚd], *fireboard*, do not have the prestige of the corresponding standard forms *kindling* and *mantelpiece* (these transcriptions are for the type of dialect in which these lexical items generally occur)—that the folk forms are generally recognized as "countrified" or "common." Folk verb forms, like *I seen what he done when he run into your car*, are under a strong social taboo, and as a rule may be used by highly cultured speakers only for deliberate, humorous effects. Even some pronunciations, such as ('aIðə(r], ['naIðə(r], instead of ['i:ðə(r], ['ni:ðə(r], *either*, *neither*, or the so-called "broad *a*" pronunciation ['haf'past] instead of the more common ['hæf,pæst], *half past*, are fairly generally known as symbols of real or fancied elegance. But there is little or no direct concern with a person's postvacalic *-r* except as part of the occupational training for such highly sophisticated crafts as elocution, pedagogy, concert singing, acting, radio announcing, and some branches of the ministry. Since the traditions of these professions generally require that their practitioners tinker with their speech in other ways, persons deliberately concerned about the presence or absence of constriction in their postvocalic *-r* would not be used as representatives of natural local usage on any cultural level. In short, constriction—or lack of it—in the speech of *Atlas* informants may be considered due to the normal operation of social forces and not to any conscious notions of elegance.

The first of the accompanying maps shows the geographical details essential to an understanding of the distribution of postvocalic *-r* in South Carolina. The tidewater area, extending inland about thirty miles through a network of

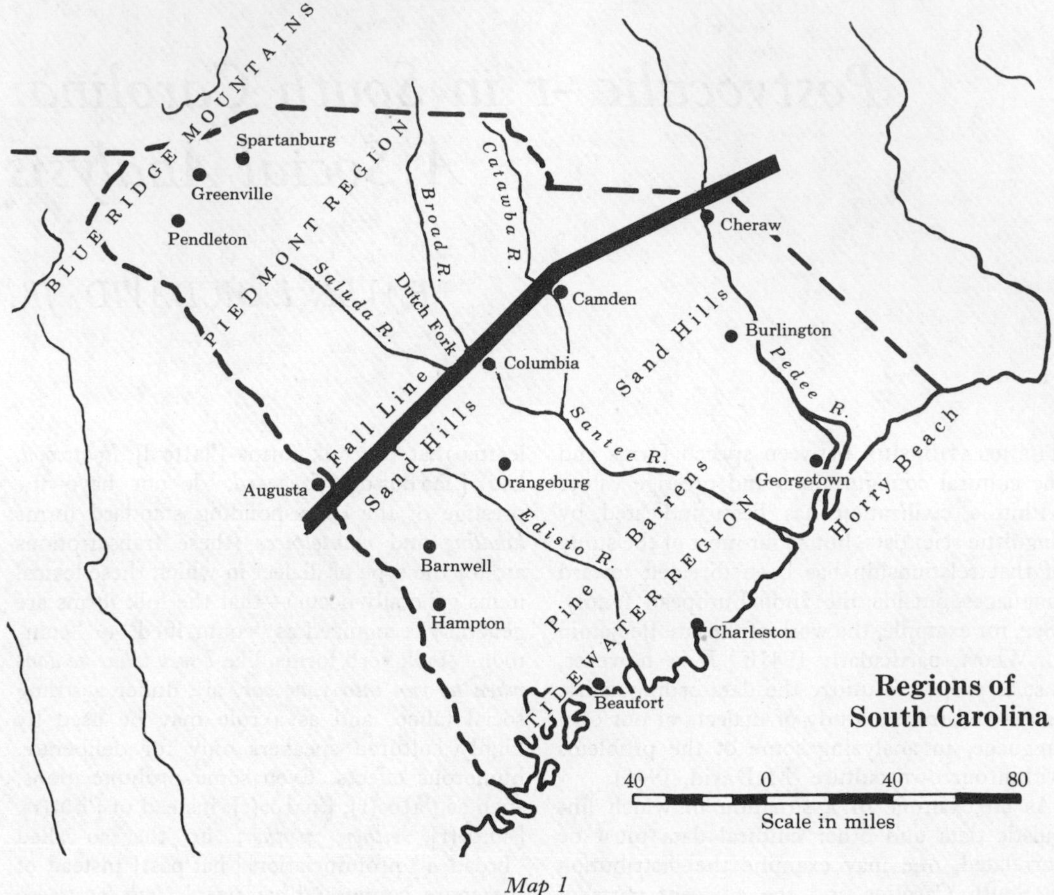

Map 1

islands and peninsulas and tidal creeks, except along the beach front of Horry County, was the area in which the first cultural centers were planted: Georgetown, Charleston, Beaufort, and Savannah. About thirty miles inland is a belt of pine barrens, which have never been suitable for large-scale plantation agriculture, and where small-scale farming is the prevailing pattern. (The difference between a farm and a plantation is not merely one of size, but rather of the attitude of the owner toward participation in the work of farming. Even on the largest farms, in the up-country and north of the Santee, the farmer and his family normally did a great deal of the manual labor; on the plantations, the work of the planters was almost exclusively managerial.) Above the pine barrens the rich coastal plain spreads inland for about seventy miles, to the infertile sand hills along and just below the fall line. Above the fall line—the old head of navigation on the rivers, and the shore line in an earlier geological period—the rolling Piedmont begins, gradually becoming more broken until in the northwestern corner of the state it merges into a fringe of the Blue Mountains. From the coast to the fall line is generally known as the low country; above the fall line, as the up-country.

The conventional statement about the Southern postvocalic *-r* is that it does not occur as constriction in words of the type here under examination. The fact that in every Southern state one may find locally rooted native speakers with constriction in at least some of these words has been either overlooked or deliberately ignored. (It is a tradition among some schools of scientific investigation not to insist on facts and examples, and to ignore them when they conflict with previously formulated theories.) The usual statement is still that Southern and New England speech differs from so-called "general American" in that the two former types do not have constriction of postvocalic *-r*. (See, for example, Krapp, 1925, Part I, p. 38; Baugh, 1935, pp. 444, 449; Ekwall, 1946, Part II, p. 13.)

However, records made for the *Linguistic Atlas of the South Atlantic States* showed very early that postvocalic *-r* does occur with constriction in many Southern communities, including several of those first investigated in South Carolina by the late Dr. Guy S. Lowman. These data led Professor Hans Kurath, director of the *Atlas*, to set off tentatively two areas in South Carolina within which constriction occurred: the middle and upper Piedmont, and the area north of the Santee River (chart accompanying talk before the annual meeting of the Linguistic Society of America, New York, 1944). A simple explanation of the evidence seemed possible at that time: The area north of the Santee was settled predominantly by Scotch-Irish planted from the coast, was adjacent to the Highlander settlements in the Cape Fear Valley of North Carolina, and could be looked upon generally as a cultural continuation of the Cape Fear settlements. The northwestern corner of the state was settled originally by the main Scotch-Irish migration southward from Pennsylvania, and would naturally represent a southward prong of the "Midland" area that Professor Kurath has set up as stemming from the Pennsylvania settlements. (The concept of the Midland group of dialects, spreading westward and southward from the Philadelphia area, is perhaps the most fruitful contribution Kurath has made to the study of American dialects. The division into Northern, Midland, and Southern types is generally a better explanation of the historical facts and the present distribution of vocabulary items than the older grouping of Eastern, Southern, and "General American," and is at least as good a framework for an analysis on the basis of phonetic types.) The explanation was still on the basis of geography and the area of original settlement.

But if a geographical interpretation of the postvocalic *-r* was the proper one, it might have been expected that further field work would substantiate and simplify the picture Instead, with further research the picture has become more complicated, as the second map indicates. Many speakers—even whole com-

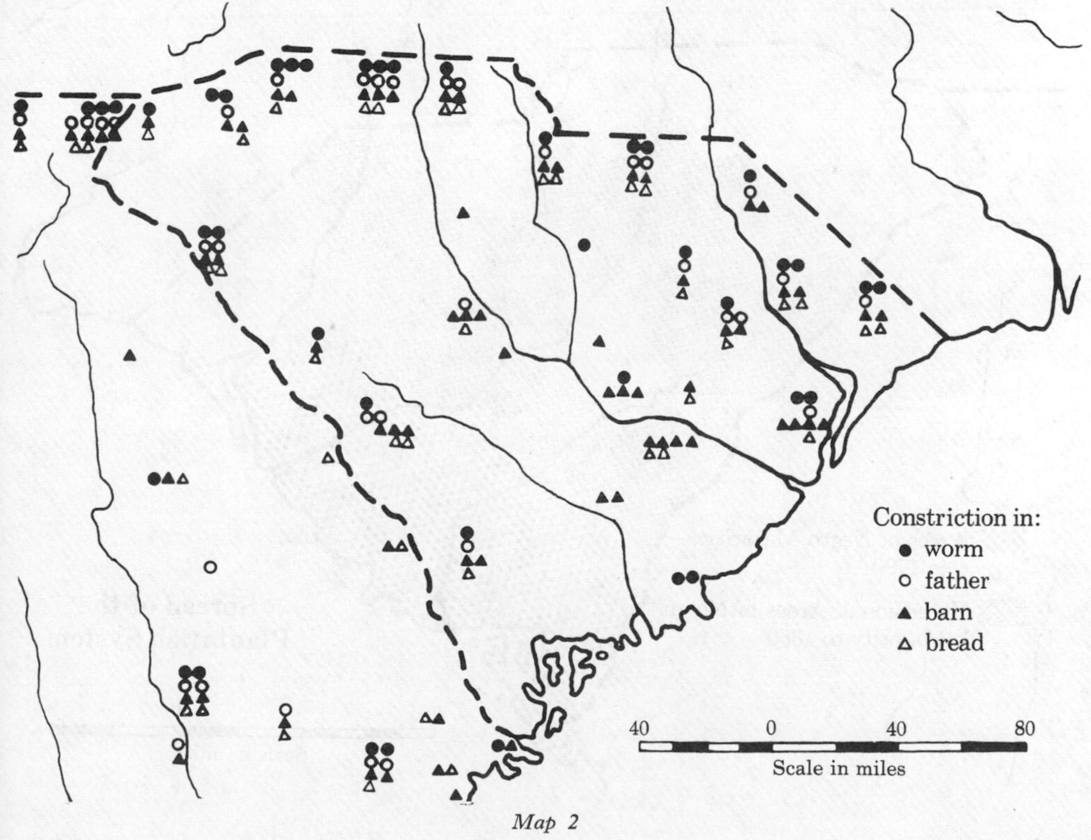

Map 2

munities—are found with constriction of postvocalic *-r* in the area where the 1941 evidence did not indicate constriction to exist, and many speakers lack constriction in areas where constriction seemed indicated as normal. A purely geographical interpretation of the distribution is likely to be meaningless: it is difficult to see how, in a geographical sense, Barnwell and Orangeburg counties can be less "Midland" than Hampton and Berkeley, where constriction occurs. It is therefore necessary to make a statement of other social phenomena in order to explain the distribution of postvocalic *-r* in South Carolina.

In the communities where postvocalic *-r* occurs with constriction, it has been noticed that three variables operate toward decreasing the amount: normally, the more education an informant has, the less constriction; and within the same cultural level, younger informants generally have less constriction than older ones, and urban informants less than rural.

Moreover, the communities in which constriction occurs have in common a proportionately large white population—generally a majority, even in 1860, when the proportion of Negroes in South Carolina was largest. (See Map 3. Since the available statistics are for counties, the large slaveholdings on the Sea Islands and the river ricelands obscure the presence of the many small farmers in the pinelands of Beaufort and Charleston districts.) These communities are counties or parts of counties where farming, often scratch-farming, was the rule, and where the cultural orientation was toward the county seat and the local religious congregation. They comprise the pine barrens, the hinterland of the Horry beach, the sand hills, and the mountain margin—lands where the plantation system could not be even temporarily profitable—and the Dutch Fork between the Saluda and Broad rivers, where a cohesive, religious-centered Lutheran community with a tradition of self-sufficient farming was able to resist the lure of alleged money crops. Constriction in the speech of textile workers in

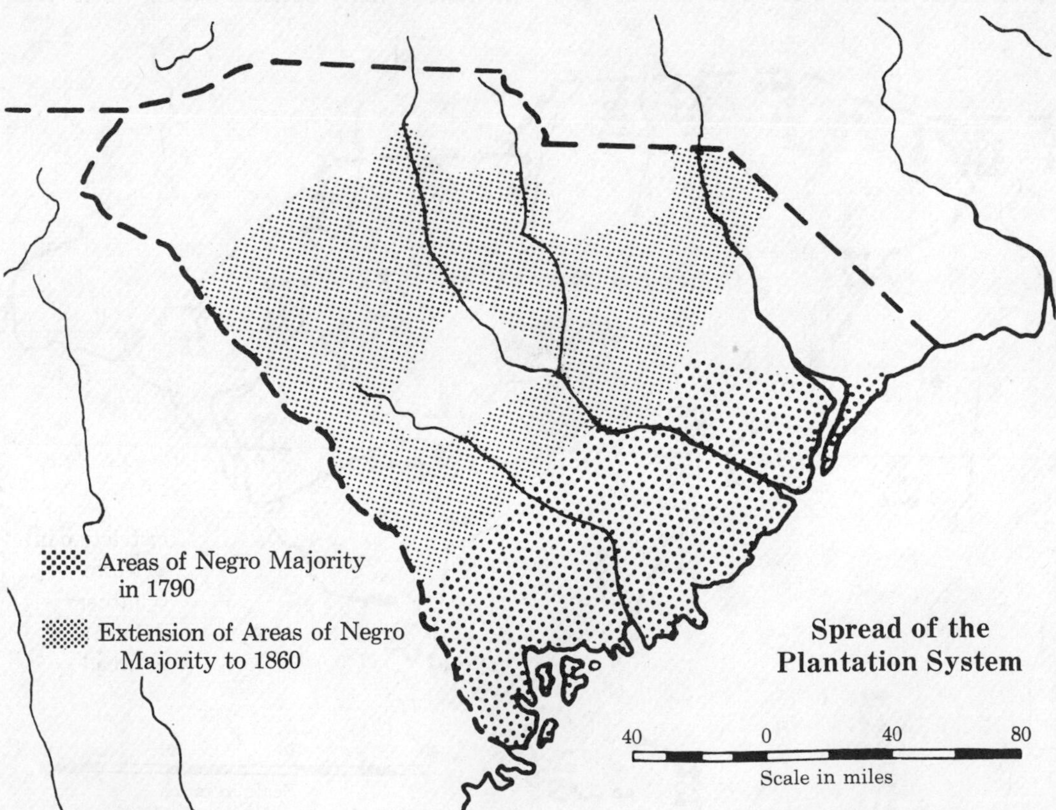

Piedmont metropolitan centers is only superficially an exception to the observation that constriction is a mark of cultural isolation: the textile workers were originally recruited from the culturally peripheral areas, and the paternalistic company village that characterizes the Southern textile industry has created a pattern of cultural segregation as real and almost as strong as that setting off whites from Negroes. (The mill villages, regardless of size—some are over ten thousand in population—are usually unincorporated, with all municipal functions handled by the mill management. The company store, with bills deducted from millworkers' wages, has existed on a scale unparalleled in any other industry, except possibly coal mining. Separate schools are provided for mill children —at Greenville, even a separate high school— and each mill village has its separate Protestant churches. See Pope, 1941. In South Carolina, the paternalistic textile village dates from the founding of the Graniteville mill, in Aiken County, by William Gregg, in 1845. Gregg is also traditionally responsible for the pattern of employing only white labor in production operations in Southern textile mills. He advocated the building up of a textile industry as a philanthropic enterprise which would provide the poor whites with a means of livelihood secure from Negro [slave] competition.)

When one studies both the early settlement history and the current distribution of speech forms other than the postvocalic *-r*, it is apparent that the original area without constriction was only a small part of the state. (The loss of initial *h-* in *wheelbarrow*, *whetstone*, *whip*—a feature of southern British "received" pronunciation today—hardly occurs outside the immediate vicinity of the coastal centers, and is by no means universal even there. Such Midland vocabulary items as *a little piece* ['a short distance'], *jacket* ['vest'], *coal oil* or *lamp oil* ['kerosene'], and *quarter till* [the hour] may still be found in many low-country communities. Original settlement from southern Britain does not necessarily imply a tendency toward loss of constriction. Field records made in England by Dr. Lowman show constriction in many southern British folk dialects today. It does not, of course, weaken the argument for the influence of prestige factors to assert that the loss of constriction occurred principally in American communities which maintained close cultural contacts with the city of London; in fact, this assertion only re-emphasized that influence.)

The area settled by southern British speakers hardly reached above tidewater; further inland, whether the settlers came in the great migration from Pennsylvania or first landed at Charleston or other ports, the early population was made up almost entirely of Scotch-Irish and Germans, who might be expected to retain their postvocalic constriction of *-r*, just as they have retained much of their characteristic vocabulary. (Expansion inland from the coast in the eighteenth century was not the work of groups within the older communities as it was in New England. Instead, frontier townships were laid out, and groups of immigrants settled directly upon them. As a rule, the townships north of the Santee were settled originally by Scotch-Irish, those south of the Santee by Germans and German-Swiss. See Meriwether, 1940.) Only in Beaufort, Charleston, and Georgetown districts—and only in the tidewater riceland sections of those districts—were the southern British settlers, in whose dialect constriction would have first been lost, the dominant group in 1790; and in those same sections plantation agriculture and large slave majorities prevailed. (See Map 3.) Clearly, the spread of the loss of constriction accompanied the spread of the plantation system, both representing the imposition on the majority of the patterns, if not the will, of a minority.

The spread inland of the minority speech pattern, so far as constriction is concerned, naturally involved several types of social readjustment. The following social forces are known to have operated; each of these forces would have tended to reinforce the prestige of the constrictionless type of speech as a model given the established prestige of the original group that lacked constriction, the tidewater plantation caste. (Although by the time of the American Revolution the bulk of the white population of South Carolina was to be found in the frontier townships and in the new settlements made by the immigrants from Pennsylvania, political power was held by the plantation group around Charleston. All the delegates to the Continental Congress and to the Constitutional Convention came from this group. The tidewater planters and merchants kept up their ties with England after the American Revolution, and a fair number of their sons were educated in England. Even today the socially elite in Charleston and Savannah tend toward uncritical admiration of things English, at least of the practices of the English upper classes.)

1. Following the establishment of American independence, the reopening of the slave trade, and the invention of the cotton gin, plantation agriculture spread inland from the coast, displacing many of the small farmers, who in their turn moved west into the frontier communities. (Under the royal government several efforts were made to restrict the importation of slaves, generally by imposing high import duties, but profits from rice and indigo plantations kept these efforts from being very effective. See Petty, 1943, pp. 50-57; and regarding the movement west, pp. 70-81.)

2. Some successful up-country farmers became planters, and intermarried with the older plantation caste. (A case history is cited by Cash, 1941, pp. 14-17.)

3. As inland towns arose, they tended to become cultural outposts of Charleston. The original fall line trading posts—Augusta, Columbia, Camden, and Cheraw—were financed by Charleston capital for the Indian trade. (See, for example, Meriwether, 1940, pp. 69-71.) As the trading posts grew into towns, the local business and financial leaders had an increasing number of contacts with the group in Charleston that has always controlled the financial life of the state. Sometimes, Charlestonians even migrated to the up-country to establish offshoots of their family banks or business houses. The cotton of the up-country was marketed through Charleston factors until well into the twentieth century. (Interest rates were usually very high. For up-country resentment toward Charleston, especially toward the symbols of Charleston influence, the merchant and the banker, see Robertson, 1942, pp. 81-84, 91-107.)

To my paternal grandfather, an up-country farmer, Charleston was a symbol of sharp business practices, if not of outright dishonesty.

Not only financial ties attached the up-country townspeople to Charleston. Both health and fashion contrived to make the low-country planters migrate inland during the malaria season to such health resorts as Aiken, Pendleton, Greenville, and Spartanburg. (See Brewster, 1942.) Some of the low-country visitors settled permanently, to become the local elite. Even the Civil War did not disturb this trend; in fact, the siege of Charleston caused many Charlestonians to become refugees in the up-country, and some did not return with the cessation of hostilities. For the Charlestonian not completely above the salt in his home town, the up-country provided a greater sense of social prestige than he could have known between the Ashley and the Cooper. Even Irish Catholics transplanted to the up-country, though remaining exotic in the Protestant environment, found that a Charleston origin and a trace of Charleston accent helped them to become accepted as part of the socially preferred group.

(Refugees from Charleston contributed particularly to the growth of Greenville. The Roman Catholic group in Greenville dates from the Civil War. Paradoxically, although the Roman Catholic Church has repeatedly served as a whipping boy for up-country Ku Klux Klan organizers, demagogues, and Protestant ministers, Roman Catholics as individuals have achieved far more complete cultural integration in Greenville than in the outwardly more tolerant culture of Charleston.

Even today, Charlestonians not fully accepted in their native city have found their origin a password to social acceptance in the up-country. Typical of the colonial attitude of the older families in up-country towns is their reverence for the exclusive balls given by the St. Cecilia Society of Charleston. In Greenville, for instance, there is much more talk of the possibility of being invited than one would hear in Charleston from people of the same social standing.)

Charleston long continued to dominate the cultural and professional life of South Carolina. The state medical college is still located in Charleston and apprenticeship in the office of a Charleston lawyer has long been considered the best type of legal training. (As for example, the apprenticeship served by the Hon. James F. Byrnes, in the firm of Mordecai and Gaston.) The moving of the state capital to Columbia, and the setting up of the state university there, did not change the picture materially; from the beginning, the dominant group in Columbia society was the plantation caste, the rulers of South Carolina.

The many Protestant colleges in the up-country did little to counteract the trend—partly because after 1830 (and almost all the up-country colleges were established after that date) there was but one approved social system and no room for competitors; partly because a rising educational institution tended to conform by way of showing its cultural legitimacy; partly because many of the founders and early faculty members of these inland institutions were themselves from tidewater areas, or at least educated in institutions located in these areas. (This was true even among the Baptists, the most loosely organized of the major Protestant sects. See McGlothlin, 1926.)

None of these influences operated alone; they make up a complex, rooted in the desire of every ambitious South Carolinian to be accepted by, and, if possible, taken into, the ruling caste. Politically, this same desire was manifested in the ardor with which many up-country leaders adopted and championed the cause of Charleston and the interests of the large slaveholders. (John C. Calhoun, the most eloquent orator for slavery and nullification and Southern separatism, was born on the South Carolina frontier, and in the early stages of his political career was a spokesman for the frontier philosophy represented nationally by Andrew Jackson. After marrying into a Charleston family, he became the spokesman for the plantation interests [Robertson, 1942, pp. 101-102].) In any event, the prestige of the old plantation caste has meant the spread inland of many of their speech ways, including the lack of constriction of postvocalic *-r*, and the trend toward the loss of constriction continues. It even serves to reinforce Southern xenophobia, for among the phonetically sophisticated the lack of constriction has become a point of caste and local pride. (A former student of mine, the son of a Darlington County informant, explained, "The reason we Southerners resent the way the Yankees roll their *-r* is that it reminds us of the way the crackers talk." In South Carolina the term *crackers* is used [though less than formerly] by the townpeople, the plantation caste, and plantation-reared Negroes as a derogatory designation for the poor whites—nonslaveholders, or decendants of nonslaveholders—in areas where large slaveholdings once prevailed.)

It is true, of course, that prestige values can change. It should not be surprising, therefore, that indications already exist that constriction of postvocalic *-r* may some day become respectable in South Carolina. The presence in local military posts of many Northern and Western servicemen, with strong constriction of their *-r*, as well as with a different and more sophisticated line of conversation, has led many Southern girls to the conclusion that a person with constriction can be acceptable as a date for the daughter of generations of plantation owners, or even possibly as a husband. Even in the heart of the low country, a number of girls in their late teens or early twenties are still speaking with a newly acquired constriction of postvocalic *-r*, long after the training camps have closed. (This phenomenon has been observed particularly in such constrictionless low-country towns as Walterboro and Sumter. The radio and the movies will probably reinforce this new trend. Similar effects may be expected from the recent and continuing migrations of Negroes northward and of up-country whites to coastal towns. Perhaps the trend is about to be reversed. An apparent tendency to replace the low-country ingliding diphthongs in *date*, *boat* [de:ᵊt, bo:ᵊt] with the up-country upgliding type [de:It, bo:Ut] also suggests a reversal of the trend in prestige values. One must remember, however, that in linguistic geography each phonological or lexical item must be judged on its own merits, and nothing could be more dangerous than to predict the fate of the postvocalic *-r* in South Carolina from the fate of the low-country diphthongs in *date* and *boat*.)

In the meantime, since practical applications of scientific information are always sought, there are some ways in which this analysis of the social distribution of postvocalic *-r* in South Carolina might be put to use by other social scientists. Just as in South Carolina, so probably in most of the other states of the Deep South, constriction is a linguistically peripheral feature found in culturally peripheral communities, generally on poor land among people who were driven onto that land—or, as with the textile workers, into their occupation—by the pressure of competition from the plantation system and Negro labor. It is among these people, whose cultural situation was originally brought about by Negro competition, that the fear of continuing Negro competition is keenest, and is most easily exploited by demagogues. It is from those people that the Ku Klux Klan, the Bleases and Talmadges and Bilbos, and the lynching mobs have tended to draw their strength. (South Carolina political observers have noticed that Horry County, the northeasternmost coastal county, has generally voted the same way as the upper Piedmont in state elections, and always gave a heavy Blease majority. Linguistic evidence—not only the preservation of constriction, but of many lexical items as well—indicates the cultural tie between the two sections.) Consequently, a Southern official whose job dealt with interracial problems might screen with a little extra care those native applicants for, say, police jobs whose speech showed strong constriction. And those interested in changing the racial attitudes of the whites might well concentrate their efforts on those areas where constriction has survived in greatest strength. Perhaps this suggestion is extreme, but it shows the possibilities. (It is not necessarily true, of course, that only those persons in the Deep South lacking postvocalic constriction of *-r* would be likely not to mistreat Negroes. Many of the plantation caste would resent the notion of equality, much as they would resist anti-Negro mob violence by poor whites. But since the revision of racial attitudes is largely a matter of education, it can hardly be without significance that in South Carolina the postvocalic *-r* loses constriction among the group with the greater amount of education. It is also worthy of note that almost every lynching in South Carolina in the last twenty-five years occurred in counties where the field work for the *South Atlantic Atlas* has disclosed strong constriction of postvocalic *-r*.) For language is primarily a vehicle of social intercommunication, and linguistic phenomena must always be examined for their correlation with other cultural phenomena—as for the correlation between the spread of the unconstricted postvocalic *-r* in South Carolina and the rise of the plantation system.

REFERENCE NOTE

This paper was presented at the symposium on linguistics and culture sponsored by Section H (Anthropology) of the American Association for the Advancement of Science at Chicago, Dec. 27, 1947. Its conclusions are substantially confirmed by W. R. Van Riper, *Postvocalic* -r *in the Eastern United States*, Doctoral dissertation, University of Michigan, 1958 (microfilm). The data for this study have been derived from the field records collected for the *Linguistic Atlas of the South Atlantic States* prior to 1941 by the late Dr. Guy S. Lowman, and since that time by McDavid. McDavid's field work was made possible first by a fellowship in 1941 from the Julius Rosenwald Fund and later by an honorary fellowship from Duke University and grants from the American Council of Learned Societies.

References are organized in two parts: (A) specific to McDavid's paper and not in the general bibliography; (B) dialectology.

A. REFERENCES SPECIFIC TO McDAVID'S PAPER

BAUGH, ALBERT C.

1935. *History of the English Language*. New York: Appleton-Century-Crofts.

BREWSTER, LAWRENCE FAY

1942. *Summer Migrations and Resorts of South Carolina Low Country Planters*. (Historical Papers of the Trinity College Historical Society.) Durham, N.C.

CASH, WILBUR JOSEPH

1941. *The Mind of the South*. New York: Knopf.

EKWALL, EILERT

1946. *British and American Pronunciation*. (The American Institute in the University of Upsala, Essays and Studies on American Language and Literature, Vol. II, No. 13.) Upsala.

KRAPP, GEORGE PHILIP
1925. *The English Language in America*. New York: Century.

MCGLOTHIN, WILLIAM JOSEPH
1926. *Baptist Beginnings in Education: A History of Furman University*. Nasville.

MERIWETHER, ROBERT LEE
1940. *The Expansion of South Carolina 1729-1765*. Kingsport, Tenn.: Southern Publishers.

PETTY, JULIAN J.
1943. *The Growth and Distribution of Population in South Carolina*. (State Planning Board, Bulletin No. 11.) Columbia, S.C.

POPE, LISTON
1941. *Millhands and Preachers; A Study of Gastonia*. New Haven: Yale University Press.

ROBERTSON, BEN
1942. *Red Hills and Cotton*. New York: Knopf.

B. DIALECTOLOGY

For general discussions of the field of dialectology, see Haugen (1956), McIntosh (1952), Pop (1950), and Weinreich (1953), all with extensive references. See also the discussions by Bloomfield (1933, chap. 19), Cohen (1956a, Part 2, Chap. 3), Ferguson and Gumperz (1960, Introduction), Gleason (1961, chap. 24). Robert A. Hall, Jr. (1960, chap. 9), Hockett (1958, chaps. 38-40, 56), Jespersen (1925, chaps. 3-4), McDavid (1946), Sapir (1921, chap. 7), Whitney (1875, chap. 9), On the concept of dialect, note Martinet (1954) and Sapir (1931d) as well.

On linguistic geography as a field, see Bottiglioni (1954), Coseriu (1956), Dauzat (1948), Jaberg (1936), Palmer (1936), Roedder (1926).

On structural dialectology, see the analyses, discussions, and references in Doroszewski (1958), Garde (1961), Ivič (1962), Moulton (1960, 1962), Stankiewicz (1956, 1957), Stockwell (1959), and Weinreich (1954, 1962).

On work in American English dialects, see Allen (1958, pp. 137-191), Atwood (1953), Kurath (1939, 1949), Kurath and McDavid (1961), McDavid (1952-1953), Pickford (1957). On work in American Indian dialects, see McQuown (1960), Swadesh (1952b), and Voegelin (1956). As a notable example of older European work, see Jaberg and Jud (1928-1940), and also see the review of Schläpfer by Moulton (1956). For work in European countries, especially for Romance languages, and to some extent the rest of the world, Pop (1950) is a monumental reference; subsequent work can be followed in the journal *Orbis*, and consult also the *Proceedings* of the International Congress of General Dialectology (first Congress held in Louvain-Bruxelles, 1960, with *Proceedings* in press).

See also references to the articles by Gumperz in Part VII, Diebold, Garvin and Bull in this Part, and Emeneau in Part IX.

References not in the general bibliography:

ATWOOD, E. BAGBY
1953. *A Survey of Verb Forms in the Eastern United States*. Ann Arbor: University of Michigan Press.

BOTTIGLIONI, G.

1954. Linguistic Geography: Achievements, Methods and Orientations. *Word, 10* (2-3): 375-387.

COSERIU, E.

1956. *La geografía linguística.* (Revista de la Faculdad de Humanidades y Ciencias, No. 14.) Montevideo. Pp. 29-69.

DAUZAT, A.

1948. *La Géographie linguistique.* Paris: Flamarrion. (1st ed., 1922.)

DOROSZEWSKI, W.

1958. Structural Linguistics and Dialect Geography. In Eva Sivertsen (Ed.), *Proceedings of the Eighth International Congress of Linguists (Oslo, 1957).* Oslo: Oslo University Press. Pp. 540-564.

IVIČ, PAVLE

1962. On the Structure of Dialectal Differentiation. *Word, 18* (1-2): 33-53.

KURATH, HANS

1939. *Handbook of the Linguistic Geography of New England.* (Linguistic Atlas of New England, Vol. 1.) Providence: Brown University Press.

1949. *A Word Geography of the Eastern United States.* (Studies in American English, No. 1.) Ann Arbor: University of Michigan Press.

KURATH, HANS, and RAVEN I. MCDAVID, JR.

1961. *The Pronunciation of English in the Atlantic States.* Ann Arbor: University of Michigan Press.

LABOV, WILLIAM

1963. The Social Motivation of a Sound Change. *Word, 19:* 273-309.

MOULTON, WILLIAM G.

1956. Review of R. Schläpfer, *Die Mundart des Kantons Baselland. Lg.,* 32: 751-760.

1962. Dialect Geography and the Concept of Phonological Space. *Word, 18* (1-2): 23-32.

PALMER, L. R.

1936. *An Introduction to Modern Linguistics.* London: Macmillan.

POP, SEVER

1950. *La Dialectologie. Aperçu Historique et Mèthodes d'Enquêtes Linguistiques.* Part I: Dialectologie Romane; Part II: Dialectologie Non-Romane. Louvain: Chez l'auteur.

ROEDDER, E. C.

1926. Linguistic Geography. *Germanic Review, 1:* 281-308.

STOCKWELL, R. P.

1959. Structural Dialectology: A Proposal. *American Speech, 34:* 258-268.

VOEGELIN, C. F.

1956. Phonemicizing for Dialect Study (with Reference to Hopi). *Lg., 32:* 110-155.

Social Influences on the Choice of a Linguistic Variant 51

JOHN L. FISCHER

During the year 1954-1955 my wife and I were engaged in a study of child-rearing in a semi-rural New England village. In the course of the study I had occasion to record two or more interviews on Audograph discs or tapes, with each of the 24 children of our sample. Previously certain inconsistencies in the children's speech had attracted my attention, especially the variation between *-in* and *-ing* for the present participle ending. (The variation in this dialect between *-in* and *-ing* in the participle ending does not extend to words with a final *-in* in an unstressed syllable in standard speech. This variation is therefore probably best viewed as a case of free alternation of two allomorphs which happen to differ in respect to one phoneme, rather than as a case of phonological free variation.) Accordingly, in transcribing the discs and tapes, I decided to note the choice of these two variants, and this paper is intended to summarize and discuss this information.

To begin with, all of the 24 children, except three, used both forms to some extent at least. The three exceptions used only the *-ing* form, and since they were less loquacious than most of the other children, it is possible that a larger sample of their speech would have revealed the use of the other variant as well. This may then be regarded as a case of so-called free variation of two linguistic forms within a local speech community, and within the speech of most individual members of our sample community. In general, the choice of one or the other of the variants would not affect the denotation of acts, states, or events by the word.

"Free variation" is of course a label, not an explanation. It does not tell us where the variants came from nor why the speakers use them in differing proportions, but is rather a way of excluding such questions from the scope of immediate inquiry. Historically, I presume that one could investigate the spread of one of these variants into the territory of another through contact and migration, and this would constitute one useful sort of explanation. However, another sort of explanation is possible in terms of current factors which lead a given child in given circumstances to produce one of the variants rather than another, and it is this which I wish to discuss here.

Before discussing the determinants of selection of the variants it will be helpful to understand a little of the general background of the data. The 24 children in our sample consisted of an equal number of boys and girls, both divided into two equal age groups, ages 3-6 and 7-10. By the time the recordings were made my wife and I had been observing the children periodically for eight to ten months and most of the children were fairly well acquainted with us. Most of the children were interviewed in an office in our house, which was located in the middle of the village. Most of the children had visited our house before, some a number of times. Four younger children who had not were interviewed in their own homes. Three general types of text were obtained:

1. Protocols for all children for a verbal thematic apperception test (TAT) in which the children were asked to make up stories starting out from short sentences given by the investigator.
2. For older children only, answers to a formal questionnaire.
3. For a few of the older children, informal interviews asking them to recount their recent activities.

I shall present first some counts of variants in the TAT protocols, since this test was administered to all the children. As is shown in Table 1, a markedly greater number of girls used *-ing* more frequently, while more boys used more *-in*.

TABLE 1

NUMBER OF CHILDREN FAVORING -ING AND -IN VARIANT SUFFIXES IN TAT PROTOCOLS ACCORDING TO SEX

	-ing > -in	-ing ⩽ -in
Boys	5	7
Girls	10	2

Chi square: 2.84; 05 <P <.1 (by two-tailed test).

This suggests that in this community (and probably others where the choice exists) *-ing* is regarded as symbolizing female speakers and *-in* as symbolizing males.

Within each sex, differences in personality are associated with the proportion of frequency of *-ing* to *-in* as illustrated in Table 2.

TABLE 2

FREQUENCY OF USE OF -ING AND -IN IN TAT PROTOCOLS OF TWO BOYS

	-ing	-in
"Model" boy	38	1
"Typical" boy	10	12

Chi square: 19.67; P< .001.

The first boy was regarded by his teacher and others as a "model" boy. He did his school work well, was popular among his peers, reputed to be thoughtful and considerate. The second boy was generally regarded as a "typical" boy—physically strong, dominating, full of mischief, but disarmingly frank about his transgressions. The "model" boy used almost exclusively the *-ing* ending here, while the "typical" boy used the *-in* ending more than half the time, as shown above.

In Table 3 one may also note a slight tendency for the *-ing* variant to be associated with higher socio-economic status, although this is not statistically significant with a sample of this size. The community studied is fairly small and does not have strong class lines, which is probably why more marked results did not appear. (Most previous studies of sociological factors connected with linguistic variants have been concerned with linguistic indices of class, cast or occupational groups. Group boundaries have been regarded, implicity or explicitly, as barriers to communication analogous to political boundaries, geographical distance, etc. The emphasis in this paper is rather on variations within a face-to-face community whose members are in frequent free communication: variations between social categories of speakers and between individual speakers, and situational variations in the speech of individual speakers, as noted below.)

TABLE 3

NUMBER OF CHILDREN FAVORING -ING AND -IN ENDINGS ACCORDING TO FAMILY STATUS

	-ing > -in	-ing ⩽ -in
Above median	8	4
Below median	7	5

Chi square (corrected): 0; P >.9.

Besides asking *who* uses which variant and how much, we may also ask whether there are situational differences in *when* a single speaker uses these variants. One variant in the situation may be described as degree of formality: in the children's terms I would think of this as degree of similarity to a formal classroom recitation. The best child to examine for this variable is the "model" boy of Table 2 since he was interviewed in all three situations mentioned above and was obligingly talkative in each. As Table 4 shows, the frequency of choice of variants changed from an almost exclusive use of *-ing* in the TAT situation to a predominance of *-in* in the informal interviews.

TABLE 4

FREQUENCY OF -ING AND -IN IN A 10-YEAR-OLD BOY'S SPEECH IN THREE SITUATIONS IN ORDER OF INCREASING INFORMALITY

	-ing	-in
TAT	38	1
Formal interview	33	35
Informal interview	24	41

Chi square: 37.07; P >.001.

Of course, these three situations should not be regarded as exhaustive of the frequency range of these variants in this boy's speech. In the interviews I myself used the *-ing* variant consistently and this probably influenced the informant's speech somewhat. Probably in casual conversation with his peers the *-in*/*-ing* ratio is even higher than in the informal interview.

Another measure similar in implication to the frequency of variants by type of interview would be differences in frequency between the beginning and later parts of a single interview. Especially in the TAT protocols, which are the most formal text, I noticed for a number of children that the *-ing* frequency was higher in the beginning of the interview and later dropped off, presumably as the child became more relaxed and accustomed to the situation. In only one child was the reverse trend noted, and there are reasons to believe that this particular child may have become more tense during the administration of the test.

A linguist might ask whether there is any association between the suffix variants and specific verbs. The corpus is not large enough to establish stable frequency indices for the suffixes of individual words, but there is certainly a trend for markedly "formal" verbs to have the *-ing* suffix and markedly "informal" verbs to have the *-in* suffix. The first boy in Table 2 above, for instance, used *-ing* in *criticizing*, *correcting*, *reading*, *visiting*, *interesting*, and used *-in* in *punchin*, *flubbin*, *swimmin*, *chewin*, *hittin*. For some common verbs, however, such as *play*, *go*, and *do* he used both alternatively. Probably only a few verbs are formal or informal enough in their connotations so that the same variant would always be used with them. Of course, the choice of verb vocabulary is itself related to personality and situational factors.

In brief, then, the choice between the *-ing* and the *-in* variants appear to be related to sex, class, personality (aggressive/cooperative), and mood (tense/relaxed) of the speakers (and doubtless of the person spoken to, although this was not investigated), to the formality of the conversation, and to the specific verb spoken. While these are "free variants" in the standard type of description of languages in which only grammatical facts and differences in none but "denotative" meaning are taken into account, if we widen our scope of study to include the meaning of these variants to the conversants we might call them "socially conditioned variants," or "socio-symbolic variants," on the grounds that they serve to symbolize things about the relative status of the conversants and their attitudes toward each other, rather than denoting any difference in the universe of primary discourse (the "outer world"). (Uriel Weinrich has suggested to me the term "symptomatic signs," after Karl Bühler, as an alternative for "socio-symbolic variant" which already has a basis in established usage. However, it seems to me that "symptomatic signs" might be in one sense too broad and in another too narrow: too broad in the sense that it might be interpreted to refer to "non-linguistic" features of speech such as general pitch, loudness, timbre, rate, etc., and too narrow in the sense that Bühler appears to regard the symptomatic function as, ideally, purely expressive of the speaker, while I am looking for a broader term which would cover this function but also include expression of the dyadic relationship between the conversants. This cannot simply be taken care of by adding in Bühler's "signal" function which deals with the "appeal" to the listener, since at least some aspects of the relationship do not exist primarily either in speaker or listener but rather *between* them, e.g., relative age, relative rank. See Bühler [1934], especially p. 28. Whether I should here introduce a term incorporating "symbol" is a further question which I acknowledge but do not discuss here, as it is complex and is not directly relevant to the main argument of the paper.)

What are the wider implications for linguistics of such an analysis of social factors influencing choice of linguistic variants? For one thing, many linguists have recognized that "free" variation is a logically necessary stage in most of all linguistic change. (I find in checking over the literature that this statement seems to be based more on my impressions of conversations with linguists than on published statements. One clear statement of this principle, however, is to be found on p. 367 of Vogt [1954]. A more general statement applying to any type of cultural element, and by implication linguistic elements can be found in Linton [1936, p. 280].) Less widely appreciated but also recognized by some is another fact: Although the mechanisms of psychic economy are becoming better understood in diachronic phonemics, they are not always sufficient to explain fully the progressive adaption of variant forms, and that people adopt a variant primarily not because it is easier to pronounce (which it most frequently is, but not always), or because it facilitates some important distinction in denotational meaning, but because it expresses how they feel about their relative status versus other conversants.

The clearest and most comprehensive statement of social factors in linguistic change which I have encountered is found in an article by Martin Joos (1952) dealing with medieval sibilants. (Others have separately recognized the importance of fashion in linguistic change, especially in the spread of standard dialects, and to a lesser degree have recognized the complementary process of using distinctive linguistic features to emphasize social exclusiveness. J. O. Hertzler (1953) gives a bibliography including studies of both sorts. Joos's statement however appears to me to be unique in his recognition that the two processes combine to constitute a self-perpetuating cycle. Since Joos is noted for his rigorous definition of the scope of linguistics proper it is perhaps all the more interesting that he should throw in this "sociological" aside.) He speaks of "the phonetic drift, which was kept going in the usual way: that is, the dialects and idiolects of higher prestige were more advanced in this direction, and their speakers carried the drift further along so as to maintain the prestige-marking difference against their pursuers. The vanity factor is needed to explain why phonetic drifts tend to continue in the same direction; the 'inertia sometimes invoked is a label and not an argument.'" This protracted pursuit of an elite by an envious mass and consequent "flight" of the elite is in my opinion the most important mechanism in linguistic drift, not only in the phonetic drift which Joos discusses, but in syntactic and lexical drift as well. (Incidentally, this flight-pursuit mechanism might be regarded as an explanation of the constant rate of decay of basic "non-cultural" vocabulary postulated by Morris Swadesh's theory of glottochronology. To make it suffice one would also need to assume that all societies possess some form of elite group—if only the "ideal conformist" in some societies—and that mass envy of the elite and ambition to join them are everywhere the same. These assumptions may seem radical and against common sense, but they are not as easy to refute as one might think. Needless to say, one would not assume that the elite is always a property or authority elite. In politically and economically undifferentiated societies, the most important criterion might be technical skill and productivity in consumer goods, admired personality traits, etc.)

The study of social factors in linguistic drift is in the field of the sociology of language rather than linguistics proper. However, this study can not reach ultimate fruition without certain linguistic studies by competent linguists. I refer here to studies of individual variations in linguistic forms in small, face-to-face speech communities, and of variations in these forms in the speech of single individuals in a range of social situations. Studies of this sort constitute tasks of respectable magnitude which have, in the main, been neglected. (The classic study in this field is Gauchat [1905]. Other references are cited by von Wartburg [1946, p. 33]. Modern techniques, of course, open entirely new perspectives for research.)

A student of social factors in the choice of linguistic variants would wish to know for a fairly large stratified sample of a speech community how often members of a given sub-group used a sizable sample of series of socially significant variants, and for at least some of the sub-groups one would want to know how these frequencies of choice of variants changed under different situations and in the presence of conversants of different social status and personal relationships. A linguist as such would not wish to analyze these social factors in great detail. But it would be well within the scope of linguistics to identify individual informants in a unitary speech community by name or code number and group them according to their similarity or dissimilarity in the use of variants in some standard situation, say, in conversation with the linguist. The psychologist and sociologist could then take these groups and see what sense they made in their terms. In practice, of course, such a rigorous separation between linguistics and the more general social sciences is not required since linguists and other laymen are presumably capable of making a number of distinctions of considerable sociological interest, such as male versus female, etc.

A word about the relation of the proposed study to dialectology is appropriate here. It has generally been the aim of dialectologists to describe linguistic variations between groups which are separated by some communications barrier, especially geography or social class. What I am advocating here is the study of linguistic variations within small groups where there is free and relatively intense communication, so that as far as possible the lack of contact between speakers is not a reason for failure to use the same forms. Of course in a large society such as ours, small closed groups are rare, and some of the variation among the individuals of any group picked for study will be due to the fact that they have different contacts outside the group. But this empirical fact does not reduce the importance of studying variation within the face-to-face community, although it suggests that the best place to study such variation would be on a remote Pacific atoll with a small, long-established population.

What I am proposing might be called comparative idiolectology rather than dialectology. Ideally, a thorough description of a single dialect would be based on the study of a sizable sample of the idiolects in a local speech community, in the same way that a through description of a language would be based on the study of a sizable sample of its dialects. In comparative idiolectology one might, as a device of field work, still concentrate on a single informant, but one would want to follow him around with a portable recording machine and note changes in his speech in different settings and situations and with different conversants. Moreover, since phenomenologically language is as much listening as speaking one would be led to analyze what was said comprehensibly to him by others as well as what he said himself.

The untrained listener will not, of course, generally be able to reproduce or identify the differences in the speech of others whom he encounters, unless he is an accomplished mimic. But he does react to these differences by making interpretations about the social situation on the basis of them and will be able to tell when a speaker is talking like a woman, like an upper class person, like a relaxed person, etc., even though he cannot specify all the variant forms on which he bases his judgment. (The "tape experiment" described by Putnam and O'Hern [1955] investigates language and social status in this manner, although the speakers were not members of a single face-to-face community, so the complication of barriers to communication is introduced.) (This is not to deny the presence or importance of other "non-linguistic" features of speech as well as things entirely unconnected with speech such as dress, physical appearance, gestures, etc., which also serve as cues for judgments of the conversational situation.)

In analyzing socio-symbolic variants there will obviously be a certain amount of association between variant series. In many of the series at least one variant could be distinguished as "formal," and another as "informal." But it is a question for empirical investigation whether this distinction applies to all variant series, and, if so, with how much force. I have suggested above a number of factors which influence the *-in*/*-ing* distinction. Conceivably they all bear on formality, that is, compliance, tenseness, femaleness, and high class all make for formal behavior. But even if this is true for these factors in American culture, are they a unitary complex in all cultures, and may there not be other social factors affecting socio-symbolic variants which are independent of the formality complex? Are variants associated with being female always associated as well with formality? In three languages with which I am acquainted, English, Japanese, and Ponapean, I can think of a number of instances where this link is found, but there also appear to be exceptions. In Ponapean, for instance, a minority of women have an unusual allophone for the *r* phoneme, but this seems to have no relation to the degree of formality. Lisping in English is regarded as feminine, but would indicate little about degree of formality.

Even where the same factor determines the choice of alternants in several series of variants, the breaking point for each series will probably be different. For instance, in the TAT texts discussed above, three of the children used the pronunciation *ey* for the indefinite article *a*. This pronunciation can be regarded as formal to the point of being artificial and is much more restricted for speakers in this community than the *-ing* variant of the present participle ending, yet the direction of social symbolism is the same, though not the intensity. In other words, *ey* in itself is more a sign of formality than *-ing* though both are signs of formality. The "formality" index of a given text would be determined by the variant chosen in several series of socio-symbolic variants, each of which would have a different socio-symbolic level with respect to formality. Presumably these series could be ordered in terms of increasingly greater thresholds of formality required to bring about the shift from the informal to the formal form.

I have been stressing here the synchronic implications of socio-symbolic variants. The diachronic implications are at least equally interesting. Obviously the threshold for a given variant does not *necessarily* remain the same, generation after generation. If a particular variant has for whatever reason greater prestige, it will gradually be adopted in more situations by more people: its threshold will be lowered. But as its threshold is lowered and approaches universality in the speech community, its socio-symbolic load is reduced and eventually vanishes. One could hardly convey much of an air of informality, for example, by saying ə for the indefinite article, though saying *ey* would be quite stilted. But presumably new series of variants keep arising to replace those which achieve uniformity in this way.

Now what is meant by "variants of greater prestige"? One could determine which of a pair of variants had the greater prestige by noting which tended to "spread" when two conversants who in other situations differed in their choice came together. But the grounds of prestige clearly vary according to individuals and societies. A variant which one man uses because he wants to seem dignified another man would reject because he did not want to seem stiff. Societies likewise have characteristic average value preferences. Using the variable of formality, it is quite possible that one society would show a tendency, at least in some situations, to show a preference for adoption of formal forms of speech, and another in analogous situations show a preference for informal forms. These preferences could in turn be related by persons so inclined to social structure. One would end up with a statement not simply of the direction of linguistic drift, but what this drift meant psychologically and what social changes might check it. It would be very interesting, for instance, to find and examine cognate variants from some related societies with differing descent practices, and see whether the current drift is in the direction of feminization or masculinization. Such data would not only illuminate the mechanism of linguistic drift, but would provide students of social structure with extremely valuable indices of the distribution of envy and cross-segmental identification in the communities speaking the language studied.

REFERENCE NOTE

For related references on variation and social perception of speech, see the article by Gumperz in Part VII.

References not in the general bibliography:

GAUCHAT, LOUIS

1905. L'Unité phonétique dans le patois d'une commune. *Aus romanischen Sprachen und Literatur*, pp. 124 ff.

WARTBURG, W. VON

1946. *Problèmes et méthodes de la linguistique*. Paris.

Interlingual Word Taboos 52

MARY R. HAAS

SOME YEARS AGO, a Creek Indian informant in Oklahoma stated that the Indians tended to avoid the use of certain words of their own language when white people were around. It turned out that the avoided words were those which bear some phonetic similarity to the "four-letter" words of English. These words were avoided even though it is doubtful that a white person not knowing Creek would, when overhearing Creek utterances delivered at a normal rate of speed for that language, be likely to catch these words and attach any special significance to them. For one thing, not understanding the language, he would be unlikely to concentrate sufficiently to notice the rather rare sequences of sounds which might cause him to think he was hearing English obscene words.

How then did the taboo develop? It may be suggested that it arose as a direct result of bilingualism among the Creeks. The more English they knew and used, the more conscious they would be of the phonetic similarity between certain Creek syllables (no full words or even morphemes coincide) and the tabooed words of English. Thus the avoidance grew as bilingualism increased among the Creeks (white people normally do not learn Creek) and as they came more and more to think in terms of the white man's taboos.

Among the words pointed out as being avoided are the following: *fákki* "soil, earth, clay," *apíswa* "meat, flesh," and *apíssi:* "fat (adj.)." Creek monosyllabic words are very rare. Hence the words given here all contain more than one syllable, only one of which bears any resemblance to an English tabooed word. The resemblance may appear to be strengthened by the fact that it is the accented syllable which bears the similarity, but composite words containing the words quoted above may also be avoided, and in such cases the accent has generally shifted to another syllable, e.g. *fakkitalá:swa* "clay," *fakkinú:ła* "brick," and *apisnihá:* "meat fat."

A few years later it became apparent that Thai students studying in this country also tend to avoid certain words of their own language which bear a phonetic resemblance to English obscene words. Here again they avoid the words only when English speakers are about, but the reason for the avoidance appears to stem from their own uncertainty about the propriety of using the words because of their knowledge of English. The tradition of avoidance is a continuous one. Thai students already residing in this country teach each succeeding group of newly arrived students about the taboo, and in this way the avoidance is kept alive from year to year. (Since the Thai do not immigrate to this country, the taboo exists only among students. Occasionally a student is found who is uninterested in observing the taboo. Such a student will usually be found to have come from a section of Thailand other than Bangkok or its environs. Elaborate gradations of politeness and vulgarity of speech are particularly characteristic of the Bangkok area.)

The phonetic nature of Thai is such that there are more words on the taboo list than there are in Creek. Furthermore, since Thai is largely, though not exclusively, monosyllabic, the words tend to bear a greater resemblance to the English tabooed words than do the corresponding avoided words of Creek.

These secondarily tabooed words of Thai include the following: *fàg* "sheath, (bean-) pod," *fág* (1) "to hatch," (2) "a kind of pumpkin or squash," *phrig* "(chili) pepper," and *khán* "to crush, squeeze out." In connection with the last word, it is to be noted that there are other words having the same sequence of sounds excepts for the tone, e.g. *khan* (1) "to itch," (2) classifier for vehicles and other objects, and *khǎn* (1) "to be funny," (2) "to crow," (3) "waterbowl," but it is only the word having the high tone that bears, to the Thai ear, a strong resemblance to the English tabooed word. The reason for this is two-fold: (1) English words with final stop consonants are borrowed into Thai with a high tone, e.g. *kéb* "(gun-) cap," *kɔ́g* "(water-) tap," and (2) the high tone on a syllable lacking a final stop is accompanied by glottal stricture when spoken in isolation or when occurring in phrase-final position. The Thai ear equates the final stop of the English word with the glottal stricture of the Thai word; hence the English word, as pronounced in English, sounds like the Thai word *khán*, whereas *khan* and *khǎn* do not.

The word *phríg* "(chili) pepper" (also used as an abbreviation for *phrígthaj* "ground pepper, esp. black pepper") caused one group of students to be faced with a dilemma, since, when eating out, it was necessary to use this word frequently. In order to observe their self-imposed taboo and at the same time provide themselves with a substitute term, this group adopted the device of translating the obscene connotation of the word (if interpreted as English) into the elegant Thai term of the same meaning, namely *lyŋ* "the lingam" (derived from the Sanskrit term). Thus in one limited circle of intimates (men), the word *lyŋ* acquired a secondary meaning "pepper" by the round-about method of translating a Thai word as if it were an English word. This example of transference of meaning is exceptionally revealing for two reasons: (1) Most types of vulgarity and familiarity of speech are not avoided by the Thai among intimates (generally persons of the samé sex- and age-group). Therefore, although *lyŋ* actually has the meaning they were trying to avoid when using it as a substitute for *phríg* (if this is interpreted as English), this particular substitution must, under the circumstances, have been virtually, if not actually spontaneous. (2) Vulgarity and familiarity of speech should be avoided in the presence of those who are not intimates. Therefore since the word *phríg* might be overheard by persons who were not intimates (in this case, speakers of English) and since, in this event, it was liable to interpretation as an obscenity, the word had to be scrupulously avoided. (The word "vulgarity" is not used here as a loose synonym for "obscenity." The Thai word *jàab*, which I translate "to be vulgar," for lack of a more adequate term, has a much wider application than "obscene." Thus, to touch the head of another person, to call attention to one's feet by kicking or any unnecessary movement, to use certain pronouns of derogatory connotation, to use any of various kinds of uncouth language, whether obscene or not, to speak loudly or laugh hilariously, all these things are *jàab*. It is in this sense, then, that the words "vulgar" and "vulgarity" are to be understood when they are used with reference to the Thai.)

Other instances of avoidance also occur in Thai. These are particularly interesting in that they are far less likely to be misinterpreted as obscenities by speakers of English than are the words quoted above. Thai has no phoneme *š* (English sh), the nearest equivalent sound being the phoneme *ch*, an aspirated palatal stop. Another sound bearing a certain resemblance to English *š*, from the Thai point of view, is *c*, an unaspirated palatal stop. In pronouncing English words the normal substitution for English *š* is Thai *ch*, but avoidance taboos, of the type mentioned above, extend also to Thai words beginning in *c*. As a consequence of this, the following words also often come into the tabooed category: *chíd* "to be close, near" and *cìd* "heart, mind" (<Pali-Sanskrit *citta*). The latter word occasionally occurs as a component of given names in Thai, and at least one man whose name was *sǒmcìd*, literally "suiting the heart" (a very pleasing name in Thai), was so embarrassed by this fact that he avoided the use of his Thai name wherever possible while residing in this country and adopted an English nickname instead. (Many others also adopt English nicknames for various other reasons.) Other examples of name-changing under somewhat comparable circumstances are taken up in a later section of this paper.

The examples of avoided words quoted in the immediately preceding paragraphs range all the way from words whose phonetic resemblance to English tabooed words is very close to others whose resemblance is so slight as to escape detection by the average speaker of English.

Therefore the careful avoidance of these words in the presence of speakers of English arises from an exceptionally acute anxiety about the proprieties and niceties of speech. This anxiety is very well reflected in the Thai language itself, for one of its most prominent characteristics is the existence of a very large number of synonymous sets of words differentiated only by the varying degrees of vulgarity and politeness associated with their use. (Thus there are at least eleven words meaning "to eat" connoting varying degrees of politeness or vulgarity. Such elaboration of speech is largely restricted to the Bangkok area. In other parts of the country other dialects are spoken, and these are marked by greater simplicity in this respect than is the Bangkok dialect.) The Thai is consequently willing to go to extreme lengths to avoid even the slightest suspicion of vulgarity. Vulgar speech, when used, is deliberate and intentional. To give the impression of vulgarity unwittingly is unthinkable.

The problem of tabooed words also exists in reverse. That is, certain perfectly harmless English words may bear a phonetic resemblance to tabooed or obscene words in other languages. A striking example of this is found in the Nootka Indian language of Vancouver Island. The English word *such* bears so close a resemblance to Nootka *sač* "*vàgina ùmens*" that teachers entrusted with the training of young Indians find it virtually impossible to persuade their girl students to utter the English word under any circumstances.

Other examples occur in Thai. The English word *yet* closely resembles the Thai word *jéd* "to have intercourse" (vulgar and impolite). The resemblance is heightened by the fact that the Thai word has a high tone. Thai taboos against the use of words which correspond in meaning to the English "four-letter" words are not puritanical in origin, as they are in English. Most of the words are at least considered printable in certain situations, for example, in dictionaries, or in textbooks designed to instruct students concerning words which must be avoided in the presence of royalty. The word under consideration here, however, is an exception—it has not been found listed in any Thai dictionary, nor in a textbook. Even so, the word is not one which would be avoided among intimates (i.e., persons of the same sex- and age-group). Nevertheless, the English word *yet* is very often a source of embarrassment to the Thai, particularly girls studying English in school, since the Thai word is definitely one of several which would be avoided in the classroom. The English word *key* also causes embarrassment to some, because of its resemblance to the Thai word *khîi* "excrement" or "to void excrement" (vulgar), and since English monosyllables not having final stop consonants are often borrowed into Thai with a falling tone; hence a Thai, when first learning English, would pronounce *key* exactly as *khîi*. However, the Thai word *khîi*, though vulgar, falls somewhat short of being obscene and its use is permissible in some circumstances. For example, words like *khîiphŷŋ* "beeswax" (lit. "bee-excrement") or *phrigkhîinûu* "bird chili or guinea pepper" (lit., "mouse-excrement pepper"), and numerous other similar words, are generally quite freely used without fear of the stigma of vulgarity. Such words would, however, be strictly avoided in the presence of royalty.

Two other examples of accidental phonetic resemblances between perfectly harmless words of one language and impolite or obscene words of another language may be cited here.

The first example involves the Chinese and Burmese languages and the locale is Rangoon. At least two common Chinese family names, Li and Chi, sound like Burmese *lî* "phallus" and *chî* "excrement." It has not been possible to ascertain the attitude of the Rangoon Chinese toward the matter beyond the statement of a Burmese informant to the effect that it is not serious enough to cause the Chinese to change their names; contrast this with the example taken up in the immediately succeeding paragraphs. Burmese Rangoonians, on the other hand, are quite aware of the interlingual similarity and cannot help but find it amusing; at the same time they feel that the resulting ambiguity is somewhat alleviated by the use of a title meaning "Mr." in front of the name.

The second example involves interlingual similarities between impolite or unflattering words and personal, that is, given names. This situation arises between Northeastern Thai and Central Thai and the locale is Bangkok. There are a number of given names of not infrequent occurrence among the Northeastern Thai which sound vulgar or impolite in the Bangkok dialect (Central Thai). Other given names sometimes used in Northeastern Thailand are of a type which is considered highly unflattering or derogatory in the Bangkok area. As a consequence, a Northeastern Thai bearing one of these given names will, on going to Bangkok, be obliged to change his name. (If he does not, he will lay himself open to constant teasing and ridicule.)

One not uncommon Northeastern Thai name is *tâw* , a personal name of a man, sometimes of a woman. (Some northeastern personal names may be given either to men or to women, some only to men, and some only to women. Each name is marked accordingly.) This is equivalent to Bankok *tâw*, which in one of its meanings is an obscene term meaning "vagina." (There are at least seven Bangkok words having this meaning; the one cited here is very nearly at the bottom of the scale in degree of vulgarity. The Bangkok word is either *tâw* or *tàw*. However, the tonal equivalences between Northeastern Thai and Central Thai are such that NE *tâw* is equivalent [in sound correspondence, not in meaning] to Bangkok *tâw* but not to *tàw*.) In northeastern Thailand animal names are sometimes used as personal names; in the Bangkok area, names of this type are strictly avoided. Thus NE *măa*, personal name (m. or w.), also means "dog"; Bangkok *măa* means only "dog" and would never be used as a name. NE *thúj*, personal name (m.), is equivalent to Bangkok *thuj* "water buffalo having abnormal or stunted horns." NE *sěen*, personal name (m.), is equivalent to Bangkok *sěen* "rufous stump-tailed monkey" (not found in Northeastern Thailand). NE *thǒon*, personal name (m.), also refers to a kind of monkey found in the northeast; there is no Bangkok equivalent, but the name would be changed in Bangkok because it refers to a kind of animal. NE *tūn*, personal name (m. or w.), also means "bamboo-rat," and is equivalent to Bangkok *tùn* which means not only "bamboo-rat" but also occurs in a common phrase *ŋôoŋâw tàwtùn* "extremely stupid."

The last example quoted above is changed not only because it refers to an animal but also because it is unflattering in its reference to stupidity. Other names are changed solely because they are unflattering, e.g., NE *kȳm*, personal name (m.), which also means "not clever." Though it has no Bangkok equivalent, it is changed because it fails to meet Bangkok concepts of suitability in a name. If the parents dislike or hate their daughter they may name her *thōom*, which also means "not pretty and not good, rather stupid." The word has no Bangkok equivalent, but its connotation in the northeast is so unflattering that it will be changed.

A few northeastern Thai personal names are changed because they are considered unpleasing in sound. Some of these have no other meaning but are changed solely because of their sound, e.g., NE *pў̌y*, a common personal name (m.). Others have other meanings besides their use as names, but they are changed because of their sound rather than because of their meaning, e.g., NE *mȳy*, personal name (m.), also "black gunpowder," and NE *mŷm*, personal name (w.), also meaning "black." ("Black," as a name, is not usually considered unflattering.)

A common stimulus for name-changing among the Northeastern Thai arises when the person bearing the name goes to Bangkok. Some persons, however, may change their names even though they remain at home, particularly upon attaining an official position. But even in this latter event, the change appears to be due to the influence of the culture of the capital, since standards for what befits a person attaining an official position are set largely in Bangkok. Note that not all instances of name-changing quoted above are the result of interlingual word taboos, i.e., word taboos arising from interlingual ambiguity. All, however, are the result of taboos imposed by another culture.

The problem of interlingual word taboos has, as far as is known, received little if any attention among linguists. Many other examples could no doubt be adduced if some attention were given to the matter. It is a type of problem that can easily escape notice, particularly if the period of field contact is short. The Creek-English and Thai-English examples cited came to attention accidentally after periods of long contact and in informal conversations, not during formalized questioning periods. The Chinese-Burmese and Northeastern Thai-Central Thai examples, on the other hand, were uncovered by direct questioning after interest was aroused in discovering more examples of such taboos. (Certain conditions, however, have to be present before the problem arises. First of all, the phonetic conditions must be present. In other words, the languages which come in contact must have certain sounds and sequences of sounds in common. For example, Japanese speakers residing in this country do not encounter this problem because Japanese is utterly lacking in the sequences of sounds which are found to occur in English "four-letter" words. Similarly, Burmese students studying in this country are likewise untroubled by the problem because Burmese lacks the necessary sounds and sound sequences.)

In general it is the speakers of the minority language who feel obliged to observe the taboo, which, though the result of contact, is not actually imposed by the speakers of the majority language; for the latter, in their ignorance of the the minority language (except when proper names are involved), are normally quite unaware of the problem.

The examples brought forth in this paper illustrate two quite different types of situations. The Creek-English example is the result of acculturation. The same is true of the Northeast Thai-Central Thai example. In both of these instances it is conceivable that in time the supposedly objectionable words of the minority language may become obsolete or obsolescent. (Of course it is also possible that Creek as a language may die out before the taboo imposed from English has had time to exercise its full effect.) The Thai-English example, on the other hand, is a matter of temporary avoidance and will never have any permanent influence on the Thai language. Thai students may try to avoid certain English-sounding Thai words while residing in this country, but they do not continue to observe the taboo after they return to their own country, even though some speakers of English also reside there. The Chinese-Burmese example is interesting for still another reason. Here, even though the interlingual ambiguity causes amusement to the majority (Burmese), the minority group (Chinese) has no inclination to be affected by this attitude and makes no attempt to effect an adaptation or change.

REFERENCE NOTE

The Creek (or Muskogee) language has the following consonants: voiceless unaspirated or weakly aspirated stops *p*, *t*, *k* and affricate *c;* voiceless spirants *f*, *s*, *ł*, *h;* voiced semivowels *y*, *w;* voiced nasals *m*, *n*, and defective *n* (of rare occurrence); voiced lateral *l*. Vowels are *i* [I], *a* [A], *u* [U], *i:* [i:], *a:* [a:], *u:* [o:], and the rare *-e-* (occurring only before *y*).

On the phonemes of Thai, see the article by Haas in Part VI. The present article notes also that "the final stops *b*, *d*, and *g* are briefly voiced but unreleased; they therefore resemble the English final stops *p*, *t*, and *k*."

In the Burmese words quoted *l* and *ch* are more or less equivalent to English *l* and *ch; i* is [i]; the tone mark (ˆ) indicates a high tone in nonfinal position or a falling tone in final position.

Northeastern Thai is not phonemically identical with Central Thai (noted above). Northeastern Thai has a consonant phoneme *n* (the palatal nasal), not found in Central Thai, and lacks *ch* and *r*, which are common in Central Thai. The vowels, on the other hand, have the same values in the two dialects, though they often differ in their distribution. Northeastern Thai has seven tones, as follows: high-falling (ˋ), lower high level (¯), lower high falling (ˆ), mid level (unmarked), low level (ˋ), very low level (˜), and rising (ˇ). The tonal equivalences between Northeastern Thai and Central Thai normally follow certain regular rules.

For examples of interlingual avoidance as a factor in change, stimulated by the present article, see Leslau (1952) and Williams-Hunt (1952).

For general discussion and case studies of taboo as a factor in linguistic change, see Bergsland and Vogt (1962, pp. 126-217), Bonfante (1939), Cohen (1956a, p. 199), Elmendorf (1951), Emeneau (1948), Estrich and Sperber (1952, chaps. 1-4), Havers (1946), Hymes (1960a, pp. 8-9), Jespersen (1922, Book 3, chap. 13, Section

2), Joffe (1948), Kunene (1958), Leslau (1959), Meillet (1926-1936, Vol. I, pp. 281-291), Mencken (1936, pp. 565-595; 639-661), reprinted in Dean and Wilson, (1959, pp. 67-78), Smal-Stocki (1950), Ullmann (1957, *passim*), Vendryes (1925, pp. 212-230). On the taboos of seaman and fisherman in particular, see Henningsen (1957), Kroeber (1960b), Lockwood (1956).

On taboo in general, see Freud (1938, pp. 807-930), Kroeber (1952, pp. 301-309), Lessa and Vogt (1958, Section 4), Mead (1928), Steiner (1956), Webster (1942).

References not in the general bibliography:

BONFANTE, G.

1939. Études sur le tabou dans les langues Indo-Européenes. *Mélanges de Linguistique offerts à Ch. Bally*. Geneva. Pp. 195-207.

ELMENDORF, W. W.

1951. Word-Taboo and Lexical Change in Coast Salish. *IJAL*, *17:* 205-208.

EMENEAU, MURRAY B.

1948. Taboos on Animal Names. *Lg.*, *24:* 56-63.

HAVERS, W.

1946. *Neuere Literatur zum Sprachtabu.* (Sitzungsberichte der Wiener Akademie, 103, No. 5.) Vienna.

HENNINGSEN, HENNING

1957. Taboo-words among Seamen and Fishermen. *The Mariner's Mirror*, *43* (4): 336-337.

JOFFE, NATALIE

1948. The Vernacular of Menstruation. *Word*, *4:* 181-186.

KUNENE, D. P.

1958. Notes on Hlonepha Among the Southern Sotha. *African Studies*, *17:* 159-182.

LESLAU, WOLF

1952. A Footnote on Interlingual Word Taboo. *AA*, *54:* 274.

1959. Taboo Expressions in Ethiopia. *AA*, *61:* 105-107.

LESSA, WILLIAM A., and E. Z. VOGT

1958. *Reader in Comparative Religion. An Anthropological Approach*. New York: Harper & Row.

LOCKWOOD, W. B.

1956. Word Taboo in the Language of the Faroese Fishermen. *Transactions of the Philological Society* (*London*, *1955*). London. Pp. 1-24.

MEAD, MARGARET

1928. *An Inquiry into the Question of Cultural Stability in Polynesia*. New York: Columbia University Press.

SMAL-STOCKI, ROMAN

1950. Taboos on Animal Names in Ukrainian. *Lg.*, *26:* 489-493.

STEINER, FRANZ

1956. *Taboo.* With a preface by E. E. Evans-Pritchard. Edited by Laura Bohannon. London: Cohen and West.

WEBSTER, HUTTON

1942. *Taboo, A Sociological Study*. Stanford: Stanford University Press.

WILLIAMS-HUNT, P. D. RIDER

1952. Comment on Interlingual Word Taboo. *AA*, *54:* 274-275.

Incipient Bilingualism 53

A. RICHARD DIEBOLD, JR.

INTRODUCTION

The past decade has seen a flurry of activity in the field of language contact, with the result that we now have many descriptive studies and several valuable theoretical reviews of the field which serve to stimulate and guide further inquiry. One of the suggestions repeatedly pressed on the reader of Weinreich's *Languages in Contact* (1953) and Haugen's *Bilingualism in the Americas* (1956) is the necessity of interdisciplinary research in studying the so-called extralinguistic factors which abound in any consideration of this subject. To be sure, linguists have made great strides in their principal area of interest in language contact viz. the study of linguistic borrowing. But these studies have been by and large descriptive of the linguistic *results* of language contact. They are not so much interested in the behavior which accounts for the observed changes (say, between two historical stages of a language) as they are in identifying and tabulating the changes. Excellent documentation of the range of variability of these linguistic results is unfortunately matched by little knowledge concerning the social factors which effect their inception.

My experience in dealing with bilingualism among American Indian groups in Mexico suggests to me that a description of the linguistic phenomena alone, while perhaps instructive in enriching a typology of linguistic borrowing, is an idle exercise if left without sociological analysis. The purpose of the present paper is to demonstrate the interdependency of linguistic and sociological factors in one situation which I have encountered: a stage in the contact between two languages which I have called incipient bilingualism.

1. PREMISES AND TERMINOLOGY

The terminology used in language contact study has fairly precise meanings, but many terms have only recently appeared in the literature. Relevant anthropological terminology is less precise, and accidents of the readers' interests may have exposed them to very casual usage of these terms or removed them from contact with these terms altogether.

1.1. CONVERGENT CHANGE

It is assumed that when there is contact between two societies whose members speak different languages, there will result certain linguistic and other cultural changes which must be attributed directly to the fact of contact. This will be evident upon examination of the change subsequent to the contact of the two groups. Language contact and culture contact universally result in the transfer of elements from one system to the other, by a process which has been variously labeled borrowing or diffusion. This transfer of elements produces systemic change which might be called *convergent*, since it involves a degree of merging of two separate systems. (Convergence based on transfer is distinct from the biological and older anthropological concept, which described the independent evolution of typologically similar forms without historical connection, or with only remote connection. Convergence in our sense is a concomitant of culture contact as well as language contact. Such merging is excluded from biological systems: speciation produces infinite bifurcation, but mutual infertility of different species prohibits subsequent biological merging. Biological change is almost totally divergent. Linguistic and cultural change, on the other hand, is rarely if ever free from convergence. The analogue of biological speciation in linguistic change is language and dialect formation; but mutual unintelligibility, unlike mutual infertility, is no block to systemic convergence.) Convergent change contrasts with the other principal process of historical change, which I call evolutionary, or *divergent*. Divergent change is not dependent on contact of two systems or transfer between them. It operates within a system and is largely observed to produce systemic change which is internal, such as that between two historical stages of the same language, or to produce bifurcation, such as the divergence of an ancestral protolanguage into descendent daughter languages.

Contact and convergence between two different languages or cultures results in a sociological situation wherein the same individual learns elements from a linguistic or cultural system other than his native system. Linguists refer to this learning situation as *language contact* and to the particular learning process as *bilingualization*. The individuals so involved are called *bilingual*. Linguistic change resulting from such contact is called *borrowing* or *interference*. Anthropologists refer to the learning situation as *culture contact* and to the particular learning process as *acculturation*. The locus is again the individual culture carrier, who, in a situation of culture contact, is sometimes called *bicultural*. Change in a culture resulting from acculturation is referred to as *borrowing*.

Thus, in both language and culture contact, there are two aspects to be considered, a sociological learning process, viz. bilingualism and acculturation, and a result of that process: change in one or both of the systems, viz. linguistic interference and cultural borrowing. The linguist has been traditionally interested only in the identification of linguistic interference, and comparative linguistics has evolved an elaborate set of analytical and descriptive procedures for the study of linguistic borrowing. But there has been until recently little interest evinced in the process; I concur with Haugen that there are further obligations: "The linguist's task is to identify and describe all cases of interference, and then to cooperate with other social scientists in accounting for them" (1956, p. 11).

1.2. BILINGUALISM

When two languages come into contact, speakers of either language may learn elements of the other language. This acquisition of the nonnative language produces *bilingualism*. While the resultant convergent change in the language systems is a purely linguistic problem, bilingualism itself is essentially sociological.

The concept of bilingualism in the literature today is a very catholic one. First, as used by Haugen (1956) and Weinrich (1953), it eschews the restriction imposed by the prefix *bi-* to learning a second language; it includes in its meaning the learning of all languages subsequent to the acquistion of one's childhood language. Nor is it restricted to Bloomfield's use of the term, viz. "native-like control of two languages," which enjoys wide distribution in the literature and in lay concepts. "Native-like control of two languages" can be included at one end of a typology of bilingualism. Weinrich adopts the term *coordinate bilingual* for any speaker learning more than one language, either during childhood acquisition of two or more native languages or later "perfect" mastery of a language other than the native one. Nonnative proficiency in the second language, which presumably can be quantified, distinguishes the *subordinate bilingual*. Haugen has suggested that the minimal qualification for bilingual status is the ability of the speaker to "produce complete meaningful utterances in the other language" (1953, vol. I, p. 7). A priori, it would appear that this measure of minimal proficiency might exclude some of the stages of initial learning, stages which would not permit the speaker a command sufficient to produce "complete meaningful utterances" either because the learning was restricted to a highly atomistic knowledge of the second language or because it remained entirely passive. I would prefer to leave open the question of minimal proficiency, reserving for the initial learning stage the term *incipient bilingualism*.

Numerous examples of languages in contact suggest that bilingualism is seldom if ever mutually balanced between the two groups of speakers. It appears, rather, that more speakers from one of the speech-groups become bilinguals than from the other. This sociological situation is matched by a concomitant one-sidedness in the actual convergent linguistic change which results from the contact (see §1.3). Bloomfield introduced the term *intimate borrowing* to cover, somewhat unfortunately, both the sociological learning situation and the linguistic results: " . . . we can usually distinguish between ordinary cultural borrowing and the *intimate borrowing* which occurs when two languages are spoken in what is topographically and politically a single community" (1933, p. 476). Bloomfield spoke of the upper or *dominant* language, which many speakers of the *lower* language learn, although few or no speakers of the dominant conversely learn the lower. "The pratical background of this process is evident. The upper language is spoken by the dominant and privileged group; many kinds of pressure drive the speaker of the lower language to use the upper language" (1933, p. 462).

Viewed historically, either of two principal sociological results can follow from language contact in a given speech community. First, there may be indefinitely prolonged bilingualism, such that both languages continue to be learned, although perhaps in determinably different contexts and functions. Alternatively, one of the two languages may fall into disuse, such that fewer and fewer and finally no new speakers learn it. In the latter case we speak of a *language shift*, and bilingualism ceases with the death of the last speaker of the language that is no longer learned.

1.3. INTERFERENCE

We consider now the linguistic aspect of language contact. Weinrich has described *interference* as "Those instances of deviation from the norms of either language which occur in the speech of bilinguals as a result of their familiarity with more than one language, i.e., as a result of language contact" (1953, p. 1).

Linguistic interference parallels the sociological situation of bilingualism. Given two languages in contact, it is discovered that the relationship of dominant to lower discussed by Bloomfield with reference to bilingualism obtains also with reference to interference: "In all cases . . . *it is the lower language which borrows predominantly from the upper*. Accordingly, if the upper language survives, it remains as it was, except for a few cultural loans, such as it might take from any neighbor . . . if the lower language survives, it bears the marks of the struggle in the shape of copious borrowings (1933, p. 464). There is, then, a recurrent imbalance for two languages in contact at any one point in time. Linguistically this is reflected in the fact that interference in the lower language is marked, while negligible or wholly absent in the dominant language.

The linguist's main concern, to describe the interference resulting from a situation of language contact, will presumably involve the detection of nonnative elements in one of the languages, i.e., "those instances of deviation" resulting from bilingualism. We speak of these nonnative elements as *replicas*, the *models* of which exist in the other language.

Weinreich has adopted in his writings the terms *primary language* (P-language) and *secondary language* (S-language). The former applies, in any discussion of a bilingual's role in language contact, to the native or earlier learned language of the two, the latter to the later learned language.

The impact of the S-language on the P-language must be considered. First, there must be some measurement of the total effect of interference from S on P; such a measure will gauge the *degree of convergence* of S-elements in the P-language. One framework for the discussion of the degree of convergence is provided by Haugen, who distinguishes (1) *switching*, "the alternate use of two languages"; (2) *interference*, "the overlapping of two languages", and (3) *integration*, "the regular use of materials from one language in another, so that there is no longer either switching or overlapping, except in a historical sense" (1956, p. 40. In this paper "interference," unspecified, will refer to the total phenomenon of linguistic interference. Subsequent sections will occasionally distinguish between integrated and non-integrated interference, but this usage will be clear from context or specification.) The choice of terms is perhaps unfortunate, since Weinreich established the usage of "interference" to cover both Haugen's "interference" and "integration," although not cases of pure code-switching. (The latter event, moreover, seems to be rare; we recognize it as a hypothetical end-point in a typology of interference.) Weinreich's discussion, in his *Languages in Contact*, of the differences between interference in *langue* and *parole* offers a very practical means for distinguishing Haugen's "integration" from other forms of interference;

this distinction is adopted here. Elements of a language which are genetically replicas of models found in another language S, but which the linguist would describe as a part of the *langue* of P, will be termed *integration*. They are those nonnative elements which the monolingual speaker of P, as well as the bilingual, learns in the childhood acquistion of his language. They are the products of completed linguistic diffusion. Interference will subsume, on the other hand, those elements in P which are replicas of models in another language S and which the speaker acquires, not through childhood learning of his P native language, but rather through subsequent contact with the S-language, i.e., through bilingualism. This material is part of the P *parole*, occurring in the speech of some but not all of the P-speakers. It is the manifestation of on-going linguistic diffusion. (Charles Hockett similarly distinguishes between what he calls the *individual* and *mass effects* of borrowing [1958, chap. 47].)

P-Replicas of S-Models	*Domain of P*	*Speakers of P*
Integration	*langue*	entire speech community
Interference	*parole*	bilinguals only

While the boundaries between the two types must necessarily remain somewhat inprecise, I believe that the distinction can be made universally. It will be useful to describe as still "unintegrated" any elements exhibiting an idiolectal range in variation with no basic alternant acquired in the *langue* (see §2.3.2).

The impact of S on P must be classified not only as to degree but as to kind. Existing typologies classify interference according to the level of linguistic structure affected; Weinreich discusses "phonic," "grammatical," and "lexical" interference. In this paper interference will be discussed in terms of *phonology* and *morphology*, including in the latter both grammatical and lexical interference.

It has been observed that interference is dependent on some sort of *interlingual identification* which the bilingual undertakes, largely unconsciously, as he acquires S models and introduces these into his own P speech. (Interlingual identification occurs when speakers equate items in one language with items in another because of their similarities in shape, distribution, or both" [Haugen, 1956, p. 67].) In reproducing S elements either in attempting to speak S or in transferring them to P, the individual perceives and reproduces the phonology of S in a manner which is structurally conditioned by his P phonological system, i.e., phonological interference occurs. But such diaphonic identifications never occur in vacuo. (Haugen [1956, p. 46] uses the term *diaphone* to describe "interlingually identified variants of phonemes" and the term *diamorph* for "interlingually identified variants of morphemes or groups of morphemes.") They are rather dependent on the phonological constituency of the meaningful elements which form the bulk of interference phenomena. One type of morphological interference can occur on the basis of diaphonic identification, i.e., where it is the phonetic shape and not the meaning of the S element which determines its transfer to P. This type of diamorph has been called "homophonous." Another type can occur purely on the basis of an identification of meaning, with no diaphonic identification; this type has been called "synonymous." There is an important distinction to be made between P replicas which are diaphonic with their S models and those *P* replicas which are synonymous only. The latter are matchings contrived of native elements, or *substitutions*; the former, depending on transfer of nonnative elements, are *importations*. We will call morphological substitutions, after Haugen, *loanshifts*, and morphological importations *loanwords*. (Haugen re *morphemic importation* and *morphemic substitution*: "In the former case a new morpheme is introduced into the language, with a phonemic shape which shows diaphonic identification with a morpheme in the source language. This is what is generally known as a *loanword*. In the latter case, however, no new morpheme is introduced, but the lexeme borrowed is translated by the redistribution of morphemes already found in the language. For this the writer has suggested the term *loanshift*" [1956, p. 52].)

2. *A CASE OF INCIPIENT BILINGUALISM*

I present here some of the materials that I collected during a linguistic and sociological investigation of bilingualism in an Indian community in Mexico. The purpose, already stated, is to demonstrate the interdependency of linguistic and sociological factors.

2.1. INDIAN-SPANISH BILINGUALISM IN MEXICO

Mexico provides an interesting laboratory for studying bilingualism. An appreciable segment of the population in certain areas learns Spanish only as a second language, or not at all; the first language is an American Indian language.

There has been considerable controversy over the sociological classification of the Mexican population into Indian and Mestizo "mixed" elements; and one of the reasons for the difficulty is language. Often enough, the term "Indian" refers to a rural peasantry, well integrated in the national economy, which has the distinction that its members first acquire an American Indian language in childhood. Thus we speak of Mayas, Zapotecs, Mixtecs, and so on. But something quite different is certainly meant here, when we say "Indian," from what we mean when we speak of our own reservation populations or of isolated tribal groups. The sociological term is merely a linguistic index. It remains true, however, that some of the most conservative elements in Mexican society are Indian-speaking and that these groups have the larger share of cultural retentions from pre-Columbian times. The confusion in terms is enlightening because it derives from a situation of "intimate borrowing" between the Mexican Indian languages, which are "lower," and Spanish, which is "dominant." (Haugen generalizes a situation of intimate contact for all the native American languages and the colonial European languages which are geographically and/or socially superimposed: "Many native speakers are sufficiently segregated to have only rare contact with the dominant languages of their area. But their political dependence makes it necessary everywhere for some of them to learn the dominant languages. The speakers of the latter seldom find it necessary to learn the native languages" [1956, p. 15].)

Acculturation and bilingualism are here clearly interdependent. It is asserted in the anthropological literature that an individual can move upward socially from an Indian to a Mestizo group by a mere juggling of linguistic and cultural symbols. (In Mexico there is little correlation of achieved status with physical or "racial" symbols.) The chief item of his Indian heritage which the individual in transition must consider is his language: he has to learn Spanish. Many isolated communitities in Mexico which are monolingually Indian-speaking find themselves engaged in greater social contact with and participation in the national life of which they are the most provincial element, and an inevitable concomitant is a greater degree of bilingualism. It is in this sociolinguistic situation that incipient bilingualism occurs. A study of predominantly monolingual communities in which some individuals are becoming bilingual should give us valuable insight into the initial stages of language contact.

2.2 BILINGUALISM IN A HUAVE COMMUNITY

San Mateo del Mar is a village of about 3000 inhabitants on the Pacific coast of the Mexican state of Oaxaca; it is one of the five Huave-speaking villages, all bordering the salt-water lagoons of the Isthmus of Tehuantepec. The Huave-speaking area is isolated physically and socially from the rest of the Isthmus. It is surrounded by two larger speech-groups, Spanish and Zapotec, which are spoken in the rural areas and the larger towns nearby, such as Salina Cruz, Tehuantepec, and Juchitán. The application of the term "Indian" to the Huave is poor, except as an index of their language. A number of cultural differences obtain between the Huave-speakers and the other peoples of the Isthmus: the Huave are ultra-conservative and, in terms of culture content, have a number of Indian traits which other groups have lost. But structurally defined, the Huave are part of the large rural peasantry; they are well integrated into the overall social structure of the area, having in particular strong ties of economic dependency with the larger Spanish-speaking towns to which they are satellite.

For eight decades the Mexican Government has conducted a national census; the last several, considering the communications problem in rural Mexico, rank with those of Europe or the United States in the quality and quantity of sociological data collected. Of particular interest is the information on bilingualism. Great stress is laid on this material, since Spanish-Indian bilingualism has priority as a national problem, being intimately bound up in the Government's efforts at improving rural education and communications. It was on the basis of the 1950 *Censo general* that I chose San Mateo. The census showed that San Mateo and a nearby hamlet (Huazontlán), together with surrounding ranching communities, had a population of 3611, less than 20 % of which was bilingual.

One of the principal field problems was to retake a village-wide census which would elicit the most data in the shortest possible time and with a minimum of resulting hostility. My census sought information on household constituency and the kinship relations involved, and on the age, sex, occupation, and language skills of the individual members of the household. Moreover, it inquired about the contacts of the head of the household with the Spanish-speaking outside world. The census was restricted to the four barrios of San Mateo itself; it excluded Huazontlán and the surrounding ranching hamlets.

San Mateo consists of 376 households with a total population of 2934. The count of bilinguals follows, tabulated by barrios to show the internal consistency of different social groups. Roman numerals designate the four barrios; succeeding columns show (A) the number of individual households in each barrio, (B) the number of coordinate bilinguals, (C) the number of subordinate bilinguals, (D) the number of monolingual Huave-speakers, and (E) the total number of persons.

	A	B	C	D	E
I	151	50	78	399	527
II	65	42	70	671	783
III	92	67	187	826	1080
IV	68	14	59	473	544
Total	376	173	392	2369	2934

Six percent of the San Mateños were coordinate bilinguals; 13 % were subordinate bilinguals; the remaining 81 % were monolingual in Huave. Any speaker was categorized by highly impressionistic measurement; native Spanish-speakers assisted in random checking of the census. They were asked to classify as coordinate bilinguals any persons in whose spoken Spanish there was no noticeable interference from Huave, i.e., who appeared to speak Spanish without "accent." Persons whose Spanish was productive but with noticeable interference from Huave were to be classified as subordinate bilinguals. Persons unable to make "complete meaningful utterances" in Spanish, after Haugen's definition, were classified as monolingual in Huave.

The census data concerning age, sex, and occupation brought out the following significant facts about Huave-Spanish bilingualism. (1) With respect to AGE, Spanish was acquired relatively late in life, rarely in childhood. This adolescent or adult acquisition has been assumed to have important bearing ont he quantitative and qualitative features of interference evinced in the second language. (See Haugen's discussion of The Age of Learning [1956, pp. 72, 73] and Weinreich's Order of Learning and Age [1953, pp. 76-77, 94-95].) Subordinate bilingualism in San Mateo involves very imperfect reproduction of Spanish, with a heavy load of interference from Huave. (2) With regard to SEX, bilingualism is predominantly a male skill, 80 % of bilinguals of both the subordinate and coordinate groups being males. Age and sex relate in turn to (3) OCCUPATION: subordinate bilinguals professed greater contact with the outside than monolingual Huave-speakers; and all coordinate bilinguals had extensive contact with the outside world, through frequent marketing trips or actual residence outside the community for various periods of time, or both.

Huave itself is rarely learned as anybody's second language. The few exceptions are North American missionaries and an occasional itinerant Zapotec merchant; but the interests which motivate this learning constitute rather special cases. Otherwise San Mateo shows an extreme example of Bloomfield's "intimate borrowing."

The impressions one receives from the census information are borne out by more detailed ethnographic description. Spanish is never the language of the home. The situation with respect to the age of acquisition and the sex of the individual is in fairly stable equilibrium: the Huave child probably could not acquire Spanish as a second childhood language since few mothers are themselves bilingual. Contact with the Spanish-speaking outside world seems to be the crucial factor involved: Spanish is learned outside of the community.

Certain features of the social structure tend to reinforce the equilibrium. Of external factors, the chief is the Huave's economic and political dependency on the Spanish-speaking outside world. The Huave economy emphasizes fishing, and surpluses are destined for outside markets; the immediate Isthmus region is dependent on the Huave for marine produce. But unfortunately for the Huave, they get little economic power from this dependency, since they in turn are at the complete mercy of the well developed Spanish and Zapotec market economy for all manufactured goods and all other foodstuffs, including even the staple starch in the diet, corn. The Spanish-speaking merchants make a conscious effort to keep the Huave in this disadvantageous position. Politically, too, the Huave village is satellite to the larger Spanish-speaking town. Much energy is devoted to forestalling any culture change which will upset the present power ratio. The Huave is thus almost a second-rate citizen. The pressures which are exerted on him make it less likely that he will leave his village, and less likely that he will have to learn Spanish or even be able to learn it. The present difficulties which the Huave encounters in attempting the transition from Indian to Mestizo are all but insurmountable. Positive external factors are varied and contradictory: there is no consistent policy of government-sponsored education in San Mateo. The community is almost wholly preliterate, and those few individuals who are literate are so chiefly in Spanish, although workers from the Summer Institute of Linguistics are instructing a small group of San Mateños in the writing and reading of Huave. These workers, members of a North American missionary group, are effecting remarkable change in the community and are no doubt facilitating contact with the outside. But their role with respect to bilingualism is difficult to evaluate, since they themselves have acquired Huave and now use it as their principal medium of communication in San Mateo.

Moreover, a number of internal factors bind the individual into the village and make it less possible for him to leave. San Mateo is markedly endogamous, and a complex web of real and fictive kinship ties limit the individual's mobility outside the community. The individual further finds himself enmeshed in the government of the community, being obliged to pass through a series of rotating political offices and to execute certain prescribed community services. Associated with the holding of political office is the sponsorship of a number of religious festivals; the economic expenditure is considerable, and the sponsor is reduced to poverty. Since everybody is supposed to participate, wealth differences in the community are levelled and the internal economic structure again binds the individual closely to his fellow villagers. The only effective way to break these social bonds is to openly defect from the community; but the rate of defection remains low, since incentive is curbed by the external pressures already described.

2.3. HUAVE-SPANISH INTERFERENCE

The present section examines the linguistic interference attendant on Huave-Spanish language contact, first in terms of integration and interference in Huave from Spanish, then in terms of the impact of Huave on the Spanish learned by Huave-speakers. The purpose is to give the reader examples of various forms of Huave-Spanish interference and not to attempt a definite classification of these phenomena.

2.3.1. *Integration in Huave.* The Spanish-derived elements of interest here are those which occur in the Huave *langue*, which are learned by monolingual and bilingual alike in the normal childhood acquisition of Huave. Although bilingual skills may later acquaint the speaker with the Spanish model, he never recognizes the relationship between that and the integrated replica.

Phonic interference in Huave *langue* is illustrated by three examples. (1) The first involves phonemic split. Pre-Spanish Huave had five vowel phonemes, **i*, **ɨ*, **e*, **a*, **o*. **ɨ* had at least two allophones, [ɨ] and [ï]. Lexical interference in the form of loanwords from Spanish early introduced the phone [u], different phonetically from [ï] with respect to lip-rounding. Unless a coexistent phonemic system is recognized, [u] then contrasted with [ï] in CV, CVC, VC and other syllable environments. (Pike and Fries [1949] argue that in Mazatec, Spanish interference sets up a definable environment which may be excluded for the purposes of description.) Thus Huave acquired a sixth vowel phoneme; cf. *čɨk* [tšïk] (a syntactic particle) and *čúk* [tšuk] 'wild dog' (Sp. *chucho*). (2) Extension of allophonic distribution is illustrated by Huave *b*, *d*, *g*, which now occur in word-initial, final, and medial positions: *b* in *bàyén* 'whale,' *mbár* 'sabalo-fish,' *àéèb* 'he smokes'; *d* in d*íòs* 'god,' *ndéóh* 'orphan,' *méèd* 'blouse'; *g* in *gástà* 'expense,' *áàgá* 'this,' *tíìg* 'seagull.' But word-initial *b*, *d*, *g* occur only in loanwords from

Spanish, cf. Sp. *ballena*, *díos*, *gasto*; so also in *báng* 'bench' (Sp. *banco*), *dás* 'dance' (Sp. *danza*), *gáyà* 'rooster' (Sp. *gallo*). (3) New phonemes are illustrated by Huave *f*, which occurs only in Spanish loanwords, e.g. *fótò* 'photograph' (Sp. *foto*), *fèbrérù* 'February' (Sp. *febrero*).

Morphological interference in Huave *langue* is most obvious in the lexicon. 15 % of the Huave nominals in my lexicon are loanwords, i.e., imported morphological elements showing diaphonic identification with their Spanish models. Examples: *àsét* 'oil' (Sp. *aceite*), *nìmál* 'animal' (Sp. *animal*), *kàwɨ́y* 'horse' (Sp. *caballo*), *kàmíš* 'shirt' (Sp. *camisa*), *kók* 'coconut' (Sp. *coco*), *kwét* 'firecracker' (Sp. *cohete*), *kùnyádà* 'sibling-in-law' (Sp. *cuñado*), *méàč* 'wick' (Sp. *mecha*), *àrɨ́ɨ̀nč* 'ranch' (Sp. *rancho*), *šèndíy* 'watermelon' (Sp. *sandía*) *tìhér* 'scissors' (Sp. *tijeras*). These loanwords are not restricted to the so-called cultural vocabulary. There are seven in the current version of the 100-word lexicostatistics list. (This is the 100-word list which appears in revised form in Swadesh [1955].) Three occur as integrated units in *langue*: *màrííl* 'yellow' (Sp. *amarillo*), *íìk* 'liver' (Sp. *hígado*) and *ìntérà* 'all' (Sp. *entero*).

Substitutive morphological interference is not prevalent in Huave *langue*. The most frequent types do not well exemplify loanshifting. They are of the type Haugen calls *induced creations*, "new words which come into being in response to foreign words, but without formal imitation of these" (Haugen, 1958, p. 783). Thus, Huave 'sheep' is *sáp*; synchronically, we describe *sáp* 'sheep' as a homonym with *sáp* 'native cotton,' but etymologically the two words are one: Huave *sáp* 'native cotton' was extended to denote 'sheep' when these animals were introduced as cultural novelties after Spanish contact; there is no loanword based on the possible Spanish model *borrego* 'sheep.' Another example is Huave *òmál-mànčíɨ̀k* 'bullet,' lit. 'tip-of-metal'; there is no replica based on the possible Spanish model *bala* 'bullet.' And so with *nàŋgáh-íɨ̀m* 'church,' lit. 'sacred house,' with no replica of Spanish *iglesia* 'church.' Some cases involve constituent elements which are themselves examples of importation. Thus, Huave has the loanword *tréŋ* 'train' (Sp. *tren*), but has not imported the word for 'railroad,' Spanish *ferrocarril*. 'Railroad' is rendered by the native Huave compound *mìtíɨ̀d-tréŋ*, lit. 'path-of-train,' while 'canal' is rendered by native *mìtíɨ̀d-ìyów*, lit. 'path-of-water,' although we infer that the latter too is an induced creation.

2.3.2. *Interference in Huave.* The Spanish-derived elements which interest us here are those which occur in the Huave *parole*, in the speech of various bilingual speakers. There are two outstanding features of interference in *parole*: (1) where there is diaphonic identification, noticeable variation in shape in the rendering of the replica in Huave, and (2) competition between a native form, if one exists, and the borrowed form, leading to marked fluctuation in frequency in occurence of the competing forms.

The first condition is limited to loanwords. Bilingual San Mateño No. 1 may use the replica *ástà* 'until' for the Spanish model *hasta*, speaker No. 2 many use *ístà*, No. 3 *íštà*, and No. 4 *ást*. At present all four replicas are in use. Since *ástà* is the most frequent form, it may displace the other three; if only *ástà* were to be learned, it would be considered an element in Huave *langue*. Other examples are *lèntérnà* ~ *lèŋktérnà* ~ *lìntérnà* for Spanish *linterna* 'lantern'; *àsúkrè* ~ *àsúkàr* ~ *àsúkà* ~ *àsúk* for Spanish *azúcar* 'sugar.' I have suggested that in such variation, when integration finally occurs the replica variant which is phonologically most similar to the Spanish model will be adopted; e.g., the variants *ástà*, *lìntérnà*, and *àsúkàr*. Unfortunately there is no historical documentation of possible earlier variants of now integrated materials which subsequently fell into disuse; we cannot state for any integrated form, e.g., *ŋgàbìlán* 'hawk' (Sp. *gavilán*), whether it was earlier represented by variant replicas such as **gàbìlá*, **ŋgàbìlá*, **ngàbìláàn*. The value, then, of recording contemporary variation in Huave *parole* is to test what properties determine the final adoption of one from a number of variant replicas.

Competition between native and partially synonymous nonnative forms is marked. "Partially synonymous" is used advisedly: although often difficult to describe, there is usually semantic specialization of native and nonnative forms. Nevertheless, the nonnative form often makes inroads in frequency of occurence sufficient to push the native form into obsolescence or into highly specialized environments. This phenomenon is illustrated by the examples of interference contained in the basic vocabulary of the 100-word lexicostatistics list; we recall that there are three Spanish-derived items in Huave *langue* from this list, and another four in *parole*. These last four are: *kéy* 'who' (Sp. *qué*), *sàmíy* 'seed' (Sp. *semilla*), *bérdè*, 'green' (Sp. *verde*), and *pyédrè* 'stone' (Sp. *piedra*). All are in competition with native forms: *kéy* with *ŋgún*, *sàmíy* with *òsáàb*, *bérdè* with *nàtéàìk*, *pyédrè* with *kàŋ*.

The native form and the competing nonnative form may undergo so much semantic specialization that there is no longer a question of synonymity. Such semantic specialization is occuring with *sàmìy* 'seed'$_1$ and *òsàáb* 'seed'$_2$: *sàmìy* connotes seed which is purchased as a commodity, for food or propagation; *òsáàb* connotes the plant part, without reference to its economic function. Even in the absence of semantic specialization we should not predict ultimate extinction, since the native form may survive as a bound constituent of a compound lexeme. In the competition between *pyédrè* 'stone'$_1$ and *káŋ* 'stone'$_2$, there is no definable semantic specialization in Huave *langue*; but *káŋ* occurs as a bound element in forms like *mìkáŋ-míš* 'anchor,' lit. 'rock-of-canoe,' and *pìl-káŋ* 'pebble,' and it is most unlikely that *pyédrè* will be substituted for *-káŋ* in these forms. In borrowings in *parole*, however, model Spanish compounds and phrases containing *piedra* are rendered by *-pyédrè* in the Huave replicas, e.g., Spanish *piedra de eslabón* 'whetstone': Huave *mìpyédrè-lìšlèàbón*. Competition between partially synonymous native and nonnative forms is of course not restricted to the basic vocabulary; it recurs throughout the lexicon, e.g., *mbáw* (Sp. *baúl* 'trunk') and *kíš* 'hamper,' *kùčíìl* (Sp. *cuchillo* 'knife') and *nìpàráŋ* 'knife,' *últà* (Sp. *último* 'last') and *téòh* 'last.'

2.3.3. *Huave Interference in Spanish.* Huave interference in Spanish might be presented in terms of the convergent change resulting in the local Spanish dialects as a result of contact with Huave; but such interference does not exist. Local Spanish-speakers rarely acquire Huave as a second language; the few speakers that have learned Huave do not enjoy the prestige or carry the communication roles which could integrate these changes in the *langue* of the local Spanish. Spanish shows Huave interference only when a Huave speaker learns it as a second language. Here we can describe certain recurrent features of phonic and morphological interference. Such phenomena as the loss of standard Spanish word- and phrase-final unstressed vowels contribute to the structure of diaphonic identifications which ultimately account for the shape of loanwords in Huave. It is through the bilingual San Mateño's version of Spanish that linguistic borrowing into Huave is mediated.

No pidgin or creole language based on convergent change results from Huave-Spanish contact. A pidgin "arises under the pressure of practical circumstances in a bilingual situation" (Hockett, 1958, p. 422). Linguistically it represents an extreme of convergent change: essentially, a new third language crystallizes as a modification of the dominant language through imperfect replication by speakers of the lower language. When this language is learned as a second language by speakers of either the lower or the dominant language, we call it a pidgin; when the pidgin begins to be acquired as a first language, we call it a creole. Typologically, the convergent change represented by the formation of pidgins parallels that which occurs in the formation of standard languages, and the sociological factors which enforce or impede the formation seem to be largely the same. The linguistic difference, of course, is that mutual unintelligibility is always a factor in pidgins, since the languages involved are different, if not actually unrelatable; standard-language formations occur with the same or closely related languages.

In the Huave-Spanish contact situation, the circumstances which might lead to the formation of a pidgin are lacking. Indeed, it is noteworthy that there are no recorded examples of Indian-Spanish pidgins in Mexico. Rather, convergent change seems to lead to one of two principal situations (§1.2): extinction of the Indian language, or bilingualism. In the latter, progressively greater amounts of interference affect the norms of the Indian language, and more and more Indian speakers learn Spanish as a second language and even teach Spanish exclusively to their children. Since we encounter a wide gamut of linguistic types in the Indian language structures of Mexico, we can only conclude that the explanation for the lack of pidgins must be sought in sociological terms (Diebold, 1958).

3. *MEASURING INCIPIENT BILINGUALISM*

The preponderance of morphological importations and the paucity of loanshifts in Huave *langue* demands comment. It has been suggested that the form assumed by interference is predetermined by the structures of the donor and recipient languages. Enough material has been collected to confirm this assertion in principle. But Huave and Spanish syntax and morphology evince remarkable typological parallels and show no differences of such a degree as to make morphological interference by substitution unlikely. Rather, the form taken by morphological interference must relate to the manner in which Spanish is learned and to the ability of the bilingual speaker to analyze Spanish structure. Furthermore, it appears contradictory that such a low percentage of bilingual skill in the speech-community should cooccur with the high percentage of interference phenomena in Huave *langue*. Clearly some measure of incipient bilingualism is needed.

Bilinguals were crudely classified by the method described in §2.2. However impressionistic the categories seem, more controls were exercised in the classification of San Mateo speakers than is ever possible on the basis of the *Censo general*, upon which much of our knowledge of Mexican bilingualism is based. (Most of our sociological information on bilingualism the world over is derived from far less reliable census data.) In particular, the ability to produce "complete meaningful utterances" in Spanish offered a pragmatically valid boundary between bilingual and monolingual which withstood random retestings. Nevertheless, I soon became dissatisfied with writing off 81 % of the San Mateños as "monolingual" on the basis of Haugen's definition of bilingual proficiency, since I had noted a minimal use of Spanish among many of these purportedly monolingual Huave-speakers. Since bilinguals are recruited from this group, it appeared that this would represent the minimal incipient situation of bilingual learning. Yet the fact remained that these individuals could not sustain even limited conversation with a Spanish-speaker, and I remained at a loss for a means of quantifying their knowledge of Spanish.

A clue finally came from the stereotypes attributed to San Mateño Spanish by local native Spanish-speakers, and from tales which the Huave tell upon themselves with regard to their difficulties in using Spanish. These folk descriptions agree that the Huave might know items of Spanish vocabulary, but is unable to combine words (or is inept at combining words) into larger phrase constructions. That this is true was dramatically proved when I elicited the 100-word lexicostatistics list from speakers chosen from each of the three groups of San Mateños, "coordinate bilinguals," "subordinate bilinguals," and "monolingual Huave-speakers."

A sample of ten household-heads from each group was chosen at random from the village-wide census. The individuals, all men, ranged in age from 27 to 52. Synoptic life-histories were collected for each subject and the lexicostatistics list was presented verbally. The list was drawn up in Huave; the subject was instructed to give a Spanish correspondence. A subject's response was scored positive if the Spanish form offered was even partially synonymous with the Huave cue-word. Thus, for Huave *nàhtáh* 'woman,' Spanish *mujer* 'woman' or *esposa* 'wife' were accepted as positive responses; Spanish *pescado* 'fish (as food)' and *pez* 'fish (as animal)' for Huave *kùét* 'fish'; and *cabello* 'hair,' *pelo* 'hair,' and even *cuero* 'pelt' for Huave *òndéàc* 'hair.' Phonic interference, no matter how great the distortion, was overlooked in scoring, save to transcribe phonetically the particular rendering—e.g., the response [k'a'be:sɨ] or [k'a'be:š] (cf. Spanish *cabeza* 'head' 'head [ka'ßesa]) for Huave *òmál* 'head.' Often more than one Huave cueword was employed, e.g., *šikónà* 'we (dual exclusive),' *ìkórà* 'we (dual inclusive),' and *ìkóòcà* 'we (plural)' to elicit Spanish *nosotros* 'we'; *nàhún* 'parched' and *nàwáàg* 'dry' for Spanish *seco* 'dry.'

The coordinate bilingual group scored a mean of 97 %, with a range of 89 %-100 %. The subordinate bilingual group scored a mean of 89 %, with a range of 61 %-94 %. Surprisingly enough, the monolingual group scored a mean of 37 %, with a range of 11 %-68 %. The sample of 10 for the last group was subsequently expanded to 20, with a mean score of 36 % and a range of 5 %-68 %.

4. *CONCLUSIONS*

I am aware that generalizations are tenuous when based on only one specific case. The modest conclusions which follow are designed to stimulate reinspection of other cases of language contact, with an eye to investigating the role which extralinguistic factors play in the observed linguistic interference.

It seems wise to pass over the more obvious examples of the interdependency of sociological and linguistic factors which occur in this paper, and to address ourselves to some wider theoretical problems. The findings of the present study suggest that at least two premises of language contact should be reexamined.

(1) The first is the now widely accepted definition of minimal skill in a second language necessary for bilingual status, i.e., the production of "complete meaningful utterances" as proposed by Haugen. The situation of incipient bilingualism has importance for both the sociologist and the linguist; it should not be lost because of an arbitrary hurdle of quantification. The present study suggests to the sociologist that much of his census data concerning bilingualism may be faulty, especially in concealing in the category "monolingual" some very real measure of bilingualism. It suggests to the linguists that the total linguistic impact of Spanish on Huave, which is very great, is not unaccompanied by fairly widespread bilingual skills in the speech-community. The analyst is thus relieved of the difficult task of reconciling the fact of the large percentage of Spanish-derived integration with the fact of a low percentage of bilingualism. If incipient bilingualism is excluded from the investigation, we further conceal the initial learning stages; yet it is here that many of the interlingual identifications are set up which profoundly affect the shape of subsequent interference. The present study also offers a possible procedure for measuring incipient bilingual skills: the use of the lexicostatistics basic vocabulary list. The procedure lends itself well to testing large numbers of speakers and is demonstrably applicable across languages.

I offer a modified definition of minimal bilingual skill: contact with possible models in a second language and the ability to use these in the environment of the native language. The definition is not normative as to the distance of correspondence between model and replica, and can include literate skills as well as so-called "passive knowledge." It has the value that it is purely formal, not bound by the pragmatic and semantic considerations inherent in "complete meaningful utterances."

(2) The second premise to be questioned is that the form assumed by interference is determined by the structures of the two languages in contact. A more modest premise would merely state that the two language structures set up limits of variability to interference. My data strongly suggest that sociological factors like the age of learning, the learning situation itself, and intergroup social relations are equally crucial factors in determining the form of Spanish-derived interference phenomena in Huave. Sociological factors account for the absence of pidgins in Huave-Spanish contact; in more specific domains of structure, they account for the preponderance of lexical interference of the importation type over both substitutive types and other higher forms of grammatical interference.

It is hoped that copious comparative material can be assembled from an area such as Mexico, where one dominant language is in contact with a number of lower languages different both typologically and in the sociological relationship of their speakers to Spanish-speakers. An area with the opportunities for laboratory-like control of variables in language contact is perhaps nowhere else as accessible.

AUTHOR'S NOTE

Part of this paper was first presented in July, 1960, at the Linguistic Institute (University of Michigan), to Paul Friedrich's seminar in Language and Culture; I am obliged to Friedrich for subsequent comments and discussion. Much of the material here presented is amplified in my doctoral dissertation, "Bilingualism and Biculturalism in a Huave Community" (ms., Yale University, 1961). The paper and my field work in bilingualism have been discussed with, Floyd Lounsbury, Laura Nader, Joan Rubin, Glenn Stairs, Morris Swadesh, Milton Warkentin, Jacqueline Wei, and Robert Weitlaner; additional comments on the paper were made by Einar Haugen and Dell Hymes. I gratefully acknowledge their interest. My field research was made possible through award of a National Science Foundation Fellowship and an appointment to the Organization of American States Fellowship Program; in addition, support was extended by the Yale Department of Anthropology. I am thankful for the aegis of the Instituto Nacional de Antropologia e Historia and the Instituto de Historia while carrying out my field investigations in Mexico.

Huave is an American Indian language; its 7000 speakers inhabit the five communities referred to. Dialect divergence is pronounced, and the three dialects have been differentially receptive to interference from Spanish; the dialects are nevertheless mutually intelligible, although there are definite weaknesses in communication which are congruent with the dialect boundaries. The genetic pedigree of Huave awaits further comparative investigation. Excellent preliminary descriptive analyses of Huave have been written by Milton and Clara Warkentin and by Glenn and Emily Stairs. The Warkentins are soon to publish some of their descriptive analyses; the Stairs are working on a lexicon and with text materials. My presentation of Huave forms has been made to conform with the Warkentin's phonemicization (Clara E. Warkentin and Evelyn G. Pike, Huave phonemics, ms., n.d.). Some differences appear in the rendering of tones and vowel length. Further alterations involve recognition of two additional phonemes *f*, *ŋ*, and deletion of *r̃*. *f* occurs in Spanish-derived loan words, [ŋ] occurs in Huave *tréŋ* ['treŋ] 'train' and contrasts with [n] in that VC+ environment, e.g., *ndén* [ˌn'den] 'shade'; elsewhere, [n] and [ŋ] are in complementary distribution. In my data flap and trill are in free variation.

Zapotec is also an American Indian language. The variety spoken here is the so-called Isthmus "dialect," actually one of a number of mutually unintelligible languages. Although this too is a lower language, the number of speakers is still very great; its displacement by Spanish is slow; and there is some interference in the Isthmus dialect of Spanish from Zapotec. All these facts indicate that Zapotec, although it is a lower language in its relationship to Spanish, enjoys greater prestige than many Indian languages in Mexico, a privilege it shares with Tarascan and Yucatec Maya. Although there is contact between Zapotec and Huave, this is negligible in San Mateo: San Mateños who are bilingual in Zapotec constitute less than 8% of the population, and the amount of Huave-Zapotec interference is minimal. I have noted only eleven instances of Huave-Zapotec-Spanish trilingualism in San Mateo.

REFERENCE NOTE

For general treatments of the problems of bilingualism and bilingual analysis, see Cohen (1956a, *passim*), Ferguson and Gumperz (1960) and the review of it by Friedrich (1961), Friedrich (1962), Haas (1953), Robert A. Hall, Jr. (1952), Haugen (1950, 1954a, 1954b, 1954c, 1956, 1958), Pike (1960), Pike and Fries (1949), Reyburn (1956), Saporta (1961, pp. 376-414, 455-459, including sections from Weinreich, 1953, and Haugen, 1956), Stewart (1962), Weinreich (1953, 1957a), Wolff (1956). The most extensive treatments are Haugen (1956, 1958) and Weinreich (1953, 1958).

On specific cases of bilingualism and its functional involvements, see Bartlett (1952), Bossard (1945), Diebold (1962b), Doob (1957, 1961), Dozier (1951), Ervin (1961), Ervin and Osgood (1954), Friedrich (1961), Graham (1956), Haugen (1953), Homeyer (1956), Lambert (1955), Lambert, Havelka, Crosby (1958), Leopold (1948), Lowie (1945), Meillet (1931, 1933b), Meillet and Sauvageot (1934), Rubin (1962), Salisbury (1962), Swadesh (1941), Weinreich (1957b).

Other functional aspects of bilingualism are involved in the articles by Haas and Herzog in Part VI, by Bloomfield, Gumperz, Ferguson, and Wolff in Part VII, and by Haas, Dozier, and the remaining authors in this part.

References not in the general bibliography:

BARTLETT, H. H.

1952. A Batak and Malay Chant on Rice Cultivation, with Introductory Notes on Bilingualism and Acculturation in Indonesia. *PAPS*, *96:* 629-652.

BOSSARD, J. H. S.

1945. The Bilingual as a Person—Linguistic Identification with Status. *American Sociological Review, 10:* 699-709.

DIEBOLD, A. RICHARD, JR.

1958. Impresiones particulares sobre el bilingüismo en México. New Haven. (Ms.)

1962b. Mexican and Guatemalan Bilingualism. In Frank A. Rice (Ed.), *Study of the Role of Second Languages in Asia, Africa, and Latin America.* Washington, D.C.: Center for Applied Linguistics of the Modern Language Association of America. Pp. 26-33.

DOOB, LEONARD W.

1957. The Effect of Language on Verbal Expression and Recall. *AA, 59:* 88-100.

ERVIN, SUSAN M.

1961. Semantic Shift in Bilingualism. *American Journal of Psychology, 74:* 233-241.

ERVIN, SUSAN M., and CHARLES E. OSGOOD

1954. Second Language Learning and Bilingualism. In Charles E. Osgood and Thomas A. Sebeok (Eds.) *Psycholinguistics, A Survey of Theory and Research Problems.* (IUPAL; Memoirs of *IJAL*, No. 10.) Bloomington. Pp. 139-146. [Also, Supplement to *JASP*, 1954, *49.*]

FRIEDRICH, PAUL

1961. Review of C. A. Ferguson and J. J. Gumperz, *Linguistic Diversity in South Asia. Lg., 37:* 163-168.

GRAHAM, R. S.

1956. Widespread Bilingualism and the Creative Writer. *Word, 12:* 356-369.

HAAS, MARY R.

1953. Bilingualism. In Claude Levi-Strauss, Roman Jakobson, C. F. Voegelin, Thomas A. Sebeok, *Results of the Conference of Anthropologists and Linguists.* (IUPAL; Memoirs of *IJAL*, No. 8.) Bloomington. Pp. 42-44.

HALL, ROBERT A., JR.

1952. Bilingualism and Applied Linguistics. *Zeitschrift für Phonetik und allgemeine Sprachwissenschaft, 6:* 13-30.

HAUGEN, EINAR

1950. Problems of Bilingualism. *Lingua, 2:* 271-290.

1954a. Some Pleasures and Problems of Bilingual Research. *IJAL, 20:* 116-122.

1954b. Review of U. Weinreich, *Languages in Contact. Lg., 30:* 380-388.

1954c. Problems of Bilingual Description. *General Linguistics, 1:* 1-9.

1958. Languages in Contact. In Eva Sivertsen (Ed.), *Proceedings of the Eighth International Congress of Linguists (Oslo, 1957).* Oslo: Oslo University Press. Pp. 771-785.

HOMEYER, HELEN

1956. Some Observations on Bilingualism and Language Shift in Italy from the Sixth to the Third Century B.C. *Word, 13:* 415-440.

LAMBERT, WALLACE E.

1955. Measurement of the Linguistic Dominance of Bilinguals. *JASP, 50.* 197-200.

LAMBERT, W. E., J. HAVELKA, C. CROSBY

1958. The Influence of Language-Acquisition Contexts on Bilingualism. *JASP*, *56:* 239-244. [Also in Sol Saporta (Ed.), *Psycholinguistics*. New York: Holt, 1961. Pp. 407-414.]

LOWIE, ROBERT H.

1945. A Case of Bilingualism. *Word*, *1:* 249-259.

MEILLET, A.

1931. Sur une Periode de bilinguisme en France. *Comptes Rendus des Séances de l'Académie des Inscriptions et Belles-Lettres*. Pp. 29 ff. [Also in Meillet, *Linguistique historique and linguistique générale*. (2nd ed.) (Collection linguistique, Société de Linguistique de Paris, No. 8.) Paris: Champion, 1926-1936. Vol. II, pp. 90-98.]

1933b. Sur le Bilinguisme. *Journal de psychologie*, *30:* 167 ff. [Also in Meillet, 1926-1936, Vol. II, pp. 99-103.]

MEILLET, A., and A. SAUVAGEOT

1934. Le Bilinguisme des hommes cultivés. *Conférences de l'Institut de Linguistique de l'Université de Paris*. Vol. 2.

PIKE, KENNETH L., and C. C. FRIES

1949. Coexistent Phonemic Systems. *Lg.*, *26:* 29-50.

STEWART, WILLIAM A.

1962. An Outline of Linguistic Typology for Describing Multilingualism. In Frank A. Rice (Ed.), *Study of the Role of Second Languages in Asia, Africa, and Latin America*. Washington, D.C.: Center for Applied Linguistics of the Modern Language Association of America. Pp. 15-25.

SWADESH, MORRIS

1941. Observation of Pattern Impact on the Phonemes of Bilinguals. In L. Spier, A. I. Hallowell, S. S. Newman (Eds.), *Language, Culture, and Personality*. Menasha, Wis.: Banta. Pp. 59-65.

WEINREICH, URIEL

1958. Languages in Contact. In Eva Sivertsen (Ed.), *Proceedings of the Eighth International Congress of Linguists (Oslo, 1957)*. Oslo: Oslo University Press. Pp. 786-797.

Two Examples of Linguistic Acculturation: The Yaqui of Sonora and Arizona and the Tewa of New Mexico 54

EDWARD P. DOZIER

THIS PAPER DEALS with an aspect of acculturation which has only recently received some attention in the literature. (For examples of such work, see Casagrande, 1954-1955; Herzog, 1941; Johnson, 1943; Lee, 1943; Spencer, 1947; Spicer, 1943; Trager, 1944.) For the most part linguists have been concerned with historical and descriptive studies, and have generally ignored studies of languages in contact. Cultural anthropologists, on the other hand, have been content to investigate acculturation in its purely nonlinguistic manifestations. Studies of linguistic acculturation, however, can furnish valuable data and may shed considerable light on the general problem of acculturation. Whether language and nonlinguistic aspects of culture change differentially, or whether in every instance language complements and reflects nonlinguistic acculturation, is a crucial problem. In the present illustrations, linguistic acculturation seems to substantiate what has taken place in other aspects of the cultures of the groups under consideration, but this may not be the case everywhere.

In line with a broader study of Spanish-Indian acculturation in the Southwest, this study attempts to elucidate the hypothesis that the contact situation, whether forced or permissive, tends to produce a situation which is correspondingly resistive or accepting of introduced cultural elements. (The following papers deal with this problem: Dozier, 1955; in press.) Two groups are examined to support the contention of this hypothesis: the Yaqui Indians of Sonora and Arizona, and the Tewa Indians of New Mexico.

Historical materials and the research of anthropologists indicate that early Spaniards among the Yaqui used little coercion in the introduction of European and Catholic cultural patterns (Perez de Ribas, 1645; Spicer, 1940, 1954a). According to ethnological accounts of theYaqui, these Indians represent a group where Spanish and Indian cultural traits are so intricately interwoven that it is virtually impossible to isolate the indigenous from the introduced traits (Beals, 1943; Johnson, 1943; Spicer, 1954b). Nor are the Yaqui themselves aware of what is Spanish and what is Indian in their culture. Yaqui culture is thus a good example of amalgamized culture.

Among the New Mexico Tewa, on the other hand, native and Spanish elements are clearly distinguishable; moreover, these Indians are conscious of what are native elements in their culture and what are Spanish. The Tewa Indians have not completely rejected Spanish elements; under compulsion they were forced to take over a great deal of Spanish culture. But they have compartmentalizd the introduced traits into a co-existing system which is essentially separate and distinct from the native system. This situation is evident in both linguistic and nonlinguistic aspects of their culture. An examination of materials in the other Rio Grande Pueblos indicates that a co-existing tradition is characteristic of all of these pueblos. The linguistic data presented in this paper, however, are restricted to the Tewa.

CONDITIONS OF CONTACT

YAQUI INDIANS OF SONORA AND ARIZONA

(This section has been summarized from Spicer 1940, 1954a.) The Yaqui number about 18,000; the population is scattered throughout the state of Sonora and southern Arizona in about seventeen communities. In the early contact period the population was concentrated in the Yaqui Valley in Sonora; it was with the advent of the Republican period and the pressure on Yaqui agricultural land and the resultant troubles with non-Yaquis that the Yaqui dispersed. These difficulties were the so-called "Yaqui Wars"; they contributed to Yaqui consciousness as Yaqui and crystallized a culture that was already a fusion of Spanish and Indian elements. The Yaqui today set themselves apart from the Mexican population, and, although their culture represents an amalgam of Spanish and indigenous traits, consider themselves Yaqui Indians and not Ladinos, Mestizos, or Mexicans.

The Yaqui first came into continuous contact with Spanish culture shortly after 1600. The early years of colonization appear to have been comparatively free of friction between the two groups. Directed cultural change came mainly at the hands of Jesuit priests, who significantly entered the area without military escort. There is also evidence that these missionaries protected their Yaqui charges against wholesale exploitation from Spanish secular authorities. Moreover, they learned the Yaqui language and spent much time in translating prayers and other religious texts, which exist today among the Yaqui as an integral part of their ceremonial ritual. The Jesuits forced the building of churches and enforced attendance at mass, but the suppression of native ceremonies and the destruction of ceremonial paraphernalia were apparently minimal; at least, this inference is suggested by the present hybridized condition of Yaqui ceremonies. In all aspects of their culture there are indications that the Yaqui were given wide latitude to rework the forms and meanings of introduced patterns.

The result of this permissive situation was that in little more than a century the syncretized nature of Yaqui culture had been established. Beginning in 1735 and culminating in the period 1870-1910, troubles began with non-Indians encroaching on Yaqui landholdings. This was the period of large-scale voluntary and forced migrations. Borrowing of cultural elements was largely resisted, so that Yaqui culture today represents a kind of crystallization of the earlier amalgam. Yaqui culture suggests a fusion of preconquest Indian elements and 16th- and 17th-century Spanish cultural traits. It seems certain that if the permissive atmosphere established in the earlier period of contact had remained, the Yaqui would have become completely Hispanized.

THE RIO GRANDE PUEBLOS OF NEW MEXICO

(This section has been summarized primarily from the writer's published materials. See especially Dozier, 1954, in press.) The contact situation will be discussed in terms of the Rio Grande Pueblos generally instead of the Tewa specifically; the acculturation phenomena appear to be similar in all these pueblos. Some twenty pueblo communities are scattered along the Rio Grande and its tributaries. The present population is about 10,000; in 1680, the date of the earliest and most complete census report, it was considerably higher, about 25,000—closer to the Yaqui number (Hodge, 1907-1910, Part 2, p. 325).

Two completely unrelated linguistic stocks occupy the Rio Grande Pueblos, Keresan and Tanoan. During the 17th and 18th centuries there were five branches of the Tanoan: Tiwa, Tewa, Towa, Tano, and Piro; the last two groups are now extinct. Of the surviving linguistic groups, the Tewa were in the center of the initial colonization area, and thus were exposed to a more intensive acculturative influence. Today there are five New Mexico Tewa villages with an overall population of about 2500.

The most significant feature of Rio Grande Pueblo culture is its extreme conservatism. Pueblo culture meets with resistance and antagonism any inroads of encroaching cultures. One student of the pueblos describes them as follows:

> The pueblos became subject to white man's rule and exploitation in the latter part of the sixteenth century. For decades the Indians chafed under the Spanish yoke. In 1680 they arose in mad and bloody insurrection. They killed or drove out every Spaniard. But is was no use. The Spaniards came back, and the pueblos were compelled to submit. But they were not wholly beaten; they did not surrender their sacred customs. They merely concealed them. Outwardly the Indians became Catholics. But underneath they have zealously preserved the faith of their forefathers (White, 1942).

When we examine the conditions of contact, we obtain an insight into the causes underlying this reaction of the Rio Grande Pueblos. The missionaries that brought the Catholic religion to the pueblos were not the sympathetic and tolerant Jesuits, but militant Franciscans with the full support of Spanish civil and military authorities. They did not learn the native languages; instead they attempted to suppress all customs that seemed to them pagan and idolatrous. They burned masks and other ceremonial paraphernalia of the Indians. They imposed physical punishment for failure to attend religious services and for participation in native ceremonial dances. In addition, both clergy and civil authorities used Pueblo Indian labor and demanded tribute from them. The colonists took the best farming lands, thus aggravating bad feeling between the two peoples.

Pueblo reaction to Spanish rule culminated in the revolt of 1680, but in 1693 the Spaniards returned with superior forces and reclaimed the pueblo country. Many Indians fled the area and joined Navaho groups, or went to live with the Hopi in Arizona. Those who remained adopted the externals of the new faith and conformed to other imposed patterns, but continued to practice their own religion and other customs in secret. With the passage of time and under constant surveillance by Spanish authorities, Spanish-Catholic practices became incorporated into the culture as an important but separate tradition. A set of values and moral concepts, essentially indigenous in character, gave coherence and integration to the two traditions (discussed in Dozier, in press).

LINGUISTIC ACCULTURATION

LINGUISTIC ACCULTURATION AMONG THE YAQUI

The following characterization is drawn and excerpted from two excellent papers on the subject (Johnson, 1943; Spicer, 1943). It is clear from these papers that linguistic acculturation among the Yaqui reflects acculturation in other aspects of culture.

Nominal loanwords in Yaqui are estimated by Spicer in the categories of domestic utensils, socials organization, and ritual as 65 per cent Spanish-derived. But Spicer interjects a word of caution as to the interpretation of this figure. He reports that a discussion by a Sonoran Yaqui in his orginal habitat about pre-Columbian items might show a lower proportion of Spanish words. Nevertheless, even half the percentage figure given by Spicer for the Yaqui would be far greater than that obtained for the Tewa and those reported for other Rio Grande Pueblo languages groups. (About 5% for Keresan and Taos. See Spencer, 1947, p. 146; Trager, 1944, p. 157.)

The technique of coining new words and the process of loan translation, which are primary linguistic processes among the Tewa, are rare among the Yaqui. Thus, Spicer reports:

> It is quite clear from the evidence that Yaquis have rarely invented words by which to call newly introduced or newly developed culture items. Occasionally there has been a compounding of roots to produce a new word, such as *liosnooka* (meaning to pray), which is made up of the Spanish *dios* (God) and Yaqui *nooka* (speak). In all cases of such compounding known to the writer, borrowing has also been involved, the new form being composed, as in the case of *liosnooka* of a Spanish and a Yaqui root. The process of loan-translation is even more rare and seems to have taken place only under somewhat artificial conditions, as when missionaries translated prayers into Yaqui and such words as *anasuale* (meaning The Credo; literally in Yaqui, "I believe it") became fixed in the language. The processes of new word building and loan-translation may definitely be listed as of minor importance in comparison with simple borrowing. (1943, p. 412).

Spanish has also produced changes in the phonology, morphology, and syntax of Yaqui. Johnson (1943) presents evidence for changes in the phonemic pattern as the result of Spanish influence. He also demonstrates changes in phrase order to approximate Spanish types and provides data to indicate the influence of Spanish indirect-object constructions on Yaqui morphological and syntactical constructions (pp. 432-434). Johnson concludes his paper with these remarks:

> The Spanish language, like the culture brought by the conquerors, has profoundly affected Yaqui language and culture to its very core, but has not destroyed its fundamental integration, nor radically changed its essential core. Yaqui has absorbed a tremendous amount of Spanish, but has not as yet shown signs of reaching that saturation point which for Linton means disintegration and breakdown in function (p. 434).

TEWA LINGUISTIC ACCULTURATION

Spanish influence on Tewa is restricted primarily to nominal designations for items of Spanish or Mexican introduction. (True also of Keresan and Taos. See Spencer, 1947, p. 144; Trager, 1944, pp. 156-157.) Tewa morphology and syntax seem not to have been affected by Spanish, nor is there evidence that Tewa phonology was changed in any way. Loanwords have undergone phonetic changes, but for the most part they are still incompatible with Tewa phonological structure. Spanish has tapped the word-building mechanisms of Tewa, however, by the introduction of unfamiliar objects and concepts. The processes are primarily of two types: (1) coinage of new words, mainly descriptive of the introduced item or concept, and (2) extension of the meanings of words already in the language to cover the new cultural acquisitions.

The fact that Tewa speakers are for the most part bilingual and recognize Spanish-derived words prompts them to find new terms, primarily descriptive designations in Tewa, when talking in the company of Spanish-Americans. This is true also when Tewa speakers are in the presence of Anglo-Americans whom they suspect of knowing Spanish. Even the younger generation, who know little or no Spanish, delete Spanish loanwords from their speech, for Spanish-derived words invariably have a phonetic form foreign to other words in the vocabulary and are therefore easily recognized. The reticence of the Tewa in this respect is paralleled by their reluctance to give out information about their way of life. This is a typical Rio Grande Pueblo trait, apparently deeply rooted. It is undoubtedly associated with the suppression of native customs by missionaries and Spanish authorities experienced by their forefathers and handed down by word of mouth to the present generation. An early student of the Tewa reports of their purist tendencies:

> There is and always has been considerable dislike for the Mexicans on the part of the Tewa, and this feeling is responsible for the purist tendencies of many Tewa speakers. The Tewa are apt to avoid the use of Spanish place-names when speaking Tewa, either translating them or using the old Tewa equivalents. When talking Tewa in the presence of Mexicans they are especially careful not to use any Spanish words, lest they be understood and the secret subject of the conversation be betrayed. Dislike for the Mexicans has tended to keep the old Tewa place-names in use, and, in general, to preserve the language (Harrington, 1916, p. 97).

The reluctance of the Tewa to use Spanish designations when Spanish speakers are present is also characteristic of Taos Indians; indeed, their language is purged of English loanwords as well. Trager reports for Taos:

> In everyday speech the Taos use many more loans, especially of English origin, but these I was never able to record because there was—once it was known that I knew something of the language—little free conversation in my presence, and what there was I could not write down but only try to remember. My informants reacted to many loan words with a kind of purism that made it difficult to get them to repeat the words. The items treated here were either recorded in texts, with no comment from me until later, or were caught on the wing, as it were (1944, p. 144).

The Tewa do not seem to mind English loanwords as much as do Taos speakers. Younger Tewa speakers, particularly, tend to interlard a Tewa sentence with English words or phrases. This seems to be because their attitudes toward Anglo-Americans are generally more favorable than toward Spanish-Americans. English, at least among the Tewa, appears to have much higher status than Spanish. We may therefore expect more influence of English on Tewa than has been the case for Spanish.

As with Taos and Keresan, only a small proportion of the vocabulary of Tewa in the writer's knowledge consists of loanwords. The number of loanwords consistently used is difficult to determine. As has been reported, all loanwords lend themselves easily to descriptive designations in the language. Some of these are stabilized in specific Tewa pueblos and even across villages, others are thought up on the spur of the moment, but are usually clear enough to allow no mistake as to their referents. Apparently all loans, Spanish or English, are on the conscious level. This is undoubtedly because all Tewa have some acquaintance with Spanish and English, and also because the loanwords have not been so altered phonetically that they cannot be identified by Tewa speakers.

Tewa linguistic acculturation differs from Keresan in one important respect: Tewa has techniques for forming new words. (Apparently this is also true of Toas: Trager, 1944, p. 157.) Indeed, the coinage of new words is the primary method for handling foreign items and concepts. In other respects Tewa linguistic acculturation is much like Keresan. Tewa like Keresan employs the technique of extending the meaning of native words to cover new cultural acquisitions. The compounding of native and Spanish words is as rare in Tewa as in Keresan. Only two such forms are in the writer's collection: *mí·sateʰ* 'church' (from *misa*, Spanish 'mass,' and *teʰ*, Tewa term for 'structure, building,'); the other is *panteʰ* 'bread oven' (from *pan*, Spanish 'bread,' and *teʰ*, as above). It is worth quoting from Spencer's paper on Spanish loanwords in Keresan for comparison with Tewa:

> . . . Keresan, unlike Athapascan, for example, has at hand virtually no mechanisms by which new words may be formed. While there is ample evidence that at one time new words might be formed by simple and derivational compounding, the present trend is the avoidance of such devices in favor of two primary alternatives. The first appears in loan translations, the extension of the meaning of native words to admit new concepts, the second in simple linguistic borrowing with consequent phonetic modification of the words borrowed. A secondary alternative is the simple compounding of native Keresan and introduced Spanish words to offer new designations. Examples of this type of word formation are rather rare, there being very few words in relatively common use (1947, p. 133).

EXAMPLES OF WORD BUILDING, LOAN TRANSLATIONS, AND LOANWORDS

First come new designations, mainly descriptive terms, developed by the Tewa as a result of Spanish influence; second are examples of terms already in the language, but now extended to cover the new cultural acquisitions; finally, there is a list of loanwords. For the sake of convenience, the examples in each of these sections have been placed in the following categories: Domesticated animals and persons, domesticated plants, religious designations, government terms, and material cultural items. In the examples of Spanish loanwords, other miscellaneous items have been added. (For a description of the phonetic symbols used in this section, see Hoijer and Dozier, 1949.)

NEW WORDS

Domesticated animals and persons: *ʔòzèʰsóyóʰ* 'mule' (*ʔòzèʰ* 'ear', *sóyóʰ* 'big'); *ʔòzèʰsóyóʔè·* 'donkey, burro' (as above, with *ʔè·* diminutive); *k'úwáʰfóʔą̀nʸę̨́ʔìʔ* 'goat' (*k'úwáʰ* 'sheep,' *fóʰ* 'hair,' *ʔànʸę̨́·ʔìʔ* 'smooth'); *kʷę̨́·zî·* 'horse' (unanalyzable; the loanword, below, is much more common [According to Harrington: "The Tewa apply *kʷę̨́·zî·* and *kavázuʰ* (loanword) to any kind of a horse, but use the former term when they talk about horses in the presence of a Mexican and fear that *kavázuʰ* will be understood" (Henderson and Harrington, 1914, p. 30).]); *kʷę̨́k'uʰ* 'Mexican, Spaniard' (= iron, perhaps from the armor worn by Spanish soldiers); *kʷę̨́k'uféndìʔ* 'Negro' (Spaniard, as above, with *féndìʔ* 'black'). In names of animals, the suffixes *sèŋ* 'man' and *kʷì.* 'woman' may be added for male and female respectively.

Domesticated plants: *pú·p'íʔ* 'beet' (*pú·* 'root, base, buttocks,' *p'íʔ* 'red'); *pú·c'ézìʔ* 'carrot' (*pú·*, as above, with *c'é·zìʔ* 'yellow'); *pú·p'á·ʔìʔ* 'mulberry' (*pú·* with *p'á·ʔìʔ* 'wrinkled'); *pú·sę̨̀·ʔìʔ* 'radish' (*pú·* with *sę̨̀·ʔìʔ* 'bitter'); *bè·fóʔìʔ* 'peach' (*bè·* 'fruit,' now narrowed in application to apple, *fóʔìʔ* 'hairy'); *θú·wìʔ* 'watermelon' ('spotted,' see also loanword); *táʰtáŋ* 'wheat' (*táʰ* from *tà·* 'grass, hay,' *táŋ* 'seed'); *táʰtâŋ fóʔìʔ* 'barley' (wheat, as above, with *fóʔìʔ* 'hairy').

Religous terms: *p'oʰp'ò·* 'baptism' (*p'óʰ* from *p'ôŋ* 'head,' *p'ò·* 'water'); *p'òʔwarep'ò·* 'holy water' (*p'òʔ* from *p'ò·* 'water,' *ware* from *wareʰ* 'to sprinkle,' *p'ò·* 'water'); *mí·satèʰ* 'church' (*mí·sa* from Spanish 'mass,' *teʰ*. Tewa 'building, structure'); *feʔwìŋ* 'cross' (*féʰ* 'wood board, timber,' *wìŋ* 'erect, standing'); *péyéqeʰ* 'hell' (falling or disposal place); *penísèndìʔ* 'devil' (*pení* 'the dead, human skeleton,' *sèŋ* 'horn,' *dìʔ* 'having the quality of'); *t'è·wóʔdìʔ* 'sin' (t'*è·* 'anger, malice,' *wóʔdìʔ* 'full of'); *ʔòxʷaʔ* 'Catholic priest' (unanalyzable).

Material items: *šùndiʔ* 'airplane' (*šùŋ* 'fly,' *dìʔ* 'having or possessing the quality of'); *wą̀·tèʰ* 'automobile' (*wą̀·* 'wind,' *tèʰ* 'structure, building'); *xʷòtèʰ* 'bed' (*xʷòʰ* 'to retire,' *tèʰ* as above); *kòféʰ* 'canoe, boat, (*kòʰ* 'swim,' *féʰ* 'wood, board, timber'); *tàʔféʰ* 'pencil' (*tàʔ* from *tà·* 'to draw a line,' *féʰ* 'wood, etc.' as above); *fà·féʰ* 'match' (*fà·* 'fire,' *féʰ* 'wood, etc.); *féfáʔ* 'shovel, spade' (*fé* from *féʰ*, *fáʔ* 'broad, flat'); *k'ùʰcę̨̀·ʔìʔ* 'hammer' (*k'ùʰ* from *k'ù·* 'stone, rock,' *cę̨̀·ʔìʔ* 'striker'); *pùwę̨̀ʔìʔ* 'mirror' (literally 'viewer'); *xʷę̨̀·tóʰ* 'plow' (*xʷę̨̀·* 'to dig a furrow,' *tóʰ* unanalyzable); *támàŋ* 'hay fork' (*tá* from *tá·* 'hay, grass,' *màŋ* 'hand'); *fébè·* 'box' (*fé* from *féʰ*, *bè·* 'enclosure'); *púweréʰ* 'chair' (*pú* from *pú·* 'root, base, buttocks,' *weréʰ* 'support'); *kʷàʰxʷę̨rèʰ* 'gun, rifle' (*kʷàʰ* from *kʷàŋ* 'rain,' *xʷę̨rèʰ* 'whipping, pelting').

EXTENSION OF OLD MEANINGS

Domesticated animals and fowl: *dì·* 'chicken' (term originally applied to fowl in general, now narrowed to domesticated chickens); *ką̀·gi*^{h} 'goose' (term for wild goose now applied to the domesticated goose); *k'úwá*^{h} 'sheep' (term formerly applied to mountain sheep, now applied to domesticated sheep).

Domesticated plants: *pò·* 'pumpkin' (native squash, but applied to all varieties of introduced squash and pumpkins); *sî·* 'onion' (wild onion, applied to introduced varieties as well); *sà·* 'tobacco' (now applied only to introduced varieties of tobacco; for the native variety the word for 'people' is prefixed); *bè·* 'apple' (term for fruit generally, but now used specifically for apple).

Religious terms: *nú·fà·* 'Christmas' (formerly and still used for winter solstice); *makówá*^{h} 'heaven' (also used for 'sky'); *hą̂·* 'soul' (term for breath).

Government terms: *xó·* 'assistant priest or leader' (means arm, limb, branch, and refers in a political or ceremonial context to an assistant leader or official; see below); *sófò*^{h} 'speaker' (mouth); *tùŋǯóŋ* 'governor' (Tewa term for leader, chief); *tùŋǯóŋxó·* 'lieutenant governor' (*tùŋǯóŋ* 'leader, chief,' *xó·* 'arm, limb, branch, assistant').

Material items: *k'ù·wí·* 'axe' (*k'ù·* 'stone, rock,' *wí·* unanalyzable; the Tewa term for stone ax, now applied to steel axes); *sú*^{h} 'ammunition, bullet' (term for arrow); *tàfén*^{y}*ìʔ* 'broom' (*tá* from *tá·* 'grass, hay,' *fén*^{y}*iʔ* possibly from *féʔn*^{y}*ę̀wè*^{h} 'weeds'; applied to commercial brooms as well as to native types made from various species of grass and brush); *cíǯó*^{h} 'knife' (possibly from *cì·* 'flint, obsidian,' *ǯó*^{h} unanalyzable; originally restricted to stone knives); *bè·sù*^{h} 'fireplace' (*bè·* 'enclosure,' *sù*^{h} unanalyzable; term for the old pueblo hearth); *xų́ʔ ʔùŋ* 'doll, play doll' (unanalyzable; native term for doll, now applied to introduced dolls).

SPANISH LOANWORDS

Domesticated animals and fowl: *besero*^{h} 'calf' (*beserro, beserra*); *mú·sa*^{h} 'cat' (*musa, musi*, Spanish forms of English 'pussy'); *wá·si*^{h} 'cow' (*vaca*); *budu*^{h} 'donkey' (*burro*); *má·cu*^{h} 'donkey stallion' (*macho*); *kavra*^{h} 'goat' (*cabra*); *kaváǯu*^{h} 'horse' (*caballo*); *ǯé·wa*^{h} 'mare' (*yegua*); *mula*^{h} 'mule' (*mulo, mula*); *periku*^{h} 'parrot' (*perico*); *peʔcure*^{h} 'pig' (probably Náhuatl *pitzotl*); *paloma*^{h} 'pigeon' (*paloma*). (Gender is usually rendered as in Spanish, but loanwords remain unchanged for number. Only one series of Tewa nominal expressions appear to be inflected for number.)

Domesticated plants: *kô·le*^{h} 'cabbage' (*col*); *serê·sa*^{h} 'cherry' (*cereza*); *cį̀di*^{h} 'chile' (*chile*); *ʔú·va*^{h} 'grape' (*uva*); *benunde*^{h} 'melon' (?); *ʔavéna*^{h} 'oats' (*avena*); *pê·ra*^{h} 'pear' (*pera*); *pápá*^{h} 'potato' (*papa*); *sandia*^{h} 'watermelon' (*sandia*); *pâŋ* 'wheat bread' (*pan*).

Religious terms: *ʔâŋhele*^{h} 'angel' (*ángel*); *ʔòví·pù*^{h} 'bishop' (*obispo*); *konfesâ* 'confession' (*confesión*); *pa*^{h}*k*^{w}*â·* 'Easter' (*pascua*); *ǯó·sì*^{h} 'God' (*Jesus* or *dios*); *kumpá·rè*^{h} 'godfather' (*compadre*); *kumarè*^{h} 'godmother' (*comadre*); *mí·sà*^{h} 'mass' (*misa*); *zû·sù*^{h} 'prayer' (probably from *Jesus*); *sakitâŋ* 'sacristan, altar boy' (*sacristán*); *santù*^{h} 'saint' (*santo*); *bî·herà*^{h} 'Virgin Mary' (*virgen*).

Government terms: *kapitâŋ* 'captain' (*capitán*); *tin*^{y}*enté*^{h} 'lieutenant governor' (*teniente*); *mayodomù*^{h} 'majordomo' (*mayordomo*; among the New Mexico Spanish-Americans and the Pueblo Indians this term designates a ditch boss); *pi*^{h}*kâ.* 'official' (*fiscal*; among the Tewa this term denotes men who are in charge of the village chapel and burials); *pìnsipâ·* 'political leaders' (*principales*); *sundaro*^{h} 'soldier' (*soldado*).

Material items: *bò*^{h}*teʔa*^{h} 'bottle' (*botella*); *p*^{w}*entè*^{h} 'bridge' (*puente*); *tenerô·* 'fork' (*tenedor*); *pi*^{h}*tô·* 'pistol' (*pistola*); *kucąda*^{h} 'spoon' (*cuchara*); *mę̂·sa*^{h} 'table' (*mesa*); *ferî·* 'train' (probably *fierro* in *fierro carril* 'railroad').

Week days: *dumiŋgu*^{h} 'Sunday' (*domingo*); *dú·ne*^{h} 'Monday' (*lunes*); *má·te*^{h} 'Tuesday' (*martes*); *m*^{y}*é·kure*^{h} 'Wednesday' (*miércoles*); *x*^{w}*é·ve*^{h} 'Thursday' (*jueves*); *b*^{y}*é·né*^{h} 'Friday' (*viernes*); *savandu*^{h} 'Saturday' (*sábado*).

Time and distance: *ʔó·ra*^{h} 'hour' (*hora*); *menuto*^{h} 'minute' (*minuto*); *segundo*^{h} 'second' (*segundo*); *mî·* 'thousand' (*mil*); *miya*^{h} 'mile' (*milla*).

SPANISH NAMES AMONG THE RIO GRANDE PUEBLO INDIANS

The Tewa, like other Rio Grande Pueblo Indians, were given surnames by Spanish priests in the initial contact period. These names are borne by their descendants today and are typically Spanish; many of them exist also as surnames among their Spanish-American neighbors. Certain names have tended to concentrate in specific pueblos: *Naranjo*, *Tafoya*, and *Gutierrez* are characteristic of Santa Clara Pueblo; *Martinez*, *Cata*, and *Archuleta* are typical surnames in San Juan Pueblo. Given names are also of Spanish derivation, and are invariably accompanied by a middle name. Names like *José Rey*, *Juan José*, and *Miguel Antonio* are common among the Tewa and Rio Pueblo Indians generally. Since these names are recorded by literate Spanish priests in the churches in which Pueblo Indians are baptized, the spelling of the names is standard Spanish. The Tewa often adjust these names in pronunciation to approximate Tewa phonological structure, but the Spanish spelling and pronunciation are retained in relations outside of the pueblos. In recent years some Tewa individuals have changed their Spanish given names to English equivalents; in some instances even the surname has been changed.

The Tewa and other Rio Grande Pueblo Indians also receive native names in accordance with special native customs and rites. It is these names, usually of native plants and animals and of the natural environment, that are translated into English and used as surnames, while the Spanish given name in its English form is retained as a first name. Names like *Tom White Cloud*, *Joseph Little Deer* are now making their appearance among Pueblo Indians. The tendency to change names reflects the general dislike for Spanish-Americans and the growing desire to identify more closely with Anglo-Americans. The new names may also indicate a pan-Indianism, since they are similar to names borne by other North American Indians. The intermingling of members of diverse American Indian peoples in such places as Indian Schools, Government Indian agencies, and summer camps and resorts has tended in recent years to give Indians a consciousness of their identity as Indians.

GENERAL CHARACTERISTICS OF SPANISH INFLUENCE ON TEWA

Spanish loanwords are in general limited to nominal forms. Only two examples of another form class are in the writer's collection: the Spanish conjunctions *si* 'if' and *porque* 'because' (the latter usually modified to *pòkeʰ*). These may be expressed, however, by Tewa equivalents; the native substitutions are typically employed when the speaker wishes to conceal the subject of his conversation in the presence of a Spanish speaker.

Only one class of nouns, a highly restricted series, appears to be inflected in Tewa, and this only for number. The class contains designations for stages in the life cycle: infant, child, pre-adolescent boy and girl, post-adolescent boy and girl, adult man and woman, etc. None of these terms has been borrowed from Spanish.

Tewa verbal and pronominal constructions are exceedingly complex. Introductions in this area would have produced radical changes in morphology. No influence is to be found anywhere in Tewa morphology or syntax.

Tewa phonology also appears not to have undergone important changes as the result of Spanish contact. Tewa phonemic consonants are more numerous than Spanish, but all Spanish consonantal phonemes with the exception of the lateral *l* are also contained in Tewa. (Reference to Spanish phonology is actually to New Mexican Spanish. For a list of New Mexican Spanish phonemes see Trager, 1944, p. 151.) For Spanish *l*, apical dental *t* and the alveolar trill *r* are substituted initially and medially. Final consonants are limited in Tewa; syllables end in only four ways: with glottal stop ʔ, open vowel (when tonal and long), breath release after short vowel *eʰ*, and velar nasal *ŋ*. Where a consonant other than *m* or *n* ends a syllable in a loanword, Tewa speakers end the sequence at the preceding vowel. For example, 'Miguel' is *migê·* and 'David' is *davî·*. The nasals *m* and *n* in medial and final positions follow the Tewa pattern: *m* before bilabials, *n* before dentals and alveolars, and *ŋ* before velars and in final position (Hoijer and Dozier, 1949).

It is clear from the examples of new word formations that Tewa has no difficulty in coining words. In this respect it is unlike Yaqui and Keresan. The technique is to compound descriptive designations. The most common method is the addition of the terminal adjectival suffix *-iʔ* or *-ʔiʔ* 'having the quality of.' The suffixes *tèʰ* 'structure, building' and *féʰ* 'wood, board, timber' are also frequent.

The ability of the language to invent words and the reluctance of Tewa speakers to use Spanish loanwords have undoubtedly restricted borrowing. In over 2000 words examined by the writer, less than five percent are of Spanish origin. The Tewa language, like the rest of Tewa culture, has vigorously resisted acculturation.

CONCLUSIONS

Evidence has been presented for two contrasting types of linguistic acculturation. The Yaqui represent a case in which borrowing from Spanish has been exhaustive: all aspects of Yaqui lexicon, morphology, and syntax show Spanish influence. The Yaqui language is not, however, simply a mixture of Spanish and Yaqui elements; it is an amalgam where Spanish and Yaqui elements have been thoroughly integrated. What has taken place in language has also occured in nonlinguistic aspects of Yaqui culture. Yaqui culture is a fusion of preconquest Indian elements and 16th- and 17th-century cultural traits, so completely reworked and modified that it is virtually impossible to trace the original affinities.

The Rio Grande Tewa, on the other hand, have resisted acculturation in language no less vigorously than in other aspects of their culture. Only a small portion of Tewa words are Spanish loanwords. Moreover, Tewa speakers are keenly conscious of these terms and tend to delete or restrict their usage in the presence of Spanish-speaking outsiders. The coinage of new words and the extension of old meanings to cover new cultural acquisitions are preferred to outright borrowings.

It is important to repeat the hypothesis to explain this situation. The initial Spanish-Yaqui contact period appears to have been a permissive one; the Indians were given an opportunity to choose introduced Spanish cultural elements and to integrate them with their own. They were apparently not coerced into taking over European and Catholic ways. The suppression of native ceremonies and customs and the destruction of ceremonial paraphernalia either did not occur or were minimal. The result was that a fusion of Spanish and Yaqui cultural elements took place in a comparatively short time.

In the Rio Grande Pueblo area the early relation of Spaniards and Indians was marked by coercion. Ceremonies and customs were suppressed, ceremonial paraphernalia were destroyed, and the Indians were fined and punished for violating regulations of church and state. Antagonistic relations between the two groups developed very early, and the Rio Grande Pueblo Indians resisted the integration of Spanish and Indian cultural elements. Under constant pressure from Spanish civil and church authorities, the pueblos fitted the Catholic religion and other Spanish cultural patterns externally to their own religion and customs, which they continued to practice in secret. A set of essentially indigenous values and moral concepts gave unity and coherence to the two traditions; but up to the present time Spanish and Rio Grande Pueblo cultural patterns have remained distinct.

These two contrasting acculturative situations, in both linguistic and nonlinguistic aspects, appear to be due to the contact situation, one permissive and the other forced. (Reed feels that the strength and tight integration of indigenous pueblo culture were responsible for resistance to acculturation. See Reed, 1944. Spicer, however, points out that historical evidence indicates that early Yaqui culture was very much like the pueblo [1954b, p. 677].)

REFERENCE NOTE

The author makes grateful acknowledgment to the Graduate School of Northwestern University and to the Social Science Research Council's Southwestern Project on Comparative Psycholinguistics, for providing an opportunity to obtain materials for this paper in the field.

References are organized in three parts: (A) specific to this paper; (B) concerning the sociocultural context of linguistic acculturation; (C) concerning language contact and acculturation proper.

A. REFERENCES SPECIFIC TO DOZIER'S PAPER

BEALS, RALPH L.

1943. The Aboriginal Culture of the Cahita Indians. *Ibero-Americana, 19:* 1-86.

DOZIER, EDWARD

1954. *The Hopi-Tewa of Arizona.* (UCP-AAE 44.) Berkeley and Los Angeles: University of California Press. Pp. 259-376.

1955. Forced and Permissive Acculturation. *The American Indian, 7:* 38-44.

In press. *Rio Grande Pueblo Values and Moral Concepts.*

HENDERSON, JUNIUS, and JOHN P. HARRINGTON

1914. *Ethnozoology of the Tewa Indians.* (BAE-B 56.) Washington, D.C.: Smithsonian Institution.

HOIJER, HARRY, and EDWARD P. DOZIER

1949. The Phonemes of Tewa, Santa Clara Dialect. *IJAL, 15:* 139-144.

JOHNSON, JEAN B.

1943. A Clear Case of Linguistic Acculturation. *AA, 45:* 427-434.

LEE, DOROTHY D.

1943. The Linguistic Aspects of Wintu Acculturation. *AA, 45:* 435-440.

PEREZ DE RIBAS, ANDRES

1645. *Historia de los Triumphos de Novestra Santa Fee en los missiones de la Nueva España.* Madrid.

REED, ERIK K.

1944. Aspects of Acculturation in the Southwest. *Acta Americana, 2:* 26-69.

SPENCER, ROBERT F.

1947. Spanish Loanwords in Keresan. *SJA, 3:* 130-146.

SPICER, EDWARD H.

1940. *Pascua: A Yaqui Village in Arizona.* Chicago: University of Chicago Press.

1943. Linguistic Aspects of Yaqui Acculturation. *AA, 45:* 410-426.

1954a. *Potam: A Yaqui Village in Sonora.* (Memoirs of the American Anthropological Association, No. 77.) Menasha, Wis.

1954b. Spanish-Indian Acculturation in the Southwest. *AA, 56:* 663-678.

TRAGER, GEORGE L.

1944. Spanish and English Loanwords in Taos. *IJAL, 10:* 144-158.

WHITE, LESLIE A.

1942. *The Pueblo of Santa Ana, New Mexico.* (Memoirs of the American Anthropological Association, No. 44.) Menasha, Wis.

B. SOCIOCULTURAL CONTEXT OF LINGUISTIC ACCULTURATION

On the sociocultural context of acculturation, see Barnett (1953), Beals (1953), Bruner (1956a, 1956b), Dozier (1951), Foster (1962), Hallowell (1945), Herskovits (1938), Linton (1940, esp. chaps 8-10), Siegel (1955), Spicer (1961), Spindler and Goldschmidt (1952), Social Science Research Council (1954), Steward (1955). Language specifically is treated in Bruner and Dozier, in Herskovits (pp. 49, 107 ff., 128), rarely in Siegel, in Spicer *passim*, and incidentally in the SSRC report.

References not in general bibliography:

BARNETT, H. G.

1953. *Innovation, The Basis of Cultural Change.* New York: McGraw-Hill.

BEALS, RALPH L.

1953. Acculturation. In Kroeber *et al.*, *Anthropology Today.* Chicago: University of Chicago Press. Pp. 621-641.

BRUNER, EDWARD M.
1956a. Primary Group Experience and the Processes of Acculturation. *AA, 58:* 605-623.
1956b. Cultural Transmission and Cultural Change. *SJA, 12:* 191-199.

FOSTER, GEORGE M.
1962. *Traditional Cultures: And the Impact of Technological Change.* New York: Harper & Row.

HALLOWELL, A. I.
1945. Sociopsychological Aspects of Acculturation. In Ralph Linton (Ed.), *The Science of Man in the World Crisis.* New York: Columbia University Press. Pp. 171-200.

HERKSOVITS, MELVILLE J.
1938. *Acculturation, The Study of Culture Contact.* New York: Augustin.

LINTON, RALPH (ED.)
1940. *Acculturation in Seven American Indian Tribes.* New York: Appleton-Century.

SIEGEL, BERNARD J. (ED.)
1955. *Acculturation: Critical Abstracts: North America.* (Stanford Anthropological Series, No. 2.) Stanford: Stanford University Press.

SPICER, EDWARD H. (ED.)
1961. *Perspectives in American Indian Culture Change.* Chicago: University of Chicago Press.

SPINDLER, G. D., and W. GOLDSCHMIDT
1952. Experimental Design in the Study of Culture Change. *SJA, 8:* 68-93.

SOCIAL SCIENCE RESEARCH COUNCIL SUMMER SEMINAR ON ACCULTURATION
1954. Acculturation: An Exploratory Formulation. *AA, 56:* 973-1002.

STEWARD, JULIAN H.
1955. *Theory of Culture Change: The Methodology of Multilinear Evolution.* Urbana: University of Illinois Press. [Reviewed, L. A. White, *AA*, 1957, *59:* 540-542.]

C. LANGUAGE CONTACT AND ACCULTURATION

For discussions focused on language contact, see the references listed with Diebold's article (pp. 495-508), especially the analyses and bibliographies of Weinreich (1953, 1958) and Haugen (1956, 1958). See also Bloomfield (1933, chaps. 25-27), Cohen (1956a, Part 4, chaps. 1, 2), Diebold (1962a), Hockett (1958, chaps. 46-49), Swadesh (1948), Vendryes (1925, Part 4, chap. 4), and Vogt (1954).

Among the many ethnographic and linguistic publications which treat of acculturation to a greater or lesser extent, note, regarding phonological aspects, besides references just indicated, Garvin (1947), Kelkar (1957), Leslau, (1957) Weinreich (1957a), Wonderly (1946).

Regarding lexical and morphological aspects, see Emeneau (1954a, Appendix I), Epstein (1959), Garvin (1949), Haugen (1950, 1953, 1956), Newman (1955), Olmsted (1954), Salzmann (1954), Swadesh (1951a), Wright (1953a); and the case studies cited by Dozier, especially Casagrande (1954-1955), the outstanding treatment of an American Indian case, and also Herzog (1941). On American Indian cases, see also Bright (1952, 1960), Dozier (1955), Malkiel (1948), Salzmann (1951), Swadesh (1948), Voegelin and Hymes (1953), and Waterhouse (1949, 1957), as representative of the problems and materials. For another New World study in which the "use of linguistic data throughout . . . as a reflection of 'the changes in cultural content and pattern' provides . . . a model for acculturation studies" (review by C. Wagley, AA, 1952, *54:* 538), see Taylor (1951). On the social matrix of innovation in an African case, see Epstein (1959). For case study of a language introduced into the United States, see the outstanding study by Haugen (1953). On English generally, see Jespersen (1905), Mencken (1936, 1945), and as a guide to treatments to date Bryant (1962); on special aspects, see the extensive case studies of Bense (1925, 1926-1939), Llewellyn (1936), and MacKenzie (1939).

For early recognition of the problem, note Powell (1880), which speaks of "the force of acculturation" and states, "The Indian method of coining new words and adapting old words to new uses is an interesting branch of philologic study. Hence, a long list of such names are called for in Schedule 24."

On the theoretical importance of the problem, see Bloomfield (1932) in which he says, "Finally, we can co-ordinate our basic assumptions about linguistic change with our knowledge of non-linguistic processes only in the matter of linguistic borrowing, which is obviously a phase of cultural borrowing in general" (p. 224).

The problems of linguistic acculturation cannot be separated from the problems treated in the articles in Part VII, especially those by Gumperz and Ferguson, and other articles in this part and in Part IX, especially those on jargons and creoles and on linguistic areas.

References not in the general bibliography:

BENSE, J. F.

1925. *Anglo-Dutch Relations from the Earliest Times to the Death of William III, Being an Historical Introduction to a Dictionary of the Low Dutch Element in the English Vocabulary*. London: Milford.

1926-1939. *A Dictionary of the Low-Dutch Element in the English Vocabulary*. London: Milford. Parts I-V.

BLOOMFIELD, LEONARD E.

1932. Review of E. Hermann, *Lautgesetz und Analogie*. *Lg., 8:* 220-233.

BRIGHT, WILLIAM

1952. Linguistic Innovations in Karok. *IJAL, 18:* 53-62.

1960. *Animals of Acculturation in the California Indian Languages*. (University of California Publications in Linguistics, Vol. 4, No. 4, pp. 215-246.) Berkeley and Los Angeles. University of California Press.

DIEBOLD, A. RICHARD, JR.

1962a. A Laboratory for Language Contact. *AL, 4* (1): 41-51.

EPSTEIN, A. L.

1959. Linguistic Innovation and Culture in the Copperbelt, Northern Rhodesia. *SJA, 15:* 235-253.

GARVIN, PAUL L.

1947. Distinctive Features in Zoque Phonemic Acculturation. *Studies in Linguistics, 5:* 13-20.

HAUGEN, EINAR

1950. The Analysis of Linguistic Borrowing. *Lg., 26:* 210-231.

1956. Review of H. Gneuss, *Lehnbildungen und Lehnbedeutungen in Altenglischen Lg., 32:* 761-766.

KELKAR, A. R.

1957. "Marathi English": A Study in Foreign Accent. *Word, 13:* 268-282.

LESLAU, WOLF

1957. The Phonetic Treatment of Arabic Loanwords in Ethiopic. *Word, 13:* 100-123.

LLEWELLYN, E. C.

1936. *The Influence of Low Dutch on the English Vocabulary*. (Publications of the Philological Society.) London.

MACKENZIE, F.

1939. *Les Relations de l'Angleterre et de la France d'après le vocabulaire*. Paris. 2 vols.

MALKIEL, YAKOV

1948. On Analyzing Hispano-Maya Blends. *IJAL, 14:* 74-76.

OLMSTED, D. L.

1954. Toward a Cultural Theory of Lexical Innovation. In Hugo Mueller (Ed.), Report on the Fifth Annual Round Table Meeting on Linguistics and Language Teaching. (Monograph Series on Language and Linguistics, No. 7.) Washington, D.C.: Georgetown University.

POWELL, S. W.

1880. New Words. *Introduction to the Study of Indian Languages*. Washington, D.C.: Government Printing Office.

SALZMANN, ZDENEK

1951. Contrastive Field Experience with Language and Values of the Arapaho. *IJAL, 17:* 98-101.

1954. Problem of Lexical Acculturation. *IJAL, 20:* 137-139.

TAYLOR, DOUGLAS MACRAE

1951. *The Black Carib of British Honduras*. (Viking Fund Publications in Anthropology, No. 17). New York: Wenner-Gren Foundation for Anthropological Research.

WATERHOUSE, VIOLA

1957. Two Oaxaca Chontal Words. *IJAL, 23:* 244-245.

WONDERLY, WILLIAM

1946. Phonemic Acculturation in Zoque. *IJAL, 12:* 92-95. [Also in Kenneth Pike, *Phonemics*. (University of Michigan Publications in Linguistics, Vol. 3.) Ann Arbor: University of Michigan Press, 1947.]

The Standard Language Problem —Concepts and Methods 55

PAUL L. GARVIN

WHEN I WAS on Ponape (Eastern Caroline Islands) some time ago as part of the Coordinated Investigation of Micronesian Anthropology, I was, in addition to straight linguistic research, concerned with the task of devising a unified orthography for Ponapean. I cooperated with a committee of five native leaders in this work, and I went one step beyond the immediate goal in that I also attempted to introduce a suitable Ponapean terminology for use in a spelling book containing the new spelling rules. This involved in part the consolidation of existing terms, in part the creation of new terms from native and borrowed sources. My native collaborators were extremely helpful not only in agreeing on terminology, but also in helping to compose a set of what I considered concise and modern-sounding statements.

I was primarily responsible for the formulation, in the sense that I would make initial suggestions and after some discussion and corrections would lead the native committee to some agreement on the final wording. In working with my Ponapean friends during and after the compilation of the new orthography and spelling book, I found that they had a keen understanding of the reasons for my suggestions and were able to make intelligent decisions under my guidance whenever a problem required a choice from among several possibilities.

I had a distinct sense of failure when, once the system was agreed upon and the spelling book was complete, I found that the members of the native committee had a great deal of trouble applying the rules and remembering the terms which they themselves had helped formulate.

The gist of my Ponapean experience can be stated quite briefly: literacy is not the same as standard language.

In an essentially folk culture, where literacy was a realistic objective, I had wanted to introduce certain elements extending beyond it and into the initial phases of language standardization—which is an essentially urban phenomenon. Specifically, I had attempted to lead the Ponapeans to achieve for their language, at least to an initial degree, the standard-language properties of flexible stability and intellectualization.

Flexible stability here refers to the requirement that a standard language be stabilized by appropriate codification, and that the codification be flexible enough "to allow for modification in line with culture change." Intellectualization here refers to the requirement of increasing accuracy along an ascending scale of functional dialects from conversational to scientific.

To bring about stability, the spelling book and certain official word lists were to serve as the beginnings of a codification. To insure flexibility, the native committee was to be developed into the embryo of a codifying agency, charged with working out the word lists and revisions of the spelling book and lists as required.

Unfortunately, the folk culture of Ponape, in spite of the existence of native schools, a money economy, and other urban elements, did not seem to have a vital need for the various functions of a standard language. Nor did my native friends, with all their good will and interest in the matter, exhibit to any great degree the attitudes which are characteristic of both nascent and established standard-language communities. Perhaps this was because they did not yet constitute the nucleus of a native urban intelligentsia. Thus, in spite of my great empathy with Ponapean culture, the presence of a single interested outsider was not sufficient to push this folk speech community further towards the urban end of the scale, although the successful completion of the spelling book was proof enough that the language qua linguistic pattern was as susceptible to standardization as any other language.

Let me now turn from the particular to the general and summarize briefly the conceptual framework which I have been using.

In a recent paper, Madeleine Mathiot and I (1960) tentatively defined a standard language as "a codified form of a language, accepted by, and serving as a model to, a larger speech community." We proposed three sets of criteria in terms of which the degree of language standardization can be discussed: "(1) the intrinsic properties of a standard language, (2) the functions of a standard language within the culture of a speech community, and (3) the attitudes of the speech community towards the standard language."

As properties of a standard language, we posited flexible stability as described by Vilém Mathesius (1932), and intellectualization as discussed by Bohuslav Havránek (1932).

We posited four functions of a standard language: the unifying, separatist, and prestige functions which we consider symbolic functions, and the frame-of-reference function which we consider an objective function.

By "unifying" we designate the function of a standard language to unite several dialect areas into a single standard-language community, by "separatist" its function to set off a speech community as separate from its neighbors. The remaining two functions refer to the prestige resulting from the possession of a standard language, and to the function of the standard language to serve as a frame of reference for correctness and for the perception and evaluation of poetic speech.

As typical standard-language attitudes we listed language loyalty as discussed by Uriel Weinreich (1953, pp. 99-102), pride, and awareness of the norm.

We differentiate between the former two by thinking of language loyalty as a protective and defensive attitude, and of pride as a positive attitude.

These attitudes are assumed to be linked to the four functions: language loyalty to the unifying and separatist functions—and with them to the broader attitude of nationalism, pride to the prestige function, and awareness of the norm to the frame-of-reference function.

In interpreting my Ponapean example, I have used these concepts to arrive at an intuitive explanation of an informally observed event, an explanation which has the status of an articulate opinion and can lay claim to a certain, perhaps high, degree of plausibility.

Let us accept that the requirements of a good methodology are (1) to discover which elements are relevant to the problem, and (2) to subject these elements to rigorous treatment.

By yielding a plausible interpretation, my conceptual framework has met the requirement of relevance.

To achieve rigor as well as relevance, I must show how these concepts can be used as a starting point for a controlled procedure which will yield products having the status of analytic results and meeting the more rigorous requirement of verifiability.

To develop such a procedure, I shall assume that my three sets of criteria reflect the nature of my subject matter, and that by studying them in detail I will arrive at an orderly description of a language situation in terms of the degree of standardization.

I can delimit my universe of data by differentiating between, on the one hand, the two sets of criteria which can be investigated directly—namely the properties of the standard language and the attitudes towards the standard language, and, on the other hand, the third set of criteria, the functions of the standard language, which can only be inferred from the observed attitudes and other cultural observations.

I can select the specific techniques from which to make up my operational steps by noting two characteristics of standard-language properties and attitudes: (1) They are continuous, sliding-scale features rather than discrete, yes-no features. That is, a given language situation can be described as meeting the criteria for a standard language to a given degree, rather than absolutely. (2) They are internally structured, that is, they are composed of multiple interrelated factors.

The major scales corresponding to standard-language properties and attitudes can then be studied by formulating a series of detailed partial scales for each in terms of the various component factors. These partial scales will be comparable to the scales of Redfield's folk-urban continuum; they will have to be sufficiently narrowly defined to be operationally viable.

The factors entering into the scales of flexible stability and intellectualization are focused on the linguistic variables of vocabulary and style; the factors entering into the attitudinal scales are focused on behavioral and situational variables.

Of these variables, vocabulary is clearly definable in terms of lexical units and easily amenable to statistical techniques. The remaining variables are not a priori definable for language as such or for culture as such, but must be stated specifically in terms of the particular linguistic and cultural pattern.

Thus, the only concrete techniques that can be listed at this point are the relatively trivial ones of specially slanted vocabulary counts. Synonym counts can serve as a measure of the stability factor in flexible stability, on the assumption that the number of synonyms for a given technical term is an inverse index of stability. Counts of specialized vocabulary, both that available in the formal code and that in actual use, as well as the ratio of both, can be worked into a measure of intellectualization.

Techniques dealing with the variable of style will have to be based on the results of morphemic analysis (primarily syntactic for those languages to which the morphology-syntax division applies); those dealing with behavioral and situational variables will have to be based on cultural and social psychological analysis.

To state such techniques in broad outline would be to belabor the obvious; to state them in detail would border on the fictitious.

Once the partial scales have been formulated and applied to organize the data, they can be considered units of a dynamic structure and structuralist method can be applied to relate them to each other, weight them, and relate them to the whole—that is the particular major scale of which they form part. In doing this, the two basic techniques of structuralist analysis—the technique of "frame and substitution" and the analysis of sequential co-occurrence—will have to be formulated in terms of the relations assumed to constitute the internal structure of each major scale, and will have to be appropriately modified to accommodate the type of units dealt with. Additional structuralist techniques may evolve from the results of this analysis, and of the preceding investigation of the partial scales.

Thus, contrary to the common assumption that structuralism is limited to the analysis of static systems only, it becomes applicable to the study of a dynamic problem.

REFERENCE NOTE

For a detailed discussion of the Ponape work, see Garvin (1954a).

The remainder of the reference note is organized in two parts: (A) general, (B) case studies.

A. GENERAL

On general aspects of the phenomena of standard languages, see Bloomfield (1933, chaps. 3.4-10, 19, 27.4-6), Ferguson (1962), Garvin and Mathiot (1960), Gumperz (1962), Kloss (1952), Meillet (1913), Ray (1961, 1962a, 1962b), Sommerfelt (1938b), Vendryes (1925, Part 4, chap. 3), Weinreich (1953, Section 4); references to literary languages with Sebeok's article in Part VI; the articles by Bloomfield, Gumperz, and Ferguson in Part VII and their references; and the article by Bull and its references in this part and the Unesco volume which is the subject of review.

On language and national feelings and attitudes, note the above and Buck (1916), Deutsch (1953) and its extensive bibliography, Dozier (1951), Hymes (1961c, 1962a), Jakobson (1945), Jespersen (1925); Kohn (1944), Ray (1962a),

Salisbury (1962), Spencer (1963), Swadesh (1948), Vendryes (1925, Part 4, chap. 4), Weinreich (1953) and its extensive bibliography, and Wolff (1959a).

References not in the general bibliography:

BUCK, CARL DARLING

1916. Language and the Sentiment of Nationality. *American Political Science Review, 10:* 44-69.

DEUTSCH, KARL

1953. *Nationalism and Social Communication; An Inquiry into the Foundations of Nationality*. New York. Wiley.

GARVIN, PAUL L., and MADELEINE MATHIOT

1960. The Urbanization of the Guarani Language—A Problem in Language and Culture. In Anthony F. C. Wallace (Ed.), *Men and Cultures*. Philadelphia: University of Pennsylvania Press. Pp. 783-790.

HAVRÁNEK, B.

1932. Ukoly spisovneho jazyka a jeho kultura (The Purposes of a Standard Language and its Cultivation). In B. Havranek and Millos Weingart (Eds.), *Spisovna cestina a jazykova kultura*. Prague. Pp. 32-84.

JAKOBSON, ROMAN

1945. The Beginnings of National Self-Determination in Europe. *The Review of Politics, 7:* 29-42.

KOHN, HANS

1944. *The Idea of Nationalism: A Study in Its Origins and Background*. New York: Macmillan.

MATHESIUS, VILEM

1932. O pozadvky stability ve spisovnem jazyce (The Requirement of Stability for a Standard Language). In B. Havranek and Millos Weingart (Eds.), *Spisovna cestina a jazykova kultura*. Prague. Pp. 14-31.

RAY, PUNYA SLOKA

1962a. Language Standardization. In Frank A. Rice (Ed.), *Study of the Role of Second Languages in Asia, Africa, and Latin America*. Washington, D.C.: Center for Applied Linguistics of the Modern Language Association of America. Pp. 91-104.

1962b. Formal Procedures of standardization. *AL, 4* (3): 16-41.

SOMMERFELT, ALF

1938b. Conditions de la formation d'une langue commune. *Actes du Quatrième Congrès International de Linguistes (1936)*. Copenhagen: Munksgaard. Pp. 42-48.

B. CASE STUDIES

For individual case studies, see those listed below by language or country, and references in Deutsch (cited above) and Weinreich (1953). See also the symposium organized by Garvin (from which the present paper is taken), "Urbanization and Standard Language," *AL*, 1959, *1* (3), with papers on German (Twaddell), Norwegian (Haugen), Neo-Melanesian (Hall), and discussion by Margaret Mead, and *AL*, 1959, *1* (5): 19-26, with a paper on Macedonian (Lunt). See also the single language studies noted with Hoijer's article on pp. 455-466 and in the volume under discussion in Bull's review. On English, see also Grove (1950) and Williams (1961).

CHINESE

DE FRANCIS, JOHN

1950. *Nationalism and Language Reform in China*. Princeton: Princeton University Press. [Reviewed, F. K. Li, *IJAL*, 1951, *17:* 255-257; M. Swadesh, *Science and Society*, 1952, *16:* 273-280; C. F. Hockett, *Lg.*, 1951, *27:* 439-445.]

ENGLISH

WILLIAMS, RAYMOND

1961. *The Long Revolution*. London: Chatto and Windus. Part II, chap. 4.

EUROPE

DAUZAT, A.

1940. *L'Europe linguistique*. Paris: Payot.

DEUTSCH, KARL W.

1942. The Trend of European Nationalism—The Language Aspect. *American Political Science Review*, *36:* 533-541.

FINNISH

SETÄLÄ, E. N.

1920. *La Lutte des langues en Finlande*. Paris: Champion.

GERMAN

BLACKALL, E. A.

1959. *The Emergence of German as a Literary Language, 1700-1775*. Cambridge: Cambridge University Press.

KLOSS, H.

1952. *Die Entwicklung neuer germanischer Kultursprachen von 1800 bis 1950*. Munich: Pohl.

LEOPOLD, WERNER F.

1959. The Decline of German Dialects. *Word*, *15:* 130-153.

HEBREW

MORAG, S.

1959. Planned and Unplanned Development in Modern Hebrew. *Lingua*, *8:* 247-263.

INDIA

BROWN, W. NORMAN

1952. The Language Problem of India and Pakistan. In J. Decastiglione (Ed.), *Report on the Third Annual Round Table Meeting on Linguistics and Language Teaching*. (Monograph Series on Languages and Linguistics, No. 2.) Washington, D.C.: Georgetown University Press. Pp. 17-30.

FRIEDRICH, PAUL

1962. Language and Politics in India. *Daedalus* (Proceedings of the American Academy of Arts and Sciences), *91* (3): 543-559.

WINDMILLER, MARSHALL

1954. Linguistic Regionalism in India. *Pacific Affairs*, *27:* 291-318.

IRELAND

CUIV, BRIAN O.

1951. *Irish Dialects and Irish-speaking Districts: Three Lectures*. Dublin: Dublin Institute for Advanced Studies.

ITALY

HALL, ROBERT A., JR.

1942. *The Italian Questione della Lingua: An Interpretive Essay*. Chapel Hill: University of North Carolina Press.

KRISTELLER, PAUL OSKAR

1946. The Origin and Development of the Language of Italian Prose. *Word, 2:* 50-65.

NORWAY

HAUGEN, EINAR

1938. The Origin and Early History of the New Norse Movement in Norway. *Publications of the Modern Language Association, 48:* 558-597.

SOMMERFELT, ALF

1942. *The Written and Spoken Word in Norway*. Oxford: Oxford University Press.

SWITZERLAND

MAYER, K.

1951. Cultural Pluralism and Linguistic Equilibrium in Switzerland. *American Sociological Review, 16:* 157-163.

WARTBURG, W. VON

1956. Origines et raison d'etre de la Suisse, pays aux divers langages. *Von Sprache und Mensch: Gesammelte Aufsätse*. Bern: Francke. Pp. 11-22. [Reviewed, Robert A. Hall, Jr., *Lg.*, 1957, *33:* 76-79.]

TURKEY

HEYD, URIEL

1954. *Language Reform in Modern Turkey*. (Oriental Notes and Studies, No. 5.) Jerusalem: Israel Oriental Society.

USSR

KOHN, HANS

1933. *Nationalism in the Soviet Union,* London. Pp. 88-106.

KUCERA, JINDRICH

1954. Soviet Nationality Policy: The Linguistic Controversy. *Problems of Communism, 3* (2): 24-29.

WEINREICH, URIEL

1953. The Russification of Soviet Minority Languages. *Problems of Communism, 2* (6): 46-57.

The Use of Vernacular Languages in Education 56

WILLIAM E. BULL

[REVIEW OF: *The Use of Vernacular Languages in Education.* (Monographs on Fundamental Education, No. 8.) Paris: Unesco, 1953.]

The present monograph approaches the ponderous problems of providing the speakers of all the vernacular languages of the world with a modern education by establishing as axiomatic three operational assumptions: first, "that every child of school age should attend school," second, "that every illiterate should be made literate," and, third, "that the best medium for teaching is the mother tongue of the pupil." Between these propositions and their realization many complex and difficult problems are bound to arise and it is primarily, though not exclusively, with the linguistic and educational aspects of these problems that this volume is concerned.

The Committee defines its usage of several socio-linguistic terms (p. 46). The two of importance here are *vernacular*, defined as: "A language which is the mother tongue of a group which is socially or politically dominated by another group speaking a different language. We do not consider the language of a minority in one country as a vernacular if it is an official language in another country"; and *world language*, defined as: "A language used over wide areas of the world."

The monograph begins with a brief introduction (pp. 8-15, aimed at the layman) which defines the nature of language, describes the three systems of writing, discusses the study of language, and attempts to define, in terms of political, linguistic, socio-cultural, and economic factors, the role of language in general education. Chapter I (pp. 16-44) is a continental survey (Africa, the American continents, Asia and the Pacific, Europe—including the USSR) which enumerates or classifies the known languages of each region and reports in considerable detail on their use in both public and private schools. Chapter II (pp. 47-75), the core of the volume, contains the report of the Unesco meeting of specialists (1951), that is, a statement of policy, a definition of problems, and a number of recommendations aimed at improving education and suggesting further Unesco action (to be discussed below). Chapter III (pp. 76-138) provides an excellent and informative series of case histories which have been selected to illustrate both the problems of education in the vernacular and some of the major attempts at their resolution. The topics discussed are: The Tarascan project in Mexico; the renovation of Arabic; developing a national language in Indonesia; the problem of "pidgin" in the Trust Territory of New Guinea; the unification of the Akan dialects of the Gold Coast; the Iloilo experiment (Philippines) in education through the vernacular, and the Finno-Ugrian experiment (primarily vocabulary expansion). There follows a tentative classification of the languages spoken in the world today (Appendix I, pp. 139-143), the resolution and instructions for the Unesco meeting of specialists, with a list of the persons attending (Appendix II, pp. 144-145), and a short bibliography (pp. 146-149).

The survey of the world language situation, presented in Chapter I, indicates that no one knows, not even vaguely, how many languages and dialects there are in the world, that only a small proportion of the known languages are actually used in formal education, and, as a partial result, that over one-half of the world's population is illiterate and vast numbers of children are forced, by circumstance, to do all or most of their formal learning in a foreign language. To achieve, as a consequence, simply the elimination of illiteracy in the world involves problems of staggering proportions. The majority of the languages of the world have no written form, a great many more lack a literature of sufficient stature to justify learning to read, and only a minority have textbooks which are adequate either for elementary school classes or adult literacy courses. To provide further, under these conditions, even a grammar school education for all children is, in all probability, a practical impossibility within the present century.

The Unesco committee's major reaction to this formidable situation and the central thesis of the volume is the proposition that every pupil should begin his formal education in his mother tongue and should continue to be taught in that language as long as the language and the supply of books and materials permit. It is asserted, in support of this thesis, that there is nothing in the structure of any language which precludes it from becoming a vehicle of modern civilization, that no language is inadequate to meet the needs of the child's first months in school, and that full self-expression can best be attained in the mother tongue. It is recognized, however, that a great many languages, probably the majority in the world, do not have a vocabulary adequate to the needs of higher and, especially, technical education. Two solutions to this problem are suggested: first, the mother tongue may be used as a bridge to learning an adequate language and, thereafter, education may be carried on in this second vehicle; second, planned expansions of the vocabulary can be undertaken, as in Arabic (pp. 87-95), Hungarian, Finnish, and Estonian (pp. 132-138). It is maintained, nevertheless, that if a child's mother tongue is not the official language of his country, or is not a world language, he needs to learn a second language. In other words, within the framework of these recommendations, a child in the Cebu province of the Philippines would, theoretically, begin his education in Cebuano. This vernacular would, then, serve as a bridge to Tagalog (the official national language) and, ultimately, either of these languages, or both, might be used to teach him English or Spanish. The child, according to this plan, would, of course, first learn to read in Cebuano and would continue to get as much of his education as possible in this language. In short, he begins his education in Cebuano because he will have fewer adjustmental problems in starting school, because it is easier on him psychologically, and because he learns more rapidly and operates more efficiently in his mother tongue; he learns Tagalog simply because he needs it as a member of the state, and finally, he must learn a world language in order to have access to knowledge not available in either Cebuano or Tagalog.

It is inevitable that the product of such an educational sequence will exhibit a mild kind of linguistic schizophrenia. He may, for example, find it easier to make love in Cebuano, discuss politics in Tagalog, and do research on thermonuclear weapons in English. In order to reduce or eliminate this confusion the Committee recommends that the mother tongue be used as the medium of instruction as far up the education ladder as possible (through college if the language is adequate), that authorities should do everything in their power to create the conditions which will make for an ever-increasing extension of schooling in the mother tongue, and that efforts should be made to persuade an unwilling public to accept education through the mother tongue.

The Committee, rather obviously, strongly believes that what is best for the child psychologically and pedagogically should be the prime point of departure in planning for universal education. This proposition appears, however, to be somewhat unrealistic. What is best for the child psychologically and pedagogically may not be what is best for the adult socially, economically or politically and, what is even more significant, what is best for both the child and the adult may not be best or even possible for the society which, through its collective efforts, provides the individual with the advantages he cannot personally attain. It would seem appropriate, as a consequence, to contemplate the fact that while getting educated is a personal matter, in contrast, providing a modern education is a social enterprise. It might, likewise, be appropriate to face the somewhat disagreeable fact that most modern states have reached their present structure through conquest, that is, in terms of the immediate problem, through the forcible integration of heterogeneous linguistic communities into a single political and economic unit. There are, consequently, at least 369 languages in the British African Territories, about 200 different Bantu languages in the Belgian Congo, approximately 558 languages in South America, some 200 different languages in Indonesia, and about 100 main languages in in Russia. Finally, it might be wise to inquire whether or not the number of existing languages is compatible with the aims, desires, and ultimately, the exigencies of the modern world. It may be pleasant for both the linguist and the anthropologist to envisage a world which permits the preservation of museum cultures and a multitude of languages, it may be profoundly distasteful to abandon the principle of linguistic self-determination, but it is apparent that the vast enterprises required to provide a modern education and to sustain a modern state cannot be carried out in excessively polyglot societies. Mexico, for example, which does not have an adequate school system even for its Spanish-speaking inhabitants, can hardly afford to support 49 more projects patterned on the Tarascan experiment (pp. 77-86). Modern Indonesia can scarcely hope to survive as a politico-economic unit without a national language (pp. 95-103), a lingua franca which will bridge the chasm between some 200 languages and dialects and make universal education an economic feasibility. It may be possible to transform Malay, the lingua franca of Indonesia, into a world language and it may be theoretically possible to convert every Indonesian language into a medium of higher education but it is surely Utopianism to hope that Indonesia can endow every speech community with a complete vernacular school system and with vernacular libraries capable of competing educationally with the great installations of the primarily monolingual nations. As a consequence, it would seem that the speakers of many vernacular languages are doomed to a kind of intellectual colonialism which can be mitigated only by some type of linguistic integration with larger speech communities and ultimately with a community whose language and resources are adequate for education in every field of human endeavor.

It would seem, in view of the foregoing discussion, that some practical compromise must be made between what is immediately best for the individual and what, in the long perspective of history, is best for the individual, his children, and his community. It would seem, furthermore, that neither the world nor any country or many individuals will eventually profit by encouraging the perpetuation of hundreds of miniature vernaculars. In place of planned heterogeneity, it would seem wise to encourage planned homogeneity. In place of more education in more vernaculars, it would seem more practical to formulate a long-range educational program aimed at a gradual reduction in the number of languages and dialects in every area of the world. Such a program would, of course, kindle some patriotic and related emotional protests (see the case of Akan dialects of the Gold Coast, pp. 115-123), but it would not, in practice, be in violent conflict with the current evolutionary process, namely, a strong tendency for the mortality rate of languages and dialects to exceed their birth rate. The actual implementation of such a program would, nevertheless, for very practical and substantial economic, nationalistic, and linguistic reasons, lead directly to some increase in education in the vernacular. It may be assumed, in view of the existing number of languages, that linguistic homogeneity is attainable in any immediate future only on a regional or national basis. This presumes, in the case of many countries and areas of the world, that some local vernacular will become the dominant language and that it will need to be converted into an adequate vehicle for modern education at all levels of schooling. This duplicates, rather obviously, in the realm of conscious planning, the actual history of the rise of all the major European languages. The problem, then, is to accomplish by programming and in a few generations what happened in many countries during a millenium or more of natural evolution. This, as the case histories and the continental survey presented by the Committee demonstrate, is a tremendous task which, if phonetics and phonemics are left to evolve naturally, may be considered under three main headings: the writing system, vocabulary, and grammar.

It is apparent, as the Committee points out, that the writing system of a number of languages does not lend itself readily to the exigencies of the modern world and, especially, to the use of typewriters and typesetting machines which are essential to the rapid and economical reproduction of educational materials. The Committee, therefore, makes a number of firm and unanimous recommendations (pp. 60-62). To encourage literacy, polygot areas might adopt a uniform system of writing for all languages used. To make learning and reading simpler, spelling should be standardized in conformity with contemporary pronunciation and the phonemic system. To increase and simplify the reproduction of texts, the system should use a limited set of symbols written in a single line, and diacritics, if equally satisfactory, should be avoided. If a language lacks symbols, digraphs should, if possible, be used in preference to new characters and, if new characters are needed, they should be derived from prevailing scientific usage.

The major problem in most vernaculars is the lack of an adequate vocabulary and, as a direct consequence, the present impossibility of providing either an adequate library of texts or actual instruction in the language. In Egypt, for example, the creation by the Royal Academy of some 10,000 technical terms has not brought Arabic to the level necessary for adequate instruction in pure science and medicine. These subjects are taught, in the higher classes, in English (p. 92). The vocabulary problem in Malay is even more pressing. The Indonesian Language Commission has fixed some 14,000 technical terms but this has not been sufficient to eliminate errors and misunderstandings even in such fundamental matters as economics and law. In addition, because of the lack of a staff which can handle technical problems in Malay, many courses on the university level are still conducted in Dutch.

The vocabulary problem in the vernaculars is, in the opinion of the Committee, a matter of sufficient gravity to justify further Unesco action and it has been recommended that this body "investigate the possibility of co-ordinating scientific and technical terminology in world languages so as to help the developing languages to create their own terminology as far as possible in conformity with the terminology in world languages" (p. 70). The Committee is not unanimous concerning practical recommendations and it spends some time debating the irrelevant question of whether or not a language has a vocabulary adequate for the expression of objects and beliefs which are of importance to its speakers. The majority opinion holds that all languages have enough words for this purpose, but the question is surely academic since it can have meaning only in terms of a closed society which is neither evolving nor accepting influences from other cultures. Morevover, to establish importance to an entire society as the criterion for judging linguistic adequacy is to deny every exploring mind the opportunity to develop the social significance of the unknown. No language is adequate if one of its speakers finds the frontiers of knowledge blocked by linguistic barriers and this, as the monograph amply demonstrates, is the characteristic state of all vernaculars. The Committee, in a sense, rejects this fact with one hand and offers a remedy with the other. Its proposals, which are not unanimous, lose some of their directness through failure to stress the fact that a vocabulary can be expanded or extended in only five different fashions: by word borrowing, by coinage, by giving new meanings to existing words, by extending the meaning of existing words, or by compounding new words from existing material taken either from the language or from it and some other tongue. With these and no other alternatives available the problem (aside from questions of phonetics, phonemics, and morphemics) cannot be meaningfully discussed without specifying the subject of discourse—a matter not considered by the committee. The terminology, for example, of political science might, quite readily, be created from the existing fund of words, roots, etc. The vocabulary of a complete pharmacopoeia could hardly be duplicated except by coinage and borrowing, the actual process by which this vocabulary was created, for example, in English. The Committee's recommendations deal with the vocabulary problem in larger generalizations. It is suggested that the vernacular be adapted as much as possible, that coinage be avoided when other means are available, that new words not be added until they are needed, that consistency in the type of formation and language of origin be maintained in borrowing scientific terms, that borrowed words be adapted to the phonemic structure and grammar of the language, and, finally, that new words be tried out to test their acceptability before they are officially adopted.

The problems of grammatical structure and of syntax (rather strangely not discussed in the monograph) have only two alternative solutions. The language can be left alone or some attempt can be made to "improve" it. The basic question is, of course, improvement in terms of what criteria ? The Committee makes no serious study of this matter and limits itself, in the majority report, to the recommendation that the language of a homogeneous speech community be left alone and that, in the case of a multilingual society, it may be useful to attempt some reconstruction of the language selected for education. Only two changes are suggested: the abolishment of irregularities and the addition of "new useful categories in order to make it (the language) a better vehicle of modern thought," (p. 67). The Committee does not exemplify the last suggestion nor does it attempt to define "useful." The whole matter, quite obviously, needs further study.

The Committee also makes a number of sound recommendations concerning general educational matters. It suggests that actual instruction in multilingual classes be delayed until all the pupils have been taught the classroom language, that adult illiterates be taught to read first in their own tongue, that a supply of reading material adequate to forestall frustation be made available before teaching people how to read, that second languages be introduced orally on the elementary level, that the amount of a second language given be increased gradually, that efficient modern techniques (not described) should be used, that a uniform system of writing be adopted in multilingual countries, that the writing system be altered to meet the requirements of printing, and that in a polygot state, which is developing a national language, the materials for teaching the language should be simplified for instructional purposes so that pupils may progress toward full mastery without anything to unlearn. In addition, the Committee calls attention to a fact of which most American institutions of higher learning seem to be woefully ignorant, to wit, "a teacher is not adequately qualified to teach a language merely because it is his mother tongue," (p. 61).

The major and final recommendations of the Committee, that is, those which call for further Unesco action, do not seem to be the product of logical progression from the description of an a enormously complex problem to a potential solution. The Committee affirms, in its first recommendation, that "the main obstacle to the use of vernacular languages is shortage of educational materials" and not the apparent fact that there are literally hundreds of languages which cannot at present carry the burden of a modern education beyond the lower elementary grades. The teachers who are to be trained to teach in these languages will, rather certainly, have to be educated in some other language and they will either stand before their classes half tongue-tied by linguistic deficiencies or they will abandon their superior knowledge in the process of accommodating themselves to the limitions of the language of their students. More paper, type, presses, and, hence, books do not, as a consequence, seem to be the prime solution except, perhaps, in those vernaculars which are on the verge of becoming major or national languages. The recommendation that the scientific and technical terminology of the world languages be co-ordinated to facilitate borrowing stems directly from the known facts and may be considered excellent. The suggestion that Unesco investigate the possibility of promoting the exchange and extension of copyrights is important but meaningful only in terms of the countries whose vernacular is adequate for translation. The last two recommendations deal with student exchanges and are directed at developing an adequate staff in younger countries. It is suggested, first, that Unesco press "for having the certificates of educational achievement granted by these countries accepted in the countries to which students normally go," and second, that "within Unesco's Exchange of Persons Programme some priority should be given to training in linguistic and in second language teaching" (p. 70).

It is important to stress, in conclusion, that the strictures which this reviewer has placed upon the recommendations of the Unesco committee stem directly from an unwillingness to accept completely both the implicit and explicit operational assumptions of the Committee. The Committee is implicitly committed to a frame of reference which produces a formulation of most problems in terms of the individual. It supports, consequently, the Wilsonian principle of linguistic self-determination and maintains that what is immediately best for the individual should determine the major features of its program. It would seem, however, first, that linguistic self-determination conceived in the face of a potential of two or three thousand languages and dialects is hopelessly unattainable when expressed in terms of the economics of a modern education, and, second, that too much stress on the immediate benefits for the individual endangers the elaboration of a long-range program compatible with the needs and the potentials of modern society.

REFERENCE NOTE

On the problems of literacy and fundamental education in the world today see, of course the general discussion and case histories in the Unesco monograph reviewed by Bull as well as other Unesco publications in the series "Monographs on Fundamental Education." Monograph II, *World Illiteracy at Mid-Century* (Paris: 1957) is "The first systematic survey of illiteracy on a world-wide scale undertaken by an international organization." The survey estimates that there are about 700 million adult illiterates in the world today, more than two-fifths of the world's adult population. The relation between world and local languages is dealt with at some length also in *African Languages and English in Education* (Paris: Unesco Education Clearing House, 1953), Spencer (1963), and Hellinga (1955). (See also the notice of Hellinga's book by Uriel Weinreich, *Word*, 1956, *12:* 493-494.)

That literacy can be a problem of language and culture in European and American society, both as to fact and quality, is indicated in such books as Hoggart (1957), Lewis (1947, 1953), Lowenthal (1961), and references therein.

Literacy and vernacular education are, of course, much affected by attitudes and methods associated with their introduction, as Dozier's paper in this part shows. On the importance of using the native language from this point of view, see Nida (1949). On the necessity of analyzing the communication situation as well as the language for success in applied linguistics, such as literacy and translation programs, see Gumperz (1957), Edward T. Hall (1959), Hymes (1961c), Nida (1960), Pike (1956, 1957-1958), Reyburn (1958b).

The task of achieving literacy has been undertaken most often and most successfully by two worldwide movements, socialism and Christianity. Socialist literature in English on the subject is not known to me, but a number of excellent works from the missionary work are available. The anthropologist, whatever his view of the missionary movement, can find a wealth of experience digested and analyzed in regard to various aspects of the problem in such works as those of Gudschinsky (1957), Nida (1947c, 1950, 1952, 1960), and Reyburn (1956). Relevant topics are frequently discussed in *The Bible Translator* (The United Bible Societies, 146 Queen Victoria Street, London, EC4); *Practical Anthropology* (Box 307, Tarrytown, New York); and in two journals not connected with the missionary enterprise, *Language Learning* (University of Michigan, Ann Arbor), and *The Linguistic Reporter* (Center for Applied Linguistics, 1346 Connecticut Avenue, N. W., Washington 6, D.C.). The latter can be had free of charge, and keeps account of work relating to language policies and programs.

Practical work in literacy and vernacular education may point to questions of general or theoretical interest. See, for example, Berry (1958), Garvin (1954a), Gudschinsky (1959), Rice (1962), Wallis (1956), and Wolff's paper in Part VII. Berry (1958) is especially valuable for its analysis of the linguistic and social factors in providing a successful orthography, and for comments and references linking practical problems to the renewed interest in the nature and analysis of writing systems. Joos (1960) is a penetrating analysis of the problems of an orthography for a standard language such as English, where the problem is posed as one of reform rather than introduction.

References not in the general bibliography:

BERRY, J.

1958. The Making of Alphabets. In Eva Siversten (Ed.), *Proceedings of the Eighth International Congress of Linguists* (*Oslo, 1957*). Oslo: Oslo University Press.

GUDSCHINSKY, SARAH C.

1957. *Handbook of Literacy*. Glendale, Calif.: Summer Institute of Linguistics.

1959. Toneme Representation in Mazatec Orthography. *Word, 15:* 446-452.

GUMPERZ, JOHN J.

1957. Language Problems in the Rural Development of North India. *Journal of Asian Studies, 16:* 251-259.

HELLINGA, W. G.

1955. *Language Problems in Surinam: Dutch as the Language of the Schools.* Amsterdam: North-Holland.

JOOS, MARTIN

1960. Review of Axel Wijk, *Regularized English. Lg., 36:* 250-262.

LEWIS, M. M.

1953. *The Importance of Illiteracy*. London: Harrap.

LOWENTHAL, LEO

1961. *Literature, Popular Culture, and Society*. Englewood Cliffs, N.J.: Prentice-Hall (Spectrum Book, 18).

NIDA, EUGENE A.

1949. Approaching Reading Through the Native Language. *Language Learning, 2:* 16-20.

1950. *Learning a Foreign Language: A Handbook for Missionaries.* New York: Foreign Missions Conference of North America.

REYBURN, WILLIAM D.

1958b. Literacy in Primitive Society. *The Bible Translator, 9:* 76-81.

ROBERTS, JANET

1962. Sociocultural Change and Communication Problems. In Frank A. Rice (Ed.), *Study of the Role of Second Languages in Asia, Africa, and Latin America.* Washington, D.C.: Center for Applied Linguistics of the Modern Language Association of America. Pp. 105-123.

SMALLEY, WILLIAM A.

1958. Dialect and Orthography in Kipende. *The Bible Translator, 9:* 63-69.

SUTHERLIN, RUTH E.

1962. Language Situation in East Africa. In Frank A. Rice (Ed.), *Study of the Role of Second Languages in Asia, Africa, and Latin America.* Washington, D.C.: Center for Applied Linguistics of the Modern Language Association of America. Pp. 65-78.

WALLIS, ETHEL EMILY

1956. Sociolinguistics in Relation to Mezquital Otomi Transition Education. *Estudios Antropológicos Publicados en Homenaje al Doctor Manuel Gamio.* Mexico, D.F.: Sociedad Mexicana de Antrópologia. Pp. 523-535.

57 Trade Jargons and Creole Dialects as Marginal Languages

JOHN E. REINECKE

I

WHEN MEN of different speech are thrown into contact and must reach an understanding, four courses are open to them. If their contact is brief and discontinuous and limited to very simple transactions, speech may be dispensed with. Dumb barter is a form of accommodation reported from many parts of the world. Nevertheless one may suspect that it does not always preclude bilingualism; it is probably more a mechanism of defence than an expedient of ignorance. In any case, it is of limited usefulness and little used. Members of two linguistic groups may speak a third language which they have already learned in other contacts, i.e., a lingua franca (Grierson, 1903). (The widespread gesture codes, such as the Sign Language of the Plains Indians, are a special form of lingua franca which may have had their origin within a single language group, and which in any case depend upon bilingualism for their spread. Drum language and similar codes have in general nothing to do with inter-group communication in this situation.) Members of one group may learn efficiently the language of a second group. In the long run one of these two accommodations usually prevails; and the social importance of effective bilingualism is hard to overestimate. But there is a fourth possible course, which in the initial stages of inter-group contact is of great importance, and which may leave a permanent mark upon linguistic and social history. Neither group may be in a position to learn the other's language or a common third tongue at all correctly, so that both will be content with an imperfect approximation to one of the languages: a debased or pidginized or jargonized form (as Jespersen terms it), a minimum or makeshift language. It is with this form of linguistic accommodation that we are concerned here.

On a small and temporary scale the use of makeshift language is a universal phenomenon, to be witnessed wherever immigrants, invaders, tourists, or sailors go. Countless little mangled dialects are spoken for a while by chance-assembled groups, only to go out of existence when the individuals who compose them are scattered. One of the most favorable situations for the formation of such dialects is found aboard merchant vessels which ply the seven seas and ship large numbers of foreign sailors—and indeed the seaman is a figure of the greatest importance in the creation of the more permanent makeshift tongues. "A sailor," says the author of that mordant sea story, *The Death Ship*, "is never lost where language is concerned. He always can make himself fairly well understood, no matter which coast he is thrown upon. He surely will find his way to an answer to the old question: when do we eat?" How sailors meet the need of communication is described by Traven in a passage which, mutatis mutandis, is applicable to many like situations.

With so many different nationalities aboard, it would have been impossible to sail the *Yorikke* unless a language had been found that was understood by the whole crew. The lingo of the *Yorikke* was English. At least that was the name the language was given, to distinguish it from any other language known under the moon. Chinese pidgin English would be considered elegant compared with the Yorikkian English. A newcomer, even a limey, a cockney, or a Pat, would have quite a lot of trouble during the first two weeks before he could pick up sufficient Yorikkian to make himself understood and to understand what was told him.

Every sailor of any nationality knows some thirty English words, which he pronounces in such a way that after half an hour you may get a rough idea of what he wishes to say. Each sailor, though, does not have the same vocabulary as the others, and hardly two have the same pronunciation of the same word. Living together and working together, each sailor picks up the words of his companions, until, after two months or so, all men aboard have acquired a working knowledge of about three hundred words common to all the crew and understood by all. This lingo, of course, is enlarged by words which are brought in by sailors who, owing to their lack of the right words, have to use occasionally words of their own home-made language. These words, used over and over again, are, after a while, picked up by others and used at the proper place. Since usually one fireman at least was a Spaniard, it had become proper to use for water and for fuel never any other words but *agua* and *carbón*. Even the engineers used these words.

Regardless of how far from the academic the Yorikkian English strayed, the fundamentals remained English; and whenever a newcomer hopped on who spoke English as his mother tongue, the Yorikkian lingo once more was purified and enriched with new words or with a better pronunciation of words which by long misuse had lost their adherence to their family. (Condensed from Traven, 1934.)

II

Out of adjustments like those which took place aboard the *Yorikke* arise the relatively widespread and permanent jargons which have long attracted popular attention and have of recent decades been the subject of several scientific studies: the forms of language known, with various degrees of accuracy, as trade languages or jargons, creole languages, mixed languages, lingua francas, minimum or makeshift languages, substitute languages, pidgins. (These expressions are popular, except for minimum and makeshift languages, terms coined by Otto Jespersen [1922, p. 232], and substitute languages a term coined by Ernst Schultze [1933].) None of these terms appears to be sufficiently exact and at the same time broad enough to be applied to all the languages under consideration. As a general appellation the present writer therefore proposes the term *marginal languages*, with the following definition: The marginal languages arise in areas of pronounced culture contacts, in situations where, broadly speaking, it is impossible or impracticable for the peoples concerned to learn each other's language well. Their structure, relative to that of the languages from which they have been derived rather recently, is greatly broken down and simplified. Largely because of this broken-down structure, but also because of the circumstances under which they are spoken, they are often held in contempt by a large section of their speakers, by speakers of the parent languages, or by both.

These jargonized languages are marginal in reference both to their parent languages and to the cultural environment in which their parent languages are spoken. By those who know the languages from which they are derived, they are usually despised as being beneath the level, not only of standard or common languages, but also of the various patois and class dialects—themselves often despised—which do at least share in the linguistic structure of the accepted standard dialects. The marginal languages are dismissed, not merely as "bad grammar" or "dialect," but as "lingoes," "hodgepodge," "*Kauderwelsch*," "no language." Often they are in fact so broken down and deviant from the parent dialects as to become new, unintelligible languages. Merely as aggregates of linguistic tools they are therefore regarded as marginal. Their speakers, too, being restricted by such divergent, and presumably imperfect, forms of language, are regarded as marginal to the main body of speakers of English, French, or whatever the parent language may be. Furthermore, the term "marginal" as developed by the Chicago school of sociologists bears the connotations of lack of full participation in a society—of standing on the border between two societies or two cultures. The languages to which the word marginal is here applied usually arise on very pronounced frontiers of culture; they are in fact a rather characteristic phenomenon of certain types of the frontier. As Schultze has pointed out (1933, pp. 391-392), those now extant are almost all closely connected with the great migrations of European peoples during the past four hundred years. They are the product of marginal conditions: generally of a primary stage in the contact of cultures, or of the violent uprooting of a great many persons from their native culture.

These marginal tongues have many points of

resemblance to regional patois, to the class dialects of the uncultivated, to many special vocabularies such as the argots, even to the languages of small, subordinate, uncultivated nationalities, especially when these are in decline. Yet to the general observer, the marginal languages have enough of a distinct character (chiefly because of their simplified, minimum-approaching rather than minimum, structure) to be treated together and for peculiar attitudes to develop regarding them. They constitute a distinct field for the study of what has been called, perhaps prematurely, *Sprachsoziologie*.

A number of tolerably good studies have been made of particular marginal dialects, but almost invariably from a strictly linguistic point of view. Historical data have been introduced usually only in order to illustrate points in the structure of the languages, and data of sociological significance is scattered and incidental at the best. Nevertheless from these studies a reasonably accurate idea may be reached of the nature of the marginal languages, of the circumstances of their formation, and thus of the divisions into which they fall.

An inductive examination of the literature on more than forty of the languages defined as marginal shows that they are divisible into several classes on the double basis of the milieu in which they took shape and of their functions. While these classes are not sharply distinguished one from another, yet it is economical to discuss the marginal languages by categories. The present writer distinguishes three important general classes, which constitute probably the only groups of relatively permanent jargons: the trade jargons, the plantation creole dialects, and the settlers' creole dialects.

Previous discussions of the so-called creole *or* trade languages have mostly suffered in clarity because they have all been lumped together—a practice perfectly justified on linguistic grounds. A common-sense dichotomy into trade jargons *and* creole dialects was adumbrated by several writers and stated in passing by the great creolist Hugo Schuchardt (Schuchardt [1842-1927] was in his time the foremost authority on the so-called creole languages. The reference is in *Zeitschrift f. romanische Philologie*, 1909, *33:* 441); but the first attempt at a formal classification of the marginal languages did not appear until 1933, in an article by Professor Ernst Schultze of Leipzig, the title of which may be translated as "Slaves' and Servants' Languages (So-called Trade Languages), an Essay in the Sociology of Language and Migration," (1933). This, as the pioneer sociological essay in its field, deserves special attention, and is a provocative piece of work, though marred by confused reasoning and an insufficient acquaintance with the source materials.

Schultze's definition of the substitute languages (*Ersatzsprachen*) as "idioms which serve to bring about an incomplete understanding between men of different tongues" (1933, p. 378; also pp. 380-381) virtually equates them with the present writer's marginal languages. He divides them into four classes: the colonial jargons, the trade jargons, the artificial international auxiliary languages of the Esperanto type, and lastly the slaves' and servants' languages. However, the artificial auxiliary languages, being quite adequate, obviously should not be included among the substitute languages. As a type of the colonial jargons, Schultze describes the Pennsylvania German, and this again, having from the beginning been used only within the immigrant group, and not as a means of inter-group communication, does not fit into his own definition of the substitute tongues. There remain the traditional categories of the trade jargons and (under a descriptive name) the creole dialects. But these Schultze attempts virtually to reduce to one category by claiming that they both arise in situations wherein one group enjoys a marked superiority over another—that is, in master-and-servant situations. "Perhaps there is no trade language in the true sense of the word," he writes in one place (1933, p. 416), though elsewhere he confines himself to the more cautious statement that the trade jargons "are a good deal more important for communication between white masters and colored servants than between white merchants and colored traders or producers" (1933, p. 393). However, as will appear in the discussion below, Schultze is correct in his original distinction between the trade jargons and the slaves' and servants' languages, and at error in his over-emphasis upon the importance of domination in all situations where jargons are spoken. Schultze also overlooks what the present writer considers the main point of difference between the trade jargons and the creole dialects (of both classes), namely that the former remain supplementary languages whilst the latter become primary languages.

III

The trade jargons may be regarded as the least developed forms of marginal language that have attained considerable fixity. Originally they arise out of the casual intercourse of traders (generally seamen) with a fixed population, although later they may be extended to serve the intercourse between the native population and resident foreigners who for some reason do not learn the native language. In the beginning they are truly makeshift, and since they tend to be short-lived, disappearing as soon as one or the other party finds it expedient to learn a standard tongue to serve as a common medium, some of them retain much of their makeshift character till their end. They remain very fluid, full of circumlocutions owing to their small vocabulary, inadequate for any but the simpler transactions. An example is the "Yokohamese" jargon of Japanese, which cannot have lasted more than four or five decades, going out of use as Yokohamans learnt a more or less adequate English. "Yokohamese" was an amorphous tongue with an inadequate word-stock. The same is true of the pidgin Eskimo spoken between whalers and natives in northern Alaska from about 1852 to early in the present century. Too much emphasis, however, must not be laid on the makeshift character and lack of development of the trade jargons as compared with the creole languages. With every year of use a trade pidgin gains in fixity of structure and in vocabulary. Some creole dialects are every whit as hyperanalytic in structure as the average trade jargon. Nevertheless, a difference probably always exists in adequacy of vocabulary. The speakers of a trade jargon use it only as a supplementary tongue for special forms of intercourse, and have their mother tongues for the more intimate and cultivated sides of their life, whereas a creole jargon must bear the whole weight of a people's culture. Thus the widely spoken Chinook Jargon of the American Northwest never employed more than 1100 root words, whilst a typical creole dialect, that of Portuguese Guinea, boasts a lexicon of 5240 words. The vocabularies of the trade jargons may be rather mixed, so that either group imagines it is speaking the true language of the other; however, contrary to early belief, the marginal languages are not for the most part any more mixed than the standard languages.

Any sudden advance of trade relations of course extends the use of some trade language, and this frequently by reason of the very abruptness of the advance is used in a jargonized form. The advance of trade may to a considerable extent be traced by mapping the jargons that arise in its path. During the twentieth century, for example, the polyglot Belgian Congo is being partitioned linguistically among somewhat jargonized forms of Swahili, Kongo, Lingala, and Kiluba. While any language on the frontiers of trade is liable to be jargonized, this happens most often to the great trade languages: Portuguese, English, French, Swahili.

At this point it is worth pointing out that the master-and-dependent relationship emphasized by Schultze does not obtain very strongly in trade situations. Between trading peoples there must be a modicum of mutual respect and freedom of action. Consequently the foreign trader may sometimes adopt the indigenous language as the basis of a jargon. Nootka and Chinook are the foundation of the Chinook Jargon, though today its vocabulary is mostly English. The Eskimo trade jargon of Alaska, the pidgin Motu of Papua, and the "Kitchen Kafir" of Natal are other examples of the adoption of a native base; so is the Tupi Lingua Geral of parts of Brazil, though this is not strictly speaking a jargon. The Pidgin English of Canton, however, to some extent illustrates Schultze's thesis, though in a different sense than he believed; for the English were originally in a position of dependence and their jargon was deliberately fostered by the Chinese in order to hold them at arm's length.

If the advance of trade is marked by the creation of jargons, the consolidation of trade relations and the foreign conquest which so often follows trade are marked by the disappearance of jargons. Those current within the past century must be but a small proportion of the total spoken within historic times, or even since the beginning of Western expansion about 1500. Alongside the speakers of any jargon are usually some persons who, enjoying special advantages, have learned the language more adequately. In case the language is akin to the native tongues or is easy to acquire, the jargonized varieties may be of limited extent and quickly yield place to the standard speech. This appears, on the strength of the scanty evidence, to be the case with Hausa and Swahili among the African tribes. On the other hand, English, so foreign in sound and structure to the Sudanese-speaking peoples, remains predominantly a pidgin in West Africa. Among literate peoples, too, the advantages of a correct writing and speaking knowledge of a trade language are obvious. While the "Russenorsk" jargon that had been current in northern Norway for four or five generations was abruptly killed by the World War, it would soon have been extinguished in any case, because young Russians connected with commercial firms saw the need of learning good Norwegian. The Lingua Franca of the Mediterranean was quickly ended by steam navigation and the French conquest of North Africa.

Only in exceptional circumstances do trade jargons gain a long lease of life, and still more exceptionally do they become established as permanent lingua francas of a region. Cantonese-English owes its tenacity (*c.* 1715 to the present) to the peculiar restrictions placed upon foreign trade before 1842, which allowed the jargon of a small community to become standardized to the point where it was even studied from textbooks by Chinese tradesmen. But since the diffusion of true English among all classes of the Chinese ports, the Pidgin is clung to only by some die-hard foreigners accustomed to use it in talking down to their servants, and its use is resented even by houseboys. The Lingua Franca, the archetype of trade jargons, had an existence of perhaps eight centuries, but this was only because the name Lingua Franca was applied to several Romance jargons differing from time to time and from place to place. Naturally, the more polygot an area, the better chance has a pidgin to spread and to remain in use for a long time. No jargon was able to gain more than a temporary footing in Polynesia, the dialects of which are mutually intelligible or nearly so. But in Melanesia and the Papuan-speaking regions, where every village may speak a distinct language, Beach-la-mar English ran like wildfire; and at present, so well has the jargon been adapted to the genius of native thought and so pressing is the need for a simple lingua franca, that administrators and missionary educators are taking hesitant steps toward adopting it as the official medium of education and rule. Similarly, in the Uele River region of the Belgian Congo, where a Bantu-based jargon, Bangala, has been carried among a polyglot Sudanese population, missionaries with the backing of the government are making it the cultural language of the country, and conceivably it may become the primary language. In nearly every case, however, the European governments encourage the use of a recognized vernacular or of their own languages in uncorrupted form, thus displacing the despised pidgins which are considered to be inadequate as well as to have no true roots among any people. In the Upper Sudan, for instance, it was decided in 1928 to use English and several important native tongues in preference to the popular lingua franca, the Sudan-Arabic jargon.

Very seldom does a trade language spontaneously become the mother tongue of a group. Perhaps the only example in the literature is that of the Chinook Jargon, which is said to have been for a time the sole language of a few children of French Canadian *voyageurs* and squaws in Oregon Territory.

Certain dialects which may be classed with the trade jargons arise, it must be admitted, from master-and-servant relationships; but, since the servant is to a large extent a free agent and is in communication with his own society while the master remains an alien in the land he rules, these dialects remain supplementary and tend to disappear without attaining a stable structure: such are the Tagalog-Spanish of Manila, the Annamese-French of Saigon, and the Tamil-English of Madras ("Butler-English") described by Schuchardt. In addition the same jargon may be used in one place for trade, in another as a language of command for planters or administrators. Thus the slaves' English of Jamaica became on the Mosquito Coast the trade jargon between Indians and Europeans.

IV

As opposed to the trade jargons, the creole languages or jargons are now primary languages, and the result of very definite domination of one people by another. Since the term "creole languages" is popularly applied to any European (especially a Romance) tongue spoken overseas in a debased form, it is, therefore, used of two distinct classes of language, sociologically considered.

One of these, the one more akin to the trade jargons in its origin, the present writer has called "settlers' creole dialects." These languages arise in situations where a small group of foreigners settle as colonists or traders in the midst of a very much larger native population. Instead of becoming assimilated linguistically, they are able because of commercial, cultural, or military-political advantages to impose their language as a lingua franca of trade—usually in a simplified and corrupted form. At the same time they assimilate a part of the native population through intermarriage, domestic slavery, and conversion to their religion and customs. (These are the only marginal languages in the formation of which intermarriage plays a direct and important rôle.) This mixed population, having apprehended the colonists' language imperfectly, reduces its flexion and introduces idioms and words from its own languages. Clearly defined local dialects take shape. With the decline of the parent language as a medium of trade and administration, the creole dialects remain in use as the domestic language of the mixed-blood groups, who now adopt some other tongue as their lingua franca with the surrounding population. The chief present examples of this type of language are the Portuguese-speaking communities of southern Asia and formerly of West Africa, débris of the Portuguese trade empire of the sixteenth and seventeenth centuries. The descendants of the *Bounty* mutineers on Pitcairn Island however, probably illustrate in miniature the same phenomenon.

That creole languages of this type are not limited to European origins is illustrated by the Sudan-Arabic. When the Egytians conquered the Upper Sudan about 1870 they built up a mercenary corps from the surrounding Nilotic tribesmen. The language of command and the camp in this mixed Islamized community was broken-down Arabic. This jargon, while remaining the military tongue of the region, also became an administrative and trade jargon. But in 1891-1894 part of these "Nubi" mercenaries were brought south to subdue Uganda, where their descendants remain, speaking Sudan-Arabic as their primary tribal language.

In those communities which remain in some touch with the parent culture and tongue, several degrees of creole are spoken. Such a community as the mixed blood Portuguese of Macao contains some persons who speak standard Portuguese on occasion, and many more who are aware of standard Portuguese and who in writing and formal speech attain a "semi-creole." Others, again—and this is the rule in isolated communities like the "Portuguese" of Malacca—know only their completely jargonized creole dialect. Finally, an even more broken Portuguese is spoken for trade purposes by the Chinese of Macao. The semi-creole in some instances is adopted, half in pride and half in sport, as a literary medium by persons conversant with the standard tongue. Less sophisticated compositions are sometimes in semi-creole, sometimes in the pure folk language. In general, however, the creole dialect is despised by Europeans and sophisticated creoles. Their attitude probably has its origin in the contempt of the European standard-speaker for the uncultivated patois of his homeland, but the elements of foreign contamination and morphological breakdown in the creole dialects put these in an even lower class than the patois. On the other hand, the necessity of imparting effective religious instruction in the folk tongue may give it a certain literary dignity. This happened during the nineteenth century to the Creole Portuguese of Ceylon; though now in decline, it boasts a considerable literature, chiefly religious.

This type of creole tongue shades into the border cases of the trade jargons, so that it is difficult to say to which class such a dialect as the Tagalog-Spanish of Manila belongs.

V

Quite distinct in their nature are the plantation creole dialects. These languages are the result of a set of circumstances which, so far as the literature indicates, are peculiar to a particular stage in the colonial exploitation of the tropics by Europeans, involving the introduction of African slave labor (*c.* 1500-1875). The West Indies, Guiana, French Louisiana, the Portuguese islands off West Africa, and the Mascarenes are the chief seats of these dialects, though the Gullah-speaking Sea Islands of

South Carolina are also included, and also perhaps at one time Bahia in Brazil. Sierra Leone and Fernando Po in West Africa, settled by liberated West Indian slaves, speak dialects derived partly from America, partly from the mistakes of assimilated African natives, which therefore are on the borderline between the two types of creole language.

The plantation creole tongues are true *Sklavensprachen*. Although they owe something to the sailors' trade jargons, they began essentially as makeshift means of communication between masters and field hands. The slaves, of very diverse origin, either quickly forgot their native languages or found them of very limited usefulness. The first creole generation was usually monolingual in an imperfectly apprehended, flexionless or at least greatly simplified dialect of their masters' language. (There were exceptions. In some colonies the major nationalities among the slaves were recruited for generations and had their slave "kings." In Brazil, for reasons not wholly clear, but which are probably connected with the early use of the Tupi Lingua Geral on the coast and the close trade connection with Guinea and Angola, no impressive Creole Portuguese dialect ever arose; but several African languages, notably Yoruba, have been maintained down to the present date. Both fetishistic and Muhammedan cults have used African tongues in their services. Some groups of independent runaway Africans, notably the Saramacca tribe in Suriname, have also retained many African expressions, particularly in their semi-esoteric religious songs.) As spoken by the raw slaves the dialect was a crude makeshift, by no means improved by the masters' efforts to talk down to their chattels. Newcomers, turned over to old hands for seasoning, learnt the jargon from them: "matty a larn matty," as an old African of Guiana phrased it. The creole Negroes, in somewhat closer touch with the whites, improved their speech, enriching their vocabulary until it was adequate for their rather simple culture, and in some cases building up a new conjugation by means of auxiliaries. A new dialect—in extreme cases, such as the Negro-"English" of Suriname, a new language—has emerged; this, if through some historic accident it can be removed from the influence of the parent language, follows the usual laws of linguistic development. But since the creole dialects are usually subject more or less to such influence, they tend even under conditions of slavery "to constant leveling-out and improvement in the direction" of the masters' tongue (Bloomfield, 1933, p. 474). Indeed, unless the slave population was overwhelmingly in the majority and fairly stable of residence (conditions obtaining especially on the sugar cane-growing islands), only the initial makeshift jargon was spoken; or, if a creole dialect did form, it was soon ironed out and the Negroes came to speak practically the same dialect as the neighboring whites. This leveling-out occured in most parts of the Southern States and Brazil, as well as in Cuba, Santo Domingo, and Puerto Rico. Especially in the Hispanic colonies, where manumission was common and the freedmen often were merged socially and racially with the whites, conditions were unfavorable to the consolidation of a creole dialect.

The whites, having to speak creole constantly in directing their establishments, and surrounded by creole-speaking nurses and playmates during early childhood, appear usually to have spoken creole more than their standard dialect, though in a somewhat refined form. Their attitudes toward the creole were ambivalent. On the one hand a greater social distance existed between master and black than between an educated person and a peasant in, say, a German patois-speaking district. So the whites, at least in some colonies—for there were differences from place to place and from time to time—despised creole as a low-caste dialect, the imperfect jargon of an inferior race. It was something that one spoke to slaves, horses, and dogs, but not to one's equals unless *en famille*. On the other hand they came to have a sentimental attachment to it as a softer, more expressive medium—at least for everyday and intimate affairs—than the European tongue. A century and a half ago a Swiss traveler in Haiti expressed his annoyance at the fond complacency with which the white creoles regarded their patois. He was sharply answered by a creole, who declared: "There are a thousand things one dares not say in French, a thousand voluptuous images which one can hardly render successfully, which the Créole expresses or renders with infinite grace (Moreau de Saint-Méry, 1797, p. 65; see Girod-Chantrans, 1785, pp. 189-191).

As long as class and caste lines nearly coincided, and all of African descent except a few mulattoes were debarred from participation in the European community, the creole language was accepted by the masses as their proper tongue. Indeed, many of the field hands must have been scarcely aware of the standard language. Then too, even after emancipation, the whites in many colonies resented as presumptuous the use of the standard dialect by a colored person. At the same time, the Negroes developed a feeling for their patois as deep if not as sophisticated as that of the whites. The creole had its own rules and nuances, of which they were aware; they ridiculed the raw Africans who spoke it brokenly, and they enjoyed manipulating it in song and proverb. (Vendryes wrote of the creole: "[The natives'] apprenticeship to this language was never completed. It was limited to its superficial characteristics, to expressions representing the ordinary objects and essential acts of life; the inner essence of the language, with its fine complexities, was never assimilated by the native" [Vendryes, 1925, p. 295]. This is much exaggerated. A new set of complexities was evolved; the creole came to have its own "inner essence" and to be applicable to social and religious concepts of considerable subtlety.)

With emancipation and the consequent increased participation of the Negroes in the whites' culture—incomplete though this still is—the attitudes of both races toward the use of creole changed. In some colonies, the liberated slaves at once saw in the acquisition of their masters' tongue a considerable step toward bridging the gap between themselves and the whites. Two years after emancipation in British Guiana a planter observed: "It is wonderful how fond they have become already of speaking like the buckras [whites], and how sharp they are in picking up phrases, although they do mispronounce the words very 'ingeniously' " ("Barton Premium," *Eight Years in British Guiana* [1850], p. 66). In general, the attitude of the colored population has come to be much like that of European patois-speakers: the patois is sentimentally dear, it is one's true mother tongue; for an ordinary person to speak any other among his own group is snobbish; but to speak crude patois before or to an educated person is impolite and displays one's ignorance. Lafcadio Hearn used to hear the colored mothers of New Orleans admonish their children: "*Allons, Marie! Eugène! faut pas parler créole devant monsieur*; *parlez Français, donc!*" (Hearn, 1885, p. 146). When an educated foreigner enters a Haitian shop, the gossip in creole ceases and everybody assumes his French, such as it may be. Conversely, an educated creole Negro is insulted if addressed in patois. (Such attitudes are, of course, possible only where interracial contact and education have been widespread. Among the tribal Bush Negroes and the isolated Haitian peasantry creole is accepted in a matter of fact way as the national tongue.)

The whites (and the educated mulattoes who pattern after them) have been slower to give up the traditional linguistic distinction between the classes. In some places they still insist that their inferiors speak creole to them. But the Colonial governments, under pressure of European democratic and nationalistic ideology, have insisted that the masses be instructed in the standard tongue. Having accepted this policy, the educated classes in still other places express their superiority by disparaging the creole and regretting its persistency.

Under the double pressure of emulation of the whites and government educational policy, the speakers of the creole dialects tend to modify their speech slowly but steadily in the direction of the standard languages—or, in case the patois is not derived from the official tongue, to drop the former completely. Thus far, however, none of the plantation creole dialects has been assimilated in structure to a standard language, and only one—the Creole Dutch of the Virgin Islands—has gone out of use. This slowness of change is attributable in the first place to the inertia of the hopelessly poor, geographically and culturally isolated colored masses, whose assimilation of European culture is still in large part superfical. Next in importance is the maintenance or development of an attitude of pride in the creole as a regional idiom. This attitude is shared by both races, though among the whites it appears to take a rather condescending aspect. Writers both white and colored have produced literature in a refined creole, and a mulatto of Cayennes even achieved the *tour de force* of a sizable novel written entirely in Guyanais French (Parépou, 1885). Only in a few areas, however, is the creole dialect generally regarded as better than a mere patois; and here the reason for its superior status must be sought in a complex of local conditions. Wide difference between the official tongue and the folk language accounts in part for the strength of Taki-taki "English" and Papiamento Spanish in the Dutch colonies of Suriname and Curaçao respectively. Missionaries, beginning their work in these colonies under slavery, before the authorities would allow the blacks to be taught Dutch, reduced the patois to writing and created a considerable religious literature, thus giving the creole a dignity which it still enjoys. In Curaçao a widely read press under ecclesiastical direction but increasingly secular in content, has kept the Papiamento vigorous in spite of its discontinuance as a medium of instruction; and the 80,000 inhabitants of all social classes, loyal Dutch subjects but conscious of at least a semi-national tradition, regard Papiamento as in a fashion a national tongue. Papiamento has for the time attained a prestige unequalled by any other creole tongue, but, spoken by so small a group and crowded by Dutch, English, and Spanish, its position is more precarious than that of the creole French of Haiti. All the two and a half million Haitians speak Créole, and most of them, being illiterate peasants, speak nothing else. Toward this dialect the handful of cultivated people display an equivocal attitude. On the one hand they pride themselves on their mastery of Parisian French, their link with the culture of France and a protection against the assimilative power of the United States. On the other hand they are attached to their patois and realize that it is the true national tongue of a considerable nation. Some believe that only in the Créole will the Haitians attain literary autonomy. The problem of lifting the masses to a knowledge of literary French is almost insoluble; and a compromise has been attempted (at least to a slight extent) through the use of school texts written in parallel Créole and French. Thus under favorable circumstances the creole dialects may attain the respectability of the minor European languages formerly spoken only by peasants, such as Estonian or Lettish. (Afrikaans, now a full-fledged language almost fanatically cultivated by a nationality fewer than the Haitians, but imperialists, was originally at least a semi-creole patois. With the Portuguese Dutch-English of the Bush Negroes there is no question of prestige or linguistic competition; it is simply their tribal language. A correspondent in Sierra Leone, where a "Sierra Leonese" English strongly colored by the Sudanese tongues is spoken by the masses, indicates that in spite of the official attitude of contempt toward it among the educated Negroes, they cherish it as a mark of their Sierra Leonese seminationality, just as they cherish English *per se* as distinguishing them from the tribal Africans.)

VI

The three major classes discussed above are the only forms of marginal language relatively stable enough to allow them to be described grammatically. Another form, the broken speech of free immigrants, is of great social significance and considerable literary importance (*cf.* the comic stage in particular, and such writings as *Hans Breitmann's Ballads*). But Italian-Spanish or Yiddish-English, for example, is not an entity with its own norms. It is an amorphous mass of what Schuchardt called "individual corruptions," attempts, varying widely in degree of success, to reach the norm of the native language. These attempts show a resemblance but have no common denominator. Under modern condition of free immigration they cannot endure, for the second or third generation of immigrant stock is exposed to so many contacts with the native stock that it becomes completely assimilated linguistically.

A partial exception may be observed only in a few places where there is already a plantation creole or a trade jargon tradition to build upon. Thus in Hawaii, where a broken English containing many Hawaiian words had long been spoken between natives and foreign seamen, Asiatic and Portuguese coolies imported to work under partially servile conditions on the sugar cane plantations gave rise to a Pidgin English of a certain stability and consistency. This has been perpetuated for sixty years from one group of immigrants to another; but the immigrants' own children, educated in in American schools, speak a dialectal but increasingly standardized English. The Hawaiian linguistic situation, therefore, falls part way between that of free immigration and that of the servile plantation colonies (see Smith, 1933, and Reinecke and Tokimasa, 1934.) (For further references to marginal languages, see Tagliavini; Göbb-Gáldi, 1934; Spitzer, 1928.)

REFERENCE NOTE

For general treatment of the nature, origin, and classification of pidgins and creolized languages, see especially Bloomfield (1933, chap. 26, section 5), Cohen (1956a, p. 290), Diebold's article in this section, Robert A. Hall, Jr. (1955, 1962), Jespersen (1922, chap. XII), Reinecke (1937), from which his article is drawn, Stewart (1962), Weinreich (1953, pp. 69-70, 104-105). See also Hall (1951, 1952, 1959a, 1959b), and the exchange among Taylor (1956), Hall (1958), and Weinreich (1958), which raises basic issues of theory and practice in historical linguistics. For earlier posing of the issue in French linguistics, see Vendryes (1925, pp. 280-311).

For descriptive information on the character of various pidgins and creolized languages, see, besides Reinecke's references and Cole's article following, Boas (1933), Robert A. Hall, Jr. (1943a,b, 1944, 1948, 1953), Jacobs (1932, 1936), Leachman and Hall (1955), Milhalic (1957), Prince (1912), Samarin (1955, 1958, 1961, 1962), Taylor (1951, 1959, 1961), Voorhoeve (1953, 1959, 1961). For a rare study of the social context of a particular case, see Rens (1953). Kleinecke (1959) and Taylor (1957, 1963) raise questions of importance for the origin of modern pidgins, as does Thompson (1961). Le Page (1961) contains valuable articles and discussions and points to the increasing richness in our knowledge of such codes which may result from modern linguistic and anthropological studies in such areas as the Caribbean, Africa, and the Pacific.

On the Haitian situation discussed by Reinecke, see Unesco (1951), partly summarized in Carroll (1956), pp. 123-124, as an example of language engineering. Hall (1955) is in origin a tract on language policy regarding pidgins and creoles. Grant (1945) presents one view on the vexed question of the aboriginal origin of the celebrated Chinook Jargon. Hockett (1958, p. 424) contributes a formula for designating pidgins and creoles, one which should help clarify discussion: "*X-Pidgin-Y* or *X-Creole-Y*, means a pidgin or creole based on Y as the dominant language which has supplied at least the bulk of the vocabulary, with X, or the languages of the X region, as the most important second contributing factor."

On lingua francas, see also Cohen on diplomatic languages (1956a, pp. 336-338), Kahane, Kahane, Tietze (1958), and Samarin (1955, 1958, 1961, and especially 1962). On koinés, see the classic treatment by Meillet (1913, Part 3) and Ferguson (1959b).

References not in the general bibliography:

BOAS, FRANZ

1933. Note on the Chinook Jargon. *Lg.*, *9:* 208-213.

FERGUSON, CHARLES A.

1959b. The Arabic Koiné. *Lg.*, *35:* 616-630.

GIROD-CHANTRANS

1785. *Voyage d'un Suisse....*

GÖBL-GÁLDI, L.

1934. Esquisse de la structure grammaticale des patois français-créole. *Zeitschrift für französische Sprache und Literatur*, *58:* 257-295.

GRANT, RENA V.

1945. Chinook Jargon. *IJAL 11:* 225-233.

GRIERSON, P. J. HAMILTON

1903. *The Silent Trade* . . . . Edinburgh.

HALL, ROBERT A., JR.

1943a. Notes on Australian Pidgin English. *Lg., 19:* 263-267.

1943b. *Melanesian Pidgin English: Grammar, Texts, Vocabulary.* Baltimore: Waverly.

1944. Chinese Pidgin English: Grammar and Texts. *JAOS, 64:* 95-113.

1948. The Linguistic Structure of Taki-Taki. *Lg., 24:* 92-116.

1951. The Genetic Relationships of Haitian Creole. *Ricerche Linguistique, 1:* 194-203.

1952. Pidgin English and Linguistic Change. *Lingua, 3:* 138-146.

1953. *Haitian Creole* (Memoirs of the American Anthropological Association, No. 75.) Menasha, Wis.: Banta.

1958. Creolized Languages and "Genetic Relationships." *Word, 14:* 367-373.

1959b. Neo-Melanesian and Glottochronology. *IJAL, 25:* 265-267.

1962. The Life Cycle of Pidgin Languages. *Lingua. 11:* 151-156.

HEARN, LAFCADIO

1885. [No title cited by Reinecke]. *Harper's Weekly.* [Reprinted in his *An American Miscellany.* Vol. 2, p. 146.]

JACOBS, MELVILLE

1932. Notes on the Structure of Chinook Jargon. *Lg., 8:* 27-50.

1936. *Texts in Chinook Jargon.* (University of Washington Publications in Anthropology, Vol. 7, no. 1, pp. 1-27.) Seattle: University of Washington Press.

KAHANE, HENRY, RENÉE KAHANE, ANDREAS TIETZE

1958. *The Lingua Franca in the Levant: Turkish Nautical Terms of Italian and Greek Origin.* Urbana: University of Illinois Press.

KLEINICKE, D.

1959. An Etymology for "Pidgin." *IJAL, 25:* 271-272.

LEACHMAN, D., and ROBERT A. HALL, JR.

1955. American Indian Pidgin English. *American Speech, 30:* 163-171.

LE PAGE, R. B. (ED.)

1961. *Proceedings of the Conference on Creole Language Studies.* (Creole Language Studies, No. 2.) London: Macmillan.

MILHALIC, F.

1957. *Grammar and Dictionary of Neo-Melanesian.* Techny, Ill.: Mission Press. [Reviewed, E. A. Nida, *Lg.*, 1959, *35:* 362-367.]

MOREAU DE SAINT-MÉRY, L. E.

1797. *Description . . . de l'isle Saint-Domingue.* Vol. 1.

PARÉPOU, ALFRED

1885. *Atipa, roman guyanais.*

PRINCE, J. D.

1912. An Ancient New Jersey Indian Jargon. *AA, 14:* 408-424.

REINECKE, J.

1937. Marginal Languages. Doctoral dissertation, Yale University.

REINECKE, J., and AIKO TOKIMASA

1934. The English Dialect of Hawaii. *American Speech, 9:* 48-58; *9:* 122-131.

RENS, L. L. E.

1953. The Historical and Social Background of Surinam Negro-English. Doctoral Dissertation, Amsterdam.

SAMARIN, W.

1955. Sango, An African Lingua Franca. *Word, 11:* 254-267.

1958. The Phonology of Pidgin Sango. *Word, 14:* 62-70.

1961. The Vocabulary of Sango. *Word, 17:* 16-22.

1962. Lingua Francas with Special Reference to Africa. In Frank A. Rice (Ed.), *Study of the Role of Second Languages in Asia, Africa, and Latin America.* Washington, D.C.: Center for Applied Linguistics of the Modern Language Association of America. Pp. 54-65.

SCHULTZE, ERNST

1933. Sklaven- und Dienersprachen (sogen. Handelssprachen), Ein Beitrag zur Sprach- und Wanderungssoziologie. *Sociologus, 9:* 377-418.

SMITH, WILLIAM C.

1933. [No title cited by Reinecke]. *American Speech, 8:* 15-19.

SPITZER, LEO (ED.)

1928. *Hugo-Schuchardt-Brevier.* (2nd ed.) Halle.

STEWART, WILLIAM A.

1962. Creole Languages in the Caribbean. In Frank A. Rice (Ed.), *Study of the Role of Second Languages in Asia, Africa, and Latin America.* Washington, D.C.: Center for Applied Linguistics of the Modern Language Association of America. Pp. 34-53.

TAGLIAVINI, CARLO

Creole, Lingue. *Enciclopedia Italiana, 11:* 833-835.

TAYLOR, DOUGLAS

1951. Structural Outline of Caribbean Creole. *Word, 7:* 43-59.

1956. Language Contacts in the British West Indies: I. A Case of Intimate Borrowing; II, On the Classification of Creolized Languages. *Word, 12:* 399-414.

1957. Spanish Contact Vernaculars in the Philippine Islands. *Word, 13:* 490-499.

1959. On Function Versus Form in Non-Traditional Languages. *Word, 15:* 485-489.

1961. New Languages for Old in the West Indies. *Comparative Studies in Society and History, 3:* 277-288.

1963. The Origin of West Indian Creole Languages: Evidence from Grammatical Categories. *AA, 65.*

THOMPSON, R. W.

1961. A Note on Some Possible Affinities Between the Creole Dialects of the Old World and Those of the New. In R. B. Le Page (Ed.), *Proceedings of the Conference on Creole Language Studies.* (Creole Language Studies, No. 2.) London: Macmillan.

[UNESCO]

1951. *The Haiti Pilot Project: Phase One.* (Monographs on Fundamental Education, No. 4.) Paris: Unesco.

VOORHOEVE, JAN

1953. *Voorstudies tot een Beschrijf van het Sranan Tongo*. Amsterdam. [Reviewed, D. Taylor, *Word*, 1955, *11:* 168-174.]

1959. An Orthography for Saramaccan. *Word*, *15:* 436-445.

1961. Le Ton et la grammaire dans le Sarammacan. *Word*, *17:* 146-163.

WEINREICH, URIEL

1958. On the Compatability of Genetic Relationship and Convergent Development. *Word*, *14:* 374-379.

Fanagalo and the Bantu Languages in South Africa 58

D. T. COLE

To ATTRACT a host of appellations, mostly scornful and uncomplimentary, seems to be the unhappy lot of that unfortunate stepchild of Creation, the hybrid. Fanagalo, also known as Kitchen-Kafir, Mine-Kafir, Pidgin Bantu, Isilololo (because of its extensive use of the "article" *lo*), Basic Bantu, Basic Nguni, Basic Zulu, Silunguboi (the type of *Isilungu* [Zulu for "European language"] which is used in speaking to the "boys"), Conversational Zulu, Isikula, etc., is a case in point. Rarely has a language been known by so many names, yet even this is by no means a complete list thereof!

In recent years, Fanagalo, as we prefer to call it, has been the subject of a considerable amount of publicity. Since 1947 at least four booklets, grammars and dictionaries of Fanagalo, have been published. In September 1948, the Bureau of Adult Education, Pretoria Technical College, started experimental leisure-time classes for the teaching of this language, and shortly afterwards began issuing a postal course as well. (These courses have subsequently been discontinued.) About this time a "student of languages" was reported in the press as having suggested, quite seriously, that Fanagalo, or, as he termed it, "Basic Bantu," should replace German as a school subject in the Transvaal. A similar suggestion was made also in Natal, and several letters and articles on the merits and demerits of this strange jargon subsequently appeared in some of our newspapers and journals. Unfortunately much of this publicity has been inaccurate and misleading. Fanagalo has been acclaimed in certain quarters as the *lingua franca* of Southern Africa, "used by millions of speakers every day," and "spoken wherever black meets white from the Cape Peninsula to the Great Lakes of Africa" (Hopkin-Jenkins, 1948, p. vii); indeed there are records even of "full-blooded Abyssinians who understood Fanagalo," and of pygmies in "the heart of the Belgian Congo," who responded to Fanagalo after "English, French, Afrikaans (in lieu of Flemish), and one or two Bantu tongues" had failed (Bold, 1949, p. 77). Attempts have been made, unfortunately not without some success, to popularize the incongruous and presumptuous term "Basic Bantu," and ill-conceived comparisons have been drawn between the development of Fanagalo and that of Afrikaans (Hopkin-Jenkins, 1948, p. vii; Bold, 1949, p. 25). What, then, are the facts about this mixture of the Indo-European English and Afrikaans, on the one hand, and Zulu and Xhosa, the two main members of the Nguni group of Bantu languages on the other? (The Bantu languages of the Union of South Africa are divided into four groups, Nguni, Sotho, Tsonga and Venda. The Nguni group includes Zulu of Natal, Xhosa of the Eastern Cape, and Swazi of Swaziland; the Sotho group includes Southern Sotho of Basutoland and the Orange Free State, Northern Sotho of Central Eastern and Northern Transvaal, and Tswana of the Bechunanaland Protectorate, Northern Cape Province Western Transvaal and Western Orange Free State.)

Concerning the place and date of origin of Fanagalo there seems to be no definite information available. One writer has suggested that ". . . it was first spoken in the Eastern Cape and Natal, between the predominantly English-speaking European settlers of these areas and Natives speaking one or other of the Nguni languages . . . " (Hopkin-Jenkins, 1948, p. vii; see also Bold, 1952, p. 6). Another has hinted at the diamond- and goldfields of Kimberley and Johannesburg as its place of origin (Lloyd, n.d., p. 3). The latter possibility must, in our opinion, be rejected immediately. Both Kimberly and the Witwatersrand are situated in Sotho areas, and, initially at least, must have depended mainly on local labour, but there is hardly anything in Fanagalo which can be derived from any of the Sotho languages. The case for the Eastern Cape is better, for it was there that the first fairly extensive contact took place between the Bantu, mainly of Xhosa stock, and the Europeans. Here however, two points must be noted. Firstly, the major proportion of the European vocabulary in Fanagalo is derived from English, whereas only a relatively small number of words is of Afrikaans or Nederlands origin. Secondly, as far as it is possible to judge, considering how similar the two languages are in basic vocabulary, the Nguni elements appear to be drawn mainly from Zulu, and there is very little which is clearly attributable to Xhosa as such. The conclusion is that Fanagalo developed primarily out of the interaction of English and Zulu, and this must have happened in Natal, some time after 1823, when the first settlement of that territory took place, mainly by English speaking people.

Perhaps the first informative reference to Fanagalo in literature was a short paper published in the journal *Anthropos* in 1908 (*3*[3]: 508-511): "Die Isikula-Sprache in Natal, Südafrika," by Brother Otto O. Trapp of the Marianhill Mission. Trapp's examples are typical of Fanagalo as we know it to-day, and we can therefore assume that it was already well established at the beginning of the present century. He described it as a mixture of English and Zulu, used mainly as a means of communication between the Indians and the Zulus, hence the name *Isikula*, the Zulu for "Coolie language." Here, I believe, we have a clue to the origin of Fanagalo—that the Zulus should have called it the "Coolie language" suggests that the Indians were its originators. The only argument against this is that Fanagalo neither contains any Indian words—a point to which Trapp himself drew attention—nor shows any other perceptible evidence of influence from the Indian languages used in South Africa, principally Tamil, Hindi, Telugu, Gujerati and Urdu. But it must be remembered that his own language was of no economic value to the Indian at the time. He had perforce to make himself understood to the Englishman and the Zulu, neither of whom spoke his language, or was even remotely interested therein. It follows therefore that the Indian, having acquired limited vocabularies of both English and Zulu, would have mixed the two in attempting to make himself understood. Certainly, if the Indians were not the first to use Fanagalo, they provided much of the impetus for its early development and diffusion; and since the importation of Indian labour into Natal commenced in 1860, I think it is reasonable to suggest that Fanagalo came into being at about this time.

It may be mentioned in passing that Fanagalo shows no evidence of direct influence from the non-Bantu Hottentot and Bushman languages. Indirectly of course, such influence does exist, for the click consonants of the Nguni languages, and a certain amount of their vocabulary, both of which have been transferred, in very limited degree, to Fanagalo, are attributable to Hottentot-Bushman.

From Natal Fanagalo spread to the diamond and gold mines, and later to other industrial and farming areas of the Union and Southern Rhodesia. Initially it must have been the Europeans who were mainly responsible for carrying the new language beyond the border of Natal; later the Indians also probably played a part in its wider dissemination. As the mining industries, more particularly, developed, labour was imported from the Nguni and other areas, with the result that Fanagalo soon became established as the means of communication between European employers or overseers and Bantu labourers. Today it is more extensively used on the Witwatersrand mines than anywhere else. Indeed, without some such *lingua franca* the gold mines would be faced with an almost insuperable language problem, for they employ Bantu labourers speaking forty or more different languages, from as far afield as Angola, Northern Rhodesia, Nyasaland and Tanganyika. On many mines new recruits are regularly put through a course of Fanagalo before being sent underground; on others they learn it while undergoing training in their various duties; but learn it they must, before becoming effective workers.

In southern Rhodesia, which has a large

population of Ndebele, a Zulu offshoot, popularly known as Matabele, Fanagalo spread rapidly, though it has many local differences owing to the influence of Shona, the predominant language. European miners and farmers, emigrating to the north, have carried Fanagalo to Northern Rhodesia and even to the mining areas of the Belgian Congo. Further than this, however, its prospects of advancing are extremely meagre, for it meets with very powerful rivals. Swahili, whose home is on the Kenya and Tanganyika coast, has a variety of debased forms which are used as *linguae francae* right across Central Africa, including Uganda, the northern portions of Portuguese East Africa, Nyasaland, Northern Rhodesia, and a large portion of the Belgian Congo. The Congo form, known as Ngwana, is but one of four such trade languages which are extensively used in that vast territory; the others are Bangala, in the north; Fiote, in the west; and Baluba, in the south and centre. But even to the south of the Swahili and Congo spheres, there are other languages which are quite extensively used outside of their own areas as *linguae francae*. These include Nyanja of Nyasaland, Umbundu of Central Angola, Lozi of Barotseland in Northern Rhodesia, and Luvale or Lwena of the Balovale District of Northern Rhodesia and adjacent areas in Angola and the Belgian Congo.

An analysis of Fanagalo vocabulary, based on material provided by existing publications, reveals that about thirty per cent of the words are of European origin, the proportion of English to Afrikaans being roughly four to one. It is of course, not always easy to determine whether a particular word is derived from English or from Afrikaans, for many cognate roots are very similar in pronunciation, e.g., *sack* / *sak*, *coffee* / *koffie*, *help* / *help*, *bottle* /*bottel*. Nevertheless, a knowledge of phonetics enables one to state with certainty that *melek* < A. *melk*, not E. *milk*; *washa* < E. *wash*, not A. *was*; *botela* < A. *botter*, not E. *butter*; while *payip* (water-pipe) < E. *pipe*, but *peyip* (tobacco-pipe) < A. *pyp*. Some words of European origin have probably come into Fanagalo via Zulu, e.g., *batala* (pay) < Z. *batala* < A. *betaal*, and *foshol* < Z. *ifosholo* < E. *shovel* (with transposition of consonants). An interesting example is *hashi* < Z. *ihhashi* < Hottentot *has* < E. *horse*. (In Hottentot, a sex-denoting language, *has* is feminine gender, *hap* masculine, and *hai* common. The Hottentot *s* is, in this case, a "lisped" sound intermediate between English *s* and *sh*, hence the appearance of *sh* in Zulu.)

In order to explain many of the peculiarities of Fanagalo, it is necessary to point out that Bantu and European languages differ radically in phonetics, word-form, grammatical structure and syntax. It is hardly surprising therefore that Fanagalo is highly inconsistent, being the product of the interacting forces of two completely divergent systems. In Bantu languages, syllables are typically open, i.e., they end in a vowel. The Bantu speaker of Fanagalo therefore tends to insert vowels between the elements of compound consonants or combinations of consonants which are foreign to him, whereas the European, who is accustomed to closed syllables (ending in consonants), tends to drop many of the vowels in words of Bantu origin. Thus A. *skroef* may become *sikulufu* in the Fanagalo of a Bantu speaker, whereas the European contracts Z. *isikhathi* (time) to *skat*. The general tendency, however, is to drop initial, final, and many intermediate vowels; in other words, the Bantu type of word form is rapidly giving place to the European pattern, even in the pronunciation of Bantu speakers of Fanagalo. Certain English and Afrikaans sounds also, are foreign to the Bantu languages, and vice versa. Thus English *th* > *d*, *t*, or *f*, and *r* > *l*, e.g., E. *this one* > *diswan* (this), E. *bath* > *baf*, A. *broer* > *blulu* or *bululu* (brother), whereas the click consonants of Zulu are frequently replaced by *k*, e.g., Z. *caɓanga* > *kabanga* (think), and Z. *AmaXhosa* > *Makosa* (Xhosa people). (The *r* sounds of English and Afrikaans do not occur in Nguni. In Shona, however, *r* occurs, but not *l*, hence E. *blanket* > *buranget*, and E. *blue* > *bru* in Rhodesian Fanagalo). Here again, alternative pronunciations occur, according as the speaker is European or Bantu, but with the Bantu type of pronounciation fighting a losing battle!

Another important feature of most Bantu languages is their semantic and grammatical use of tone, e.g., Zulu *inyanga* (doctor, tones High-Low-Low), but *inyanga* (moon, tones High-Low-High). This usage has completely disappeared in Fanagalo, which is spoken with an intonation similar to that of English. Again, in Zulu the penultimate syllable of each word and sentence is characteristically accentuated by pronouncing it with greater length than its fellows, whereas in English and Afrikaans certain syllables are accentuated by stressing them, (stress in English and Afrikaans is usually associated with increased length and raised tone), e.g., *óbject* (noun), but *objéct* (verb). As one might expect, in Fanagalo the penultimate length-accent of Zulu is replaced by a stress-accent similar to that of English and Afrikaans. Hence Zulu *izinkomo* (cattle), with long and low-toned penultimate syllable *nko*, becomes *lo zinkomo*, with longstressed and high-toned *ko*.

The following are a few miscellaneous examples of Fanagalo words which are derived from English and Afrikaans: *aina* (press, iron) < E. *iron*; *basopa* (take care, look after) < A. *pas op*; *bulughwe* (bridge) < A. *brug*; *bontshis* (beans) < A. *boontjies*; *fesklas* (good, excellent) < E. *first class*; *langwan* (tall, long) < E. *long one*; *mbaimbai* (later on, presently) < E. *bye and bye*; *mosha* (spoil, mess, waste) < A. *mors*; *nikis* (nothing) < A. *niks*; *nyuwan* (new) < E. *new one*; *shova* (push) < E. *shove*; *skop* (head) < A. *kop*; *skiti* (pound) < A. *skut*; *skafu* (food) < E. *scoff* (South African English, "from Dutch *schoft*, quarter of a day (hence, meal)," O.E.D.); *Sonto* (Sunday, week, church) < A. *Sondag*; *stin* (brick) < A. *steen*; *stes* (stairs) < E. *stairs*; *stoplayit* (robot) < E. *stop light*.

Most of the words listed above are fairly easy to identify, even for the layman, but some "Fanagalized" words are distorted almost beyond recognition, e.g., *klabish* (cabbage) < E. *cabbage*; *vodlela* (carrot) < A. *wortel*; *sikwelete* (debt) < A. *skuld*; *sihlutula* (key, lock) < A. *sleutel*; *skrumpat* (tractor) < A. *skilpad* (tortoise). In some cases the original European word is camouflaged by the addition of a Bantu formative element, e.g., *layisha* (load) < A. *laai* plus verb-forming suffix *-sha*; *bitshan* or *mbitshana* (a little, slightly) < A. *bietjie* plus diminutive suffix *-ana; bitshanisa* (make small, reduce) < *bitshan* plus causative suffix *-isa*; *tshipisa* (cheapen, reduce price) < E. *cheap* plus *-isa*. No less interesting are some of the compound words in which one part is of European origin and the other Bantu, e.g., *tshisa-stik* (fuse lighter) < Z. *shisa* (set alight, burn) and E. *stick*; *makaza-mbitshan* (cool) < Z. *amakhaza* (cold) and *mbitshan* (slightly); *tshisa-mbitshan* (warm) < Z. *shisa* (burn) and *mbitshan*; *sokismude* (stocking) < E. *socks* and Z. *omude* (long); *hayikona-stelek* (weak) < Z. *ayikhona* (it is not there) and A. *sterk* (strong). Intriguing and amusing also are the associations of ideas which have produced the following: *strongimani* (circus) < E. *strong man*; *injin-faya* or *injin-fayif* (racing-car) < E. *fire-engine* (with inverted word-order); and *tayimholo* (town hall). To the Bantu the feats of the "strong man" are apparently more impressive than any other item on the circus programme; a speeding fire-engine is more spectacular and exciting than a racing-car in action; and however the English may choose to pronounce the word, we know that it is from the clock of the *tayimholo* that we can get the correct time!

As in other "pidgin" languages, certain words do much more than their fair share of work. Thus *stelek* < A. *sterk* (strong) expresses *hard*, *well*, *very*, *strongly*, *thoroughly*; and *skelem* < A. *skelm* (rogue, scoundrel) is used in reference to anything unreliable, dangerous or destructive, e.g., *skelem smok* (carbon monoxide, poisonous gas; *smok* < E. *smoke*). Undoubtedly one of the most hard-worked words in Fanagalo is *pikanin*, which expresses *small*, *short*, *narrow*, *young*, *child*, *junior*, etc., as in *pikanin hashi* (foal); *pikanin tshopa* (hatchet; *tshopa* < E. *chopper*); *pikanin mes* (pen-knife; *mes* < A. *mes*); *pikanin sicogo* (cap; *sicogo* < Z. *isigqoko*, *hat*); *pikanin foloman* (young foreman, small foreman, junior foreman); *basop pikanin* (nurse or look after a child); *figa pikanin* (shrink; *figa* < Z. *fika*, arrive).

Grammatically and syntactically Fanagalo retains hardly any Bantu characteristics. Of several more or less unique features of the Bantu languages, there are two which stand out as the hallmarks of this family. The first is the system of noun prefixes. In Zulu there are fifteen regular prefixes, some singular, others plural, which are arranged in eight classes, e.g., 1. *umu-ntu/aɓa-ntu* (person/people); 2. *umu-thi/imi-thi* (tree/trees); 3. *i-qanda/ama-qanda* (egg/eggs); 4. *isi-hlalo/izi-hlalo* (chair/chairs); 5. *in-kaɓi/izin-kaɓi* (ox/oxen) etc. However, except for a few remnants, this system of noun classes had disappeared in Fanagalo. The great majority of nouns have no specialized singular prefix, and assume *ma-* in the plural, e.g., *skatul/maskatul* (shoe/shoes; cf. Z. *isicathulo/izicathulo*); a few retain the *mu-/ba-* prefixes, e.g., *muntu/bantu* (person/people), and the Zulu class 5 is preserved in quite a number of forms such as *nkabi/zinkabi* (ox/oxen).

The second major characteristic of Bantu languages is the system of "concords." Every word is grammatically related to a noun, be it pronoun, adjective (of which there are several different types), possessive or verb, must show that relationship by assuming a prefixal formative which agrees concordially with the noun prefix. There is a full set of these concords for each class of nouns, singular and plural, and usually the same or similar consonant or vowel as appears in the noun prefix is repeated in the concords, producing a delightful alliterative effect. For example in Zulu we find:

Aɓa-	*ɓa-*	*aɓa-*	*ɓa-*	*ɓo-*
fana	*mi*	*khulu*	*yasebenza*	*nke*
Sons	of-me	big	are-working	all

All my big sons are working.

Izin-	*za-*	*ezin-*	*zi-*	*zo-*
komo	*mi*	*kulu*	*yaklaɓa*	*nke*
Cattle	of-me	big	are-grazing	all

All my big cattle are grazing.

Of this fascinating system of concords, which puts music and poetry into every Bantu sentence, nothing at all remains in Fanagalo! It is perhaps in a sub-conscious attempt to compensate for this loss, and to accommodate the European preference for a definite or indefinite article (there are no articles in the Bantu languages), that speakers of Fanagalo acquired the habit of putting *lo* before every noun, and a "personal pronoun" before every verb, even if the subject be expressed. Thus we have: *Lo foloman yena funa lo nyuzipepa na lo ti* (The foreman he want the newspaper and the tea); *Lo wil ga lo motokali yena pontshiwe* (The wheel of the motorcar he punctured); *Lo Mary yena deka lo taful* (The Mary he lays the table). There is no indefinite form corresponding to the so-called "definite article" *lo*, and it is noteworthy that the latter is used also before proper names! By origin *lo* is a Zulu demonstrative pronoun, one of a concordial series, meaning *this*. In the name *Fanagalo* we have it retaining its demonstrative significance—*fana* (be like, resemble), *ga* (with, of), *lo* (this), hence *fanagalo* (thus, like this). Since *Enza fanagalo!* (Do like this! Make like this!) is one of the most commonly used expressions in the language—certainly the new and inexperienced "boy" has it dinned into his ears from morning till night—it is hardly surprising that the language has come to be known as Fanagalo.

The "personal pronouns" are *mina* (I), *tina* (we), *wena* (thou), *nina* (you) and *yena* (he, she, it, they), and are taken from the full concordial series of "Absolute Pronouns" which occurs in Zulu.

The fate of the noun class and concord systems has been suffered also by the various other structural peculiarities which characterize the Bantu languages; either they have disappeared completely or only remnants thereof remain in Fanagalo. Of the extensive system of verbal prefixes and suffixes which express distinctions of mood and tense and other specialized ideas in Nguni, only a very few such as the passive *-wa*, causative *-isa* and past *-ile*, are still retained, and even then irregularly and inconsistently; examples of their use are *pentwa* (be painted) < *penta* < E. *paint; figisa* (bring, cause to come) < *figa* (come, arrive); *shefile* (have shaved) < *shefa* < E. *shave; Yinindaba wena hayikona shefile namhla?* (Why have you not shaved to-day?).

As regards syntax, the simple Bantu sentence is fundamentally the same in word-order as that of English or Afrikaans, i.e., Subject-Verb-Object / Adverb, and Fanagalo naturally conforms thereto. One outstanding difference, however, is that Bantu adjectives follow the noun which they qualify; Fanagalo has adopted the European pattern and puts the adjective first e.g., *makaza manzi* (cold water), cf. Z. *amanzi, amakhaza; maningi santi* (much sand), cf. Z. *isihlaɓathi esiningi; zonke skafu* (all the food), cf. Z. *ukudla konke; nyuwan motokali* (a new motorcar), cf. Z. *imoto entsha*. Again, whereas interrogative words in English and Afrikaans are usually placed first in the sentence, they usually follow the verb in Zulu. In Fanagalo the European word-order is used, e.g., *Bani wena funa?* (Whom do you want?), cf. Z. *Ufuna uɓani? Ipi wena sebenza?* (Where do you work?), cf. Z. *Useɓenza-phi?*

Many more comparisons of this type could be made, but they would involve us in further lengthy explanations of Bantu word and sentence structure. The evidence already adduced is more than sufficient to show quite conclusively that Fanagalo lacks the main features by which linguists recognize and identify languages as being Bantu. It is true that the bulk of its vocabulary, i.e., about 70 per cent, is of Nguni-Bantu origin and it is interesting, by way of comparison, to note that modern classical Swahili contains over 30 per cent of foreign vocabulary, acquired mainly from Arabic. The difference is that in all other respects Swahili is essentially Bantu, whereas Fanagalo is not. In any case, for Fanagalo even the criterion of vocabulary, taken alone, would be inconclusive, for Nguni is by no means typical of Bantu in this respect, as is shown by the extensive occurrence therein of non-Bantu clickwords.

It is important to emphasise that Fanagalo is not a Bantu language, for its champions persist in stating or implying that it is. Apart from using such phrases as "a really easy Bantu language" and "like other Bantu languages" in reference thereto, some of them have had the effrontery to call it "Basic Bantu," "Basic Nguni," etc. The term *Bantu* is correctly applied to a family of some 200 or more separate languages, apart from dialects, which extend from the Cameroons, Congo, Uganda and Kenya in the north to the Union and South West Africa in the south. Obviously therefore, it is no more possible to produce a "Basic Bantu" than it would be to do the same for the vast Indo-European family of languages. The selection of a basic vocabulary can be done, of course, for any individual Bantu language, as it has been for English by C. K. Ogden and for Afrikaans by Barnes; however, were any Bantuist to produce a "Basic Zulu" or even a "Basic Nguni," which is possible, it would bear extremely little resemblance to Fanagalo.

Another important point is that the Bantu do *not* automatically understand Fanagalo; they have to learn it, just as the Europeans do. Having learned it, the unsophisticated Bantu fondly imagine that they are speaking the language of the White man (this is naively quoted as a "standing joke" by Bold, 1949, p. 77)—so different is it from their own languages! From the Bantu point of view therefore, Fanagalo, which serves mainly as a means of communication with Europeans, might with equal justification be called "Basic English" or "Basic Afrikaans" or "Basic European"—which is patently ridiculous!

Equally ridiculous and ignorant is any suggestion that the origin and development of Fanagalo are comparable with those of Afrikaans. The latter has developed out of the natural and spontaneous modification of the phonetic, morphological and syntactical structures of its Nederlands parent, with some accretions from other members of the same language family, in the same way as modern English and other European languages have developed from earlier forms. Fanagalo, on the other hand, is not a spontaneous or natural outgrowth from Zulu, but a disintegrated mixture of mutilated elements from two entirely different language families.

It is hardly surprising, considering the nature of its development and its function, that Fanagalo has an extremely limited range of expression; that the recently published *Fanagalo Dictionary*, by J.D. Bold, contains only a little over 1,200 entries in the Fanagalo-English section is convincing proof of this. (". . . although a couple of vocabularies giving the Fanagalo equivalents of some English words have appeared, there has been no attempt to compile a comprehensive dictionary. This two-way dictionary . . . is therefore a pioneering effort" [Bold, 1952, p. 5]. Nevertheless, Lloyd's *Kitchen-Kafir Grammar and Vocabulary*, also "two-way," seems to contain two or three hundred more entries.) Lest we forget, this "language," with its total vocabulary of under 2,000 words, has been proposed for study in our schools, as a substitute for German! The following examples, taken from the literature on Fanagalo, will illustrate what clumsy methods must be employed to express anything more than the most straight-forward ideas; note that relative clause constructions, for example, are expressed by mere juxtaposition of sentences. In each case a literal translation is given, followed by the "idiomatic" rendering of the original text.

Mina funa lo muntu yena sebenza stelek (I want the person he work strong; "I want a boy who works well")

Biza mina lo skati lo telefom yena kala (Call me the time the telephone he cry; "Call me when the telephone rings")

Ngaganani pezulu lo muti? (How-big above the tree?; "How high is the tree?")

Tina funa yidla lo skafu nbada tina lambile (We want eat the food affair we hungry; "We want to eat the food because we are hungry")

Mina yazi nombola yena tshela hamba kanjani (I know number he tell travel how; "I know what the speed limit is")

Lo skati wena pega lo nyama ga lo ngulube, pega yena stelek (The time you cook the meat of the pig, cook him well; "Don't eat underdone pork!")

After this—and many more such examples could be quoted—it is probably superfluous to mention that Fanagalo is almost incapable of expressing abstract concepts.

One cannot resists the temptation, in conclusion, to quote the following remarks on Fanagalo, translated from a recently published article by Prof. J. A. Engelbrecht and Dr. D. Ziervogel, of the Department of Bantu Languages in the University of Pretoria:

> The champions thereof commend it as the desirable *lingua franca* between European and Native; . . . About the value thereof as a means of getting by, no one wishes to quibble. It is a makeshift in the same sense as a sequence of strung-together French words can be when a Russian and an Englishman meet; yet no one would assert that these two people were engaged in speaking French. So also with Fanagalo: it is a hotch-potch of words which is born out of the necessity and quandary of the moment, and which therefore never replaces the genuine article. . . . The champions of Fanagalo still regard the Bantu as a hewer of wood and drawer of water, and not as a person with his own emotions, culture and traditions, thus he is to them merely *Wena boy, tshetshisa enza lo ti!* (You boy, hurry make the tea!). If this is to be our approach to the Native problem, it must remain a problem. If on the contrary, our aim is to make the Bantu individual a good and independent fellow-countryman, we shall have to address him in something better than this jargon before he becomes convinced of our good intentions (1951, pp. 29-30).

Lest there be any doubt about the validity of this statement the following entries, but a few of many in similar vein, are quoted from *So! You Want To Learn the Language! An Amusing and Instructive Kitchen Kaffir Dictionary*, by S. E. Aitken-Cade (1951):

As, adv. . . . *sa.* Unbelievable but true. Proves that the native mind works in the opposite direction to ours . . .

Beat, vb. . . . *chaiya.* "I'll beat you." "Mena chaiya wena." If you are going to get any effect do it first and talk later.

Go, vb. int. . . . *hamba* (hortative—footsack).

Lie, vb. . . . It is extraordinary that there are so few words to describe this national pastime of the native Africans . . .

Scandal, n. . . . Cannot find a word in K.K. Possibly nothing scandalous in K.K. Just natural.

Shame, vb. int. . . . Is there such a word?

Tie, vb. tr. . . . *bopa.* "Tie him to that baling press until the police come." "*Bopa yena lapa screw paka fika Mapolisa.*"

Trunk, n. (of elephant) . . . *hands ga lo njobvu.*

Zebra, n. . . . *donkey ga lo football jersey.*

In the present circumstances Fanagalo fulfils a real need on the mines and in certain other industries where the multiplicity of languages creates an enormous problem of communication. It is of great value in the normal prosecution of the work, in the prevention of accidents, and in the maintenance of satisfactory relations between the workers, for lack of mutual understanding may lead to friction and violence. Wherever possible, however, its use is to be discouraged, for to address the Bantu in this debased jargon, if not insulting, is certainly not courteous. The future progress and prosperity of South Africa are dependent on the establishment of goodwill and mutual respect between the different peoples of the country, and one of the prerequisites for mutual understanding is the knowledge of one another's languages; therefore the introduction of Bantu languages as subjects for study in European schools must be heartily welcomed —but Fanagalo is not one of these.

REFERENCE NOTE

Cole's article was originally prepared at the request of Professor Abel Coetzee, for publication in the *Tydskrif vir Volkskunde en Volkstaal*, of which he is the editor, and appears under the title "Fanagalo en die Bantoe-tale van Suid-Afrika" (1953, *9* [3].) It draws on shorter items and "Letters to the Editor" in South African newpapers as well as the references cited.

For other examples of pidgins and general discussion, see the references listed with Reinecke's article on pp. 534-546. Turner (1949) is an important, instructive study, showing how widespread views in our own society about speech patterns of creolized origin can be mistaken, yet reinforce social stereotypes.

References not in the general bibliography:

AITKEN-CADE, S. E.

1951. *So! You Want to Learn the Language! An Amusing and Instructive Kitchen Kaffir Dictionary*. Salisbury, Southern Rhodesia: Centafrican Press.

BOLD, JOHN D.

1949. Fanagalo Is Becoming the Lingua Franca of Southern Africa. *The Outspan*, May 13.

1952. *Fanagalo Dictionary*. Central News Agency.

COLE, DESMOND T.

1949. South Africans Are Taking More and More Interest in Bantu Languages. *The Outspan*, September 9.

ENGELBRECHT, J. A., and D. ZIERVOGEL

1951. Die Keuse van die Vantoetaal op Skool. *Journal of Racial Affairs*, *2:* 29-30.

HOPKINS-JENKINS, K.

1948. *Basic Bantu*. Pietermaritzburg: Shuter and Shooter.

LLOYD, D. C.

n.d. *Kitchen Kafir Grammar and Vocabulary*. Central News Agency.

PRETORIA TECHNICAL COLLEGE, BUREAU OF ADULT EDUCATION

1948-1949. *Fanagalo Postal Course*. Pretoria.

RAND MUTUAL ASSURANCE CO. LTD., PREVENTION OF ACCIDENTS' COMMITTEE

1920. *Miners' Companion in Zulu* (*and Kitchen Kaffir*). Johannesburg.

1938. *Miners' Companion in English, Afrikaans, Sesuto and Mine Kafir*. Johannesburg.

[TURNER (1949)] [Cf. review by McDavid, *Lg*. 26.323-33 (1950), andannotations by H. P. Blok, *Lingua*, 1959, *8:* 306-321.]

VAN DER WATT, P. J.

1950. Leer 'n Nuwe Taal Binne Drie Weke. *Die Brandwag,* October 6, pp. 26-27.

A Planned Auxilary Language 59

NORMAN A. MCQUOWN

[Review of: H. Jacob, *A Planned Auxiliary Language.* With a Preface by Harold E. Palmer. London: Dobson, 1947.]

This book, written by a man who has had considerable first-hand experience with a number of artificial international auxiliary languages, bears on what seems to be a perennial problem, with innumerable suggested solutions, but with no universally accepted one.

The fact that Jacob has had direct experience with international languages makes his commentary on the five type-languages reviewed in the first part of the book anything but academic, as too many critiques of international languages have been in the past (Brugmann and Leskien, 1907). On the other hand, one can also detect a certain lack of objectivity, perhaps inevitable from someone who has the opportunity to play a direct role in some of the rather heated controversies among impassioned adherents of one or the other system. It is also regrettable that the criteria used for judging the various systems are not more in conformity with the generally recognized body of linguistic knowledge. Notwithstanding these minor defects, however, the book presents a very useful survey of the chief characteristics of the most important international languages (Part I), a sketch of the structural differentiae of these languages and the problems connected with them (Part II), and a consideration of the international language problem from the point of view of the technician and scientist, together with an account of the attempts of the International Auxiliary Language Association to solve the problem (Part III).

In his Preface, Harold E. Palmer sets up the contrast between "artificial" and ethnic languages, emphasizing the use of "artificial" not in any pejorative sense, but only in the sense of man-made, consciously constructed. Palmer emphasizes the practical in his treatment of the question: "Quaintness and oddity may enhance the beauty of a work of literature or art, but not the utility of an instrument of precision." He points out that there are no processes going on in artificial languages which are not also in constant operation in ethnic languages, and that processes such as the borrowing of international words from one language to another (almost all words in the vocabulary of an international language consist of such borrowings), or word-coining (some few analogically formed coinages are used in some of the international languages), make the life and growth of an international language much like that of an ethnic language. He describes a common medium of communication as "an indispensable condition of international understanding and harmony." He cites the need for such a medium in international congresses ("Let the handicap be fair, and the language-learning task be the same for all"), for the language-learner ("Let it be a language that I can learn in the minimum of time"), the educationist (who holds "that one should know something of the structure and nature of languages"), the scientist ("Let us . . . do for vocabularies in general what has already been done for vocabulary in particular [in international scientific terminology]"), and the businessman (who now resorts to commercial "codes"). He mentions the long search of the philosopher for a "more perfect instrument of thought." He lists five general characteristics of all modern constructed languages: (1) a minimum of speech sounds, most of them common to all languages, (2) perfectly phonetic spellings, (3) adequate but simple vocabularies, (4) regular and logical systems of derivation, (5) the minimum of rules of grammar and syntax, all regular. From these it is "only to be expected that an artificial language can be mastered in from one quarter to one twentieth of the time needed for mastering any natural language." Palmer himself confesses to having learned two of the artificial languages, Esperanto and Ido, and expresses his preference for the latter. (The disconcerting consequence of attempting to limit the phonemes of an artificial language to the types present in most [not all] of the more important ethnic languages is set forth by Troubetzkoy [1939]. Palmer's assumption that most of the phonetic types used in "modern constructed languages" [not to mention the combinations and clusters in which they occur there] are "common to all languages" is a piece of unwarranted optimism.—Bernard Bloch, editor of *Language*.)

In the Introduction, discussing the function of an international language, Jacob suggests certain minimum requirements: (1) an international language "must answer to the needs of the vast scientific and social life as it exists today," and must further be "adaptable to any demands which might be made upon it in the future." (2) "We require nothing less than a complete and autonomous language . . . ." (3) Monosignificance of linguistic elements is highly desirable, but the principle should be applied NOT to the word (which would entail much too large a vocabulary), but to the "smallest, but complete unit of thought, the sentence." Like Palmer, he points out that the contrast of "artificial" and "natural" is hardly valid today: "Today language is no longer the product of nature alone, but the more deliberate result of the human mind, shaping and forming it to suit the growing needs of our civilization." But even though both ethnic and artificial languages are in a sense "planned," the ethnic language is at a considerable disadvantage because it is bound by its inherited structure, whereas the planning of the structure of an artificial language "may be *a priori* even though its elements are based on the known root material of the European languages." This a-priorism of the structure of an artificial language makes it possible for such a language to be "precise where natural languages are vague" and "regular where the natural tongue is irregular."

E. Allison Peers' "bilinguism" (English and Spanish) is rejected as complicating rather than simplifying the present situation. Sir Richard Paget's "sign language" is rejected as inadequate. This inadequacy had previously been pointed out by R. A. Wilson in his book *The Miraculous Birth of Language*: "If each gesture is to represent one notion, we should require as many gestures as we possess notions. The two hands cannot form this number of gestures." The larynx and associated "organs of speech" are inherently much more flexible than the hands. The vocal medium of communication is capable of the high degree of differentiation without which linguistic systems would not be possible. The same objection applies to systems of pictures (Neurath, 1936) as a means of international communication. The British Association Committee on Post-War University Education arrives at the conclusion that "any auxiliary means of education will have to be closely related to the English language and to be such that the learning of it is a direct step toward learning English." This clearly looks forward to an Anglo-American condominium, but it seems to this reviewer to be over-sanguine in its prognosis of the predominant role to be played by English-speaking peoples in the world of tomorrow: "English is one of two languages of the Anglo-Soviet treaty and the common language of Generalissimo Chiang Kai Shek and the peoples of India." Russian is the other (180,000,000 speakers), and although English may be playing the role of lingua franca in the Far East, it happens that Chiang himself does not speak it. Jacob approvingly quotes Margaret Schlauch (1943) as taking professional linguists to task for their exclusive devotion to "the purely analytical study of language" and their non-participation in the working out of a solution to the international language problem "as citizens of the world."

In Part I, Jacob outlines five of the more or less successful constructed languages. ESPERANTO (Chap. I), invented by Dr. L. L. Zamenhof, appeared in 1887, under the author's pseudonym of Doktoro Esperanto. The first book contains the sounds, the grammar, and a lexicon of 921 "root" elements. The phonemic system and the grammatical framework are as follows:

Sounds

Consonants					*Vowels*		
p	t	c	ĉ	k	i		u
b	d	dz	ĝ	g	e		o
f		s	ŝ	ĥ h		a	
v		z	ĵ				
m	n				[Stress, on the penult, is non-phonemic.]		
ŭ			j				
	l						
	r						

Forms

Noun -o	Pl. -j (Noun, Adj.)	Acc. -n (Noun, Adj., Adv.)		
Adj. -a				
Adv. -e				
Inf. -i				
Pres. -a-	Fin. -s (Pres., Past, Fut., Cond.)	Act. Ptc. -nt- (Pres., Past, Fut.)	Pass. Ptc. -t- (Pres., Past, Fut.)	
Past -i-				
Fut. -o-				
Cond. -u-				
Impv. -u				

If the stress, in Esperanto or any other language, regularly falls on a particular syllable of the word, it can be regarded as non-phonemic only if the word-boundary is phonemically marked by some other feature. Needless to say, the space between words in writing is not a phonemic feature; at most it is an indirect (but perfectly legitimate) device for indicating the position of the phonemic stress.—B.B.

Esperanto roots are inherently nominal, adjectival, adverbial, or verbal, although this fact was not theoretically recognized for some time. The noun ending *-o*, the adjective ending *-a*, the adverb ending *-e*, and so on, are pleonastic when added to roots which are already inherently nouns, adjectives, adverbs, etc. When added to other roots (*-o* to an adjective root, *-i* to a noun root, and so on), they are derivative in function (nominalizing the adjective, verbalizing the noun, etc.): *bel-a* 'beautiful' > *bel-o* 'beauty,' *martel-o* 'hammer' > *martel-i* '(to) hammer.' The resulting forms are not very precise, but may be made more so, if necessary in a given context, by means of specific additional suffixes: *bel-ec-o* 'beauty,' *bel-ul-o* '(a) beauty,' *bel-aĵ-o* 'a beautiful thing.' The very pleonasm of the *-o*, *-a*, *-e*, *-i* endings has led to their acquiring a vitality of their own, so that, for example, although properly speaking *hodiaŭ* 'today' is self-sufficient, one may add adverbial *-e*, resulting in *hodiaŭe* 'nowaday.' One may also speak of *l'o* [*la -o*] '(the) essence, entity.' The derivational affixes proper may also be used independently: *eco* 'quality,' *ulo* 'person,' *aĵo* 'thing.' The result is a language which, although superficially flexional, is actually agglutinative in its structure. Each of its basic elements is semi-independent, and constructions are simple concatenations of these basic elements in conventional orders. In the sixty-odd years of its life, the Esperanto vocabulary has increased, by adding common-European roots, from its original 921 to over 6000 officially recognized, and between forty and fifty thousand unofficial roots, if one includes the non-official but already internationalized scientific terminology.

In his commentary, on the credit side, Jacob mentions the modesty of its inventor, in launching the project without any personal ties, and in refusing to exert his personal influence to bring about modifications in the language, although he himself was perfectly amenable to criticism, and quite willing to suggest changes (as he did in 1894) in conformity with what seemed to him to be the consensus of opinion. The suggested basic changes were rejected, however, by the users of the language, and in 1905, at the first international Esperanto-Congress at Boulogne-sur-Mer, in France, the decision was reached to make no changes in the basic structure until the language was officially recognized and adopted. The members of the Congress hoped thereby to gain in stability what they might lose in retaining imperfections inherent in the original instrument. Jacob comments that "Esperanto has consequently never been, and is not today, open to fundamental changes or adjustments based on new proposals in the fields of interlinguistics, though it does develop according to its own laws." This characteristic of Esperanto, as over against the other systems (which were, in general, very amenable to change), makes it of peculiar interest to the general linguist, who may be interested in observing the principles of growth and development, from known beginnings, under more or less sharply determinable conditions, of such a type-language.

On the debit side, Jacob mentions the reversed Czech ˇ, i.e.ˆ, invented by Zamenhof as a common diacritic for the Esperanto alphabet, as a serious defect. To the linguist, accustomed to dealing with phonetic and phonemic writing systems, it seems a minor item, and certainly the advantages to be gained (by the use of a uniform diacritic and by unit-symbol representation of phonemes) should easily outweigh any purely esthetic considerations. Jacob, furthermore, criticizes Zamenhof for not using *x* ("internationally known as a character and as a sound"). It seems that here Zamenhof showed himself a better linguist than Jacob, for his solution to the *x*-problem (*ks* or *kz*) is in complete conformity with the phonetic facts and with the principle of one phoneme one letter. From the phonemic point of view, on the other hand, it is not improbable that *dz* (so written by Zamenhof) is a unit phoneme, and should, therefore, be respresented by a unit symbol. A more general criticism might have been made of the whole group *c dz ĉ ĝ* as offering some difficulty to the native speakers of a considerable number of languages. In his criticism of *ĥ* (*monarĥo*, *ĥemio*) Jacob implies that only in the Esperanto-derived system Ido have such forms been replaced by forms with *k*. As a matter of fact, such replacement (*monarko*, *kemio*) is now almost universal in Esperanto itself, through its normal processes of development. With respect to the system of "correlatives" in Esperanto, Jacob concludes that it "lacks the natural elements familiar to so many Europeans" and that it is "largely arbitrary and artificial." It might be pointed out that in the system (consisting of combinations of five stems *i-* 'some, any,' *ki-* 'what,' *ti-* 'that,' *ĉi-* 'all,' *neni-* 'no' with nine endings, *-a* 'kind,' *-al* 'reason,' *-am* 'time,' *-e* 'place,' *-el* 'manner,' *-es* 'one's,' *-o* 'thing,' *-om* 'quantity,' *-u* 'person') not all the elements are arbitrary: *ki-*, *ti-*, and *neni-* remind one of Indo-European interrogatives, demonstratives, and negatives; *-a* is the Esperanto adjective ending, *-e* the adverbial ending (limited here, it is true, to place), and *-o* the noun ending; *-es* reminds one of Germanic possessives. Interesting, likewise, is the fact that, far from feeling uncomfortable in the presence of these "artificialities," the users of the language have attempted to extend the system to other elements not originally included in it: from *alia* 'other' have been derived *alies* 'someone else's,' *alie* 'elsewhere,' and so on. There seems to be a certain advantage to having a large number of analogous forms made up from a small number of roots and affixes—the effort required to learn them is much less than that necessitated by a large number of unrelated forms. The chief objection seems to fall again on the esthetic side: they look "queer" and they are not immediately intelligible to people familiar with Latin. Jacob criticizes the variability (singular and plural, general and accusative) of the adjective in Esperanto: "this variability does not add to the clarity of the language"; objects to the plural ending *-j* /y/ as "inelegant and heavy," suggesting that *-i* be substituted for it; and objects to the use of the accusative: "it does in no way contribute to the clarity of the phrase except in inversion." Jacob does not realize that word-order, far from being "logical" or "natural," is just as highly conventional as the use of particular endings for number and case, and that for a language which is to be of maximum worth to peoples all over the world, the "normal" word orders of English and French are of little value, that the flexibility of order and reference obtained by the use of the plural and accusative for adjectives, the accusative for nouns, might very well compensate for the additional learning effort involved. It is likewise not true, at least unofficially, to say that the use of the accusative in Esperanto is "obligatory," although a writer who omitted it would certainly be considered stylistically deficient. The reference to the plural *-j* /y/ as "inelegant and heavy," if valid for Esperanto, would be equally valid for Classical Greek, where /oy/ endings are frequent. In criticizing specific vocabulary choices, and particularly some of the the results of the extremely liberal word-formational usages of Esperanto, Jacob makes much of accidental homonymy with words of different meaning in some of the West European languages. Accidental homonymy in a world-wide linguistic framework is unavoidable. Why should we be more seriously concerned when it strikes closer to our West European center? The form *fraŭlo* 'master' is obviously a back-formation from *fraŭlino* 'miss,' just as is *edzo* 'husband' from *edzino* 'wife,' and this in turn from a re-analyzed *kronprincedzino* 'crown princess' (< German *Kronprinzessin*). Such processes are "natural" in all ethnic languages. Why should they be forbidden in an artificial language? The free use of *mal-* 'direct opposite' (*malbona* 'bad,' *malbela* 'ugly,' etc.), the free use of "affixes" as independent roots (*eta* 'small'), the processes of compounding (even when they result in such "unfortunate" forms as *foresto* 'absence' not 'forest') are all devices which contribute to the vitality and flexibility of an auxiliary language. To restrict them on the grounds of unnaturalness is to confine the developmental processes of the international language within the same narrow tradition-bound framework as those of the ethnic languages. One of the chief advantages of an international language is that one cannot make a "mistake" in giving free rein to the normal analogizing tendencies: to limit the results of the analogizing process to those forms which happen to be sanctioned by tradition in the West European languages is to lose that advantage. Jacob introduces his commentary on Esperanto with the statement that "Esperanto is today the only artificial language which has been able to form and to maintain a mass movement [of the order of 100,000 practicing users]" and concludes with the remark that "Esperanto cannot be considered the solution of the problem of communication." Yet, except for the criticisms listed and commented on above, he gives no further justification for this conclusion. Esperanto (and a number of other candidates as well) seems to meet Jacob's own criteria for such a solution (listed in my comment on the Introduction, above). One can only conclude that for unstated reasons, Jacob personally prefers one of the other candidates.

How, then, do these other systems compare with Esperanto?

Ido (Chap. II) "started as a reformed Esperanto," the creation of Louis de Beaufront, Zamenhof's personal representative to the Délégation pour l'adoption d'une Langue Auxiliaire Internationale, formed in 1901 on the initiative of Léopold Leau, and including a number of well-known linguists (Baudouin de Courtenay, Otto Jespersen, and Hugo Schuchardt). The Délégation rendered its decision in 1907, and "decided to adopt in principle Esperanto, on account of its relative perfection, and of the many and varied applications which have been made of it," but with the proviso that "certain modifications" be made along the lines indicated by the project of Ido (de Beaufront's pseudonym). These modifications were designed to meet the objections to Esperanto (specified by Jacob) which I have cited and commented on above. The effect of the changes was to make the new language (in Jacob's words) "more immediately comprehensible and more natural in aspect."

A number of Jacob's specific statements with respect to Ido are misleading. For example, he refers to Ido grammars, dictionaries, and textbooks available immediately after the first world war as "the most complete works of their kind for any system of planned language." Esperanto works such as Eugen Wüster's *Enzyklopädisches Wörterbuch* (Leipzig, 1923– ; four volumes to date, *a-kor*), the *Plena·Vortaro de Esperanto* (Paris, 1930) by Grosjean-Maupin and others, and the *Plena Gramatiko* (Budapest, 1935) by Kalocsay and Waringhien, are at least as exhaustive as anything published in Ido.

The modifications of Esperanto, eventually incorporated into Ido, have two general tendencies: one, to make the language more natural, that is, more like the ethnic languages; and two, to make it more "logical," that is, to conform more rigorously to a predesigned system of derivation. Concessions to naturalness involved the introduction of digraphs *ch sh* (unit phonemes) *qu* /kw/, the use of *x* (a single symbol for two phonemes), relaxing of the penult accent rule to permit exceptions (last syllable of the infinitive: *pensár*, and third-from-the-last vowel in words ending in *iV*: *família*), variability (for number) of the article (*la* sg., *le* pl.), optional adjective ending *-a*, special rules of word order for S V O and for adjectives (since the "obligatory" use of the accusative and adjective agreement had been abolished). Adaptations in the direction of "logicality" involved the rule of "reversibility," stated by Courturat: "Every derivative must be *reversible*; that is to say, if one passes from one word to another of the same family in virtue of a certain rule, one must be able to pass inversely from the second to the first in virtue of a rule which is exactly the reverse of the preceding" (1907). From the verbal root *labor-* 'to work' one derives *laboro* 'works, working,' whence *laboristo* 'worker.' From *laboristo*, by successively removing the noun ending *-o* and the suffix *-ist-*, one arrives again at the root *labor-*. This principle seems to be subsumed by most linguists under the label "regular," and as such works just as well in Esperanto as in Ido. On the other hand, certain of the derivative forms in Ido are restricted in meaning: *richo* (noun from an adjective root) 'a rich person' (Esp. *riĉulo*). In Esperanto *riĉo* is multi-significant: "richness" (*riĉeco*), "riches" (*riĉaĵo*), 'rich person' (*riĉulo*), but can be made specific where the context makes it necessary (by using the forms indicated). In Ido, an attempt was made to make precision obligatory, in Esperanto it has always been optional. Many of the new affixes introduced into Ido have subsequently been adopted by Esperantists, but as permissible aids to precision, rather than as obligatory straitjackets. In practice, not even in Ido was the obligatory feature carried out. Critics of Ido, according to Jacob, have advanced the following points:

1. "In Ido the application of logic has led to a certain amount of artificial rigidity."
2. "the planned language should have an analytic conjugation" (*me vil protektar* instead of *me protektos* 'I will protect').
3. There is no suffix equivalent to *-ation*, and no direct derivation for desubstantive verbs (Ido *martel-ag-ar* = Esp. *martel-i* 'to hammer').
4. Ido derived forms are not "natural" enough (Ido *inspektisto* instead of **inspektoro*). This objection had been applied by Idists to Esperanto; apparently Ido did not go far enough in the direction of "naturalness" to satisfy everyone.

OCCIDENTAL (Chap. III), put forward in 1922 by Edgar de Wahl, is a more independent effort than Ido, although its author was acquainted with both Esperanto and Ido. It attempts to meet the fourth objection to both Esperanto and Ido, listed above, and goes very far in the direction of naturalness. Instead of creating a system of derivation, it attempts to abstract from the international vocabulary its own system of derivation. It tries not to alter in any way forms already existent in the ethnic languages. Immediate comprehensibility for those who are familiar with these languages is a principal aim. But it cannot create regularity—a prime requisite in an auxiliary language—where regularity does not exist. Jacob concludes that "to use Occidental correctly a fairly wide knowledge of the international words of the European languages is required." But, if such a language is to be of value outside Europe, or, for that matter, even to most Europeans, it should be so designed as to eliminate the necessity for such knowledge. An artificial language should be designed to function as a SECOND language; if its use presupposes the knowledge of other languages, it is not fulfilling its function. Although de Wahl's project met with little success, his ideas were influential, not only on subsequent languages (such as Novial), but also on the further development of Esperanto and Ido. His idea that an international language "should be an organic, autonomous entity, living and growing according to its own laws, harmonizing and assimilating new elements" had been one of Zamenhof's guiding principles. But all post-Esperanto international languages, including Occidental, have been constantly subject to personal tinkering by their individual authors, so that they were not given the opportunity for such development as de Wahl prescribes.

NOVIAL (Chap. IV), advanced in 1928 by Otto Jepersen, constituted a new synthesis, based on the same general principles as previous international languages, but incorporating Jespersen's ideas on analytic linguistic structure, which he believed essentially "superior" to the agglutinative type. With respect to its general make-up, Jacob concludes that "Novial can be said to be midway between the extremes of naturalness and autonomy."

INTERLINGUA or Latino sine flexione (Chap. V), initiated in 1903 by Giuseppe Peano, represents an effort somewhat off the path beaten by Esperanto, Ido, Occidental, and Novial, in the sense that its grammatical structure is based directly on that of a single ethnic language, Latin; but its vocabulary, like that of the others, admits all elements common to the languages of Europe. Latin flexion is reduced to a minimum: only the noun plurals end in *-s*, and even this may be omitted where some other word indicates plurality. For all other forms the Latin stem is used. Grammatical constructions are indicated by conventions of word-order and by the use of particles. Derivation is "natural," again in the sense that no derivative may be used which tradition (Latin or international) does not sanction: "Peano suggests the frequent reading of Interlingua literature for the acquisition of a correct and good style." Here again, as with Occidental, the other extremely naturalistic international language, one cannot construct new forms freely, and so one of the great advantages of an auxiliary language is lost.

Having concluded his brief sketches of Esperanto, Ido, Occidental, Novial, and Interlingua, the only international auxiliary languages, out of the hundreds that have been put forward, which "claim any following in different countries and a literature and magazines of their own," Jacob, in Part II of his book, reviews comparatively the chief points at issue among the various international languages.

In Part III (Chaps. XIII and XIV), he discusses the relationship of the problem of an international system of technical nomenclature to the broader problem of au international auxiliary language.

The International Federation of the National Standardizing Associations (ISA), founded in 1926, received a proposal in May 1934, from the Soviet-Russian Standardizing Commission (SRSC), that work should be started on an international code for the technical sciences. A full report on the problem was presented in September 1934 at a meeting of ISA in Stockholm, and was unanimously accepted by representatives of nineteen national standardizing associations. The SRSC formed a special committee for the preparation of a code project, submitted in June 1935. It embodies the following principles:

1. a Latin-based alphabet, supplemented by devices such as those of Esperanto or Czech (*ĉ* or *č*)
2. international root words, common and technical
3. an Esperanto-based affix-system
4. an Esperanto-based grammar

The discussion of this project has been interrupted, first by the second world war, and now the "cold war." The problems are the same, in general, as those for the various proposed international languages, and the final solution will be found in one of those languages into which all internationally agreed-on technical vocabulary will be incorporated.

The last chapter is devoted to the work of the International Auxiliary Language Association (IALA), founded in 1924, at the instance of the Committee on International Language of the International Research Council. IALA has sponsored a continuing series of experiments and studies on various aspects of the language problem. It has assumed from the beginning that no national language could meet the need, and has devoted itself to a program with two main objects: (1) "to obtain agreement on one definite planned language system and to obtain official sanction for that language," and (2) "to secure the general acceptance of the sanctioned language which would include its teaching in the schools." It has attempted "to build upon the fund of experience and knowledge furnished by the languages which have been tested by time and use." Edward L. Thorndike determined, in experiments carried on at Columbia Univeristy, that "on the whole, with expenditures of from ten to a hundred hours, the achievement [presumably of English-speakers] in a synthetic language [Esperanto in this case] will be from five to fifteen times that in a natural language, according to the difficulty of the latter."

Among works sponsored by IALA are the following: *Totality*, by Edward Sapir (Language Monograph No. 6, 1930); *The Expression of the Ending-point Relation in English, French, and German*, by Edward Sapir and Morris Swadesh, ed. by Alice V. Morris (Language Monograph No. 10, 1932); *Indication: A Study of Demonstratives, Articles, and Other "Indicators,"* by William Edward Collinson (Language Monograph No. 17, 1937); *Cosmopolitan Conversation: The Language Problems of International Conferences*, by Herbert N. Shenton (New York, 1934); and *Semantic Frequency List for English, French, German, and Spanish*, by Helen S. Eaton (Chicago, 1940). For a time IALA entertained the idea of selecting one of the international languages (probably Esperanto) as a base language "from which a definitive form of language might be developed." Since the Second World War, however, that idea has been abandoned in favor of a plan of working anew with the basic elements from which these languages have been constructed. The present plan is to create various type-languages, embodying the various conflicting principles, with a view toward subsequent testing in practice to determine which type may eventually prove to be most desirable. The vocabulary, however, is now to be selected only from elements common to English, French, Italian, Spanish, and Portuguese (eliminating German and Russian, which have figured in some of the established languages).

IALA's work will certainly play an important part in the ultimate determination of the nature of the language to be accepted as the international auxiliary language.

In the opinion of the reviewer, however, the chief difficulty in the way of final solution of the problem has been a political and social one.

Until the world is ready, no amount of hashing and rehashing of minuscule details of the various shemes will affect in the slightest their ultimate acceptance. When the time is ripe, any one of the established schemes—say Esperanto, the earliest of them, or Novial, the most recent—will prove structurally adequate to meet the demands put upon it. A scheme which has had wide practical use, and in which large technical vocabularies, internationally agreed upon, are already available, will have a great advantage. In the meantime, cross-fertilization has taken place on a large scale; and once the factor of competition has been eliminated, the language chosen will be able to benefit from the past experience of all the projects (as Esperanto, for example, has already benefited by the criticisms of Ido, Experantido, and numerous other schemes). When the final choice is made, the problems will be practical ones, and in the face of these, the theoretical divergences, which now seem so important, will evaporate.

REFERENCE NOTE

For recent comment by a leading linguist, see Martinet (1946, 1949, 1952). Pei (1958) is an optimistic advocate rebutted by a participant in the IALA (Gode, 1958). On the general topic, see Burney (1962), Carroll (1953, pp. 125-132), Cohen (1956a, Part 4, chap. 4), and Jacob (1946). For the history of the movement and the nature of some of the systems, see Brinton (1889), Guerard (1922), Jespersen (1928). Sapir (1931e) and Shenton, Sapir, Jespersen (1931) are vigorous arguments. That some degree of practical success has been achieved is shown by Griggs and Rulon (1953), among others.

For Basic English as a solution to the problem of international communication, see Ogden (1930, etc.) Carroll (1953), and Whorf's critique in his article on pp. 129-141 of this book. That article, and others by Whorf (e.g., 1942) represent another approach to international communication and understanding.

References not in the general bibliography:

BRINTON, DANIEL G.
1889. *Aims and Traits of a World-Language*. New York.

BRUGMANN, KARL, and AUGUST LESKIEN
1907. *Zur Kritik der Künstlichen Weltsprachen*. Strassburg.

BURNEY, PIERRE
1962. *Les Langues internationales* ("Que Sais-je?" Le Point des Connaissances Actuelles, No. 968.) Paris: Presses Universitaires de France.

COURTURAT, LOUIS
1907. *Étude sur la dérivation en Esperanto*. Paris.

GODE, A.
1958. Review of M. Pei, *One Language for the World and How to Achieve It*. *Science*, *28*: 194.

GRIGGS, T., and P. J. RULON
1953. *International Language for Aviation: Instrument Flight*. Cambridge. [Cf. Joshua Whatmough, *Language*. London: Secher & Warburg; New York: St. Martin, 1956. (Reprinted, New York: Mentor [209], 1957.)]

GUERARD, A. L.
1922. *A Short History of the International Language Movement*. London.

JACOB, H. (ED.)
1946. *On the Choice of a Common Language*. London. D. Dobson

JESPERSEN, OTTO
1928. *An International Language*. London: G. Allen & Unwin.

MARTINET, ANDRÉ

1946. "La Linguistique et les langues artificielles." *Word, 2:* 37-47.

1949. Comments. *Actes du VIe Congrès Internationale des Linguistes (1948).* Paris: Hincksieck. Pp. 93-112, 585-600.

1952. Review of *Interlingua-English: Interlingua. Word, 8:* 163-167.

NEURATH, OTTO

1936. *International Picture Language, the First Rules of Isotype.* London: Kegan Paul, Trench and Trübner.

OGDEN, C. K.

1930a. *Basic English: A General Introduction with Rules and Grammar.* London: Kegan Paul, Trench and Trübner.

1930b. *The Basic Vocabulary: A Statistical Analysis, with Special Reference to Substitution and Translation.* London: Kegan Paul, Trench and Trübner.

1931. *Debabelization.* London: Kegan Paul, Trench and Trübner.

1932. *The Basic Dictionary, Being the 7,500 Most Useful Words with Their Equivalents in Basic English, for the Use of Translators, Teachers, and Students.* London: Kegan Paul, Trench and Trübner.

1934. *The System of Basic English.* New York: Harcourt, Brace.

1935. *Counter-offensive; An Exposure of Certain Misrepresentations of Basic English.* Cambridge, England, and Peiping. [Appendix: monograph by M. West *et al.* A Critical Examination of Basic English. 1934.]

PEI, MARIO

1958. *One Language for the World and How to Achieve It.* New York. [Reviewed, A. Gode, *Science*, 1958, *28:* 194.]

SAPIR, EDWARD

1931e. The Function of an International Auxiliary Language. *Psyche, 11:* 4-15. [Also in H. Shenton *et al., International Communication.* London: 1931. Pp. 65-94; and David G. Mandelbaum (Ed.), *Selected Writings of Edward Sapir in Language, Culture, and Personality.* Berkeley and Los Angeles: University of California Press, 1949. Pp. 110-121.]

SHENTON, H., EDWARD SAPIR, OTTO JESPERSEN

1931. *International Communication.* London. Kegan Paul, Trench and Trübner.

TROUBETSKOY, N. S.

1939. Wie soll das Lautsystem einer Künstlichen internationalen Hilfsprache beschaffen sein? *Travaux du Cercle Linguistique de Prague, 8:* 5-21.

part IX

RELATIONSHIPS IN TIME AND SPACE

Introduction

In dealing with languages in much of the world, anthropology often must infer past processes of change from their present results. To a large extent, such inference is part of the place of linguistics in historical anthropology. The progress of Indo-European studies has permitted attention in European anthropology to quite refined culture-historical inferences. The state of work in most of the world is such that anthropology continues to focus on the initial questions of the facts of relationship and classification.

The work of classification entails a conceptual model shared by all of anthropology. Underlying it is the fundamental question: How are resemblances and differences among peoples (their cultural, racial, linguistic characteristics) to be interpreted? The answers ultimately become part of a general theory of the nature and dynamics of human life, but the first task is sorting and mapping, ordering the universe with which one is dealing. Thus, while historical linguistics is often undertaken for its intrinsic interest, it also provides essential context for other work. To take a prominent example, linguistic classifications enter into determining historical independence of cases in cross-cultural studies.

The classic anthropological approach to ordering has been to begin in terms of time and space. The work involves distinguishing four kinds of source for resemblances and relating these to the principal kinds of classification of units that show resemblance, always of course within some specified frame of reference.

In terms of source, resemblances either are due to a historical connection or are not. If not due to a historical connection, resemblances may be *generic* (inherent in all units within the frame of analysis) or *convergent* (due to chance, because of the limits of possible divergence, or some recurrent positive tendency such as sound symbolism or a functional correlation of traits). If due to historical connection, resemblances may be *genetic* (continuously transmitted to the units in question from a common ancestor) or *diffusional* (transmitted from one unit to another subsequent to the period of any common ancestor). Work based on this conception of resemblances proceeds by successively sorting out, first, the historical from the nonhistorical resemblances, and, second, the genetic from the diffusional resemblances, genetic classification being fundamental to other lines of historical work.

Turning to kinds of classification, a *generic* classification would, of course, be equivalent to identifying the units in question as properly members of the same universe of discourse. It would precede the usual kinds of historical work, either as warrant for their application within the generic classification or to provide a unit for classification within a larger universe of discourse. (Thus, a generic classification of all natural languages might serve to exclude questions as to the place of logically constructed languages or to characterize natural languages in relation to forms of communication among other species.) A *genetic classification* is based exclusively upon resemblances due to a genetic historical connection whatever the location of the units in space and time may be. (Thus it may lead to the inference that a migration has taken place.) An *areal classification* considers resemblances due to either kind of historical connection, provided there is proximity in space and time. A *typological classification* may consider any resemblances, without regard to historical connection or to proximity (except insofar as such must be considered when seeking a representative sample of types). In effect, genetic classification sorts out lines of historical connection that converge in the past; areal classification, lines of historical connection that converge in the present; typological classification, lines of convergence of whatever sort.

The study of relationships in space and time and the study of processes of change (Part VIII) are, of course, interdependent. One can say that, in sociolinguistic terms, genetic classification deals with the results of the weakening or loss of contact among speech communities once intimate if not identical; areal classification deals with the results of the establishment and maintenance of contact among speech communities, even if once remote or independent; and typological classification deals with the results of the functional as well as historical interdependence, either of linguistic traits among themselves or of linguistic traits and traits common to some or all speech communities.

It should be noted that any diffusional resemblance might be taken as defining an area, that of its distribution, but that one ordinarily speaks simply of diffusion and borrowing, and introduces the concept of *area* when there is coincidence of several traits, contiguity has been maintained, and more than two groups are involved. Such an area may pertain only to one sector—a phonetic, morphological, syntactic, or lexicosemantic area—or to all. And while the term is most often used for the notable case in which the languages are originally independent, logically it also covers the mapping of dialects and contiguous subgroups whose provenience is originally the same parent speech community. The degree and type of similarity among dialects and related languages is generally a function both of retentions and interinfluence.

These types of resemblance and classification are easier to distinguish conceptually than in practice, and the history of anthropology and linguistics has been marked by considerable controversy in these regards. (A good deal of it, especially on the American scene, is discussed in the articles in this part and in the article on Kroeber in Part X.) Controversy has flurried over criteria, over what should count as evidence of the criteria, and over the interpretation of particular facts of resemblance as belonging to one or another class. Certain general points of special pertinence to anthropological work may be noted here.

First, typological resemblance may have historical significance, but if so, one is using typology heuristically for other purposes, and must go on to invoke the criteria proper to one of the other kinds of classification.

Second, genetic and areal classification and the proof of genetic and diffusional resemblance are each interdependent. To establish a resemblance as genetic implies elimination of the possibility that it is diffusional *and the converse*. Positive evidence is needed in either case. Too much ink has been spilled in the senseless cause of trying to place the burden of proof solely on one or the other.

Third, in genetic classification it is important not to confuse *proof* with *establishment*. To establish a relationship is to provide the systematic analysis of resemblances which makes possible reconstruction of the proto language in some detail, including details of protocultural vocabulary. Even in the most favorable circumstances, the job of establishment is never complete, as continuing Indo-European studies show. The theoretical requirement for proof of relationship, on the other hand, is simply that chance and borrowing be ruled out as sources of the resemblances in question, leaving genetic connection as the only probable explanation. Controversy sometimes involves the mistake of requiring what is in effect some degree of establishment before the *fact* (*i.e.*, proof) of relationship can be asserted.

Fourth, the validity and value of research in such a historical field is cumulative, both within linguistic work and in the relation between it and other lines of anthropological evidence. The net is often stronger than the threads of which it is woven, for in history anything is possible, but not everything is probable. Possibilities must reinforce each other, and the whole must make a consistent story. Thus cooperation between branches of anthropology on historical problems is essential.

Fifth, the work of historical anthropology, including that of linguistics, is largely in terms of accumulated experience and rules of thumb. Little systematic research on the theoretical and empirical bases of work in an area such as, for example, genetic relationship has been undertaken. Besides its own intellectual interest and contribution to the solution of particular problems, such basic research would offer help in unifying historical anthropology by making generally known how results and methods of different lines of work were grounded, and by exploring the relationships among them. Critical discussion and exchange of methods, as well as of results, among the different branches of historical anthropology would add a unity in logical foundations to their existing unity in ultimate goals. (On linguistic and archaeological parallels in method, note Hymes, 1958b, and Rowe, 1959.)

In "Linguistics as an Instrument of Prehistory," Swadesh speaks to the need for cooperation in prehistoric research, especially among linguists and archaeologists. After tackling the problem of linguistic mapping, much neglected in American anthropology although of profound effect in the communication of results, Swadesh turns to the three types of linguistic result of most immediate interest to prehistory, genetic classification, evidence of diffusion, and reconstruction of vocabulary. He discusses criteria of proof and inference, the use of lexicostatistics, and chain relationships, and concludes with recommendations for research with comparative study as its primary purpose.

The comparative method, as developed in Indo-European work, is often cited as the standard for historical work in other language families. In an essay written especially for the volume, one of the leading scholars in the Indo-European field, Paul Thieme, sets forth the principal features of the comparative method as he practices it, especially in relation to the reconstruction of semantic systems.

Note the probabilistic and in a sense, experimental, nature of the conclusions; the weight given morphological resemblances; the basis of proof in the arbitrary (noniconic) relation between linguistic signs and their meaning; the elimination of chance and borrowing as explanations; and the interdependence of semantic and phonetic correspondences. The importance of systemic and cumulative evidence in proof appears throughout, not least in the concluding review of some of the characteristic semantic systems or fields that can be reconstructed for Proto-Indo-European.

In his explication of Bloomfield's work in comparative Algonquian, Hockett gives a stimulating account, not only of principles of comparative method, but also of the importance of the anthropological contribution to it. Although comparative work was hailed as one of the triumphs of the nineteenth century, dispute persists as to its interest, generality, and validity. To the historically oriented anthropologist, its interest is clear. American anthropology has already provided a striking demonstration of its applicability to unwritten languages (Sapir, 1931c). Ultimate demonstration of its generality and validity depends upon work in language families in parts of the world in which anthropologists have primary interest. Comparative work in the New World and in Africa, for example, offers a large number of independent cases (independent at the time-depth of Indo-European). In addition, anthropological needs for progress in so much of the world in the initial steps of prehistoric linguistics may provide a stimulus for effective extension of the depth of comparative work in time as well as in space. Extensions of horizon as to genetic relationship in recent years have come principally from anthropologically oriented linguists (see the article by Kroeber and its refererence note on pp. 654-663).

Note Hockett's general scheme of types of research with three types of analysis cross-cutting three of method. The scheme, as Hockett remarks, is generally applicable in anthropology. Necessary modifications would be to recognize an additional mode of analysis, one that states changes in speech habits from one point in *space* to another, and also an additional form of comparative method, one that extrapolates in space as well as in time (as in reconstructing features of a dialect or language from knowledge of other forms of speech contemporaneous with it or providing a general framework for describing related dialects). Since research involving space and research involving time may be interdependent (see Stankiewicz, 1957), the two may properly be linked under a single heading. As has been implied, "comparative" remains an adequate term for both within the category of method, but the category of analysis poses a problem. Strictly speaking, Hockett's stated definition of "diachronic" properly excludes its "diatopic" counterpart, while his definition of "synchronic" improperly implies the inclusion of "syntopic" as well. Perhaps "diachronic" and "synchronic" may still serve as general terms, if it is understood that they do so by metonymy, as does "man" when used for both men and women.

Some aspects of the use of glottochronology are discussed by Swadesh in his articles in this part. Gudschinsky here presents the best exposition available of how the glottochronologic test list is applied in a given case.

There is no concise summary of the extensive and growing literature on this controversial subject. A few points must be made here to supplement Gudschinsky's account. First, the revised, 100-item list (see Swadesh, 1955) should now be used, replacements, if needed, being taken from a 100-item supplementary list... Second, the cognates (better, "glottochronologic sames") to be counted are a special subset of all true cognates between the languages concerned, namely, those retained in the same common meanings. (Thus, English *head* [Old English *heafod*] is a true cognate to German *haupt*, but the two do not count for the purpose in hand; on the test lists, *head* would be paired with the present-day common German term for that meaning, *Kopf*.) Third, the time depths obtained are usually *minimum* estimates (on the factors involved, see Swadesh, 1955; Hymes, 1960a). In a family of languages, the greatest divergence time between any pair is the best estimate of the time depth of the whole. Fourth, the various factors that make the time depths statistical estimates having ranges of error (a point well stressed by Gudschinsky) are such that the range of error drastically reduces the value of results outside the span between 500 and 2500 years.

Fifth, the results can even so provide only a rough chronology, for a recent study (Bergsland and Vogt, 1962) has shown that the tendency for basic vocabulary to change at a constant rate is not universal. The glottochronologic and lexicostatistic studies can still give some estimates of unique value not possible by other means (cf. Kroeber, 1955), but it is more than ever necessary to check the results, as Swadesh has said, with other lines of evidence in reaching conclusions as to a particular case.

The Bergsland and Vogt study underscores two aspects of the present state of glottochronology: the need for further basic research in both the theory and application of the method as a linguistic instrument, and the need to recognize more clearly and to investigate the *socio*linguistic character of the phenomena involved. Clearly the rate of retention is not independent of sociocultural context. The clustering of rates of retention in a good many cases, on the one hand, and the existence of outright exceptions, on the other (such as perfectly conservative Icelandic and rapidly deviating pidginized Neo-Melanesian), show that the tendency to uniform retention is the empirical manifestation of a complex of underlying factors, a "near universal" of the sort described by Greenberg (1957c, pp. 86 ff.) and by Osgood (in Greenberg, 1963).

The need for basic research has implications beyond glottochronology itself, for the method is novel only in the explicitness of its assumptions and procedures. Much of historical linguistics, especially genetic classification and subgrouping, has used a concept of basic vocabulary essentially the same as that manifested in the glottochronologic list and has implicitly assumed a correlation between degree of lexical divergence and time elapsed since separation. Moreover, the semantic difficulties of using the list cross-culturally inhere in any attempt at standardized, objective study of lexical relationship and rates of change.

At the same time, the need for continued applications remains—that is why the article by Gudschinsky has been selected for this part. Applications not only may give useful results in the particular historical case, but supply the extended base of empirical data needed to refine the method, regarding the behavior of test-list items, the criteria for choosing test-list equivalents, the fit of results with other lines of evidence, and the sociolinguistic factors affecting retention.

Two byproducts of glottochronology and lexicostatistics should be noted. First, the comparative study of the semantic aspects of the lists, synchronically and diachronically, is proving of considerable interest for the light it can shed on lexicosemantic universals and on the semantic habits of particular language groups (cf. Kroeber 1961; Hymes 1960e; Weinreich, 1963). Second, the test list has been found useful, not only as an eliciting device, but also as an instrument in a variety of sociolinguistic studies (see Hymes, 1962b, pp. 136, 140).

In "Diffusional Cumulation and Archaic Residue as Historical Explanations," Swadesh explicates a famous dispute in American anthropology and proceeds to resolve it by analyzing a documented case and generalizing the result. Such basic research, testing New World problems against Indo-European data where the answer is known, is all too rare. The paper provides additional insight into processes of change and the application of the comparative method to the results of these processes. An important point is the treatment of the linguistic issue as one case in the general problem of culture history.

While recognizing that linguistic data must be interpreted in relation to the map, if their full contribution to historical anthropology is to be realized (cf. Kroeber, 1955), Voegelin shows that the data must first be analyzed in linguistic terms, i.e., in terms of genetic classification, including subgrouping. An examination of five New World cases brings out various ways in which the historical picture may be obscured or clarified, depending on whether or not proper linguistic classification precedes attempts at correlation with geography. The lesson holds for other external factors, such as race and culture. At the same time Voegelin points out the value of taking area as a specialized point of departure, granted the necessary preliminaries, a challenge which has yet to be taken up in the New World.

Whereas Swadesh stressed the recognition of archaic residue, Emeneau emphasizes the occurrence of diffusional cumulation, demonstrating particularly the diffusion of features of morphology and syntax significant enough to constitute a grammatical linguistic area. It is important to remember that a balance can be struck, since Swadesh's argument was not to deny diffusion, but to show that it could be discriminated from genetic retention, and since Emeneau's masterful exposition of diffusion presupposes that the pertinent genetic groups and traits have been identified. The inference of prolonged and intimate contact which must result from such a demonstration of grammatical diffusion must be of considerable interest to the general study of culture history in any area.

Kroeber raises some general issues of taxonomy in anthropology, combining a retrospective view with prospects for the future. Note especially the emphasis on the need for systematic classification, as well as the characteristic interest in quantitative approaches, and the hope that methods of typology may give results of historical significance. Here Kroeber puts his finger on a crux. In genetic and areal classification, the great need is more work. The work may be difficult, but the significance of the questions and answers is clear. In typological classification, the work is often relatively straightforward, and, in any case, the great need is clearer significant questions and answers. A good deal of current activity is limited to ways of cataloguing data and to the particular insights that can be gained from contrastive studies of two or a few languages. Both are useful, but the typological tradition of the nineteenth century flourished because it spoke to major theoretical concerns. It was indeed the great tradition of general linguistics in its time, although the fact has been forgotten, together with its underpinnings in concepts of evolution and psychology. It may be that the revitalized anthropological interest in cultural evolution, cognitive psychology, and general linguistics will nourish a revitalized linguistic typology as well.

Linguistics as an Instrument of Prehistory 60

MORRIS SWADESH

1. *THE PROBLEM*

Prehistoric research today benefits from an accumulation of techniques for discovering, correlating and interpreting data about the past. Each of them has its value and some are quite remarkable, but it is well to remember that no one technique can begin to compare in effectiveness with a balanced combination of all research means. Since only scattered small fragments of the past are preserved in the ground or reflected in the living cultural and physical forms of the present, it is necessary to bring to bear every possible line of evidence on each problem of prehistory. Specialists in each field of research should try to fight free from any tendency to limit their efforts to a favorite procedure or to close their minds to the clues derived from other forms of study and from other disciplines. However, open-minded receptiveness to the findings of other specialists is not sufficient, because, even when one wants to know what has been achieved in other fields, it is often practically impossible to find out, short of suspending one's own research for a period of years while one learns the language, the literature and the complex customs of what is reported and what is left unreported among the practicants of each speciality. Hence, what we mostly need is for each of us to develop a full awareness of what his discipline has to contribute to prehistory, to concentrate on essential problems and to learn to translate out of the specialists' dialect into the general lingua franca of prehistory. In the present paper, we propose to discuss, we hope in clear language, the potential contribution of linguistics to prehistory, on the basis of the present state of development of this field, and the possibilities of further increasing its value.

There are three main ways in which linguistics can illuminate prehistory: (a) by establishing facts concerning the common origin and subsequent divergence of languages, implying the earlier unity and subsequent separations of peoples; (b) by discovering diffused features (of phonetics, structure or vocabulary) among languages which bear evidence of prehistoric culture contacts; and (c) by reconstructing the vocabulary of old stages of languages so as to bring out suggestions of the physical environment and content of prehistoric cultures. In each of these connections, matters of time and place are of prime importance both as intrinsic facts and as points of coordination between the linguistic and other lines of evidence. For all three aspects—time, place and cultural fact—it is essential to have an evaluation of the reliability, so that users of the real or supposed evidence can distinguish the barely possible from the highly probable and in general to note the different degrees of probability needed to guide them in drawing conclusions from the totality of evidence.

2. *LINGUISTIC MAPPING*

If there is any part of linguistics which archeologists are aware of, it is the matter of classification as represented on maps showing genetic classification. These they evidently consult as a routine procedure, but their use of them is of necessity a hit-or-miss proposition. Sometimes the linguistic relationships prove to be enlightening with respect to archeologic problems and sometimes not, so the scholar as a rule uses the data when it fits and disregards it when it does not. He assumes that there is an obscure culturological complication which explains the apparent contradiction or that the linguistic classification is wrong. However, in many cases the only real problem is that the map does not show time depth or shows it in inadequate fashion. Related languages which were a single tongue a thousand years ago may be shown in the same way as languages which have been separate for over five thousand. Maps which attempt to distinguish different degrees of linguistic divergence often do so with an uncertain and undefined scale of value or use a representational technique that is not readily grasped by the non-linguist. The problem of adequate determination of time depth has to be discussed apart; here we offer a few thoughts, not necessarily original, on how the facts may be shown.

If one wishes to make a map readily usable by the non-linguistic prehistorian, it is necessary to base it upon a definite conception of time depth or at least on a clear notion of linguistic divergence, which is the linguist's means of inferring time depth. The scale may be based on estimated minimum centuries of separation or on such general degrees of divergence as close, distant and remote, or on an equivalent differentiation of language groups into "families" (close relationship), "Stocks" (distant) and "phyla" (remote).

One then selects a mapping technique to show such degrees. For example, one may represent each phylym with a distinctive color, differentiate stocks of each phylum by a distinctive hachure shown over the phylum color, and indicate the families by outline boundaries. Of course, in some cases the area of the family may be divided, but this will happen less often than in the case of phyla and stocks. As we shall see, setting up degrees of relation, if accurately done, is certain to run into the problem of overlap. Perhaps this can be shown on the map by the crossing of colors, hachures and boundaries by some other special handling of the ambiguous areas. Up to now maps have generally avoided the problem of overlap, either arbitrarily to avoid difficulties in mapping or because linguists have not known how to evaluate it.

Instead of trying to show all the levels of classification on the map itself, it may be more convenient to indicate only the lowest level of grouping and to supply the rest of the scheme in the map legend. If one wishes to show smaller gradations of degrees of relationship, such as those estimated in "minimum centuries," with all the complexity of interlocking connections, one form of representation which is simple enough to be included in a map legend or in an accompanying key, is the divergence diagram. As an illustration we offer a diagram of Amerindian relations insofar as the author's present research permits defining them. Each linguistic group having an internal divergence up to 50 mc. (minimum centuries) by lexico-statistic estimate is enclosed in a box. The box is subdivided by means of a broken line if the group has discrete divisions separated from each other at their point of greatest similiarity by 31-40 mc. The maximum internal divergence, in minimum centuries, is written below the name within the box. Next to each other are placed the boxes representing linguistic groups which at their point of greatest similarity have a separation of 51-60 mc. from each other. Where the nearest affinity of a group is even more remote, falling between 61 and 70 mc. an additional broken line is interposed. Even more remote relations could be shown, if necessary, by adopting still other symbols. If the relationships prove too complicated at some point to be diagrammed, presumably a few additional notes could be added or some reduction may be made in what the diagram attempts to show. In the accompanying example, [omitted here], the fact that only the points of greatest affinity are shown is a simplification adopted to prevent excessive complication.

The use of the diagram in connection with a map can be facilitated by using the same identifying symbols, for example letters of the alphabet, on both. Insofar as possible, one should try to make top, bottom, right and left of the diagram correspond with the location of the groups on the map. Repeating the colors and hachures used on the map in the diagram will also help.

During our efforts to define linguistic relations at all levels, we have sometimes been asked by archeologists specializing in recent time horizons as to the value of the more remote connections. Those who concern themselves with "early man," on the other hand, require the data of ancient relationships and particularly need a clear demarcation of these from the more recent. The general rule must be that the prehistorian needs linguistic information for all periods back to the horizon of his particular problem plus one additional time stage, the latter being necessary to clarify the background. Since all time depths make up the total body of prehistory, comparative linguistics must study all periods, insofar as the present development of the science admits, and must at the same time bend a portion of its efforts toward devising means of penetrating to farther horizons.

3. *PROVING COMMON ORIGIN*

The principal requirement for good linguistic mapping is of course satisfactory linguistic classification. And logically basic to this is the matter of proving common origin. However, the fact is that in many cases the genetic connection of languages is so obvious that proving it is not a problem. Ordinarily, two languages which have separated say two thousand years ago still have so much common vocabulary, general structure and specific morphologic elements that even a layman would know they are related. If one or both of them have undergone unusually great phonetic changes, it may require the insight of a practiced comparative linguist to recognize the cognate forms but for him they do not remain long hidden. If phonetic and morphologic change has been unusually small, the relation may be obvious for up to five or six thousand years. With greater effects of change and with greater time periods, the fact of relationship may still be fairly obvious if the comparativist has the good fortune to have available for study a large number of languages with interlocking relationship. Because of variable factors—affecting principally amount of phonetic and structural change and the number and pattern of interlocking relationship—a classification like that of Powell and his associates is uneven in scale, failing to note separations of 3000 years in a few cases and recognizing others up to about 6000 years of time depth. It is convenient to have a methodology for resolving doubtful cases.

The most powerful technique for proving relationship in difficult cases would appear to be the systematic search for points of greatest concordance among the totality of languages. Where we cannot easily convince ourselves of the common origin of two languages or linguistic groups, we can look for other entities more closely related to each until we have built up a series of links involving unquestionable relationship, finally drawing our conclusion on the principle that languages which have a common origin with the same language must have the same relationship with each other.

Where there are fairly great divergences in the chain of relationship, leaving a certain amount of doubt, it is helpful to set about building up a comparative dictionary. A collection of evident cognates linking various languages in the total set may add up to convincing proof of common origin. This was the method used by Sapir in demonstrating the Hokan phylym to the satisfaction of most comparative linguists. However, since a few insist that the number of cognates is insufficient or that the presumed proto-language is insufficiently reconstructed phonologically, it is well to examine the matter of the quantitative requirements of proof.

It has been asserted that "phonetic laws" and not sheer quantity of resemblances demonstrate linguistic relationship. This is a half truth that requires clarification. It is of course true that comparative linguistics requires that supposed cognates (words or affixes of common origin going back to the common period of related languages), in order to be accepted as real ones, must show correspondences of their component phonemes that are consistent with a unified and realistic theory of phonological development. Nevertheless, there has to be a scientific determination of the number of instances needed to prove the phonological theory in its totality and in its parts. Sapir's comparisons were strictly based on a conception of historic phonology and he reconstructed that of Hokan in general and even with some minor details; the doubt cannot then be of the nature of the proof but of the amount. Since the first essential is to eliminate the chance factor (see below for the question of diffusional similarities), we need to calculate the number of agreements which might be contributed by sheer chance and still fit the phonological assumptions of the reconstruction. This can be done by taking into account the number of phonemes in each of the compared languages and their rules of combination into syllables and morphemes. We also need a criterion as to how far the actual cases have to exceed the chance factor to guarantee within reason against the complicating factor of the fluctuation of chance. This problem has been solved at least in a preliminary way (for example, see Swadesh, 1956a). The general prehistorian can therefore be reasonably confident of genetic connections when he knows that they have met objective tests, as well as in the cases where the time depth of the relationship is too limited to create the problem.

There has been much discussion of whether common vocabulary or common structure is the proper basis of proving common origin. This led Hymes (1955, 1956b) to the idea of a technique for calculating chance in the sheer order of elements in the word, whereby it is possible to prove common origin beyond reasonable doubt by structure alone in many cases. In the instances covered by the experiments, the matter could at the same time be proved by vocabulary. This confirms what linguistic science would lead us to expect, that common origin is reflected for long periods both in vocabulary and structure. There may be some structures that lend themselves less well to mathematical proofs than others, just as the phonetic aspect is variable in this respect. Nevertheless, the existence of two separate techniques greatly increases the security and considerably extends the time depths and the number of specific cases that can be covered.

How far back can we trace linguistic connections with reasonable certainty? If in some areas the bulk of the comparative linguists confine themselves to problems belonging to the last five or six thousand years of time depth, this is only because of personal predilections and established areas of research. There can be no doubt that there are already successful probings of time depths far greater than 5000 years, possibly up to 15,000, and that even more can be achieved by a systematic and careful application of already known techniques.

We have so far omitted specific mention of the complicating factor of borrowed elements, whether of lexicon or structure, which may sometimes give the superficial appearance of common origin between two languages. This problem can generally be met by distinguishing levels of stability in language material. Minor details of morphology and "cultural" vocabulary are more easily borrowed than broad structural features and "basic" vocabulary. Therefore, if the resemblances between two languages lie primarily in the area of what is readily diffused, the relationship must be due to borrowing; if it is primarily in the area of the most stable, it must be due to common origin. Often enough one finds both types of similarity, and sometimes along with them two different sets of phonological correspondences which permit us to distinguish what is due to common origin from the over-lay of later borrowing. There is a need for much careful study of this problem, to improve our capacity for judging specific cases.

4. *GENETIC CLASSIFICATION*

The main service of comparative linguistics to prehistory is not simply asserting the common origin of languages but defining the degree of their divergence and relating it to two variables, time and separation. Time is a variable related to divergence in the sense that, under like circumstances, the longer the time the greater the divergence. Separation is variable in that it has different degrees of completeness from little more than zero to essentially complete; if parts of an original language community become completely separated the language in each of them will tend to diverge from that in the other less slowly than if they continue in occasional or frequent contact. Both time and degree of separation are of vital concern to prehistory, and we must try to determine to what extent each is involved in the observed linguistic divergence.

Not all forms of linguistic differentiation are equally related to time and separation. It can be shown from specific instances that phonetic change sometimes moves with relative rapidity and sometimes is practically suspended. A condition favoring phonetic change is often the presence of a neighboring language or dialect with different sounds or with a given trend of sound change; consequently the presence or absence of the ouside stimulus may determine the occurrence or non-occurrence of the change. Something similar is true of structural change, except that it is usually slower and less contagious. In vocabulary, we have to make a very sharp difference between the "cultural" and the "basic," the former being relatively sensitive to and the latter largely independent of outside contacts and cultural changes. Thus "basic" vocabulary taken in sum is the one part of language which most truly reflects the mere passage of time and is least affected by special factors in the history of each group except that the specific changes may be influenced by the linguistic surroundings, particularly with reference to adjacent variant dialects of the same language. And because of this the lexico-statistic method is a logical means of obtaining an index of the combined effect of time and separation (see Swadesh, 1955, 1956a; Kroeber 1955). Based on the study of control cases and the determination of a norm of retention with respect to passage of time, the percent of cognates in the diagnostic lists of two compared languages is translated into a divergence measure called "minimum centuries," abbreviated mc., and representing the amount of time necessary for such a divergence to develop between two languages when they are not in a position of contact to influence each other. To the extent that the two compared languages have in fact been in contact, particularly in the earlier period while they are still mutually intelligible, the actual time may be from little to very considerably longer than the minimum centuries of the divergence figure.

To some extent it is possible to distinguish the time and separation factors from a consideration of the pattern of divergence figures in a complex of related languages. When there are more than two languages and hence more than one measure of divergence in the group, the largest number of minimum centuries must be the closest to actual time. If two or a larger set of languages are relatively close to each other linguistically and if they all show essentially equal divergences with relation to other more distantly related languages, one may infer that they were an undifferentiated dialect until after they lost contact with each other; their divergence with respect to the closest outside language must then represent a maximum measure of the time depth of their original unity. By using such hints in the pattern of divergences one can partially define actual time, but it is unlikely that a final answer can come directly from the linguistic facts alone. To complete the reconstruction it is well to make a coordinated use of the non-linguistic data.

The difficulty of separating the time and separation factors may appear to be a limitation on the usefulness of linguistic time depth, but there is an even more valuable compensation in the possibility it opens for reconstructing the old dialect geography. The picture may be blurred due to the complexity of varying degrees of contact over space and time, but it is usually possible to translate a collection of divergence figures into a relational diagram which must bear some relation to the spatial collocation of the early dialects except that the order may be symmetrically reversed, giving a mirror image, and the orientation with respect to map directions cannot be known from the internal pattern of divergences alone. By broadening the comparison to include more distantly related languages, by considering the present location of all the languages, and by taking into account archeological and other data, it may be possible to correct the orientation of the diagram and perhaps to fit it to a specific geographic area.

In the use of lexico-statistics as an instrument of prehistory, it should be born in mind that it is a new method still needing much research and refinement (Swadesh, 1955). The indices of divergences should be used with the necessary caution, and every effort should be made to check the results by other linguistic and non-linguistic evidence. In applying the method to divergences upwards of three or four thousand years, it is necessary to allow for a tendency to foreshorten long time periods. There also appears to be a "drift" factor, leading to a certain underestimation in shorter periods. Moreover, although diffusional influences do not ordinarily affect the basic vocabulary in sufficient degree to essentially modify the total retention rate, nevertheless special situations may occasionally modify this general rule; the distorting effect would be to exaggerate the divergence between the affected language and its congeners.

Before the advent of lexico-statistics, specific "isoglosses" were used to reconstruct old dialect geography. If two languages reflect the same archaic feature of phonetics, structure or word usage, this may indicate that they were neighboring dialects in the old days. If two or more isoglosses give the same indications of dialect proximity, this constitutes confirmation of the reconstruction. Where a language shares isoglosses with two others, it may have been a geographically intervening dialect. The difficulty with isoglosses is simply that there may not be enough of them to fully reconstruct the old dialect map, and lexico-statistics has the advantage that it can be uniformally applied to each pair of languages in a group. Nevertheless, the use of the new method should not eliminate the old one but on the contrary the two should be used as counter-checks upon each other. In certain cases, the method of isoglosses will amplify the picture, reflecting later contacts after the initial period of dialectal relationship.

5. *EVIDENCE OF DIFFUSION*

It is often possible to prove, or at least to suggest with a certain probability, that common features in two languages are not due to common origin of the two languages but to diffusion from one to the other or to both from the same outside source. Such common features include sounds or the fact of undergoing the same sound change, relatively superficial details of structure, words of like form and meaning, similar associations of meanings in one morpheme (e.g., using the same word for *seed* and *eye*) or the same derivative formation to express a given meaning (e.g., *leg-head* for *knee*). If enough or sufficiently complex common elements are found to eliminate the possibility of chance, we may have evidence of cultural contact. The determination of when, where and under what circumstances the contact took place may have to depend on other than linguistic evidence. There is sometimes the possibility of dating the contact linguistically. For example, borrowed words may show phonetic changes, whose relative date is known, and it follows that they came into the language before that time. Incomplete assimilation in phonetics or morphological treatment is usually a mark of recency.

The meaning of borrowed words is often an important clue as to the period, place and nature of prehistoric culture contacts. If a language has many borrowed terms for local flora and fauna, it is an indication that it is new to the region and the source language has been longer in the region. Similar considerations apply to place names. Often one finds that the bulk of the place names are in the present-day language of the area, but that a certain number have no meaning in that tongue. These may be suspected of being borrowings taken from an earlier group of people. If possible one should try to find the source language. In certain regions, the bulk of the place names come not from the local languages but from a politically dominant group. In such cases, these names can help map the area of influence of that group.

The use of a borrowed culture term almost always implies the diffusion of the corresponding culture trait, and is therefore a fairly direct clue to a fact of prehistory.

6. *RECONSTRUCTION OF CULTURE*

Once a group of languages has been found to be of common origin, their vocabularies can be examined for cognate elements that give evidence of the cultural content and physical environment of the old community. The number of helpful words will bear a relation to the recency of the differentiation, the cultural conservatism of the peoples, and the number of languages and the richness of the vocabularies available for comparison. One should not hesitate to apply the method no matter how divergent the languages may be, because even a few hints of early culture are worth having, but much more detail is normally recoverable in more limited time depths. Where the present populations have simple archaic cultures which are fairly similar one to another, the yield may be higher than in cases of advanced and much varied cultures. In making studies of this type, one should try to obtain material from as many related languages as possible and to get very complete vocabularies. It is well not to limit the languages to those going back to a common form precisely at the time horizon being studied, but to include also more distantly related tongues with a common period even farther back, since these may add to the clarity and completeness of the reconstruction. The parallel study of unrelated groups sharing the cultural area of languages in the reconstruction, may also be helpful by bringing out evidence of cultural borrowings and of interlocking cultural development.

The technique of cultural reconstruction from vocabulary is a complicated and delicate one, requiring imagination and care in the linguistic aspect along with a good knowledge of contemporary and archeological cultures of the areas concerned and a theoretical understanding of culture change. Collaboration between linguists and culturologists is to be recommended (see, for example, Schrader, 1890).

Two chief problems from the linguistic point of view are distinguishing real cognates from accidental similarities, and borrowings from old common vocabulary. Some cognates will have a probability so high that they cannot be reasonably doubted unless there is overwhelming cultural evidence against their antiquity. Others may be moderately reliable, moderately doubtful or just barely possible. All should be assembled, because there may be other ways of verifying their archaic character but it is well to set down an estimate of the probability of each case, based on phonological considerations and upon the spread of occurrences among the related languages (see, for example, Longacre and Millon, 1961), the latter not so much on the basis of present geography but rather in terms of linguistic differentiation. As for interdialect borrowing, it is necessary to consider the possibility of this circumstance at every time level from the common period to the present. In many cases it is possible to recognize recent borrowings by the phonology, but this is less and less easy as one goes back to the common horizon. In the first period of mere dialects, the process of borrowing among local forms is hardly to be distinguished from the development of the language as a single undifferentiated whole, and unless the cognate element is also found in separate languages dating back to a still earlier common period, one cannot be sure it was already in use in the earliest phase of the period being reconstructed.

Cognates do not necessarily have the same meanings in the present languages. The instances of varying meanings may in some instances be the most enlightening of all, since they may reveal culture traits now gone from all of the contemporary groups. The process of inferring original meanings from a variety of later ones, the semantic reconstruction, is thus just as important and just as demanding of caution as the phonological one.

Culture terms should be compared not only with words of the same category but also with noncultural vocabulary. Where an artifact or cultivated product bears a name traceable to a common object of nature, this may be evidence of relative recency of the trait. The etymology may also reveal something of the original provenience, procedure of production or customary uses. In addition to culture terms, words describing plants, animals, terrain features and phenomena of the weather (e.g., snow) may tell something of the ancestral home. A cognate place name may pin it down even more exactly.

7. *POINT AND AREA*

Ninety years after Johannes Schmidt (1872) pointed out the impossibility of the family-tree conception of language development, some comparative linguists are still trying to trace language groups back to single points of space and time from which a previously undifferentiated parent language sent out colonies to develop into a series of daughter languages; family tree diagrams are still made; and the outline form of presenting divisions and subdivisions of a linguistic group is still used even by scholars who reject the theory on which it is based. These procedures fit only the exceptional case of a language carried from one point to a far off new location where it immediately loses contact with the old community, but normally the spread of peoples is gradual, with the old and new areas maintaining contact from generations to thousands of years. Innovations appearing in one part of a dialect community tend to spread all around, in some cases being eventually adopted everywhere and in others reaching to various portions of the whole. Out of the complex series of processes arise dialects and separate languages, but the old continuity of dialects may be reflected thousands of years afterwards in the chain of interlocking relations among the derived languages.

The size of dialect and language areas and the reach of the uniformizing tendency evidently vary according to terrain and the level of economy and organization of the group. From a study of linguistic maps, it would seem that hunting-gathering groups, when not too much impeded by terrain, may long maintain a relatively uniform type of speech over a large area despite a low concentration of population and slow means of travel.

When dialect differentiation appears, as it must in time, it takes on the typical chain formation. Where the continuity is broken, it may be the result of the expansion of one group into adjacent territory, thus eliminating intermediate dialects.

In early stages of agriculture, with the appearance of fixed settlements, local differences develop in each nucleus of population, with gradations evidently maintained by the movement of people for trade and other purposes mainly among neighboring towns. Advanced commerce and political organization open the way to broader areas of linguistic unity, resulting either through the establishment of common trade languages, which eventually may become regional languages, or from colonization. Yet the kinds of development here suggested are merely broad generalizations, whose actual application has to be studied in each individual case.

The application of these general observations to comparative linguistics requires that we get away from family tree diagramming and classification, develop techniques for handling chain relationships and adapt our conceptions of divergence, contact phenomena and time depth to the realistic possibilities of linguistic development. Instead of trying to force language into discrete large groups, each subdivided into its set of smaller separate groups, we must look for evidence that will indicate what actually happened. The relational diagram, already mentioned as a technique for showing interlocking relationships of divergence, may be taken as a rough reconstruction of dialect geography, to be used together with reconstructed vocabulary and with non-linguistic evidence to help determine the location of the dialects and the subsequently developing languages in each period of prehistory.

8. *NEEDS*

Comparative linguistics, to make its proper contribution to prehistory, needs a great deal more knowledge of languages and of detailed genetic relationships than it now has, and much more than it even can hope to have at the present rate of accumulation of data. That we need more people competent in this field and funds for field and subsequent research, is all too obvious. However, even with increased personnel and facilities, a vital requirement is the development of more efficient methods of work.

Our field linguists must learn to collect good material faster—to obtain a working phonemic analysis in hours instead of months and to determine the main structural features of a language in days instead of years. In each aspect of the work—phonemics, structure, vocabulary—there should be an order of priority, putting principal emphasis on that part which is most essential for comparative purposes. Instead of trying to do a few languages with commendable thoroughness, we should find ways of making the data of all of them available with commendable speed. Survey and sampling techniques should be broadly used, and methods of exhaustive research applied at leisure, after a survey, not necessarily to all the languages surveyed but primarily to those which appear to be of strategic value to comparative research and to those which are in danger of being lost.

One of the great problems in efforts at comparing languages is that we may have very different coverages of material for the compared languages. We have the word for *horn* in one language and seek its equivalent in the next only to find that the recorder of that language did not obtain the word. In our linguistic surveys we should use standard vocabularies, well selected to obtain on the one hand basic words helpful in establishing genetic relationships and on the other hand culture terms useful in tracing old diffusional influences and in reconstructing ancient culture.

The use of standard vocabulary lists on printed (or mimeographed) forms reduces tremendously the work of the comparativist, since laying a set of lists down side by side on a flat surface will reveal cognates at a glance which would take hours or days to locate in dictionaries or in ordinary field notebooks. However, since cognates often have different meanings, one needs in addition a guide to likely near synonyms and other related meanings based on knowledge of general semantics and the specific tendencies of particular groups of languages. These notions have led to the following technique of locating cognates, which the author has seen used with great saving of time and increased thoroughness. Word lists for a set of languages are placed side by side, and all apparent cognates of the same meaning are put on a slip of paper; if no cognates are observed separate slips are made for each word in each language. A carbon copy of the slips is retained in the original numerical order as a finder list; since the word lists are in topical order an alphabetical index by meanings is needed for locating the slips when needed. The originals are regrouped to bring together all those of related meaning, and cognates thus found are joined by stapling the slips together. Sometimes different semantic groupings are tried until all the possibilities have been examined. Tentative reconstructions of phonetic form are written in for each set of cognates. The slips are re-filed according to the phonetic form of the reconstructions, allowing the comparativist to study the correctness of the phonologic equations and also sometimes revealing additional cognates with unexpected meanings. Corrections in cognate identification and reconstruction are made whenever the accumulating information requires it. The file prepared for one linguistic group may be collated with another one to build up broader and broader comparisons. The technique we have described could be easily adapted to use with the simpler types of filing machinery, with the comparativist intervening at the critical points.

Prior to the operation of the foregoing technique, it is convenient to have a preliminary idea of what languages go together. This can be done by making tentative counts of possible cognates and grouping together all lists which show a given minimum percent of agreements.

REFERENCE NOTE

This article also appears in a collection of essays (Swadesh, 1960a, pp. 93-128), translated and with fresh illustrative material by Professor Leonardo Manrique. The three figures of the original article have been omitted here, because they do not reflect the author's most recent views on the interrelations of Amerindian languages. The text has been modified slightly accordingly. Other works by the author on linguistic prehistory are noted with his article on pp. 624-637 and with the article by Gudschinsky.

For general views on linguistics and prehistory, see further Swadesh (1960a, 1960b, 1960c, 1960d), the remaining articles and references in this part, whose substantive contributions involve general considerations, and Hoijer's article and references in Part VIII. See also, for general views, Boas (1911), De Saussure (1916, Part 5, chap. 4), Greenberg (1953; 1957c, chaps. 3-6), Hockett (1958, chaps. 55-61), Hymes (1956a, 1958b, 1960a), Krahe (1954), Kroeber (1940, 1941, 1955, 1960a), Lehmann (1962), Malkiel (1962c), Meillet (1933a), Milke 1955), Pulgram (1958), Romney (1958), Sapir (1916; 1921, chap. 10), Tovar (1954), Trager (1955b), Whitney (1875, chap. 13), and the conference *Kultur und Sprache.*

References not in the general bibliography:

KRAHE, HANS

1954. *Sprache und Vorzeit.* Heidelberg: Winter, Universitätsvorlag.

KROEBER, A. L.

1940. Conclusions: The Present Status of Americanistic Problems. In C. L. Hay *et al.* (Eds.), *The Maya and Their Neighbors: Essays in Honor of Alfred Marston Tozzer.* New York: Appleton-Century. Pp. 460-489.

[KULTUR UND SPRACHE]

1952. *Kultur und Sprache;* mit Unterstützung des Bundesministeriums für Unterricht, der Osterreichischen Akademie der Wissenschaften und der Wenner-Gren Foundation for Anthropological Research. (Wiener Beiträge zur Kulturgeschichte und Linguistik, 9.) Vienna: Herold.

MILKE, WILHELM

1955. *Theorie der Kulturellen Ähnlichkeit.* Soest/Westfallen, Germany: published by the author.

PULGRAM, ERNST

1958. *The Tongues of Italy: Prehistory and History.* Cambridge: Harvard University Press.

SWADESH, MORRIS

1960c. Problems in Language Salvage for Prehistory. *International Committee on Urgent Anthropological and Ethnological Research, Bulletin 3*. Vienna: International Union of Anthropological and Ethnological Sciences. Pp. 13-19.

1960d. On Interhemisphere Linguistic Connections. In Stanley A. Diamond (Ed.), *Culture in History*. New York: Columbia University Press. Pp. 894-924.

The Comparative Method for Reconstruction in Linguistics 61

PAUL THIEME

THE COMPARATIVE method in linguistics as a tool for reconstructing prehistoric linguistic data, developed chiefly, though not exclusively, by an investigation of the so-called Indo-European languages, is a procedure that emerged from the science of comparative grammar (founded by Franz Bopp in 1816: *Über das Conjugationssystem der Sanskritsprache, in Vergleichung mit jenem der griechischen, lateinischen, persischen und germanischen Sprache . . .*). It was August Schleicher who first clearly formulated its program (*Formenlehre der kirchenslawischen Sprache*, 1852) and attempted to carry it out. The reconstruction of prehistoric linguistic data can be of the greatest help to prehistoric ethnological reconstruction.

THE NATURE OF PREHISTORIC RECONSTRUCTION

All prehistoric reconstruction is of course purely hypothetical, that is, it is based on conjectural assumptions. Strictly speaking, any conjectural assumption is a guess. This can, however, not be inverted: it is not true that every guess is a scientific hypothesis. A scientific guess must serve the specific purpose of explaining the nature and mutual relation of observed facts. It value is in strict correlation, first, to the accuracy of the factual observation and, second, to its being demonstrably evident that there is no other guess that would serve this purpose better or just as well. A characteristic feature of a scientific hypothesis lies therein, that it makes possible predictions and hence can be tested by experiments. An experimentally verified hypothesis is considered "proven."

The procedure of a prehistorian may be likened to that of a detective. He hunts for clues. He puts them together into a meaningful whole, discovering the secret of their disposition by relating them to a hypothetical picture. He goes on, after this, looking for further clues and testing them one by one to see whether they fit, all the while correcting and complementing —if necessary, altogether changing—his initial conception. Once he has a sufficient number of significant clues, he will be able to make certain definite predictions as to the nature of further clues and as to precisely what will happen if certain tests are applied. His success depends on the watchfulness and correctness of his observation, on the methodical strictness of his inferences, and of course on his imagination, which is not a dreamer's or a poet's fantasy, but a capacity, trained by experience, to visualize a possible sitation. There is, in all this, no secret magic involved, no uncanny gifts: "Elementary, my dear Watson."

It is obvious that the certainty of a hypothetical assumption is related to the nature and significance of the clues. The immediate facts of the prehistoric ethnologist are concrete objects that can be handled, looked at, and put in museums. His hypothetical reconstruction consists in filling in the gaps in the information that are left by his necessarily fragmentary facts. From the specific material and shape of prehistoric tools and weapons, or whatever else is at his disposal, he proceeds to make inferences to types of civilizations and their distributions. His complaint will be the scarcity and lack of variety of his prehistoric facts, otherwise unassailable in their reliable substantiality.

The immediate facts of the prehistoric linguist—called in to supply subsidiary information—are of a vastly different kind. They are neither concrete nor prehistoric—prehistoric being, by definition, a culture or a situation from which no, or no decipherable, linguistic records are available. Speaking of prehistoric linguistic data, we mean in fact hypothetically postulated items. The linguist seems, then, to be at a considerable disadvantage from the outset. This disadvantage, however, is outweighed by the peculiar nature of the historical material at his command. It permits him to reconstruct prehistoric facts with a precision unequalled in any other branch of humanistic studies. It is the particularity of linguistic facts and the characteristic processes of language change that enable him to ask questions for which there are operational answers: he can test his hypothetical predictions, within methodically defined limits, by accurate experiments.

THE PARTICULARITY OF LINGUISTIC FACTS

The particularity of linguistic facts is determined by the symbolic nature of the linguistic sign: the connection between the significans and the significandum is not natural and necessary ("symptomatic"), but factual and arbitrary. Its factuality is historical: it derives from a unique event, unrepeatable except by accident, and is kept alive by tradition. Its arbitrariness is not that of an individual, but that of society: it derives from and is maintained by social convention. Comparing languages means, then, comparing social conventions. Other traditional conventions lending themselves to a comparative examination are, for example, religions, mythologies, legal institutions, cultural patterns. The specific forms of religious or social conceptions, however, can be derived throughout from understandable motives; those of linguistic signs cannot. There are, to be sure, certain traditional conventions in language that are on precisely the same level as other traditional conventions. Among these are, for example, the fairly widespread distinction of a masculine and feminine gender, ascribed to all sorts of objects that are, in reality, without sex. The origin of this conventional distinction can be found in a general tendency of humanity to look at the world in analogy to its own kind. The almost universal custom of naming measurements after parts of the human body ("foot," etc.) can be motivated in the same manner: *ánthrōpos métron hapántōn* 'man is the measure of all things.' Appellations of certain concepts (actions like murmuring, objects like drums, animals like birds) can also be motivated as stylizations of acoustic impressions (onomatopoetica). By no means, however, can the particular forms of the great bulk of words be motivated: no reasonable motive besides its being an established convention is detectable for calling a horse *horse* (or *cheval* [French] or *Pferd* [German] or *lošad* [Russian], or *ghoṛā* [Hindi]), or for choosing a specific sound to express a grammatical function: *-s* is no more suitable for expressing the so-called nominative function and the singular of a living being (in Proto-Indo-European) than *-m* is for expressing that of the accusative singular.

If the form of the signs with an appellative function (roots, stems) and of those with a designative function (particles, conjunctions, suffixes, endings) correspond closely in different languages, this cannot be explained, consequently, as the result of an analogous motivation. If the nature of the correspondences is, further, of a kind that they can be assumed to be due neither to borrowing nor to chance, the conclusion is evident that the compared languages are developments of one single language: they are "historically related."

The special situation created by a linguistic correspondence, in contradistinction to that created by a religious analogy, may be illustrated by an example.

In many religions, all over the world, we find a conception of the sky/heaven as "father" and of the earth as "mother." The motive is easy to gauge. The sky sends down the rain that causes fertility like semen, and the earth brings forth, as it were from its womb, plants and fruits. This leads to the personification and divinization of sky and earth as "father" and "mother." Since the analogous facts can thus result from a general human way of viewing nature, they do not permit a historical conclusion. If we find this conception in different religions, it need by no means be due to either borrowing or common inheritance. The analogy cannot even be called an "accident" or a "chance," as the idea is of so obvious a motivation that its independent reoccurrence in different religions lacks the element of surprise.

The Sanskrit (Vedic) term *Dyaúṣ pitā́* (nom.) 'Father Sky/Heaven' is strikingly similar to the Greek (Homeric) term *Zeûs patér* (nom.) 'Father Zeus,' and to archaic Latin *Diēspiter* (nom.) 'Jupiter.' Here we have a fact that cannot be explained as due to a possible analogous motive for choosing corresponding symbols for similar independently in different languages. It is significant in a specific way: it cries for an interpretation in terms of history or prehistory.

THE DEMONSTRATION OF GENETIC RELATIONSHIP

An explanation of similarities as the result of chance can be eliminated on the axiom that chance does not repeat itself indefinitely. Similarities between two given languages, that are in nature and quantity conspicuously different from those prevailing between *any* two languages, must be accounted for by a specific assumption. This is the line of reasoning that was adopted by Sir William Jones, when he asserted (in 1786) that Sanskrit, Greek, and Latin had "sprung from some common source," Sanskrit "bearing to both of them [Latin and Greek] a stronger affinity, both in the roots of verbs and in the forms of grammar, than could possibly have been produced by accident." Since then, the explicit or implicit decision, "This cannot have been produced by accident," has been the basis for any assertion of genealogical linguistic relationship.

The elimination of an explanation by borrowing, on the other hand, requires some technical linguistic skill and, for certain instances, may even prove difficult. The first step will be to get a clear conception of what kind of similarity we are dealing with. To be of value for our purposes—that is, to admit of a precise inference to a genealogical relationship—a given similarity must be shown to be a *correspondence* that can be defined in specific terms as obtaining between the sounds (phonemes) and the appellative and formative elements (morphemes), as well as between the methods of formation and the semantic functions. This means that we have to replace the observation of a more or less vague resemblance of words by the technique of comparative grammar. The salient feature of this technique—introduced by Franz Bopp in 1816—is the analysis of words, that is, of the practical units of speech, into their abstract elements (roots, suffixes, endings, in the case of Indo-European languages). Its necessary complement is the investigation of correspondences between sounds, that is, the "clay" of which the "bricks" (the functional elements) are fashioned. Only if several of these different types of correspondences are established, are we in a position to interpret particular words of "similar" aspect in different languages as the reflexes of a particular original identity.

Now in principle, any individual speaker is able to change, arbitrarily, the pronunciation of particular sounds or particular words, the pattern of a particular construction, the use of a particular term; he may even coin new words. However, such individual innovations are nothing better than more or less serious proposals. They become part of a linguistic system when, and only when, they are accepted, that is, imitated, by the speech community. And the speech community will change its established conventions only if an individual proposal suits a general tendency or is capable of meeting a specific want. Some changes introduced into a given linguistic system in the course of a given period of time can be described systematically according to types that correlate familiar types of behavior: assimilation, dissimilation, prolepsis, haplology, for example, can be explained as due to anticipation, perseverance, overaccuracy or inaccuracy in making distinctions.

More difficult to motivate are sound changes proper. Yet it is just this kind of change that seems most regular in its ways and hence most suited to rigorous description and exact inference. By "sound change" we understand the substitution of a new pronunciation, not for a particular word, but for a particular sound (phoneme). This means that, for example, the substitution of a *th* for a *t*, though it must of course first have become manifest in the pronunciation of single words, will in fact be executed everywhere where formerly a *t* appeared under the same conditions. Looking at the single words where the new sound appears, we get the impression of the working of a "law." In reality, it is of course a single act which then shows its effect in many different instances. What we actually have are sets of *regular correspondences* that are of the greatest value for reconstruction.

Correspondences between languages could, in principle, be described without making use of any hypothesis. They become meaningful, however, only on the assumption that they are due to original identities, changed into differences by historic developments for which strict analogies can be found in the development of linguistic facts that is observable in the bright light of history. The changes we can trace in the development of Vulgar Latin to the modern Romance languages (Italian, French Spanish, Rumanian, etc.) are of exactly the same kind as those we presuppose from Proto-Indo-European to the oldest attested Indo-European languages. The system of describable correspondences that can be established between the Romance languages has its exact counterpart in the correspondences of the oldest Indo-European languages.

TYPES OF CORRESPONDENCE

A. SOUND CORRESPONDENCES

One of the simplest types of sound correspondences is the following:

	Indo-Iranian	*Slavic*	*Greek*	*Latin*	*Germanic*
1	a	o	a	a	a
2	a	e	e	e	e
3	a	o	o	o	a
4	i	o	a/e/o	a	a

In order to do something with these four correspondences, we have to interpret them. Our interpretation proceeds on the assumption that they are the reflexes of four particular identities. We might designate them by figures: 1, 2, 3, and 4; but this notation would give no hint as to the nature of our postulates, which obviously consists in their being particular sounds, presumably vowels. A reconstruction of the type a_1, a_2, a_3, A, as was proposed originally, evidently comes nearer to reality, as it involves an attempt at a description that does not leave out the most characteristic feature. Since there is no particular reason for choosing the vowel *a* as a symbol, this series could be replaced immediately by a series **a*, **e*, **o*, **ə* (the asterisk denoting the hypothetical character of the designated vowels).

For choosing these particular values, considerations of probability are primarily responsible: except where we must, we do not assume changes. In reconstructing **a*, we need to assume a change for Slavic only; in reconstructing **e*, a change for Indo-Iranian only; and in reconstructing **o*, a change for Indo-Iranian and Germanic only. The last series alone requires the reconstruction of a sound that was not preserved in any of these languages, since none of them distinguishes its correspondence from some other sound with other correspondences (Indo-Iranian *i* corresponds also to an *i* in all the other languages). The symbol **ə* is chosen to indicate a vowel that, like *i* and *u*, cannot bear the high-pitch accent in Proto-Indo-European, and is similar to these sounds also in that it may appear as the second part of a dipthong. Its color is not immediately definable. Only if we look very closely, do we seem to be able to suggest that Greek, with its three different correspondences, *a*, *e*, *o*, for **ə*, has preserved an old distinction of which traces are preserved elsewhere. Certain facts of the last Indo-European language to be deciphered, Hittite, suggest, moreover, that the pronunciation of our vowel **ə* was characterized by a laryngeal pronunciation. Hence we may replace **ə* by **H*, or rather by $*H_a$, $*H_e$, $*H_o$, or similar symbols.

In other words, our reconstruction follows the principle of choosing the path of least resistance. Fortunately, we have independent evidence that can be used to check our probabilistic reconstructions. First, the sounds we reconstruct cluster together in systems, similar in principle to those observable in living languages; we obtain systematic structures that are free from contradictions. For example: our reconstructed series **a*, **e*, **o* is matched by another series, reconstructed by the same method: **ā*, **ē*, **ō*. Second, we find that in the prehistory of certain Indo-European languages, our **e* has effects on certain preceding sounds ($*k^w$, $*g^w$, etc.) similar to those of **i* ("palatalization"), and that **o* has effects similar to those of **u*. This demonstrates that we were right in reconstructing a palatal vowel for $*a_2$ and a nonpalatal vowel for $*a_3$, while the presence of an **i* and an **u* in our reconstructed vowel system vindicates the choice of **e* and not of **i*, of **o* and not of **u* for our particular series. Our reconstruction of **H* for **A* is confirmed by the observation that in certain cases (before vowels) where **H* seems to have disappeared, a preceding unvoiced stop (especially *t*) is aspirated in Indo-Iranian.

If, armed with the results of a thorough and comprehensive examination of the sound correspondences of the Indo-European languages, one looks at the above-mentioned "similarity" of Sanskrit *Dyaúṣ pitā́*, Greek *Zeûs patḗr*, Latin *Diēspiter*, one can ascertain that these terms indeed correspond phonologically in a predictable and strictly accountable manner. We are permitted—even more, we are compelled—to reconstruct an original identity, a little Proto-Indo-European phrase: **Dyḗus pH$_a$tḗr*.

B. MORPHOLOGICAL CORRESPONDENCES

Any language may borrow from any other language a word of an appellative meaning, but rarely, if ever, elements of a designative function, and almost never methods of formation. In simple terms: we readily borrow the Russian word *sputnik*, but we should not dream of inflecting it, or deriving an adjective from it, in the Russian way. The reason is obvious: case endings and derivative suffixes make sense and can be understood only as parts of an overall pattern that permeates the structure of the whole language. Morphological correspondence is, then, the safest indication of genealogical relationship.

The inflection of Sanskrit *ásmi* 'am,' *asti* 'is,' *sánti* 'are' corresponds with strict phonological regularity to pre-Greek **esmi* (won by inner Greek reconstruction from the correspondence Attic-Ionic *eimi* [pronounced *ēmi*], Aeolic *emmi*), *esti*, **henti* (won by inner Greek reconstruction from Attic-Ionic *eisi* [pronounced *ēsi*] and Boeotic *enthi* [< **henti*, with metathesis of the aspirate]); to Gothic *im*, *ist*, *sind*, and so on. We are compelled to reconstruct a Proto-Indo-European paradigm: **és-mi* 'am,' **és-ti* 'is,' *s-énti* 'are,' that cannot have spread by borrowing.

We must add a further essential observation. If we compare this reconstructed paradigm with other, seemingly disparate, paradigms of other verbs, it emerges that only the reconstructed Proto-Indo-European forms have a recognizable rationale: they turn out to conform to certain simple principles that can be derived only partly, sometimes not at all, from a study of any single Indo-European language. For example, the change in the form of the root—*és-* before a singular ending, *s-* before a plural ending—is in strict concordance with parallel changes in other roots (*ei:i*, *eu:u*, *ye:i*, *ve:u*, etc.); it fits into the general morphological pattern of Proto-Indo-European as a case of "ablaut," of which every single daughter language has preserved traces, that, however, become fully meaningful only when related to Proto-Indo-European word-forming procedures.

Here it is necessary to insert a word of warning. While it is possible to reconstruct a great many Proto-Indo European morphological elements (roots, suffixes, endings) and the abstract principles of word-forming processes, it would of course be wrong to attempt to trace back every word or form of any Indo-European language to a Proto-Indo-European prototype. Like the system of sounds, the systems of word formation are subject to continuous change—with the result that old forms are constantly given up and new forms created. It is, in fact, hardly possible to reconstruct any full "paradigm" for any "declension" or "conjugation"; we must be satisfied with understanding the principles and with getting certain characteristic forms. To tell the truth, this is quite enough—at least for the prehistorian who is not interested in grammar for grammar's sake, but in grammar as a tool for reconstructing linguistic reflexes of prehistoric cultural items.

A few practical instances may make clear the essential value of morphological correspondences for prehistoric reconstruction.

1. The words for 'sheep' in almost all Indo-European languages correspond phonologically in a predictable way:

Sanskrit *ávis*, Lithuanian *avìs*, Greek *ó(u)is*, Latin *ovis*, Irish *oi*, Old High German *ouwi* [pronounced *owi*], 'ewe' (Gothic *avi-str* 'sheepfold'); Sanskrit *avi-kā* 'ewe,' Old Slavic *ovĭ-ca* 'ewe.'

Now, it may be—in fact, it has been—maintained that, in view of the uncomplicated nature of the phonological correspondence, this word may be a loan that spread to the different languages independently from an unknown source. Morphology answers this proposition unambiguously in the negative: Sanskrit *ávis* forms a genitive *ávyas*—almost without parallel in Sanskrit—and Greek *ó(u)is* forms, in Homer, a genitive *oî(v)os* (from an earlier **óvyos*) quite unique in Greek. The reconstructible, peculiar paradigm: nominative **óvis*, genitive **óvyos*, warranted by Sanskrit and Greek, together with the derivation **ovi-kā* 'ewe,' warranted by Sanskrit and Slavic, vouches for a Proto-Indo-European age of the stem-form *óvi-* 'sheep.'

A further weight can be thrown in the balance by referring to the fact that the formation of the genitive **óvyos* from an *i*-stem **óvi-*, has an analogy in reconstructible genitives from *u*-stems (like **peku-* 'small cattle,' gen. **pekvos*). It conforms to a Proto-Indo-European pattern.

2. Possibly still more compelling is the evidence for a Proto-Indo-European *g^{u}ōus 'cattle' (masc. 'bull,' fem. 'cow'), reconstructed from the corresponding nominative forms: Sanskrit *gaúṣ*, Greek *boûs*. It is confirmed as Proto-Indo-European by the accusative *g^{u}ōm: Sanskrit *gām*, Homeric *bō̃n*, Umbric *bum* (the Latin nominative *bōs*, which does not correspond to *g^{u}ōus phonologically, presupposes an old accusative **bōm*, after which the nominative was innovated); a stem form *g^{u}ou- (before a consonant): Sanskrit instr. plural *gó-bhiṣ*, Latin *bū-bus*, and *g^{u}ov- (before a vowel); Sanskrit dat. sing. *gav-ḗ*, Homeric nom. pl. *bó(v)-es*; a stem form *g^{u}u- (before a consonant): Sanskrit *śata-gu-* 'of a hundred cows'; and *g^{u}v- (before a vowel): Sanskrit *śatá-gv-in* 'winning a hundred cows,' Homeric *hekatómbv-ē* '[sacrifice] winning a hundred cows.'

The different stem forms: *g^{u}ōu-, *g^{u}ou-/g^{u}ov-, *g^{u}u-/g^{u}v- again make full sense only when fitted into the framework of Proto-Indo-European "ablaut," while neither the Greek nor the Latin forms, when looked at in isolation, unite into a recognizable pattern.

3. In the end, we return once more—though not for the last time—to the correspondence *Dyaúṣ pitā́*, *Zeũs patḗr*, *Diēspiter*, and the reconstructed *Dyḗus pH$_a$tḗr, in order to look at it from the morphological point of view. For both words we can reconstruct characteristic paradigmatic forms and adjective derivations that confirm the presumption that we are dealing not with a loan, but with an item inherited from a common source. This is easiest to show of **dyḗus*:

Accusative singular	**dyēm/diyēm*	Sanskrit *dyā́m*, Greek (Homeric) *Zē̃n*, Latin *diem* (< **diyēm*)
Genitive singular	**divós*	Sanskrit *divás*, Greek *di(v)ós*
Dative singular	**divéi*	Sanskrit *divé*, Greek *diveí* (in the Cyprian name *Diveíphilos* 'dear to Zeus')
Locative singular	**dyévi*	Sanskrit *dyávi*, Latin *Jove*
Adjective	**deivós*	Sanskrit *devás* 'heavenly,' Latin *dīvos* 'heavenly,' Germanic (Old Norse) *tīv-ar* (nom. pl.) 'gods'

Of special interest is the vocative singular *Dyéu pH$_a$ter, warranted by Greek *Zeû páter* and Latin *Jūpiter* (also used a nominative), as it shows that *Dyéus pH$_a$tér was addressed as a person, that is, invoked like Zeus and Jupiter in Greek and Latin.

The relation of the different stem forms can be understood, exactly like those of the word for 'cattle,' within the pattern of Proto-Indo-European "ablaut," whereas, viewed in isolation in Greek and Latin, their relation would remain altogether puzzling: *Zeũs*, *Di(v)ós*, *Zē̃n* and *Diēspiter*, *Jūpiter*, *Jove* have to be crammed as "irregular" paradigms by classicists who lack a training in Indo-European comparative grammar.

C. SEMANTIC CORRESPONDENCES

To establish sound correspondences between different languages is possible only if we have corresponding words or corresponding morphological elements.

Only after getting several series like:

Sanskrit *ajrás* Greek *agrós* Latin *ager* Gothic *akrs*

can we establish the sound correspondence:

1. Sanskrit *a* Greek *a* Latin *a* Germanic *a*

and only after getting several series like:

Sanskrit *asti* Greek *esti* Latin *est* Old Russian *estĭ*

can we establish the sound correspondence:

2. Sanskrit *a* Greek *e* Latin *e* Slavic *e*

and only after getting several series like:

Sanskrit *ávis* Greek *óvis* Latin *ovis* Gothic *awi-str* Old Slavic *ovĭ-ca*

can we establish the sound correspondence:

3. Sanskrit *a* Greek *o* Latin *o* Gothic *a* Slavic *o*

and only after getting series like:

Sanskrit *pitā́* Greek *patḗr* Latin *pater* Gothic *fadar*

can we establish the sound correspondence:

4. Sanskrit *i* Greek *a* Latin *a* Gothic *a*

To establish correspondences of words and morphological elements between languages, on the other hand, is possible only if we have corresponding semantic values.

1. The correspondence of the words Sanskrit *ajrás*, etc., is established only because their semantic value in the different languages corresponds closely: they are all used in the sense of 'pasturage' or 'field.'

2. Sanskrit *asti*, etc., can be shown to correspond only because they are all used in the sense of 'is.'

3. Sanskrit *ávis*, etc., can be shown to correspond only because they are all used in the sense of 'sheep.'

4. Sanskrit *pitā*, etc., can be shown to correspond only because they are all used in the sense of 'father.'

The establishment of corresponding semantic values is thus the starting point and mainstay for the exploration of all other linguistic correspondences—so much so that no sound correspondences can possibly be discovered between languages that are not understood. But it is the sound correspondences that create the evidence of relationship—so much so that no semantic correspondences can prove anything if it is not accompanied by sound correspondences: for the purpose of reconstruction, the sound correspondences are the starting point and mainstay of all other work.

A comparison of the two basic types of correspondence reveals another paradoxical feature. Investigating a semantic correspondence will seem at first glance much easier than investigating a sound correspondence, which sometimes presupposes considerable technical training and skill. Actually, the former task is a much more delicate one; it is, if attempted with a view to arriving at a valid judgment, by far more exacting than the latter, which can rely on strictly mechanistic procedures.

It is true, there are a number of semantic correspondences that seem to offer no difficulty. If the Sanskrit stem *ávi-* 'sheep' appears in phonologically and morphologically exactly corresponding forms in almost all other Indo-European languages, and is used everywhere likewise in the sense of 'sheep,' the probability that a reconstructed Proto-Indo-European stem **óvi-* (with the equally reconstructible forms: nom. sing. **óvi-s*, acc. **óvi-m*, gen. **óvy-os*; nom. pl. **óvey-es*, acc. **ovi-ns*, etc.) was used in the same sense and hence must be assigned the meaning 'sheep,' is indeed so strong that nobody, let us hope, will have the unrealistic courage of refusing to consider it a certainty.

Matters become more complicated, however, as soon as we turn to the correspondence Sanskrit *ajrás* 'pasturage' and Greek *agrós*, Latin *ager*, Gothic *akrs*, all 'field' and 'acre.' Of course, it will readily be admitted that the concepts 'pasturage' and 'field,' and the concepts 'field' and 'cultivated field, acre,' are of sufficient affinity to make it understandable if they are not kept strictly asunder, and hence to permit the assumption that a word, originally naming one of them, was used first occasionally and then exclusively to designate the other one. More ticklish is the question, whether it is possible to establish a reasonable probability for one particular use as the original one. Can we reconstruct the meaning of Proto-Indo-European **agrós* as either 'pasturage' or 'cultivated field, acre'? It is obvious that the answer may be of considerable interest to an ethnological prehistorian.

Unfortunately, in a case like this, it is not immediately feasible to apply the simple method of just choosing that value which occurs most frequently in different languages, as it was in reconstructing sounds. For one thing, a new meaning is not substituted in the way a new sound is, by a single act, so that the substitute appears in all contexts equally: "a new meaning" is really only our abstract formula for the fact that a word is used in certain contexts in which it was not used before and does not appear in others in which it did. New and old usage patterns may exist side by side for a long time.

Looking at our instance from this angle, we notice that Sanskrit *ajrás* is never used in the sense of 'cultivated field, acre,' but that, for example, Greek *agrós* may designate, in Homer, the obviously not cultivated field where the herdsman is with his sheep (*Iliad v.* 137). If we tentatively accept this fact as a cue and follow the direction to which it appears to point, we encounter other traces that confirm our orientation as correct. We find a compound *agraulós* 'spending the night on the *agrós*,' again said of a shepherd (*Iliad xviii.* 162), of which the denominative verb *agrauléō* 'spend the night in the open' is used as late as Luke 2:8 of shepherds: the St. James version says 'abiding in the field,' but might equally well have said 'abiding on the pasturage.'

In Latin, we have an adjective *agrārius*, most obviously derived from *ager* in the sense of 'cultivated field, acre,' as a look in any Latin dictionary will teach. But there is another adjective: *agrestis* (an ancient compound from *agro* + *st-i-* 'standing [root *stā*] on the *ager*'), which is used is the sense of 'wild' (in contrast to 'domestic' and 'cultivated'). Accurately corresponding is the use of two Greek derivatives: *agrios* and *agróteros*, both 'wild.' The Latin adverb *peregrē* 'abroad' (its contrast: *domi* 'at home') and adjective *peregrinus* 'foreign', which must be analyzed as 'beyond the *ager*' and 'coming from/living beyond the *ager*,' presuppose a use of *ager* in the sense 'the known land (region) around the settlement,' with the connotation 'cultivated' obviously lacking.

Thus, a more careful analysis of the actual use of the word and its derivatives in different languages leads one to posit as a probable original value 'uncultivated field, pasturage' rather than 'cultivated field, acre': it is actually the former use that is revealed as more widespread if we look at the oldest available sources —Sanskrit, early Greek, early Latin—though the latter is more common in Later Greek and Latin and is the only one in Germanic. Yet more than a strong probability cannot be obtained by purely semantic procedures, it must be conceded.

As it turns out, we are lucky. In this particular instance, as in a number of others, though by no means in all, we are able to pursue an entirely different line of argument, that arrives at the same point and thus converts our "probability" into a "proven assumption." The Proto-Indo-European word stem **agró-* can be etymologically analyzed as root **ag-* + suffix *-ro*. *ag-* is 'lead, drive,' and its descendants are used of the action of 'driving' animals to the pasturage: Latin *agere* (with objects like: *tauros* 'bulls,' *armentum* 'cattle,' *capellas* 'goats,' *bovem/bovēs* 'cattle,' *pecora* 'small cattle,' etc.), Vedic Sanskrit root *aj* (frequent object: *gā́s* 'cows'); the same must have been the case in Pre-Greek, as is evinced by *ag-élē* 'herd' ('what is driven').

The very complexity of the semantic facts, which makes impossible the application of a foolproof mechanical procedure, enables us to formulate a hypothesis that accounts for its particular features by explaining them as the result of a prehistoric semantic development and is confirmed by etymological analysis: Proto-Indo-European *agró-* 'pasturage,' then 'land lying around the settlement,' then—in some daughter languages, spoken by people with a developed agriculture, but not in Vedic Sanskrit, spoken by a society of settled cattle breeders with only little cultivation of land— 'cultivated field, acre.'

Our Proto-Indo-European **Dyḗus pH$_a$tḗr* and its correspondences in Sanskrit, Greek, and Latin create a similarly complex semantic problem. We translate hypothetically *'Father Sky/Heaven.' This is the undoubtable meaning of Sanskrit *Dyaúṣ pitā́*. Greek *Zeũs* is a divine proper name, which we had better not translate. Its bearer is much more than a personified sky/heaven: he is the father of men and gods, who sits on his throne; when he nods, his ambrosial hair waves from his head (*Iliad i.* 529 f.). But, again, there are cues that betray his original nature: he sends the lightning, the thunder, and the rain. And the Greek idiom *Zeũs húei* 'it rains,' literally 'Zeus rains,' is etymologically understandable as 'the sky rains.' *Diēspiter/Jūpiter*, also, is the proper name of a god, strikingly similar to the Greek *Zeũs*: to *Zeũs huétios* 'the rain-giving Zeus' corresponds the Roman *Jūpiter pluvius*. Most significant is the idiom *sub Jove* 'in the open,' historically interpretable only if we insert our reconstructed value, 'under (*sub*) the sky'. Latin *diēs* 'day' (in contrast to *nox* 'night') reveals itself as a development of **dyēus* *'(day-)sky,' for which Sanskrit offers an analogy (Vedic instrumental *divā* 'during the day', *div-asa* 'day,' etc.). An independent confirmation of our reconstruction *'Father Sky/Heaven' can be had, in this instance, from a comparative study of religions, which teaches us that the idea expressed in this phrase is indeed worldwide and hence a predictable possibility.

In discussing the probable meaning of Indo-European **óvis* 'sheep,' I used the expression "unrealistic courage." Now, there may be some who would be inclined to level it at our own procedure. All right, then. I shall recant the use of it: actually, it does not constitute a scientifically relevant argument. Courage is an explorer's indispensable requirement—I should say his most splendid asset—and "unrealistic" is a qualification so strongly redolent of subjective bias that it is worthless as a criterion. Examples are legion for scientific progress being achieved by courageous questioning of what seemed to be self-evident facts, by demolishing answers that seemed to be plain common sense, and by destroying an accepted view of reality.

Let us be radical and concede that the reconstructed semantic value *'sheep' is no more than a probability vouched for by the questionable judgment of common sense, but still waiting to be verified by an independent argument. Our evidence, being circumstantial by nature, must be *cumulative* in order to be convincing. Etymological analysis yields no argument here. Is there any other way of approaching our problem?

What we call a "linguistic system" is in reality composed of different systems, independent of each other: a sound system, a system of morphemes and morphological processes, a system of semantic values. Each of these is further composed of smaller units: the sound system comprises a vowel system and a system of consonants, further subdivided into systems of stops, sibilants, liquids, etc.; the system of morphemes comprises systems of primary and secondary suffixes, nominal and verbal endings, etc.; the system of semantic values, the richest and most variegated one, consists of groups (abstracta, concreta; actions, objects; logical and grammatical relations) that may be subdivided practically ad infinitum.

This situation opens up the possibility of asking an experimental question: does a reconstructed 'sheep' fit into the semantic system of Proto-Indo-European; does it form a unit with other semantic values reconstructed by the same probabilistic procedure? The answer is: yes, it does; it fills a necessary place within a well-knit, characteristic semantic context. For we obtain, for example, a Proto-Indo-European word for 'lamb': **veren-/uren-/urn-* (Sanskrit *úraṇas*, Greek **[v]arén*, gen. *[v]arnós*, both 'lamb'), and for 'wool': **vl̥nā* (Sanskrit *ūrṇā*, Old Slavic *vluna*, Lithuanian *vìlnōs* [pl.], Gothic *wulla*, Latin *lānā*, etc., all phonologically corresponding and all 'wool'). It goes together, further, with Proto-Indo-European words for 'goat' and 'he-goat' and a word for 'small cattle' (**peku-*) comprising, in all languages where its descendants appear, sheep and goats. Even if we didn't have the correspondence Sanskrit *ávis*, etc., the reconstruction of a semantic value *'sheep' beside the values *'lamb' and *'wool' would be inescapable.

That we can trust this kind of experiment becomes evident by a countertest. The phonologically corresponding Sanskrit *asis* masc. '(iron) sword' and Latin *ēnsis* masc. '(iron) sword' would seem to permit the reconstruction of a **n̥sis* masc. *'(iron) sword.' Now here is an item that could not be accommodated within a Proto-Indo-European semantic group. While we are able to reconstruct words for the metals gold, silver, and copper or (?) bronze, a reconstructible word for iron is conspicuously lacking. Each of the Indo-European languages or language groups has a different expression: Greek *sidēros*; Latin *ferrum*; OSlavic *želēzo*, Lithuanian *gelezis* (permitting a Balto-Slavic, but not a Proto-Indo-European reconstruction); Old Irish *ēaru* (<**eisarn*, borrowed into Germanic). The probabilistic **n̥sis* 'sword' is, as it appears, not confirmed, rather, gainsaid. The two approaches—reconstruction by individual correspondences and examination of reconstructed patterns—have led not to one, but to different results; we are confronted with two contradictory probabilitites. Hence we conclude that somewhere we made a mistake.

Once we are alerted to the dilemma, the mistake is easily discovered. The apparently perfect semantic correspondence (Sanskrit *ásis* masc. 'iron sword': Latin *ēnsis* masc. 'iron sword') does not stand up to close examination. To the Ṛgveda, the oldest document of Sanskrit literature, which is full of the noise of battle, the sword is unknown as a weapon. The earliest passages where *ásis* occurs belong to comparatively late layers of the Ṛgveda, and here *ásis* is '(a butcher's) knife.' The value 'sword' occurs only later; consequently, it is not inherited, but the result of a development within the history of Sanskrit. This conclusion is in agreement with the fact that Homer, who speaks of swords (*xíphos* n.) and daggers (*mákhaira*) all the time, never uses in this context an expression that could be connected with a Proto-Indo-European **n̥sis* or any other reconstructible word.

Now it is possible to assign the Proto-Indo-European stem **n̥si-* a convincing place within a morphological and a semantic pattern, if we drop the idea that it was either 'sword' or 'dagger.' Sanskrit *asi-* can be related to *asi-ta-* 'black,' as *rohi-* 'red' is to *rohi-ta-* 'red,' *hari-* 'yellow' to *hari-ta-* 'yellow,' which means that we are entitled to reconstruct a Proto-Indo-European adjective **n̥si-* *'black.' Sanskrit *ásis* masc. and Latin *ēnsis* masc. would then be independent, parallel nominalizations: 'the black one,' designating in Vedic Sanskrit the iron knife and later the iron sword, in Latin the iron sword. Greek *ásis* fem. 'river mud' can be explained as a nominalization of the same adjective and assigned the original value 'the black one.'

Nouns used in the sense of 'quagmire, sludge, mud' are often, indeed with characteristic frequency nominalizations of color adjectives (beside 'black,' also 'grey,' 'red,' 'white,' 'variegated'). That iron, in contradistinction to other metals, is black, seems so obvious that it hardly calls for a proof. Nor is there any want of purely linguistic evidence: the oldest word for 'iron' in Sanskrit is *kṛṣṇāyasa*, literally 'black metal' (it contains the inherited **ayes-* *'metal' [*'copper' or (?) *'bronze']); Hesiod (*opera* 15 f.) when speaking of the copper/bronze age, tells us:

> There were bronze weapons and bronze houses;
> With bronze [for tools] they worked; but there was no black (*mélās*) iron (*sídēros*).

In *Atharva Veda* 9.5.4., another word for 'black' (*syāma*) is used in the sense of 'a butcher's knife'; the Indian epic (*Mahābhārata*) has a story of how the sword (*ásis*) was created. The very first qualification of this new 'being' (*bhūta-*) is the adjective *nīlotpalasavarṇābha-* 'having a shine of the same color as a dark-blue lotus' (*Śāntiparvan* [ed. Belvalkar], 160.38). Incidentally, both Hesiod and the *Mahābhārata* serve witness that in their time iron and the iron sword were still traditionally considered comparatively late acquisitions of mankind.

THE RECONSTRUCTION OF SEMANTIC SYSTEMS

If the final proof for the correctness of case-by-case reconstructions lies therein, that they close together into consistent and compact systems, the very fact that we do get such coherent units is a confirmation of the soundness of our procedure as a whole. It will also give us confidence in judging such reconstructed items as happen to remain isolated, if they are arrived at by the same method as the others. Our method of operation can best be likened to the restoration of a mosaic, consisting of a great number of minute stones, some of which have disappeared irretrievably, and all of which have lost their color. We start by working on the single pieces, attempting to restore, by technical processes, their original hues. If our procedures work correctly, it will appear that the colored stones are arranged in a particular, significant way: we obtain parts of a coherent whole and in certain instances can make a definite assumption as to what kind of stones must have been in the gaps. It is obvious that, finally, the meaning of the mosaic representation is of much greater interest than all the single details taken by themselves: the total is more than the sum of its parts. This will become clear if we gather up into brief review some of the characteristic semantic systems that can be reconstructed for Proto-Indo-European. We recognize certain general outlines and certain particular features of a meaningful picture.

1. The simplest, most neatly intertwined semantic system is formed by the numbers. The numerals from 1 to 10 can be reconstructed with exactness; all others, up to 100, can be shown to be formed either by additive or multiplicative composition, or by the formation of collective nouns (e.g., **dékm̥t-* '10,' *dkm̥t-ó* 'ten-hood' = '100'); though we do not always get single expressions, the formative processes are reconstructible in the abstract. The fundamental method of counting, consequently, must have been decimal (that is, proceeding with the help of the fingers). The numerals 1-4 were treated grammatically as adjectives (with differentiation of gender); their peculiar character points to an archaic type of counting by applying the thumb to the other four fingers. Certain traces of a duodecimal counting betray the existence of a third system: passing the thumb along the 12 finger joints.

2. Exactly reconstructible designations of relatives are not limited to the most elementary —father, mother, husband, wife, brother, sister, son, daughter—but comprise: daughter-in-law, mother of the husband, father of the husband, brother of the husband, sister of the husband, wife of the husband's brother. Much less precise correspondences or no correspondences at all are available for nonimmediate relations—except for grandson—and for the blood relations of the wife. The Proto-Indo-European family quite evidently was a patriarchally organized joint family; upon marriage, the wife entered her husband's clan, acquiring new relatives, while the husband was not officially connected with his wife's family. The

linguistic system is characteristic and without gap if interpreted in the light of this assumption.

3. Proto-Indo-European designations of visible parts of the human and animal body: head, face, ear, eye, eyebrow, mouth, tooth, lips, nose, chin, shoulder, arm, elbow, nail claw, hips, arse, penis, foot.

The reconstruction of the exact form of the word for 'tongue' makes difficulties; each language or language group has a different expression for 'hand' (Latin *manus*, Greek *kheír*, Germanic *handus*, Balto-Slavic *roka/rankà*, Indo-Iranian *hasta-/zasta-*). The situation with respect to 'palm' and 'finger' is similar. The reason seems to be that these organs play a particular and essential role for man (the tongue in talking and tasting; the hand in working, taking, and counting). They could be named from different standpoints so that an abundance of imaginative designations developed that was simplified in the different languages independently.

Proto-Indo-European designations of the inner parts of the body: blood, intestines, heart, liver, milt, lungs.

There is no safely reconstructible term for 'stomach.' Its function was certainly unknown, for it can be established by the witness of earliest tests of an Indo-European tongue that it was erroneously ascribed to the heart. Expressions for 'liver,' 'milt,' 'lungs' show that animals were slaughtered, which is confirmed by the etymological meaning of the Proto-Indo-European word for 'lungs': **pleumon-* 'swimmer' characterizes the behavior of the organ when thrown into water after the dissection of the butchered animal.

4. The personification and subsequent divinization of the concept 'sky/heaven' that is inferable from the reconstructed term nom. **Djḗus pH$_a$tḗr*, voc. *Djéu pH$_a$ter*, fits together with an equally reconstructible feminine nom. *áusōs*, gen. *usós* 'dawn,' celebrated as a goddess in the Ṛgveda (*uṣás-* fem. '[goddess of] dawn,' qualified as 'of reddish breath') and in Homer (*ḗōs* '[goddess of] dawn,' qualified as 'of rosy fingers'), and further confirmed by Latin *aurōra* fem. 'dawn.' According to expectation, we obtain several feminine nouns for 'earth.'

A great number of other natural phenomena can be designated as a masculine or feminine gender, that is, as "animate"; they may also be looked upon optionally as "inanimate": sometimes there are available neuter expressions for the same phenomena. For example: 'fire' and 'water' may be named either by neuter stems (cf., e.g., Greek *pûr* n., Old High German *fuir/fiur* n., Hittite *pah̯h̯uuar*, gen. *pah̯h̯uenos* : Indo-European **peuer-, peuen-*; Greek *húdōr* n., gen. *húdatos*, Old English *waeter* n., Gothic *watō*, gen. *watins*, Hittite *uātar*, gen. *uetenas* : Indo-European **vedor-, veden-*) or by a different masculine (Sanskrit *agni-*, Latin *ignis*, Old Slavonic *ognjĭ*) or feminine noun (Sanskrit *ap/āp*, Latin *aqua*, Gothic *ahva* : Indo-European **ap-/āp-, /ap-q^{u}ā-* 'water'). In other cases, a masculine or feminine derivative stands beside an original neuter stem. For example, the neuter **suvel* 'sun' (Sanskrit *s[u]var* n., Gothic *sauil* n. 'sun,' treated as a masculine in Latin *sol* 'sun' and as a feminine in Old Icelandic *sól* 'sun') has beside it a nominalized adjective: **sū́liyo-* masc. 'Sun-god' (Sanskrit *sū́r[i]ya-* masc. 'Sun') and **sāvéliyo-* (Homer *ēélios* 'Sun').

The Indo-European language has a clear opposition between 'divine,' literally 'celestial': **deivo-*; **divyo-*; **diviyo-* (Sanskrit *devá-*, Latin *dīvus*, Lithuanian *dievas*, etc.; Sanskrit *divya*, Greek *dīos*; Sanskrit *div(i)yá-*, Latin *dīus*) and 'earthly' (Latin *homō/hemō*, Gothic *guma* 'man,' derived from Indo-European **ghem-* fem. 'earth'); between 'immortal': **n̥mr̥to-* (Sanskrit *ámr̥ta*, Greek *ámbrotos*) and 'mortal': *morto/mortiyo-* (Sanskrit *márta*, *mártiya*, Greek *mórtos*). The 'celestials,' that is the 'gods,' are the 'givers of good things' (Greek *dotē̃res eáōn*, Sanskrit *dātāro vásūnām*).

The oldest religious rites of Indo-European peoples do not presuppose temples or idols. Nor is there a reconstructible term for 'temple.' But there is a 'worship,' conceived as a hospitable reception with a meal, consisting of slaughtered animals, and accompanying recitation of poetry, the 'celestials' coming, as it were, on a visit to the 'earthly ones.' The Greek *hekatómbē* 'sacrificial meal' goes back to an earlier **km̥togv-ā* 'meal that wins a hundred cows (from the 'givers of good things')' (cf. Sanskrit *śatagv-ín-* consisting of a hundred cows'). The complicated ritual of the old Indian sacrifice can and must be understood as a stylization of a hospitable meal.

It seems characteristic that we cannot reconstruct any divine proper names—like Greek *Apollōn*, Latin *Māvors/Mars*, Indo-Iranian

Indra—but only appellatives like 'heaven,' 'dawn,' etc., used as designations of divine beings. On the whole, there is a conspicuous lack of particulars that would fill in the recognizable, but rather general, ideological framework. We largely obtain abstract methods of grammatical personification and thereby possibilities of divinization of natural phenomena rather than concrete details; the linguistic material for the expression of a specific religious Weltanschauung rather than its particular terms. *Zḗus pH$_a$tḗr* is, as a practical detail, almost an exception—but it is an exception that makes perfect sense within the theoretical outlines that are recognizable as a rule.

The situation allows of a probable inference: our reconstructions reach into times where there was no common national religion with an official cult. It is not possible to reconstruct a term for 'priest,' for the alleged equation of Sanskrit *brahmán* masc., originally 'poet,' and Latin *flamen* 'fire-priest' is untenable. Each family, it appears, was its own religious center, the 'father' of the house functioning as the family priest, in his practical role as butcher and his ideological role as host. What we reconstruct are then, naturally, only the most general ideas that were common, in contradistinction to the particulars that were individual.

5. The reconstruction of Proto-Indo-European flora and fauna poses special problems and has to take into account particular conditions. At the moment Indo-European languages enter the light of history, they are spoken in regions of a vastly different animal and plant life: India, Iran, Mediterranean countries, Middle Europe —to name the most important. It is evident that their botanical and zoological vocabularies cannot be expected to show the same strict term-by-term correspondence as the numerals or the designations of relatives.

Starting from the probability that the mother language was spoken in one of the regions occupied by later Indo-European languages, we can eliminate those for whose characteristic plants and animals no reconstructible designations are available, that is: India (no Proto-Indo-European words for elephant, tiger, monkey, fig, tree, etc.), Iran (no Proto-Indo-European words for camel, donkey, lion, etc.), the Mediterranean countries (no Proto-Indo-European words for: donkey, lion; olive, vine, cypress, etc.). Which leaves us practically with the regions north of the Black or south of the Baltic Sea. There exists an a priori likelihood for the latter, because it is here we find, in historic times, the densest accumulation of diverse Indo-European languages: Germanic, Baltic, Slavic. We may contrast the situation in India and Iran: all Indian and Iranian Indo-European languages can be demonstrated to have descended from one single Indo-European speech form: Proto-Indo-Iranian. Very much the same is true for Greece and Italy. This kind of linguistic condition is typical for countries with an immigrant population, as the example of the practical linguistic unity of the U.S.A. shows.

The system of trees (and plants) we can reconstruct fits well into the country south of the Baltic Sea. Enumerating according to decreasing certainty, we obtain the following items, for all of which there exists at least a possibility of reconstruction, as it does not for items like elephant, donkey, lion, etc.: barley, birch, beech, aspen, oak, yew-tree, willow fir, spruce, alder, aspen.

This makes a tableau that is not only not self-contradictory, but characteristic: birch, beech, and aspen are common in our region; the beech does not cross a line that can be drawn from Königsberg (Kaliningrad) on the Baltic Sea to Odessa on the Black Sea; the aspen does not occur in more southern regions. The only one of the trees named that is found in India (in the Himālaya) is the birch; it bears an Indo-European name (*bhūrja*: Slavic *brēza*, Baltic *béržas*, English *birch*, Proto-IE **bherHgo-* fem.), in contrast to every single other tree in the Sanskrit dictionary. As to animals, we obtain:

Domesticated animals: dog, cattle, sheep (besides lamb and wool), horse (and mare), pig (and pigling), goat (and he-goat).

Animals of prey: wolf, bear, lynx, fox.

Other wild animals: stag, hare, mouse, snake (but not its characteristic enemy in India, the mongoose), hedgehog, turtle.

Birds: eagle, falcon, owl, crane, thrush.

Aquatic birds: goose, duck, diver.

Other aquatic animals: salmon, otter, beaver.

Insects: fly, hornet, wasp, bee (beside honey), louse, flea.

This is, again, a tableau that—though obviously far from being complete—is without inner contradictions and seems to let us recognize the most essential points: there is lacking no domestic animal and no big animal of prey that we can otherwise prove to have lived in the later Stone and the Copper and Bronze Age, in the Baltic and North German plains. Especially characteristic is the term for 'salmon.' This fish is found (together with beech, birch, and turtle) only in the rivers that go into the Baltic and German Sea. While the expression for 'beech' lets us fix the eastern border of the region of Proto-Indo-European speech, that for 'turtle,' which is foreign to Scandinavia (as was, originally, the beech), excludes the Scandinavian countries.

The clear-cut character and the harmonious consistency of this picture of the Proto-Indo-European flora and fauna confirms in its own way the soundness of our methods of reconstruction. It makes it possible to locate the area where our postulated language was spoken—within the domain of salmon rivers and their tributaries, to the west of the "beech line," outside of Scandinavia, that is, in the region of the rivers Vistula, Oder, and Elbe, approximately around the point where representatives of eastern (Baltic, Slavic) and western (Germanic) Indo-European languages meet.

REFERENCE NOTE

This article is in origin an expansion of points made in two reviews, one of Hugh Hencken, *Indo-European Languages and Archaeology* (*Lg.*, 1957, *33:* 183-190), and the other of Albert Carnoy, *Dictionnaire Étymologique du Proto-Indo-Européen* (*Lg.*, 1958, *34:* 510-515), together with results based on the author's monograph, *Die Heimat der indogermanischen Gemeinsprache* (1954). (Cf. Thieme, 1958.)

For semantic reconstruction in Indo-European, see also Bender (1922), Bosch-Gimpera (1960), Meillet (1926-1936, 1934), Schrader (1890, 1906), and Schrader and Nehring (1917-1929). For semantic reconstruction in New World language families, see Hoijer (1956), Hymes and Driver (1958), Law (1961), Longacre and Millon (1961), Matthews (1959), Sapir (1916, 1936), Swadesh (1960a, 1960b); and see also the Algonquian example in the next article, together with Hockett (1957). For views on general method and problems, see Benveniste (1954), Bonfante (1945), Gleason (1959), Hockett (1958, pp. 523-525), Hoenigswald (1960), Hymes (1955, 1956b), Pike (1950), the important series of articles on etymological research by Malkiel (1954a, 1954b, 1956, 1957, 1962a) and his exemplary review of Hubschmid's prehistoric probings (1962c), Meillet (1933a), Sapir (1916), Swadesh's article on pp. 575-584 and its references, Trager (1955b), and see references on semantic change with Hoijer's article on pp. 455-466.

For inference of the homeland of a linguistic group from the evidence of distribution, rather than reconstructed cultural content, see the recent theoretical analysis by Dyen (1956), its application with New World examples (Salishan, Mayan) by Diebold (1960), the classic paper by Sapir (1916), the related papers by Voegelin (1945b, 1958), and the inference of an historical process affecting a number of groups in a particular environment by Jacobs (1937).

References not in the general bibliography:

BENVENISTE, EMILE

1954. Problèmes sémantiques de la reconstruction. *Word*, *10* (2-3): 251-264.

BONFANTE, G.

1945. On Reconstruction and Linguistic Method. *Word*, *1:* 83-94, 132-161.

BOSCH-GIMPERA, P.

1960. *El Problema Indoeuropa*. With an appendix by M. Swadesh. (Universidad Nacional Autonoma de Mexico, Publicaciones del Instituto de Historia, Primera serie, Num. 45.) Mexico: Direccion General de Publicaciones.

DIEBOLD, A. RICHARD, JR.

1960. Determining the Centers of Dispersal of Language Groups. *IJAL, 26:* 1-10.

DYEN, ISIDORE

1956. Language Distribution and Migration Theory. *Lg., 32:* 611-626.

HOCKETT, C. F.

1957. Central Algonquian Vocabulary: Stems in /k-/. *IJAL, 23:* 247-268.

HOIJER, HARRY

1956. Athapaskan Kinship Systems. *AA, 58:* 309-333.

HYMES, DELL H., and H. E. DRIVER

1958. Concerning the Proto-Athapaskan Kinship System. *AA, 60:* 152-156.

JACOBS, MELVILLE

1937. Historic Perspective in Indian Languages of Oregon and Washington. *Pacific Northwest Quarterly, 28:* 55-74.

LAW, HOWARD W.

1961. A Reconstructed Proto-Culture Derived from Some Yuman Vocabularies. *AL, 3* (4): 45-52.

LONGACRE, ROBERT E., and RENÉ MILLON

1961. Proto-Mixtecan and Proto-Amuzgo-Mixtecan Vocabularies: A Preliminary Analysis. *AL, 3* (4): 1-44.

MALKIEL, YAKOV

1954a. Etymology and the Structure of Word Families. *Word, 10:* 251-264.

1954b. The Place of Etymology in Linguistic Research. *Bulletin of Hispanic Studies, 31:* 78-90.

1956. The Uniqueness and Complexity of Etymological Solutions. *Lingua, 5:* 225-252.

1957. A Tentative Typology of Etymological Studies. *IJAL, 23:* 1-17.

MATTHEWS, G. H.

1959. Proto-Siouan Kin Terms. *AA, 61:* 252-278.

PIKE, KENNETH L.

1950. *Axioms and Procedures for Reconstruction in Linguistics. An Experimental Syllabus.* Glendale, Calif.: Summer Institute of Linguistics.

THIEME, PAUL

1958. The Indo-European Language. *Scientific American*, October, pp. 63-74.

VOEGELIN, C. F.

1945b. Relative Chronology of North American Linguistic Types. *AA, 47:* 232-234.

1958. The Dispersal Factor in Migrations and Immigrations of American Indians. In R. H. Thompson (Ed.), *Migrations in New World Culture History*. (University of Arizona Social Science Bulletin, No. 27.) Tucson: University of Arizona Press. Pp. 47-61.

Implications of Bloomfield's Algonquian Studies 62

CHARLES F. HOCKETT

IT IS GENERALLY known that one of Leonard Bloomfield's life works is the descriptive and comparative study of Algonquian. (Bloomfield's publications on Algonquian are listed here, approximately in order of publication. They will be referred to hereafter as "Ref. 1," and so on, except that the third and twelfth items will be termed, respectively, the Sound System and the Sketch. The latter includes a bibliography of Algonquian which is complete save for a few items which have appeared since 1941.

1. Review: Truman Michelson, *The Owl Sacred Pack of the Fox Indians*, *American Journal of Philology*, *43*:276-281 (1922).
2. The Menomini Language, *Proceedings of the Twenty-first International Congress of Americanists*. (The Hague, 1924), pp. 336-343.
3. On the Sound-System of Central Algonquin, *Lg. 1*:130-156 (1925).
4. The Word-Stems of Central Algonquian, *Festschrift Meinhof* (Hamburg, 1927), pp. 393-402.
5. Notes on the Fox Language, *IJAL*, *3*:219-232 (1924); *4*:181-219 (1927).
6. A Note on Sound Change, *Lg.*, *5*:99-100 (1928).
7. The Plains Cree Language. *Proceedings of the Twenty-second International Congress of Americanists* (Rome, 1928), pp. 427-431.
8. *Menomini Texts* (Publications of the American Ethnological Society, Vol. 12; New York, 1928).
9. *Sacred Stories of the Sweet Grass Cree* (National Museum of Canada, Bulletin 60; Ottowa, 1930).
10. *Plains Cree Texts* (Publications of the American Ethnological Society, Vol. 16; New York, 1934).
11. Proto-Algonquian *-iit-* "Fellow," *Lg.*, *17*:292-297 (1941).
12. Algonquian, *Linguistic Structures of Native America* (Viking Fund Publications in Anthropology, No. 6; New York, 1946), pp. 85-129. [See now Hockett, 1953b.]

Many of the non-Algonquian references given in the footnotes of this paper were found with the assistance of Robert A. Hall, Jr. For my understanding of the "almost mystical" version of the drift theory [see Section 8], I am indebted to Gordon H. Fairbanks [who is not a proponent of this version of the theory]. All of my colleagues at Cornell have participated in instructive discussion of this paper, and to all of them I express my thanks.)

It is also generally conceded that his work in this field is of considerable importance. ('A remarkable contribution,' says Sturtevant [1947] of Bloomfield's Sketch.) But most of those who are quite willing to admit this do so on indirect evidence: since Bloomfield's other work proves him a sound scholar, his Algonquian studies must be sound too. Algonquian, after all, is an out-of-the-way language family, and few have concerned themselves with it. In view, particularly, of Bloomfield's endeavors in this field, this neglect is unfortunate. To the writer the following points seem beyond dispute: (1) careful study of Algonquian as Bloomfield has described it can be a fascinating, enlightening, and rewarding experience even for established comparatists and historical linguists; (2) for the newcomer to linguistics, a reading of Bloomfield's Algonquian works is one of the finest indoctrinations into the best of linguistic method.

In a sense, any body of data on any group of languages can serve in both these roles. But if, for example, the would-be linguist attempts to learn the elementary principles of comparative method in terms of Indo-European, or even of Germanic or Romance, the external difficulties are great: the material is widely scattered and bulky, some of it is old and hard to interpret, some of it is excellent but some is extremely bad. On the other hand, even though the

Algonquian languages are "exotic" (whatever that may mean), they are phonetically simple, not too widely divergent from the familiar Indo-European languages in structure—remarkably similar, in some ways, to older Germanic—and Bloomfield's treatment is compact, uniform in approach, and uniformly excellent. (Bloomfield has noted the resemblance to older Germanic several times in conversation but not, so far as I know, in print; in Ref. 5, 4:191, the comparison is rather with Indo-European as a whole. Needless to say, the attempts of Reider T. Sherwin [1940-1946] to establish a genetic connection between Algonquian and Germanic are entirely misguided.)

Most of the lessons which can be learned from Bloomfield's Algonquian are apparent to anyone who reads, with suitable diligence, his Sketch. There are, in addition, a few important points which are not apparent from that paper alone, nor even necessarily from that paper together with his other writings in this field, save to someone who had some independent first-hand contact with the extant Algonquian languages and with earlier efforts, mainly by missionaries, to describe this or that language of the group. It is our purpose here to list those principles and procedures of historical and comparative linguistics which seem to emerge with especial clarity and force from Bloomfield's Algonquian studies. It is the writer's hope that this listing and discussion will serve to focus more attention on the work dealt with, and to be of some assistance to the person who does undertake the study recommended. (The principles itemized in this paper are by no means intended to constitute a complete canon of historical or comparative linguistics. The choice is based on the nature of the Algonquian material, not on a general analysis of linguistic method.)

We shall discuss the following points:

1. Description and history
2. The evaluation of written records
3. The use of phonemic notation
4. Preliminary internal reconstruction
5. Assumptions about directions of linguistic change
6. The assumption of regular sound change
7. The *Wörter-und-Sachen* technique
8. Drift
9. Significance of starred forms
10. Negative lessons

On each of these there has been, and is, disagreement among those who occupy professional posts in which they purport to deal with language. On each point (save the last), Bloomfield's Algonquian material unambiguously indicates one answer, to the exclusion of the various alternatives that have been proposed.

1. *DESCRIPTION AND HISTORY*

There are still extremists who say that descriptive linguistics is balderdash, and a few, equally extreme, who scorn the comparative method in historical linguistics as irrelevant antiquarianism and, at best, guess work. (On the former, Whatmough, 1943, 1944; also the implications of Harris, 1940; on the latter, *Acta Linguistica*, 1940-1941, 2:1-22; Jakobson, 1944, pp. 192-193; and see Robert A. Hall Jr., 1946. [Cf. now also, 1953, pp. 52-108—D.H.H.]) Some of the disagreement is genuine; but some stems simply from the insufficient complexity of our terminology for different types of linguistic operation. In order to see the genuine issue we must clear away the terminological obscurities.

A SYNCHRONIC analysis describes the speech habits of an individual or a relatively homogeneous group at a particular time. (The terms "synchronic" and "diachronic" date at least from Ferdinand de Saussure [1916].) It ignores what interpersonal differences may be known, and makes no mention of changes in habits that take place during the period from which the evidence dates. A CONTRASTIVE study compares the speech habits of different individuals or groups and tallies the similarities and differences—regardless of the relative position of the speakers or groups in space or time. ("Contrastive" is Whorf's proposal [see Whorf, 1941a] made because the more natural term "comparative" is already pre-empted for a different technical use.) A DIACHRONIC analysis states the changes in speech habits in a single community from one point in time to a later period. Occasionally one can observe marked personal differences even in a small community, or clear instances of change of habit during a very short span of time; when such observations are included in a monograph which is mainly synchronic, that does not necessitate any change in the definition of "synchronic," but simply means that the content of the monograph is not purely synchronic. This comment should not be interpreted as an objection to the practice, which is often valuable. (Good illustrations of the value of mixed synchronic and diachronic discussion are Ref. 4, 401—which includes also some extremely penetrating remarks on the relation between the synchronic and diachronic points of view—and Bloomfield's paper "Literate and Illiterate Speech" [Part VII, pp. 391-396].)

In the gathering of information, for synchronic, contrastive, or diachronic purposes, there are several different methods. The CONTACT method consists in first-hand observation of the speakers. The PHILOLOGICAL method consists in the interpretation of written records. The COMPARATIVE method extrapolates backwards from the earliest evidence available (or the earliest used) from two or more dialects or languages which seem to be related. Between these methods there is no sharp line of demarcation. The field worker, though he uses the contact method, later studies his own notes and in so doing involves himself in a kind of philological method; another linguist may read the notes, or the completed report, of the first, and so places himself in a position somewhat analogous to that of the interpreter of written records which date from earlier generations. The close intertwining of the philological and comparative methods is obvious. (This three-by-three categorization of types of linguistic activity is more general in its application than here indicated: it applies, as a matter of fact, to all the subject-matter of cultural anthropology, of which linguistics is logically a subdivision. This is clearly indicated in Sapir [1916]. There are doubtless some types of fruitful and valid investigation, of language or of culture as a whole, not subsumed in the classification.)

The extraneous sources of argument about "description" and "history" stem from the ambiguity in the use of those two terms (or of others used in place of them). "Description" sometimes refers to synchronic analysis, sometimes to contact method. "History" sometimes means diachronic analysis, sometimes philological or comparative method or both. With the more narrowly defined terms, the logical interrelationships are easy to see. (The methodological points of "principles" drawn from the discussion are lettered serially through the paper, from *a* to *p*.)

a. Synchronic analysis may be based on any of the three methods, or on combinations of them. Synchronic analysis of a language no longer spoken, obviously, cannot involve the contact method; that of a language for which there are no direct records has to be based on the comparative method. In this sense, "description" is not logically prior to "history."

b. Either diachronic or contrastive analysis involves prior synchronic analysis. In this sense, "description" is logically prior to "history."

c. The comparative method has to involve comparison of something. The data to which the comparative method is applied consist of bodies of synchronic descriptions of related languages. The assumptions which underlie the comparative method are distilled from diachronic analyses of bodies of synchronic material, all of which are based, in turn, on a method other than the comparative method. (That is, we derive our notions of linguistic change in the first instance from the history of those languages, such as English, French, and German, for which there is documentary evidence over a considerable span of time. We then make a comparative analysis of some group of languages whose common ancestor is known to us independently—for example, Romance—assuming the kinds of linguistic change discovered by the first operation, and comparing our reconstruction with the documentary evidence for the parent. Since our inverted predictions in such cases have a considerable degree of accuracy, we feel confident of at least statistically accurate results when the same comparative method is applied to a group of languages for whose parent there is no other evidence. It is true that linguistic science in the 19th century did not follow this course in its chronological development; but this does not invalidate the logical statement. Until the logical interrelationships had clearly emerged, the statements of historical linguistics were somewhat more tentative than afterwards.)

These interrelations are complex. The virtue of Bloomfield's Algonquian studies on this score is that the interrelations not only are perfectly clear to Bloomfield, but are made equally clear to his reader. His Sketch, for example, is at one and the same time all of the following: (1) a brief synchronic outline grammar of four Algonquian languages still extant; that is, Fox (F), Cree (C), Menomini (M), and Ojibwa (O). (The abbreviations indicated will be used in the rest of this paper, together with "PA" for Proto-Algonquian, the reconstructed parent, but see Section 10.); (2) a brief synchronic outline grammar of their parent; (3) a contrastive analysis of the four modern languages and the parent language; (4) an outline of the diachronic analysis of the continuum from the parent to each of the modern languages; and (5) a demonstration of the application of the comparative method to the modern data for the reconstruction of the parent language. The Sketch does not take up these problems one by one, but rather gives a composite picture. A single careful reading produces an accurate and realistic general impression of Algonquian structure. A subsequent reading with special attention to any one of the facets listed above can give more detailed information. In such successive readings, one is never at a loss to know the range of application of each individual statement: it applies just to F, or just to the development of F from PA, or just to PA, or to all the languages, and so on.

Bloomfield's Sketch, then, is a model useful to anyone who faces the task of organizing information about a family of languages into an arrangement that makes synchronic, diachronic, and contrastive sense.

2. *THE EVALUATION OF WRITTEN RECORDS*

The documentary material on which Bloomfield bases his Algonquian analysis is of several types: (1) his own field records of M and C, made with full benefit of phonemic theory; (2) F records from William Jones, a native speaker of F who was trained under Boas and Michelson in phonetics, but not in phonemics (For references see the Sketch. Later contributions by Michelson use approximately the same notation. It is not clear whether this notation was a joint product of Jones and Michelson, or was worked out by one and passed on to the other.); (3) O records from the same person; (4) earlier records by missionaries and traders, without benefit of either phonetics or phonemics, and with English or French as native language, but with the advantage of long residence with the Indians and constant practical use of the languages. Since Bloomfield's first publications, others trained under him or within his sphere of influence have recorded F and O, and Bloomfield himself has recorded O. (F: at least J. M. Cowan, Carl F. Voegelin, and the present writer; O: the latter two, J. A. Geary (other dialects), F. T. Siebert, Jr., and—in the summers when O was the language studied in the field-methods course at the Linguistic Institute—a good many others.) We thus have a check on the accuracy of older reports, except for the negligible extent to which speech patterns may have changed between missionary times and the present.

Jones' F materials are overloaded with superfluous diacritics, indicating evanescent distinctions or subphonemic differences, but in general no phonemic contrast is omitted. O materials from the same observer have the same unnecessary indication of minutiae, but in addition obscure certain phonemic contrasts which are of considerable comparative importance—for example, the contrast between *sk* and *šk*. Certainly there is a relationship between these facts and Jones' background. F does not have the contrast *sk:šk*; it is not surprising that as a native speaker of F, Jones missed the contrast when listening to the rather similar O. His phonetic training, without phonemics, led to the overly minute recording of what he had happened to be trained to hear; his native control of F prevented omission of contrasts that were relevant there. (It would be tempting to generalize as follows. If a native speaker of a language is trained in phonetics in such a way that he will hear, in any language, at least all those contrasts, which are distinctive for his own speech, and will have the symbols easily at hand to record them, he will, in recording his own language, sometimes include subphonemic contrasts, but will never omit contrasts that count. But this statement is far from obviously true. Suggestions of this kind were made by Sapir in "Sound Patterns in Language" [1925] and more elaborately in "La realité psychologique des phonèmes" [1933b], but Twaddell's discussion, "On Defining the Phoneme" [in Joos, 1957] raises serious doubts.)

As might be expected, the missionary records are much less satisfactory. Some of them consistently fail to indicate such important features as vowel length; some of them write subphonemic distinctions heard at one time or another, because those distinctions were present phonemically in French or in English; sometimes certain contrasts are recorded irregularly. As a result of the last, when one desires to check on some feature of a particular word, one often finds that the missionary recording is unreliable on that point. (Some such cases are discussed in Geary [1941].)

We may distill from this the following methodological observation:

d. The extent to which one can use written records made by an untrained person can only be determined by direct observation of the language by a trained person. For a language no longer spoken, this is of course impossible.

e. When a direct check is impossible, records made by a native speaker are more trustworthy than those made by a foreigner; those made by a person with some training (as Jones' training in phonetics to the exclusion of phonemics) are more trustworthy than those from a person with no training at all; obviously, records from a person with long practical contact, other things being equal, are more trustworthy than those from the casual passer-by.

3. *THE USE OF PHONEMIC NOTATION*

If one compares Bloomfield's Sketch with the recent paper by Geary, one difference is striking. All forms cited in Bloomfield's paper are phonemicized, and the choice of symbols for each language is such as to render the switch from one language to another as easy as possible for the reader. Geary could not validly do this; for his object was to cull from all sources, including the missionary records, forms which are evidence for a particular PA consonant cluster; of necessity he cites each form from an older record in the graphic shape in which it was found. Anyone can read Bloomfield; only an Algonquianist can really read Geary.

Further scrutiny of these two papers, and of some of the older records, shows that the close relationship of the Algonquian languages is immediately apparent from the missionary records; but it would be almost impossible to attempt the reconstruction of PA on the basis of missionary records alone. On the other hand, once something is known of the structure of PA, many of the missionary records can be used, though sometimes with uncertainty, to find additional cases of this or that correspondence.

This further supports point (d) and (e) and suggests the following:

f. Written records are a means to an end, and there is no justification for holding them in high esteem, or even in reverence (as is sometimes the case) except as indirect evidence for what one is trying to discover (Lane, 1946, p. 256; *French Review,* 1944, *17:* 168-170).

g. When his only evidence consists of written records, the analyst should attempt a phonemic interpretation of the material. He can achieve accuracy in his synchronic description, in his diachronic deductions, and in his use of the material for comparative purposes, only to the extent that the phonemic interpretation of the written records is feasible without ambiguity. (Disagreements about methods of phonemicization are another matter. If "phonemic solutions" are non-unique, as seems likely to me at the present moment, any alternative one will do. There is a gain in clarity and simplicity if each of a set of languages to be compared is phonemicized by the same principles, but if this is not done reconstruction is still perfectly feasible. Against phonemics of any kind: *Archivo Glottologico Italiano, 1940, 31:*159—one instance of many.) Furthermore, he should make his phonemic interpretation clearly recognizable to his readers, by including for every form cited, explicitly or by implication, a possible phonemicization (Bloomfield, 1933, Section 5.10). Failure to do the former impairs his own results; failure to do the latter hampers his readers.

Some of the undue esteem in which written records are held has probably been supported by the following additional principle, which is not deducible from Bloomfield's Sketch, but does appear in some of his earlier writings and quite clearly in Geary's paper:

h. When the interpretation of written records cannot be completely free from ambiguity, the graphic shape actually occurent in the source should be included along with the attempted phonemicization—or, when more convenient, a transliteration of the original graphic shape. The reader is then in the best possible position to re-examine the evidence and draw his own conclusions.

4. *PRELIMINARY INTERNAL RECONSTRUCTION*

The statement made above that in Bloomfield's Sketch all forms are phonemicized now has to be modified. His notation for O, and possibly for M and F, deviates from the phonemic "ideal" in being somewhat more than phonemic.

In Southern O occur three varieties of vowels: long /*ii ee aa oo*/, short /*i a o*/, and ultra short /*ə u*/. Within the limits of a word, the distribution of short and ultra-short vowels is almost, but not quite, predictable in terms of environment. Since the predictability is not complete, the distinction is phonemic: one must write /*i a o*/ and /*ə u*/ as they are heard. Bloomfield does not do so: he writes only *ii ee aa oo* and *i a o*, e.g., *mittik* instead of *məttik* 'tree.' For most Southern O dialects, one cannot tell whether the vowel in the first syllable—an ultra-short one—is /*i*/ or /*a*/, and phonemically one would have to use a special symbol /*ə*/; the same symbol would have to be used in a completely phonemic transcription of what Bloomfield transcribes as *akkikk* 'kettle,' rather than the initial *a* of that form. O itself, and the diachronic analysis of the continuum from PA to O, are treated by Bloomfield in terms of this normalized notation. Can this procedure be justified?

The answer is yes. Bloomfield's notation is based on the preliminary internal reconstruction (Hoenigswald, 1944, 1946; see also, 1960) of an O dialect-type that must have preceded the current dialects by only a relatively short period of time. The reconstruction is internal, not based on comparison of dialects, since the earlier stage can be postulated with validity on the basis of the data for any one dialect. If one compares phonemic /*məttik*/ 'tree' with /*nəmittəkoom*/ 'my tree,' and /*əkkikk*/ 'kettle' with /*nəntakkəkkoom*/ 'my kettle,' one observes that /*ə*/ alternates (under statable conditions of word-rhythm) with both /*i*/ and /*a*/. There are a few cases in which no larger form can be found of the right rhythmic pattern to determine whether the alternation is with /*i*/ or with /*a*/, and in most of the dialects there are a few cases in which ultra-short vowels have disappeared altogether. Even in a synchronic description of O, however, the restoration of /*i*/ and /*a*/ rather than /*ə*/ in all such cases, with statements on the reduction of short vowels in words of each rhythmic pattern, is a necessary step for efficient treatment. One's working notation then becomes morphophonemic rather than purely phonemic; from the graphs /*mittik*/, /*nimittikoom*/, /*akkikk*/, /*nintakkikkoom*/, and the statements, one can infer the actual phonemic shape with very little difficulty.

In other words, what Bloomfield does in the case of O is to use a morphophonemically regularized notation instead of a straight phonemic transcription. There is evidence of such regularization in M and F too. F forms are given with intervocalic /*w*/ and /*y*/, which are morphophonemically correct and which must have been phonemically correct in a slightly earlier stage, rather than with the curious alternation and evanescence that those morphophonemes now exhibit. (Obvious from Jones' texts; observed by the present writer in the Kickapoo and Sauk dialects of Fox.) M is cited with five short and five long vowels, though Bloomfield himself has said that in actual pronunciation the three-way distinction of /*i*/ : /*e*/ : /*ε*/ is partly obscured. (Ref. 8, xiv: "The texts are here recorded as they struck my ear. Analysis shows that this record [and therefore, if I heard aright, the actual pronunciation] largely obscures the distinction between three short front-vowel phonemes, which here appear as i and e." Since Bloomfield became a fluent speaker of Menomini [a fact which he does not admit, but which is fairly obvious from his discussions], his recording is probably accurate. Nowadays we would cast his statement in the terminology of morphophonemics rather than phonemics, but the fact stated would not be altered.)

We deduce the following principle:

i. Before comparative analysis is undertaken, each body of synchronic data should be examined carefully to see whether there are not internal clues, mainly morphophonemic, to the structure of the language at a slightly earlier stage. When there are, any possible internal reconstruction should be undertaken, since it will dispose of later innovations in each language, getting them out of the way for a clearer view of the deeper time-perspective of external comparison.

5. *ASSUMPTIONS ABOUT DIRECTIONS OF LINGUISTIC CHANGE*

Bloomfield's description of Proto-Algonquian reveals it as a language of approximately the same degree of complexity as any one of the modern languages. Each of the modern languages has retained some of the features of the parent, lost some, and developed some new ones. F has the vocalic system of PA; C and O have one vowel fewer than PA; M has two more. The number of individual consonants in PA (excluding first members of clusters, section 9) is greater than in any of the modern languages; it seems highly probable however, that θ and *s*, and similarly *t* and *c*, which stand in close morphophonemic relation in PA, were at a slightly earlier stage allophones of single phonemes—perhaps, indeed, this was true even in PA times. The larger number of consonants in PA, then, was a temporary matter, the result of certain phonemic and analogic changes, and the number was later reduced in each line of development. The modal systems of verbs in the daughter languages correlate exactly only in a few cases. One suspects that some of the modes present in PA have split in some of the modern languages, and have been lost in others; certainly the total number of modes in PA did not exceed the rather large number in present-day F (Sketch, Section 33).

j. In undertaking a reconstruction, there is no justification for any of the following a priori assumptions: (1) that the parent language was simpler than the descendants; (2) that it was more complex than the descendants; or (3) that it manifested about the same degree of complexity as the descendants.

The first of these a priori assumptions is the old theory of the "primitiveness" of "early" language, and of contemporary languages spoken by "simple" peoples. (Max Muller's myth of speakers with vocabularies of only a few hundred words is related. W. von Humboldt [1836, Section 19] gives three stages in the history of language: "growth" before IE, a "state of perfection" in IE, and "decay" since then; for other early references see *Lg.*, 1936, *12:*101 and *Italica*, 1941, *18:*145-154. Later survivals of these older notions: the subject of review in Kent, 1935; Bonfante, 1935, esp. 272, 274-275; Sommerfelt, 1938.) The second is the inversion of the first brought about primarily by Jespersen's discussion (1894). (See also his *Efficiency in Linguistic Change* [1941] and the review in *Lg.*, 1941, *17:*350-353. Bernhard Karlgren [1926], in reconstructing ancient and archaic Chinese, posits extremely complex phonological structure for those stages of Chinese, and seems [though without explicit reference] to justify this greater complexity for the older stage in terms of Jespersen's theory. Cf. now Koenraads, 1954, with reviews of it in *Language and Word.*) More concrete suggestions, akin to one or the other, are also found. All such theories derive from a hope which a hundred years ago was legitimate: that comparative linguistics might in time push our perspective on the history of language appreciably nearer the beginnings of human speech. Now that we realize how old is human speech, and what a scratch on the surface of that depth is our deepest reconstruction, the hope must be abandoned.

Bloomfield's PA reconstruction speaks not only against assumptions (1) and (2), but against any a priori assumption of this kind whatsoever. In his paper of 1925 (Ref. 3), Bloomfield postulated two more vowels and one more consonant for PA than are included in the Sketch. Since then he has discovered the analogical bases, in certain of the individual languages, for the complications that had earlier led him to assume these additional phonemes. The first, more complex system was not set up because Bloomfield thought that an older language "should be" more complex; nor did he later simplify the picture through any conviction that an older language "should not be" more complex. In each case the assumed degree of complexity was simply an inference from the facts known about the modern languages.

6. *THE ASSUMPTION OF REGULAR SOUND CHANGE*

One story in the slow development of our understanding of PA is worth telling in detail, even though it is already perhaps the most generally known phase of Algonquian linguistics.

In his Sound System (Ref. 3), Bloomfield postulated the PA cluster *çk* (F O *šk*, C M *hk*) on very slim evidence. There was only one stem, meaning 'red,' to be found which showed just this correspondence in the extant languages, and each of those languages had the cluster in question also as a reflex of one or more other PA clusters. Yet there seemed to be no analogical basis in any of the languages whereby a reconstruction could be made with a better attested PA cluster, and borrowing seemed unlikely in view of the meaning of the stem. There were a few other sets of apparently related words showing unique correspondences of cluster—'spoon' has F C *hk*, as though from PA *hk*, but M has *sk* instead of the *hk* which would arise from the latter. But these other cases are in morphologically isolated words, whereas the PA stem 'red' underlies many derivatives in every language.

A year or so later, it was discovered that Swampy Cree, a dialect from which records had not earlier been available, had in words containing this stem not *hk* but *htk*, a cluster not found in Swampy Cree as the reflex of any other PA cluster so far set up. Here was not merely an exceptional correspondence between usual clusters, but an extant dialect in which the postulated PA cluster is kept separate from all others. Bloomfield published a note giving this as evidence for the productivity of the assumption of regular sound change (Ref. 6). Sapir cited the case, together with a similar one from his own Athabascan work, in an article on the comparative method as one of the methods of social science (1931c; see also Bloomfield, 1933, Section 20.8).

But the story did not end there. New investigators (listed on p. 602) discovered that Jones had consistently misheard the O forms: the O words with this stem have *sk*, not *šk*, and this *sk* is not found as a reflex of any other PA cluster. Swampy Cree no longer stood as the only extant dialect to keep PA *çk* separate; O was now known to do so too. Geary examined the missionary sources and discovered a number of other cases of the same correspondence, so that the stem for 'red' was no longer isolated —even though PA *çk* still seemed to be relatively rare. In his Sketch, Bloomfield indicates a footnote: "The fuss and trouble behind my note in Language [see above] . . . would have been avoided if I had listened to O, which plainly distinguishes *sk* (< PA *çk*) from *šk* (< PA *šk*); instead, I depended on printed records which failed to show the distinction" (Sketch, n. 10).

It should be clear that the wording of Bloomfield's note detracts in no way from the importance of the sequence of events outlined above as evidence for the productivity of the assumption we are discussing. After the publication of the Sound System, events might conceivably have taken a different turn. Instead of discovering additional cases of the same correspondence, Jones' error, and the special reflex in Swampy Cree, Algonquianists might have found an analogical basis or an opportunity for borrowing whereby PA *çk* could be eliminated. This turn of events would also have proved the fruitfulness of the assumption.

For what we mean in this case by "productivity" or "fruitfulness" is just what Bloomfield states in his book *Language* (1933, Section 20.5): residual forms, not accounted for at a particular stage in the history of the reconstruction of a particular parent borrowing, or accounted for by postulated changes for which there is very little evidence—such residual forms *stimulate further investigation.* As a basis for further investigation, the linguist sets up hypotheses to explain what might have been the past history of certain forms. Many such hypotheses remain unproved, because additional investigation reveals no additional evidence; others are disproved by new evidence that is uncovered. But some of them are proved right. Slowly but surely the stock of residual forms is reduced, though it may never be exhausted. The contrary fundamental assumption—that sound changes proceed at random—produces nothing at all, because there are never any problems; given any form that won't fit the sound changes so far observed, one simply assumes a sporadic change of a different sort.

k. We must assume regularity of sound change.

7. *THE* WÖRTER-UND-SACHEN *TECHNIQUE*

(Bloomfield, 1933, Section 18.14 and references.) Bloomfield reconstructs PA *paăskesikani* 'gun' and *eškoteewaapoowi* 'whisky,' both on the basis of perfectly normal correspondences between whole words in the extant languages. The items named by these terms, of course, are post-Columbian. The forms are compound; Bloomfied says in a footnote to the first that "here, as in some other examples, the meaning is modern, but the habit of formation is old" (Sketch, n. 13).

If only this is to be ascribed to pre-Columbian times, then each of the modern languages concerned has coined new terms for the new items of material culture, using identical (Cognate) morphemes according to identical patterns of formation, in such a way that the phonetic correspondences between the whole words are perfect. But it might also be that the terms themselves date from PA times, and that since the introduction of whisky and guns by Europeans the semantic shifts have been parallel in the various languages. Or, as European influence spread, the forms may have been invented by the speakers of one language and then borrowed by loan-translation into the other languages. (The English expression "fire-water" may be a loan-translation from Algonquian; if the former is older, then one or more Algonquian languages may have loan-translated the English.)

It does not matter, for our present purposes, which of these alternatives is true. The fact that from well-attested modern forms one can reconstruct PA forms with meanings that were obviously impossible for PA is a clear indication of danger in the *Wörter-und-Sachen* technique. We deduce the following composite principle:

l. Attempts to infer the culture of the speakers of a reconstructed parent language wholly from the forms and meanings of the daughter languages are always dangerous. The danger is less, though probably still considerable, if the forms compared are morphologically simple than if they are compounds.

8. *DRIFT*

There are two versions of the theory of drift. One is almost mystical: in a particular linguistic continuum the same sound shifts may happen over and over again; there is something in the genius of the language which leads to these sound shifts rather than to others (Prokosch, 1939, especially pp. 34 ff.). The other is realistic and fairly simple: when a speech community has split, inherited speech habits are for a while fairly similar, and may lead to the independent analogical development of forms which look like inherited cognates. If at a later date the descendant languages are compared with a view to reconstruction of the parent, some such pseudo-cognates may be falsely ascribed to the parent language. (The discussion in Sapir's *Language*, [1921, chaps. 7-8] is sufficiently broad to justify [apparently] either interpretation; for the realistic theory, see pp. 184-185 in particular.) The Algonquian words for 'gun' and 'whisky,' in all probability, are illustrations of this, though we cannot be absolutely sure.

m. Any *individual* reconstructed form is suspect because of the possible influence of drift (in the second sense). In comparative linguistics one may achieve only statistical accuracy.

9. *THE SIGNIFICANCE OF STARRED FORMS*

There have been two theories of reconstructed forms. (Cogently discussed by C. D. Buck [1926]. Buck says: the purpose of reconstructions "is not to furnish a picture of the parent speech for its own sake, but as a background of the historical relations" [p. 102]. This is in part an answer to the charge of "irrelevant antiquarianism" sometimes leveled at the comparative method; even so, we should say that "a picture of the parent speech for its own sake," to the degree attainable, is also a legitimate aim. When this problem was discussed at Yale in the late thirties, one person cited Sapir as a proponent of the realistic theory, in contrast to Bloomfield as a supporter of formulas. It will be clear from the present discussion that this interpretation of Bloomfield was wrong.) The so-called "realistic" theory holds that in reconstructing the phonemic pattern of a parent language, one should try to arrive at a set of phonemes bearing a relation to each other of the kind that is known to exist in languages more directly observed. The "formula" theory, on the other hand, holds that reconstructions are simply short notations representing sets of correspondences.

Bloomfield's Algonquian reconstructions show clearly the circumstances under which the first practice is possible, and those under which the second is necessary. The vowel system postulated for PA is certainly phonemically realistic, being identical with that of one modern language, F. The fundamental consonant system is also: *p t č* (possibly an allophone of *t*) *k s θ š* (possibly an allophone of *θ*) *h l m n w y* (the last two possibly allophones respectively of *o* and *i*). Of these, *l m n* (*w y*) were in all probability voiced; the others may have been voiced or voiceless, or perhaps were sometimes one and sometimes the other, without phonemic distinction (Sketch, Section 6). *θ* may have been a voiceless lateral rather than an interdental spirant, or, again, perhaps both, depending on dialect or on environment. The phonetic details are naturally obscure; it is the phonemic pattern which we claim to be "realistic." (In several recent papers Herbert Penzl [1944, 1947] has demonstrated, in connection with problems of early English, the difference between phonemic realism and what might be meant by phonetic realism.) The only type of doubt which could be raised as to the status of these elements as the actual phonemes of PA would be purely logistic: if, for example, every daughter language had, independently, changed PA *m* to *n* and PA *n* to *m*, no one could be the wiser. One could even claim that such a change would be subphonemic; in any case such possibilities need not disturb us.

When it comes to medial clusters, the situation is different. Medial clusters consist of two members; the second is always clearly identifiable as one of the ordinary consonants; but the multiplicity of correspondences requires the postulation of a somewhat larger munber of purely arbitrary elements as prior members (Sketch, Section 7). Thirty-one different medial clusters are attested; no one of them has identical reflexes in all four of the modern languages. (Since the phonemic systems of the modern languages are different, "identical" must be interpreted relatively: since F and O *š* and *k* are elements in differing sets of contrasts, F *šk* and O *šk* are not in any absolute sense "identical.")

In this case all one can do is to choose for the prior members a set of symbols which will have, if possible, some mnemonic value; e.g., PA *mp nt nč nk ns nš nθ nl* for clusters which in O have a nasal as first element, especially since such clusters in O occur only as reflexes of this set in PA.

Similarly, instead of writing *çk* for the PA cluster which gives F *šk*, C M *hk*, O *sk*, one could write *sk*, which is not otherwise used. It may well be that the PA clusters customarily written *mp*, *nt*, etc., actually had a nasal as first element. It may also be that PA *çk* was phonemically *sk*, the first elements being phonemically identical with the independently occuring PA *s*. But the use of these notations for mnemonic reasons is *not evidence* for such a phonemic interpretation: one may attain a spurious appearance of realism, but the actual phonemic nature of the first members of the clusters is still as obscure as before.

That the number of medial clusters in PA was larger than the number in any descendant language is surprising only to one who is not familiar with aspects of Algonquian linguistics other than phonology. In most of the modern languages there is a sandhi habit whereby an element ending in a consonant, when due to be followed in the same word by one beginning with a consonant, is separated therefrom by a non-morphemic i (Sketch, Section 16). This habit existed in PA times, but was then apparently rather new. The new habit prevented the re-formation of many clusters that had formerly existed; but compounds surviving from an earlier stage retained the more complex consonantism. The trend towards simplification of the cluster system was a characteristic of PA which continued in the various separate dialects after their split, but the details varied from one dialect to another. Some of the pre-PA compounds are reconstructible from the modern languages, giving an essential clue to the statements just made; most, however, remain obscure (Sketch, Section 17).

Thus it is quite possible that Algonquian research may in time produce evidence that will make the interpretation of the prior members of PA consonant clusters less purely algebraic. Only a deeper time-perspective, achieved by more detailed comparisons with Algonquian languages not of the Central Algonquian type, can do this. In the meantime, to underscore the point, "realism" in this phase of the reconstruction of PA can only be spurious.

n. Reconstruction should be phonemically realistic whenever possible.

o. When realistic reconstruction is not possible, arbitrary indices of correspondences must be used. The fact that they are arbitrary, and the reasons which necessitate that arbitrariness, should be clearly stated. This practice will prevent a spurious impression of realism on the reader, and will obviate futile speculation on his part as to what the arbitrarily symbolized elements may "really" have been.

10. *NEGATIVE LESSONS*

This paper could not serve its purpose fully without mentioning a few points on which, in the present writer's opinion, Bloomfield's Sketch can be misleading.

1. Bloomfield labels his reconstructed prototype "Proto-Algonquian." It is based mainly on the comparisón of F, C, M, and O; eastern Algonquian and the three groups of Plains languages are not often brought into the picture. Indeed, it would be difficult to include more mention of them in the present state of our knowledge. In feeling that the PA reconstructed in his Sketch will take care of the Plains languages, Bloomfield gives Michelson's work in the comparative analysis of the latter languages more credit than it deserves (Sketch, Section 2, referring to Michelson, 1935. The implication here is not that Michelson's study is not "brilliant," as Bloomfield terms it, but that the synchronic information on Plains Algonquian available to Michelson was unsatisfactory.) The course of wisdom for the reader

of Bloomfield's Sketch is to replace "PA" everywhere by "PCA," standing for "Proto-CENTRAL-Algonquian," and to withhold judgment on the status of the eastern and Plains languages until a good deal more of descriptive and comparative work has been done.

2. Bloomfield says, "before syllabic vowels, PA *i, o* are non-syllabic; we write *y, w*" (Sketch, Section 4). The phonemic status of *y* and *w* is another on which judgement is best reserved. Bloomfield's notation (with all four symbols *i o y w*) is good; his statement seems hasty.

3. Bloomfield cites Penobscot forms for Siebert, following Siebert's orthography except that accent marks are omitted. This conceals the fact that a number of the eastern languages of the family have an accentual system, more or less complex but definitely phonemic; these accentual systems have to be taken care of in the reconstruction of anything that can be called Proto-Algonquian. Exact citation of Siebert's forms, including the accent marks (perhaps with a footnote), would have been more in line with the general principles on which Bloomfield's work is based.

Point (3) turns on the discussion of Sections 2 and 3 in this paper. Point (2) is connected with the content of Section 9. From point (1) we derive our last principle:

p. A parent language reconstructed from the comparison of a certain set of daughter languages can be regarded as the parent only of the languages so used. Information from languages not previously used may change the reconstruction, deepen the time-perspective with a new reconstruction of an earlier stage, or demonstrate that the reconstruction already made is capable of handling the new data also. (Thus Potawatomi is probably historically analyzable on the basis of Bloomfield's P [C] A without modification thereof [Hockett, 1942], but Delaware is probably not [Voegelin, 1941].)

CONCLUSION

The sixteen principles which have been listed in the course of our discussion are not new or startling; indeed, by this time each of them ought to be so generally agreed upon that any mention of them, save in the most elementary textbooks of linguistics, would be ridiculous. We have unhappily not yet reached such uniformity of opinion about fundamentals. Yet if, for any one of the sixteen, Bloomfield's Algonquian evidence stood alone—if there were no comparative Germanic, comparative Romance, comparative Indo-European, comparative Semitic, and so on—that isolated support for the principle would still be persuasively solid.

REFERENCE NOTE

A few references have been added with the author's permission, and others completed, and the term "sound change" has been substituted in section 6 at his request, in keeping with the terminology of his *A Course in Modern Linguistics* (1958).

To Bloomfield's Algonquian publications may now be added the posthumous *Eastern Ojibwa* (1957) and *The Menomini Language* (1963). For other recent work on comparative Algonquian, consult articles and references in *IJAL*.

For general treatments of the comparative method and historical linguistics, consult references with the article by Hoijer in Part VIII and with the other articles in this Part, especially those of Swadesh, Thieme, and Kroeber. See especially Bloomfield (1933, chaps. 18 ff.), Gray (1939), Greenberg (1953, 1957c), Hoenigswald (1960), Lehmann (1962), Meillet (1925, 1926-1936, 1934), Paul (1960), Pedersen (1931), Sturtevant (1947), Swadesh (1954c, 1956a), Vendryes (1925, Part 4, chap. 5). See also Malkiel's essay in Part X. Handbooks and monographs on comparative work in Indo-European and other language families are regularly reviewed in the journals *Language* and *Word*. For an extended exchange on the nature and validity of comparative linguistics, see Allen (1953) and Ellis (1958); Allen takes the negative side and Ellis the positive.

References not in the general bibliography:

ALLEN, W. S.

1953. Relationship in Comparative Linguistics. *Transactions of the Philological Society*. London. Pp. 52-108.

BLOOMFIELD, LEONARD

1957. *Eastern Ojibwa: Grammatical Sketch, Texts, and Word Lists*. Edited by Charles F. Hockett. Ann Arbor: University of Michigan Press. [Reviewed, C. F. Voegelin, *Lg.*, 1959, *35:* 109-125.]

1963. *The Menomini Language*. Edited by Charles F. Hockett. (William Dwight Whitney Linguistic Series, Special Publications of the Linguistic Society of America.) New Haven: Yale University Press.

BONFANTE, G.

1935. Sobre la función de la heteroclisis en la formación de los termas nominales Indoeuropeos. *Emerita*, *3:* 257-276.

GEARY, J. A.

1941. Proto-Algonquian *çk:* Further Examples. *Lg.*, *17:* 304-310.

HARRIS, ZELLIG S.

1940. Review of Louis H. Gray, *Foundations of Language*. *Lg.*, *16:* 216-231.

HOCKETT, CHARLES F.

1942. The Position of Potawatomi in Central Algonkian. *Papers of the Michigan Academy of Sciences, Arts, and Letters*, *28:* 537-542.

1953b. Errata in Bloomfield's Algonquian Sketch. *IJAL*, *19:* 78.

HOENIGSWALD, HENRY M.

1944. Internal Reconstruction. *Studies in Linguistics*, *2:* 78-87.

JESPERSEN, OTTO

1894. *Progress in Language*. London.

KARLGREN, BERNHARD

1926. *Philology and Ancient China*. Oslo. Especially pp. 16-18.

KENT, ROLAND G.

1935. Review of Hermann Hirt, *Indogermanische Grammatik, Teil VI: Syntax I*. *Lg.*, *11:* 154-160.

KOENRAADS, W.

1954. *Studien über Sprachökonomische Entwicklung im Deutschen*. Amsterdam: Meulenhoff. [Reviewed, H. Hoenigswald, *Lg.*, 1954, *30:* 591-593; U. Weinreich, *Word*, 1955, *11:* 327-330.]

LANE, GEORGE S.

1946. Review of Stephen Einarsson, *Icelandic Grammar, Texts, Glossary*. *Lg.*, *22:* 249-259.

MICHELSON, T.

1935. Phonetic Shifts in Algonquian Languages. *IJAL*, *8:* 131-171.

PENZL, HERBERT

1944. Miscellanea: A Phonematic Change in Early Old English. *Lg.*, *20:* 84-86.

1947. The Phonemic Split of Germanic *k* in Old English. *Lg.*, *23:* 34-42.

PROKOSCH, E.

1939. *A Comparative Germanic Grammar*. Philadelphia.

SHERWIN, REIDER T.

1940-1946. *The Viking and the Red Man*. New York. 4 vols. to date.

STURTEVANT, EDGAR LEE

1947. Linguistics and the American Council of Learned Societies. *Lg.*, *23* (3): 313-317.

VOEGELIN, C. F.

1941. Proto-Algonquian Consonant Clusters in Delaware. *Lg.*, *17:* 143-147.

WHATMOUGH, J.

1943. Review of B. Bloch and G. L. Trager, *Outline of Linguistic Analysis*. *Classical Philology*, *38*: 210-211.

1944. Up from Gilgal: A Rejoinder. *Classical Philology*, *39:* 218-222.

63 The ABC's of Lexicostatistics (Glottochronology)

SARAH C. GUDSCHINSKY

INTRODUCTION

1. Lexicostatistics is a technique which attempts to provide dates for the earlier stages of languages much as carbon 14 dating provides dates for archaeological finds. This contrasts with previous linguistic methods which, although able to reconstruct to some extent the history of language, have been unable to provide dates apart from written historical records.

2. By simple inspection of comparable word lists, for example, the fact of the relationship of closely related languages can be discovered. But no one can say on the basis of simple inspection precisely how closely related two languages are (Swadesh, 1950, pp. 157, 164).

3. By the methods of comparative linguistics, it is possible to chart the phonemic changes by which contemporary languages have developed from a common parent language, and to reconstruct some of the vocabulary of the parent language (see Paragraph 15). This method permits the investigator to decide, to some extent, the historical order of dialect differentiation. That is, he can say that languages A and B diverged from each other before such and such a phonological change, which is peculiar to language B, took place. Or he can say that the separation of languages A and B from each other must have taken place after their separation from language C, because they share phonological features which do not occur in C. The method does not, however, permit the investigator to say at what date the separation of languages A and B took place (Hockett, 1953).

4. A method for determining the chronological relationships of cultural elements to one another by use of various kinds of linguistic evidence has been suggested by Sapir (1916, pp. 434-436). The relative antiquity, for example, of the culture items *bow*, *arrow*, and *spear* is attested by the fact that these terms cannot be analysed into constituent morphemes as can the morphologically transparent terms *railroad* or *capitalist* which represent recent additions to the culture. The assumption is that sound changes and shifts of meaning over a long period of time have obscured the original morphemic content of the older terms. Similarly, the archaic *-en* plural of *oxen* attests the ancient use of these animals, since it is assumed that words using archaic morphological processes, and the cultural elements to which the words refer, are of ancient origin. Although these and other linguistic clues discussed by Sapir have considerable value in determining something of the relative age of cultural items, and the chronological order in which they became a part of a given culture pattern, this method does not provide any exact dates. At best this method can provide the basis for such statements as: "This element was probably a part of the culture pattern before such and such sound changes took place in the language." or "This item probably entered the culture pattern of tribe A during a period of close contact with the culture of tribe B from whose language the terminology was borrowed."

5. Sapir also suggested (1921, pp. 217-220) that marked similarities in the basic morphological structure of otherwise dissimilar languages indicated remote common origin of the languages, since the effects of borrowing or other influence of one language on another seldom penetrate to the structural core or nucleus of the language affected. The use of this principle increases the number of languages that can be postulated as belonging to a given

linguistic grouping, and gives insight into linguistic relationships at deep time depths but it cannot tell us when the languages whose relationship is postulated began to diverge from one another.

6. Such historical estimation is not sufficient for the needs of anthropologists, historical linguists, and archaeologists, who want to know at just what date linguistic changes took place, and who also want to know just how the language developments correlate with cultural changes, migrations, etc., of which there is evidence from other lines of investigation (Swadesh, 1950, p. 157). Lexicostatistics is an attempt to provide the more precise dating that is needed.

BASIC ASSUMPTIONS OF LEXICOSTATISTICS

7. The first basic assumption of lexicostatistics is that some parts of the vocabulary of any language are assumed, on empirical evidence, to be much less subject to change than other parts (Swadesh [1951a], p. 12). This basic core vocabulary includes such items as terms for pronouns, numerals, body parts, geographical features, etc. This concept is similar to Sapir's idea of a basic nucleus of morphological structure discussed in Paragraph 5. Terms for new items in the material culture, on the other hand, are frequently borrowed along with the cultural items. Such terms are also easily lost with a change in the material culture, or the borrowing of a new item, or for other reasons. The contrast between the basic core vocabulary and general vocabulary may be seen in the following illustration of French loan words in English: "As against perhaps 50 percent of borrowed correspondences between English and French in the general vocabulary, we find just 6 percent in the basic vocabulary. Residual correspondences are found to be 27 percent. Thus the archaic residuum after 5000 years turns out to be five times greater than 2000 years of accumulated borrowings" (Swadesh, [1951a] p. 13).

8. The second basic assumption of lexicostatistics is that the rate of retention of vocabulary items in the basic core of relatively stable vocabulary is constant through time. That is, given a certain number of basic words in a certain language, a certain percentage of these words will remain in the language after a thousand years of vocabulary loss; that same percentage of the residue of words will remain after a second thousand years; and after a third period of a thousand years, the same percentage of the words remaining at the end of the second period will remain; and so on. Complete empirical evidence that the rate of loss is constant through time is still lacking (Lees, 1953, pp. 121-122), since the assumption has not yet been checked for a time span greater than 2,200 years and this span does not provide adequate evidence for a constant rate of loss over a long period of time.

9. The third basic assumption of lexicostatistics is that the rate of loss of basic vocabulary is approximately the same in all languages. This assumption has been tested in thirteen languages in which there are historical records. The results range from a retention of 86.4 % to 74.4 % per thousand years—an average of 80.5 % (Lees, 1953, pp. 118-119). This is not, however, conclusive evidence that all languages change at this rate, especially since all but two of the thirteen languages tested are Indo-European. (See also Kroeber, 1955, p. 91).

10. The fourth assumption of lexicostatistics is a corollary of the third, namely, that if the percentage of true cognates within the core vocabulary is known for any pair of languages, the length of time that has elapsed since the two languages began to diverge from a single parent language can be computed (Lees, 1953, pp. 116-117), provided that there are no interfering factors through migrations, conquests, or other social contacts which slowed or speeded the divergence (Swadesh, 1950, pp. 158-160; Gudschinsky, 1955, p. 149).

TECHNIQUES OF LEXICOSTATISTICS

11. In applying the lexicostatistical techniques developed from the basic assumptions, the steps are: collecting of comparable word lists from the relatively stable core vocabulary (Paragraphs 12-14); determining the probable cognates (Paragraphs 15-23, 25-28); computing the time depth (Paragraphs 31-36); computing the range of error (Paragraphs 37-45); and, optionally, computing the dips (Paragraphs 50-52).

WORD LISTS

12. The first essential in making a lexicostatistical comparison of two or more languages

is the collection of comparable word lists in the various languages. (Lexicostatistics provides a quick way of estimating linguistic relationships on the basis of a relatively small body of data. For this reason it is a useful tool in linguistic surveys. For a detailed description of gathering data in a number of dialects in minimum time, see Swadesh, 1954a.) A convenient list for this purpose is Swadesh's 200 word list. The use of this list has several advantages: it is made up of noncultural items that have been specifically chosen as a part of the core vocabulary. These items have been tentatively tested (see Paragraph 9) for percentage of retention in languages with written historical records. Later tests may well indicate that a different assortment of words would be more useful, but any revised list must be tested to ascertain whether or not the same rate of vocabulary loss applies. Meantime, this list has been used in a number of comparisons, and will yield results that can easily be compared with studies already made. It does not seem wise to start with a list shorter than 200 words, since the shorter the list of words used, the greater the probable error (see Paragraph 41). Furthermore, it is sometimes impossible to get the entire list in all of the languages investigated so that the comparisons must be made with fewer items than in the original list. For these reasons it would be good if a longer list of satisfactory items could be worked out. Swadesh is at present experimenting with the use of a list of only 100 items (see Swadesh, 1955, for a detailed analysis of the 200 word list and the suggested revision to 100 words). The reasons given for eliminating some of the items (e.g., the repetition of some roots in such pairs as woman-wife, the non-universality of such words as ice and snow, etc.) seem valid to this author. The gain in quality of test items, however, is balanced by some loss in terms of statistical accuracy. Kroeber (1955, p. 97) has suggested that a list of 1000 items would be preferable, and doubts that deep time depths can be explored by use of a list as small as 200 words. (Anyone choosing to use Swadesh's new list of 100 items must use .86 as the "constant" in the time depth formula of Paragraph 32.)

13. In gathering the data, each English word should be translated by the most common conversational equivalent (Swadesh 1951a, p. 13). If there is an equal choice of two or more expressions, one should be chosen purely at random (by flipping a coin if necessary) to avoid any bias in the direction of choosing known cognates, since nonrandom choice could considerably skew the final results. It is essential, for statistical reasons, that the error be random error, so that the accumulating errors tend to cancel each other out instead of compounding each other.

The same meaning of each English word should be translated in each case. For example "know" is understood as referring to facts rather than to persons. Translation from English of isolated forms in general insures that the resultant forms in each language will be comparable root stems rather than affixes or other items which are not comparable (Lees, 1953, p. 115). This is not, however, always the case, and the procedure of Paragraph 18 is used to eliminate the irrelevant material.

14. Greater time depths may be explored by the methods of lexicostatistics if the list is filled in with the reconstructed forms of the postulated common parent language of a linguistic family or stock (Swadesh, 1953a, pp. 41-42). A comparison of Proto-Romance with Proto-Germanic, for example, might be expected to give a more accurate picture of the historical facts than a comparison of modern French with modern German. Such comparisons are dependent on preliminary comparative studies (see Paragraph 15), and are limited by the fact that reconstructed forms for the entire list are seldom available.

COGNATE COUNT

15. When the word lists have been compiled, the next step is to compare the words of the two lists in order to ascertain how many of the pairs of words are probable cognates (Swadesh, 1950, pp. 157-158). True cognates are developed from the same word in a common parent language, and only true cognates are conclusive evidence of genetic relationship. The most accurate estimate of whether or not the pairs of words in a given comparison are cognate is arrived at by the careful use of the comparative method in reconstructing the proto-language. The major assumption of the comparative method is that while the phonemes of the parent language develop differently in the different daughter languages, the development

is consistent in each kind of linguistic environment within each daughter language. The investigator working on reconstruction matches the words of two (or more) languages by similarity of form and meaning. The phonemes in the same relative position in both members of a matched pair are compared—as initial consonant with initial consonant. If the two languages are related, the same pairs of phonemes will occur in many pairs of words (e.g., many words in language A beginning with t^y may be matched in language B by words of similar meaning which begin with *č*). Each such recurring pair of phonemes is assumed to represent a different phoneme or allophone of the common parent language. The investigator on the basis of his data postulates what phoneme is represented by each pair. He also postulates the phonemic system of the parent language and on this basis reconstructs the probable form of the morphemes from which the observed forms in the daughter languages have developed. A full discussion of this method is beyond the scope of this paper, but the interested student should read Bloomfield (1933, pp. 297-320) and Pike (1950). (For a listing of additional sources, see Pike, 1950, bibliography.)

16. When detailed comparative studies are not available, probable cognates can be estimated by an "inspection method," which, although cruder and subject to a greater margin of error, can be used for time depth estimates. The careful use of the following procedures will in general discover the pairs of words which may be considered as probable cognates within a margin of error not great enough to invalidate the method or render the results useless, even though in any one particular instance the conclusion might not reflect the actual historical facts. (Fairbanks [1955] has experimented with an "inspection method" [the term is his], testing the number of dissimilar cognates and similar noncognates in eight comparisons within Indo-European. His criteria were somewhat less strict than those suggested is this paper. For example he ignored vowels, he required agreement in only two consonants of each word, and he made no provision for regularly recurring correspondences [criterion d of this paper]. In his experiment two of the eight cases showed considerable skewing because of cognates which were not similar [pp. 118-119]. This does not completely invalidate the method, but it shows the need of caution especially in deeper time depths. Both Fairbank's experiment and Taylor's work on Arawak [see Taylor and Rouse, 1955, p. 106, in which Taylor uses criteria more strict than those presented here] imply that the skewing from the use of the inspection method rather than careful reconstruction tends to be in the direction of overestimation of time depth, since after long divergence, cognates frequently lose much of their similarity.) The procedures are based in part on the improbability of the chance occurrence of the same sequence of phonemes with the same meaning in two different languages, and in part on the assumptions of comparative linguistics discussed in Paragraph 15.

17. *Procedure 1.* Register as probable noncognates the words which are similar because one language has borrowed from the other, or because both have borrowed from a common source. Borrowings from a common source are recognizable if the forms are very similar to a word of the same or similar meaning in a language which is known to be unrelated, but with which there has been cultural contact. The Mexican Indian languages of Mazatec and Ixcatec, for example, are clearly not closely related to the Indo-European Spanish, but for some centuries, Spanish has been the official language of Mexico. Therefore such words as Mazatec ni^4ma^4 and Ixcatec $ʔa^2ni^1me^3e^3$ 'heart' are registered as noncognate because of the strong probability that they are common borrowings from Spanish *anima* rather than descendents of a native word in their common parent language.

Borrowings of related languages from each other or from a closely related common source may be more difficult to detect. In comparing the Huautla and San Miguel dialects of Mazatec, for example, the only evidence that the San Miguel word $nʔai^3$ 'father' is a borrowing and not a true cognate with the Huautla word $nʔai^{4\ 3}$ 'father' is the fact that the vowel cluster *ai* occurs in the San Miguel dialect only in a limited number of religious terms, whereas it is normal in the Huautla dialect (Gudschinsky, 1955, p. 148). Such clues may indicate some, though probably not all, of the borrowings from related languages or dialects.

In languages whose probability of close relationship is small, all identical or very similar words are suspect as loan words unless clearly proved otherwise (see Paragraph 20, criterion a). The apparent closeness of the dialects as ascertained by lexicostatistical methods will be greater in proportion to the number of undiscovered loans that are registered as cognates. The probability, however, is that in most cases the number of such loans will not be great enough to seriously skew the results.

18. *Procedure 2.* Isolate the equivalent morphemes in each pair of words. If equivalent morphemes are not isolated, the investigator may be misled by the complexity of the words he is comparing. The similarity of affixes marking person, number, class, aspect, etc., may obscure the fact that the basic stem morphemes are not true cognates. For example, the person marker *-le*^{4} in the forms *me*^{3}*-le*^{4} (Huautla dialect of Mazatec) and *me*^{3}*hę*^{3}*-le*^{4} (San Mateo dialect of Mazatec) 'he wants' is irrelevant to the comparison of the stems meaning 'want.' If both members of a pair of words are compounds, one pair of the constituent morphemes may be cognate even though the words as a whole are not cognate. For example, Ixcatec *r̃a*^{2}*yi*^{2}*ʔe*^{3} and Mazatec *nʔo*^{1}*yʔe*^{4} 'guts' are not cognate in spite of the very similar *yi*^{2}*ʔe*^{3} and *yʔe*^{4} since these are the morphemes meaning 'dung'; the morphemes which distinguish between 'dung' and 'guts' are *r̃a*^{2}- 'skin' and *nʔo*^{1} 'rope' and are clearly not cognate. (For a further illustration of the need for isolating equivalent morphemes see Taylor and Rouse, 1955, p. 107.)

If the investigator finds it impossible to isolate all of the morphemes in the languages he is comparing, he should proceed with the best guess he can make from the data available to him, recognizing that the comparing of nonrelevant morphemes may cause him to register a number of false cognates which will tend to skew final results in the direction of lesser time depth and closer relationship than is the true hisorical fact. (See Paragraph 30 for an illustration of such skewing in the comparison of Ixcatec and Mazatec.) The increased margin of error from failure to identify morphemes is not so great as to invalidate the method if the results are used with caution, and not treated as absolutes.

19. *Procedure 3.* Test the pairs of equivalent morphemes isolated by procedure 2 to determine whether or not they are sufficiently similar to be considered probable cognates. This testing is done by comparing the phonemes or phoneme clusters occurring in comparable position within the equivalent morphemes. For example, in comparing Ixcatec *cu*^{2} with Mazatec *co*^{2} 'say,' *c* is compared with *c* and *u* is compared with *o*; in comparing Ixcatec *ku*^{2} with Mazatec *kao*^{4} 'and,' *k* is compared with *k* and *u* is compared with *ao* since *ao* occurs in the position comparable to the *u*; in comparing Ixcatec *šu*^{2}*wa*^{2} with Mazatec *ṇčoa*^{21} 'come,' *š* is compared with *ṇč* and *uwa* is compared with *oa*. (Tone is ignored in this example and others in this study because the discussion of the complicated tone problems are beyond the scope of this paper.)

Any pair of equivalent morphemes may be registered as probable cognates if a minimum of three pairs of comparable phonemes or phoneme clusters are found to "agree" according to one or more of the criteria given below. In cases in which one or both members of the pair of morphemes being tested is constituted of fewer than three phonemes, the pair can be considered as probably cognate only if all the phonemes or phoneme clusters of the shorter morpheme of the pair agree with the phonemes or phoneme clusters in comparable position in the other morpheme. (For different sets of criteria for determining probable cognates, see Fairbanks, 1955, and Swadesh, 1954c, p. 308.)

20. *Criterion a.* Identical members of a pair of phonemes occurring in comparable position in a pair of equivalent morphemes may be considered as agreeing except that complete identity between languages whose relationship is suspected of being remote may suggest recent borrowing rather than genetic relationship. (Criterion d, Paragraph 23, may be used to determine whether or not the identity of any given pair of phonemes is in accord with a pattern in the language, or whether it is peculiar to this instance. In the latter case, the morpheme pair should be registered as probable noncognates.)

21. *Criterion b.* Phonetically similar members of a pair of phonemes in comparable position in a pair of equivalent morphemes may be considered as agreeing. "Phonetically similar" here means that the two phonemes of the pair must be sufficiently alike phonetically to render them suspect as possible allophones

of a single phoneme if they occurred in the same language. In general, the members of a pair of phonemes are phonetically similar if they differ in such ways as: the presence or absence of vocal vibration as *t* and *d*; the speed of articulation as *r̃* (pronounced with a quick flap of the tongue) and *t*; a slight variation of tongue position as *t* and *ṭ* (pronounced with the tongue tip curled back), or *i* (pronounced as in 'meat') and ɪ (pronounced with the tongue slightly lower and more lax as in mitt'); the presence of secondary activity modifying one of the sounds as *k* and k^w (pronounced with the lips rounded); the extent of interruption of the air stream as *θ* (pronounced with partial interruption of the air stream) and *t* (pronounced with complete interruption of the air stream). For a fuller discussion of phonetic similarity, see Pike, 1947, pp. 69-71. (This criterion should be used with caution if it yields many agreements which are not substantiated by criterion d.)

22. *Criterion c.* A conditioned member of a pair of phonemes occurring in comparable position in a pair of equivalent morphemes may be considered as agreeing with a phonetically dissimilar member. That is, phonetically dissimilar phonemes agree if their environment is such that it could be considered a conditioning factor responsible for the present phonetic shape of one member of the pair of phonemes even though, arbitrarily, it has not had the same effect on the other member of the pair. For example, in comparing the forms *či*^{4}*kį*^{1} (Huautla dialect of Mazatec) and *ča*^{4}*kį*^{1} (San Mateo dialect of Mazatec) 'firewood,' the *i* and *a* are considered as agreeing since it is possible that the *č* might have been responsible for the change from *a* to *i* (which is pronounced with the tongue closer to the palate than *a*) in the Huautla dialect, even though the change did not occur in the San Mateo dialect. A discussion of conditioning factors may be found in Pike (1947, pp. 84-96).

23. *Criterion d.* Regularly corresponding members of a pair of phonemes occurring in comparable position in equivalent morphemes may be considered as agreeing even though they are not phonetically similar. By regularly corresponding is meant that the same pair of phonemes or phoneme clusters occur in comparable position in a number of different pairs of equivalent morphemes. For example, the Ixcatec phoneme *š* agrees with the Mazatec phoneme *l* because this pair regularly corresponds in such pairs of morphemes as: Ixcatec *šˀwi*^{2} and Mazatec *lˀi*$^{1\ 3}$ 'fire,' Ixcatec *šu*^{3} and Mazatec *lao*^{4} 'rock.'

24. In reading the work of specialists in this field, the reader should bear in mind that they differ in the degree of conservatism in their work. The reader can assess the conservatism and solidity of the work by the application of the criteria suggested in Paragraph 20-23 to the pairs of cognates which the author offers as evidence. The inclusion of a quantity of comparative data which is solid in terms of these criteria indicates that the data are conservative and reliable. If, however, only reconstructed forms (marked with an asterisk) are given, without careful documentation, the reader should realize that the proposed reconstructions and the conclusions based on them may in fact be of a highly tentative nature, and should not be accepted as conclusively proved. (See also Kroeber, 1955, p. 97.)

. . . .

29. *In Summary.* A total of 192 pairs of words in Ixcatec and Mazatec were compared in Paragraph 28. (Eight of the original list of words were lacking in one or the other of the languages.) Of these 192 pairs, the procedures of Paragraphs 17-23 give a total of 74 probable cognates and 118 probable noncognates. The time depth based on these figures is computed in Paragraphs 34-36; the range of error of the time depth is computed in Paragraphs 44-45; the Ixcatec-Mazatec lexical relationship in dips is computed in Paragraphs 50-51.

30. A careful comparative study would probably result in an estimated 78 cognates and 114 noncognates, since in the author's opinion it is likely that two of the 74 pairs registered as probable cognates are not true cognates, and it is also likely that six of the pairs registered as probable noncognates can be proved to be true cognates on the basis of reconstruction. On the other hand, an investigator completely unacquainted with both languages and unable to isolate the equivalent morphemes and without additional data beyond the 200 word list would be expected to arrive at a total of 72 probable cognates and 120 probable noncognates, since failure to isolate the equivalent morphemes would have resulted in registering four noncognates as probable cognates, but

lack of additional data would have resulted in registering as probable noncognates six pairs which may well be true cognates. See Paragraphs 46-48 for a discussion of the degree to which the time depth estimate is skewed by such inaccurate registering of probable cognates.

COMPUTATION OF TIME DEPTH

31. For use in the time depth formula, the number of probable cognates ascertained by the techniques of Paragraphs 17-23 must be converted to percent of cognates. This is done by dividing the number of probable cognates by the total number of pairs of words compared (Swadesh, 1950, p. 158).

32. Time depth is computed by the formula $t = \log C/(2 \log r)$ (Lees, 1953, p. 117). In this formula t stands for indicated time depth in millenia; C stands for the percent of cognates (Paragraph 31); r stands for the "constant" (also called "index" in Swadesh, 1955, p. 122), that is, the percent of cognates assumed to remain after a thousand years of diverging (Paragraph 8). (In the illustrative material in this paper the value .805 has been used for r, following Lees [1953, p. 119].) Log means "logarithm of" so that log C means the logarithm of the percent of probable cognates registered, and 2 log r means twice the logarithm of the constant.

33. The formula is solved by the following steps: (a) The logarithm of C and the logarithm of r are ascertained from Table 1. (For any who may be rusty on the use of logarithms, the following example is given. The logarithm of .38 is .968; it is found at the point where a line from .3 on the vertical scale of Table 1 meets a line from .08 on the horizontal scale. The logarithm of .39 is found at the point where a line from .3 on the vertical scale of Table 1 meets a line from .09 on the horizontal scale. The logarithm of .385 is halfway between these; half the difference between .968 and .942 subtracted from .968 gives .955 which is the logarithm of .385. Table 1 has been included in the text as more convenient to use than a full logarithmic table; it contains only those values of N that are necessary for computing the time depth.)
(b) The logarithm of r is multiplied by two.
(c) The product of the multiplication in (b) is divided into the logarithm of C.
(d) The quotient of the division in (c) is the indicated time depth in millenia. It may be changed to years by multiplying by 1,000.

COMPUTATION OF TIME DEPTH ILLUSTRATED

34. In the comparison of Ixcatec and Mazatec, 74 of the 192 pairs were registered as probable cognates (Paragraph 29). Dividing 74 by 192 gives .385 (38.5 %). This is the value to be used for C in the time depth formula.

35. The formula may now be filled in to read $t = \log .385/(2 \log .805)$. It is solved as follows: (a) The logarithm of .385 is found from Table 1 to be .955. The logarithm of .805 is

TABLE 1. NATURAL LOGARITHMS

N	.00	.01	.02	.03	.04	.05	.06	.07	.08	.09
.1	−2.303	−2.207	−2.120	−2.040	−1.966	−1.897	−1.833	−1.772	−1.715	−1.661
.2	−1.609	−1.561	−1.514	−1.470	−1.427	−1.386	−1.347	−1.309	−1.273	−1.238
.3	−1.204	−1.171	−1.139	−1.109	−1.079	−1.050	−1.022	−.994	−.968	−.942
.4	−.916	−.892	−.868	−.844	−.821	−.799	−.777	−.755	−.734	−.713
.5	−.693	−.673	−.654	−.635	−.616	−.598	−.580	−.562	−.545	−.528
.6	−.511	−.494	−.478	−.462	−.446	−.431	−.416	−.400	−.386	−.371
.7	−.357	−.342	−.329	−.315	−.301	−.288	−.274	−.261	−.248	−.236
.8	−.223	−.211	−.198	−.186	−.174	−.163	−.151	−.139	−.128	−.117
.9	−.105	−.094	−.083	−.073	−.062	−.051	−.041	−.030	−.020	−.010

To obtain the natural logarithm of numbers less than .1:
multiply the number by 10 and subtract 2.303 from the ln (natural logarithm) obtained,
or multiply by 100 and subtract 4.605 from the ln obtained,
or multiply by 1,000 and subtract 6.908 from the ln obtained, etc.

NOTE: In the operations described in the text, it is possible to leave out of account the negative value of the logarithms; one negative number divided by another gives a positive quotient.

SOURCE: By permission from *Introduction to Statistical Analysis*, by Wilfrid J. Dixon and Frank J. Massey, Jr., copyright 1951, McGraw-Hill Book Company, Inc.

found to be .217. (b) The product of 2 x .217 (that is 2 log *r*) is .434. (c) The quotient of .434 (2 log *r*) divided into .955 (log *C*) is 2.200; that is, the indicated time depth, *t*, for Ixcatec-Mazatec is 2.2 millenia or (multiplicd by 1,000) 2,200 years.

36. The indicated time depth for Ixcatec-Mazatec computed in Paragraph 35 may be stated in either of the following ways: Ixcatec and Mazatec are estimated to have been a single homogeneous language 2,200 years ago; Ixcatec and Mazatec are estimated to have begun to diverge from a common parent language about 245 B.C. (In the computations given here for illustrative purposes, the time depths, and the dates arrived at by subtracting the time depth from the present date, are not rounded off. It should be noted, however, that the range of error computed in Paragraphs 44-45 indicates that these dates must be taken at best as an approximation somewhere within a few years of correct. The dates have no significance in terms of single years or even decades.)

COMPUTATION OF RANGE OF ERROR

37. It is exceedingly improbable that any two successive random samplings of the basic vocabulary of a pair of languages would yield exactly the same percent of probable cognates. For this reason it is necessary to qualify the statement of time depth in such a way as to give an estimate of its accuracy. The usual way of qualifying a time depth statement is to state it as a range of years rather than as a specific number of years, and to state the degree of probability (or level of confidence) at which the range of years was computed. For example the time depth for Mazatec Ixcatec may be stated as 2,200 years $\pm$ 200 years at 7/10 confidence level (see end of Paragraph 45). (The computation of range of error is based on the assumption that all changes in the basic vocabulary are random, producing a "normal curve.")

38. Statistical methods permit computation of range of error at any level of confidence or probability. Computations are usually made, however, at one of three levels: "standard error" which is 68 % confidence level; (For convenience, standard error will be referred to as 7/10 confidence level) (see Paragraphs 39 and 44); 9/10 (90 %) confidence level; or 5/10 (50 %) confidence level which is also called "probable error." The higher the level of confidence (i.e., the more certainly the true answer lies within the range cited) the wider the range of years. Narrowing the range of years lessens the probability that it includes the true answer.

39. The first step in computing range of error at any level of confidence is the computation of "standard error" (7/10 confidence level). Standard error is computed by the formula $\sigma = \sqrt{C(1\text{-}C)/n}$ (Lees, 1953, p. 124, formula 11). In this formula σ stands for standard error in terms of percent of cognates; *C* means the percent of cognates (see Paragraph 34—this is the same *C* used in working the time depth formula); *n* means the number of pairs of words compared. The formula is solved by the following steps: (a) *C* is subtracted from 1. (b) The remainder of the subtraction in (a) is multiplied by *C*. (c) The product of the multiplication in (b) is divided by *n*. (d) The square root of the quotient of the division in (c) is found. (e) The square root found in (d) is the range of error of the percent of cognates at the 7/10 confidence level.

40. Standard error in years is computed by the following steps: (a) The range of error of the percent of probable cognates (found in step (e) of Paragraph 39) is added to *C* (found in Paragraph 31). (b) The sum of the addition in (a) is worked through the time depth formula exactly as the original *C* was (Paragraph 32). (c) The new time depth obtained from (b) is subtracted from the original time depth as computed in Paragraph 32 to give the number which is added to and subtracted from the original time depth as computed in Paragraph 32 to give the range of error in years at 7/10 confidence level. (The range of error at 9/10 confidence is obtained by multiplying the standard error of the percent of cognates [found in Paragraph 39] by 1.645 [Dixon and Massey, 1951, Table 4]. The product of this multiplication is the range of error, at 9/10 confidence level, for the percent of cognates. From it, the range of error in years at the 9/10 confidence level can be computed by the same steps used for the computation of the range of error at 7/10 confidence level (Paragraph 40]. The range of error at 5/10 confidence level is obtained by the same steps, using the figure .674 instead of 1.645.)

41. Note that standard error, and therefore any range of error, is larger if the number of

comparisons made is small, but decreases as the number of cases increases because there is division by the number of cases. This makes it important to use a list of words of sufficient length (Lees, 1953, p. 126).

42. An improved word list and more careful collection of data and ascertaining of probable cognates will reduce the actual error, but these will not show up in this method of computing the range of probable error since the accuracy of the investigator cannot be included in the formula. Lexicostatistics operates admittedly with a wide margin of error due to inaccuracy in choice of words, mistakes in determining cognates, etc. This is the price of using the method at all, and is legitimate if one does not abuse it by relying on it for a degree of accuracy that is not basically possible.

43. In very deep time depths where the percent of cognates is small the choice of a single false cognate or the rejection of a single true cognate may make considerable difference in the resulting date (Swadesh, 1953a, p. 41). If, for example, in a list of 200 comparisons there is only one cognate (.5%) the estimated time depth is 12.2 millenia, but if there are two cognates (1%) the time depth is 10. 6 millenia. This is a difference of sixteen centuries dependent on the recognition of a single cognate.

COMPUTATION OF RANGE OF ERROR ILLUSTRATED

44. The range of error at 7/10 confidence level can now be computed for the Ixcatec Mazatec time depth by the formula $\sigma = \sqrt{C\,(1\text{-}C)/n}$ as follows (see Paragraph 39 for the steps followed here): (a) The percent of cognates computed in Paragraph 34 is .385. This number subtracted from 1.000 leaves a remainder of .615 (1-C). (b) .615 multiplied by .385 gives a product of .236775 [$C\,(1\text{-}C)$]. (c) .236775 divided by 192 (the number of pairs of words compared) gives a quotient of .0012332 [C (1-C)/n]. (d) The square root of .0012332 is .03511 [$\sqrt{C\,(1\text{-}C)/n}$]. (The simplest way to find square root is by reference to a manual of mathematical tables.) This is rounded off to give a standard error at 7/10 confidence level of .035.

45. The range of error in years, at 7/10 confidence level, is computed as follows (following the steps outlined in Paragraph 40): The range of error computed in Paragraph 44 (which is the range of error of the percent of cognates) is added to the original percent of cognates computed in Paragraph 34; that is, .385 plus .035 is .42. (b) This new C is worked through the time depth formula $t = \log C/(2 \log r)$; $t = \log .42/2 \log .805$; $t = .868/.434$; $t = 2.000$ millenia or 2,000 years. (c) The new time depth is subtracted from the time depth computed in Paragraph 35 that is 2,200 years minus 2,000 years is 200 years. (d) The range of error at 7/10 confidence level may now be stated in any of three ways: Ixcatec and Mazatec were a single homogeneous language 2,200 ± 200 years ago; Ixcatec and Mazatec were a single homogeneous language between 2,000 and 2,400 years ago; Ixcatec and Mazatec began to diverge from a common parent language between 445 B.C. and 45 B.C. From the standard error the range of error at 9/10 confidence level is computed as 2,200 ± 324 years. The range of error at 5/10 confidence level is 2,200 ± 140 years (see Paragraph 40).

46. The percent of cognates likely to be verified by comparative study, and the percent of probable cognates likely to be registered by a person with no knowledge of the two languages involved are given in Paragraph 30. At this point we are ready to work these two estimates through the time depth formula and from the results to estimate the probable degree of skewing of time depth figures due to weakness in the criteria or to the inexperience of the investigator.

47. The more conservative estimate is 78 probable cognates (rather than the 74 probable cognates on which the illustration has so far been based). 78 probable cognates out of 192 comparisons is .406 (40.6 %). Worked through the time depth formula (Paragraphs 32-33) this gives an estimated time depth of 2,078 years. The range of error computed at 7/10 confidence level is .035 (computed according to the steps in Paragraph 39) or 191 years (following the steps of Paragraph 40). This makes the most conservative estimate for the time of Mazatec Ixcatec divergence 2,078 ± 191 or 1,887-2,269 years ago. Note that the figure 2,200 years (Paragraph 36) obtained by the criteria of Paragraphs 20-23 is within this range.

48. The least accurate estimation of cognates, that arrived at by the use of the criteria suggested in this paper, by an investigator without

sufficient knowledge of the language to isolate the equivalent morphemes, without help from the comparative method, and without data beyond the 200 word list, is 72 probable cognates (Paragraph 30). This is .375 (37.5 %) and gives a time depth of 2260. Note that this figure also is within the range of error, at 7/10 confidence level, of the most conservative estimate (Paragraph 47).

49. On the basis of Paragraphs 47 and 48, it is evident that in this particular comparison, the result arrived at by the use of the criteria in this paper are only very slightly skewed from the results arrived at by the use of the more conservative methods. In other comparisons the skewing may be greater, but the investigator can, in general, estimate the direction of the skewing, and take account of it in assessing the reliability of his results.

DIPS

50. As has been demonstrated, the dating arrived at by lexicostatistical techniques is very tentative, and can be seriously misleading to anyone who assumes that the dates are absolutes in terms of years or months, and uses them without due caution. For this reason it may be convenient to consider the data in terms of dips (i.e., degrees of lexical relationship) rather than in terms of historical dates, so that the relative lexical relationships can be discussed apart from any implication of absolute time (Gudschinsky, 1955, pp. 141-142) which may be more confusing than helpful. The dip expresses a true degree of objective lexical relationship even though borrowing or other factors has destroyed the time relationship. A knowledge of this present relationship is invaluable in practical decisions regarding homogeneity of speech areas for vernacular schools, production of literature, etc.

51. The formula for computing lexical relationship in dips is $d = 14$ (log C/2 log r). Having once worked the time depth formula, however, the results may be converted to dips by multiplying the time in millenia by 14, or the time in years by .014. In the Ixcatec Mazatec example used in this study, the lexical relationship expressed in Paragraph 36 as 2,200 years may be expressed as 30. 8 dips.

Similarly, the range of error in years may be converted by multiplication to range of error in dips. The range of error at 7/10 confidence level is given in Paragraph 45 as 200 years. Multiplied by .014 this gives a range of error of 2.8. dips; that is to say, at 7/10 confidence level, the Ixcatec Mazatec relationship is 30.8 ± 2.8 dips.

52. Swadesh has suggested a classification of dialects, languages, stocks, and phylums on the basis of lexicostatical results (1954c, p. 326), as follows:

Term	*Divergence Centuries*	*Cognate Percent*
language	0-5	100-81
family	5-25	81-36
stock	25-50	36-12
microphylum	50-75	12-4
mesophylum	75-100	4-1
macrophylum	over 100	less than 1

(Swadesh has used .81 as the constant in determining the value in centuries of the various percents.) These labels may be defined in terms of dips as: language, 0-7 dips; family, 7-35 dips; stock, 35-70 dips; microphylum, 70—105 dips; mesophylum, 105-140 dips; macrophylum, more than 140 dips.

This particular classification is, of course, still tentative. Its empirical usefulness with a large number of languages remains to be demonstrated. But without question, the quantified data resulting from this technique makes possible a more objective classification of lexical relationships than has hitherto been possible (Swadesh, 1950, pp. 162-163).

THE VALUE OF LEXICOSTATISTICS

53. For the anthropologist and historian, the lexicostatistical data suggest the order of the development of languages and dialects. That is, by studying a number of pairs of languages or dialects within a related group, or within a dialect area, those pairs which show greatest time depth are assumed to be representative of older splits in the dialects, and those showing lesser time depth show more recent splits so that a progressive splitting is implied (Gudschinsky, 1955). This suggested order of splitting may help in correlating the linguistic data with known or suspected migrations, cultural developments, etc.

54. The lexicostatistical data also imply the geographical location and cultural contacts

of ancient dialects, since the dialects were presumably relatively homogeneous until the time at which the evidence shows the beginning of their divergence. Then the dialects closest linguistically must have been closest geographically and longest in cultural contact. Such linguistic geographical relationships have been charted by Swadesh (1950, pp. 164-167) and Hirsch (1954). (For an extensive discussion of time depth and geographical location see Kroeber [1955]. For use of the principles of Paragraphs 53 and 54 see Taylor and Rouse, 1955.)

55. In using lexicostatistical data, it must be remembered that even when further experiment with the word list and the constant make possible a greater degree of accuracy, no individual study will be more accurate than the data available and the care used in ascertaining the probable cognates. Also, regardless of the degree of accuracy possible in determining when certain languages or dialects diverged from each other, it is not possible to determine by lexicostatistics what language was spoken by the people responsible for the artifacts found in any given place (Swadesh, 1954b; Kroeber, 1955, p. 104).

56. The archaeologist or nonlinguist who is curious to try this material is urged to do so. All that he needs beyond what is given here is the historical records or informants from which to obtain the lexical data.

REFERENCE NOTE

The problems and literature of lexicostatistics and glottochronology are discussed generally in Hymes (1960a, 1960e), in Bergsland and Vogt (1962) and in the comments to these articles (esp. Hymes, 1962b) by a variety of scholars. For recent comment, see also Hoijer (1961). For recent work of new scope, see Dyen (1962a, 1962b, 1962c) and Carroll and Dyen (1962), and cf. Elmendorf (1962b). Elmendorf (1962a), Diebold (1960), and Dyen (1962b) restate Salish relationships discussed in Swadesh (1950) and indicate the importance a well-worked body of data may acquire. For recent work on lexicostatistics, apart from glottochronology, see also Cowan (1959), Ellegard (1959), Gleason (1959), and Kroeber (1960a).

References not in the general bibliography:

CARROLL, JOHN B., and ISIDORE DYEN

1962. High Speed Computation of Lexicostatistical Indices. *Lg.*, *38:* 274-278.

COWAN, H. K. J.

1959. A Note on Statistical Methods in Comparative Linguistics. *Lingua*, *8:* 233-246.

DIXON, WILFRID J., and FRANK J. MASSEY, JR.

1951. *Introduction to Statistical Analysis*. New York: Wiley.

DYEN, ISIDORE

1962a. The Lexicostatistical Classification of the Malayopolynesian Languages. *Lg.*, *38:* 38-46.

1962b. The Lexicostatistically Determined Relationship of a Language Group. *IJAL*, *28:* 153-161.

1962c. Lexicostatistically Determined Borrowing and Taboo. *Lg.*, *38:* 60-66.

ELLEGARD, ALVAR

1959. Statistical Measurement of Linguistic Relationship. *Lg.*, *35:* 131-156.

ELMENDORF, W. W.

1962a. Lexical Innovation and Persistence in Four Salish Dialects. *IJAL*, *28:* 85-96.

1962b. Lexical Relation Models as a Possible Check on Lexicostatistic Inferences. *AA*, *64:* 760-770.

FAIRBANKS, GORDON H.

1955. A Note on Glottochronology. *IJAL*, *21:* 116-124.

FERNANDEZ DE MIRANDA, MARIA TERESA

1951. Reconstrucción del Protopopoluca. *Revista Mexicana de Estudios Antropológicos*, *12:* 61-93.

GREENBERG, JOSEPH H., and MORRIS SWADESH

1953. Jicaque as a Hokan Language. *IJAL*, *19:* 216-222.

GUDSCHINSKY, SARAH C.

1955. Lexico-statistical Skewing from Dialect Borrowing. *IJAL*. *21:* 138-149.

HIRSCH, DAVID I.

1954. Glottochronology and Eskimo and Eskimo-Aleut Prehistory. *AA*, *56:* 825-838.

HOCKETT, CHARLES F.

1953. Linguistic Time-Perspective and Its Anthropological Uses. *IJAL*, *19:* 146-152.

LEES, ROBERT B.

1953. The Basis of Glottochronology. *Lg.*, *29:* 113-127.

SWADESH, MORRIS

1951b. Kleinschmidt Centennial III: Unaaliq and Proto Eskimo. *IJAL*, *17:* 66-70.

1953a. Mosan I: A Problem of Remote Common Origin. *IJAL*, *19:* 26-44.

1953b. Comment on Hockett's Critique. *IJAL*, *19:* 152-153.

1953c. The Language of the Archaeologic Huastecs. *Notes on Middle American Archaeology and Ethnology*, *4:* 223-227.

1954a. On the Penutian Vocabulary Survey. *IJAL*, *20:* 123-133.

1954b. Time Depths of American Linguistic Groupings. With Comments by G. I. Quimby, H. B. Collins, E. W. Haury, G. F. Ekholm, and Fred Eggan. *AA*, *56:* 361-377.

TAYLOR, DOUGLAS, and IRVING ROUSE

1955. Linguistic and Archaeological Time Depth in the West Indies. *IJAL*, *21:* 105-115.

64 *Diffusional Cumulation and Archaic Residue as Historical Explanations*

MORRIS SWADESH

IF TWO CULTURES have traits in common to an extent that cannot be explained by sheer coincidence, a historic basis must be assumed. There are two principal possibilities. The sum of common traits may be the cumulative result of a long series of separate borrowings, or they may be all that is left of a once extensive complex anciently shared by forerunners of the two cultures. The problem of distinguishing between the two types of cases is important for every aspect of culture history but for certain reasons is most clear-cut with reference to language, where it has been formulated as the question of diffusion versus common origin. The classic controversy on this subject between Franz Boas and Edward Sapir resulted in considerable clarification of the main problem, even though there was a limited area in which these two scholars never agreed. The present paper attempts to resolve or to narrow the moot point, and to develop the general theoretical implications of the problem. This is done by reëxamining the main arguments of Boas and Sapir and by experimenting with the use of objective tests for distinguishing diffusional cumulation from archaic residue. We discuss linguistic phenomena primarily, but attempt to see them in the perspective of the general cultural problem.

I

Language is a cultural complex. It has its special characteristics, of course, but it is nonetheless a body of customary forms transmitted from generation to generation and from society to society in the same way as other cultural forms. Both Boas and Sapir recognized this, as shown, for instance, in the following quotations.

> Speech is a human activity that varies without assignable limit as we pass from social group to social group, because it is a purely historical heritage of the group, the product of a long-continued social usage (Sapir, 1921, p. 2).

> Thus it appears that language has behaved in the same way as all other cultural traits. . . . (Boas, 1938b, p. 140).

Now, since language behaves in the same general way as other aspects of culture, it is interesting that the problem of common origin versus diffusion has been raised only in connection with language. There seem to be two reasons for this. First, the special characteristics of language make the problem more apparent. And second, the question has been inaccurately formulated in such a way as to obscure its general application.

The crucial fact that distinguishes language among cultural forms is suggested by Sapir in the following words:

> Language is probably the most self-contained, the most massively resistant of all social phenomena. It is easier to kill it off than to disintegrate its individual form (1921, p. 220).

As these remarks indicate, language is different in degree, not in kind, with reference to a quality which Sapir describes as being "self-contained" and which results in strong resistance to structural change. Societies have been known under special circumstances to drop the use of traditional languages and to adopt new languages. Examples are the tribes of Gaul and Iberia which took over Latin or the American Indian groups which now use English, Spanish, or Portuguese. In this process, it sometimes happens that the new language is modified in the direction of the old language.

However, more often than not the effect of the old language on pronunciation, vocabulary, and phraseology is eventually ironed out.

Why is language so self-contained? For one thing, languages are large highly organized systems, involving hundreds or thousands of conventional symbols (words or morphemes) which are combined in conventional sequences (sentences, phrases, complex or compound words). Secondly, language is an archaic human invention probably developed concomitantly with the earliest definitely human society. As far back as history and prehistoric reconstruction permit us to penetrate, we find fully developed languages comparable with those existing today. Thirdly, the communicative function of language is possible only on the basis of a body of conventions that is preponderantly stable. By its nature, elemental communication is largely neutral to social upheaval. An advanced technology, a new economic system, or a more complex social organization will generally be reflected in a changed and enlarged vocabulary but without necessary changes in the phonetics or structure of the language or in the basic vocabulary.

These are the facts that make languages more resistant to radical changes than other social phenomena. However, it must be emphasized that the difference is not an absolute one. Other complex patterned social forms also admit superficial modifications more readily than fundamental change.

II

A general examination of the main processes of culture history will prove helpful in clarifying our problem.

Diffusion is the spread of culture traits or complexes from one group to another. A contrasting process is tradition, whereby culture is handed down from generation to generation.

The life of every cultural feature is accompanied by fluctuation and change, which sometimes proceed so slowly as to be imperceptible but in principle are constantly going on. Changes are especially apt to take place in the process of diffusion. The borrowing culture often sluffs off or replaces traits in a borrowed complex. Frequently the borrowing culture takes over single traits, incorporating them into native complexes. A society, usually over a period of generations, may take on a new language and let its original language fall into disuse. Or it may incorporate into the native speech one or more individual vocabulary elements or even a phonetic or morphological feature from a neighboring language. In general separate traits are borrowed more readily than complexes; subordinate patterns within a larger complex are more readily diffused in inverse proportion to their complexity. Of the component traits, some are bound into the entire system in particularly intimate fashion and are consequently less likely to pass from one culture to another independent of the complex.

While diffusion carries culture from one society to another, societies themselves experience considerable flux, marked by growth or diminution of population and by splitting up or coalescence with other groups. The growth of a group may involve territorial changes, either in the form of gradual expansion or contraction of the area or by relatively abrupt migrations of portions of the group to new areas. As long as conditions of close internal communication prevail in the society, the culture tends to remain uniform throughout; changes appearing in one part of the area either spread quickly through the whole territory or are dropped because of the cultural influence of the bulk of the society. Where the size of the territory or other circumstances prevent the fullest internal contact of the group, there is a tendency to develop local variations of the culture which may eventually amount to major differences.

The processes of gradual change and regional differentiation and the interweaving effect of migration and diffusion can be clearly observed in connection with language. For example, Latin, having spread through Italy, Iberia, Gaul, and Dacia, developed local dialects which eventually differentiated into Italian, Spanish, French, Rumanian, and other Romanic languages. These tongues are of common origin because they all started out as variations of a single original language. Their development involved the full gamut of historical processes: migration, development of regional differences, diffusion of the whole complex to new populations, diffusional borrowing of separate elements from different neighboring languages.

The processes shown here affecting language operate in essentially the same way with regard to other culture complexes. While Latin was spreading and differentiating, many features of Roman industry, ceremonialism, art, government, and economy were carried by migration and diffusion and went through local changes comparable to what took place in language. In this way, non-linguistic culture patterns now found in France, Spain, Italy, and Rumania are of common origin. However, the other complexes did not necessarily show the same limits of diffusion as the Latin language; they generally went much farther. Wine culture, military organization, and the alphabet are especially good examples of Mediterranean culture features that traveled much farther than the Latin language. Many individual features of the language, particularly vocabulary, also went much farther.

It is clear that diffusion and common origin are not opposites. Instead, the former refers to the process of conveyance and the latter to the source. Diffusion along with migration accounts for the occurrence in different places of complexes having a single origin. In a strict sense, therefore, there is no such thing as a problem of diffusion versus common origin either in language or in any other aspect of culture. The question which occupied Boas and Sapir was actually not diffusion versus common origin but diffusional cumulation versus archaic residue.

III

The theoretical differences between Boas and Sapir on the subject of language history were not as great as is sometimes supposed. It is not by any means that the one believed in diffusion and the other did not. On the contrary both were keen students of diffusion both as a general cultural phenomenon and in its application to language. Nor must one imagine that Boas did not accept the concept of common origin of groups of languages. The question rather turned on the extent to which science can trace groups of languages back to such prototypes. Boas' notion is simply that deceptive cases can arise as a cumulative result of the diffusion process, so that in some instances he considered it impossible to be certain that a group of languages has or has not a common origin. Sapir, on the other hand, is convinced that a careful examination of the evidence will definitely establish the prehistory of the supposedly ambiguous cases.

Here is Boas' statement of the problem:

> . . . the whole theory of an "Ursprache" for every group of modern languages, must be held in abeyance until we can prove that these languages go back to a single stock and that they have not originated, to a large extent, by the process of acculturation.
>
> From this point of view I should not be inclined to claim, for instance, that Tlingit and Athabascan are members of the same linguistic family. There is not the slightest doubt that the morphology of the two groups shows the most far-reaching similarities. Since, furthermore, the two languages are contiguous, the inference is inevitable that these similarities must be due to historical causes. It is, however, another question whether we are to infer immediately that these differences [read *similarities*] are due to the fact that in very early times the two groups had a common "Ursprache." The vocabularies of Tlingit and Athabascan are fundamentally distinct, and it does not seem to me that Dr. Sapir has proved his case of relationship between the two languages by the comparison of a limited number of words that show slight phonetic similarities. The question would remain to be answered, why there should be such fundamental dissimilarities between by far the greater number of words, and the question should still be asked how these dissimilarities are to be explained (1920a, pp. 374-375).

Sapir's answer is as follows:

> . . . The theory of "borrowing" seems totally inadequate to explain those fundamental features of structure, hidden away in the very core of the linguistic complex, that have been pointed out as common, say, to Semitic and Hamitic, to the various Soudanese languages, to Malayo-Polynesian and Mon-Khmer and Munda, to Athabascan and Tlingit and Haida.
>
> . . . certain languages have, in all probability, taken on structural features owing to the influence of neighboring languages. An examination of such cases, however, almost invariably reveals the significant fact that they are but superificial additions on the morphological kernel of the language. So long as such direct historical testimony as we have gives us no really convincing examples of profound morphological influence by diffusion, we shall do well not to put too much reliance in diffusion theories. On the whole, therefore, we shall ascribe the major concordances and divergences in linguistic form—phonetic pattern and morphology—to the autonomous drift of language, not to the complicating effect of single, diffused features that cluster now this way, now that (1921, p. 219).

Boas years later, in 1938, restates his position in very reserved fashion:

> It follows from all this that for many distantly related languages the history of which is unknown, a cate-

gorical answer in regard to their genetic relationship cannot be given. In many cases historical relation must be assumed, but whether we are dealing with mixture languages or with divergent branches of an ancient stock will remain doubtful (1938b, p. 139).

Thus, Boas limits the problem to certain cases of "distantly related languages," and insists that in some of these cases one cannot know with certainty whether one is dealing with a residue of similarities from a single earlier language or an accumulation of common features through borrowing of single traits. Sapir maintains the possibility of distinguishing the "morphological kernel" of a language from "superficial additions." Basing himself on documented cases ("direct historical testimony") he holds that no accumulation of features of the kind that may be diffused singly is likely to add up to the appearance of an essential core of morphological features.

Stated in this fashion, it is easy to see that the problem of accumulation versus residue in language is not unlike familiar problems in other branches of culture. For example, myths belonging to two cultures are compared. It is found that myth A of one culture has a number of points in common with myth X in the other culture. Are we dealing with the same original myth which has diverged in two directions until only the given number of common details remain, or have these details recently been incorporated into originally distinct myths? Normally such a problem can be easily solved on the basis of internal evidence. Do ambiguous cases occur? Folklorists may attempt to answer this question on the basis of their experience. In the present paper we attempt a definitive answer with reference to language. We do not know to what extent the answer holds for industrial complexes, ceremonial forms, art, social organization, and so forth, but we are satisfied that the general facts have a great deal in common with language. Perhaps, also, our approach to the problem may suggest something of interest for the other aspects of culture.

IV

Sapir singles out morphology as the most fundamental component of language and among morphological features he points out that some are relatively superficial while others enter into the "morphological kernel" of the language. This gives the key to the problem of accumulation and residue. The inference is that the sharing of superficial features may reflect single-trait borrowing while the sharing of fundamental features, particularly if a number of them go together, demonstrates common origin. The validity of this criterion can be tested by examining various controlled cases, where we have a relatively complete developmental record of known end-products. Such knowledge may come from written samples of the languages from a succession of periods or from a detailed reconstruction made by systematic comparison of several related languages.

A convenient as well as very adequate test for our purposes is provided in the two-fold relation existing between English and French, which involves both ancient common origin and long recent contact. Systematic comparison and detailed reconstruction have demonstrated beyond doubt that a whole series of languages of the ancient world, including Latin and Teutonic, were divergent developments from an earlier single language, known as primitive Indo-European. The period of common Indo-European—when its divergent forms presumably did not constitute more than local dialects—may have been about 5000 years ago. Present-day French is a modern continuation of Latin. English as we know it today is the modern form of Anglo-Saxon, belonging to the Teutonic group. Thus French and English are the end-products of two lines of divergent development from a common origin and have had perhaps 5000 years in which to develop their present divergent characteristics. In the last 2000 years these two historical streams have been in contact under conditions very favorable for diffusion. A striking measure of the close contact of the two languages is the fact that about half of the English vocabulary corresponds with French on the basis of recent borrowings. This includes loans from French at different stages of its history, from Latin down to the modern speech; elements possessed in common with French because the latter has borrowed from English or from older forms of Teutonic; and words which both languages have from some source, including classical written Latin and Greek, and a miscellaneous variety of modern languages (Italian, Arabic, American Indian, African, etc.). However, it may not be assumed that structural borrowings have been as extensive as those in the vocabulary, and it is the structural relationships we must now examine.

The historic data of the recent centuries shows progressive gradual loss of residual common features of morphology. For example, in the earliest records both historic lines, that is Latin and Anglo-Saxon, have nouns inflected for case by means of suffixes; there are analogies in the usage of the cases and even a few similarities of endings. In recent centuries French has lost its case endings entirely and English preserves only the genitive. Noun plural formations are maintained in English but are vestigial in French, occuring only in phrase "liaison." French preserves the person distinctions in the verbal endings of the plural while English has lost them in the plural. Thus we see in process the slow changes which have been reducing the inventory of residual common features. On the other hand we find some new common features acquired by diffusional influence. We can therefore pose the test question: How does the inventory of common residual features compare with the present accumulation of traits acquired by diffusion? We present for consideration lists of typical features in each category. As will be recognized, the lists are intended to be representative rather than complete.

Features of modern English and French which go back to their ancient common form, that is Indo-European, include such traits as the following:

1. Separate noun and verb inflection. Verb-stems in some instances identical with noun-stems.
2. Inflectional categories of singular and plural number; past and present tenses (perhaps based on an original aspect system); past and present participles. Inflection shown by endings. The actual formatives show phonetic similarities in some instances.
3. Substantival rather than verbal-type adjectives. This contrasts with Chinese and many other languages, even though it is not exclusively Indo-European.
4. Adjectival forms of pronouns, e.g., *we–our*, *nous–nôtre*.
5. Inflectional irregularities including the first person pronoun (*I–me*, *je–moi*) and the use of two stems in the predicative verb (*is–be*, *est–fus*), though the places where each stem is used agree only in part.
6. Relational and local prepositions. The same elements also used in association with verbs in directional or derived senses, e.g., *in-come*, *en-tendre*.

Common structural features of French and English which reflect diffusional influences of recent centuries include:

1. Use of definite and indefinite articles developed in Teutonic and Romanic languages out of demonstratives and the unitary numeral; the articles are preposed in most languages of both groups but are postposed in Scandinavian and Rumanian. Historic evidence suggests that Latin may have led the way in this development, with Teutonic influenced by it, even though the actual forms are developed out of native elements in each language group.
2. Genitive relation shown by preposition (English *of*, French *de*), universal in Romanic, restricted in English.
3. A few freely used affixes in English, including *re-* as in *re-do*, *ex-* as in *ex-fighter*, *-able* as in *lovable*. Borrowed from French.
4. Bound prefixes used only with stems of Latin origin, as in *extract–retract–subtract–contract–distract–protract*. English has adopted these elements in their characteristic combinations partly from French but mainly from the learned use of Latin.
5. Formative suffixes added, with consonant changes, to non-independent stem-forms in such series as *electric–electricity–electrify–electrification* or *delicate–delicious–delicacy*. In French this process belongs partly, in English largely, to the field of learned late borrowings from classic Italian and Greek.
6. Limited instances of untypical word order with modifier second in such names as *Cafe Boston* (instead of *Boston Cafe*) in English or with modifier first in French as in the newspaper name *Paris Express* (instead of *Express de Paris*).

If nothing were known of the history of two languages and they were found to have in common only such features as are given in our second list, would one have any doubts as to whether these were residual or cumulative similarities? Obviously not. The similarities in word order are very limited and obviously represent exotic rather than normal usage. The bound prefixes and suffixes are mostly used with learned or refined vocabulary, and generally exist side by side with more everyday elements; for example, *ex* in *extract* serves the same function as *out* in *to pull out* and the latter is the simple every-day equivalent of the former; similarly *shiny* is the down-to-earth equivalent of *lustrous*. The prepositional genitive in English shares the function of the suffixal form, and the latter corresponds to the irregularly made pronominal forms (*his*, *her*, *my*, *our*, *your*). Of the two genitives, therefore, the prepositional is the less archaic; only if the suffixal genitive went entirely out of use might the resemblance to French be suspected of being residual. The freely used affixes (*re-*, *ex-*, *-able*) cannot be taken for residual correspondences with French because their forms coincide too closely with the latter; if they were residual after a long period of separate development their phonetic forms would have diverged considerably more. Only one feature, the use of articles, could possibly be regarded as pointing toward common origin. But, standing alone, it would have no force. It is not the kind of feature that might be expected to persist longer than any other a period of time sufficient to remove all other vestiges. Moreover, it is a simple enough trait to be taken over under diffusional influence.

We have seen that residual common traits after some 5000 years still constitute an impressive array. The number is not so great, but their relation to the languages is intimate. And they involve formational irregularities that could hardly come over with borrowed words. But what would happen after a much longer time? Suppose twelve or twenty-four thousand years had elapsed since the common history of the two languages. Would not the structural similarities become less and less in number and more and more attenuated in form until they are reduced to perhaps only one recognizable but very vague similarity? In this case, would the situation be indistinguishable from one in which a single trait had been taken over by borrowing? Not necessarily. If the last vestigial similarity involved a deep-seated coincidence in formation, such as that between English *I–me* and French *je–moi*, then even one common feature would be strongly suggestive of common origin rather than borrowing. If the common feature were more superficial, say like the use of preposed articles, it could just as easily be a borrowed feature. However, it could also constitute a chance coincidence with no necessary historical relationship at all. It therefore can be concluded that in any instance where morphological similarities between two languages force the conclusion that they have some kind of historical connection, there should be no difficulty in determining whether that connection is residual from a common origin or cumulative from a series of borrowings.

We can test this conclusion on the case which Boas regarded as probably unresolvable, the relationship between Tlingit and Athabaskan. To do so we list the structural similarities as noted by Sapir (1915c):

1. Frequent stem form CV (C), that is consonant followed by vowel and perhaps by another consonant. Tlingit also has CVCC. Comparison with Haida seems to indicate that the initial consonant is in some instances reduced from a consonant cluster, particularly groups beginning in *s* and *l*.
2. Absence of reduplication. A negative feature but a striking one among languages of the Northwest Coast, where reduplication is typical.
3. Noun and verb distinct, but some stems function as both.
4. Very little affixing on nouns. Possessive prefixes, largely identical with object prefixes of the verb. Suffixes include plural of humans and a diminutive.
5. Noun plus noun compounds, with a qualifying element first.
6. Verb complex involves a single verb stem, at or near the end. Prefixes for pronominal object and subject, mode, adverbial elements of instrument, direction, place. Adverbial prefixes often identical with or related to nouns.
7. A few temporal-modal and aspectival suffixes used with verbs.
8. Postpositions used with pronominal prefixes and with nouns in the manner of second-position elements in compounds. Postpositions often identical with nouns, e.g., Tlingit *wan* meaning "edge" or "around," Athabaskan *man* meaning "edge" or "close

to." Some postpositions also used with verbs.

9. Use of relative suffix (Tlingit *-yi*, Athabaskan *-ye*) with verbs. Identical element also added to nouns when used with pronominal prefix in possessive usage, except for relationship terms and most body parts.

The foregoing list of common structural features bears out Boas' statements that "There is not the slightest doubt that the morphology of the two groups shows the most far-reaching similarities" and further that "the inference is inevitable that these similarities must be due to historical causes" (1920a, p. 374). However, in the light of our control case, we no longer need have any doubts as to the kind of historical causes which gave rise to this array of structural similarities. It is clearly of the same general order as that shown by the residual similarities of English and French. In fact, Tlingit and Athabaskan show a distinctly closer structural affinity than English and French. With this as a basis of comparison we see that it would be fantastic to imagine such a body of fundamental structural affinities coming about by a series of borrowings.

Similar to our use of a control case is Truman Michelson's pointed observation: "Thus Athapascan, so far as we know, has been in just as intimate contact for a very long period with Salishan and Esquimauan as with Tlingit; but there is not the slightest resemblance structurally between Athapascan, Salishan and Esquimauan" (1921, p. 236).

Salishan and Eskimo thus confirm Sapir's thesis, even though we know little about their past history. The relation of French and English is both well documented and convenient for the purposes of illustration. However, several other control cases might have been taken, such as the influence of Chinese on Japanese, of Arabic on Persian, of Indic on Burmese or Malay, of Latin on Albanian, of Greek on Russian, etc. Any of these cases would give essentially the same general results as those we have seen.

V

In his treatment of "how languages influence each other," Sapir (1921, pp. 205-220) discusses the borrowing of words at some length but does not mention the possibility of using vocabulary as a criterion of residual and cumulative relationships. However, as is reflected in Sapir's discussion and as is well known, there is a gamut of probability in word borrowings. And this fact can be very effectively used in studying relationships. Properly handled, vocabulary becomes a highly reliable criterion, just as reliable in fact as morphology, and it has the special advantage that it can be converted into percentages with consequent advantages in objectivity. The chief significance of employing vocabulary as a measure of relationship is that it affords an additional separate test, capable of verifying the results of the morphological criterion.

The use of vocabulary in historical studies is based on the same general principle as that used in morphology, namely that some elements are more fundamental and therefore more stable than others. The stability of words is related not only to the structure of the language but also to their place in the life of the people using the language. Culture words are borrowed readily, basic words much more rarely. Though this fact is generally recognized, the degree of difference objectively measured may prove surprising. We can take the same control languages we used for morphology.

There are few languages that have borrowed so liberally as has English. The bulk of the borrowings has been from Romanic, both through spoken Latin and French and through learned borrowings from the written tradition of Latin. English has also taken vocabulary from classical Greek, from Arabic, American Indian, African, and many other languages. On the other hand, the Romanic languages have received many vocabulary influences from Teutonic in the old days and from English in modern times. And they have shared in cultural terms (e.g., *café*, *coffee*) which English has from exotic tongues. As a result of these factors about half of the general English vocabulary coincides with French on the level of borrowing, either of one language from the other or of both from a common source. Against this large percentage of borrowings in the general vocabulary, loans in the basic vocabulary are all but negligible.

In order to obtain an index of diffusional influence on the basic vocabulary, we have used a list consisting of 215 items empirically chosen for their relatively stable character. The test list, designed as a general measure of affinity between related languages (Swadesh, 1950), is not fully satisfactory in its selection of stable items, but will serve our purposes. The procedure in using any such technique has to be standardized so that one may always get approximately the same results from the same material. We have operated as follows. Each item is expressed in English and a series of notes narrows the meaning in the event of ambiguity; for example, "know" is understood to refer to facts rather than persons, so that the French equivalent is *savoir* not *connaître*. For each item we enter the most common simple form used in the given language, avoiding the complication of having to deal with a choice of words. After the lists are filled in for two languages, one compares them for correspondences and non-correspondences. For the present study, the correspondences are marked either residual or borrowed as the case may be. A correspondence is an instance in which the compared elements derive, in whole or in part, from a common prototype; affixes and composite elements are disregarded, e.g., French *avoir peur* is considered to correspond with English *to fear* despite the difference of formation. Phonetic changes have to be taken into account in terms of the regular developments known to have taken place, based on historically recorded facts or the best available reconstructions. We confine ourselves to the words entered for each item, disregarding correspondences which do not fit the meaning; for example, French *uns* and English *some* must be counted a non-correspondence even though another English word, *ones*, is related to the French word.

The results of the test are dramatic. As against perhaps 50 percent of borrowed correspondences between English and French in the general vocabulary, we find just 6 percent in the basic vocabulary. Residual correspondences are found to be 27 percent. Thus the archaic residuum after 5000 years turns out to be five times greater than 2000 years of accumulated borrowings. Similar results are found between German and French, except that the borrowings are only 3 percent. The residual relations between German and English, with only about 2000 years of independent development, are much closer than those between French and English. Here are the comparative figures:

	Borrowed	*Residual*	*Unrelated*
English and German	2%	60%	38%
English and French	6%	27%	67%
French and German	3%	29%	68%

If suitable dictionaries were available it would be a simple matter to measure basic vocabulary correspondences among the Nadene languages in order to compare the results with English-German-French. In the absence of adequate dictionaries we can make shift with the comparative vocabulary which Pliny Earle Goddard gives in his attempt to disprove the relationship of Tlingit and Athabaskan (Goddard, 1920). Goddard includes all the items for which he had available both a Tlingit form and an Athabaskan form, taken from Hupa, Kato, Chasta Costa, Chipewyan, Jicarilla, or Navaho. Since his list is intended to be as complete as he could make it, giving whatever forms it was "possible to match," and was not chosen to exaggerate the similarities of Tlingit and Athabaskan, we can take it to be representative and unbiased for our purposes. From his comparisons we take all items which coincide with our test list, amounting to 82. Of these, 36 show phonetic correspondence suggestive of common origin. This amounts to 44 percent. (The 36 items in Goddard's list which coincide with our test list and which show similarity consistent with historic connection are: brother, tooth, offspring, trail, night, heart, stone, feather, name, rain, bone, bird, head, song, cloud, ear, hair, husband, mother, fly, sleep, count, shoot, push, old, hunt, kill, think, drink, tell, burn, large, dark, look, sit, deep.) Even allowing a liberal margin for errors in determining the correspondences and for chance resemblances, this figure is far too high to be explained by accumulation of borrowings. More than that, it is clearly within the range of residual correspondences found in our examination of German, English, and French, exceeding the 27-29 percent residuum found persisting after 5000 years, but less than the 60 percent persisting between English and German after 2000 years of separate development. The inference is that Tlingit and Athabaskan have diverged from a single language, and that they separated more than 2000 and less than 5000 years ago. This conclusion corroborates what is indicated by the morphological criterion.

VI

Diffusional cumulation of basic vocabulary is counteracted by the universal trend of gradual vocabulary displacement. That is, once foreign words are brought into the basic vocabulary of a language they are subject to being subsequently displaced in the same way as all other vocabulary elements. As a result only a small fraction of the basic vocabulary can ever be loanwords. It is possible to calculate the approximate size of this fraction.

The study of basic vocabulary change as a phenomenon of culture history has barely begun, but there are already indications that the rate of change is not indefinitely variable. Since the test vocabulary has not yet been perfected and some problems of statistical technique have not been standardized, there is little point in presenting a detailed report of the results to date. Instead we note that the figures we have cited for English, German and French are fairly typical of other languages with reference to the rate of basic vocabulary change they indicate. For present purposes we may operate simply with these figures.

The percentage of change in successive time periods applies to the vocabulary at the beginning of each period, not to the original common vocabulary. Our comparison of English and German shows that 40 percent of the original common basic vocabulary has been displaced in one or the other or both languages in 2000 years. If the same percentage of the original vocabulary were affected in subsequent time periods, then in 5000 years two diverging forms of an original language would no longer have any common basic vocabulary. But this does not happen. If 60 percent of the original basic vocabulary is still held in common after 2000 years, then after a second like period there remains 60 percent of those 60 percent, that is 36 percent. To obtain the percentage after an additional 1000 years, making 5000 in all, one must multiply 36 percent by the square root of 60 percent. The calculated percentage in then 28 percent. [Swadesh's notes on vocabulary retention have been omitted here, since they reflected an early and transitional stage in the development of his calculation of retention rates. The estimates he arrived at were almost immediately superseded.] Since the actual percentage for English-French is 27 percent and for German-French 29 percent after approximately 5000 years, we have here a corroboration of the general correctness of this approach.

Applying this rate of retention to the maximum rate of borrowing, we can determine the maximum percentage of diffusional cumulation in the basic vocabulary. There is small likelihood in culture history that conditions favoring maximum borrowing of vocabulary will persist indefinitely over thousands and thousands of years. Nevertheless, for the purpose of calculating a statistical limit, let us proceed on the assumption that in successive periods of 2000 years 6 percent loan correspondences appear between two languages. During the second such period, while 6 percent of new borrowed correspondences are accumulating, the first 6 percent reduces to 60 percent of itself or 3.6 percent. This gives a total of 9.6 percent at the end of the second 2000 year period. For the third period we take 60 percent of 9.6 percent and add 6 percent. Continuing thus, the total would reach 15 percent in 12,000 years, after which the total would increase no further, because the rate of loss would just equal the maximum rate of cumulation.

To accumulate 44 percent of common elements through borrowing is thus utterly out of the question. Even reaching 15 percent of borrowed correspondence is so remote a possibility as to be negligible, since it could come about only if the same two languages continue to exist side by side under the most favorable kind of culture contact for a tremendous span of time. It would assume that no migrations separate the two languages, that neither of them displaces the other in all this time and that neither gives way to a third language.

By recognizing the diagnostic significance of basic vocabulary, we reduce almost to the vanishing point the uncertainty which Boas saw in the problem of diffusional cumulation versus archaic residue. Tlingit-Athabaskan, which he felt epitomized the problem, is found to be completely removed from the category of doubtful cases. It is conceivable that the area of uncertainty reappears at a much greater time-depth, but even this possibility must not be taken for granted. We must look into it further. However, it is worthwhile to first examine some questions of stable vocabulary and of phonetic change.

VII

A few points regarding stable vocabulary need to be clarified.

We have presented a mathematical test of the common origin of languages based upon the use of an empiric basic vocabulary. But we do not claim that only this particular list may be used for such a purpose, nor can we hold that the proof has to be narrowly statistical. Normally any substantial array of correspondences among stable vocabulary elements constitutes adequate proof of genetic relationship. By this token, Sapir's demonstration of the Nadene stock was fully successful. He listed ninety-eight comparisons of structural morphemes and basic vocabulary in at least two of the three branches of the new stock—Tlingit, Athabaskan, and Haida. Not more than one or two of his comparisons can be considered to be of doubtful stability. Therefore, Harry Hoijer gives undue weight to illusory counterarguments when he says: "The complete evidence for this classification is not yet available. It has, however, been attacked by Boas and Goddard, who point out that the similarities listed by Sapir as evidence of genetic relationship may have resulted from borrowing" (1946, p. 12). Hoijer's reservations are unjustified because, as we have seen, it would be impossible for such a substantial number of correspondences among stable vocabulary items to accumulate through borrowing.

It is understood that stability, whether of basic vocabulary or of formative elements, means relative and not absolute stability. Pronouns, for example, can and do change. English and German pronouns do not agree at all points. English and French have only their first-person singular in common. Tlingit and Athabaskan show less correspondence than English and German but more than English and French. Athabaskan and Haida are almost completely unrelated in their pronouns. However, Mattole *ya-* "third person plural prefix, meaning 'all' " may be residually related to Haida *ga* "they (indef.)" (Li, 1930, p. 65; Swanton, 1911) and other relationships may appear when the phonology of the Nadene languages is better known. In any event, the small number of personal pronoun elements demonstrably comparable between Haida and Athabaskan may prove that Haida is more distantly connected than Tlingit but does not destroy the case for including Haida in the Nadene stock.

In the Indo-European languages, the numerals from one to ten show remarkable stability. From this, we may conclude that counting had developed into a very fixed form in common Indo-European. But we cannot conclude that all stocks must show the same stability in their numbers. Many tongues have only five primary numbers, with the remainder built on these. Some have only four, and the word for "four" may be built on the word for "two." This seems to be the case in Tlingit and Haida. The word for "five" in all three branches seems to be related to "hand," even though the actual forms are not the same in all three (Athabaskan *dla*, Tlingit *-djin*, Haida *tli'l*). There seem to be two numerals that correspond among the Nadene languages, "one" and "four," and this should be regarded as positive evidence.

Boas lays a great deal of emphasis on divergent vocabulary, declaring that "The question would remain to be answered, why there should be such fundamental dissimilarities between by far the greater number of words, and the question should still be asked how these dissimilarities are to be explained." However, our examination of control cases has already provided the explanation. We have seen that divergences accumulate approximately in proportion to the lapse of time. The only explanation that is needed to account for 60 percent divergent basic vocabulary in Tlingit-Athabaskan is a separate development of about 4000 years.

VIII

To study cultural correspondences, one needs to understand and allow for minor changes of form and function, which affect all traits in the course of their cultural life. In linguistics this means giving attention to changes in the phonetics and meanings of elements. Since it is known that phonetic changes tend to operate with complete consistency, so that all like sounds in like phonetic surroundings are uniformly affected, these are the easiest of all cultural changes to study. By painstaking comparison of divergent modern forms, it is possible to reconstruct the ancient prehistoric forms of words with a high degree of accuracy.

Cultural comparison which fails to take the

factor of change into account is bound to fall wide of the mark. By failing to consider phonetic and semantic change, particularly the former, Goddard was able to let pass through his hands a large body of overwhelming evidence of the genetic unity of Tlingit and Athabaskan and yet come away with the belief that only a handful of words showed any appreciable similarity. Here is his conclusion:

> Morphologically, Tlingit is very similar to Athapascan. . . . With this striking likeness in morphology, one would expect lexical similarity leading to the definite conclusion that the languages were originally one, or sprang from the same source. The comparisons made of the lexical content, however, do not justify this conclusion. The similarities are few, forming but a slight percentage of the whole. They might be attributed to accident were there not at hand a more acceptable solution. The few nouns that are common are probably due to borrowing. It would be a remarkable thing if fully the number noted had not been borrowed in the course of the generations that Tlingit and Athapascan peoples have been neighbors (1920, p. 270).

Goddard's whole discussion shows that he does not consider elements comparable unless they are identical or nearly so in form and meaning. For example he belittles Sapir's comparison of Tlingit *s'axw* "hat" with Chipewyan *c'ah* on the ground that the Athabaskan word refers to "dance hat." Thus, he fails to take into account the shifting that takes place in the meaning-association of linguistic elements in the course of time. By such an approach, one might reject the comparison of German *hund* with English *hound*, since the former refers to dog in general while the latter refers to a given type of dog. But Goddard's phonetic rigidity is an even more serious drawback to meaningful comparative work. His approach applied to French and English might mistakenly conclude that French *feu* and English *fire* are related, even though correct reconstructive method would show this to be impossible because the sounds, though similar, are inconsistent with other known correspondences; the actual historic fact is that the French word is derived from Latin *fokus* "hearth" and has developed a purely secondary and accidental similarity to the English word. On the other hand, Goddard's standard would miss a considerable number of superficially obscured relationships, like English *tooth*, French *dent*, which could be proved by comparative linguistic methods to be of common origin even if we did not possess documental intermediary forms, like Greek *dont-*, Gothic *tunth-*.

In general the process of reconstruction consists of positing and testing for each of the related languages a series of prehistoric phonetic changes by which the contemporary forms may be derived from reconstructed original prototypes. The procedure involves making hypotheses on the basis of one or more instances and then looking for further examples to confirm or contradict the hypotheses. In other words it is a matter of guided guesses followed by a rigid check-up as to the correctness of each guess.

In his comparison of Tlingit, Athabaskan, and Haida, Sapir assembled a large number of elements of similar form and meaning in the three languages. Of these he published only about one hundred in his article, intended as a preliminary report. Among the compared forms he showed consistent relationships of sounds, in some instances involving identity, in some instances consistent divergence. For example, several compared elements shows *n* in each of the languages. In another set of comparisons, *y* of the Athabaskan and Tlingit was found to coincide with *g* of Haida. The fact that the same relationship obtains in a fair number of examples tends to substantiate and to demonstrate historic linguistic processes as against chance similarity. The present author has carried Sapir's exploration a bit farther and continues to find more and more corroboration of the genetic relation indicated by Sapir. However, even the limited data contained in Sapir's published material is fully convincing.

IX

Phonology, besides being a necessary concomitant of any effective study of vocabulary correspondences, constitutes an additional criterion for the differentiation of residual and cumulative similarities. If the phonologies of compared languages are such as to admit their being derived by realistic regular formulas of change from a realistic reconstructed prototype language, one cannot doubt the fact of common origin and residual relation. The interwoven fabric of a reconstructed speech-sound pattern is too complex to be pulled together out of thin air. While a few words can be forced to fit a reconstruction, and while a few historically unjustified correspondences may creep into any reconstructive effort, there are no tricks of the trade that could give a realistic explanation for any large number of forms unless the languages are actually related in the way assumed by the general theory.

Foreign words taken into a language at a given time tend to follow a consistent pattern of phonologic adjustment to the borrowing language. Once these words become part of the language, they share all the phonologic changes that may affect the whole system from that time forward. In consequence it is possible to discover strata of diffusion differentiating elements that came in early from those which were adopted more recently. For example, English *village* is marked by its accent and sounds to be an earlier borrowing from French than the word *garage*.

This consideration removes the last possibility of confusing diffusional overlay with residual relationship. Suppose two languages show correspondences in, say, 15 percent of their basic vocabularies as measured by the standardized list which we have used. As we have seen, it is conceivable though not likely that such a figure might accumulate over a period of many thousands of years, but it is impossible for such a large portion of the basic vocabulary to be adopted in a few generations or even a few centuries. Therefore, in reconstructing the earlier phonetic forms of accumulated borrowings, it is impossible to treat them all on the same level. Some are only slightly divergent, others profoundly different. The reconstructions and the assumed shifts necessary for one group of correspondences do not work out with the next. The material thus falls into a series of strata, and one thereby detects that there has been an accumulation of borrowing over a long time span. Only if a substantial percentage of common elements of stable type can be reconstructed by a unified theory of sound changes may one conclude common origin of the compared languages.

If two languages have, say, 5 percent of basic vocabulary in common, this could be due either to relatively recent borrowing or to very ancient original identity. These two cases can easily be distinguished through phonologic criteria. If it is a recent diffusional relationship, the elements in the two languages will be phonetically fairly close. In fact the main distinction is likely to be due to the lack of given sounds in one of the languages, necessitating substitution of the next closest sounds. On the other hand the reduction of an originally identical basic vocabulary to only 5 percent in common through gradual divergence would require something like 12,000 years. During such a time span no language can escape suffering a whole series of phonologic shifts. The cognate words in the two languages would therefore be phonologically very divergent. Indeed, unless there were several languages that could be brought into the comparison, it might prove impossible to demonstrate historical relationship at all.

X

By way of conclusion, we may then say that in the structure of complex cultural features, some component traits are relatively fundamental and others relatively superficial. This fact makes possible dependable inferences as to prehistoric relationships whenever divergent forms of the same original traits are found in two or more cultures. If a number of similarities are found in the corresponding complexes of two cultures, the criterion of essentiality enables the culture historian to determine whether the similarities are residual from an originally identical complex or cumulative from continued borrowing of individual traits.

Languages, constituting extensive self-contained complexes operating to a considerable extent on a non-conscious level, lend themselves particularly well to historical study. Highly dependable separate tests can be developed in the three areas of structure, basic vocabulary, and phonology. These three criteria, moreover, are mutually confirmatory.

The effectiveness of this method is shown by applying it to Tlingit-Athabaskan, a case which Boas regarded as impenetrable by comparative linguistics. We are able to demonstrate by qualitative and statistical evidence far beyond the minimum requirements, that these languages are of common origin on an ancient level. Their common period may go back as much as 4000 years. However, the possibility of establishing archaic against diffusional relationship exists even when the time period is far greater than this.

REFERENCE NOTE

For Boas' position in the classic controversy, see his articles and comments (1917, pp. 3-5; 1920a; 1929a; 1938b, pp. 135-138). For Sapir's position, see especially his *Language* (1921, pp. 205-220), and the methodological statements and exemplifications in some of his comparative studies (1913a, 1913b, 1915b, 1915c, 1917a, 1917b, 1921a, 1925a), as well as his reply to Michelson (1915a).

Among later comments on the classificatory views of the two men, note Emeneau (1956), Hoijer (1941, 1954c), Hymes (1956a, 1956b, 1959c), Kroeber (1955, 1960a), Swadesh (1961). An adequate account of the history of genetic classification in American anthropology has yet to be written; an overview is sketched in Hymes (1963c).

On lexicostatistics and glottochronology generally, see references to the paper by Gudschinsky on pp. 612-623; on comparative method, see Thieme's article and its references (pp. 585-598); on classification, see Kroeber's article and references (pp. 654-663).

References not in the general bibliography:

GODDARD, PLINY EARLE

1920. Has Tlingit a Genetic Relation to Athapascan? *IJAL, 1:* 266-279.

HOIJER, HARRY

1946. Introduction. In Hoijer *et al.*, *Linguistic Structures of Native America.* (Viking Fund Publications in Anthropology, Vol. 6.) New York: Wenner-Gren Foundation. Pp. 9-29.

1954c. Some Problems of American Indian Research. *Papers from the Symposium on American Indian Linguistics* (University of California Publications in Linguistics, No. 10). Berkeley and Los Angeles: University of California Press. Pp. 3-12.

LI, FANG KUEI

1930. *Mattole, An Athapaskan Language of California.* Chicago: University of Chicago Press.

MICHELSON, TRUMAN

1921. The Classification of American Languages. *AA, 23:* 236-237; *IJAL 2:* 73.

SAPIR, EDWARD

1913a. Southern Paiute and Nahuatl, a Study in Uto-Aztekan, Part I. *Journal Société des Americanistes de Paris, 10:* 379-425.

1913b. Wiyot and Yurok, Algonkin Languages of California. *AA, 15:* 617-646.

1915a. Algonkin Languages of California: A Reply. *AA, 17:* 188-194.

1915b. Southern Paiute and Nahuatl, a Study in Uto-Aztekan, Part II. *AA, 17:* 98-120, 306-328. [Also in *Journal Société des Américanistes de Paris 11:* 443-488 (1914).]

1915c. The Na-Dene Languages, a Preliminary Report. *AA, 17:* 534-558.

1917a. The Status of Washo. *AA, 19:* 449-450.

1917b. Linguistic Publications of the Bureau of American Ethnology, Review. *IJAL, 1:* 76-81.

1921a. A Characteristic Penutian Form of Stem. *IJAL, 2:* 58-67.

1925a. The Hokan Affinity of Subtiaba in Nicaragua. *AA, 27:* 402-435, 491-527.

SWADESH, MORRIS

1961. The Culture Historic Implications of Sapir's Linguistic Classification. In *A William Cameron Townsend en el Vigésimoquinto Aniversario del Instituto Lingüístico de Verano*. Mexico, D.F. Pp. 663-671.

SWANTON, JOHN R.

1911. *Haida*. (BAE B 40, Part I.) Washington, D.C.: Smithsonian Institution. Pp. 205-212.

65 *Influence of Area on American Indian Linguistics*

C. F. VOEGELIN

1. THE TITLE OF THIS PAPER suggests Franz Boas' observation that certain areas have in common phonetic features or morphological features lacking in other areas. It is possible to question the influence, the fact, and the source of interest of Boas' linguistic areas. (It is also possible to say that these linguistic areas anticipated the work of the Prague school, or that they are spiritually allied to that work. See Jakobson, 1944.)

1.1 Boas' general observations about phonetic areas have been independently made and reaffirmed, or at least not denied, by other workers in the field. But, perhaps significantly, they have never received monographic treatment. It might be said, therefore, that they had exerted no special influence in the field. Or it might be said that Boas had found yet another fertile research lead, but that by chance neither he nor his students had had time or opportunity to work it out in detail. Then the status of the phonetic area problem would appear to be like the larger problem of dialect-geography in Native America—awaiting investigators.

1.2. Whether there are clearly delimited phonetic areas in North America has been questioned, apparently, in only one published paper (Voegelin, 1941a, p. 30). The detailed statement, when made, may be less in terms of areas than in distributions of phonetic features.

1.3. Boas' own interest in phonetic and morphological areas did not spring from an interest in dialect-geography, as such, but lay rather, in finding an alternative answer to theories of genetic relationships between language-families. (For another statement of the value and danger of such theories, see Kroeber, 1941.) If the observable similarities are a result of diffusion, they do not indicate a differentiation from a single prototype. Thus, the phonetic area may be at bottom only an indirect answer to the numerous attemps by Americanists to find genetic relationships between language-families, generally prior to doing comparative work on the constituent language-families in the larger relationship-schemes (as though, in the Old World, scholars attempted to demonstrate that Indo-European and Semitic were genetically related without first making reconstructions in Indo-European and in Semitic).

2. This is not to say that comparative work within single families has not been undertaken. It has, and for at least five language-families: Athabascan, Salish, Uto-Aztecan, Algonquian, and Siouan. In each case the problem of area obtruded itself in connection with stating subdivisions of the language-family in question. The lack of documentary sources in American Indian comparative work is perhaps most clearly reflected in the difficulty of stating subdivisions comparable to Italic, Indic, and other subdivisions of Indo-European. In one sense, area-groupings of languages within American Indian language-families have been almost regarded as a sort of substitute for the documentary sources of Indo-European (Latin, Sanskrit, etc.).

2.1 Athabascan languages are spoken in three discontinuous areas, one in the Mackenzie River region of northwest interior Canada, another on both sides of the Oregon-California border, and a third in the Southwest (chiefly Arizona and New Mexico). Having worked with the northern languages, Goddard came to survey the half dozen languages of the Southwest. (That is to say, subsequent work revealed that there are six separate Athabascan languages in the Southwest area [Hoijer, 1938].) Expecting a homogeneous linguistic result, Goddard suggested that Southern Athabascan was one language, with the possible exception of Navaho and Lipan (Goddard, 1911, p. 8).

2.2. Salish languages have an essentially continuous distribution in British Columbia, on the coast of Puget Sound, and in the interior of Washington and Idaho. The culture of this linguistically continuous region is, however, sharply contrastive, that of the coast being variously influenced by the North Pacific Coast culture, and that of the interior falling in a part of Kroeber's Intermountain culture-area which was recently exposed to Plains influence (Kroeber, 1939, pp. 56-57). The one comparative paper on Salish languages constantly relates and groups linguistic features in terms of coastal dialects and interior dialects (Boas and Haeberlin, 1927). It does not, however, pretend to find a linguistic cleavage parallel to the cultural contrast between coast and interior.

2.3 Uto-Aztecan languages are distributed from the International Boundary at the Rocky Mountains as far south as the Panama Canal. Most of the Uto-Aztecan languages in the United States are continuously distributed, and have come to be known as Shoshonean, without benefit of linguistic evidence: "Taking even the largest geographical division, Shoshonean, does it mean anything linguistically? Are there any traits that distinguish 'Shoshonean' from the rest of Uto-Aztecan? If there are, I do not know what they are" (Whorf, 1935, p. 608). The group of Uto-Aztecan languages between the Shoshonean to the north and Nahuatlan to the south have come to be known and defended as Sonoran. D. G. Brinton first divided all of Uto-Aztecan into three parts; J. W. Powell did not recognize the Shoshonean, Sonoran, and Nahuatlan grouping; E. Sapir definitely established the fact of genetic relationship in Uto-Aztecan; Kroeber and Mason have independently brought linguistic evidence to formulate sub-groupings of the Sonoran group; Whorf would take some of these sub-groupings as sub-groupings of the whole Uto-Aztecan family rather than of the Sonoran group, which would then be reduced to a geographic area (without linguistic unity) within the wide-flung range of Uto-Aztecan languages (Mason, 1936).

2.4. Algonquian languages are spoken both along the Atlantic coast and in the Great Lakes region, with some speakers passing between these two semi-separate regions in historic times; and at the present time there are three geographically separate Algonquian languages in the western Plains. This geographic distribution of the family into four areas may appear to have influenced Michelson's classification of the family into four major divisions, the three divergent western Algonquian branches, and a fourth half-unified branch: Eastern-Central languages spoken in the semi-separate region of Atlantic Coast-Great Lakes (Michelson, 1912, p. 229). But Michelson based his classification wholly on linguistic data, contrasting his approach with the purely geographic classification of his predecessors, J. Mooney and C. Thomas, C. C. Uhlenbeck, and F. N. Finck (Michelson, 1912, p. 226), and did not hesitate to include the Massachusetts language (Natick) and Delaware in the Central substyle of his Eastern-Central branch. Systematic reconstructions were first based on four languages of the Great Lakes group (Bloomfield, 1925). These reconstructions must include nothing more than an additional consonant cluster to account for certain Atlantic Coast languages (Siebert [1941] discovered the need for the additional consonant cluster), and can also, apparently, account for the reflexes of the divergent western languages. (Michelson [1935] demonstrated more correspondence between the divergent western languages and the Central dialects than Algonquian students had expected.)

Some recent attempts have been made to state earlier geographic positions of the languages in terms of relative chronology of sound-changes. For example, one group of languages, Delaware and Ojibwa and Miami, share in the preservation of the *n*-stop clusters; another group of Great Lake languages, including Delaware again, share in a later development, the coincidence of θ and *l* as *l*; but for subsequent developments, Delaware does not follow the innovations of Great Lakes languages but rather those of Atlantic coast languages, and hence we may make an inference of Delaware movement from Great Lakes to the Atlantic coast (Voegelin, 1941b, p. 147); Siebert (1941, p. 302) also makes this kind of historical assumption.

2.5. Siouan languages are scattered in three widely separated regions. Of the larger western group, Hidatsa and Crow were early recognized as being linguistically distinct; Winnebago and Iowa-Oto-Missouri were set up as a Chiwere group, although the linguistic basis of Chiwere might include Dakota and Dhegiha (Omaha-Kansas-Osage-Quapaw). Swanton's crystallized opinion was that Tutelo and Catawba (the only Atlantic coast Siouan languages) do not in any sense belong to the same group; furthermore, the Tutelo of the Atlantic coast appears to belong in the same linguistic group as that which includes Ofo and Biloxi, linguistic neighbors in the lower Mississippi region (Voegelin, 1941c, citing Swanton and others). It is possible here to make an historical assumption of prior adjacent residence of Tutelo, Ofo, and Biloxi.

2.6. The fact of area-groupings obtruded itself in different ways in the formulation of the comparative work of the five language-families here reviewed. Where the location of languages in certain areas influenced postulates which appealed to linguistic data to substantiate, the work was misleading (2.1), or diverted attention to essentially irrelevant considerations (2.2), or the results were controversial (2.3). Conversely, where an examination of linguistic features suggests a subdivisional classification first, and where this classification is then projected against the distribution of languages in areas, historical interpretations of movements (2.4) or former locations (2.5) of languages can be made with the assistance of linguistic data.

3. With structural linguistics as the chief interest of some workers, area may be expected to play a more central role—to be, in effect, a specialized point of departure. (Velten uses the term Linguistic Area for this; see Sebeok's review of his paper [1944].) Rather than being a specialist in Athabascan languages, a student might become a specialist in Southwest languages. Such area-students might be expected to observe borrowing not only between Athabascan languages and Taos, for example, but between Taos and Jemez and Spanish and English and other languages of the Southwest, irrespective of whether the languages are related or belong to the same cultural tradition; and ultimately to state structural features which appear to offer resistance or make for acceptance of change in the area studied.

REFERENCE NOTE

Since this paper was written, work in each of the language families cited so succinctly (Athapaskan, Salishan, Uto-Aztecan, Algonquian, Siouan) has progressed in understanding the details of subgroupings, but the points of principle remain valid. The history of areal interpretation in American anthropology is discussed further in Hymes (1961e, pp. 22-23). For areal work generally, including specific reference to American Indian languages, see Emeneau's article and its references (pp. 642-653).

References not in the general bibliography:

BLOOMFIELD, LEONARD

1925. On the Sound System of Central Algonquian. *Lg.*, *1:* 130-156.

BOAS, FRANZ, and H. HAEBERLIN

1927. Sound Shifts in Salishan Dialects. *IJAL*, *4:* 118-136.

GODDARD, PLINY EARLE

1911. *Jicarilla Apache Texts.* (American Museum of Natural History, Anthropological Papers, No. 8.) New York.

MASON, J. ALDEN

1936. The Classification of the Sonoran Languages. With an appendix by B. L. Whorf. In *Essays in Anthropology in Honor of Alfred Louis Kroeber*. Berkeley: University of California Press. Pp. 183-198.

MICHELSON, TRUMAN

1912. Preliminary Report of the Linguistic Classification of Algonquian Tribes. *BAE-AR*, *28:* 221-290.

1935. Phonetic Shifts in Algonquian Languages. *IJAL*, *8:* 131-171.

SIEBERT, FRANK T., JR.

1941. Certain Proto Algonquian Consonant Clusters. *Lg.*, *17:* 298-303.

VOEGELIN, C. F.

1941b. Proto-Algonquian Consonant Clusters in Delaware. *Lg.*, *17:* 143-147.

1941c. Internal Relationships of Siouan Languages. *AA*, *43:* 246-249.

66 *India as a Linguistic Area*

MURRAY B. EMENEAU

THE AMERICAN ANTHROPOLOGISTS who have been linguistic scholars as well—I would mention Boas, Sapir, and, last but not least, Alfred L. Kroeber, whom we delight to honor in this issue of *Language*—have been catholic in their approaches to linguistics. Descriptive linguistics on this continent owes a tremendous amount to these men. But none of them has ignored historical problems, and in their various ways and even with radically different points of view on subjects which were open to dispute, they have contributed much to both detailed genetic problems, especially of the North American continent, and to the discussion of certain general questions. One of the latter is a problem that arises again and again in any region of the world where the linguistic picture is complicated, and it is particularly fitting, as will appear, if I attempt to add something to it as an offering to Kroeber.

The problem is that of diffusion of linguistic traits across genetic boundaries. Boas raised the problem (whether it was original with him, does not matter—for I do not intend to be bibliographically complete) in several places, including especially the introduction to *Handbook of American Indian Languages* (1911, pp. 47-53) and two articles (1920a, 1929a). One of his conclusions was that "in a considerable number of native languages of the North Pacific Coast [of North America] we find, notwithstanding fundamental differences in structure and vocabulary, similarities in particular grammatical features distributed in such a way that neighboring languages show striking similarities. . . . It seems . . . almost impossible to explain this phenomenon without assuming the diffusion of grammatical processes over contiguous areas" (1929a, p. 6). In the preceding exposition he had taken it to be a matter of general agreement (as it patently is) that words may be borrowed, and probably also that phonetic traits may be borrowed. He was particularly concerned to demonstrate that morphology also may diffuse, and he brought forward a rather considerable number of instances that seem convincing. This for us is the important point of his treatment. We may find it more difficult to accept the phraseology of his general theory ("hybridization of languages"), as being a little too simple, too unsubtle, and as ignoring (as we know he did) genetic relationships that were not clear at first inspection; but at the moment we are not concerned with this.

Sapir treated the problem especially in Chapter 9 of his book *Language* (1921, pp. 205-220). He ranged much more widely for his examples than Boas had done, drawing in material from his immensely broad linguistic experience. He, like Boas, accepted the borrowing of words as commonplace, though he pointed out and discussed the varying tolerances of languages for such borrowings. He accepted also the borrowing of phonetic traits; his discussion introduced the bilingual individuals who are the social carriers of change. More important as prefiguring what his attitude would be when he took up morphology, was his insistence that phonetic borrowings are not random but are regulated (as by a sort of "governor") by "the phonetic drift" of the language: "so long as its main phonetic concern is the preservation of its sound patterning, not of its sounds as such, there is really no reason why a language may not unconsciously assimilate foreign sounds that have succeeded in worming their way into its gamut of individual variations, provided always that these new variations (or reinforced old variations) are in the direction of the native drift," (1921, p. 214). This is essentially a reluctance to accept such borrowings without qualification; whether the qualification is always demonstrable in Sapir's terms, will depend on the historical data available (and of course on the ingenuity of the scholar). The method is surely that of our present-day structuralists. In the final section of the chapter (1921, pp. 215-220) Sapir examined morphological borrowings. His argument ran: English has borrowed a certain number of affixes from French, Latin, Greek (*-ess*, *-ize*, *-able*), but these are merely additions to the old stock of affixes and are hardly different from the borrowings of words. They make no difference "to the essential build of the language." To generalize: "nowhere [i.e., in no language] do we find any but superficial morphological interinfluencings." He summed up: "We may infer one of several things from this:—That a really serious morphological influence is not, perhaps, impossible, but that its operation is so slow that it has hardly ever had the chance to incorporate itself in the relatively small portion of linguistic history that lies open to inspection; or that there are certain favorable conditions that make for profound morphological disturbances from without, say a peculiar instability of linguistic type or an unusual degree of cultural contact, conditions that do not happen to be realized in our documentary material; or, finally, that we have not the right to assume that a language may easily exert a remolding morphological influence on another." In some cases of morphological similarities Sapir pointed out that they are vestiges of genetic relationship, and he was willing (as he showed elsewhere in setting up the superstocks for North America) to use this solution rather freely. Finally, he frankly said of diffusion that we have "no really convincing examples of profound morphological influence by diffusion," and he characterized language as "probably the most self-contained, the most massively resistant of all social phenomena." The well-known conflicting attitudes of Boas and Sapir are clearly at work here—Sapir's 1921 statement is reaction to Boas' skeptical attitude toward genetic relationships; Boas' 1929 article is his rebuttal of Sapir, even though only tacitly so. It is to be emphasized that Sapir makes a distinction between two types of morphological influence, one "superficial," the other "profound." This is, in spite of its specious attractiveness, a highly subjective differentiation and one that it will be very difficult to apply in specific cases; it will undoubtedly give rise to disagreement between scholars who handle the same data, and it may in the long run not be at all a usable distinction, just since it is a value judgment and not quantifiable.

Sapir's attitude has come to be widely held in this country. Kroeber in his presidential address to the Linguistic Society in 1940 (1941) calls it a "usual dictum" that "words can be borrowed freely between distinct languages, but grammar with difficulty if at all." Hoijer (1948c, p. 335) says: "Traits of language are not readily borrowed." A Boasian point of view has been and is, however, apparently more favored in Europe (cf. Sebeok, 1950a, and the bibliography given by him; Troubetekoy, 1939b; Jakobson, 1944; etc.). It has, moreover, never been totally abandoned here. Leonard Bloomfield in his book *Language* (1933, pp. 468-471) certainly favored it. Kroeber (1941, p. 290) thought that "the time has come to reexamine this (i.e., Sapir's] dictum," led to this statement by Ray's hypothesis that the Melanesians have borrowed from Malayo-Polynesian more formal structure than vocabulary. Whatever may be the correct solution for this last specific problem, it would seem that more evidence bearing on the general problem would be welcome. Probably the most useful approach to a solution would be the provision of material of a kind that would allow historical examination with a considerable time-depth. India provides such material. Some of it has been examined from this point of view by earlier scholars, but little of it has penetrated into the realm of general linguistics, since it was published in specifically Indological outlets. (The first phonetic trait that I shall examine below is quoted, e.g., by Bloomfield 1933, pp. 469 f., relying on *Linguistic Survey of India* [hereafter *LSI*], *4*:278 ff. Of the two other suggested influences mentioned by Bloomfield, the first, that the confusion of Indo-European *l* and *r* in Sanskrit is pernaps due to a substratum language which possessed only one of these sounds, has nothing to recommend it, since we know of no language in India with this characteristic. The remaining one will be discussed below; it concerns the use of distinct singular and plural stems to which the same case endings are added.) Perhaps this reexamination will have a better fate.

The Indian subcontinent is inhabited by a very large population who speak languages belonging to three major families, Indo-Aryan (a subfamily of Indo-European), Dravidian, and Munda. Indo-Aryan speakers in 1931 numbered about 255 million; by 1951 they must have numbered nearly 330 million. Dravidian speakers in 1951 numbered approximately 90 million. Munda speakers must number well over 5 million. This does not take account of all the languages that are included geographically in this area. There are Burushaski in Gilgit, Khasi in the hills of Assam, Nicobarese, Andamanese, and many languages of the Tibeto-Burmese group in the Himalayas and in Assam. Our attention will be focussed primarily on Indo-Aryan, Dravidian, and Munda.

For Indo-Aryan and Dravidian our historical knowledge is considerable. Sanskrit speech, that important member of the Indo-European family, has been in India and recorded voluminously since the second millennium B.C. Middle Indo-Aryan in a number of varieties is well known, and Modern Indo-Aryan, in its dozen or more major languages and innumerable local dialects, is also fairly well known. Of the four literary Dravidian languages, Tamil has voluminous records dating back at least two millennia. These four languages are well known, and the remaining fifteen or sixteen nonliterary Dravidian languages are on record to some extent. The dozen or so Munda languages are on the whole not well known—they are not literary languages—but for a few of them there are preliminary accounts that tell us a considerable amount.

The historical relationships between the three families are largely a matter of reconstruction (see Emeneau, 1954a). It is clear from the geographical nature of the boundaries between the three families in Central India that the northern boundary of Dravidian is and has been for a long time retreating south before the expansion of Indo-Aryan, and that the small islands of Dravidian speech north of the main boundary are isolated patches that have not yet become extinct. Similarly with the Munda languages; they are all islands of greater or less extent surrounded by and pressed upon by Dravidian or by Indo-Aryan. This should mean a much greater spread both for Munda and for Dravidian at an earlier period. We know in fact from the study of the non-Indo-European element in the Sanskrit lexicon that at the time of the earliest Sanskrit records, the Ṛgveda, when Sanskrit speakers were localized no further east than the Panjab, there were already a few Dravidian words current in Sanskrit. This involves a localization of Dravidian speech in this area no later than three millennia ago. It also of course means much bilingualism and gradual abandonment of Dravidian speech in favor of Indo-Aryan over a long period and a great area—a process for which we have only the most meager of evidence in detail. (This is the historical process to be invoked, rather than the too facile and unrealistic one of a general displacement of populations through expansions. Undoubtedly there were expansions involved, in the shape of marauding bands and of missionaries, but neither of these agencies had an interest in getting rid of earlier populations; it was to their advantage, political, economic, religious, to have subjects and proselytes. Absorption, not displacement, is the chief mechanism in radical language changes of the kind we are considering). Similar relationships must have existed between Indo-Aryan and Munda and between Dravidian and Munda, but it is still almost impossible to be sure of either of these in detail.

The question of vocabulary borrowings between the three families need not be more than mentioned. The Dravidian languages all have many Indo-Aryan items, borrowed at all periods from Sanskrit, Middle Indo-Aryan, and Modern Indo-Aryan. The Munda languages likewise have much Indo-Aryan material, chiefly, so far as we know now, borrowed from Modern Indo-Aryan, though this of course includes items that are Sanskrit in form, since Modern Indo-Aryan borrows from Sanskrit very considerably. That Indo-Aryan has borrowed from Dravidian has also become clear; Burrow (1955, pp. 379-388), gives a sampling and a statement of the chronology involved (see also Emeneau, 1954a). It is noteworthy that this influence was spent by the end of the pre-Christian era, a precious indication for the linguistic history of North India: Dravidian speech must have practically ceased to exist in the Ganges valley by this period. Borrowings from Munda into the other two families must have taken place, but are difficult to identify (Burrow, 1955, pp. 377-379).

Other features than vocabulary items are of more interest in this connection. It has long been recognized that even our earliest Sanskrit texts show features that historically are un-Indo-European in their nature, but that resemble features of the Dravidian languages, and that as time went on, more such features appeared in Indo-Aryan. The late Jules Bloch collected and discussed all such points that he knew in the concluding chapter of his book *L'indo-aryen du Veda aux temps modernes* (1934, pp. 321-331). I shall discuss these and can add several more and more detail. Three general tendencies emerge: either specifically an "Indianization" of Indo-Aryan, or, in a few instances, the appearance of a trait in contiguous languages (but not all the languages) of all three major families, without the possibility of one's being sure where it originated, or a similar situation to this last, but with evidence for the original source.

Most of the languages of India, of no matter which major family, have a set of retroflex, cerebral, or domal consonants in contrast with dentals. The retroflexes include stops and nasal certainly, also in some languages sibilants, lateral, tremulant, and even others. Indo-Aryan, Dravidian, Munda, and even the far northern Burushaski, form a practically solid bloc characterized by this phonological feature; since, however, one of the Munda languages, viz. So:ra:, which there is a good chance is archaic, does not have it, it is at least possible that it is not Proto-Munda (so Burrow, 1955, p. 95). Even our earliest Sanskrit records already show phonemes of this class, which are, on the whole, unknown elsewhere in the Indo-European field, and which are certainly not Proto-Indo-European. In Sanskrit many of the occurrences of retroflexes are conditioned; others are explained historically as reflexes of certain Indo-European consonants and consonant clusters. But, in fact, in Dravidian it is a matter of the utmost certainty that retroflexes in contrast with dentals are Proto-Dravidian in origin, not the result of conditioning circumstances. In Southern Dravidian, moreover, several languages have three phonemic series in the front of the mouth—dental, alveolar, retroflex—a possibility hardly envisaged by the framers of the International Phonetic Association's alphabet; the comparative evidence looks to similar distinctions in Proto-Dravidian. This being so for Dravidian, it is beyond doubt that, even where Indo-European material yields Sanskrit retroflexes, pre-Indo-Aryan and pre-Dravidian bilingualism provided the conditions which allowed pre-Indo-Aryan allophones to be redistributed as retroflex phonemes. Certainly as time went on, Middle Indo-Aryan showed more such phonemes than old Indo-Aryan, and in consequence Modern Indo-Aryan does so too. This is a clear instance of Indianization of the Indo-European component in the Indic linguistic scene.

A phonological example of more limited inter-influence—an isogloss, for which the historical solution is not yet at hand, is the following. In Marathi the palatals of Old Indo-Aryan are represented by *tš* and *dž* affricates before front vowels, by *ts* and *dz* affricates before back vowels; there are so many exceptions to this statement of distribution (because of recent borrowings from Sanskrit which always have *tš* and *dž*, and for other reasons) that it is necessary to postulate two sets of phonemes. A similar distribution is found in southern Oriya (Indo-Aryan; *LSI*, *5*(2):379), in Telugu and northern Kannaḍa (Dravidian; Sreekantaiya, 1954) and, according to Bloch (following the *LSI*, *4*:169, but the distribution is completely uncertain), in Kurku (Munda). These languages form a continuous band across central India, and the trait undoubtedly originated in one language and spread to the others from it; which was the originator is, as I said, unknown. One can, however, guess from the distribution, which shows a very wide gap between southern Oriya (on the northeast) and Marathi (on the northwest), and from the fact that the feature appears only in northern dialects of Kannada, that the feature originated in either of the two contiguous languages which show it in all dialects, viz. in Marathi or in Telugu. The only possibility of a decision between these two lies in philological work, which may possibly be successful in establishing a relative chronology. Kashmiri shows a similar phenomenon; this can only be of independent origin.

On the side of morphology and syntax, it may be well to quote Bloch's summary statement and then to enlarge on a few details. Bloch indicates that in what follows Dravidian and Indo-Aryan have more traits in common than Munda has with Indo-Aryan.

Dans le mot, usage constant de la suffixation et absence (en ce qui concerne l'aryen, perte) des préfixes et infixes, lesquels sont courants en munda; dans le groupe, absence (perte) des prépositions et des préverbes comme tels. Dans la flexion, absence (perte) du numbre duel, courant en munda. Dans les noms, double thème, le thème oblique étant susceptible de valeur génitive, et se faisant suivre de mots plus ou moins vides de leur sens propre; pronoms personnels à deux thèmes: celui de nominatif, et celui de régime direct et indirect (un seul thème en munda). Dans le verbe, troisième personnes de forme nominale et variables en genre; présence d'un gérondif (qui manque au munda) tenant un rôle important dans la liaison des phrases et dans la création de locutions composées á valeur stylistique au grammaticale. . . . Quant aux expressions comparables, et par exemple les mots doubles et á écho on en ferait aisément de longues listes dans toutes les familles de langues dravidiennes (1934, pp. 327-328).

[In the word, constant use of suffixation and absence (where Aryan is concerned, loss) of prefixes and infixes, which are present in Munda; in the phrase, absence (loss) of prepositions and of preverbs, as such. In the inflexion, absence (loss) of the dual number, present in Munda. In nouns, double theme, the oblique theme being capable of genitive function, and following words more or less devoid of their proper meaning; personal pronouns having two themes: that of the nominative, and that of direct and indirect rection (a single theme in Munda). In the verb, three persons nominal in form and variable in gender; occurrence of a gerundive (which Munda lacks) having an important role in the linking of phrases and in the creation of compound phrases with stylistic or grammatical function. . . . As for comparable expressions, such as, for example, double words and echo words, one could easily make long lists in all the families of Dravidian languages.]

Not all of these will seem to be of equal cogency. Loss of the dual in Sanskrit is paralleled by its loss all over the rest of the Indo-European domain. Loss of infixation, which occurs after all only in a certain verb type, is similarly paralleled everywhere. The disuse of verbal prefixes as a living set of morphemes in Modern Indo-Aryan is closely tied up with the general shift of accent to initial syllables (whatever the exact chronology of this may be). The absence of prepositions is striking to an Indo-Europeanist or a speaker of a Western Indo-European language; it should be remembered, however, that in Sanskrit itself (and it inherits this trait from Proto-Indo-European) there is no class of "prepositions"—the morphemes in question are rather "adverbs in immediate constituency with nouns," the position being postpositional probably rather more often than prepositional. If these are replaced in Modern Indo-Aryan by noun forms invariably following the oblique form of the head noun, the construction is not too different from that of Sanskrit. Parallel constructions in Dravidian may possibly have helped toward the shift. The two themes of personal pronouns are paralleled by Dravidian phenomena; but Indo-European in general is marked by double stems in the personal pronouns (e.g., English *I:m-* [*me*, *my*]; Sanskrit *aham:ma-* [*mām*, *mayā*, *mahyam*, *mat*, *mama*, *mayi*, *me*]). It has been pointed out by others (*LSI*, *4*:280, whence Bloomfield, 1933, p. 470) that Modern Indo-Aryan, like Dravidian, adds the same inflexional (case) morphemes to distinct stems for singular and plural, which is unlike general Indo-European inflexional practice. This is convincing and to be interpreted as evidence of borrowing from Dravidian, even though similar structure is seen in Tocharian.

The phenomena pointed out by Bloch for the verb are more impressive. Especially am I impressed by the Sanskrit form which he calls the "gérondif," which, following Whitney, is usually called in English "gerund" (otherwise "absolutive," "indeclinable participle," "conjunctive participle," "adverbial participle"). All three major stocks show constructions in which verb stems or nonfinite verb forms are strung together in series which are closed by a finite verb form (or other predicate-ender). This is a prominent feature of Dravidian; it is well known in Munda also and in Indo-Aryan. It is one of the syntactic features of Sanskrit that distinguishes it from other Indo-European languages, even though the actual forms used are relatable to Indo-European morphological material. We must look to the syntax of the non-Indo-European languages of India for the stimulus that brought about this re-use in India of older material. It might be expected that an attempt would be made to find priority between Dravidian and Munda for this type of construction. Such a discussion would be fruitless in the present stage of our knowledge of Munda, and especially moreover since such strings of verb stems or nonfinite forms are a common feature of so many other languages and language families, e.g., Vietnamese, Chinese, Japanese, Korean, Altaic, Finno-Ugric (at least Hungarian); it is Indo-European and Semitic, if I mistake not, that are aberrant in this matter in Eurasia.

Bloch (1934, p. 328) also mentions that Marathi, Oriya, and Sinhalese have constructions based on a nominalized or adjectivized form of a verb (or rather of a predication ending in a verb) followed by a postposition. I have available only material from Marathi (cf. Bloch 1920, pp. 260 f., §263), such as: *tujhī āī vārlyā-pāsūn* 'since (*pāsūn*) your mother (*tujhī āī*; subject) died (*vārlyā*).' I have pointed out (1954b, p. 484) that there are in Buddhist Hybrid Sanskrit and in Pali constructions like this, in which the first member of a compound is a participle and the second a noun which is not the (syntactic) subject of the participle (e.g., *āgatakāle* 'at the time of [his] having come'). This is all parallel to the pan-Dravidian construction in which a predication ending in an adjectivized or nominalized form of a verb is in attributive construction with a following noun (e.g., Kota *a:m unčvd unyp* 'the thought (*unyp*) which we (*a:m*) have thought (*unčvd;* adjective form of past paradigm).' Bloch failed to note that Munda also has the construction. There are many parallels to this construction in languages of Asia outside of India. We cannot decide priority as between Dravidian and Munda; we need only note that the Indo-Aryan tentatives in the direction of this construction (in all probability under Dravidian stimulus) are an Indianization, for there is nothing parallel to it elsewhere in Indo-European.

The echo-word construction mentioned by Bloch has been written about in some detail, both by a number of Indian scholars in early circulars of the Linguistic Society of India and by myself (1938). It is generally a construction in which a basic word formulated as CVX is followed by an echo-word in which CV is replaced by a morpheme *gi-* or *u-* or the like (or C is replaced by *m-* or the like), and X echoes the X (or VX echoes the VX) of the basic word. The meaning of the echo-word is 'and the like'; e.g., *puli gili* 'tigers and the like.' There are many variations, though it is notable that nearly all the Dravidian languages have *gi-*. Most notable is the fact that the construction is found in all three families, there being good evidence for Dravidian, fairly good evidence for Indo-Aryan, and good evidence for at least So:ra: in the Munda family (G. V. Ramamurti (1931) pp. 150 ff.). The chief So:ra: echo-morpheme is *m-*, which is evidenced also for Brahui, Kolami, Parji, Telugu, Tamil-Malayalam, and for various Indo-Aryan languages such as Ḍogrī. We need more detailed evidence and analysis, but it is clear already that echo-words are a pan-Indic trait and that Indo-Aryan probably received it from non-Indo-Aryan (for it is not Indo-European).

Finally, I would present in detail a matter which has not been noticed before. The phenomenon is of limited areal range, but appears in all three families, having spread from Indo-Aryan, though it is not an Indo-European phenomenon. This is the use of "classifiers" or "quantifiers." In constructions marked by these, when a noun is numerated by means of a numeral or a similar word, the construction contains also one of a smallish class of words or morphemes which we can call by either of these terms. The term "classifier" indicates that there are as many classes of nouns as there are classifiers; the term "quantifier" indicates that in numeration of nouns there is always specification of the type of unit by which the species indicated by the noun is counted. The units indicated are of various kinds, either measured units of nondiscrete entities (e.g., a quart of liquid, an acre of land) or discrete entities as classed by various criteria (e.g., human vs. animal, animate vs. nonanimate, long and thin vs. flat and thin vs. spherical). Such quantifiers are, to be sure, used in probably all languages; English has *a ton of coal*, *two acres of land*, *three head of cattle*, etc. But the languages under discussion at the moment are not those in which only nouns denoting nondiscrete entities and a few others are classified or quantified, but those in which all or nearly all nouns are treated thus. Conspicuous as having such systems are Chinese, Japanese, Korean, Vietnamese, Khmer, Thai, Burmese, and Malay.

The existence of classificatory systems in some of the languages of India has hardly been noted and is, as a matter of fact, difficult to get information on. They have been reported for the Magadhan languages of Modern Indo-

Aryan, viz. Bengali, Assamese, Oriya, and in Bihari for some dialects (e.g., Maithili). The systems in these closely related languages involve a half-dozen or more classes. The morpheme order is noun + numeral + classifier, or numeral + classifier + noun; there is no information on different meanings for the two constructions. According to S. K. Chatterji, since all the languages use practically the same morphemes, the modern systems are all descendants of a system that originated in the Magadhan Apabhraṃśa at the end of the Middle Indo-Aryan period.

Less attention has been paid to the fact that Marathi has a meager suggestion of this system with one classifier, viz. *jaṇ* [dzʌn] 'person,' fem. *jaṇī*, when nouns denoting persons are numerated by numerals higher than four (and optionally for two to four). This is historically related to one of the Magadhan classifying morphemes (Bengali *jan*, etc.), but the word order in the construction is fixed in Marathi (numeral + classifier + noun) as opposed to the variation in the Magadhan languages. This, combined with Marathi's having only one classifier, seems to argue for a certain degree of independence in the development of the systems in the two Indo-Aryan branches, at least since Middle Indic times, though it is not ruled out that the Marathi construction owes its inception to some stimulus ultimately deriving from the full-fledged system of Magadhan. For some of the village Hindi dialects show a use of *janā* like that of Marathi. The construction is not described in the grammars of Hindi, which deal essentially with urban forms. The Nepali dictionary also records such a use for Nepali *janā*. Until better descriptive accounts are available for Modern Indo-Aryan languages and dialects, it will be impossible to map the present use of classificatory systems in this section of India, and until a more searching study has been made of the various stages of Middle Indo-Aryan, the history of the systems will remain a matter of speculation.

Classificatory systems have been found also in some of the Dravidian and Munda languages. Of the former, Kolami (Wardha dialect), Parji, the Kui-Kuwi dialects, and Kuru<u>kh</u> and Malto have such systems, and in each instance it has been borrowed from Indo-Aryan neighbors.

The Wardha dialect of Kolami classifies persons when they are numerated by the numerals six and over. These numerals are borrowed from Marathi, as well as the Marathi classifier in the form *zen* [dzen], with feminine *zenikul*, i.e., Marathi fem. *jaṇi* plus the Kolami plural suffix *-kul*. This applies also to the numeral five, when the Marathi numeral is optionally used instead of the Kolami numeral. This Kolami dialect is in predominantly Marathi-speaking country. The Adilabad Kolams have not borrowed so many numerals and do not use the Marathi classifier with the Kolami numerals, which are the only ones that have been reported.

In the account of Parji no statement is given about the matter, but the texts provide a few examples that indicate that *jan* is used for persons and that in addition *gŏṭa* is used for certain nouns denoting nonpersons. The neighboring Indo-Aryan language is Halbi, for which our information is not good. The Indo-Aryan classifier represented by Parji *gŏṭa* presumably is found in Halbi (so *LSI*, *7*, Standard List item 114, would seem to indicate); it certainly is not Marathi, just as certainly is Magadhan, and is also found in Chhattīsgaṛhī dialects of Eastern Hindi (*LSI*, *6*:215, 225). The account of Parji says that the numerals from six on are borrowed from Halbi; apparently the classifiers are used only with these numerals of Halbi origin.

The Kuwi dialect described by Schulze has a system like that of Parji, with Oriya numerals from three on and the classifiers *zāna* (*z* = *j*) for nouns denoting male persons and *gotta* for all others (corresponding to the Kui-Kuwi gender system). The language is spoken at the boundary between Oriya and Telugu. The accounts of other Kui-Kuwi dialects, one of which is to the north in Oriya territory, do not speak of a system of classifiers. However, in Fitzgerald's account of Kuwi there is one phrase with the classifier for persons (1913, p. 126) *tīnijoṅa māska* 'three girls'). Winfield (1928, p. 37) describes Kui forms for the numerals from three on, which are very like those of Bengali which have the classifier enclitic *-ṭā*; the order too is Magadhan (noun + numeral + classifier). These few examples are sufficient evidence that all the Kui-Kuwi dialects have borrowed the classificatory system of Oriya.

The Kurukh system shows very close similarities to the system of the Magadhan languages, including an option in word order, and a number of classifying morphemes, most, if not all, of which are borrowings from the contiguous Magadhan languages Bihari and Oriya (Chhattīsgaṛhī Hindi is also a neighbor, but does not have so elaborate a classificatory system) (e.g., *jhan*, *goṭaŋg*, *ṭhur* [cf. Bengali -*ṭu*]). The classifiers are used not merely with the Indo-Aryan numerals which have been borrowed from four on, but also with the Dravidian numerals two to four.

The Malto system is the most complex of all these. With the numerals from three on, which it has borrowed from the surrounding Bengali or Bihari, it uses a number of classifiers and the order numeral + classifier + noun. The classifiers are in part at least borrowed from a Magadhan system and include *jen* and *goṭa*. In addition there are used *ḍaṉṛa* for long objects (roads, bamboos, articles of clothing; < Modern Indo-Aryan **ḍaṇḍ*- < Sanskrit *daṇḍa*- 'stick'), *paṭa* for 'objects distinguished for surface' (plates, combs, ponds, clouds, bedsteads; < Modern Indo-Aryan **paṭ*-, **paṭṭ*-, **pāṭ*-, cf. Sanskrit *paṭṭaka*-'board'), *kaḍa* for tendril-like things (hair, wire, grass stalks; etymology not yet found), and several others whose etymologies have not yet been found. In addition to this, the Dravidian numerals for one and two, when they enumerate nouns denoting nonpersons, are used with some of the same set of classifiers just listed (*paṭ*, *kaḍ*, *ḍaṉṛ*, etc.) plus several others, e.g. *páṉṛ* for round objects (no etymology yet found) and *maq* for animals (Dravidian in origin). In this last construction many nouns are used as their own classifiers (e.g., *man-ond manu* 'one tree'). A unique feature of this construction for one and two is the order: classifier + numeral + noun, found nowhere else in any of the systems in India and presumably a Malto invention. It is to be noted too that the numeral forms -*ond* 'one' and -*is* 'two' in this construction are found nowhere else but in this construction (cf. *ort* 'one person,' *ivr* 'two persons'), and that for 'one' the closely related Kurukh has the forms *ort* 'one person' and *oṇṭā* 'one animal or thing,' the latter of which may either precede or follow a noun (contrasting with the single order in Malto). Malto, then, presumably began by borrowing numerals and classifiers from a neighboring Magadhan language, and subsequently elaborated the system independently, chiefly on the basis of inherited material.

For the Munda languages the evidence is less good. Koṛowa certainly uses *jhan* and *gwoṭ*/*gwoṭaŋ*, borrowings from Indo-Aryan, as well as others, like *ho?* 'head of cattle' and *hoṛ* 'person,' which are not borrowed; *hoṛ* and *jhan* seem to be in free variation. The numerals involved are not borrowings. The order is numeral + classifier + noun. It is fairly clear from the accounts of Santali and Mundari that they use a similar system; it is quite clear that So:ra: does not.

Here then is a large area of India, especially eastern and central India, with this feature. My reconstruction, relying on the fact that some, if not only, Indo-Aryan classifier morphemes are used in all the languages involved and on the further fact that these morphemes are used only with Indo-Aryan numerals in some of the non-Indo-Aryan languages, is that the construction (so far as India is concerned) is originally Indo-Aryan. It spread thence to the other languages as a total construction consisting of numeral + classifier, and then was elaborated in some of the languages with native material, the native numerals, native morphemes as additional classifiers, etc.

The problem of Telugu and Kannaḍa is difficult. In certain dialects of Telugu the numerals from eight to ten are followed by the classifier *mandi* when persons are numerated; e.g., *enimidi mandi manuṣulu* 'eight men.' Up to ten this morpheme is in complementary distribution with the suffix -*guru* found in the forms denoting persons from three to seven (e.g. *mug-guru manuṣulu*, *nalu guru manuṣulu*, etc.) and the suffix -*aru* in *idd-aru manuṣulu* 'two men." I do not know whether *mandi* is to be classed as a free form or as a suffix; presumably complete analysis of the language will answer this question. The morpheme is of Dravidian origin. Taken by itself it might be thought that Telugu had developed this construction under the stimulus of Oriya; without a complete mapping of dialects and philological work to determine chronology one cannot be sure about this possibility. Another problem is why the use of *mandi* should start only with eight. Perhaps the statement of it as in complementary distribution with -*aru* and -*guru* is the answer; these suffixes do not occur from eight to ten and perhaps *mandi*, as it were, makes up for their absence. But such an explanation is uncomfortably teleological and ad hoc, and the fact that there seems to be some free variation above ten is disturbing. It is hardly possible to dissociate the Telugu facts from those of Kannaḍa. About the latter we are told that in the modern language and occasionally in the medieval one, *mandi* is added to the cardinal numerals to replace special forms for numerating persons. It is uncertain at what point the series starts; one authority says at four, a better one gives the form for three as an example. The special political interrelation between Telugu and Kannaḍa in the medieval period (Vijayanagar kingdom, A.D. 1336-1565) allowed extensive borrowing between them in both directions. Telugu in all probability owes the construction and the form to Kannaḍa. It is not impossible that the Kannaḍa construction might be a calque from Marathi.

We must note too that Tamil, presumably the colloquial, uses *pēr* 'name' as classifier in numerating persons from two on; e.g., *nālu pēr tiruṭar* 'four thieves.'

I am at a loss to say more about these Tamil, Kannada, and Telugu examples. But certainly we must not ascribe the use of classifiers to Proto-Dravidian.

The use of classifiers can be added to those other linguistic traits previously discussed, which establish India as one linguistic area for historical study. (This term "linguistic area" may be defined as meaning an area which includes languages belonging to more than one family but showing traits in common which are found not to belong to the other members of [at least] one of the families. It is perhaps not quite satisfactory as a technical term, though it has the virtue of having been used previously in this sense by H. V. Velten [1943] as a translation of Troubetzkoy's *Sprachbund*. [My attention was called to this by Sebeok (1944) and Voegelin (1945, p. 58).] Among the disadvantages of the term is the lack of an adjective and the impossibility of using the reverse phrase "areal linguistics," since this is preempted by the Italian neolinguistic school in another sense. Perhaps however it will do for the moment, until some more ingenious scholar invents better terminology.) The evidence is at least as clear-cut as any that has been advanced in the establishment of a linguistic area in any part of the world, and in fact a good deal more so than much that has been offered. It is to be hoped that it will not be neglected henceforth when the question is raised whether linguistic features, especially those of morphology and syntax, can diffuse across genetic boundaries. Some of the features presented here are, it seems to me, as "profound" as we could wish to find (if we must attempt to apply Sapir's value criteria). Certainly the end result of the borrowings is that the languages of the two families, Indo-Aryan and Dravidian, seem in many respects more akin to one another than Indo-Aryan does to the other Indo-European languages. We must not, however, neglect Bloch's final remark and his reasons therefor: "Ainsi donc, si profondes qu'aient été les influences locales, elles n'ont pas conduit l'aryen de l'Inde . . . à se différencier fortement des autres langues indo-européennes" (1934, p. 330). [Thus, as profound as local influences have been, they have not led Indo-Aryan . . . to diverge greatly from the other Indo-European languages.]

In another place I adumbrate an attempt to include the linguistic area India in the larger linguistic area of East, Southeast, and South Asia. The evidence so far found concerns the use of classifiers and makes it at least possible that this trait reached the Indo-Aryan languages of the Magadhan area from Southeast Asia; but the demonstration of this is not as clear as that of the relationships within India and need not be given here to obscure the clear outlines of the matter discussed in this paper.

REFERENCE NOTE

Emeneau's extensive identification of and running commentary on sources unfortunately has had to be omitted, and should be consulted in the original publication.

A. REFERENCES SPECIFIC TO LANGUAGES DISCUSSED

BLOCH, JULES

1920. *La Formation de la langue marathe*. (Bibliothèques de l'École des Hautes Études; Sciences historiques et philologiques, no. 215.) Paris.

1934. *L'Indo-Ayren du Veda aux temps modernes*. Paris. Adrien-Maisonneuve.

BURROW, T.

1955. *The Sanskrit Language*. London: Faber and Faber.

EMENEAU, M. B.

1938. Echo-words in Toda. *New Indian Antiquary*, *1:* 109-117.

1954b. Review of Franklin Edgerton, Buddhist Hybrid Sanskrit grammar and dictionary; Buddhist Hybrid Sanskrit vocabulary. *Lg.*, *30:* 474-485.

FITZGERALD, A. G.

1913. *Kuviñga bassa: The Khond Language as Spoken by the Parjas . . . of the Madras Presidency*. (1st ed.) Calcutta: M. Apel.

RAMAMURTI, G. V.

1931. *A Manual of the So:ra: or Savara Language*. Madras.

SREEKANTAIYA, T. N.

1954. Affricates in Kannada speech. *Indian Linguistics*, *15:* 83-90.

WINFIELD, W. W.

1928. *A Grammar of the Kui Language*. Calcutta.

B. GENERAL REFERENCES

For discussion of concepts and principles of areal interpretation of linguistic phenomena, see Bartoli (1925), Becker (1948), Bonfante (1947; 1950, p. 114), Bonfante and Sebeok (1944), Gołab (1959), Robert A. Hall, Jr. (1946), Hymes (1956a), Jakobson (1931b, 1938), Pulgram (1954, p. 500), Sandfeld (1930), Sebeok (1944, 1950a), Troubetzkoy (1931, 1939b), Wolff (1959b). For more specific works on American Indian languages, see Bartoli (1934, 1937), Devoto (1947, p. 215, n. 14), Jacobs (1954), Kroeber (1955), Swadesh (1952b), Trager (1939). For areal interpretation of typological relationships, note Milewski (1954) and Voegelin (1961b), concerning American Indian languages, and compare the principles discussed by Wolff (1959b, Section 4).

The question of the mechanisms underlying areal phenomena raises the subject of substratum, one of the most vexed issues of historical linguistics. But interest in the subject is reviving with fresh definitions of types of strata (ad-, super-, etc.) and methodological constraints. See Catalán (1957-1958) and the reviews by Fowke and Jungemann, Dyen (1956), Hoenigswald (1962), Jespersen (1922, chap. 11), Jungemann (1956), Malkiel (1962c), Meillet (1932), Pulgram (1957), Raun (1953), and Sebeok (1948). See also the references on the closely related questions of linguistic geography, bilingualism, and acculturation, with the articles by McDavid, Diebold, and Dozier, respectively, in Part VIII.

References not in the general bibliography:

BARTOLI, MATTEO

1925. *Introduzione alla Neolinguistica*. Geneva: Olschki.

1934. Le Origini degli Indiani d'America lumeggiate dalle aree linguistiche. *Annali dell'Istituo Superiore di Magistero di Torino*. Pp. 335-352.

1937. Ancora delle origini dei linguaggi precolombiani alla luce delle norme spaziali. *Mélanges van Ginneken*. Paris. Pp. 123-133.

BECKER, H.

1948. *Der Sprachbund*. Berlin and Leipzig.

BONFANTE, G.

1947. The Neo-linguistic Position. *Lg.*, *23:* 344-375.

1950. The Prepositions of Latin and of Greek. *Word*, *6:* 106-116.

BONFANTE, G., and THOMAS A. SEBEOK

1944. Linguistics and the Age and Area Hypothesis. *AA*, *46:* 382-386.

DEVOTO, G.

1947. Matteo Bàrtoli. *Word*, *3:* 208-216.

DYEN, ISIDORE

1956. The Ngaju-Dayak "Old Speech Stratum." *Lg.*, *32:* 83-87.

GOŁAB, SBIGNIEW

1959. Some Arumanian-Macedonian Isogrammatisms and the Social Background of Their Development. *Word*, *15:* 415-435.

JACOBS, MELVILLE

1954. The Areal Spread of Sound Features in the Languages North of California. *Papers from the Symposium on American Indian Linguistics* (University of California Publications in Linguistics, No. 10). Berkeley and Los Angeles: University of California Press. Pp. 46-56.

JAKOBSON, ROMAN

1931b. Über die phonologischen Sprachbünde. *Travaux du Cercle Linguistique de Prague*, *4*. [Also in Jakobson, *Selected Writings*. Vol. I, *Phonological Studies*. The Hague: Mouton. Pp. 137-143.]

1938. Sur la Theorie des affinities phonologiques entre les langues. *Actes du quatrième Congrès international de linguistes* (*Copenhagen, 1936*). Pp. 48-58. Copenhagen: Munksgaard. [Also in N. S. Troubetzkoy, *Principes de Phonologie*. Translated by J. Cantineau. Paris: Klincksieck. Pp. 351-365; Jakobson, *Selected Writings*. Vol. I, *Phonological Studies*. The Hague: Mouton. Pp. 234-246.]

JUNGEMANN, F. H.

1956. *La Teoria del Sustrato y los Dialectos Hispano-Romances y Gascones*. (Biblioteca Romanica Hispanica, Tratados y Monografias, No. 7.) Madrid: Gredos. [Reviewed, L. Prieto, *Word*, 1957, *13:* 372-378; D. F. Solá, *Lg.*, 1957, *33:* 461-465.]

MEILLET, A.

1932. Sur les Effets des changements de langue. *Scientia*, pp. 91 ff. [Also in Meillet, *Linguistique Historique et Linguistique Générale*. (2nd ed.) (Collection Linguistique, Societé de Linguistique de Paris, No. 8.) Paris: Champion. Vol. II, pp. 104-112.]

MILEWSKI, TADEUSZ

1954. Phonological Typology of American Indian Languages. *Lingua Posnanensis*, *4:* 229-276.

PULGRAM, ERNST

1954. Review of L. R. Palmer, *The Latin Language*. *Lg.*, *30:* 499-503.

1957. Linguistic Expansion and Diversification. *Studies Presented to Joshua Whatmough on His Sixtieth Birthday*. The Hague: Mouton. Pp. 239-252.

RAUN, ALO

1953. Review of L. Posti, *From Pre-Finnic to Late Proto-Finnic*. *Studies in Linguistics, 11:* 83-90.

SANDFELD, K.

1930. *Linguistique Balkanique*. (Collection Linguistique, Société de Linguistique de Paris, No. 31). Paris: Klincksieck.

SEBEOK, THOMAS A.

1948. Review of B. Malmberg, *L'Espagnol dans le Nouveau Monde—Problème de Linguistique Générale*. *IJAL, 14:* 278-279.

TROUBETZKOY, N.

1939b. Gedanken über das Indogermanen Problem. *Acta Linguistica, 1:* 81-89.

VELTEN, H. V.

1943. The Nez Perce Verb. *Pacific Northwest Quarterly, 34:* 271-292.

67 On Taxonomy of Languages and Cultures

A. L. KROEBER

DEVELOPMENT AND VALUE OF TAXONOMY

. . . .

The reason evolutionary, phylogenetic, and strictly genetic biology have made such rapid and productive progress since Darwin is because of the sound taxonomy that biology had built up in the century and more between Linnaeus and Darwin. At the critical moment, accumulated pressures broke the dam of combined inertia and religious doctrine, and a rich static system was rapidly converted into a richer dynamic one, without waste and with enormous gain in understanding.

TAXONOMY OF LANGUAGES AND CULTURES

Linguistics, very exceptionally, about seventy years before the *Origin of Species*, became diachronically genetic through discovering evidence of Indo-European language relationship. This genetic relationship remained its overwhelming preoccupation through the nineteenth century, along with minor or nominal replicas of Semitic, Hamitic, Ugric, and Altaic relationship. The nature of the changes diversifying this genetic unity was investigated with increasing refinement and accuracy, but without serious progress toward understanding of the causality of the changes. The line of investigation was pursued autonomously, and was scarcely affected by the revolutionary shift of biological science to a diachronic and genetic approach after 1859. Within the sociocultural sciences genetic linguistics long remained unique in pursuing its way by point-for-point comparison of "homologous" evidence and refraining from speculative leaps with evolutionistic stages, the constituent members of each of which may be only analogously alike.

Contrariwise, the study of society, through the philosophic addictions of Comte and Spencer, did not turn really diachronic because it substituted the qualitative and normative concept of progress for the chronology of history and the definable genetic affinities of linguistics (D. G. Macrae, in "Darwinism and the Social Sciences," says: "What, in all probability, sociology most needs at the moment is not either a Newton or a Darwin, but a Linnaeus to elaborate a really workable classification of social structures and of the range and variety of institutional patterns and sequences" [in S. A. Barnett (Ed.), *A Century of Darwin*, 1958, p. 311].)

The study of culture, however, which was just beginning to emerge at the time of the Darwinian breakthrough, was tremendously stimulated by this revolution. Only, possessing inadequate knowledge, and less taxonomic ordering of it, the early anthropology substituted lunges at absolute "origins" for the relativities of historic development. Its first phase, as exemplified by Morgan, Bachofen, and in a measure Tylor, was a wholly placeless and timeless construct. A second phase, led by Frazer, added a psychological emphasis that led to its wide popularity and influence; but it was also placeless and timeless, in keeping with its principle of spontaneous psychic unity. Before the energy of this wave was spent, it was overtaken by a third, pseudohistoric one. In this, Graebner and Schmidt more or less specified the places of development though the times were left vague; Elliott Smith was more reckless in guessing and specified both, so that his scheme broke down more quickly.

The Bachofen-Morgan and the Frazerian evolutionistic speculations did have some counterpart in linguistics in the typological sequences culminating with Schleicher, which were outrightly speculative as well as normative and ethnocentric; but these failed to deflect the genetic direction of comparative evidential linguistics.

Contemporaneously with the speculative pseudohistories of culture, in fact beginning somewhat before them, the sternly critical intellect of Boas, inspired more by physical than by organic precedent but containing covert humanistic impulses such as his interest in languages, had overtaken the preceding speculatively evolutionistic movements and soon swamped them, at least within scientific confines. But criticism seems antithetical to taxonomy, which may labor ploddingly but labors constructively, and overt systematic classification was something that Boas could somehow never bring himself to undertake. Boas' successors, in turn, tended to throw their energies into semiesthetic physiognomic characterizations of individual cultures, which may be good historian's material but are neither quite history nor taxonomy. I participated in this along with Malinowski and Lowie, and Evans-Prichard and Ruth Benedict and Margaret Mead have carried it farther. Of late, anthropologists have been largely given to testing hypotheses, which is again a procedure that seems to leave little room for taxonomic efforts, whether in physics or biology or in cultural studies.

So what Ellegård finds for linguistics, that it "has not yet developed more than the rudiments of a taxonomy," I find for the anthropological study of culture. We do have some solid and modern beginnings in anthropology by Murdock and Driver, though they stand pretty isolated. For language, Greenberg has started something equally promising with his typological index, though his work on this remains so scant, so meager in labor and effort, as to make one wonder whether he has the necessary convincing faith in his own idea.

One quality these three just-mentioned endeavors share: they are all unafraid of quantitative formulations. Because both anthropology and linguistics root in humanistic soil, they have long tended to look askance at statistics as a bogey, forgetting that their activities involve natural science as well as humanism. I agree that a quantitative approach will require a more systematic linguistic and cultural taxonomy for its own proper development in regard to man as a species. Beyond that, whether it comes statistically or in patterning or by qualitative description, I feel that the study of both culture and language is in crying need, in its own right, of far more systematic classification of their multifarious phenomena. Perhaps we have had a surplus of bright ideas and a shortage of consistent ordering and comparison of our data.

GENETIC INQUIRY INTO LANGUAGE AND CULTURE

It is evident that linguistics has differed from the systematic study of culture and society not so much in being more directly interested in taxonomic classification (which none of the three disciplines really pursued systematically) as in the fact that those phenomena which we call Indo-European—and which linguists (who were Europeans) were most concerned with because they included the languages of Europe —obtruded and forced upon the inquiring observer the fact of genetic relationship. To this event there was little or no active counterpart in the study of culture or society. Moreover, after a century and a half, increased study still continues to increase and clarify the evidences of relationship within genetic families. Contrariwise, the investigation of culture, until nearly the turn of the century (and in belated quarters until well after it), continued to operate largely with speculation bolstered by selected evidence. When genuinely inductive and impartial use of evidence on culture began to prevail, what it more and more tended to establish was the wide spread of interinfluencing by contact diffusion and induced ("stimulus") diffusion, which muddied and overlaid such pictures as there might also be of more or less pure-line autonomous developments of culture, comparable to the diversification within Indo-European.

In part this difference in the history of language and culture seems due to a difference between the nature of language and the nature of the rest of culture. Superficially, language has seemed on the whole to be less permeable by alien contacts, and more conditioned by and retentive of its own past, so long as a particular language survives at all. But it is increasingly becoming evident that the difference is far from complete, that alien and kindred contacts measurably influence language also, and that the belief in the seeming prevalence of automatic, orderly, slow genetic differentiation as the sole or even dominant process in the history of linguistic change must be questioned and perhaps abandoned. This belief has to date been built up and reenforced by the fact that comparativists have ordinarily confined themselves to dealing only with such part of linguistic phenomena as manifested genetic differentiation. This part of the phenomena showed orderly correspondences, which could be construed by the enthusiastic as a sort of predictable laws; whereas the effects of alien impingements were, as in culture history or in any history of man, much less regular, orderly, or conformable to a pattern. All the indications are that with reorientation of interest and objective, we shall find that the general course of linguistic change is considerably more like that of long-range cultural change than linguists have heretofore assumed. Historical accidents, including impingements from outside, must be allowed a place in addition to spontaneous or "causeless" differentiation out of immanent genetic unity.

(This view of the situation during the last century and a half sheds considerable light on the anomaly of linguistics having successfully operated on a genetic basis without having concerned itself seriously with a general taxonomy. It suggests that the assumption of genetic unity in linguistics was partly parallel to the positing of hypothetical origins in culture—although better evidenced. The whole tangle of the complexity of actual history was thereby avoided in both cases. I am not implying that the positive results of the comparative study of Indo-European, Semitic, Sino-Tibetan, Malayo-Polynesian, or Athabascan are about to be overthrown or discarded. They are founded and they will stand. But they may be considerably modified by the recognition of other processes which comparativists have mostly ignored; and the hitherto accepted results will at any rate have to be viewed as forming only part of a larger web of causes and effects.

In twentieth-century study of culture, solid and positive results of assumptions of unitary origin and unfolding development have been very much fewer than in linguistics, and the impending revision in understanding may accordingly be smaller, or even in reverse direction. This would be so because, first, the cultural findings of development from a single origin have usually been world-wide and universal, but linguistic ones have been limited to one family of speech at a time out of many; and second because the cultural findings have been supported by less systematic evidence. Still, it does seem possible that some portions of Tylor's, Morgan's, and Frazer's findings may ultimately be revindicated, now that there is no longer danger that the massive effects of contact and diffusion will be underweighted as they used to be on the ground of being perhaps undeniable but also accidental, random, of little significance, and discardable.)

THE BOAS POSITION

On this point, credit for the most consistent championing of the probable parallelism of the historic behavior of language and culture must be accorded to Boas. He took the attitude that all taxonomy of languages should be deferred—except for the inspectionally most obvious and accepted cases like Indo-European and the Powellian stocks in North America. This was on the ground that without historic documents we were not in a position to determine what came into most languages from inside and from outside, out of their past history or through alien influences. I remember discussing Boas' attitude on this matter with Sapir and agreeing with the latter's formulation that while outside influencing (corresponding to diffusion in culture) must indeed be accepted for languages, such influencing ordinarily was a definitely minor factor, which should not be played up in order to negate the possibility of genetic classification and reconstructive history in linguistics. I certainly felt that Boas was oriented against further classificatory efforts in linguistics, and that it was this orientation that led him to pit contact effects against genetic diversification. And I had the impression that Sapir agreed with this opinion of mine. Boas certainly consistently pushed the securing and presentation of new linguistic data very much harder than any comparative work. Yet it may be that with his negative and critical bent he saw farther ahead than most linguists of his day, and that he was actuated less by a generic antipathy to comparison and classification as such than by the perception that genetic reconstructions would be increasingly interfered with and sullied by diffusions and influences between originally distinct genetic units.

THE INFLUENCE OF LEXICOSTATISTIC COMPARISONS FOR CHRONOLOGY

It would also seem that a similar change in viewpoint is now occurring as a by-product of the increase of time-depths claimed to result from application of lexicostatistics, and the accompanying findings, especially by Swadesh and Greenberg, of ancient cross-family relationships in the ancient levels of many established "families." It is true that most linguists still refuse to accept many of these findings: the periods involved are too long, the percentages of similar forms altogether too low for satisfactory reliability, and the forms themselves too truncated for likeness and unlikeness to be soundly distinguishable. The whole picture of what is genetic and what is secondarily acquired has become turbid; the genetic units have become few but vast, and undefined at the edges, without the intrusions into the genetic units being clear as to what happened, or how and when. At the same time linguists who do not use the summary comparative methods of Swadesh and Greenberg, but operate with comparisons of the long valid sort, are discovering more limited but perhaps more significant cross-ties between genetic groups heretofore rated as wholly unconnected—such as Mary Haas's Muskogian elements shared with Algonkian and Ritwan (1958b). The overall picture, at least among linguists in America, is fast becoming chaotic. When in 1919 Paul Radin assembled fifteen pages of evidence to show that all native American languages were probably interrelated, he was shrugged or laughed off. Now it is a group of Sapir-trained linguists who are making much more voluminous findings by newer methods to the same effect as Radin, and the results of their more conservative colleagues seem to point in the same direction of overall anarchy. It does begin to look as if time were beginning to justify Boas in his contention that all but the more obvious reconstructive and historic classifications of unwritten languages contained elements of unreliability.

TAXONOMY AS THE WAY OUT OF THE CONFUSION

The exit from this confounding of the long established order seems to be more comparison and more taxonomy, and let the genetic and the influencing chips lie where they fall. In native America, and no doubt for many unwritten languages on other continents also, the genetic families most in use have generally been first established by little more than inspection only: by evidence which a layman would accept as reasonably indicative of kinship. Sapir long ago made it plain, in spite of his premature death, that these simple findings would be transcended; he suggested probably reduction to six phyla in North America. Parts of these six have been reasonably validated by others since. But all such modifications have been still in the genetic framework. Where genetic similarity is strong enough to be certain, its findings should of course continue to be accepted. But when the similarity dilutes into mere possibilities which are so scant or scattering that they might be due to remnants of original unity, or to contact influences or borrowings, or to both sets of causes, some broader strategy of attack is indicated.

THE TYPOLOGICAL INDEX

Here is where Greenberg's typological index might be of use, or some extension of it. It is the one general classificatory tool yet devised in linguistics, other than the sense-and-sound homologies of the genetic comparative method. There are of course the older typings of whole languages—isolating, agglutinating, inflectional, sometimes polysynthetic—from which Sapir's 1921 revised classification took off, and which it was intended to supersede, just as Greenberg took off from this otherwise unutilized whole-language typing by Sapir. But the older classifications are too valuative and ethnocentric for modern use; and both they and Sapir result in too few fundamental classes—three or four—for these to embody more than gross distinctions. In fact, up to Schleicher the formulations were not so much in terms of embracive classes as they were high-point types—and ideal types at that. This does not apply to Sapir, who was evidently trying to evolve a system that would take care of all known languages more or less adequately. But

Sapir's sensitive empiricism and honesty would have revolted at any forcing of actual languages into four Procrustean patterns. So he ended up with a good many languages belonging to two or more subclasses; which inspires confidence in Sapir's integrity, but diminishes the operational utility of his results. (Thus, Simple Mixed-Relational French, which "might nearly as well have come under D," Complex Mixed-Relational, is also Fusional and mildly synthetically Analytical; Complex Mixed-Relational Nootka is "very nearly Complex Pure-Relational" and is also Agglutinative with a symbolic tinge and Polysynthetic; Chinook is Complex Mixed-Relational, Fusional-Agglutinative, and mildly Polysynthetic; Polynesian and Haida are both Complex Pure-Relational and Agglutinative-Isolating but differ in being respectively Analytic and Polysynthetic [Sapir, 1921, pp. 150-151].)

The fundamental virtue and originality of Greenberg's essay is that he has broken away altogether from classifying languages as wholes and has substituted ten features—the number could be increased—each expressible for each language by a simple numerical index. The simultaneous employment of these ten features potentially gives a considerable number of classes, and more subclasses if needed; and the fitting of particular languages into such seriating subclasses would be aided by the measure of objectivity provided by the index being quantitative.

Here then we have at last a possible means for providing the needed taxonomy of extant languages. It would not be genetic classification; but that would be in its favor, since we have begun to get some notion of the temporal distance at which the genetic classifying of language dissolves into tenuous mistiness, as well as an increasing awareness of the likely amount of alien intrusion into any genetic linguistic stream.

It is true that in biology a good "natural" classification regularly proves to be a genetic one, with true homologues. But in the field of language and culture we shall evidently have to reconcile ourselves to a different and normally more complex situation, because of the contact influencing, the intrusions and absorptions, the hybridizing current on this level. When we get to the limits of even only reasonably probable genetic taxonomy, what have we got? An indefinite but presumably fairly considerable number of genetic units, irreducible, fading out into diffuse open ends, with an unknown number of inter-influencings presumable between them, not only in their beginnings but later in their courses.

It would seem that our only hope of achieving a sound linguistic taxonomy of breadth and depth is by operating with mechanisms that transcend the concept of genetic unity. And what tool of that sort is there extant, other than something along the lines of Greenberg's indices and extension of them? True, we shall have to renounce then, temporarily at least, tracing regular correspondences of sound and of meaning, and shall have to deal instead with functional "meanings," or perhaps more accurately, forms of linguistic mechanisms irrespective of similarity of sound. When these have resulted in some kind of intelligible taxonomy, this may show significant groupings that can perhaps be interpreted as histories of trends of what happened. Or, the emergent groupings may connect with some of the open-ended genetic ones we have already reached now, and the two may confirm each other. We cannot predict; we do have reason to expect that the trial will bear some fruit. And while some hopes will be dashed and results remain confused or obscure or negative, there are likely to be other spots in the terrain where unexpected positive findings will emerge.

The century-and-a-half-old comparative genetic technique, the pride of linguistics, older than biological phylogenies, with its innumerable firm homologies of sense and sound, is still a valuable tool; but our problems have grown so that we are beginning to realize that there are many questions which this method cannot even try to answer. It is a splendid tool for confirming similarities within diversifications that have been going on for some millennia—perhaps up to 5,000 years, perhaps to 7,000. But there comes a point in the past—perhaps 10,000 years ago, perhaps less—at which the method no longer yields reliable results. (It might be suggested, if comfort is needed, that even in biology, where phylogenies are simple in that mainly they only diversify, and we do have extinctions but no positive complications through convergences and recombinations—even in biology the natural genetic system of life branches or classes works clearly for the Vertebrates, and nearly as well for the Arthopods, but breaks down if we try to trace the connection of the Chordate and Arthropod phyla.) And there, for a while at least, new methods of investigation must take over; and Greenberg's indices of characteristics and trends are one method that should certainly be given systematic try-out. If other methods too develop, so much the better.

REFERENCE NOTE

References are organized in two parts: (A) genetic classification, and (B) typological classification.

A. GENETIC CLASSIFICATION

For comment on Kroeber's discussion, see the last article in Part X. For a recent survey of the present state of genetic classification, see Hymes (1959c). For Swadesh's classificatory work, including a provisional formulation of world relationships, see his papers and references on pp. 575-584, 624-637; see especially (1960b) for a claim counter to Kroeber's evaluation of the limited time depth at which genetic relationship can be traced. For Greenberg's work, see his methodological articles (1953, 1957a) and his studies in several areas of the world, partly reported in the paper of 1953. His most famous contribution, a classification of African languages has been reissued in revised form (1963); see the review of the original version by Welmers (1956) and remarks by Gleason (1960). Greenberg's survey classification of Latin American indigenous languages has been used in several publications (1959c, 1960a, Tax 1960); and a novel classification of Pacific and South Asian languages has been presented to a 1960 meeting of the Association for Asian Studies in New York. Present problems of genetic classification in Oceania are well brought out in Capell (1962) and the associated discussion by Chrètien, Goodenough, Grace, Milke, *et al.* The studies by Mary Haas involving Algonquian (1958a, 1958b, 1959, 1960), referred to by Kroeber, like those of Swadesh and Greenberg, point toward deeper and broader historical connections among languages than heretofore established.

On problems of genetic classification, see further the general references to Hoijer's article in Part VIII; the articles on classification of creoles by Hall and Taylor listed on pp. 543ff.; and the articles, and references thereto, by Swadesh Thieme, and Hockett in this part. See also the discussions by Hymes (1956a, 1956b, 1957, 1960a, 1964), Gleason (1961, chap. 27), Lamb (1959), McQuown (1955, especially pp. 501-511, 556-566), Meillet (1926-1936, vol. I, pp. 19-35, 76-101, 102-109; vol. II, pp. 44-46, 47-52, 53-69), and Pedersen (1931, *passim*).

Genetic classification involves the vexed problem of determining subgroupings of the languages and dialects proven related. On the issues and methods of subgrouping, see, besides the general references already cited, the references on dialect distance with Wolff's article in Part VII; on dialectology and linguistic geography with McDavid's article in Part VIII; and on lexicostatistics and glottochronology with the articles by Gudschinsky and Swadesh in this part, especially those by Dyen, Ellegard, Elmendorf, and Gleason. See also Dyen (1953, 1960), Garde (1961), Greenberg (1957c, chap. 4) and the review by Dyen (1959), Gudschinsky (1958), Hamp (1958), Pilch (1954), Porzig (1954), Stankiewicz (1957), Swadesh (1959b).

References not in the general bibliography:

CAPELL, ARTHUR

1962. Oceanic Linguistics Today. *CA*, *3* (4): 371-431.

DYEN, ISIDORE

1953. Review of O. C. Dahl, *Malgache et Maanjan*. *Lg.*, *29:* 577-590.

1959. Review of Joseph H. Greenberg, *Essays in Linguistics*. *Lg.*, *35:* 548-550.

1960. Comment to Hymes, *Lexicostatistics So Far*. *CA*, *1* (1): 34-38.

GLEASON, H. A., JR.

1960. Review of G. P. Murdock, Africa: Its Peoples and Their Culture History. *Lg.*, *30:* 470-475.

GREENBERG, JOSEPH H.

1957a. Genetic Relationship Among Languages. *Essays in Linguistics*. (Viking Fund Publications in Anthropology, No. 24.) New York: Wenner-Gren Foundation; Chicago: University of Chicago Press. Pp. 35-45.

1959c. [Classification of Aboriginal Languages of Latin America.] In J. H. Steward and L. C. Faron, *Native Peoples of South America*. New York: McGraw-Hill. Pp. 22-23.

1960a. The General Classification of Central and South American Languages. In Anthony F. C. Wallace (Ed.), *Men and Cultures*. Philadelphia: University of Pennsylvania Press. Pp. 791-794.

GUDSCHINSKY, SARAH

1958. Mazatec Dialect History: A Study in Miniature. *Lg.*, *34:* 468-481.

HAAS, MARY R.

1958a. Algonkian-Ritwan: the End of a Controversy. *IJAL*, *24:* 159-173.

1958b. A New Linguistic Relationship in North America: Algonkian and the Gulf Languages. *SJA*, *14:* 231-264.

1959. Tonkawa and Algonkian. *AL*, *1* (2): 1-6.

1960. Some Genetic Affiliations of Algonkian. In Stanley A. Diamond (Ed.), *Culture in History*. New York: Columbia University Press. Pp. 977-992.

HAMP, ERIC P.

1958. Protopopoloca Internal Relationships. *IJAL*, *24:* 150-153.

HYMES, DELL H.

1957. Some Penutian Elements and the Penutian Hypothesis. *SJA*, *13:* 69-87.

1964. Evidence for Penutian: Lexical Sets in [c] and [s]. *IJAL*, *30*.

LAMB, SYDNEY M.

1959. Some Proposals for Linguistic Taxonomy. *AL*, *1* (2): 33-49.

MCQUOWN, NORMAN A.

1955. Indigenous Languages of Native America. *AA*, *57:* 501-570.

PILCH, H.

1954. Review of E. Schwarz, Goten, Nordgermanen, Angelsachsen. *Word*, *10:* 98-103.

PORZIG, WALTER

1954. *Die Gliederung des indogermanischen Sprachgebiets*. Heidelberg: Winter. [Reviewed, A. Martinet, *Word*, 1955, *11:* 126-132.]

RADIN, PAUL

1919. The Genetic Relationship of the North American Indian Languages. *UCP-AAE, 14* (5): 489-502.

SWADESH, MORRIS

1959b. The Mesh Principle in Comparative Linguistics. *AL, 1* (2): 7-14.

TAX, SOL

1960. Aboriginal Languages of Latin America. *CA, 1:* 430-436.

WELMERS, W.

1956. Review of Joseph H. Greenberg, Studies in African Linguistic Classification. *Lg., 32:* 556-563.

B. TYPOLOGICAL CLASSIFICATION

For some of the history of typological classification, see Greenberg (1957b) and Jespersen (1922, Book I, *passim*); concerning American anthropology particularly, see Hymes (1961a).

On typology with special reference to grammatical properties, see Bazell (1949, 1958), Forchheimer (1953), Greenberg (1954a, 1957b), A. A. Hill (1941), Hockett (1958), Hymes (1961a), IJAL (1960), Jakobson (1957b), Kroeber (1960b), Milewski (1950a, 1951, 1953), Sapir (1921, chap. 6), Togeby (1951, p. 266), Voegelin (1961b).

On typology with special reference to phonological properties, see Ferguson and Chowdhury (1960, pp. 51-59) for comparison of typological approaches to one language; Hockett (1955, Section 2) for a world survey, Jakobson (1958); Kramsky (1959); Lyons (1962) for interpretation of methodological differences as implication of typology; Milewski (1954, 1955); Saporta (1957); Voegelin (1954, 1957); Yegerlehner and Voegelin (1957).

On typology with special reference to lexical material, see Menzerath (1950), Ullmann (1953), Whorf (1938).

For general discussions of typology, see Bazell (1958), Greenberg (1957b), Hymes (1961a), Jakobson (1958), Milewski (1950b), Pierce (1962), Spang-Hanssen (1958), Voegelin (1955, 1956), Voegelin and Yegerlehner (1956), Wells (1954), Whorf (1938); also, IJAL (1954, 1960).

On Kroeber's interest in typology, see the article by Hymes in Part XI.

References not in the general bibliography:

BAZELL, C. F.

1949. Syntactic Relations and Linguistic Typology. *Cahiers Ferdinand de Saussure, 8:* 5-20.

1958. *Linguistic Typology*. (Inaugural Lecture.) London: School of Oriental and African Studies, University of London.

FERGUSON, CHARLES A., and MUNIER CHOWDHURY

1960. The Phonemes of Bengali. *Lg., 36:* 22-59.

FORCHHEIMER, P.

1953. *The Category of Person in Language.* Berlin: de Gruyter. [Reviewed, F. W. Householder, Jr., *Lg.*, 1955, *31:* 93-99; D. H. Hymes, *IJAL*, 1955, *21:* 294-300.]

HILL, A. A.

1941. Incorporation as a Type of Language Structure. In *Humanistic Studies in Honor of John Calvin Metcalf*. (University of Virginia Studies, No. 1.) Charlottesville: University of Virginia Press. Pp. 65-79.

[IJAL]

1954. "Archiving Issue." *IJAL, 20* (2).

1960. "Typology Papers." *IJAL, 26* (3).

KRAMSKY, JIRI

1959. A Quantitative Typology of Languages. *Language and Speech, 2:* 72-85.

KROEBER, A. L.

1960b. Typological Indices I: Ranking of Languages. *IJAL, 26:* 171-177.

LYONS, JOHN M.

1962. Phonemic and Non-Phonemic Phonology: Some Typological Reflections. *IJAL, 28:* 127-134.

MENZERATH, PAUL

1950. Typology of Languages. *Journal of Acoustical Society of America, 22:* 698-701.

MILEWSKI, TADEUSZ

1950a. La Structure de la phrase dans les langues indigènes de l'Amerique du Nord. *Lingua Posnanensis, 2:* 162-207. [Reviewed, C. F. Voegelin, *Lg.*, 1952, *28:* 405-410.]

1950b. Podstawy Teoretyczne Typologii Jezyków [The Theoretical Basis of the Typology of Language]. *Bulletin de la Société Polonaise de Linguistique, 10:* 122-140.

1951. The Conception of the Word in the Languages of North American Natives. *Lingua Posnanensis, 3:* 248-267.

1953. Typologia Syntaktyczna Jezyków Amerykanskich [The Syntactic Typology of American Languages]. *Bulletin de la Société Polonaise de Linguistique, 12:* 1-24.

1954. Phonological Typology of American Indian Languages. *Lingua Posnanensis, 4:* 229-276.

1955. Comparaison des systèmes phonologiques des langues Caucasiennes et Américaines. *Lingua Posnanensis, 5:* 136-165. [1950b, 1951, 1955 reviewed, D. H. Hymes, *IJAL*, 1956, *22:* 281-287.]

NEWMAN, S. S.

1954. Suggestions on the Archiving of Linguistic Material. *IJAL, 20:* 111-115.

PIERCE, JOE E.

1962. Possible Electronic Computation of Typological Indices for Linguistic Structures. *IJAL, 28:* 215-226.

SAPORTA, SOL

1957. Methodological Considerations Regarding a Statistical Approach to Typologies. *IJAL, 23:* 109-113.

SPANG-HANSSEN, H.

1958. Typological and Statistical Aspects of Distribution as a Criterion in Linguistic Analysis. In Eva Sivertsen (Ed.), *Proceedings of the Eighth International Congress of Linguists (Oslo, 1957)*. Oslo: Oslo University Press. Pp. 182-194.

TOGEBY, KNUD

1951. *Structure Immanente de la Langue Française.* (Travaux du Cercle Linguistique de Copenhague, No. 6.) Copenhagen: Nordisk Sprog-og Kulturforlag.

VOEGELIN, C. F.

1954. Inductively Arrived at Models for Cross-genetic Comparisons of American Indian Languages. *University of California Publications in Linguistics, 10:* 27-45. [Reviewed, D. H. Hymes, *Lg.*, 1956, *32:* 585-602.]

1955. On Developing New Typologies and Revising Old Ones. *SJA, 11:* 355-360.

1956. Subsystems Within Systems in Cultural and Linguistic Typologies. In *For Roman Jakobson.* The Hague: Mouton. Pp. 592-599.

1957. Six Statements for a Phonemic Inventory. *IJAL, 23:* 78-84.

1961a. Typology of Density Ranges II: Contrastive and Non-Contrastive Syntax. *IJAL, 27:* 287-297.

VOEGELIN, C. F., and JOHN YEGERLEHNER

1956. The Scope of Whole System ("Distinctive Feature") and Sub-System Typologies. *Word, 12:* 444-453.

WELLS, RULON

1954. Archiving and Language Typology. *IJAL, 20:* 101-107.

YEGERLEHNER, JOHN, and F. M. VOEGELIN

1957. Frequencies and Inventories of Phonemes from Nine Languages. *IJAL, 23:* 85-93.

part X

TOWARD HISTORICAL PERSPECTIVE

Introduction

THOSE WHO STUDY LANGUAGE AND CULTURE can see their work as itself a part of their subject-matter. From a long-range viewpoint, the rise of special disciplines, such as linguistics and anthropology, can be seen as an advance to a novel stage in the interrelations of language and culture. The stage is one of increased explicit awareness of language as part of culture, of appeal to more adequate criteria and evidence for conceptions of language, and of work with practical consequences that partly shape it. It was especially of the last development that Bloomfield wrote, "linguistic science is a step in the self-realization of man" (1914, p. 325).

All societies have some conceptions and awareness of the nature and uses of language. As specialists, our beliefs and attitudes are but part of the spectrum in our own society. and not wholly independent of the rest.

Seen comparatively, conceptions and awareness of language are a significant, unfortunately neglected part of ethnography and cross-cultural studies. Nonliterate peoples are not wholly unconscious of linguistic habits, even of structural detail, as occasional reports of native terms for phonemic tonal contrasts, the distinctive feature of nasality, and the like, attest. Hence it becomes an empirical matter of some interest to determine the varying degree of explicit awareness and the factors on which it depends. For that matter, writing systems form part of the evidence, since their invention or adaptation is prima facie indication of some sort of structural analysis.

Seen in a broadly evolutionary perspective, conceptions and awareness of the nature and uses of language can be taken as having progressed. The contents of a book such as this, when compared to what could have been chosen even a generation ago, are indication of that fact. Yet in a given case, advance appears as contingent upon the same sorts of factors that affect the place of language in any society: existing knowledge, values, and beliefs; existing resources of data, procedure, and equipment; the organization of relevant activity in relation to the social structure of the whole; focuses of cultural interest; types and particular cases of personality and motivation. Advance in any particular line of study may be irregular, and relations between lines of study may be out of phase.

Historical perspective, then, gives the student of linguistics and anthropology a long-range sense of his place in the advance of knowledge, in sociocultural evolution, or history (whichever phrasing one prefers). At the same time it induces a measure of humility in regard to his immediate role, as he becomes aware of how his own context may appear when analyzed in terms of particular factors and functions and of the dependence of published work and statement on particular, contingent relations among senders and audiences, sharers of a code, conformity to norms of message-form, differential access to channels, and the like. It would be unfortunate and ironic if those who adopted relativity as a working perspective on the verbal behavior of others should lack it with regard to their own.

An additional advantage gained from the cultivation of historical perspective is that it contributes to continuity and cumulativeness and to economy of effort (a good many things turn out to be new bottles for old wine). Moreover, the past of a discipline may play an ideological role in current disputes, so that an objective understanding of it is needed for balanced judgment. Some evaluations of Boas miss the mark by overlooking the role of linguistic work *within* his anthropological career and thought. The extremes of posthumous flurry over Whorf's ideas might have been avoided, if the century and a half of interest in the problem (in connection with Amerindian languages at that) had not been seemingly forgotten.

More generally, we sometimes forget that the kinds of work and thought that we recognize as anthropological precede by several decades the professional disciplines devoted to them. The experience of field work in an exotic tongue; the publication of grammar, text, and dictionary to make such a tongue known to scholarship; interest in languages as evidence of the origins and characteristics of the peoples speaking them—all these have a significant development antedating our present journals, organizations, and culture heroes, and sometimes that development has helped shape subsequent work. Some of the earliest descriptive work is of first quality, and good accounts of individual languages are scattered through the centuries since the sixteenth. Moreover, the notion of describing a language *sui generis* has at least as long a history, and has either been transmitted or independently invented throughout that time. The record shows not a past which lacked the notion and a present which has gained it, but a recurrent struggle for its proper recognition. One further example from a theoretical line of development is particularly worth mention. A decade ago many scholars would have written the history of the study of language in terms of the successive triumphs of comparative linguistics in the nineteenth century and descriptive or structural linguistics in the twentieth, both conceived in a rather positivistic and particularistic spirit. Recent currents of renewed interest in general linguistics and general grammar have seen a revival of the reputations of Wilhelm von Humboldt and George de Gabelentz. The work of these two men, at the beginning and end of the nineteenth century, respectively, had almost been lost from sight, but they cultivated an outlook, distinct from the nineteenth century comparative linguistics celebrated in the standard histories, which anticipated the basic questions of structural linguistics today. Bloomfield (1914, p. 310) had signalled von Humboldt's work as leading the way both to the special philologies of the various language families of the world, and "the study of the conditions and laws of language: its psychic and social character and its historical development"; but subsequent American linguistics seemed to forget von Humboldt until after the Second World War and the interests awakened by discussions centered around Whorf.

The twin moral, of course, is that the latest work is not always or exclusively the best and that triumphs and reputations are seldom fixed. Both points need to be taken to heart in disciplines such as linguistics and anthropology, whose scope and intersection and productive work have so often been shaped by fashion, so that continuity and cumulativeness seem as much the exception as the rule.

No history of linguistic anthropology exists, although one may emerge as part of the growing professional interest in the history of anthropology generally. Aspects of its history are indicated in the introductions to the preceding parts. The two articles included in this part contribute to historical perspective. both by their content and by the contrast their content affords.

Malkiel's delineation of a tradition of linguistic work, important but unfamiliar to most of us, not only has a special contrastive value, but brings out a number of the considerations which must enter into the historical study of any branch of scholarship. His paper serves as a model for compact treatment. Moreover, although historical, the paper speaks also to current interests. It calls attention to a major European tradition of joint work in linguistics and ethnography, concerned with the study of folk or peasant communities. These joint field investigations of dialects and artifacts and the consequent analyses, such as in *Wörter-und-Sachen* studies, broach topical problems of increasing interest to linguistic ethnographers working in other areas. Given this fact and the revival of the study of European rural communities by American anthropologists, one may expect the experience of the Romance field in these respects to gain considerable general attention. (The significance of the Romance field for questions of long-range historical process and methodology has, of course, been long well known.)

The discussion of Kroeber's work in the study of language exemplifies the genre in which most of the contributions to the history of linguistics and anthropology by linguists and anthropologists themselves have been made. Because of Kroeber's long productive career and the breadth of his interests, such a discussion touches upon a large part of the development of linguistic anthropology in this century.

Distinctive Traits of Romance Linguistics 68

YAKOV MALKIEL

THE SCOPE OF THE PROBLEM

At the critical borderline between physical sciences, social sciences, and humanities, general linguistics has become one of the rallying points for particularly ambitious mid-century scholars. Earlier systems of analysis are being appraised and mostly repudiated on the strength of their insufficient applicability to the widest possible range of differently structured languages. Under these conditions, is it feasible and advisable for workers in a neatly bounded subfield of linguistics to strive for limited autonomy, i.e., for their right to use a private scale of values, not incompatible with the broad principles and aims of the chosen science, but neither necessarily identical with such tastes and emotional preferences as have in actual life become inextricably tangled with those theoretical foundations? Many will hasten to deny this privilege without further hearing, for disciplinary reasons that can readily be anticipated, but the problem has too many ramifications to be summarily dismissed. Indeed, the chances are that the most effective answer that can be provided will be neither a flat denial nor an exuberant affirmation, but an unhurried tracing of the limits beyond which the autonomy of a part cannot be stretched without impairing the common weal.

Let Romance linguistics serve as a test case of a defensible share of "separatism," in a climate of debate free from apology and inculpation. Once a strong case for a partial autonomy of one meaningfully delimited subdiscipline has been established, spokesmen for any other comparable smaller unit may legitimately invoke this principle, adjusting its implications to varying circumstances.

This paper contends that most distinctive traits of Romance linguistics may be deduced from an inventory of its characteristic resources. The chief advantage of this strategy is the reduction of subjectively colored choices to a reasonable modicum. This platform does not force one to disregard the agency of other powerful determining factors. At least three such additional ingredients seem worthy of mention: the specific evolutionary stage that the subdiscipline has reached, the matrix of the national (or continental) culture that gave it birth and initially sheltered it, and the impact of magnetic personalities among its leaders, past and present. The discussion of these supervenient influences will be relegated to the concluding section.

CHARACTERISTICS TRACEABLE TO THE MATERIAL

THE AVAILABLE RECORDS

The peculiar ambit and even the tone of Romance linguistics have to an astonishing extent been predetermined by the abundant material—either relatively well-preserved petrifacts or elements still in a state of flux and accessible to direct scrutiny—which generations of competent workers have become accustomed to handling. The bulk of these raw data, in its bare essentials, includes several standard languages, observable over periods of from four to ten centuries and known to have served as carriers of influential literatures; a wide variety of not too sharply differentiated clusters of dialects, a few of them lacking archival documentation, hence explorable through field work alone; scattered vestiges of ancestral lexical material in less closely related media, e.g., stray Latin words fossilized in Numidian (Berber), Germanic, or Celtic dialects; plus—a priceless possession—the thoroughly documented parent language itself, Latin. This language, used at widely discrepant social levels, counted among its speakers many who were in the process of gradual assimilation to Graeco-Roman culture; it occupied a far-flung expanse of territory fringed by ever fluctuating contours, an area subjugated in the course of four centuries of almost relentless warfare. An inwardly corroded Roman empire started falling apart at its seams in the third century; it is plausibly argued that as a result of its piecemeal dismemberment in the following two hundred years, colloquial Latin, except possibly among the highly literate, began to adopt several regionally colored forms in ever quickening tempo.

Scarcely any reliable records of the suspected varieties of spoken Latin have been directly transmitted, with the probable exception of the early comedy (Plautus), phrased in an idiom true to life, and of Petronius' sensitive rendition of conversations held by a motley crowd at Trimalchio's Banquet. However, an impressive mass of circumstantial evidence enables the experienced "restorer" to piece together a few of the fleeting or (as we sometimes know from retrospect) lasting features of that submerged Latinity. Between the gradual extinction of a relatively unified, if finely graded, Latin and the emergence of the earliest, awkwardly styled texts in the major vernaculars (ninth to twelfth century), there lies a critical gap ranging, according to zone and language, from four to six hundred years, with Portuguese, Spanish (except in its archaic Mozarabic garb), and Italian trailing conspicuously behind French and Provençal. Texts (legal, historiographic, religious, didactic, and epistolary) dating from this transitional period (the tag "dim" rather than "dark" would most eloquently characterize such a twilight age) were often composed in some kind of semiconventional minimum Latin, affording occasional glimpses of the presumable actual speaking habits of writers, copyists, and notaries.

Eventually the vernaculars were recognized as fitting media for at least some literary genres and for charters; their coming of age was exceedingly slow in entailing the recession of medieval Latin as a favorite vehicle of writing, a vehicle subject, not unlike many other immobilized and slightly rusty prestige languages, to periodic attempts at "purification" imposed from above. This strained situation nourished a protracted osmosis between, on the one hand, an artificially maintained Latin seemingly almost arrested in its development but in fact never quite immune to steady erosive infiltration, and, on the other, a constellation of local dialects each almost free (but at no time entirely so) to follow its own natural bent or drift. In short, early Romance in all its protean manifestations is the very image of shackled spontaneity.

OVERLAPPING OF PHILOLOGY AND LINGUISTICS

At this point a short terminological digression is in order. Whether one takes philology in its narrow, archaeological sense (bibliography, paleography, textual criticism, epigraphy, numismatics, toponymy) or in its broader meaning of cultural history moored to the meticulous examination of records, there are many temptations for moderns to establish valid contrasts, as regards definition and characterization, between this "antiquarian" branch of knowledge and a thoroughly refurbished linguistics.

The provinces of the two disciplines are not exactly coterminous, their respective degrees of abstractness are incongruous, their appeals to imagination are unequal in intensity and in direction, their affinities to other lines of learning could not, one is at intervals sharply reminded, be less germane. But granted this pervasive divergence between the two climates of research, it still remains true that a radical, unhealable break between the two approaches cannot be seriously advocated in a subfield as clearly predestined to yield a perfect testing ground for experiments in diachronic research as is the Romance domain.

In this privileged precinct ancient idiosyncrasies of spelling (suggestive, if deftly interpreted, of otherwise unobservable or elusive vocal habits) and present-day patterns of dialect speech, lending themselves to advanced techniques of recording and analysis, are at bottom mutually complementary and invite systematic comparison. One can, then, with a measure of justification set off philology from historical linguistics in formal presentation (much as in Ernout and Meillet's admirable etymological dictionary the unexciting inventory of recorded and readily inferrable Latin forms has been neatly segregrated from the corpus of hazardous reconstructions relating to a nebulous past); but one cannot, in actual operations, expect to enforce this disentanglement without grave damage to the chosen inquiry.

THE CHANGING HIERARCHY OF APPROACHES (ARRANGEMENT VS. SEQUENCE)

In theory most linguists are likely to admit the perfect equality of status between synchronic and diachronic studies. Yet in practice powerful currents of fashions in scholarly thinking have tended to upset this equilibrium in favor of some kind of hierarchization. Fifty years ago, under the aegis of historicism refined by evolutionism, the dominant perspective in language study was diachronic. Today's heightened concern with exotic languages—many of them lacking a knowable past—and a general shift of focus in the direction of behavioral sciences, reinforced in some tone-setting milieus by an emotionally nurtured indifference to history, are jointly giving tremendous impetus to synchronic studies and concomitantly tend to discourage large-scale undertakings along the time axis. Romance linguistics can only profit from increased sophistication in structural analysis, but its stock of precious material is so distributed as to have inescapably predetermined the greatest potential services that its practitioners can hope to render to the advancement of knowledge. These services lie unequivocally along the path of diachronic inquiries. To put it differently: the patterns of arrangement in Romance languages and dialects seem less diversified, hence conceivably less thought-provoking, than those discovered in other not quite so prominent families. In contrast, the patterns of temporal sequences can here be recognized in all their complexity with such uniquely gratifying precision as to lead one to expect from the Romance quarters particularly weighty contributions to this phase of general linguistic theory.

SOME SPECIAL IMPLICATIONS OF HISTORICISM

Just as some perceptive theorists make it a point to discriminate between the labels "general," "synchronic," "descriptive," "functional," "structural," and "static" applied to closely allied perspectives in linguistics, so the three tags used in the opposite camp, "diachronic," "historical," and "dynamic," though practically interchangeable in informal scholarly discourse, deserve each to evolve a slightly distinctive connotation. Diachrony preeminently implies unilinear reconstruction of earlier stages by means of linguistic comparison alone, a procedure reminiscent in its rigor of logical and mathematical analyses. Historicism may well with equal force suggest a scholar's indebtedness to all sources of historical information (external and internal evidence alike) and presuppose on his part a special virtuosity in tapping these disparate sources as well as a liberal endowment of judiciousness in weighing them against one another. Dynamics, though inconclusive with regard to the selection of sources, seems closer to historicism, being chiefly attuned to the interplay of such forces as shape (or forcibly keep intact) a closely cohesive mobile mass of linguistic molecules.

Granted that much, one may thus elaborate upon the preference which most Romance linguists display for the time perspective. Theirs tends to be a truly historical approach with all the heavy implications of this qualifier rather than purely diachronic extrapolation; consequently the grasp of the dynamic formula presiding at each juncture over the combination of forces and counterforces locked in a ceaseless struggle is to them a goal worthy of earnest endeavor.

To be sure, it is hazardous to introduce non-linguistic assumptions into the reconstruction of most hypothetical parent languages, which the analyst is rarely in a position to assign, on independent grounds, to specific primeval habitats and itineraries, still less to definite ethnic stocks; few who have played with this avenue of approach have entirely eschewed the risk of circular thinking. On the other hand, the events surrounding the gestation of Romance languages were for a long time in the limelight of ancient and medieval historiography, hence merited rough dating and localization at the hands of articulate and literate contemporaries, including not a few eyewitnesses. Also, archaeology and physical anthropology, furnishing their evidence under so tightly controlled conditions, may act as fairly trustworthy handmaidens to "linguistic paleontology" (to use G. I. Ascoli's and W. Meyer-Lübke's favorite term). For these reasons numerous Romance linguists, to round out their training, have striven to acquire additional skills in ancillary disciplines and have cheerfully put these skills to good use in linguistic projection.

This proclivity toward an intricate argument, involving frequent and adroitly executed shifts from one discipline to another, in turn explains why most Romanists have tacitly avoided an austerely isolationist theoretical platform. Their policy, on the tactical and the strategic levels, has rather been interventionist (at times excessively so for their own good), that is, geared to the exploration, by free imaginative blends of all devices legitimate in identification, of the constant interaction between language and nonverbal culture. Hence a Romance linguist is more likely than not to deprecate any rash equation between linguistics and straight grammar, while acknowledging a flair for formulating grammatical relationships as a desirable part of one's professional equipment.

LEXICAL EMPHASIS

Heightened alertness to concrete detail, viewed at close range in multidimensional projection, calls for sharpness of focus balanced by narrowness of scope. Applied to linguistic conditions and translated into the appropriate terminology, this kind of curiosity ordinarily signifies keener concern with the loosely split-up lexicon than with close-knit sound-systems or with fairly tight morphological scaffolding. In fact, Romance linguistics has lately perfected to an enviable degree lexicography (the art of cogently arraying lexical data in reference works of varying size), lexicology (stage-by-stage analysis of bundles of lexical trajectories), and etymology (inquiry into the inceptive phases of lexical evolutions), pouring out lavishly documented monographs on individual words of rich associative potentialities, striking cultural implications, or unusual areal configurations; on intricately ramified word families; on neatly delineated semantic clusters (including anatomic designations, kinship terms, and especially names of tools, containers, vehicles, buildings, and textiles examinable in the graphic *Wörter-und-Sachen* style). Other researches revolve around strings of secondary formations tied together by powerful morphological bonds, e.g., sharing a prefix, a suffix, or an "interfix," a compositional pattern, a characteristic distribution of sounds in "expressive" words. Regrettably, this praiseworthy sustained excellence on the lexical side has sometimes been gratuitously achieved at the painful cost of relative indifference to equally thought-arresting grammatical patterning.

VISUAL ASPECTS OF LANGUAGE

Like all linguists, Romance scholars recognize a flexible pattern of auditory symbolism as the primeval origin and continued foundation of all speech. Yet their special preoccupation with the lexicon, in particular with semantic extensions and restrictions, has furthermore sharpened their awareness of visual problems in language. (Visual is here taken in the psychological or poetic sense of imagery, not in the pragmatic sense of written records or of any comparable artificial devices.)

At the present stage of scientific progress the student of imagery finds himself at a disadvantage, since he lacks apposite machinery or even an unassailable rule of thumb that would lend authority to his observations, whereas the auditory base of speech invites a dual set of precise descriptions: one on the articulatory and one on the acoustic level. But even impressionistic work, with its unavoidable margin of subjectivity, may be rewarding as long as its limitations (calling for further revision) are expressly recognized and as it is superadded to more rigorous dissections. Moreover, within the fabric of our culture this pictorial approach, for all its imprecision or even, paradoxically, on account of it, has acquired a certain inherent charm which attracts into the fold of linguistics not a few artistically sensitive and imaginative intellectuals who might feel discouraged by an accumulation of unmitigated severity.

Pictorial analysis can be of great usefulness for any investigation into the metaphoric extensions of a word's limited semantic ambit. Thus, in studying the names of the flail across language and dialect borders, one needs a statement that would set this tool apart from others displaying comparably sharp and suggestive contours, like the ax, the pickax, the shovel, the pitch fork, the saw, and the comb. The typical features of a European flail, reduced to its bare essentials, include a long slender bar (handle) at one end of which a stouter or shorter stick (swingle), occasionally curved or rounded, is so attached as to swing freely. Normally it serves to beat the grain out of the ear, but it may equally well qualify for separating beans from their pods, for handling flax, and for comparable subsidiary functions. There are many variables: the connection between the two sticks shows several degrees of elaborateness, the material out of which the sticks are carved is mostly, but not always, wood (for instance, in the medieval military weapon called flail the swingle was replaced by a metal ball or a piece set with spikes and the short handle was generally of metal). The irreducible elements that make up the pattern, then, are three: (1) difference in length between the two bars, ordinarily in favor of the handle; (2) irreversible distribution of functions between them; (3) provision for free swinging, yet solid attachment. This last-named condition explains such figurative uses in English as (obs.) *flail* 'swinging part, as a gate bar or the lever of a press'; (anat., surg.) *flail joint* 'joint showing abnormal mobility'; (coll.) *to flail about* (*one's arms*, etc.). One may similarly go about defining with utmost economy the basic design of a comb, to appreciate its use, in numerous languages, as a designation not only of certain toothed tools and adornments for separating, cleaning, and keeping well-groomed human hair (primarily, the woman's hair), but also of a miscellany of characteristically shaped instruments adopted in traditional crafts and trades no less than in modern industry for the processing of wool, flax, oakum, etc., for weaving fabrics and mats, and for embroidering. Moreover, the local word for comb denotes a musical instrument (in classical Portuguese); parts of the human or animal body ('crest of a cock' in English; 'pubes' in Latin and Ibero-Romance); the top of a wave or a hill (in Germanic); an aggregation of cells for honey (in English); several plants, some of them expressly described as prickly (in Brazilian Portuguese), etc.

THE GEOGRAPHIC DIMENSION AND THE DIFFUSIONIST DOCTRINE

The general propensity of Romance linguists toward concreteness, plus their prominent representation among the pioneer dialect cartographers and fieldworkers have sensitized most younger workers in their ranks to the crucially important geographic factor in every ensemble of causes-and-effects bearing on language. In their consciousness a given linguistic form and its neatly pinpointed locus belong as intimately together as do the numerator and the denominator of any vulgar fraction. Other teams of linguists may have displayed a more impressive degree of attention to such variables as oscillations on the social scale, the tempi of speech, the intonational curves, the controlling phrasal environment of words at issue; on the credit side of Romance scholarship one must place progressive alertness to localization.

This flair for static ordering of restricted or vast zones, in conjunction with a vivid grasp of the subtle interlocking of historical events, has made Romance dialect geographers experts in stratigraphy, centering their attention on patterns of successive layers, and, indirectly, the staunchest advocates—and most enthusiastic practitioners—of the diffusionist doctrine outside the Boasian school. The major risk that one runs in putting these ideas into practice lies in calculating on the scale of increasing abstractness the precise degree beyond which any appeal to them may become more of a liability than of an asset. The staking-out of minor self-contained linguistic zones (*Sprachlandschaften*) bounded by an approximate consensus of isoglosses is an unimpeachable procedure. The identification of recurrent specific areal patterns in the linguistic growth of a major territory (say, the pervasive aloofness of Gascony vis-à-vis the remainder of Gallo-Romance or the coincidences, too frequent and striking to be discounted as fortuitous, between Leonese and Aragonese on either flank of Old Castilian) also deserves unqualified endorsement. But Bàrtoli's attempt to advance one step further by extracting, from the comparison of some such concrete situations, a set of generally valid norms for the reconstruction of hidden sequences of events on the sole basis of resultant areal configurations ("Age-and-Area" Hypothesis") has failed to outgrow the stage of a stimulating experiment.

LITERARY LANGUAGES AS OBJECTS OF STUDY

The earlier variety of anthropological linguistics, which crystallized at a moment when anthropologists were mainly engrossed by primitive, exotic societies lacking any sustained tradition of literacy, militantly emphasized not only the temporal priority of speech over script, but—less persuasively—also its supremacy in other respects, the chief argument being the customary omission from most conventional notations of such prosodic key features as pitch and stress (also of juncture). In some quarters this attitude of diffidence toward any kind of records coalesced with cultivated indifference toward the study of fine literature, possibly as a recoil from the excessive subjectivism in aesthetic appreciation or in tacit protest against the glaring disparity in recognition which our society bestows on broadly literary as against stringently linguistic pursuits.

Romance linguists here stand apart almost en bloc: they cherish treating the spoken and the written on a par, delight in tracing their interactions (including the increasingly frequent surrender of speech habits to the pressure of spelling), and refuse to abjure their active interest in literary analysis, again along the axes of time and of arrangement. In fact, joint concern with spontaneous dialect speech and with stylized, sophisticated discourse, and purposefully developed deftness in examining their complicated interactions have become the hallmark of Romance scholarship at its most satisfying. Such specialists as choose to concentrate exclusively on the one or on the other unwittingly relegate their researches to some fringe of our domain.

There are numerous reasons for this idiosyncrasy. For one thing, the Romanist—unlike, say, the Latinist—witnesses no gradual spread of a single, fairly homogeneous city dialect over a widening expanse of territory, but rather protracted rivalry between clusters of cognate dialects vying for the privilege of serving the needs of a written standard, especially at the opening period of the vernacular literatures and with particular regard to the frequently conflicting preferences of authors, revisers, and copyists. With the possible exception of the Old Provençal troubadour lyric couched from the outset in a fairly undifferentiated idiom (a leveling of form that matches the exquisite conventionality of much of its content), the early Romance texts from France proper, Italy, and Spain all show a high incidence of regional features, and those transmitted through devious routes often display a confusingly erratic intermingling of such traits. Though medieval and modern dialect literature, despite its spontaneous ring, uses a vehicle not entirely immune to inroads of convention, the distance separating unpremeditated utterances from polished written statements is here conspicuously short.

For another thing, in such complexly structured and tradition-ridden societies as those of the northwestern and central Mediterranean it would be naïve to reckon with the consistent preservation of parochial speech habits, transmitted from mouth to mouth, except in a few almost hermetically isolated nooks. All over the plains, in hilly terrain, along the coasts, and especially down the valleys of navigable rivers it is perfectly normal for trends of local and regional drift to have been disturbed by the infiltration not only of patches of neighboring dialect speech, but also of chunks of the prestige language (which, in the last analysis, merely represents the sublimation, through deliberate sifting, of just another humble rural dialect); to this formula add, for the earlier periods, the ever-present unweakening grip of Latin, especially in the ecclesiastic domain. Symptomatic of this ceaseless bidirectional oozing is the presence, by the hundreds, of original dialect words in the most selective standard languages: Tuscan, for example, is replete with words drawn from Lombard and other northern dialects, Spanish and Galician-Portuguese are, at least lexically, a classic illustration of communicating vessels, and the French vocabulary teems with patois words, despite early political centralization and aloofness to rusticity. By way of compensation, as it were, rural and partially rural dialect speech has absorbed a vast amount of "semilearned" features, often not immediately recognizable in their new disguises: combinations of sounds—typically, jarring diphthongs or unfamilar medial consonant clusters—garbled pretentious affixes, half-understood sesquipedalian words, syntactic constructions clumsily imitative of classical Latin, even accentual schemes and pitch contours. These linguistic tradingposts are ideal breedingplaces for folk etymology and hypercorrection.

Two final considerations. First, no coolheaded Romance linguist would deny the chronological priority and continued preeminence of the actual flow of speech, provided one makes due allowance for the fact that the written language, whether living or dead, may at any propitious moment have acted as a powerful force (a stimulant or a barrier) in the shaping of that speech and will in all likelihood continue to leave its impress on the colloquial medium at an accelerated rhythm. In not a few instances spelling has demonstrably deflected pronunciation from its predictable course (a fact gratuitously played down in some quarters), while the luxuriant growth of hyperurbanism reveals in what direction the pressure of social forces is most effectively at work. In modern western societies average speakers, for scientifically valid or indefensible reasons, are eager to attach to their pronunciation a cachet of respectability, i.e., of a certain conformity to recognized spelling habits, and correspondingly to mould their grammar and vocabulary, as best they can, by standards officially encouraged or enforced. If linguists are sincere in confining themselves to the role of detached observers and analysts rather than of active participants, they should refrain scrupulously from either abetting or obstructing this controversial trend.

Second, the fully grown literary language, whatever trickling or torrential sources and tributaries may have fed it, tends to fall into a system, or subsystem, of its own, laying itself open to analytical inspection no less than does any representative corpus of elicited utterances. In some respects (nonobligatory features of lexicon and clausal architecture) this stylized language may display a greater abundance of resources or more delicately graded patterning, bordering on the ornamental. As an intricate but ordered whole (if one discounts the rare occurrences of intentional obfuscation), it invites individuating study at the same levels—sounds, forms, constructions—as any adequate speech specimen and is available in various sizes, ranging from a single passage, stylistically uniform or split, via an extant text, fragmentary or complete, to the collected works of a given author, to a genre, or to the cross-section or even the sum total of writings attributable to a certain period.

ROMANCE SCHOLARSHIP AND THE STRUCTURAL APPROACH

Do these deeply rooted, in part immutable, traits of Romance linguistics create a barrier to the establishment of fruitful liaison with structuralism? Divorced from surrounding circumstances, the two approaches are not mutually exclusive; on the contrary, the injection into Romance researches of a reasonable dosage of structuralistic thinking—bent on the redefinition of basic concepts, relativistic, and intent on subordinating the irrelevant to the relevant—would act as a wholesome corrective to any measure of lopsidedness and staleness that might otherwise develop and would thus produce an effect at once remedial and rejuvenating. Under adverse conditions an overflow of primary data and a plethora of uncoordinated studies bearing on them may constitute two focuses of acute danger; the reintroduction of a compelling hierarchy would, at least temporarily, tend to restore the balance. Historical grammar, in particular, might profit from some degree of tightening through integration of myriads of disconnected details not into a congeries of gross facts, but, after meticulous distillation, into elegantly designed chain reactions, such as have been proposed by economy-minded phonologists. The scrupulous, but excessively detailed dialect studies bearing the hallmark of Romance workmanship may profit from streamlining through diminishing resistance to the phonemic principle, refined through increased attention to contrasts in the chain and in the system. Yet in those domains in which Romance materials happen to flow most copiously, e.g., the lexicon, one hesitates to apply structuralistic thinking except cautiously and, lest it cause more harm than good, without detriment to other viewpoints. Effects of analogy (associative interference), which, until after one learns how to handle with assurance raw statistical data, do not seem to fall into comparably clear-cut patterns, excite the Romance scholar not one whit less than does the establishment of schemas, while familiarity with geographic shifts doubles his awareness of temporarily unstable, oscillating systems. As a result of these cautioning experiences, he is not quite at ease in an environment where stringency and trenchancy of static classification alone are judged matters of overruling importance. It is not the essence of functional thinking traceable to Saussure that seems difficult to reconcile with the finest traditions of Romance research, but, on the one hand, strident demands for a new orthodoxy pressed by certain reformers, which clash with the ideal of elasticity and with the standards of tolerance cherished by most Romanists, and, on the other, the well-founded realization that structuralism at its most daring and successful has come to full fruition in descriptive inquiries into exotic languages, with whose unique conformation it seems impossible to cope intelligently in other terms, whereas in the Romance domain, given the peculiar slant of its data, structuralism at best is apt to play a powerful supporting rôle. The full implications of this briefly sketched suspicion would require a thorough discussion of the seldom admitted correlation and mutual conditioning between favored method and the material at hand.

MODERN ALTERNATIVES TO FORMAL ANALYSIS

It has been occasionally suggested that the inescapable alternative to standard structuralistic practice is utter chaos, a haphazard array of colorful odds and ends, a bric-à-brac shop. This description of the choices facing a beginner might be partially correct if it did not operate with a straw man. The conventional type of Romance linguist—a scholar versed in philology, old-style historical grammar, a conservative variety of dialect geography, and an etymology heavily mortgaged with conjectures —may have shied away from steeper altitudes of abstract reasoning and stopped short in his phonological pursuits at the precise unambitious point where they served to localize a text, to circumscribe a dialect, or to identify a word-origin; measured by modern demands, his semantics and esthetics may appear homespun. Yet a program of studies conducive to this meaningful blend of diverse interests and techniques, with a perceptibly heavier emphasis on the unassuming establishment of sober facts, or approximations to facts, than on pretentious experiments with untried explicative or classificatory methods, has distinct virtues of its own, and future generations may some day declare our hasty retreat from this program to have had deleterious consequences.

Richer in potential repercussions is the fact that Romance scholars (and others in their company) have tried out significant patterns of ordering fairly removed from the prime concerns of organized structuralism. The most exacting and promising among such experimental groupings has been the attempt to present sound shifts of a particular language not in a routine enumeration based on articulatory conditions (or, worse, on the alphabetical order), but in their presumable chronological succession. In broad outline, Meyer-Lübke essayed this tour de force for proto-French as early as 1908; a quarter of a century later, E. Richter embroidered on his master stroke. The elaboration of such relative chronologies may be extended to inflection, derivation, syntax, etc., and seems perfectly compatible with research in diachronic phonology. Other scholars have endeavored to segregate certain sound shifts as particularly illustrative of a unique nonlinguistic sequence of events, so as to weave them into the fabric of specific demographic processes and cultural developments. This Menéndez Pidal strove to accomplish for the period of the early *reconquista* (eighth to eleventh century) in the bulk of his masterly treatise *Orígenes del español* (1926); W. von Wartburg matched his effort for the prehistory of French, Provençal, and Italian, in a proliferation of books and monographs issuing from his famous programmatic article (1936) on the fragmentation of Late Latin. The theoretical justification for this preferential treatment of assorted features, to the neglect of others, rebellious to the favored pattern, a treatment without explicit vindication of the criteria of selection, remains to be provided.

A third cogent marshaling of disjointed facts, eminently characteristic of the historical method, would be to arrange them roughly in the order of decreasing transparency. Thus, an etymologist grappling with thousands of equations of unequal complexity may procede from relatively simple cases involving no (or just a few easily eliminable) unknowns to progressively intricate tangles, ending up with a residue of issues inextricably confused or wholly recalcitrant. (He may at least toy with this grading at the operational stage, if not in the definitive product which, like most dictionaries, should be alphabetical to satisfy the layman's need for maximum speed in casual consultation.) This rational arrangement presupposes, on the worker's part, the ability to denude each situation of its frills, reducing it to an algebraic formula, and a concurrent willingness to deemphasize, without ruling them out entirely, the ingredients of intuition and of chance that have undeniably presided over some etymological discoveries.

Finally, to reconcile the various causes of linguistic change so far adduced (phonological drift, which may run afoul of inertia or of morphological obstacles; a state of bilingualism created by ethnic sub-, ad-, and superstrata, by intermarriages, by economic inducements, by religious habits, or by intellectual aspirations; diffusion; social upheavals; unconscious internal economy revolving around minimum effort, evenness of distribution, and a desirable degree of clarity; "expressivism," sensuous delight in certain well-developed features; deliberate search for reputed betterment), one may attempt to excogitate some system of possible alliances, concomitancies, mergers, or mutual hindrances and exclusions between these discrete forces.

These are just a few possibilities that can, at first glance, be successfully tried out within a limited subfield; a broader frame would invite other, more tempting experiments, such as the audacious survey of well-established categories across language families, a type of monograph launched by Humboldt, or the discovery, delimitation, and labeling of new categories, either static (witness É. Benveniste's newly identified "delocutive verbs") or dynamic (such as E. Schwyzer's overstated "hypercharacterization" or B. Migliorini's neatly delimited "synonymic radiation").

CHARACTERISTICS TRACEABLE TO THE STAGE OF THE DISCIPLINE

TRANSITION FROM LEARNING TO SCIENCE

The absolute age of a semiautonomous discipline and the stage that it has currently reached in its development are matters of great moment in any inventory of its salient features. There is no denying that Romance linguistics has irreversibly outgrown its adolescence. As a fully developed discipline, conscious of its topical independence and later also of its methodological originality, it is at least 130 years old. Even certain ingredients of markedly older Renaissance scholarship can hardly be brushed aside as prescientific, inasmuch as traditional linguistic "learning" and modern linguistic "science" have failed to drift apart from each other with anything like the same speed as, say, alchemy and chemistry. (Even some of the etymological lore of Antiquity and the Middle Ages, if adroitly winnowed by discriminating minds, continues to be grist to our mills, and for the external history of pronunciation we still rely heavily, if with reluctance, on the quaintly phrased statements of the old normative grammarians, foreign language teachers, and missionaries.)

CYCLES OF EMPHASIS

Even if one restricts his observation to the probings of indisputably solid science, certain recurrent cycles of emphasis become discernible. Thus rough grammatical sketches, diachronically slanted, became available for most Romance languages under the Neo-grammarians and their immediate followers in an atmosphere of austere isolationism and unquestioning dogmatism not very different from the atmosphere prevailing until all too recently among all too many straight descriptivists. After the richest yield of this method had become exhausted, the pendulum began swinging in the opposite direction, when the talented generation of Gauchat, Jaberg, and Jud, sated with schematization which at best had merely accounted for a privileged portion of the total stock of data, started exploring with great alacrity those attractive problems of erratic growth that had slipped through the wide meshes of the Neo-grammarians.

This new trend, at least among the levelheaded, did not entail the abandonment of phonetic correspondences (though their magic glitter had become tarnished) or the neglect of the edifice of historical grammar built on this foundation. But it implied diversion of the focus of attention toward other goals: word biographies replete with cultural content, welters of dialectal cross-currents, fireworks set in motion by homonymic clashes, and lexical masquerades unleashed by folk etymology became the staple food of the most imaginative Romanists. Among the sound changes examined at rare intervals, most were of an abnormal nature; they included either broad, tendential, recurrent transformations (metathesis, haplology, assimilation, dissimilation, echoing of nasal resonance; in short, Ascoli's "accidenti generali"), reaching athwart such basic shifts as are sharply limited, by definition, in space and time; or they were confined to the language of the educated and the gifted and spiced by some manner of cultural piquancy, i.e., again cutting across the major drift. The new watchword was the reconstruction of the unique set of circumstances, not a few of them extraneous to linguistics proper, that govern the trajectory of each separate word.

This vigorous reaction to schematization, aside from filling in countless factual gaps, tended to place linguistic research in another academic (and marginally even artistic) context; it made itself felt not in Romance quarters alone, but nowhere did its impact produce a more powerful jolt. Still later, abstractionism became again the irresistible fashion in general linguistics, geared by definition to ceaseless search for constants, even universals, and, in the New World, concerned primarily with skeletal sketches of unexplored indigenous languages. At this point the smaller pendulum in the restricted Romance field was temporarily delayed, failing to swing back into its initial position; the retardative force was, of course, the special commitment of this team of workers to the ideals of concreteness, plasticity, and individualism.

An inherent affinity between the Neo-grammatical and the (American-style) descriptive approach explains the curious paradox that to the Romance scholar, steeped exclusively in the tradition of his subdiscipline, some elements of the most advanced speech analysis (e.g., the schematization, the evasion or postponement of references to meaning, the emphatic divorce from other cultural analyses) may smack of reaction, insofar as they remind him of premature generalizations in Neo-grammatical practice, i.e., of errors which he was cautioned to avoid or trained to correct. Conversely the shortsighted avant-garde descriptivist is not unlikely to deride the present-day Romanist for being behind the times in clinging so tenaciously to minute concrete details. By the same token, half a century from now students of exotic languages (by then, let us hope, no longer in critical need of provisional sketches) may very well, in their predictable anxiety to cover each "skeleton" with flesh and skin, fall back, perhaps unknowingly, on many assumptions and techniques that now hold sway in the Romance camp.

Couched in more general terms: aside from its pivotal theoretical postulate the unvarnished Neo-grammatical position (or some of its modern derivatives) need not be regarded as something absolutely right or wrong, but rather as a method which at fairly early stages of a typical inquiry is apt to yield optimal results. Beyond that stage, once the requisite sound correspondences have been set up, the usefulness of the method diminishes rapidly, since such painstaking operations, for instance, as must be brought to bear on the hard core of refractory etymologies demand a program of research at the opposite pole of isolationism, presupposing close integration with kindred disciplines, if attainable without loss of identity. Granted that this cyclic argument has any merit, then a tolerant (though by no means lax) attitude of relativism, which for decades has been the stock-in-trade of any enlightened anthropologist and linguist analyzing the raw data of a culture not his own, however aberrant, should at long last be extended to the serene appraisal of heterodox linguistic doctrines.

DEGREE OF SPECIALIZATION

The age of a subdiscipline carries with it one peculiarity which some may deem an asset and others, a liability: the tendency, on the part of each successive generation, to examine under a more powerful microscope a commensurately smaller sliver of material. The reason for this temptation is obvious. As a rule, the pioneers have no qualms about surveying, as best they can, a vast slice of territory, at the risk of a high quota of errors. Their successors, on the average more scrupulous but less daring, set about to eradicate these flaws by allowing themselves more leisure to examine a smaller piece from all possible angles. An ambitious generation of workers will always succeed in weeding out a crop of inaccuracies, oversimplifications, and plain slips in the research of their immediate predecessors by concentrating on more narrowly staked out assignments.

But such victories may turn Pyrrhic through the concurrent loss of perspective and of evenly spread competence in the broader field. By cutting up a language into countless subdialects and analyzing each to the limit of one's patience one merely succeeds in scratching a surface with ever greater effectiveness. Some of the truly important problems plaguing a historically-minded linguist do not even acquire shape except through reference to closely and even distantly related languages. And yet, pathetically, wide-ranging comparatism has been on the decline. The full magnitude of this danger of excessive shrinkage has begun to dawn upon us, but no infallible means has yet been devised for underpinning the entire discipline without disrupting the flow of useful small-scale operations.

Another peculiarity—which again may constitute an advantage or a drawback—flowing from the respectable age of Romance linguistics is the overgrowth of earlier pronouncements on many crucial issues. In extreme cases (for instance, to etymologize certain words that have exercised or merely titillated the imagination of generations of conjecturers, such as Fr. *aller*), up to twenty or even thirty irreconcilably different hypotheses have been advanced over the years. Points of syntax prominently represented in practical language teaching, such as the use of the subjunctive in French, have been mercilessly labored, for the most part by unqualified analysts.

To what extent should a modern scholar, before or after frontally attacking a chosen problem, attempt to disentangle this complicated skein of previous opinions? No entirely satisfactory answer to this ever-present question has been offered in the past or seems to be forthcoming. Some escapists from bibliography, infatuated with the idea of a clean slate, altogether disregard the toiling of their predecessors. Other scholars apologetically relegate the digest of earlier researches to some kind of supplement or annotated bibliography (which a last-minute decision may then prompt them to omit). Still others, in an effort to draw a line somewhere, confine their curiosity to a limited span of time, starting from, say, the threshold of the twentieth century or from the publication date of some revolutionary book. A minority may decide on the selective coverage of a long period, using as the prime criteria of choice the originality, accessibility, temporary influence, or continued relevance of pertinent statements. A very few are likely to aim at exhaustiveness, and among these an occasional virtuoso may present the expected meandrous account with such zest and incisiveness as to afford fresh insights into turning-points in the history of linguistic science. From case to case, considerations of expediency and economy may dictate the most opportune course of action. Generally speaking, a subfield like Romance is not a suitable maneuvering terrain for scholars emotionally reluctant to examine with patience, sympathy, and humility the gropings of their elders.

THE MATRIX OF NATIONAL CULTURES

The remaining determinants need not detain us long. A particular national culture fostering a line of inquiry on a grandiose scale inevitably leaves its impress on nomenclature, tone of phrasing, and even slant of analysis. During its critical growing years Romance linguistics was preponderantly under the tutelage of Central European scholarship, entrenched far beyond the boundaries of the German-speaking countries proper. This style of learning displays a peculiar cleavage of accumulated knowledge—especially at the standard-setting level of the Academies—into a "physical" and a "spiritual" realm, the latter roughly coincident with the Humanities (minus their concern with pedagogy and the arts), to the virtual exclusion, especially at the outset, of some such stretch of middle-ground as is suggested by the social sciences. Without hesitation linguistics, initially embedded in philology, was assigned to the domain of the flourishing *Geisteswissenschaften* and so tailored and weighted as to fit its surroundings with a minimum of rough edges.

For a while this classic design was indiscriminately imitated in other countries, from St. Petersburg to Chicago and Santiago de Chile, even though the academic edifice of some was quite differently designed, until it became clear that an immediate transfer of isolated pursuits of knowledge from one citadel of learning to another, reflecting divergent tastes and dissimilar aims, was impracticable, at least in fluid disciplines lending themselves to multiple classification. This discovery came as a shock and has ever since provoked considerable and, all told, unnecessary irritation, inasmuch as a few workers hypersensitive to differences in national taste and regional traditions have magnified out of all reasonable proportion the importance of clashing integuments, oblivious of the incomparably more significant common pith. The smoothest way of producing within a locally underdeveloped subfield a style of research that harmonizes with the broader trends of a self-conscious national culture, instead of violently impinging on them (and grating on some participants' nerves), is to channel unobtrusively as much talent as possible in that neglected direction. The prompt acquisition of apposite styling will then presumably take care of itself.

Outside Central Europe there crystallized some minor styles, in part ephemeral and hardly qualifying for exportation. In his memorable essay on "The Spaniards in History," Menéndez Pidal, musing on Spain's destiny, remarked that his country was apparently foredoomed to regale the world with the late, exquisitely mellow fruits of cultural attitudes and endeavors elsewhere long extinct. It certainly is true that the recipe for this century's Spanish linguistics, a few drops of which spilled over into Latin America, represents a blend of studies in folklore, literature (down to Gongorism), straight history, and linguistics proper that calls to mind the Germany of Jakob and Wilhelm Grimm, propelled by philological curiosity. Peculiar to romantic Germany and to neo-romantic Spain alike is further the close and, on the whole, gratifying liaison between current creative literature and organized research in philology and linguistics, a spontaneous harmony comparable to that which exists between deep undercurrents of modern American civilization and the fine flowering of professional anthropological inquiries.

The Italian scene is quite different. The character of linguistics has there been cosmopolitan and polygot, its ambit encompassing with undiminished intensity Latin and Greek, but rarely extending beyond the ancient and modern Near East, in accord with Italy's severely limited commitments to, and investments in, overseas territories (aside from immigration). Two facts give extra touches of authenticity to that country's native school of Romance linguistics. First, knowledge of Latin (as a member of the Indo-European family), of the "Mediterranean substratum," and of the neo-Latin, i.e., Romance, languages is typically imparted by the same chair of *glottologia*, a state of affairs maintaining a vital cross-connection severed or curtailed elsewhere. Second, dialectology, long fostered by political conditions and to no appreciable extent thwarted by the late unification, until very recently here enjoyed almost the same prestige as the study of the literary language.

The inclusion of a given language in a nation's collegiate curriculum may act as a stimulant or as a deterrent to its liberal utilization in advanced linguistic inquiry. The former possibility undoubtedly points to a healthy climate; the alternative, to some conflict of loyalties, some exaggerated fascination for the unknown, or some morbid revulsion against the known mistaken for the stale and banal. Many hope that the almost complete divorce of advanced linguistic investigation not only from Latin and French, less thoroughly explored than the voice of rationalized indifference avers, but also from Spanish and Portuguese, which boast enormous stretches of uncharted territory, will not harden into an unremovable characteristic of progressive British and American scholarship, otherwise so elastic and versatile.

THE IMPACT OF POWERFUL PERSONALITIES

As the final component, whether or not one inclines to consider it an imponderable, it is fitting to mention the impact of magnetic personalities. Diez, Schuchardt, Ascoli, Cuervo, Meyer-Lübke, Leite de Vasconcelos, Gilliéron, Menéndez Pidal, Bally, Jaberg, and Jud are some of the luminaries in the ranks of Romance linguists who have each opened up new vistas, set or raised standards, and for decades left the stamp of their private and public performance on a wealth of significant output. On the debit side of the ledger let us readily admit that among these splendid thinkers, writers, and teachers only very few have cultivated in more than casual fashion either languages not included in, or bordering upon, the Romance domain (Ascoli) or linguistic theory for its own sake (Bally); the incomparable Schuchardt, dynamically curious along both lines, represents the great exception. In this single respect of deplorable self-sufficiency the logbook of Romanists has lately been in less than satisfactory shape, particularly if one wistfully contrasts the glorious elasticity and ability for forceful synthesis of a Jespersen, a Troubetzkoy, or a Sapir; here alone they may do well to chart their future course with a livelier spark of imagination.

THE CONTRIBUTION OF ROMANCE SCHOLARSHIP TO LINGUISTICS

The distinctive features of Romance linguistics as here projected from four vantage points are by no means immutable. Very opportunely they contain, caught in an attractive balance, both variables and near-invariables, thus offering the dual guarantee of flexibility and continuity. Easily the most precious gifts that

Romance scholarship has so far tendered to general linguistics include an almost oversubtle approach to dialect geography, a firm grasp of the osmosis between literary languages and the corresponding gamuts of vernaculars, and a vast reservoir of practice in etymology, with a record of meticulous, zestfully conducted monographic researches not yet welded into a single thoroughly integrated doctrine. At this critical point Romance linguistics happens to represent a highly atypical subdiscipline. But is typicality a measure of inherent value ? And may not a closer rapprochement with general linguistics be smoothly achieved through mutual concessions ? Thus far Romance linguists have handled with astonishing assurance slivers of concrete, unique, historically controllable material, at the crossroads of language and nonverbal culture and at the opposite pole from that of sweeping schematization. No general theory of language nor, indeed, any history of linguistic science is complete that fails to treat understandingly such a privileged store of experiences and experiments.

The recognition that one major subdiscipline may, under favorable conditions, quite legitimately develop certain unmistakable characteristics of its own carries with it the significant implication that linguistic research at its most engaging and rewarding need not, indeed should not, be conceived as monolithic. There must, of course, exist a hard core of agreement on essentials of purpose, assumptions, and techniques; it may be useful, in times of stress, to set limits to the margin of tolerable individual departures from the common standard. But the leeway left to individual taste and initiative and to the preferences of well-defined groups must be more than minimal and should take into account such factors as peculiarities of material, stage of research, academic traditions, and personal leanings. A community of linguists at its best calls to mind a fine symphony orchestra in which, enviably enough, each instrument and each group of instruments retains a perceptible measure of individuality while contributing its share to the tonal effect of the whole.

REFERENCE NOTE

The supporting bibliography supplied by Professor Malkiel is presented here intact, despite an occasional duplication of an item in the general bibliography, because of occasional additional information and, especially, because of the importance and interest of each entry as part of the whole.

BIBLIOGRAPHY

This highly selective reading list includes all items mentioned or alluded to in the article; moreover, a few titles selected on the basis of distinction, typicality, and self-explanatory usefulness to anthropologists. Thus, Kahane-Tietze and Vidos exemplify techniques of charting diffusion over sea lanes, while Gamillscheg combines the study of settlement, toponymy, and loan words; Tappolet focuses on kinship terms, Zauner on anatomical terms, Maçãs on zoonymy; Hasselrot (in his monograph on the apricot), Herculano de Carvalho, Krüger, Livingston, and Wagner illustrate so many facets of the fruitful *Wörter-und-Sachen* approach; Gilliéron and Orr emphasize the chain reactions of homonymic clashes; Rohlfs blends folklore with dialectology. Of the available textbooks only Tagliavini's, the latest, has been included; of methodological guides, as many as four, Meyer-Lübke's, Millardet's, Jaberg's, and Wartburg's; to these one may add the surveys by Iordan and Orr, Kuhn, and Quadri. In some instances, "Collected Papers" by a leading scholar were deemed most helpful (Migliorini, Rohlfs, Schuchardt); in others, influential or representative miscellanies of papers in honor of a scholar (Gauchat, Jud, Wartburg); both genres frequently contain helpful bibliographies.

Translations, primarily from German, are listed for the benefit of those readers more familiar with English, French, or Spanish (Iordan, Meyer-Lübke, Vossler, Wartburg). Other aids, especially for those largely dependent on their command of English, include references to extended book reviews, review articles, and elaborations published in American journals (Bartoli, Herculano de Carvalho, Kuhn, Maçãs, etc.).

AEBISCHER, PAUL

1948. *Estudios de toponimia y lexicografía románica.* Barcelona: Escuela de Filología.

ALONSO, AMADO

1951. *Estudios lingüísticos; temas españoles.* (Biblioteca románica hispánica; 2. Estudios y ensayos, Vol. II.) Madrid: Gredos. (New printing, 1954.)

1953. *Estudios lingüísticos; temas hispano-americanos.* (Biblioteca hispánica románica; 2. Estudios y ensayos, Vol. XII.) Madrid: Gredos.

ASCOLI, GRAZIADIO ISAIA

1873. Saggi ladini. *Archivio glottologico italiano, 1:* 1-556 and folding map.

BALLY, CHARLES

1913. *Le Langage et la vie.* Geneva: Atar. (Reprinted, Paris: Payot, 1926; rev. 2nd ed. [Romanica Helvetica, Series Linguistica, Vol. I], Zurich: Niehans, 1935; 3rd ed. [Société de publications romanes et françaises, Vol. XXXIV], Geneva: Droz, 1952; translated by A. Alonso, *El lenguaje y la vida,* Buenos Aires: Losada, 1941.)

1932. *Linguistique générale et linguistique française.* Paris: Leroux. (rev. 2nd ed., Bern: Francke, 1944; 3rd ed., 1950.)

BARTOLI, MATTEO

1925. *Introduzione alla neolinguistica; principi, scopi, metodi.* (Biblioteca del "Archivum Romanicum," Series II, Vol. XV.) Geneva: Olschki.

1945. *Saggi di linguistica spaziale.* Turin: Rosenberg & Sellier.

BENVENISTE, ÉMILE

1958. Les verbes délocutifs. *Studia philologica et litteraria in honorem L. Spitzer.* Bern: Francke. Pp. 57-63.

BUBEN, VLADIMIR

1935. *Influence de l'orthographe sur la prononciation du français moderne.* (Spisy filosofické fakulty University Komenského v Bratislavě, Vol. XIX.) Bratislava.

CUERVO, RUFINO JOSÉ

1867. *Apuntaciones críticas sobre el lenguaje bogotano.* Bogotá: Guarin. (2nd ed., 1876; 3rd ed., 1881; rev. 4th ed., Chartres: Durand, 1885; 5th ed., Paris: Roger & Chernoviz, 1907 [title lengthened: . . . *con frecuente referencia al de los países de Hispano-America*]; 6th ed., Paris, 1914; 9th ed., Bogotá: Instituto Caro y Cuervo, 1955.)

1950. *Disquisiciones sobre filología española.* Edited by R. Torres Quintero. (Publicaciones del Instituto Caro y Cuervo, Vol. IV.) Bogotá.

DIEZ, FRIEDRICH

1853. *Etymologisches Wörterbuch der romanischen Sprachen.* Bonn: Marcus. (3rd ed., 2 vols., 1869-1870.)

DURAFFOUR, ANTONIN

1941. *Lexique patois-français du parler de Vaux-en-Bugey* (*Ain*) (*1919-1940*). Grenoble: Institut de phonétique.

GAMILLSCHEG, ERNST

1934-1936. *Romania Germanica; Sprach- und Siedlungsgeschichte der Germanen auf dem Boden des alten Römerreichs*. (Grundriss der germanischen Philologie, edited by H. Paul, Vol. XI: 1-3.) Berlin and Leipzig: de Gruyter.

GARCÍA DE DIEGO, VICENTE

1923. *Contribución al diccionario hispánico etimológico* (Revista de Filología Española, Suppl. II.) Madrid.

GAUCHAT, LOUIS

1926. *Festschrift Louis Gauchat*. Aarau: Sauerländer.

GILLIÉRON, JULES

1912. *Études de géographie linguistique d'après l'Atlas Linguistique de la France*. (With Mario Roques.) Paris: Champion. [On homonymics see also *Lg*., 1952, *28:* 299-338; *Hispanic Review*, *21:* 20-36, 120-134 (1953).

1918. *Généalogie des mots qui désignent l'abeille, d'après l'Atlas Linguistique de la France*. (Bibliothèque de l'École des Hautes Études, Vol. CCXXV.) Paris: Champion.

HASSELROT, BENGT

1957. *Études sur la formation diminutive dans les langues romanes*. (Uppsala Universitets Årsskrift, Fasc. XI.) Uppsala.

1940-1941. L'Abricot; essai de monographie onomasiologique et sémantique. *Studia Neophilologica*, *13:* 45-79, 226-252.

HERCULANO DE CARVALHO, JOSÉ GONÇALO C.

1953. Coisas e palavras: Alguns problemas etnográficos e linguísticos relacionados com os primitivos sistemas de debulha na Península Ibérica. *Biblos*, *29:* 1-365 and 11 folding maps. [Reviewed, *Lg*., 1957, *33:* 54-76.]

IORDAN, IORGU

1937. *An Introduction to Romance Linguistics, Its Schools and Scholars*. Revised, translated, and in parts recast by John Orr. London: Methuen.

JABERG, KARL

1936. *Aspects géographiques du langage. Conférences faites au Collège de France* (*Décembre 1933*). (Société de publications romanes et françaises, Vol. XVIII.) Paris: Droz.

1957-1958. The Birthmark in Folk Belief, Language, Literature, and Fashion. *Romance Philology*, *10:* 307-342.

JUD, JAKOB

1914. Probleme der altromanischen Wortgeographie. *Zeitschrift für romanische Philologie*, 38 (1): 1-75 and five folding maps.

1943. *Sache, Ort und Wort. Jakob Jud zum sechzigsten Geburtstag 12. Januar 1942*. (Romanica Helvetica, Vol. XX.) Geneva: Droz.

KAHANE, HENRY, RENÉE KAHANE, ANDREAS TIETZE

1958. *The Lingua Franca in the Levant; Turkish Nautical Terms of Italian and Greek Origin*. Urbana: University of Illinois Press.

KRÜGER, FRITZ

1925. *Die Gegenstandskultur Sanabrias und seiner Nachbargebiete; ein Beitrag zur spanischen und portugiesischen Volkskunde.* (Hamburgische Universität; Abhandlungen aus dem Gebiet der Auslandskunde, Vol. XX.) Hamburg: Friederichsen.

KUHN, ALWIN

1951. *Romanische Philologie.* Vol. I, *Die romanischen Sprachen.* (Wissenschaftliche Forschungsberichte, Geisteswissenschaftliche Reihe, Vol. VIII.) Bern: Francke. [Reviewed, *Lg.*, 1952, *28:* 509-525.]

1947-1948. Sechzig Jahre Sprachgeographie in der Romania. *Romanistisches Jahrbuch*, *1:* 25-63.

LEITE DE VASCONCELOS, JOSÉ

1928. *Antroponímia portuguesa; tratado comparativo da origem, significação, classificação e vida do conjunto dos nomes próprios, sobrenomes e apelidos, usados por nós desde a idade-média até hoje.* Lisbon: Imprensa Nacional.

LERCH, EUGEN

1925-1934. *Historische französische Syntax.* Leipzig: Reisland. 3 vols.

LIVINGSTON, CHARLES H.

1957. *Skein-winding Reels. Studies in Word History and Etymology.* Ann Arbor: University of Michigan Press. [Reviewed, *Romance Philology*, 1958-1959, *12:* 262-282.]

MAÇÃS, DELMIRA

1950-1951. *Os animais na linguagem portuguesa.* (Publicações do Centro de Estudos Filológicos, Vol. II.) Lisbon. [Reviewed, *Hispanic Review*, 1956, *24:* 115-143, 207-231.]

MARTINET, ANDRÉ

1955. *Économie des changements phonétiques; traité de phonologie diachronique.* Bibliotheca romanica. Ser. I, Manualia et commentationes, Vol. X.) Bern: Francke. [Reviewed, *Romance Philology*, 1956-1957, *10:* 350-362; 1961-1962, *15:* 139-153.]

MENÉNDEZ PIDAL, RAMÓN

1926. *Orígenes del español; estado lingüístico de la Península Ibérica hasta el siglo XI.* (Revista de Filología Española, Suppl. XI.) Madrid: Hernando. (2nd ed., 1929; 3rd rev. ed., 1950 [=*Obras*, Vol. VIII].)

MEYER-LÜBKE, WILHELM

1901. *Einführung in das Studium der romanischen Sprachwissenschaft.* Heidelberg, Winter. (rev. 2nd ed., 1909; rev. 3rd ed., 1921; translated by A. Castro: *Introducción a la lingüística románica, con notas y adiciones*, Madrid: Centro de Estudios Históricos, 1926.

1908-1921. *Historische Grammatik der französischen Sprache.* (Sammlung romanischer Elementar- und Handbücher. Ser. I, Grammatiken, Vol. I.) Heidelberg: Winter. 2 parts. (5th ed. of Part I, 1934.)

MIGLIORINI, BRUNO

1927. *Dal nome proprio al nome comune; studi semantici sul mutamento dei nomi propri di persona in nomi comuni negl'idiomi romanzi.* (Biblioteca dell' "Archivum Romanicum," Ser. I, Vol. XIII.) Geneva: Olschki.

1957. *Saggi linguistici.* Florence: Le Monnier.

MILLARDET, GEORGES

1923. *Linguistique et dialectologie romanes; problèmes et méthodes.* (Société des Langues Romanes, Publications Spéciales, Vol. XXVIII.) Montpellier.

ORR, JOHN

1953. *Words and Sounds in English and French.* (Modern Language Studies.) Oxford: Blackwell.

QUADRI, BRUNO

1952. *Aufgaben und Methoden der onomasiologischen Forschung; eine entwicklungsgeschichtliche Darstellung.* (Romanica Helvetica, Vol. XXXVII.) Bern: Francke.

RHEINFELDER, HANS

1933. *Kultsprache und Profansprache in den romanischen Ländern; sprachgeschichtliche Studien, besonders zum Wortschatz des Französischen und des Italienischen.* (Biblioteca dell' "Archivum Romanicum," Ser. II, Vol. XVIII.) Geneva: Olschki.

RICHTER, ELISE

1934. *Beiträge zur Geschichte der Romanismen; chronologische Phonetik des Französischen bis zum Ende des 8. Jahrhunderts.* (Zeitschrift für romanische Philologie, Suppl. LXXXII.) Halle: Niemeyer. [Cf. E. Gamillscheg, *Zeitschrift für französische Sprache und Literatur*, 1937-1938, *61:* 89-106.]

ROHLFS, GERHARD

1952. *An den Quellen der romanischen Sprachen; vermischte Beiträge zur romanischen Sprachgeschichte und Volkskunde.* Halle: Niemeyer.

RONJAT, JULES († 1925)

1930-1937. *Grammaire historique des parlers provençaux modernes.* Montpellier: Société des Langues Romanes. 3 vols.

SALVIONI, CARLO

[Scattered monographs, articles, and notes; for complete list see Robert A. Hall, Jr., *Bibliography of Italian Linguistics*, Baltimore: Linguistic Society of America, 1941, pp. 486-488.]

SCHUCHARDT, HUGO

1922. *Hugo Schuchardt Brevier; ein Vademekum der allgemeinen Sprachwissenschaft, als Festgabe zum 80. Geburtstag des Meisters zusammengestellt.* Edited by L. Spitzer. Halle: Niemeyer. (rev. 2nd ed., 1928.)

SCHWYZER, EDUARD

1941. Sprachliche Hypercharakterisierung. *Abhandlungen der Preussischen Akademie der Wissenschaften.* (Phil.- hist. Klasse, No. 9.) Berlin. [For a different interpretation, see my article, Diachronic Hypercharacterization in Romance, *Archivum Linguisticum*, 1957, *9:* 79-113; 1958, *10:* 1-36.]

TAGLIAVINI, CARLO

1952. *Le origini delle lingue neolatine.* (rev. 2nd ed.) Bologna: Pàtron. [Reviewed, Robert A. Hall, Jr., *Romance Philology*, 1953-1954, *7:* 193-197.] (Rev. and enl. 3rd ed., 1959.)

TAPPOLET, ERNST

1895. *Die romanischen Verwandtschaftsnamen, mit besonderer Berücksichtigung der französischen und italienischen Mundarten; ein Beitrag zur vergleichenden Lexikologie.* Strassburg.

ULLMANN, STEPHEN

1952. *Précis de sémantique française.* (Bibliotheca Romanica. Ser. I, Manualia et Commentationes, Vol. IX.) Bern: Francke.

VIDOS, B. E.

1939. *Storia delle parole marinaresche italiane passate in francese; contributo storico-linguistico all'espansione della lingua nautica italiana.* (Biblioteca dell' "Archivum Romanicum," Ser. II, Vol. XXIV.) Florence: Olschki.

VOSSLER, KARL

1921. *Frankreichs Kultur im Spiegel seiner Sprachentwicklung; Geschichte der französischen Schriftsprache von den Anfängen bis zur klassischen Neuzeit.* (Sammlung romanischer Elementar- und Handbücher, Ser. IV, Vol. I.) Heidelberg: Winter. (Translated by A. Juilland, *Langue et culture de la France; histoire du français littéraire des origines à nos jours*, Paris: Payot, 1953.)

WAGNER, MAX LEOPOLD

1921. *Das ländliche Leben Sardiniens im Spiegel der Sprache; kulturhistorisch-sprachliche Untersuchungen.* (Wörter- und- Sachen; Kulturhistorische Zeitschrift für Sprach- und- Sachforschung, Suppl. IV.) Heidelberg: Winter.

WARTBURG, WALTHER VON

1936. Die Ausgliederung der romanischen Sprachräume. *Zeitschrift für Romanische Philologie, 56:* 1-48, with 7 maps. (Elaborated in book form with the same title, Bern, 1950.)

1943. *Einführung in Problematik und Methodik der Sprachwissenschaft.* Halle: Niemeyer. (Translated by P. Maillard, *Problèmes et méthodes de la linguistique*, Paris: Presses Universitaires de France, 1946; translated by D. Alonso and E. Lorenzo, *Problemas y métodos de la lingüística*, Madrid: Instituto Miguel de Cervantes, 1951.)

1958. *Etymologica. Walther von Wartburg zum siebzigsten Geburtstag, 18. Mai 1958.* Tübingen: Niemeyer.

WEIGAND, GUSTAV

1909. *Linguistischer Atlas des dacorumänischen Sprachgebietes.* Leipzig: Barth.

ZAUNER, ADOLF

1903. Die romanischen Namen der Körperteile. *Romanische Forschungen, 14:* 339-530. [Cf. H. R. Kahane, Designations of the Cheek in the Italian Dialects, *Lg.*, 1941, *17:* 212-222.]

Alfred Louis Kroeber 69

DELL H. HYMES

ALFRED LOUIS KROEBER'S contributions to knowledge, sustained over some sixty-four years, are remarkable not merely in number, but for scope and quality. He was probably the greatest general anthropologist that American anthropology has known. His contributions to linguistics, archaeology, ethnography, and ethnology could each have earned him an enviable reputation as a major figure, and he made noteworthy contributions to biological anthropology and folklore as well. He was a prolific fieldworker, a master systematizer, an independent and provocative theorist and critic. Something of his scope is reflected in the monographs and books he has occasionally listed as major publications: *The Arapaho* (1902), *The Yokuts Language of South Central California* (1907), *Zuni Kin and Clan* (1916), *Peoples of the Philippines* (1919, 1928), *Anthropology* (1923, 1948), *Handbook of the Indians of California* (1925), *Cultural and Natural Areas of Native North America* (1939), *Peruvian Archaeology* (1944), *Configurations of Culture Growth* (1944), *The Nature of Culture* (1952), *Style and Civilization* (1957).[1]

Kroeber delighted in quantative estimate as a heuristic device: of eight paragraphs of preface to *The Nature of Culture* three set forth fractions that characterize the papers collected therein; and so it is worth noting that his publications ultimately will total 460 or more, and that of this number, some 70, slightly less than a sixth, are wholly or in important part contributions to linguistics. (This does not count reviews or comments in published records of conferences.) It is appropriate, too, to put the figures in temporal perspective: the linguistic contributions are not evenly spaced throughout his career, but cluster at its beginning and end. Somewhat more than half come in the first two decades in California, a dozen or so are distributed among the next three decades, and then, beginning with 1952, there are about half again as many in his last ten years.

The roots of Kroeber's linguistic interests go deep. His first remembered purely intellectual pleasure, as a boy of ten, was the demonstration of pattern of the classes of English strong verbs. As to his professional work, he observed: "I came from humanistic literature, entered anthropology by the gate of linguistics" (*Nature of Culture* 173). When Kroeber began graduate study at Columbia, Boas had announced courses in statistical theory and American Indian languages. The two courses were to remain fundamental to Boas' program for forty years, and the two subjects, sometimes in conjunction, were to be lifelong interests of his great student. Indeed, the course in American Indian languages seems to have been Kroeber's first graduate course, and he frequently mentioned the experience, speaking of Swanton as having "cut his teeth first on Chinook like so many of us,"[2] elsewhere describing himself[3] as "an anthropologist who found his way into his profession by being shown how to analyze Boas' Chinook Texts into grammar," and describing with pleasure

> Boas' first linguistic class, which met Tuesday evenings at his home around the cleared family dining table, [and] consisted of an archaeologist from the Museum, a teaching assistant of English, and an adventurous nondescript who soon after rolled himself out of anthropology as suddenly as he had rolled in, and who required some quarts of beer in a can from the nearest saloon to overcome the tension of a two hours' session with Chinook or Eskimo.[4]

The effect on the teaching assistant of English, Kroeber, is implicit in his praise of Boas for instituting the first productive teaching of American Indian linguistics by

> setting his students to discover the structure of a language by analysis of texts. This equivalent of laboratory method introduced the student to an attitude of independent research. It also served as specific training for new field investigation, which was subsequently provided whenever possible. This method naturally proved to be intensely stimulating to capable students.[5]

That the study of language should have played an important part at the outset of Kroeber's career is not surprising: in the school of Boas it almost could not have been otherwise. With Kroeber the linguistic interest was to prove abiding and individual. Partly this was because of a personal attraction to linguistic data, but it was also because of Kroeber's conception of anthropology. He sets forth this conception and his commitment to it in the sections of introduction written for *The Nature of Culture* and in the appendix to the report of his week-long symposium in the summer of 1960 on "Anthropological horizons" (the report is to be published by the Wenner-Gren Foundation). In *The Nature of Culture* Kroeber presents his anthropology almost as a matter of personal style, involving both a way of working and a perspective. To sketch its character, one can perhaps best say that it joined a capacity for a broad view with love of concrete data; desire to discover patterns intrinsic to data with belief that patterns must be understood in context; a giving of primacy to cultural data and cultural frames of reference with continuous effort to extend cultural patterns and contexts to the limits of their relevance in space and time; that much of his work had its roots in a natural-history approach to the materials of the humanities; that his preference was for characterization rather than dissection; for ordering rather than manipulating data; for theory sweated out of empirical studies rather than proclaimed in advance. There was almost no side of culture but subtended his angle of vision; to change the metaphor, there was little in cultural phenomena that could not come as grist to his mill. For such an approach there was a natural place for the study of language in its own right as part of culture, and for the sake of its contribution to other, sometimes general problems; and there was of course much in language that lent itself to his way of working.

These qualities of Kroeber's anthropology could perhaps be inferred from the body of his linguistic work alone, for it is a microcosm of the whole. It has, indeed, a certain unity. Problems of the earliest years reappear in the writings of the last decade, appropriately recast; and several of the themes that run through his linguistic work are often enough combined in one publication, so that any point of entry to his work is likely to lead, chronologically and bibliographically, into much of the rest. To a considerable degree, *tout se tient*. Much of the work has been forgotten, yet it is worth while to survey it with some care, not only in tribute to a great scholar, but also because some of the problems still wait to be carried beyond the point to which Kroeber brought them, and because the significance of the man and work as an example for the future relations between linguistics and anthropology lies so much in the details seen as part of the whole.

The matrix is the early period in California. There the first two decades of the century saw the bulk of Kroeber's linguistic field work, and the appearance of his characteristic interests and mode of interpretation.

A pattern of combined ethnographic and linguistic investigation had begun with Kroeber's first major field work, among the Arapaho. His dissertation related their decorative art to a theoretical controversy, but he also obtained material for a valuable monograph on Arapho dialects, *UCP-AAE*, 1916, *12:*71-138. This pattern continued in his almost single-handed labors in California in the first part of the century. The tribes of California were many, diverse, and little known. With the support of Mrs. Hearst, Kroeber undertook an "ethnological and archaeological survey" of the state (ethnology included linguistics). He was joined in the linguistic work by Goddard (Athabaskan), and, for varying periods, by Dixon (Maidu, Wintu, Shasta, Achomawi), Sapir (Yana), Waterman (Yurok), Barrett (Pomo, Miwok), Radin (Wappo), and others, but the sustained bulk of the work was his, culminating, ethnographically, in the monumental *Handbook* (completed in 1918, but not published until 1925).

Much of the work was in response to the obvious need to fill gaps in knowledge before too late. Already some of the languages and dialects were extinct, and for them philology of a sort with early materials was all that could be done,[6] if that. Since the description of disappearing languages has often not seemed an obvious need at all, despite being the only contribution to the future of linguistics that future linguistics cannot make for itself, Kroeber's extensive service in this task deserves full praise. Sometimes his reports mention absence of other knowledge of a dialect as a reason for publishing imperfect data obtained in the course of an ethnographic field trip.[7] Opportunities for obtaining linguistic data that would remedy a lack were seized.[8] Sometimes native speakers were brought to Berkeley to be worked with or trained to write their own language.[9] As much as could be done was done, given the opportunity. Voegelin tells the story of Kroeber waiting for a train, noticing an Indian, and promptly taking a vocabulary in the time available. Kroeber's descriptive experience during this period embraced Arapaho, Zuni, Marshallese, and, of the languages of California and the adjacent west, Atsugewi, Bannock, Chumash, Costanoan, Diegueno, Esselen, Karok, Luiseno, Miwok, Mohave, Pomo, Salinan, Shoshonean, Ute, Washo, Wiyot, Yokuts, Yuki, Yurok; altogether some 33 languages.

Throughout Kroeber's work with language as with other phenomena, there runs a remarkable capacity to observe and to seize opportunities for doing so. At Zuni in 1915 he encountered what was observable to all, surface finds of archaeological materials, but it was Kroeber who first ordered the stylistic variations of surface finds into a series, and thus invented a method of chronology. This by-product of his Zuni work was matched by another, apparently the only observations on the speech development of an American Indian child ever published. He had occasion to hear the daily speech of the youngest son of the family with whom he lived, and recorded the changes over a two-month interval; the record is still worth noting, for its details and general summary.[10]

A little-known series of phonetic studies shows Kroeber's attentiveness to empirical detail,[11] and his eagerness to make use of aids to precision. He himself had moderate phonetic gifts, and he worked when what to expect in the native languages of western America was still uncertain. The identification of segmental sounds was being sweated out mostly by men without much phonetic training,[12] and Kroeber welcomed application to Amerindian languages of

> principles and methods of phonetic research established by European scholars . . . largely through the entrance into this field [Amerindian] of several students trained in the study of Indo-European philology.[13]

Kroeber's empirical work was never data-gathering for its own sake. There was always in mind an immediate question or a larger frame of reference, and his phonetic studies show this. They were undertaken to provide orientation and grounding for further descriptive work, to answer questions current at the time about the phonetic characteristics of American languages, and also because phonetic data were cultural data whose distribution and historical interpretation were of interest in themselves. One of the questions of the day concerned the so-called "intermediates," consonants variously perceived as voiced and voiceless by field-workers. As part of the phonetic instability considered characteristic of "primitive" language, the matter had been analyzed by Boas in a brilliant paper.[14] In the case of "intermediates," Kroeber suspected a specific phonetic cause in the sounds themselves, voiceless onset of otherwise voiced stops (*UCP-AAE*, 1911, 10:8); and when a German trading schooner with a crew of Marshall Islanders docked at San Francisco in April 1911, he seized the opportunity. His earlier recordings of Caroline Islands dialects had showed such inconsistency in writing surd and sonant as to make him suspect that "intermediates," widespread in western America, might be found in Polynesia too. About 409 tracings revealed surds in final position, sonants intervocallically, and initial "intermediates" that began surd and invariably became voiced approaching the following vowel. Kroeber goes on to summarize the study as a whole in characteristic fashion, placing the phenomena as a type in a broader geographical and genetic context.[15]

The California linguistic field work had indeed an overall problem orientation from its beginning. Against the background of the number and distribution of linguistic stocks in the rest of North America, California stood out as a great exception. Nearly half the stocks (according to the Powell classification) in the country were represented in the one state (22 out of 52). Explaining this extreme diveristy was seen as "the fundamental problem of California linguistics" (*AA*, 1903, *5*:2). When similarity in grammatical structure was glimpsed between a number of languages whose vocabularies seemed unrelated, there seemed an obvious bearing on the problem of diversity.

> An attempt was therefore made by the writers [Dixon and Kroeber] to secure, through field investigation, information concerning the grammatical structure of all Californian languages. This task was rendered necessary by the fact that with one or two exceptions the grammar of these languages was wholly unknown.[16]

The background of the problem orientation was a natural-history approach to the data of ethnology. Languages, like cultures, were units to be ordered, their connections traced and explained, and in this period of American anthropology the value of linguistics for ordering the ethnological data was at a peak. With historical documents lacking, archaeological time perspective not yet available, and no uniform way of determining political or cultural units amidst the mass of data, the qualitative units of linguistic classification were seized upon by many, and became a primary framework for description and interpretation. Subsequent work has modified the role of genetic classification to that of one line of evidence to be integrated with others, but its value remains a main source of anthropology's vested interest in linguistics.

When Kroeber began his California work, the Powell classification was so well established and so rightly valued that the temper of the times was not inclined toward more than incidental tinkering with it.[17] Also, Kroeber was well aware of the necessity of lexical correspondences for proof of genetic connection,[18] and the California vocabularies did not manifest connections not already considered by Powell. With the data and analyses available, the apparent resemblances among languages were in structural outlines and subsystems, and these were the lines pursued in search of further ordering. Since the connections that appeared were traced typologically in space rather than genetically in time, the correlative principle of explanation was diffusion, convergence through areal contiguity.

The first result of the field work inspired by the notion of typological resemblances was the first areal classification of a set of New World languages according to grammatical type. The four chief diagnostic features (pronominal incorporation, syntactical [pure-relational] cases, material [mixed-relational] cases, morphophonemics [Sapir's typological feature of technique, here contrasting agglutinative vs. fusional combination]) would not today seem sufficient, even with the additional minor features, such as marking of number and reduplication, that were noted; but a classification according to these features was one that the data could support, and the results made sense: the California languages fell into three broad types correlated with geographical location, cultural groupings seemed more or less to coincide, and comparison with languages outside California showed the types to be indeed distinctive. Interpretation of the typology was carefully restrained, and its application to languages outside California on which it had not been based was not assumed. Moreover, it was a remarkably original step in the study of New World languages, one that has never adequately been followed up.

Kroeber collaborated with Dixon in another pioneering typological survey, one of California numeral systems. A major point was to note correlations between features and to show the inadequacy of some existing conceptions: decimal and quinary-vigesimal could not be set up as absolute types for whole systems, since the character of a system might change at 10, and indeed, the California material showed more cases of shift at 10 (from quinary to decimal or from decimal to vigesimal) than of continuity (quinary becoming vigesimal or decimal remaining decimal). The great diversity of radicals below 10 within even the most closely related languages was shown, the contrast with the uniformity within Indo-European made, and the moral for comparative method drawn:

> Altogether it would appear that numerals occupy a very different place in California languages from their philological position in Indo-European and other great linguistic families of the old world, and that

> on the whole they cannot be given the importance in comparison and in questions of determination of genetic relationship that they occupy in these languages.[19]

The California diversity was explained in terms of the use of arithmetical operations and compounding in the numerals below 10, and the systems related to the corresponding counting practices. This study has stood almost alone in the Americanist literature since its publication more than a half-century ago.[20]

The thrust of the first of the two papers (Native Languages of California) is such as to define what are to all intents and purposes grammatically based linguistic areas, and the principle of areal relationship is clearly stated in both.[21]

The phonetic studies of this period show the same interest in tracing types of phenomena in the contexts of geographical distribution and genetic affiliation. The Marshallese paper concludes with the summary:

> In all essentials, these phonetic traits are duplicated in the Pima-Papago language of Arizona, and several individual features recur in a number of American languages; but as regards the allied tongues of Malayo-Polynesian stock, the Marshall dialect seems to be phonetically greatly specialized.[22]

With the California phonetic studies, the Marshallese study raises the prospect of a typological and areal survey of phonetic traits; but like the German trading ship that supplied Kroeber's informants, the prospect was soon lost from sight. (The ship sank 24 hours after sailing; the crew was saved, and Kroeber's informants had deserted before the vessel left San Francisco.) For many years, Kroeber's California paper [23] remained the only detailed survey for any part of the New World. Areal groupings and "the fundamental problem whether the linguistic families of America possess any underlying or general features peculiar to themselves as a class" (*UCP-AAE*, 1911, *10*:2) remained untackled.

The typological interest informed many of Kroeber's reports on individual languages at this time, and his study of Washo was expressly to determine its place and areal connections as a type.[24] But about 1910 the focus of linguistic interpretation shifted to genetic relationships, as a decade began that was not to be paralleled until that of the nineteen-fifties for rapid unfolding of new connections and disruption of established perspectives. Kroeber has himself recorded the excitement of the period.[25] Swanton showed Natchez to be Muskogean, and compared Athabascan, Haida, and Tlingit; Kroeber linked Miwok and Costanoan again (Powell having separated them) and with Dixon joined Maidu, Wintu, and Yokuts with them to form Penutian; by a quick series of steps, aided by Harrington and Sapir, Hokan came into being, comprising first Karok, Chimariko, Shasta, Pomo, Yana, Esselen, (with Chumash and Salinan separate as "Iskoman," then joined in to Hokan through Sapir's comparisons and Harrington's affirmation of the unity of Chumash and Yuman), and incorporating Seri and Tequistlatecan through Kroeber's work, and Washo through that of Harrington and Sapir. Yurok and Wiyot were joined in Ritwan by Dixon and Kroeber, and then connected with Algonquian by Sapir. In addition, Sapir demonstrated the unity of Uto-Aztekan to the satisfaction of all and of Na-Déné to the satisfaction of some, and traced Penutian northward into Oregon and Canada. In passing, Kroeber had also forecast the linking of Salishan, Wakashan, and Chemakuan. No wonder that in the midst of this period Kroeber asserted: "We may accordingly be confident that the language map of North America will be thoroughly recolored in a few years."[26] One could not then foresee that the breaking of the Powell log-jam was to release a tide of discovery and controversy that shows no sign yet of subsiding. But the genetic connections discovered by Kroeber and Dixon have stood the test of subsequent work, and today the necessarily slow establishment in detail of comparative Hokan, Penutian, and Ritwan is one of the healthiest parts of Amerindian linguistics.

Of particular interest is the way in which the two men came to perceive the relationships. Structural similarities had suggested connections such as that of Miwok and Costanoan, and of Yurok and Wiyot, but, adhering to the Powell framework, they wrote of all lexical connections among recognized families as due to diffusion. Attempting to interpret the accumulating lexical evidence, they made a mass comparison of the equivalents in 67 dialects (of the 21 California stocks) for a list of 225 meanings appropriately "basic" for the area. The considerable number of resemblances that appeared made no sense on any hypothesis of diffusion.

> Finally, in a mood rather of baffled impotence, an interpretation of the cases of most abundant resemblance as due to genetic relationship was applied. At once difficulties yielded, and arrangement emerged from the chaos.[27]

The method (involving a table of interrelationships) anticipated the statistical analyses of cultural and linguistic similarities that were to be one of Kroeber's main interests in the nineteen-thirties and later, and it has been credited by Swadesh as an independent earlier invention of lexicostatistics.[28] Perhaps the most important legacy of the work is in its tactic of careful progress, its attitude of scrupulous boldness. Too narrow a concern with purity of method was rejected as sterile, but essential methodological safeguards were observed. There was no clinging to conventional classifications, but new findings were built up step by step, and not projected beyond the accessible horizon.

The 1919 monograph culminates the first period of Kroeber's linguistic work, and marks its end. On the theoretical plane the period is outlined by the shift in the dominant mode of interpreting historical connections, genetic retention replacing convergence through diffusion. The 1919 monograph is the chief product of this shift; following it, there is a sharp drop in linguistic publication for three decades, and also little or no conceptual change with regard to historical interpretation. Indeed, insofar as periods of Kroeber's linguistic work can be defined, it is jointly by amount of activity (great or small) and state of historical perspective (stable or in development). In the first and last periods there is both extensive activity and development in historical perspective; in the middle period, as stated, there is little of either. His textbook chapter on language, mostly concerned with historical perspective, hardly changes from the first edition to the last (1923-1948). That is a tribute to its soundness (it is still worth reading), but also a symbol of Kroeber's lack of involvement in the main linguistic developments of the period.

From about 1920 to 1950, Kroeber's linguistic publications consist of a few reviews of linguistic books; some ethnological monographs containing linguistic material; treatment of linguistic topics in general books (*Anthropology*, *Handbook*, *Cultural and Natural areas*, *Configurations*); subgroupings of known language families (with development of statistical techniques); and a scattering, topically and chronologically, of papers. Most of the topics are not confined to the period, and indeed, except for instrumental phonetics and child language, which seem wholly part of the first period, it is hard to find one of Kroeber's linguistic interests that does not persist throughout his career. Mode of historical interpretation becomes vital again in the last period, so it seems best to consider it there, while considering now the range of other topics not yet discussed.

Ethnology led Kroeber into dialectology almost at the start. An early paper treats the degree of dialect differentiation within California languages.[29] Kroeber noted conflicting assumptions about the nature of the unusual Californian diversity, as projected at the dialect level, and made an empirical test. The paper also takes up the relations between dialects and political, social, and cultural units, showing how the relation differs as between such groups as the Maidu and Yokuts. As elsewhere, he states that collection of uniform materials by a single investigator is needed to resolve problems. Much dialect material was obtained adventitiously, but he twice made special field trips, one for the Moquelumnan (Miwok) study just noted, another for systematic coverage of the many Yokuts languages and dialects. The Yokuts material was first dealt with in part of his major linguistic monograph, *The Yokuts Language* (1907), and the full data, promised there, form part of a monograph completed late in the summer of 1960. Dialect work involved interest in the historical information gleaned from place names, as shown in the Moquelumnan paper and throughout the *Handbook*. In addition one paper is devoted solely to toponymy, California Place Names of Indian Origin.[30]

As a concomitant of ethnography, Kroeber noted social variation in speech. Information is scattered through the *Handbook*, and that for the Yurok is collected in a special article.[31] Such study was never intensive on Kroeber's part, and the early ethnographic work that is most important for linguistics today is that on kinship. In Classificatory Systems of Relationships,[32] he defined eight principles (or categories) as basic to the classification of kin by relationship terms, and in so doing, showed the way for the semantic (componential) analysis of kinship that has only now come into its own.[33] In this paper Kroeber showed himself not only a brilliant analyst, finding principles that could order a mass of data, but also a polemical theorist. Here and in subsequent writings on kinship, he insisted (as against Rivers, Radcliffe-Brown, and their followers) on the linguistic dimension of kinship. For Kroeber this meant that kinship systems could not be explained entirely by fit to social institutions and practices, but must also be understood as systems of classificatory logic with a partly independent history of their own. That kin terms are linguistic facts was taken as warrant for this view,[34] and as showing historical linguistics to be essential to kinship study. Belief in the latter point led him to make a trial reconstruction of Athapaskan kin terms and later to urge Hoijer to undertake a more nearly definitive study. The conclusion of his Athpaskan paper puts the historical matter clearly:

> Since kinship systems are, first of all, systems of classificatory logic expressed in words which are parts of languages, the analysis and comparison of such systems without reference to their linguistic history, so far as this may be available, is an arbitrary limitation on understanding.[35]

The point is especially pertinent, for the best effort so far to reconstruct the evolution of kinship terms on a purely sociological base seems to have gone wrong in two cases where it has been linguistically checked.[36]

Like other American anthropologists, Kroeber was concerned from the first to destroy misconceptions about the "primitive" languages he studied. Part of his early work in typology (and of his praise of Sapir's *Language*)[37] was directed against overgeneralizations and prejudices current among scholars (and still remarkably alive, even among linguists).[38] For the *Popular Science Monthly* (then an intellectual rather than mechanical journal), Kroeber wrote a special article exploding notions of Amerindian languages as rapidly changing, barbarous in sound, and the like, and many of the points were incorporated into his textbook.[39] Here he showed his persistent concern not only for objectivity in science, but also for its communication to the general society, as part of a desire to maintain the public relevance of scientific work. Although never a reformer or political activist, Kroeber more than once expressed such concern. It is reported from his student days,[40] and it enters as an argument against the esoteric consequences of Powell's principles of priority in the nomenclature of linguistic families,[41] in the note struck in the introduction to his monumental *Handbook*, in his praise of Sapir's book as uniquely a successful popularization,[42] in the organization of his classic textbook, whose first eighty-six pages, preceding the chapter on language, concern the lack of objective evidence for belief in racial inferiority, particularly, as regards the Negro.[43]

Kroeber's substantial interest in the phenomena and science of biology impinged upon his interest in language. In the first years of the century he was mainly concerned, like most American anthropologists, to separate the biological from the cultural realm, but, this accomplished, Kroeber took up, unlike most anthropologists, problems of comparison and continuity. In the first edition of his textbook he defined anthropology as concerned with the interplay of biological and cultural factors,[44] and gave special attention to the emergence of language in the course of human evolution and its comparison to animal communication.[45]

The latter interest shows in his response to the theoretical implications of von Frisch's work.[46] Most important are his articles Sub-human Cultural Beginnings and On Human Nature.[47] With renewal of interest in such questions, Kroeber has been singled out as a pioneer.[48]

It is not certain when Kroeber first became interested in systems of communication other than speech. The development of writing and the alphabet was long a subject of special interest, both in its own right and as an example of processes of cultural change and growth. (Language phenomena always appealed to Kroeber in this regard.) The alphabet has a prominent place in both editions of his textbook, and the spread of writing systems provides several case histories for his concept of stimulus diffusion.[49] Linguistic phenomena indeed provide most of the examples in this article, for several other cases deal with the development of grammatical traditions (in Japan, in China, and in Greece vis-a-vis India), and the diffusion of patterns of quantitative meter and rime. His interest in sign language appears first in a review, later in a discussion of the theoretical import of the first results from research on sign language that he helped sponsor.[50]

Kroeber's interest in literature came early and continued throughout his life. His first publication was a short story, and one activity of his last years was to experiment with translating Heine into English, Housman into German. He was a conscious stylist in all his writing. Of poetry, he once said, "I soon learned that I had nothing to say—in verse," but he returned to creative prose in "Earth-maker," a fictional (Mohave) biography written for Elsie Clews Parson's collection of such, *American Indian Life* (1922), and he included it in his collected essays, as an experiment that was not repeated, to be sure, but yet one with perhaps untried possibilities.[51] His field work resulted in publication of many myths and tales from American Indians, of which the most significant for comparative literature (and linguistics in relation to it) are probably the later Mohave pieces.[52] In the second Mohave work he states his conception of stylistic analysis, a critical comment on the linguistic inadequacy of most of what has passed for stylistic study of Amerindian materials:

> Of course, in any strict sense of the word, style is choice of language and can therefore be fully conveyed only in the original idiom. Even considered translation from a text in the original by one who knows the language well will successfully seize only part of the style. . . . However, the majority of American Indian narrative material has been recorded in English or some other European language. And even the smaller fraction written and published in text in the original idiom has practically never been subject to genuinely stylistic word-by-word analysis. . . . The one outstanding exception is the description of Yokuts linguistic style by Stanley Newman. . . . Occasional other references to "style" in Indian narrative or song usually boil down essentially to matters of form or content . . . and not with linguistically selective form, which, it seems to me, is what literary style above all means.[53]

It is unfortunate that such comment should be necessary, but Radin's Winnebago work is almost the sole exception, half a century after Boas had insisted that stylistic study had to be undertaken with linguistic tools. Kroeber's other late publications reflect his interest in long-range perspective,[54] sometimes linked with statistics, especially as stimulated by the research of Josephine Miles.[55] She tells of his delight at discovering the possibility of tracing long-range temporal patterns in use of words through the concordances of the major English poets; a study in which he found such a pattern for the frequencies of *death*, *dead*, *die*, *dying* is now published.[56]

As to the history of linguistics, Kroeber of course contributed partly as a participant observer. Passages in his writings on predecessors and contemporaries such as Brinton Powell, Boas, Swanton, and Sapir are indispensable to the historian of American linguistics; and his personal correspondence with Sapir should be edited (as he himself wished) for the material of scientific relevance. His participation engaged him eventually in full-scale discussion of the authorship of the Powell classification, after allusions throughout his career to the role of the ornithologist Henshaw.[57] He contributed an historical sketch to the final report of the Committee on Research in Native American Languages,[58] and has helped place the discovery of Indo-European relationships in the context of general sience.[59] His chief contribution to the history of linguistics is his treatment of it as part of the general problem of the clustering of peaks in human achievement.[60] Most of the chapter, dealing with single lines of national philology, is successful, forming one of the best starting points for the student of history of linguistics. The end of the chapter, dealing with the recent period under the two main headings of "linguistics" and "comparative philology" suffers from closeness to our own time; the lists of great scholars seem partly arbitrary and incomplete. But if the general method were applied to lines of scholarship defined more precisely and consistently, the results would be quite valuable.

Two characteristic interests were statistics and style, as ways of ordering and grasping significance in phenomena. The 1919 monograph with Dixon sorted counts of cognates in tables. In the 1930's Kroeber's ethnology and linguistics took a decidedly statistical turn as he collaborated with H. E. Driver and later S. Klimek on the ethnological side, and with C. D. Chrétien on the linguistic side. The general mode of approach was the same, seeking statistical techniques for grouping historically related data, whether California Indian ethnological traits or Indo-European dialect features. The statistics in the middle period was part of its most solid single line of linguistic work, subgroupings within known language families.[61] And statistics played a large part in his later linguistic activity, as he encouraged its use by others,[62] and employed it in critical and constructive work himself.[63]

The word and concept of style came increasingly to the fore as Kroeber's work unfolded. It played a great part in his contributions to archaeology, entered into his treatment of other cultural problems (e.g., the stage of development of New World civilizations at time of conquest in *Cultural and Natural Areas* [1939]), and reached its fullest statement in his Messenger lectures at Cornell (1956). Much of the attention is to art; his doctoral dissertation had been on Arapaho decorative art, and a concern for art history found expression throughout his life. But the stylistic interest goes deeply into his linguistic work as well, and language figures in his major application of the concept of style to civilizations. In the central chapter among the published lectures, Kroeber concluded:

> I have faith that a greatly enlarged understanding of civilizations as macrophenomena is attainable, and that it will include comprehension of the part played in their constitution by style.[64]

And in reaching that conclusion, he stated:

> That the members of our civilization and of others are very little aware of total style need not discourage us much. Every human language has such a patterned style—we call it its grammar—of which the speakers are unaware while speaking, but which can be discovered by analysis and can be formulated. The coherence of a grammar is never total or ideal, but is always considerable; it certainly much exceeds a catalogue of random items. Cultures are larger, more varied and complicated sets of phenomena than languages, as well as more substantive and less autonomous. But the two are interrelated—in fact, language is obviously a part of culture, and probably its precondition. So the structure of cultures, like that of languages, also seems potentially describable in terms of an over-all patterning.[65]

For the most part, style is a humanistic concept, statistics a scientific tool, but for Kroeber there was no clash between the two. Statistics sometimes served in the description of style, and both were means to the main end of discovering the order in phenomena. Indeed, Kroeber's work stands as an example of how the clash between the two cultures of science and the humanities, of which Sir Charles Snow has written, can be resolved in the pursuit of linguistics and anthropology, the two disciplines which have both humanistic and scientific roots. Unlike narrow partisans of science, Kroeber never rejected significant data on the grounds of maintaining the purity of certain methods; unlike narrow partisans of the humanities, he never rejected useful methods on the grounds of maintaining the purity of certain data. He often commented on the importance of linguistics as an example for anthropology and the study of culture, as providing a model and hope for the scientific treatment of humanistic materials,[66] sometimes with regard to historical, sometimes descriptive work. It is notable that the "Index of principal topical cross-references" to his book, *The Nature of Culture*, contains as its only linguistic item: "Language as an example for culture." The citations are mostly to the argument that the study of language exemplifies the study of cultural phenomena in purely cultural terms, and their understanding through pattern and historical context.

As the dean of American anthropology, Kroeber became involved in its discussions of linguistic questions at conferences and in various volumes. Two such questions were the general relation of language to culture, and the special relation proposed by Whorf. Kroeber was senior author of the chief American treatment of the concept of culture, wherein literally hundreds of authors are cited; but strangely, the section on the general relation of culture to language does not mention Kroeber's own statements.[67] His view is manifest, however, in his textbook and many other writings: though often distinct in practice, language is part of culture, sometimes an especially significant part. In his textbook chapter on language emerge his views on the unconscious nature of cultural patterns, the role of the individual in history, and the sane attitude toward cultural relativism (1923, 125-33). And the concluding review of the *Culture* monograph has an important section that begins: "The clearest case is furnished by linguistics."[68]

On the hypothesis associated with Whorf, Kroeber took always a cautious view, as shown in his direct comments at the Wenner-Gren conference of 1952, and at the special conference in Chicago in 1953.[69] His last comments were.

> As soon as we learn how to approach the problem with varying depth of focus . . . it will probably prove both "true" and "false" at different levels. . . . I do not believe that at the present time the Whorfian problem can be solved by tests or experiments any more than by analysis: both evidence and arguments simply do not meet counterevidence or argument . . . a new basic approach will be needed for a pertinent answer to this intriguing and important problem.[70]

Whorf's proposed language-culture correlations called to Kroeber's mind such attempts at supersummative patterns as those of Spengler, and his book on style and civilization suggests that his own new basic approach to the problem would have been to trace linguistic and cultural patterns historically, looking for congruences but not determinisms. The gist of his thought seems to have been to regard language as an example of culture, and for the study of culture, but not as its matrix. Certainly his bent was toward the working out of linguistic patterns in their own terms with larger correlations or summations to follow. This is especially clear in his treatment of two problems. One is parallel: reviewing an attempt at cultural and psychological interpretation of music, he wrote:

> The author appears to have had a feeling that a song could best be studied in relation to its place in the culture. Ultimately, this feeling is correct. But in its first aspect a song presents a musical problem and must be brought into relation with other musical material. It is probably only after the music and the religion of the Sioux have been separately worked out with some care that endeavors to determine the relation between the two can be seriously fruitful. . . . In other words, a piece of music associated with a certain cultural activity is first of all music, secondly a piece of culture, and only lastly and indirectly an expression of personal emotion.[71]

The parallel (*mutatis mutandis*) to G. L. Trager's formulation of the Whorfian problem is almost exact.[72] And Kroeber dealt just this way with the cognitive aspect of kinship, which is perhaps the language-and-culture problem par excellence of American anthropology. He insisted on the cognitive import of kin terms as part of language, but also on their degree of autonomy of other parts of culture, such that the problem was always, having worked out the pattern of each in its own terms, to discover the degree of fit, rather than to take one as determinant of the other. Again, the concept of style and historical context enter: kin terms, as unconscious systems of classificatory thought, are "styles of logic in a limited field of universal occurrence.[73]

The several conferences and volumes during the early part of the nineteen-fifties involved Kroeber in fresh currents of anthropological discussion about language, and therein is the prelude or turning point for his increased linguistic activity. In the first half of the decade his published linguistic work consisted mostly of comments and discussions for such occasions, although he had begun to work again on early field data. (In 1951 he obtained a grant to aid completion of linguistic and ethnologic researches on California Indians.) The second five years of the decade saw a spurt of linguistic publication. Some of it was the bringing out of California materials.[74] Most striking were the papers on new results and approaches in lexicostatistics and typology.[75]

Kroeber was responding to, and helping to encourage, an emerging trend. What he perceived is best summarized in his own words: "Linguistics has begun the return to (1) typology and classification, (2) semantics."[76] The interest in semantics, or meaning, was a serious one; in his own contribution to the question of the differential stability of semantic classes of stems, he praised lexicostatistics for helping bring meaning back into linguistics more definitely,[77] and in a discussion of relations between linguistics and anthropology, singled out meaning for consideration as "one kind of content, one body of phenomena, which language and culture indubitably share.[78] But fresh ideas on classification and historical interpretation were what engaged him most, and the changing content of his engagement illuminates his life's work. What began as a continued concern with statistical methods of subgrouping and achieving time depth within a genetic perspective led into a new typological perspective (with increased weight given to diffusion). This was a development that had come full circle, for the California work had begun with typological and diffusional interpretation.

The narrative sequence is somewhat misleading, however, and to understand fully Kroeber's historical work (his chief linguistic love) and to appreciate its value as a legacy, one must realize that each of the three main modes of historical interpretation for linguistic resemblances, genetic, areal, typological, had for him deep and lasting roots, the typological in his love of extrication of pattern, the areal in his ethnology, the genetic in his regard for its ordering power.[79] All had a part to play in his concern for understanding through classification and context. The key to the shifts in priority of attention is that Kroeber, never a partisan of one mode of interpretation against another, worked and recommended according to his sense of the weight of evidence as to the most productive direction of effort at a given time. He was quick to sense diminishing returns; at the same time he seldom abandoned an interest, but kept it at hand (or let it lie fallow).

This capacity for a mixed strategy is one enduring significance of his historical work, and there are other values for us now in his use of each mode of interpretation. In typological work he had a skill for concise characterization of a language that is worth emulating, and he demonstrated an approach still waiting further development in Amerindian linguistics, when he aligned Yokuts and Yuki, point-for-point, putting differences of structure into relief and also showing a commonalty of type within the wider North American context.[80] His last ethnological monograph applied the same approach, and, although he had known Yurok culture for half a century, he found that the controlled comparison gave him a deeper insight into it. He hoped the approach would be developed by others, so organizing in a new way the accumulated rich data on North American cultures, a hope that was part of his general concern in his last writings for the extension of taxonomy, in culture and language, as the indispensable task.[81] And in relating typology to diversity, Kroeber maintained a balance between extremes that it would be well to emulate. In much of the present century there has been a tide toward uniqueness and incomparability; now there is a swelling of emphasis on the essential sameness of languages. Kroeber consistently related his descriptions of individual languages to the concepts and terms of the general linguistics of the time, and where the facts required, participated vigorously in the trend (set by Boas in the Introduction to his *Handbook of American Indian Languages*) to highlight relativity and explode biased generalizations;[82] and one of his last statements cautioned against premature statement of universals, and against stretching recognition of their importance into a tacit claim that they are of sole or even primary concern.[83] Yet he made no fetish of diversity or exceptions; inadequate general concepts and terms had to be attacked, so that more adequate ones could replace them. Indeed, he maintained that the goal of an individual description was to place the language in the context of general linguistics. The attitude is clear in early critiques of typological terminology. He rejected biased use of a general term such as "incorporation":

> It is thoroughly misleading to designate the same process respectively "composition" and "incorporation" according as one has in mind his own or other forms of speech. Some day philologists will approach their profession not with the assumption that language must differ in kind or in being relatively better or worse, but with the assumption that exactly the same fundamental processes run through them all, and with the realization that it is only by starting from the conception of their essential unity of type and method that their interesting and important diversities can be understood.[84]

But he likewise rejected ad hoc machinery to fit each case, and in doing so went beyond Boas (or beyond Boas as commonly interpreted and followed) to a position just beginning to be occupied by the advance guard of American linguistics at the present time. In a discussion of the structure of the Algonkin verb, Kroeber maintained that to describe each language sui generis was not enough, that the repudiation of frameworks misleadingly extended from other languages was only a first step. If traditional Indo-European categories did not fit Algonkin, it would be meaningless to invent a novel set for Algonkin alone:

> The determination of what they [Indo-European and Algonkin] have in common, involving as it does the recognition of that in which they are different, is an essential purpose of the study of both: for whether our interest lies in the problem of the nature or that of the origin of human speech, a classification is involved. In its widest ultimate aspect philology is concerned not with Algonkin as such nor with Indo-European as such but with all languages. Only when speech in general, its scope and its methods, are

better understood will both Algonkin and Indo-European, or for that matter any particular group of languages be more truly understandable. The real aim of the study of any American tongue, as well as the aim of any deeper research in Indo-European philology, must therefore be the more precise and fundamental determination of their relations to all other languages: and this necessitates concepts and terms which are applicable in common. It is impossible to characterize the wolf in terms of his skeleton, the elephant of his embryology, the whale of his habits, and then to construct a classification which will help to reveal the inherent nature, the development, or the origin of the animal kingdom.[85]

The point of view of the concluding metaphor is of a piece with that of his last article in *Language*. The typological perspective was there, if largely latent, through the intervening period. Similarly the areal perspective persisted, in the broad sense of tying linguistic phenomena to the map and inferring significance from their geographical relationships. As a matter of principle, Kroeber insisted on language as one criterion in the areal classification of cultures, as against primarily ecological approaches.[86] And areal perspective led him to an original contribution to lexicostatistic theory.[87] Salishan had been recognized as a family very early, Hokan late and with dispute, yet glottochronology showed similar time depths for both. Pointing out the contiguity of most Salishan languages, the isolation of most Hokan languages, Kroeber argued that the percentages of retention could be the same, but the sources of the replacement different. For a Salishan language most innovations would be shared with other Salishan languages, most borrowings Salishan in origin, keeping relationship apparent; while for a Hokan language, most borrowings would be non-Hokan, innovations unique, obscuring relationship. Geographical distribution thus explained the disparity between the traditional classification and impression of internal diversity, based on inspection of vocabulary lists, and the new glottochronologic time depths. A later article made use of another connection between time perspective and areal distribution, using the principle that "close uniformity of speech throughout wide areas must be due to recency of spread" to interpret a number of North American cases (Algonkin, Teton within Dakota, Navaho within Apachean, Chemehuevi and Kawaiisu within Southern Paiute, Northern Paiute and Mono, Yokuts, Wintu).[88] Nor was the diffusional aspect of areal resemblances lost from sight. He pointed up the problem of grammatical diffusion as the final topic of his presidential address,[89] He was sensible of Boas' contention against Sapir that grammar might be significantly diffused, but took it as a methodological counter-argument for which Boas had never developed sufficient evidence. He saw the problem as an empirical one that warranted systematic investigation to decide among the alternative interpretations of Ray's work (that IE was exceptional as a group, that Melanesian was exceptional, or that Ray's analysis was wrong). Thus it is no surprise that in his last article in *Language* he responded to increasing evidence from his Berkeley colleagues of the importance of diffusion with reappraisal of Boas as possibly right.

It must be noted here that Kroeber's role with regard to genetic and areal interpretation in Amerindian linguistics has been largely ignored or misinterpreted. The usual picture is one of Boas holding out almost in isolation for the importance of diffusion and areal interpretation against Sapir and others hell-bent for long-range genetic connections, later being consoled by news of the areal perspective of many European scholars.[90] Because Kroeber helped discover new genetic relationships beyond those of Powell, accepted many of Sapir's results, and criticized Boas' refusal to consider new evidence or value historical reconstruction,[91] it has been overlooked that he stood as a third party to the dispute. Not only was his approach pragmatic rather than partisan, but the principle of areal relationships in language was stated clearly in his work far earlier than the writings of the Prague school on Sprachbünde, and earlier, so far as I can ascertain, than in any writing of Boas.[92] And, unlike Boas, who acted mainly as a methodological critic, Kroeber helped make substantive contributions to areal interpretation in language. Indeed, the kind of work that he did with Dixon in the first decade of the century still largely waits to be taken up again; the mapping of Amerindian linguistic traits is almost all still to be done.

In genetic classification, Kroeber's middle view is a healthy legacy, as has been noted; he was open to new findings, yet distinguished carefully between the proven and the prophetic,[93] and sought to work within the range where consolidation and integration with other lines of historical evidence were possible.

In reappraising Boas' views on diffusion more sympathetically, Kroeber implied that the new genetic results of Haas and others led only to anarchy, not in time to an ordered, if novel, overall picture. He withdrew the implication,[94] but the heart of his view would seem still to be in the passage beginning:

> The exit from this confounding of the long established order seems to be more comparison and more taxonomy, and let the genetic and the influencing chips lie where they fall. . . . When genetic similarity is strong enough to be certain, its findings should of course continue to be accepted. But when the similarity dilutes into mere possibilities which are so scant and scattering that they might be due to remnants of original unity, or to contact influences or borrowings, or to both sets of causes, some broader strategy of attack is indicated.[95]

Kroeber's developing views, as presented in the conclusion of this article, need some clarification. The conclusion, for example, seems directed primarily to persuasion of those whose main interest is genetic connection, by suggesting that other taxonomic methods may probe historical connections even further into the past, whereas the earlier portions of §8 (15-18) are general, implying a systematic taxonomy in both language and culture that would apply at all time levels, remote and near. But it is a tribute to the man that his latest work has the vigor of growth. What beside Greenberg's typological indices he would have accepted into a program for "achieving a sound linguistic taxonomy of breadth and depth . . . by operating with mechanisms that transcend the concept of genetic unity" (21), we cannot now know. Clearly, however, the core of the program is that with which he began: to extract all possible historical significance from linguistic phenomena, operating within known genetic relationships, transcending them with typology, always interpreting in reference to the place of things in time and space, always seeking the largest accessible context in time.

Kroeber's lasting contribution is almost wholly through his own substantive work and example, not, as with Boas and Sapir, also through an impact on descriptive method and on students trained by himself. Kroeber seemed always somewhat shy of the technical core of "philology" or linguistics, as containing methods whose rigor he admired but with which he did not feel wholly conversant, or free, certainly not to the point of modifying them (his use of statistics is the one exception). He referred to himself as "something of a philologist (= linguist)" in his review of Sapir's *Language*, and at most claimed no hesitancy with regard to a content he thoroughly knew, that of California Indian language (*Handbook*, vi). In this hesitancy to claim the mantle of full-fledged linguist, he was but honest. His training in linguistic analysis came from a self-taught pioneer well before the codification of descriptive methods, and his student contact with the comparative method was not, like Sapir's, first-hand. Whether his bilingualism in German and English helped or hurt, he had no special phonetic gift, and told stories on himself in this regard; nor was extensive phonetic training adequate to the western Amerindian languages available to him at the time. Moreover, his task in his years of field work was never solely linguistics, for had it been, he undoubtedly would have set himself to master and develop descriptive linguistic methods, rather than use those at hand; but he was responsible for a broad range of data, and his personal sweep of interest reinforced this commitment. Here again is the lesson that something of a double standard must be invoked in judging the linguistic contributions made by field workers in the course of other duties, the value of the information being set against the imperfections of the record or the lack of excitement in the method.

Kroeber's massive contributions of data and interpretation show how greatly he felt the fascination of linguistics, despite his hesitancy. If any serious criticism can be fairly made of his California career, it is that he did not see to the technical training of others during so much of the period in which he dominated the Berkeley department. In later years he insisted that no anthropology department could claim to be first-rate without an active linguistic specialist, but not so in practice during his middle years.[96] In the first years of the Berkeley department, linguistics was a major part of the instruction offered, reflecting concern with Amerindian languages and Goddard's interest in instrumental phonetics. After Goddard left in 1909, no other linguist was hired, except for Sapir's presence as Lecturer in the summer of 1915. Native speakers were given encouragement and training, and many students did incidental linguistic work, but the only specialists were J. Alden Mason (Univeristy Fellow in 1910 1911, Research Fellow in 1916-1917), L. S. Freeland at the turn of the 1920's, and C. F. Voegelin in the early 1930's. The Hearst memorial volume (1923) and Kroeber's festschrift (1936) contain but a sprinkling of linguistic contributions, a sharp contrast to the quantity and, in some measure, the quality of the special number of *Language* (1956). In the first years there were few or no graduate students, but the influx of the middle years coincided with a period in which anthropology was one of the few settings in which linguistics could be carried on at the university (philology was under a cloud there for some time after the First World Far). The influx unfortunately coincided also with the dip in Kroeber's own linguistic activity.

In the first half-century of work with Amerindian languages at the University of California, then, after the extensive activity in the first two decades by Kroeber, supplemented by that of Dixon, Goddard, Sapir, and Harrington, there came decades that saw field work by Harrington of the BAE, by a Boas student (Reichard on Wiyot), Sapir students (Li on Mattole, Newman on Yokuts), Sapir himself (a summer with Hupa), and other friends and associates of the department (especially Paul Radin, Jaime de Angulo and his wife Nancy Freeland, and Hans Uldall); but, except for Freeland and Voegelin, none were the University's own products. A fresh, sustained impetus to the increasingly critical rescue work, and to the training of linguists to do it, had to wait until the formation of the Survey of California Indian Languages by Mary Haas and Murray Emeneau early in the 1950's. In the intervening period Kroeber and his department concentrated on ethnology and culture history. Kroeber still listed himself as actively instructing in Indian languages (*ACLS Bull.*, 1939, *29:*119), but it was the Committee on Research in American Native Languages, sparked by Boas, that supported and fought for the urgently needed descriptive work in California and elsewhere, whereas Kroeber conceived and carried through a massive and effective ethnographic salvage program, that of the Culture Element Surveys. It would be jejune to note all this, were it not that students are part of a scholar's record, and that the record here involves Kroeber's role in American linguistics. When the study of language in future years shows the fruit of seeds sown by him, it will be through the work of men, trained by others, who have responded to his insights and perspective. So far as this will be due to the dip in linguistic activity of his middle years, it is compensated by his encouragement of younger men in his last years, and his attraction of them by his own youthful freshness of mind, for which there are countless anecdotes and illustrations. And if with him a whole historical period has passed,[97] much of its value he consciously transmitted in his person. He knew well how much a value must change to remain the same.

The dip in linguistic activity must be seen in proportion. The middle period was scant only relative to the standards of productivity of someone like Kroeber—not like an artist's period of silence, but like a period with few portraits from a painter who had turned most of his attention to murals. Like Boas, Kroeber ranged so widely and individually that any conventional framework is too narrow, and to estimate him within one is an error. Perhaps he will not suffer like Boas, who has often been judged anachronistically by social anthropologists who forget that his major chosen fields were physical anthropology, folklore, and linguistics. Yet to evaluate Kroeber one must bring to mind so many contributions in method, theory, and data in so many lines of work that the imagination can hardly hold them all together, although the character and greatness of the man lie in the whole. He was in his own right a cultural world of values, pattern, and distinctive style, a world that teaches that value and meaning may sometimes emerge more from the whole of a dedicated career than from any one striking event. This is perhaps the core of his significance for the future relations of linguistics and anthropology. Kroeber's work embodies the view that linguistic research is intrinsic to (and a responsibility of) anthropology. His work carries implicit definitions of linguistic anthropology as, simply and broadly, study of language within an anthropological context, and of the linguistic anthropologist as one who uses linguistic techniques and data to answer anthropological questions. Sometimes these questions are straightforwardly descriptive ("What is that language like?"), or classificatory ("Where does that language belong?"), sometimes more complex; but language being part of culture, language data are cultural data, and there is no necessary chasm between the study of the two. Almost any general anthropological question can be asked of language, some can be best asked of language, and some cannot be answered without the aid of language. The implicit definition of linguistic anthropology, the "figure in the carpet" of Kroeber's linguistic work, accounts for the diversity of his studies, varying across phonetic detail, grammatical typology, semantic components, speech development of children, statistical subgrouping, and more. All were germane to anthropological questions. Kroeber is the best example to set against the attitude of some anthropologists that linguistics is something apart, reserved for those with a miraculous ear or the mind of a mathematical genius. He respected the rigor of linguistics, but he also practiced it wherever he could, and showed that the main thing is a sense of problem. The need in anthropology is not so much to give anthropologists a training in linguistic techniques, although that is important, practically and intellectually. The great need is for anthropologists to have a sense of anthropological problems in the data of linguistics. Where this sense exists, the rest can follow.

1. A full bibliography of Kroeber's writings appears in the *American Anthropologist* (Gibson and Rome, 1961). At the request of the Editor of *Language* I have not tried to duplicate part of that bibliography, but cite particular writings as they are discussed. The abbreviations used include *AA: American Anthropologist*; *SJA: Southwestern Journal of Anthropology*; *UCP-AAE: University of California Publications in American Archaeology and Ethnology*; *UCP-AR: University of California Publications, Anthropological Records*; and, as short titles for some of the books cited above, *Handbook, Cultural and Natural Areas, Configurations.*

Although in the other articles in this book, footnotes have been incorporated into the text, as a practical necessity the nearly 100 notes of Hymes' original article have been retained as such. Also the style of the original publication has been retained in some respects. The first four notes have been omitted and the remainder renumbered accordingly.

2. The work of John R. Swanton, in Essays in Historical anthropology of North America, *Smithsonian Miscellaneous Collections, 100:*2 (1940); a graduate student at Harvard, Swanton had come to Columbia to learn linguistics, and wrote his dissertation, one of Harvard's first in anthropology, on the morphology of the Chinook verb.

3. Foreword, in D. H. Hymes (Ed.), *Language in Culture and Society: A Reader in Anthropology and Linguistics.*

4. Franz Boas, The Man, *AA, 45*(3):7 (1943).

5. An Outline of the History of American Indian Linguistics, *ACLS Bulletin, 29:*119 (1939).

6. E.g., in The Chumash and Costanoan Languages, *UCP-AAE, 9*(2):237-271 (1910).

7. Thus, "Since there is practically no Nisenan linguistic material accessible beyond old word lists, the vocabulary obtained is given in full"—The Valley Nisenan, *UCP-AAE, 24:*289 (1929); "There was no intention of presenting the imperfect lexical material thus obtained, until it was realized that no vocabulary of Washo has ever been published, and that the determination of the language by Powell as constituting an independent family, however correct it may be, has never been rendered verifiable by the general availability of the information used for the determination"—The Washo Language of East Central California and Nevada, *UCP-AAE, 4:*308 (1907), and Notes on the Ute Language, *AA, 10:*74 (1908).

8. E.g., "Consequently an occasion for obtaining information as to these two languages, presented by the visit to San Francisco . . . of a number of Shoshoni and Bannock was made use of"—The Bannock and Shoshoni Languages, *AA, 11:*266 (1909).

9. E.g., Juan Dolores (a Papago) and Gilbert Natchez (a Paiute); see *UCP-AAE, 20* (1923).

10. The Speech of a Zuni Child, *AA, 18:*529-539 (1916).

11. Phonetic Constituents of the Native Languages of California, *UCP-AAE, 10:*1-12 (1911); Phonetic Elements of the Mohave Language, *UCP-AAE, 10:*45-96 (1911); Phonetics of the Micronesian Language of the Marshall Islands, *AA, 13:*380-393 (1911); Phonetic Elements of the Diegueno Language, *UCP-AAE, 17:*177-188 (1914); cf. also, Visible Speech, *Scientific American, 112:*471 (1915).

12. A good example is found in the history of gradual recognition of the members of the voiceless lateral order; the matter is mentioned by Kroeber (*UCP-AAE, 10:*11 [1911]) and is salient in Boas' work on the Northwest Coast.

13. He had particularly in mind his first colleague at Berkeley, Pliny Earle Goddard, who, fresh from a degree in philology with Benjamin Ide Wheeler, combined Athabaskan field work and laboratory phonetics, using equipment modelled on that current

in French research. Goddard's study of Hupa (*UCP-AAE, 5:*1-20 [1907]) was probably the first instrumental phonetics done with an American Indian language, and Kroeber, wishing to extend the use of such methods with American languages, chose Mohave because of familiarity with it through earlier fieldwork (*UCP-AAE, 10:*45-46 [1911]).

14. On Alternating Sounds, *AA, 2:*47-53 (1889), reprinted in Frederica de Laguna (Ed.), *Selected Papers from the American Anthropologist, 1888-1920* (New York: Harper & Row, 1960), partly at Kroeber's recommendation. Boas used psychophysical data to explain the supposed alternation of pronunciation as due to alternating apperception of a fixed sound partly resembling each of two different sounds in the observer's speech. The paper, although falling short of a phonemic conception, is a remarkable anticipation of modern work on phonic interference.

15. *AA, 13:*393 (1911): in all essentials the Marshallese phonetic traits "are duplicated in the Pima-Papago language of Arizona, and several individual features recur in a number of American languages; but as regards the allied tongues of Malayo-Polynesian stock, the Marshall dialect seems to be phonetically greatly specialized."

16. Native Languages of California, *AA, 5:*2 (1903).

17. The convenience of the first exhaustive and entirely definite classification was so great that it was soon looked upon as fundamental, and the incentive to tamper with it was lost"—Kroeber, *UCP-AAE, 11:*288 (1915); cf. *UCP-AAE, 16:*49 (1919).

18. The Determination of Linguistic Relationship, *Anthropos, 8:*389-401 (1913), and statements in other writings of the period, e.g., *UCP-AAE,* 9:415 (1911).

19. The Numeral Systems of California, *AA, 9:*690 (1907).

20. Its only successor as a systematic study was inspired by two former students of Kroeber; see V. D. Hymes, Athapaskan Numeral Systems, *IJAL, 21:*26-45 (1955).

21. "A principle that appears prominent in the facts that have been presented is that of territorial continuity of characteristics. A feature is rarely found in only one language. When it does occur in several stocks, as is usually the case, these are not scattered at random and more or less detached from each other, but generally form a continuous or nearly continuous area, however irregular its outline may be. This principle applies as well to types of languages as to single characteristics"—*AA, 5:*21 (1903); "The accompanying maps showing the geographical distribution by linguistic families of the various methods of numeral formation, sum up the material collected and the generalizations stated. They are in no need of a commentary beyond a notice of the extent to which the principle of territorial continuity of characteristics obtains. While diversity and irregularity seem the chief features of the maps, yet the areas in which similar numeral methods occur are not randomly scattered, but with few exceptions are geographically continuous. This makes it clear that, with but little borrowing of specific words distinct families have considerably influenced each other as regards their processes of numeral formation"—*AA, 9:*671 (1907).

22. *AA, 13:*319 (1911). (The passage was quoted in n. 19 above.)

23. *UCP-AAE, 10*(1):1-12 (1911).

24. Introduction, *UCP-AAE, 4:*252-253 (1907).

25. *UCP-AAE, 11:*287-289 (1915) are pages of special value for understanding this period; see also *SMC, 100:*7 (1940).

26. *UCP-AAE, 11:*288 (1915). Kroeber's contributions to this work are found in The Chumash and Costanoan Languages, *UCP-AAE, 9:*237-271 (1910), on Miwok and Costanoan; The Languages of the Coast of California North of San-Francisco, *UCP-AAE, 9:*273-435 (1911), on presumption of Yurok-Wiyot connection; Relationship of the Indian Languages of California, *AA, 14:*691 (1912; with Dixon); The Relationship of the Indian languages of California, *Science, 37:*225 (1911); New Linguistic Families in California, *AA, 15:*647-655 (1913: with Dixon); Chontal, Seri, and Yuman, *Science, 40:*448 (1914); Serian, Tequistlatecan, and Hokan, *UCP-AAE, 11:*279-290 (1915); and the principal statement, Linguistic Families of California, *UCP-AAE, 16:*47-118 (1919; with Dixon).

27. *UCP-AAE, 16:*50 (1919).

28. *Lg., 32:*17-18 (1956).

29. The dialectic divisions of the Moquelumnan family in relation to the internal differentiation of other linguistic families of California, *AA, 8:*652-663 (1906).

30. *UCP-AAE, 12:*31-69 (1916).

31. Yurok Speech Usages, in Stanley A. Diamond (Ed.), *Culture in History: Essays in Honor of Paul Radin* (New York: Columbia University Press, 1960), pp. 993-999.

32. *JRAI, 39:*77-84 (1909).

33. See the papers by Lounsbury and Goodenough in the issue of *Language, 32*(1) (1956), dedicated to Kroeber. Kroeber's other important discussions of the problem are in his California Kinship Systems, *UCP-AAE, 12:*339-396 (1916); Kinship and History, *AA, 38:*338-341 (1936); Yurok and Neighboring Kin Term Systems, *UCP-AAE, 35:*15-22 (1934); Athabascan Kin Term Systems, *AA, 39:*602-608 (1937). The 1909, 1934, 1936, and 1937 papers are reprinted in *The Nature of Culture* (the 1937 paper only in part), with introductory comment (172-173).

34. " . . . the patterns have had each a history of its own as a pattern, just as the languages in which

they occur have had each a history of its own"—*Nature of Culture*, p. 200.

35. *AA*, *39:*608 (1937); *The Nature of Culture*, p. 209.

36. The sociological reconstructions are in G. P. Murdock, *Social Structure* (New York: Macmillan, 1949); the linguistic checks are H. Hoijer, Athapaskan Kinship Systems, *AA*, *58:*309-333 (1956), which give bifurcate collateral terms in the first ascending generation as against the generation type of terminology proposed by a follower of Murdock (see discussion in D. H. Hymes and H. E. Driver, On Reconstructing Proto-Athapaskan Kinship Terms, *AA*, *59:*151-155 [1957]), and G. H. Matthews, Proto-Siouan Kin Terms, *AA*, *61:*252-278 (1959), which gives an Omaha system where Murdock inferred a Crow.

37. *The Dial*, *72*(3):314-317 (March, 1922).

38. E.g., W. J. Entwistle, Pre-grammar? *Archivum Linguisticum*, *1:*117-125 (1949), and *Proceedings VII*[th] *International Congress of Linguists* (London, 1956), pp. 96, 392, 411; see pp. 394-396 of the latter for a statement in refutation by Bernard Bloch.

39. The Languages of the American Indian, *Popular Science Monthly*, *78:*500-515 (1911); *Anthropology* (1923), pp. 112-119.

40. *Essays*, xvii.

41. *AA*, *7:*579-593 (1905).

42. "The technique of modern philology has something superb about it. It is as austere as anything in the world. The work of an accepted leader like Brugmann is of an order unsurpassed in any branch of learning. But it cannot be popularized . . . [Here is where Sapir's book is new] . . . It is unique in its field, and is likely to become and long remain standard"—*The Dial*, *72*(3):314, 317 (1922).

43. This in 1923. Kroeber's distaste for antiquarianism and insistence on public relevance appear most strongly here: "obviously the heterogeneous leavings of several sciences will never weld into an organized and useful body of knowledge. . . . As a co-laborer on the edifice of fuller understanding, anthropology must find more of a task than filling with rubble the temporarily vacant spaces in the masonry that the sciences are rearing"—*Anthropology*, p. 2.

44. "Here, then, is a specific task and place in the sun for anthropology: the interpretation of these phenomena into which both organic and social causes enter. The untangling and determination and reconciling of these two sets of forces are anthropology's own. They constitute, whatever else it may undertake, the focus of its attention and an ultimate goal."—*Anthropology*, pp. 3-4.

45. Sections on The Biological and Historical Nature of Language, Problems of the Relation of Language and Culture, Period of the Origin of Language, *Anthropology*, pp. 106-110.

46. Sign and Symbol in Bee Communication, *Proceedings of the National Academy of Science*, *38:*753-757 (1952).

47. *Quarterly Review of Biology*, *3:*325-342 (1928); *SJA*, *11:*195-294 (1955).

48. *The Evolution of Man's Capacity for Culture*, Edited by J. N. Spuhler (Detroit, 1959), is inscribed as bringing up to date Kroeber's 1928 paper, and within the volume, Hockett's chapter on animal communication vis-à-vis language is dedicated to him.

49. *AA*, *42:*1-20 (1940).

50. Review of W. Tomkins, *Indian Sign Language*, in *AA*, *29:*127 (1927); Sign Language Inquiry, *IJAL*, *24:*1-9 (1958).

51. *The Nature of Culture*, pp. 263 ff.

52. Seven Mohave Myths, *UCP-AR*, *11:*1-70 (1948); A Mohave Historical Epic, *UCP-AR*, *11:*76-171 (1951).

53. A Mohave Historical Epic, *UCP-AR*, *11:*133 (1951).

54. The Novel in Asia and Europe, *UCP in Semitic and Oriental Studies*, *11:*233-241 (1951).

55. Parts of Speech in Periods of English Poetry, *PMLA*, *73:*309-314 (1958), a discussion of Miss Miles's work.

56. Theodora and A. L. Kroeber, Shropshire Revisited, *KASP*, *25:*1-18 (1961).

57. Kroeber, Systematic Nomenclature in Ethnology, *AA*, *7:*580 (1905); Some Relations of Linguistics and Ethnology, *Lg.*, *17:*288 (1940); Concluding Review, in Sol Tax *et al.* (Eds.), *An Appraisal of Anthropology Today* (Chicago: University of Chicago Press, 1953), p. 369; Powell and Henshaw: An Episode in the History of Ethnolinguistics, *AL*, *2*(4):1-5 (1960). The full-scale discussion in the last paper was prompted by W. C. Sturtevant, Authorship of the Powell Linguistic Classification, *IJAL*, *25:*196-199 (1959). The basis of the matter is a visit to Kroeber by Henshaw early in the century. In date and content Kroeber's own 1905 paper (cited above) corroborates his memory of the event 55 years later.

58. An Outline of the History of American Indian Linguistics, *ACLS Bulletin*, *29:*116-120 (1939).

59. Evolution, History, and Culture, in Sol Tax (Ed.), *Evolution after Darwin* (Chicago: University of Chicago Press, 1960), vol. 2, pp. 1-16; the section is "An Exception: Philology," pp 8-9.

60. Philology, *Configurations of Culture Growth* (Berkeley and Los Angeles: University of California Press, 1944), chap. 4, pp. 215-238.

61. Relationships of the Australian Languages, *Proc. Royal Sec. New S. Wales*, *57:*101-117 (1923); Uto-Aztecan Languages of Mexico, *Ibero-Americana*, *8* (1934); *Quantitative Classification of Indo-European Languages*, *Lg.*, *13:*83-103 (with Chrétien); of Mayan languages, in *Cultural and Natural Areas* (1939), pp. 112-114; The Statistical Technique and Hittite,

Lg., *15:*69-71 (1939; with Chrétien); Classification of the Yuman languages, *UCPL*, *1:*21-40 (1943).

62. E.g., "[there are] two new developments to chronicle, both of interest to cultural anthropologists in their results, and both using quantitative expression" (referring to lexicostatistics and Greenberg's typological indices)—History of Anthropological Thought, in W. L. Thomas (Ed.), *Current Anthropology* (Chicago: University of Chicago Press, 1955), pp. 296-297.

63. In lexicostatistics: Linguistic Time Depth Results So Far and Their Meaning, *IJAL*, *21:*91-104 (1955); Romance History and Glottochronology, *Lg.*, *34:*454-457 (1958); Reflections and Tests on Athabascan Glottochronology, *UCP-AAE*, *47:*241-258 (1959); Semantic Contribution of Lexicostatistics, *IJAL*, *27:*1-8 (1961). On Greenberg's quantitative typology, besides encouragement in Critical Summary and Comment, in R. E. Spencer (Ed.), *Method and Perspective in Anthropology: Papers in Honor of Wilson D. Wallis* (Minneapolis: University of Minnesota Press, 1954), pp. 273-299, and in *Lg.*, *36:*20-21 (1960), the first paper of an intended series, Typological Indices I: Ranking of Languages, *IJAL*, *26:*171-177 (1960).

64. *Style and Civilizations*, p. 107.

65. *Ibid.*, p. 106.

66. E.g., "Linguistics is a genuine natural science dealing with intangible phenomena. That it grew out of culture-bound contexts augurs well for the study of culture"—concluding review, in Sol Tax *et al.* (Eds.), *An Appraisal of Anthropology Today* (Chicago: University of Chicago Press, 1953), p. 368.

67. Kroeber and Clyde Kluckhohn, Culture: A Critical Review of Concepts and Definition, *Papers of the Peabody Musueum of American Archaeology and Ethnology* (Harvard University), *47*(1):115-124 (1952).

68. *Culture*, p. 188.

69. Concluding Review, in Sol Tax *et al.* (Eds.), *An Appraisal of Anthropology Today* (Chicago: University of Chicago Press, 1953), p. 370 (the Whorf correlations are not proved); comments passim in H. Hoijer (Ed.), *Language in Culture* (Chicago: University of Chicago Press, 1954), such as that the Whorf insights are very interesting but hard to prove (pp. 231-232) and need certain kinds of testing (p. 274).

70. Prepared comments on Clyde Kluckhohn, Notes on Some Anthropological Aspects of Communication, *Wenner-Gren Foundation Symposium*, *7* (1960). I am much indebted to the director of the Foundation, Paul Fejos, for copies of the paper and the comments.

71. Review of Frances Densmore, Teton Sioux Music, *AA*, *20:*446-450 (1918).

72. G. L. Trager, The Systematization of the Sapir-Whorf Hypothesis, *AL*, *1*(1):31-38 (1959).

73. *AA*, *38:*340 (1936).

74. An Atsugewi Word List, *IJAL*, *24:*203-204 (1958); Northern Yokuts, *AL*, 1(8):1-19 (1959); *The Sparkman Grammar of Luiseno*, (UCPL 16; 1960; with George Grace); Yurok Speech Usages (see n. 35); and two Yokuts monographs now in press. Kroeber also resumed work on Yuki, and one note reached print: Possible Athapaskan Influences on Yuki, *IJAL*, *25:*59 (1959).

75. Linguistic Time Depth Results So Far and Their Meaning, *IJAL*, *21:*91-104 (1955); Romance History and Glottochronology, *Lg.*, *34:*454-457 (1958); Reflections and Tests on Athabascan Glottochronology, Ethnographic Interpretations 8, *UCP-AAE*, *47:*241-258 (1959); Statistics, Indo-European, and Taxonomy, *Lg.*, *36:*1-21 (1960); Typological Indices I: Ranking of Languages, *IJAL*, *26:*171-177 (1959); Semantic Contribution of Lexicostatistics, *IJAL*, *27:*1-8 (1961).

76. Addendum, *Report on Anthropological Horizons* (preliminary version) 70 (Wenner-Gren Foundation for Anthropological Research, 1960).

77. *IJAL*, *27:*8 (1961).

78. Foreword, *Language in Culture and Society: A Reader in Anthropology and Linguistics*.

79. E.g., "The situation is one of those not infrequently arising in which the philologist, and only he, can come to the ethnologist's or historian's rescue. A dozen randomly preserved facts from the history of civilization of a nation are almost certain to be so disconnected as to allow only of the most general or doubtful inferences; the same number of words, if only they and their meanings are carefully written down, may, if there are more fully cognate tongues, suffice to determine with reasonable assurance the provenience and the main outlines of the national existence of a lost people. The student of history who permits the difference of material and technique of the sister science philology to lead him into the lax convenience of disregarding it as something alien and useless, withdraws his hand from one of the most productive tools within his reach—on occasion his only serviceable instrument"—*Handbook*, p. 281; Kroeber considered the *Handbook* a history.

80. The Yokuts and Yuki Languages, *Boas Anniversary Volume* (New York: 1906), pp. 64-79: The conclusion states in part: "the degree to which their similarities are fundamental is quickly and convincingly apparent when they are even superficially compared with such languages as Iroquois, Algonquin, Shoshonean, Eskimo, Nahuatl, Wakashan, Chinook, Salish, or Siouan" (p. 78),

81. E.g., "I feel that the study of both culture and language is in crying need, in its own right, of far more sytematic classification of their multifarious phenomena. Perhaps we have had a surplus of bright ideas and a shortage of consistent ordering and comparison of our data"—*Lg.*, *36:*17 (1960); "The situation is made more difficult by the fact that

anthropologists still tend to value personal expertise, technical virtuosity, cleverness in novelty, and do not yet clearly recognize the fundamental value of the humble but indispensable task of classifying—that is, structuring—our body of knowledge, as biologists did begin to recognize it two hundred years ago"—Evolution, History, and Culture, in Sol Tax (Ed.), *Evolution after Darwin* (Chicago: University of Chicago Press, 1960), vol. 2, p. 11.

82. His repeated discussions of the use of suppletive stems for number in verbs, of the relations of objective and subjective forms to each other and to verbs, of the presence or absence of pronominal incorporation, are all with an eye toward then current typological generalizations about Amerindian languages.

83. Prepared comment on Clyde Kluckhohn, Notes on Some Anthropological Aspects of Communication (1960).

84. Noun Incorporation in American Languages, *Verh. der XVI. Internationalen Amerikanisten-Kongress* (Wien, 1909), pp. 569-576; Noun Composition in American Languages, *Anthropos, 5:*204-218 (1910). When Sapir then showed that "incorporation" could be given precise descriptive content (The Problem of Noun Incorporation in American languages, *AA, 13:*250-282 [1911]), Kroeber, noting that Sapir's explication related it to stem-compounding, offered a fourfold typology of stem-compounding in terms of parts of speech that did away with need for the term "incorporation" altogether: Incorporation as a Linguistic Process, *AA, 13:*577-584 (1911).

85. Arapaho Dialects, *UCP-AAE, 12:*71-138, esp. 93, (1916), In the monograph Kroeber accepts rehabilitation of terms such as "incorporation" and "polysynthetic," as convenient designations for particular applications of general processes (pp. 91-92).

86. "Language itself is a natural part of culture from one point of view, though it can also be separated off for other purposes of study. I have therefore not hesitated to put Paiute and Walapai into separate subareas and even main areas in my maps. It is true that Yuman speech (Walapai) would be as practicable north of the Grand Canyon as south of it or for that matter in the Colorado River bottomlands; any historically particularized language is in its nature impervious to such interadaptation with environment. Consideration of speech may therefore tend to blur the sharpness of classificatory conceptualization of culture. But as long as speech is in culture, and cultures are what we are classifying, speech obviously belongs in the picture"—Comments to P. Kirchoff, Gatherers and Farmers, *AA, 56:*556-559 (1954).

87. Linguistic Time Depth Results So Far and Their Meaning, *IJAL, 21:*91-105 (1955).

88. Recent Ethnic Spreads, *UCP-AAE, 47:*235-310 (1959).

89. *Lg., 17:*290-291 (1940), regarding Ray's work on Melanesian; Kroeber had reviewed Ray's book a quarter-century before, *AA, 29:*705 (1927).

90. Roman Jakobson, Franz Boas' Approach to Language, *IJAL, 10:*188-195 (1944). The disagreement between Boas and Sapir and the theoretical issue have been explicated by Morris Swadesh, Diffusional Cumulation and Archaic Residue as Historical Explanations, *SJA, 7:*1-21 (1951).

91. E.g., in *IJAL, 21:*92-93 (1955), and *SMC, 100:*7 (1940).

92. See n. 25.

93. Cf. *Lg., 17:*289 (1940); *SMC, 100:*7 (1940).

94. "I do not think the overall anarchy will be permanent—more like a turn of the tide: still flowing out and the new flood coming in. I'm not in the least pessimistic over it; stimulated rather"—Personal communication, July 12, 1960.

95. *Lg., 36:*19-20 (1960).

96. Sapir spent a year before his degree as Research Fellow at Berkeley, but: "Sapir's stay fell in the terminal year of a second period of affluence and research activity provided for the Department and Museum of Anthropology by Regent Phoebe Apperson Hearst. In the summer of 1908 came a renewed and deeper cut in resources, with the University assuming responsibility for all staff salaries; this circumstance rendered a continuation of Sapir's connection with the University impossible. In fact the staff of Anthropology—Museum and Department—was reduced to the two original academic appointees: Goddard and myself. A year later, Goddard, depressed by the contracted prospects at Berkeley, accepted an appointment with the American Musuem in New York."—Kroeber's preface, E. Sapir and M. Swadesh, *Yana Dictionary*, edited by M. R. Haas (UCPL 22. v; 1960).

97. C. Lévi-Strauss, *L'Express* (Paris, October 20, 1960), pp. 32-33,

REFERENCE NOTE

This note is organized in two parts: (A) concerning Kroeber; (B) concerning the history of linguistics and of linguistic work in anthropology.

A. KROEBER

For a brief but excellent discussion of Kroeber's linguistic work, see Hoijer

(1960). For discussion of other aspects of his work, see Rowe (1962) and Steward (1961). For his complete bibliography as of mid-1961, see Gibson and Rowe (1961).

References not in the general bibliography:

GIBSON, ANN J., and JOHN H. ROWE

1961. A Bibliography of the Publications of Alfred Louis Kroeber. *AA, 63:* 1060-1087.

HOIJER, HARRY

1960. Alfred L. Kroeber 1876-1960. *AL, 2* (8): 31-32.

ROWE, JOHN H.

1962. Alfred Louis Kroeber 1876-1960. *American Antiquity, 27:* 395-415.

STEWARD, JULIAN H.

1961. Alfred Louis Kroeber 1876-1960. *AA, 63:* 1038-1060.

B. HISTORY OF LINGUISTICS AND LINGUISTIC WORK IN ANTHROPOLOGY

The present surge of interest in the history of linguistics will result in a number of new and valuable treatments. At present no really satisfactory general study is available, but a number of relatively adequate and accessible accounts can be consulted, such as Arens (1955), Benfey (1869), Bloomfield (1914, chap. 10), Carroll (1953, pp. 15-23, 246-268), Cassirer (1923, chap. 1 [pp. 117-176 in the 1953 translation]; 1944, chap. 8), Gray (1939), Jakobson (1933), Jespersen (1922, Book I), Kroeber (1944, chap. 4), Meillet and Cohen (1952, pp. xvii-xlii), Pedersen (1931), Sandys (1903, 1908), Steinthal (1863), Thomsen (1927), White (1896, chap. 17). Accounts more limited in scope are also found in W. Sidney Allen (1949, 1953), Brough (1951), Bloomfield (1933, chap. 1), Cassirer (1945), Emeneau (1955), *Grundriss* (1916), Meillet (1934, Appendix), Robins (1951, 1958), Verburg (1949, 1952). T. A. Sebeok (Ed.), *Profiles of Linguists by Linguists* (in preparation) will be an especially valuable resource. In general, consult obituary articles in linguistic journals and the section on the history of linguistics in the issues of the *Linguistic Bibliography*.

On the history of linguistic work in anthropology, and hence, of linguistic anthropology, see the general discussions in Boas (1904), Hymes (1963c), Kroeber (1950), Levi-Strauss (1949, 1953b, 1960d), Pennimann (1952, pp. 195-204, 435); with particular reference to American anthropology, also see Frederica De Laguna (1960, pp. 380-383), Hallowell (1960, pp. 23-34), Kroeber (1939b), and Wissler (1942). See also, of course, the introductions to the Parts of this book, especially to Part I and the articles and references therein.

References not in the general bibliography:

ALLEN, W. SIDNEY

1949. Ancient Ideas on the Origin and Development of Language. *Transactions of the Philological Society* (*London, 1948*). Pp. 35-60. London.

1953. *Phonetics in Ancient India.* (London Oriental Series, No. 1.) London: Cumberlege, Oxford University Press, for the School of Oriental and African Studies, University of London.

ARENS, HANS

1955. *Sprachwissenschaft. Der Gang ihrer Entwicklung von der Antike bis zur Gegenwart.* Munich and Freiburg: Alber.

BENFEY, THEODOR

1869. *Geschichte der Sprachwissenschaft und Orientalischen Philologie in Deutschland seit dem Anfange des 19. Jahrhunderts mit einem Rückblick auf die früheren Zeiten.* (Geschichte der Wissenschaften in Deutschland, herausgegeben durch die Historische Commission bei der Königl. Academie der Wissenschaften, No. 8.) Munich: Cotta'schen Buchhandlung

BOAS, FRANZ

1904. The History of Anthropology. *Science, 20:* 513-524.

BROUGH, JOHN

1951. Theories of General Linguistics in the Sanskrit Grammarians. *Transactions of the Philological Society (London).* Pp. 27-46. London.

[GRUNDRISS DER INDOGERMANISCHEN SPRACH- UND ALTERTUMSKUNDE]

1916–. [Series of histories of linguistics with extensive bibliography.] Strassburg; then Berlin and Leipzig: de Gruyter.

HALLOWELL, A. IRVING

1960. The Beginnings of Anthropology in America. In Frederica De Laguna (Ed.), *Selected Papers from the American Anthropologist, 1888-1920.* New York: Harper & Row. Pp. 1-90.

KROEBER, A. L.

1944. *Configurations of Culture Growth.* Berkeley and Los Angeles: University of California Press.

PENNIMAN, T. K.

1952. *A Hundred Years of Anthropology.* 2nd rev. ed. London: Duckworth.

ROBINS, R. H.

1951. *Ancient and Medieval Grammatical Theory in Europe.* London: Bell. [Reviewed, H. Hoenigswald, *Lg.*, 1953, *29:* 179–182.]

1958. Dionysius Thrax and the Western Grammatical Tradition. *Transactions of the Philological Society (London, 1957).* Pp. 67-106. London.

SANDYS, SIR JOHN EDWYN

1903. *A History of Classical Scholarship.* Vol. I, *From the Sixth Century B.C. to the End of Middle Ages.* Cambridge: Cambridge University Press. (3rd rev. ed., 1921.)

1908. *A History of Classical Scholarship.* Vol. II, *From the Revival of Learning to the End of the Eighteenth Century;* Vol III, *The Eighteenth Century in Europe and the United States of America.* Cambridge: Cambridge University Press. [Reprinted, New York: Hafner, 1958, vols. I-II, III.]

STEINTHAL, HEYMANN

1863. *Geschichte der Sprachwissenschaft bei den Griechen und Römern mit Besonderer Rücksicht auf die Logik.* Berlin: Dümmlers Verlagsbuchhandlung. (2nd rev. ed., 1890; reissued 1961.)

THOMSEN, VILHELM L. P.

1927. *Geschichte der Sprachwissenschaft bis zum Ausgang des 19 Jahrhunderts; Kurzgefasste Darstellung der Hauptpunkte.* Translated from the Danish by Hans Pollak. Halle: Niemeyer. (Original Danish edition, 1919; translated with prologue and epilogue by Javier de Echave-Sustaeta,

Historia de la lingüística. [Collección Labor, Sección 3, Ciencias literarias, 418.] Barcelona, Madrid, Buenos-Aires, Rio de Janeiro: Editorial Labor, 1945.)

VERBURG, P. A.

1949. The Background to the Linguistic Conceptions of Bopp. *Lingua*, *2:* 438-468.

1952. *Taal en Functionaliteit*. Wageningen: Veenman and Sons. [Reviewed, R. G. Faithfull, *Archivum Linguisticum*, 1955, *7:* 144-150.]

WHITE, A. D.

1896. *A History of the Warfare of Science with Theology in Christendom*. New York. (Reprinted, New York: Dover, 1960, 2 vols.)

WISSLER, CLARK

1942. The American Indian and the American Philosophical Society. *PAPS*, *86:* 189-204.

General Bibliography

Articles marked with an asterisk are included (complete or in part) in the text.

ABERLE, DAVID F.

1960. The Influence of Linguistics on Early Culture and Personality Theory. In Gertrude E. Dole and Robert L. Carneiro (Eds.), *Essays in the Science of Culture in Honor of Leslie A. White*. New York: Crowell. Pp. 1-29.

ADAMS, JOHN BOMAN

*1957. Culture and Conflict in an Egyptian Village. *AA*, *59:* 225-235.

ALLEN, HAROLD B. (ED.)

1958. *Readings in Applied English Linguistics*. New York: Appleton-Century-Crofts. [2nd ed., enlarged, 1963.]

ASCH, SOLOMON E.

1958. The Metaphor: A Psychological Inquiry. In R. Tagiuri and L. Petrullo (Eds.), *Person Perception and Interpersonal Behavior*. Stanford: Stanford University Press. Pp. 86-94.

AUSTIN, WILLIAM M. (ED.)

1960. *Report of the Ninth Annual Round Table Meeting on Linguistics and Language Study; Anthropology and African Studies*. (Monograph Series on Languages and Linguistics, No. 11.) Washington, D.C.: Georgetown University Press.

BALLY, CHARLES

1950. *Linguistique générale et linguistique française*. (3rd ed. [same as 2nd].) Bern: Francke. (1st ed., 1932.)

1951. *Traité de stylistique française*. (3rd ed.) Geneva: Georg; Paris: Klincksieck. 2 vols. (1st ed., 1909.)

1952. *Le Langage et la vie*. (3rd ed.) (Société de Publications Romanes et Françaises, No. 34.) Geneva: Droz; Lille: Giard. (Previous editions, 1925, 1935.)

BARKER, GEORGE C.

1945. The Social Functions of Language. *ETC.: A Review of General Semantics*, *2:* 228-234.

1950. *Pachuco: An American Spanish Argot and Its Social Functions in Tucson, Arizona*. (University of Arizona Social Science Bulletin, No. 18.) Tucson: University of Arizona Press.

BARKER, ROGER G., and LOUISE BARKER
1961. Behavior Units for the Comparative Study of Cultures. In Bert Kaplan (Ed.), *Studying Personality Cross-Culturally*. New York: Harper & Row. Pp. 457-476.

BARKER, ROGER G., and HERBERT F. WRIGHT
1954. *Midwest and Its Children*. New York: Harper & Row.

BASCOM, WILLIAM R.
1949. Literary Style in Yoruba Riddles. *JAF*, *62:* 1-67.

BASILIUS, HAROLD
1952. Neo-Humboldtian Ethnolinguistics. *Word*, *8:* 95-105.

BAZELL, C. F.
1954. The Choice of Criteria in Structural Linguistics. In Martinet (Ed.), *Linguistics Today*. Pp. 126-135. [Same as *Word*, *10:* 2-3.]

BECKWITH, MARTHA W.
1922. Hawaiian Riddling. *AA*, *24:* 311-331.

BENDER, HAROLD H.
1922. *Home of the Indo-Europeans*. Princeton: Princeton University Press.

BERGSLAND, KNUT, and HANS VOGT
1962. On the Validity of Glottochronology. *CA*, *3:* 115-158.

BERNSTEIN, BASIL
*1961. Aspects of Language and Learning in the Genesis of Social Process. *Journal of Child Psychology and Psychiatry*, *1:* 313-324.

BLACK, MAX
1949. *Language and Philosophy*. Ithaca: Cornell University Press.
1962. *Models and Metaphors*. Ithaca: Cornell University Press.

BLOCH, BERNARD, and GEORGE L. TRAGER
1942. *Outline of Linguistic Analysis*. (Special Publications of the Linguistic Society of America.) Baltimore: Linguistic Society of America.

BLOCH, JULES
1910. Castes et dialectes en Tamoul. *Mémoires de la Société de Linguistique de Paris*, *16:* 1-30.

BLOOMFIELD, LEONARD
1914. *An Introduction to the Study of Language*. New York: Holt.
1925. Why a Linguistic Society? *Lg.*, *1:* 1-5.
1926. A Set of Postulates for the Science of Language. *Lg.*, *2:* 153–164, [Reprinted in *IJAL*, *15:* 195-202 (1949); also in Martin Joos (Ed.). *Readings in Linguistics*. Washington: American Council of Learned Societies. Pp. 26-31.]
*1927a. Literate and Illiterate Speech. *American Speech*, *10:* 432-9.
1933. *Language*. New York: Holt.
1942a. Philosophical Aspects of Language. In *Studies in the History of Culture. The Disciplines of the Humanities*. (Published for the Conference of Secretaries of the American Council of Learned Societies.) Menasha, Wis.: Banta. Pp. 173-177.
1942b. *Outline Guide for the Practical Study of Foreign Languages*. Baltimore: Linguistic Society of America.

1943a. Meaning. *Monatshefte für deutschen Unterricht*, *35:* 101-116.
1944. Secondary and Tertiary Responses to Language. *Lg.*, *20:* 45-55.

BOAS, FRANZ
1889. On Alternating Sounds. *AA* (o.s.), *2:* 47-53. [Also in Frederica De Laguna (Ed.), *Selected Papers from the American Anthropologist, 1888-1920*. New York: Harper & Row. Pp. 385-402.]
1904. The History of Anthropology. *Science*, *20:* 513-524 (October 21).
1907. Language. In F. W. Hodge (Ed.), *Handbook of American Indians North of Mexico*. (BAE-B 30.) Washington, D.C.: Smithsonian Institution, 1907-1910. Vol. I, pp. 757-759.
*1911. Introduction. *Handbook of American Indian Languages*, (BAE-B 40, Part I.) Washington, D.C.: Smithsonian Institution. Pp. 1-83.
1914. Mythology and Folk-tales of the North American Indians. *JAF*, *27:* 374-410. [Also in Boas, 1940, pp. 451-490.]
1917. Introductory. *IJAL*, *1:* 1-8. [Also in Boas, 1940, pp. 199-210.]
1920a. The Classification of American Languages. *AA*, *22:* 367-376. [Also in Boas, 1940, pp. 211-218.]
1920b. The Methods of Ethnology. *AA*, *22:* 311-321. [Also in Boas, 1940, pp. 281-289.]
1925. Stylistic Aspects of Primitive Literature. *JAF*, *38:* 329-339. [Also in Boas, 1940, pp. 491-502.]
1929a. Classification of American Indian Languages. *Lg.*, *5:* 1-7. [Also in Boas, 1940, pp. 219-225.]
1929b. Metaphorical Expressions in the Language of the Kwakiutl Indians. In *Verzameling van Opstellen door Oud-Leerlingen en Bevriende Vakgenoten opgedragen aan Mgr. Prof. Dr. Jos. Schrijnen, 3 Mei 1929*. Chartres. Pp. 147-153. [Also in Boas, 1940, pp. 232-239.]
*1934. *Geographical Names of the Kwakiutl Indians*. (Columbia University Contributions to Anthropology, No. 20.) New York: Columbia University Press.
1937. Some Traits of the Dakota Language. *Lg.*, *13:* 137-141. [Also in Boas, 1940, pp. 226-231.]
1938a. *General Anthropology*. New York: Heath.
1938b. Language. In Boas, *General Anthropology*. New York: Heath. Pp. 124-145.
1939a. A Report of the Committee on Research in American Native Languages, 1927-1937. *American Council of Learned Societies Bulletin*, no. 29: 105-115.
1940. *Race, Language and Culture*. New York: Macmillan.
1942. Language and Culture. In *Studies in the History of Culture. The Disciplines of the Humanities*. (Published for the Conference of Secretaries of the American Council of Learned Societies.) Menasha, Wis.: Banta. Pp. 178-184.

BOGATYREV, P., and ROMAN JAKOBSON
1929. Die Folklore als eine besondere Form des Schaffens, *Donum Natalicium Schrijnen*. Nijmegen-Utrecht. Pp. 900-913.

BONFANTE, GIULIANO
1947. The Neolinguistic Position. *Lg.*, *23:* 344-375.

BONFANTE, GIULLIANO, and THOMAS A. SEBEOK

1944. Linguistics and the Age and Area Hypothesis. *AA, 46*:382–386.

BRIGHT, WILLIAM O.

1960a. Linguistic Change in Some Indian Caste Dialects. In Charles A. Ferguson and John J. Gumperz (Eds.), *Linguistic Diversity in South Asia.* (RCAFL-P 13; *IJAL, 26* [3], Part III.) Bloomington. Pp. 19-26.

*1960b. Social Dialect and Language History. *CA* 1 (5-6): 424-425.

1963. Language. In B. J. Siegel (Ed.), *Biennial Review of Anthropology 1963*. Stanford: Stanford University Press. Pp. 1-29.

BROWER, REUBEN A. (ED.)

1959. *On Translation.* (Harvard Studies in Comparative Literature, No. 23.) Cambridge: Harvard University Press.

BROWN, ROGER W.

1956. Language and Categories. In J. S. Bruner, J. J. Goodnow, and G. A. Austin, *A Study of Thinking*. New York: Wiley. Pp. 247-312.

1957. Linguistic Determinism and the Parts of Speech. *JASP, 55:* 1-5.

1958. *Words and Things.* Glencoe, Ill.: Free Press.

BROWN, ROGER W., and MARGUERITE FORD

*1961. Address in American English. *JASP, 62:* 375-385.

BROWN, ROGER W., and A. GILMAN

1960. The Pronouns of Power and Solidarity. In Thomas A. Sebeok (Ed.), *Style in Language*. New York: Wiley; Cambridge: Technology Press. Pp. 253-276.

BROWN, ROGER W., and ERIC H. LENNEBERG

1954. A Study in Language and Cognition. *JASP, 49:* 454-462.

1958. Studies in Linguistic Relativity. In Eleanor Maccoby, T. H. Newcomb, and E. L. Hartley (Eds.), *Readings in Social Psychology*. (3rd ed.) New York: Holt. Pp. 9-18.

BRUNER, J. S., J. J. GOODNOW and G. A. AUSTIN

1956. *A Study of Thinking*. New York: Wiley.

BRYANT, MARGARET M.

1962. *Modern English and Its Heritage.* (2nd ed.) New York: Macmillan. (1st ed., 1948.)

BÜHLER, KARL

1934. *Sprachtheorie*. Jena: Fisher.

BULL, WILLIAM A.

*1955. The Use of Vernacular Languages in Fundamental Education. *IJAL, 21:* 288-294.

BURKE, KENNETH

1945. *A Grammar of Motives*. New York: Prentice-Hall.

1951a. *A Rhetoric of Motives*. New York: Prentice-Hall.

1957. *The Philosophy of Literary Form. Studies in Symbolic Action.* (Rev. ed. abridged by the author.) New York: Vintage Books (K-51). (1st ed., 1941.)

1958. The Poetic Motive. *The Hudson Review, 11:* 54-63.

1961. *The Rhetoric of Religion*. Boston: Beacon.

1962. What Are the Signs of What? *AL, 4* (6): 1-23.

BURLING, ROBBINS

1962. A Structural Restatement of Njamal Kinship Terminology. *Man, 62:* 122-124 (Article 201).

CARNAP, RUDOLPH

1942. *Introduction to Semantics*. Cambridge: Harvard University Press.

CARPENTER, EDMUND, and MARSHALL MCLUHAN (EDS.)

1960. *Explorations in Communication. An Anthology*. Boston: Beacon.

CARROLL, JOHN B.

1953. *The Study of Language*. Cambridge: Harvard University Press.

1958. Some Psychological Effects of Language Structure. In P. Hoch and J. Zubin (Eds.), *Psychopathology of Communication*. New York: Grune and Stratton. Pp. 28-36.

CARROLL, JOHN B. (ED.)

1956. *Language, Thought, and Reality. Selected Writings of Benjamin Lee Whorf*. New York: Wiley; Cambridge: Technology Press.

CARROLL, JOHN B., and JOSEPH B. CASAGRANDE

1958. The Function of Language Classifications in Behavior. In Eleanor Maccoby, T. H. Newcomb, and E. L. Hartley (Eds.), *Readings in Social Psychology*. (3rd ed.) New York: Holt. Pp. 18-31.

CASAGRANDE, JOSEPH B.

*1948. Comanche Baby Language. *IJAL, 14:* 11-14.

1954-1955. Comanche Linguistic Acculturation, I, II, III. *IJAL, 20:* 140-151, 217-237; *21:* 8-25.

CASSIRER, ERNST

1923. *Philosophie der symbolischen Formen: Die Sprache*. Berlin: Bruno Cassirer. (Translated by Ralph Mannheim, *The Philosophy of Symbolic Forms*, Vol. I, *Language*. New Haven: Yale University Press, 1953.)

1944. *An Essay on Man. An Introduction to a Philosophy of Human Culture*. New Haven: Yale University Press. (New York: Doubleday Anchor Books [A3], 1953.)

1945. Structuralism in Modern Linguistics. *Word, 1:* 99-120.

CATALÁN, DIEGO (ED.)

1957–1958. *Miscelánea homenaje a André Martinet: Estructuralismo e historia*. (Biblioteca filológica de la Universidad de la Lagune.) Tenerife, Canarias: Universidad de la Laguna (Distribución, Editorial Gredos, Madrid). [Reviewed, F. H. Jungemann, *Word, 15:* 465-484 (1959); R. A. Fowkes, *Lg.*, 1959, *35:* 78-90.]

CHAFE, WALLACE (ED.)

1963. *Aspects of Language and Culture*. (Proceedings, American Ethnological Society, Washington, D.C., 1962.) Seattle: University of Washington Press.

CHAO, YUEN-REN

1931. Eight Varieties of Secret Language Based on the Principle of Fanch'ieh. *Academia sinica, National Research Institute of History and Philology, Bulletin, 2:* 312-354. Peiping. [Text in Chinese.]

1956. Chinese Terms of Address. *Lg., 32:* 142-149.

CHERRY, COLIN

1957. *On Human Communication. A Review, a Survey, and a Criticism.* Cambridge: Technology Press. (New York: Science Editions, 1961.)

CHOMSKY, N.

1957. *Syntactic Structures.* The Hague: Mouton.

CHOWDHURY, MUNIER

1960. The Language Problem in East Pakistan. In Charles A. Ferguson and John J. Gumperz (Eds.), *Linguistic Diversity in South Asia.* (RCAFL-P 13; *IJAL, 26* [3], Part III.) Bloomington. Pp. 64-78.

COHEN, MARCEL

1950. *Le Langage, structure et évolution.* Paris: Éditions Sociales.

1956a. *Pour une Sociologie du langage.* Paris: Paris Editions, Albin Michel.

1956b. Social and Linguistic Structure. *Diogenes, 15:* 38-47.

COLE, D. T.

*1953. Fanagalo and the Bantu Languages in South Africa. *Africa Studies, 12:* 1-9.

CONKLIN, HAROLD C.

*1955. Hanunóo Color Categories. *SJA, 11:* 339-344.

1956. Tagalog Speech Disguise. *Lg., 32:* 136-139.

1957. *Hanunóo Agriculture.* Rome: Food and Agriculture Organization of the United Nations.

*1959. Linguistic Play in Its Cultural Context. *Lg., 35:* 631-636.

1962. Lexicographical Treatment of Folk Taxonomies. In Fred W. Householder and Sol Saporta (Eds.), *Problems in Lexicography.* (RCAFL-P 21; *IJAL, 28* [2], Part IV.) Bloomington. Pp. 119-141.

COWAN, GEORGE

*1948. Mazateco Whistle Speech. *Lg., 24:* 280-286.

DAUZAT, ALBERT

1929. *Les Argots: caractères—evolution—influence.* Paris: Delagrave.

DANEHY, J. S., C. F. HOCKETT, and R. PITTENGER

1960. *The First Five Minutes.* Ithaca: Martineau.

DE CAMP, DAVID

1961. Social and Geographical Factors in Jamaican Dialects. In R. Le Page (Ed.), *Proceedings of the Conference on Creole Language Studies.* (Creole Language Studies, No. 2.) London: Macmillan. Pp. 61-84.

DE LAGUNA, GRACE

1927. *Speech, Its Function and Development.* New Haven: Yale University Press. [Also, Bloomington: Indiana University Press, 1963.]

DE LAGUNA, FREDERICA (ED.)

1960. *Selected Papers from the American Anthropologist, 1888-1920.* New York: Harper & Row.

DE SAUSSURE, FERDINAND

1916. *Cours de linguistique générale.* Paris: Payot. (Translated by Wade Baskin, *Course in General Linguistics.* New York: Philosophical Library, 1958.)

DEAN, LEONARD F., and KENNETH G. WILSON
1959. *Essays on Language and Usage*. New York: Oxford University Press. [2nd ed., enlarged, 1963].

DEVEREUX, GEORGE
*1949. Mohave Voice and Speech Mannerisms. *Word*, *5:* 268-272.
1951. Mohave Indian Verbal and Motor Profanity. In Géza Róheim (Ed.), *Psychoanalysis and the Social Sciences*. New York: International Universities Press. Chap. 3, pp. 99-127.

DIAMOND, STANLEY A. (ED.)
1960. *Culture in History: Essays in Honor of Paul Radin*. New York: Columbia University Press.

DIEBOLD, A. RICHARD, JR.
1960. Determining the Centers of Dispersal of Language Groups. *IJAL*, *26:* 1-10.
*1961. Incipient Bilingualism. *Lg.*, *37:* 97-112.

DIMOCK, EDWARD C.
1960. Literary and Colloquial Bengali in Modern Bengali Prose. In Charles A. Ferguson and John J. Gumperz (Eds.), Linguistic Diversity in South Asia. (RCAFL-P 13; *IJAL*, *26* [3], Part III.) Bloomington.

DOROSZEWSKI, W.
1933. Quelques remarques sur les rapports de la sociologie et de la linguistique: Durkheim et F. de Saussure. In Pierre Janet and Georges Dumas (Eds.), *Psychologie du Langage*. Paris: Alcan. [*Journal de psychologie: normale et pathologique*, *30* (1-4).]

DOZIER, EDWARD P.
1951. Resistance to Acculturation and Assimilation in an Indian Pueblo. *AA*, *53:* 56-66.
1955. Kinship and Linguistic Change Among the Arizona Tewa. *IJAL*, *21:* 242-257.
*1956. Two Examples of Linguistic Acculturation. *Lg.*, *32:* 146-157.

DU BOIS, CORA (ED.)
1960. *Lowie's Selected Papers in Anthropology*. Berkeley and Los Angeles: University of California Press.

DUNCAN, HUGH DALZIEL
1962. *Communication and the Social Order*. New York: Buckminster.

DUNDES, ALAN
1963. Structural Typology of North American Indian Folktales. *SJA*, *19:* 121-130.

DURKHEIM, EMILE
n.d. *The Elementary Forms of the Religious Life*. Translated from the French by Joseph Ward Swain. Glencoe: Free Press.

ELLIS, J.
1958. General Linguistics and Comparative Philology. *Lingua*, *7:* 134-174.

EMENEAU, MURRAY B.
1937. Toda Marriage Regulations and Taboos. *AA*, *39:* 103-112.

1941. Language and Social Forms: A Study of Toda Kinship Terms and Dual Descent. In L. Spier, A. I. Hallowell, and S. S. Newman (Eds.), *Language, Culture, and Personality*. Menasha, Wis.: Banta.
1950. Language and Non-Linguistic Patterns. *Lg., 26:* 199-209.
1953. Dravidian Kinship Terms. *Lg., 29:* 330-353.
1954a. Linguistic Prehistory of India. *PAPS, 98:* 282-292.
*1955. India and Linguistics. *JAOS, 75:* 145-153.
*1956. India as a Linguistic Area. *Lg., 32:* 3-16.
*1958. Oral Poets of South India: the Toda. *JAF, 71:* 312-324.

EMPSON, WILLIAM
1951. *The Structure of Complex Words*. London: Chatto and Windus.

ESTRICH, ROBERT M., and HANS SPERBER
1952. *Three Keys to Language*. New York: Rinehart.

EVANS-PRITCHARD, E. E.
1929. Some Collective Expressions of Obscenity in Africa. *JRAI, 59:* 311-332.
1934a. Imagery in Ngoh Dinka Cattle Names. *BSO(A)S, 7:* 623-628.
1940. *The Nuer*. Oxford: Oxford University Press.
*1948. Nuer Modes of Address. *The Uganda Journal, 12:* 166-171.
1949. Nuer Curses and Ghostly Vengeance. *Africa, 19:* 288-292.
1954a. A Problem of Nuer Religious Thought. *Sociologus, 4:* 23-41.
1956. *Sangi*, Characteristic Feature of Zande Language and Thought. *BSO(A)S, 18:* 161-180.

FEARING, FRANKLIN
1954. An Examination of the Theories of Benjamin Whorf in the Light of Theories of Perception and Cognition. In Harry Hoijer (Ed.), *Language in Culture*. (Comparative Studies of Cultures and Civilizations, No. 3; Memoirs of the American Anthropological Association, No. 79.) Chicago: University of Chicago Press. Pp. 47-81.

FERGUSON, CHARLES A.
1956. Arabic Baby Talk. In *For Roman Jakobson*, pp. 121-128.
*1959a. Diglossia. *Word, 15:* 325-340.
1962. The Language Factor in National Development. *AL*, *4* (1): 23-27.

FERGUSON, CHARLES A., and MUNIER CHOWDHURY
1960. The Phonemes of Bengali. *Lg., 36:* 22-59.

FERGUSON, CHARLES A., and JOHN J. GUMPERZ (EDS.)
1960. *Linguistic Diversity in South Asia: Studies in Regional, Social, and Functional Variation*. (RCAFL-P 13; *IJAL, 26* [3], Part III.) Bloomington.

FIRTH, J. R.
*1935. The Technique of Semantics. *Transactions of the Philological Society* (London), pp. 36-72. [Also in Firth, 1957b, pp. 7-35.]
1937. *The Tongues of Men*. London: Watts.
1950. Personality and Language in Society. *Sociological Review*, 42 (sect. II.): 8-14. [Also in Firth, 1957b, pp. 177-189.]
1951. General Linguistics and Descriptive Grammar. *Transactions of the Philological Society* (*London* , pp. 69-87. [Also in Firth, 1957b, pp. 216-228.]

1957a. Ethnographic Analysis and Language with Reference to Malinowski's Views. In Firth, R. (Ed.), *Man and Culture*. London: Routledge & Kegan Paul. Pp. 93-118.

1957b. *Papers in Linguistics 1934-1951*. London: Oxford University Press.

FIRTH, RAYMOND (ED.)

1957. *Man and Culture. An Evaluation of the Work of Bronislaw Malinowski.* London. Routledge & Kegan Paul.

FISCHER, JOHN L.

*1958. Social Influences in the Choice of a Linguistic Variant. *Word, 14:* 47-56.

FOCK, NIELS

1958. Cultural Aspects and Social Functions of the "Oho" Institution Among the Waiwai. *Proceedings of the Thirty-second International Congress of Americanists (Copenhagen, 1956)*. Copenhagen: Munksgaard. Pp. 136-140.

[FOR ROMAN JAKOBSON]

1956. *For Roman Jakobson: Essays on the Occasion of his Sixtieth Birthday*. The Hague: Mouton.

FRAKE, CHARLES O.

*1961. The Diagnosis of Disease Among the Subanun of Mindanao. *AA, 63:* 113-132.

1962a. The Ethnographic Study of Cognitive Systems. In Thomas Gladwin and William C. Sturtevant (Eds.), *Anthropology and Human Behavior*. Washington, D.C.: Anthropological Society of Washington. Pp. 72-85.

1962b. Cultural Ecology and Ethnography. *AA, 64:* 53-59.

FREUD, SIGMUND

1938. *The Basic Writings of Sigmund Freud*. Edited and Translated by A. A. Brill. New York: Modern Library.

FRIED, MORTON H. (ED.)

1959. *Readings in Anthropology*. Vol. I, *Physical Anthropology, Linguistics, Archaeology*. New York: Crowell.

FRIEDRICH, PAUL (Organizer)

1962. Multilingualism and Socio-Cultural Organization. (Symposium presented at the 1961 meetings of the American Anthropological Association.) *AL, 4* (1).

FRIES, CHARLES CARPENTER

1952. *The Structure of English. An Introduction to the Construction of English Sentences*. New York: Harcourt, Brace.

GARDE, PAUL

1961. Réflexions sur les différences phonétiques entre les langues slaves. *Word, 17:* 34-62.

GARDINER, ALAN H.

1919. Some Thoughts on the Subject of Language. *Man, 19:* 2-6.

1932. *The Theory of Speech and Language*. Oxford: Oxford University Press. (2nd ed., 1951.)

GARVIN, PAUL L.

1949. Standard Average European and Czech. *Studia Linguistica, 3:* 65-85.

1954a. Literacy as a Problem in Language and Culture. In Hugo Mueller (Ed.), *Report on the Fifth Annual Round Table Meeting on Linguistics and Language Teaching*. (Monograph Series on Languages and Linguistics, No. 7.), Washington, D.C.: Georgetown University Press. Pp. 117-129.

1955. Problems in American Indian Lexicography and Text Edition. *Anais do XXXI Congres Internacional de Americanistas*. São Paulo. Pp. 1013-1028.

*1959. The Standard Language Problem: Concepts and Methods. *AL*, *1* (2): 28-31.

1963. *Natural Language and the Computer*. New York: McGraw-Hill.

GARVIN, PAUL L. (ED.)

1957. *Report of the Seventh Annual Round Table Meeting on Linguistics and Language Study*. (Monograph Series on Languages and Linguistics, No. 9.) Washington, D.C.: Georgetown University Press.

GARVIN, PAUL L., and S. RIESENBERG

1952. Respect Behavior on Ponape: An Ethnolinguistic Study. *AA*, *54:* 201-220.

GAYTON, ANNA H.

*1940. Narrative Style. In Gayton and Newman, 1940, pp. 7-11.

GAYTON, ANNA H., and STANLEY S. NEWMAN

1940. *Yokuts and Western Mono Myths* (UCPAR 5.) Berkeley and Los Angeles: University of California Press.

GLADWIN, THOMAS, and WILLIAM C. STURTEVANT (Eds.)

1962. *Anthropology and Human Behavior*. Washington, D.C.: Anthropological Society of Washington.

GLEASON, H. A., JR.

1955. *Workbook in Descriptive Linguistics*. New York: Holt. (Rev. ed. 1961.)

1959. Counting and Calculating for Historical Reconstruction. *AL*, *1* (2): 22-32.

1961. *An Introduction to Descriptive Linguistics*. (Rev. ed.) New York: Holt, Rinehart and Winston.

1962. Linguistics in the Service of the Church. *Practical Anthropology*, *9:* 205-219.

GLUCKMAN, MAX

1959. The Technical Vocabulary of Barotse Jurisprudence. *AA*, *61:* 743-759.

GOFFMAN, ERVING

1959. *The Presentation of Self in Everyday Life*. New York: Doubleday Anchor Books (A174).

1961. *Encounters. Two Studies in the Sociology of Interaction*. Indianapolis: Bobbs-Merrill.

GOLDSCHMIDT, WALTER (ED.)

1959. *The Anthropology of Franz Boas. Essays on the Centennial of His Birth*. (The American Anthropological Association, Vol. 61, No. 5, Part 2; Memoir 89.) Menasha, Wis.: San Francisco: Chandler.

GONDA, J.

1948. The Javanese Vocabulary of Courtesy. *Lingua*, *1:* 333-376.

GOODENOUGH, WARD H.

*1951. *Property, Kin and Community on Truk*. (Yale University Publications in Anthropology, No. 46.) New Haven: Yale University Press.

1956. Componential Analysis and the Study of Meaning. *Lg.*, *32:* 195-216.

*1957a. Cultural Anthropology and Linguistics. In Paul L. Garvin (Ed.), *Report of the Seventh Annual Round Table Meeting on Linguistics and Language Study*. (Monograph Series on Languages and Linguistics, No. 9.) Washington, D.C.: Georgetown University Press.

1957b. Review of F. M. Keesing and Marie M. Keesing, *Elite Communication in Samoa*. *Lg.*, *33:* 424-429.

GOTTSCHALK, LOUIS, CLYDE KLUCKHOHN, and ROBERT ANGELL

1945. *The Use of Personal Documents in History, Anthropology, and Sociology*. (Social Science Research Council, Bulletin 53.) Washington, D.C.

GRANET, MARCEL

1934. *La Pensée chinoise*. (L'Évolution de l'Humanité, Synthèse Collective, No. 25.) Paris: Albin Michel.

GRAY, LOUIS H.

1939. *Foundations of Language*. New York: Macmillan.

GREENBERG, JOSEPH H.

*1948a. Linguistics and Ethnology. *SJA*, *40:* 140-148.

1948b. The Classification of African Languages. *AA*, *50:* 24-30.

1949-1954. Studies in African Linguistic Classification, I-VIII. *SJA*, *5:* 79-100, 190-198, 309-317; *6:* 47-63, 143-160, 223-237, 388-398; *10:* 405-415. [Also published in book form, New Haven: Compass, 1955.]

1949. The Logical Analysis of Kinship. *Philosophy of Science*, *16:* 58-64.

1953. Historical Linguistics and Unwritten Languages. In A. L. Kroeber *et al.*, *Anthropology Today*. Chicago: University of Chicago Press. Pp. 265-286.

1954a. A Quantitative Approach to the Morphological Typology of Language. In Robert Spencer (Ed.), *Method and Perspective in Anthropology*. Minneapolis: University of Minnesota Press. Pp. 192-220. [Also, *IJAL*, 1960, *26:* 178-194.]

1954b. Concerning Inferences from Linguistic to Non-linguistic Data. In Harry Hoijer (Ed.), *Language in Culture*. (Comparative Studies of Cultures and Civilizations, No. 3; Memoirs of the American Anthropological Association, No. 79.) Chicago: University of Chicago Press. Pp. 3-19.

1957b. The Nature and Uses of Linguistic Typologies. *IJAL*, *23:* 68-77.

1957c. *Essays in Linguistics*. (Viking Fund Publications in Anthropology, No. 24.) New York: Wenner-Gren Foundation for Anthropological Research; Chicago: University of Chicago Press. [Chicago: Phoenix Books 119, 1963.]

1959a. Current Trends in Linguistics. *Science*, *130:* 1115 ff. (October 30).

1959b. Language and Evolution. In Betty Meggers (Ed.), *Evolution and Anthropology: A Centennial Appraisal*. Washington, D.C.: Anthropological Society of Washington. Pp. 61-75.

1963. *The Languages of Africa*. (RCAFL-P 24; *IJAL*, *29* [1], Part 2.) Bloomington.

GREENBERG, JOSEPH H. (ED.)

1963. *Universals of Language*. Cambridge: M.I.T. Press.

GREENOUGH, J. B., and G. L. KITTREDGE

1961. *Words and Their Ways in English Speech*. New York: Macmillan. (First published, 1900-1901.)

GROOTAERS, W. A.

1952. Language Behavior of an Individual During One Day. *Orbis, 1:* 126-129.

GROVE, VICTOR

1950. *The Language Bar.* London: Routledge & Kegan Paul.

GUDSCHINSKY, SARAH C.

*1956. The ABCs of Lexicostatistics (Glottochronology). *Word, 12:* 175-210.

1958a. Native Reactions to Tones and Words in Mazatec. *Word, 14* (2-3): 388-345.

GUIRAUD, PIERRE

1958a. *La Sémantique.* (2nd ed.) ("Que Sais-Je?" Le Point des Connaissances Actuelles, No. 655.) Paris: Presses Universitaires de France. (1st ed., 1955.)

1958b. *L'Argot.* (2nd ed.) ("Que Sais-Je?" Le Point des Connaissances Actuelles, No. 700.) Paris: Presses Universitaires de France. (1st ed., 1956.)

1961. *La Stylistique.* (3rd ed.) ("Que Sais-Je?" Le Point des Connaissances Actuelles, No. 646.) Paris: Presses Universitaires de France. (1st ed., 1954.)

GUMPERZ, JOHN J.

1958a. Dialect Differences and Social Stratification in a North Indian Village. *AA, 60:* 668-682.

1958b. Phonological Differences in Three Western Hindi Dialects. *Lg., 34:* 212-224.

*1961. Speech Variation and the Study of Indian Civilization. *AA, 63:*976–988.

1962. Types of Linguistic Communities. In Paul Friedrich (Organizer), Multilingualism and Socio-Cultural Organization. (Symposium presented at the 1961 meetings of the American Anthropological Association.) *AL, 4* (1).

GUMPERZ, JOHN J., and C. M. NAIM

1960. Formal and Informal Standards in Hindi Regional Language Area. In Charles A. Ferguson and John J. Gumperz (Eds.), *Linguistic Diversity in South Asia.* (RCAFL-P 13; *IJAL, 26* [3], Part III.) Bloomington. Pp. 92-118.

HAAS, MARY R.

*1944. Men's and Women's Speech in Koasati. *Lg., 20:* 142-149.

*1951. Interlingual Word Taboos. *AA, 53:* 338-344.

*1957. Thai Word Games. *JAF, 70:* 173-175.

HALL, EDWARD T.

1959. *The Silent Language.* New York: Doubleday.

HALL, EDWARD T., and GEORGE L. TRAGER

1953. *The Analysis of Culture.* Washington, D.C.: American Council of Learned Societies.

HALL, ROBERT A., JR.

1946. Bartoli's Neolinguistica. *Lg., 22:* 273-283.

1955. *Hands Off Pidgin English!* Sydney: Pacific Publications.

1959a. Pidgin Languages. *Scientific American, 200* (2): 124-134.

1960. *Linguistics and Your Language.* [2nd rev. ed. of *Leave Your Language Alone!*] New York: Doubleday Anchor Books (201).

HALLE, MORRIS
1962. Phonology in a Generative Grammar. *Word*, *18* (1-2): 54-72.

HALPERN, A. M.
1942. Yuma Kinship Terms. *AA*, *44:* 425-441.

HARRAH, DAVID
1960. The Adequacy of Language. *Inquiry*, *3:* 73-88.

HARRINGTON, JOHN P.
1916. The Ethnogeography of the Tewa Indians. *BAE-AR* (1907-1908), *29:* 29-618.

HARRIS, ZELLIG S.
1940. Review of L. H. Gray, *Foundations of Language*. *Lg.*, *16:* 216-231.
1951a. Review of David G. Mandelbaum (Ed.), *Selected Writings of Edward Sapir in Language, Culture and Personality*. *Lg.*, *27:* 288-333.
1951b. *Methods in Structural Linguistics*. Chicago: University of Chicago Press. [Also, *Structural Linguistics*. Chicago: University of Chicago Press (Phoenix Books, P52).]
1954. Distributional Structure. *Word*, *10* (2-3): 146-162.

HAUDRICOURT, ANDRÉ
1961. Richesse en phonèmes et richesse en locuteurs. *L'Homme*, *1* (1): 175-208.

HAUGEN, EINAR
1953. *The Norwegian Language in America: A Study in Bilingual Behavior*. Philadelphia: University of Pennsylvania Press. 2 vols.
1956. *Bilingualism in the Americas: A Bibliography and Research Guide*. (American Dialect Society, No. 26.) Alabama: University of Alabama Press.
1957. The Semantics of Icelandic Orientation. *Word*, *13:* 447-60.

HENLE, PAUL (ED.)
1958. *Language, Thought, and Culture*. Ann Arbor: University of Michigan Press.

HERSKOVITS, MELVILLE J.
1950. *Man and His Works*. New York: Knopf.

HERTZLER, J. O.
1953. Toward a Sociology of Language. *Social Forces*, *32:* 109-119.

HERZOG, GEORGE
1934. Speech Melody and Primitive Music. *Musical Quarterly*, *20:* 452-466.
1935. Speech Melody and Primitive Music. *Africa*, *8:* 375-377.
1941. Culture Change and Language: Shifts in the Pima Vocabulary. In L. Spier, A. I. Hallowell, and S. S. Newman (Eds.), *Language, Culture, and Personality*. Menasha, Wis.: Banta.
*1945. Drum-Signaling in a West African Tribe. *Word*, *1:* 217-238.
1946. Some Linguistic Aspects of American Indian Poetry. *Word*, *2:* 82.
1949. Linguistic Approaches to Personality. In S. Stanfield Sargent and Marian W. Smith (Eds.), *Culture and Personality*. New York: Wenner-Gren Foundation for Anthropological Research. Pp. 93-102.

HERZOG, GEORGE, and C. G. BLOOAH
1936. *Jabo Proverbs from Liberia*. London: International Institute of African Languages and Cultures.

HEWITT, J. N. B.

1893. Polysynthesis in the Languages of the American Indians. *AA* (o.s.), *6:* 381-407.

HILL, A. A.

*1952. A Note on Primitive Languages. *IJAL, 18:* 172-177.

HILL, TREVOR

1958. Institutional Linguistics. *Orbis, 7:* 441-455.

HILL, W. W.

1943. Navaho Humor. *General Series in Anthropology, 9:* 1-28.

HJELMSLEV, LOUIS

1935–1937. La Catégorie des Cas. Étude de Grammaire Générale, I, II. *Acta Jutlandica, 7* (1); *9* (2).

1943. *Omkring Sprogteoriens Grundlaeggelse.* Copenhagen. [See 1953, 1961.]

1953. *Prolegomena to a Theory of Language.* Translated from the Danish by Francis Whitfield. (IUPAL; Memoirs of *IJAL,* No. 7.) Bloomington.

1959. *Essais Linguistiques.* (Travaux du Cercle Linguistique de Copenhague, No. 12). Copenhagen: Nordisk Sprog—og Kulturforlag.

1961. *Prolegomena to a Theory of Language.* Revised translation. Madison: University of Wisconsin Press.

HOCART, A. M.

1917. The Psychological Interpretation of Language. *British Journal of Psychology, 5:* 267-280.

1918. A Point of Grammar and a Study in Method. *AA, 20:* 265-279.

HOCKETT, CHARLES F.

*1948a. Implications of Bloomfield's Algonquian Studies. *Lg., 24:* 117-131. [Also in Martin Joos (Ed.), *Readings in Linguistics.* Washington, D.C.: American Council of Learned Societies. Pp. 281-289.]

1948b. A Note on "Structure." *IJAL, 14:* 269-271. [Also in Martin Joos (Ed.), *Readings in Linguistics.* Washington, D.C.: American Council of Learned Societies, 1957. Pp. 279-280.]

1948c. Biophysics, Linguistics, and the Unity of Science. *American Scientist, 36:* 558-572.

1950. Age Grading and Linguistic Continuity. *Lg., 26:* 449-457.

1954a. Two Models of Grammatical Description. *Word, 10,* (2-3): 210-231. [Also in Martin Joos (Ed.), *Readings in Linguistics.* Washington, D.C.: American Council of Learned Societies, 1957. Pp. 386-399.]

1954b. Chinese Versus English: An Exploration of the Whorfian Thesis. In Harry Hoijer (Ed.), *Language in Culture.* (Comparative Studies of Cultures and Civilizations, No. 3; Memoirs of the American Anthropological Association, No. 79.) Chicago: University of Chicago Press. Pp.: 106-123. [Also in Morton H. Fried (Ed.), *Readings in Anthropology.* Vol. I, *Physical Anthropology, Linguistics, Archaeology.* New York: Crowell, 1959. Pp. 232-248.]

1955. *A Manual of Phonology.* (IUPAL; Memoirs of *IJAL,* No. II.) Bloomington.

1958. *A Course in Modern Linguistics.* New York: Macmillan.

1959. Animal "Languages" and Human Languages. In J. N. Spuhler (Arranger), *The Evolution of Man's Capacity for Culture*. Detroit: Wayne University Press. Pp. 32-39.

1960a. The Origin of Speech. *Scientific American*, September, pp. 3-10.

1960b. Ethno-linguistic Implications of Studies in Linguistics and Psychiatry In W. Austin (Ed.), *Report of the Ninth Annual Round Table Meeting on Linguistics and Language Study*. Pp. 175-193. Washington, D.C.: Georgetown University Press.

HODGE, F. W. (ED.)

1907-1910. *Handbook of American Indians North of Mexico*. (BAE-B 30.) Washington, D.C.: Smithsonian Institution. 2 vols. (Re-issued, New York: Pageant Books, 1959.)

HOENIGSWALD, HENRY M.

1946. Sound Change and Linguistic Structure. *Lg.*, *22:* 138-143. [Also in Martin Joos (Ed.), *Readings in Linguistics*. Washington, D.C.: American Council of Learned Societies, 1957. Pp. 139-141.]

1950. The Principal Step in Comparative Grammar. *Lg.*, *26:* 357-364. [Also in Martin Joos (Ed.), *Readings in Linguistics*, Washington, D.C.: American Council of Learned Societies, 1957. Pp. 298-302.]

1960. *Language Change and Linguistic Reconstruction*. Chicago: University of Chicago Press. [Reviewed, W. L. Chafe, *Lg.*, 1961, *37:* 113-120; F. W. Householder, Jr., *IJAL* 1962, *28:* 69-79.]

1962. Bilingualism, Presumable Bilingualism, and Diachrony. *AL*, *4* (1): 1-5.

HOGGART, RICHARD

1957. *The Uses of Literacy: Changing Patterns in English Mass Culture*. London. Chatto and Windus; Fair Lawn, N.J.: Essential Books. (Boston: Beacon [Paperback 120], 1962; with subtitle, *Aspects of Workingclass Life with Special Reference to Publications and Entertainments*, London: Pelican [A431], 1962.)

HOIJER, HARRY

1938. The Southern Athapaskan Languages. *AA*, *40:* 75-87.

1941. Methods in the Classification of American Indian Languages. In L. Spier, A. I. Hallowell, and S. S. Newman (Eds.), *Language, Culture, and Personality*. Menasha, Wis.: Banta. Pp. 3-14.

*1948c. Linguistic and Cultural Change. *Lg.*, *24:* 335-345.

*1951. Cultural Implications of Some Navaho Linguistic Categories. *Lg.*, *27:* 111-120.

1953. The Relation of Language to Culture. In A. L. Kroeber *et al.*, *Anthropology Today*. Chicago: University of Chicago Press. Pp. 554-573.

1954b. The Sapir-Whorf Hypothesis. In Hoijer (Ed.), *Language in Culture*. (Comparative Studies of Cultures and Civilizations, No. 3; Memoirs of the American Anthropological Association, No. 79.) Chicago: University of Chicago Press. Pp. 92-105. [Also in Morton H. Fried (Ed.), *Readings in Anthropology*. Vol. I, *Physical Anthropology*, *Linguistics*, *Archaeology*. New York: Crowell, 1959. Pp. 219-231.]

1961. Anthropological Linguistics. In Christine Mohrmann, Alf Sommerfelt, and Joshua Whatmough (Eds.), *Trends in European and American Linguistics, 1936-1960*. Utrecht and Antwerp: Spectrum. Pp. 110-127.

HOIJER, HARRY (ED.)

1946. *Linguistic Structures of Native America.* (Viking Fund Publications in Antropology, No. 6). New York: Wenner-Gren Foundation for Anthropological Research, Inc.

1954a. *Language in Culture.* (Comparative Studies of Cultures and Civilizations, No. 3; Memoirs of the American Anthropological Association, No. 79.] Chicago: University of Chicago Press.

HOUSEHOLDER, FRED W., JR.

1957. Rough Justice in Linguistics. In Paul L. Garvin (Ed.), *Report of the Seventh Annual Round Table Meeting on Linguistics and Language Study.* (Monograph Series on Languages and Linguistics, No. 9.) Washington, D.C.: Georgetown University Press. Pp. 153-160.

HOUSEHOLDER, FRED W., and SOL SAPORTA (EDS.)

1962. *Problems in Lexicography.* (RCAFL-P 21; *IJAL, 28* (2), Part IV.) Bloomington.

HULME, HILDA M.

1962. *Explorations in Shakespeare's Language. Some Problems of Word Meaning in the Dramatic Text.* London: Longmans.

HUMBOLDT, WILHELM VON

1836. *Über die Kawisprache.* Part I, *Über die Verschiedenheit des Menschlichen Sprachbaues und Ihren Einfluss auf die geistige Entwickelung des Menschengeschlechts.* (Abhandlungen der Akademie der Wissenschaften zu Berlin, as of 1832, 1836-1839.) Berlin. (Reprinted, Bonn: Dümmlers Verlag, 1960.]

HYMES, DELL H.

1955. Positional Analysis of Categories: A Frame for Reconstruction. *Word, 11:* 10-23.

1956a. Review of Papers from the Symposium on American Indian Linguistics held at Berkeley, July 7, 1951. *Lg., 32:* 585-602.

1956b. Na-Dene and Positional Analysis of Categories. *AA, 58:* 624-638.

1958a. Linguistic Features Peculiar to Chinookan Myths. *IJAL, 24:* 253-257.

1958b. Tradition Trend in Archaeology and Linguistics. *SJA, 14:* 152-155.

1959a. Myth and Tale Titles of the Lower Chinook. *JAF, 72:* 139-145.

1959b. Field Work in Linguistics and Anthropology [Annotated bibliography]. *Studies in Linguistics, 14:* 82-91.

1959c. Genetic Relationship: Retrospect and Prospect. *AL, 1* (2): 50-66.

1960a. Lexicostatistics So Far. *CA, 1* (1): 3-44.

1960b. Phonological Aspects of Style: Some English Sonnets. In Thomas A. Sebeok (Ed.), *Style in Language.* New York: Wiley; Cambridge: Technology Press. Pp. 109-131.

1960c. Ob-Ugric Metrics. *Anthropos, 55:* 574-576.

1960d. Discussion of the Symposium on Translation Between Language and Culture. *AL, 2:* 81-85.

1960e. More on Lexicostatistics. *CA, 1:* 338-345.

1961a. On Typology of Cognitive Styles in Language (with Examples from Chinookan). *AL, 3* (1): 22-54.

1961b. Linguistic Aspects of Cross-Cultural Personality Study. In Bert Kaplan (Ed.), *Studying Personality Cross-Culturally*. New York: Harper & Row.
1961c. Functions of Speech: An Evolutionary Approach. In Fred Gruber (Ed.), *Anthropology and Education*. Philadelphia: University of Pennsylvania Press. Pp. 55-83.
1961d. Abstract of Vachek, The London Group of Linguistics. *IJAL, 27*: 166-167.
*1961e. Alfred Louis Kroeber. *Lg., 37:* 1-28.
1961f. Review of Walter Goldschmidt (Ed.), *The Anthropology of Franz Boas*. *JAF, 74:* 87-90.
1962a. The Ethnography of Speaking. In Thomas Gladwin and William C. Sturtevant (Eds.). *Anthropology and Human Behavior*. Washington, D.C.: Anthropological Society of Washington. Pp. 13-53.
1962b. [Comment]. *CA, 3:* 136-141.
1963a. Objectives and Concepts in Linguistic Anthropology. In David Mandelbaum et al. (Eds.), *Teaching Anthropology*. (Memoirs of the American Anthropological Association, No. 93.) Berkeley and Los Angeles: University of California Press. Pp. 275-302.
1963b. Toward a History of Linguistic Anthropology. *AL, 5* (1): 59-103.
1964. A Perspective for Linguistic Anthropology. In Sol Tax (Ed.), *Horizons of Anthropology*. Chicago: Aldine. Pp. 92-107.

JABERG, KARL
1936. *Aspects géographiques du langage*. Paris: Droz.

JABERG, KARL, and JACOB JUD
1928-1940. *Sprach und Sachatlas Italiens und der Sudschweiz*. Zofingen, Switzerland: Ringmiret.

JACKSON, KENNETH
1953. *Language and History in Early Britain: A Chronological Survey of the Brittonic Languages First to Twelfth Century A.D.* Cambridge: Harvard University Press.

JAKOBSON, ROMAN
1929. Remarques sur l'évolution phonologique du russe comparée à celle des autres langues slaves. (*Travaux du Cercle Linguistique de Prague, 2*. [Also in Jakobson, 1962, pp. 7-116.]
1931a. Prinzipien der historischen Phonologie. *Travaux du Cercle Linguistique de Prague, 4:* 247-267. [Also in Jakobson, 1962, pp. 202-220.]
1933. La Scuola Linguistica di Praga. *La Cultura, 12:* 633-641.
1939. Observations sur le classement phonologique des consonnes. *Proceedings of the Third International Congress of Phonetic Sciences* (*Ghent, 1938*). Ghent. Pp. 34-41. [Also in Jakobson, 1962, pp. 272-279.]
1942. *Kindersprache, Aphasie und allgemeine Lautgetsetze*. Uppsala: Spräkvetenskapliga Sällskapets i Uppsala Förhandlingar, 1940-1942 (=Uppsala Universitets Arsskrift, 1942, No. 9.) [Also in Jakobson, 1962, pp. 328-401.]
1944. Franz Boas' Approach to Language. *IJAL, 10:* 188-197.
1949. Principes de phonologie historique. In N. S. Troubetzkoy, *Principes de Phonologie*. Translated by J. Cantineau. Paris: Klincksieck, Pp. 315-336. [Also in Jakobson, 1962, pp. 202-220.]

1953. [Chapter Two.] In Claude Levi-Strauss *et al.* (Eds.), *Results of the Conference of Anthropologists and Linguists.* (IUPAL; Memoirs of *IJAL*, No. 8.) Bloomington.

1957a. The Cardinal Dichotomy in Language. In Ruth Nanda Anshen, (Ed.), *Language: An Inquiry into Its Meaning and Function.* New York: Harper & Row. Pp. 155-173.

1957b. *Shifters, Verbal Categories, and the Russian Verb.* Cambridge: Harvard University, Russian Language Project.

1958. Typological Studies and their Contribution to Historical Comparative Linguistics. In Eva Sivertsen (Ed.), *Proceedings of the Eighth International Congress of Linguists* (*Oslo, 1957*). Oslo: Oslo University Press. Pp. 17-35. [Also in Jakobson, 1962, pp. 523-531.]

1959. Boas' View of Grammatical Meaning. In Walter Goldschmidt (Ed.), (1959), pp. 139-145.

1960a. Concluding Statement: Linguistics and Poetics. In Thomas A. Sebeok (Ed.), *Style in Language.* New York: Wiley; Cambridge: Technology Press. Pp. 350-373.

1962. *Selected Writings.* Vol. I, *Phonological Studies.* The Hague: Mouton.

JAKOBSON, ROMAN, C. GUNNAR M. FANT, and MORRIS HALLE

1952. *Preliminaries to Speech Analysis. The Distinctive Features and Their Correlates.* (Acoustics Laboratory, Massachusetts Institute of Technology, Technical Report 13.) Cambridge.

JAKOBSON, ROMAN, and MORRIS HALLE

1956. *Fundamentals of Language.* The Hague: Mouton. [Also in part in Jakobson, *Selected Writings.* Vol. I. *Phonological Studies.* The Hague: Mouton. Pp. 464-504.]

JANET, PIERRE, and GEORGES DUMAS (EDS.)

1933. *Psychologie du langage.* Paris: Alcan [*Journal de psychologie: normale et pathologique, 30* (1-4).]

JESPERSEN, OTTO

1894. *Progress in Language.* London: Sonnenschein; New York: Macmillan.

1905. *Growth and Structure of the English Language.* New York: Stechert. (Reprinted, New York: Doubleday Anchor Book [A46], 1955.)

1922. *Language, Its Nature, Development, and Origin.* London: Allen & Unwin.

1924. *The Philosophy of Grammar.* London: Allen & Unwin.

1925. *Mankind, Nation and Individual from a Linguistic Point of View.* Oslo. [Also, Bloomington: Indiana University Press, 1964.]

1941. *Efficiency in Linguistic Change.* (2nd Ed.) (Det. KGL. Danske Videnskabernes Selskab Historisk-Filologiske Meddelelser, Vol. 25, No. 4.) Copenhagen: Ejnar Munksgaard (Reprinted 1949).

JOHANSEN, SVEND

1949. La notion de signe dans la glossématique et dans l'esthétique. *Recherches structurales.* (Travaux du Cercle Linguistique de Copenhague, No. 5.) Copenhagen: Nordisk Sprog-og Kulturforlag. Pp. 288-303.

JOOS, MARTIN

1950. Description of Language Design. *The Journal of the Acoustical Society of America, 22:* 701-708. [Also in Joos (Ed.), *Readings in Linguistics.*

Washington, D.C.: American Council of Learned Societies, 1957. Pp. 349-356.]

1952. The Medieval Sibilants. *Lg.*, *28:* 222-231. [Also in Joos (Ed.), *Readings in Linguistics*. Washington, D.C.: American Council of Learned Societies, 1957. Pp. 377-382.]

1958a. Semology: A Linguistic Theory of Meaning. *Studies in Linguistics*, *13:* 53-70.

JOOS, MARTIN (ED.)

1957. *Readings in Linguistics*. Washington, D.C.: American Council of Learned Societies.

KAINZ, F.

1946-1954. *Psychologie der Sprache*. Vienna. 4 vols. (Vol. 5 in preparation.)

KAISER, L. (ED.)

1957. *Manual of Phonetics*. Amsterdam: North-Holland.

KANTOR, J. R.

1936. *An Objective Psychology of Grammar*. Bloomington: Indiana University Press. (Reprinted, Bloomington: Principia Press, 1952. [Reviewed, H. V. Velten, *Lg.*, 1938, *14:* 66-68; S. S. Newman, *IJAL*, 1953, *19:* 312-313; N. G. Esteres, *Word*, 1955, *11:* 117-122.]

KAPLAN, BERT (ED.)

1961. *Studying Personality Cross-Culturally*. New York: Harper & Row.

KEESING, FELIX M., and MARIE M. KEESING

1956. *Elite Communication in Samoa: A Study in Leadership*. Stanford: Stanford University Press. [Reviewed, Ward H. Goodenough, *Lg.*, 1957, *33:* 424-429.]

KENYON, JOHN S.

1948. Cultural Levels and Functional Varieties of English. *College English*, *10:* 31-36. [Also in Harold B. Allen (Ed.), *Readings in Applied English Linguistics*. New York: Appleton-Century-Crofts, 1958. Pp. 215-221.]

KLAUSNER, SAMUEL Z.

1955. Phonetics, Personality and Status in Israel. *Word*, *11:* 209-215.

1956. Reply to Haim Blanc's "A Note on Israeli Hebrew 'Psychophonetics' " (*Word*, *12:* 106-113). *Word*, *12:* 113-114.

KLOSS, H.

1952. *Die Entwicklung neuer germanischer Kultursprachen von 1800 bis 1950*. Munich: Pohl.

KLUCKHOHN, CLYDE

1945. The Personal Document in Anthropological Science. In Louis Gottschalk, Clyde Kluckhohn, and Robert Angell, *The Use of Personal Documents in History, Anthropology, and Sociology*. (Social Science Research Council, Bulletin 53.) Washington, D.C.

1954. Culture and Behavior. In Gardner Lindzey (Ed.), *Handbook of Social Psychology*. Cambridge: Addison-Wesley. Pp. 921-976.

1956. Some Navaho Value Terms in Behavioral Context. *Lg.*, *32:* 140-145.

1961. Notes on Some Anthropological Aspects of Communication. *AA*, *63* (5): 895-909 (With comment by A. L. Kroeber, pp. 910-912).

KROEBER, A. L.

1909. Classificatory Systems of Relationship. *JRAI*, *39:* 77-84. [Also in Kroeber, 1952, pp. 175-181.]

1936. Kinship and History. *AA*, *38:* 338-341. [Also in Kroeber, 1952, pp. 202-205.]

1937. Athabascan Kin Term Systems. *AA*, *39:* 602-608. [Also in Kroeber, 1952, pp. 206-209.]

1939a. *Cultural and Natural Areas of Native North America.* (UCP-AAE 38.) Berkeley and Los Angeles: University of California Press. Pp. 1-242.

1939b. An Outline of the History of American Indian Linguistics. *American Council of Learned Societies*, *Bulletin*, no. 29, pp. 116-120.

1941. Some Relations of Linguistics and Ethnology. *Lg.*, *17:* 289-290.

1943. Structure, Function and Pattern in Biology and Anthropology. *The Scientific Monthly*, *56:* 105-113. [Also in Kroeber, 1952, pp. 85-94.]

1950. The History and Present Orientation of Cultural Anthropology. Paper prepared for 49th Annual Meeting, American Anthropological Association, Berkeley. In Kroeber, *The Nature of Culture.* Chicago: University of Chicago Press, 1952. Pp. 144-151.

1952. *The Nature of Culture*. Chicago: University of Chicago Press.

1955. Linguistic Time Depth Results So Far and Their Meaning. *IJAL*, *21:* 91-104.

*1960a. Statistics, Indo-European, and Taxonomy. *Lg.*, *36:* 1-21.

1960b. Yurok Speech Usages. In Stanley A. Diamond (Ed.), *Culture in History*. New York: Columbia University Press. Pp. 993-999.

1961. Semantic Contribution of Lexicostatistics. *IJAL*, *27:* 1-8.

KROEBER, A. L., *et al.*

1953. *Anthropology Today. An Encyclopedic Inventory*. Chicago: University of Chicago Press.

KRONASSER, H.

1952. *Handbuch der Semasiologie. Kurze Einführung in die Geschichte, Problematik, und Terminologie der Bedeutungslehre.* (Bibliothek der allgemeinen Sprachwissenschaft, No. 1; Reiche: Handbücher.) Heidelberg: Winter.

KURYLOWICZ, J.

1945-1949. La nature des procès dits "analogiques." *Acta Linguistica*, *5* (1): 15-37.

LADO, ROBERT

1957. *Linguistics Across Cultures*. Ann Arbor: University of Michigan Press.

LANDAR, HERBERT J.

1962. Fluctuation of Forms in Navaho Kinship Terminology. *AA*, *64:* 985-1000.

LANGER, SUZANNE K.

1942. *Philosophy in a New Key*. Cambridge: Harvard University Press. (Various subsequent editions, including Mentor Books and Penguin Books, 1948.)

LEACH, E. A.

1958. Concerning Trobriand Clans and the Kinship Category "Tabu." In Jack Goody (Ed.), *The Developmental Cycle in Domestic Groups.*

(Cambridge Papers in Social Anthropology, No. 1.) Pp. 120-145. Cambridge: Cambridge University Press.

LEACH, MARIA (ED.)

1949-1950. *Funk and Wagnall's Standard Dictionary of Folklore, Mythology and Legend*. New York: Funk and Wagnall. 2 vols.

LEHMANN, WINFRED P.

1962. *Historical Linguistics: An Introduction*. New York: Holt, Rinehart, and Winston. [Reviewed, W. Diver, *Word*, 1963, *19:* 100-106; W. Chafe, *AA*, 1963, *65:* 757-759.]

LENNEBERG, ERIC H.

1953. Cognition in Ethnolinguistics. *Lg.*, *29:* 463-471.

1960. Language, Evolution, and Purposive Behavior. In Stanley A. Diamond (Ed.), *Culture in History*. New York: Columbia University Press. Pp. 869-893.

LENNEBERG, ERIC H., and JOHN M. ROBERTS

1956. *The Language of Experience: A Case Study*. (IUPAL, Memoirs of *IJAL*, No. 13.) Bloomington.

LEOPOLD, WERNER F.

1939-1949. *Speech Development of a Bilingual Child: A Linguist's Record*. (Northwestern University Studies, Humanity Series, Nos. 6, 11, 18, 19.) Evanston, Ill.: Northwestern University Press. 4 vols.

1948. The Study of Child Language and Infant Bilingualism. *Word*, *1:* 249-259.

LESSER, ALEXANDER

1961. Social Fields and the Evolution of Society. *SJA*, *17:* 40-48.

LEVI-STRAUSS, CLAUDE

1949. Histoire et ethnologie. *Revue de Métaphysique et de Morale*, *54:* 363-391.

1951. Language and the Analysis of Social Laws. *AA*, *53:* 155-163.

1953a. [Chapter One.] In Levi-Strauss *et al.*, *Results of the Conference of Anthropologists and Linguists*. (IUPAL; Memoirs of *IJAL*, No. 8.) Bloomington. Pp. 1-10.

1953b. Social Structure. In A. L. Kroeber *et al.*, *Anthropology Today*. Chicago: University of Chicago Press. Pp. 524-553.

1955. The Structural Study of Myth. *JAF*, *68:* 428-444. [Also in Thomas A. Sebeok (Ed.), *Myth: A Symposium*. (American Folklore Society, Bibliographical and Special Series, No. 5.) Bloomington: Indiana University Press, 1958.]

1956. Structure et dialectique. In *For Roman Jakobson*. The Hague: Mouton. Pp. 289-294.

*1958a. L'Analyse structurale en linguistique et anthropologie. *Anthropologie Structurale*. Paris: Plon. Pp. 37-62. [Revised from, *Word*, 1945, *1:* 33-53.]

1958b. *Anthropologie Structurale*. Paris: Plon. [Including revised versions of earlier papers.] [Translated as *Structural Anthropology* by C. Jacobsen and B. G. Schoepf (New York: Basic Books, 1963).]

1960a. Four Winnebago Myths: A Structural Sketch. In Stanley A. Diamond (Ed.), *Culture in History*. New York: Columbia University Press. Pp. 869-893.

1960b. L'Analyse morphologique de contes russes. *International Journal of Slavic Linguistics and Poetics, 3:* 122-149.

1960c. La Structure et la forme. *Cahiers de l'Institut de Science Economique Appliquée*, No. 99, Série M, No. 7.

1960d. L'Anthropologie sociale devant l'histoire. *Annales*, 15: 4. 625-637. Paris: Armand Colin. [Extrait de la leçon inaugurale de la chair d'Anthropologie sociale, faite le 5 janvier 1960 au Collège de France.] [Extract published in *Diogenes*, 1960, *31:* 19-28, as "The Problem of Invariance in Anthropology."]

1961. La Geste d'Asduvàl. *Les Temps Modernes*, March, 1961, No. 179, pp. 1080-1123. (First published in l'annuaire 1958-1959 de l'École Pratique de Haute Études, VIe Section.)

1962. *La Pensée sauvage*. Paris: Plon.

LEVI-STRAUSS, CLAUDE, ROMAN JAKOBSON, C. F. VOEGELIN, and THOMAS A. SEBEOK

1953. *Results of the Conference of Anthropologists and Linguists.* [IUPAL; Memoirs of *IJAL*, No. 8.] Bloomington.

LEWIS, M. M.

1947. *Language in Society. The Linguistic Revolution and Social Change*. London: Nelson. (New York: Social Science Publishers, 1948.)

LINGUISTIC BIBLIOGRAPHY FOR THE YEARS 1939-1947.

Published by the Permanent International Committee of Linguists. Utrecht and Antwerp: Spectrum. 2 vols. Bibliographies published for each subsequent year with supplement for previous years.

LINTON, RALPH

1936. *The Study of Man.* New York: Appleton-Century.

LOMAX, ALAN

1959. Folk Song Style. *AA, 61:* 927-954.

LONGACRE, ROBERT E.

1958. Items in Context: Their Bearing on Translation Theory. *Lg., 34:* 482-491.

LONGACRE, ROBERT E., and RENÉ MILLON

1961. Proto-Mixtecan and Proto-Amuzgo-Mixtecan Vocabularies: A Preliminary Cultural Analysis. *AL, 3* (4): 1-44.

LOTZ, JOHN

1950. Speech and Language. *The Journal of the Acoustical Society of America, 22:* 712-717.

*1955. On Language and Culture. *IJAL, 21:* 187-189.

LOUNSBURY, FLOYD

1953. Field Methods and Techniques in Linguistics. In A. L. Kroeber *et al.*, *Anthropology Today*. Chicago: University of Chicago Press. Pp. 401-416.

1956. Semantic Analysis of the Pawnee Kinship Usage. *Lg., 32:* 158-194.

1960a. Language. In Bernard J. Siegel (Ed.), *Biennial Review of Anthropology 1959*. Stanford: Stanford University Press. Pp. 185-209.

1962. Language. In Bernard J. Siegel (Ed.), *Biennial Review of Anthropology 1961*. Stanford: Stanford University Press. Pp. 279-322.

LOWIE, ROBERT H.

1935. *The Crow Indians*. New York: Rinehart.

1937. *The History of Ethnological Theory*. New York: Rinehart.

1950. Observations on the Literary Style of the Crow Indians. *Beiträge zur Gesslungs-und Volkerwissenschaft, Festschrift Dr. Richard Thurnwald zu seinen achtzigsten Geburtstag gewidmet.* Berlin. Pp. 271-283. [Also in Cora Du Bois (Ed.), *Lowie's Selected Papers in Anthropology.* Berkeley and Los Angeles: University of California Press. Pp. 165-176.]

LURIA, A. R.

1959a. The Directive Function of Speech, I: Its Development in Early Childhood. *Word, 15* (2): 341-52.

1959b. The Directive Function of Speech, II: Its Dissolution in Pathological States of the Brain. *Word, 15:* 453-64.

LURIA, A. R., and F. I. YUDOVICH

1959. *Speech and the Development of Mental Processes in the Child.* London: Staples.

MACCOBY, ELEANOR, T. H. NEWCOMB, and E. L. HARTLEY (EDS.)

1958. *Readings in Social Psychology.* (3rd ed.) New York: Holt.

MCCORMACK, WILLIAM

1960. Social Dialects in Dharwar Kannada. In Charles A. Ferguson and John J. Gumperz (Eds.), *Linguistic Diversity in South Asia.* (RCAFL-P 13; *IJAL, 26* [3], Part III.) Bloomington. Pp. 79-91.

MCDAVID, RAVEN I., JR.

1946. Dialect Geography and Social Science Problems. *Social Forces, 25:* 168-172.

1948. Postvocalic /-r*/ in South Carolina: A Social Analysis. *American Speech, 23:* 194-203.

1952-1953. Some Social Differences in Pronunciation. *Language Learning, 4:* 102-116. [Also in Harold B. Allen (Ed.), *Readings in Applied English Linguistics.* New York: Appleton-Century-Crofts. Pp. 174-185.]

MCINTOSH, ANGUS

1952. *Introduction to a Survey of Scottish Dialects.* Edinburgh: Nelson.

MACLAY, HOWARD

1958. An Experimental Study of Language and Non-Linguistic Behavior. *SJA, 14:* 220-229.

MCLUHAN, MARSHALL

1962. *The Gutenberg Galaxy. The Making of Typographic Man.* Toronto: University of Toronto Press.

MCQUOWN, NORMAN A.

*1950. A Planned Auxiliary Language. *Lg., 26:* 175-185.

1954a. Analysis of the Cultural Content of Language Materials. In Harry Hoijer (Ed.), *Language and Culture.* (Comparative Studies of Cultures and Civilizations, No. 3; Memoirs of the American Anthropological Association, No. 79.) Chicago: University of Chicago Press. Pp. 20-31.

1960. American Indian and General Linguistics. *AA, 62:* 318-326.

MALINOWSKI, BRONISLAW

1920. Classificatory Particles in the Language of Kiriwina. *BSO(A)S, 1* (4): 33-78.

1922. *Argonauts of the Western Pacific.* London: Routledge.

1923. The Problem of Meaning in Primitive Languages. In C. K. Ogden and I. A. Richards, *The Meaning of Meaning*. London: Kegan Paul. Pp. 451-510. [Also in Malinowski, *Magic, Science and Religion and Other Essays*. Glencoe: Free Press, 1948. Pp. 451-510.]

1935. *Coral Gardens and Their Magic. A Study of the Methods of Tilling the Soil and of Agricultural Rites in the Trobriand Islands*. Vol. II, *The Language of Magic and Gardening*. New York: American; London: Allen & Unwin.

*1937. The Dilemma of Contemporary Linguistics [Review of M. M. Lewis, *Infant Speech*], *Nature, 140:* 172-173.

MALKIEL, YAKOV

1960a. Paradigmatic Resistance to Sound Change. The Old Spanish Preterite Forms *vide*, *vido* Against the Background of the Recession of Primary *-d-*. *Lg.*, *36:* 281-346.

1962a. Etymology and General Linguistics. *Word*, *18* (1-2): 198-219.

1962b. Weak Phonetic Change, Spontaneous Sound Shift, Lexical Contamination. *Lingua*, *11:* 263-275.

1962c. Review of Johannes Hubschmid, *Schläuche und Fässer; Substratprobleme*. *Lg.*, *38:* 149-185.

*1964. Distinctive Features of Romance Linguistics. [Written for this volume.]

MANDELBAUM, DAVID G. (ED.)

1949. *Selected Writings of Edward Sapir in Language, Culture, and Personality*. Berkeley and Los Angeles: University of California Press.

MAROUZEAU, J.

1949. *Quelques Aspects de la formation du latin littéraire*. (Collection Linguistique, Société de Linguistique de Paris, No. 53.) Paris: Klincksieck.

MARETT, R. R.

1912. *Anthropology*. London.

MARSH, GORDON H., and WILLIAM S. LAUGHLIN

1956. Human Anatomical Knowledge Among the Aleutian Islanders. *SJA*, *12:* 38-78.

MARTIN, SAMUEL

*1958. Speech Levels and Social Structure in Japan and Korea. Paper read at annual meeting, Asian Studies Association, New York City.

MARTINET, ANDRÉ

1953. Structural Linguistics. In A. L. Kroeber *et al.*, *Anthropology Today.*, Chicago: University of Chicago Press. Pp. 574-586.

1954. Dialect. *Romance Philology*, *8:* 1-11.

1955. *Economie des changements phonétiques*. (Bibliotheca Romanica. Ser. prima, Manualia et Commentationes, Vol. X.) Bern: Francke.

1960. *Éléments de linguistique générale*. (Collection Armand Colin, Section de Litterature, No. 349.) Paris: Colin.

1962. *A Functional View of Language*. (The Waynflete Lectures.) London: Oxford University Press.

MARTINET, ANDRÉ, and URIEL WEINREICH (EDS.)

1954. *Linguistics Today*. [*Word, 10*: 2-3. Published on the occasion of the

Columbia University Bicentennial.] New York: Linguistic Circle of New York.

MATHIOT, MADELEINE
*1962. Noun Classes and Folk Taxonomy in Papago. *AA*, *64* (2): 340-350.

MAUSS, M.
*1923. Discussion. *Journal de psychologie; normale et pathologique*, *20*: 944-947. [Also in A. Meillet, *Linguistique historique et linguistique générale*. (2nd ed.) (Collection Linguistique, Société de Linguistique de Paris, No. 8.) Paris: Champion. Vol. II, pp. 24-28. (Reprinted, 1938-1948.)]

MAY, L. CARLYLE
1956. A Survey of Glossolalia and Related Phenomena in Non-Christian Religions. *AA*, *58*: 75-96.

MEILLET, A.
1906a. L'État actuel des études de linguistique générale. [Leçon d'ouverture du cours de Grammaire comparée au Collège de France, lue le mardi 13 février 1906.] In Meillet, 1926-1936, Vol. I, pp. 1-18.
1906b. Comment les mots changent de sens. *L'Année Sociologique* (*1905-1906*). [Also in Meillet, 1926-1936, pp. 230-271]; partially translated in Talcott Parsons *et al.*, *Theories of Society*. Glencoe: Free Press, 1961. Vol. II.]
1913. *Aperçu d'une histoire de la langue grecque*. Paris: Hachette.
1918. Linguistique historique et linguistique générale. *Revista di Scienzia*, *4* (8). [Also in Meillet, 1926-1936, Vol. I, pp. 44-60.]
*1923. Le Genre feminin dans les langues Indo-Européennes. *Journal de psychologie: normale et pathologique*: *20*: 943-944. [Also in Meillet, 1926-1936, Vol. II, pp. 24-28.]
1925. *La Méthode comparative en linguistique historique*. (Instituttet for Sammenlignende Kulturforskning. Ser. A; Forflesninger, No. 2.) Oslo: Aschehoug (Nygard). (Reissued, Paris: Ancienne Honoré Champion, 1954.)
1926-1936. *Linguistique historique et linguistique générale*. (2nd ed.) (Collection Linguistique, Société de Linguistique de Paris, No. 8.) Paris: Champion. 2 vols. (Reprinted, 1938-1948.)
1933a. Linguistique et anthropologie. *L'Anthropologie*, *43*: 41 ff. [Also in Meillet, (1926-1936), Vol. II, pp. 84-89.]
1934. *Introduction à l'étude comparative des langues Indo-Européennes*. (7th ed.) Paris: Hachette. (New edition augmented and corrected by Emile Benveniste, 1953].

MEILLET, A., and MARCEL COHEN
1952. *Les Langues du monde*. By a group of linguists under the direction of Meillet and Cohen. (Rev. ed.) (Société de Linguistique de Paris.) Paris: Centre National de la Recherche Scientifique. (1st ed., 1924.)

MENCKEN, H. L.
1936. *The American Language. An Inquiry into the Development of English in the United States*. (4th ed.) New York: Knopf.
1945. *Supplement I* to *The American Language*. New York: Knopf.

MILLER, GEORGE A.
1951. *Language and Communication*. New York: McGraw-Hill.

1954. Psycholinguistics. In Gardner Lindzey (Ed.), *Handbook of Social Psychology*. Cambridge: Addison-Wesley. Pp. 693-708.

1956. The Magical Number Seven, Plus or Minus Two: Some Limits on Our Capacity for Processing Information. *The Psychological Review*, *63:* 81-97.

MILNER, G. B.

1961. The Samoan Vocabulary of Respect. *JRAI*, *91:* 296-317.

MOHRMANN, CHRISTINE, ALF SOMMERFELT, JOSHUA WHATMOUGH (EDS.)

1961. *Trends in European and American Linguistics, 1930-1960*. (Edited on the occasion of the Ninth International Congress of Linguists, Cambridge, Massachusetts, August 27–September 1, 1962, for the Permanent International Committee of Linguists.) Utrecht and Antwerp: Spectrum.

MORICE, A. G.

1933. Carrier Onomatology. *AA*, *35:* 632-658.

MORRIS, CHARLES W.

1939. *Foundations of the Theory of Signs*. (International Encyclopedia of Unified Science, Vol. 1, No. 2.) Chicago

1946. *Signs, Language and Behavior*. New York: Prentice-Hall.

MOULTON, WILLIAM G.

1960. The Short Vowel Systems of Northern Switzerland: A Study in Structural Dialectology. *Word*, *16:* 155-182.

MUELLER, HUGO (ED.)

1954. *Report on the Fifth Annual Round Table Meeting on Linguistics and Language Teaching*. (Monograph Series on Languages and Linguistics, No. 7.) Washington, D.C.: Georgetown University Press.

MULLER, HENRI F.

1945. Phénomènes sociaux et linguistiques. Un cas démontrable de concordance entre phénomènes d'ordre social et phénomènes d'ordre linguistique. *Word*, *1:* 121-131.

MURDOCK, GEORGE P.

1959. Cross-Language Parallels in Parental Kin Terms. *AL*, *1* (9): 1-6.

NADEL, S. F.

1951. *The Foundations of Social Anthropology*. London: Cohen and West.

*1954. Morality and Language Among the Nupe. *Man*, *54:* 55-57.

NELLIS, JANE GOODNER

1947. Sierra Zapotec Forms of Address. *IJAL*, *13:* 231-232.

NEWMAN, STANLEY S.

1939. Personal Symbolism in Language Patterns. *Psychiatry*, *2:* 177-182.

*1940. Linguistic Aspects of Yokuts Narrative Style. In Anna H. Gayton and Stanley S. Newman, *Yokuts and Western Mono Myths*. (UCPAR 5.) Berkeley and Los Angeles: University of California Press. Pp. 4-7.

1941. Behavior Patterns in Linguistic Structure: A Case Study. In L. Spier, A. I. Hallowell, and S. S. Newman (Eds.) *Language, Culture, and Personality*. Menasha, Wis.: Banta. Pp. 94-106.

1944. Cultural and Psychological Features in English Intonation. *Transactions of the New York Academy of Science*, *7:* 45-54.

1954. Semantic Problems in Grammatical Systems and Lexemes: A Search for Method. In Harry Hoijer (Ed.), *Language in Culture*. (Comparative Studies of Cultures and Civilizations, No. 3; Memoirs of the American Anthropological Association, No. 79.) Chicago: University of Chicago Press. Pp. 82-91.

*1955. Vocabulary Levels: Zuni Sacred and Slang Usage. *SJA*, *11:* 345-354.

NEWMAN, STANLEY S., and VERA G. MATHER

1938. Analysis of Spoken Language of Patients with Affective Disorders. *American Journal of Psychiatry, 94:*913-942.

NIDA, EUGENE A.

*1945. Linguistics and Ethnology in Translation Problems. *Word*, *1:* 194-208.

1947a. Field Methods in Descriptive Linguistics. *IJAL*, *13:* 138-146.

1947b. *Linguistic Interludes*. Glendale, Calif.: Summer Institute of Linguistics.

1947c. *Bible Translating: An Analysis of Principles and Procedures with Special Reference to Aboriginal Languages*. New York: American Bible Society.

1949. *Morphology: The Descriptive Analysis of Words*. (2nd ed.) (University of Michigan Publications, Linguistics II.) Ann Arbor: University of Michigan Press.

1952. *God's Word in Man's Language*. New York: Harper & Row.

1952-1953. Selective Listening. *Language Learning*, *6:* 17-23.

1958. Analysis of Meaning and Dictionary Making. *IJAL*, *24:* 279-292.

1960. *Mission and Message: The Communication of the Christian Faith*. New York: Harper & Row.

1961. Some Problems of Semantic Structure and Translation Equivalence. In *A William Cameron Townsend en el vigésimoquinto aniversario del Instituto Lingüístico de Verano*. Mexico, D.F. Pp. 313-325.

NYGARD, HOLGER OLOF

1958. *The Ballad of Heer Halewijn. Its Forms and Variations in Western Europe*. Knoxville: University of Tennessee Press.

OGDEN, C. K., and I. A. RICHARDS

1923. *The Meaning of Meaning*. London: Kegan Paul.

ÖHMAN, SUZANNE

1951. *Wortinhalt und Weltbild. Vergleichende und Methodologische Studien zu Bedeutungslehre und Wortfeldtheorie*. Stockholm.

1953. Theories of the "Linguistic Field." *Word*, *9:* 123-134.

OLIVER, D. L.

1949. *Human Relations and Language in a Papuan-speaking Tribe of Southern Bougainville, Solomon Islands*. (Peabody Museum Papers, Vol. 29.) Cambridge. Harvard University Press.

OPIE, IONA, and PETER OPIE

1959. *The Lore and Language of Schoolchildren*. Oxford: Oxford University Press.

OPLER, MORRIS E.

1937. Apache Data Concerning the Relation of Kinship Terminology to Social Classification. *AA*, *39:* 201-212.

OPLER, MORRIS E., and HARRY HOIJER
1940. The Raid and War-Path Language of the Chiricahua Apache. *AA, 42:* 617-634.

OSGOOD, CHARLES E.
1953. *Method and Theory in Experimental Psychology.* New York: Oxford University Press.

OSGOOD, CHARLES E., and THOMAS A. SEBEOK
1954. *Psycholinguistics, A Survey of Theory and Research Problems.* (IUPAL, Memoirs of *IJAL*, No. 10.) Bloomington. [Also, Supplement to *JASP*, 1954, *49*.]

OSGOOD, CHARLES E., GEORGE J. SUCI, and PERCY H. TANNENBAUM
1957. *The Measurement of Meaning.* Urbana: University of Illinois Press.

PARSONS, TALCOTT
1951. *The Social System.* Glencoe: Free Press.
1961. Language as a Groundwork of Culture. In Parsons *et al.* (Eds.), *Theories of Society.* Glencoe: Free Press. Pp. 971-976.

PARSONS, TALCOTT, EDWARD SHILS, KASPAR NAEGELE, and JESSE PITTS (EDS.)
1961. *Theories of Society.* Glencoe. Free Press. 2 vols.

PAUL, HERMANN
1960. *Prinzipien der Sprache Geschichte.* (6th unaltered ed.) Tübingen: Niemeyer.

PEDERSEN, H.
1931. *Linguistic Science in the Nineteenth Century.* Translated by J. Spargo. Cambridge: Harvard University Press. [Reissued as, *The Discovery of Language.* Bloomington: Indiana University Press, 1962.]

PETTITT, G. A.
1946. *Primitive Education in North America.* (UCP-AAE 43.) Berkeley and Los Angeles: University of California Press.

PHILLIPS, HERBERT B.
1959-1960. Problems of Translation and Meaning in Fieldwork. *Human Organization, 18:* 184-192. [Reprinted in R. N. Adams and J. J. Press (Eds.), *Human Organization Research, Field Relations and Techniques.* Homewood, Ill.: Dorsey. Pp. 290-307.]

PICKFORD, GLENNA R.
1957. American Linguistic Geography: A Sociological Appraisal. *Word, 12:* 211-233.

PIKE, KENNETH L.
1943. *Phonetics. A Critical Analysis of Phonetic Theory and a Technic for the Practical Description of Sounds.* (University of Michigan Publications, Language and Literature, No. 21.) Ann Arbor: University of Michigan Press.
1947. *Phonemics: A Technique for Reducing Languages to Writing.* (University of Michigan Publications in Linguistics, Vol. 3.] Ann Arbor: University of Michigan Press.

1948. *Tone Languages. A Technique for Determining the Number and Type of Pitch Contrasts in a Language, with Studies in Tonemic Substitution and Fusion.* Ann Arbor: University of Michigan Press.

1950. *Axioms and Procedures for Reconstructions in Comparative Linguistics: An Experimental Syllabus.* Glendale, Calif.: Summer Institute of Linguistics.

1952. More on Grammatical Prerequisites. *Word, 8:* 106-121.

1954–1955–1960. *Language in Relation to a Unified Theory of the Structure of Human Behavior*, Parts I, II, III. (Preliminary ed.) Glendale, Calif.: Summer Institute of Linguistics.

*1956. Towards a Theory of the Structure of Human Behavior. In *Estudios Antropológicos Publicados en Homenaje al Doctor Manuel Gamio.* Mexico, D.F. Pp. 659-671.

1957-1958. *Language and Life.* (W. H. Griffith Thomas Memorial Lectureship for 1956, Dallas Theological Seminary and Graduate School of Theology.) Glendale, Calif.: Summer Institute of Linguistics. [Reprinted from *Bibliotheca Sacra, 114:* 141-156, 255-262, 347-362; *115:* 36-43.]

1959. Language as Particle, Wave, and Field. *The Texas Quarterly, 2* (2): 37-54.

1960. Toward a Theory of Change and Bilingualism. *Studies in Linguistics, 15:* 1-7.

PILLAI, M., SHANMUGAM

1960. Tamil—Literary and Colloquial. In Charles A. Ferguson and John J. Gumperz (Eds.), *Linguistic Diversity in South Asia.* (RCAFL-P 13; *IJAL, 26* [3], Part III.) Bloomington. Pp. 27-42.

PITTENGER, ROBERT E., and HENRY LEE SMITH, JR.

1957. A Basis for Some Contributions of Linguistics to Psychiatry. *Psychiatry, 20:* 61-78.

PITTMAN, RICHARD S.

1948. Nahuatl Honorifics. *IJAL, 14:* 236-239.

POOL, ITHIEL DE SOLA (ED.)

1959. *Trends in Content Analysis.* Urbana: University of Illinois Press.

POTTER, SIMEON

1960. *Language in the Modern World.* Baltimore: Penguin (Pelican Books, A470).

PROPP, VLADIMIR

1958. *Morphology of the Folktale.* Edited by Svatava Pirkova-Jakobson; translated from the Russian by Laurence Scott (RCAFL-P 24; *IJAL, 24* [4], Part III; Bibliographical and Special Series of the American Folklore Society, No. 9.) Bloomington. (Original edition, 1928.)

PUTNAM, GEORGE N., and EDNA M. O'HERN

1955. *The Status Significance of an Isolated Urban Dialect.* (Language Dissertations, No. 53; Supplement to *Lg., 31* [4], Part II.) Baltimore: Linguistic Society of America.

QUINE, WILLARD V.

1959. Meaning and Translation. In Reuben A. Brower (Ed.), *On Translation.* (Harvard Studies in Comparative Literature, No. 23.) Cambridge: Harvard University Press. Pp. 148-172.

RADCLIFFE-BROWN, A. R.

1957. *A Natural Science of Society*. Glencoe: Free Press and Falcon's Wing Press.

RADIN, PAUL

1933. *The Method and Theory of Ethnology. An Essay in Criticism*. New York: McGraw-Hill.

1949. *The Culture of the Winnebago: As Described by Themselves*. (IUPAL; Memoirs of *IJAL*, No. 2.) Bloomington.

1950. *The Origin Myth of the Medicine Rite: Three Versions*. (IUPAL, Memoirs of *IJAL*, No. 3.) Bloomington.

RAY, PUNYA SLOKA

1961. The Value of a Language. *Lingua, 10:* 220-233.

REICHARD, GLADYS

1930. The Style of Cœur d'Alêne Mythology. *International Congress of Americanists, 24:* 244-253.

1944. *Prayer: The Compulsive Word*. (Monographs of the American Ethnological Society, No. 7.) New York: Augustin.

1945. Linguistic Diversity Among the Navaho Indians. *IJAL, 11:* 156-168.

1947. *An Analysis of Cœur d'Alêne Indian Myths*. (Memoirs of the American Folklore Society, No. 41.) Philadelphia.

REINICKE, JOHN

*1938. Trade Jargons and Creole Dialects as Marginal Languages. *Social Forces, 17:* 107-118.

REYBURN, WILLIAM O.

1956. *Problems and Procedures in Ethnolinguistic Surveys. An Outline Based on a Pilot Study in a Multilingual Area*. New York: American Bible Society.

1958. Don't Learn That Language. *Practical Anthropology, 5:* 151-178.

RICE, FRANK A. (ED.)

1962. *Study of the Role of Second Languages in Asia, Africa, and Latin America*. Washington, D.C.: Center for Applied Linguistics of the Modern Language Association of America.

RICHARDS, I. A.

1936. *Philosophy of Rhetoric*. New York and London: Oxford University Press.

ROBERTS, JOHN M., and BRIAN SUTTON-SMITH

1962. Child Training and Game Involvement. *Ethnology, 1:* 166-185.

ROBINS, R. H.

1959. Linguistics and Anthropology. *Man, 59:* 175-178 (Article 283).

ROMNEY, A. K.

1958. The Genetic Model and Uto-Aztekan Time Perspective. *Davidson Journal of Anthropology, 3:* 35-41.

ROSS, ALAN S. C.

1954. Linguistic Class Indicators in Present-Day English. *Neuphilologische Mitteilungen, 55:* 20-56.

ROWE, JOHN H.

1959. Archaeological Dating and Cultural Process. *SJA, 15:* 317-324.

RUBIN, JOAN

1962. Bilingualism in Paraguay. *AL*, *4* (1): 52-58.

RUESCH, JURGEN, and GREGORY BATESON

1951. *Communication. The Social Matrix of Psychiatry.* New York: Norton.

RUESCH, JURGEN, and WELDON KEES

1956. *Nonverbal Communication. Notes on the Visual Perception of Human Relations.* Berkeley and Los Angeles: University of California Press.

SALISBURY, R. F.

1962. Notes on Bilingualism and Linguistic Change in New Guinea. *AL*, *4* (7): 1-13.

SAPIR, EDWARD

[*SWES.* = *Selected Writings of Edward Sapir in Language, Culture, and Personality.* Edited by David G. Mandelbaum. Berkeley and Los Angeles: University of California Press, 1949.]

1910. Song Recitative in Paiute Mythology. *JAF*, *23:* 455-472. [Also in *SWES*, pp. 463-467, in part.]

1912. Language and Environment. *AA*, *14:* 226-242. [Also in *SWES*, pp. 89-103; Frederica De Laguna (Ed.), *Selected Papers from the American Anthropologist, 1888-1920.* New York: Harper & Row, 1960. Pp. 434-450.]

1915. *Abnormal Types of Speech in Nootka.* (Canada, Department of Mines, Geological Survey, Memoir 62; Anthropological Series No. 5.) Ottawa: Government Printing Bureau. [Also in *SWES*, pp. 179-196.]

1916. *Time Perspective in Aboriginal American Culture: A Study in Method.* (Canada, Department of Mines, Geological Survey, Memoir 90; Anthropological Series, No. 13.) Ottawa: Government Printing Bureau. [Also in *SWES*, pp. 389-462.]

1921. *Language.* New York: Harcourt, Brace.

1924a. The Grammarian and His Language. *American Mercury*, *1:* 149-155. [Also in *SWES*, pp. 150-159.]

1924b. Culture, Genuine and Spurious. *American Journal of Sociology*, *29:* 401-429. [Also in *SWES*, pp. 308-331.]

1925. Sound Patterns in Language. *Lg.*, *1:* 37-51. [Also in *SWES*, pp. 33-45; Martin Joos (Ed.), *Readings in Linguistics*, Washington, D.C.: American Council of Learned Societies, 1957. Pp. 19-25.]

1927a. Speech as a Personality Trait. *American Journal of Sociology*, *32:* 892-905. [Also in *SWES*, pp. 533-543.]

1927b. The Unconscious Patterning of Behavior in Society. In E. S. Dummer (Ed.), *The Unconscious: A Symposium.* New York: Knopf. Pp. 114-142. [Also in *SWES*, pp. 544-559.]

1929a. Central and North American Languages. *Encyclopaedia Britannica* (14th ed.), *5:* 138-141. [Also in *SWES*, pp. 169-178.]

1929b. Male and Female Forms of Speech in Yana. In St. W. J. Teeuwen (Ed.), *Donum Natalicium Schrijnen.* Nijmegen-Utrecht: Dekker and Van de Vegt. Pp. 79-85. [Also in *SWES*, pp. 206-212.]

1929c. The Status of Linguistics as a Science. *Lg.*, *5:* 207-214. [Also in *SWES*, pp. 160-166.]

1930. *Totality*. (Language Monographs, No. 6.) Baltimore: Linguistic Society of America.

1931a. Communication. *Encyclopaedia of the Social Sciences, 4:* 78-81. [Also in *SWES*, pp. 104-109.]

*1931b. Conceptual Categories in Primitive Languages. *Science, 74:* 578.

1931c. The Concept of Phonetic Law as Tested in Primitive Languages by Leonard Bloomfield. In Stuart A. Rice (Ed.), *Methods in Social Science: A Case Book*. Chicago: University of Chicago Press. Pp. 297-306. [Also in *SWES*, pp. 73-82.]

1931d. Dialect. *Encyclopaedia of the Social Sciences, 5:* 123-126. [Also in *SWES*, pp. 83-88.]

1931e. The Function of an International Auxiliary Language. *Psyche, 11:* 4-15. [Also in *SWES*, pp. 110-121; H. N. Shenton, Edward Sapir, and Otto Jespersen (Eds.), *International Communication: A Symposium on the Language Problem*. London. pp. 65-94.]

1933a. Language. *Encyclopaedia of the Social Sciences. 9:* 155-169. [Also in *SWES*, pp. 7-32.]

1933b. La Réalité psychologique des phonémes. In Pierre Janet and Georges Dumas (Eds.), *Psychologie du langage*. Paris: Alcan. Pp. 247-265. [*Journal de psychologie: normale et pathologique, 30* (1-4).] [Also in *SWES*, pp. 46-60, in English translation.]

1936. Internal Linguistic Evidence Suggestive of the Northern Origin of the Navaho. *AA, 38:* 224-235. [Also in *SWES*, pp. 213-224.]

1944. Grading: A Study in Semantics. *Philosophy of Science, 11:* 93-116. [Also in *SWES*, pp. 122-149.]

1947. The Relation of American Indian Linguistics to General Linguistics. *SJA, 3:* 1-4.

1957. *Culture, Language, and Personality*. (Selections from the larger *Selected Writings of Edward Sapir*.) Ed. by David G. Mandelbaum. Berkeley and Los Angeles: University of California Press.

SAPIR, EDWARD, and HARRY HOIJER

1942. *Navaho Texts*. (William Dwight Whitney Linguistic Series; Special Publications of the Linguistic Society of America.) Iowa City: University of Iowa, Linguistic Society of America.

SAPIR, EDWARD, and MORRIS SWADESH

*1946. American Indian Grammatical Categories. *Word, 2:* 103-112.

SAPORTA, SOL (ED.)

1961. *Psycholinguistics. A Book of Readings*. With the assistance of Jarvis Bastian. New York: Holt, Rinehart and Winston.

SCHLAUCH, MARGARET

1943. *The Gift of Tongues*. New York: Modern Age.

1946. Early Behaviorist Psychology and Contemporary Linguistics. *Word, 2:* 25-36.

1955. *The Gift of Language*. (Rev. ed. of *The Gift of Tongues*.) New York: Dover.

SCHNEIDER, DAVID, and G C. HOMANS

1955. Kinship Terminology and the American Kinship System. *AA, 57:* 1194-1208.

SCHRADER, O.
1890. *Prehistoric Antiquities of the Aryan Peoples*. London: Griffen. (Translation of *Sprachvergleichung und Urgeschichte* [2nd ed.].)
1906. *Sprachvergleichung und Urgeschichte*. (3rd ed.) Jena.

SCHRADER, O., and A. NEHRING
1917-1929. *Reallexikon der indogermanischen Altertumskunde*. (2nd ed.) Berlin: De Gruyter. 2 vols.

SEBEOK, THOMAS A.
1944. Review of H. V. Velten, *The Nez Perce Verb*. *IJAL*, *10:* 213-214.
1950. The Meaning of "Ural-Altaic." *Lingua*, *2* (2): 124-139.
*1953a. Structure and Content of Cheremis Charms. *Anthropos*, *48:* 369-388.
1960a. Folksong Viewed as Code and Message. In Sebeok (Ed.), *Style in Language*. New York: Wiley; Cambridge: Technology Press. Pp. 220-235.
1962. Coding in the Evolution of Signalling Behavior. *Behavioral Science*, *7:* 430-442.
1963. The Informational Model of Language. Analog and Digital Coding in Animal and Human Communication. In Paul Garvin (Ed.), *Natural Language and the Computer*. New York: McGraw Hill.

SEBEOK, THOMAS A. (ED.)
1960b. *Style in Language*. New York: Wiley; Cambridge: Technology Press.

SERVICE, ELMAN R.
1960. Kinship Terminology and Evolution. *AA*, *62:* 747-763.

SHIMKIN, DMITRI B.
*1947. Wind River Shoshone Literary Forms. *Journal Washington Academy of Sciences*, *37:* 329-352.

SIMMONS, DONALD C.
1960a. Tonality in Efik Signal Communication and Folklore. In Anthony F.C. Wallace (Ed.), *Men and Cultures*. Philadelphia: University of Pennsylvania Press. Pp. 803-808.
1960c. Tonal Rhyme in Efik Poetry. *AL*, *2* (6): 1-10.

SINCLAIR, ANGUS
1951. *The Conditions of Knowing*. London: Kegan, Routledge, Paul.

SIVERTSEN, EVA (ED.)
1958. *Proceedings of the Eighth International Congress of Linguists* (*Oslo, 1957*). Oslo: Oslo University Press.

SKINNER, B. F.
1957. *Verbal Behavior*. New York: Appleton-Century-Crofts.

SLAMA-CAZACU, TATINA
1961. *Langage et contexte*. The Hague: Mouton.

SMITH, HENRY LEE, JR.
1952. *An Outline of Metalinguistic Analysis*. Washington, D.C.: U.S. Department of State, Foreign Service Institute.

SMITH, M. G.
1957. The Social Functions and Meaning of Hausa Praise Singing. *Africa*, *27:* 26-44.

SMITHERS, G. V.
1954. Some English Ideophones. *Archivum Linguisticum*, *6*: 73-111.

SOKOLOV, Y. M.
1950. *Russian Folklore*. New York: Macmillan.

SOMMERFELT, ALF
1938a. *La Langue et la société. Caractères sociaux d'une langue de type archaique.* (Instituttet for Sammenlignende Kulturforskning [L'institut pour l'étude comparative des civilisations (Oslo), Sér. A, No. 18.] Oslo.
1960a. The Interrelationship Between Language and Culture. *Texas Studies in Literature and Language*, *1*: 449-456.
1961. The French School of Linguistics. In Christine Mohrmann *et al.* (Eds.), *Trends in European and American Linguistics, 1936-1960*. Utrecht and Antwerp: Spectrum. Pp. 283-293.

SPANG-HANNSEN, H.
1954. *Recent Theories of the Linguistic Sign*. (Travaux du Cercle Linguistique de Copenhague, No. 9.) Copenhagen: Nordisk sprog-og Kulturforlag.

SPENCER, JOHN
1957. Received Pronunciation: Some Problems of Interpretation. *Lingua*, *7*: 7-29.

SPENCER, JOHN (ED.)
1963. *Language in Africa. Papers of the Leverhulme Conference on Universities and the Language Problems of Tropical Africa*. Cambridge: Cambridge University Press.

SPIER, L., A. I. HALLOWELL, and S. S. NEWMAN, (EDS.)
1941. *Language, Culture, and Personality: Essays in Memory of Edward Sapir*. Menasha, Wis.: Banta.

STANKIEWICZ, EDWARD
1956. The Phonemic Patterns of the Polish Dialects: A Study in Structural Dialectology. In *For Roman Jakobson*, The Hague: Mouton. Pp. 518-530.
1957. On Discreteness and Continuity in Structural Dialectology. *Word*, *13*: 44-59.

STERN, GUSTAV
1931. *Meaning and Change of Meaning. With Special Reference to the English Language*. (Göteborg Högskolas Arsskrift, 1932, *38* [1].) Göteborg.

STERN, THEODORE
1957. Drum and Whistle Languages: An Analysis of Speech Surrogates. *AA*, *59*: 487-506.

STEWARD, J. L.
1960. *The Problem of Stuttering in Certain North American Indian Societies*. (*Journal of Speech and Hearing Disorders*, Monograph Supplement 6.) Washington, D.C.: American Speech and Hearing Association.

STONE, LEO
1954. On the Principal Obscene Word ot the English Language. *International Journal of Psycho-Analysis*, *35*: 30-56.

STOUT, D. B.
1947. Ethnolinguistic Observations on San Blas Cuna. *IJAL*, *13*: 9-13.

STREHLOW, T. G. H.

*1947. *Aranda Traditions*. Melbourne: Melbourne University Press.

STURTEVANT, EDGAR LEE

1947. *An Introduction to Linguistic Science*. New Haven: Yale University Press. (Reprinted, Yale University Press paperbound, 1960.)

SWADESH, MORRIS

1934. The Phonemic Principle. *Lg.*, *10:* 117-129. [Also in Martin Joos (Ed.), *Readings in Linguistics*. Washington, D.C.: American Council of Learned Societies. Pp. 32-37.]

1937. A Method for Phonetic Accuracy and Speed. *AA*, *39:* 728-732.

1948. Sociologic Notes on Obsolescent Languages. *IJAL*, *14:* 226-235.

1950. Salish Internal Relationships. *IJAL*, *16:* 157-167.

*1951a. Diffusional Cumulation and Archaic Residue as Historical Explanations. *SJA*, *7:* 1-21. [Also in Morton H. Fried (Ed.), *Readings in Anthropology*. Vol. I, *Physical Anthropology*, *Linguistics*, *Archaeology*. New York: Crowell, 1959. Pp. 199-218.]

1952a. Lexico-statistic Dating of Prehistoric Ethnic Contacts. *PAPS*, *96:* 453-462.

1952b. Salish Phonologic Geography. *Lg.*, *28:* 237-248.

1954c. Perspectives and Problems of Amerindian Comparative Linguistics. *Word*, *10* (2-3): 306-332.

1955. Towards Greater Accuracy in Lexicostatistic Dating. *IJAL*, *21:* 121-137.

1956a. Problems of Long-range Comparison in Penutian. *Lg.*, *32:* 17-41.

*1959. Linguistics as an Instrument of Prehistory. *SJA*, *15:* 20-35.

1960a. *Estudios sobre lengua y cultura*. (Acta anthropologica, 2a. Epoca II-2.) Mexico, D.F.: Escuela Nacional de Antropologia e Historia, Sociedad de Alumnos.

1960b. *Tras la huella linguistica de la prehistoria*. Mexico: Universidad Nacional de México.

THIEME, PAUL

1954. *Heimat der indogermanischen Gemeinsprache*. Wiesbaden: Akademie der Wissenschaften und der Literatur in Mainz in Kommission bei Franz Steiner Verlag GMBH.

*1963. The Comparative Method in Linguistics. [Written for this volume.]

THOMPSON, STITH

1946. *The Folktale*. New York: Dryden.

TOVAR, ANTONIO

1954. Linguistics and Prehistory. *Word*, *10* (2-3): 333-350.

TRAGER, GEORGE L.

*1939. "Cottonwood" = "Tree": A Southwestern Linguistic Trait. *IJAL*, *9:* 117-118.

1943. The Kinship and Status Terms of the Tiwa Languages. *AA*, *45:* 557-571.

1949. *The Field of Linguistics*. (Studies in Linguistics, Occasional Papers, No. 1.] Norman, Oklah. Battenburg.

1955a. Language. *Encyclopaedia Britannica, 13:* 696-703.

1955b. Linguistics and the Reconstruction of Culture History. In *New Interpretations of Aboriginal American Culture History*, Washington, D.C.: Anthropological Society of Washington. Pp. 110-115.

1956. Linguistics. *Encyclopaedia Britannica, 14:* 162A-H, 163.
*1958. Paralinguistics: A First Approximation. *Studies in Linguistics, 13:* 1-12.
1959. The Systematization of the Whorf Hypothesis. *AL, 1:* 31-35.

TRAGER, GEORGE L., and EDWARD T. HALL, JR.
1954. Culture and Communication: A Model and an Analysis. *Explorations, 3:* 157-249.

TRAGER, GEORGE L., and HENRY LEE SMITH, JR.
1951. *An Outline of English Structure.* [Studies in Linguistics, Occasional Papers, No. 3.] Norman, Okla.: Battenburg. (2nd printing, Washington, D.C.: American Council of Learned Societies, 1956; 3rd printing, 1957.)

TROUBETZKOY, N. S.
1931. Phonologie et geographie linguistique. *Travaux du Cercle Linguistique de Prague, 4:* 228-234. [Also in Troubetzkoy, 1949, pp. 343-350.]
1933. La Phonologie actuelle. In Pierre Janet and Georges Dumas (Eds.), *Psychologie du langage.* Paris: Alcan. Pp. 227-246. [*Journal de psychologie: normale et pathologique, 30* (1-4).]
1939a. Grundzüge der Phonologie. *Travaux du Cercle Linguistique de Prague, 7.*
1949a. Phonologie et géographie linguistique. *Principes de phonologie.* Translated by J. Cantineau. Paris: Klincksieck. Pp. 343-350.
1949. *Principes de phonologie.* Translated by J. Cantineau. Paris: Klincksieck.

TURNER, LORENZO DOW
1949. *Africanisms in the Gullah Dialect.* Chicago: University of Chicago Press.

TYLOR, EDWARD BURNETT
1871. *Primitive Culture.* London: Murray. 2 vols. [Reprinted as *The Origins of Culture* (Vol. 1) and *Religion in Primitive Culture* (Vol. 2). New York: Harper Torchbooks, 1958.]
1881. *Anthropology. An Introduction to the Study of Man and Civilization.* London and New York. (Also, London: Watts, The Thinker's Library [No. 14], 1930.)

UHLENBECK, E. M.
1960. The Study of the So-Called Exotic Languages and General Linguistics. *Lingua, 9:* 417-434.

ULDALL, HANS
1957. *Outline of Glossematics, Part I.* (Travaux du Cercle Linguistique de Copenhague, Vol.II.) Copenhagen: Nordisk Sprog-og Kulturførlag.

ULLMANN, STEPHEN
1952. *Précis de sémantique française.* (Bibliotheca romanica. Series I, Manualia et commentatimes, No. 9.) Berne: Francke.
1953. Descriptive Semantics and Linguistic Typology. *Word, 9:* 225-240.
1957. *The Principles of Semantics. Linguistic Approach to Meaning.* (2nd ed.) Glasgow: Jackson; Oxford: Blackwell.
1962. *Semantics: An Introduction to the Science of Meaning.* New York: Barnes and Noble; Oxford: Basil Blackwell.
1963. *Language and Style.* Oxford: Basil Blackwell.

VENDRYES, J.
1921. *Le Langage. Introduction linguistique à l'histoire.* Paris: La Renaissance

du Livre. Translated by Paul Radin as *Language. A Linguistic Introduction to History*. New York: Knopf, 1925. (2nd rev. ed., Paris: Michel, 1950.)

VIGOTSKY, L. S.

1939. Thought and Speech. *Psychiatry*, *2:* 29-54.

1962. *Thought and Language*. Edited and translated by Eugenia Hanfmann and Gertrude Vakar. New York and London: The M.I.T. Press, Massachusetts Institute of Technology, and Wiley. (Original edition, 1934.)

VOEGELIN, C. F.

1941a. North American Indian Languages Still Spoken and Their Genetic Relationships. In L. Spier, A. I. Hallowell, and S. S. Newman (Eds.) *Language, Culture, and Personality*. Menasha, Wis.: Banta. Pp. 15-40.

*1945. Influence of Area on American Indian Linguistics. *Word*, *1:* 54-58.

1952a. The Boas Plan for the Presentation of American Indian Languages. *PAPS*, *96:* 439-451.

1960. Casual and Noncasual Utterances within Unified Structure. In Thomas A. Sebeok (Ed.) *Style in Language*. New York: Wiley; Cambridge: Technology Press. Pp. 57-68.

1961a. Anthropological Linguistics in the Context of Other Fields of Linguistics. *A William Cameron Townsend en el Vigesimoquinto Anniversario del Instituto Linguístico de Verano*, Mexico, D.F. Pp. 673-686.

1961b. Culture Area: Parallel with Typological Homogeneity and Heterogeneity to North American Language Families. *KASP*, *25:* 163-180.

VOEGELIN, C. F., and Z. S. HARRIS

1945. Linguistics in Ethnology. *SJA*, 1: 455-465.

1947. The Scope of Linguistics. *AA*, *49:* 588-600.

1951. Methods for Determining Intelligibility Among Dialects of Natural Languages. *PAPS*, *45:* 322-329.

1952. Training in Anthropological Linguistics. *AA*, *54:* 322-327.

VOEGELIN, C. F., and D. H. HYMES

1953. A Sample of North American Indian Dictionaries with Reference to Acculturation. *PAPS*, *97:* 634-644.

VOEGELIN, C. F., and F. M. VOEGELIN

1957. *Hopi Domains: A Lexical Approach to the Problem of Selection*. (IUPAL; Memoirs of *IJAL*, No. 14.) Bloomington.

VOGT, HANS

1954. Language Contacts. *Word*, *10* (2-3): 365-374.

WALLACE, ANTHONY F. C.

1961. The Psychic Unity of Human Groups. In Bert Kaplan (Ed.), *Studying Personality Cross-Culturally*. New York: Harper & Row. Pp. 129-164.

WALLACE, ANTHONY F. C. (ED.)

1960. *Men and Cultures. Selected Papers of the Fifth International Congress of Anthropological and Ethnological Sciences* (*Philadelphia, 1956*). Philadelphia: University of Pennsylvania Press.

WALLACE, ANTHONY F. C., and JOHN ATKINS

1960. The Meaning of Kinship Terms. *AA*, *62:* 58-80.

WATERHOUSE, VIOLA

1949. Learning a Second Language First. *IJAL, 15:* 106-109.

WATERMAN, J. T.

1957. Benjamin Lee Whorf and Linguistic Field Theory. *SJA, 13:* 201-211.

WEINREICH, URIEL

1953. *Languages in Contact.* New York: Linguistic Circle of New York.

1954. Is a Structural Dialectology Possible? *Word, 10* (2-3): 388-400.

1955. Review of S. Ullmann, *Précis de semantique française. Lg., 31:* 537-543.

1957a. On the Description of Phonic Interference. *Word, 13:* 1-11.

1957b. Functional Aspects of Indian Bilingualism. *Word, 13:* 203-233.

1962. Multilingual Dialectology and the New Yiddish Atlas. *AL, 4* (1): 6-22.

1963. On the Semantic Structure of Language. In Joseph Greenberg, (Ed.), *Universals of Language.* Cambridge: M.I.T. Press. Pp. 114-171.

WELLEK, RENÉ, and AUSTIN WARREN

1949. *Theory of Literature.* New York: Harcourt, Brace.

WELLS, RULON S.

1954. Meaning and Use. *Word, 10:* 235-250. [Also in Sol Saporta (Ed.), *Psycholinguistics.* New York: Holt, Rinehart and Winston, 1961. Pp. 269-283.]

WERNER, HEINZ, and BERNARD KAPLAN

1956. The Developmental Approach to Cognition. *AA, 58:* 866-880.

WHATMOUGH, JOSHUA

1956. *Language.* London: Secker & Warbur; New York: St. Martin. (Reprinted, New York: Mentor [209], 1957.)

WHITE, LESLIE A.

1940. The Symbol: The Origin and Basis of Human Behavior. *Philosophy of Science, 7:* 451-463. [Also in White, 1949, chap. 2.]

1944. A Ceremonial Vocabulary Among the Pueblos. *IJAL, 10:* 161-167.

1949. *The Science of Culture.* New York: Farrar, Strauss, and Cudahy. (Reprinted, New York: Grove [Evergreen Books E105], n.d.)

WHITNEY, WILLIAM DWIGHT

1875. *The Life and Growth of Language.* New York: Appleton.

WHORF, BENJAMIN LEE

[*LTR = Language, Thought, and Reality. Selected Writings of Benjamin Lee Whorf.* Edited by John B. Carroll. New York: Wiley; Cambridge: Technology Press, 1956.]

1935. The Comparative Linguistics of Uto-Aztekan. *AA, 37:* 600-608.

1936. The Punctual and Segmentative Aspects of Verbs in Hopi. *Lg., 12:* 127-131. [Also in *LTR*, pp. 51-56.]

1938. Some Verbal Categories of Hopi. *Lg., 14:* 275-286. [Also in *LTR*, pp. 112-124.]

1940a. Gestalt Technique of Stem Composition in Shawnee. In C. F. Voegelin, *Shawnee Stems and the Jacob P. Dunn Miami Dictionary* (Prehistory Research Series, Indiana Historical Society), *1* (9): 393-406. [Also in *LTR*, pp. 160-172.]

1940b. Science and Linguistics. *Technological Review, 42:* 229-231, 247-248. [Also in *LTR*, pp. 207-219.]

1940c. Linguistics as an Exact Science. *Technological Review*, *43:* 61-63, 80-83. [Also in *LTR*, pp. 220-232.]

1941a. Languages and Logic. *Technological Review*, *43:* 250-252, 226, 268, 272. [Also in *LTR*, pp. 233-245.]

1941b. The Relation of Habitual Thought and Behavior to Language. In L. Spier, A. I. Hallowell, S. S. Newman (Eds.), *Language, Culture, and Personality*. Menasha, Wis.. Banta. Pp. 75-93. [Also in *LTR*, pp. 134-159.]

1942. Language, Mind and Reality. *Theosophist* (Madras, India). [Also in *LTR*, pp. 246-270.]

1945. Grammatical Categories. *Lg.*, *21:* 1-11. (Written *ca.* 1937.) [Also in *LTR*, pp. 87-101.]

1950. An American Indian Model of the Universe. *IJAL*, *16:* 67-72. (Written *ca.* 1936.) [Also in *LTR*, pp. 57-64.]

1953. Linguistic Factors in the Terminology of Hopi Architecture. *IJAL*, *19:* 141-145. (Written 1940.) [Also in *LTR*, pp. 199-206.]

*1956a. A Linguistic Consideration of Thinking in Primitive Communities. In *LTR*, pp. 65-86. (Written *ca.* 1936.)

1956b. Language: Plan and Conception of Arrangement. In *LTR*, pp. 125-133. (Written 1938.)

WOLFF, HANS

1956. Phonemic Structure and the Teaching of Pronunciation. *Language Learning*, *6:* 17-23.

*1959a. Intelligibility and Inter-Ethnic Attitudes. *AL*, *1* (3): 34-41.

1959b. Subsystem Typologies and Area Linguistics. *AL*, *1* (7).

1962. Rárà: A Yoruba Chant. *Journal of African Languages*, *1:* 45-56.

WRIGHT, ARTHUR F.

1953a. The Chinese Language and Foreign Ideas. In Wright (Ed.), *Studies in Chinese* Thought. (Comparative Studies of Cultures and Civilizations, No. 1; Memoirs of the American Anthropological Association, No. 75.) Chicago: University of Chicago Press. Pp. 286-304.

WRIGHT, ARTHUR F. (ED.)

1953b. *Studies in Chinese Thought*. (Comparative Studies of Cultures and Civilizations, No. 1; Memoirs of the American Anthropological Association, No. 75.) Chicago: University of Chicago Press.

ŽINKIN, N. I.

1962. Four Communicative Systems and Four Languages. *Word*, *18* (1-2): 143-172.

INDEXES

Index of References Not in General Bibliography

The references indexed here are all those that occur *once* in a bibliography or list of references somewhere in the book, and hence are not to be found by consulting the General Bibliography. Such references are indexed alphabetically by name of author (or authors), and the number of the page on which each occurs. If a page contains more than one such reference for an author (or authors), the name is followed by parentheses containing the number, e.g., "Alonso, Amado, 684 (2)."

Index to Topical Bibliographies

Index of Authors

Index of Language Names

All languages for which the articles of the volume give substantive information are listed here, together with the number(s) of the articles concerned. Pertinent groups of languages are also entered. Where groups are discussed as such, the entry reads "family" in the case of genetic groups, "languages" in the case of geographical groups. Where the entry reads "languages" in the case of a genetic group, it simply lists constituent languages, so far as represented in the volume, as an additional convenience.

Group entries are italicized, and comprise: African languages; Algonquian family; Algonquian languages; American Indian languages: general; American Indian languages: specific; Athapaskan family; Athapaskan languages; Australian languages; Austronesian (= Malayo-Polynesian) family; Austronesian (= Malayo-Polynesian) languages; Bantu family; California Indian languages: general; California Indian languages: specific; Chinookan family; Dravidian family; Dravidian languages; Finno-Ugric family; Hokan family; Hokan languages; Indo-Aryan (= Indo-Iranic) family; Indo-Aryan (= Indo-Iranic) languages; Indo-European family; Indo-European languages; Indo-Iranic (= Indo-Aryan) family; Indo-Iranic (= Indo-Aryan) languages; Malayo-Polynesian (= Austronesian) family; Malayo-Polynesian (= Austronesian) languages; Munda family; Munda languages; Muskogean family; Muskogean languages; Na-Déné family; Na-Déné languages; Nigerian languages; Penutian family; Penutian languages; Romance family; Romance languages; Salishan family; Siouan family; Tanoan family; Uto-Aztecan family.

74 75 10 9